FROMMER'S
COMPREHENSIVE TRAVEL GUIDE
GERMANY '91

W9-CYV-743

by Darwin Porter
Assisted by Danforth Prince

PRENTICE
HALL
PRESS

NEW YORK • LONDON • TORONTO • SYDNEY • TOKYO • SINGAPORE

FROMMER BOOKS
Published by Prentice Hall Press
A division of Simon & Schuster Inc.
15 Columbus Circle
New York, NY 10023

ISBN 0-13-326802-0
ISSN 1044-2405

Manufactured in the United States of America

CONTENTS

PART TWO

EAST GERMANY

MAPS

A Disclaimer

Readers are advised that prices fluctuate in the course of time and that travel information changes under the impact of the varied and volatile factors affecting the travel industry. The author and publisher cannot be held responsible for the experiences of the reader while traveling. Readers are invited to write the publisher with ideas, comments, and suggestions for future editions.

Readers should also note that the establishments described under Readers' Selections or Suggestions have not in all cases been inspected by the author and that opinions expressed there are those of the individual reader(s) only and do not in any way represent the opinions of the publisher or author of this guide.

Travel Alert

Because of the fast-changing political situation in both East and West Germany, travel conditions, regulations, and certainly prices will change. Although we have quoted prices in East Germany in Deutsche Marks and dollars in this edition, these prices will undoubtedly rise to the level of prices in West Germany. The wise traveler will consult a travel agent, and the German National Tourist Board, before planning a trip to East or West Germany.

FROMMER'S GERMANY

A new, wealthy, industrial—yet beautiful—Germany awaits you.

Many of its treasures were lost during the war, but many remain and much has been rebuilt in the old style. Natural scenery, particularly such places as the Black Forest, the Mosel Valley, the Harz Mountains, and the Bavarian Alps, was and is a potent lure for any prospective traveler to Germany, either East or West.

I have set for myself the task of seeking out Germany at its best, basing this book on the premise that the best need not be the most expensive. My aim, beyond that of familiarizing you with the offerings of Germany, is to stretch your dollar, to reveal that you need not always pay scalper's prices for charm, top-grade comfort, and first-rate food.

I'll devote a great deal of attention to Munich, Frankfurt, Heidelberg, Hamburg, and both West and East Berlin, focusing on both obvious and hidden treasures. But important as these places are, they do not represent completely the diverse and complicated country that is Germany. To seek out the wonders of this often perplexing land, you must also go to the Bavarian Alps, Lake Constance, the Rhine and Mosel valleys, and the coast of the North Sea.

Fast-changing developments in East Germany have opened up new prospects of tourism. A trip there is a chance to see history in the making—to visit the old cities of Potsdam, Leipzig, Dresden, Meissen, and Weimar; to travel through the Harz Mountains, with its legendary past.

USING THIS GUIDE

This is a guidebook giving specific, practical details (including prices) about Germany's hotels, restaurants, sightseeing attractions, and nightlife. Establishments in all price ranges have been documented and described, from the extravagant chambers of the Vier Jahreszeiten (Four Seasons) in Hamburg to a moderately priced 12th-century knight's castle commanding a spectacular view of the Harz Mountains.

In all cases, establishments have been judged by the strict yardstick of value. If they measured up, they were included in this book, regardless of price classification.

But the major focus of the book is on neither the impecunious nor the affluent. Rather, my chief concern is the average, middle-income voyager who'd like to patronize establishments that offer maximum value.

SOME "VORSPEISEN" OF BARGAINS

Borrowing the word that means an array of tempting beginnings to a German meal, I'll preview some of the most delectable establishments awaiting you. In my journeys through every section of Germany, including its large cities and small villages, I have discovered surprising luxury offered for little cost, or establishments where the creative touch of their proprietors lifted them far above the ordinary.

You'll find dozens more in the pages ahead—and perhaps discover others on your own when you go to Germany.

In the Mosel Valley at **Traben-Trarbach,** you can stay at the Bellevue, a heavily Germanic structure right on the banks of the river. It was created in an ornamental style around 1900, with elaborate timberwork, a domed tower, a highly pitched roof, gables, and dormers. Warmly decorated double rooms with baths cost from $83.

Or on Germany's famed Romantic Road, in the medieval town of **Dinkelsbühl,** still surrounded by ancient walls, you can stay in the Deutsches Haus, an inn whose fascinating carved and painted facade dates from 1440. In the individually furnished bedrooms, you're likely to find a ceramic stove in one room, a Biedermeier desk in another. For this you'll pay from $77 double.

What about restaurants? In the Bavarian capital is the Weinstadl, reportedly the oldest house in **Munich,** tracing its history back to 1468. But in spite of its antique look, it's no museum. Waitresses in regional dress hurry across the brick floor, serving hearty Bavarian fare at scrubbed wooden tables lit by candles. Typical main dishes include pork cutlet with vegetables and a salad. A complete, filling meal costs from $12.

In the large Black Forest city of **Freiburg im Breisgau,** you can dine in the Oberkirchs Weinstuben, where you can saturate yourself with the food and flavor of the old town. The restaurant's situation is picture-postcardy, on a little square, with step-gable-roofed houses. An old wrought-iron sign hangs over the restaurant's entrance, and red and white tables are set out front for wine sampling or meals. A memorable lunch in the dark-paneled Weinstube costs as little as $18.

THE DEUTSCHE MARK AND THE DOLLAR

The unit of German currency is the **Deutsche Mark (DM),** which is subdivided into **pfennigs.** What the Deutsche Mark is worth in terms of U.S. money is a tricky question, the answer to which you determine by consulting the market quotations from day to day, in this case the money market.

The best advice is to consult a broker immediately before you leave or upon arrival to determine the most up-to-the-minute rate of exchange.

Still, some idea of what you'll be spending will be useful as you read these pages, so I've prepared a DM-to-dollar chart to be used *only as a gauge.* It is based on an exchange rate of approximately $1.68 DM to $1 U.S.

DM	U.S.$	DM	U.S.$
0.25 (25 pfennigs)	.14	20	11.88
0.50 (50 pfennigs)	.29	25	14.85
1	.59	50	29.69
2	1.19	75	44.54
5	2.97	100	59.38
7.50	4.45	125	74.23
10	5.94	150	89.07
15	8.91	200	118.76

SOME DISCLAIMERS

No restaurant, inn, hotel, Gasthaus, shop, tour agency, or nightclub paid to be mentioned in this book. What you read are entirely personal recommendations. In many cases, proprietors never knew their establishments were being visited or investigated for inclusion in a travel guide.

A word of warning: Unfortunately, costs change—and they rarely go down. All prices quoted in this book are subject to change.

Always, when checking into a hotel, inquire about the price. This policy can save much embarrassment and disappointment when the time comes to settle your bill. You cannot insist on being charged the precise prices quoted in this guide, although much effort has been made to secure accurate tariffs.

An additional note: The price quoted for double or twin hotel rooms is the rate for both persons, unless otherwise indicated.

AN INVITATION TO READERS

Like its companion Frommer guides, *Frommer's Germany* hopes to maintain a continuing dialogue between its writer and its readers. All of us share a common aim—to travel as widely and as well as possible, at the best value for our money. In achieving that aim, your comments and suggestions can be of aid to other visitors. Therefore if you come across an appealing hotel, restaurant, nightclub, shopping bargain, or sightseeing attraction, please don't keep it to yourself. And the letters need not apply only to new establishments: hotels and restaurants already recommended in this guide are also fair game. The fact that a listing appears in this edition doesn't give it squatter's rights in future publications. If its services have deteriorated, its chef grown stale, its room prices risen unfairly, whatever, these failings need to be known. Even if you enjoyed every place and found every description accurate, a letter letting me know that too can cheer many a gray day. Send your comments to Darwin Porter, c/o Prentice Hall Travel, 15 Columbus Circle, New York, NY 10023.

TIME OUT FOR A COMMERCIAL

The very fact that you've purchased a guide to Germany (both East and West) puts you in a special, sophisticated category of traveler—that is, the one who wants to explore and get to know a single country or two, as opposed to the "Grand Tour" individual who wants to do not only Belgium on Tuesday, but Rome on Wednesday, and perhaps the North Cape by Friday.

Even so, in your tour of Germany you come to the very doorstep of major attractions in other countries that you may want to explore. Since I had to set some limitations on the number of pages in this book, it was impossible to devote separate chapters to neighboring attractions.

I'll cite only an example or two to prove my point. As you tour Bavaria, you'll be on the doorstep of Switzerland, Liechtenstein, and Austria, with sunny Italy just a short drive away. As you tour along the western section of West Germany, you'll be passing the old provinces of Alsace and Lorraine, and may want to explore some of eastern France. North from Hamburg, as you go through Schleswig-Holstein, you'll be near the border of Denmark, with all of Scandinavia opening up to you.

Because of the geography of Germany, and depending on which sections of the country you plan to travel in, you may want to take along some of our other guides as traveling companions. Some that might appeal to you include: *Frommer's Switzerland and Liechtenstein, Frommer's Austria and Hungary, Frommer's Italy, Frommer's France, Frommer's Scandinavia on $60 a Day.*

• • •

Frommer's Dollarwise Travel Club—How to Save Money on All Your Travels

In this book we'll be looking at how to get your money's worth in Germany, but there is a "device" for saving money and determining value on all your trips. It's the popular, international Frommer's Dollarwise Travel Club, now in its 31st successful year of operation. The club was formed at the urging of numerous readers of the $-A-Day and Frommer Guides, who felt that such an organization could provide continuing travel information and a sense of community to value-minded travelers in all parts of the world. And so it does!

The club publishes a quarterly newspaper, *The Dollarwise® Traveler,* that keeps you up to date on fast-breaking developments in low-cost travel in all parts of the world, and brings you not only the latest money-saving information, but new ideas for travel with a difference as well as all the new information about your favorite, familiar places. For details, write to Frommer's Dollarwise Travel Club, 15 Columbus Circle, New York, NY 10023.

PART ONE

WEST GERMANY

I

GETTING THERE

1. TRAVELING TO WEST GERMANY
2. TRAVELING WITHIN WEST GERMANY
3. WHERE TO GO
4. ALTERNATIVE AND SPECIAL-INTEREST TRAVEL

You couldn't choose a more central place than Germany to start your European experience. Germany is in the heartland of Europe. Not only is it jam-packed with atmosphere, nightlife, and sightseeing interests, but it's also a perfect gateway to the rest of Europe. The Eastern European countries beckon, while to the south are storybook Austria and Switzerland, as well as tantalizing Italy. Directly to the west is France; to the north lie the Scandinavian countries. You can use Germany as your starting point to explore any of these countries with comparative ease.

Moreover, in planning a trip to Germany, there are several available methods of cutting your air transportation costs, previewed here.

1. Traveling to West Germany

PLANE ECONOMICS

The best strategy for securing the most economical airfare is to shop around. Keep calling the airlines. Sometimes you can purchase a ticket that is lower in price at the very last minute, because if the flight is not fully booked, an airline will discount tickets to try to achieve full passenger capacity.

For those who don't want to or can't leave everything to the last minute, there are certain things that you should know about airfare structures. Most airlines charge different fares according to seasons. Peak season, usually during the summer months if you're flying to Europe, is most expensive; basic season, during winter months, except during the Christmas holidays, offers the least expensive fares. Shoulder season is in between. Most airlines also offer an assortment of fares from first class, the most expensive, through business class to economy class, the lowest-priced regular airfare carrying no special restrictions or requirements. Most airlines also offer promotional fares, which carry stringent requirements such as advance purchase, minimum stay, and cancellation penalties. The most common such fare is the APEX (Advance Purchase Excursion).

Also note that prices are higher on weekends (around $50 usually) and also over the Christmas holidays (about $100 usually).

THE AIRLINES

Five airlines currently fly directly to Germany. They are Lufthansa (the national flag carrier of West Germany), American, Delta, Pan Am, and TWA.

Of the five, **Lufthansa** operates the most frequent service, flies to the greatest number of cities in Germany, and gives the best introduction to the kinds of service and experience that will be waiting for you once you land in Germany. As a safety note, passengers are usually relieved to learn that Lufthansa has one of the newest fleets of any airline, with an average aircraft age of 7.8 years.

From the United States and Canada, Lufthansa serves 17 North American gateway cities (13 of them in the U.S.). In any season there are more than 100 weekly flights from these cities to Germany. Lufthansa, which estimated its 1990 volume at more than 20 million passengers, has placed its U.S. gateways in cities well serviced by domestic airlines, so that getting from even the smallest North American town to Germany is usually convenient and easy. The largest of these gateways is New York's John F. Kennedy International Airport, which has daily flights to Frankfurt, Munich, Düsseldorf, and Stuttgart. From the New Jersey's Newark International Airport, Lufthansa offers daily flights to Frankfurt, Hamburg, and Cologne. Other gateway cities include Boston, Philadelphia, Atlanta, Miami, Chicago, Houston, Dallas/Fort Worth, Los Angeles, San Francisco, Washington, D.C., Anchorage, and San Juan, Puerto Rico. Charlotte, North Carolina, will soon be added. From Canada and Mexico, Lufthansa flies to Germany from Montréal, Toronto, Vancouver, Calgary, and Mexico City.

Several of the gaps within Lufthansa's service are hotly contested by some excellent airlines that give Lufthansa stiff competition, especially from the American Southeast and Midwest. **Delta Airlines,** long known as a strong regional airline, now offers frequent service from its headquarters in Atlanta to Hamburg, Munich, Stuttgart, and Frankfurt. It also has frequent service to Frankfurt from Cincinnati (a city that Delta has helped to transform into a major midwestern hub), Orlando, and Dallas.

American Airlines flies to four West German cities (Frankfurt, Munich, Hamburg, and Düsseldorf, with intermediate stops at some of them along the way) from its gateway cities of New York, Chicago, and Dallas.

TWA flies every day from New York to Frankfurt.

Pan Am flies from New York to six West German cities, with preliminary stopovers in each case except for the daily routes into Frankfurt and its five-times-per-week flights into Munich.

Least Expensive Fares

The airlines compete in offering the most economical rates with the least number of restrictions. Any promotional fare announced without advance notice by one will probably be quickly matched by its competitors. Insofar as airline fares go, the early bird almost always merits lower fares, since price structures are specifically geared to reward travelers who reserve and arrange payment for their tickets in advance. Watch the newspapers, and consult with your travel agent, for last-minute changes in the price wars.

For example, at press time Lufthansa offered a complicated series of promotional fares for high-season travel from all of its North American gateway cities to each of its destinations in Europe, requiring that tickets be paid for before March 14 and that travel be completed before a certain date (usually in late June). Only a dialogue with a reservations agent could have determined a price for your preferred itinerary. However, as an example, a high-season promotional round-trip transit from New York to Frankfurt averaged about $500, depending on which day you wanted to fly. Unfortunately, this and most other promotional fares were completely nonrefundable in the event that your plans changed.

Delta announced a similar arrangement to Germany from Atlanta, Cincinnati, Orlando, and Dallas. Defined as a "Promotional Early Sale" ticket, it offered midsummer round-trip passage from Atlanta to Frankfurt for an average price of about $620, depending on the day of the week you wanted to fly. The equivalent arrangement for a round-trip flight in low season averaged around $440. As at Lufthansa, Delta's early-sale tickets were nonrefundable, although the return date from Germany, if space was available, could have been rearranged for a payment of an extra $100.

This type of promotional fare changes as rapidly as the political scene in Central Europe, so be alert and flexible to new developments.

APEX Fares

The tickets mentioned above are suitable only for passengers lucky enough to have planned their trips many months in advance. For passengers who find that type of clairvoyance difficult, Lufthansa offers a cost-conscious Advance Purchase Excursion Fare (APEX), which requires prepayment only seven days in advance and a relatively nonrestrictive delay of between seven days and three months before you must use the return half of your round-trip ticket. If you cancel one of these tickets more than seven days before departure, you'll pay a penalty of $100. Despite that rule, this type of APEX ticket (or one of those roughly similar to it) has been among the most popular fare options in all of airline history.

On Lufthansa, as on all the airlines, midweek travel is less expensive than weekend travel. (Lufthansa defines "midweek" as Monday to Thursday, and "weekend" as Friday, Saturday, and Sunday.)

Lufthansa's low-season (January to late March) APEX fares for round-trip travel between New York and Germany's busiest airport, Frankfurt, cost $626 (midweek) and $679 (weekend). Its high-season APEX fares for the same route cost $904 (midweek) and $957 (weekend). For a different routing, say Chicago to Munich, low-season round-trip APEX fares cost $766 (midweek) and $819 (weekend). High-season fares for the same itinerary cost $1,075 (midweek) and $1,128 (weekend).

American's flights from Chicago to Munich include an excursion fare that has many restrictions (most notably a 30-day advance-purchase requirement and a nonrefundability—under any circumstances—clause). Passengers willing to accept these restrictions pay lower prices commensurate with the risk; i.e., an average of $800 in high season and an average of $615 in low season, with slight variations depending on the day of intended travel.

Business-Class and First-Class Fares

Each of the airlines recognizes that a part of its profits comes from business travelers who need to be as rested and awake as possible upon arrival for what might be a tightly scheduled set of meetings and business problems. Each of them offers a category of service midway between tourist class and the most luxurious class of service, first class. Known as business class, it has bigger seats, upgraded food and service, and more room to spread out papers, calculators, briefcases, and that novel you keep meaning to read but never get the chance to. Since business travelers travel in any season, the prices are the same year-round. Lufthansa charges $1,162 each way for transit from New York to Munich, but imposes absolutely no restrictions about either the length of time spent abroad or the prepayment of tickets.

First class offers extra comforts and extra services, whose benefits can only be determined by your values, your pocketbook, and your need for privacy and discretion during your travels. The first-class Lufthansa fare from New York to Munich costs $2,110 each way, and the amenities and luxuries that accompany it, while nonessential, can be very, very pleasant.

The competition for first- and business-class passengers is hotly contested throughout the industry. American's first-class fare from Chicago to Munich costs $2,368 each way; its business fare for the same route is about $1,400 each way.

For Toll-Free Information

Each of the airlines maintains toll-free reservation numbers that anyone can call to learn more about promotions, dates of departure, and fares. Call Lufthansa at 800/645-3880, Delta at 800/221-1212, American at 800/443-7300, Pan Am at 800/221-1111, and TWA at 800/221-2000.

Important Note

All fares, rules, and regulations are subject to change.

CHARTER FLIGHTS

To many travelers, the convenience, flexibility, and dependability provided by scheduled airlines outweigh the cost advantages of charter travel. In recent years, however, there have been changes in the charter concept that may make charter travel more attractive. Today, many charter flights are offered in conjunction with economical land packages featuring hotel accommodations and tours to popular tourist attractions. Most such packages also include car rentals or railpasses for land transportation.

Schwaben International, Inc., a German-based charter operator, maintains a U.S. office at Suite 1145, 1 World Trade Center, New York, NY 10048 (tel. 212/432-0116). From the northeastern United States, outside of New York City, call toll free 800/457-0009. Schwaben is one of the sales agents for Condor Charters, the charter subsidiary of Lufthansa. Condor runs charters to Stuttgart or Frankfurt from eight U.S. cities, usually departing from New York once a week. Currently, round-trip passage from New York to Stuttgart costs $379 to $619, depending on the season.

Other charter specialists are **Council Travel,** a division of the Council on International Educational Exchange (CIEE), 205 East 42nd St., 16th floor, New York, NY 10017 (tel. 212/661-1450); and **Access International,** 250 West 57th St., Suite 511, New York, NY 10107 (tel. 212/333-7280 or 1-800/333-7280). For additional assistance, check with a travel agent.

BY FREIGHTER

Many people think travel by freighter might be fun, something out of a Humphrey Bogart movie. Actually, it's more prosaic than that. If you're interested, try **Anytime, Anywhere Travel,** 35 King St., Chappaqua, NY 10514 (tel. 914/238-8800). Only 12 passengers are allowed on board, and a freighter voyage to Europe takes 9 to 10 days. Reservations must be made at least six months in advance. Ships leave several times a month from Newark to Bremerhaven. Not only will you enjoy a cabin with private bath, but you will get to dine with the officers. Cost is about $1,100 one way, not exactly a cheap means of transport when compared to flying.

Lykes Brothers Steamship Co., Lykes Center, 300 Poydras St., New Orleans, LA 70130 (tel. toll free 800/535-1861). Owned and operated by a Florida-based family, this American-registered shipping company runs four freighters, plying goods every six days between New Orleans and Rotterdam and Bremerhaven. On the way back from Bremerhaven, vessels stop at an English port, at Le Havre in France, at Norfolk, Virginia, then at Galveston, Texas, before returning to New Orleans. No more than 12 passengers are accommodated at one time. They dine in the saloon with the officers and crew, mingling in the alcohol-free lounge. There is no entertainment of any kind, and there are six double cabins on these vessels.

For more information on freighter travel, write to **Fords Freighter Travel Guide,** 19448 Londelius St., Northridge, CA 91324, asking for information about their specialty travel guide.

TOURS
Is this the year for your first trip to Europe? If you are not absolutely certain of just what country you want to visit, what sights to see, how to get around, and all the factors that go into making such a trip a success, my advice to you is to consider taking a good tour. Such a tour can give you a look at one or more countries, a taste of what Europe has to offer, so that by the time you go on a second or third trip, you know what to expect and what you'd like to see at your leisure.

2. Traveling Within West Germany

AIR SERVICES
More than 60 international airlines serve the Federal Republic of Germany, but the most frequent connections to and from the greatest number of destinations are operated by **Lufthansa.** Its globe-spanning network links more than 100 cities throughout the world.

West Germany's international airports are at West Berlin, Bremen, Cologne/ Bonn, Düsseldorf, Frankfurt am Main, Hamburg, Hannover, Munich, Nürnberg, Stuttgart, and Saarbrücken. Visitors arriving at West Berlin by air merely require the documents necessary for travel to the Federal Republic. The commercial airports of West Germany are linked with one another by scheduled Lufthansa services and other carriers. For example, from Frankfurt am Main, all Lufthansa destinations in Germany can be reached in an average of 50 minutes, with at least four flights daily. Contact your Lufthansa travel agency or Lufthansa town office for the most economical current offers.

All West German cities with commercial airports have their own **airport shuttle service,** offering reduced fares and fast connections between the city and the airport. Departure points are usually the airlines' town offices and the main railway terminal. Luggage can be turned in at the DB (GermanRail) baggage counter at the airport for delivery to all railroad stations in Germany.

Once in Germany, many visitors take advantage of the efficient Lufthansa Airport Express, a high-speed train that travels between the Frankfurt and Düsseldorf airports, with stops at Bonn and Cologne, giving the traveler an opportunity to view the beautiful Rhine Valley.

GERMAN FEDERAL RAILROAD
Whether you travel first or second class, you'll find that GermanRail's trains deserve their good reputation for comfort, cleanliness, and punctuality. They are modern and fast, running smoothly over welded tracks. Both first- and second-class trains carry smoker and nonsmoker compartments. A snackbar or a dining car serving German dishes and international cuisine, as well as good wines and beers, will usually be on your train (unless you're taking a "local"), and you can enjoy the landscape through picture windows.

Actually, GermanRail's customer service begins long before you board the train. Special features of major rail stations include information desks and ticket offices, pictorial directional signs (eliminating language problems), and posted timetables listing departures and arrivals of trains chronologically. In addition, each car carries signs, inside and out, describing its routing, point of origin, destination, and important stops en route. Restaurants, snackbars, post and money-exchange offices, newsstands and bookstores, flower shops, beauty parlors, pharmacies, and often a cinema are just some of the facilities major railroad stations offer. And they're usually located right in the center of the city.

For city sightseeing, you can leave your baggage in a locker or check it at the station's baggage counter. In many cities GermanRail provides door-to-door baggage service, allowing passengers to have their luggage picked up at or delivered to their hotels. Accompanying baggage can be checked for a nominal fee. Suitcases, baby carriages, skis, bicycles, and steamer trunks are permitted as baggage. Insurance policies of various kinds, even a travel medical plan, may be obtained in addition to your ticket (inside Europe only).

About 20,000 passenger trains per day comprise the network of first-class Inter-City (IC) trains offering express service every hour among some 50 major German cities. IC trains carry first as well as coach class. These trains require a surcharge (but not from holders of the Eurailpass and the first-class GermanRail Tourist Card). The luxurious interiors of IC trains have cushioned, adjustable seats and individual reading lights. Business travelers appreciate the telephone and secretarial services offered on most of these trains. Bars, lounges, and dining rooms are available too. A network of EuroCity trains in 13 countries of Europe, designated EC, offers the same high standards of service as those of IC.

A high-speed InterCity Express (ICE) train will go into service in June 1991 between Hamburg and Munich. Reaching speeds of 165 m.p.h., an ICE significantly reduces travel time from point to point, making same-day, cross-country travel possible. It's been called state-of-the-art transportation. ICE units include both first- and second-class cars, sleek bistro or formal dining cars, and other special features.

Advance reservations for sleeping accommodations on GermanRail trains are necessary. Travelers wanting to avoid the fatigue of long-distance driving can reach their destination on special car-sleeper trains (Auto Trains). Some daytime automobile trains are also operated.

Children below the age of 4, provided they do not require a separate seat, travel free; those between the ages of 4 and 12 pay half fare.

The Eurailpass, Eurail Saverpass, Eurail Flexipass, and Eurail Youthpass are well-known travel bargains. These passes are valid in most Western European countries, excluding Great Britain and Yugoslavia.

But before I go into specifics about these passes, I should certainly mention that GermanRail runs trains directly from the Düsseldorf and Frankfurt airports to the Düsseldorf and Frankfurt am Main main railroad stations, Wiesbaden, and Mainz. Travel time is all of 30 minutes, and the usual hassle of getting yourself from airport to town is considerably lessened.

Before leaving for Germany, you can get complete details about the German Federal Railroad and the many plans it offers, as well as information about Eurailpasses, at the following offices: 747 Third Ave., New York, NY 10017 (tel. 212/308-3100); 625 Statler Office Bldg., Boston, MA 02116 (tel. 617/542-0577); 9575 W. Higgins Rd. (Suite 505), Rosemont, IL 60018 (tel. 312/692-4209); 222 West Las Colinas, Suite 1050, Irving, TX 75039 (tel. 214/402-8377); 3400 Peachtree Road NE, Lenox Towers, Suite 1229, Atlanta, GA 30326 (tel. 404/266-9555); 323 Geary St./Union Square, Suite 501, San Francisco, CA 94102 (tel. 415/362-6206); and 11933 Wilshire Blvd., Los Angeles, CA 90025 (tel. 213/479-2772). In Canada: 1290 Bay St., Toronto, Ontario M5R 2C3 (tel. 416/968-3272).

GermanRail Tourist Passes

The German Federal Railroad offers discount fares to Americans and Canadians who buy tickets before leaving home, as well as cheaper round-trip fares for long-distance trips inside West Germany if you buy your tickets in advance. Tourist passes are available from travel agents and GermanRail offices in the United States.

Most popular is the GermanRailpass. A pass for 4 days in first class costs $135; for 9 days, $202; and for 16 days, $285. In second class, 4 days cost $90; 9 days, $135; and 16 days, $190. A GermanRailpass "Junior" is for second class only: 9 days for $85 or 16 days for $110.

Like Eurail, GermanRail has its own Flexipass. This pass gives you 4 days of first-class travel for $180; 9 days, for $270; and 16 days, for $375. In second class, the 4-day ticket costs $120; the 9-day ticket, $180; and the 16-day ticket, $250.

There's also a GermanRail Junior Flexipass, but for second-class travel only. It costs $65 for 4 days, $100 for 9 days, and $135 for 16 days.

Reservation fees for sleepers/couchettes and seats are extra, of course.

Other GermanRail Options

In addition to these travel plans, GermanRail offers various other programs that can be purchased at railroad ticket offices and authorized travel agencies—but within West Germany only.

Physical fitness enthusiasts, overworked managers, and nature lovers have long heeded GermanRail's advice to take the train to the countryside and enjoy the landscape "bike-back." More than 300 railroad stations in scenic areas participate in the "Bicycle at the Station" plan. The cost per day, including insurance, is 10 DM ($5.95). There is a charge of only 5 DM ($2.95) for holders of the GermanRail Tourist Card. Together with your bike ticket, you receive an area map with tour suggestions, telling you where to stop and visit a baroque church, a historical site, or some other attraction. You do not have to return the bicycle to the starting station—you can leave it at another station (having made certain that its baggage counter is still open).

Other travel plans include programs for senior citizens as well as "junior citizens," city-to-city weekend tours, and district tickets. In addition, GermanRail offers reduced fares for minigroups of more than six passengers, holiday tickets (Vorzugskarte), conference compartments in IC trains, or even conference cars.

EURAILPASS

This ticket, restricted to persons living outside Europe or North Africa, gives unlimited first-class rail travel over the more than 100,000-mile national railroad networks of Western European countries (not including Great Britain or Yugoslavia). You travel first class on any GermanRail train (subject to first class availability, of course), making as many stops as you please en route at no extra fare. A Eurailpass also entitles you to free or reduced-rate travel on many bus lines, lake and river steamers, and ferries. Reservation fees and sleeping accommodations are extra. The Eurailpass, together with the Eurail Saverpass, Eurail Flexipass, and Eurail Youthpass (see below), must be purchased before you go to Europe. Half fare is charged for children 4 to 12 years of age.

Vacationers planning a trip can purchase a 15-day Eurailpass for $340; otherwise, prices are $440 for 21 days, $550 for one month, $750 for two months, and $930 for three months. A pass must be used within six months of its date of issuance. The first day of validity must be stamped at the railroad station where travel begins; validity expires at midnight on the last day of the period for which the pass was purchased.

Eurail Saverpass

This ticket offers discounted 15-day travel, but only if groups of three persons travel constantly and continually together between April and September, or if two persons travel constantly and continually together between October and March. The price of a Saverpass, valid all over Europe, good for first class only, is $240 per person for the 15 days.

Eurail Flexipass

A time-flexible Eurailpass, the Flexipass gives travelers yet another option. After you have validated your pass, you do not lose travel days (as you do with some passes) if you elect to stay in one place a little longer. Countdown begins the first time you use the pass. Five days of travel in a 15-day period costs $198; 9 days of travel in 21 days costs $360; and 14 days of travel within one month goes for $458.

Eurail Youthpass
If you're under 26, you can purchase a Eurail Youthpass offering a true travel bargain. It gives you one or two months of unlimited second-class (coach) rail travel in the Eurailpass countries. Rates are $380 for one month, $500 for two months.

As mentioned above, before you leave for Europe you can get complete details on the GermanRail Tourist Cards and Eurailpasses from travel agents or from the German Federal Railroad at addresses given under "German Federal Railroad," above.

WEEKEND EXCURSIONS
Many German cities and towns offer weekend packages with reductions on hotel accommodations, restaurants, and admissions to nightclubs and museums. The list of such excursions is extensive, and I have, unfortunately, not the space to review them all. The "Munich Weekend Key," however, is a particularly exciting example. It's run by the Munich Tourist Office and is offered in three price ranges, from economy to deluxe, for one, two, or three days. Included in the prices are hotel room and breakfast, a sightseeing tour of Munich or a tour of Upper Bavaria, a free ride to the top of Olympia Tower, free admission to all museums and galleries in Munich, and a host of further reductions (on car rentals and admission to the Krone Circus, to name but two).

These excursions can be booked through local tourist offices only. The best way to find out about weekend excursions is to ask at the various local tourist offices as you travel around Germany. (See information under "Fast Facts" for other listings.)

TRAVELING BY CAR
If more than one person goes along for the ride, travel by car becomes economical. When four share expenses, it makes for a particularly good bargain. American car-rental organizations provide rental services, or else you might rent from one of the big German companies. Car operators arriving from most European countries need only their national driving license and permit. Otherwise, an international license and permit must be obtained. In Germany, drive on the right-hand side of the road.

Car Rentals
All the big U.S. firms, including **Budget, Hertz,** and **Avis,** are represented in West Germany. You can make reservations and do comparison shopping before you go to Germany by calling their toll-free numbers in the United States: Budget at 800/527-0700, Avis at 800/331-2112, and Hertz at 800/654-3001.

Many visitors to Germany who plan to visit other countries might want to drop off a rented car there. That is possible in many cases, but of course the agreement has to be made in advance. Budget rental vehicles, for example, can be picked up in one West German city and returned in another for no additional charge. Likewise, if you keep the car for more than a week, and plan to return it to a city in a neighboring country (Zurich or Innsbruck, for example), there is only a nominal charge (if any). If you return it to, say, Naples, the charge will be a lot more, of course.

Insurance is all-important in selecting a car-rental firm. A collision damage waiver (CDW) is an optional insurance policy that can be purchased when you sign a rental agreement. For an extra fee, the rental agency agrees to eliminate your financial responsibility for liability and collision damage in case of an accident. If you don't have a CDW and you have an accident, you'll pay between $500 and the full value of the damages to the car, depending on your contract.

Certain credit-card companies, such as American Express and Diners Club, agree to reimburse card-users for the deductible in the event of an accident. Because of that, many renters have chosen to waive the extra CDW. However, payments have often been delayed with such coverage and the car renter involved in an accident has had to pay cash on the spot, leaving some vacationers financially strapped.

To avoid such misunderstanding, some car-rental companies, notably Hertz and Avis (but not Budget), have begun automatically including a CDW as part of the standard rental agreement, even though some renters object to what they consider "double coverage." Double coverage or not, it has prevented hundreds of renters from having to shell out cash while waiting for their reimbursement.

If you forego the CDW, then Budget is much less expensive than its major contenders. However, if you take the full CDW coverage with Budget, then its prices are approximately the same as those charged by Hertz and Avis. Of course, all this could change by the time you arrive in Germany, so you should do some last-minute checking.

Midsummer rates at the Frankfurt airport for Budget's least expensive car requires a 14-day advance booking and a minimum driver's age of 18. A cramped but peppy Fiat Panda with unlimited mileage costs around $125 for a one-week rental, or $117 per week if you keep the car 14 days. Full payment is required in advance. If a reservation is canceled, a $30 fee is assessed. However, if you pay a bit more, about $10 per week, no prepayment is required and no penalty is assessed should you cancel. To all prices, a 14% tax is added in Germany.

The least expensive car at Hertz is a Ford Fiesta, renting for $245 per week with insurance included. It requires a 21-day advance reservation and full prepayment. Budget, on the other hand, with a 14-day advance reservation, offers the same car at the same location for a more reasonable $144 per week, but only if you forego the CDW. The cost of the least expensive car at Avis is a Volkswagen Polo Coupe at $243 per week, including the CDW.

Don't overlook the availability of cars with automatic transmission, which is still viewed as somewhat of a luxury in Europe. At Budget, for example, you'll pay $200 per week for a four-door Volkswagen Golf with automatic transmission—but without the CDW.

Motor Homes

If you're keeping costs really low, you might want to rent a motor home from **Executive Motorhomes,** 28 Opelstrasse, D-6082 Moerfelden (tel. 06105/3037). It offers up-to-date vehicles, airport pickup and return, and reserve vehicles in case of a breakdown. (The dinnerware in the little kitchens is Rosenthal china.) Established in 1964, this is the oldest and largest camper and motor home rental company in Europe. Its location is only about 9 miles from the Frankfurt airport. Depending on the camper desired, fixed rates, including unlimited mileage, range from $99 to $160 daily, plus 14% VAT. Off-season reductions are granted, and there are extra charges made for such things as cooking gas and cleaning.

Fuel

Gasoline is readily available throughout the Federal Republic, and service stations appear frequently along the Autobahns. As of this writing, the average cost for gasoline or petrol is about 1.50 DM (90¢) per liter.

Traffic Signs

Easy-to-understand international road signs are used throughout Germany.

Crossing Points

The border-crossing points into the Federal Republic are open day and night, including those to West Berlin. In the case of West Berlin, foreign visitors always need a passport and a transit visa, which is issued at the border. This costs nothing for coach and rail travelers, but tourists going by car are charged 10 DM ($5.95) for the return journey. Short-term third-party insurance must also be taken out at

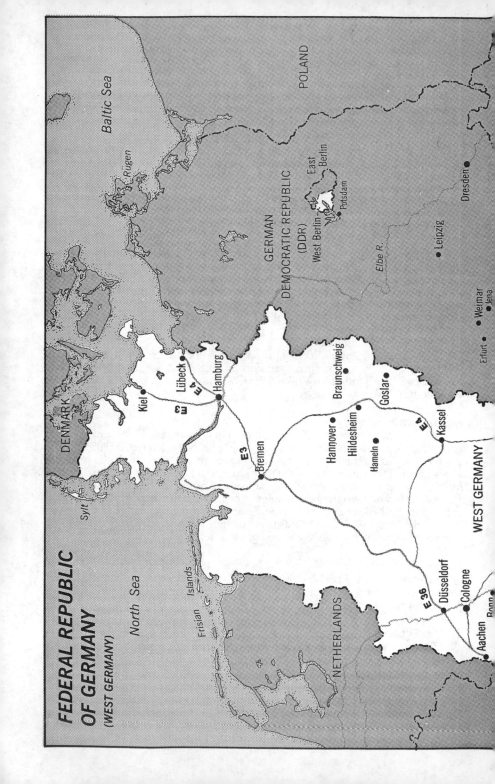

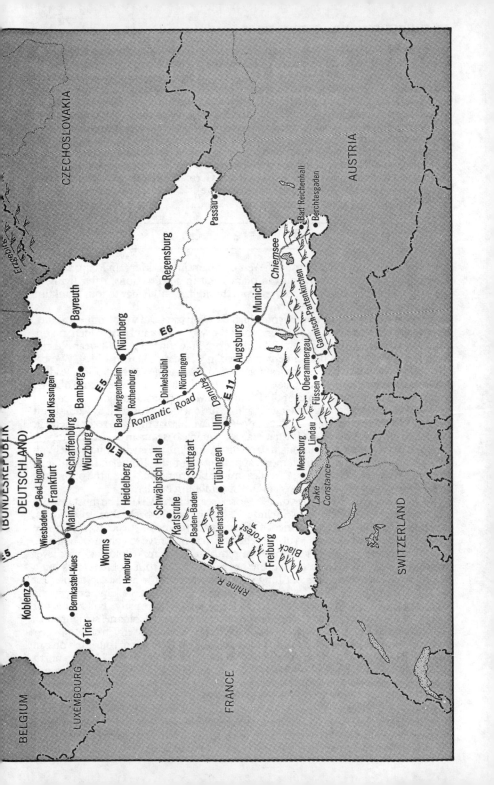

border-crossing points for all foreign cars. (Of course, this data could become out-of-date, depending on the timing of German reunification.)

Hitchhiking

Germany offers some of the best hitchhiking possibilities in Europe. Seemingly every West German owns an auto, and there is a splendid network of Autobahns. *Der Weg-Wanderer,* as hitchhikers are known, aren't frowned upon here, as they are in some countries. However, you should never hitch a ride while actually on an Autobahn or freeway. It is also illegal to hitch a ride near an exit or entrance to a freeway. Therefore, you'll have to stand far enough away so you won't get picked up by the police. You'd better have a sign (always use the German name for a city, not the English one—for example, Köln instead of Cologne).

---

3. Where to Go

Most visitors begin their tour of West Germany in Frankfurt am Main, which is a convenient center because you can branch out in all directions. After flying to Frankfurt, you'll need a day to recover from the flight, another day to tour Frankfurt itself.

If you are touring by car, on your third day, you can head west from Frankfurt, paying visits to two famous stopovers along the way: Mainz and Wiesbaden, on opposite banks of the Rhine. Mainz, 24 miles from Frankfurt, is a 2,000-year-old city founded by the Romans (Gutenberg invented movable type here in 1440). Wiesbaden, on the opposite bank, 8 miles north of Mainz, is one of the world's leading belle-époque spas. From Wiesbaden it is a 64-mile drive northwest to Koblenz, which stands at the confluence of the Rhine and Mosel rivers. On the way there you can go through the famous Rheingau, whose little wine towns such as Rüdesheim are known around the world. Koblenz doesn't have all that much to recommend it, but because of its strategic position it makes a suitable base for an overnight stop.

On the morning of your fourth day, you can explore the enchanting Mosel Valley, which many visitors find more appealing than the Rhineland. Your final destination, a distance of some 77 miles, might be Trier, considered the oldest city in Germany, lying some 6 miles from the Luxembourg border.

You can also take boat trips on the Mosel (see Chapter VIII). The most intriguing stopovers along the way include Zell, Traben-Trarbach, Bernkastel-Kues, Beilstein, Cochem, and Eltz Castle. Of course, many motorists spend a week or more exploring the Mosel. But on a rushed schedule, you may have to confine it to a day.

On the fifth day, I suggest that you return to Koblenz (exploring whichever riverbank of the Mosel you missed the preceding day). From Koblenz, it is but a 55-mile trip north to Cologne. Along the route you can stop at the capital of West Germany, Bonn, only 17 miles south of Cologne. Cologne is the largest city in the Rhineland, and also one of the premier attractions of Germany. Following our "slow" route, you will need to spend at least a day getting to Cologne, so figure on a two-night stopover there, the second day spent discovering the city itself.

On the seventh day, which will have made for a total week of touring, you can press north to Düsseldorf, a city of haute couture and culture, lying 24 miles north of Cologne, or else you can return to Frankfurt, where yet another exciting tour is recommended.

If you'd like to take a "Grand Tour," beginning in Frankfurt and working your way eventually to Munich, via Heidelberg, the Black Forest, the Romantic Road, and the Bavarian Alps, you can motor along the following suggested route. Count on spending at least eight nights before you reach Munich. Even so, you'll only have skimmed the highlights, but modern schedules have to be dealt with realistically.

Most of the run between Frankfurt and Heidelberg can be made by Autobahn. There are more scenic routes, but if you wish to spend as much time in Heidelberg as possible, you can be there in about an hour and a half, covering a distance of some 60 miles.

Spend your first night in Heidelberg exploring its castle of *Student Prince* fame and visiting one of the student taverns in the evening. Leave the next day along the Autobahn heading south toward Basel (Switzerland). If you have time, stop off for a visit to the internationally famous spa of Baden-Baden, with its casino and baths. Visitors settle in here for days or weeks, but, again, if time is very limited you can continue along the Autobahn until you reach Freiburg im Breisgau, the capital of the Black Forest, a distance of 70 miles from Baden-Baden. Filled with charming inns and cozy wine taverns, Freiburg makes an ideal stopover.

The next day, your third, you can travel northeast to Stuttgart, a distance of 129 miles, with some stopovers along the way. The first morning visit might be to Triberg, home of the cuckoo clock, lying 38 miles from Freiburg. Here you can visit the highest waterfall in all of Germany. From Triberg, you can head east to Schwenningen, where you can take a major artery north to Tübingen, an old university town on the upper Neckar River, which is often compared to Heidelberg. If it's getting late, you can spend the night here; otherwise, motorists can press on to Stuttgart, 29 miles to the northeast.

After a night in Stuttgart, continue northeast to Würzburg, stopping off for lunch at either Schwäbisch Hall or Bad Mergentheim. Würzburg, lying some 102 miles from Stuttgart, is one of the loveliest baroque cities of Germany. It lies about 60 miles from Frankfurt.

After a night there, you can begin on your fifth day to explore the Romantische Strasse, or Romantic Road, which stretches for 180 miles between Würzburg in the north and Füssen at the foothills of the Bavarian Alps. Some motorists cover this route in just one day, but to do so you will be able only to see the sights passing in review from your car window. It's better to head first for Rothenburg, which is considered one of the finest medieval cities in Europe—some say *the* finest. It lies 40 miles south of Würzburg. After time spent there, you might settle in for the rest of the day and evening, or head instead for Dinkelsbühl or Nördlingen; each of these picture-book towns is considered an irresistible stopover along the Romantic Road. Each has old-fashioned inns.

To begin your sixth day, I'd leave either Dinkelsbühl or Nördlingen, paying a morning visit to the old city of Augsburg, which, incidentally, is only 42 miles from Munich if you've run out of time. Otherwise, you can continue along the Romantic Road south to Füssen. At this point you'll be near the Austrian frontier.

On the morning of your seventh day, you can explore the royal castles of Bavaria, including Hohenschwangau (built by Ludwig II's father, Maximilian II) and Neuschwanstein, the fairy-tale castle of the "mad king." For accommodations that evening, it's an easy drive east to Garmisch-Partenkirchen, Germany's leading alpine resort and the largest city of the Bavarian Alps. I suggest two nights there. First, the visit to the royal castles will have eaten up your first day, and Garmisch deserves the minimum of a day to itself. Not only that, you may be tempted to visit Berchtesgaden, which is set below the summits of the Watzmann Mountain. You can drive from Berchtesgaden to Obersalzberg, one of the most scenic routes in Bavaria.

On the morning of the ninth day, you can head north to Munich, a distance of 55 miles, where you'll want to spend at least three days—much more if you can afford the time.

What about Berlin? West Berlin, as covered in Chapter XVII, is a destination unto itself.

By taking the tour I've outlined, you will not have seen Germany, but you will have seen a good part of it, at least the section that tourists have praised for centuries. Other cities, such as Hamburg and Nürnberg, are outlined in detail in the chapters ahead for those with more time; and other areas, such as the famed Harz Mountains, await exploration by the visitor with time to venture into the less trampled parts of Germany.

Chances are you can't see Germany in one visit—so you may want to return again and again.

---

4. Alternative and Special-Interest Travel

Mass tourism of the kind that has transported vast numbers of North Americans to the most obscure corners of the map has been a by-product of the affluence, technology, and democratization that only the second half of the 20th century was able to produce.

With the advent of the 1990s, and the changes this decade promises to bring, some of America's most respected travel visionaries have perceived a change in the needs of many of the world's most experienced (and sometimes jaded) travelers. There has emerged a demand for specialized travel experiences whose objectives are clearly defined well in advance of an actual departure. There is also an increased demand for organizations that can provide like-minded companions to share and participate in increasingly esoteric travel plans.

Warning: Under no circumstances is the inclusion of an organization in this section to be interpreted as a guarantee either of its creditworthiness or its competency. Information about the organizations coming up is presented only as a preview, to be followed by your own investigation should you be interested.

INTERNATIONAL UNDERSTANDING

Servas, 11 John St., New York, NY 10038 (tel. 212/267-0252). Servas (translated from the Esperanto, it means "to serve") is a nonprofit, nongovernmental international, interfaith network of travelers and hosts whose goal is to help build world peace, goodwill, and understanding. They do this by providing opportunities for deeper, more personal contacts among people of diverse cultural and political backgrounds. Servas travelers are invited to share living space in a privately owned home within a community, normally staying without charge for visits lasting a maximum of two days. Visitors pay a $45 annual fee, fill out an application, and are interviewed for suitability by one of more than 200 Servas interviewers throughout the country. They then receive a Servas directory listing the names and addresses of Servas hosts who will allow (and encourage) visitors in their homes.

International Visitors Information Service, 733 15th St. NW, Suite 300, Washington, DC 20005 (tel. 212/783-6540). For $4.95, this organization will mail anyone a booklet listing opportunities for contact with local residents in foreign countries. Germany is featured. Checks should be made out to Meridian House IVIS.

TRAVEL AND LEARNING

An international series of programs for persons over 50 years of age who are interested in combining travel and learning is offered by **Interhostel,** developed by the University of New Hampshire. Each program lasts two weeks and is escorted by a university faculty or staff member, arranged in conjunction with a host college, university, or cultural institution. Participants can extend a stay beyond two weeks if they wish. Interhostel offers programs that consist of cultural and intellectual activities, with field trips to museums and other centers of interest. For information, get in touch with the University of New Hampshire, Division of Continuing Education, 6 Garrison Ave., Durham, NH 03824 (tel. 603/862-1147). It's best to phone between 1:30pm and 4pm EST. You can also call toll free at 800/733-9753.

WEST GERMANY
Mileage Between Major Cities
(in Miles)

	Berlin	BONN	Bremen	Bremerhaven	Cologne	Constance	Düsseldorf	Frankfurt	Hamburg	Kiel	Koblenz	Lübeck	Munich	Nürnberg	Stuttgart	Trier	Wiesbaden
Berlin		375	243	277	357	200	350	343	184	226	379	200	363	272	392	479	361
BONN	375		214	250	17	318	45	109	282	335	52	318	348	243	215	89	95
Bremen	243	214		36	197	504	180	276	74	128	262	110	466	360	398	301	273
Bremerhaven	277	250	36		232	543	216	312	84	115	298	144	499	394	432	337	309
Cologne	357	17	197	232		329	24	116	264	317	66	300	355	250	226	104	102
Constance	200	318	504	543	329		354	230	526	588	273	562	140	239	114	252	236
Düsseldorf	350	45	180	216	24	354		141	248	301	91	284	380	275	251	129	127
Frankfurt	343	109	276	312	116	230	141		304	366	76	340	244	138	127	123	24
Hamburg	184	282	74	84	264	526	248	304		60	331	41	483	378	415	369	322
Kiel	226	335	128	115	317	588	301	366	60		155	57	544	439	477	422	384
Koblenz	379	52	262	298	66	273	91	76	331	155		366	301	210	170	77	63
Lübeck	200	318	110	144	300	562	284	340	41	57	366		519	414	451	405	358
Munich	363	348	466	499	355	140	380	244	483	544	301	519		102	136	324	264
Nürnberg	272	243	360	394	250	239	275	138	378	439	201	414	102		128	259	158
Stuttgart	392	215	398	432	226	114	251	127	415	477	170	451	136	128		193	133
Trier	479	89	301	337	104	252	129	123	369	422	77	405	324	259	193		102
Wiesbaden	361	95	273	309	102	236	127	24	322	384	63	358	264	158	133	102	
Würzburg	309	180	300	334	185	203	210	73	317	379	145	353	173	68	92	192	180

TRAVEL COMPANIONS

If you're between the ages of 50 and 90, and need a travel companion, **Golden Companions,** P.O. Box 754, Pullman, WA 99163 (tel. 208/883-5052), might provide the answer. Research economist and writer Joanne R. Buteau founded this helpful service—and is quick to point out it's not a dating game. The service provides the means whereby travelers can seek introductions to possible travel companions through a confidential mail network service. Members, once they have "connected," make their own travel arrangements. Created in 1987, this organization has members from many walks of life, including professional types and retirees, as well as the single, divorced, widowed, or married. Members also receive a bimonthly travel newsletter, *The Golden Traveler,* which outlines travel discounts for senior citizens, vacation home exchanges, and other data. Membership for a full year costs $60 per person.

SENIOR CITIZEN VACATIONS

One of the most dynamic organizations promoting postretirement studies for senior citizens is **Elderhostel,** 80 Boylston St., Boston, MA 02116 (tel. 617/426-7788), established in 1975. Elderhostel maintains programs throughout Europe, including Germany. Most courses last for around three weeks, representing good value, considering that airfare, hotel accommodations in student dormitories or modest inns (or perhaps with a private family), all meals, and tuition are included. Courses involve no homework, are ungraded, and are especially concerned with liberal arts. In no way is this to be considered a luxury vacation, but rather an academic fulfillment of a type not possible for senior citizens until several years ago. Participants must be more than 60 years of age. However, if a pair of members go as a couple, only one member need be over 60. Anyone interested in participating in one of Elderhostel's programs should write for a free newsletter and list of upcoming courses and destinations.

SPAS

Some 260 registered spas and health resorts are to be found in Germany. They feature the most modern therapeutic facilities and provide numerous medical treatments, sports, and amusements for recuperation, weight reduction, and rest. Information on spas and health resorts may be obtained by writing **Deutscher Bäderverband e.V.,** Schumannstrasse 111, D-5300 Bonn. Also refer to Chapter V in this guide, "Leading Spa Resorts."

HIKING

In the German uplands, a network of marked hiking trails (approximately 81,840 miles) is serviced by regional hiking associations organized under the **German Hiking and Climbing Association** (Verband Deutscher Gebirgs-und-Wandervereine), Reichsstrasse 4, D-6600 Saarbrucken (tel. 0681/39-00-70). The associations provide information about trails, shelters, huts, whatever, in their respective regions. A directory of local hiking associations may be requested by writing to the above address.

MOUNTAIN CLIMBING

Some 252 huts in the uplands and in the Alps, owned and operated by the **German Alpine Club** (Deutscher Alpenverein), Praterinsel 5, D-8000 München 22 (tel. 089/23-50-90-0), are open to all mountaineers. In addition to the huts, the association maintains a 15,000-mile network of alpine trails.

OPERA TOURS

On a cultural note, **Dailey-Thorp Travel,** 315 West 57th St., New York, NY 10019 (tel. 212/307-1555), in business since 1971, is probably the best-regarded organizer of music and opera tours operating in America. Because of its "favored" relations with European box offices, it is often able to purchase blocks of otherwise unavailable tickets to such events as the Bayreuth Festival in Germany and the Salzburg Festival in Austria, as well as to performances at the Vienna, Milan, Paris, and London opera houses. Tours range from 7 to 21 days and include first-class or deluxe accommodations and meals in top-rated restaurants. Dailey-Thorp is also known for its breakthrough visits to opera houses in Eastern Europe and in the less traveled cities of Italy.

II

SETTLING INTO GERMANY

1. THE GERMANS

2. THE CULTURE

3. FOOD AND DRINK

4. FAST FACTS FOR WEST GERMANY

The people of Germany are complex, the descendants of varied cultural backgrounds. Distinguishing differences can be noted among the Westphalians, the Lower Saxonians, the Bavarians, and the Rhinelanders. Don't expect to find a nation of happy, laughing beer drinkers running around in lederhosen with feather-topped hunting caps resting jauntily on their heads. However, enough of these tradition-minded souls exist to reinforce the stereotype. All in all, it's a land that knows how to harmonize contrasts.

1. The Germans

Until World War II, Germany was a unified whole and the German people displayed a close kinship. The division of the country into East and West Germany wrought political and economic changes. But both Germanys share a common history and culture, and as unification approaches, the likenesses rather than the differences appear to be coming to the fore. The history presented here, of course, applies to both East and West Germany. But it is a history still unfinished.

HISTORY

The land that today is Germany—both West and East—has been inhabited for eons, ever since the Paleolithic period 600,000 to 10,000 years before Christ. Tribes ranged through the forested country, where they found plentiful streams, rivers, fish, and game. At Mauer near Heidelberg, at Steinham an der Murr, and in the Neander valley near Düsseldorf, remains of human beings dating from 500,000 to 150,000 B.C. have been found.

These were rootless people, moving as crops were exhausted or animals migrated. It wasn't until between 8000 B.C. and the arrival of the Bronze Age, about 1800 B.C., that the early people began to settle in more or less permanent spots.

They cultivated crops, raised animals they could domesticate, and eventually established some commerce with their neighbors.

These early tribes were called **Celts,** and they had the whole Central European area to themselves until Indo-Europeans known as **Teutons,** or **Germanic tribes,** began to move in. The newcomers established themselves in the Rhine and Oder valleys and southern areas that today comprise southern Germany and northern Italy. The Celts and their hilltop forts were overrun, and they were forced to flee to the west across the Rhine. They were replaced by the Germanic tribes—**Alemanni, Burgundians, Franks, Lombards, Ostrogoths,** and **Visigoths.** Then, a couple of centuries before Christ, **Romans** came with a view to extending their empire north. They succeeded briefly, building forts at strategic spots, including Cologne, Trier, Mainz, Wiesbaden, and Passau. The inhabitants of the area resisted ferociously, forming large, combined West Germanic tribes whose descendants are still in the land. They stopped the Romans; later, some of these tribes invaded Italy and eventually helped destroy the Roman Empire. This meant that neither Latin culture nor Christianity gained much foothold in early times.

Beginning about A.D. 300, the Huns came from the east into central Europe. The Huns didn't make lasting inroads into what is today Germany, but the migration signaled permanent fixing of home ground by the Bavarians in the south, Alemanni in Swabia, Thuringians in central Germany, Franks in the west, and Saxons and Frisians in the north. Gradually, Christianity spread, and the former tribes took on the gloss of civilization and culture. By A.D. 800, a Frankish king, Charlemagne, was crowned as emperor, ruling the entire area. Emperors who followed Charlemagne did not match him in ability and power, and control decentralized. The Holy Roman Empire came into existence with the coronation of Otto I in 962; within it arose little nations, dukedoms, bishoprics, and principalities. As the might of the Holy Roman Empire declined, emperors were forced to seek alliance with rich German cities and with such powerful political and commercial city leagues as the Swabian League and the Hanseatic League. The later Middle Ages were marked by continual conflict between the emperors and their subjects.

When Martin Luther ushered in the Reformation by nailing his theses on the church door at Wittenberg in 1517, he created political as well as religious schism. The Reformation divided the Catholic emperors from the Protestant princes and set the stage for the devastating Thirty Years' War (1618–1648), from which Germany emerged more fragmented than ever. The only powerful German state to emerge from these conflicts was the little kingdom of Prussia in the northeast on the Baltic Sea. The rise of Prussian power continued throughout the 18th century; under Frederick II (the Great) it became a major kingdom with Berlin as its capital.

The Congress of Vienna (1814–1815), following the Napoleonic wars, redrew the map of Germany, giving more territory to Prussia, but making Austria the leader in a German Confederation. During these events, there was a rising spirit of nationalism, exploited to good effect by Prince Otto von Bismarck when he became Prussia's chief minister in 1862. In the Austrian-Prussian War of 1866, Prussia triumphed over its rival to create a North German Confederation with Prussia as its leader. After the Franco-Prussian War, Bismarck succeeded in his goal: William I was crowned emperor of Germany, and the German Empire was established in 1871. Unity was achieved and a strong Germany took shape; an advanced social welfare system was adopted, and industrial production as well as technical and scientific pursuits advanced to new heights. The nation also grew in military might, but Bismarck kept the country out of wars.

At the accession of Wilhelm II in 1888, Bismarck came into conflict with the ambitions of the emperor, whose efforts to make Germany a world power upset the fragile balance in Europe. The result was World War I, with disastrous results: Germany was forced to disarm and pay heavy reparations. The empire became a republic with a liberal constitution, but social dislocation, postwar inflation, and the Great

Depression combined to weaken the political structure of the republic and to prepare the ground for Adolf Hitler and the Third Reich.

Hitler and his National Socialist (Nazi) Party came to power in 1933, promising at first implicitly and later loudly and clearly to restore Germany to its position as a world power and to avenge the ignominy heaped on the nation by the 1918 Treaty of Versailles. The Nazis quickly changed the form of government into a dictatorship with Hitler at the helm, eliminated democratic institutions, and set out on a program of genocide against so-called "inferior" people. These actions were accompanied by moves to restore Germany's economic and military power. Hitler took Germany a short way along the path of glory, but he plunged the nation quickly into war, destruction, and degradation. After World War II there was some hope that Germany, after a suitable period, could be restored as a unified nation, but it was a vain hope at the time.

At the war's end, Germany and its capital city were divided. The nation shrank in size, losing long-held territories (among them East Prussia). The United States, Great Britain, France, and the USSR divided the country into four zones of occupation, with Berlin lying in the Soviet area. However, it was decided that the capital would also be divided among the four powers. The Soviet Union tried to cut off access by the other three nations into Berlin in the early 1960s, but the attempt failed. The Soviet-directed government of East Germany erected the Berlin Wall and sealed off the borders to stop emigration from East to West, at the same time making visits to the East very difficult for the people of the West. That wall stood until 1990.

Starting in 1949, Great Britain, the United States, and France allowed their zones of occupation to be self-governing. The USSR, on the other hand, made its zone into a virtual police state, severely limiting the freedom of its citizens until the momentous events that began in 1989.

Regardless of the old zones of occupation, the destruction caused to Germany by World War II was stupendous, mostly in the cities. The task of rebuilding has been one of the miracles of the 20th century. Much was reconstructed in the old style, although much of the Germany of old was lost forever.

Once thought only a remote possibility—"not in our lifetime"—German reunification dominated the headlines in 1990 as the Berlin Wall came tumbling down, and the idea of a united Germany sent shock waves through Europe all the way to Washington. Poland, having gained former German territory in East Prussia, eagerly sought for some sign that a unified Germany would respect the border established in the postwar era.

A unified Germany would bring together as a nation some 78 million citizens in the heart of Europe. As we go to press, negotiations concerning the many complex questions of reunification are continuing, and probably will continue for some time.

West Germany

Governmental affairs of the Bundesrepublik Deutschland (BRD), Federal Republic of Germany, are centered in its capital, Bonn. The country comprises ten Länder (states): Baden-Württemberg, Rhineland-Palatinate (Rheinland-Pfalz), the Saar, Bavaria (Bayern), North Rhine-Westphalia (Nordrhein-Westfalen), Lower Saxony (Niedersachsen), Schleswig-Holstein, Hamburg, and Bremen (the latter two have been city-states since the days of the Hanseatic League in medieval times).

Berlin was the capital of Germany from 1871 to the end of World War II. After the war, the three parts of the city occupied by the Allies became West Berlin, technically not part of West Germany. Political commentators, however, think that in the future it might once more become the German capital.

Since its establishment, the BRD government has been stable. It is parliamentary in structure, with a democratic constitution. The chief of state is the president, with mainly ceremonial duties. The chancellor (prime minister) heads the executive branch of government. The two houses of parliament are the Bundestag (lower chamber, with the most power) and the Bundesrat (upper chamber).

Since the 1950s, West Germany has seen healthy economic progress, with occasional setbacks. The West German population is about 62 million.

THE PEOPLE

The nature and appearance of the German people vary from region to region, ranging from the highland denizens of the south to the gregarious Rhinelanders to the more reserved inhabitants of the industrialized north. Descended from the several Germanic tribes mentioned above, the people of Germany today reflect the religious and cultural traditions of their forebears.

Prussian characteristics are *not* admired or emulated among the West Germans, especially among young people. They do tend, in the main, to be conformists, although some of the more progressive political and environmental movements in Europe have arisen in Germany. Among the people of the southern parts, you'll find an informality and a joie de vivre that are sometimes lacking in the Germans of the north. As a rule, the people of Germany are methodical, hard-working, and also hard-playing at such scheduled times as Oktoberfest, carnivals, weddings, and other festive occasions. Germany long ago pretty well did away with the class system, and the people as a whole are genial, outgoing, and friendly and helpful to visitors.

Many old traditions are still followed. You can see age-old costumes at folk festivals, particularly in Bavaria, the Black Forest, and Hesse. The land of castles and fairy tales, cuckoo clocks, oompah bands, and beerhall frivolity still exists, although sometimes you may be startled at the regimentation of German festivities.

The Germans are nature lovers, treasuring their woods and parklands. Physical fitness is almost a religion to many, from childhood until they can no longer hike along mountain trails or follow the fitness courses laid out in most parks and playgrounds. They are also neat, tidy, and esthetically oriented, as you'll appreciate when you observe their almost litter-free and flower-decked public places, and even more, their homes and their immediate surroundings.

LANGUAGES

High German is the official language, but some dialects persist. In the North German coastal regions and the Frisian islands, Lower Saxony, and Westphalia, the Low German dialect (Plattdeutsch) is both spoken and written, while the distinctive Frisian tongue is almost gone, used in only a tiny area. The Alemanni dialect is heard in the Black Forest, mingling with Franconian in the north and Swabian in the east.

In East Germany, the Wendish language is occasionally used. The Wends (Sorbs), descended from Western Slav tribes, live in the southeastern part of the country. Low German is also heard along the Baltic coast and islands.

---

2. The Culture

Their businesslike lifestyle hasn't stifled the creative spirit of the German people. Their admiration of and devotion to the arts has existed from early times. Kings, dukes, and even wealthy merchants encouraged and gave financial aid to talented painters, musicians, and artisans. Ordinary citizens staged morality plays, participated in folk dancing and singing, and honored their compatriots who showed creative abilities.

MUSIC

Music has been an important facet of life in Germany from tribal times, although there is no written record proving this until the Middle Ages. Presumably, there was music-making among tribal peoples in ancient times, and folk music in Germany today derives much from the tunes of long-past ages. Some sources claim that such instruments as clappers, rattles, scrapers, bells, lyres, and crude lutes probably encouraged Stone Age warriors in combat. In the Bronze Age, the long horns called *Lurs,* known throughout Europe, were added to the list. Ritual songs, shepherds' tunes, magic songs, and songs recounting tribal tradition were part of Celtic and Teutonic life.

In the Middle Ages, the folksongs varied, some being influenced by the imperial court, the Roman Catholic Church, and urban and village life. Dances followed in the same tradition, with tribal circle forms melding into couple steps. Peasant dances of the Middle Ages included an elaborate *Moresche* similar to the English morris dance. Bagpipes, shawms, hurdy-gurdies, and dulcimers sounded the tunes. In the towns, *Stadtpfeifer* (professional musicians) guilds played trumpets and drums to accompany dances and religious processions. In monasteries, the plain chant of Roman origin came into use, and art music slowly took shape. Latin was the language used by the monks, but from their chants the early vernacular hymns (religious folk songs) developed.

From about the 11th century, the *Minnesang* (love song) became widely known, the courtly love lyrics sung in the manner of the troubadours of France, accompanied by bowed and wind instruments. The Minnesang traditions were kept alive in later centuries by the *Meistergesang* (master song), a conservative form used by singing schools (guilds) in such towns as Augsburg and Nürnberg, bringing music into focus in middle-class culture. Development of the organ, an instrument known from the 8th century, was rapid as history goes. By the end of the 15th century, its use in Germany was widespread and was the most highly developed in Europe.

Musical establishments began to spring up based on church, court, and town. Court musicians, usually made up of a number of different groups, performed both sacred and secular music. One group was the ecclesiastical court *Kapelle,* with choirboys and clerics, replaced after the Reformation in Lutheran courts by *Kantorei* (professional voices). Vocalists were much higher up the social ladder than instrumentalists, except for trumpeters, the highest-ranking players, who were paid by the military. In cities and towns without courts, professional musicians' guilds were formed, sometimes paid by the town council. These performed for civic entertainment and also were used to sound the hours of the day from a tower in the town. The idea for the fable, "The Town Musicians of Bremen" by the Brothers Grimm, was based on such performers.

In the 16th century, music came to play a major role in university curricula in the Protestant north of Germany, both as a discipline and as a practical subject, with emphasis on church music. Martin Luther, who wrote both words and music of hymns, was an important influence on church music. Protestant hymns, borrowing from the style of secular tunes, gained popularity through much of Germany with the spread of music printing, although not in the Catholic south. The organ dominated the instrumental music of the 16th century, becoming larger, more sophisticated, and more widely used. A 17th-century leader in the field of church music was **Heinrich Schütz.**

German baroque music that developed from an adoption and fusing of foreign ideal and native tradition prepared the way for the great works that date from the 18th century on, especially in the art of the harpsichord and other keyboard instruments. In the course of about a century, German opera grew from vernacular works on religious and moral subjects to the operatic masterpieces of Wagner.

Early in the 18th century, in the baroque period, the names of musical geniuses whose works are known throughout the world began to resound in Germany. Ensembles became a part of life among university and town groups, one of which was started at Leipzig by **Georg Philipp Telemann,** whose descriptive music became popular. This ensemble later was headed by **Johann Sebastian Bach** (the Brandenburg Concertos), who was a master of all musical forms of his time. The baroque church cantata was one of the main German musical genres of the century, and Bach produced many fine ones for the Lutheran churches in which he served as cantor. After his death, he grew still more influential in German music in the last half of the 18th century because of his keyboard works, the tradition of which was maintained especially by his two talented sons. During the baroque period also, **George Frideric Handel** (*Messiah* and other fine oratorios) rose to prominence in his role as musician to the courts of Hanover and St. James, which resulted in his writing many of his compositions in London. Another famous German musician of this time was **Christoph Willibald Gluck,** who lived and worked in Vienna and Paris, producing *Orfeo ed Euridice* and *Iphigénie en Aulide*. **Wolfgang Amadeus Mozart** and **Franz Joseph Haydn,** though mainly connected with Vienna, cannot be omitted from any discussion of German music.

Musical theater was developing in Germany in the 18th century, a specialty of the stage being the *Lied,* an art song used with chamber instrumental music in its early stages and then with symphony orchestras. The German musical stage produced the *Singspiel,* which combined dialogue with music, following introduction of the form in Vienna. The hearty acceptance of the Singspiel became the base for the popularity of 19th-century German opera. Mozart's *Die Zauberflöte* (*The Magic Flute*) was the point of departure for German opera.

Ludwig von Beethoven, working in Vienna, helped usher in romanticism in music, his works showing that music could be a personal statement. Major examples are his symphonies, and he also produced the opera *Fidelio* in this period. Riches of music poured across Germany in the 19th century. **Franz Schubert** developed the song (Lieder) to a high art. **Felix Mendelssohn-Bartholdy, Robert Schumann,** and **Johannes Brahms** all produced masterworks.

Carl Maria von Weber is credited with giving definition to the form of opera for Germany. A giant in the music world, **Richard Wagner** embodied the love of the country's heritage in his operas, bringing German romantic opera to new heights in *Lohengrin, Tristan und Isolde, Der Ring des Nibelungen,* and *Parsifal,* among others. Following in his footsteps in the 19th and early 20th centuries was **Richard Strauss** (*Salome, Elektra,* and *Der Rosenkavalier*). The works of Strauss and **Max Reger,** both living and working in the 20th century, showed trends toward contemporary music.

During the Nazi era, several eminent composers had to leave their homeland and work abroad. Among these were **Paul Hindemith, Kurt Weill,** and **Arnold Schoenberg.**

In the present day as in the past, music is important in Germany. Notable modern and experimental composers working today are **Karlheinz Stockhausen, Carl Orff,** and **Hans Werner Henze.**

The Länder and cities keep alive the music of the masters and encourage modern composers by holding operatic weeks and various music festivals. Among major events is the Bayreuth Festival instituted by Wagner, who made the town a music landmark. Throughout the country, music lovers can pretty well take their pick of what to hear at most times, with opera, symphonic music, chamber music, vocal recitals, and choral singing—and just about everything else—available.

ART AND ARCHITECTURE

The earliest known Germanic art, as in many prehistoric tribes, was bone ornament, later replaced by metal objects. This applied art changed in northern Germany during the Bronze Age, from simple circles and other geometric forms to objects decorated with spirals and scrolls, also found in Ireland and southern Scandinavia. When the Germanic tribes spread out over the plain in what is today North Germany, different tribal cultures arose, each adding to the art forms of its people. Grotesque animal figures made their appearance among these pagan tribes of the north on ornaments and sculpture a few centuries after the birth of Christ.

The Romans left traces of their stay in southern Germany between the Danube and Rhine rivers. The ruins of buildings, little statues, earthenware, and glass have been found in the area.

In the Christian era, which took a firm hold under the auspices of Charlemagne and the Holy Roman Empire, new architectural forms came into play. German art, as we know it today, had its beginning during the 10th and early 11th centuries—known as the Ottonian period, for Emperor Otto I. The **Romanesque** period was roughly from 1000 to 1300. German architects, virtually all of whom are anonymous, built churches that were adaptations of the Roman basilica style. **St. Michaelis-Kirche** in Hildesheim (refer to Chapter XIV, on Lower Saxony and North Hesse) is often cited as the most outstanding example from this period. The present structure was reconstructed after World War II damage.

Decorative ivories, crucifixes, and book illumination were also characteristic of the period. Monasteries set up painting schools, and wall paintings of the time—around A.D. 1000—still exist on the island of Reichenau in Lake Constance.

The typically Romanesque **Cathedral of Speyer** was the 12th-century prototype for the imperial cathedrals in Mainz and Worms. Door carvings, bronze figures of Christ, and stained glass from this period show striking force despite their crudity.

Gothic architecture flowered in Europe, notably in France, from the 13th to the 16th centuries. The Romanesque influence was still strong, however, and Gothic did not establish as strong a foothold in Germany. The greatest of the German Gothic cathedrals, the **Dom** at Cologne, was started in 1284 but was not completed, as astonishing as it may sound, until 1880. The cathedral needed restoration after World War II. High Gothic is best represented by the **Münster** at Freiburg im Breisgau (see Chapter IX on the Black Forest), which is famous for its pierced octagonal belfry crowned by a delicate openwork spire.

Perhaps more representative of the period is the hall-type church, which had its origins in Westphalia. Called **Hallenkirche,** this type of church was characterized by aisles constructed at the same height as the nave. They were separated from the nave by tall columns. Many of these churches were built during the late Gothic period, the 14th and 15th centuries, which was a period of great artistic growth in Germany.

The Renaissance, which began around 1520 and lasted a century, did not take hold in Germany as it did in Italy. While Italy basked in its sunny glow, much of Germany still clung to the clouds of the Middle Ages. The finest German Renaissance town is perhaps Rothenburg (see Chapter XI "The Romantic Road").

The Thirty Years' War turned the country into a wasteland. But **baroque style,** an Italian import, brought a different kind of renaissance to Germany. The baroque swept southern Germany, especially Bavaria, though builders in the north tended to resist it. Perhaps because it was Italian, it was too closely associated with the Catholic Church in the Protestant strongholds of the north.

The baroque period in Germany began about 1660 and continued into the 18th century. Architectural forms no longer followed regular patterns. There was more freedom and more variety in design. The German and Danubian baroque artists, such as those of the Vorarlberg School, sought to give an impression of movement to their florid building designs. The splendor of the period is exemplified in the designs of such architects as **Lukas von Hildebrandt** and **J. B. Fischer von Erlach.** Berlin, as the center of an emerging Prussian state, moved into prominence as a seat of art and architecture. The baroque movement eventually dipped its brushes into the flippant paint of the rococo, and that movement brought even greater freedom and gaiety.

By the 19th century, many members of the rising and prosperous middle class in Germany preferred to decorate their homes in the **Biedermeier** style, with its lighter designs and flowing lines. By now the baroque and rococo styles were dead (the French Revolution had seen to that). Neoclassicism was strong. Once again, the south of Germany brought a lighter touch to this style than did the north. The

Romantic Movement followed the neoclassical period. For inspiration in this Neo-Gothic era, architects looked back to medieval days.

Historicism is a word often used to describe an era that characterized German architecture in the latter 1800s. No one represented this flamboyant movement better than **Ludwig II** of Bavaria at his palace **Neuschwanstein,** which even today is one of the major tourist attractions of the country.

By the end of the 19th century, the art nouveau movement—called Jugendstil in German—swept the country. It can be said to mark the beginning of contemporary architecture. It was characterized by mass production and solid construction, as architects used such materials as glass, steel, and concrete.

In the aftermath of World War I, the name of **Walter Gropius,** as leader of the **Bauhaus** movement, became prominent. Art and technique were wed at this architectural school whose primary aim was to unify arts and crafts in architecture. Founded at Weimar and directed there by Gropius from 1919, it moved to Dessau in 1925 (Gropius eventually settled in the United States). This movement was dissolved in 1933.

By then the so-called National Socialist, or "Third Reich," architecture was the law of the land, and under Hitler and his lieutenants, architecture as well as art became a form of propaganda. The Führer's dream of rebuilding Germany collapsed, of course. One of the sad legacies of World War II, aside from the loss of human life and the unbelievable suffering, was that many of Germany's greatest architectural treasures were virtually leveled by Allied bombing raids. Notable among these tragedies was the destruction of the city of Dresden, one of the most beautiful cities of Europe until 1945.

In the years after the war, both Germanies, East and West, have set for themselves the formidable task of rebuilding. In some cases, the past was swept away in war rubble, never to be rebuilt. On the other hand, many cathedrals and other buildings were restored in the old style, even though they were extensively damaged. In some instances, entire buildings have been carefully reconstructed in their original style.

As Germany advances through the 1990s, rebuilding continues on some structures. Cologne, for example, has already reconstructed a dozen Romanesque churches that had been destroyed. Buildings, both domestic and commercial, erected immediately after the war were hastily put up for convenience more than for architectural grandeur. However, in the prosperous Germany of today, there has also been a renewed interest and concern for style in modern architecture. The country weds a respect for its past with the expanding needs of a growing population.

The Artists and Architects

Before the 1400s, the names of individual German artists did not stand out. But by the 15th century, individual artists and sculptors, as well as architects, began to enter the art history books. Notable among these was **Tilman Riemenschneider** (1460–1531), "the master of Würzburg." A sculptor, he carved splendid altars at Würzburg, Bamberg, and Rothenburg.

Veit Stoss (1445–1533), another sculptor, was often called a "tormented genius." His celebrated *Annunciation* is displayed in the Gothic church of St. Lawrence in Nürnberg. **Stephan Lochner,** who died in 1451, was a leading member of the Cologne school. Lochner's altarpiece is today one of the outstanding artistic treasures of the cathedral at Cologne.

The premier name of the 16th century—indeed the best-known and most praised artist of the German school—was **Albrecht Dürer** (1471–1528), who was noted for his very imaginative, often symbolic, works and his incredible attention to detailed workmanship. Not only was this Nürnberg artist a master of painting, but he excelled at drawing and the woodcut, and he wrote a treatise on his theories of art.

No roster of 16th-century German artists would be complete without the name of **Lucas Cranach the Elder** (1472–1553), who is known for having painted the portraits of the leaders of the Reformation, most notably Martin Luther. His son, called **Cranach the Younger** (1515–86), followed in his father's footsteps. The other major member of this Danubian school was **Albrecht Altdorfer** (1480–1538). **Matthias Grünewald,** or Mathis Gothart Nithart, continued to show a healthy respect for the Middle Ages even though he lived from 1460 to 1528. A master colorist, he excelled in realistic studies of the crucifixion of Christ. His greatest work, the *Isenheim Altar* is in Colmar, in France. Another portrait painter, **Hans Holbein the Younger** (1497–1543), also turned to religious themes for his strikingly realistic works. With his graceful and inventive mature style, he became court painter to Henry VIII of England. He was the son of the famous German painter **Hans Holbein the Elder** (1460–1524), whose works included the *Altar of St. Sebastian.*

The 17th century produced fewer great artists and architects than the 16th. An exception was **Elias Holl** (1573–1646), a Renaissance architect whose notable works included the large Rathaus at Augsburg with its golden chamber. The building (see Chapter XI), was hit by bombs in 1944 but has been restored. Among sculptors in North Germany, **Andreas Schlüter** (1660–1714), praised for his virile style, is represented today by such works as the bronze equestrian statue of the Great Elector, his masterpiece, in the Court of Honor at Charlottenburg in West Berlin.

While painting and sculpture in the 18th century was not so outstanding as it was in the great 16th century, nonetheless many artists and architects left a rich legacy. **Dominikus Zimmermann** (1685–1766) was the master of the Bavarian rococo style. On the slopes of the Ammergau Alps, he created his masterpiece, the Wieskirche, or Wies Church, completed in 1754. Another architect (and in this case an engineer as well) was **Balthazar Neumann** (1687–1753), who was a master at creating both religious and secular buildings. He is today remembered for his pilgrimage church, Vierzehnheiligen (northeast of Bamberg), and his Residenz at Würzburg, one of the biggest baroque palaces in the country.

Often in the baroque era, an architect would work with a painter or sculptor. One of the most successful collaborations was that of the **Asam** brothers. **Egid Quirin Asam** (1692–1750) was a sculptor; his brother, **Cosmas Damian Asam** (1686–1739), a painter. They worked on churches at Weltenburg, Rohr, and Munich.

Arguably, the 19th century didn't produce many world-class artists in Germany. However, many artists, representing various movements of that century, from romantic to realist, distinguished themselves. These included **Wilhelm Leibl** (1844–1900), a master of the realist school, known for his scenes of common life in Bavaria, and **Caspar David Friedrich** (1774–1840), the most acclaimed painter of the Romantic Movement.

The often dreary, imitative art of the 19th century in Germany gave way in the 20th to schools and movements noted for their vigor and vitality. Often deliberately "revolutionary" and shocking (at least for their time), the works of many of these artists were destroyed or labeled decadent during the Third Reich, when painters were commanded to turn out works that espoused the "ideals" of National Socialism.

The new century began with the **expressionist school,** whose haunted, tormented view of the world was inspired by Van Gogh as well as Scandinavia's greatest painter, Edvard Munch. Expressionism grew out of **Die Brücke (The Bridge)** group founded in 1905. Until the outbreak of World War I, this controversial but influential group brought together such artists as **Karl Schmidt-Rottluff, Erich Heckel,** and **Ernst Ludwig Kirchner.** Kirchner, who committed suicide in 1938, did pictures that were sharply patterned and colored, with distorted figures.

For a time, Emil Hansen (1867–1956) was a member of the group. Better known by the name **Emil Nolde,** the painter lived in a house in the marsh in Seebüll in Schleswig-Holstein. He was known for his aggressive use of color and for his juxtaposition of the sacred and the profane. One of the most prominent expressionists was **Ernst Barlach,** a sculptor who was born in 1870 and died a year before the outbreak of World War II. His large, tormented works in bronze and wood include *Man in Doubt* and *The Avenger.*

Another major artistic movement, **Der Blaue Reiter** (The Blue Rider), was developed in Munich in 1911 by **Franz Marc** and **Wassily Kandinsky,** a Russian. Later, **August Macke** and **Paul Klee** reinforced the movement. Absorbed by the romantic and the lyrical, their dreamy works influenced abstract painting in the decades to come.

If the "Blue Riders" wanted to free art from rigid constraints, the **Dadaists** carried such a desire to the ultimate extreme. However, at the same time, such eminent artists as **George Grosz** (1893–1959) practiced a brutal realism. This painter and graphic artist, who came to the U.S. in 1932, was noted for his satirical pictures of German society and of war and capitalism.

Gropius' Bauhaus also attracted a number of painters and sculptors, such as **Wassily Kandinsky** and **Lyonel Feininger.**

As mentioned, art deteriorated under the Third Reich but bounced back in the postwar era with a number of movements. For example, **Max Ernst,** a German painter (born in 1891) who lived for many years in the U.S., was a leader in the Dada and surrealist movements and is credited with adapting the cubist technique of collage in a highly original manner. There is a lively art scene in West Germany today, with many important younger artists.

LITERATURE
Even before Gutenberg invented the first printing press in the Western world in the 15th century, German literature, both oral and written, was being produced. The first written literary work known is *The Lay of Hildebrand,* a narrative poem handed down by ancient storytellers and copied by monks at the Benedictine Abbey at Fulda. Such tales of valor, love, sorrow, and death were strong in oral tradition, with the Rhine Valley giving rise to many legends and songs through the centuries —Lohengrin, Roland, the Lorelei, and the Nibelungen being among the subjects.

The age of chivalry gave birth to lyric poetry in Germany. Like the troubadors in France, *Minnesingers* of the Holy Roman Empire roamed the land singing songs of love and derring-do inspired by the Crusades. One of these, **Walter von der Vogelweide,** a knight of the late 12th and early 13th centuries, is seen as the father of lyric poetry in Germany. Another early 13th-century poet of note was **Wolfram von Eschenbach,** whose epic, *Parsifal,* glorifies chivalry and religious devotion. By the 16th century, another "hero" had joined German folklore and literature, Til Eulenspiegel, a clownish fellow whose life around 1300 became the subject of story and song.

From the time of the Reformation (16th century), **Martin Luther**'s influence can be traced in many fields of the German life of the mind and spirit. His translation of the Bible into modern German was hailed as the first great literary work in the language. A Luther contemporary, **Hans Sachs,** a *Meistersinger,* was a prolific author of stories, poems, plays, and songs.

Publication of a picaresque novel, *Simplicissimus,* by **Hans Jakob Christoffel von Grimmelshausen** (17th century), marked the start of production of long prose narratives in the country. The Age of Enlightenment in German literature dawned in the late 17th century, inaugurated by **Friedrich Gottlieb Klopstock** in his epic, *Der Messias,* and his *Odes,* and it continued into the 18th century. Rationalization was the watchword in this period. Also in this era, the principles of German drama were laid out by **Gotthold Lessing.**

As a reaction to rationalization, a literary movement known as Sturm und Drang was born in the 18th century, marked especially by poetry and drama extolling both sentiment and grand passions and rejecting previous social, political, moral, and literary authority. It was at this time, that **Johann Wolfgang von Goethe** arrived on the scene, a giant of letters. Dramatist, novelist, philosopher, and

Germany's greatest poet, Goethe followed the pattern of the times in youth and early manhood (the *Urfaust* [or *Early Faust*], *Egmont,* and *The Sorrows of Young Werther*). However, he soon became disenchanted with Sturm und Drang, turning in mid-life after a stay in Italy to a classical mode (*Nausikaa*). During this period, he reworked *Faust,* so that the final product begins with storm and stress and then levels off into tranquil classicism. It was after his sojourn in Italy that he also produced *Wilhelm Meisters Lehrjahre,* a novel that served for decades as the prototype of the best German fiction.

Another literary immortal, **Friedrich von Schiller,** playwright and poet, a contemporary and friend of Goethe, also turned away from Sturm und Drang with the presentation of *Don Carlos,* a powerful historical drama honoring liberty. Similar dramas were *Wallenstein* and *William Tell.* Schiller's outlook placed his interests in the fields of history and philosophy.

As the literary world moved on from classicism to romanticism to historical romanticism, such names of world note appear as the brothers **Jakob** and **Wilhelm Grimm,** famous for their collection of fairy tales, folk tales, and myths, and **Heinrich Heine,** second only to Goethe as Germany's greatest poet.

A poet who became known for his work in the first quarter of the 20th century was **Rainer Maria Rilke.** Another German, the novelist **Erich Maria Remarque** (*All Quiet on the Western Front*), moved to the United States to escape the political conditions of his homeland. **Franz Kafka** became known for his novels of the absurd. **Bertolt Brecht** (*The Threepenny Opera* and *Mother Courage*) chose to live in East Germany after World War II.

Germany's winners of the Nobel Prize for Literature have been **Theodor Mommsen** (1902), classical scholar and historian; **Rudolf C. Eucken** (1908), philosopher; **Paul J. L. Heyse** (1910), novelist, dramatist, and poet; **Gerhart J. R. Hauptmann** (1912), dramatist; and novelists **Thomas Mann** (1929), **Hermann Hesse** (1946), and **Heinrich Böll** (1972).

The influence of German thought on the Western mind has been powerful, from as far back as the 13th century when **Albertus Magnus** became known as a scholastic philosopher, naturalist, and theologian. Through the centuries, other notable philosophers have been **Wilhelm von Leibniz, Immanuel Kant, Moses Mendelssohn, Arthur Schopenhauer, Friedrich Hegel, Karl Marx, Friedrich Engels,** and **Friedrich Wilhelm Nietzsche** (*Thus Spake Zarathustra*).

---

3. Food and Drink

The Germans like to eat, and they take food preparation and consumption seriously. Calorie- and cholesterol-conscious Americans may recoil at the sight of meals of dumplings, potatoes, some of the hundreds of Würste (sausages), breads, and pastries. The beer that may accompany such a meal is not in the "light" category, and helpings of food served in this country are not small. Heavy meals, however, do not keep many of the German people from their 4pm cream cake and coffee break, considered a compulsory afternoon event.

The German love affair with sausage is of ancient lineage, Wurst having been a major part of the national diet almost since there were people in the area. However, Germans get German cooking at home, and so more and more restaurants are offering foreign foods and Neue Küche (cuisine moderne), although the people of the country still like large helpings. Young people have become health-conscious, and are eschewing the overrich, overabundant fare of their ancestors. Health food shops are seen more and more frequently, and it is considered chic to patronize them. Young chefs, trained in Switzerland, France, or Italy, are returning to Germany in droves and opening Continental restaurants. Italians, many who came originally to Germany as "guest workers," have stayed to open up trattorias.

You can get German cookery as well. Every region has its own specialties, ranging from A (Aalsuppe, or eel soup) to Z (Zwiebelbrot, or onion bread). You might begin with a Hamburg herring dish, then follow with red-wine soup from the Palatinate and (for a main course) Berlin liver with Bavarian potato dumplings, then some Allgäu cheese, with some Zwetschenkuchen (plumcake) for dessert, rounded off by a glass of cherry brandy from the Black Forest. Fish comes from two seas in the north and also from the south, and from the many lakes.

The most common German food is the already mentioned sausage (or Wurst), and not Sauerkraut, as the world often mistakenly assumes. Germans take their Wurst with a bun and a dab of mustard (often smokey). Every region of Germany has its own sausage, but everybody's favorite seems to be Bratwurst from Nürnberg, made of seasoned and spiced pork. White sausage is called Weisswurst, and it's often a medley of veal, calves' brains, and spleen. As tradition has it, this sausage should be eaten only between midnight and noon. Bauernwurst, or farmer's sausage, and Knockwurst are variations of the Frankfurter. The Frankfurter originated in Frankfurt, although another country made it even more famous as the hot dog. Small Frankfurters, which are called wieners or Vienna sausages in the U.S. and Wienerwurst in Germany, are, surprise of surprises, known as Frankfurters in Austria. Leberwurst is a specialty of Hesse. Rinderwurst and Blutwurst, beef sausage and blood sausage, are specialties of Westphalia, and are often consumed with Steinhäger, or corn brandy.

Bavarians are hearty eaters, devouring such dishes as Züngerl (pig's tongue) or Wammerl (pig's stomach), most often with cabbage. Potato dumplings, or Klösse, also are served with many dishes, and Leber (liver) dumplings enjoy a great popularity. Semmel (bread) dumplings most often accompany the most famous meat dish of Bavaria, Schweinebraten, or roast pork. Also with their devotees are Kalbshaxen (veal shank) and Schweinshaxen (roast knuckle of pork). At Altmühl, carp is praised by gastronomes, as is a superb trout, Forelle. Lake Constance has almost three dozen types of fish, of which the salmonlike Felchen is the most prized.

Berlin has its own hearty cuisine, no dish being more famous than Eisbein (knuckle of pork). The "back-up" dishes to this main course are Sauerkraut and Pease pudding, the latter a thick pea purée. Soul food to a Berliner is Erbsensuppe (yellow split pea soup) served with Bockwurst. If you're not a true carnivore, you might skip the Berliner Schlachtplatte, most often containing pig's kidneys, boiled pork, along with liver and fresh blood sausage. Goose, prepared in several different ways, is popular in Germany, especially Berlin. A favorite of the famed Berlin conductor, Herbert von Karajan, was Königsberger Klopse, pingpong meatballs with capers and herring. A leg of pork with red cabbage is also a classic.

Along with Wurst, herring has long enjoyed a place on the German table. It is prepared in countless ways, including herring tartare or Bismarck. Perhaps the most common is Matjeshering, served with boiled potatoes.

From the Lüneburg Heath comes the most delectable lamb in Germany. Called Heidschnückenbraten, it is most often served roasted. Most visitors will prefer this lamb to such local dishes as Braunkohl mit Brägenwurst, or kale with brain sausage.

The chefs of Bremen and Hamburg are known for an Aalsuppe, or eel soup, which is often cooked with fruit. Neptune rules on the tables of the East Frisian islands, where local tables feature everything from fresh crab to eggs laid by seagulls. Fish is also a staple of the diet of Schleswig-Holstein, along with that sailors' favorite, Labskaus, a medley of such ingredients as potatoes, pickled meat, beer, and herring. The Holstein Schnitzel from this region is similar to the Wiener Schnitzel. From Lübeck comes the famed Marzipan.

Westphalia is best known for its delectable hams, which often weigh as much as 30 pounds, but it also produces a number of other plates. Ham is invariably accompanied by a dark pumpernickel bread. A highly spiced boiled beef, Pfefferpotthast, is the peppery local goulash. From the many freshwater rivers of the area come a wide variety of fish.

One dish from the Rhineland that has crossed the oceans of the world is Sauerbraten, which is braised pickled beef. This dish is often marinated for three days in a spicy vinegar before it is slowly cooked in robust red wine. Rotkohl, or red cabbage, another famous German dish, is its usual accompaniment. Himmel und Erde (heaven and earth) is a medley of potatoes and apples with blood sausage, and Hase im Topf is a tasty rabbit pâté flavored with various "brews."

Pork is king in Hesse. Everything from that animal goes into the pot, including pig's trotters and ears. Bacon pie, or Speckkuchen, is a tasty concoction, as is Kasseler Rippchen, or smoked pickled loin of pork.

Swabia and Franconia enjoy their own cuisines and if you indulge in them you may need to start a *Diät*, or diet, when you return home. The most popular soup of the region is Flädlesuppe (crêpelike pancakes are cut into strips and added to this soup). Instead of dumplings, Spätzle (pasta made of eggs, salt, and flour) often accompanies the Sunday roast. This noodle dish is a golden yellow in color. The Swabians have their own version of ravioli, Maultaschen, which are filled with minced meat and often flavored with onions and spinach. This is served in a rich broth or browned in fat. One of the best-known German confections comes from the Black Forest; a cherry cake called Schwarzwälderkirschtorte, it is usually eaten with afternoon coffee. The people of this region also consume a lot of Speck, or smoked bacon.

The people of Franconia are known for their honest cookery—that means it's rather plain and homelike fare without a lot of fancy adornments. This cuisine is represented by such dishes as the Bamberger Krautbraten, meat-stuffed cabbage served with potato dumplings.

BEER

Nowhere else are there so many good and different kinds of **beer**. Nowadays, many inns brew their own. The world's oldest brewery is in Bavaria, but the Bavarians are not the only ones who know about beer, which in Germany, incidentally, comes straight from the barrel. Export beers and the rather more bitter Pils, the most popular kinds, are also produced in Berlin, Hamburg, the Ruhr, Hesse, and Stuttgart. Altbier, a very early product of the brewer's art, is today to be found all over Germany. Berliner Weisse is another kind of beer (made from wheat, like a Bavarian white beer), but with a dash of raspberry or woodruff syrup. Malt beer is dark and sweet and contains hardly any alcohol, whereas "March beer" is also dark but considerably stronger.

In Germany, if you go into a beerhall and ask the bartender for *ein Bier,* you'll probably get the standard stock beer, Vollbier, which is 4% proof. More potent is Export at 5% or Bockbier at 6%. Helles Bier is light and brewed from malt that the local brewery, or Brauerei, has dried and baked. When the malt has been darkly roasted and fermented for much longer, it becomes dunkles Bier, or dark beer. Pils, or Pilsener, beers are light and contain more hops. Dortmund has earned a reputation in this field. In summer, Bavarians flock to beer gardens to enjoy their local brews, which are sometimes accompanied by white or red radishes and crisp pretzels.

WINES OF GERMANY

For centuries, Germany has made delightful, thirst-quenching wines, renowned for their natural lightness and their balance of sweetness and acidity. Climate, soil, and grape varieties all contribute to the success of the wine industry. Most vineyards flourish on steep hillsides, with protection from harsh winds provided by wooded neighboring hills. These vineyards rise mainly from the Rhine River and its tributaries, profiting by the reflected warmth from the sunlit water. Slow maturing of the grapes gives the German wines their typical fresh, fruity acidity.

There are 11 German wine-growing districts: Ahr, Mosel-Saar-Ruwer, Mittelrhein, Rheingau, Nahe, Rheinhessen, Rheinpfalz, Hessische Bergstrasse,

Franken, Württemberg, and Baden. Their wines range from vigorous reds to fragrant, aromatic whites, with Rheingau being the home of one of the most popular and best known, Riesling. There are German wines for every taste and occasion. "Trocken" (dry) and "Halbtrocken" (semidry) are often indicated on the labels, which also give other vital statistics about the bottles' contents, such as the growing region, the year the grapes were harvested, the town and vineyard from which the grapes came, the grape variety, the quality level, and other data.

There are two basic categories of wine allowed in Common Market countries: table wine and quality wine from specified regions. In addition, Germany produces its famed Qualitätswein mit Prädikat (quality wines with special attributes). This latter category includes Kabinett, Spätlese, Auslese, Beerenauslese, Eiswein, and Trockenbeerenauslese, the crowning achievement of German viticulture. Qualitätswein b.A. is a light, fruity wine, which, along with Kabinett, is good with lightly seasoned dishes. Spicy dishes call for Qualitätswein (quality wines) or Prädikat Spätlese, while such dishes as roasts and game go best with white and red wines: Riesling, Ruländer, Spätburgunder, or Lemberger. Delicate, medium-dry wines are best with mild cheeses, spicy or fragrant ones with strong cheeses. For a leisurely drink after your meal, perhaps with savory snacks, try a noble, full-bodied wine such as a fine Spätlese or Auslese.

Choosing the right wine to go with your meal is no longer governed by rigid rules, and there are a wide variety of bottles from which to select. Drink the wine you like best with your meal, and you can be helped in your choice by knowing some of the basic facts given above.

A visit to Germany is not complete without a tour of one of the wine-growing districts, which stretch from the middle Rhine at Bonn south to Lake Constance, filled with classic scenery of imposing castle ruins, cathedrals, black-and-white gabled houses, elegant spas, and little Brothers Grimm villages. For information on a trip through one or more of these regions, ask at the **German Wine Information Bureau,** 79 Madison Ave., New York, NY 10016 (tel. 212/213-7028), or at the **German National Tourist Office,** 747 Third Ave., New York, NY 10017 (tel. 212/308-3300).

OTHER LIBATIONS

A clear corn brandy and juniper Schnapps are made in North Germany and Westphalia and are often served in earthenware bottles. From the Black Forest come clear fruit brandies and delicate herb liqueurs, often produced in places where, centuries ago, they were invented by monastic friars.

---

4. Fast Facts for West Germany

For the first-time visitor, being armed with some "facts of life" can ease adjustment not only into Frankfurt and Munich but into the fascinating countryside itself.

Such problems as tipping must be faced even before you check into your hotel room. There are any number of situations that could mar your trip. Included in this is a medical emergency, of course. I don't promise to answer all your needs in a small section of this guide, but there are a variety of services available in Germany that you need to know about.

In a large establishment, a concierge is usually reliable for dispensing information, getting theater tickets, arranging tours, whatever. In many of the smaller third-class hotels and pensions listed in this guide, you're pretty much on your own, as the proprietor is generally overworked. Therefore, the following summary of pertinent facts may prove helpful.

Many practical facts, such as transportation within Munich, the address of a local U.S. consulate, or the location of the local American Express, are given under the individual chapter headings.

BANKS AND EXCHANGES: Banks are open Mon. to Fri. from 8:30am to 1pm and 2:30 to 4pm (Thurs. until 5:30pm). They are closed Sat., Sun., and holidays. Money exchanges at airports and border-crossing points are generally open daily from 6am to 10pm. Exchanges at border railroad stations are kept open for arrivals of all international trains.

CAMPING AND CARAVANING: Some 2,100 German camping sites, located in the most beautiful and popular resort districts, and with all the necessary facilities, welcome visitors from abroad. Blue signs bearing the international camping symbol—a black tent on a white background—make it easy to find camping sites. Some 400 camping sites are kept open during the winter. Information on camping matters and camping sites is available on request from the **Allgemeiner Deutscher Automobil-Club** (ADAC), Am Westpark 8, D-8000 München 70, and the **Deutscher Camping-Club,** Mandlestrasse 28, D-8000 München 40.

CASINOS: Roulette and baccarat are just some of the international games that can be played at the spa resorts of Germany, the most famous of which is Baden-Baden in the Black Forest. It was from Bad Homburg, close to Frankfurt, that roulette was "exported" to Monte Carlo. Other famous casinos are at Wiesbaden and at Garmisch-Partenkirchen, south of Munich. Admission tickets are available to persons over 21 years of age upon presentation of a valid passport.

CLIMATE: It can be very cold in winter, especially in January, and very warm in summer. But even in July and August, there may be days when it's cool and rainy. You have to dress for "all occasions." For example, on the same trip you can be chilled on a Bavarian Alp, yet the next day be running around in a bikini at Lake Constance. Winters tend to be mild, springs "stretched out," and summers most agreeable. In fact, I've enjoyed many a Bavarian-style "Indian summer" until late in October. The most popular tourist months are May to October, although winter travel to Germany is becoming increasingly popular, obviously to the ski areas in the Alps.

CLOTHING: There are no dress regulations to speak of. Collars, ties, and jackets are worn in the evening in first-class bars and restaurants.

CLOTHING SIZES: German clothing and footwear sizes often vary slightly from international standards. Sometimes the sizes are quite different. Therefore you should always try on or at least ask for the appropriate continental size.

CURRENCY: Refer to "The Deutsche Mark and the Dollar," in the Introduction.

CUSTOMS: In general, items required for your personal and professional use or consumption may be brought in duty free. No duty is levied for your private car, provided that it is reexported. Gifts are duty free up to a total value of 620 DM ($316.15), to include a maximum of 115 DM ($68.30) in items from non-

Common Market countries. This limitation covers all commodities, including food, imported as gifts or for your personal use or consumption.

The following items are permitted into West Germany duty free (imports from Common Market countries in parentheses): 200 (300) cigarettes or 100 (150) cigarillos, or 50 (75) cigars, or 250 (400) grams of tobacco. Americans or Canadians not residing in Europe may import double the tobacco allowance. You are also allowed 1 (1.5) liter(s) of liquor above 44 proof, or 2 (3) liters of liquor less than 44 proof, or 2 (3) liters of sparkling wines and 2 (4) liters of other wines; 50 (75) grams of perfume and .25 (.375) liters of eau de cologne; 250 (750) grams of coffee, 100 (150) grams of tea. The duty-free tobacco and alcoholic beverage allowances are authorized for persons age 17 and above only, the coffee quota for persons age 15 and above only. All duty-free allowances are authorized only when the items are carried in the traveler's personal baggage.

On returning to the United States, American citizens who have been out of the country for at least 48 hours or more are allowed to bring back to their home country $400 worth of merchandise duty free—that is, if they haven't claimed a similar exemption within the past 30 days. Beyond this free allowance, the next $1,000 worth of merchandise is assessed at a flat rate of 10% duty. If you make purchases in Germany, it is important to keep your receipts. The duty-free limit on gifts sent from abroad has been increased to $50.

DOCUMENTS FOR ENTRY: U.S. and Canadian citizens need only a valid passport to enter the Federal Republic of Germany and West Berlin.

DRUGSTORES: There are two types: the Apotheke, which sells pharmaceuticals, and the Drogerie, which sells cosmetics and over-the-counter drugs. German pharmacies are open during regular business hours. All post lists of pharmacies that are open nights, on Sunday, and on holidays. It's always possible to get a prescription filled outside of business hours.

ELECTRICAL APPLIANCES: In most places the electrical current is 220 volts AC, 50 cycles. Therefore, adapters will be needed for your U.S. appliances. Many of the leading hotels will supply you with an adapter if you ask for one, or you can bring one along with you.

EMBASSIES: The **U.S. Embassy** is at Deichmans Avenue, D-5300 Bonn–Bad Godesberg (tel. 0228/33-91); the **Canadian Embassy,** Friedrich-Wilhelmstrasse 18, D-5300 Bonn (tel. 0228/23-10); and the **British Embassy,** Friedrich-Ebert-Allee, D-5300 Bonn (tel. 0228/34-40).

FILM: German film is among the best in the world, and is readily available in all cities and small towns. If you want color, as most visitors do, the price is tripled.

HOLIDAYS: Public holidays are January 1; Easter (Good Friday through Easter Monday); May 1 (Labor Day); Ascension Day (10 days before Pentecost); Corpus Christi (10 days after Pentecost); June 17 (Unity Day); November 1 (All Saints Day); November 17 (day of prayer and repentance); and Christmas (lasting through December 26).

INFORMATION: Nearly all major towns and certainly all cities in the Federal Republic have tourist offices. The headquarters of the **German National Tourist Board** is at Beethovenstrasse 69, D-6000 Frankfurt am Main (tel. 069/75-72-0). Before you go, you'll find the German National Tourist Office in New York at 747 Third Ave., New York, NY 10017 (tel. 212/308-3300); in Los Angeles at 444 So. Flower St., Los Angeles, CA 90017 (tel. 213/688-7332); and in Montréal at 2 Fundy, Place Bonaventure, Montréal, PQ H5A 1B8 (tel. 514/878-9885).

LANGUAGE: The official language, of course, is German, but English is commonly spoken, at least at major hotels and restaurants and in the principal tourist areas.

LAUNDRY: Upper-bracket hotels have facilities for having your clothes laundered, but the service is very expensive. To cut costs, you can use a laundromat, available in all major cities and towns. They are called Wäscherei in the telephone directories. Coin laundries are called Münzwäscherei.

MAIL DELIVERY: General delivery—mark it "poste restante"—can be used in any major town or city in the Federal Republic. Your mail may be picked up upon presentation of a valid identity card or passport.

MEDICAL: Most major hotels in West Germany have a doctor on staff or on call. If you can't get hold of a doctor, the best thing to do is to dial the emergency service, which is open day and night. The number is listed in every telephone directory under the heading of **Ärztlicher Notdienst** (Emergency Medical Service). The Red Cross can also help in cases of illness or accident. Medical and hospital services in the Federal Republic and West Berlin aren't free. It is therefore advisable, before departure, to be sure you have appropriate insurance coverage.

METRIC CONVERSION: In Germany, you will likely face a whole new way of measuring. Germany uses the metric system of measurement, and even the temperature will be expressed differently, in centigrade.

NEWSPAPERS: The *International Herald Tribune* is widely distributed throughout the Federal Republic. News magazines such as *Time* and *Newsweek* are sold at major newsstands in the big cities.

PETS: Leave Fido or Morris at home. Germany has rigid controls on pets. If you're traveling with a pet, you must have proof of a rabies vaccination.

POSTAGE: An airmail letter to the United States or Canada costs 1.40 DM (85¢) for 5 grams and 1.60 DM (95¢) for 10 grams. Postcards sent airmail to the United States or Canada cost .90 DM (50¢). Domestic letters sent from West Germany to points within West Germany cost .80 DM (45¢), postcards sent within the country cost .60 DM (35¢). These rates are subject to change, of course, and should be verified on the spot in case there is a postal increase by the time of your visit. Post offices are generally open Mon. to Fri. from 8am to 6pm and on Sat. from 8am to noon. Railway terminal post offices, found in all principal cities, are open weekdays until late evening.

RELIGIOUS SERVICES: Roman Catholic and Protestant churches are found throughout Germany. Your hotel should be a helpful source in locating a church near you.

REST ROOMS: Women's toilets are usually marked with an "F" for Frauen, and men's toilets are marked with an "H" for Herren. Germany, frankly, doesn't have enough public toilets, except in transportation centers. The locals have to rely on bars, cafés, or restaurants, which isn't always appreciated unless you're a paying customer. In a public toilet, tipping is customary, usually .30 DM (16¢). If you need soap and towel, give something extra.

ROMANTIK HOTELS: Throughout Germany you'll encounter hotels with a "Romantik" in their names. This is not a chain, but a voluntary association of small inns and guesthouses that have only one element in common: they are usually old and charming, and romantic in architecture. If you like a traditional ambience as opposed to bandbox modern, then a Romantik Hotel might be for you. The requirement is that the hotel be in a historic building (or at least one of vintage date) and personally managed by the owner. Usually you get a regional cuisine, and good, personal service, along with an old-fashioned setting and cozy charm. Whenever possible, I always book myself into one, savoring a life known to travelers years ago. Sometimes the plumbing could be better, and standards of comfort vary widely, but all of them have been inspected.

SAFETY: Whenever you're traveling in an unfamiliar city or country, stay alert. Be aware of your immediate surroundings. Wear a moneybelt or keep your wallet in an inside pocket. Don't sling your camera or purse over your shoulder; wear the strap diagonally across your body. This will minimize the possibility of your becoming a victim of crime. Every society has its criminals. It's your responsibility to be aware and alert even in the most heavily touristed areas.

SHOPPING AND SOUVENIRS: No one wants to return home without an attractive or useful souvenir, and small "typically German" articles can be obtained at reasonable prices. And as you travel throughout the country, you can often buy direct from the manufacturer: jewelry in Idar Oberstein, china in the Bavarian Forest, stoneware in Westerwald, woodcarvings in Upper Bavaria, cuckoo clocks in the Black Forest, and wine from the growers.

SHOPPING HOURS: These can vary slightly from state to state. Shops are generally open from 9am to 6:30pm Mon. to Fri. and from 9am to 2pm on Sat. (except the first Sat. of the month, when they remain open till 4pm).

SWIMMING: Nearly every town, especially the popular tourist resorts, has one or more outdoor and indoor pools (some heated). More and more hotels also have their own facilities for guests. German beaches are found along the North and Baltic seas. Thermal- and mineral-water swimming pools may be found in a great number of health resorts and spas.

TAXES: As a member of the Common Market, the Federal Republic of Germany imposes a tax on most goods and services known as a value added tax (VAT) or, in German, *Mehrwertsteuer.* You can get a refund of approximately 10% of the Mehrwertsteuer when you leave the country. Most large establishments have the appropriate forms to fill out for the refund—look for the sign "tax free" and request these when you make purchases. At the airport before departure, take the forms and receipts to the customs office, which will stamp them for you. Attach the receipts to the forms and mail them to the stores where you made the purchases. You should receive your refunds through the mail.

Tax for books and materials of educational or cultural content is only 7%, but nearly everything else is taxed at 14%. That includes everything from a vital necessity such as gas to luxury items such as jewelry. Note that the purchase of goods, such as a German camera, has the 14% already factored into the price, whereas services, such as paying a garage mechanic to fix your car, will have the 14% added to the bill.

TELEGRAMS: The post office runs the telegraph service. You can go directly to a post office or else file a telegram at your hotel desk.

TELEPHONES: Local and long-distance calls may be placed from all post offices and coin-operated public telephone booths. The unit charge is .20 DM (14¢) or two 10-pfennig coins. All towns and cities in the Federal Republic may be dialed directly by using the prefix listed in the telephone directory above each local heading. Telephone calls made through hotel switchboards can double, triple, or *whatever,* the charge. Therefore try to make your calls outside your hotel. For telephone information within West Germany, dial 1188. For international telephone information, phone 0118.

TELEX AND FAX: These most often are sent through your hotel.

TIME: West Germany is six hours ahead of Eastern Standard Time in the United States. Germany operates on Central European Time, which places it one hour ahead of Greenwich Mean Time. Summer time begins in West Germany in April and ends in September—there is a slight difference in the dates from year to year—so there may be a period in early spring and in the fall when there is a seven-hour difference between U.S. Eastern Standard Time and Central European Time. Always check carefully if you're traveling at these periods, especially if you plan to catch a plane.

TIPPING: In restaurants, if the bill says "Bedienung," that means a service charge has already been added, so just round up to the nearest mark. If not, add 10% to 15%. Round up to the nearest mark for taxis. Bellhops get 2 DM ($1.20) per bag, as does the doorman at your hotel, restaurant, or nightclub. Maids aren't tipped in Germany, but tip the concierge if he or she did some special favor such as obtaining hard-to-get theater or opera tickets. Tip hairdressers or barbers 5% to 10%.

WINTER SPORTS: More than 300 winter-sports resorts are found in the German Alps and such wooded hill country as the Harz Mountains, the Black Forest, and the Bavarian Forest at altitudes of up to 1,500 meters. In addition to outstanding ski slopes, trails, lifts, and jumps, toboggan slides, and skating rinks, many of the larger resorts also offer ice hockey, ice boating, and bobsledding. Curling is very popular, especially in Upper Bavaria. The Olympic sports facilities at Garmisch-Partenkirchen enjoy international renown, as do the ski jumps of Oberstdorf and the artificial-ice speed-skating rink at Inzell. More than 250 ski lifts are found in the German Alps, the Black Forest, and the Harz Mountains. Information on winter-sports facilities is available from local tourist bureaus and the offices of the German National Tourist Board.

YOUTH HOSTELS: Germany has some of the finest youth hostels in the world. There are 537 of them, many in old castles or bucolic settings. Visitors up to 26 years of age pay 11 DM ($6.55) to 22.50 DM ($13.35) per night. Persons over 26, provided there is room, are charged 13.50 DM ($8) to 24 DM ($14.25). Space allowing, adults are given a bed only after 6pm. In Bavaria, adults over 27 years of age may not stay in youth hostels. For young people up to age 26, a junior membership card is issued for 15 DM ($8.90); an adult membership costs 24 DM ($14.25). Membership cards stamped for families also cost 24 DM. These are annual dues. An additional 2 DM ($1.20) is charged when the card is first issued.

Membership cards of associations affiliated with the International Youth Hostel Federation are regarded as the equivalent of German membership cards. Foreigners who are not members of an association affiliated with the IYHF, and who are only temporarily in Germany, must obtain an international guest card at 30 DM ($17.80). The average price for a meal in one of these hostels is 7 DM ($4.15). Breakfast, however, is included in the rate.

Application should be made in writing to Deutsches Jugendherbergswerk (German Youth Hostel Association), Postfach 220, D-4930 Detmold 1, or to the American Youth Hostel Association, 132 Spring St., New York, NY 10012 (tel. 212/431-7100).

FRANKFURT AM MAIN AND ENVIRONS

Your first glimpse of Germany will very likely be this thriving industrial metropolis. Only the country's seventh-largest city, Frankfurt am Main is Germany's most important transportation center. Its huge airport, Flughafen Frankfurt/Main, welcomes every major international airline. More than 1,200 trains run in and out of its massive 19th-century station, the largest in Germany.

As the home of the Bundesbank (Federal Bank), Frankfurt is also the financial center of the Federal Republic. Since the Rothschilds opened their first bank here in their hometown in 1798, it has been a major banking city, currently containing more than 220 banks and the third-largest stock exchange in the country. It is also a heavily industrial city, with more than 2,450 factories operating around the ford (*Furt*) on the Main where the Frankish tribes once settled.

Frankfurt has also been the home of Germany's most important trade fairs since way back around A.D. 1200. The international Frankfurt fairs in spring and autumn bring some 1.2 million visitors to the city, causing a logjam in its hotels. Fairs include the Motor Show, the Textile Fair, the Chemical Industries Fair, the Cookery Fair, and the International Book Fair. The International Book Fair, perhaps the best known, is the most important meeting place in the world for the acquisition and sale of book rights and translations, drawing some 5,500 publishers from nearly 100 countries.

But in spite of its commerce and industry, Frankfurt is also a tourist city, offering numerous attractions to its many visitors. One out of 11 persons in Frankfurt on any given day is actually a stranger to the city.

1. Orientation

When arriving in Frankfurt by air, the best way to get from the airport to Frankfurt is by the airport train. A taxi will charge from 30 DM ($17.80), maybe more, but the train costs only 4 DM ($2.40) in peak hours, 3.40 DM ($2) at other times. Tickets for the train must be purchased in advance at automatic ticket-vending machines. Every 10 minutes a district train (S-Bahn) heads for the Hauptbahnhof, and every 20 minutes one leaves for the Hauptwache in the city center. Travel time is between 11 and 15 minutes, making this far faster than other means of transport. Every 15 to 30 minutes a no. 61 city bus runs between the airport and the Sudbahnhof in Frankfurt Sachsenhausen. One-way fare for the bus is 4 DM ($2.40) in peak hours, 3.40 DM ($2) at other times.

To and from the airport, there are direct connections with 14 other S-Bahn stations in the direction of Mainz and Wiesbaden and also direct intercity connections with 64 main stations between Amsterdam and Munich, as well as the special Lufthansa Airport Express to Bonn, Cologne, and the Düsseldorf airport.

The large, bustling main railway station, the Hauptbahnhof, may be the arrival point for Eurailpass holders and others traveling by train. At the western edge of the center of town, it opens onto the Am Hauptbahnhof. As you walk out of the station, Düsseldorferstrasse will be on your left, Baselerstrasse on your right, heading south toward the Main River. From this rail square, you have a choice of three streets heading east to the center of the old town: Taunusstrasse, Kaiserstrasse, and Münchnerstrasse. Münchnerstrasse leads directly into the heartbeat Theaterplatz, with its opera house. The most northerly street, Taunusstrasse, leads to three of the major squares of the Altstadt (old town) in the southern part of the city: Goetheplatz, Rathenauplatz, and (most important) the Hauptwache, with its good subway (U-Bahn) connections. In this section of Frankfurt, along Kaiserstrasse, some of the best shops are found; and major attractions, including Goethe-Haus, are nearby.

The Main River runs slightly south of the Altstadt. Many bridges, including Alte Main-Brücke and Ober Main-Brücke, cross this vital river. On the left bank of the Main is a popular district, Alt Sachsenhausen, center of the apple-wine taverns (more about them later). For other major attractions, you'll have to branch out, heading east to the Frankfurt Zoo or northwest to the Palmengarten (both easily reached by public transportation).

GETTING AROUND

The city of Frankfurt and its surrounding area, up to a radius of 24 miles, are connected by a number of fast, modern means of transport, under the Frankfurt Transport Federation (FVV). City and overland buses, trams, subways, and district trains can be used within fare zones at one price, including transfers. Tickets are obtained at *blue* coin-operated automatic machines labeled Fahrscheine. These machines will change up to 5 DM ($2.95). A 24-hour ticket with unlimited travel costs 8 DM ($4.75), half price for children. Zone charts and additional information in six languages are displayed on all the automatic machines. Be sure to buy your ticket before you board the transport conveyance. If you are caught traveling without the proper card, you are subject to a fine of about 60 DM ($35.65).

Tickets for the GermanRail within a 30-mile radius of Frankfurt, plus necessary additional tickets, may be obtained from the *red* coin-operated machines in the main section foyer of the railway station in front of the platforms. The machines return your change.

If for some reason public transport is not feasible, you'll have to rely on taxi service. Radio taxis are on call day and night, either at marked taxi stands or by calling 23-00-01, 25-00-01, or 23-00-33. There is no extra charge for pickup. The fare is charged per trip, not per passenger or per piece of luggage transported. The flat rate is 3.60 DM ($2.15) plus 1.80 DM ($1.05) per kilometer.

FAST FACTS

American Express: Offices are centrally located at Steinweg 5 (tel. 069/2-10-51), open Mon. to Fri. from 8:45am to 5:30pm (Sat. from 9am to noon). Unless

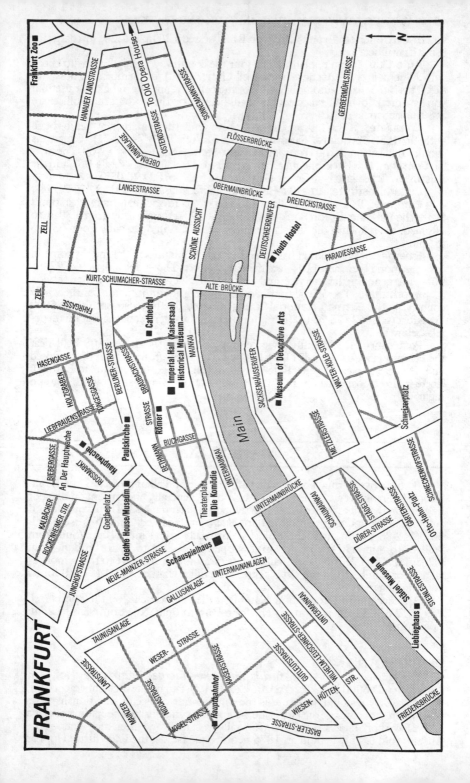

you have an American Express card, you'll be assessed a 2-DM ($1.20) surcharge for using its mail services.

Auto Club: If you're planning to tour the country, you might want to check with **Allgemeiner Deutscher Automobil-Club (ADAC)** for membership possibilities. This is the major automobile club of the country, and it can be most useful if you have breakdowns or experience other difficulties on the road. Its main offices are at Schumannstrasse 6 (tel. 069/74-30-1).

Consulates: If you lose a passport or have some such emergency, get in touch with the **U.S. Consulate,** Siesmayerstrasse 21 (tel. 069/74-00-71). Canadians should contact **Kandische Fremdemveikehr-Samt,** Taunusstrasse 52-60. The **British Consulate** is at Bockenheimer Landstrasse 61-3 (tel. 06102/72-04-06), and the **Australian Consulate** is at Grosse Gallusstrasse (tel. 06102/20-057).

Cultural institute: Amerika-Haus is at Staufenstrasse (tel. 06102/72-27-94).

Currency: To exchange dollars into marks, go to the main railway station's **Deutsche Verkehrs-Kredit Bank** (tel. 069/264-82-01), open daily from 6:30am to 10pm, or the branch at the airport (tel. 069/690-35-06), open daily from 7:30am to 9pm.

Emergencies: Frankfurt has several emergency numbers that might come in handy. Among them are: 110—accident; 112—fire; 112—first aid; 069/792-02-00—emergency medical service; and 069/660-72-71—emergency dental service.

Information: The official tourist office, dispensing information for the whole country, is the **German National Tourist Board,** Beethovenstrasse 69, D-6000 Frankfurt (tel. 069/75-72-0). (For information bureaus, refer to the section on hotels, below.)

Post office: In Frankfurt, the central post office is at Zeil 108-110, near the Hauptwache (tel. 069/211-44-17), which is open from 8am to 6pm; closed Sun. Go here to pick up general delivery mail (called "poste restante" in Europe). There is also a post office in the main railway station, which is open both day and night.

2. Where to Stay

If you arrive during a busy trade fair, you may find all of the better hotels full. Rooms in Frankfurt are rather expensive. You can generally find a room on the spot by going to the tourist office in the railway station, near track 23. There you will find an office of **Verkehrsamt Frankfurt am Main,** Im Hauptbahnhof, Nordseite (tel. 069/212-88-49). In summer the office is open daily from 8am to 10pm (Sun. from 9:30am to 8pm). In the off-season it is open from 8am to 9pm (on Sun. from 9:30am to 8pm). During a particularly busy season you may have to take a room as far as 2 or 3 miles from the city's center. The office charges 3 DM ($1.80) for its hotel-finding services.

Another tourist information center is at the Hauptwache, on the B level (tel. 069/212-87-08), open Mon. to Fri. from 9am to 6pm, Sat. from 9am to 2pm; closed Sun.

DELUXE HOTELS

The grand hotel of Frankfurt is the **Steigenberger Frankfurter Hof,** Am Kaiserplatz, D-6000 Frankfurt (tel. 069/2-15-02), run by the Steigenberger chain. This massively restored structure is the number-one choice of traditionalists. Its position in the center of the city is ideal for visitors and businesspeople alike, as it's just a few short blocks from the main railway station and near the sights of the Altstadt (old town). Behind an 1876 neobaroque facade, the Frankfurter Hof has successfully combined the classic and the modern. Its art collection, particularly its Gobelin tapestries, is outstanding. In spite of its size, this well-maintained hotel offers both comfort and a personalized atmosphere. The 360 rooms and suites, all with well-equipped baths, are furnished in a restrained and dignified modern style. The cost varies with size and location of your room: singles range from 245 DM ($145.50) to 435 DM ($258.30) daily; doubles begin at 340 DM ($201.90), going up to 485 DM ($288). An American breakfast is included in all room prices.

In keeping with the management's belief that a fine hotel is "more than just a place to sleep," the Frankfurter Hof boasts several fine attractions. There is the Restaurant Français, decorated in Empire style, and the thatch-roofed Hofgarten Restaurant, which has fine grilled meats. The Kaiserbrunnen offers light meals and the finest of wines and champagne in a cozy setting with a Biedermeier decor. The hotel's Lipizzaner Bar is regarded by discerning visitors as the most elegant in the city (see my nightlife recommendations). The favorite spot in the hotel is the provincial-style Frankfurt Stubb, recommended in the upcoming restaurant section.

Hotel Gravenbruch-Kempinski-Frankfurt, Neu-Isenburg 2, D-6078 Frankfurt (tel. 0610/50-50), located in the suburbs a 20-minute haul from the center of the city, is recommended for guests wanting to escape the bustle of a commercial setting. Here you'll find luxury combined with rural charm. Only 10 minutes from the Frankfurt airport, the hotel is set back from Highway 459 on 37 acres of parkland, complete with a lake. (A free limousine transfer service takes hotel guests to and from the airport and city center.) The structure was built on the foundation and old walls of a former manor house dating from 1568. More modern residential wings are positioned along the lakeshore. Some touches of the old country-mansion character remain, as exemplified by the large atrium-style courtyards. Today the hotel provides 298 attractive, sleep-inducing bedrooms; amenities include color TVs, minibars, phones, radios, and adjustable air conditioning. Singles with baths cost 270 DM ($160.35) to 405 DM ($240.50) daily, while twin-bedded rooms go for 405 DM ($240.50) to 455 DM ($270.20).

Many in-the-know Frankfurters journey here just to sample the cuisine. The elegant Restaurant Forsthaus, with a view of the park, was converted from a 16th-century hunting lodge. It serves meals costing 50 DM ($29.70) to 85 DM ($50.45). And better still is the Gourmet-Restaurant, seating only 40 diners, with meals that begin at 75 DM ($44.55) and range up to 135 DM ($80.15). The Torschänke has a stone-slab floor, as well as draft beer from a barrel, and is housed in what were horse stables in the 16th century. The hotel bar offers dancing to music from international trios and entertainers. Other facilities include heated indoor and outdoor swimming pools, a fitness center, a sauna, a solarium, tennis courts, boutiques, and a hairdressing salon; golf and horseback riding are available nearby. A beauty and fitness farm is also on the premises.

Hessischer Hof, Friedrich-Ebert-Anlage 40, D-6000 Frankfurt (tel. 069/7-54-00), is a private, traditional hotel with an elegant atmosphere. All 120 rooms are comfortably furnished, and all have private bathrooms. Singles range from 255 DM ($151.40) to 455 DM ($267.20) daily, and twin-bedded rooms cost 395 DM ($234.55) to 515 DM ($305.80). Suites are more expensive, of course. Always bearing in mind the well-being of its guests, the Hessischer Hof has chosen a quotation from Goethe as its slogan: "Here I feel like a human being." The furnishings in the public rooms, including gilt-framed oil paintings and a museum-level collection of Sèvres porcelain in the dining room, give the hotel character.

EXPENSIVE HOTELS

Frankfurt Marriott Hotel, Hamburger Allee 2, D-6000 Frankfurt (tel. 069/7-95-50), stands across the street from the Messenglände (fairgrounds). It is packed to the rafters during Frankfurt's book and trade fairs, with top publishers reserving rooms a year in advance. This chain-run hotel, one of the most inviting in Frankfurt, is within walking distance of the heart of town, the Palmengarten (Botanical Gardens), and the Senckenberg Museum (just around the corner). Its 591 bedrooms have private baths and are equipped with radios, color TVs, in-house videos, direct-dial phones, minibars, trouser presses, hairdryers, and air conditioning. Singles cost 250 DM ($148.45) to 410 DM ($243.45) daily, with doubles going for 290 DM ($172.20) to 410 DM ($243.45). Traffic noise is left far below in this multistory building, and you can look out over the city and the surrounding countryside, framed against a backdrop of the Taunus Mountains. The hotel offers two restaurants, the luxuriously appointed Geheimratsstube and the Bäckerei, where you can watch the hotel's bakers turn out fresh bread and rolls each morning.

Mövenpick Parkhotel Frankfurt, Wiesenhüttenplatz 23-28, D-6000 Frankfurt (tel. 069/2-69-70), considered by many discriminating travelers to be one of the finest hotels in Frankfurt, provides not only warmth but personal attention for each of its guests. Near the station, it opens onto a quiet square, offering parking (the underground garage has additional space for 50 cars). The hotel has been built in two sections—an ornately decorated, recently renovated 19th-century building right alongside a sleek 1970s wing. In the older part, rooms have a luxurious atmosphere and are individually designed; the largest suite is done in the style of Louis XVI. The newer section boasts a more modern style. All of the 303 rooms and suites are in the five-star category. A single with either shower or complete bath costs 238 DM ($141.30) to 298 DM ($176.95) daily, a double with bath going for 388 DM ($230.40) to 438 DM ($260.10). The hotel's gourmet restaurant, La Truffe, dishes out some of the best hors d'oeuvres in Frankfurt and has one of Germany's best wine lists, recognized by the Deutsche Sommelier Union. The Mövenpick restaurant offers German regional cooking.

Hotel National, Baselerstrasse 50, D-6000 Frankfurt (tel. 069/23-48-41), with an ambience unmatched by larger, more impersonal hotels, will appeal to the traditionalist. A first-class hotel of Best Western affiliation, the 95-bedroom hostelry lies only 2 minutes from the central station, from which the Rhein-Main airport can be reached in just 12 minutes by electric train. The fairgrounds are also nearby. The hotel has antiques or handsome reproductions in both its public and private chambers. Many of the rooms are spacious, with decoration enhanced by Oriental carpeting. Singles come in a wide range, those with little or no plumbing going for a rock-bottom 86 DM ($51.05) daily, those with private showers or baths ranging from 140 DM ($83.15) to 169 DM ($100.35). Doubles with showers cost 237 DM ($140.75) to 238 DM ($141.30), those with baths going for 260 DM ($154.40). All rates include a buffet breakfast. If you don't want to venture out into the station area at night, you might want to dine at the hotel, in a beautifully appointed room where an international menu features a 45-DM ($26.70) dinner. There are à la carte selections as well. The recently installed lobby bar, decorated in classical style, invites you to a protected, comfortable rendezvous before dinner as well as after the theater.

Pullman Savigny Hotel, Savignystrasse 14-16, D-6000 Frankfurt (tel. 069/7-53-30), has undergone extensive upgrading. The foyer, restaurant, and bar have been renovated and redesigned; and the newly furnished bedrooms are equipped with luxury modern baths. The 124 accommodations, with direct-dial phones, radios, color TVs, and minibars, cost 190 DM ($112.80) to 280 DM ($166.25) daily for a single, 240 DM ($142.50) to 325 DM ($193) for a double. The restaurant offers inventive cuisine and outstanding service, with meals priced from 50 DM ($29.70) to 80 DM ($47.50). The elegant hotel bar has a welcoming atmosphere. The hotel is an eight-minute walk from the main railway station and the fairgrounds, but the location is quiet despite being central.

Scandic Crown Hotel, Wiesenhüttenstrasse 42, D-6000 Frankfurt (tel. 069/27-39-60), formerly the Frankfurt Savoy, has been given a new lease on life under the baton of Scandic Crown management. In 1988 the entire hotel was renovated, providing first-class comfort and a lighthearted ambience only 300 yards from the main railway station. Swedish furnishings are used throughout, and the 144 guest rooms contain color TVs, radios, minibars, direct-dial phones, trouser presses, hairdryers, and, of course, private baths or showers. Rooms cost 215 DM ($127.65) daily for a single, rising to 275 DM ($163.30) for a double. Included in these prices is a plentiful breakfast buffet. Guests can enjoy a Continental menu with many international dishes in the Rhapsody, or they can head for the hotel's premier (and more expensive) restaurant, the Savoy, honoring the old name of the establishment. Facilities include a fitness club with an indoor pool, along with a sauna and solarium. A multistory car park is nearby if you're driving.

MODERATELY PRICED HOTELS

Leader among middle-bracket hotels in the vicinity of the railway station is the **Hotel Continental,** Baselerstrasse 56, D-6000 Frankfurt (tel. 069/23-03-41). Founded in 1889, it enjoyed its heyday in the belle-époque era. From the ashes of World War II, it was reconstructed in 1952 and then refurbished in 1985. Around the corner are lively bars, but serenity prevails inside this hotel, some of whose chambers—especially those with more modern plumbing—are most comfortable. Windows, mercifully, have been soundproofed to keep out traffic din. A single ranges in price from 140 DM ($83.15) to 160 DM ($95) daily; a double costs 185 DM ($109.85) to 270 DM ($160.35). The 117-bedroom hotel—the choice of many businesspeople, including Japanese clients—has a pleasant restaurant with an international cuisine. À la carte orders can be very expensive; however, a table d'hôte is a potent bait, costing from 35 DM ($20.80).

Mozart, Parkstrasse 17, D-6000 Frankfurt (tel. 069/55-08-31), is a honey, perhaps the best of the small hotels in Frankfurt. It stands on the periphery of the Botanical Gardens, right off the busy Fürstenbergerstrasse, near the Alte Oper. The 35-bedroom hotel is recognized by its marble facade, softened by the curtains at the windows. Everything inside—walls, furniture, bed coverings—is white or pink. The breakfast room, incidentally, could easily pass for an 18th-century salon with its crystal chandeliers and Louis XV–style chairs. The cheaper rooms are those with showers and toilets; the more expensive ones offer tubs with showers. All have TV sets, radios, and refrigerators. A single ranges in price from 125 DM ($74.25) to 145 DM ($86.10) daily, and a double goes for 195 DM ($115.80). Members of the staff are polite and helpful.

Turm Hotel, Eschersheimer Landstrasse 20, D-6000 Frankfurt (tel. 069/15-40-50), is a six-story structure with 75 compact, boxy rooms where, as the Germans say, *"Der Komfort ist gut."* The lines in the bedrooms are sleek and uncluttered, in spartan taste. A single with bath or shower costs from 120 DM ($71.25) daily, and a double with bath costs 175 DM ($103.90) to 225 DM ($133.60); these rates include breakfast, service, and VAT. The innkeeper has a helpful staff to run this centrally located structure, the most winning part of which is its restaurant. Attracting local folk as well as hotel residents, it's done in a rustic style and features dishes from an international kitchen. Hotel parking is also available.

Hotel an der Messe, Westendstrasse 104, D-6000 Frankfurt (tel. 069/74-79-79)—its white facade pierced by smoked-glass windows and a canopied entrance—is in a quiet location just a five-minute walk from the university and the railway terminal, and the banking district. The staff does much to make guests feel comfortable in the 46 bedrooms, all with private baths or showers, toilets, color TVs, direct-dial phones, radios, and minibars. Only half a dozen singles are rented, at 170 DM ($100.95) to 260 DM ($154.40) daily, and they're hard to come by unless you reserve well in advance. Doubles cost 200 DM ($118.75) to 400 DM ($237.50). All tariffs include breakfast, served in a light, airy room. There is an underground garage.

Hotel Falk, Falkstrasse 38a, D-6000 Frankfurt (tel. 069/70-80-94), may be stark outside, but inside there is much to recommend it. Bright and modern, it has enough traditional touches to make it warm and cozy. Opened in 1972, the Falk has been a success ever since. It rents 32 bedrooms—small, compact, and uncluttered —that are spotlessly maintained. A single with shower costs 105 DM ($62.35) to 115 DM ($68.30) daily; a double, 165 DM ($98) to 180 DM ($106.90). These prices include taxes, service, and breakfast. A rustic bar with Spanish tiles and hanging lights is called the Toledo-Stil.

Frankfurt Luxor Hotel, Allerheiligen Tor 2-4, D-6000 Frankfurt (tel. 069/29-30-67), modern and reliable, offers good, middle-class comfort right in the heart of the city. It has a quiet urbanity that appeals to many travelers, and the staff gives guests personal attention. Each of the 46 small, modern rooms has a private bath, toilet, color TV, minibar, and phone. A single costs 80 DM ($47.50) to 125 DM ($74.25) daily, with a double going for 120 DM ($71.25) to 165 DM ($98); all tariffs include a buffet breakfast. Of course, during fair periods prices climb, as they do all over Frankfurt. The hotel has a cozy bar and a TV lounge. A tram stops right in front of the Luxor.

BUDGET HOTELS

Just across from the entrance to the zoo, **Hotel am Zoo,** Alfred-Brehm-Platz 6, D-6000 Frankfurt (tel. 069/49-07-71), is a modern 85-bedroom hotel with a nice restaurant. The rooms are clean and furnished with simple but comfortable modern pieces. Singles with showers and toilets rent for 95 DM ($56.40) daily, and doubles with baths go for 145 DM ($86.10). The breakfast room on the street level is the hotel's most charming feature, with linen-covered tables and stained-glass windows. Parking facilities are available behind the hotel. The tram stops just across the street, and the subway connects with the train station and the airport.

Hotel Jaguar, Theobald-Christ-Strasse 17-19, D-6000 Frankfurt (tel. 069/43-93-01), is felt by its management to be "the leading hotel garni in the city" ("garni" refers to the fact that no meals other than breakfast are offered). The location is near the zoo. The decor is bright and cheerful, especially in the breakfast room, and the staff is pleasant and helpful. The price is attractive too: a single without bath costs 94 DM ($55.80) daily, rising to 112 DM ($66.50) for a room with complete bath. Doubles, all with private baths, range in price from 125 DM ($74.25) to 142 DM ($84.30). The 37 rooms are compact. The TV and reading room is inviting, and you can store your car in an underground garage.

Admiral, Hölderlinstrasse 25, D-6000 Frankfurt (tel. 069/44-80-21), is often favored by families, including many connected with the U.S. military forces in Germany. Perhaps they like its location near the zoo, a short haul from the center of Frankfurt. The hotel serves breakfast only. It rents 67 plainly but comfortably furnished bedrooms, with a natural wood decor in the style of the Nordic countries. Units come equipped with private baths (often showers) and TVs, and they cost 80 DM ($47.50) to 110 DM ($65.30) daily for a single and 120 DM ($71.25) to 150 DM ($89.05) for a double.

Schwille, Grosse Bockenheimerstrasse 50, D-6000 Frankfurt (tel. 069/28-30-54), is a 50-bedroom establishment with a popular café well known for its pastries. All rooms are quiet, despite the fact that the hotel is in the center of the city. Accommodations have radios, and most have been completely renovated with new furnishings, minibars, and color TVs (receiving the AFN programs in English). Bathless singles rent for 80 DM ($47.50) daily, singles with showers for 125 DM ($74.25), and singles with complete bathrooms for 170 DM ($100.95). Doubles with complete baths cost 180 DM ($106.90) to 250 DM ($148.45). All prices include breakfast, service, and taxes. The first-floor breakfast room faces the trees of the pedestrian zone. The U-Bahn is a one-minute walk from the hotel. A private parking garage holds about 20 cars.

Hotel Niedenau, Niedenau 5, D-6000 Frankfurt (tel. 069/72-25-36), is a find—a well-kept family-style hotel with only 10 rooms. The atmosphere is intimate, and the well-furnished rooms have been individualized to make them more inviting. A single without bath goes for 60 DM ($35.65) daily, rising to 95 DM ($56.40) for a room with bath. Most doubles (except one) have private baths, and they cost 150 DM ($89.05) nightly. Though a Continental breakfast is included in the prices, you can also order a special breakfast with egg, sausage, even an omelet, for an additional charge. The hotel stands in the vicinity of the railway station.

Neue Kräme, Neue Kräme 23, D-6000 Frankfurt (tel. 069/28-40-46), stands on a street of the same name in the heart of the pedestrian area, right off Berlinerstrasse, not far from Römerberg. Modest and strictly functional, it serves breakfast only, but many visitors like it because of its strategic location. If you lodge here, you can cover much of the shopping area and a lot of the sightseeing attractions on foot. The 24 modernized rooms are pleasantly decorated, ranging in price from 110 DM ($65.30) daily for a single to 160 DM ($95) for a double. A Continental breakfast buffet is included.

Hotel Diana, Westendstrasse 83-85, D-6000 Frankfurt (tel. 069/74-70-07), spotless and homey, stands as a leader in its price class. A copy of a private villa, with a drawing room and an intimate breakfast salon, it is situated in the West End on a pleasant residential street, where it maintains a tone of quiet dignity. The Diana is a postwar building, but in the surrounding neighborhood are many 19th-century houses that were at least partially spared the Allied bombings. Each of the Diana's 29 quite comfortable rooms comes with a bath or shower, toilet, TV, and phone. A single costs 63 DM ($37.40) to 78 DM ($46.30) daily, with doubles going for 106 DM ($62.95).

Pension Uebe, Grüneburgweg 3, D-6000 Frankfurt (tel. 069/59-12-09), is a mother-daughter venture—and a successful one. Both Elizabeth Kern and her daughter, Andrea, speak English. They have named each room after a European city, carrying out the motif of each particular city with prints and decorative objects. Reached by elevator, the pension occupies three floors over a bakery and a butcher shop and is entered through a covered passageway with window displays for an adjoining clothing store. The rooms are quiet, having windows insulated against noise. Of the 18 bedrooms, 14 have showers (4 with showers and toilets), and the rest have only hot and cold running water (with a bath and toilet available on the same floor). Most units have refrigerators, and color TVs are available on request. A single costs 50 DM ($29.70) daily without shower, or else 65 DM ($38.60) to 75 DM ($44.55) for a room with shower or with shower and toilet. A double with shower goes for 80 DM ($47.50) to 90 DM ($53.45), peaking at 110 DM ($65.30) for a room with shower. A large selection is offered in the country-style breakfast room. The pension —for those seeking a warm, gentle, homelike atmosphere—is centrally located, with a subway station and taxi stand across the street; a garage and parking spaces are available in the courtyard.

Hotel am Kurfürstenplatz, Kurfürstenplatz 38, D-6000 Frankfurt (tel. 069/ 77-78-16). The English-speaking owner has decorated this 34-bed hotel in a mixture of styles, perking up each room with bright, cheerful colors and boxes of plants at the windows. The combination breakfast room and lounge sparkles. The front rooms face a park complete with fountain, church spire, and lots of baby carriages. The hotel provides one bath and toilet for every three rooms. Singles rent for 60 DM ($35.65) daily; doubles go for 110 DM ($65.30). There are some rooms with showers, and for these a single costs 95 DM ($56.40) daily; a double, 150 DM ($89.05). Rates include breakfast, taxes, and service.

Hotel Pension West, Gräfstrasse 81, D-6000 Frankfurt (tel. 069/77-80-11), occupies part of an old house just off a busy street opposite the university. The atmosphere is that of a private home, and the managers see that everything is clean and orderly. Single rooms with showers cost 73 DM ($43.35) to 85 DM ($50.40) daily.

Doubles with showers are priced at 156 DM ($92.55). Breakfast, included in the rates, is served in a room on the ground floor. There are no parking facilities, but metered parking is usually available on the nearby streets.

Hotel Hübner, Westendstrasse 23, D-6000 Frankfurt (tel. 069/74-60-44), solid and modern, lies about 500 yards from the main railroad station. However, the house is on a one-way street, and at night all is quiet here, noises sometimes absorbed by the small gardens of the neighboring houses. (The yard of the hotel offers parking space.) Guests are made to feel welcome in this well-run 48-bed hotel, all of whose pleasantly comfortable rooms have phones and hot and cold running water. A single without bath costs 54 DM ($32.05) daily, rising to 70 DM ($41.55) for a room with shower or bath and toilet. A double with shower goes for 120 DM ($71.25), increasing to 150 DM ($89.05) for a room with bath and toilet. These rates include a Continental breakfast. Rooms are reached by elevator. Although in theory the hotel serves only breakfast, drinks can be ordered at any time, and if a guest so desires, he or she can request a small snack in the evening.

Württemberger Hof, Karlstrasse 14, D-6000 Frankfurt (tel. 069/23-31-06), has the family style of a Germanic Gasthof, even though it's on a busy commercial street close to the main station. The bedrooms, 67 in all, are functional and modern, those overlooking the street being equipped with special soundproof windows. A single without bath costs 55 DM ($32.65) daily, increasing to 88 DM ($52.25) for a room with bath. A double without bath goes for 88 DM ($52.55), going up to 123 DM ($73.05) for a room with bath. Tariffs include Continental breakfast. This is a good, standard overnight stop.

Westfälinger Hof, Düsseldorfer Strasse 10, D-6000 Frankfurt (tel. 069/23-47-48), has been in the same family for some 60 years. It is a modern 60-room hotel in the vicinity of the railroad station. The neat and clean accommodations are comfortable but cramped. A single room without bath but with direct-dial phone rents for 60 DM ($35.65) daily, the cost rising to 90 DM ($53.45) for a room with complete bath. Twin-bedded or double rooms, with complete baths and phones, cost 140 DM ($83.15).

Corona Hotel, Hamburger Allee 48, D-6000 Frankfurt (tel. 069/77-90-77), is a hotel garni (a breakfast-only hotel) whose pleasant central location is 10 minutes from the main railway station and 20 minutes from the airport. The 27 rooms are modern and well kept. Singles rent for 60 DM ($35.65) to 120 DM ($71.25) daily, doubles for 120 DM ($71.25) to 180 DM ($106.90). The tariffs include breakfast. The hotel is closed from December 10 through the beginning of January.

Kolpinghaus, Langestrasse 26, D-6000 Frankfurt (tel. 069/28-85-41), is a modern 48-bedroom hotel whose most winning feature is the little garden out back where café tables are placed in fair weather. The rooms are small, some of them reminding me of a modern American university dormitory, but they are well maintained and cared for. The sheets are crisp and white. Both singles and doubles come with almost no plumbing, with showers and toilets, or with complete baths. Singles range from 58 DM ($34.45) to 83 DM ($49.30) daily, and doubles go from 88 DM ($52.25) to 118 DM ($70.05). The location is within walking distance of the zoo and the shopping street, the Zeil.

LEFT BANK HOTELS

Opening onto a small park in the apple-wine district, **Hotel Maingau,** Schifferstrasse 38-40, D-6000 Frankfurt (tel. 069/61-70-01), just across the Main from the Altstadt, is just right for those who want to live among the Frankfurters rather than with their fellow visitors on the right bank. Plenty of blond-wood Nordic furnishings characterize both the old building and the annex. Bathless singles rent for 83 DM ($49.30) daily, increasing to 108 DM ($64.15) for rooms with private showers or baths. Bathless doubles cost 103 DM ($61.15), and those with private baths will run to a high of 150 DM ($89.05). The 100-bedroom Maingau is a good point from which to launch a nighttime pub crawl of the apple-wine district, beginning at the restaurant and Bierstube next door.

Hotel Schiff, Triftstrasse 33, D-6000 Frankfurt (tel. 069/67-70-12), is a well-run 55-bedroom hotel on the left bank, catering to large numbers of German business and professional women. A single room costs 100 DM ($59.40) daily, a double 155 DM ($92.05), with buffet breakfast, service, and taxes included. The well-appointed accommodations have showers and toilets. Service here is excellent, and the desk staff shows concern for the well-being of guests.

HOTELS NEAR THE AIRPORT

Your best bet is the **Novotel Frankfurt Rhein-Main,** Am Weiher 20, D-6092 Kelsterbach (tel. 06107/7-50-50), one of the best representatives in Germany of this increasingly popular French chain. Its rooms are often full when some better-known hotels are half empty. The reason is not only the reasonable prices but the services and amenities, including a location a short distance from the Frankfurt airport. To cut costs, guests wheel their own luggage to the rooms—149 in all, renting for 190 DM ($112.80) daily for a double, or 170 DM ($100.95) if it is used as a single. Each room contains generous desk space, private bath, double beds (plus a sofa that can also sleep a third person), TV, ample closet and storage space, and functional modern furniture.

In the lobby of the hotel is a convivial bar, as well as a fireplace. The hotel's grill, which opens early in the morning for a copious breakfast buffet and serves late into the night, also offers excellent food at moderate prices. You can peruse the constantly changing daily menu for specials or else order from an à la carte listing, with many regional dishes or hearty French fare. In summer, tables overflow onto a terrace overlooking the lake. Sports are also near at hand, including a swimming pool, sauna, and fitness room (ideal for limbering up after those long transatlantic flights). Tennis and jogging are also available. The hotel maintains a shuttle bus service, taking guests to and from the airport or into the center of Frankfurt.

---

3. Where to Dine

At the crossroads of European travel, Frankfurt's restaurants reflect a sophisticated international flavor. You can find everything here, from haute cuisine to cuisine moderne (new German cooking), to great French and Italian restaurants, to the city's sausage namesake. The best wines are also readily available, but many Frankfurters still prefer beer or Apfelwein. A three-block-long pedestrian mall, Grosse Bockenheimerstrasse, cuts through the heart of the center of Frankfurt. Frankfurters humorously refer to this street as Fressgasse, meaning "grub alley." In a way, they have a point. Several restaurants along this street do serve what might be called "grub." You'll do much better by dining on one of the side streets such as Kaiserhofstrasse.

THE TOP RESTAURANTS

Restaurant Français, Steigenberger Frankfurter Hof, Am Kaiserplatz 17 (tel. 069/2-21-502), on the main floor of the previously recommended hotel, is by far the most outstanding restaurant in Frankfurt today. As the name suggests, the cuisine is French, more haute than nouvelle. The stress, in the main, is on cookery from Lyon and Provence (Lyon, the gastronomic capital of France, you anticipate, while Provence might come as a bit of a surprise).

The chef is a perfectionist, insisting that dish after dish reflect not only professionalism but enthusiasm. One of my favorites is a stuffed quail in a truffle butter sauce. You might begin your meal with a velvety-smooth cream of wild mushroom soup or a gâteau of mostelle, a delicately flavored fish found mainly in the Mediterranean, covered with orange butter. Breast of chicken is also served with a truffle butter sauce, and a magret of duckling is prepared with blackcurrants and a confit of onions. Try also the Angus beef grille Villette or roast pork "like your grandmother used to make." In season, game is a specialty.

The chairs in the restaurant are Louis-Philippe in style, with peach-colored upholstery, and the vivid forest-green walls have impeccably white trim. For lunch, costing from 70 DM ($41.55) to 130 DM ($77.20), the place largely fills up with businesspeople. Dinner is more romantic, à la carte meals averaging 80 DM ($47.50) to 125 DM ($74.25). The restaurant is open Tues. to Sat. from noon to 2pm and 7 to 11pm; closed July and on holidays.

Weinhaus Brückenkeller, Schützenstrasse 6 (tel. 069/28-42-38), is also a leading restaurant, perhaps the favorite watering spot of North American visitors. In the heart of the old town, you dine under medieval-looking arches at candlelit tables. Strolling musicians encourage singing and gaiety. Franconian carvings adorn the alcoves, and huge wooden barrels are decorated with scenes from Goethe's *Faust* and from the life of Martin Luther. The food is a happy mix of German and French cuisine. A typical meal might begin with cream of sorrel soup or a more substantial goose liver terrine, followed by saddle of venison or saddle of young lamb. For a perfect finish, you might order a soufflé of strawberries with vanilla sauce. Their Tafelspitz (prime cut of boiled beef) is the best in town, as good as any you might have in Vienna. It's served with a sauce made with herbs and fresh vegetables such as spinach. Count on parting with 100 DM ($59.40) for an evening repast, which includes homemade sourdough bread. The wine cellar holds an excellent collection of German wines, some 180 in all, including the best from the Rhineland. The Brückenkeller is invariably crowded, so reservations are imperative. Personal attention and efficient service are hallmarks here. It's open for dinner only, from 6pm to 1am; closed Wed. and Sun.

Humperdinck, Grüneburgweg 95 (tel. 069/72-21-22), is named after the composer Engelbert Humperdinck, not the British singer. The composer once lived at this fashionable address near the Botanical Gardens in the western sector of Frankfurt. The setting, under the supervision of H. Willi Tetz and Edmund Teusch, is classical, refined, and elegant; tones of subtle ivory and dove gray complement the cracklewood paneling. An eight-course menu is offered for 135 DM ($80.15), and you can also order à la carte, with meals costing from 75 DM ($44.55) to 100 DM ($59.40)—or much higher, depending on what you order. Specialties are likely to include ravoli stuffed with crayfish in the chef's special sauce, a rich herb soup with butter croutons, or a salmon Schnitzel with a vegetable risotto. The cuisine is French, both traditional and modern. Dress is more relaxed in hot weather but consciously fashionable in winter. Hours are noon to 2pm and 7 to 10:30pm; closed Sun. and for Sat. lunch.

Erno's Bistro, Liebigstrasse 15 (tel. 069/72-19-97), a chic midtown rendezvous between the Alte Oper and the Palmengarten, draws everybody from visiting film stars to bank executives. For all its big reputation, Erno's Bistro is a little place where the staff speaks English; fine service and appointments, plus a commendable French cuisine that seems to improve year by year, are hallmarks of this establishment. The menu changes daily, and the kitchen serves only the fish brought fresh from Paris by air or from European waters. The chef offers both cuisine moderne and what is known as *cuisine formidable*. The most exciting—and also the most expensive—appetizer is his foie gras natural à l'ombre. For a main course, I'd suggest the grilled brill, whose flesh is very delicate and light, served with a special, rare type of mushroom. Lunches cost from 90 DM ($53.45) and dinners from 100 DM ($59.40). Hours are noon to 2pm and 6 to 10pm Mon. to Fri.; closed mid-June to mid-July. Never show up without a reservation.

OTHER LEADING RESTAURANTS

Less than a mile from the heart of the city, **Bistrot 77,** Ziegelhüttenweg 1 (tel. 069/61-40-40), in Frankfurt-Sachsenhausen, is one of the most chic restaurants in town. The overall impression is one of lots of light and glass; a black-and-white tile floor and an airy latticework ceiling also set the scene. In summer the preferred tables are on the terrace. Dominique and Guy Mosbach, two French citizens, have made a name for themselves in Frankfurt with their nouvelle cuisine, and the food here is a frequently changing array of imaginatively prepared fish and meat dishes, along with intriguing appetizers and desserts. The bill of fare depends on the shopping of the day. A seven-course menu here costs from 110 DM ($65.30); a set menu is offered at 65 DM ($38.60). The place is open Mon. to Fri. from noon to 2pm and 7 to 10pm; Sat. from 7 to 10pm only; closed Sun. You must reserve in advance for one of the dozen tables.

Mövenpick am Opernplatz, Opernplatz 2 (tel. 069/2-06-80), is the spot where the Swiss have invaded Frankfurt and have given Hesse cuisine a real challenge in the process. Having long enjoyed an outstanding reputation for cooking in their own country, the Mövenpick interests have created dramatic dining in this German city. In the main restaurant, Baron de la Mouette, the roast rib of Angus beef with horseradish cream, Warwick mustard sauce, beef pan gravy, and baked potato is the daily specialty. More seductive dishes of the French and international cuisine include scampi in a tarragon sauce and entrecôte Bordelaise. The restaurant, open daily from 11:30am to 3pm and 5pm to midnight, serves apéritifs, liquors, steaks, warm snacks, seafoods, and salads; specialties include a crayfish cocktail and Angus entrecôte. Meals come in a wide price range here, from 36 DM ($21.40) for a business lunch all the way to 80 DM ($47.50) for a big dinner.

Jacques Offenbach, Opernplatz 1 (tel. 069/284-820), is the perfect place for an after-theater supper, in a setting that Offenbach himself might have found stimulating. Surely the composer of *The Tales of Hoffmann* would gravitate to the dusty-pink and beige walls with globe lights, the brass belle-époque lighting fixtures, and the comfortably upholstered oval-backed chairs that look as if they belonged in a Renoir painting. Both classical fare and cuisine moderne are served here, the elegant service matching the elegant decor. Visitors gaze at Frankfurt's music lovers, their fellow diners, across the long expanse of the large room. There is a brigade of talent in the kitchen, turning out such delicacies as cream of broccoli soup, a perfectly done tournedos with Roquefort sauce, loin of veal with fresh cabbage, scallops with fennel, and frogs'-legs salad in the style of the Camargue in Provence. A gourmet supper costs 60 DM ($35.65) to 85 DM ($50.45), and the menu is in both French and German. Hours are 6pm to midnight daily; closed in July.

MODERATELY PRICED RESTAURANTS

A dependable dining spot, **Frankfurter Stubb,** Kaiserplatz (tel. 069/2-15-02), in the Steigenberger Frankfurter Hof, specializes in regional German cooking of the past century. The food here is straightforward and honest. The ambience is that of an elegant wine cellar, with cozy dining nooks. The attentive English-speaking waitresses in regional garb are most helpful in translating the German menu. For openers, try the excellent lentil soup with Frankfurters. One of the house specialties is boiled beef (Tafelspitz) with Frankfurt green sauce, served with potatoes cooked in bouillon. The featured dessert is Rote Grüte, a jelly of fresh fruit served with either vanilla sauce or cream. Expect to spend 40 DM ($23.75) to 70 DM ($41.55) for a complete meal here. The Stubb, a favorite with visitors, is open from noon to midnight; closed Sun.

Henninger-Turm, Hainer Weg 60-64 (tel. 069/606-36-00), is a dining oddity. Located across the Main River in Sachsenhausen, it has three functions: as a brewery with one of the largest storage facilities in the region, as a museum devoted to the exposition of brewery-related artifacts, and as a revolving restaurant set atop the rectangular skyscraping headquarters of the company that owns it. The place is the pride of Henninger Brewery. To go up in its elevator costs 3.50 DM ($2.10). On the upper part is a lookout platform with a panoramic sweep of the city. In the restaurant, Hessian specialties are featured 357 feet above ground. The soup of the day is usually good and filling. Look also for local seasonal specialties such as medallions of hare in a juniper cream sauce. Desserts include fresh strawberries in season. Expect to spend 35 DM ($20.80) to 60 DM ($35.65) for a meal here. Hours of food service are from 10am to 11pm. The Frankfurter Brauerei Museum, however, is open from 10am to 9pm (to 7pm from October to March); closed Mon.

Börsenkeller, Schillerstrasse 11 (tel. 069/28-11-15), is an oasis in the austere metropolis, concealing its old-world atmosphere behind a deceptively modern exterior. It is a favorite choice of stockbrokers and bankers. Dining takes place on the lower level, with arched cellar rooms and lots of nooks and recessed areas. During the evening, accordian music is played. Typical dishes include rumpsteak Rothschild with croquettes, and pork chops in the Swiss style. Tabs begin at 35 DM ($20.80), ranging upward to 75 DM ($44.55). If you've just arrived in Germany, a memorable meal at the Börsenkeller will whet your appetite for exploring the countryside. Hours are 11am to 11pm Mon. to Fri.; closed Sat. and Sun.

Gallo Nero, Kaiserhofstrasse 7 (tel. 069/28-48-40), the leading and most refined Italian restaurant in Frankfurt, is chic, expensive, and worth it. Guests often have a drink in the stand-up bar, admiring the strawberry-pink colors and the stained-glass representations of roosters, before being shown to a beautifully set table in a trio of intimate dining rooms. Only the freshest of ingredients are used. You might begin with one of their interesting appetizers, such as a ricotta-stuffed crêpe, then select from such dishes as a rack of lamb perfectly seasoned with herbs, filet of sea wolf grilled with garlic, or sole with "fruits of the sea." Meals cost from 60 DM ($35.65) and are served from noon to 2:30pm and 6 to 10pm, closed Sun.

Firenze, Bergerstrasse 30 (tel. 069/43-39-56). Very popular for late dining, this fine Tuscan restaurant is noted mainly for its antipasti. Fish is also a specialty, and the pasta dishes are homemade and good. A favorite is saltimbocca (literally, "jump-in-your-mouth") alla romana; try also the filet steak à la chef with Gorgonzola. The table wines are good, and the bottled red ones excellent. Expect to part with anywhere from 42 DM ($24.95) to 75 DM ($44.55) for dinner. The place is open from noon to 2:30pm and 6 to 11pm; closed Mon.

BUDGET RESTAURANTS

Zum Bitburger, Hochstrasse 54 (tel. 069/28-03-02), stands near the Alte Oper in the center of Frankfurt. Run by the Bitburger Brauerei, it is one of the finest brewery-operated restaurants in Frankfurt, with a long and proud tradition. The place is often packed, and it's open weekdays only, from 11:30am to 1am. Waiters hurry back and forth with mugs of beer, and somehow they also manage to slip through with hearty platters of food, including such standard but well-prepared dishes as grilled rumpsteak, scampi in a Riesling sauce, filet steak with herb-flavored butter, and the veal steak Cordon Bleu. Meals cost from 30 DM ($17.80). You can begin with a soup of the day, and there is always a fresh seasonal salad. The kitchen serves hot food until midnight.

Churrasco, Domplatz 6 (tel. 069/28-48-04), is where Frankfurters go for succulent Argentine beefsteaks. The black sign with the steer outside marks this dimly lit tavern, just next door to the cathedral. The Argentine beef filet comes in two sizes: 180 grams and 250 grams. Cheaper orders of rumpsteak are also available. All cuts are charcoal-grilled to your specifications. Rounding out the menu are fresh salads and a limited list of desserts. A steak-and-salad meal costs 25 DM ($14.85) to 40 DM ($23.75). Hours are 11:30am to 11:30pm daily.

BUDGET APFELWEINSTUBEN

For your best dining bargains, head across the Main to a district known for its apple-wine taverns, or Apfelweinstuben. These taverns—there are dozens of them —are in the **Alt-Sachsenhausen** section of the left bank. It was here that the composer Paul Hindemith lived in a watchtower dating from the 1400s. Sachsenhausen was once called the most *frankfurtish* neighborhood in the city. But the main drag, Schweizerstrasse, is now filled with bistros, cafés, and boutiques catering to tourists. The area, especially in summer, is often overrun with buses filled with passengers on the nightlife tour, so much of the old character is gone. Here you drink local apple wine, which some Frankfurters enjoy and some foreigners consider a cousin to vinegar. My verdict: an acquired taste. Tradition says that you won't like the apple wine until you've had three big steins. After that, what does taste matter?

You can go on a tavern crawl, stopping off at the **Zum Grauen Bock,** Grosse Rittergasse 30-54 (tel. 069/61-80-26), which is run by the Elsässer family. It's open only from 5pm to 1am (closed Sun.). A gemütlich atmosphere prevails in this smoke-filled tavern. Sometimes the communal singing is so robust it's necessary to slide back the roof on a summer night. An accordionist goes from table to table, involving everyone in his song. Contact is made, instant friendships formed, at least for the evening. Featured on the menu is something known as Handkäs mit Musik (cheese with vinegar, oil, and onions). You may want to let the locals enjoy the subtle pleasures of this repast, selecting instead a Germanic specialty known as Schweinhaxen, a huge pork shank with Sauerkraut and boiled potatoes. A good beginning is the Frankfurter Bohnensuppe (bean soup). A simple menu begins at only 22 DM ($13.05).

Zum Gemalten Haus, Schweizerstrasse 67 (tel. 069/61-45-59). Don't bother to call—no one takes reservations around here. You simply arrive, and chances are you'll share a table with some of the other patrons, perhaps in the garden if the weather is fair. Both of you will have the same aim: ample portions of good Hessian cooking. If your taste dictates "Frankfurter Platte" (specialties of the house) with Sauerkraut or perhaps Knockwurst with Kraut or potato salad, you won't be disappointed. The Eisbein, or pork chops with Kraut and mashed potatoes, washed down with the local apple wine, is the cook's specialty. The apple wine is homemade, and the patrons of the restaurant love it. The portions of food are gigantic. The raw or cooked Sauerkraut is very healthful, making this place a spot even for the diet-minded. And don't forget to taste the various types of sausages. An entire repast is likely to cost no more than 30 DM ($17.80), a great bargain. Hours are 10am to midnight, Wed. to Sun.

A RUSTIC INN ON THE OUTSKIRTS

Some 8 miles south of the center of Frankfurt, **Gutsschänke Neuhof,** 6072 Dreieich-Götzenhain (tel. 06102/32-00-14), between Neu Isenberg and Götzenhain, is a dining adventure. Surrounded by woods, meadows, and fields of flowers, the inn is part of a huge farm estate (Hofgut Neuhof) dating from 1499. In summer, tables are set out on the wide terrace overlooking the pond. Inside, the former manor farmhouse is a maze of connecting rooms for dining. It's a totally rustic atmosphere, with pewter candlesticks and fresh-cut field flowers on the tables; on the walls hang antlers, maps, swords, rifles, and old prints. English-speaking waiters proffer excellent service, and the food is exceptional, beginning with the Vorspeise Neuhof, an assortment of hors d'oeuvres including such delicacies as fresh crayfish with dill. Served at your table from a cart, the array of appetizers is priced by size. Venison is a popular main course in season, and two house specialties are gespickte Rehkeule Hubertus (leg of venison) and roast duck. The owner of Neuhof supplements the excellent wine cellar with wines from his own Herzheim/Weinstrasse (Rhenish Palatinate) vineyards. Expect to spend from 75 DM ($44.55) for a complete meal. Guttschänke Neuhof is open every day, serving lunch from noon to 2:30pm and dinner from 6 to 9:30pm.

While you're visiting Neuhof, stop in and browse in the gift shop on the premises, which sells pottery and linens as well as homemade sausages, candy, applecakes, and aromatic breads.

THE CAFÉS

Not as firmly entrenched in the Frankfurter's daily life as it is in Vienna, the café is still a pleasant place for people-watching, light (or full) meals, and drinks, along with pastries, of course.

The one nearly everybody finds without any guidance is **Zur Hauptwache,** An der Hauptwache (tel. 069/28-10-26), which dates from 250 years ago. Standing in the strategic heart of Frankfurt, the present building was reconstructed after World War II bombings. The menu appears in English, among other languages. On a warm evening the street level, attracting coffee-drinkers and pastry-eaters, is a delight. The pedestrian zone has been completed, making it more pleasant for a stroll. Don't fail to ask for the special beer, Römer Pilsner. Daily meals range from 10 DM ($5.95) to 40 DM ($23.75). Hours are 7:30am to 7pm; closed Sun. Coffee costs 2.80 DM ($1.65) per cup.

If you have a sweet tooth, head for the **Café Schwille,** Grosse Bockenheimer-strasse 50 (tel. 069/28-30-54), the most famous place in Frankfurt for pastries and sweets. The hotel there was already recommended. Light snacks begin at 7 DM ($4.15). The café is open Mon. to Sat. from 7am to 7:30pm; Sun. from 12:30 to 7pm. In summer, if the weather's good, it stays open as late as 11pm.

Café Laumer, Bockenheimer Landstrasse 67 (tel. 069/72-79-12), enjoys an enviable location between the Palmengarten and the Alte Oper. The service is helpful and welcoming, and the habitués often have their favorite marble-topped tables. There they enjoy a light lunch for 18 DM ($10.70), or snacks and a selection of cakes and tortes throughout the afternoon. Hours are 8am to 7pm Mon. to Sat.; from 11am to 7pm Sun. In summer, try for a table on the open-air terrace.

---

4. The Sights

When bombs rained on Frankfurt in 1944, nearly all the old half-timbered buildings were leveled to mere piles of rubble. In what must have been a record reconstruction, however, the Frankfurters not only built up their city into a fine mélange of modern and traditional architecture but faithfully restored some of their most prized old buildings as well.

Goethe-Haus, Grosser Hirschgraben 23 (tel. 069/28-28-24), is among them. It's been a shrine for Goethe enthusiasts since it was opened to the public in 1863. Goethe was born in the house in 1749. The house was faithfully restored after it was bombed in 1944. One critic wrote that the restoration was carried out "with loving care and damn-the-expense craftsmanship."

Reflecting the fashion trends of the 18th century, the house was decorated in different styles: neoclassical, baroque, rococo. You can view the library where Goethe's father worked and often watched the street for the return of his son. A portrait of the severe-looking gentleman hangs behind the door of his wife's room.

On the second floor is an unusual astronomical clock built about 1749 and repaired in 1949 to run again for another 200 years. One room also contains a picture gallery with paintings collected by Goethe's father. Most of them painted by contemporary Frankfurt artists, these works influenced Goethe's artistic views for a great part of his life. The poet's rooms contain a puppet theater that was one of Goethe's most important childhood possessions and played a significant role in his *Wilhelm Meister.*

Annexed to the house is the **Frankfurter Goethe-Museum,** built after the war on the site of its predecessor. The museum contains a library of 120,000 volumes and a collection of about 30,000 manuscripts, as well as 16,000 graphic artworks and 400 paintings associated in some way with Goethe and his works. The house and museum are open Mon. to Sat. from 9am to 6pm in summer (to 4pm in winter); Sun. from 10am to 1pm. Admission is 3 DM ($1.80), year round.

The **Altstadt** centers around three Gothic buildings with stepped gables, known collectively as the **Römer.** These houses were originally built in 1305 and bought by the city a century later for use as the town hall. The second floor of the center house is the **Imperial Hall** (Kaisersaal), lined with the rather romanticized portraits of 52 emperors. Thirteen of the emperors depicted celebrated their coronation banquets here. You can visit this hall Mon. to Sat. from 9am to 1pm and 1:30 to 5pm, on Sun. from 10am to 4pm. Tickets can be purchased at the entrance to the Römer building. The cost is 1 DM (60¢).

The elaborate facade of the Römer, with its ornate balcony and statues of four emperors, overlooks **Römerberg Square.** On festive occasions in days gone by, the square was the scene of oxen roasts and flowing wine. Today, unfortunately, the Justitia Fountain pours forth only water, but oxen are still roasted on special occasions.

Towering over the opposite side of the square is the belfry of St. Nicholas, but the dominating feature of the old town is the 15th-century red-sandstone tower of the **cathedral,** Domplatz 14 (tel. 069/28-43-24), in whose chapel German emperors were elected and crowned for nearly 300 years.

The architecture of many buildings in the old town has changed over the centuries, through enlargement or reconstruction, and since the war many buildings have been rebuilt along more modern lines. The oldest structure left unscathed by the bombings of 1944 was the 12th-century chapel of the Saalhof, constructed as a palace for Frederick Barbarossa. Goethe-Haus, described above, also in the Altstadt, has been carefully reproduced. The Carmelite Convent and 13th-century St. Leonard's Church have a few modifications in their restorations.

At the northern edge of the old town is the **Hauptwache,** an old guard house, which is the heart of modern Frankfurt. Under it is the main subway station with a modern shopping promenade, but the Hauptwache remains serene in spite of the traffic whirling around and underneath.

On the south bank of the Main stands the **Städel Museum,** Schaumainkai 63 (tel. 069/61-70-92), Frankfurt's most important art gallery, containing a fine representative collection of most European schools and periods of paintings. The French impressionists are represented on the first floor by Renoir and Monet, mixed in with the most notable German painters of the 19th and 20th centuries. One of the best of these is Ernst Ludwig Kirchner (1880–1938); see in particular his *Nude Woman with Hat.* Also on the first floor is Johann Heinrich Wilhelm Tischbein's portrait of Goethe in the Campagna in Italy. If you're short on time, however, go directly to the second floor to view the outstanding collection of Flemish primitives, Dutch paintings from the 17th century, and German masters of the 16th century. Works by Dürer, Grünewald, Memling, Hans Holbein, Mantegna, Elsheimer, Rembrandt, Vermeer, Claude Lorrain, Tiepolo, and many others have been brought together here. One of the most impressive paintings is Jan Van Eyck's *Madonna* (1433). Lucas Cranach is represented in several works, including a large winged altarpiece and his rather impish nude *Venus.* The museum also includes a display of works from the Italian school, including a *Madonna* by Bellini. There is a department of prints and drawings containing 30,000 drawings and 70,000 prints of European schools. Recent acquisitions include Jean Antoine Watteau's *L'Île de Cythère* (1709). In the Department of Modern Art are works by Bacon, Dubuffet, Tapiès, and Yves Klein. The museum is open Tues. to Sun. from 10am to 5pm (on Wednesday to 8pm); closed Mon. Admission is 3 DM ($1.80); free Sun.

Liebieghaus, Schaumainkai 71 (tel. 069/63-89-07), contains the city's largest collection of sculpture, spanning thousands of years, from ancient Egyptian to baroque. One of the most impressive works is a bas relief by Andrea della Robbia. Outside of the Bargello in Florence, this museum is considered one of the most important sculpture museums in Europe. The museum is open Tues. to Sun. from 10am to 5pm; Wed. to 8pm. Admission is free. The house was built at the turn of the century, and it's surrounded by a garden. At a tiny café on the premises you can order tasty little fruit pies baked by the woman caretaker.

The **Frankfurt Zoo** (Zoologischer Garten), Alfred-Brehm-Platz 16, (tel. 069/212-33715), is a multifaceted institution intent on education rather than entertainment, and because of this, it is unique and interesting for both young and old. Most of the animals are in enclosures that resemble their native habitats: one of the best examples is the African Veldt Enclosure, landscaped with hills and bushes so that the animals living there can avoid encounters with other breeds. In this single exhibit, antelopes and ostriches roam freely; in the Exotarium, fish and various reptiles live under special climatic conditions; and in an artificially cooled polar landscape, king and gentoo penguins swim and dive. In keeping with its educational policy, the zoo has, in addition to many typical animal exhibits, a nursery where young apes are cared for by zookeepers (this is done only when the mother cannot care for the baby properly), as well as a breeding aviary where you can watch birds preparing unusual nests. A building for small mammals, with a nocturnal section, opened in 1978. It is one of the largest and most diversified of its kind in the world and also contains many educational facilities. The zoo is open daily from 8am to 5pm in winter, to 7pm in summer. The Exotarium is open until 9pm. Admission to the zoo is 7 DM ($4.15) for adults, 3 DM ($1.80) for children aged 2 to 17. For the Exotarium, admission is 3.50 DM ($2.10) for adults, 1.50 DM (90¢) for children. You can purchase a combined ticket for both the zoo and the Exotarium for 8.50 DM ($5.05) for adults, 4 DM ($2.40) for children.

The **Palmengarten,** Siesmayerstrasse 61 (tel. 069/212-339-39), is more than a botanical garden. It is a public park area for recreation throughout the year. During the last decade, the gardens have been totally renewed and conservatories completely reconstructed, as were the historical greenhouses. All year, many thousands of flowers bloom. A garden for perennials, an expanded rock garden, a beautiful rose garden, and rich and varied beds of annuals at all seasons can be admired. The old palmhouse from 1869 is now surrounded by a huge gallery that serves as an exhibition hall for flower shows as well as for botanical exhibitions from early spring to Christmas. During recent years, a complex of conservatories, the Tropicarium, has been built. It has seven parts: semidesert, thorn forest, savannah, monsoon forest, lowland rain forest, highland rain forest, and mangrove with tropical waterplants. A lot of tropical plants can be viewed. Huge collections of orchids, palms, bromeliads, succulents, waterlilies, insectivorous plants, and many others are on display. In summer, concerts are given in the bandshell, and evening events include open-air dancing, jazz, and fountain illumination. Some facilities for food are provided in the garden. It is open daily from 9am to dusk. Admission is 4.50 DM ($2.65).

The **Senckenberg Museum of Natural History,** Senckenberganlage 25 (tel. 069/75-41-1), is considered one of the most significant natural history collections on the Continent. The much-visited ground floor contains fossils of extinct animals —none more notable than the dinosaur—and there's an impressive exhibit of giant whales. Important human fossils are also on display, as well as birds from all over the planet, including, regrettably, some that are already extinct. Hours are 9am to 5pm daily, and admission is 5 DM ($3) for adults, 2 DM ($1.20) for children.

ORGANIZED TOURS

In addition to seeing the sights of Frankfurt on foot or by tram, you can enjoy many attractions from a comfortable coach seat on one of the two daily tours sponsored by the Tourist Information Office. The 2½-hour tours depart in season from the Tourist Information Office in front of the Hauptbahnhof at 10am and 2pm. From November 1 to February 28, the tours depart Mon. to Sun. at 10am from the

Frankfurt International Airport, Arrival Hall B; at 10:30am from the Hauptbahnhof; and at 10:45am from the Tourist Information Office at the Römer.

The English-speaking guide provides a running commentary as you drive through old and new Frankfurt. You'll get brief glimpses of the Altstadt and some of the more interesting modern buildings, with stops at Goethe-Haus and the telecommunications tower. If you prefer a longer or more detailed look at any of the major sights, you'll have to visit them on your own. But the tour provides a good general look at Frankfurt for 28 DM ($16.65), 14 DM ($8.30) for children. Bus tours are made to the Bad Homburg gambling casino.

Tram tours, organized by Stadtwerke Frankfurt am Main, Borneplatz 3 (tel. 069/13-68-24-25), often aboard the **Apple Wine Express,** an old-fashioned streetcar, pass through the city center and Sachsenhausen. Regular trips start on the half hour from the eastern railway station (Ostbahnhof, Danziger Platz), daily from 1:30 to 5:30pm, or from the zoo station Sat. and Sun. from 1:35 to 5:40pm. You can get on at any of the tram stops. The tour costs 3 DM ($1.80), which includes a glass of apple wine or juice and pretzels. Children aged 4 to 14 pay 2 DM ($1.20).

5. Shopping

For shoppers, Frankfurt has everything—the specialty shops are so much like those back in the States that most visitors from America will feel right at home. Shops in the downtown area are open Mon. to Fri., 9am to 6:30pm and Sat. from 9am to 2pm.

In Frankfurt the street or area rather than the specific shop is important. For example, the **Zeil** is one of the most famous shopping streets on the Continent. A pedestrian zone lying between the Hauptwache and the Konstablerwache, it has the highest business turnover of any shopping area in Germany. It was a cattle round-up market as early as the 14th century; by the 19th century it had become a major shopping center. Destroyed in the war, it was redesigned in the 1980s but has not regained its former prestige. Here you will find department stores, clothing shops, shoe stores, and furniture outlets. Nearby is the **Kleinmarkthalle,** a covered market with international grocery products from all over the world.

In the center of Frankfurt, the **Hauptwache** consists of two shopping areas, one above and one below the ground. Groceries, flowers, clothing, tobacco, photo supplies, records, and sporting equipment abound. In the Hauptwache-Passage are found numerous restaurants, travel agencies, and banks.

Schillerstrasse, another pedestrian zone, lies between the Hauptwache and Eschenheimer Turm, near the Stock Exchange. From Schillerstrasse northeast toward Eschenheimer Tor, you'll pass many elegant boutiques and specialty shops.

Southwest of the Hauptwache is the Alte Oper. You can reach it by taking either **Goethestrasse,** with its exclusive stores, evocative of Paris or Milan, or else make your way via the parallel **Grosse Bockenheimerstrasse,** traditionally nicknamed "Fressgasse." Most of the wine dealers, delis, and butcher shops here look back on a long and venerable past. At Opernplatz you find a variety of restaurants and cafés. Going west from the Hauptwache is the Rossmarkt, leading to **Kaiserstrasse.** It passes the BFG skyscraper, which has three floors of exclusive retail stores, boutiques, and restaurants, and directly connects the downtown area to the Hauptbahnhof. Kaiserstrasse is known for its specially large selection of stores selling clothing, hi-fi and photography equipment, and stainless-steel ware. The heart of the fur trade in Frankfurt is **Düsseldorfer Strasse,** opposite the Hauptbahnhof. Most book dealers are located around the Hauptwache and **Goetheplatz.** You will find a large selection of antiques, old books, etchings, and paintings in Braubachstrasse near the Römer, at the Dom, and in Fahrgasse.

Art and antiques are the domain of **Old Sachsenhausen.** In this appealing and original part of Frankfurt, the famous **Frankfurt Flea Market** takes place every Sunday morning at the Schlachthof, where anything and everything are for sale. The Flea Market is an El Dorado where fervent collectors of every creed and color congregate.

Kinderhaus Pfüller, Goethestrasse 12 (tel. 069/28-45-47), concentrates on children's wear, from baby clothes all the way up to teenage fashions. It also sells bath towels and linen.

Modelhaus Pfüller, Goethestrasse 15-17 (tel. 069/28-45-47), is a specialist in traditional fashions for women, offering a line of exclusive lingerie and beachwear, among other merchandise.

Lorey, Schillerstrasse 16 (tel. 069/29-99-50), carries one of the best selections of Hummel and Meissen figurines.

On the same street, check out **Foto Netthold,** Schillerstrasse 13, (tel. 069/28-25-61), for your photo needs.

One of the best bookstores in Frankfurt is **Blazek & Bergmann,** Goethestrasse 1 (tel. 069/28-86-48).

Finally, one of the best centers of elegant jewelry in Frankfurt is **Gerhard Wempe,** An der Hauptwache 7 (tel. 069/29-17-77). They also have one of the biggest collections of watches for sale anywhere in Germany, with all the famous Swiss brands heavily featured.

---

6. After Dark

CLUBS AND BARS

St. John's Inn, Grosser Hirschgraben 20 (tel. 069/29-25-18), is found across from Goethe-Haus, a short walk from the Hauptwache. Its cozy old-world ambience is created in part by its large brick-and-timber fireplace with raised hearth, Windsor chairs, and candlelit tables. It's possible to drop in just for drinks, but you may order food as well; the house specialty is a pot of Irish stew. Meals cost 25 DM ($14.85) to 55 DM ($32.65). A disc jockey plays international favorites. Often it's so crowded that you can't get in. Open from 9pm to 4am; closed Sun. (open Sun. if there's a fair on in Frankfurt).

Jimmy's, Hotel Hessicher Hof, Friedrich-Ebert-Anlage 40 (tel. 069/75-40-0), will greet you with a luxurious atmosphere. It opens daily at 8pm, serving snacks and other specialties until 4am in an atmosphere of candlelit calm and soft background music. You can enjoy drinks, with prices beginning at 12 DM ($7.15), in the midst of a social gathering or while you relax after a busy day.

Jazz Haus, Kleine Bockenheimerstrasse 12 (tel. 069/28-71-94), which used to attract some of the big names of international jazz, now offers only recorded music. No one dances here, yet it's known as a "discotheque for jazz." Enthusiasts prefer the smoky, permissive, and relaxed ambience of the club, which has a distinctive personality. There's no cover, but a medium-size beer goes for 3.30 DM ($1.95). Hours are 6pm to 1am daily. The only food served is a selection of small snacks.

For jazz, try **Jazz-Kneipe,** Berlinstrasse 70 (tel. 069/28-71-73), which has some lively jam sessions. It's considered the number-one place in Frankfurt for traditional swing. It's open daily from 8pm to 4am, with live music from 10pm to 3am. The cover charge ranges from 5 DM ($3) to 8 DM ($14.75).

Paradieshof, Paradiesgasse (tel. 069/62-40-53), is a Henninger Brau house in the apple-wine district. This establishment is divided into two parts, including a street-level dancing restaurant where food and music begin at 8pm every night of the week. Food can be ordered until 12:30am, and the music (contemporary) stops at 1am. There's a cover charge of 3 DM ($1.80) on Thurs., Fri., and Sat. Full meals, costing from 35 DM ($20.80), include such dishes as herring, snails in garlic butter, barbecued rumpsteak, filet mignon, and lamb cutlets. The disco in the basement operates on Thurs., Fri., and Sat. from 8pm to either 2am or 3am. Entrance is 9 DM ($5.35).

Maier Gustl's Bayrisch Zell, Münchnerstrasse 57 (tel. 069/23-20-92), is one of the best-known beerhalls in Frankfurt. It's perfect for a checkered-tablecloth kind of Teutonic nostalgia in a heavily timbered re-creation of a mountain chalet. Two bands play nightly, one a typical Bavarian brass group and one a modern show band, changing every half hour so that the music is nonstop. Some 1,000 persons can be fitted into the two dance floors. Some of the tables have private phones for electronic assignations with a person you fancy. The place even has a shooting gallery. Meals are available, with the famous leg of pork (Eisbein mit Sauerkraut), the most expensive dish, going for 15 DM ($8.90). Beer, depending on the size, costs 6 DM ($3.55) to 10 DM ($5.95). The place is open daily from 7pm to 4am.

Lipizzaner Bar, Steigenberger Frankfurter Hof, Am Kaiserplatz (tel. 069/2-15-02), is regarded as the most elegant bar in town, with crystal mirrors, wood paneling, and international drinks and cocktails that cost from 14 DM ($8.30). There is nightly live entertainment by a pianist. The bar is open daily from 10pm to 2am.

In the catacombs of the Frankfurt airport is **Dorian Gray** (tel. 069/69-15-21), on O Level of Section C, reached from the heart of the city in about 15 minutes aboard an S-train, departing from the Hauptbahnhof every 20 minutes or so. (This place should not be confused with Dorian Gay, a self-styled "gaymen sexshop" in another part of the city.) Dorian Gray is a disco that enjoys a wide popularity, as well as a Continental bistro, with well-appointed lounges and clubroom, often drawing an elegant, well-dressed crowd. You can order from a wide range of drinks. Beer is the cheapest, of course, costing from 6 DM ($3.55) a mug. The club is open Wed. and Thurs. 9pm to 4am; Fri. from 9pm to 6am; Sat. 9am to noon the following day.

Cooky's, Am Salzhaus 4 (tel. 069/28-76-62), presents live music every Mon., including rock, acid, funk, and the blues. Acts change frequently. The club opens nightly at 10:30pm, until about 4am. On Fri. and Sat., it closes at 6am. Though the entrance price depends on the act booked, it is usually in the range of 6 DM ($3.55) to 12 DM ($7.15). You can dance, eat, drink, or just listen to the music.

In a 16-square-block area in front of the Hauptbahnhof, you will find a rowdier kind of entertainment. Here you'll discover what the Germans call *erotische Spiele*. Doormen will practically pull you inside to view porno movies, sex shows, sex shops, even discos teeming with prostitutes. *Warning:* This area is dangerous; don't go there alone.

CULTURAL ENTERTAINMENT

Alte Oper, Opernplatz (tel. 069/13-40-400), is the pride of Frankfurt, even though opera is presented elsewhere today. This building was reopened in 1981 following its reconstruction after World War II bombings. The original building was officially opened in 1880 by Kaiser Wilhelm I. At that time, it was hailed as one of the most beautiful theaters in Europe. Today, the "old opera" is part of the intrinsic cultural life of the city, the site of frequent symphonic and choral concerts.

To hear the city's opera company perform, go to Städtische Bühnen/Oper, Theaterplatz 1–3 (tel. 069/212-374-34). Productions of the Frankfurt Municipal Opera in this newly built theater have received worldwide recognition in recent years.

If your German is adequate, you can attend a performance at the same address of the Städtische Bühnen/Schauspiel, Theaterplatz 1–3 (tel. 069/212-374-35), which is a forum for classic German plays as well as modern drama. One auditorium at this cultural center is devoted to opera, another two stages for drama.

There are some two dozen or so theaters in Frankfurt. These include the **Fritz Rémond Theater im Zoo** at the Frankfurt Zoo, Alfred Brehm Platz (tel. 069/43-51-66), which often stages American and British productions in German. For tickets, call 069/44-40-44.

Light comedy—often called "boulevard theater"—is presented at **Die Komödie,** Theaterplatz at Neue Mainzerstrasse 18 (tel. 069/28-45-80).

Hessischer-Rundfunk, Bertramstrasse 8 (tel. 069/15-51), has a changing repertoire of musical events, including chamber music concerts.

You can purchase tickets at the tourist office for many of these major cultural presentations, or at the theater box offices.

---

7. Exploring the Environs

Unless you're rushed beyond reason, you should allow an extra day or two in Frankfurt to take a look at some of the attractions of the surrounding countryside. Here you'll stumble on little medieval towns, or you'll be awed by the sophisticated spas of the Taunus. I'll highlight some of the best attractions below.

THE TAUNUS

These wooded hills north of Frankfurt include peaks of the ancient mountain range cut by the Rhine and its tributaries. The geological formations have created a number of mineral springs along the periphery of the range. Entrepreneurs have developed these springs into spas; two of the most active Taunus spas, Bad Homburg and Bad Nauheim, are described separately in Chapter V. From the Taunus's highest peak, the **Grosser Feldberg,** the towers of Frankfurt, 15 miles away, become part of the panoramic view. Because of its altitude, this peak is an important telecommunications post for the German post office. A few miles south of the Grosser Feldberg is one of the Taunus's most popular landmarks.

Kronberg im Taunus

Nine miles northwest of Frankfurt, **Schloss Hotel Kronberg,** Hainstrasse 25, D-6242 Kronberg (tel. 06173/70101), comes as close as one can get to living in a royal castle. The former home of Queen Victoria's eldest daughter, the German Empress Victoria Friedrich, it was turned into a hotel in 1954. Architecturally, the hotel is Wagnerian in scope, with towers, turrets, and stone terraces overlooking the vast forest (where there is an 18-hole golf course, once used by General Eisenhower). The Schloss attracts everyone from presidents to kings to international bankers and industrialists, including on one occasion President Nixon and King Constantine of Greece. Throughout the salons, drawing rooms, and dining halls, there are abundant antiques and a number of valuable tapestries. Guests enjoy the English library and the petite salon. Everywhere you turn, even in the intimate drinking lounge, you'll see paintings worthy of a museum. The hotel boasts the only bar in the world with originals by Turner, Sir Thomas Lawrence, and Sir Joshua Reynolds.

The hotel's 57 rooms, 7 of which are suites, all contain private baths. In 1967 the castle was swept by a devastating fire and during the restoration, 20 rooms and some modern furnishings were added; most of the rooms still have real antiques, however. The price of a single room is 263 DM ($156.15) to 363 DM ($215.55) daily, and doubles go for 396 DM ($235.15) to 591 DM ($350.95). The hotel is open year round. The hotel's dining room serves good food, and the service is superb, almost courtly. The menu is à la carte, a dinner costing 55 DM ($32.65) to 125 DM ($74.25). Diners arriving just to enjoy the classic, French-oriented cuisine can do so daily from noon to 2:30pm and 6:30 to 10:30pm. Since space is limited, reservations are imperative.

Königstein im Taunus

Surrounded by fields of wildflowers and wooded hills, **Sonnenhof Königstein,** Falkensteinerstrasse 9, D-6240 Königstein im Taunus (tel. 06174/2-90-80), is ideal for nature lovers seeking a peaceful interlude. If you're just passing through Königstein on a tour of the Taunus, you may want to stop here for dinner after viewing the feudal ruins of the Königstein fortress overlooking the town. The hotel's menu is an international one. Roast dishes are a specialty, such as a haunch of stag in cream, and there are a number of seafood items on the menu. Meals cost 50 DM ($29.70) to 80 DM ($47.50).

If you plan to stay over, the hotel offers 45 comfortable rooms, all overlooking the Main Valley and Taunus hills. Singles rent for 100 DM ($59.40) to 142 DM ($84.30) daily, and doubles go for 145 DM ($86.10) to 240 DM ($142.50). But whether you're staying for dinner or for the night, you'll find the whole staff attentive and the atmosphere one of relaxed elegance. Tennis, swimming pool, and a sauna are additional attractions.

THE ODENWALD

Odin, chief of the Nordic gods, could probably still identify his forest today. Many of the landmarks in this farm country south of Frankfurt date from legendary beginnings. For instance, the well in the forest where Siegfried met his death at the hand of Hagen stands today in a tiny village on the Siegfriedstrasse, one of the best roads for exploring the Odenwald.

The climate here is among the warmest in Germany, owing to the shelter of the surrounding mountains. Blossoms appear early on trees and vines, and abundant harvests are celebrated in the otherwise quiet little German towns. To reach the Odenwald, drive south from Frankfurt to Darmstadt, then take the Bergstrasse (Rte. 3) running toward Heidelberg. This scenic route leads along the western slopes of the mountains to some charming old towns.

Bensheim

Just 30 miles south of Frankfurt, Bensheim could be an inspiring place even for a short flying visit from Frankfurt if you're between planes and want to see a typical German town. Here the old timbered and plastered buildings, clustered about tiny squares and fountains, look as if they've been copied from a Christmas card. The vineyards around the town indicate that this is wine country. Each September, Bensheim is the scene of the most exuberant wine festival in the Odenwald, the Bergstrasse Wine Festival.

Just west of Bensheim is its major sightseeing attraction, the ruins of the great abbey at **Lorsch,** at the edge of the Rhineland Palatinate. The monastery was built in Carolingian style in the eighth century, with a massive Königshalle (King's Hall), adorned with huge columns and walls covered with mosaics.

The best place to stay in the area is the **Parkhotel Krone,** Darmstädterstrasse 168, D-6140 Bensheim (tel. 06251/73081), which is the center of social life and business conferences in the area. Since 1655 there has been an inn on this spot, and wayfarers to Frankfurt have often stopped here before venturing on to the big Hessian city. Today it is completely modernized and updated, with 55 streamlined bedrooms. Single rooms rent for 135 DM ($80.15) nightly, and doubles go for 175 DM ($103.90). In addition to its comfort, special features of the Krone include an indoor pool, a sauna, and a fitness room. The hotel's restaurant, the Auerbacher, ranks as the best in the area. If it is featured on the menu, try the duck breast in a cream sauce laced with Calvados, a specialty of Normandy. Meals range in price from 40 DM ($23.75) to 60 DM ($35.65), depending on what you order.

Erbach im Odenwald

This town's reason for being seems to be the magnificent baroque palace of the Erbach-Erbach family, **Schloss Erbach** (tel. 06062/3700). The present structure, dating from 1736, was built on the site of an earlier, 14th-century castle, of which only an ancient round watchtower has survived. The palace is a museum, with its huge knight's hall, endless corridors, and Gothic painted windows. But even more remarkable are the collections exhibited within the castle halls: art treasures of the

Erbach-Erbach family, including medieval sculptures and ivory displays. The castle and its museums are open from March 1 to October 31, daily from 8:30 am to noon and 1:30 to 5pm, charging 5 DM ($3) for admission.

Michelstadt

In a valley just 3 miles north of Erbach, Michelstadt resembles a prosperous and commercial medieval town. Around the marketplace are old houses and the 15th-century town hall, a half-timbered structure with oriel windows and a pointed roof supported by wooden pillars.

Just outside the town is the ancient fortified **Fürstenau Castle** (tel. 06068/2221), built in the 14th century for the Archbishopric of Mainz. In the 16th century it was expanded into a Renaissance palace, with an unusual archway connecting it to the courtyard. The castle sits in a huge English-style park dating from 1756. The courtyard can be visited by the public. Daily visiting hours are 9am to noon and 1 to around 5:30pm (to 4pm in winter).

For meals or lodgings in Michelstadt, the inn described below is the most logical choice.

Drei Hasen, Braunstrasse 5, D-6120 Michelstadt (tel. 06061/71017), is a glamorized tavern, first established in 1830. From his post at the cash register, the innkeeper makes frequent appearances at the tables to wish his guests "bon appétit." The hotel rents 20 bedrooms, furnished in Directoire style; each room comes with shower, toilet, TV, and phone. Including a breakfast buffet, singles cost 72 DM ($42.75) daily, with doubles going for 110 DM ($65.30). The best rooms have a view of the market square. In true inn fashion, the meals are more of a source of revenue than the beds. Be sure to sample the specialty, original Nürnberger Rostbratwurst; other recommended and featured items include Schweinhaxen and Holsteiner Schnitzel. Menus cost 28 DM ($16.65) to 55 DM ($32.65).

THE SPESSART

Separated from the Odenwald by the snakelike Main River, the oak-covered Spessart Mountains are much more rugged than the rolling hills to the west, broken here and there to make room for an old village or castle. Most of the towns in the Spessart lie along the Main, their link to the outside world. At the confluence of the Main and the Tauber stands our first stop.

Wertheim

Towering over the medieval town are the ruins of the ancient castle of the feudal counts of Wertheim. The town is much better preserved than the castle, with a marketplace dating from the 16th century and narrow brick streets sheltered by overhanging timbered houses. Beside the Tauber stands the ancient city gate of Wertheim, the Kittstein Tower, a reminder of the 14th-century days when Wertheim was an important city and not the sleepy community of today.

Hotel Schwan, Mainplatz 8, D-6980 Wertheim (tel. 09342/12-78), is an enchanting inn, part of it incorporating the previously mentioned medieval stone tower. Only a roadway separates it from the river. The innkeeper has considerably upgraded the Schwan, including the plumbing, and the 32 upstairs accommodations are comfortable. Doubles with baths rent for 140 DM ($83.15) daily. Singles with baths cost 100 DM ($59.40). À la carte meals start at 30 DM ($17.80), going up to 55 DM ($32.65). The Schwan is easy to spot, with its ornate wrought-iron sign projecting over the front dining terrace.

In the environs, in-the-know Frankfurters flock to **Hotel Schweizer Stuben,** Geiselbrunnweg 11, D-6980 Wertheim-Bettingen (tel. 09342/3070), a *Relais & Châteaux* establishment, which is a gourmet mecca renowned throughout Germany. Set in a resort that sprawls across 14 acres of sporting facilities, the deluxe hotel is the personification of country elegance. It offers a trio of restaurants: Swiss, Italian, and French. The famous one is French, serving food prepared by master chef Dieter

Müller. The decor is modern yet rustic, and from a table by the window a view is possible over the meadow to the Main. A five-course menu is offered at 160 DM ($95), a seven-course repast at 190 DM ($112.80). To begin with, order Guglhupf, a goose liver terrine in aspic for which the chef is justly acclaimed. Try such entrees as chicken in a Chardonnay sauce with truffles, or pigeon breast au jus with truffles.

The hotel also offers 33 bedrooms, individualized in a traditional Swiss chalet–style decor. The wooden furnishings are tasteful, and there is a beautiful garden. Breakfast is among the most sumptuous you'll be served in Germany, including such dishes as steak tartare and chicken liver pâté with brioches. Instead of coffee, you can wash it all down with champagne. Prices are 200 DM ($118.75) to 345 DM ($209) daily for a single, 250 DM ($147.50) to 395 DM ($233) for a double.

Mespelbrunn

Just 3 miles from the Weibersbrunn exit of the Frankfurt-Würzburg Autobahn, the little village of Mespelbrunn seems far removed from the reality of 20th-century living.

The chief attraction of the town is the well-preserved Renaissance castle of the counts of Ingelheim. The **Schloss Mespelbrunn** is a lake palace, more common in France than in Germany, completely surrounded by water. The rooms are open to the public from March to November, daily from 9am to 6pm. The admission price is 5 DM ($3). Included is a museum devoted to the history of the ruling family.

The best restaurant close at hand is **Schlossgaststätte,** Schlossalle 25, D-8751 Mespelbrunn (tel. 06092/2-56). Lots of natural stone graces the facade of this hotel, which is run with discreet care and attention. It has a garden terrace and a café, serving good, reasonably priced food. Set meals range from 21 DM ($12.45) to 40 DM ($23.75), or you can order from a more expensive à la carte menu. The hotel also has 40 pleasantly furnished bedrooms, costing 60 DM ($35.65) to 95 DM ($56.40) daily for a single, 80 DM ($47.50) to 125 DM ($74.25) for a double. Many of these tranquil units open onto a lovely view of the forest, only 55 yards from the hotel. Closed in January and February.

MUNICH

To Münchners, beer has been the core of existence for centuries. Songs were written in praise of the brew, festivals were organized in its honor, and beerhalls were the scenes of all major events.

The people of Munich don't need much of a reason for celebrating. If you arrive here in late September, you'll find them in the middle of a festival in honor of Ludwig I's engagement to Princess Theresa—and that took place in 1810! The Oktoberfest, for which more than 7 million may show up, starts on a Saturday, lasts 16 days, and ends the first Sunday in October. Although this great Oktoberfest, where beer flows as freely as water, is the most famous of Munich's festivals, the city is actually less inhibited and more individualistic during the pre-Lenten **Fasching** (Carnival). Even the most reserved Germans are caught up in this whirl of colorful parades, masked balls, and revelry.

Between these two festival seasons, Munich remains lively all year—fairs and holidays seem to follow one on top of the other. But no "oompah" town this. You'll find the most sophisticated clubs, the best theaters, and the finest concert halls as well. Don't go to Munich to rest—it's a city mainly for having fun.

1. Munich—Past and Present

One of Europe's most visited cities, filled with monuments and fabulous museums, Munich is a city with memories of yesterday, both good and bad, but it is very much a city living in its present, with hopes for a great future. Don't worry about feeling lost and bewildered here. You'll be like most everybody else: two-thirds of the population are newcomers.

WHAT IT WAS

Munich owes its name to a tiny settlement of monks near the banks of the Isar River more than 1,200 years ago. Their cloister and the little villages that grew up around it were referred to as *Munichen*, the little monks. In modern German, that nickname has become *München*. A little monk is incorporated into the city's coat-of-arms—he raises his hands as if he wants to speak. If so, he'll probably say, "Gruss Gott!" the welcome still used around here.

Munich lay on the Salzstrasse (salt route) linking Augsburg with Salzburg, and in 1158, when Duke Henry the Lion of the house of Wittelsbach, diverted the salt trade over the bridge "by the monks," Munich began to thrive as the trading center for Upper Bavaria. In time the little town grew into a walled city with entrance through five gates. One was near what is now the Alte Rathaus (or old town hall) on Marienplatz; this was once the grain market, and very early in the city's history formed its heartbeat. By the end of the 13th century, the city had increased its size fivefold. The Wittelsbachs were to retain power until the end of World War I (1918). Autocratic and proud, they ruled with an iron hand, though many historians have called them "benevolent despots."

During the centuries that followed, Munich went through many vicissitudes. From 1314 to 1347, it was an imperial city when its duke, Ludwig IV, called "Ludwig the Bavarian," became German emperor. In 1327, a great fire destroyed much of the city. During the Reformation period, Munich remained loyal to the Roman Catholic religion, and became the chief city of the Counter-Reformation in Germany.

In 1799 Bavaria became a sovereign state when Napoleon Bonaparte crowned Maximilian IV Joseph as King Maximilian I, a position it held for the better part of the 19th century. It was in the 19th century that real growth took place, and the art-loving kings, Ludwig I, Maximilian II, and Ludwig II built it up into "a modern Athens." Ludwig I attracted artists, writers, sculptors, and painters to the city, but his notorious love affair with the dancer Lola Montez (subject of countless movies) threatened his reign. Finally, in 1848, Ludwig abdicated, Ms. Montez fled to Mexico, and Ludwig's son, Maximilian, assumed power.

Interested in the arts and sciences, Maximilian II ushered in a liberal era, which included the founding in 1855 of the Bavarian National Museum. The railway arrived in 1839. When Maximilian II died in 1864, Ludwig II became the ruler. He is the Bavarian king best known around the world today, mainly because of his "fairytale castles."

In 1871, under the unification plan for Germany, Bavaria lost its status as an independent state. Ludwig died by mysterious drowning in 1886. Under his successor, Prince Regent Luitpold, Munich became known as a cultural city, and played an important part in the development of art in the 19th and early 20th centuries, attracting such artists as Wassily Kandinsky and Paul Klee. By this time the city had gained a reputation for drinking, merrymaking, and festivals.

World War I brought hunger and deprivation to the city. Demonstrations and social unrest followed the war. A Munich republic was established, but it did not last long. Reaction set in. Julius Streicher, later to become a colleague of Hitler's, founded the anti-Semitic German Freedom Party. Unemployment and inflation plagued the city, problems to be exploited by Hitler. In 1923 Hitler's "beerhall putsch" attempted—and failed—to overthrow the government. He was sentenced to five years in prison, during which time he wrote *Mein Kampf*. After he was released in 1924, he established his headquarters in the city.

By 1933 Munich was in the grip of a National Socialist dictatorship. The Bavarian government, led by Heinrich Held, was dissolved, the first concentration camp, Dachau, was established outside Munich, and a torture chamber was set up in the former Wittelsbach Palace. The city at the time had 10,000 Jews, but only 200 were to survive.

Hitler and Chamberlain came to the city in 1938 to sign the infamous Munich Pact. Then came World War II, and the face of Munich was to be changed forever. Air raid followed air raid, especially in 1942, and nearly half the city had been destroyed by the time American troops arrived on April 30, 1945. Over 200,000 people had lost their lives.

WHAT IT IS NOW

With something approaching a miracle, Munich bounced back from the disaster of World War II. Rubble was cleaned up, the city rebuilt. In 1949, upon establishment of the Federal Republic of Germany, it became the capital of the Federal Land of Bavaria. It was to be—and still is—a major economic city, a center of north–south trade in Europe. The largest industrial city of the Federal Republic, it soon attracted such famous names as Siemens and BMW, becoming a center for hi-tech microelectronics. It has the biggest publishing empire in Germany, as well as a burgeoning film industry, and is the largest university town in Germany.

By 1957 the population had jumped from 470,000 to 1 million. In 1972 the city played host to the Olympic Games.

Today, with some 1.2 million inhabitants, of which 16% are foreigners, Munich is the third-largest city in Germany. It is also the Germans' first choice as a place to live, according to various polls. Still a city of art and culture, it remains one of the most beautiful of German cities—although much of the older beauty is gone forever.

It's been called "the secret capital of Germany."

---

2. Orientation

Munich is just slightly smaller than Berlin and Hamburg. Trying to see all of it would be a major undertaking; however, you can explore the heart of Munich on foot. Many of its attractions are in its environs, and you'll have to rely on public transportation (see "Getting Around") to take in such sights as Schloss Nymphenburg.

ARRIVAL IN MUNICH

The **international airport** is at Riem, some 5 miles from the center of Munich. Once you've cleared customs, you can take an airport bus for 5 DM ($2.95), which will bring you to the Hauptbahnhof, the city's main railway terminal. Buses depart about every 15 minutes—they are, of course, far cheaper than cabs.

You may also arrive at the Hauptbahnhof by train. In either case, you'll be in the very heart of Munich, and from that central point you can avail yourself of various means of public transportation, discussed below. For general information about the German Federal Railroad, call 089/194-19. And if you want to check on your flight, the number to call at Airport Munich-Riem is 089/92-112-27.

A QUICK OVERVIEW

Munich's **Hauptbahnhof,** the main railway station, lies just to the west of the center of town and opens onto Bahnhofplatz. From the square (hardly the most attractive part of Munich), you can take Schützenstrasse to one of the major centers of Munich, Karlsplatz (nicknamed Stachus). Many streetcar lines converge on this square. From Karlsplatz, you can continue east along the pedestrian-only streets of Neuhauserstrasse and Kaufingerstrasse until you reach Marienplatz, where you'll be deep in the old town of Munich (for a more complete description of this sector, refer to the "The Sights" later in this chapter).

From Marienplatz, with its daily Glockenspiel performance, you can take a

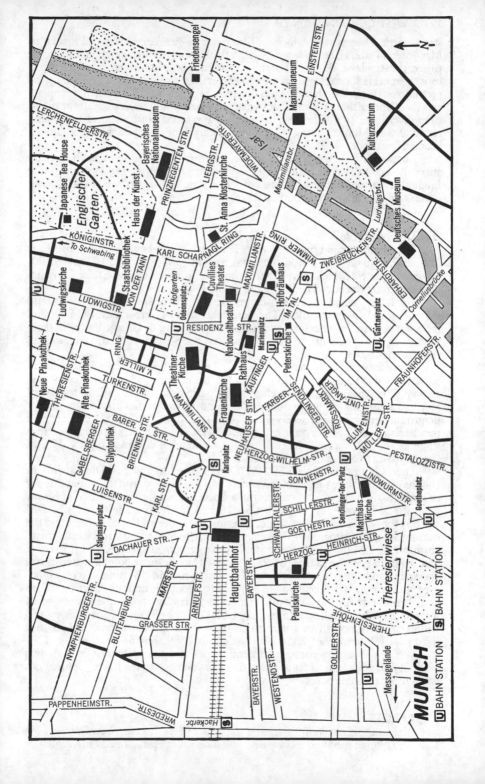

MUNICH

S BAHN STATION
U BAHN STATION

street north, Dienerstrase, which will lead you to Residenzstrasse and finally, to Max-Joseph-Platz, a landmark square, with the Nationaltheater and the former royal palace, the Residenz. To the east of this square runs Maximilianstrasse, which is perhaps the most fashionable shopping and restaurant street of Munich, containing the prestigious Hotel Vier Jahreszeiten Kempinski München. Between Marienplatz and the Nationaltheater is the Platzl quarter, where you'll want to head for nighttime diversions, as it's the seat of some of the finest (and some of the worst) restaurants in Munich, along with the landmark Hofbräuhaus, the most famous beerhall in Europe.

North of the old town is Schwabing, a former bohemian section whose main street is Leopoldstrasse. The large, sprawling municipal park grounds, the Englischer Garten, are found due east of Schwabing. To the northwest of Schwabing is the Olympic complex (more about that later).

GETTING AROUND

The city has a rapid transit system. The subway is to be preferred to streetcars and certainly to the high-priced taxis, which cost 7 DM ($4.15) to 10 DM ($5.90) for an average ride. However, if you want one in an emergency, they are radio-dispatched and can be reached by calling 2-1611.

The underground network contains many convenient electronic devices, and the rides are relatively soundless. The same ticket entitles you to ride the U-Bahn and the S-Bahn, as well as streetcars and buses. The U-Bahn, or Untergrundbahn (subway), is the line you will use most frequently; the S-Bahn, or Stadtbahn, services suburban locations.

At the transport hub, Marienplatz, U-Bahn and S-Bahn rails crisscross each other. It's possible to use your Eurailpass on S-Bahn journeys, as it's a state-owned railway. Otherwise, you must purchase a single-trip ticket or a strip ticket for several journeys at one of the blue vending machines positioned at the entryways to the underground stations. These tickets entitle you to ride both the "S" and "U" lines, and they're also good for rides on streetcars and buses. If you're making only one trip, a single ticket will average 2.40 DM ($1.40), although it can go as high as 12 DM ($7.15) to go to one of the outlying areas.

The 24-hour ticket costs 7.50 DM ($4.45) for adults and 2.50 DM ($1.50) for children for the entire metropolitan system and can be used with no limitations day or night. Sign the ticket and cancel it when you begin your first journey. It is now good for 24 hours. A 24-hour ticket for 15 DM ($8.90) for adults and 4.50 DM ($2.65) for children is also available, covering the entire metropolitan area and the outside S-Bahn territory. Strip tickets, called Streifenkarte, come in 10 blue strips, costing 9.50 DM ($5.65) for five rides in the metropolitan area. A blue strip ticket with 16 strips goes for 15 DM ($8.90). A trip within the metropolitan area costs you two strips, and your two strips are valid for two hours. In that time, you may interrupt your trip and transfer as you like, traveling in one continuous direction. When you reverse your direction, you must cancel two strips again. Children aged 4 to 14 use the red Kinderstreifenkarte costing 4.50 DM ($2.65) for six strips. For a trip within the metropolitan area, they cancel only one strip. Above the age of 15, they must pay adult fares. For S-Bahn information, dial 089/55-75-75.

Where the subway comes to an end, buses and streetcars take over. As was pointed out, you can transfer as many times as you need to reach your destination, while using the same ticket.

FAST FACTS

Besides the general information given under "Fast Facts for West Germany" in Chapter II, some specific data may help you have a more pleasant stay in Munich.

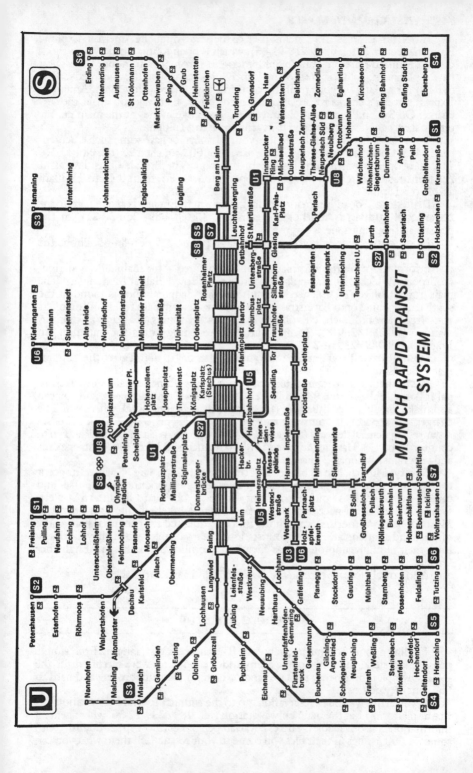

MUNICH RAPID TRANSIT SYSTEM

American Express: Your lifeline back to the States might be American Express, Promenadeplatz 6 (tel. 089/219-91-45), which is open for mail pickup and check cashing Mon. to Fri. from 9am to 5:30pm, on Sat. from 9am to noon. Unless you have a platinum, gold, or green American Express card, you'll be charged 2 DM ($1.20) for picking up your mail. If you don't have a card, show them American Express traveler's checks to prove you're a customer; that way you avoid the surcharge. On Sat. and Sun. or at night, you can exchange money at the main railway terminal exchange, which is open daily from 6am to 11:30pm.

Consulate: In case you should lose your passport, or have some such emergency, the **U.S. Consulate** is at Königinstrasse 5, D-8000 München 22 (tel. 089/2-30-11). It is open Mon. to Fri. from 8am to noon. The **British Consulate** is at Amalienstrasse 62 (tel. 089/3940-15); open Mon. to Fri. from 8:45 to 11:30am and 1 to 3:15pm.

Drugstore: For an international drugstore where English is spoken, go to **International Ludwig's Apotheke,** Neuhauser 8 (tel. 089/260-30-21), in the pedestrian shopping zone.

Emergencies: For emergency medical aid, phone 089/55-86-61. Phone the police at 110.

Information: Tourist information can be obtained at the main railway station, at Airport Munich-Riem (arrivals hall), and at the Town Hall at Marienplatz. The main tourist office (Fremdenverkehrsamt) at the Hauptbahnhof is found at the south exit opening onto Bayerstrasse. It is open daily from 8am to 11pm and offers you a free map of Munich. This office will also reserve rooms (see below). For information, call 089/239-11. To find out about opening hours for museums (in English), call 089/2391-62.

Laundromat: If you want to wash your clothes day or night, go to the laundromat at Landshuter Allee 77, near Rothreuzplatz.

Post office: The Postamt München stands across from the main railway terminal at Bahnhofplatz 1 (tel. 089/5388-27-30). It's open day and night, and you can also make long-distance calls here (far cheaper than at your hotel, where you'll be charged for service). If you want to have your mail sent to you, mark it "poste restante" for general delivery (take along your passport to reclaim any mail and go to counter 16 or 17). Have it addressed D-8000 München 32. For long-distance calls and telegrams, it is open 24 hours.

Safety: Munich, like all big cities of the world, has its share of crime. Innocent tourists are often victims. The major crimes are pickpocketing and purse- and camera-snatching. It is your responsibility to keep your guard up and to be alert. Wear a moneybelt. If necessary, store valuables in a hotel safe if one is provided. Most robberies of tourists occur in the much-frequented tourist areas, such as the one around Marienplatz. Many tourists lose their valuables when they carelessly leave their clothing unprotected as they join the nude sunbathers in Englischer Garten.

And now, before we take on the town, let's find a place to stay.

---

3. Where to Stay

Finding a room is comparatively easy. The choice is vast, ranging from simple pensions to sleek, modern hotels. Many older candidates were facelifted for the 1972 Olympics. In general, the tabs tend to be high. Bargains are few and hard to find, but they do exist.

If you arrive without a reservation, go to the **Munich Tourist Information Office** at platform 11 at the main railway station (tel. 089/239-12-56, where general information is also available). There, Bavarian personnel (most speak English) with some 34,000 listings in their files will come to your rescue. Tell them what you can afford, pay a fee, and get a receipt—as well as a map with instructions on how to reach the accommodation into which they have booked you. You pay a fee of about 3 DM ($1.80) per room. Keep your receipt. If you don't like the room to which you have been sent, go back to the tourist office and they will try to find you another lodging at no extra charge. The tourist office at the Hauptbahnhof is open daily from 8am to 11pm; the one at the airport arrivals hall (tel. 089/239-12-66), Mon. to Sat. from 8:30am to 10pm (Sun. from 1 to 9pm); and the one at the Town Hall, next to the elevator to the tower, Mon. to Fri. from 9am to 5pm (closed Sat. and Sun.). Correspondence, however, should be addressed to the administration offices at Sendlingerstrasse/Ruffinihaus, D-8000 München 2. These offices are open Mon. to Fri. from 9am to 4pm.

DELUXE HOTELS

The most elegant place to stay in Munich is the **Hotel Vier Jahreszeiten Kempinski München,** Maximilianstrasse 17, D-8000 München 22 (089/230-39-0), a grand hotel with a tradition stretching back to 1858. King Maximilian II took a personal interest in the establishment of this hotel and helped the founder, restaurateur August Schimon, financially. The hotel gained worldwide fame under the ownership of the Walterspiel family, who brought it to the peak of its prominence and still owned it when it was mostly destroyed in a 1944 air raid. They rebuilt it and brought it back to its number-one position, selling it in 1970 to its present proprietors, Kempinski AG and Lufthansa German Airlines. Das Restaurant, its finest dining spot (open nightly), is recommended separately. Other features of the Four Seasons, as the name translates, are the magnificent glass roof (with emblems representing the four seasons of the year) above the lobby, an indoor swimming pool and sauna, a solarium, an underground garage, and courteous service. Guests like to linger in the Jahreszeiten Bar, where piano music is played nightly during the cocktail hour, with an international trio performing until 2am.

The completely refurnished Bisto Eck surprises guests with its modern yet classical atmosphere. It overlooks Munich's elegant Maximilianstrasse. The newly designed Theaterkeller welcomes you at night to a comfortable setting; every Sat. from 6pm to midnight, a romantic candlelit buffet awaits you there. On Sun. from 10:30am to 2:30pm, the Theaterkeller invites you to a buffet brunch.

The 340 guest rooms and suites, which have hosted royalty, statesmen, and famed personalities from all over the world, combine the charm of days gone by with the amenities of the modern world. Each of the bedrooms is air-conditioned and contains a bath/shower, minibar, TV, radio, and direct-dial phone. Singles cost 265 DM ($157.35) to 385 DM ($228.60) daily, and doubles rent for 410 DM ($243.45) to 530 DM ($314.70). The windows of rooms opening onto Maximilianstrasse are double-glazed, and quiet is assured in the units facing the three inner courts. The hotel is not connected to other Vier Jahreszeiten hotels found throughout Germany.

Considered by many travelers a Bavarian version of New York's Waldorf-Astoria, the **Bayerischer Hof und Palais Montgelas,** Promenadeplatz 2–6, D-8000 München 2 (tel. 089/2-12-00), is in a swank location, across from American Express, opening onto a little tree-filled square. The tastefully decorated central lounge, with English and French reproductions and Oriental rugs, is practically the living room of Munich: "Meet you in the lounge of the Bayerischer Hof" is heard often. The integration of the sumptuously decorated Palais Montgelas into the hotel brought deluxe suites and double rooms, as well as a number of conference and banqueting rooms. The 440 bedrooms all have baths or showers, phones, radios, TVs, and minibars. Singles rent for 220 DM ($130.65) to 270 DM ($165.35) daily, depending on size, bath facilities, and view. Doubles cost 350 DM ($207.85) to 450 DM ($267.20). Some rooms are air-conditioned. All major credit cards are accepted.

The major dining room evokes the grandeur of a small palace, with ornate ceiling, crystal chandeliers, and French provincial chairs. Generous drinks and charcoal specialties from the rôtisserie are served in the clublike bar, where the tables are lit by candlelight and the reflected glow from the octagonally paned stained-glass windows. Other facilities include a rooftop swimming pool and garden with a bricked sun terrace, the Kleine Komödie Theater, a sauna, massage rooms, a Trader Vic's, and the best nightclub in Munich, recommended separately.

Grand Hotel Continental, Max-Joseph-Strasse 5, D-8000 München 2 (tel. 089/55-15-70), is perhaps the nicest place to stay in Munich if you appreciate a stylish, antiques-filled hotel run in a personal manner. It belongs to a small deluxe hotel chain, Royal Classic Hotels, and is just five minutes from the railway station. The formal lounge, with an overscale tapestry, sets the tone. A formal dining room has a wood-beamed ceiling, an open château fireplace, and high antique cupboards. That the Continental deserves its "Grand" appellation is reflected everywhere: in the French provincial coffee and card room; in the formal sitting salon, with ornate Louis XVI–style furniture, brocaded walls, and baroque doors; in the garden room, with its arbor, vines, and planters of red geraniums. In fair weather, guests seek the inner garden for dining. Breakfast is served at tables near the fish pond, splashing fountain, and ivy-covered wall. Each of the 149 bedrooms has style. A single with shower/bath costs 243 DM ($144.30) to 318 DM ($188.85) daily, a double with shower/bath going for 306 DM ($181.70) to 426 DM ($252.95). Several elegant, antiques-filled apartments are more expensive.

Park Hilton München, Am Tucherpark 7, D-8000 München 22 (tel. 089/3-84-50), is a modern 15-story hotel between the Isar River and the English Garden. Built in 1972 in the center of the former Tivoli park, it's about a 10-minute ride from the downtown shopping areas. The hotel's 477 bedrooms contain floor-to-ceiling picture windows, plus balconies affording a distant view of the Alps. Units are contemporary yet elegant, with dark Macassar-wood furniture perfectly complementing the autumnal colors used throughout. Each accommodation is equipped with color TV and a self-service refrigerator/bar, plus air conditioning and direct-dial phone. Depending on floor and location, singles range from 230 DM ($136.55) to 390 DM ($231.60) daily, doubles from 316 DM ($187.65) to 430 DM ($255.35). Opened in 1988 was a deluxe Executive Floor, providing handsomely decorated guest rooms and a private lounge where Continental breakfasts, drinks, and small snacks are served.

Overlooking the pool is the hotel's popular-priced restaurant, which offers a buffet and an à la carte menu. In summer the restaurant opens onto the hotel's garden. International and creative dishes are offered in the grill on the ground floor. The Piano Bar features a pianist and the best martinis in town. You can relax in the health club facing the English Garden, with a heated indoor swimming pool, sauna, and solarium.

München Sheraton, Arabellastrasse 6, D-8000 München (tel. 089/9-26-40). If you're in Munich on a convention, chances are good that you'll be housed here. In the Bogenhausen section, east of the heart of Munich, the 22-story structure, with 650 attractively furnished bedrooms, opens onto the English Garden. All rooms, many quite large, contain baths, toilets, air conditioning, TVs, radios, and phones. A single ranges in price from 195 DM ($115.80) to 345 DM ($204.85) daily; a double goes for 290 DM ($172.20) to 430 DM ($255.35). The hotel places a strong emphasis on keeping fit. In addition to a health club, there are a 65-foot swimming pool, solarium, fitness room, sauna, and massage parlor. The Sheraton is almost a world unto itself, offering two bars, three restaurants, a beer garden, coffee shop, nightclub, shopping arcade, car-rental agency, and 260-car garage. In the nightclub, international bands and disco music entertain guests until 4am. With all this action, it's hardly necessary to leave, but if you do, you'll find bus and tram connections nearby; the center of town is less than 10 to 15 minutes away.

Hotel Königshof, Karlsplatz 25, D-8000 München 2 (tel. 089/55-13-60), in the heart of Munich, overlooks the famous Stachus (Karlsplatz) and the old part of the city, where interesting walking and shopping areas are found. Opened in 1862, the 160-room hotel has enjoyed great renown, and the proprietors, the Geisel family, have done much to see that it maintains its legend. Completely facelifted for the 1972 Olympics, the hotel offers traditional comfort plus up-to-date facilities. All of its sleekly styled rooms have private baths, air-conditioning, and soundproofing, and feature TV sets and picture windows. Singles rent for 210 DM ($124.70) to 250 DM ($148.45) daily, and doubles cost 270 DM ($160.35) to 320 DM ($190). On the second floor is a well-known restaurant, serving French and international cuisine. The lobby houses an intimate club bar, the Königshof-Bar. An underground garage shelters 180 cars.

München Penta Hotel, Hochstrasse 3, D-8000 München 80 (tel. 089/448-55-55), one of the largest hotels in the city, is rated four stars by the government. It enjoys a prime location in the city center, a 10-minute walk from Marienplatz. The S-Bahn, which stops at the hotel complex (station: Rosenheimer Platz), will whisk you to wherever you're going. Renovated in 1987, the hotel offers 583 bedrooms and 12 suites, each with first-class comfort. Amenities include private baths, hairdryers, cable TVs, air conditioning, minibars, and direct-dial phones. The attractively furnished rooms cost 230 DM ($136.55) to 260 DM ($154.40) daily for a single, 275 DM ($163.30) to 300 DM ($178.15) for a double. However, when you're booking, ask if weekend discounted rates are in effect, as they often are. The hotel also has a wide array of services, including three restaurants and an indoor swimming pool. A Lufthansa check-in counter is found in the hotel lobby, as is a Sixt Budget Rent-a-Car agent.

EXPENSIVE HOTELS

When it opened in 1989, **City Hilton München,** Rosenheimerstrasse 15, D-8000 München (tel. 089/480-40), became the second Hilton to grace the Munich skyline and the second-largest hotel in the city. Owned by a Dutch pension fund, it opted for four-star status, which means it can offer the business and vacation traveler Hilton management and comfort at prices considerably less than tariffs charged by the city's deluxe palaces. The location is to the side of both the Deutsches Museum and the performing arts center, Gasteig. It was designed in a low-rise format of red brick, shimmering glass, and geometric windows divided by white bands of metal reminiscent of a Mondrian painting. The historic center of Munich is an invigorating 30-minute walk across the river. On the premises are a pair of well-designed restaurants, a lobby-level café, a bar, and a staff sensitive to the needs of visitors. A total of 483 comfortably traditional bedrooms are rented, each containing modern adaptations of Biedermeier furniture, plush carpeting, air conditioning, phone, radio, cable-reception color TV, and minibar. Singles range from 200 DM ($118.75) to 260 DM ($154.40) daily, with doubles costing 250 DM ($148.45) to 300 DM ($178.15). The hotel offers good drinking and dining facilities, including Zum Gasteig, a Bavarian restaurant decorated in a typical style; Löwen-Schanke, a Bavarian pub; and Café Lenbach, where you can order a leisurely breakfast.

Arabella Hotel, Arabellastrasse 5, D-8000 München 81 (tel. 089/92-32-0), is situated in the Bogenhausen section, 10 minutes from the city center. The Arabella has a freewheeling contemporary design, with many dramatic public rooms. The pool on the 23rd floor, with a view over the city, is in Caribbean style; it has a waterfall, five whirlpools, three Roman steam baths, two saunas, solariums, a health club, palm trees, and a pool bar. All of the 478 chic accommodations have private baths, direct-dial phones, radios, color TVs with English-language programs, minibars, trouser presses, hairdryers, and balconies. Singles range from 185 DM ($109.85) to 260 DM ($154.40), doubles from 235 DM ($139.55) to 300 DM ($178.15). The two restaurants serve Bavarian and international cuisine daily until 11:30pm. The hotel is 3 miles from the airport, with good transportation connections and easy access to all major motorways. A subway connection links the hotel to the city center and the exhibition park.

Eden-Hotel-Wolff, Arnulfstrasse 4–8, D-8000 München 2 (tel. 089/55-11-50), opposite the railway station, misleads with its sedate exterior. The interior is warmly attractive, decorated in a richly traditional style. In the main dining room the theme is Bavarian—natural pine ceiling, gleaming brass lantern sconces, and thick stone arches. Another, paneled dining room has oil paintings and brass chandeliers. The 214 bedrooms are also in Bavarian style, with polished woods, TV sets, and radios. Single rooms cost 165 DM ($98) to 240 DM ($142.50) daily, and twin-bedded units go for 260 DM ($154.40) to 350 DM ($207.85). All prices include a buffet breakfast. An underground garage is on the premises.

Splendid, Maximilianstrasse 54, D-8000 München 22 (tel. 089/29-66-06), is one of the most attractive old-world hotels in Munich. Each of the 40 rooms reflects the owner's ability to combine antiques with good reproductions, achieving a harmonious style that evokes the aura of a country home. Room prices are scaled according to size, furnishings, and plumbing. A single without bath costs 105 DM ($62.35) to 130 DM ($77.19) daily, with a double in the same category going for 165 DM ($98) to 210 DM ($124.70). For a double with bath, the charge ranges from 225 DM ($133.60) to 290 DM ($172.20); for a single with bath, from 165 DM ($98) to 195 DM ($115.80). A tasty breakfast is included. On sunny mornings many guests prefer to have their morning meal on the paved and trellised patio.

Austrotel München, Arnulfstrasse 2, D-8000 München 2 (tel. 089/53-86-0), is a high-rise that has been refurbished and upgraded to four-star status. The 174 modern bedrooms all have complete baths or showers, radios, direct-dial phones, and minibars, as well as views across the city. Singles rent for 185 DM ($109.85) to 195 DM ($115.80) daily, with doubles going for 270 DM ($160.35) to 280 DM ($166.25)—all tariffs including a buffet breakfast and service. The handsome Belvedere restaurant on the 15th floor serves international menus, including Austrian and Bavarian specialties. As you dine, you can look out on Munich—with the Alps visible in the distance on clear days. A coffee bar, Amadeus, and a gift shop are also on the premises. The Austrotel is at the main railway station and air terminal, as well as the U- and S-Bahn stations.

Hotel Preysing, Preysingstrasse 1, D-8000 München 80 (tel. 089/48-10-11). If you don't mind the inconvenience of a hotel on the outskirts, one of the best places to stay in Munich today is the Preysing, across the Isar near the Deutsches Museum. A short train ride will whisk you into the center of the city, and you can leave your car safely in their underground garage. When you first view the building, a seven-story modern structure, you may feel I've misled you. However, if you've gone this far, venture inside for an amazing surprise.

The family who runs it has one of the most thoughtful staffs in Munich: not only the service but the smiles will warm your day. The style of the hotel is most agreeable, with dozens of little extras to provide homelike comfort. Fresh flowers are everywhere, and the furnishings, traditional combined with modern, have been thoughtfully selected. Furthermore, the location is quiet, far removed from the city's noisy downtown section. Each room has a private bath and costs 165 DM ($98) to 265 DM ($157.35) daily for a single, from 300 DM ($178.15) for a double. The 76 rooms are also air-conditioned, containing such extras as radios, direct-dial phones, color TVs, and well-stocked refrigerators. A grand breakfast is included in the tariffs. Facilities include an indoor swimming pool with a sauna, solarium, and hot whirlpool. If you're still not tempted to cross over the river, know that the Preysing's restaurant is one of the finest in Munich (we'll call on it in the restaurant section to follow).

MODERATELY PRICED HOTELS

You can have your own homelike setup, perfect for entertaining friends, at the **Ambassador Hotel,** Mozartstrasse 4, D-8000 München 15 (tel. 089/53-08-40). For a reasonable outlay you get a studio apartment decorated in functional style, including a complete sitting room with sofa, coffee table, reading lamp, armchairs, desk, TV, and three-channel radio. Silk draperies draw across a bed recess, with night-light and telephone. In a corridor leading to an all-tile bath is your own little bar and refrigerator (stocked with basic materials). Singles run from 100 DM ($59.40) to 170 DM ($100.95) daily; doubles, from 180 DM ($106.90) to 270 DM ($160.35). In addition to all this, there's an intimate lounge-bar on the lower level, plus a dignified wood-paneled dining room. Another asset: The Ambassador lies only a few blocks south of the railway station. Garage space is available. The hotel rents 65 units.

Hotel Reinbold, Adolf-Kolping-Strasse 11, D-8000 München (tel. 089/59-79-45), is a no-nonsense, no-frills hotel that delivers what it promises: a clean, decent room and quiet, efficient, and polite service. If that's what you're after, then you'll find it right in the heart of Munich, about a three-minute walk from the main rail terminal and only a five-minute stroll from the fair and exhibition site. Its 61 compact, comfortably (but not lavishly) furnished rooms contain a variety of plumbing, as well as refrigerator/bars, radios, phones, color TVs, hairdryers, trouser presses, and air conditioning. A single with hot and cold running water and toilet is 92 DM ($54.65) daily, going up to 142 DM ($84.30) for a room with shower. Likewise, the low double rate starts at 144 DM ($85.50), rising to 192 DM ($114) for a room with complete private bath. Tariffs include a substantial Continental breakfast, and for only 12 DM ($7.15) you can use the underground garage.

Hotel an der Oper, Falkenturmstrasse 11, D-8000 München 2 (tel. 089/290-02-70), is located just off Maximilianstrasse, in the vicinity of Marienplatz. It's superb either for sightseeing or shopping in the traffic-free malls. In spite of its basic, clean-cut modernity, there are touches of elegance: the crystal chandeliers in the little reception area, for example. Adjoining the luxurious cellar bar, the Opern Taverne, is one of Munich's most prestigious restaurants, the Bouillabaisse. The 55 bedrooms offer first-class amenities, each containing a private bath, phone, refrigerator, and small sitting area with armchairs and tables for breakfast. Traditional and modern elements have been combined. Including breakfast, a single rents for 115 DM ($68.30) to 130 DM ($77.20) daily, a double for 175 DM ($103.90) to 192 DM ($114).

Hotel Metropol, Bayerstrasse 43, D-8000 München 2 (tel. 089/53-07-64), a modern businessperson's hotel, stands in a "you-can't-miss-it" location directly across from the main railway station. English-speaking receptionists literally roll out the red carpet in the cavernous lobby and reception area. Sleek, contemporary lines and styling attract those who are tired of the rustic and traditional. The 275 bedrooms are furnished in a "sober" style, nothing grand in any way, but nothing overlooked either. In high season, a double with complete bath costs 157 DM ($93.25) to 185 DM ($109.85) daily, dropping to 164 DM ($97.40) for a room with shower and toilet. The cheapest single has a shower—no toilet—and costs 85 DM ($50.45) nightly, rising to 128 DM ($76) for a room with complete bath. The windows have been soundproofed, and each unit has a phone and radio; some have TVs. In all, the Metropol at peak capacity can shelter 370 guests. In addition, a garage holds 200 cars. The hotel also has a restaurant if you (wisely) don't want to venture out into the railway station area at night.

Adria, Liebigstrasse 8a, D-8000 München 22 (tel. 089/29-30-81), is a revamped hotel, offering many special appointments that remove it from the ordinary. With red-shaded lamps, global maps behind the reception desk, wood panels, planters of greenery, and Oriental rugs, the lobby sets the stylish contemporary look. Some of the 53 rooms have TVs as well as refrigerators filled with cold drinks. Armchairs or sofas and small desks add to the comfort. A single without bath costs 83 DM ($49.30) daily, increasing to 175 DM ($103.90) for a room with bath. A double with private bath or shower costs 144 DM ($85.50) to 190 DM ($112.80). Breakfast, included in the room rate, is the only meal served in the garden room.

Germania, Schwanthalerstrasse 28, D-8000 München 2 (tel. 089/5-16-80), conservative and sedate on the outside, has many winning design touches inside. Special features include automatic air conditioning, soundproofing, boxes for shoes in the vestibule, and bathrooms lined either with pearl-gray, black, or blue tiles or with Venetian glass mosaic. Usually there is a sitting room adjoining the bedroom, with original paintings, etchings, Oriental rugs, and fruitwood furnishings. Large windows let in plenty of light. A single with bath costs 170 DM ($100.95) to 244 DM ($144.90) daily, and a double with bath is 220 DM ($130.65) to 285 DM ($169.25). All these rates include breakfast, service charge, and taxes. The hotel rents 100 bedrooms.

BUDGET HOTELS

Making up part of the railway station complex—in fact, right inside it—is the **Intercity-Hotel München,** Bayerstrasse 10, D-8000 München 2 (tel. 089/55-85-71). However, it shuts out that dreary world as soon as you enter its doors. A dignified, traditional lounge—but one with contemporary flair—greets you. You can unwind in the snug leather-coated bar, or enjoy good German cooking in the Bavarian restaurant. More important, however, are the 199 bedrooms. The accommodations, all behind soundproof windows and each with its own personality, combine French and art nouveau designs; all have private baths or showers. Prices differ, depending on arrangement and size. Singles cost 130 DM ($77.20) to 164 DM ($97.40) daily, and doubles rent for 166 DM ($98.55) to 218 DM ($129.45).

Europäischer Hof, Bayerstrasse 31, D-8000 München 2 (tel. 089/55-15-10), a nine-floor hotel opposite the railway station, was originally built by a group of Catholic sisters and is now run by the Stürzer family. (There's even a chapel on the premises.) It's one of the best buys in Munich. Many of the 156 accommodations overlook an inner courtyard, with a subterranean parking area. A bathless single costs 65 DM ($38.60) daily, one with full bath going for 100 DM ($59.40) to 130 DM ($77.20). A bathless twin-bedded room costs 108 DM ($64.15); one with full bath, 138 DM ($81.95) to 180 DM ($106.90). Suites for two are 220 DM ($130.65). Most of the rooms are of fair size, with built-in headboards, double-glazed windows, radios, TV, direct-dial phones, desk tables, sofas, armchairs, coffee tables, luggage racks, and entry-hall wardrobes. Despite its dreary station location, the hotel couldn't be more immaculate: constant dusting, polishing, buffing, and waxing make spring cleaning a year-round activity here.

Hotel-Pension am Markt, Heiliggeiststrasse 6, D-8000 München 2 (tel. 089/22-50-14), a Bavarian hotel with many decorative trappings that reflect the glory of another era, stands in the heart of the older section. It's not that easy to get in here, but it's worth a try. The hotel is not luxurious, and owner Harald Herrler has wisely maintained an interesting, nostalgic decor in the entrance lobby and dining room. Behind his reception desk is a wall of photographs of friends or former guests of the hotel, including the late Viennese chanteuse Greta Keller. As Mr. Herrler points out, when you have breakfast here, you are likely to find yourself surrounded by opera and concert artists who like to stay here because they're close to the houses in which they perform. The 31 bedrooms are basic modern—quite small, but trim and neat. Many have private baths, and all units have hot and cold running water, with free use of the corridor baths and toilets. The cost for a single is 50 DM ($29.70) to 52 DM ($30.90) daily; for a double the rate is 90 DM ($53.46) to 120 DM ($71.25).

Kraft Hotel, Schillerstrasse 49, D-8000 München 2 (tel. 089/59-48-23), is a neat, modern 39-bedroom hotel. Set back from a busy street, about five minutes from the railway station, it has just enough space in front to park four cars. The reception lounge is inviting, but you guessed it—absolutely tiny. The emphasis is on streamlined bedrooms, which are well kept and up-to-date, with many built-in units. Depending on the bath facilities, singles range in price from 105 DM ($62.35) to

140 DM ($83.15) daily, and doubles from 130 DM ($77.20) to 180 DM ($106.90). Included in these tariffs are taxes, service, and breakfast.

Hotel Mark, Senfelderstrasse 12, D-8000 München 2 (tel. 089/59-28-01). This 91-bedroom hotel, near the south exit of the railway station, should be considered for its comfort and moderate prices. Rebuilt in 1956, it offers serviceable amenities and modern plumbing. Included in the rates are taxes, service, and breakfast. A single with basin and toilet costs 117 DM ($69.45) daily, increasing to 125 DM ($74.25) for a room with bath. A double with shower rents for 160 DM ($95); a double with bath, from 180 DM ($106.90). Many rooms have TVs. You can park your car in an underground garage. The tavern-style dining room has good food.

Hotel Habis, Maria-Theresa-Strasse 2a, München 80-Haidhausen (tel. 089/47-05-071), wins my respect as a small hotel of special character. The location is across from Isarpark overlooking the river; across the bridge are some of Munich's leading museums. The renovated 40-bed hotel, built on a corner, has five floors of individualized bedrooms and a wine restaurant. Also on the premises is the unusual Komödientheater, where shows are presented nightly except Monday. The hotel's general decor, especially that of the entrance with its gracious, curving staircase, is in modified art nouveau style. The bedrooms have strong earth colors, with painted built-in pieces, trim beds, casual wicker armchairs, and balloon lights; all rooms have private baths. Singles cost from 110 DM ($65.30) daily and doubles from 150 DM ($89.10), with a buffet breakfast included.

Novotel München, Rudolf-Vogel-Bogen 3, D-8000 München 83 (tel. 089/63-80-00 or toll free 800/221-45-42). Distinguished by its trademark, an illuminated Novotel sign colored a vivid azure, this comfortable hotel is a member of a worldwide French chain that has enjoyed startling success since it was launched in the 1960s. It is a well-established favorite with business travelers and families who appreciate the Novotel formula of standardized bedrooms, extended restaurant hours, no-nonsense efficiency, and easy access to motorways. This is the biggest Novotel in Germany, with 254 bedrooms and a desirable location not far from the center of the city, about 3 miles southwest of the airport. A subway station (U-Bahn and S-Bahn) lies within walking distance, and on the grounds are a swimming pool, sauna, and solarium. A well-managed restaurant, with attentive service and a warmly comfortable decor, serves generously portioned and well-prepared meals, and the bar also does a brisk business. Each of the bedrooms contains a private bath, a large desk, color TV, phone, and radio. Singles cost from 195 DM ($115.80) daily, and doubles rent for 235 DM ($139.55). Children up to 16 can sleep free in their parents' room.

Hotel Ariston, Unsöldstrasse 10, D-8000 München 80 (tel. 089/22-26-91), is a modern hotel in the center of Munich, not too far from the Haus der Kunst and the Bavarian National Museum. It's a straightforward, no-frills type of place, with 60 rooms in all, furnished in a very simple style. In every room, however, you'll find a private bath or shower, toilet, radio, and direct-dial phone. Singles range in price from 120 DM ($71.25) to 160 DM ($95) daily, and doubles go for 136 DM ($80.75) to 195 DM ($115.80). These tariffs include the standard buffet breakfast. A small entryway to each unit allows for greater quietness and privacy.

City Hotel, Schillerstrasse 3a, D-8000 München 2 (tel. 089/55-80-91), just a few minutes from the main railway terminal, the Stachus, and the exhibition ground, likes to think of itself as your "cozy home in Munich." The 65 rooms are compact, with all the necessities and a decorative touch or two; all units contain private baths, toilets, radios, phones, minibars, TVs, and air conditioning. A single rents for 138 DM ($81.95) daily, and a double costs 198 DM ($117.60), these tariffs including a buffet breakfast, service, and taxes.

Hotel Torbräu, Tal 37, D-8000 München 2 (tel. 089/22-50-16), an inviting choice, stands in the center of old Munich, near the Isartor subway station, within easy reach of the Rathaus, the pedestrian shopping mall, the Deutsches Museum, the

Residenz, and the opera house. It's much more charming than some of the bandbox modern hotels we've been considering so far. The staff rents 92 traditionally furnished bedrooms, all with private baths and toilets. The rate for a single, with Continental breakfast included, ranges from 160 DM ($95) to 180 DM ($106.90) daily; the rate for a double, from 220 DM ($130.65) to 260 DM ($154.40). The restaurant is bright and festive, serving Bavarian specialties, and there's also a Café-Conditorei on the premises.

Hotel Königswache, Steinheilstrasse 7, D-8000 München 2 (tel. 089/52-20-01), though not as regal as its name, has much to recommend it. The location, about a 10-minute ride from the train station and only 2 minutes from the technical university, is between the Stachus and Schwabing—a section of Munich preferred by many clients who find the railway station area dangerous, especially at night. The 39-bedroom Königswache is warmly decorated, and the hospitable staff speaks English. Rooms are modern and comfortable, with private baths, color TVs, radios, minibars, and writing desks with direct-dial phones. A single costs 125 DM ($74.25) to 155 DM ($92.05) daily, and a double costs 165 DM ($98) to 225 DM ($133.60). These tariffs include a buffet breakfast with champagne. The attractive restaurant serves Korean food, offered by a Korean staff, and the hotel bar is decorated in a cozy, rustic style.

Hotel Domus, St.-Anna-Strasse 31, D-8000 München 22 (tel. 089/22-17-04), may sound like a university dormitory, but it isn't. Sleekly modern, this 45-room hotel near the English Garden and the Haus der Kunst is about a 10-minute ride from the main railway terminal and 20 minutes from the airport. After a hectic day of sightseeing, you return here to comfort as you would to a private home, even though the Domus is a good-size hotel. A single room with a private bath costs 160 DM ($95) a night, rising to 200 DM ($118.75) if there is a private terrace attached. A double with bath goes for 190 DM ($112.80), jumping up to 250 DM ($148.45) for an apartment with bath, toilet, and terrace. Tariffs include breakfast, color TV, service charge, and taxes. To give you an undisturbed night's rest, the hotel pays special attention to the quality of its carpeting and doors. You can breakfast in your room or downstairs. There's an underground garage.

Hotel Wallis, Schwanthalerstrasse 8, D-8000 München 2 (tel. 089/59-16-64), is almost like a Bavarian inn, with 54 compact bedrooms that may not be a decorator's showcase but are nonetheless warm and inviting. The management is cooperative—and filled with suggestions about touring or "survival" in Munich. Rooms have baths, color TVs, and phones. A buffet breakfast is included in the prices: singles for 119 DM ($70.65) to 199 DM ($118.15) daily, doubles for 149 DM ($88.50) to 229 DM ($136).

Hotel Concorde, Hernstrasse 38, D-8000 München 22 (tel. 089/22-45-15), is a suitable oasis for those seeking an intimate hotel in the center of Munich. Though not very well known, and located on a side street, it's only a few minutes' walk from some of the major sightseeing attractions of the Bavarian capital. The hotel has 73 guest rooms with large and comfortable beds, along with such amenities as private baths, direct-dial phones, color TVs, radios, and minibars. A single with shower rents for 150 DM ($89.05) daily, the price rising to 210 DM ($124.70) for a room with private bath. A double with shower goes for 200 DM ($118.75), increasing to 300 DM ($178.15) for a twin-bedded room with bath.

Arabella-Central Hotel, Schwanthalerstrasse 111, D-8000 München 2 (tel. 089/510-83-0), managed by the Arabella conglomerate, is called in German *das kleine Grosstadthotel,* or "the little metropolitan hotel." A hotel garni (meaning it serves only breakfast), it lies only five minutes from the Messegelände (exhibition grounds) and the Oktoberfest grounds, a distance of half a mile from the main railroad station. Everything is modern, often attractively so. The 103-room hotel was designed for convenience, and each unit is equipped with a private bath, balcony, color TV, radio, minibar, alarm clock, and direct-dial phone. A single room rents for 170 DM ($100.95) to 230 DM ($136.55) daily, and a double goes for 220 DM

($130.65) to 280 DM ($166.25). Some apartments are also available, and tariffs include a breakfast buffet, service, and taxes.

THE PICK OF THE PENSIONS

Just three blocks from the Hauptbahnhof, the **Hotel Uhland Garni,** Uhlandstrasse 1, D-8000 München 2 (tel. 089/53-92-77), is a stately town mansion that stands in its own small garden. A well-run family hotel directed by the Hauzenbergers, it offers 30 good accommodations at fair prices and could easily become your home in Munich. Accommodations contain either showers or baths, toilets, mini-bars, and color TVs. A sliding price scale is based on the location and size of your room. Singles with showers rent for 85 DM ($50.45) to 120 DM ($71.25) daily, doubles with showers for 120 DM ($71.25) to 160 DM ($95), doubles with baths for 130 DM ($77.20) to 170 DM ($100.95), triples with showers for 150 DM ($89.05) to 180 DM ($106.90), and four-bedded rooms with showers for 170 DM ($100.95) to 230 DM ($136.55). During the Oktoberfest, rates are about 20% higher.

Pension Westfalia, Mozartstrasse 23, D-8000 München 2 (tel. 089/53-03-77), stands only two blocks from the meadow where the annual Oktoberfest takes place. The four-story town house, near Goetheplatz and reachable by taking bus no. 58 from the main railway station, is one of the best pensions in Munich, offering 19 immaculately maintained rooms, 11 with private baths. Bathless doubles cost 70 DM ($41.55) daily; bathless singles, 50 DM ($29.70). With a shower, a single costs 70 DM ($41.55) and a double 95 DM ($56.40). Rates include breakfast, service, and taxes. Owner Bertram Hoos, who was trained at the Hilton in Berlin, speaks English.

Audrey Bauchinger (bed-and-breakfast), Zeppelinstrasse 37, D-8000 München 80 (tel. 089/48-84-44), is across the street from the Deutsches Museum on the bank of the River Isar, with its jogging and biking paths. It is convenient to public transportation and a 15-minute walk from Marienplatz; parking is available. This is a private home, with clean, quiet, and tastefully decorated bedrooms. Mrs. Bauchinger has four double rooms, one very tiny single (a favorite of backpackers), and one triple. Maid service and an honor refrigerator are available. Rooms with private showers cost 90 DM ($53.45) to 100 DM ($59.40) daily for two persons, while a double with full private bath goes for 120 DM ($71.25), including a large American-style breakfast. Rooms with shared baths run from 55 DM ($32.65) to 65 DM ($38.60) daily, with an optional breakfast. Singles range from 35 DM ($20.80) to 75 DM ($44.55). Mrs. Bauchinger, a former teacher from Virginia, and her husband, Alfred, will help clients plan their tour of Munich, dispensing city maps. Credit cards carry a 5% surcharge.

Hotel Pension Utzelmann, Pettenkoferstrasse 6, D-8000 München 2 (tel. 089/59-48-89), is an impersonal building, but the atmosphere inside is familylike. Its owner, Hermann Ernst, has freshened everything with furniture, carpeting, and modern toilets. The 11 large accommodations are well kept, airy, and bright; all units are suitable as doubles. Without bath, the rate is 85 DM ($50.45) for two. With shower or complete private bath, the charge goes from 95 DM ($56.40) to 125 DM ($74.25).

Pension Schubert, Schubertstrasse 1, D-8000 München 2 (tel. 089/53-50-87), lies one floor above street level in a baroque-style villa in a tree-covered residential section of Munich. Guests climb a wide and elegant staircase to the entrance. The owners, the Fürholzner family, have only six bedrooms to rent. With breakfast included, the charge is 45 DM ($26.70) daily for a single without bath, 70 DM ($41.60) for a double without bath, rising to 85 DM ($50.50) for one with bath. Only breakfast is served, and the pension is open all year. Take the U-Bahn to Goetheplatz.

Pension Diana, Altheimer Eck 15, D-8000 München 2 (tel. 089/260-31-07), set behind a grand stone facade, occupies a section of what used to be a grand palace in an interesting central district of Munich. There's no elevator, so you'll have to climb a wide baroque staircase to the third floor. There you'll find a total of 17 bright, sunny bedrooms, each with simple but comfortable pinewood furnishings. None has a private bath, however. With breakfast included, singles rent for 60 DM ($35.65) daily, doubles for 90 DM ($53.45). Each unit has hot and cold running water, and showers cost extra.

Pension beim Haus der Kunst, Bruderstrasse 4, D-8000 München 22 (tel. 089/22-21-27), noted for its ideal location near the English Garden, its copious breakfasts, and its warm hospitality, is one of the most inexpensive and well-run small pensions of Munich. There are only nine rooms, so reserving early is important here. The cost for a single is 60 DM ($35.65) daily, rising to 75 DM ($44.55) for a double. Only the apartment contains a private bath; guests in the other rooms must share the facilities in the hallways. Built in 1956, the hotel is low-key and decent.

HOTELS IN SCHWABING

A breath of fresh modernity in Schwabing is provided at **Residence,** Artur-Kutscher-Platz 4, D-8000 München 40-Schwabing (tel. 089/38-17-80). A corner honeycomb structure, it contains 153 rooms on eight floors, most of which have balconies. The lounge is attractive, its vibrant colors intermixed with chalk white and wood paneling. There's even a sauna-style swimming pool, with a wall and ceiling of natural pine, subtropical plants, and lounge chairs. Color and style are also notable features of the spacious bedrooms. Prices are set according to the floor you're assigned—those nearer the ground are cheaper. All rooms have private baths, balconies, refrigerators, and radios. Singles cost 193 DM ($114.60) to 250 DM ($148.45) daily, going up to 268 DM ($159.15) to 320 DM ($190) for a double; breakfast is extra. An underground garage is available. You can dine here at the elegant Le Pavillon restaurant, with its glass-globe lighting, bentwood chairs, and filmy white curtains; patronize the cozy bar-restaurant, Die Kutsche (air-conditioned); or meet for drinks in the wood-paneled bar.

Holiday Inn, Leopoldstrasse 194, D-8000 München 40-Schwabing (tel. 089/38-17-90), acquainted Munich with this American motel chain. And this one's quite a glamorous introduction. Long a leading Munich hotel, it was created originally to lure business in the year of the Olympics. Every one of its 363 rooms is air-conditioned, with private bath and shower, queen-size bed (two in doubles), TV, and direct-dial telephone. The decor is streamlined, with natural woods and picture windows. Singles cost 215 DM ($127.65) to 285 DM ($169.25) daily; doubles, 375 DM ($222.70). A copious buffet breakfast is included. A distinctive plus is the no-cost policy for children under 12, who occupy the same room as their parents. Guests are invited to use the marble-edged indoor swimming pool, the Old Munich cocktail bar, the restaurants Omas Küche and Altstuben-Grill, and the Aquarius nightclub. The inn is near the Olympic area, right at the Autobahn Nürnberg–Berlin–Frankfurt.

International Hotel, Hohenzollernstrasse 5, D-8000 München 40-Schwabing (tel. 089/33-30-43), ranks as one of the best-run little hotels in Schwabing. The owners have created a hospitable environment, with up-to-date comfort.

Each of the 70 modern rooms has a private bath, shower, toilet, radio, direct-dial phone, TV, and carpeting, along with a little balcony. A single rents for 130 DM ($77.20) to 180 DM ($106.90) daily, and a double costs 170 DM ($100.95) to 210 DM ($124.70). Children up to 12 years of age sharing a room with their parents stay free. The location is only a few steps away from Leopoldstrasse and near the English Garden, which we'll visit later. A two-minute walk from the hotel leads you to the underground station. A cozy café provides informal dining, and in summer, tables are placed out on the sidewalk.

Gästehaus Englischer Garten, Liebergesellstrasse 8, D-8000 München 40-Schwabing (tel. 089/39-20-34), ranks among my most preferred stopovers in the

Bavarian capital. An oasis of charm and tranquility, named for its proximity to the English Garden, this ivy-covered villa was once the site of a mill. It later became a private villa, but for some two decades now it has been operated as a hotel by Frau Irene Schlüter-Hübscher. All but 3 of her attractively furnished bedrooms, 24 in all, contain private baths. Half of the units lie in an annex across the street. Try for room 20, a particular favorite. Depending on the plumbing, singles rent for 78 DM ($46.30) to 146 DM ($86.70) daily. Doubles range from 100 DM ($59.40) to 172 DM ($102.15). In fair weather, breakfast is served in a rear garden.

Consul, Viktoriastrasse 10, D-8000 München 40-Schwabing (tel. 089/33-40-35), is a bright, welcoming hotel whose innkeeper employs a fine staff. The public areas have warming touches—Oriental carpets, "comfy" chairs—and many of the 27 bedrooms have sitting areas; decorative accessories help avoid the impersonal look. The hotel has a bar and a cozy little breakfast room. To save marks, you can ask for a single without shower for 80 DM ($47.50) daily, the price rising to 130 DM ($77.20) should you want a private shower. Doubles contain private showers and rent for 100 DM ($59.40), the cost rising to 170 DM ($100.95) for a room with complete bath plus phone. These tariffs include a Continental breakfast.

Tourotel, Domagkstrasse 26, D-8000 München 40-Schwabing (tel. 089/36-00-10), in north Munich, is slightly outside the Schwabing district, close to the Olympic stadium. The nearby Mittlerer Ring makes it quick and easy to reach the airport and the motorway. The hotel is big, with 230 well-furnished rooms in all; each has a full private bath, phone, color TV, minibar, and radio. A single costs 139 DM ($82.54) daily, a double going for 179 DM ($106.30), including a buffet breakfast, service, and taxes. As an added attraction, the hotel has plenty of health facilities, including an indoor swimming pool and sauna. There's also a garage, plus outdoor parking facilities. Bavarian food and Munich beer are served in the Schmankerin restaurant, along with international dishes. All day long you can order snacks or full meals in their own Bierstüberl. It's open daily from 6 am to 1 am.

Leopold, Leopoldstrasse 119, D-8000 München 40-Schwabing (tel. 089/36-70-61), is a unique hotel in Schwabing. A 1924 villa, it offers a modern annex behind its garden, connected to the main building by a glassed-in passageway. Passing the hotel is the exit road of the Autobahn Nürnberg–Würzburg–Berlin. Think of the Leopold as a kind of motel, with plentiful parking. Two subway stations are 250 yards from the hotel; a bus and tram stop is in front of the door, allowing you access to the city center in about 10 minutes. Finally, the English Garden is only a few minutes away by foot. Most of the public rooms are furnished in Bavarian style, with wooden wing chairs and pine dado. The 80 bedrooms are nicely designed, many with built-in beds and all with armchairs and sofas. Bathless doubles are 105 DM ($62.35) daily, rising to 150 DM ($89.05) to 175 DM ($103.90) if they contain showers or baths. Breakfast is included. Whether in the old or new wing (which has an elevator), you'll have a telephone, as well as doors that have been double-soundproofed.

Hotel Gebhardt, Goethestrasse 38, D-8000 München 2 (tel. 089/53-94-46), lies only three minutes from the main railway station, right in the center of town. Frau Gebhardt, the helpful, hospitable owner, has 30 rooms that are pleasantly and attractively decorated, usually in autumnal colors. A bathless single costs 70 DM ($41.55) daily, rising to 90 DM ($53.45) for a room with shower. Bathless doubles cost 92 DM ($54.65), those with showers going for 130 DM ($77.20). Some units, ideal for families, are rented as triples and quadruples.

AT OLYMPIA PARK

Right at Europe's biggest sports and recreation center stands **Arabella Olympiapark Hotel München,** Helene-Mayer-Ring 12, D-8000 München 40 (tel. 089/351-60-71). The hotel is near the stadium, site of so many major sports events. For fitness-minded souls who want to be near all the action, the Olympiapark Hotel is appealing. Its rooms are among the most modern and well kept in the city, and sports heroes, both European and American, casually stroll through the lobby. They are lodged in 102 bedrooms, which cost 155 DM ($92.05) to 180 DM ($106.90) daily for a single and 195 DM ($115.80) to 225 DM ($133.60) for a double. These units contain complete baths, color TVs, and toilets, and a buffet breakfast is included in the tariffs. There's also plenty of free parking, and there's no need to drive into the city center: the U-bahn will whisk you there in minutes. The airport is about 20 minutes away, maybe more, depending on traffic conditions. If you want to unwind after a tough night in the beerhalls, you'll find a refreshing swimming pool, sauna, and massage room.

INNS NEAR MUNICH

South of Munich, **Schloss-Hotel Grünwald,** Zeillerstrasse 1, D-8022 Grünwald (tel. 089/641-79-35), is a favorite hotel and restaurant for motorists who'd like to escape the congestion of central Munich. If you don't have a car, you can take streetcar no. 25 from Grünwald or the rapid city train (S7) to Hollriegelskreuth. Allow about half an hour or more for the journey. If you're driving, follow the signs from the airport toward Autobahn Salzburg, which will lead in the direction of Garmisch-Partenkirchen. Exit at Oberhaching/Grünwald.

The Schloss has had a long history, sometimes glorious, sometimes sad. In 1293 Duke Ludwig built Castle Grünwald as a hunting lodge. Royalty came and went during its heyday, but eventually it fell into neglect and was used as a prison and arsenal. By 1892 it had been turned into a restaurant. However, fire destroyed it. It reopened again but this time to offer a refuge for victims of World War I and, later, World War II. Once again, in 1948, it was reopened as a hotel.

Today visitors come to relax in the beer garden underneath the old chestnut trees, enjoying the garden terrace overlooking the Isar Valley. Guests can also enjoy food in the Knights' Hall, with its old ceramic stove and arched windows. The hotel rents 16 handsomely furnished guest rooms, each decorated in the old style but containing such amenities as a private bath or shower, toilet, color TV, radio alarm, and direct-dial phone. The suites have their own minibars. Rates, including a buffet breakfast, range from 110 DM ($65.30) to 145 DM ($86.10) daily for a single, rising to 170 DM ($100.95) to 230 DM ($136.55) for a double, with suites for two costing 195 DM ($115.80) to 250 DM ($148.45). You'll note that the most expensive double is costlier than the least expensive suite.

Brauereigasthof Hotel Aying, Zornedinger Strasse 1, Aying bei München, D-8011 Aying (tel. 080/957-05), a country inn owned by the famous Aying Brewery, is all hearts-and-flowers alpine. Everything is traditional, except for the 18 excellent bathrooms, which have 20th-century comfort. Beds are as large as Ping-Pong tables, and colors are coordinated. Large double accommodations rent for 175 DM ($103.90) daily, including breakfast; some smaller doubles are offered for 150 DM ($89.05). The dining room pleases both palate and eye. On chilly days, a fire burns in the fireplace, and soft candles light the meals. A well-cooked dinner might range in price from 30 DM ($17.80) to 75 DM ($44.55). Directions: Take the Autobahn toward Salzburg, leaving it at the second exit. Aying is about 18 miles from the center of Munich.

Insel Mühle, Von-Kahr-Strasse 87, D-8000 München 50-Untermenzing (tel. 089/8-10-10), contains 40 bedrooms, but this time-honored establishment is better known as a restaurant than as a hotel. Built in 1506 as a mill, the L-shaped building beside the Würm River has a plank-covered wharf where parasols shield diners from the midsummer sun. The real beauty of the place, however, can be seen in the massive beams of the dining room and in the mellow brick vaults of the basement's wine cellar. Meals are served daily from noon to 2pm and 6:30 to 10pm. A set lunch costs 28 DM ($16.65) and an evening menu goes for 78 DM ($46.30). Specialties include shrimp in a dill-flavored cream sauce, medallions of veal in a mushroom-flavored cream sauce with fresh vegetables, rack of venison, beef filet in a red-wine sauce, roast goose with black-currant dressing, and a selection of such fresh fish as salmon, halibut, and monkfish. Reservations are recommended.

Despite its nearness to the center of Munich, many clients consider this a country-inspired retreat for a quiet weekend away from home. Each of the establishment's bedrooms is slightly different from its neighbor, although each contains a private bath, TV, and phone. A few have sloping garretlike ceilings or large comfortable floor spaces upholstered with thick carpeting. With breakfast included, singles cost 150 DM ($89.05) to 190 DM ($112.80) daily, with doubles going for 220 DM ($130.65) to 300 DM ($178.15).

4. Where to Dine

It is said that the good people of Munich consume more beer and food than the people in any other city of Germany. If the cuisine isn't exactly delicate, it's certainly plentiful, so if you like food, and plenty of it, you've come to the right city.

In many restaurants, especially the beerhalls, you'll find that the gemütlich atmosphere prevails until the early hours of the morning. Stamina is needed if you're going to live life as the locals do. Bernd Boehle once wrote: "If a man really belongs to Munich he drinks beer at all times of the day, at breakfast, at midday, at teatime; and in the evening, of course, he just never stops."

Some of the local fare may frighten the timid: "spleen" Wurst, calves' feet, pigs' trotters, and pork and liver "cheese." But if your palate requires careful attention, you needn't fear. Many of the restaurants of Munich, admittedly the upper-bracket ones, feature international cuisine, with emphasis on French dishes. A number of specialty restaurants exist. The most classic dish of Munich, however, is Weisswürste, herb-flavored white veal sausages that have been blanched in water. Traditionally, they are consumed before noon. Munich is definitely the place to practice *Edelfresswelle* ("high-class gluttony").

Our main interest is lunch and dinner, and the spots where you'll find the best meals for the best value in Munich.

THE TOP RESTAURANTS

Discreet and distinguished, **Aubergine,** Maximilianplatz 5 (tel. 089/59-81 71), is a citadel of fine taste, good food, impeccable service, and lethal tariffs. It's chic, elegant, and fashionable. The owner-chef, Austria-born Eckart Witzigmann, studied with the famous Paul Bocuse of Lyon, France. His cuisine is a mixture of classic dishes along with cuisine moderne offerings. One food expert has divided West German's gastronomic history into two parts—"before Witzigmann and after." The extraordinary chef has been called a "culinary messiah." There are many experts who consider the Aubergine the finest restaurant in West Germany today. The great chef told Craig Claiborne of the *New York Times* that "the important things are slow cooking and patience and freshness of ingredients." Sometimes his guests at the Aubergine are very special indeed, as when the master prepared a private banquet for King Carl XVI Gustaf of Sweden and his queen.

At lunch you can order a set menu for 165 DM ($98), although the cost of the table d'hôte dinner rises to 195 DM ($115.80). The set menu is almost invariably good, and contains an array of widely varying specialties, including a sorbet served between courses to clear your palate. Menus change every day, and can't be written until the owner returns from the market after having decided what was fresh and good that day. Fresh ingredients and top-quality produce are keys to the success of the Aubergine. You can also order à la carte, selecting such tempting treats as sole filet in a champagne sauce or crab salad with broccoli in vinaigrette. Many specialties are for two persons, including the venison with wild berries. Hours are noon to 2pm and 7 to 11pm Tues. to Sat. Closed on public holidays, Christmas, New Year's Day, and usually for the first three weeks in August.

Tantris, Johann-Fichte-Strasse 7 (tel. 089/36-20-61), in Schwabing, serves some of the best food in Munich—and it's French. The setting is unlikely—near the Holiday Inn and an Esso station—but once you're inside the restaurant's doors, you're transported into an ultramodern atmosphere with fine service. Incidentally, don't arrive without reservations, as many of the leading members of Munich's business colony like to entertain here, not only their families and friends but foreign associates as well.

The food is a treat to the eye as well as the palate, with the soups especially interesting. Among the main courses, I'd recommend the roast lamb with herbs; you also might enjoy suprême de turbot Marguery or a salmon soufflé. The choice of dishes is wisely limited, and everything is served and prepared with the utmost care. The cooking is both subtle and original, the beautiful interior adding to one's enjoyment. The head chef is Heinz Winkler, who was the former sous-chef for Eckart Witzigmann of Aubergine. Like Mr. Witzigmann, Mr. Winkler is Austrian, and he learned to cook mainly in France. An eight-course menu that changes daily is offered for about 187 DM ($111.04); a five-course table d'hôte, served at noon, costs 138 DM ($81.95). Hours are noon to 3pm and 6:30pm to midnight; closed for lunch Mon. and Sat. Tantris is closed on Sun. and public holidays, as well as for annual holidays in January and May.

OTHER LEADING RESTAURANTS

Another gourmet citadel, **Restaurant Sabitzer,** Reitmorstrasse 21 (tel. 089/29-85-84), is a devotee of cuisine moderne but serves classical specialties as well. The Austrian head chef, Herwig Sabitzer, made his debut on the Munich restaurant scene in 1981, and within months he was the "talk of the town." Mr. Sabitzer is assisted by his wife, Dorothea, and together they offer seasonal specialties and only the freshest of products, based on the shopping of the day. The menu changes so frequently one hesitates to recommend a specific dish. However, turbot is often cooked en paupiette and salmon in a saffron sauce. Open from noon to 3pm and 7pm to 1am (hot food is available only from noon to 1:30pm and 7 to 10pm); closed Sun. and for lunch Sat. A fixed-price menu is likely to cost about 140 DM ($83.15).

Restaurant Le Gourmet, Ligsalzstrasse 46 (tel. 089/50-35-97), is an evening restaurant specializing in cuisine moderne. The classical and elegant decor has a restful color scheme of burgundies and beiges, plus many antiques. The chef and owner, Otto Koch, is the motivating force behind the success of this place. He graciously circulates in the restaurant, attending to the well-being of his guests. Your meal might have such outstanding specialties of the moment as mushroom cake Le Gourmet with truffle sauce; sautéed goose liver with red cabbage; filet of plaice fried in rice paper with warm vegetable vinaigrette; tenderloin of veal in black olive sauce; or rack of lamb roasted in mustardseed. The soufflé café chocolat makes a luscious dessert. A seven-course menu costs about 130 DM ($77.20), or you can add another two courses, bringing the price to 155 DM ($92.05). You can spend less by ordering from the à la carte offerings. The restaurant is open from 6pm, with the last orders taken for a full meal at 10:15pm; closed Sun.

Das Restaurant, Maximilianstrasse 17 (tel. 089/23-03-90), in the Hotel Vier Jahreszeiten, is in a quiet, elegant location within walking distance of the opera house. The atmosphere is dignified and refined, the service extremely competent, and the food prepared along classic lines, with many imaginatively original variations. Appetizers are likely to include smoked and home-marinated salmon on blinis with caviar cream, truffled rabbit jelly, essence of black truffles with goose liver, and small marmite with filet of venison. For a main course, you might choose aiguillettes of duck and medallions of crayfish in Calvados, saddle of hare with stuffed plums in Armagnac sauce, or filet of beef à la nage with white shallot sauce. Desserts include such delicacies as whisky parfait with hot moss berries and, for two persons, a warm soufflé croquant with walnuts and orange sauce. Lunch is served daily from noon to 3pm and dinner from 6pm to midnight. Expect to pay 100 DM ($59.40) to 150 DM ($89.05) for an evening meal. A business lunch costs only 40 DM ($23.75).

Käfer-Schänke, Schumannstrasse 1 (tel. 089/41-68-1), is famous for its cookery, and you have to make reservations if you want a seat here. In one room on the main floor there is a deluxe gourmet shop. The decor suggests the home of a wealthy country gentleman, with a few antiques placed here and there. You select your own hors d'oeuvres, the most handsome and dazzling display in Munich, and are billed according to how many pâtés or croûtes you made off with. The main dishes are served by waiters. Often Käfer-Schänke features a week devoted to a particular country's cuisine. On one visit I enjoyed the classic loup (sea bass) with fennel as presented on the French Riviera. The salads have what one reviewer called "rococo splendor." From a cold table, you can select such temptations as smoked salmon or smoked eel. Venison, quail, and guinea hen are regularly featured. You've surely had beef Wellington, but have you tried veal Wellington? And the wild duck in truffle sauce is definitely worth writing home about. Service is from 11:30am to midnight; closed Sun. and holidays. Meals begin at 60 DM ($35.65), going up to 95 DM ($56.40)—or maybe a lot more.

Kay's Bistro, Utzschneiderstrasse 1 (tel. 089/260-35-84), is arguably the most sophisticated dining rendezvous in the Bavarian capital. It's filled nightly with a glamorous (sometimes media-related) clientele that appreciates the value of being seen in the right places. Reservations are important. The decoration is changed four or five times a year—perhaps you'll be there when the walls are laden with Hollywood souvenirs. The cuisine is light, nouvelle, and avant-garde; many ingredients are shipped in fresh daily from the wholesale food market, Rungis, in Paris. You might on any night be presented with veal cutlets with mango, carpaccio with parmesan, turbot with fresh asparagus in a Riesling sauce, followed with a white chocolate mousse with a mocha sauce. Kay Wörsching greets his guests from 7pm to 1am; closed Sun. A gracious, welcoming host, he writes for the German version of *Penthouse* magazine. He closes his restaurant for several weeks in midsummer. A fixed-price meal costs 100 DM ($59.40), and you can easily spend 120 DM ($71.25) ordering à la carte. The location is off the market of Munich, the Viktualienmarkt.

Weinhaus Schwarzwälder, Hartmannstrasse 8 (tel. 089/22-72-16), is an old Munich wine restaurant. Loyal habitués come here to order meals accompanied by fine German wines from an extensive list. From the moment you enter, the atmosphere evokes a warm and hospitable charm that sets the mood for a fine meal. The menu is international, but in season, game is the specialty—prepared with flair by the chef. Freshwater fish and shellfish are other specialties. For dessert, try the walnut parfait with nougat sauce or Viennese-style apple pie. Meals begin at 28 DM ($16.65) and can easily climb to 100 DM ($59.40). Set menus cost from 55 DM ($32.65) to 95 DM ($56.40). Open Mon. to Sat. from noon to 2:30pm and 6 to 11:30pm, the restaurant lies only a short walk from the Bayerischer Hof and American Express, both of which open onto Promenadeplatz.

Hotel Königshof, Karlsplatz 25 (Am Stachus) (tel. 089/55-13-60). Münchners have become increasingly sophisticated in their taste for food, and the owners of this deluxe hotel (already surveyed) want the Königshof to surface near the top in culinary delights. The Geisel family has made major renovations to the dining room, with its oyster-white panels of oak, polished bronze chandeliers, silver candelabra, and porcelain. The black-jacketed waiters in long white aprons are among the most polite and skilled in the city. Wolfgang Abrell, the chef, is one of the most inventive and creative in Germany today. His "culinary masterpieces" depend on his whim of the moment and, almost as important, upon what is available in season. He likes extremely fresh ingredients, and the food here reflects his passion. Perhaps you'll get to try his foie gras with sauternes, a lobster soufflé, loin of lamb with fines herbes, lobster with vanilla butter, or sea bass suprême. Meals begin at 42 DM ($24.95). If you go for the more expensive selections, your bill could easily climb to 135 DM ($80.15). Hours are noon to 3pm and 6:30 to 11pm daily.

Preysing-Keller, Innere-Wiener-Strasse 6 (tel. 089/48-10-15), is a "find," but you have to cross the Isar to discover its superb cookery and wines. It's connected to the Hotel Preysing, already previewed. Go only for dinner, served nightly from 6pm to 1am, and be sure to make a reservation. You dine in a 300-year-old cellar, with massive beams and high masonry arches; the decor is simple, with wooden tables and chairs. The head chef is Gottfried Lenz, and he's a good one. Under his direction, daily excursions to the market are made by the staff, who are told to select only the freshest ingredients. The fish and seafood served here are stored in aquariums on the premises prior to cooking. The goose-liver pâté is a specialty, as is lobster in butter sauce and a steak tartare of venison. Pigeons in basil sauce with lettuce might be on your menu, perhaps beef filet in beaujolais with artichoke hearts. In addition to original recipes, the chef also prepares old-fashioned Bavarian dishes. Meals begin at 65 DM ($38.60). A seven-course menu is offered for 110 DM ($65.30).

Bouillabaisse, Falkenturmstrasse 10, Hotel an der Oper (tel. 089/29-79-09), is highly rated in local gourmet circles. The restaurant prepares beautiful food in a lovely setting near the Hofbräuhaus and across from Harry's Bar. The peppersteak is served Madagascar style, but the chef's specialty is bouillabaisse, honoring the name of the restaurant. You can have a small plate as an appetizer or a large order. An unusual hors d'oeuvre for Munich is the specially prepared squid. The menu generally remains the same from day to day, and the kitchen manages to secure some of the finest sole in Munich, which the chef prepares in several ways. For dessert, I suggest the peach Melba. Meals begin at 65 DM ($38.60), averaging around 100 DM ($59.40). Hours are noon to 2:30pm and 6 to 11:30pm; closed Sun., and for lunch Mon. The restaurant is closed in August.

A. Boettner, Theatinerstrasse 8, off Marienplatz (tel. 089/22-12-10), is one of the choicest special restaurants in Munich. It's tiny and totally intimate, and at times everybody seems to know everybody else. Here you're assured of such savory fare as saddle of venison and fried goose liver on green beans. Lobster is a specialty. For dessert, the chocolate mousse makes a particularly velvety choice. Meals begin at 75 DM ($44.55), going up to 125 DM ($74.25)—and beyond that if you should go crazy with the caviar and lobster. The restaurant is open Mon. to Fri. from 11am to midnight; Sat. from 11am to 3pm; closed Sun. The wine cellar is excellent, the relatively unadorned surroundings pleasant, and the service polite and skilled. It's for the discriminating gourmet only. Reservations are required.

MODERATELY PRICED RESTAURANTS

The Fauchon's of Munich is **Alois Dallmayr,** Dienerstrasse 14 (tel. 089/213-51-00), tracing its history back to 1700. Near the City Hall, it is perhaps the most famous delicatessen in Germany and actually is one of the most renowned in the world. After walking through it, looking at its tempting array of delicacies from all around the globe, you'll think you're lost in a millionaire's supermarket. Dallmayr has been a purveyor to many royal courts. Here you'll find the most elegant consumers in all of Munich, looking for that "tinned treasure," perhaps Scottish salmon, foie gras, English biscuits, wines and spirits, as well as fashionably out-of-season fresh produce.

It's possible to dine upstairs. The food is a subtle German version of Continental cuisine, owing a heavy debt to France. The food array is dazzling, ranging from the best herring and sausages I've ever tasted, to such rare treats as perfectly vine-ripened tomatoes flown in from Morocco, to papayas from Brazil. The famous French poulet de Bresse, believed by many gourmets to be the finest in the world, is also shipped in. The smoked fish such as eel is particularly outstanding. The soups are superb (especially one made with shrimp). Your bill is likely to be *anything* here, depending on your selection. Count on paying 50 DM ($29.70) to 85 DM ($50.45) for a satisfying meal. If you're dining alone, you might prefer to anchor at the counter instead of a table. The bustling restaurant is crowded at lunchtime. Open Mon. to Fri. from 9am to midnight; on Sat. from 9am to 3pm; closed Sun.

Austernkeller, Stollbergstrasse 11 (tel. 089/29-87-87), is the "oyster cellar" of Munich, a delight to both visitors and the local trade. Of course, as promised by the name, you get the finest oysters and the largest selection in town. Many gourmets make an entire meal of them, eating them raw. Others prefer them elaborately prepared, for example, oysters Rockefeller. One delectable beginning to a meal would be to order the shellfish platter with fresh oysters as well as mussels, clams, scampi, and sea snails. Or else you might begin with one of the excellent soups or one of the cold hors d'oeuvres. French meat specialties, such as roast leg of lamb with herbs, are offered, but most guests prefer one of the fish dishes— everything from lobster thermidor to shrimp grilled in the shell. Meals cost 50 DM ($29.70) to 90 DM ($53.45), and are served from 6pm to 1am; closed Mon. The decor, under a vaulted ceiling, is a collection of kitsch—everything from plastic lobsters to old porcelain.

Gasthaus Glockenbach, Kapuzinerstrasse 29 (tel. 089/53-40-43), offers consistently competent traditional cookery in a half-paneled and vaulted dining room awash with sunlight from arched windows. Menu items include skillful preparations of whatever fresh fish was available that day in the marketplace. You might enjoy a potato-and-fresh-lettuce salad garnished with strips of grilled salmon, or perhaps a flavorful ragoût of freshwater fish, or a confit of goose, followed by an array of tempting desserts. Full meals cost from 55 DM ($32.65) to 110 DM ($65.30) Tues. to Sat. from noon to 3pm and 7pm to 1am. Reservations are strongly recommended. The restaurant is closed for 10 days at Christmas and for two weeks in July.

Halali, Schönfeldstrasse 22 (tel. 089/28-59-09), can be roughly translated as "tallyho." The huntsman-style decor and the traditions of this old-fashioned and charming restaurant are about as authentically Bavarian as anything in Munich. Full à la carte meals cost 50 DM ($29.70) to 75 DM ($44.55). You can also order a fixed-price lunch at 35 DM ($20.80) or a dinner extravaganza at 90 DM ($53.45). Hours are 11am to 11pm; closed Sun., for Sat. lunch, and holidays. Typical dishes, derived from the Germanic traditions of game and fish, might include a terrine of smoked fish, a salad of braised quail, and filets of veal in a mustard sauce, plus the kind of desserts that, in spite of their caloric input, might prove tempting.

Zum Alten Markt, Am Viktualienmarkt, Dreifaltigkeitsplatz 3 (tel. 089/29-99-95), is snug and cozy, serving a fresh, beautifully presented cuisine at a good price. Located on a tiny square just off the large outdoor food market of Munich, the restaurant has a mellow charm, and the welcome is from its owner, Josef Lehner. The interior decor, with its intricately coffered wooden ceiling, came from a 400-year-old Tyrolean castle that was torn down. In summer, tables are placed outside. Like a little village inn, the restaurant is open from 11am to 2:30pm and 6 to 10:30pm; closed Sun. Meals cost from 50 DM ($29.70). The fish and fresh vegetables come from the nearby market. You might begin with one of their tasty homemade soups, such as cream of carrot, or perhaps black-truffle tortellini in a cream sauce with young onions and tomatoes. The chef makes some of Munich's best Tafelspitz (the elegant boiled beef dish so beloved by Emperor Franz Joseph of Austria). You can also order such classic dishes as Bavarian goose or roast suckling pig. It's wise to call for a reservation.

Madrigal, Herzog-Rudolph-Strasse 1 (tel. 089/22-33-55), at the corner of Maximilianstrasse, one of the most sophisticated restaurants in Munich, draws a pleasure-loving younger set. Besides the main floor, with its closely packed tables, there are a downstairs piano bar and a bowling and video room. The cuisine is French, as is the wine list. You might begin the action with a salmon crêpe with caviar or a shrimp and avocado salad. Try the steak tartare (it's very good and reliable here), or ask the waiter to recommend whatever is especially fresh on any particular day. Meals cost from 55 DM ($32.65). The place is open Mon. to Fri. from noon to 2am, Sat. and Sun. from 7pm to 2am. Always make a reservation.

A lot of Swiss gastronomic know-how has been poured into the **Mövenpick Restaurant,** Im Künstlerhaus, Lenbachplatz 8 (tel. 089/55-78-65), a cluster of five different dining spots in a historic building that used to be called "the house of the artists," where the literary élite once gathered for coffee. Posted at the door is a menu bulletin for each of the restaurants, allowing you to select in advance. In summer the terrace, seating 250 patrons, is one of the most popular rendezvous places in Munich. Depending on which restaurant you select, meals can range from 20 DM ($11.90) to 45 DM ($26.70). Open daily from 10am to midnight.

Restaurant Krukenberg im Weinhaus Neuner, Herzogspitalstrasse 8 (tel. 089/260-39-54), is an *Ältestes Weinhaus Münchens* divided into two parts. Its history dates back to the end of the 15th century, and it is the only building in Munich that has its original Tyrolean vaults. Once young priests were educated here, but after secularization by Napoleon the place became a wine tavern and a meeting place for artists, writers, and composers, including Richard Wagner. Fortunately, the restaurant survived World War II. Its rooms have been renovated and its paintings restored. The less expensive place to dine in is the Weinstube, which has lots of local atmosphere. Here you can order typical Bavarian dishes, with meals costing from 35 DM ($20.80). Dress is casual. The Restaurant, on the other hand, is elegant with candles and lots of flowers. The chef makes a happy marriage between cuisine moderne and regional specialties. All food is fresh and prepared *à la minute,* with the menu changing weekly. The room offers a daily three-course lunch menu at 30 DM ($17.80) or a five-course dinner menu at 75 DM ($44.55). The wine list has excellent selections from both France and Germany. The establishment is open Tues. to Sat. from noon to 2pm and 6pm to 1am, and Mon. from 6pm to 1am.

THE FOREIGN COLONY

Riding the crest of the wave of the French-food craze that long ago overtook Munich is **La Belle Epoque,** Maximilianstrasse 29 (tel. 089/29-33-11). Returning to the nostalgic style of the turn of the century, the restaurant has a low-key atmosphere, a first-class cuisine, and deft, efficient service. It is open for dinner Mon. to Sun. from 6pm to midnight, for lunch Mon. to Fri. from noon to 2pm. The restaurant closes the first two weeks in January and in August. The menu changes daily, but a satisfactory meal is offered for 60 DM ($35.65). Always call for a reservation.

El Toulà, Sparkassenstrasse 5 (tel. 089/29-28-69). Whenever you see this name, know that you will be in a showcase of haute Italian cuisine. This elegant Munich restaurant is one of the finest links in a chain that stretches from Rome to Tokyo. The decoration is in turn-of-the-century style, with wickered bentwood chairs, and prominently featured is a work of the well-known artist Dudovic, called *Woman with Hound.* All pasta is homemade on the premises, and the fish and meat specialties use only the finest, freshest ingredients. The style of cookery ranges across Italy from the Piedmont to Lombardy, with a stopover in Venice. Care is taken with the vegetables as well, and desserts are luscious in the Italian tradition. Prices are also a bit luscious as well, a meal costing 75 DM ($44.55) to 100 DM ($59.40). Hours are from noon to 2:30pm and 7pm to 1am; closed Mon. and for lunch on Sun. Also closed for the first three weeks in August.

Chesa Rüegg, Wurzerstrasse 18 (tel. 089/29-71-14), beside the Vier Jahreszeiten, has rough white plaster walls, a beamed ceiling, and a collection of large cow bells. Red-shaded kerosene lamps on the tables, plus vases of red roses, further enhance the alpine-tavern theme. The star of the intimate dining theater is the Swiss chef. From start to finish, your repast is carefully planned and served; it might consist of a rich-tasting soup, followed by crab with lobster sauce or perhaps a venison steak. A complete meal here could easily top 60 DM ($35.65). Hours are noon to 3pm and 6pm to 1am, Mon. to Fri.; closed holidays.

Goldene Stadt, Oberanger 44 (tel. 089/26-43-82). Come here for the finest Bohemian specialties in Bavaria. The setting is sedate, much like the ground floor of a town house. You're given a choice of three dining rooms (the central one is the most often reserved). Against a background of scenic etchings and a mural depicting scenes of Czechoslovakia, the savory cuisine from Germany's neighboring country has been served since 1961. A gracious English-speaking host takes your order. Borscht is the classic beginning, but not the type you're served in New York. Bohemian specialties include roast goose and duckling. After dinner it's customary to order apricot brandy, served in a glass that looks like a bud vase. A complete meal will cost 40 DM ($23.75) to 70 DM ($41.55) per person. Hours are 11:30am to 3pm and 6pm to midnight; closed Sun.

At the **Csarda Piroschka,** Prinzregentenstrasse 1 (tel. 089/29-54-15), the Hungarian cuisine is absolutely first-rate. The location is decidedly offbeat: the ground floor of the Haus der Kunst art museum. The service is as smooth as the food is good, in a mellow candlelit ambience. Featured is a traditional Hungarian orchestra with violins and a cimbalon player. The menu is placed before you by one of the most gracious proprietors in Munich, who is the epitome of Hungarian charm. The house specialty, served to two persons only, is called Husarenspiess flambiert; another good dish is the Hungarian farmer's steak. A fine beginning is the Bohnensuppe (bean soup) Jókai or the Goulashsuppe. A bottle of the sweet-tasting Hungarian wine Tokaji rounds things out nicely. Count on spending 40 DM ($23.75) to 70 DM ($41.57) for a full meal. Hours are from 6pm to 1:30am; closed Sun. Be sure to reserve a table in advance.

BUDGET BAVARIAN RESTAURANTS

The coziest and warmest of Munich's local restaurants is **Nürnberger Bratwurst Glockl am Dom,** Frauenplatz 9 (tel. 089/22-03-85). You sit in chairs that look as if they came from some carver's shop in the Black Forest, and the wide-ranging collection of memorabilia includes pictures, prints, pewter, and beer steins. Upstairs, reached through a hidden stairway, is a dining room decorated with Dürer prints and memorabilia. Open daily from 9am to midnight. The restaurant has a strict policy of shared tables. The homesick Nürnberger comes here just for one dish: Nürnberger Schweinwurstl mit Kraut—those delectable little sausages. A robust meal here will cost 25 DM ($14.85) to 35 DM ($20.80). The service is on tin plates. A short walk from Marienplatz, the restaurant faces the cathedral of Munich.

Palais Keller, Palais Montgelas, Promenadeplatz 2 (tel. 089/21-20-990), lies deep within the cellar of one of Munich's finest hotels, but its prices are easily competitive with those of beerhalls and Weinstubes in far less desirable places. You descend a flight of stone steps to reach the massively beamed and wood-sheathed interior of this charming restaurant. Waitresses speak English and wear frilly aprons and genuine smiles. The restaurant serves daily from 11:30am to 1am, with full meals costing from 30 DM ($17.80). There is a tempting array of German dishes, including, for example, veal in sour cream sauce with glazed turnips, cabbage, and carrots; breast of chicken in almond coatings; pike balls on buttery leaf spinach with shrimp sauce; and prime boiled beef (Tafelspitz) with a vinaigrette sauce. A wide selection of German wines is sold by the bottle or by the glass.

Weinstadl, Burgstrasse 5 (tel. 089/22-10-47), has been a Weinhaus since 1850. Reputedly the oldest house in Munich, it was built in the 15th century for use as a municipal wine cellar. Luckily, this antique building survived World War II. First glance might lead you to mistake this for a museum, but not so. Real old-world charm is to be found here: vaulted ceilings, coats-of-arms, a trompe l'oeil facade, and wrought-iron sconces. Dining is on three levels. Hearty Bavarian food and Palatinate wines are served; especially hearty is the bean soup with ham. A typical main dish is roast pork with potato dumplings and mixed salad. Meals cost 20 DM ($11.90) to 40 DM ($23.75). A beer garden is popular in summer. Hours are 10am to midnight, Mon. to Sat.; 10am to 4pm, Sun.

Restaurant zum Bürgerhaus, Pettenkoferstrasse 1 (tel. 089/59-79-09), dates from 1827 and has furnishings typical of that era. Little known to North American visitors, it has a loyal German patronage attracted to its good home-style cookery from the Bavarian region. There are about two dozen or so tables seating about 65 diners, and this place can really fill up. A set lunch costs 30 DM ($17.89), with dinners going for 55 DM ($32.65) to 72 DM ($42.75). Hours are noon to midnight Mon. to Fri. and 6pm to midnight on Sat.; closed Sun.

Haxnbauer, Münzstrasse 8, at Sparkassenstrasse (tel. 089/22-19-22), more than 100 years in the same family, could get by on atmosphere alone. One of the most typical Bavarian restaurants in Munich, with a devoted following, it offers the patron a choice of dining rooms. A specialty is Radi mit Hausgeräuchertem Schinken—razor-thin slices of ham with white radishes and chive bread, a traditional appetizer. Other specialties of the house are Schweinhaxen and Kalbshaxen (pork or veal shank), priced according to weight; you can also order Truthahnhaxen (turkey shank). They are spit roasted, the skin cooked to a crusty brown. The meat or poultry is guaranteed fresh, as the restaurant has its own butcher. For dessert, the chef's pride is Apfelkucherl flambé. You can easily spend 25 DM ($14.85) to 45 DM ($26.70) here for a complete meal, served daily from 11am to midnight.

Hundskugel, Hotterstrasse 18 (tel. 089/26-42-72), reportedly the oldest tavern in the city, dates back to 1440. Built in an alpine style, it is within easy walking distance of Marienplatz. Perhaps half the residents of Munich at one time or another have made their way here, to be wined and dined in style. The cookery is honest Bavarian with no pretensions. Though the chef makes a specialty of Spanferkel, or roast suckling pig with potato noodles, you might prefer Tafelspitz (boiled beef) in dill sauce or roast veal stuffed with goose liver. To begin, try one of the hearty soups, made fresh daily. Meals cost 35 DM ($20.80) to 50 DM ($29.70). Service is daily from 10am to 1am, and reservations are necessary.

Weisses Bräuhaus, Tal 10 (tel. 089/29-98-75), right in the heart of the city, is big, bustling, and Bavarian with a vengeance. Not for the pretentious at heart, this informal place does what it has for centuries: serves its home-brewed beer. At one time the famous salt trade route between Salzburg and Augsburg passed right by its door, and salt traders were mighty thirsty back then. In a world of smoke-blackened dark-wood paneling and stained glass, you have a choice of rooms. The front part is for drinking (and lots of it) and informal eating; the back room has white tablecloths and black-outfitted waitresses, and here you can sample typical Bavarian dishes.

Begin with smoked filet of trout or a rich-tasting potato soup, then try roast pork with noodles and Sauerkraut or Viennese veal Gulasch with mushrooms and cream sauce. Meals cost 20 DM ($11.90) to 40 DM ($23.75). Service is daily from 11am to midnight, and if you'd like a table in the rear, you should call ahead. Nevertheless, you'll invariably share your table with others. But that's part of the fun of going here.

Spatenhaus, Residenzstrasse 12 (tel. 089/22-78-41), is one of the best-known beer restaurants in Munich. Its wide windows overlook the opera house on Max-Joseph-Platz. Of course, to be loyal, you'll accompany your meal with the restaurant's own beer, called Spaten-Franziskaner-Bier. You can choose to sit in the intimate, cozy, semiprivate dining nooks or at a big table. The Spatenhaus has old traditions, offering typical Bavarian food, and it is known for its generous portions and reasonable prices. The cost range is from 30 DM ($17.80) to 70 DM ($41.55). Open daily from 11am to midnight.

Donisl, Weinstrasse 1 (tel. 089/22-01-84), is reputedly the oldest beerhall in Munich, dating from 1715. Some readers praise this Munich-style restaurant as gemütlich, with its relaxed and comfortable atmosphere. Seating capacity is about 350, and in summer one can enjoy the hum and bustle of Marienplatz while dining in the garden area out front. The restaurant has two levels, the second of which is a gallery. English is spoken. The standard menu offers traditional Bavarian food as well as a daily-changing specials menu. (International cuisine is, of course, always available.)

Specialties include Weisswürste, the little white sausages that have been a tradition of this place for decades. Others will try the Bavarian meatloaf (Leberkäs), grilled sausages, or a traditional Sauerbraten. Select beers from Munich's own Hacker-Pschorr Brewery top the evening. An average meal will cost about 10 DM ($5.95) for appetizers and 21 DM ($12.45) for a main course. A zither player at noon and an accordian player in the evening entertain the guests. The Donisl is open daily from 8am to 12:30 am, and hot meals are served at all times.

St. Georg Weinhaus, Prinzregentenplatz (tel. 089/47-30-38). Here you dine under the massive beams of a 500-year-old farmhouse, in one of five vaulted cellar rooms in the Upper Bavarian style. As you enter, a bar is on the left; to the right are candlelit tables with colorful napkins. The restaurant is owned by a former wine merchant, Herr Hummert, who stocks the finest Rhine, Franconia, and Mosel bottles. This family-run winehouse has been going for more than a quarter of a century, and is noted for its simple yet tasty dishes. Try the lentil soup with bacon. Depending on your taste, you can spend from 10 DM ($5.95) to 50 DM ($29.70) for a meal here. Hours are 7pm to 3am daily.

Ratskeller, Im Rathaus, Marienplatz 8 (tel. 089/22-03-13). Many visitors discover the tradition of the German "Ratskeller" in Munich. Throughout Germany you'll find these cellar restaurants in the basements of town halls, serving inexpensive good food and wine. Although not as celebrated as some (the one at Bremen, for example), the Munich Ratskeller holds its own. Bavarian music adds to the ambience. The decor is much what you'd expect, with lots of dark wood and carved chairs. The most interesting tables, and the ones staked out first by the in-the-know locals, are at the rear, under vaulted, painted ceilings. One mural depicts a Bavarian choking a dragon to make the monster swallow poison. The ideal table is in a cozy, semiprivate dining nook in the rear. A large wine vat suggests that Bavarians don't drink only beer.

The menu is a showcase of regional fare, but it also includes some international dishes. A freshly made soup of the day is always featured, and you can help yourself from the salad bar. Specialties include ragoût of venison in red wine, served with juniper berries, and a sausage platter with four homemade broiled sausages of beef, veal, and pork, served with mashed potatoes and Sauerkraut. Good desserts are the chocolate Bavarian cream tart and the Black Forest tart. The chef has prepared a menu in English especially for North American guests. Complete dinners, costing 30 DM ($17.80) to 55 DM ($32.65), include soup or dessert and a choice of four typical dishes. The waiters are helpful, and most speak English. Ice water is served at the beginning of the meal—unusual in Europe unless specifically requested. The Ratskeller is open daily from 9am to midnight.

A VEGETARIAN RESTAURANT

Cantina Vegetarische Imbiss, Weissenburgerstrasse 39 (tel. 089/447-09-22), is more sophisticated in its offerings than the word Imbiss (snackbar) suggests. One of its co-owners is the architect who designed the place, including the chairs and tables (lots of chrome and nickel). The food is completely vegetarian, served cafeteria style, with inspiration from culinary traditions around the world, including Mexico. Tortillas, for example, cost from 6.50 DM ($3.85); a Lebanese falafel (chick peas and olive oil), served pizza style, goes for 7 DM ($4.15). You can eat very well for only 11 DM ($6.55); the place is closed Sun. and on national holidays. The nearest subway stop is S-Bahn Ostbahnhof.

DINING IN SCHWABING

This district of Munich, which used to be called "Bohemian," overflows with restaurants, many of them cheap, attracting a youthful clientele. It has a few exceptional choices, which we'll dine at, in case you decide to make the most recommended trek up here. Nighttime is the best time for a visit.

La Mer, Schraudolphstrasse 24 (tel. 089/272-24-39), is a French restaurant that deserves its well-earned reputation. A decorator went wild here with gilt mirrors, crystal chandeliers, candelabra, ceramics, and flowers. If you can take your eyes off the trappings long enough to order, you'll find a truly superb cuisine. Only the freshest seafood is offered—the menu depends on the day's catch. Specialties are turbot in champagne and duck-liver mousse. A menu dégustation is a regular feature. Service and reception are first-class. La Mer is expensive, a daily set menu costing from 115 DM ($68.30) per person. You can also order an á la carte meal, costing from 75 DM ($44.55). Go only for dinner, from 7 to 11:30pm; closed Mon. The restaurant closes from mid-July through mid-August and shuts down for one week at Christmas.

Walliser Stuben, Leopoldstrasse 33 (tel. 089/34-80-00), is like a Hollywood version of a Swiss tavern. Because of its skill with the Helvetian cuisine, it attracts many visitors to Schwabing. It not only serves some of the best food in the area, but is one of the leading Swiss-style restaurants in Germany. The atmosphere is an inviting one, with an open fireplace, copper pans, and carved wooden chairs. The master chef enchants his patrons with such classic dishes as fondue Bourguignonne. Popular and very good are the flambé desserts. The price of an average meal will range from 50 DM ($29.70) to 75 DM ($44.55). Walliser Stuben is open from 5pm to 1am; closed Sun.

Bistro Terrine, Amalienstrasse 89 (tel. 089/28-17-80), has an inviting outdoor terrace where you might like to sit in warm weather. Locals, however, request a table in the art nouveau interior, even in summer. This is a popular bistro where small tables are set between high-ceilinged walls festooned with old mirrors, tasselbottomed lamps, and cozy turn-of-the-century bric-a-brac. The chef uses the freshest possible ingredients in his cuisine moderne. Menu items vary, depending on the season and the day's shopping. A main course may sate your hunger without benefit of an appetizer, but few guests are able to resist one of the tempting light desserts. A fixed-price noon meal, costing about 35 DM ($20.80), is a good value. An à la carte dinner is likely to cost from 75 DM ($44.55). Lunch is served from noon to 2:30 pm and dinner from 6:30pm to 1am, to accommodate the after-theater crowd. The bistro is closed Sat. at lunch and all day Sun. and Mon.

Badische Weinstuben, "Rolandseck," Viktoriastrasse 23 (tel. 089/30-94-38), next to the underground station of U3, Bonner Platz, in Schwabing, is open daily from 4pm to midnight. It serves traditional dishes accompanied by an impressive array of wines from Baden or the famous Arco Brau beer. A menu ranges from "a little bite" to a complete meal, costing from 7.80 DM ($4.65).

Weinbauer, Fendstrasse 5 (tel. 089/39-81-55), off Leopoldstrasse, is one of the preferred budget favorites in the area. It's a rather small Gaststätte full of students and smoke. No bright accessories are found here, just wood tables and passable food. Generous platters range from a Wurst and Leberwurst (liver sausage) platter at 8.50 DM ($5.05) to a filet steak at 19 DM ($11.30). The restaurant is open from 9am to 1am; closed Wed.

THE BEER GARDENS

If you're in Munich anytime between the first sunny spring day and the last fading light of a Bavarian-style Indian summer, make a beeline for one of the city's celebrated beer gardens (Biergärten). Hopefully, you will have learned the words to the famous German drinking song, "Ein Prosit," before heading to one. These beer gardens are literally "soaked with suds" throughout the long Bavarian summer. Traditionally, beer gardens were tables placed under the chestnut trees that were planted above the storage cellars to keep the beer cool in summer. People, naturally, started to drink close to the source of their pleasure, and the tradition has remained. Lids on beer steins, incidentally, originally were meant to keep out the flies.

It is estimated that today Munich has at least 400 beer gardens and cellars. My favorite one, however, is in the Englischer Garten, the park lying between the Isar River and Schwabing. The biggest city-owned park in Europe, it has several beer gardens, of which the **Biergarten Chinesischer Turm,** Englischer Garten 3 (tel. 089/ 39-50-28), is preferred. It is the largest and most popular of its kind in Europe, taking its name from its location at the foot of a pagodalike tower, a landmark that is easy to find. Beer and Bavarian food, and plenty of it, are what you get here. A large glass or mug of beer (ask for ein Mass Bier), enough to bathe in, costs 7 DM ($4.15). It will likely be slammed down still foaming by a waitress carrying 12 other tall steins as well. Food is very cheap, a simple meal costing about 15 DM ($8.90). Homemade dumplings are often a specialty, as are all kinds of tasty sausages. You can get a first-rate Schweinbraten (a braised loin of pork served with a potato dumpling and rich brown gravy), which is Bavaria's answer to the better-known Sauerbraten of the north. Leberknödl is classic, served in a broth with fresh chives. Huge baskets of pretzels are passed around, and they are eaten with Radi, the large, tasty white radishes famous in these parts. Oompah bands often play, and it's most festive. Hours are 10am to midnight daily in summer.

Space is too tight to allow me to document and describe too many beer gardens of Munich. However, I'll cite a few more favorites. In all, the food, drink, and atmosphere have much in common, and the price structure is about the same.

Bamberger Haus, Brunnerstrasse 2 (tel. 089/308-89-66), in a century-old house northwest of Schwabing at the edge of Luitpold Park, is named after the city most noted for the quantity of its beer drinking. Most visitors head for the street-level restaurant where meals are served. Specialties include well-seasoned soups, grilled steak, veal, pork, and sausages. If you want only to drink, you might visit the beerhall in the cellar. A set lunch costs 24 DM ($14.15), and a substantial à la carte platter of food begins at 18 DM ($10.70). In midsummer, the restaurant is open daily from 10am to midnight. From November to May, it is open only from noon to 3pm and 6pm to midnight. The cellar beer hall is open daily from 6pm to 1am.

If you're going to the zoo, which I'll recommend later, you might want to stop over for fun and food at the **Gaststätte zum Flaucher,** Isarauen 1 (tel. 089/72-32-677), which is close by. "Gaststätte" tells you that it's a typical Bavarian inn. This one is mellow and traditional, with tables set out in a tree-shaded garden overlooking the river. Here you can order that local specialty, Leberkäse, which many foreigners mistakenly think is "liver cheese." It's neither—rather, a large loaf of sausage eaten with black bread and plenty of mustard, a deli-delight. Beer costs 7 DM ($4.15) for a large mug, and the most expensive platter of food goes for 15 DM ($8.90). Full meals range from 10 DM ($5.95) to 20 DM ($11.90). The place is open daily from 10am to 10pm from May to the end of October. The rest of the year it closes on Thurs.

If you're motoring, you might visit a hunting lodge that was once owned by the kings of Bavaria. It's **Zum Aumeister,** Sondermeierstrasse 1 (tel. 089/32-52-24), which lies off the Frankfurter Ring at Munich–Freimann. It offers a daily list of seasonal specialties, and you might end up with cream of cauliflower soup or perhaps a rich oxtail. Meals cost from 25 DM ($14.85). Open from 11:30am to 9:30pm; closed Mon.

Another one to try is **Hirschgarten,** Hirschgartenstrasse 1 (tel. 089/17-25-91), in the Nymphenburg Park sector of the city (near one of Munich's leading sightseeing attractions, Schloss Nymphenburg), west of the heart of the town. It is part of a nearly 500-acre park with hunting lodges and lakes. Try to go here on any day except Monday so you can visit the palace as well. This is the largest open-air restaurant in Munich, seating some 8,000 beer drinkers and Bavarian merrymakers. Full meals cost from 25 DM ($14.85). A one-liter stein of Augustiner tap beer goes for 5 DM ($2.95). Hours are 9am to midnight daily. To reach Hirschgarten, take the tram to Romanplatz or the S-Bahn to the Laim station.

AT THE OLYMPIC GROUNDS

A choice of dining experiences is offered at the **Olympia Tower** (tel. 089/308-10-39). The television tower, open daily from 9am to midnight, is 950 feet in height, and it costs 5 DM ($2.95) for adults and 3 DM ($1.80) for children to take the speediest elevator on the Continent to its summit. Parking is 3 DM ($1.80).

The most expensive dining spot in the tower is the **Tower Restaurant,** featuring a selection of international dishes. Food is served daily from 11am to 5:30pm and 6:30 to 10:30pm, a complete dinner costing 35 DM ($20.80) to 50 DM ($29.70). Before or after dinner you'll want to take in the view, including the alpine mountain chain. Four observation platforms look out over the Olympiapark. The Tower Restaurant revolves around its axis in 36, 53, or 70 minutes, giving the guests who linger a changing vista of the entire Olympic Grounds.

At the base of the tower is the **Am Olympiasee** (tel. 089/30-61-32-90), serving genuine Bavarian specialties, with meals costing from 15 DM ($8.90). Favored items include half a roast chicken and various hearty soups, and food is served daily from 9am to 7pm. The restaurant is popular in summer because of its outdoor terrace.

CAFÉS AND PASTRIES

About 10:30 am or before (to make sure you have a good seat), head for the **Café Glockenspiel,** Marienplatz 28 (tel. 089/26-42-56), right in the heart of Munich. There you'll have a good perch for watching the miniature tournament staged each day by the clock on the Rathaus facade. In addition to its view, the café has good coffee and pastries, which cost from 5.30 DM ($3.15). It is open daily from 10am to 8pm.

Café Luitpold, Briennerstrasse 11 (tel. 089/29-28-65), is even better known. Opened in 1888, in its day it attracted such notables as Ibsen, Kandinsky, Johann Strauss the Younger, and other great musicians, authors, and artists as well as members of the royal court of Bavaria. Rebuilt after World War II, it's a favorite rendezvous with Münchners, who enjoy its whipped-cream-laden pastries, costing from 5 DM ($2.95). Coffee goes for about 3.50 DM ($2.10). The café is open daily from 9am to 8pm. The Grill Restaurant on the same premises serves meals continuously from 11:45am to 8:30pm, from 9am to 5:30pm on Sat., with meals costing from 35 DM ($20.80). Closed Sun.

Café Extrablatt, Leopoldstrasse 7 (tel. 089/33-33-33), in Schwabing, is very much like a Parisian café. It's complete with Piaf recordings, bentwood chairs, and a wide outdoor terrace. Operated by Michael Greter, a well-known newspaper columnist, the café is open for drinks or open-air dining. Light meals cost from 12 DM ($7.15), drinks from 3.50 DM ($2.10). The Extrablatt is open Mon. to Fri. from 7am to midnight; Sat. from 9am to 1am; and Sun. from 9am to midnight. Inside, you can admire the photo gallery of celebrities.

Roses, Leopoldstrasse 9 (tel. 089/39-64-38). To honor the old "roses are red" rhyme, the decor features roses-patterned walls, lampshades, whatever. Swathes of bright red create the overall impression of tongue-in-cheek Victoriana. A large beer costs 5.50 DM ($3.25), and it can be enjoyed in the company of a convivial crowd. A limited menu, containing about 10 different items (including soups and pastas) is also served. The café is open nightly from 6pm to 2am.

---

5. The Sights

Munich is stocked with so many treasures and sights, the visitor who plans to "do" the city in one or two days makes a mistake. Not only will such a person miss many of the highlights, but he or she will also fail to grasp the spirit of Munich and to absorb fully its special flavor, unique among the cities of the world. But faced with an enormous list of important attractions and a time clock running out, the visitor may have to limit sightseeing to a few of the more vital attractions, especially in the area of museums and galleries, with which Munich is generously endowed. After a quick trip through the old city center, with its numerous sights, I'll survey the most important of Munich's museums and churches, and then add a few interesting excursions from the city.

THE CITY CENTER

Try to arrive at **Marienplatz** before 11am. This square, dedicated to the patron of the city, whose statue stands on a huge column in the center, is the heart of the old town. On its north side is the **Rathaus,** built in 19th-century Gothic style. Each day at 11am, and also at noon and 5pm in the summer season, the **Glockenspiel** on the facade performs a miniature tournament, with little enameled copper figures moving in and out of the archways. Since you're already at the Rathaus, you may wish to climb 55 steps to the top of its tower (an elevator is available if you're conserving your energy) for a good overall view of the city center. The Altes Rathaus, with its plain Gothic tower, is to the right. It was reconstructed in the 15th century, after being destroyed by a fire.

To the south of the square you can see the oldest church in Munich, **St. Peter's.** To the north lies **Odeonsplatz,** Munich's most beautiful square, surrounded by the **Residenz** (Royal Palace) and the **Theatinerkirche.** Adjoining the Residenz is the restored **Nationaltheater,** home of the acclaimed Bavarian State Opera.

Running westward from Odeonsplatz is the wide shopping avenue, Briennerstrasse, leading to **Königsplatz.** Flanking this large Grecian square are three classical buildings constructed by Ludwig I—the **Propyläen,** the **Glyptothek,** and the **Antikensammlungen.** Returning to Odeonsplatz, take the busy Ludwigstrasse north to the section of Munich known as **Schwabing.** This is the Greenwich Village, Latin Quarter, or Chelsea of Munich, proud of its artist and writer element, numbering among its own such literati as Ibsen and Rilke. The Blue Rider group, which so influenced abstract art in the early 20th century, was originated here by Kandinsky, along with Marc and Klee. Today it still retains a frankly offbeat flavor, with racks of handmade jewelry for sale along the streets and sidewalk tables filled with young people from all over the world.

Bordering Schwabing on the east and extending almost to the Isar River is Munich's city park, the 18th-century **Englischer Garten** (English Garden), laid out by Sir Benjamin Thompson. Here you can wander for hours along the walks and among trees, flowers, and summer nudes, even stopping for tea on the plaza near the Chinese pagoda.

MUSEUMS AND GALLERIES

The museums and galleries of Munich contain some of the finest and most varied collections of art found anywhere. If you have time to visit only one of these during your stay, it definitely should be the **Alte Pinakothek.**

Alte Pinakothek

Art lovers come to Munich just to gaze at the hundreds of famous works exhibited in this huge neoclassical building at Barerstrasse 27 (tel. 089/23-805-215) (tram no. 18, U-Bahn no. 2, or bus no. 53). The nearly 900 paintings on display (many thousands more are in storage) represent the greatest European artists of the 14th through the 18th centuries. Begun as a small court collection by the royal Wittelsbach family in the early 1500s, the collection is now the largest and most important in Germany. There are only two floors with exhibits, but the museum is immense, and I do not recommend that you try to cover all the galleries in one day. If you have only a few hours to spend here, however, see the works below.

The landscape painter par excellence of the Danube school, Albrecht Altdorfer, is represented by no fewer than six monumental works. The works of Albrecht Dürer include his greatest—and final—self-portrait (1500). Here the artist has portrayed himself with almost Christ-like solemnity. Also displayed is the last great painting of the artist, his two-paneled work called *The Four Apostles* (1526).

Several galleries are given over to the works by Dutch and Flemish masters. The *St. Columba Altarpiece* (1460–62), by Roger van der Weyden, is one of the greatest of these, in size as well as importance. Measuring nearly 10 feet across, this triptych is a triumph of van der Weyden's subtle linear style, and one of his last works (he died in 1464).

A number of works by Rembrandt, Rubens, and van Dyck, are displayed. Included are a series of religious panels painted by Rembrandt for Prince Frederick Hendrick of the Netherlands. A variety of French, Spanish, and Italian artists are found in both the larger galleries and the small rooms lining the outer wall. The Italian masters are well represented by Fra Filippo Lippi, Giotto, Botticelli, Raphael (*Holy Family*), and Titian.

You'll also find a *Madonna* by da Vinci, a famous self-portrait by the young Rembrandt (1629), and a number of works by Lucas Cranach, one of Germany's Renaissance painters. Cranach's *Venus* is displayed. Pieter Brueghel's *Land of Cockaigne,* where nothing has to be done and where food simply falls into one's mouth, is on view too. Brueghel has taken a popular subject of European folk literature and satirized it in this painting. Note the little egg on legs running up to be eaten, and the plucked and cooked chicken laying its neck on a plate. In the background you'll see a knight lying under a roof with his mouth open, waiting for the pies to slip off the eaves over his head.

Important works are always on display, but exhibits are changed in two rooms on the first floor. You'd be wise to buy a map of the gallery to guide you through the dozens of rooms. The museum is open daily from 9:15am to 4:30pm, with additional hours on Tues. and Thurs. evenings from 7 to 9pm. Closed Mon. Admission is 4 DM ($2.40); free Sun.

Neue Pinakothek

The Neue Pinakothek offers a survey of 18th- and 19th-century art. Across the Theresienstrasse from the Alte Pinakothek, the museum at Barerstrasse 29 (tel. 089/23-80-51-95) was reconstructed after its destruction in World War II, reopening again in 1981. Closed Mon., it may be visited other days from 9:15am to 4:30pm (on Tues. it is also open in the evening from 7 to 9 pm). A combined ticket to both the Alte Pinakothek and the Neue Pinakothek costs 7 DM ($4.15) per person.

The museum has paintings by Gainsborough, Goya, David, Manet, van Gogh, and Monet. Among the more popular German artists represented are Wilhelm Leibl and Gustav Klimt; you should encounter a host of others whose art is less well known. Note particularly the genre paintings by Carl Spitzweg.

Placed throughout the gallery are sculptures, mainly in bronze, by German artists, with a Degas and Rodin here and there. I've especially enjoyed the French paintings, including several Cézannes, Corots, and Gauguins.

Deutsches Museum (German Museum)

On an island in the Isar River, in the heart of Munich, the Deutsches Museum of Masterpieces of Science and Technology, Museumsinsel 1 (tel. 089/2-17-91), is the largest museum of its kind in the world. It possesses a huge collection of priceless artifacts and historic originals such as the first electric dynamo (Siemens, 1866), the first automobile (Benz, 1886), the first diesel engine (1897), and the laboratory bench at which the atom was first split (Hahn, Strassmann, 1938), to mention just a few. There are hundreds of buttons to push, levers to crank, and gears to turn, as well as a knowledgeable staff on hand in every department to answer questions and demonstrate the workings of steam engines, pumps, or historical musical instruments.

Among the most popular displays are those on mining, with a series of model coal, salt, and iron mines, as well as the electrical power hall, with high-voltage displays that actually produce lightning. There are also exhibits on transportation, printing, photography, textiles, and many other activities, including demonstrations of glass-blowing and paper-making. The air-and-space hall is the largest in the museum. Recently the Deutsches Museum opened another hall, for high-tech exhibits: computer science and automation, microelectronics, and telecommunications.

The Deutsches Museum is open daily except for major holidays. Hours are 9am to 5pm except on the second Wed. in December, when it closes at 2pm. Admission is 5 DM ($3) for adults, 2 DM ($1.20) for children over 6. There are a good restaurant and a museum shop on the premises. The museum is easily reached by S-Bahn. Go to Isartor station.

The Residenz

When a member of the royal Bavarian family said he was going to the castle, he could have meant any number of places, especially if he was Ludwig II. But if he said he was going home, it could only be the Residenz to which he referred. This enormous palace, with a history almost as long as that of the Wittelsbach family, was the official residence of the rulers of Bavaria from 1385 to 1918. Added to and rebuilt over the centuries, this complex of buildings is a conglomerate of various styles of art and architecture. Depending on the direction from which you approach the Residenz, your impression can be one of a German Renaissance hall (the western facade), a Palladian palace (on the north), or a Florentine Renaissance palace (on the south facing Max-Joseph-Platz).

The Residenz has been completely restored since its almost total destruction in World War II and now houses the Residenz Museum, a concert hall, the Cuvilliés Theater, and the Residenz Treasure House.

The **Residenz Museum,** Max-Joseph-Platz 3 (tel. 089/22-46-41), takes up the whole southwestern section of the palace, some 100 rooms of art and furnishings collected by centuries of Wittelsbachs. To see the entire collection, you'll have to take two tours, one in the morning and the other in the afternoon. You may also visit the rooms on your own.

The Ancestors' Gallery is designed almost like a hall of mirrors, with one important difference: where the mirrors would normally be, there are portraits of the members of the Wittelsbach family, set into gilded, carved paneling. The largest room in the museum section of the palace is the Hall of Antiquities, possibly the finest example of interior Renaissance styling in Germany (outside of churches, that is). Frescoes seemingly adorn every inch of space on the walls and ceilings alike, painted by dozens of 16th- and 17th-century artists. The room is broken into sections by wall pillars and niches, each with its own bust of a Roman emperor or a Greek hero. The hall contains pieces of furniture dating from the 16th century as well, but the center of attraction is the two-story chimney-piece of red stucco-marble. Completed in 1600, it is adorned with Tuscan pillars and a large coat-of-arms of the dukes of Bavaria.

On the second floor of the palace, directly over the Hall of Antiquities, the museum has gathered its enormous collection of Far Eastern porcelain. Note also the fine assemblage of Oriental rugs in the long narrow Porcelain Gallery.

Many of the rooms have been organized as exhibit salons with glass cases and pedestals, and some have been furnished as they were when the palace was actually a residence. The best example is the Elector's bedroom (1730) on the second floor. Several tapestries adorn the walls, and the room is lit by carved and gilded sconces as well as by the massive cut-glass chandelier. The focal point is the ornate bed enclosed by a balustrade.

Entrance to the museum—open Tues. to Sat. from 10am to 4:30pm, on Sun. from 10am to 1pm—costs 3.50 DM ($2.10). You'll have to pay another 3.50 DM ($2.10) to visit the **Schatzkammer** (Treasure House) of the Residenz, open the same hours. If you've time to see only one item here, it should be the Renaissance statue of *St. George Slaying the Dragon* (16th century). The equestrian statue is made of gold, but you can barely see the precious metal for the thousands of diamonds, rubies, emeralds, sapphires, and semiprecious stones imbedded in it.

One room is devoted to sacred objects, including several icons and numerous crucifixes, carved in ivory or ebony, or hammered in gold. The Wittelsbach equivalent to the Crown Jewels is in another room, with scepters and royal orbs. The crown of the realm is also on display.

Both the Residenz Museum and the Treasure House are entered from Max-Joseph-Platz on the south side of the palace. From the museum, for another 2 DM ($1.20), you can visit the **Cuvilliés Theater,** whose rococo tiers of boxes are supported by nymphs and angels. Directly over the huge center box, where the royal family sat, is a crest in white and gold topped by a jewel-bedecked crown of Bavaria held in place by a group of cherubs in flight. In summer this theater is the scene of frequent concert and opera performances. Mozart's *Idomeneo* had its first performance here in 1781.

Bavarian National Museum

King Maximilian II in 1855 began an ever-growing institution that today presents the largest and richest display of the artistic and historical riches of Bavaria. So rapidly has its collection grown in the past 100 years that the museum has had to move into larger quarters several times. Its current building, at Prinzregentenstrasse 3 (tel. 089/21-68-1), near the Haus der Kunst, contains three vast floors of sculpture, painting, folk art, ceramics, furniture, and textiles, as well as clocks and scientific instruments.

Entering the museum, turn to the right and go into the first large gallery (called the Wessobrunn Room). Devoted to early church art, from the 5th through the 13th centuries, this room holds some of the oldest and most valuable works. The desk case contains ancient and medieval ivories, including the so-called Munich ivory, from about A.D. 400. The carving shows the women weeping at the tomb of Christ while the resurrected Lord is gingerly stepping up the clouds and into heaven. The adjoining room is named for the stone figure of the *Virgin with the Rose Bush,* from Straubing (c. 1300). This is one of the few old Bavarian pieces of church art to be influenced by the spirit of mysticism.

The Riemenschneider Room is devoted to the works of the late-15th-century sculptor Tilman Riemenschneider and his contemporaries. Characteristic of the sculptor's works is the natural, unpainted look of his carvings and statuary. Note especially the 12 apostles from the Marienkapelle in Würzburg (1510), St. Mary Magdalene, the central group of the high altar in the parish church of Münnerstadt (1490–92), and the figure of St. Sebastian (1490). Also on display are famous collections of arms and armor from the 16th to the 18th centuries.

Other salons on the main floor are devoted to various periods of German and northern Italian art (which is closely tied to the cultural evolution of Bavaria).

The second floor contains a fine collection of stained and painted glass—an art in which medieval Germany excelled. Other rooms on this floor include historic glassware, Meissen porcelain, and ceramics. One of the novelty additions to the museum is the collection of antique clocks, dating from as early as the 16th century. One gallery is occupied by scale models of important Bavarian towns as they looked in the 16th century.

In the east wing of the basement level are many Christmas Cribs, not only from Germany but also from Austria, Italy, and Moravia. The variety of materials competes with the styles themselves—wood, amber, gold, terra-cotta, and even wax were used in making these nativity scenes. Also on this level is a display of Bavarian folk art, including many examples of woodcarving. The museum is open from 9:30am to 5pm; closed Mon. Admission is 3 DM ($1.80); free on Sun. To reach the museum, take streetcar no. 20 or bus no. 53 or 55.

Munich Antikensammlungen and Glyptothek

After 100 years of floating from one museum to another, the Museum of Antiquities finally found a home in the 19th-century neoclassical hall on the south side

of the Königsplatz, at no. 1 (tel. 089/59-83-59). The collection grew around the
vase collection of Ludwig I and the Royal Antiquarium, both of which were incorporated after World War I into a loosely defined group called the Museum Antiker
Kleinkunst (Museum of Small Works of Ancient Art). Many of the pieces may be
small in size, but never in value or artistic significance.

Entering the museum, you find yourself in the large central hall. The five halls
of the main floor house more than 650 Greek vases, collected from all parts of the
Mediterranean. The pottery has been restored to a near-perfect condition, although
most of it dates as far back as 500 B.C. The oldest piece is "the goddess from Aegina," dating from 3000 B.C. Technically not pottery, this pre-Mycenaean figure,
carved from a mussel shell, is on display along with the Mycenaean pottery exhibits
in Room I. The upper level of the Central Hall is devoted to large Greek vases discovered in Sicily and to the art of the Etruscans.

Returning to the Central Hall, take the stairs down to the lower level to see the
collection of Greek, Roman, and Etruscan jewelry. Note the similarities of today's
fashions in design. Included on this level as well are rooms devoted to ancient colored glass, Etruscan bronzes, and Greek terra-cottas.

The Glyptothek, Königsplatz 3 (tel. 089/28-61-00), is the ideal neighbor for
the Museum of Antiquities. It supplements the pottery and smaller pieces of the
main museum with an excellent collection of ancient Greek and Roman sculpture.
Included are the famous pediments from the temple of Aegina. Both the Glyptothek
and the Antikensammlungen are open Tuesday to Sunday from 10am to 4:30pm.
Antikensammlungen is open Wed. and Glyptothek on Thurs. from noon to
8:30pm. A 6-DM ($3.55) ticket admits you to both. Separate admissions cost 3.50
DM ($2.10) each. Free on Sun. Take U-8 to Königsplatz.

Haus der Kunst

Munich's **Staatsgalerie Moderner Kunst** (State Gallery of Modern Art),
Prinzregentenstrasse 1, in the west wing of the Haus der Kunst (tel. 089/29-27-
10), is considered one of the 10 finest repositories of art in the world. It shows about
400 paintings, sculptures, and art objects from the beginning of the 20th century to
the present. The largest selection is devoted to German art. You'll see paintings by
Klee, Marc, Kirchner, and Beckmann. Italian art—with stars such as Marino Marini
and Renato Guttuso—American abstract expressionism, minimalist art, and a host
of celebrated artists from Bacon to Braque, de Chirico to Dali, Dubuffet to Giaco-
metti, Matisse to Mondrian, round out the collection. Picasso is especially honored,
with 14 works, the earliest dating from 1903. There are also examples of fauvism
and surrealism. The gallery is open Tues. to Sun. from 9:15am to 4:30pm; additional hours Thurs. from 7 to 9pm; closed Mon. and on important holidays. Admission
is 3.50 DM ($2.10); free on Sun. The underground station to head for is
Odeonsplatz. Bus no. 53 stops right in front of the gallery.

The east wing of the Haus der Kunst, Prinzregentenstrsse 1 (tel. 089/22-26-
51-3), is entered separately and requires a separate ticket, costing 5 DM ($3) (or
more depending on the show). It is devoted to changing exhibitions, which often
consist of the works of exciting new artists whose canvases are for sale as well as display. Many traveling exhibitions of worldwide importance are shown. It's open daily
from 9:30am to 6pm.

Münchner Stadtmuseum

Munich's Municipal Museum is to the city what the Bavarian National Museum is to the whole of the province. In what was once the armory building at St.
Jakobsplatz 1 (tel. 089/233-23-70), its collections give you an insight into the history and daily lives of the people of this unique community. A wooden model shows
how Munich looked in 1572. Special exhibitions about popular arts and traditions
are frequently presented. The extensive collection of furnishings is changed annually so that visitors will have a chance to see various periods from the vast storehouse.

The museum's main exhibit is its Moorish Dancers (Moriskentänzer) on the ground floor. These 10 figures, each 2 feet high, carved in wood and painted in bright colors by Erasmus Grasser in 1480, are among the best examples of secular Gothic art in medieval Germany. In the large Gothic hall on the ground floor you can admire an important collection of armor and weapons from the 14th to the 18th centuries.

The photo museum on the second floor traces the early history of the camera back to 1839. Cabinet after cabinet of early cameras line the walls. Every day, at 6 and 9pm, the film museum shows two different films from its extensive archives.

One salon is devoted to the replica of an old brewery, with effective models, vats, and other equipment. An adjacent room shows the modern technique of bottling, depicted in large photo murals and other exhibits, right down to the beer cans.

Some readers have found the displays on the fourth floor even more impressive. The historical collection of musical instruments is one of the greatest of its kind in the world. In addition, there is an ethnological collection of instruments from Africa, Oceania, the Americas, the Far East, the Middle East, Byzantium, and early Europe.

Enter the Municipal Museum through the main courtyard with its cafeteria. It is open from 10am to 5pm, on Wed. to 8:30pm; closed Mon. Admission is 4 DM ($2.40); free on Sun. and holidays.

Städtische Galerie im Lenbachhaus

The ancient villa of Franz von Lenbach, this gallery exhibits works by that 19th-century artist (1836–1904) and others. Entering the gold-colored mansion at 33 Luisenstrasse (tel. 089/52-10-41) through the gardens, you'll first be greeted with a large collection of early works by Paul Klee (1879–1940)—mainly those predating World War I. There's an outstanding group of works by Kandinsky, leader of the Blue Rider movement in the early 20th century. There are many 19th-century paintings throughout the villa, along with a few earlier works. The enclosed patio is pleasant for a coffee break. The gallery is open from 10am to 6pm except Mon. Admission is 4 DM ($2.40). Take U-8 to Königsplatz.

Schack-Galerie

Near the Haus der Kunst, the Schack Gallery, Prinzregentenstrasse 9 (tel. 089/23805-224), houses a collection of art bequeathed to the German Emperor by Prussian civil servant Count Schack. The comprehensive collection is devoted to 19th-century German art and has paintings by such artists as Böcklin, Lenbach, Spitzweg, Schwind, and others. The building, erected in 1907, also housed the headquarters of the Prussian Embassy in Bavaria. The gallery can be visited from 9:15am to 4:30pm (9am to noon on Fasching Sunday and December 31); closed Tues. and some public holidays. Admission is 2.50 DM ($1.50); free on Sun.

CHURCHES OF MUNICH

As Germany's largest Catholic city, Munich naturally contains a number of outstanding churches. For those interested in ecclesiastical art and architecture, I offer a trio of the finest.

Frauenkirche (Cathedral of Our Lady)

When the smoke cleared from the bombings of 1945, only a fragile shell remained of Munich's largest church. Workmen and architects who restored the 15th-century Gothic cathedral used whatever remains they could find in the rubble, along with modern innovations. The overall effect of the rebuilt Frauenkirche is strikingly simple, yet dignified.

The twin towers (which remained intact), with their strangely un-Gothic onion domes, have been the city's landmark since 1525. The red-brick exterior of the cathedral has retained its Gothic appearance. Instead of the typical flying buttresses, the edifice is supported by huge props on the inside that separate the side chapels. The Gothic vaulting over the nave and chancel is borne by 22 simple octagonal pillars.

Entering the main doors at the west end of the cathedral, you first notice no windows (they are actually hidden, except for the tall chancel window, by the enormous pillars). According to legend, the devil thought so too, and you can still see the strange footlike mark called "the devil's step" in the entrance hall where he stamped in glee at the stupidity of the architect. As you enter the left aisle of the three-aisled nave, you'll see photographs showing the cathedral as it looked after it was destroyed in the air raids of World War II. Many of the works of art formerly housed in the church were safely put away before that time, and are displayed in the chapels along the nave and behind the chancel.

In the chapel directly behind the high altar is the most interesting painting in the cathedral: *The Protecting Cloak,* a 1510 work by Jan Polack, showing the Virgin holding out her majestic robes to shelter all humankind. The collection of tiny figures beneath the cloak includes everyone from the pope to peasants. At the entrance to the vestry, just to the left of the choir, is a huge painting of *The Ascension of the Virgin Mary* by Peter Candid. In the south chapel adjoining the Chapel of the Holy Sacrament is one of the modern works, *The Immaculate Virgin,* a graceful bronze statue (1959) hung over a simple altar.

The Baptistry, to the right of the choir, contains the cathedral's oldest work, a stone sculpture of the suffering Christ, dating from 1380.

Returning to the entrance via the south nave, you'll pass the mausoleum of Emperor Ludwig IV, built in 1622. The elaborately carved tomb is guarded at each corner by armored soldiers with banners of the realm. In the front stands a sculpted likeness of the emperor, sword in hand. The cathedral is open daily from 6am to 6:30pm. Entrance is on Frauenplatz.

Peterskirche (St. Peter's Church)

Munich's oldest church (1180), at the Rindermarkt, has turned over a new leaf, and it's a gold one at that. The white-and-gray interior has been decorated with painted medallions of puce and lots of gilded baroque. It contains a series of murals by Johann Baptist Zimmermann, but nothing tops the attraction of the bizarre relic in the second chapel on the left: the gilt-covered and gem-studded skeleton of St. Mundita staring at you with two false eyes in its head, which rests on a cushion. Jewels cover the mouth of rotten teeth, quite a contrast to the fresh roses usually kept in front of the black-and-silver coffin.

Near the Town Hall, St. Peter's, known locally as Old Peter, also has a high steeple, although you may be discouraged from going up it by the lack of an elevator. The colored circles on the lower platform will tell you whether the climb is worthwhile, however. If the circle is white, you can be assured of a spectacular view as far as the Alps. Admission is 2 DM ($1.20), and the tower is open Mon. to Fri. from 9am to 5pm; Sat. from 8:30am to 7pm; and Sun. from 10am to 7pm.

Theatinerkirche

Named for a small group of Roman Catholic clergy (the Theatines), this church is the finest example of Italian baroque in Munich. Dedicated to the scholar-saint Cajetan, it was begun in the mid-17th century by two Italian architects, Barelli and Zucalli. It was completed in 1768 by the son of the dwarf court jester–cum–architect, François Cuvilliés. The facade and the interior are both studded with cherubs. Some of them are quite mischievous, especially the "Angel of Silence," which points the way to the interior with one hand while he holds the other to his lips to form an obvious "shh."

The arched ceiling of the nave is supported by fluted columns lining the center aisle. Above the transept dividing the nave from the choir, the ceiling breaks into an open dome with an ornate gallery decorated with large but graceful statues. Nothing seems to detract from the whiteness of the interior, except the dark wooden pews and the canopied pulpit.

SCHLOSS NYMPHENBURG

When the call of spring made city life unbearable, the Wittelsbachs would pack up their bags and head for their country house, the summer residence at Nymphenburg. A more complete, more sophisticated palace than the Residenz in Munich, it was begun in the style of an Italian villa in 1664 by Elector Ferdinand Maria and took more than 150 years and several architectural changes to complete. The final plan of the palace was due mainly to Elector Max Emanuel, who in 1702 decided to enlarge the villa by adding four large pavilions connected by arcaded passageways. Gradually, the French style took over, and today the facade is a subdued baroque.

The interior of the palace is less subtle, however. Upon entering the main building, you're in the Great Hall, decorated in rococo colors and stuccos. The frescoes by Zimmerman (1756) depict incidents from mythology, especially those dealing with Flora, goddess of the nymphs, for whom the palace was named. This hall was used for both banquets and concerts during the reign of Max Joseph III, elector during the mid-18th century. Concerts are still presented here in summer. The smaller rooms are devoted to tapestries, paintings, and period furniture.

From the main building, turn left and head for the arcaded gallery connecting the northern pavilions. The first room in the arcade is the Great Gallery of Beauties, painted for Elector Max Emanuel in 1710, containing portraits of five of the loveliest ladies in the court of Louis XIV. More provocative, however, is Ludwig I's Gallery of Beauties in the south pavilion (the apartments of Queen Caroline). Ludwig commissioned no fewer than 36 portraits of the most beautiful women of his day. The paintings by J. Stieler (painted from 1827 to 1850) include the *Schöne Münchnerin* (lovely Munich girl) and one of the dancer Lola Montez, whose "friendship" with Ludwig I caused such a scandal that it was a factor in the Revolution of 1848.

To the south of the palace buildings, in the rectangular block of low structures that once housed the court stables, is the **Marstallmuseum,** containing carriages, coaches, sleighs, and riding accessories from the 18th and 19th centuries. As soon as you enter the first hall, look for the coronation coach of Elector Karl Albrecht. Built in Paris in 1740, this glass coach is ornamented with everything from acanthus leaves to dolphins. The few flat panels on the side of the coach are filled with oil paintings of Justitia, Bellona, and Ecclesia. From the same period is the hunting sleigh of Electress Amalia, with the statue of Diana, goddess of the hunt. Even the runners of the sleigh are decorated with shellwork and hunting trophies.

The coaches and sleighs of Ludwig II are displayed in the third hall. In keeping with his constant longing for the grandeur of the past, his state coach was ornately designed for his marriage to Duchess Sophie of Bavaria, a royal wedding that never came off. The fairy-tale coach wasn't wasted, however, since Ludwig often rode off through the countryside to one of his many castles in it, creating quite a picture. The coach is completely gilded, inside and out. Rococo carvings cover every inch of space except for the panels, faced with paintings on copper. In winter the king would use his state sleigh, nearly as elaborate as the Cinderella coach.

Nymphenburg's greatest attraction is the park. Stretching for 500 acres in front of the palace, it is divided into two sections by the canal that runs from the pool at the foot of the staircase to the cascade at the far end of the gardens. From the palace steps, you can see the formal design of the gardens, laid out in an English style, with lakes, greenery, and beds of flowers.

Within the park are several pavilions. On the guided tour, you begin with the **Amalienburg,** whose plain exterior belies the rococo decoration inside. Built as a hunting lodge for Electress Amalia (1734), the pavilion carries the hunting theme through the first few rooms and then bursts into salons of flamboyant colors, rich carvings, and wall paintings. The most impressive room is the Hall of Mirrors, a symphony of silver ornaments on a faintly blue ground.

The **Badenburg Pavilion** sits at the edge of the large lake of the same name. As its name implies, it was built as a bathing pavilion, although it's difficult to visualize Ludwig dashing in from the water with swimming suit dripping on those elegant floors. A trip to the basement, however, will help you appreciate the pavilion's practical side. Here you'll see the unique bath, surrounded by blue and white Dutch tiles. The ceiling is painted with several frescoes of bathing scenes from mythology.

The octagonal **Pagodenburg,** on the smaller lake on the opposite side of the canal, looks little like a Chinese pagoda from the outside. The interior, however, is decorated with pseudo-Chinese motifs, often using Dutch tiles in place of the Oriental ones.

The **Magdalenenklause** may look like a ruin, but it was intended that way when it was built in 1725. Also called the Hermitage, it was planned as a retreat for prayer and solitude. The four main rooms of the one-story structure are all paneled with uncarved, stained oak. All the furnishings are simple and the few paintings religious. It's really a drastic change from the other buildings.

You can park your car beside the Marstallmuseum and walk through the palace and gardens. Those arriving by tram no. 12 or bus no. 41 can get off at Auffahrtsallee and go along the small canal to the palace. If you have the better part of a day, buy the 5-DM ($2.95) ticket to the palace, carriage museum, and the pavilions in the park. From October 1 to March 31, the collective ticket costs only 4 DM ($2.40), as the Badenburg Pavilion, Pagodenburg, and Magdalenenklause are closed during this period. All buildings are closed on Mon. all year long. From April 1 to September 30, the main palace is open Tues. to Sun. from 9am to 12:30pm and 1:30 to 5pm; the Amalienburg from 9am to 12:30pm and 1:30 to 5pm; the Marstallmuseum from 9am to noon and 1 to 5pm; the Badenburg, Pagodenburg, and Magdalenenklause from 10am to 12:30pm and 1:30 to 5pm. In winter Tues. to Sun.; the main palace building is open from 10am to 12:30pm.; the Amalienburg from 10am to 12:30pm; and the Marstallmuseum from 10am to noon and 1 to 4pm. For information, call 089/17-90-81.

OTHER SIGHTS

About 4 miles south of the city center, the **Hellabrunn Zoo** stands in the Tierpark Hellabrunn, Tierparkstrasse 30 (tel. 089/62-50-80). It is one of the largest zoos in the world, and may be visited daily from 8am to 6pm (off-season, from 9am to 5pm), for an admission of 5 DM ($3) for adults and 3 DM ($1.80) for children. To reach the park, you can take a bus leaving from Marienplatz, no. 52, or U-Bahn 3. Hundreds of animals roam in a natural habitat. A walk through the park is so attractive it's recommended even if you're not a zoo buff. There is also a big children's zoo, as well as a large aviary whose inhabitants are allowed "free flight" (relatively speaking).

Right in the heart of the city, the **Viktualienmarkt** has been the gathering place of Munich since 1807. Here citizens go not only to buy fruits, vegetables, honey, meats, and cheese, but to gossip, browse, and snack as well. The location is off Marienplatz, around the corner from St. Peter's Church. Many of the vendors are from the farming areas, selling their white asparagus and their fresh strawberries in season. If you've got the munchies, this is the place to sample the wares, any day except Sunday. Try one of Munich's sour pickles or the famous Weisswurst, with spicy, sweet mustard. Thick soups are also sold, along with liver dumplings and lots of beer.

THE OLYMPIC GROUNDS

The Olympiapark, site of the 1972 Olympic Games, is a 740-acre plot of land at the northern edge of the city. More than 15,000 workers from 18 countries transformed the site into a park of nearly 5,000 trees, 27 miles of roads, 32 bridges, and a lake.

Olympiapark has its own railway station, subway line, mayor, post office, churches, even an elementary school. It broke the skyline of Munich by the addition of a 960-foot television tower in the center of the park.

The showpiece of this city is a huge stadium, capable of seating 80,000 spectators, and topped by the largest roof in the world—nearly 90,000 square yards of tinted acrylic glass. The supports for the stadium are anchored by two huge blocks, each capable of resisting 4,000 tons under stress. The roof serves the additional purposes of collecting rainwater and draining it into the nearby Olympic lake.

Nearly 5,000 apartments and cottages were built on the grounds to house members of the Olympic staffs and teams. After the games were over, these were turned into modern housing for some 10,000 residents.

Smaller halls throughout the park are used for exhibitions and such competitive events as wrestling, judo, fencing, and weight lifting. The covered swimming stadium, with four large pools, is now open to the public. Take the U-2 and U-3 subway.

Near Olympiapark, you can visit the **BMW Museum,** Petuelring 130 (tel. 089/38-95-33-07), where the history of the automobile is stunningly displayed in an atmosphere created by Oscar winner Rolf Zehetbauer, a "film architect." The museum, housed in a demisphere of modern architecture, takes you both into the future and the past. You can also view 10 video films and 13 slide shows (an especially interesting one shows how people of yesterday imagined the future). Cars, motorcycles, plane engines, and the tools of the automobile industry range from the days of the "oldies" to the age of robots. The museum is open daily from 9am to 4pm, charging no admission. While there, you might also ask about tours of the BMW factory. Take U-3 or U-8 to Olympiazentrum.

TOURS

Blue buses, with conducted sightseeing tours in both German and English, leave from the square in front of the main train station (Hauptbahnhof), corner of Prielmayerstrasse, all year round. Tickets are sold on the bus, and no advanced booking is necessary.

A short 1-hour tour, costing 15 DM ($8.90), leaves daily at 10am, 11:30am, and 2:30pm from May 1 to October 31. Winter departures are daily from 10am and 2:30pm. A 2½-hour tour, including the Olympic Tower, costs 26 DM ($15.45) from May 1 to October 31. Departures are at 10am and 2:30pm. In winter, November 1 to April 30, the cost is 23 DM ($13.65), and departures are at 10am and 2:30pm.

A 2½-hour tour, costing from 26 DM ($15.45), visits Nymphenburg Palace and the Schatzkammer every day, except Mon., at 2:30pm.

If you'd like to go farther afield and visit some of the major attractions in the environs of Munich, you can get information from **Panorama Tours,** an affiliate of Gray Line. The office is at Arnulfstrasse 8 (tel. 809/59-1504), to the north of the railway station. Hours are 7:30am to 6pm Mon. to Fri. and 7:30am to 2:30pm on Sat. and Sun.

EXCURSION TO DACHAU

In 1933 what had once been a quiet little artists' community just 20 miles from Munich (tel. 08131/17-41) became what was to be a tragic symbol of the Nazi era. Himmler and the SS set up the first German concentration camp in March of that year, on the grounds of a former ammunition factory. Dachau saw countless prisoners arrive between 1933 and 1945. Although the files show a registry of more than 206,000, the exact number of people imprisoned here is unknown.

Entering the camp today, you are faced by three memorial chapels—Catholic, Protestant, and Jewish—built in the early 1960s. Immediately behind the Catholic chapel is the "Lagerstrasse," the main camp road lined with poplar trees, once flanked by the 32 barracks, each housing 208 prisoners. Two of these barracks have been rebuilt to give visitors an insight into the horrible conditions endured by the prisoners.

The museum is housed in the large building that once contained the kitchen, laundry, and shower baths where prisoners were often brought for torture by the SS. Photographs and documents show the rise of the Nazi regime, the super-power of the SS, as well as exhibits depicting the persecution of Jews and other prisoners. Every effort has been made to present the facts. The tour of Dachau is a truly moving experience.

You can get to the camp by taking the frequent S-Bahn trains (train S-2) from the Hauptbahnhof to the Dachau station (direction: Petershausen), and then bus no. 722 from the station to the camp. Admission is free and the camp is open, except Mon., from 9am to 5pm. The English version of a documentary film, *KZ-Dachau*, is shown several times daily. All documents are translated in the catalogue, available at the entrance of the museum.

---

6. Shopping

The most interesting shops are concentrated on Munich's pedestrians-only street, lying between Karlsplatz and Marienplatz at the Rathaus. In general, Munich is the most varied shopping city in Germany, with merchandise-loaded shops lining many intriguing streets.

The following recommended stores keep the same hours: 8:30am to 12:30pm and 3 to 6pm Mon. to Fri. On Sat., they operate "half days"—that is, 8:30am to noon; closed Sun.

Rosenthal, Theatinerstrasse 8 (tel. 089/22-04-22), near the Rathaus, is the prestige shop for porcelain and glass in imaginative designs. It attracts everybody from the pope to Queen Juliana of the Netherlands. Ask for Dr. or Mrs. Hans Zoellner. Several factories in Bavaria combine to produce high-quality china, such as Rosenthal with its Classic Rose collection, the Studio Linie, and the collection of Hutschenreuther. In this Munich outlet you will also find matching crystal, cutlery, and many gift items. Dr. Zoellner's china export store also does a lot of mail-order business and sends gift parcels all over the world.

In optical goods, Germany has been famed since the birth of that industry. For contact lenses and other eye aids, I suggest you patronize **Söhnges,** Briennerstrasse 7 and Kaufingerstrasse 34. For information about either store, phone 089/27-29-02.

Germany's cameras are magnificent, and Leica is perhaps the most famous name. **Kohlroser,** Maffeistrasse 14 (tel. 089/22-10-19), carries a good assortment of cameras and equipment. The location is within an easy walk of the Bayerischer Hof and American Express. Look also for the Minox cameras (sometimes referred to humorously as "spy cameras"). The shop also carries Japanese cameras.

Dirndl Ecke, Am Platzl 1 (tel. 089/22-01-63), across from the famous Hofbräuhaus, gets my unreserved recommendation as a stylish shop specializing in high-grade dirndls, feathered alpine hats, and all clothing associated with the alpine regions. Everything sold here is of fine quality—there is no tourist junk. Other merchandise includes needlework hats, beaded belts, and pleated shirts for men. You may also be attracted to the stylish capes, the silver jewelry in old Bavarian style, the shoes in leather, or the linen and cotton combinations, such as skirts with blouses and jackets.

For folk art and handcrafts, **Wallach,** Residenzstrasse 3 (tel. 089/22-08-71), is preferred. In fact, I consider it the finest place in Germany to obtain handcrafts, both newly made and antique. It can save much time in your search for a memorable object that will remind you of your trip to Germany. You'll find such items as antique churns, old kitchen ware, brass hunting horns, rag rug lengths sold by the yard, paintings on glass, charmingly hand-painted wooden boxes and trays, milking stools, painted porcelain clocks, wooden wall clocks, doilies, napkins, and towels.

Kunsthandlung Timberg, Maximilianstrasse 15 (tel. 089/29-52-35), in the central shopping mall, has the best collection of new and antique Meissen and Dresden porcelain. It's almost a miniature museum. Look for both an old or new Meissener coffee set with the blue-and-white onion design. The shop has access to Dresden porcelain denied to other retail stores. *Important:* Any purchase here can be packed and shipped safely. They've had a lot of experience in doing just that.

Ludwig Beck am Rathauseck, Am Marienplatz (tel. 089/236-91-0), is a four-floor shopping bazaar selling handmade crafts from all over Germany, both old and new. You'll find it a feast of tasteful, colorful items to purchase. Items offered for sale include decorative pottery and dishes, beer steins and vases of etched glass, painted wall plaques depicting rural scenes, and decorative flower arrangements. There is much unusual kitchenware, colored flatware, calico hot pads and towels, plus a stunning collection of leather-trimmed canvas purses that are casually chic. The shop also offers fashions and textiles.

Andreas Huber, Weinstrasse 8 (tel. 089/29-82-94), sells all the big names in Swiss and other European wristwatches as well as clocks. They offer some jewelry, but their main focus is on timepieces.

Bayerischer Kunstgewerbeverein (Bavarian Association of Artisans), Pacellistrasse 7 (tel. 089/29-35-21), is another good choice for handcrafts. At this showcase for Bavarian artisans, you'll find excellent ceramics, glasses, jewelry, wood carvings, pewter, and Christmas decorations.

At **Karl Storr,** Kaufingerstrasse 25 (tel. 089/22-95-14), you'll find the finest selection of Bavarian wood carvings, both machinemade and hand-carved items.

Hugendubel, Marienplatz 22 (tel. 089/23-89-1), is the biggest bookstore in Munich and enjoys a central location.

Gebrüder Hemmerle, Maximilianstrasse 14 (tel. 089/22-01-89), is the place for jewelry. The original founders of this stylish place made their fortune designing bejeweled fantasies for the Royal Bavarian Court of Ludwig II. Today, within a shop paneled in southern baroque pastel-painted wood, you can buy some of the most desirable jewelry in the capital. All pieces are designed and made in-house by Bavarian craftspeople whose editions are limited. The company also designs a wristwatch of its own, the Hemmerle, and distributes what is said to be one of the world's finest watches, the Brequet.

Loden-Frey, Maffeistrasse 7-9 (tel. 089/23-69-30). The twin domes of the Frauenkirche are visible above the soaring glass-enclosed atrium of this shop's showroom. Go here for the world's largest selection of Loden clothing and traditional costumes (lederhosen, dirndls, and the like), as well as for international fashions from top European designers such as Armani, Valentino, and Ungaro, among others.

Elly Seidl, Am Kosttor 2 (tel. 089/22-15-22), is the premier shop for delectable homemade chocolates. Whatever your taste in chocolate, this store can generally meet your demand.

Frankonia, Maximilianplatz 10 (tel. 089/22-58-81), has one of the most prestigious collections of traditional Bavarian dress (called Tracht in German) in Munich. If you see yourself dressed hunter style, this place can outfit you well. It has a fine collection of wool cardigan jackets with silvery buttons as well.

Bogner Haus, Residenzstrasse 15 (tel. 089/22-17-24), is the place to stop for the latest in ski clothing and styles before you head for the slopes. All this flamboyant attire is sold by Willy Bogner, the filmmaker and Olympic downhill racer.

Biebl, Karlsplatz 25 (tel. 089/55-75-05), sells the widest assortment of Solingen carving sets, silverware, along with many other items, including Austrian crystal, Swiss army knives, and Hummel figurines.

Nymphenburger Porzellanmanufaktur, Nördliches Schlossrondell 8 (tel.

089/17-24-39), is at Nymphenburg, about 5 miles northwest of the heart of Munich. This is one of the most famous porcelain factories in Germany, lying on the grounds of Schloss Nymphenburg, already previewed as a sightseeing attraction. You can visit its exhibition and sales rooms, where shipments can be arranged if you make purchases, Monday to Friday only from 8am to noon and 12:30 to 5pm.

Ileana Ellenbogen, Frauenstrasse 12 (tel. 089/29-27-98), is a small shop selling some of Europe's most beautiful stained-glass windows. It stands across the street from one of Munich's best-known outdoor vegetable markets. This Romanian-born art historian sells glass carefully extracted from old houses and public buildings in Belgium, Germany, France, and Austria, with a scattering from 19th-century America as well.

7. Kids' Munich

It's fun all the way for children in Munich. From the Circus Krone to the Marionetten Theater, to the Bavarian Film Studio, kids tend to love Munich.

Take your children to the **Münchner Stadtmuseum** (Municipal Museum), St. Jakobsplatz 1 (tel. 089/233-23-70). On the third floor is an array of puppets from around the world, with star billing going to the puppeteer's art. The comical and grotesque figures include both marionettes and hand puppets. Like a Lilliputian version of the world of the stage, the collection also includes detailed puppet theaters and miniature scenery. A special department is devoted to fairground art, including carousel animals, shooting galleries, models of rollercoasters, and wax and museum figures. The main exhibit contains the oldest known carousel horses, dating from 1820. For opening hours, see the previous write-up.

If children have a favorite museum in Munich, it's the **Deutsches Museum,** Museumsinsel 1 (tel. 089/21-791). It's been called a "hands-on" museum. For details, refer to the previous write-up.

The **Spielzeugmuseum** in the Altes Rathaus is a historic collection of toys. Open Mon. to Sat. from 10am to 5:30pm; Sun. 10am to 6pm.

At the **Münchner Marionetten Theater,** Blumenstrasse 29a (tel. 089/26-57-12), you can attend puppet shows and the *théâtre de marionnettes.* Adults as well as children are delighted with these productions, many of which are of operas. Performances are Wed., Thurs., Sat., and Sun. at 3pm. Admission is 8 DM ($4.75) for adults and 6 DM ($3.55) for children. To reach the theater, take the U-Bahn (underground train) to Sendlinger Tor.

The **Bavaria Film Studio** is the largest filmmaking center in Europe. It is Munich's version of Hollywood. Guided tours are possible from March 1 to October 31, daily from 9am to 4pm. The tour lasts 1½ hours. Take streetcar no. 25 to Bavariafilmplatz. The entrance fee is 12 DM ($7.15).

Hellabrunn Zoo, already described, has a large children's zoo where children are allowed to pet the animals.

8. After Dark

Munich is a city with a lively and quite inexpensive nightlife. It won't take you long to realize that most of it centers around the golden brew.

THE BEERHALLS

A legend among beerhalls, **Hofbräuhaus am Platzl,** Am Platzl 9 (tel. 089/22-16-76), is the most famous in the world. Visitors with only one night in Munich usually target the Hofbräuhaus as their number-one nighttime destination. Owned by the state, the present Hofbräuhaus was built at the end of the 19th century, but the tradition of a beerhouse on this spot dates from 1589. In the 19th century it attracted artists, students, and civil servants. It was called the Blue Hall, because of its dim lights and smoky atmosphere. When it grew too small to contain everybody, architects designed another hall in 1897. This one was the 1920 setting for the notorious meeting of Hitler's newly launched German Workers Party. Fistfights erupted as the Nazis attacked their Bavarian enemies right in the beer palace.

Today 4,500 beer drinkers can crowd in here on a given night. They eat about 10,000 meals a day, and consume nearly 3,000 gallons of beer. There are several rooms spread over three floors, including one on the top floor for dancing every night of the week in summer. But with its brass band (which starts playing in the afternoon), the ground-floor Schwemme is most typical of what you always expected of a beerhall—here it's eternal Oktoberfest. In the second-floor restaurant, strolling musicians, including an accordian player and a violinist, entertain you. Dirndl-clad waitresses place mugs of beer at your table between sing-alongs. For a liter, expect to pay 7.20 DM ($4.25); meals are in the 12-DM ($7.15) to 25-DM ($14.85) range. In season, from mid-March to October, Hofbräuhaus am Platzl presents a typical Bavarian show in its fest-hall every evening, starting at 7 and lasting till midnight. The entrance fee is 7 DM ($4.16), and the food is the same as that served in the other parts of the beer palace. Beer here will be more expensive, costing around 8 DM ($5.05) for a liter. Hours are 10am to midnight daily.

Augustinerbräu, Neuhauserstrasse 16 (tel. 089/55-199-257), on the principal pedestrians-only street of Munich, offers generous helpings of food, good beer, and mellow atmosphere. Dark-wood panels and ceilings in carved plaster make the place look even older than it is. It's been around for less than a century, but beer was first brewed on this spot in 1328, or so the literature about the establishment claims. The long menu changes daily, and the cuisine is not for dieters: it's hearty, heavy, and definitely starchy, but that's what the customers want. Meals average 15 DM ($8.90) to 25 DM ($14.85). Hours are 10am to midnight daily.

Platzl, Am Platzl 1 (tel. 089/23-70-30), faces its more famous competitor, the Hofbräuhaus. It presents a Bavarian folk program nightly in the large beerhall area. The women dancers wear dirndls, the men dress in lederhosen, loden jackets, and felt hats. Together they perform the Schulplattler, the thigh-slapping folk dance of the Bavarian Alps. The show lasts two hours, and the entrance charge is 11.50 DM ($6.85). The inn offers fine Bavarian food and sausages; Platzl draft beer in a keg is placed at the table. The Platzl is open Mon. to Sat. from 11:30am to 2pm and 6:30pm to midnight; closed Sun.

Mathäser Bierstadt, Bayerstrasse 5 (tel. 089/59-28-96), is a rough and rowdy beer city, filled both afternoons and evenings with happy imbibers. To reach the Bierhalle, walk through to the back, then go upstairs. Featured is a brass band oomphaing away. The largest of all Bavarian taverns, the Mathäser contains tables and tables of drinkers joining in the songs. Even at midafternoon the place is often packed, making you wonder if anybody is working in the entire city. In addition to the main hall, there is a rooftop garden and a downstairs tavern. Löwenbräu kegs spill out onto the sidewalk for stand-up sausage and Kraut nibblers. Specialties of the house include knuckles of veal and pork. At certain times of the year you can order soups made with fresh white asparagus. Meals cost 15 DM ($8.90) to 25 DM ($14.85).

During the spring "strong beer season," two weeks after the end of Fasching, and during Oktoberfest, the Mathäser holds a special program featuring a big brass band and yodeling. The place is also famous for its Bavarian breakfasts with Weisswürste and beer. Open daily from 8am to midnight.

Zum Pschorrbräu, Neuhauserstrasse 11 (tel. 089/260-30-01), is the showcase of the Pschorrbräu interests. It's a good place for both food and entertainment. Live music is played daily in the wine cellar, St. Michael, from 7pm to midnight; the cellar, however, opens at 4:30pm. The wine list provides 60 different varieties, and hot food is served until closing. Actually, the Pschorrbräu offers a more toned-down introduction to a Bavarian beer restaurant than does, say, the Hofbräuhaus. And the food is better than that usually found in such places. It's not expensively priced; for example, set lunches range from 15 DM ($8.90) to 25 DM ($14.85). Hours are 8am to midnight daily.

Löwenbräukeller, Nymphenburgerstrasse 2 (tel. 089/52-60-2). This beerhall should be better known. Admittedly, it's somewhat removed from the center of town, yet it offers one of the best gemütlich evenings in Munich. On the à la carte menu, a typical main dish would be Sauerbraten with dumplings and red cabbage. Such Bavarian specialties are served in the open-air beer garden. A simple meal might cost 15 DM ($8.90), but you could spend a lot more, of course—from 25 DM ($14.85) and beyond. The Löwenbräukeller is especially known for its individual Bavarian evenings and royal Bavarian nights, when live entertainment is offered. Hours are 9am to 1am daily.

Waldwirtschaft Grosshesslohe, Georg-Kalb-Strasse 3 (tel. 089/79-50-88), a popular summertime rendezvous, is a Bavarian beer garden with seats for some 2,000 drinkers. The gardens are open daily from 10:30am to 10pm (they have to close early because of complaints from neighborhood residents). However, music ranging from Dixieland to English jazz to Polish bands is played throughout the week. Entrance is free and you bring your own food, paying 8 DM ($4.75) for a large mug of beer. The location is above the Isar River in the vicinity of the zoo.

A MEDIEVAL FEAST

From 6pm to midnight every day, **Welser Küche,** Residenzstrasse 27 (tel. 089/29-69-73), offers hearty medieval feasts. Guests can come early (but no later than 8pm), and they must be prepared to stick around for three hours, as they are served by "Mägde" and "Knechte" (or wenches and knaves) in 16th-century costumes, as was the custom 450 years ago. In many ways this is like a takeoff on one of the many medieval Tudor banquets that enjoy such popularity with tourists in London. Food is served in hand-thrown pottery, and guests eat these medieval delicacies with their fingers, aided only by a stilettolike dagger.

You can order a six- or ten-course menu, called a Welser Feast, costing 55 DM ($32.65) to 70 DM ($41.55). For smaller appetites, four-course meals are also served, beginning at 35 DM ($20.80). Many of the recipes were found in a cookbook that belonged to Freiin von Zinnenburg, the wife of the Habsburg Archduke Ferdinand II. Discovered in 1970, the cookbook serves as a culinary guide. Most of the guests accompany their meals with a special dark beer. The place can be good fun if you're in the mood, but because it is likely to be overflowing, reservations are recommended. If you call ahead, don't use the restaurant's direct number; instead, call 089/29-65-65.

THE TOP NIGHTCLUB

The ground-floor cellar nightclub the **Bayerischer Hof,** Promenadeplatz 2–6 (tel. 089/2-12-00), in the deluxe hotel, offers the most gilt-edged entertainment in Munich. The orchestras are the smoothest in town, and so is the clientele. Dancing goes on in front of the bandstand (the combo wisely varies the pace from fast to slow); some of the tables are placed above the dance floors, others are right in the center of the action. Large drinks are served, and most whiskies average about 20 DM ($11.90) a drink. The club opens nightly at 8:30pm and closes at 3am.

FAVORITE BARS

Located on Munich's most desirable shopping street, **Schumann's,** Maximilianstrasse 36 (tel. 089/22-90-60), doesn't waste any money on decor. It doesn't have to, as it depends on the local beau monde to keep it fashionable. In cold weather, guests retreat inside, but once the sun heats up, they prefer the terrace that spills out onto the street. Schumann's is known as "a thinking man's bar." Charles

Schumann, author of two bar books, is one of the best-known bar men in Europe, and his bar has been called one of the best in the world. Mr. Schumann conceived of a bar that would serve as an artistic, literary, and communicative social focus of the metropolis. Popular with the film, advertising, and publishing worlds, his place is said to have contributed to a remarkable renaissance in bar culture in the city. Drink prices start at 12 DM ($7.15). Open from 5pm to 3am; closed Sat.

Harry's New York Bar, Falkenturmstrasse 9 (tel. 089/22-27-00), is near the Hofbräuhaus. The establishment, which is managed by its owner, Bill Deck, takes its name from the first American bar in Paris in the 1920s and features such drinks as the Sidecar cocktail, created in 1931, and the Monkey's Gland, created in 1930. Attentive waiters will bring you food as well, including grade-A sirloin, chili tacos, and a shrimp plate. Beer is available on tap at 6 DM ($3.55). Open from 4pm to 3am; closed Sun.

Once a literary café, **Alter Simpl,** Türkenstrasse 57 (tel. 089/272-30-83), takes its name from a satirical revue of 1903. There is no one around any more who remembers that revue, but Alter Simpl remained on the scene and was made famous by its legendary owner, Kathi Kobus. Lale Andersen, who made the song "Lili Marlene" famous, frequented the café when she was in Munich. Today it attracts a wide segment of the local population, including a lot of young people, even counterculturists and *Gastarbeiters* (guest workers). The place is open, except Sun., from 6pm to either 3 or 4am. A whisky costs from 9 DM ($5.35). Food is served, including sausages, potato salad, Wiener Schnitzel, rumpsteak, and omelets. The real fun of the place occurs after 11pm, when the iconoclastic artistic ferment is more reminiscent of Berlin than Bavaria.

Schultz, Barerstrasse 47 (tel. 089/271-47-11), is a New York–style bar in Schwabing popular with a clientele of theater people who crowd in as they do at Schumann's for lots of smoke-filled chatter. It is open daily from 5pm to 1am. A large beer costs 4.60 DM ($2.75), a whisky beginning at 9 DM ($5.35). The food is uncomplicated, including grilled steaks, smoked trout platters, and salads. The decor, as they say here, is "unobvious and understated."

WINE DRINKING

Since about 1400, Münchners have patronized the ancient winehouse, **Weinschenke am Markt,** Dreifaltigkeitsplatz 1 (tel. 089/22-61-33). At the edge of the city's huge outside vegetable and fruit market, the Viktualienmarkt, the winehouse has arched ceilings and hand-painted country furnishings. You can have cheese, Black Forest ham, and herb bread to accompany one of the Austrian, French, or German wines, which cost about 8 DM ($4.75) a glass. The establishment is open, from 11am to 1am.; closed Sun.

JAZZ

A center for jazz in Munich is **domicile,** Leopoldstrasse 19 (tel. 089/39-94-51), in the Schwabing district. It also features rock music. The best artists seem to perform there from late April through early October, and everything or everyone from big bands to solo performers can be heard nightly from 9pm to 4am. Students and artists are drawn to the place, a typical jazz cellar, its walls decorated with enlarged transparencies of many performing jazz artists. Whisky goes for around 12 DM ($7.15) and open wine for the same price.

Schwabinger Podium, Wagnerstrasse 1 (tel. 089/39-94-82), offers different entertainment nightly. Some evenings are devoted to jazz, and on other occasions I've been entertained by Dixieland as well as rock. Hours are 8pm to 1am daily, with beer priced at 6.50 DM ($3.85). On some weekends the cover charge is 5 DM ($3).

Jazzclub Unterfahrt, Kirchenstrasse 96 (tel. 089/448-27-94), the leading jazz club of Munich, lies near the Ostbahnhof in the district of Haidhausen. Within a Gemütlich ambience of pinewood paneling and flickering candles, its management presents live music every night of the week but Monday. Off to one corner of the

120-seat establishment is an art gallery where a changing collection of paintings and sculpture are sold. The doors open daily from 6pm to 1am, and live music begins at 9. A beer costs 4.20 DM ($2.50), and wine, small snacks, and hard drinks are sold as well. Sunday night there's a special jam session for improvisation, while every Sunday morning (from October to April only) brings a "jazz breakfast" concert beginning at 10:30am.

CABARET

In Munich when you "come to the cabaret"—political, that is—you may end up at the **Rationaltheater,** Hesseloherstrasse 18 (tel. 089/33-50-40). It has existed since 1963, and some critics claim its political satire is so pointed that it has the power to topple governments. The show is performed every day except Mon., starting at 8:30pm. Tickets must be reserved by phone, beginning at 10am. Prices range from 18 DM ($10.70) to 28 DM ($16.65).

DISCOS

Babalu, Ainmillestrasse 1 (tel. 089/39-89-64), corner of Leopoldstrasse, was originally built in the 1950s as a striptease bar. In its reincarnation, the owners deliberately retained the red-flocked wallpaper, gilt accents, dark paneling, and kitsch when they transformed it into a basically straight disco—geared to a clientele whose ages range from 20 to 40. Sometimes it's rhythm and blues, sometimes live jazz, sometimes new or old soul—all in an electronic mishmash the owners call "commercial." If you have strong tastes in music, it's best to phone ahead to find out what's on the program. Babalu is open nightly from 8pm to 4am. On Tuesday there is a live concert with a 5-DM ($2.95) cover charge. Beer costs from 5.50 DM ($3.25).

Nachtcafé, Maximilianplatz 5 (tel. 089/59-59-00). It hums, it thrives, and it captures the nocturnal imagination of everyone: no other nightspot in Munich attracts such an array of soccer stars, film celebrities, literary figures, and, as one employee put it, "ordinary people, but only the most sympathetically crazy ones." It is open nightly from 7pm to 5am. Waves of patrons appear at different times of the evening: at midnight, when live concerts begin; at about 2am, when restaurants close; and at about 4am, when diehard revelers seek a final drink as they face the predawn hours. There are no fewer than five bars and lots of tiny tables. There's no cover charge, and a bottle of beer goes for 4.80 DM ($2.85). Full meals range from 10 DM ($5.95) to 30 DM ($17.80). The decor is updated 1950s (lots of neon), the music a sort of "retro-fun" beat, with electric rhythms.

Park-Café, Sophienstrasse 7 (tel. 089/59-83-13), a Tanzpalast (dance palace) with a disc jockey, is located near the Hauptbahnhof in an imposing building whose massive neoclassical porch belies the theatrical kitsch decor within. The only cover imposed is on Friday and Saturday, when you pay 15 DM ($8.90). Once you're inside, a beer costs 7.50 DM ($4.45); sandwiches are the only food served. Open nightly from 10:30pm to 4am.

CULTURAL ENTERTAINMENT

Perhaps nowhere else in Europe, other than London and Paris, will you find so many musical and theatrical performances. And the good news is the low cost of the seats—so count on indulging yourself and going to several concerts. You'll get good tickets if you're willing to pay anywhere from 15 DM ($8.90) to 70 DM ($41.55).

Gasteig Kulturzentrum, Rosenheimer Strasse 5 (tel. 089/480-980), or Gasteig Cultural Center, is the home of the Münchner Philharmoniker (Munich Philharmonic Orchestra), which was founded in 1893. Its new home, which opened in 1985, also shelters the Richard Strauss Conservatory of Music. The orchestra performs in Philharmonic Hall, which has the largest seating capacity of the center's four performance halls. In the district of Haidhausen, Gasteig stands on the bluffs of the River Isar. It is reached by taking the S-Bahn or bus no. 51. You can purchase tickets to events at the ground-level Glashalle, Mon. to Fri. from 10:30am to 2pm and 3 to 6pm and on Sunday from 10:30am to 2pm. The Philharmonic season begins in mid-September and runs to July. The orchestra, however, is heavily subscribed, so tickets are hard to come by.

Practically any night of the year, except August to mid-September, you'll find a performance at the opera house, the **Nationaltheater,** on Max-Joseph-Platz (tel. 089/21-85-1), the home of the Bavarian State Opera, one of the world's great companies. The Germans give their hearts, perhaps their souls, to opera. Productions are beautifully mounted and presented, and sung by some of the world's greatest singers. Hard-to-get tickets may be purchased Mon. to Fri. from 10am to 1pm and 3:30 to 5:30pm, and one hour before each performance (during the weekend, only on Sat. from 10am to 12:30pm). For ticket information, telephone 089/22-13-16.

The regular season of the **Deutsches Theater,** Schwanthalerstrasse 13 (tel. 089/59-34-17), lasts from March to June and July to December. Musicals are popular, but operettas, classical plays, ballets, and international shows are performed as well. It's the only theater in Germany that is both a theater and a ballroom. During the carnival season in January and February, the seats are removed and stored away, replaced by tables and chairs for more than 2,000 guests. Handmade decorations by artists combined with lighting effects create an enchanting ambience. Waiters serve wine, champagne, and food. There are costume balls and official black-tie festivities, famous throughout Europe.

Staatstheater am Gärtnerplatz, Gärtnerplatz 3 (tel. 089/201-67-67), is yet another theater where the presentations are varied and entertaining. The programs include ballet, operettas, and musicals. The ticket office is open during the same hours as those of the Nationaltheater.

Altes Residenztheater (Cuvilliés Theater), in the Residenz (entrance at Residenzstrasse 1; tel. 089/22-46-41), is a sightseeing attraction in its own right. The Bavarian State Opera and the Bayerisches Staatsschauspiel (Bavarian National Theater) perform smaller works here in keeping with the more intimate character of the unique baroque architecture of the tiny theater. Box-office hours are the same as those for the Nationaltheater. The theater is celebrated as the most outstanding example of a rococo tier-boxed theater in the country. Seating an audience of 550, it was designed by court architect François de Cuvilliés in the mid-18th century. During World War II, the interior of the theater was dismantled and stored; after the war it was reassembled in the reconstructed building. For an admission of 1.50 DM (90¢), visitors can look at the theater Mon. to Sat. from 2 to 5pm, Sun. from 10am to 5pm. To reach it, take U-3, U-5, or U-6 to Odeonsplatz.

If you speak German, you'll find at least 20 theaters offering plays of every description: classic, comedic, experimental, contemporary—take your pick. The best way to find out what current productions might interest you is to go to a theater-ticket agency. The most convenient one is at Marienplatz at the entrance to the underground S-Bahn.

The **Residenztheater,** Max-Joseph-Platz 1 (tel. 089/22-57-54), is the home of Bayerisches Staatsschauspiel, which presents classical drama (including Shakespeare) as well as modern plays.

Special mention should be made of an unusual theater: **Theater Rechts der Isar,** Wörthstrasse 9 (tel. 089/45-58-13), which presents contemporary and experimental plays, by such playwrights as Peter Handke and Bertolt Brecht.

Not to be ignored is the **Circus Krone,** Marstrasse 43 (tel. 089/55-81-68). It might be compared to London's Albert Hall, its productions are so varied—one night, a jazz festival; the next night, a hard rock concert; yet another night, gospel singers; and from December 25 to March 31, a circus show every night. In season, performances are at 3pm and 8pm daily, and admission is 5 DM ($3) for children and 7 DM ($4.15) for adults. To reach the circus, take S-Bahn to Hackerbrücke.

GAY MUNICH

New York, Bonnenstrasse 25 (tel. 809/59-1056). The strident rhythms and electronic sounds might just have been imported from New York, Los Ángeles, or Paris. The sound system is sophisticated, and the shows of laser-derived lighting amazing. This is the premier gay (male) disco of Munich. Most clients, whose ages range from 20 to 30, wear jeans. There's no cover charge, but beer costs 6 DM ($3.55). The disco is open nightly from 11pm to 4am.

More mature and perhaps bizarre gay taste is catered to by **Ochsengarten,** Müllerstrasse 47 (tel. 089/26-64-46), which is open Sun. to Thurs. from 9pm to 1am, on Fri. and Sat. from 9pm to 3am. There's no cover charge, and beer costs 3.50 DM ($2.10). The wearing of leather isn't mandatory to get in, but it helps.

Teddy Bar, Hans-Sachsstrasse 1 (tel. 089/260-33-59), is a gay bar—no disco, no dancing, just 100% gay. This small, cozy bar is decorated with teddy bears. Beer costs from 4 DM ($2.40), and it's served nightly from 8pm to 1am.

Around the corner is the best women's bar in Munich: **Mylord,** Ickstattstrasse 2a (tel. 089/59-83-13). Established in 1964, it is run by its English-speaking owner, the very charming Marietta Gruneberg, whose style and impeccable manners set the tone for a series of rooms filled with oil paintings, antique odds and ends, and photographs of artists, movie stars, and devoted friends. Most of the clients are women, although "boys and their friends" are "very, very welcome." A beer costs from 3.50 DM ($2.10), although in the early hours—usually from 6 to 10pm on Wed., Fri., and Sat.—drinks are half price. There is no cover. Disco favorites, rock and roll, electronic music, and nostalgic oldies are heard on the small dance floor. The club is open nightly from 6pm to 1am (on Sat. to 3am).

LEADING SPA RESORTS

Even if you wander into the most out-of-the-way places in Germany, you'll never get away from one of the greatest of all Teutonic institutions, the spa. Dozens are spread throughout the country; some have been known since Roman times, while others are of much more recent vintage, but they all have one thing in common—"healing" waters.

From seawater to thermal or radioactive springs, the Germans have learned to make the best use of all types of water for all types of ailments. Ever since the Kneipp treatment, commonly called hydrotherapy, was formulated by a Bavarian pastor, natural mineral springs are no longer a prerequisite for the establishment of a spa. Spas exist in every imaginable location, from seaside resorts to mountaintops in the Bavarian Alps. Besides mud baths and hydrotherapy, they offer a wide range of activities and facilities. From the casinos in Baden-Baden, Bad Homburg, and Westerland to golf courses and horse racing, there's never a dull moment during the busy summer spa season. Some of the larger spas are active all year.

In this chapter I'll sample some of the variety to be found among the spas. In addition to the ten spas detailed, you'll find other important German resorts, such as Baden-Baden, Bad Godesberg, and Westerland, in other chapters.

1. Bad Pyrmont

This attractive spa, 104 miles from Hannover, has enjoyed a reputation for more than 2,000 years. Its springs are of different kinds, from the brine variety in the fields to the medicinal iron waters on the southern side of the valley of the Weser Hills. In the center of town you can drink a medicinal cocktail from the fountain at the Hyllige Born spring. Another popular pastime is taking mud baths. But Bad Pyrmont is a good place to vacation even if you don't come to take the waters. Horseback riding in the hills, hiking, tennis, and swimming, as well as concerts and shows, make the resort a lively place.

The spa gardens are among the most beautiful in Germany, with little temples, flowering trees, and even a palm garden, an unusual touch in the temperate climate. The concert house in the Kurpark has shows during the busy summer. At night the central promenade is glamorously lit, giving the spa a festive air, while guests sit at sidewalk tables drinking beer.

WHERE TO STAY AND DINE

Bergkurpark, Ockelstrasse 11, D-3280 Bad Pyrmont (tel. 05281/40-01), is the most distinguished hotel at the spa, certainly the most glamorous architecturally. Its entryway has a thatched roof, covering a combination hewn-stone and stucco facade with half-rounded picture windows—most dramatic. After checking in, you're shown your room, which might be in a modern block with private terraces overlooking a park. The 57-room hotel rents singles for 59 DM ($35.05) to 148 DM ($87.90) daily. Twin-bedded rooms with baths or showers begin at 158 DM ($93.80), climbing to 360 DM ($213.75) for the best in the house. The hotel has its own park, a forest, a heated swimming pool, and a terrace with sun parasols overlooking the garden. There are also exercise rooms and a sauna. Its restaurant serves the best food at the spa (see below). The hotel also has an elegant café, Sans Souci, and the rustic-style Wilhelm Busch–Stube, where beer, wine, and good food are served.

Park-Hotel Rasmussen, Kirchstrasse 8, D-3280 Bad Pyrmont (tel. 05281/44-85), a completely renovated 12-room villa in the heart of Bad Pyrmont, stands on the traffic-free promenade. The spacious rooms are well furnished, with phones and color TVs; beds are comfortable, and many rooms have balconies overlooking the promenade. Prices are 150 DM ($89.05) to 196 DM ($116.40) daily for a double with bath, 75 DM ($44.55) to 140 DM ($83.15) for a single with bath. The staff is pleasant. The hotel's quiet dining room offers set lunches costing from 35 DM ($20.80). In the evening, diners are offered more expensive dishes, including trout au bleu and wild game (in season) for two. The bar adjoining the dining room has a clublike atmosphere.

Hotel Bad Prymonter Hof, Brunnenstrasse 32, D-3280 Bad Pyrmont (tel. 05281/60-93-03), is a 45-room hotel that provides a personal atmosphere, good service, and comfort. The place has been considerably modernized, especially the bedrooms, which are immaculate and restful. Depending on the plumbing, singles range from a low of 65 DM ($38.60) daily to a high of 80 DM ($47.50), the latter with complete private baths. Twin-bedded rooms with private baths go for 120 DM ($71.25) to 150 DM ($89.05). A Continental breakfast is included. All units contain color TV, and direct-dial phones.

Hotel Kaiserhof, Kirchstrasse 1-2, D-3280 Bad Pyrmont (tel. 05281/1-81-20), is like an overscale villa, a pinkish structure with elegant multipaned windows on a tree-shaded street not far from the Kurpark and the Casino. The elegant dance café on the ground floor is the best-known one at the spa. The 50 private rooms are well furnished, each with private bath or shower, phone, and TV. Many accommodations have balconies opening onto the promenade. Singles rent for 70 DM ($41.55) to 95 DM ($56.40) daily, with doubles costing 120 DM ($71.25) to 170 DM ($100.95). For half-board terms, add another 15 DM ($8.90) to the rates quoted.

Restaurant Separée, Hotel Bergkurpark, Ockelstrasse 11 (tel. 05281/40-01), is part of the finest hotel in town, already previewed. In summer many diners, both foreign and domestic, like to eat on the beautifully decorated terrace. Otherwise, food is served in an elegantly decorated restaurant, with large, comfortable chairs. I was impressed by the size and cleanliness of the kitchen, which turns out an array of international specialties. Trout and lobster are kept in a tank. The restaurant offers eight different fixed-price menus, costing 35 DM ($20.80) to 75 DM ($44.55). Service is daily from noon to 2:30pm and 6 to 10pm.

---

2. Bad Wildungen

The healing mineral springs of Bad Wildungen have long attracted northern Europeans to the rolling hills and deep forests of the Waldeck region southwest of Kassel. Thousands of annual visitors, seek treatment for kidney and gallbladder disorders, or simply come for rest and relaxation and the numerous cultural activities.

The spa gardens augment the natural wooded surroundings with carefully planted flowers from all parts of the world, as well as with several attractive buildings, including two bandshells where outdoor concerts are frequently given. Lawn chairs are placed throughout the grounds for the convenience and comfort of strollers. The modern horseshoe-shaped arcade houses the Georg-Viktor spring, plus several exclusive shops and a small auditorium.

Bad Wildungen is more than 700 years old. Rising above the Altstadt is the massive tower of the 14th-century **Stadtkirche,** the most impressive (and oldest) structure in the town. The highlight of the church is not its interesting Hallenkirch architecture, however, so much as its remarkable *Niederwildungen Altarpiece,* one of the best examples of early German painting. Painted in 1403 by Master Konrad von Soest, the wing-paneled altarpiece contains a large dramatic scene of the Crucifixion, flanked by six smaller scenes depicting the birth, passion, and resurrection of Christ. The work shows an obvious French influence in the use of delicate colors and figures, made even more dramatic by the use of actual gold.

WHERE TO STAY AND DINE

Right at the entrance to the gardens, in the Kurpark, the **Staatliches Badehotel,** Dr.-Marc-Strasse 4, D-3590 Bad Wildungen (tel. 05621/8-60), is located in the center of the clinical and cultural activities. Evoking the grandeur of another era, the Badehotel is large and rambling, branching out in two great wings from the circular, domed entrance. It has its own private clinic and sanitorium, providing diagnostic and therapeutic facilities, including carbon dioxide baths, massages, and complete medical attention by a fine professional staff.

The hotel's 74 rooms (43 more in the sanitorium) are large, sunlit, and airy, all with views of the Waldeck woodlands and spa gardens. Furnishings are sleek, comfortable, and modern. Prices of rooms vary according to size and location. Singles rent for 100 DM ($59.40) to 130 DM ($77.20) daily; doubles, 150 DM ($89.05) to 200 DM ($118.75). Room rates include breakfast, service, taxes, and use of the large indoor heated pool. Garage facilities are available. The hotel's restaurant is just what the doctor ordered—that is, if you're not worried about calories. Special diets are available. Veal dishes are the specialty, and the Kalbsschnitzel (veal scallops) cooked with herbs is a tasty choice. Other dishes include trout au bleu, filet of sole, and nasi-goreng (Indonesian fried rice cooked with various spices and ingredients). A carafe of Mosel wine goes with most meals, which cost 38 DM ($22.55) to 70 DM ($41.55).

Hotel-Pension Die Hardtmühle, Im Urfftal 5-7, D-3590 Bad Wildungen (tel. 05621/7-41), at Bergfreiheit, is my favorite spot in the area, and it's the most suitable for motorists. Set in the countryside, with lazy cows grazing the pastureland, this family-run hotel places a strong accent on sports, including swimming in an indoor pool, tennis, and other activities. The 36 rooms are cozy and warmly inviting, and there are many accommodations suitable for three to five people. Singles rent for 60 DM ($35.65) to 70 DM ($41.55) daily, doubles for 100 DM ($59.40) to 140 DM ($83.15). Family rooms rent for 194 DM ($114.45) and an apartment suitable for four guests costs 204 DM ($120.35). Sometimes a buffet is set out, or the cook may have a barbecue. Meals cost from 30 DM ($17.80). English is spoken. This place is so popular in summer that reservations should be made well in advance. Closed from January 10 to February 15.

Hotel-Café Schwarze, Brunnenallee 42, D-3590 Bad Wildungen (tel. 05621/40-64), was founded in 1876, and for decades it has been one of the most popular rendezvous points at the spa. You can drink and dine al fresco at one of the tables in front of the large main building. Antiques and typical furnishings of the region have been used, giving the place a rustic character. A total of 26 comfortably furnished rooms are rented, and at very reasonable rates. Singles range in price from 38 DM ($22.55) to 48 DM ($28.50) daily, depending on the plumbing, and doubles go from 64 DM ($38) to 80 DM ($47.50); all tariffs include breakfast.

For meals, most guests dine at their hotel. However, there is one good independent eatery. It's **La Camarque,** Brunnenallee 12 (tel. 05621/23-23), a specialty restaurant and rôtisserie-grill serving both classical and cuisine moderne dishes. The food is temptingly presented and there's a large wine list. A choice of 10 wisely selected main courses is offered, along with fixed-price menus that range from 28 DM ($16.65) to 55 DM ($32.65). The restaurant is open from noon to 2pm and 6 to 10pm; closed Mon.

---

3. Wiesbaden

A health resort has been firmly entrenched in this sheltered valley between the Rhine and the Taunus Mountains since Roman times. Though part of its success as a spa is due, of course, to its 26 hot springs, with temperatures ranging from 117° to 150°F, its proximity to Germany's larger cities and transportation centers has made Wiesbaden the most international of spas. It lies only 20 minutes away by car from the Frankfurt International Airport, or a 30-minute run by frequent train service. Retaining much of its turn-of-the-century splendor, Wiesbaden competes with Baden-Baden as Germany's most fashionable resort. It is also one of the most important cultural centers in the country. Every spring it plays host to the International May Festival of music, dance, and drama. Most of these cultural activities take place in Wiesbaden's Bath Quarter, around the Kurhaus and Kurhauskolonnade (also called Theaterkolonnade). The major concert halls are in the Kurhaus, a big, lively structure centering around a cupola-crowned hall that opens into rooms in all directions. In addition to concerts, the complex hosts plays and ballets, plus a variety of social gatherings. Since its complete renovation in 1988, it has established itself as a center for international conferences, congresses, exhibitions, and trade fairs. There is also a casino.

If you prefer the outdoors, Wiesbaden offers horseback riding, a golf course, indoor and outdoor swimming, tennis, and hiking. The streets of the city are enjoyable for rambling, and the spa section has a lake surrounded by old shade trees. It is especially beautiful at night, when the lights of the spa and the huge fountains in the lake are reflected in the water.

WHERE TO STAY

Expensive Hotels

A 500-year-old tradition in the area, **Schwarzer Bock** (Black Ram), Kranzplatz 12, D-6200 Wiesbaden (tel. 0611/155-0), traces its history back to 1486. Most of its public rooms are treasure troves of Teutonic architecture and are filled with Empire, Biedermeier, and Louis XVI antiques. It's a world of wood paneling, gilt, and crystal. If you like cozy nooks, then this is your hotel. There's a Chinese tea room, for example, with screens, lanterns, vases, and a teak dragon table. Dining facilities include the Restaurant Elisabeth (see below), the Austern Bar (Oyster Bar) with live piano entertainment, and the Brasserie Côte d'Azur with its southern French appeal. A New Orleans jazz brunch is held every Sunday from 11am to 2:30 pm. There are 150 individually appointed rooms with baths, direct-dial phones, color TVs, radios, and minibars, as well as 20 luxuriously styled suites. Singles range from 188 DM ($111.65) to 278 DM ($165.10) daily, doubles from 241 DM ($143.10) to 351 DM ($208.40). The Health Care Department offers kinesthetic exercises, fango-packs, carbon dioxide baths, a sauna, a solarium, and massages. To wind down after all this strenuous activity, guests retreat to the restful roof garden terrace.

Nassauer Hof, Kaiser-Friedrich-Platz 3-4, D-6200 Wiesbaden (tel. 0611/133-0), is an old favorite with up-to-date conveniences. In 1987, renovations preserved the baroque facade, but the interior was completely modernized. With the addition of two restaurants, this hotel now ranks with the most appealing in Germany. The Orangerie features local German specialties at moderate prices, while Die Ente vom Lehel boasts the finest deluxe fare in Wiesbaden. The cozy Nassauer Hof Bar has an open fireplace and piano entertainment. The staff provides cordial service in understandable English, and the spacious rooms feature baths, TVs, stocked minibars, and soundproof windows. Singles range from 290 DM ($172.20) to 370 DM ($219.70) daily, and twins cost 445 DM ($264.25) to 490 DM ($290.95), including service and taxes. The hotel stands in the city center, within walking distance of the Kurhaus, Spielbank, theaters, and the shopping area.

Aukamm Hotel, Aukamm-Allee 31, D-6200 Wiesbaden (tel. 0611/57-60), built in 1970, is one of the leading deluxe hotels in Wiesbaden, in a fashionable residential area across from the spa gardens and next to the Clinic for Diagnostics. The 160 comfortable rooms all have full baths, balconies, color TVs, in-house videos (some in English), radios, phones, and minibars. There are also 12 luxury suites with two to five rooms. Singles rent for 275 DM ($163.30) daily, and doubles for 310 DM ($184.10), tariffs including a hot and cold buffet breakfast, service, and taxes. The hotel has a Japanese restaurant; a European restaurant; a day bar for snacks and drinks; a cocktail bar serving international drinks, draft beer, and light meals; and the Bierkathedrälsche, a rustic pub with regional dishes as well as live organ music. A cosmetic studio, an underground garage, and ample parking on the hotel premises are plus factors at the Aukamm. The hotel lies only about 15 miles from the Frankfurt airport.

Wiesbaden Penta Hotel, Auguste-Viktoria-Strasse 15, D-6200 Wiesbaden (tel. 0611/37-70-41), can't be beat at the spa for up-to-date amenities. A Penta chain member, it stands in the heart of Wiesbaden, opposite Rhein-Main-Halle, a five-minute walk from the main station. Glamorously modern, it offers 200 well-furnished and soundproof rooms, all with private baths, direct-dial phones, color TVs, radios, minibars, and individual balconies, many of which overlook the gardens that surround the hotel. The cost for a single ranges from 180 DM ($106.90) to 205 DM ($121.75) daily; a double goes for 205 DM ($121.75) to 235 DM ($139.55). A buffet is served in the split-level restaurant and coffee shop or, in summer, on the terrace. German beer and snacks are the feature of the hotel's Bierstube. Recreation is important here, with a health club, sauna, plunge pool, and tanning studio.

Moderately Priced and Budget Hotels

A three-minute walk from the Schloss and the Marktkirche (Market Church), the **Hotel Bären,** Bärenstrasse 3, D-6200 Wiesbaden (tel. 0611/30-10-21), is standard modern. The 58 bedrooms are clean, efficiently appointed, and comfortable. A bathless single costs 80 DM ($47.50) daily; with private bath or shower, 120 DM

($71.25) to 140 DM ($83.15). Two persons pay 190 DM ($112.80) in a bathless double, or 240 DM ($142.50) in a double with private bath. All these tariffs include a breakfast buffet, service, and the use of the thermal swimming pool. The cocktail bar and the restaurant, König im Bären, take care of your well-being.

Hotel Klee am Park, Parkstrasse 4, D-6200 Wiesbaden (tel. 0611/30-50-61), is a square, modern hotel in a tranquil setting at the edge of a park, surrounded by its own informal gardens. The theater is nearby, as are the casino and shopping area. All of the hotel's 60 bedrooms, which have French doors opening onto balconies, have color TVs, phones, minibars; some rooms have a sitting area large enough for entertaining. The baths are tiled, many containing double sinks. Singles range in price from 125 DM ($74.25) to 165 DM ($98) daily, and twins and doubles go for 175 DM ($103.90) to 240 DM ($142.50). Guests will find a café and restaurant, where French cuisine is served, and a comfortable English-style bar. The hotel is highly recommended for those who find the older, superluxurious hotels a bit too monumental.

Forum Hotel Wiesbaden, Abraham-Lincoln-Strasse 17, D-6200 Wiesbaden (tel. 0611/797-0), is in a region where top-name companies make their homes. Lots of businesspeople stay here instead of in Frankfurt, as it is only 20 minutes from the Frankfurt airport. Its 157 guest rooms have been redecorated, and each has a private bath, minibar, direct-dial phone, color TV and video, and air conditioning. A single costs 149 DM ($88.50) to 285 DM ($169.25) daily, and a double rents for 189 DM ($112.25) to 325 DM ($193); these rates include taxes and service. For recreation, a swimming pool, sauna, and solarium are available. The restaurant, Friesenstube, offers a variety of regional and international dishes. Try a glass of Rhine wine or draft beer in the Bierpumpe Bar, or a snack on the terrace bordering the indoor pool.

Hotel am Kochbrunnen, Taunusstrasse 15, D-6200 Wiesbaden (tel. 0611/52-20-01), might be your "home in Wiesbaden." It has long been a favorite of mine because of its belle-époque atmosphere. Cozy and snug, it offers 24 comfortable and attractively furnished bedrooms. Address your request for reservations to the director, K. D. Rogall, who speaks English. Doubles with showers and toilets, along with TVs and minibars, cost 120 DM ($71.25) to 145 DM ($86.10) daily, with singles going for 80 DM ($47.50) to 110 DM ($65.30). These tariffs include the breakfast buffet, which in fair weather is served at tables set out in the courtyard.

Hotel am Landeshaus, Moritzstrasse 51, D-6200 Wiesbaden (tel. 0611/37-30-41), is under the same management as the previously recommended Am Kochbrunnen. In central Wiesbaden, within walking distance of the railroad station, this 21-room hotel opened in the spring of 1984 and has since become recognized as one of the spa's best moderately priced hotels. Completely modern, with an elevator, the place is warm, cozy, and inviting, a choice for the traditionalist. The well-kept rooms are all doubles, each equipped with shower/toilet or complete bath, along with direct-dial phone. Doubles cost 145 DM ($86.10); rented as singles, they are 100 DM ($59.40) daily. These tariffs include a breakfast buffet, service, and taxes. Guests can enjoy drinks in a rustic ale tavern.

Hansa Hotel, Bahnhofstrasse 23, D-6200 Wiesbaden (tel. 0611/3-99-55), near the Rhein-Main-Halle, is like a big town house, offering 86 comfortable rooms, each with a shower (or bath) and toilet, phone, TV, and radio. Singles cost 100 DM ($59.40) daily, with doubles going for 150 DM ($89.05) to 160 DM ($95). A real German pub, dark and mellow, serves good beer and Continental food. The hotel is closed from mid-December to January.

Fürstenhof-Esplanade, Sonnenbergerstrasse 30-32, D-6200 Wiesbaden (tel. 0611/52-20-91), is one of the warmest, most inviting, and traditional of the spa hotels. In a quiet part of town, the 74-room hotel stands near the casino, spa park, theater, and shopping center. It's central and convenient, and most important, reasonable. Rooms with baths or showers cost 85 DM ($50.45) to 110 DM ($65.30) daily for a single and 130 DM ($77.20) to 200 DM ($118.75) for a double. For rooms without private baths, the singles rate is lowered to 45 DM ($26.70) to 75 DM ($44.55) and the doubles rate to 90 DM ($53.45) to 110 DM ($65.30). All these tariffs include breakfast.

Hotel Oranien, Platterstrasse 2, D-6200 Wiesbaden (tel. 0611/52-50-25), dating from 1879, is an 85-room hotel right in the center of the spa, surrounded by a small park near a shopping center. It offers immaculate, traditionally furnished rooms. Singles with shower bath, toilets, and phones cost 98 DM ($58.20) to 115 DM ($68.30) daily, and doubles go for 148 DM ($87.90) to 158 DM ($93.80). Breakfast and taxes are included.

Hotel im Park, Danziger Strasse 104, D-6200 Wiesbaden (tel. 0611/54-11-96), is a 14-room bed-and-breakfast accommodation next to the Café Hahn and the lovely Kurpark. Run by English-speaking hotelier Christian Kollman, the place is quiet, inviting, and maintained in good taste. Each of the bedrooms has a wash basin. Singles rent for 59 DM ($35.05) to 65 DM ($38.60) daily and doubles for 89 DM ($52.85) to 95 DM ($56.40).

WHERE TO DINE

An intimate restaurant seating 85 persons on two levels, **Die Ente vom Lehel,** in the Hotel Nassauer Hof, Kaiser-Friedrich-Platz 3-4 (tel. 0611/13-36-66), is where the innovative Hans-Peter Wodarz prepares a cusine as pleasing to the eye as to the palate. Often he combines the pulp of the freshest fruits with meat or fish such as in his mousse of pike with tree tomatoes. His unusual dishes include a calf's head with blue carp in a Riesling sauce and breast of woodcock with goose-liver sauce. One of the most interesting desserts I've ever seen is called Dialogue of Fruits, consisting of different colored fresh fruit purées served elegantly in an octagonal dish. The ultimate look resembles an abstract painting by Jasper Johns. Meals cost 80 DM ($47.50) to 155 DM ($92.05), and hours are 7pm to 1am Tues. to Sat.

A boutique, delicatessen, wine cellar, and bistro are attached. The bistro offers some two dozen menu choices, served Tues. to Sat. from 10am to midnight, with meals costing 60 DM ($35.65) to 90 DM ($53.45). The wine cellar, Entenkeller, is open Tues. to Sat. from 6pm to 1am.

Elegantly modern, **Le Gourmet,** Bahnhofstrasse 42, (tel. 0611/30-16-54), is unusual in specializing in both French and Turkish cookery. Although the combination may sound bizarre, this citadel of good food achieves harmony between the cuisines. The Turkish coffee is divine, naturally, as is the eggplant kebab over grilled lambsteak. Full of Oriental charm, this restaurant is run by Akin Soykandar, who is proud of his large wine and champagne list. Expect to spend 60 DM ($35.65) to 85 DM ($50.45) for a meal. Hours are noon to 2pm and 6 to 10pm; closed Sun.

Restaurant Elisabeth, Hotel Schwarzer Bock, Kranzplatz 12 (tel. 0611/155-0), is renowned, a favorite of *tout Wiesbaden.* As you enter, you're immediately dazzled by an incredible array of priceless 15th-century woodcarvings, the type of delicate work that made German craftsmen famous throughout Europe. The Ingelheimer Zimmer, considered by some the most attractive dining room in Germany, serves haute French cuisine. Meal costs begin at 78 DM ($46.30), going up to 120 DM ($71.25). Service is daily from noon to 2:30pm and 6 to 11pm.

Restaurant de France, Taunusstrasse 49 (tel. 0611/5-12-51), has become one of Germany's top 30 restaurants under the direction of Alois Köpf, the young, ambitious chef de cuisine. The place has an elegant and tasteful decor with a touch of art deco. Here you'll find cuisine moderne at its best, which has made it a favorite with sophisticated gourmets. The menu carries many variations of shellfish (changing daily); and the filet of baby lamb is excellent, too, as are the desserts. A selection of more than 400 French and Continental wines complements the menu. Lunch costs 89 DM ($52.85), and is served from noon to 2pm. Dinner, served from 7pm until closing, costs 115 DM ($68.30) to 155 DM ($92.05); closed Sun., Sat. for lunch, and for two weeks in July. Reservations are essential.

Ristorante Lanterna, Westendstrasse 3 (tel. 0611/40-25-22), is both rustic and elegant, featuring nuova cucina (Italian) and cuisine moderne (French). A big wine list accompanies the menu, which offers at least 15 entrees, including such light dishes as seafood salad with lemon sauce and, the specialty, wild game (particularly woodcock and pheasant) in season. A six-course meal is also available, at the cost of 108 DM ($64.15); or you can spend more—or less—if you order à la carte, from 60 DM ($35.65) to 90 DM ($53.45). Hours are noon to 2pm and 6 to 11pm; closed Fri. As there are only a dozen tables, reservations are necessary. In summer, request a table on the fully planted terrace, which seats another 20 diners.

Alt-Prag, Taunusstrasse 4 (tel. 0611-52/04-02), is for Bohemian specialties. Three salons and two different restaurants are housed in this baroque country place, which pays homage to the culinary specialties of "Old Prague," as its name suggests. A daily menu changes frequently, offering three fixed-price meals costing 38 DM ($22.55) to 80 DM ($47.50). During Bohemian and German festivals, elaborate specialties such as bear meat Gulasch and roast goose are offered. The restaurant serves from noon to 2pm and 6pm to midnight; closed Mon. You can also try a piano-bar nightclub, Charles, on the second floor, which is open nightly from 10pm to 4am.

ENTERTAINMENT

"Rien ne va plus" is the call when the ball starts to roll on the gaming tables at **Spielbank Wiesbaden** (Wiesbaden Casino), Im Kurhaus (tel. 06121/52-69-54), which is open daily from 3pm to 2am and charges an admission of 5 DM ($2.95). Roulette and baccarat are the featured games. Here the great Russian writer, Fyodor Dostoyevski, attempted to win a fortune. A gourmet restaurant of subdued elegance, **La Belle Epoque** (tel. 0611/52-69-37), offers meals nightly from 6:30pm to 1am (last orders at 11:30pm). Expect to spend from 68 DM ($40.40) to 95 DM ($56.40) there. It can be reached only through the casino, and reservations are advised. If you prefer, you can eat outside the casino but still within the Kurhaus, where **Le Bistro** is open from noon to midnight daily. Meals here cost 35 DM ($20.80) to 60 DM ($35.65).

On a more cultural note, the greatest event, already mentioned, is the **International May Festival** throughout the month of May. The festival features artists of international statue from all over Europe, and comprises instrumental music, opera, dance, drama, folk music, and other offerings.

Music and theater flourish at Wiesbaden throughout the year. For information on what performances are available at the time of your visit (plus the availability of tickets), check at the **Wiesbaden Tourist Office,** Rheinstrasse/Ecke Wilhelmstrasse 15 (tel. 0611/31-28-47 or 0611/37-43-53). It's open Monday to Friday from 8am to 6:30pm. There's another office at the main railway station (tel. 0611/31-28-48), open daily from 8am to 9pm.

The **Hessisches Staatstheater** (Hessian State Theater), Christian-Zais-Strasse (tel. 0611/30-68-08), is part of the Kurhaus compound. Built in 1984, this theater presents a program of operas, musicals, ballets, and plays by its resident companies.

For information about any facility within the Kurhaus compound, such as the casino or the theater, telephone 06121/31-28-33.

At the **Brunnenkolonnade,** which dates from 1825, you can enjoy not only thermal waters but concerts and dancing. There is also a café.

If you're in Wiesbaden on a summer night, you can wander in the **Kurpark,** enjoying the concerts and the garden festivals—the latter with illumination and fireworks displays that beat most after-dark activity likely to be going on behind any nearby walls.

Wiesbaden even has its own version of the Via Veneto. Here it's called **Wilhelmstrasse.** On this street you can find a café where you can stake out a post to people-watch, a favorite pastime of both locals and visitors.

4. Bad Nauheim

Like many similar spas throughout Germany, Bad Nauheim grew popular in the early part of this century when the railroad became a convenient and inexpensive means of transportation. Still going strong today, the resort at the northern edge of the Taunus Mountains is a center for golf, tennis, and water sports, as well as the beginning point for energetic hikers to scale the 773-foot Johannisberg, towering over the town.

The warm carbonic acid springs of the spa are said to be beneficial in the treatment of heart and circulatory disorders. The Kurpark is attractive, well maintained, and filled with promenaders all summer long.

Bad Nauheim offers a number of hotels that sprouted up to cater to the turn-of-the-century crowds who flocked to "take the waters," as well as some hostelries of a more recent vintage.

WHERE TO STAY

Expensive Hotels

Built of starkly angled planes of concrete, the **Parkhotel am Kurhaus,** Nördlichen Park 16, D-6350 Bad Nauheim (tel. 06032/30-30), is pierced with big sliding glass windows and expanses of balconies. This modern hotel, the finest in town, is located in the middle of the park that rings the resort's thermal springs. Inside, public rooms are filled with green plants, arching windows, and two restaurants and a café, in addition to a Bierstube, wine tavern, and bar. You get all the calm, quiet, and conservative comfort you expect in a spa hotel here. The management offers 99 attractively furnished bedrooms, renting for 120 DM ($71.25) to 160 DM ($95) daily for a single, 190 DM ($112.80) to 270 DM ($160.35) for a double.

In a quiet location near woodlands, **Hotel am Hochwald,** Carl-Oelemann-Weg 9, D-6350 Bad Nauheim (tel. 06032/34-80), is a stylish modern hotel with facilities ranging from a swimming pool with a bar to a sauna, solarium, massage room, and table tennis. The 124 bedrooms, each comfortably furnished, contain private baths or showers, balconies, direct-dial phones, radios, TVs, and minibars, plus many other thoughtful touches. Singles cost 116 DM ($68.90) to 149 DM ($88.50) daily, with doubles renting for 150 DM ($89.05) to 194 DM ($115.20). The hotel offers interesting dining possibilities at its Hessenstube and Terrassen Restaurant.

Moderately Priced Hotels

A huge, classic-style villa, **Blumes Hotel am Kurhaus,** Auguste-Viktoria-Strasse 3, D-6350 Bad Nauheim (tel. 06032/20-72), is recommended for its tranquil setting in a residential district at the edge of the spa gardens. The furnishings are a mixture of modern and traditional. Many of the 19 rooms have terraces, but those with the best views go quickly and are usually reserved in advance. Singles range from 55 DM ($32.65) to 95 DM ($56.40) daily, with doubles running from 115 DM ($68.30 to 135 DM ($80.15). Interesting food is served in the dining room, which has a baronial fireplace straight out of a castle.

Haus Grünewald, Terrassenstrasse 10, D-6350 Bad Nauheim (tel. 06032/22-30), is a pink baroque confection of a building where Elvis Presley stayed for six weeks in 1961 when he was doing his military service in Friedberg/Hessen. Its lounges are decorated in an eclectic style, with a collection of 19th- and 20th-century furniture. Framed needlepoint in pinks and beiges show idealized French huntresses chasing deer through a forest. The 11 bedrooms are charmingly furnished, often with crystal chandeliers and swag draperies. Singles are priced at 85 DM ($50.45) to 108 DM ($64.15) daily, with doubles at 176 DM ($104.50), or you can rent an apartment for 142 DM ($84.30) to 150 DM ($89.05) for two persons. Breakfast is included.

Hotel Inter-Europa, Bahnhofsallee 13, D-6350 Bad Nauheim (tel. 06032/20-36), is a lively modern 35-room hotel. Oriental carpets and antique paintings add warmth to the public areas. Rooms are compact, clean, and comfortable, each with shower, toilet, color TV, and phone. Doubles range from 140 DM ($83.15) to 160 DM ($95) daily, and singles go for 100 DM ($59.40) to 125 DM ($74.25), including a buffet breakfast. There is a restaurant and a grill room that serve many international specialties, a Weinstube, and a popular café.

A Budget Hotel

Known mainly for its restaurant, **Hotel-Restaurant Gaudesberger,** Hauptstrasse 6, D-6350 Bad Nauheim (tel. 06032/25-08), offers eight bathless rooms for rent. Singles cost 38 DM ($22.55) to 43 DM ($25.55) daily, and doubles go for 70 DM ($41.55) to 80 DM ($47.50), all with breakfast included. Even if you don't stay here, you might want to patronize the dining room (see below).

WHERE TO DINE

A large menu of dishes, well prepared by the chef, is offered at **Restaurant Gaudesberger,** Hauptstrasse 6 (tel. 06032/25-08). You can stick to the tried-and-true specialties, such as a chateaubriand with a béarnaise sauce or a mixed grill. Or you can dip into the international specialties: pork in a curry cream sauce, or ox tongue in a madeira sauce. At lunch you can order set menus costing from 25 DM ($14.85), while at night the charge for dinner can run up to 52 DM ($30.90). Hours are 11:30am to 2:30pm and 6:30 to 10:30pm; closed Wed. The restaurant, part of the Hotel Gaudesberger, shuts down annually in February. The English-speaking manager, Kurt Berger, is most cooperative and courteous to guests.

Rosenau—La Rose, Steinfurtherstrasse 1-5 (tel. 06032/8-60-61). Contained within a 39-room hotel, this restaurant is known as one of the best dining spots in town. Open daily from noon to 2pm and from 6 to 10pm, it serves two fixed-price lunch menus for 25 DM ($14.85) and 35 DM ($20.80), and à la carte evening meals from about 23 DM ($13.65). The cuisine, international and flavorful, might include such dishes as cream of tomato and young vegetable soup, roasted breast of young hen, and filet of salmon with fresh herbs, plus several different pork and game dishes, depending on the season.

Am Hochwald, Carl-Oelemann-Weg 9 (tel. 06032/34-80), offers good service in a modern decor with country-cousin accents. The menu includes all the typical German dishes as well as a selection of international specialties. Fixed-price meals begin around 38 DM ($22.55), although depending on what you order the tab can run to almost three times that. You can also be served a beer and a cold snack or salad throughout the day. Warm food is served daily from 11:30am to 2:30pm and 6:30 to 11:30pm. The restaurant is in one of the town's larger hotels, recommended previously.

5. Bad Homburg

Ten miles north of Frankfurt lies one of Germany's most attractive spas, still basking in the grandeur of turn-of-the-century Europe. Actually, Bad Homburg has been a popular watering spot since Roman times. Royalty from all over the world have visited the spa and left their mark. King Mongkut, immortalized in *The King and I*, was so impressed by it that he built a Siamese temple in the Kurpark. Czar Nicholas I erected an onion-domed Russian chapel nearby. The name of the town was popularized by Edward VII of England when, as Prince of Wales, he visited the spa and introduced a new hat style, which he called the homburg. The town became the gaming capital of Europe when the Blanc brothers opened the casino in 1841.

The spa park is an oasis in the middle of a large, rather commercial town. The spa's saline springs are used in the treatment of various disorders, especially heart and circulatory diseases. The Kurpark extends into the foothills of the Taunus Mountains, stretching in front of the Kurhaus. The gardens are filled with brooks, ponds, and arbors.

"Alpina-Airport-Express" is Bad Homburg's special hourly nonstop shuttle service (deluxe motor coach) to and from Frankfurt airport. It operates between 5am and 8pm.

WHERE TO STAY

As a world-famous spa, Bad Homburg can house you well.

Steigenberger Hotel, Kurpark, Kaiser-Friedrich-Promenade, D-6380 Bad Homburg, launched late in 1990 (too late to be reviewed in this edition), is slated to be a deluxe hotel with 150 bedrooms and 20 suites, all offering maximum comfort. For information or reservations, call 800/223-5652 toll free in the United States or 800/882-4777 toll free in New York State. In New York City, dial 212/593-2988. Its array of conference facilities and restaurants is designed to be the finest at the spa.

Maritim Kurhaus-Hotel, Kurpark, Ludwigstrasse, D-6380 Bad Homburg (tel. 06172/2-80-51), has modern spa facilities nearby and an adjacent hotel, constructed in 1984. Visitors are treated to plushly comfortable accommodations, many illuminated with tall bay windows. Some units have balconies or terraces, permitting wide-angle views over the greenery of the surrounding park. The hotel's big-windowed indoor swimming pool tempts guests with the opportunity to exercise away any weight they might gain in either of the well-managed restaurants or at the café-terrace. There's a sauna for additional relaxation. Copious buffet breakfasts are a part of the many offerings at this attractive place. Prices range from 187 DM ($111.05) to 297 DM ($176.35) daily for a single, from 248 DM ($147.25) to 368 DM ($218.50) for a double.

Parkhotel, Kaiser-Friedrich-Promenade 53a, Am Kurpark, D-6380 Bad Homburg (tel. 06172/80-10). At least some of the appeal of this hotel derives from its position in the middle of the Kurpark's well-maintained gardens, near the thermal springs at the spa. Although its design is modern and angular, its edges are softened with flowerboxes. Each of the 90 accommodations contains a cable-connected TV, phone, private bath or shower, radio, and minibar, along with comfortably conservative furnishings. With a buffet breakfast included, singles rent for 168 DM ($99.75) to 238 DM ($141.30) daily, with doubles costing 228 DM ($135.40) to 288 DM ($171). On the premises are a bar and a sunny room devoted to the writing of letters and postcards.

Hardtwald Hotel, Philosophenweg, D-6380 Bad Homburg (tel. 06172/8-10-26), resembles a chalet set in a forest. Run by the Kurze family since 1868, the hotel is an ideal retreat near the spa gardens. Its 39 rooms, overlooking the forest, all have phones, TVs, radios, minibars, and baths or showers. Prices are 105 DM ($62.35) to 155 DM ($92.05) daily for a single, 138 DM ($81.95) to 240 DM ($142.50) for a double. The hotel's dining room, planted with flowers, is noted for its food. It is closed on Friday. In summer, tables are set outdoors on the large patio.

Haus Daheim, Elisabethenstrasse 42, D-6380 Bad Homburg (tel. 06172/2-00-98), is in a pinkish corner building only a short stroll from the Kurhaus. The innkeeper, Horst Stiegmann, sees to your needs, and his is one of the finest of the small hotels of the spa. All 18 of the comfortable rooms have good beds, baths or showers, toilets, phones, and radios. Singles range from 58 DM ($34.45) to 128 DM ($76) daily, with doubles costing 135 DM ($80.15) to 185 DM ($109.85). These tariffs include breakfast, taxes, and service.

Villa Kisseleff, Kisseleffstrasse 19, D-6380 Bad Homburg (tel. 06172/2-15-40), lies in the Kurpark, close to the curative springs. Tastefully renovated in 1976, it's a symmetrical four-story baroque villa with 14 rooms. A restful atmosphere pervades the place, which is run by Frau Helena Klein. The rooms are comfortable, some equipped with baths, showers, and toilets. A bathless single costs 35 DM ($20.80) to 50 DM ($29.70) daily, rising to 80 DM ($47.50) for a room with shower. A double without bath rents for 80 DM ($47.50), rising to 120 DM ($71.25) to 130 DM ($77.20) for a room with shower or private bath. The service is good, from breakfast in your room (the only meal served) to your final good night from the receptionist.

WHERE TO DINE

One of the best restaurants at the spa is called simply **"Table,"** Kaiser-Friedrich-Promenade 85 (tel. 06172/2-44-25). Located in the Kurpark, not far from a Russian Orthodox chapel, it offers cuisine moderne. The chef prepares a series of creative dishes that change from day to day, depending on ingredients available at the market; he has a marvelous touch with oysters, goose liver, and lobster. À la carte meals cost from 80 DM ($47.50). The "Table" is set Wed. to Mon. from 6 to 10pm. Reservations are important.

Casino-Restaurant, Im Kurpark (tel. 06172/170-10), maintains a traditional style of decor and service, with a good selection of modern and classic dishes. The daily changing fixed-price meals cost from 35 DM ($20.80) to 50 DM ($29.70), with seasonal and daily specialties. Head chef Günther Schwanitz begins each workday in the market. He turns out such outstanding dishes as sautéed chicken with sweetbreads in a mushroom cream sauce, accompanied by a dandelion salad. Hot food is served daily from 6 to 11pm. It's necessary to reserve a table.

Assmann's Restaurant im Römerbrunnen, Kisseleffstrasse (tel. 06172/2-47-10), is another fine restaurant. Its beautiful roofed terrace (only used in summertime) is surrounded by big old trees amid the green of the Kurpark. The restaurant and the bistro, both completely renovated in 1988, offer a wide range of excellent French cuisine. (A wine boutique with delicatessen is attached.) Mr. Assmann himself stays in the kitchen, and his cookery is as pleasing to the eye as to the palate. Meals cost 39 DM ($23.15) to 98 DM ($58.20). Open from noon to midnight. Hot cuisine is offered only from noon to 2:30pm and from 6 to 10:30pm; closed Wed.

Oberle's Restaurant, Obergasse 1 (tel. 06172/246-62), owned and operated by the Weitzel-Oeth family, is considered one of the best restaurants of Bad Homburg. Surrounded by an art nouveau and art deco decor, you are served full meals that range from 50 DM ($29.70) to 85 DM ($50.45) depending on your menu selections. The restaurant is open from noon to 2:30pm and from 6:30 to 12pm; closed Mon. Reservations are necessary.

If you're driving, you can patronize a restaurant in the environs. It's called **Darmstadter Hof mit Schoppe-Stübche,** Frankfurter Landstrasse 77, at Gonzenheim (tel. 06172/4-13-47). Reservations are suggested before heading here. It's a rustic grill restaurant with a large menu of many specialties, including (if you're there at the right time of year) trout, venison, or pheasant. This is also a popular gathering place in the evening for the locals. It serves from 11am to 2pm and 6pm to midnight, with meals costing 38 DM ($22.55) to 60 DM ($35.65); closed Sun.

THE SIGHTS AND ENTERTAINMENT

The **Bad Homburg Palace,** Schlossverwaltung (tel. 06172/2-60-91), a few short blocks from the spa gardens, was the residence of the Landgraves of Hesse-Homburg from its construction in 1680 until the mid-19th century. Its builder,

Prince Friedrich II von Homburg, preserved the White Tower from the medieval castle that stood on the site and incorporated it into the structure of his baroque palace. In the late 19th century, the palace became a summer residence for Prussian kings and, later, German emperors. After World War I the state assumed ownership.

The interior of the palace contains furniture and paintings of the 18th century, including a bust of Prince Friedrich II by Andreas Schlüter, Germany's greatest baroque sculptor. The former "telephone room of the empress" includes a *Cleopatra* by Pellegrini. The palace and formal gardens are open daily from 10am to 4pm in season, with guided tours every 40 minutes. Admission is 2 DM ($1.20).

Spielbank (Casino), Im Kurpark (tel. 06172/170-10), called the "Mother of Monte Carlo," is especially popular in summer. Roulette, blackjack, and baccarat are the games people play. The entrance fee is 5 DM ($2.95). The Spielbank opens at 3pm; closing time varies.

The **Taunus Therme,** Seedammweg (tel. 06172/48-78), is a large fascinating recreation area with several pools, a sauna, solarium, and health center, plus TVs, cinemas, and two restaurants. It is open daily from 9am to 11pm (to midnight Wed., Fri., and Sat.).

Close to the Spielbank, the **Tennis Bar,** Im Kurpark (tel. 06172/2-60-41), is the most famous spot in town, with dancing and live music. Many Frankfurters visit it just for the evening, arriving around 9pm. The Chinese restaurant, **Bambusgarten,** Im Kurpark (tel. 06172/2-31-02), stays open daily from noon to 3pm and from 6pm to midnight (Fri. and Sat. to 3am). Meals begin at 18 DM ($10.70).

6. Bad Wiessee

If you've always believed that the best medicine is the worst tasting, you should feel right at home in Bad Wiessee—the mineral springs of this popular spa on the Tegernsee are saturated with iodine and sulfur. But the other attractions of this small town more than make up for this discomfort. Just 30 miles south of Munich, this spa, with a huge lake at its feet and towering Alps rising behind it, is a year-round resort. In summer, swimming and boating are popular pastimes; in winter, you can ski on the slopes or skate on the lake.

The springs are used for the treatment of many diseases, including rheumatism and heart and respiratory conditions. In spite of its tiny size, Bad Wiessee is sophisticated in its medicinal facilities as well as in accommodations and restaurants. There's even a small gambling casino.

The main season begins in May and ends in October. Bad Wiessee in recent years has become increasingly popular with holidaymakers. During these busy times, you should definitely make a reservation. Many hotels close in winter, so be warned if you're an off-season visitor.

WHERE TO STAY AND DINE

Clearly the most distinguished choice in the town is the **Hotel Lederer am See,** Bodenschneidstrasse 9–11, D-8182 Bad Wiessee (tel. 08022/82-91). It's a spa and holiday hotel, and from the balcony of your room you'll most likely look out onto Tegernsee and the Lower Bavarian Alps. The 98-room establishment has a pleasant atmosphere, good service, and comfortable rooms. Including half board, the daily singles rate ranges from 127 DM ($75.40) to 185 DM ($109.85). Two persons pay 230 DM ($136.55) to 324 DM ($192.40). The hotel stands in a large park, and there's a dock for bathing and a meadow for sunbathing. However, if the weather is bad, the place also has an indoor swimming pool. Sometimes there is a barbecue on the terrace facing the lake, followed by entertainment or dancing in the Martinsklause. The hotel has its own medical staff and "beauty farm." The kitchen turns out an international cuisine of good standard, meals costing 35 DM ($20.80) to 75 DM ($44.55). Closed from November 1 to mid-December.

Kurhotel Rex, Münchnerstrasse 25, D-8182 Bad Wiessee (tel. 08022/8-20-91), is a modern 62-room hotel of much charm and character, set against a backdrop of the Lower Bavarian Alps. Run by the Beil family, it's one of the nicer choices at the spa—in fact, an ideal choice for a holiday by the lake. There is a lavish use of wood and discreet lighting, and some decorator tried to make the place as warm and inviting as possible. Doubles rent for 140 DM ($83.15) to 210 DM ($124.70) daily, and singles cost 75 DM ($44.55) to 130 DM ($77.20). For half board, add another 18 DM ($10.70) per person daily. Apartments, even more expensive, are also rented. The hotel has good food and also caters to special dieters. Its Bierstüberl is often a lively gathering place for holidaymakers. Open April to October.

Hotel Marina, Furtwänglerstrasse 9, D-8182 Bad Wiessee (tel. 08022/8-60-10), is a typical Bavarian house with encircling balconies and a roof overhang. Potted plants grace the balconies in summer, making it even more colorful, in keeping with the character of the region. Every guest here (well, almost) seems on a fitness campaign, swimming in the indoor pool or patronizing the solarium and sauna (no one shrieks at a little nudity around here). In summer the place has a lovely gardenlike setting, and on a cold winter's night it's ablaze with lights. The service is personal. Rates in the 49 bedrooms range from 65 DM ($38.60) to 85 DM ($50.45) daily for singles, from 140 DM ($83.15) to 150 DM ($89.05) for doubles. The hotel is closed from mid-November to mid-December.

Landhaus Hotel Sapplfeld, Im Sapplfeld 8, D-8182 Bad Wiessee (tel. 08022/8-20-67), is another typical Bavarian inn, with geranium-filled balconies and a roof overhang. It's a real alpine resort, and people come here to have a good time when they're not involved in a fitness program or swimming in the indoor pool. Men go nude with women into the sauna, sprawling out on the hot wooden benches. The 17-room hotel is bi-seasonal, attracting scenery lovers in summer, skiers in winter. Rooms are completely modern and up-to-date, and each one has a private bath, radio, TV, and a balcony. A single costs 100 DM ($59.40) to 120 DM ($130.65) daily, and a double rents for 160 DM ($95) to 220 DM ($130.65). Breakfast is included.

Hotel Terrassenhof, Adrian-Stroop-Strasse 50, D-8182 Bad Wiessee (tel. 08022/86-30), is exceptional in many ways. Attracting a largely German clientele, it delivers a lot for what it charges. It has attractively furnished rooms, both public and private, and its lakeside setting makes for an idyllic retreat. Daily rates are 74 DM ($43.95) to 114 DM ($67.70) for a single, 160 DM ($95) to 230 DM ($136.55) for a double. In summer, guests enjoy a tree-shaded terrace overlooking the lake. The 82-room hotel is open all year—indeed, a hotel "for all seasons."

Hotel Resi von der Post, Zilcherstrasse 14, D-8182 Bad Wiessee (tel. 08022/8-27-88), an enduring favorite, has been around much longer than many of its fast-rising competitors. The 35-room hotel has character, and has been considerably modernized. Inside, the atmosphere is often bustling, as diners who live nearby fill up the place; many show up in Bavarian costumes. They know they can get fresh fish from the lake, as well as good, hearty Bavarian fare. Ask for a special cheese of the Tegernsee district, Miesbacher. Each bedroom has a bath and phone, plus many thoughtful amenities. Singles range in price from 38 DM ($22.55) to 95 DM ($56.40) daily, while doubles go for 95 DM ($56.40) to 130 DM ($77.20). These tariffs include breakfast.

Wiesseer Hof, Sanktjohanserstrasse 46, D-8182 Bad Wiessee (tel. 08022/8-20-61). Most of the 56 rooms in this modern hotel have balconies that in summertime are festooned with boxes of geraniums. The style of the place is like an overgrown chalet, with four floors of rooms, many with views over a lawn dotted with greenery, leading up to the blue expanse of the Tegernsee. The bedrooms are cheerfully up-to-date, and the stuccoed wooden walls of the public rooms create a gemütlich warmth. The Eberle family, which runs the Wiesseer Hof, has a healthy respect for traditional styles. The kitchen features many Bavarian specialties, and an elevator comes in handy when you've overindulged in them. Singles range from 40 DM ($23.75) to 100 DM ($59.40) daily, doubles from 75 DM ($44.55) to 170 DM ($100.95).

St. Georg, Jägerstrasse 20, D-8182 Bad Wiessee (tel. 08022/81-97-00, is a hotel garni, serving breakfast only. This is a traditional-style three-story chalet with heavy overhanging timbered eaves and window boxes filled with geraniums. The modern interior is designed in a comfortably rustic style, and everything is kept spotlessly clean. Many of the 19 bedrooms open onto views of the Tegernsee. Singles cost 90 DM ($53.45) to 135 DM ($80.15) daily, and doubles go from 150 DM ($89.05) to 210 DM ($89.05).

Kurhotel Edelweiss, Münchnerstrasse 21, D-8182 Bad Wiessee (tel. 08022/8-12-87). The main body of this 42-room chalet guesthouse is skillfully ornamented with wooden balconies and painted detailing around its doors and windows. Additional units are available in the motel-like outbuildings that stretch beside the main structure, affording comfortable and well-maintained lodging for guests in summer and winter. The colorfully modern public rooms have a certain German kitsch. The charges for single rooms range from 45 DM ($26.70) to 65 DM ($38.60) daily; doubles cost 88 DM ($52.25) to 110 DM ($65.35). Closed from mid-November to Christmas.

---

7. Bad Reichenhall

Only the most excellent German spas can call themselves Staatsbad, and Bad Reichenhall bears that title with pride. This old salt town, lying 84 miles from Munich, is the most important curative spa in the Bavarian Alps. Mountain chains surround it, protecting it from the winds. It's brine springs, with a salt content as high as 24%, are the most powerful saline springs in Europe, and the town has been a source of salt for more than 2,400 years. The combination of the waters and the pure air has made Bad Reichenhall a recognized spa for centuries.

In 1848 King Maximilian of Bavaria stayed here, doing much to popularize Bad Reichenhall as a fashionable resort. Today visitors come from all over the world to take the waters, which are supposedly effective in the treatment of asthma and other respiratory ailments. Treatment sessions are almost exclusively in the morning at the seven resort institutes, therapy ranging from simply drinking the water to pneumato-therapy—even electronic lungs for the most serious cases. But although Bad Reichenhall takes the medical side of the cure seriously, spa authorities encourage visitors to enjoy its many attractions as well.

There's a wide choice of activities, from symphony concerts to folklore presentations. The State Gaming Rooms are popular, and the ideal climate permits a complete spectrum of outdoor events, from excursions into the mountains for hikes or skiing to tennis tournaments. Incidentally, the spa gardens are unusual in that the sheltered location of the town amid the lofty Alps permits the growth of several varieties of tropical plants, giving the gardens a lush, exotic appearance.

The Bad Reichenhaller Quellenbau, **Alte Saline** (Old Salt Works) (tel. 08651/70-02-51), just a short walk from the Kurgarten, is the home of the ancient industry responsible for the growth and prosperity of Bad Reichenhall from Celtic times to the present. Parts of the old plant still stand today, but most of it was reconstructed in the mid-19th century in the troubadour style by Ludwig I of Bavaria. The large pumps and huge marble caverns are impressive. Tours are provided daily from April 1 to October 31; hours are 10 to 11:30am and 2 to 4pm. Admission is 6 DM ($3.55) for adults, 3 DM ($1.80) for children.

The great fire of 1834 destroyed much of the town, but many of the impressive churches survived. One outstanding memorial is **St. Zeno,** a 12th-century Gothic church showing a later baroque influence. Its most remarkable feature is the painted interior, centering on the carved altarpiece of the *Coronation of the Virgin.*

WHERE TO STAY

Expensive Hotels

In an excellent position in its own 7½-acre garden, **Steigenberger Hotel Axelmannstein,** Salzburger Strasse 2-6, D-8230 Bad Reichenhall (tel. 08651/40-01 or toll free 800/223-5652), is a first-class hotel attracting a mature clientele. It offers a cure department, sauna, solarium, fitness center, cosmetic studio, haridresser, minigolf, indoor pool, and a tennis court. Many of the rooms have views of the encircling Bavarian Alps, and each of the 151 well-furnished accommodations contains a private bath, color TV, radio, direct-dial phone, and a minibar. Prices are 175 DM ($103.90) to 225 DM ($133.60) daily for singles, 242 DM ($143.70) to 470 DM ($279.10) for doubles.

The public rooms are traditionally furnished with antiques and reproductions, including some Gobelin tapestries. The Parkrestaurant, opening onto a garden, attracts many nonresidents, as does the cozy wood-paneled Axel-Stüberl, offering regional dishes as well as daily live entertainment. The cozy wood-paneled Axel-Bar offers live entertainment daily.

Luisenbad, Ludwigstrasse 33, D-8230 Bad Reichenhall (tel. 08651/604-0), is a world unto itself. It's an older hotel with a newer bedroom wing in a garden setting, making a total of 87 rooms. Its most outstanding feature is its indoor swimming pool, with a glass wall bringing the outdoors inside. The lounges and atmosphere are inviting—nothing austere here, as the emphasis is on informality and comfort. The more modern bedrooms are quite handsome, with bold colors and tasteful furnishings; all contain showers. Singles range in price from 157 DM ($93.25) to 233 DM ($138.35) daily, including full board. Doubles with baths cost 300 DM ($178.15) to 440 DM ($261.25), including full board. There are facilities for thermal baths, inhalations, massages, and mud baths, plus a Finnish sauna.

Hotel Panorama, Baderstrasse 6, D-8230 Bad Reichenhall (tel. 08651/6-10-01), in a pristine modern style, overlooks the spa, with a scenic mountain backdrop. The hotel is for those who demand the latest in spa facilities, and the many it offers range from a large swimming pool to a sauna to cure treatments. Accommodations, compact and sleekly contemporary, are divided into category "A" and category "B." Naturally, the most expensive of the 83 rooms are those with the better views. The hotel offers rooms with balconies, private baths, toilets, and radios, with singles costing 110 DM ($65.30) to 130 DM ($77.20) daily and doubles going for 185 DM ($109.85) to 275 DM ($163.30). The hotel serves good meals in an attractive setting, and has a café and bar you can enjoy when you've finished your fitness program for the day.

Moderately Priced Hotels

One of the best buys if you're shopping for a moderately priced hotel is the **Salzburger Hof,** Mozartstrasse 7, D-8230 Bad Reichenhall (tel. 08651/20-62). Though recently built and architecturally contemporary, most of the public rooms have been given an overlay of old Bavarian charm. Public lounges have been sacrificed to make room for unique dining rooms and nooks. Best of all are the 25 compact bedrooms, most of which contain streamlined sofas, window desks, beds with built-in headboards, and armchairs around a breakfast table. All of the accommodations open onto tiny balconies, and all have baths, phones, and minibars. Single rooms with half board range in price from 88 DM ($52.25) to 108 DM ($64.15) daily, doubles with half board from 154 DM ($91.45) to 194 DM ($115.20). Your hosts, the Helmut Herkommer family, speak English.

Hotel Bayerischer Hof, Bahnhofplatz 14, D-8230 Bad Reichenhall (tel. 08651/60-90), modern and inviting, is in the center of the spa. The staff is well trained, and those at the reception desk are helpful in arranging excursions to such places as Obersalzberg, Berchtesgadener Land, and Salzburg. If you're there in winter, they'll help arrange such sports as cross-country and downhill skiing. They rent 34 single rooms and 30 two- and three-room apartments, each fitted out with elegant Bavarian furniture. Single rooms rent for 74 DM ($43.95) to 111 DM ($65.90) daily, including a breakfast buffet, and the more expensive units contain private balconies. Likewise, the doubles rate (for two persons) goes from 130 DM ($77.20) to 200 DM ($118.75). Each unit contains a private bath, minibar, radio, and direct-dial phone. The hotel is equipped with such facilities as a roof-garden indoor swimming pool with Finnish sauna and a salon for massage and cosmetic treatments. In addition to the main restaurant, there is a café with live music as well as the Tiffany Bar and a nightclub with international acts.

Tiroler Hof, Tirolerstrasse 12, D-8230 Bad Reichenhall (tel. 08651/20-55), and its annex on the corner, lie within "ten minutes of everything." There has been an eating place on this spot ever since 1634. Affiliated with Germany's Ringhotels, the 37-room Tiroler Hof is run in a personal way. It is warm and inviting, with a swimming pool and a wood-beamed restaurant on the premises. Singles rent for 65 DM ($38.60) to 90 DM ($53.45) daily, and doubles go for 115 DM ($68.30) to 165 DM ($98). The most expensive units contain complete private baths and balconies.

Hotel Garni Alfons Maria, Schillerstrasse 19, D-8230 Bad Reichenhall (tel. 08651/20-88), lies about two blocks from the railway station, offering breakfast only. The modernity of this elongated three-story building is relieved by the use of weathered wood on the balcony railings, and the rows of geraniums in windowboxes along the length of the building's facade. Inside, guests will find 26 comfortable rooms, many with balconies or small terraces. Singles cost 50 DM ($29.70) to 60 DM ($35.65) daily, and doubles rent for 110 DM ($65.30). You can meet your fellow visitors in the Bauernstube, with a small bar and rustic tables and chairs. In addition, there's a communal sun terrace and an informal breakfast room. They close the place from November to March.

Budget Hotels

The ornate facade at **Brauerei Bürgerbräu,** Waaggasse 2, D-8230 Bad Reichenhall (tel. 08651/24-11), features groups of dancers. Inside, the vaulted dining rooms have an ambience typical of the popular breweries of Bavaria. The food is good, copious, and inexpensive. A range of menus, costing from 22 DM ($13.05) to 45 DM ($26.70), is offered daily. An elevator whisks you up to immaculate modern and functional bedrooms with up-to-date plumbing. The hotel charges 75 DM ($44.55) to 105 DM ($62.35) daily for a single, and 135 DM ($80.15) to 170 DM ($100.95) for a double.

Hansi am Kurpark, Rinckstrasse 3, D-8230 Bad Reichenhall (tel. 08651/31-08), is a late-19th-century building of pleasing symmetry with a tile mansard roof and flower-bedecked verandas. The owners of this well-maintained establishment offer their guests a good cuisine, with vegetarians and dieters catered to. For the 18 rooms, charges depend on size and comfort, the rate going from 60 DM ($35.65) to 90 DM ($53.45) daily for a single, from 120 DM ($71.25) to 130 DM ($77.20) for a double.

Hotel Kurfürst, Kurfürstenstrasse 11, D-8230 Bad Reichenhall (tel. 08651/27-10), is under the personal management of its conscientious owner, Renate Voitz. Hers is a 16-room family-run hotel near the outskirts of Bad Reichenhall, close to the river and about a 20-minute walk to anywhere else in town. A trim and well-maintained modern facade in white stucco opens into a lobby with Oriental rugs and a staircase that curves up to the upper floors. The rooms are spacious and sunny, some of them having terraces with tables and chairs. Lunch can be served here. The price for a single is 45 DM ($26.70) to 65 DM ($38.60) daily, rising to 86 DM ($51.05) to 106 DM ($62.95) for a double. Closed from December 15 to January 15.

Excelsior, Paepkestrasse 12, D-8230 Bad Reichenhall (tel. 08651/25-48), is a 36-room hotel open year-round, and many visitors find that their favorite time here is winter. Across from the Kurpark, this 19th-century building has a red-tile mansard roof, green shutters, and encircling double verandas. If you want a calm, comfortable lodging at a good price, the rather pretentiously named Excelsior is a good bet. Singles with showers or private baths and balconies rent for 60 DM ($35.65) to 100 DM ($59.40) daily, and doubles cost 140 DM ($83.15) to 170 DM ($100.95).

Hotel-Pension Erika, Adolf-Schmid-Strasse 3, D-8230 Bad Reichenhall (tel. 08651/30-93), is a 19th-century gingerbread-bedecked villa. This grand four-story, 36-room edifice welcomes guests into the high-ceilinged splendor of a renovated palace, now updated into a modern hotel. The rooms are warm and comfortably furnished. Singles in a unit with showers and toilets cost 52 DM ($30.90) to 90 DM ($53.45) daily; two persons are charged 105 DM ($62.35) to 145 DM ($86.10). The Erika, known for its garden, is open from February 20 through October.

If you have a car, you'll find some of the most engaging accommodations—and some of the best food—in the environs of Bad Reichenhall.

The choice spot to seek out is **Neu-Meran,** D-8230 Bad Reichenhall 3-Nonn (tel. 08651/40-78), a little satellite of Bad Reichenhall. This modern 20-room rendezvous has been run by the Weber family for three generations, and its two beflowered and balconied wings stretch off at right angles to one another. The Neu-Meran nestles at the foot of a wooded mountain, with a view of the Lower Bavarian Alps in the distance. The windows are oversize, even in the comfortable bedrooms, which are tastefully appointed in pleasing earth tones. The hotel boasts a swimming pool where you wear your bathing suit and a sauna where you do not. It also has a "sun studio" and a whirlpool bath. Single rooms range in price from 45 DM ($26.70) to 126 DM ($74.80) daily, and doubles go from 138 DM ($81.95) to 170 DM ($100.95). The hotel's cuisine is both Bavarian and international. Even if you're not staying here, perhaps you'd like to drive out for a meal, costing 15 DM ($8.90) to 35 DM ($20.80). A gourmet meal goes for 69 DM ($40.95). Hours are 11:30am to 11pm daily.

WHERE TO DINE

In Bad Reichenhall, most guests dine on *en pension* terms. However, if you can slip away from your hotel for a meal, perhaps you'll try one of the following selections.

The **Parkrestaurant** and the **Axel-Stüberl** are in the Steigenberger Hotel Axelmannstein, Salzburger Strasse 2-6 (tel. 08651/40-01), previewed above. The Parkrestaurant is known for international specialties, while the Axel-Stüberl features original Bavarian and Austrian cooking. The head chef uses his skills to prepare cuisine moderne specialties—tasty and of low calorie count. The fish served in both restaurants is particularly good, as is the standing rack of lamb provençal, with fresh herbs and homemade bread. A gourmet meal costs around 95 DM ($56.40); otherwise, most meals go for 52 DM ($30.90) to 80 DM ($47.50). Hot food is served at the Parkrestaurant daily from noon to 2pm and 6:30 to 9pm, and at the Axel-Stüberl from noon to 2pm and 6 to 11pm.

Restaurant Die Holzstube, Hotel Luisenbad, Ludwigstrasse 33 (tel. 08651/60-40), serves some of the best food at the resort. Its old-fashioned tradition and service have always had a seductive pull on me. It's a place where you can watch the flowers bloom and enjoy a world-class cuisine (with many diet-conscious selections). You might try one of the original recipes developed here in the kitchen: for example, marinated and roasted medallions of venison Königin Luise, served with bacon, chanterelles, and whortleberries. The hotel restaurant is open daily from noon to 2pm and 6:30 to 10pm, offering fixed-price menus ranging from 45 DM ($26.70) to 85 DM ($50.45).

Schweizer Stuben, Thumseestrasse 11 (tel. 08651/27-60). If you want to throw a party, this is the place to do it. The cook will feed "any number of guests," or so he promises. However, even if your "party" is confined just to yourself or one or two others, Messrs. Schwab and Anfang will open to you the delights of what is known as Bad Reichenhall's "rendezvous point for gourmets." They feature a light cuisine, along with specialties from Bavaria and the Berchtesgaden region. The decor is appropriately rustic, the ambience gemütlich, and the choice of food attractively poised between international and regional. Fixed-price menus begin at 45 DM ($26.70), while a seven-course gourmet meal costs 80 DM ($47.50). The restaurant serves from 11am to 3pm and 6pm to 1am; closed on Thurs.

---

8. Bad Neuenahr

Lying in the foothills of the Eifel Mountains, near the confluence of the Ahr and Rhine rivers, this modern spa has a mild climate and wide range of facilities suitable to the international clientele who gather here. Twenty miles south of Bonn, Bad Neuenahr attracts a diplomatic crowd from the capital to its fashionable gambling casino, one of the largest in Germany. It's called the **Spielbank Bad Neuenahr,** at Felix-Rütten-Strasse 1 (tel. 02641/22-41). Roulette, American roulette, baccarat, and blackjack are played here daily from 2pm to 2am. The entrance fee is 5 DM ($2.95).

Besides the spa installations, including facilities for the Kneipp hydrotherapy, Bad Neuenahr is a popular gathering spot for relaxation and sport. Businesspeople often hold conferences here, combining decisions with golf, entertainment, fine food, and wines. The spa is also a good starting point for day trips and hiking expeditions into the Ahr Valley, one of the Rhine's most attractive tributaries. The river is lined with old wine-growing villages, crumbling castles, and wooded hills.

WHERE TO STAY

Expensive Hotels

Right in the heart of the spa, 550 yards from the main station, the **Steigenberger Kurhotel,** Kurgartenstrasse 1, D-5483 Bad Neuenahr (tel. 02641/22-91 or toll free in the U.S. 800/223-5652), is a Wilhelmian hotel with a modern extension. When the newer wing was added, an interior decorator was given a free hand to create a completely contemporary look. This is especially reflected in the 171 spacious bedrooms, all containing sitting areas. A single room with shower or bath ranges in price from 160 DM ($95) to 178 DM ($105.70) daily; a double with bath goes for 220 DM ($130.65) to 290 DM ($172.20); prices include a buffet breakfast. Guests at this chain hotel are given a choice of dining places, including the Kupferkessel (Copper Kettle), the Kurhaus Restaurant, and the gambling casino. (The chef specializes in diets for diabetics, by the way.) Elaborate meals are offered, a three-course lunch going for 50 DM ($29.70), a three-course dinner for 82 DM ($48.70). The spa facilities here are exceptional, including therapeutic installations, plus an indoor swimming pool with thermal water.

Dorint Hotel, Am Dahliengarten, D-5483 Bad Neuenahr (tel. 02641/89-50), is a modern first-class hotel situated between the Dahlia Garden and the River Ahr. All year round it's lively with activities. The 180 bedrooms, all with balconies, are comfortably and attractively furnished. Each has a private bath/shower, toilet, minibar, phone, radio, and color TV. Including breakfast, service, and taxes, a single room rents for 150 DM ($89.05) to 170 DM ($112.80) daily, and a double goes for 210 DM ($124.70) to 220 DM ($130.64). The hotel has a large swimming pool with massage jets and a waterfall, as well as a sauna area with a diving pool. It also has a "Kneipp corner," with health-promoting water applications. Other facilities include massage and medical water treatments, a sun studio, a "beauty farm," and a children's playroom. The Dancing Bar is a popular nighttime rendezvous, with disco music played daily from 8pm. Among the drinking and dining facilities: Weinstube zum Roten Ahrburgunder (a wine tavern), Restaurant Ahrpromenade, with a terrace overlooking the Ahr, and Restaurant Dahliengarten.

Moderately Priced Hotels

On a quiet street only 100 yards from the Kurpark stands **Giffels' Goldener Anker,** Mittelstrasse 14, D-5483 Bad Neuenahr (tel. 02641/80-40). Founded in 1869, it's still managed by the Giffels family, and the present (fifth-generation) operators carry on with the same personalized manner that has always been a hallmark of the hotel. On one recent occasion, one of their "repeaters" admitted to having patronized the establishment for 47 years. A traditional four-story building in the spa center, the hotel offers 91 comfortable bedrooms. Singles cost 95 DM ($56.40) to 110 DM ($65.30) daily; doubles, 150 DM ($89.05) to 250 DM ($148.45). All units have complete baths, TV/videos, phones, radios, and minibars. Facilities include a large restaurant, two bars, a sauna, a fitness center, two bowling lanes, and convention facilities, as well as an indoor pool and equipment for therapeutical treatments.

Hotel Fürstenberg, Mittelstrasse 4-6, D-5483 Bad Neuenahr (tel. 02641/23-17). The most prominent feature of this four-story hotel is the brightly lit Restaurant Habsburg jutting onto the sidewalk, welcoming visitors in for a good meal and a comfortable room on the floors above. The overflow from the main building spills into the Beethovenhaus annex, an older structure next door. The strollers from the neighboring public gardens sometimes eat in the restaurant, with its colorful ambience. The Wilhelmian touches in the lobby show in the 19th-century moldings and the gold-and-black striped wallpaper. The 27 bedrooms are tastefully and comfortably furnished; all have baths or showers, phones, and TVs. Singles cost 55 DM ($32.65) to 68 DM ($40.40) daily. Doubles are 95 DM ($56.40) to 125 DM ($74.25). Breakfast, service, and taxes are included in the tariffs.

Hotel Elisabeth, Georg-Kreuzberg-Strasse 11, D-5483 Bad Neuenahr (tel. 02641/2-60-74), has a modern exterior whose white facade is relieved by balconies and colorful awnings stretching over the ground-level sun terrace. The public rooms of the interior are warmly decorated, with comfortably upholstered armchairs in the sitting room and in the Weinstube, with its red brick walls, wooden ceilings, and chalet furniture. The restaurant has one of those panoramic photographs of an autumn forest splashed across a windowless wall, red medallion chairs, and spotlessly white linen tablecloths. Many of the attractive bedrooms come with sun terraces. You can stay in a single for 92 DM ($54.65) to 136 DM ($80.75) daily, in a double for 156 DM ($92.65) to 188 DM ($111.65). Special features of the hotel include an indoor swimming pool, sauna bath, and solarium. The hotel is open from March through November.

Budget Hotels

Architectural detail has been preserved in the double columns of the entrance to the twin-building **Villa Aurora,** George-Kreuzberg-Strasse 8-10, D-5483 Bad Neuenahr (tel. 02641/2-60-20). The public rooms are an adaptation of the salons of this former private house, with high ceilings and windows opening onto a view of a well-maintained garden. Many of the 50 rooms are fairly new—added, it seems, onto the roof of the Wilhelmian structures. All are sunny and comfortably furnished. Depending on the plumbing, singles range from 73 DM ($43.35) to 99 DM

($58.80) daily, doubles from 160 DM ($95) to 250 DM ($148.45). The hotel is closed from mid-November to mid-December. Special features include an indoor swimming pool, sauna bath, and solarium.

Haus Ernsing, Telegrafenstrasse 30, D-5483 Bad Neuenahr (tel. 02641/22-21)—painted white, decorated with flowerpots, and boasting a wide and welcoming sun terrace—is a 24-room hotel situated in a quiet neighborhood. Rooms are furnished in a modern style, and some open onto private balconies. Singles are priced at 38 DM ($22.55) to 60 DM ($35.65) daily and doubles at 95 DM ($56.40) to 110 DM ($65.30). A popular place for breakfast is an al fresco terrace shaded by parasols. The hotel has good food, and plenty of it. Closed mid-November until just before Christmas.

Hotel und Kurpension Krupp, Poststrasse 2-4, D-5483 Bad Neuenahr (tel. 02641/22-73), a baroque "great house," is one of the most charming buildings in Bad Neuenahr, with a modern annex. Located only a block from the Kurpark, it offers convenient comfort to some 50 guests in 35 rooms. The hotel has been in the same family since 1883, offering good service and individualized cooking for every taste, including dieters and vegetarians. The price range for rooms depends on size and whether or not you request a private balcony. Singles begin at 63 DM ($37.40) daily, climbing to 75 DM ($44.55); doubles cost 120 DM ($71.25) to 140 DM ($83.15). These prices include breakfast, and for another 22 DM ($13.05) to 40 DM ($23.75) per person daily, you can order lunch or dinner.

WHERE TO DINE

Well worth a trip to the environs is **Romantik-Restaurant Brogsitter's Sanct Peter,** Walporzheimer Strasse 134 (Route B 267; tel. 02641/38-99-11). Some restaurants give off a sense of history and this winehouse, whose walls date from 1246, is one of them. The exterior is white stucco, with a steep tile roof, jutting dormers, and the traditional windowboxes of geraniums. The menu revolves around whatever fresh products are available at the time. Fish is imported—frequently from the North Sea, the Mediterranean, or the Atlantic—and turned into delicately seasoned specialties. Diners have a choice of rooms in which to eat, including an elegant gourmet restaurant with a superb French cuisine, a Weinkirche Restaurant with classical regional cuisine, or a Kaminstube with an open fireplace and homemade local specialties. The wines are from the best vineyards and are supplied by the cellars under the same ownership as the restaurant. Meals cost 65 DM ($38.60) to 120 DM ($71.25) depending on which restaurant you choose. Food is served daily from noon to 2:30pm and 6 to 10pm.

Back in the center of the spa, the **Ratskeller,** Casinostrasse 8 (tel. 02641/2-54-66), is about your best bet. The head chef is Rolf Hanssen; his wife, Helga, helps serve the tables. This husband-and-wife team have maintained a ten-year tradition of feeding visitors and locals alike, serving them classic specialties and cuisine moderne, such as fish soup with dill, baby turbot in cider, and tournedos du chef, either veal or beef. An average meal will cost about 55 DM ($32.65) to 80 DM ($47.50), with selections made from a handwritten menu. This attractively decorated bar and restaurant is open for dinner from 7 to 10:30pm; closed Tues. Lunch is served Sat. and Sun., noon to 2pm. The Ratskeller shuts down in summer for three weeks. Check before going there.

9. Bad Oeynhausen

The Jordan spring at Bad Oeynhausen, 49 miles from Hannover, is considered the world's greatest carbonic acid thermal salt spring, said to be beneficial for heart and vascular diseases as well as rheumatism. Lying between the Wiehen and Weser mountains at the northern edge of the Teutoburger Wald, the resort contains attractive spa gardens.

WHERE TO STAY

A Moderately Priced Hotel

Overlooking the spa gardens, **Kur-und-Badehotel Wittekind,** Am Kurpark 10, D-4970 Bad Oeynhausen (tel. 05731/2-10-96), stands like a sunny Italian villa. The emphasis is more on homey comfort than on stylized decor, and the rooms—some of them quite large—are furnished in a mixture of traditional and contemporary styles. All 22 rooms have private baths or showers, plus toilets. With Continental breakfast, taxes, and service included, singles cost 68 DM ($40.40) to 90 DM ($53.45) daily and doubles 140 DM ($83.15) to 160 DM ($95), depending on their size and location.

Budget Hotels

Westfälischer Hof, Herforderstrasse 14-16, D-4970 Bad Oeynhausen (tel. 05731/2-29-10). The hotel offers 25 rooms decorated for the most part in shades of terra-cotta and sienna. It has been under the direction of the same family for more than a century, and the new establishment was built in 1975. Charges are 45 DM ($26.70) to 58 DM ($34.45) daily for singles, 105 DM ($62.35) to 110 DM ($65.30) for doubles, including breakfast. The hotel also has a little Bierstube. Closed from December through mid-January.

Hotel Stickdorn, Wilhelmstrasse 17, D-4970 Bad Oeynhausen (tel. 05731/2-11-41). The sunny bar area of this three-story hotel is a popular rendezvous spot for many of Bad Oeynhausen's local citizens. The restaurant serves good, filling meals in a modern high-ceilinged room. Each of the 24 bedrooms has such conveniences as a phone, toilet, and bath or shower. Breakfast, included in the tariffs, is served either in the dining room or, in fair weather, on a white-flagstone terrace. The charge is 138 DM ($81.95) to 158 DM ($93.80) daily for a double, 95 DM ($56.40) to 115 DM ($68.30) for a single.

Hotel Bosse, Herforderstrasse 40, D-4970 Bad Oeynhausen (tel. 05731/2-80-61). The unadorned facade of this modern hotel is built on the acute angle of a street corner, centrally located between the Kurpark and the Kaiser-Wilhelm-Platz. The 22 rooms are in fresh colors, and all have phones. Singles with showers and toilets cost 49 DM ($29.10) to 90 DM ($53.45) daily, while doubles with showers or baths and toilets rent for 98 DM ($58.20) to 140 DM ($83.15). The hotel has a little bar.

WHERE TO DINE

On the outskirts of town, a distance of some 1½ miles, you'll find good food at the **Romantik Hotel Hahnenkamp,** Alte Reichsstrasse 4, D-4970 Bad Oeynhausen (tel. 05731/50-41). It stands on Route B 61, the road to Minden. The restaurant, typical of a "romantisch" hotel, is decorated with hunting trophies and a rustic mixture of woods, many of them hand-carved. Food is well prepared and handsomely presented by a helpful staff. The cheapest way to dine here is to order the fixed-price menu, costing from 40 DM ($23.75). If you're feeling ravenously hungry and have a well-stuffed wallet, you can order the gourmet menu at 65 DM ($38.60) to 110 DM ($65.30), which is adjusted seasonally depending on the available ingredients. For golf guests, there are two special menus, at 40 DM ($23.75)—the so-called "birdie"—and at 55 DM ($32.65). The restaurant serves from noon to 2pm and 6 to 10pm year-round; closed Sun. It also rents about 24 bedrooms: singles go for 99 DM ($58.80) to 149 DM ($88.50) daily, and doubles cost 139 DM ($82.55) to 189 DM ($112.25).

10. Bad Kissingen

Of the many spas in the Franconian basin north of Bavaria, Bad Kissingen, 38 miles from Würzburg, stands out as the most attractive and most popular. Aside from its modern cure installations for the treatment of liver and stomach disorders, the town is a major attraction. It's a quiet village, nestled in the valley of the Saale River. The sleepy little marketplace is flanked by old shops and the medieval Rathaus. Parks and gardens surround the town, including the Kurgarten with its palms, extensive walks, and Rosengarten.

The huge Kurhaus is one of the most impressive buildings in the town, with arcades stretching to the mineral springs and the huge promenade hall. In summer, there is always plenty to do besides taking the cure—tennis, golf, chess. This is probably the only place where chess is as much a test of the body as the mind—the board is nearly 35 feet square, with gigantic pieces that must be picked up and carried to the next square. For the less energetic, spectator games include horse racing at the track. At night, the track receives heavy competition from the gambling casino and the paneled concert hall.

WHERE TO STAY

A Deluxe Hotel

The leading hotel at the spa, **Steigenberger Kurhaushotel,** Am Kurgarten 3, D-8730 Bad Kissingen (tel. 0971/8-04-10), has direct access to the baths. Built in 1738, it was once a meeting place for some of the VIPs of Europe, including Bismarck, Tolstoy, and Russian and Austrian royalty. The serene public rooms offer maximum comfort to the well-seasoned spa habitués who gather in comfortably upholstered chairs to exchange notes on cures. The 100 bedrooms are pleasant; most are spacious enough to have sitting areas, and all have color TVs. A single with bath ranges from 119 DM ($70.65) to 199 DM ($118.15) daily. A double costs anywhere from 186 DM ($110.45) to 330 DM ($195.95), depending on the size and location of the room. Breakfast is served in a private enclosed garden at the rear of the hotel; afterward, guests take a morning stroll by the pond with its musical fountain. A meal at the hotel is elegant, enhanced by an elevated garden in the center of the two dining rooms. Meals are also served on the balconies, which overlook the park and are bordered with flowers. The specialty of the executive chef is French haute cuisine, but he's quite used to some of the most esoteric dietary requests. There is a choice of three menus, including one geared to dieters, beginning at 40 DM ($23.75). Guests gather to drink and relax in the intimate bar.

Moderately Priced and Budget Hotels

Favored by many is **Das Ballinghaus,** Martin-Luther-Strasse 3, D-8730 Bad Kissingen (tel. 0971/12-34). A neoclassic building, it is prim and proper, lying only a few minutes from the Kurhaus Gardens and across the street from a row of boutiques. Actually, spa devotees who come here for liver and stomach cures need never leave the grounds, as Das Ballinghaus has its own gardens and indoor swimming pool with medical baths. Behind the sedate town-house look lies a classic interior. Semimodern furnishings enhance the air of quiet dignity, and the 70 rooms are both comfortable and immaculately kept. A bathless single with toilet starts at 80 DM ($47.50) daily, going up to 110 DM ($65.30) for a room with private bath or shower. All double accommodations have been equipped with private baths or showers, costing 178 DM ($105.70) to 195 DM ($115.80), including taxes, service charge, and a buffet breakfast. The hotel is closed November to mid-March.

Rixen Hotel, Frühlingstrasse 1, D-8730 Bad Kissingen (tel. 0971/82-30), stands two minutes away from the Kurpark. A quiet hotel, it looks a bit like an American Holiday Inn, but with a row of international flags flying out front. A host of domestic and foreign visitors stop in here for "the cure," everybody defining it differently. The decor is modern and as attractive as you might wish. There's also a wide range of health and sports facilities, including a sauna, whirlpool, solarium, and other equipment. The kitchen turns out French, German, and international dishes. The 94 accommodations contain private baths, phones, balconies, TVs, radios, and minibars. Including a breakfast buffet, a single rents for 94 DM ($55.80) to 104 DM ($61.75) daily, a double or twin going for 158 DM ($93.80) to 174 DM ($103.30). In addition to the restaurant, there is a gemütlich Bitstube.

Kurhaus Tanneck, Altenbergweg 6, D-8730 Bad Kissingen (tel. 0971/40-36), is a real Germanic type of institution, a health-spa hotel, again emphasizing "the cure" that clients can take for health problems, real or imagined. Modern, efficient, and businesslike, the hotel has a long wing of rooms, rising three stories, where guests have their own balconies with a view of the garden. Diet specialties are featured in the dining room, which also has a perpetually laden buffet table. With the cuisine served here, you might not lose weight unless you can resist temptation. The philosophy is to relax, breathe deeply, and enjoy it here. An incredible array of massages are available, all of them priced separately from the room charge. You might have an underwater massage or an electrogalvanizing bath. There's a large indoor swimming pool and many other winning features, including the good-size bedrooms, 48 in all. Christian and Lilo Zoll charge from 110 DM ($65.30) to 140 DM ($83.15) per person daily, single or double, for full board. A beauty farm also operates on the premises. The hotel is open from mid-February to November.

Hotel Diana, Bismarckstrasse 40, D-8730 Bad Kissingen (tel. 0971/91-60), enjoys a woodland setting that would have made even its namesake, the mythical huntress, feel at home. Its hillside prospect, on the edge of Luitpoldpark, looks out over the valley of Bad Kissingen. The 75-room hotel is warm and appealing, the glass walls of the tasteful dining room giving a panoramic view of the hillside greenery. Also on the premises are a swimming pool, sun terrace, and bar area for meeting other guests. Room prices are based on plumbing, the cheapest accommodations containing a toilet but no private bath or shower. Singles range from 80 DM ($47.50) to 115 DM ($68.30) daily, while doubles cost 158 DM ($93.80) to 230 DM ($136.55). The hotel is closed from November to March.

Arkadenhof, Von-Humboldt-Strasse 9, D-8730 Bad Kissingen 1 (tel. 0971/6-11-11), is a family-run hotel with gemütlich service and rustic ambience in a four-story balconied hotel where there should be a room for every taste. My favorites are the wood-ceilinged, white-walled smaller units up under the eaves, where illumination comes from a slanted skylight that gives a view of the forest and the hills in the distance. Singles range from 65 DM ($38.60) to 75 DM ($44.55) daily, and doubles rent for 130 DM ($77.20) to 140 DM ($83.15). The hotel, lying less than a mile from the center of town, rents 21 bedrooms.

WHERE TO DINE

The Spielbank dining room, **Casino-Restaurant "le jeton,"** Im Luitpoldpark (tel. 0971/40-81), features an international cuisine and a carefree attitude on the part of diners, making for an interesting evening. The bartender knows how to make a good, stiff drink, and the wine list is far above average. A good and proper dinner costs from 50 DM ($29.70), which is reasonable considering the setting. This elegant rendezvous is open from 6pm until the last call for the roulette wheel; closed Tues. It's also the hottest after-dark diversion (well, almost), as dancing begins at 7pm. The restaurant closes from January to mid-February. The café is a good place at which to spend a summer afternoon, and it opens at 2pm.

Schubert Restaurant und Weinstuben, Kirchgasse 2 (tel. 0971/26-24), has more antique charm and rustic ambience than any other dining spot in Bad Kissingen. Since the beginning of the 19th century, it has been run by the Schubert family. Local Franconian specialties and classics of French cuisine are harmoniously blended here. Service is polite, but they'll also let you alone if you want to sit and drink awhile. Fixed-price menus begin at 25 DM ($14.85), but you might find your meal costing 50 DM ($29.70) with extras. In season, it is open daily from 10am to 2:30pm and 5pm to midnight.

Bratwurstglöckle, Grabengasse 6 (tel. 0971/44-06), is your best bargain. Franconia is famous for its sausages, and you'll find several varieties here, along with 10 kinds of beer. The restaurant has a comfortably rustic decor, and you can come here either to drink or dine. You can eat for as little as 15 DM ($8.90), but chances are you'll spend from 25 DM ($14.85). The place is small, with only 12 tables. Food is served from 11am to 11pm; closed Wed. The restaurant is closed from December 1 to March 1.

THE RHINELAND

Few rivers of the world claim as important a role in the growth of a nation as does the Rhine. It is the greatest single contributor to the history, legend, wealth—even the art—of Germany; along its banks parades a capsule version of the past, present, and future of Western Europe.

The Rhine begins in Switzerland (as a trickling mountain stream), and ultimately passes through the Netherlands in its search for the sea, but most of its 850 miles snake and stretch through the mountains and plains of West Germany. For more than 2,000 years it has been a chief trade route, its deep waters enabling the most modern of sea vessels to travel upstream from the North Sea as far as Cologne.

Trade was not the only commodity carried along the waters of the Rhine. From the earliest times, it was also the magnet for the intellectual, artistic, and religious minds of Europe. It has been called "a triumphal avenue of the muses," and a trip along its banks today reveals historic and artistic treasures. Cathedrals and castles, huge modern cities, and sleepy little wine villages dot the landscape. Legends and history seem to wait around every bend of the river.

From Mainz to Koblenz stretches the most scenic section of the Rhine Valley; the winding river cuts through steep vine-covered hillsides dotted with towns whose names are synonymous with fine German wines. In this section is the rock of the legendary Lorelei, from which the siren lured men to their doom. The saga of the Nibelungen, the best known of the Rhine legends, is associated with the topography along the Rhine, from the Seven Mountains near Bonn, where Siegfried slew the dragon, to the city of Worms, where Brünnhilde plotted against the dragon-slayer.

The Rhine is also the home of many of Germany's largest and most modern cities. Cologne and Düsseldorf vie for the prestige of trade and tourism; Bonn continues as the provisional capital of West Germany.

RHINE CRUISES

The best way to get a really intimate look at the Rhine Valley is by taking a boat along the Rhine River. A wide range of cruises is offered by several shipping lines, from a 500-mile tour in a luxury liner complete with cabins, restaurant, deck, and swimming pool, to one-day cruises between selected scenic points via smaller tour boats. The KD German Rhine Line runs its liners all year (less frequently in winter, of course) between Amsterdam at the North Sea and Basel, Switzerland, with all the elegance of a tropical island cruise. These tours usually last four days (one way) and vary in price according to the ship and season.

For the visitor to Germany, however, the popular tours are the one-day cruises between Mainz and Cologne, also operated by the KD German Rhine Line. This short trip takes in the Rhine's most scenic portion, including the Lorelei, the best Rhine castles, and interesting wine villages. Cruise tours are also available between almost any two major points along the full length of the Rhine. Special tickets enable you to leave or join a cruise at any of these points.

KD, which has operated for more than 160 years, has a fleet of 22 vessels. To give you an example of fares, a four-day Amsterdam–Strasbourg cruise goes from $535 to $1,300. A five-day Basel–Cologne trip costs from $455 to $1,120. However, one of the shorter trips, such as Cologne to Koblenz, costs only around 65.60 DM ($38.95) for a single one-way fare. By this relatively inexpensive method, you can decide which stretch of the Rhine you find the most beautiful, enjoy it by boat, and then return by train. Children up to 4 years of age travel free on all KD excursion boats, and older children, up to 14 years of age, pay only half fare. Cruises are free to holders of a Eurailpass.

Travel agents will book you on any of these cruises, or you'll find the main headquarters of the **KD German Rhine Line** at Frankenwerft 15, D-5000 Köln 1 (tel. 0221/2-08-80).

BY CAR

The advantage of seeing the Rhine by car, of course, is being able to stop and start whenever and wherever you want without the restrictions of train or boat schedules or the locations of stations or ports. If your schedule can possibly accommodate the time, allow at least a week. Know then that you will have only scratched the surface, and promise yourself a return whenever possible.

If you wish, you can settle yourself in one of the big towns, such as Düsseldorf or Cologne, with its wide range of accommodations. But you may prefer to seek out a village with an old inn where the pace is less frenetic, the food worthy of the finest tables in Germany.

---

1. Bonn

Until 1949 Bonn was a sleepy little university town, basking in its glorious 2,000 years of history. Suddenly it was shaken out of this quiet life and made the provisional capital of the Federal Republic of Germany. The city has adjusted to its important new position in the country's affairs, but many of the older citizens still long for the relaxed and unhurried days before the war.

Within sight of the Seven Mountains, the home of the Nibelungen legends, Bonn has been a strategic city since Roman times. From the 13th through the 18th centuries it was the capital of the electors of Cologne, princes of the Holy Roman

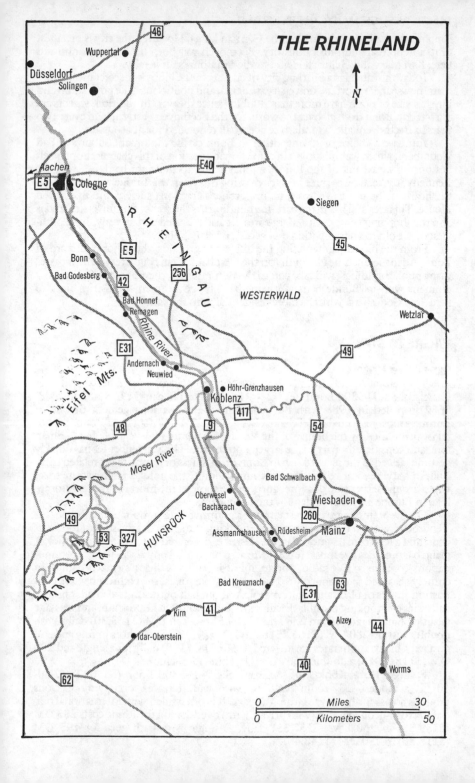

THE RHINELAND

N

Düsseldorf
Wuppertal
Solingen

46

E40

Aachen
E5
Cologne

Siegen

R H E I N G A U

45

Bonn
E5
Bad Godesberg

256

WESTERWALD

42

Bad Honnef
Remagen

Rhine River

Wetzlar

E31

Eifel Mts.

Andernach
Neuwied

49

Höhr-Grenzhausen
Koblenz

417

48

9

54

Mosel River

Bad Schwalbach

Oberwesel
Bacharach

Wiesbaden

HUNSRÜCK

260

49

Assmannshausen
Rüdesheim
Mainz

53

327

Bad Kreuznach

63

E31

Kirn

41

44

Idar-Oberstein

Alzey

62

40

Worms

| 0 | Miles | 30 |
| 0 | Kilometers | 50 |

Empire who had the right to elect the German kings. However, the city is proudest of its intellectual and musical history. Beethoven was born here, Schumann lived here, Karl Marx and Heinrich Heine studied in Bonn's university.

Today the capital is a bustling city of civil servants, lobbyists, secretaries, diplomats, newspaper reporters, university students, and politicians. The population and physical size of Bonn have more than doubled since the war. In addition, visitors are attracted to Bonn from all over the world for the Beethoven Festival, held every two years in Beethovenhalle, a modern concert hall renowned for its acoustics.

You have a choice of staying either in Bonn or the diplomatic suburb of Bad Godesberg, which we will look at in the following section of this chapter. Bonn itself lies on the west bank of the Rhine; its major link to the right bank is across the Kennedybrücke. One of three bridges crossing this river, this bridge will lead you to the heart of the old town, with its important attractions such as the Beethoven House. This area still has many baroque buildings, is the seat of the university, and is also the shopping center, with a large area set aside for pedestrians only. Just southwest of the old town, but within easy access, is the Bahnhof.

From the old town, bypassing the university grounds, the major boulevard of Bonn, Adenauerallee, heads south (on the west bank). This big artery, which passes many public buildings, will take you to the Bonn Center, the seat of the federal government with its Bundeshaus (Parliament). The government ministries are also here. Bad Godesberg, which is more residential, is to the south.

WHERE TO STAY

Expensive Hotels

The elegant and intimate **Steigenberger Hotel Venusberg,** An der Casselsruhe 1, D-5300 Bonn (tel. 0228/28-80 or toll free in the U.S. at 800/223-5652), opened in 1988 with 86 bedrooms under the management of one of Europe's most respected hotel chains. Lying some 2½ miles south of Bonn, the hotel is surrounded by the beauty of the Venusberg nature reserve, fabled in German lore, and considered a part of the larger Kottenforst. The Steigenberger has quickly become viewed as the place to stay in Bonn on business or government-related trips. Built in a style evocative of a French country home, the hotel extends symmetrical wings around either side of a forecourt, where some of the most luxurious automobiles in Europe are likely to deposit their occupants.

On the premises are two restaurants; a gourmet dining room called Restaurant Venusberg, with an outdoor terrace overlooking the seven nearby hills of local legends; and a less formal wine cellar, Casselsruhe, decorated with rustic accessories. A piano bar provides live music (except Mon.) from 5 to 11pm. Each of the accommodations contains a TV, radio, phone, minibar, and a well-accessorized bathroom entirely sheathed in cream-colored marble. (In the suites, the bathrooms have contrasting shades of black and white marble.) About half of the units also offer private balconies overlooking the hills. Facilities include a sauna, a health club, and massage facilities. Singles range from 235 DM ($139.55) to 275 DM ($163.30) daily, with doubles costing 280 DM ($166.25) to 360 DM ($213.75). Visitors in July and August get a break: room rates are lowered to 165 DM ($98) daily for a single and 200 DM ($118.75) for a double, and a breakfast buffet is included.

Pullman Hotel Königshof, Adenaueralle 9, D-5300 Bonn (tel. 0228/2-60-10), is a modern 137-room building, with wide terraces, occupying spacious grounds across the boulevard from the park. It is often filled with international officials. A twin-bedded room (with private bath) overlooking the Rhine costs 235 DM ($139.55) to 260 DM ($157.35) daily. A single with bath goes for 195 DM ($115.80) to 250 DM ($148.45).

Bristol, Prinz-Albert-Strasse 2, D-5300 1 (tel. 0228/2-69-80), is one of the most luxurious hotels in Bonn, perched right in the heart of the capital near the railway station. A popular sun terrace and an elegant indoor pool are just two of its attractions. All 120 of its attractive and up-to-date units are air-conditioned, with their own phones, toilets, and private baths or showers; windows are soundproofed. Regular singles are at the rate of 270 DM ($160.35) daily, and doubles range from 340 DM ($201.90) to 370 DM ($219.70), including breakfast.

Schlosspark Hotel, Venusbergweg 27–31, D-5300 Bonn (tel. 0228/21-70-36), lies a few minutes by car from the center of Bonn, just off the Autobahn B9. There you'll find a quiet and elegantly modern hotel set across the street from Bonn's botanical gardens, which surround the Poppelsdorfer Schloss. The innkeeper, Herr Eichholz, has 70 bedrooms in the hotel itself as well as a number in a modern guesthouse nearby. In the hotel, singles cost 95 DM ($56.40) to 160 DM ($95) daily, and doubles 135 DM ($80.15) to 260 DM ($154.40). In the guesthouse, singles are 90 DM ($53.45) and doubles are 140 DM ($83.15). It's open from Mon. to Fri. The main hotel has a swimming pool, sauna, and solarium, as well as a garage.

Hotel Domicil, Thomas-Mann-Strasse 24–26, D-5300 Bonn (tel. 0228/72-90-90). Built in 1985, this modern and convenient hotel lies about four blocks north of the cathedral in the center of town. It announces itself with a glass-and-steel portico stretching over the sidewalk in front. The hotel offers one of the most elegantly decorated interiors in the capital, including a stylishly angular lobby and an art deco bistro. Hotel Domicil has 42 handsomely designed bedrooms, each with private bath, phone, radio, and TV. Singles range from 160 DM ($95) to 280 DM ($166.25) daily and doubles from 230 DM ($136.55) to 380 DM ($225.65), with a well-stocked breakfast buffet included in the price.

You can enjoy a drink here in the piano bar before heading for the Krull restaurant, where meals run from about 50 DM ($29.70) to 75 DM ($44.55). Specialties include fresh fish, well-seasoned lamb, noodles laden with crabmeat, marinated salmon and Tafelspitz (the famed boiled beef of Vienna). Meals are offered from noon to 2:30pm and 7 to 11:30pm. There's no food served on Sun. and for several weeks in midsummer. The hotel also has a nightclub, Joyce Evening Club.

Kaiser Karl, Vorgebirgsstrasse 56, D-5300 Bonn (tel. 0228/65-09-33), is one of the gems of Bonn. Its stately, symmetrical facade is illuminated at night. Constructed in 1905 as a private town house, it was converted in 1983 into one of the most stylish hotels of Bonn, with 42 bedrooms. The attractive decor includes lacquered Japanese screens, English antiques, Oriental carpets, Venetian mirrors, and Edwardian potted palms. Special amenities include a garden where you can order drinks and an indoor swimming pool. Breakfast, however, is the only meal served. One of the most relaxing corners is near the piano in the elegant piano bar. Each beautifully furnished bedroom has a TV with video, a safe for valuables, and a phone in both bedroom and private bath. Singles cost 185 DM ($109.85) to 320 DM ($190) daily; doubles, 255 DM ($151.40) to 340 DM ($201.90).

Moderately Priced Hotels

One of the best of Bonn's hotels in the moderately priced category is the **Sternhotel,** Markt 8, D-5300 Bonn (tel. 0228/726-70). It's right in the heart of town, next door to Bonn's most colorful building, the baroque town hall. The 70-room Stern has been in the hands of the Haupt family since 1902, and they offer an informal, homelike place for guests. A reception lounge has been combined with a cafeteria; furnishings harmoniously blend the traditional and the contemporary. Equally homelike are the bedrooms, the larger of which have sitting areas. A single with shower and toilet costs from 98 DM ($58.20) daily, from 120 DM ($71.25) with complete bath. A twin-bedded room with shower costs from 150 DM

($89.05), increasing to 180 DM ($106.90) for a room with complete bath. Meals are served in the dining room.

Astoria, Hausdorffstrasse 105–113, D-5300 Bonn (tel. 0228/23-95-07), is a 50-room hotel frequented by traveling businesspeople, members of Parliament, and diplomats. The hotel lies in the heart of "Greater Bonn," about a 10-minute walk from the Bundeshaus. Each bedroom is well furnished, with private shower, bathtub, toilet, minibar, radio, and TV. Singles with showers cost 95 DM ($56.40) daily, going up to 140 DM ($83.15) for rooms with complete baths. Doubles with showers go for 140 DM ($83.15), those with complete baths for 180 DM ($106.90). A buffet breakfast is included in the tariffs quoted. In the evening some hot meals are served.

Hotel Beethoven, Rheingasse 24–26, D-5300 Bonn (tel. 0228/63-14-11), stands across the street from the Stadttheater, with one of its wings facing the Rhine. Its main attraction is a panoramic view of the river traffic from the high-ceilinged dining room, where first-class meals are served, supervised by the owner himself, Karl Heinz Lipper. Double-glazed windows prevent urban noises from disturbing the calm in this hotel's 59 comfortable bedrooms, which go for anywhere from 70 DM ($41.55) to 140 DM ($83.15) daily for a single, depending on the plumbing, and from 139 DM ($82.55) to 159 DM ($94.40) for a double. Triple units with private toilets and showers are available for 159 DM ($94.40) also. The location is a 10-minute walk from the main station.

Hotel Continental, Am Hauptbahnhof, D-5300 Bonn (tel. 0228/63-53-60), is refreshing for a railway station hotel. Of modern construction, it has gone out of its way to have some character. The 11 rooms are attractively decorated and well kept, costing 135 DM ($80.15) to 170 DM ($100.95) daily for a single and 180 DM ($106.90) to 240 DM ($142.50) for a double with bath or shower; these tariffs include breakfast, service, and taxes. From its panoramic terrace there's a view of Bonn's forested skyline.

Budget Hotels

In the precincts of the Hofgarten and within walking distance of the Rhine are hotels offering modest accommodation at moderate tariffs.

Haus Hofgarten, Fritz-Tillmann-Strasse 7, D-5300 Bonn (tel. 0228/22-34-82), is one of these. A hardworking couple presides over this unique establishment, furnished with antiques. The look is slightly cluttered, but it's ideal if you appreciate the charm of another era. A good-size breakfast room makes it a bit like living in a private home. A wide dark mahogany staircase leads to the 15 bedrooms. Large doubles with baths go for 150 DM ($89.05) daily; if bathless, 90 DM ($53.45). Singles with baths are 98 DM ($58.20); if bathless, 58 DM ($34.45).

Römerhof, Römerstrasse 20, D-5300 Bonn (tel. 0228/63-47-96), is not known to many travelers, but it's a suitable accommodation on a busy street close to the northern exit of the Autobahn to Cologne. In reality it's a 26-room Gasthof-type inn, where the owner puts up overnight guests. The rooms are kept in good shape. Prices, including a Continental breakfast, are 86 DM ($51.05) to 98 DM ($58.20) daily for a single with shower, rising to 142 DM ($84.30) to 160 DM ($95) for a double with shower or bath. The hotel closes in July.

Rheinland Bonn, Berliner Freiheit 11, D-5300 Bonn (tel. 0228/65-80-96), is centrally located, near the Stadttheater and the Beethovenhalle. It's a modern, efficiently run hotel owned by Wolfgang Seiler. The cost is 70 DM ($41.55) to 98 DM ($58.20) daily for a single and 100 DM ($59.40) to 140 DM ($83.15) for a double, depending on the room size. A fortifying breakfast is included in the rates. Units have private showers/baths, toilets, minibars, phones, and TVs.

Hotel Weiland, Breite Strasse 98a, D-5300 Bonn (tel. 0228/65-50-57), is great for a tight budget—a 17-room guesthouse not far from Kölnstrasse. It's as fresh as violets, and the welcome from the Weiland family, who run it, is warm. If the decor is uninspired, the rates, including breakfast, are commensurately low: singles cost 48 DM ($28.50) to 80 DM ($47.50) daily and doubles 115 DM ($68.30) to 125 DM ($74.25) with shower and toilet.

WHERE TO DINE

Tracing its origin back to the year 1389, **Em Höttche,** Markt 4 (tel. 0228/65-85-96), has a long and colorful history. Next to the baroque town hall, it has been restored by the Mieboch-Grunwald family, with carved wood paneling and columns, natural brick, old beamed ceilings, decoratively painted plaster, grandfather clocks, and curlicued chandeliers. Favored as a dining spot are the tables set inside the walk-in fireplace. The front room is mostly for drinks. On the à la carte list, you'll find filet Gulasch Stroganoff and specialties for two persons, including entrecôte. Fresh salmon is often available. You can complement your meal with a carafe of local wine—the best buy in the house. If you order à la carte, you're likely to spend 35 DM ($20.80) to 75 DM ($44.55). The restaurant is open noon to 2:30pm and 6pm to midnight; closed Sun.

Restaurant Schaarschmidt, Brüdergasse 14 (tel. 0228/65-44-07), is a desirable international rendezvous for dining. Run by the Schaarschmidt family, the restaurant does a flourishing business and enjoys an enviable reputation for its kitchen. Specialties include sweetbreads and Bresse chicken, pheasant from Normandy in season, and veal filet in tarragon-flavored cream sauce. On nice days, you can eat outside at one of the sidewalk café tables. Since the place is popular, it's best to phone ahead for a table. Meals are served from noon to 3pm and 6:30 to 10:30pm; closed Sun. At noon, a three-course luncheon costs from 48 DM ($28.50). Dinner can get quite expensive, especially if you order the five-course banquet at 95 DM ($56.40). The restaurant closes the last two weeks in July.

Restaurant am Tulpenfeld, Heussallee 2–10 (tel. 0228/21-90-81), is a first-class restaurant popular with journalists and government officials. You might begin your meal with white herring or a soup made with morels. The chef makes the famed boiled beef dish of Vienna, Tafelspitz, exceedingly well. Saddle of venison is often featured. The restaurant is open from noon to 3pm and 6:30 to 11pm (closed Sat., closes Sun. 3pm). A typical dinner will begin at 45 DM ($26.70) but could range as high as 90 DM ($53.45).

Le Petit Poisson, Wilhelmstrasse 23a (tel. 0228/63-38-83), reflects the personality of the couple who own it. Ludwig Reinarz and his wife, Johanna, have decorated this place elegantly in an art nouveau bistro style. They don't get frantic about cuisine moderne, but that cookery has made itself felt here. All ingredients are fresh, and many concoctions are temptingly light. Try the cream of fish and mushroom soup. Some savory meat and game dishes are available, including venison in a vermouth sauce. Fixed-price menus cost 78 DM ($46.30) to 115 DM ($68.30), and you could spend 65 DM ($38.60) to 90 DM ($53.45) if you order à la carte. Hours are noon to 2:30pm and 6 to 10pm, Tues. to Sat. Call to reserve one of the 11 tables.

Im Bären, Acherstrasse 1–3 (tel. 0228/63-32-00), is a very old Gasthaus dating from 1385. The quality of the hearty food is high, and the antique atmosphere is in keeping with the style of the building. It's one of the best bargains of Bonn, with fixed-price menus costing from 25 DM ($14.85). Open daily from 10am to midnight.

Weinhaus Jacobs, Friedrichstrasse 18 (tel. 0228/63-73-53), is a traditional winehouse decorated with lots of hand-carved wood and serving an unusual array of local specialties—many recipes date from the days of the Holy Roman Empire. The food and drink are reasonable in price as well, a meal costing 15 DM ($8.90) to 25 DM ($14.85). The place is open from 4:30pm to 1am; closed Sun. It is closed in July.

Im Stiefel, Bonngasse 30 (tel. 0228/63-48-06), is located a few doors down the street from the Beethoven House. This atmospheric restaurant is a favorite with students, with dining at bare bleached tables in several rooms. The decor is rich in butterscotch and brown shades, with wood paneling, pewter plates, and stained glass. There's even a stand-up bar for mugs of beer. Try oxtail soup, along with typical German specialties, including schnitzels, roast pork, and wursts. Meals cost 22 DM ($13.05) to 32 DM ($19). Hot meals are served from noon to 3pm and 6 to 11pm; closed Sun.

Le Marron, Provinzialstrasse 35 (tel. 0228/25-32-61), is at Lengsdorf, 3 miles southwest of Bonn. Reservations are strongly recommended because of the popularity of this place. It's a warmly rustic restaurant where, in wintertime, an open fireplace burns in the intimate dining room. A favorite dish is fresh mussels in a truffle butter sauce or with chervil and wild mushrooms, or Norwegian salmon in a Riesling sauce. Meals range from 48 DM ($28.50) to 100 DM ($59.40). Service is from noon to 2pm and 7 to 10pm; closed Sun., Sat. for lunch.

Zur Lese, Adenauerallee 37 (tel. 0228/22-33-22), is a wine restaurant with a terrace café, one of the finest in Bonn, attracting the diplomatic corps. Hartmut Wicht, your English-speaking host, believes that care and precision should go into a cuisine, and he's imbued his staff with that feeling. Zur Lese opens every day except Mon., at 10am for morning coffee and serves throughout the day until 10pm. It's especially popular in the afternoon, when visitors drop in for coffee and cakes. On a summer night the view of the Rhine from the terrace is dramatic. A menu of international specialties is presented (with very rough English translations). You might begin your meal with French onion soup or smoked salmon from Norway (my favorite is crayfish soup laced with cognac). Among the specialties, pork is served with curry sauce, and the chef prepares a superb filet Gulasch Lese. You can also choose rainbow trout or lobster from the terrace aquarium. Meals cost 35 DM ($20.80) to 65 DM ($38.60).

Ristorante Grand'Italia, Bischofsplatz 1 (tel. 0228/63-83-33), right off the old market square, is rightly considered one of the best Italian restaurants along the Rhine. It makes an excellent change of pace, and the service is good. Fish soup is a savory offering, and pasta is prepared with a number of sauces. The pizza oven turns out many different sizzling pies. In season, the chef buys the white truffle of Piedmont to use in a variety of ways and also prepares pheasant. For dessert, you may want to sample the classic Italian zabaglione. Meals cost 35 DM ($20.80) to 70 DM ($41.55). Hours are noon to 2:30pm and 6 to 11:30pm daily.

THE SIGHTS

The best way to become oriented to what Bonn has to offer is to take a guided sightseeing tour. From April to October, tours are offered daily from 10am to 12:30pm; from July to September, the hours are 2 to 4:30pm daily except Sunday. The meeting point is the **Bonn Tourist Information Office,** Cassius-Bastel, Münsterstrasse 20 (tel. 0228/77-34-66). From April to October, it's open Mon. to Sat. from 8am to 9pm; from November to March, Mon. to Sat. from 8am to 7pm; Sun. and public holidays, 9:30am to 12:30pm. For those who prefer to explore on their own, a description of some of the city's fine attractions follows.

Bonn's pride and joy, the **Beethoven House,** is in the old section of town, just north of the marketplace, Bonngasse 20 (tel. 0228/63-51-88). Beethoven was born in 1770 in the small house in back, which opens onto a little garden. On its second floor is a simple marble bust of the composer, the only decoration in the room where he was born. Within the house are many personal possessions of Beethoven, including manuscripts and musical instruments. In the Vienna Room, in the front of the house overlooking the street, is Beethoven's last piano. The instrument was custom-made, with a special sounding board meant to amplify the sound enough so that the composer might possibly hear it in spite of his deafness. The house is open Mon. to Sat. from 10am to 5pm, Sun. from 10am to 1pm. Admission is 5 DM ($2.95).

The **government quarter,** along the west bank of the Rhine, is a complex of modern white buildings, rather nondescript when compared to the architecture of the old town. The two most impressive structures, both along Koblenzerstrasse, are the residences of the president and chancellor (prime minister). These Empire villas are more reminiscent of old Bonn, long before it became an international center of diplomatic activity. They are not open to the public. Running north along the Rhine from the government buildings is a promenade, lined with trees and flowers as far as the **Alter Zoll**, an ancient fortress whose ruins make a good viewing point from which visitors can see across the Rhine to the Seven Mountains and the old village of Beuel.

Rhineland Museum, Colmantstrasse 14–16 (tel. 0228/7-29-41), contains a fine collection of art and artifacts from the Rhine Valley, including the first skull of Neanderthal man ever discovered, found in 1856 a few miles east of Düsseldorf. The most interesting collection, however, is in the department devoted to the Roman period, with altars, stones, glass, and artifacts found in the Roman settlements in the Rhineland. The most fascinating exhibit is the altar to the Aufanic Matrons, a group of deities worshipped by the landowners of the Rhine. The galleries continue with the Frankish period and with the art and applied arts of the Middle Ages to modern times, including paintings by noted German, Dutch, and Flemish artists, furniture, earthenware, glass, goldsmiths' art, and sculpture. Ten galleries exhibit contemporary Rhineland art. The museum is open Tues. and Thurs. from 9am to 5pm; Wed. from 9am to 8pm; Fri. from 9am to 4pm; and Sat. and Sun. from 11am to 5pm. Admission is 4 DM ($2.40).

AT BRÜHL-SÜD

From Bonn, if you're driving, it's easy to take an excursion to the German version of Disney World, **Phantasialand.** Directly on the B51 road off the A553 Autobahn, northwest of Bonn, it is between Brühl and Euskirchen. Many road signs point the way, so it's hard to miss. It is also easy to reach by railway or bus. This fantasyland takes up more than 280,000 square yards of space, making it the biggest amusement park in Europe, a record that also applies to the water-flume ride. The monorail is the major attraction, but crowds also flock to shows such as the Starparade electronic presentation, the Acapulco Death Divers, the prehistoric animals display, and the Castle of Horrors. My favorite part is Alt-Berlin, a designer's rendition of what Berlin was like at the turn of the century, complete with an old-time bus and a hurdy-gurdy man.

You can plan to have lunch here, as there are five restaurants on the grounds, seating 2,000 holidaymakers. Phantasialand is open April 1 to September 31, daily from 9am to 6pm. Admission is 19 DM ($11.30) for adults, 17 DM ($10.10) for children under 12. Rides cost extra. For information, phone 02232/3-20-84.

2. Bad Godesberg

Bonn's diplomatic suburb 4 miles to the south is a modern town built around one of the Rhine's oldest resorts. Just opposite the Siebengebirge (Seven Mountains), it has a view of the crag Drachenfels (Dragon's Rock) where Siegfried slew the dragon. The dragons are gone from the Rhine, but you can still see some ancient castle ruins on the hills. The most interesting is the Godesberg castle, built in the 13th century by the electors of Cologne (its ruins have been incorporated into a hotel; see below). From the promenade along the Rhine, you can watch a constant flow of boats and barges wending their way up and down the river.

Most of the spa's activity centers around the Redoute Palace, a small but elegant 18th-century castle. Beethoven Hall, the main ballroom, was the scene of the meeting between the young Beethoven and Haydn. Although the town is mainly a residential center for the representatives of many nations in Bonn, including the United States, there is seemingly no end to the entertainment and cultural facilities here. Theaters, concerts, and social functions offer a constant whirl of events.

WHERE TO STAY

Sitting among its own gardens and terraces, the **Rheinhotel Dreesen,** Rheinstrasse 45–49, D-5300 Bonn 2-Bad Godesberg (tel. 0228/8-20-20), is a traditional five-story building directly on the Rhine. It has been receiving guests since 1893 and is a sentimental favorite of old-timers, as well as a preferred accommodation for businesspeople and families using it as a holiday resort center. The 68 bedrooms and two suites, all recently renovated, contain TVs, radios, phones, and showers or baths. The units are elegant and of generous size with prices based on plumbing and view. Singles rent for 132 DM ($78.40) to 225 DM ($133.60) daily and doubles for 188 DM ($111.65) to 250 DM ($148.45). Breakfast is included in the tariffs. The restaurant features a view of the river. Among the amenities are room service until 11pm, valet and laundry service, an elevator, and space for parking.

Zum Adler, Koblenzerstrasse 60, D-5300 Bonn 2-Bad Godesberg (tel. 0228/36-40-71), provides a 19th-century cultural atmosphere. This prestigious 39-room hotel, dating back to 1860, is modest considering the caliber of guests who have either stayed or dined here. The Zum Adler was once a private villa, built right on the street, with a small rear garden. It is furnished with good antiques. The plumbing has been completely renewed and improved, although a few bathless singles still remain, costing 95 DM ($56.40) daily. For singles with showers or baths, the tariff is 140 DM ($83.15). Doubles with showers or complete baths go for 140 DM ($83.15) to 180 DM ($106.90). A substantial breakfast is included in the prices, but no other meals are served.

Insel Hotel, Theaterplatz 5–7, D-5300 Bonn 2-Bad Godesberg (tel. 0228/36-40-82), is a comfortable medium-priced establishment right in the heart of this spa city. If you perch here, you'll be but a short car ride from the Rhine. The hotel has 66 pleasantly furnished rooms, each with private bath or shower. A single rents for 107 DM ($63.55) to 195 DM ($115.80). A double goes for 175 DM ($103.90) to 195 DM ($115.80). In the restaurant or at the sidewalk café terrace, you can find both German dishes and international specialties, served with a fine selection of Rhine wines. There are ample free parking facilities.

Godesberg Castlehotel, Auf dem Berg 5, D-5300 Bonn 2-Bad Godesberg (tel. 0228/31-60-71), is a comfortable place to stay. A winding road leads up to this hilltop castle ruin, converted into a 14-room hotel. It's distinctive and highly recommended. Its tall tower and many of its rugged stone walls were erected in 1210 by the archbishop of Cologne and are still intact. A lounge, built against one of the stone walls, provides a sunny perch and a view of the spa and the river. There's also a roof terrace, with tables for drinks. The bedrooms have been designed with zigzag picture windows, allowing for views. Various kinds of woods have been used in the units, each of which has a shower or bath. Singles range in price from 120 DM ($71.25) to 135 DM ($80.15) daily, the difference based on your view or lack of it. Doubles with showers or complete baths go for anywhere from 150 DM ($89.05) to 170 DM ($100.95), breakfast included. The food is especially good here (see my restaurant recommendations).

WHERE TO DINE

The best cuisine in Bad Godesberg is served at **Wirtshaus St. Michael,** Brunnenallee 26 (tel. 0228/36-47-65). The beautifully coffered ceiling of this elegant and revered restaurant is painted white, and century-old antiques and intimate lighting are also part of its charm. In summer you can dine on the terrace with a view of the Godesberg castle. Diners feast on lobster, shrimp, and homemade goose liver pâté, perhaps Norwegian salmon on a bed of freshly picked spinach leaves. You can spend from 46 DM ($27.30) to 70 DM ($41.55 for an à la carte meal. Hours are 7 to 11pm; closed Sun. Reservations are necessary.

Cäcilienhöhe, Goldbergweg 17 (tel. 0228/32-10-01). Besides a panoramic view, this restaurant offers an array of classic German dishes along with Tuscan specialties and fish from both the Atlantic and Mediterranean. Top-quality natural and fresh ingredients are used in the kitchen. Meals begin at 50 DM ($29.70), but most diners will probably spend more. With hours from noon to 2:30pm and 6:30 to 11pm, the place closes Sat. at noon, all day Sun., and for the first two weeks in August. Call for one of the dozen tables. The hotel also has 11 pleasantly furnished rooms attached, renting for 100 DM ($59.40) to 130 DM ($77.20) daily for a double.

Halbedel's Gasthaus, Rheinallee 47 (tel. 0228/35-42-53), is a turn-of-the-century villa with a 12-table restaurant. Amid such nostalgic souvenirs as a slowly ticking grandfather clock and antique tables and chairs, you are likely to be greeted by courtly owners and genteel waiters. The kitchen prides itself on its usage of mostly German-grown ingredients. Menu choices might include a flavorful and stylish array of light-textured modern dishes (including a soup made of wild mushrooms), rack of lamb prepared in the French style, and a salad of dandelion greens and wild lettuce, followed by flavorful desserts. Full meals priced from 55 DM ($32.65) are served only in the evening, 6pm to midnight; closed Mon. Last food orders are accepted at 10:30pm. Reservations are recommended.

Zur Korkeiche, Lyngsbergstrasse 104 (tel. 0228/34-78-97), lies outside Bad Godesberg in the village of Lannesdorf, but it's such a tranquil and satisfying choice that it's worth arming yourself with a road map to find. Advertised as a wine and sherry house, it's a well-maintained half-timbered building with two stories of gemütlich comfort and tradition; the decor is rustic in a country-elegant way. The head chef prepares a light cuisine, including a delicately seasoned smoked salmon in champagne sauce. Meals range from 50 DM ($29.70) to 80 DM ($47.50), depending on your selection of items and your appetite, of course. Dinner is served from 7pm to midnight; lunch, noon to 2pm, Tues., Wed., Thurs., and Sun.; closed Mon. Sometimes in the summer there is a four-week shutdown—so always call first before heading here.

Weinhaus Maternus, Löberstrasse 3 (tel. 0228/36-28-51), with its plush tavern atmosphere, has attracted a diplomatic crowd ever since 1950. The cuisine and service are superb, and there are some excellent à la carte suggestions: onion soup, deer steak (in season), and veal piccata alla milanee. For your dessert, splashy crêpes Suzette for two is alluring. Menus begin at 35 DM ($20.80), rising to 55 DM ($32.65). Service is from noon to 3pm and 6pm to midnight, closed Sun. The winehouse is easy to find—opposite the railway station, with sidewalk tables in warmer weather. Unquestionably, Weinhaus Maternus offers some of the best food in the spa.

Godesberg Castlehotel Restaurant, Auf dem Berg 5 (tel. 0228/31-60-71), offers excellent meals in a romantic situation. It's part of the previously recommended 13th-century castle that was turned into a hotel. The former knights' hall has been converted into a spacious dining room with picture-window views—the true eagle's-nest style. The adjoining Weinstube is warmer in tone, with its inner wall paneled in grainy wood. Meals range in price from 45 DM ($26.70) to 65 DM ($38.60). The international menu appeals to the widest possible tastes. Hours are noon to 2pm and 6 to 9pm daily.

3. Cologne (Köln)

The largest city in the Rhineland is so rich in antiquity that every time a new foundation is dug, the excavators come up with new relics from its past. Tragic though the World War II devastation of Cologne was—nearly all the buildings of the Altstadt were damaged—it brought to light a period of Cologne's history that had been steeped in mystery for centuries. When the rubble was cleared away, evidence was found that Cologne was as important and powerful a city during the early Christian era as it was during Roman times and the Middle Ages.

Cologne (Köln in German) traces its beginning back to 38 B.C., when Roman legions set up camp here. As early as A.D. 50 it was given municipal rights as a capital of a Roman province by the emperor Claudius.

Findings from the early Christian era indicate that Cologne became a city of martyrs and saints, including the patron of the city, St. Ursula. During the Middle Ages, as Cologne became a center for international trade, the Romanesque and Gothic churches of Cologne were built with prosperous merchants' gold. There is much to see from every period of the city's 2,000-year history—from the old Roman towers to the modern opera house.

The city was the birthplace of Jacques Offenbach, and the Offenbachplatz, a large square in front of the Cologne Opera, commemorates that fact. Offenbach was born on June 20, 1819, at Grosser Griechenmarkt 1; a plaque on the building there honors that occasion.

The very word Cologne has become a part of the common language since the introduction to the world many years ago of the scented water called *eau de cologne,* first made by the Italian chemist Giovanni Maria Farina, who settled in Cologne in 1709. Cologne water is still produced in the city.

ORIENTATION

The major sightseeing attractions of this ancient city lie within the Altstadt, the section along the Rhine in the shape of a semicircle. The streets enclosing the old town follow the route of the original medieval city wall, remnants of which remain in three gates. Today one houses a traditional carnival association. Cutting through the center of the town is **Hohestrasse,** a straight street connecting the north and south Roman gates. This main shopping artery of Cologne is so narrow that vehicles are prohibited, enabling shoppers to move freely from one boutique or department store to the next.

The silhouette of the cathedral is prominent as you cross any of Cologne's eight bridges spanning the Rhine. The major ones are Hohenzollernbrücke, Deutzer Brücke, and Severinsbrücke. The Hauptbahnhof, or railway station, lies slightly north of the cathedral, but still very conveniently situated to the center of town.

The already mentioned Hohestrasse runs south into Gürzenichstrasse. If you take this west, it becomes Schildergasse, another pedestrian zone leading into the huge Neumarkt area. Most of the hotels, shops, attractions, nightlife possibilities, and sightseeing attractions lie within this central area, and are therefore within walking distance of one another.

GETTING AROUND

For 1.50 DM (90¢) to 2.40 DM ($1.45), depending on where you're going, you can purchase a ticket allowing you to travel on Cologne's excellent bus, tram, or underground (subway) connections. A day ticket for 7 DM ($4.15) allows you to travel on the transportation network of the city for 24 hours. You buy your ticket from a dispensing machine on any of these vehicles. Tickets are interchangeable. You stick the ticket into a cancellation machine to show that it's been used.

Cologne and Bonn share the same airport, a distance of some 11 miles from the heart of Cologne. Regularly scheduled airport buses make the run into Cologne in about 15 minutes on the Autobahn if the traffic isn't bad. Buses leave from the main railway station in Cologne for the airport about every 20 minutes from 7am, costing 3.60 DM ($2.15) for a single ticket.

To solve transportation and other problems, head for the **Verkehrsamt,** Am Dom, D-5000 Köln 1 (tel. 0221/221-33-45), the tourist information office, which in summer is open Mon. to Fri. from 8am to 10:30pm, on Sat., Sun., and holidays from 9am to 10:30pm. In winter, this office is open Mon. to Sat. from 8am to 9pm, on Sun. and holidays from 9:30am to 7pm.

WHERE TO STAY

Expensive Hotels

On the banks of the Rhine, the **Hyatt Regency,** Kennedy-Ufer 2a, D-5000 Köln 21-Deutz (tel. 0221/828-12-34 or toll free in the U.S. at 800/228-9000), is the best, most spectacular, and up-to-date hotel in Cologne. Owned by a Dutch company, but managed by one of North America's finest hotel groups, it is considered an architectural triumph. It lies across the river from the world-famous cathedral. The hotel is a shimmering mixture of reddish granite, huge expanses of glass, and a facade incorporating elements of Neo-Aztec and art deco. The location is next to the Messe/Exposition halls, near Lufthansa's headquarters, and a short walk from the train station. You can take the Hohenzollernbrücke across the Rhine to the Dom and the old city.

The glass-ringed lobby is considered one of the most dramatic in the region, with a 12-foot waterfall cascading into a reflecting pool. Among the dining facilities, Graugans is the specialty restaurant, offering a Germanic version of cuisine moderne, with meals beginning at 65 DM ($38.60). You can also dine in the lobby café, Glas Haus, with its views of the river, the cathedral, and old town. The intimate bar, Schael Sick, serves the locally brewed Koelsch beer, which can also be enjoyed, along with a selection of international wines, on the garden terrace. Facilities include a fitness center with a swimming pool, sauna, steam room, massage facilities, solarium, whirlpool, and fully equipped exercise room. A business center is also part of the offerings.

Each of the 307 bedrooms is comfortably and stylishly furnished with plush carpets, richly grained hardwood furniture, air conditioning, minibar, color TV, and phone. Many have views of the Rhine and of the cathedral rising across the river. A total of 35 Regency Club guest rooms are in five suites occupying the top floor. Either single or double rooms rent for 245 DM ($145.50) to 495 DM ($293.95) daily.

Standing within the shadow of Germany's most famous cathedral, the **Dom Hotel,** Domkloster 2a, D-5000 Köln 1 (tel. 0221/2-02-40), is almost assured a steady clientele because of its location alone. Few hotels in Germany, however, have been so consistently awarded five stars or have so consistently maintained such a standard of excellence.

It was founded in 1857 by Theodore Metz, whose afternoon concerts welcomed such artists as Paganini and Mendelssohn, who played for luminaries from around the world. Since then, it has been rebuilt a number of times, including in 1945, when it was destroyed in one of the final air raids in Europe in 1945. The hotel received a boost and an elegant redecorating in 1987, shortly after its reservations facilities were acquired by Trusthouse Forte. Today the hotel's wide portico overlooking the square to the side of the cathedral is filled in summer with sun worshippers, who enjoy the café tables. To reach it, drive your car into the square to the side of the Dom's flying buttresses and unpack your baggage with the help of porters. Inside, each of the 125 guest rooms contains all the modern conveniences you'd expect from such a citadel: bath, TV, minibar, phone, radio, and an interesting collection of period furniture. A single rents for 280 DM ($166.25) to 330 DM ($195.95) daily, and a double costs 395 DM ($234.55) to 485 DM ($288), including a buffet breakfast, service, and taxes. On the premises is an elegant French restaurant, ringed with lustrous dark paneling and upholstered in golden beige, plus a newly opened winter-garden bistro.

Excelsior Hotel Ernst, Domplatz, D-5000 Köln 1 (tel. 0221/27-01), is Cologne's long-time prestige hotel. It faces the cathedral square, has plenty of traditional style and ambience, and is situated right in the center of the city's finest shopping and business area, only a couple hundred yards from the railway station. The 165 bedrooms are spacious, with many facilities for comfort, including built-in wardrobes, bedside reading lamps, and traditional furnishings mixed with reproductions, as well as showers or baths, phones, minibars, color TVs, and radios. Doubles are priced according to size and location, costing 360 DM ($213.75) to 550 DM ($326.60) daily for those overlooking the cathedral. Singles rent for 295 DM ($175.15) to 360 DM ($213.75). Tariffs include service, taxes, and a Continental breakfast. The hotel has an outstanding restaurant, Hanse-Stube (see my dining recommendations), and guests can enjoy the intimate and cozy Piano Bar as well as the Excelsior Keller, where regional and seasonal delicacies are served amid elegant rustic surroundings. The hotel has shopping arcades, a hairdresser, and a barber shop.

Moderately Priced Hotels

Only four blocks from the cathedral, **Haus Lyskirchen,** Filzengraben 26–32, D-5000 Köln 1 (tel. 0221/20-97-0), is unusual in that it offers a rustic country decor in a 95-room inner-city hotel. The facade has one of those baroque yellow-stuccoed step-gabled rooflines. The units, with unfinished wood planking on parts of the ceilings and walls, look more like something from a chalet in the Alps than a room in central Cologne. The hotel has a 19-foot by 37-foot heated swimming pool, a sauna, and a solarium, along with two warmly decorated restaurants and an attractively masculine wood-paneled pub. The bedrooms all have color TV, radios, minibars, hairdryers, and trouser presses. Singles rent for 135 DM ($80.15) to 165 DM ($98) daily and doubles for 176 DM ($104.50) to 220 DM ($130.65).

Pullman Hotel Mondial, Kurt-Hackenberg Platz 1, D-5000 Köln 1 (tel. 0221/20-63-0), is a modern, large-scale international hotel in the heart of the city facing the cathedral and the Roman-Germanic Museum. Quite near the shopping area, it is about 200 yards from the pier of the Köln-Düsseldorfer Rhine steamers. The hotel's 204 rooms are well kept and comfortable, all with private baths, direct-dial phones, radios, color TVs, and minibars. Singles rent for 174 DM ($103.30) to 272 DM ($161.50) daily and doubles for 210 DM ($124.70) to 330 DM ($195.95), with a buffet breakfast included. The Symphonie Restaurant offers well-prepared meals with good service, and the hotel also has a bar, a beer pub, and a terrace for drinks and relaxation.

Hotel Savoy, Turinerstrasse 9, D-5000 Köln 1 (tel. 0221/12-04-66). Residents of this recently renovated hotel need walk only a short distance to either the railway station or the Dom. The hotel, designed in an angular format of strong horizontal lines and sweeping bands of glass, includes 71 comfortably furnished bedrooms, each with a modern tile bath. The streamlined decor includes warmly monochromatic color schemes, French-style armchairs, and green plants. The Intermezzo Bar offers a warmly wood-lined hideaway for a drink, and lunch and dinner are served in a restaurant decorated with artworks. A sauna and solarium are available for the use of hotel guests. Singles cost 140 DM ($83.15) to 220 DM ($130.65) daily, and doubles go for 185 DM ($109.85) to 350 DM ($207.85).

Hotel Bristol, Kaiser-Wilhelm-Ring 48, D-5000 Köln 1 (tel. 0221/12-01-95), is unusual and exceptional in that each of its 43 rooms is furnished with genuine antiques, either regal or rustic. There is a different antique bed in almost every room, ranging from French baroque and rococo to something reminiscent of High Rhenish ecclesiastical art; the oldest four-poster dates from 1742. The hotel is conveniently located near an underground stop, within walking distance of the cathedral, and it charges 125 DM ($74.25) daily for a single and from 185 DM ($109.85) for a double, each with bath or shower; breakfast is included. Bathroom amenities include hairdryers and magnifying makeup mirrors. The hotel now has a

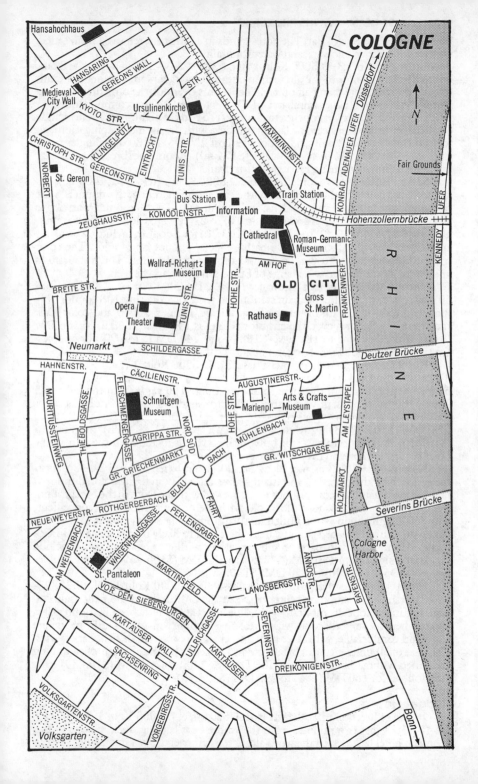

bar for guests, the Bristol Bar. The hotel stands in a little park removed from traffic, with lots of greenery, flowers, and water fountains.

Eden, Am Hof 13, D-5000 Köln 1 (tel. 0221/23-61-23), opposite the Dom, brings a light, airy note to the old section of the city with its sunny colors and architectural design. More than half of its 33 bedrooms overlook the cathedral; each has its own bath, phone, radio, minibar, and TV (on request). The accommodations are well conceived, with twin couches that convert to beds at night. Rates here include breakfast, taxes, and service. The largest doubles, with sitting and sleeping room, go for 280 DM ($166.25) daily; other doubles cost 220 DM ($130.65). Singles range from 175 DM ($103.90) to 260 DM ($154.40). Room and breakfast only are provided, although there's a Herren Bar for drinks.

Senats Hotel, Unter-Goldschmied 9, D-5000 Köln 1 (tel. 0221/2-06-20), lies in a secluded corner within the heart of the city shopping center, five minutes' walk from the cathedral, the Rhinegardens, and the Altstadt. The 60 rooms are attractive and comfortable. Rates are 145 DM ($86.10) to 230 DM ($136.55) daily for a single and 195 DM ($115.80) to 275 DM ($163.30) for a double, including breakfast and service charge. All rooms have baths, toilets, phones, and radios. The color scheme throughout is brown, beige, and other natural colors. The restaurant is known for its cuisine and wide range of European wines and beverages.

Hotel Altea Baseler Hof, Breslauer Platz 2, D-5000 Köln 1 (tel. 0221/1-65-40), lies directly opposite the main station and the Dom, offering 108 comfortably furnished rooms, all with private baths, minibars, phones, radios, and color TVs. Including a buffet breakfast, the tariff for singles is 145 DM ($86.10) to 186 DM ($110.45) daily, rising to 182 DM ($108.05) to 244 DM ($144.90) for doubles. On the premises are a French restaurant and a bar.

Hotel Ludwig, Brandenburgerstrasse 24, D-5000 Köln 1 (tel. 0221/12-30-31), much improved and upgraded in recent years, enjoys a central location, directly by the north entrance of the main station and only 100 yards from the cathedral. The 62 rooms are pleasantly and attractively furnished and have private baths, color TVs, radios, and phones. For singles, the overnight charge is 100 DM ($59.40) to 175 DM ($103.90) daily, while doubles cost 155 DM ($92.05) to 255 DM ($151.40). A buffet breakfast, the only meal served, is included in the tariffs. The hotel has an elevator, and there is space to park your car.

Kommerz-Hotel, Breslauer Platz, D-5000 Köln 1 (tel. 0221/12-40-86), is in the center near the cathedral and main train station. A tangerine-colored modern hotel, it looks glaringly conspicuous when viewed with the Dom in the background. But despite this juxtaposition of the old with the new, the rooms are convenient, with full-length windows and utilitarian furnishings. The sunny, wood-paneled bar has an attractive U-shaped serving area where you're likely to meet anyone in Cologne. All units contain bath or shower, along with a toilet, and tariffs include breakfast: singles from 130 DM ($77.20) to 170 DM ($100.95) daily and doubles from 180 DM ($106.90) to 220 DM ($130.65).

Hotel am Augustinerplatz, Hohestrasse 30, D-5000 Köln 1 (tel. 0221/23-67-17), stands in a shopping center between the cathedral and the main train station. It is internationally modern, with some effort at Gemütlichkeit in the breakfast room, where the staff will cook, within reason, anything you want. The 56 rooms are clean and comfortable, with large beds and chairs upholstered in rich, dark fabrics. The cost of all units includes breakfast, and depends on the amount of plumbing contained within. Singles rent for 105 DM ($62.35) to 275 DM ($163.30) daily and doubles for 160 DM ($95) to 295 DM ($175.15).

Budget Hotels

In the old section, the **Alstadt-Hotel,** Salzgasse, D-5000 Köln 1 (tel. 0221/23-41-87), is just two minutes from the Rhine boat-landing dock. Guests of this 29-room hotel have passed the word along to their friends, making it a big success.

Herr Olbrich learned about catering to international guests while a steward on the German-America Line, and he has furnished his little hotel beguilingly. Each of his rooms is immaculate and individually decorated, a restful haven with a telephone and a refrigerator, and radio and television available on request. Singles with showers rent for 80 DM ($47.50) to 85 DM ($50.45) daily. Doubles with showers are priced at 95 DM ($56.40) to 140 DM ($83.15). All rates include a buffet breakfast, service charge, and taxes. A sauna is on the premises. Space is not easy to obtain, and reservations are recommended.

Stapelhäuschen, Fischmarkt 1–3, D-5000 Köln 1 (tel. 0221/21-30-43), was originally built in the 1100s near the city site where fish was sold by Benedictine monks from Scotland. Since then, it figured in occasional references in the city's chronicles as the home of one or another of Cologne's leading merchants until it was converted into a hotel in 1950. Today, amid paneling and an occasional portrait of Irish-born St. Brigit, you'll find a richly evocative decor of beamed ceilings clustered within a pair of medieval buildings set on a street corner on a historic square. Each building is a tall and narrow town house whose ironwork announces the year of its construction—1235. Not all of the 33 bedrooms contain private baths; each, however, offers an old-fashioned decor of busily patterned wallpaper and clean, if slightly faded, furniture. Depending on the plumbing, singles rent for 45 DM ($26.70) to 85 DM ($50.45) daily, with doubles costing 70 DM ($41.55) to 150 DM ($89.05), including breakfast. On the premises is a good restaurant, recommended separately.

Hotel Tourist Thielen, Brandenburgerstrasse 1–5, D-5000 Köln 1 (tel. 0221/12-33-33), is a pleasant family-run hotel with fair-size rooms that lies only a block behind Cologne's main railway terminus. The guest list is definitely international. The best and most economical way to stay here is in a room with no private bath. That way, a single costs 45 DM ($26.70) daily, and a double goes for 68 DM ($40.40). Guests can shower free in one of the hallway facilities. With a shower, a twin-bedded room goes up in price to 85 DM ($50.45), and a triple-bedded unit rents for 110 DM ($65.30). In all, there are 120 good clean beds up for grabs.

Brandenburger Hof, Brandenburgerstrasse 2, D-5000 Köln 1 (0221/12-28-89), is a 45-room family-style hotel where you can get cheaper rates in accommodations sheltering three or four persons. Singles without baths cost 45 DM ($26.70); doubles go for 55 DM ($32.65) to 65 DM ($38.60) if bathless, for 85 DM ($50.45) for rooms with showers and toilets. Triples are priced at 85 DM ($50.45) and a four-bedded room at 95 DM ($56.40). All rooms are small, warm, and equipped with running water, and there's a bath on each floor. Breakfast with orange juice and eggs, included in the price, is served in a cozy room. The hotel is behind the railway station, about three blocks from the river and within walking distance of the cathedral. There's no charge for parking your car in the hotel's space.

Hotel Lenz, Ursulaplatz 9, D-5000 Köln 1 (tel. 0221/12-00-55), advertises itself as "your home in Cologne," and for many overnight guests it's just that. The hotel was totally renovated in 1982, and now is better than ever with more up-to-date facilities. Most of the 110 rooms have private baths, are pleasantly and comfortably furnished, and have color TVs, minibars, and phones. Bathless singles are rented for 55 DM ($32.65) daily, those with private baths or showers going for 96 DM ($57) to 154 DM ($91.45). Doubles cost 96 DM ($57) to 220 DM ($130.64), depending on the plumbing. All tariffs include breakfast, taxes, and service. The hotel contains one of the most colorfully decorated winehouses in Cologne, with intricate woodcarvings—almost a Black Forest fantasy, everything brightened by panels of red. The Lenz is convenient to the railway station, the cathedral, and other major points of interest.

Hotel Berlin-Sunset, Domstrasse 10, D-5000 Köln 2 (tel. 0221/12-30-51), is a sister hotel of the Lenz (see above). On the other side of the railway station, yet quietly located, it offers 78 well-furnished rooms, each with private bath or shower, minibar, cable color TV, radio, and phone. Singles rent for 96 DM ($57) to 154 DM

($91.45) daily, with twins or doubles costing 146 DM ($86.70) to 220 DM ($130.65), including a rich buffet breakfast, taxes, and service. The hotel also operates a rustic restaurant decorated in the style of an old farmhouse.

WHERE TO DINE

The Top Restaurants

On the outskirts in the suburb of Merheim, the **Goldener Pflug,** Olpener Strasse 421 (tel. 0221/89-55-09), should be visited for "that special occasion." Owned by Ludwig Robertz, it's one of the top restaurants in all of Germany. The chef appreciates impossibly demanding clients with jaded palates, and takes pleasure in sending them away satisfied. Top-quality ingredients are used in his imaginative blend of classical repertoires. Try, for example, any of his truffled specialties, ranging from soups to a wide choice of delicately seasoned main courses. For dessert, the most exciting choices are an apple cake flambé and a soufflé à la Rothschild with strawberries. The decor of what was a former tavern is simple, with a golden motif repeated in the walls, draperies, and upholstery. A fixed-price gourmet "surprise" menu costs 180 DM ($106.90) for eight courses. If you order à la carte, expect to spend 110 DM ($65.30) to 175 DM ($103.90) or more for a meal. However, a set lunch is offered for 55 DM ($32.65). Hours are noon to 3pm and 6pm to midnight; closed Sun. and for three weeks in summer. Always call for a reservation and ask for directions.

Chez Alex, Mühlengasse 1 (tel. 0221/23-05-60), is the finest restaurant in the city itself. A festive vista of hot-pink linen greets guests who enter this elegant "Maison de Champagne." The decor is belle époque, with paneled walls and dark velvet banquettes. Established in 1978, Chez Alex quickly moved to the foreground of Cologne restaurants serving cuisine moderne. The menu is in French with German subtitles. Among the offerings, you're likely to find coquilles St-Jacques en feuilletage or a mousse of smoked salmon with caviar. In season you can order a suckling lamb marinated in Pauillac. A nine-course menu gastronomique goes for 135 DM ($80.15), and other dinners begin at 80 DM ($47.50). Hours are noon to 2:30pm and 7 to 11pm and Sat. for lunch; closed Sun. Also closed on holidays.

Hanse-Stube, Domplatz (tel. 0221/27-01), on the ground floor of the Excelsior Hotel Ernst, is rightly considered one of the best restaurants in Cologne. The cuisine and service are top-drawer. The setting is that of a tavern, which you can enter through the hotel. The restaurant provides food and beverages daily from noon to midnight, with meals costing 70 DM ($41.55) to 95 DM ($56.40). Main-dish specialties include poached salmon in sorrel sauce and filet of veal Excelsior style. For dessert, try the parfait of hazelnut with Rémy Martin sauce.

Restaurant Bado–La Poêle d'Or, Komödienstrasse 52 (tel. 0221/13-41-00). The idea of a new philosophy in French cookery is nothing new to the chef of this sophisticated restaurant. Jean-Claude Bado has used fresh ingredients and a lighter approach to classical French recipes for years. Try the salmon in lemon sauce, or the goose salad with wild mushrooms, or perhaps filet of John Dory in caviar sauce. Meals cost 90 DM ($53.45) to 140 DM ($83.15). The decor is elegantly simple, the service impeccable. Hours are noon to 2pm and 6:30 to 10pm; closed Sun., Mon. for lunch, and holidays. The 12-table restaurant shuts down in July.

Rino Casati, Ebertplatz 3 (tel. 0221/72-11-08). The trappings of this elegant restaurant are rich and old-world. The cuisine is light and modern, the entire show orchestrated with flair and panache by Guerino Casati, who diligently supervises the service and advises clients on the freshest delicacies available on his seasonally adjusted Italian menu. Dining does indeed resemble an evening's entertainment, and "the production" isn't cheap—from 70 DM ($41.55) to 100 DM ($59.40) for a meal. But local gourmets insist that the price is worth it. Hours are noon to 2:30pm and 6 to 10pm; closed Sun. and Mon. Always call for a reservation.

Die Bastei, Konrad-Adenauer-Ufer 80 (tel. 0221/12-28-25), is the favored spot for your "watch on the Rhine," the trick being to aim for a window table. The split-level dining room is on the second floor of a circular, towerlike building jutting out into the river, and the view is dramatic. The restaurant is as high-class as its prices, with no meals under 65 DM ($38.60) and some reaching heavenward to 120 DM ($71.25)—the latter for the seven-course gourmet menu. In addition to German specialties, many dishes are presented from neighboring Switzerland, Austria, and France. Hours are noon to midnight; closed Sat. for lunch. Dinner and dance music is played on Saturday evening.

Moderately Priced Restaurants
A comfortable, classy place, **Bistro 1900,** Kettengasse 1A (tel. 0221/21-28-83), is decorated in a turn-of-the-century style, with bentwood chairs and art nouveau accessories. It's the creation of Gerry Zoethout. At noon the cuisine is uncompromisingly *gutbürgerlich* (traditional), but it becomes tantalizingly French at night. The noontime menu, served till 3pm daily, could consist of any one of a dozen or so Germanic specialties, costing 15 DM ($8.90) to 25 DM ($14.85). The evening menu, beginning at around 50 DM ($29.70) and ranging upward, is prepared with subtle blends of seasonings. Try, for example, chicken stuffed with shrimp and covered with a delicately seasoned lobster and crab sauce. Dinner is served daily from 6pm to midnight. Most intimate, the restaurant holds only eight tables.

Soufflé, Hohenstaufenring 53 (tel. 0221/21-20-22). As its name suggests, the restaurant incorporates about a dozen versions of soufflés into its menu. You might begin with a spinach soufflé as an appetizer, finishing with one of the dessert soufflés. However, the creative chefs here also produce such typical dishes as rack of lamb, many variations of lobster, a rosy-pink preparation of calves' liver, a ragoût of sweetbreads and kidneys in a champagne-flavored mustard sauce, and succulent desserts —the last likely to include whatever fresh fruit happens to be in season served with an amaretto sabayon. Full meals are offered from noon to 2:30pm and 6:30 to 11pm; closed Sat. and for Sun. lunch. Full meals cost 50 DM ($29.70) to 65 DM ($38.60), and reservations are needed.

Börsen Restaurant, Unter Sachsenhausen 10 (tel. 0221/13-56-26), near the stock exchange, is also not too far from the cathedral. This busy place welcomes the clerks, clients, and administrators of Cologne's financial community. It offers not only good value but a glimpse of everyday Cologne life, particularly at noon. Seasonally adjusted fixed-price menus range from 60 DM ($35.65) to 95 DM ($56.40). You get classic and conservative cookery from noon to 3pm and 6 to 10pm; closed for dinner Sun. Closed in July.

"baguettchen," Hochstadenstrasse 35 (tel. 0221/21-57-24). If you are looking for a good little French restaurant with an interesting menu, the "baguettchen," owned by Ulla Wegener, should be on your itinerary for Cologne. In a rustic, cozy atmosphere, the chef concocts what might be called a country-style modern cuisine. You will find delicacies to satisfy even the fastidious gourmet, as well as savory provincial dishes, all served on white damask tablecloths. The three complete, fixed-price meals range from 35 DM ($20.80) to 70 DM ($41.55). You can, of course, order à la carte. Service is from noon to 2pm and 7pm to 1am; closed Sun. Reservations are required.

Dining in the Altstadt
Dating back to 1626, **Weinhaus in Walfisch,** Salzgasse 13 (tel. 0221/21-95-75), is a step-gabled inn with a black-and-white timbered facade behind which you'll find the leading atmospheric choice for dining. More important, it serves some of the best food in the city. Not too easy to find, it's on a narrow street set back from the Rhine. There are many German specialties, or you might try the sole meunière or venison for two. Your final bill is likely to total about 35 DM ($20.80) to 65 DM ($38.60) per person. Hours are noon to 3pm and 6 to 10pm; closed Sat. and Sun.

Im Stapelhäuschen, Fischmarkt 1–3 (tel. 0221/21-30-43), is one of the most popular wine taverns in Cologne. Just a few minutes from the cathedral, it's housed in an office building, opening onto the old fish market square and the Rhine. The two-story-high dining room and service bar are antique in style, and provincial cabinets hold a superb wine collection behind the service bar. A carved Madonna attached to the wall, brass objects hanging against paneled wainscoting, a copper coffee urn—everything here is rustic. A wide wooden cantilevered staircase leads to mezzanine tables. While wine is the main reason for coming here (it's that special), the cuisine is excellent. Soups are hearty and full of flavor, and main dishes such as medallions of veal in a creamy sauce are well prepared. A specialty is Rheinischer Sauerbraten with almonds, raisins, and potato dumplings. Desserts are appropriately luscious. A complete meal costs from 35 DM ($20.80). Hours are from noon to 11:30pm daily.

The Beer Taverns

Within the cathedral precincts is **Früh Am Dom,** Am Hof 12–14 (tel. 0221/ 21-26-21), a beer tavern restaurant—the best all-around choice for economy and hearty portions. The denizens of Cologne congregate here for well-cooked meals served on scrubbed wooden tables, with a different German specialty offered every day of the week. Meals cost up to 25 DM ($14.85). To make things easier, the menu is in English. A favorite dish is a Cologne specialty of cured knuckle of pork cooked in root-vegetable broth and served with Sauerkraut and potato purée; apple purée and dumplings go well with this dish. Hot meals are served daily from noon to midnight. Früh-Kölsch, a very special beer, is available. It's a top-fermented brew with a dry, inimitable taste and a tradition stretching back 1,000 years.

Alt-Köln am Dom, Trankgasse 7–9 (tel. 0221/13-46-78), seemingly can feed half the visitors to Cologne on any busy day. Its location across from the cathedral and the railway station, right in the heart of the city, is hard to miss. It has a mechanical clock on its face; when it chimes the hour, a parade of figures emerges and disappears. Alt-Köln is a re-creation of a group of old taverns, including one done in the Gothic style. You can come here for a beer or a good hot meal. Some of the upper-floor tables provide box-seat views of the cathedral. The favorite main dishes include Wiener Schnitzel, Schweinehaxen (pork knuckle), and a platter of sausage specialties with spicy mustard. Try also the braised beef Rhineland style. Meals begin at 15 DM ($8.90). Hours are 11am to 11 or 11:30pm daily.

Brauhaus Sion, Unter Taschenmacher 5 (tel. 0221/21-42-03). If you want a traditional local Brauhaus where the wood paneling is a little smoky with time and frequent polishings, where the portions are inexpensive and generous, where you can sit alone or with friends and enjoy a few glasses of draft beer, this is the place. It's an institution that has been around for a long time, and will change only under great pressure. Traditional and filling fixed-price menus range from 12 DM ($7.15) to 25 DM ($14.85). You'll get such hearty fare as pigs' knuckles with Sauerkraut or the inevitable Bratwurst with savoy cabbage and fried potatoes. But the traditional dish to order here is Kölsch Kaviar (blood sausage decorated with onion rings). You can also ask for halve Hahn, which translates as "half a rooster." On tap is the famed local beer, Kölsch, which is light with an alcohol content of about 3%. It is served in Stangen (rods) about 7 inches tall. The Brauhaus is open every day of the year (except Christmas Eve) from 10am to midnight.

Dining in the Environs

A historic villa, **Remise,** Wendelinstrasse 48 (tel. 0221/49-18-81), lies in the suburbs of Müngersdorf. It has an apéritif bar where, if you feel like it, you can stop in just for a drink. The menus change weekly, according to what's available at the market and what's in season. Dinners range from 65 DM ($38.60) to 90 DM ($53.45). Nine tables seat some two dozen diners in friendly intimacy (or at least I hope so). Hours are noon to 3pm and 6pm to midnight; closed for Sun. and Sat. lunch.

THE SIGHTS

If you walk northward on Hohestrasse, you'll soon reach Cologne's major attraction.

Cologne Cathedral (Dom), Domplatz, is the spiritual and geographical heart of the city, the most overwhelming edifice in the Rhine Valley. Built on the site of a pagan temple and earlier Christian churches, the majestic structure is the largest Gothic cathedral in Germany. Construction was begun in 1248 to house the relics of the Magi brought to Cologne by Archbishop Reinald von Dassel, chancellor of Frederick Barbarossa in 1164, but after the completion of the chancel, south tower, and north side aisles (about 1500), work was halted and not resumed until 1823. In 1880 the great 632-year enterprise was completed, and unlike many time-consuming constructions that change styles in midstream, the final result was true to the Gothic style as in the original plans.

For the best overall view of the cathedral, stand back from the south transept, where you can get an idea of the actual size and splendor of the edifice. Note that there are no important horizontal lines—everything is vertical. The west side (front) is dominated by two towering spires, perfectly proportioned and joined by the narrow facade of the nave. The first two stories of the towers are square, gradually merging into the octagonal form of the top three stories and tapering off at the top with huge finials. There is no great rose window between the spires, so characteristic of Gothic architecture, as the designers insisted that nothing was to detract from the lofty vertical lines.

Entering through the west doors (main entrance), one is immediately caught up in the grandeur of the cathedral. Although this portion of the church is somewhat bare, the clerestory and vaulting give an idea of the size of the edifice. The towering windows on the south aisles include the Bavarian Windows, donated by King Ludwig I of Bavaria in 1848. Typical of most windows in the nave, they are colored in portraitlike pigments, which have been burned on rather than stained. In the north aisles are the stained-glass Renaissance windows, which were made in the years 1507–09.

When you reach the transept, you become aware of the actual size of the cathedral. Here are the organ and choir loft, just south of the Treasury, with its liturgical gold and silver pieces. In the center of the transept—and the cathedral—is an elegant bronze and marble altar, which can be seen from all parts of the cathedral. This was to have been the site of the Shrine of the Three Kings, but the reliquary actually stands behind the high altar in the chancel.

The Shrine of the Three Magi is the most important and valuable object in the cathedral. Designed in gold and silver in the form of a triple-naved basilica, it is decorated with relief figures depicting the life of Christ, the Apostles, and various Old Testament prophets. Across the front of the chancel are two rows of choir stalls divided into richly carved partitions. The unpainted oak choir dates from 1310 and is the largest extant in Germany.

Surrounding the chancel are nine chapels, each containing important works of religious art. The Chapel of the Cross, beneath the organ loft, shelters the painted, carved oak cross of Archbishop Gero (969–976), the oldest full-size cross in the Occident. Behind the altar in Our Lady's Chapel, directly across the chancel from the Chapel of the Cross, is the famous triptych masterpiece painted by Stephan Lochner (1400–51). When closed, the Dombild, as it is called, shows the Annunciation, and when opened, it reveals the Adoration of the Magi in the center, flanked by the patron saints of Cologne, St. Ursula and St. Gereon.

The cathedral (tel. 0221/23-10-25) welcomes visitors daily from 7am to 7pm, except during religious services. Daily tours take place at 10 and 11am, and 2:30, 3:30, and 4:30pm. Visitors are welcome to visit the Treasury and Cathedral Tower daily from 9am to 5pm in summer, from 9am to 4pm in winter; on Sun. and holidays, opens at noon. Admission to each is 2 DM ($1.20).

The **Dionysos-Mosaik,** from the third century, was discovered in 1941 when workmen were digging an air-raid shelter. Near the cathedral, this mosaic once was the decorative floor of the oecus (main room) of a large Roman villa. It was named Dionysos because most of the octagons and squares within the elaborately decorated and colored work are pictures dealing with the Greek god Dionysus, god of wine and dispeller of care. The mosaic is housed in the **Roman-Germanic Museum,** Roncalliplatz 4 (tel. 0221/221-23-01). On the second floor is an unusual collection of Roman antiquities found in the Rhine Valley, including Roman glass from the first to the fourth centuries, as well as pottery, marble busts, and jewelry. The museum and mosaic are open daily from 10am to 5pm. Admission is 3 DM ($1.80); closed Mon.

Wallraf-Richartz Museum/Museum Ludwig, Bischofsgartenstrasse 1 (tel. 0221/221-23-79), just a short walk from Domplatz, is Cologne's oldest museum, begun in the 19th century with a collection of Gothic works by Cologne artists. That group of works is still one of the main attractions, although today the Wallraf-Richartz shows art from 1300 to 1900, and the Ludwig, art from 1900 until today. Representative of the Gothic style in Germany is Stephan Lochner, best shown in his *Madonna in the Rose Garden,* painted in 1450. Several works from the cathedral are exhibited here, including the triptych of the *Madonna with the Vetch Flower* (1410). The museum is proud of its collection of German artists, spanning more than 500 years. It houses Germany's largest collection of works by Wilhelm Leibl as well as paintings by Max Ernst, Paul Klee, and Ernst Ludwig Kirchner. There is also a representative collection of nearly every period and school of painting, from the Dutch and Flemish masters to the French impressionists to American art of the 1960s and 1970s (the famous Ludwig Donation). The museum is open from 10am to 6pm; closed Mon. Admission is 3 DM ($1.80).

Schnütgen Museum, Cäcilienstrasse 29 (tel. 0221/221-23-10), is a curator's dream: Cologne's best collection of religious art and sculpture displayed in an original setting, the Church of St. Cecilia. The church is a fine example of Rhenish Romanic architecture. The works displayed include several medieval tapestries, especially one showing rosy-cheeked Magi bringing gifts to the Christ child (1470). There are many Madonnas, of all sizes and descriptions, carved in stone, wood, and metal. The museum is open Tues. to Sun. from 10am to 5 pm (on the first Wed. of every month until 8pm). Admission is 3 DM ($1.80).

Museum of Applied Art, An der Rechtsschule (tel. 0221/221-38-60), opened in 1989 in the museum vacated by the removal of Wallraf-Richartz and Museum Ludwig (see above). In mothballs since World War II, this museum has an impressive collection of arts and crafts from medieval days up to today. It is open Wed. to Sun. from 10am to 5pm; Tues. until 8pm; closed Mon. Admission is 3 DM ($1.80).

Cologne has 12 Romanesque churches, all lying within the medieval city wall, which are considered the most important in their category. Much devastated during World War II, they have been almost completely restored and again recapture Cologne's rich medieval heritage. **St. Pantaleon,** one of the oldest, was built in 980 on the site of a monastery founded by Archbishop Bruno, the brother of Emperor Otto the Great. On Waisenhausgasse, near Barbarossaplatz, this church has an imposing west end and nave, as well as the oldest cloister arcades remaining in Germany, to the north of the choir. Other features of St. Pantaleon are the side aisles (1175), the choir (1621), and a 17th-century organ case above a 16th-century decorated roodscreen.

Claiming an even older basis is **St. Gereon,** on Gereonsdriesch/Christophstrasse. In the late 4th century, a classical Roman memorial church, reputedly dedicated to St. Gereon and his companions in martyrdom, was built on a graveyard outside the Roman city wall. The oval-shaped structure was converted into the present-day decagon in 1227. **St. Severin,** on Severinstrasse, originated in a late 4th-century memorial chapel in a Roman-Frankish graveyard. The present church dates from the 13th to the 15th centuries and contains a 14th-century plague crucifix, 13th-century mosaic floor and choir stalls, and panel paintings depicting the life of St. Severin.

The church of **St. Ursula** (1135), on Ursulaplatz, is on the site of a Roman graveyard where virgin martyrs were interred. Among its unique features are the baroque Golden Chamber from the 17th century, where relics of the saints were collected; and the upper parts of the walls, which are completely covered with bones arranged to form decorations and sayings. On Pippinstrasse, near Heumarkt, **St. Maria im Kapitol** is in the place where Plectrudis, wife of Pippin, built a church in the early 8th century on the foundation of the walls of the Roman capitol. The cloverleaf choir of the present structure was modeled on that in the Church of the Nativity in Bethlehem. Of special interest is the carved wooden door from the 11th century. Two of the city's other Romanesque churches, **St. Aposteln,** in Neumarkt, and **Gross St. Martin,** on the Rhine in the Altstadt, also have the cloverleaf choir design.

St. Georg, Am Waidmarkt, the only remaining Romanesque pillared basilica in the Rhineland, contains an impressive forked crucifix from the early 14th century. **Cäcilienkirche,** on Cäcilienstrasse, near Neumarkt, the site of the Schnütgen Museum for sacred art, was formerly a ladies' collegiate church. **St. Andreas,** on Komödienstrasse, near the cathedral, is the former collegiate church, the present parish church, and a Dominican monastery. It contains a wealth of late Romanesque architectural sculpture. The remaining two Romanesque churches are on the Rhine —**St. Kunibert,** between Hohenzollernbrücke and Zoobrücke, and **St. Maria Lyskirchen,** between Deutzer Brücke and Severinsbrücke, both of 13th-century origin.

Visitors can take the only **cable railway** across a river to be found in Europe. It spans the Rhine from the zoo in Cologne-Riehl to the Rhine Park in Cologne-Deutz, a total of about 1,000 yards. The part actually over the river is about 525 yards. The cable railway operates daily from Easter to the end of October from 11am to 9 or 10pm, depending on business. A one-way trip costs 4 DM ($2.40), a round trip going for 7 DM ($4.15). For further information, phone 0221/76-42-69.

Organized Tours

The easiest way to get a comprehensive look at Cologne's many attractions is to take one of the tours departing from the Verkehrsamt (tourist information office), opposite the cathedral. From May 1 to October 31, two-hour tours in English are offered daily at 10 and 11am, and at 1, 2, and 3pm. From November 1 to April 30, tours are from noon to 2pm. Costing 18 DM ($10.70), they cover the major sights, including a large number of Gothic and Romanesque churches, a Roman tower, the medieval city gates, the Gothic (15th-century) town hall, the Roman Praetorium, and the modern opera house. The tour also includes a stop at one of the major museums.

Guided walking tours, offered daily from June 1 to August 31, also lasting two hours, start from the tourist information office at 4:30pm, with commentary in English. They cost 7 DM ($4.15) per person.

From July through August 31, evening tours of the city are offered every Fri. and Sat., departing from the tourist information office at 8pm. The price of 40 DM ($23.75) includes a cold platter.

SHOPPING

The pedestrian precincts of the city—ideal for shoppers—are an example to town planners. The traffic-free Hohestrasse, as mentioned, is the main shopping artery. The major mecca along this street is the **Kaufhof Department Store,** Hohestrasse 41 (tel. 0221/22-51), which is said to have a little bit of everything.

Cologne is a city of menswear, with about 100 shops. Typical of these is

Daniels, which has a branch not only at Hohestrasse 60 (tel. 0221/21-06-52), but another at Schildergasse 1 (tel. 0221/24-26-41).

For smart, stylish fashions in leather, head for **Offermann,** Hohestrasse 135 (tel. 0221/23-44-21).

Women interested in hair styling should head for **Michaelis,** Komödienstrasse 107 (tel. 0221/13-41-69).

One of the finest bookstores in Cologne is **Bücherstube am Dom,** Zeppelinstrasse 2 (tel. 0221/23-42-34).

For your perfume needs in this "city of cologne," **Dr. Bataille,** Hohestrasse 148 (tel. 0221/21-13-82), is the preferred choice. Throughout the world, cologne water is practically synonymous with 4711, the most famous name in cologne. For your selection, head for **4711 Ferdinand Mühlens Pärfumerie Fabrik,** Domkloster 2 (tel. 0221/23-47-11).

AFTER DARK

Cultural Entertainment

Cologne is one of the major cultural cities of Germany.

The **Oper der Stadt Köln,** Offenbachplatz (tel. 0221/22-18-400), seating 1,400 patrons, is one of Europe's finest modern opera houses, built between 1954 and 1957. The city's **Philharmonic Concert Hall** is a circular building with a beamless roof 130 feet in diameter. It has a changing repertoire of some of the finest classical music, and it also presents pop and jazz programs. Tickets are available at Roncalliplatz (tel. 0221/23-38-54).

For drama and comedy (if you speak German), it's the **Schauspielhaus** (tel. 0221/22-18-40), next door to the opera. Another theater is the **Kammerspiele,** Ubierring 45 (0221/21-26-51). The **Kefka,** Albertasstrasse (0221/24-01-688), is the only theater in Europe devoted to pantomime.

Nightlife

Maxwell, Pfeilstrasse 25 (tel. 0221/24-16-24), in the vicinity of Neumarkt, is both a café and bistro with a Jugendstil look to it. A port of call for models, journalists, and advertising people, along with a host of other persons, it is open daily from 10am to 1am. Light meals cost from 25 DM ($14.85), but you can spend a lot more, of course. Some of the chef's best dishes include roast woodcock, tortellini with ham, and broccoli-and-asparagus salad with vinaigrette.

Papa Joe's Jazzlokal "Em Streckstrump," Buttermarkt 37 (tel. 0221/21-79-50), is the best center of jazz in Cologne. It's open Mon. to Sat. from 7pm to 3am and on Sun. from 11am to 4pm. Every night another band plays. The walls are hung with "Berliner Illustrirte" from 1903. Beer costs 5 DM ($2.95), and admission is free.

Papa Joe's Biersalon "Klimperkasten," Alter Markt 50-52 (tel. 0221/21-67-59), is Cologne's most unusual beerhall in turn-of-the-century style. Its center of attraction is a collection of mechanical instruments that play every night, in the original sound. And from 8pm on, well-known pianists provide background music. The Biersalon is open daily from 11am to 3am. Beer costs 5 DM ($2.95), and admission is free.

---

4. Aachen (Aix-la-Chapelle)

Just 40 miles west of Cologne, where the frontiers of Germany, Belgium, and the Netherlands meet, is the ancient Imperial City of Aachen (Aix-la-Chapelle), inseparably associated with Charlemagne, who selected this natural spa as the center of his vast Frankish empire.

As a spa, Aachen has an even longer history than it does as an imperial city. Roman legionnaires established a military bath here in the first century A.D. At the end of the 17th century it became known as the Spa of Kings, attracting royalty from all over Europe. In 1742 Frederick the Great took the cure here, and in 1818 the "Congress of Monarchs" brought Czar Alexander from Russia. After World War II, which badly damaged the town, the spa was rebuilt and today enjoys a mild reputation as a remedial center. Its springs are among the hottest in Europe. The treatment includes baths and the *Trinkkur* (drinking of water). The spa gardens are the center of the resort activity, with attractive ponds, fountains, and shade trees.

Most travelers visit Aachen on a day trip from Cologne, via the Cologne-Aachen Autobahn, usually having dinner at the Ratskeller before returning to the larger city on the Rhine. However, those interested in the spa facilities can stay at one of the hotels described below.

The old town of Aachen is small enough to be covered on foot. Marktplatz, or market square, is in the heart of town, overshadowed by the Gothic Rathaus. From here, you can head down one of the most popular and busiest pedestrian precincts in the city, Krämerstrasse, which will lead to Münsterplatz and the famous cathedral, one of the masterpieces of architecture in the western world.

From Cathedral Square you can go through the great iron gate to the Fischmarkt, with its old merchants' houses and the Fischpuddelchen fountain with its spouting fish. On the other side you can see Aachen's town hall, which today houses the city archives. Past the Dom you reach the Elisengarten, bordered to the south by the symbol of Bad Aachen, the Elisenbrunnen, a rotunda with a thermal drinking fountain.

The Wingertsberg Kurgarten and the Stadtgarten with its thermal bath and casino lie to the northeast of town, and the Hauptbahnhof is on the southern ring, opening onto Römerstrasse.

WHERE TO STAY

A Deluxe Hotel

A palacelike structure in a tranquil setting, the **Steigenberger Hotel Quellenhof,** Monheimsallee 52, D-5100 Aachen (tel. 0241/15-20-81 or toll free in the U.S. at 800/223-5652), is as inviting as it is impressive. It was built from 1914 to 1916, even though World War I was raging at the time. Originally it was intended as a residence for the king of Germany. That didn't happen, but it was a favorite rendezvous of royalty for decades after its completion. Architecturally neoclassical, it's furnished with a combination of antique reproductions and modern pieces. True to spa tradition, it is stately and elegant, with a large indoor thermal pool overlooked by picture windows that also allow a view of the garden. All of the 200 comfortable, tastefully furnished bedrooms have baths or showers, direct-dial phones, and radios; most have TVs. Singles rent for 175 DM ($103.90) to 250 DM ($148.45) daily, twin-bedded rooms for 260 DM ($154.40) to 340 DM ($201.90). Most of the accommodations are large-scale.

The large Parkrestaurant Quellenhof, the best of the hotel's several eating places, is known for its modern cuisine. Seating more than 80 guests, it combines elegance and refined service with stylistic harmony; in summer, windows open onto the terrace, and cakes and coffee can be enjoyed under bright sun umbrellas. Both international and regional dishes are served, and a complete wine list is featured. A meal costs 50 DM ($29.70) to 95 DM ($56.40). The Parkrestaurant is open daily from noon until shortly before midnight. Nonresidents are welcome to dine here but should make reservations first. You can also eat in the Parkstube bar, where meals cost from 40 DM ($23.75). The Nationenbar is a good place to enjoy a drink from an almost unlimited variety of libations.

Expensive Hotels

On a downtown street corner in Aachen, the **Aquis Grana City Hotel,** Büchel 32, D-5100 Aachen (tel. 0241/4-43-0), a good piece of urban architecture, offers all the modern amenities of a 90-room city hotel. Rooms are warm, comfortable, and inviting, with quilts in autumnal colors on the single or twin beds. All units contain complete modern baths or showers, and rent for 155 DM ($92.05) to 170 DM ($100.95) daily for a single, 195 DM ($115.80) to 225 DM ($133.60) for a double, including a buffet breakfast. Children up to 10 years stay free in the same room as their parents.

Novotel, Am Europaplatz, Joseph-von-Görres-Strasse, D-5100 Aachen (tel. 0241/1-68-70), has up-to-date comfort and amenities. It offers 119 well-furnished rooms with private baths, direct-dial phones, radios, color TVs, and minibars. The charge is 163 DM ($96.80) daily for a single, 191 DM ($113.40) for a double, with a buffet breakfast included. The hotel's swimming pool is open from May to September, and it also has a flower garden and a terrace. The restaurant is open daily from 6am to midnight.

Moderately Priced Hotels

On a quiet street, **Hotel Krott,** Wirichsbongardstrasse 16, D-5100 Aachen (tel. 0241/4-83-73), built of brown brick with insulated climate-resistant windows, is a family-run hotel within walking distance of the historic center of Aachen. The 20 rooms might be called "cozy," with lots of overstuffed armchairs. Single rooms, depending on the plumbing accessories, run anywhere from 110 DM ($65.30) to 150 DM ($89.05) daily, and doubles rent for 150 DM ($89.05) to 215 DM ($127.65), with breakfast included.

Hotel Buschhausen, Adenauerallee 215, D-5100 Aachen (tel. 0241/6-30-71), can be easily reached by car from the center of Aachen (get off the Autobahn at the Lichtenbusch exit in the direction of Aix-la-Chapelle). The innkeeper, Roger Thomas, rents rooms that are peaceful and quiet, owing to the double-glazed windows and the surrounding woods. The hotel has a swimming pool and two saunas, and its 80 immaculate rooms are decorated in a modern style. Breakfast is included in the rates, which depend on the plumbing: from 88 DM ($52.25) daily for the cheapest single, climbing to 98 DM ($58.20). Doubles begin at 125 DM ($74.25), rising to 175 DM ($103.90).

Hotel Royal, Jülicherstrasse 1, D-5100 Aachen (tel. 0241/1-50-61), is modern, its brick facade curving slightly to follow the contour of one of Aachen's peripheral ringed streets. The 31-room hotel offers cozy comfort within 200 yards of the casino. Rooms are carpeted, with colorfully tiled baths. A double room with shower and toilet costs 175 DM ($103.90) to 195 DM ($115.80) daily, and a single on the same arrangement rents for 125 DM ($74.25) to 150 DM ($89.05), including breakfast. Triple glazing on the windows keeps out the noise. In the attractive bar of the Royal, you can order a drink or a light meal.

Budget Hotels

The warm and inviting **Hotel Benelux,** Franzstrasse 21, D-5100 Aachen (tel. 0241/2-23-43), is tastefully decorated and personalized. It's a small family-run hotel, my personal favorite for those watching their marks. Americans from the West will feel at home in the lobby/reception area—it has probably the only cactus collection in Aachen. Antiques are scattered throughout the corridors, and the rooms are streamlined, each with a shower or bath (tiled in earth tones) and toilet. The Benelux is centrally located within walking distance of most everything. The hotel is also reasonably priced: from 98 DM ($58.20) to 110 DM ($65.30) daily for a single and from 120 DM ($71.25) to 160 DM ($95) for a double, breakfast included. On the premises is a Chinese restaurant.

Hotel Baccara, Turmstrasse 174, D-5100 Aachen (tel. 0241/8-30-05), relaxed and inviting, lies a few minutes from central Aachen. The 33 rooms are contemporary, clean, and comfortable, with blond-wood furniture and a predominant use of black and white. Some of the units contain private balconies, and all of them have toilets and showers (or complete baths). Singles rent for 90 DM ($53.45) to 120 DM ($71.25) daily, and doubles go for 120 DM ($71.25) to 140 DM ($83.15), breakfast included. Parking is available.

Hotel Danica, Franzstrasse 38, D-5100 Aachen (tel. 0241/3-49-91), is a "breakfast only" 26-room hotel that is modern, efficient, clean, and centrally located. It has a family atmosphere and a small staff. Singles rent for 80 DM ($47.50) to 100 DM ($59.40) daily, doubles for 120 DM ($71.25), and triples for 150 DM ($89.05), these rates including breakfast, service, and taxes. If no room is available at the Danica, the same Adang family also owns the very similar **Hotel Danmark,** Lagerhausstrasse 21, D-5100 Aachen (tel. 0241/3-44-14), with almost the same prices.

Am Marscheirtor, Wallstrasse 1-7, D-5100 Aachen (tel. 0241/3-19-41), stands in the center of Aachen, not far from the main station and next to the medieval town gate, Marschiertor—a beautiful and historical part of town. It's in a quiet position, with a courtyard and a view over the old city and the cathedral. Run by the Bott family, the hotel has an attractive lobby and connecting hall with antique furniture. The 50 recently furnished rooms have a cozy atmosphere, as well as showers or complete baths and toilets. Singles cost 98 DM ($58.20) to 120 DM ($71.25) daily, doubles going for 140 DM ($83.15) to 165 DM ($98), all tariffs including a large buffet breakfast. Parking facilities are available opposite the hotel.

WHERE TO DINE

One of the best dining places in Germany is the **Restaurant Gala,** Monheimsallee 44 (tel. 0241/15-30-13). Light plays merrily through the crystal-draped decor onto the oak-paneled walls of this elegant restaurant, which is loosely linked to one of the country's busier casinos. Some of the paintings are by Salvador Dali. The Gala, owned by Gerhard Gartner, is reputed to be able to soothe the frayed nerves of even the heaviest gamblers. The kitchen turns out such frequently updated menus as gamecock in a Calvados and mustard sauce or filet of venison in blood sauce. Cookery here is a "reformed regional style." The food is trucked in daily from Rungis in Paris. The wine list is impressive, the confections French and delicious. A set dinner costs from 130 DM ($77.20), and you can also order à la carte for 80 DM ($47.50) to 105 DM ($62.35). The Gala serves from 7pm to midnight; closed Mon.

Ratskeller, Am Markt (tel. 0241/3-50-01), is a charming place to dine, with its rustic atmosphere of brick and stone, oak benches and tables. There are three major dining rooms. Most intimate and attractive is an extension containing a pub where patrons gather to drink and play cards. Little drinking nooks upstairs are for other games. Among main dishes are such chef's specialties as pork filet chasseur, veal fricassée, and steak done eight different ways. A dessert specialty is a cream of hot cherries flambé with Kirsch. Meals range in price from 35 DM ($20.80) to 65 DM ($38.60). Hours are noon to 3pm and 6pm to midnight daily.

La Bécasse, Hanbrucherstrasse 1 (tel. 0241/7-44-44), is a modern restaurant with much greenery, serving a pleasing combination of traditional German recipes and light, modern specialties. Daily and seasonal dishes are served. Christof Lang, realizing early his "calling" of reproducing the fine foods of France, has been the owner since 1981. The food is imported every day from the wholesale markets at

Rungis, outside Paris. Try, for example, his ragoût of fish or his cassoulet. Meals range from 75 DM ($44.55) to 95 DM ($56.40). La Bécasse is open for lunch from noon to 2:30pm and for dinner from 7 to 10:30pm; closed Sun.

Elisenbrunnen, Friedrich-Wilhelm-Platz 13a (tel. 0241/2-97-72), belongs to one of Germany's biggest concerns, offering a large and well-maintained terrace for summertime dining. The menu boasts more than 50 items, with complete meals costing 28 DM ($16.65) to 70 DM ($41.55). Many of them will appeal to those who are vegetarian or calorie-conscious. On a warm day, seated on the terrace in the shade of the Kaiserdom and the historic Rathaus, a diner can dream of the splendors of the old city. In the kitchen you'll find Hans Holland whipping up the latest in a light, modern cuisine. Service is daily from 9am to 10:30pm.

On the outskirts, **Restaurant Schloss Friesenrath,** Pannekoogweg 46 (tel. 02408/50-48), stands at Friesenrath, about 7 miles southeast of Aachen. There's plenty of venerable atmosphere, as this was a castle with a garden terrace. Reservations are highly recommended, especially on weekends, when it's very popular with local residents. Specialties are deer (in season) and fish, and here one can enjoy the culinary arts with visual pleasure. You can dine here for around 58 DM ($34.45) if you really watch it, or else you could go wild for 82 DM ($48.70) by ordering some of the upper-grade specialties. Try the loup de mer (sea bass) in champagne sauce. Service is from noon to 2pm and 6 to 9pm; closed Mon. The Schloss is closed annually for a period in June.

Restaurant St. Benedikt, Benediktusplatz 12 (tel. 02408/28-88), is found in Kornelimünster, about 6 miles from Aachen. Owners Gisela and Hans-Joachim Kreus welcome their guests into the intimate 1755 town house, painted a terra-cotta red with blue-gray trim. The restaurant is actually a baroque-style house, with a wrought-iron sign discreetly announcing the entrance to this intimate family-run restaurant. They offer attentive service and a thoughtful preparation of modern and classical dishes. Reservations are essential, as there are only five tables. A varied menu of six meat dishes and four fish selections is offered, with an additional choice of two menus featuring ever-changing specials. Try, for example, salmon in champagne sauce, the filet of veal, or, in season, pheasant. A spectacular dessert tray features sherbet mousses, pastries, and exotic fruits. In the kitchen, Gisela Kreus devotes herself to her work with zeal, soul, and fire, and is known throughout the town for her confections. Meals range from 70 DM ($41.55) to 95 DM ($56.40). Open Tues. to Sat. from 7 to 9pm.

THE SIGHTS

About A.D. 800 the emperor built the octagon, the core of the **Imperial Cathedral.** Within the cathedral stands the marble "Königsstuhl," Charlemagne's throne, considered one of the most venerable monuments in Germany. For 600 years the kings of Germany were crowned here, until Frankfurt became the country's coronation city in the mid-16th century.

The cathedral is an unusual mixture of Carolingian (the well-preserved dome), Gothic (the choir, completed in 1414), and baroque (the roof), all united into a magnificent upward sweep of architecture. The **Treasury,** in the adjoining treasure house, is the most valuable and celebrated ecclesiastical treasure store north of the Alps. But the cathedral holds its own share of wealth. The elaborate gold shrine in the chancel contains the relics of the Emperor Charlemagne. The pulpit of Henry II is copper studded with precious gems. Visitors to the cathedral can view the throne of Charlemagne only with a guide (request one at the Treasury). The Treasury may be visited between April and October, Tues., Wed., Fri., and Sat. from 10am to 6pm; Mon. from 10am to 2pm; Thurs. from 10am to 8pm; and Sun. from 10:30am to 5pm. In winter it is open Sat. from 10am to 5pm; Sun. from 10:30am to 5pm; and Mon. from 10am to 2pm. Admission is 3 DM ($1.80) for adults, 2 DM ($1.20) for children. For more information, phone 0241/477-09-27.

The 14th-century **Rathaus,** Am Markt (tel. 0241/432-73-10), was built on the original site of Charlemagne's palace. Part of the old structure can still be seen in the so-called Granus Tower at the east side of the hall. The richly decorated facade of the Rathaus facing the marketplace is adorned with the statues of 50 German rulers, 31 of them crowned in Aachen. In the center, standing in relief, are the "Majestas Domini" and the two most important men in the Holy Roman Empire, Charlemagne and Pope Leo III.

On the second floor of the Rathaus is the double-naved and crossbeamed **Imperial Hall,** dating from 1330, the scene of German coronation meals from 1349 to 1531, built as the successor to the Carolingian Royal Hall. This hall today contains exact replicas of the Imperial Crown Jewels, true in size and material to the originals, presently in the Vienna Secular Treasury. On the walls are the Charlemagne frescoes, painted in the 19th century by Alfred Rethel, illustrating the victory of the Christian Franks over the Germanic heathens. The hall is open Mon. to Fri. from 8am to 1pm and 2 to 5pm; on Sat. and Sun. from 10am to 1pm and 2 to 5pm. Official events at the Town Hall sometimes make visits impossible. Admission is 1 DM (60¢).

Couven Museum, Hühnermarkt 17 (tel. 0241/432-44-21), is a lovely rococo residence filled with elegant household furnishings from the 1600s and 1700s. On the ground floor is a dispensary set up as it existed in the 1700s, and on the second landing there is a spacious chamber with a chimney of decorated sculptured wood. In fact, there's a little bit of everything here: lots of hidden treasures. The museum is open Tues. to Fri. from 10am to 5pm; it closes on Sat. and Sun. at 1pm. Admission is only 1 DM (60¢). Closed Mon.

Suermondt-Ludwig Museum, Wilhelmstrasse 18 (tel. 0241/432-44-00), offers an impressive collection of medieval German sculpture—one of the finest in the land, in fact, although it seems little known. It has some exceptional art, including a *Madonna in Robes* from 1420 from the Swabian school and a *Virgin and Child* from the 14th-century Tournai school. The second landing has a good collection of primitive Flemish and German works, along with 17th-century Dutch and Flemish paintings. Look for works by major masters such as Van Dyck and Rubens. The museum also has modern works, everything from Picasso to Roy Lichtenstein. Open from 10am to 5pm; closed Mon. (closes on Sat. and Sun. at 1pm). The museum charges only 1 DM (60¢) for admission.

Additional information is available at the **Tourist Office Aachen,** Haus Löwenstein, Markt 39 (tel. 0241/180-29-60).

AFTER DARK

Behind the portals of what were formerly pump rooms is **Spielcasino Aachen,** Kurpark, Monheimsallee 44 (tel. 0241/18-080), where many gaming possibilities are offered in spacious, elegant surroundings. Roulette, blackjack, and baccarat are played by international rules, from 3pm to 2am daily, and to 3am on Fri. and Sat. Visitors, who must be over 18 years old, are required to show their passports to enter. Jackets and ties are required for men. Minimum stakes are 5 DM ($2.95) to 20 DM ($11.90) for roulette, 10 DM ($5.95) for blackjack, and 60 DM ($35.65) for baccarat. There are also slot machines. The casino has a large underground garage.

The most elegant club in Aachen, **Zero,** Kurpark, Monheimsallee 44 (tel. 0241/18-080), is on the ground floor of the Casino. It offers drinks from 17 DM ($10.10) in an elegant setting of black pillars and mirrors. You can dance the night away to disco music. Open only on Fri. and Sat. nights, 10pm to 4am.

5. Düsseldorf

Although Düsseldorf got its start as a settlement on the right bank of the Rhine, today it is built on both sides—the older sections on the right bank and the modern, commercial and industrial parts on the left. The two parts are connected by five bridges, the most impressive being the Oberkassle. Parks and esplanades line the riverbanks. After 85% of the right bank city was destroyed in World War II, it could have easily grown into just another ugly manufacturing town, but Düsseldorf followed a modern trend in reconstruction, and today it is the most elegant metropolis in the Rhine Valley.

As in most German cities, there is the **Altstadt,** with its marketplace, a Gothic town hall, and a few old buildings and churches. Near the town hall in Burgplatz, two of the city's most famous landmarks can be seen: the twisted spire of **St. Lambertus Church** and the round **Castle Tower,** both of 13th-century origin.

The Altstadt has been called "the longest bar in the world" because of the some 200-plus bars and restaurants found there. The favorite drink here is a top-fermented Althier (old beer), a dark, mellow brew that must be drunk fresh soon after it's made.

A walk up **Königsallee,** affectionately called the "Kö" by Düsseldorfers, will give the outsider a quick look at what the city and its residents are like. This street flanks an ornamental canal, shaded by trees and crossed by bridges. While one bank is lined with office buildings and financial centers, the other is filled with elegant shops, cafés, and restaurants. Here you'll see women dressed in the latest styles, as Düsseldorf is also the fashion center of Germany. It is known for its Fashion Weeks, attracting designers and buyers from all over Europe. Retail shops are generally open Mon. to Fri. from 9am to 6:30pm, Sat. from 9am to 2pm. On the first Sat. in every month, shops stay open until 6pm.

As the capital of North Rhine-Westphalia, Düsseldorf is a wealthy city—the richest in Germany. It's a big, commercial city full of banks and industrial offices, yet it's surprisingly clean. It has managed to incorporate parks and gardens throughout the city, some of them wedged comfortably between skyscrapers. The most impressive of these buildings is the **Thyssen House,** in the bustling center of town. Residents call the office tower the *Dreischeibenhaus* (three-slice house), because it actually looks like three huge monoliths sandwiched together.

GETTING THERE AND GETTING AROUND

Lufthansa flies from New York to Düsseldorf on a daily nonstop flight. There is service also from Miami and Toronto. You land at Lohausen Airport, five minutes away. It's about a 20-minute taxi ride to the Municipal Air Terminal at the railway station. Therefore, it's cheaper to go by an S-Bahn commuter train from the airport, which will take you to the Hauptbahnhof as well. Departures are about every 20 minutes.

For questions about transportation, boat trips, or other matters, ask at the tourist office, the Verkehrsverein, Konrad-Adenauer-Platz (tel. 0211/35-05-05).

Düsseldorf is a big, sprawling city, and you can't get around on foot too easily. Therefore, you'll need to rely on public transportation. The Hauptbahnhof, or railway station, lies in the southeastern sector, opening onto Konrad-Adenauer-Platz.

Düsseldorf and its environs are served by a network of S-Bahn railways that fan out to the suburbs, along with buses and streetcars, called Strassenbahn. An underground system went into operation in 1988. Ask at the tourist office about purchasing a 24-hour visitor's ticket. The cost is 8.50 DM ($5.05).

WHERE TO STAY

Expensive Hotels

One of the most outstanding Hiltons in the chain, and one of the best run, is in Düsseldorf. Both the **Düsseldorf Hilton,** Georg-Glock-Strasse 20, D-4000 Düsseldorf 30 (tel. 0211/43-77-0), and its adjoining congress centers are between the Kennedy Damm and the Rhine, close to the city, airport, and fairgrounds. It is exactly what you would expect from a Hilton, and a lot more. A total of 374 well-

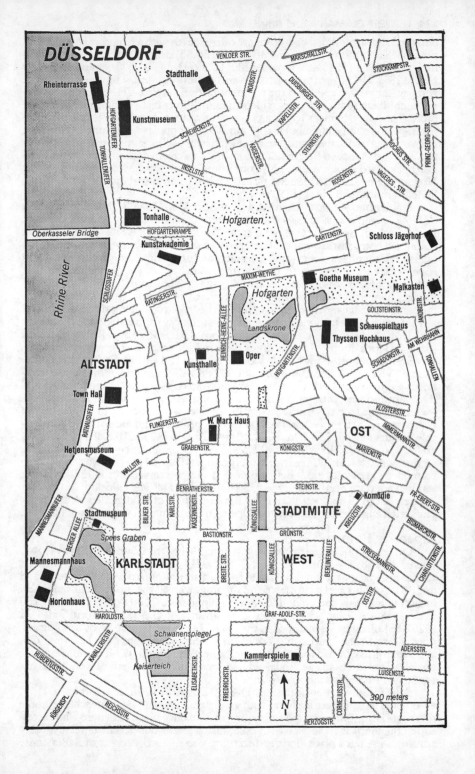

designed and streamlined bedrooms are offered, each with a handsomely equipped tile bath. Single rooms cost from 230 DM ($136.55) daily, although they may go as high as 410 DM ($243.45). Doubles start at 276 DM ($163.90), going up to 480 DM ($285). The most expensive rooms are on the upper floors. But no matter what you pay, the view is good and the rooms attractively styled. Those added conveniences are there too: color TVs, videos, radios, direct-dial phones, minibars, and more. The public lounges reflect a progressively ultramodern decor, utilizing freeform sculpture and contemporary paintings. Most popular is Neptune's Club, with its swimming pool, sauna, and massage facilities, as well as a fitness center and solarium. The San Francisco Restaurant is known for its creative cuisine, and at the Club 1001 it's disco time every night from 10pm until 4am. Most agreeable is the Hofgarten-Restaurant, a glassed-in garden room for informal dining. It sponsors a Sunday brunch for 32 DM ($19).

Breidenbacher Hof, Heinrich-Heine-Allee 36, D-4000 Düsseldorf 1 (tel. 0211/130-30), seems to have been designed to coddle the well-heeled German. Dating back to 1806 (although rebuilt after World War II), it is Düsseldorf's leading traditional hotel, just around the corner from Königsallee. Everything for plush living is to be found here, including a South Seas restaurant and nightclub and a grill room with background music during the cocktail hour. The Breidenbacher Eck, with its intimate atmosphere, is also a magnet. The main drawing rooms and lounges have traditional furnishings, glamorized by antiques, gilt mirrors, paintings, and bronze chandeliers. Each of the 135 bedrooms is differently decorated, but all have private baths, phones, radios, and TVs. You pay from 290 DM ($172.20) to 410 DM ($243.45) daily for a single, from 420 DM ($249.40) to 590 DM ($350.35) for a double. Tariffs include breakfast and taxes. The service is excellent.

Steigenberger Park-Hotel, Corneliusplatz 1, D-4000 Düsseldorf 1 (tel. 0211/86-51 or toll free in the U.S. at 800/882-4777), is one of the deluxe traditional German hotels that survived World War II. Completely modernized and reequipped to meet modern demands, it is a prestige hotel maintaining a high service level in the true old-world style. The lounges were renewed in 1982. All 160 bedrooms, refitted to the latest standards with private baths, are cozy and comfortable. Singles rent for 255 DM ($151.40) to 375 DM ($222.70) daily, and doubles go for 370 DM ($219.70) to 490 DM ($290.95). Both prices include breakfast, service, and taxes. The Rôtisserie attracts gourmets from all over the world, drawn to its modern French cuisine. Before-dinner drinks are served in the Étoile Bar. In summer a terrace overlooking the parks and gardens of Düsseldorf invites you for leisurely meals. The hotel is right at the beginning of Königsallee, overlooking Hofgarten Park, next to the German Opera on the Rhine, a few steps from the river.

Expensive Hotels

Owned by one of Germany's largest hotel chains, the **Günnewig Savoy Hotel,** Oststrasse 128, D-4000 Düsseldorf 1 (tel. 0211/36-03-36), gives personalized service in a gracious setting. Its facade is of heavily sculptured white limestone, and its 130 bedrooms are comfortable and inviting, with all the modern conveniences, including minibars and color TVs. Singles range from 200 DM ($118.75) to 250 DM ($148.45) daily, with doubles going from 290 DM ($172.20) to 350 DM ($207.85). Breakfast is included in the rates. Guests can use the Savoy's swimming pool. Bierhoff, the court confectioners in the Savoy, is more than 125 years old. When the old Savoy had to make way for the new underground, this famous city café was relocated in Oststrasse. Today, in its reincarnation, the Bierhoff Konditorei has reemerged with most of its old splendor.

Saga Excelsior, Kapellstrasse 1, D-4000 Düsseldorf 30-Derendorf (tel. 0211/48-60-06). Finally, here's a hotel with an imaginative classical color scheme: some rooms are beautifully carpeted and wallpapered in olive-green with pure-white accessories; the lobby is royal blue with gold, plus a few antiques. The hotel justifiably advertises itself as a place "for the discerning guest." At the corner of Kaiserstrasse and Kapellstrasse, it offers six floors and 65 rooms of air-conditioned comfort to travel-tired guests for anywhere from 150 DM ($89.05) to 160 DM ($95) daily for a single and from 240 DM ($142.50) to 275 DM ($163.30) for a double. Tariffs include breakfast.

Börsenhotel, Kreuzstrasse 19a, D-4000 Düsseldorf (tel. 0211/36-30-71), in the heart of Düsseldorf, stands almost at the front door of the stock exchange. It is reasonable, considering how attractively furnished it is, with a marble-floored lobby and high-ceilinged bedrooms that are comfortable and well proportioned. All have color TVs, direct-dial phones, and radios. Thermopane windows keep out the noise of the city. A single ranges in price from 140 DM ($83.15) to 190 DM ($112.80) daily; a double goes for 200 DM ($118.75) to 260 DM ($154.40).

Holiday Inn, Graf-Adolf-Platz 10, D-4000 Düsseldorf 1 (tel. 0211/38-73-0), stands at the very center of Königsallee, offering 177 attractively furnished, air-conditioned rooms, with large beds, private baths, radios, color TVs, direct-dial phones, and double-glazed windows. A single rents for 275 DM ($163.30) to 340 DM ($201.90) daily, a double room costs 320 DM ($190) to 385 DM ($228.60). The Düsseldorfer bistro-bar-restaurant serves national and international dishes. The hotel also has an indoor swimming pool, sauna, and solarium. Children up to 18 stay free in their parents' room.

Hotel Esplanade, Fürstenplatz 17, D-4000 Düsseldorf 1 (tel. 0211/37-50-10), convenient for motorists, lies less than a mile from the central railway station, 5 miles from the Autobahn in the Friedrichstadt section. The Esplanade has an excellent restaurant, the Rib-Room, and a hotel bar. All the public rooms are air-conditioned. The large heated indoor swimming pool with solarium and Finnish sauna can be reached from each floor by elevators. The 80 rooms are comfortably furnished, with direct-dial phones, radios, color TVs, private baths, and soundproof windows. Singles, depending on the plumbing, cost 155 DM ($92.05) to 250 DM ($148.45) daily. Doubles are 198 DM ($117.55) to 380 DM ($225.65). Prices include a buffet breakfast, service, and taxes.

Moderately Priced Hotels

The centrally located **Eden,** Adersstrasse 29-31, D-4000 Düsseldorf 1 (tel. 0211/3-89-70), in spite of its name, is more solid than lush. A lot of care has gone into making the 130 completely renovated bedrooms comfortable. They're all equipped with baths or showers, toilets, color TVs, radios, direct-dial phones, and minibars. Singles cost 177 DM ($105.10) to 266 DM ($157.95) daily, and doubles go for 252 DM ($149.65) to 352 DM ($209). All rates include a buffet breakfast, taxes, and service. The hotel has a lobby bar, a hairdresser, a flower shop, and space for parking. The Eden is in a good location, only two minutes from the Kö shopping area and five minutes from the main railway station.

Rema-Hotel Fürstenhof, Fürstenplatz 3, D-4000 Düsseldorf 1 (tel. 0211/37-05-45), has been totally revamped and renamed. Modern but not glaringly so, it opens onto an attractive tree-filled square. All its 43 handsomely furnished bedrooms are equipped with private showers or baths, toilets, color TVs, radios and minibars. Nonsmoker rooms are available, and half of the breakfast room is reserved for nonsmoking guests. A single room rents for 190 DM ($112.80) daily, a double for 260 DM ($154.40), these tariffs including one of the best buffet breakfasts in town. This hotel is a good, comfortable, safe choice in the center of town.

Lindenhof, Oststrasse 124, D-4000 Düsseldorf 1 (tel. 0211/36-09-63), is an 80-year-old five-story hotel on a tree-shaded street, within walking distance of central Düsseldorf. All 43 rooms have showers/baths, toilets, phones, radios, and color TVs, and breakfast is included in the rates, which run anywhere from 130 DM ($77.20) to 195 DM ($115.80) daily for single and from 170 DM ($100.95) to 215 DM ($127.65) for a double. Children are lodged in their parents' room free.

Hotel am Rhein Schnellenburg, Rotterdamerstrasse 120, D-4000 Düsseldorf 30 (tel. 0211/43-41-33), on the outskirts, was built on the ruins of a medieval castle opening directly onto the Rhine. In a traditional style, with window boxes of flowers in summer, it is an engaging choice, lying about 2½ miles from Düsseldorf's international airport and within walking distance of both the Convention Center and the Japanese Garden. All 50 rooms are completely modern, with such amenities as refrigerator-bars, direct-dial phones, color TVs, and good-size baths with showers. Rates are 140 DM ($83.15) to 220 DM ($130.65) daily for a single, rising to 180 DM ($106.90) to 280 DM ($166.25) for a double. The hotel has a good restaurant with a terrace overlooking the river. Sightseeing boats leave from the hotel's own pier. The place manages to be both sophisticated and cosmopolitan, yet still comfortably informal. English is spoken.

Lancaster, Oststrasse 166, D-4000 Düsseldorf 1 (tel. 0211/35-10-66), is attractively situated in the center of town. The mirrored reception area efficiently registers guests before packing them off to 40 comfortable and often sunny rooms with private baths. Breakfast is included in the rates, with an assortment of sausages that might make a Wurst fan of you. Singles go for 135 DM ($80.15) to 165 DM ($98) daily and doubles for 175 DM ($103.90) to 195 DM ($115.80).

Central, Luisenstrasse 42, D-4000 Düsseldorf (tel. 0211/37-90-01), in the heart of the business and fair world, is well located, lying near Königsallee. Its 75 rooms are modern and clean, with phones, TVs, baths (or showers), and toilets. With breakfast included, units rent for 170 DM ($100.95) to 270 DM ($160.35) daily for a single and from 240 DM ($142.50) for a double.

Hotel National, Schwerinstrasse 16, D-4000 Düsseldorf 30 (tel. 0211/49-90-62), lies 1½ miles from the downtown section. Modern and efficient, it was pleasantly renovated a few years ago. All the 32 comfortably furnished units are equipped with private baths, color TVs (English channel available), radios, direct-dial phones, minibars, and balconies. The rates, often reduced in July and August, are 115 DM ($68.30) to 175 DM ($103.90) daily for a single, 160 DM ($95) to 225 DM ($133.60) for a double.

One of the better links in the Best Western chain in Germany is the **Hotel Graf Adlof,** Stresemannplatz 1, D-4000 Düsseldorf (tel. 0211/36-05-91). It offers a superclean, reasonably priced accommodation about three blocks from the railway station and a five-minute walk from the Königsallee shopping area. All 100 bedrooms have private baths or showers, and the units facing the street have soundproof windows. Singles rent for 165 DM ($98) to 220 DM ($130.65) daily and doubles for 250 DM ($148.45) to 295 DM ($175.15), with breakfast included in the tariffs. The breakfast room on the first floor offers you a fair view of the morning crowd rushing to work.

Budget Hotels

In a five-story stucco building, close to the Graf-Adolf-Strasse and about four blocks from the railway station, the **Wurms Hotel,** Scheurenstrasse 23, D-4000 Düsseldorf 1 (tel. 0211/37-50-01), offers 28 bedrooms that are most recommendable. The accommodations are done in dark wood offset by bright bedspreads and curtains. Bathless singles are 95 DM ($56.40) daily, increasing to 130 DM ($77.20) for rooms with showers. Doubles come only with baths or showers, costing 130 DM ($77.20) to 180 DM ($106.90).

Hotel Grosser Kufürst, Kufürsterstrasse 18, D-4000 Düsseldorf (tel. 0211/35-76-47), is housed in a modern building. The 22 rooms are well organized, but there's no furniture to spare. Rates include breakfast, and singles with private baths or showers range in price from 85 DM ($50.45) to 125 DM ($74.25) daily; doubles go for 105 DM ($62.35) to 185 DM ($109.85). Accommodations are equipped with phones, minibars, and radios (in some cases, TVs).

Rheinpark, Bankstrasse 13, D-4000 Düsseldorf 30-Golzheim (tel. 0211/49-91-86), is an antiseptically modern little hotel, about three blocks from the Rhine, in the Golzheim section. You are quite far away from the center, but a streetcar stopping nearby will quickly bring you to the Königsallee. The hotel's in a colorless concrete building, with no proper reception area, but the 30 rooms are comfortable and nicely decorated with old pictures. All rooms have running water, and there's a shower on each floor. Singles cost 60 DM ($35.65) to 115 DM ($68.30) daily; doubles, 100 DM ($59.40) to 130 DM ($77.20).

WHERE TO DINE

The Top Restaurants

Ranked as one of the most outstanding independent restaurants in the city is the **Orangerie,** Bilkerstrasse 30 (tel. 0211/13-18-28). For elegant dining and high prices, the haute cuisine of the Orangerie is, in my opinion, almost without equal. Inviolately aristocratic, it draws the fashion moguls of the city on the see-and-be-seen circuit. Everything here is of the highest quality, including the service. The owner, Horst Weigandt, specializes in such dishes as a gratin of crayfish and suprême de turbot. Try especially the medaillon de veau à la périgourdine—that is, veal with a garnish of truffles to which foie gras has been added. The establishment's well-deserved reputation among gourmets is perpetuated by its exclusivity—generated, to a large extent, by the rarefied prices. A complete dinner can cost anywhere from 65 DM ($38.60) to 100 DM ($59.40), and a lot more if you select an expensive wine. This place gets very busy at the time of the international fashion trade fair, held four times a year. It's open from noon to 2:30pm and 6:30 to 10:30pm; closed Sun. Reservations are absolutely necessary.

Victorian Restaurant, Königstrasse 3a (tel. 0211/32-02-22). Set behind a sign richly lettered with gilded characters, this establishment has a meticulously crafted environment of sparkling crystal, black leather banquettes, and masses of flowers. The food represents the best of both traditional and modern schools of cuisine. Examples include deep-fried zucchini flowers stuffed with lobster mousse and flavored with a sauce of champagne vinegar and coriander; apple salad with slices of goose liver; John Dory with fennel sauce (served with a cucumber-flavored spaghetti); gamecock braised in butter with rosemary, exotic mushrooms, and celery; and a trio of vegetable purées. The delectable desserts change with the inspiration of the pastry chef but might include a terrine of oranges served with raspberry liqueur and fresh mint.

A fixed-price meal costs from 60 DM ($35.65) at lunch and from 125 DM ($74.25) at dinner. À la carte meals cost from 60 DM ($35.65) at either lunch or dinner. Reservations are vital, and meals are served from noon to 3pm and 7 to 11pm; closed Sun. and holidays.

Between May and August, less expensive and simpler variations of the cuisine are served in the Victorian Lounge. Here meals costing from 50 DM ($29.70) might include such typical dishes as Tafelspitz, goose liver terrine flavored with aged cognac, and apple strudel.

San Francisco, Georg-Glock-Strasse 20, Düsseldorf Hilton (tel. 0211/4-37-70). Whoever designed this international restaurant must have lost his heart somewhere on the West Coast of the United States, because the decor is turn-of-the-century "San Francisco." The chef uses the best produce Düsseldorf can offer, imports his beef directly from Hilton slaughterhouses in the United States, and produces prime rib with a distinctive taste. Other specialties are parfait of salmon and sole in a cress foam, soufflé of baby turbot in red-wine butter, and terrine of chocolate in a mint sauce with wild strawberries. Meals cost 85 DM ($50.45) to 120 DM ($71.25). Dinners are served from 7 to 11pm; closed Mon. and in July. The ambience, cuisine, and service are among the finest along the Rhine.

Restaurant Savini, Stromstrasse 47 (tel. 0211/39-39-31), is a rustically elegant gathering place run by a cheerful Italian, Carlo Caputo. In a white-walled room with tastefully striped banquettes, diners are served from a menu that includes classical French and Italian cuisine. Herr Caputo does everything he can to see that his produce is as fresh as the local markets can provide and that the service is personalized and attentive. Try a time-honored dish such as Bresse chicken in a tarragon sauce or a four-fish platter garnished with four different sauces. À la carte meals cost 75 DM ($44.55) to 90 DM ($53.45). Hours are noon to 2:30pm and 6 to 10:30pm; closed Sun. and Sat. for lunch. There are only 10 tables, so you must reserve in advance.

De' Medici, Ambosstrasse 3 (tel. 0211/59-41-51), on the outskirts at Oberkassel, is elegantly modern, serving two culinary traditions, French and Italian. The oversize menu reflects the constant array of tried-and-true dishes, with concessions to whatever was available in the market that day. An unusual choice might be marinated sweetbreads over sautéed eggplant, or medallions of veal in puff pastry. A tab of 50 DM ($29.70) is about the cheapest possible. The restaurant is open from noon to 3pm and 6pm to midnight; closed Sun.

Im Schiffchen, Kaiserwerther Markt 9 (tel. 0211/40-10-50), on the outskirts at Kaiserwerth, offers what many gourmets consider the finest food in Düsseldorf, if you don't mind the journey here to enjoy it. The featured piece of decor in this 18th-century house is the steering wheel from an old Rhine cruiser, and looking past it through the large windows, one has the feeling of being in a boat. The menu, in German and French, features such cuisine moderne delights as homemade goose liver pâté with green peppercorns, Norwegian salmon in a Vouvray sauce, lobster cooked in camomile tea, and pike or perch in puff pastry. For dessert, you might try a granulated fruit mélange with almond cream. For a complete meal, expect to spend 110 DM ($65.30) to 120 DM ($71.25). Hours are 6pm to 1am; closed Sun. and holidays. The restaurant is also closed from mid-July to early August.

Rheinturm-Top 180 Restaurant, Stromstrasse 20 (tel. 0211/84-85-80). The food is competently served and decently prepared, but most of the restaurant's clients consider the view as important as the cuisine. Set atop a spool-shaped summit of the city's tallest tower, its futuristic design incorporates a 360-degree panorama of Düsseldorf, its buildings, and its parks. Many of the people who share the elevator with you might only intend to use the tower's observation lookout. It costs 4.50 DM ($2.65) to go up in the elevator. The establishment serves drinks and snacks daily from noon to midnight, and full hot meals from noon to 2:30pm and 6:30 to 10:30pm. Full meals cost from 50 DM ($29.70), although a fixed-price meal is sometimes offered for 52 DM ($30.90). Menu items include grills, game dishes, fish, and soups. Reservations are a good idea, since many of the establishment's tables might be occupied by groups.

Moderately Priced Restaurants

There's plenty of atmosphere at **Zum Schiffchen,** Hafenstrasse 5 (tel. 0211/13-24-21). A golden model ship on top of the step-gabled building reminds you of its location, only a block from the Rhine. The interior of the 1628 structure relies heavily on the Germanic tavern tradition of scrubbed wooden tables and rustic artifacts. Good, hefty portions are the rule of the kitchen, open daily from noon to 3pm and 5pm to midnight. The Schiffchen roast plate is served for two. To eat here, expect to spend from 32 DM ($19) to 60 DM ($35.65) per person. The menu's large, and the service rather hectic. Zum Schiffchen is the perfect place to sample Düsseldorf's own beer. Over the years, it has attracted a host of famous diners, ranging from Napoleon to Henrich Heine, from Curt Jürgens to Arthur Miller.

Carl Maassen's Zur Auster, Bergerstrasse 9 (tel. 0211/32-44-04), is the latest reincarnation of one of the most venerable shellfish restaurants of Düsseldorf. Lying one floor above street level, this place specializes in oysters; its name, in fact, means oyster in German. In addition, it offers many kinds of fish, including some so rare you'll need an unabridged German dictionary to translate the names. Zur Austur has a list of faithful habitués who know many of the waiters—and who insist, for example, on the unique blend of ingredients that goes into the ragoût of squid. Oysters are prepared in about a dozen different ways. The restaurant is open from noon to midnight; closed Sun. and holidays. Meals cost from 55 DM ($32.65). You could spend far more, of course, by ordering the most expensive shellfish platters. Reservations are always necessary.

Budget Restaurants with Atmosphere

On the original site of the famous Gatzweilers Alt brewery is **Zum Schlüssel,** Gatsweilers beer hall, Bolkerstrasse 43-47 (tel. 0211/32-61-55). The decor is that of a classic German Gasthaus, with an abundance of wood, ceramics, and pictures, capturing the aura of a country inn. The service, proffered by courteous, shirtsleeved waiters, is swift. The food has both aroma and taste, and there's plenty to eat. Try the Eisbein (pigs' knuckles) or a huge bowl of soup. This establishment is as Germanic as the Rhine. Set lunches, running from 15 DM ($8.90) to 30 DM ($17.80), are featured. Actually, there are more than 30 meals from which to choose. If you want only to drink, there's a side bar. Try a quarter of a liter of the house beer, Gatzweilers Alt. The place is open daily from 10am to 11pm, with hot food being served only from 11am to 10pm.

Im Alten Bierhaus, Alt-Niederkassel 75 (tel. 0211/55-12-72), is on the outskirts. The centuries-old look of this guesthouse dates from 1641, when much of the place was built. Connoisseurs of German handcrafts will recognize the style of the Rhine's left bank (as opposed to the right). Typical German specialties, many of them sautéed, are served here, where meals cost about 25 DM ($14.85). This is actually more a Weinstube than a restaurant. Open from 3pm to 11pm; closed Mon. Also closed for four weeks in summer. On Sun., however, the beer drinkers pile in at 11am.

When you tire of Germanic cookery, **Zum Csikos,** Andreastrasse 9 (tel. 0211/32-97-71), makes a refreshing change of pace with its Hungarian cuisine and music, and a name that translates as "Hungarian cowboy." The structure dates from 1697. This charming place is arranged on three different levels; candlelight gives the place (and the diners) a mellow glow. The home-style Hungarian food is well prepared and the portions are hefty. The beef Gulasch is excellent, as is the chopped liver. Only dinner is served, costing from 35 DM ($20.80). The restaurant is open daily from 6pm to 3am, following the Hungarian tradition of late-late closing. It shuts down in July. Always call ahead for a reservation, as it's likely to be crowded on certain nights.

THE SIGHTS

If you walk up the Kö toward the triton fountain at the northern end of the canal, you'll reach the **Hofgarten,** a huge, rambling park. You could wander along the walks or just sit and relax for hours amid shade trees, gardens, fountains, and statues, almost forgetting you're in the very center of the city. Among the monuments is one to Düsseldorf's favorite son, the poet Heinrich Heine. The Hofgarten is a good central point for seeing the city's major attractions. Nearly all the museums and cultural attractions are on the perimeter of the park.

Kunstsammlung Nordrhein-Westfalen, Grabbeplatz 5 (tel. 0211/13-39-61), opposite the Kunsthalle, has an outstanding collection of modern art, including works by Picasso, Braque, Juan Gris, Fernand Léger, Max Ernst, Salvador Dali, René Magritte, Joan Miró, Kirchner, Kandinsky, Chagall, Jackson Pollock, Mark Tobey, Robert Rauschenberg, Roy Lichtenstein, Andy Warhol, Frank Stella, and others, plus a big collection of works by Julius Bissier. The museum also has 94 works by Paul Klee—so many, in fact, that the Klee exhibition is rotated at regular intervals since all the works cannot be shown at the same time. Furthermore, there are about six temporary exhibitions of contemporary art in the large exhibition hall every year. The museum is open from 10am to 6pm; closed Mon. Admission is 5 DM ($2.95) for adults, 3 DM ($1.80) for children.

Goethe-Museum Düsseldorf, Schloss-Jägerhof, Jacobistrasse 2 (tel. 0211/ 899-62-62), housed in the 18th-century Jägerhof Castle at the Hofgarten, near the city, sponsored by the Anton and Katharina Kippenberg Foundation, is a literary museum dedicated to the memory of Goethe's life and work. It emerged from the Kippenbergs' private collection of Goetheana containing some 35,000 items, consisting of autographs, books, busts, paintings, coins, medals, plaques, and china, among other objects. Anton Kippenberg, the owner and managing director of the Insel publishing house in Leipzig from 1904 to 1945, began collecting Goethe memorabilia when he was a young bookseller. About a thousand pieces of his collection are shown in the permanent exhibition, including the first draft of Goethe's poem "Noble Be Man"; a special copy of the fifth *Roman Elegy,* which Goethe sent to his friend Jacobi from Düsseldorf; the love poem "Ginkgo Biloba" from *The Divan;* and the world-famous "Chorus Mysticus" from *Faust II.* The displays present a chronology of Goethe's life and work. There are also exhibits on certain topics of the Goethe era. The museum is open Tues. to Fri. from 11am to 5pm, Sat. from 1pm to 5pm; and Sun. from 11am to 5pm; closed Mon. Admission is 2 DM ($1.20) for adults, 1 DM (60¢) for children.

Kunstmuseum Düsseldorf, Ehrenhof 5 (tel. 0211/899-24-60), is one of the largest and most comprehensive museums in the Rhineland. The museum is famous for its collection of paintings (Rubens, Caspar David Friedrich, Brücke, the Blue Rider school) and sculpture from the late Middle Ages to the 20th century, and for its print room with a collection of Italian drawings. There are also early Persian bronzes and ceramics, textiles from late antiquity to the present, a glass collection with a strong showing of art nouveau, Jugendstil, and art deco items. The museum is open from 11am to 6pm; closed Mon. Admission is 5 DM ($2.95).

Heinrich-Heine-Institut, Bilker Strasse 14 (tel. 0211/89-95-71), has more than 4,000 volumes as well as the manuscript bequest of this Düsseldorf-born poet (1797–1856). One of Germany's greatest lyric poets, he is the author of the famous "Die Lorelei." Many of his lyrics were set to music, notably by Schubert and Hugo Wolf. He also wrote satires that were pointed criticisms of the society of his time, as well as travel sketches, *Reisebilder.* Born into a Jewish family, he nominally converted to Christianity so that he could attend law school. His work was prohibited during the Nazi era, and "Die Lorelei" officially attributed to an unknown author. The institute is open to the public Tues. to Sun. from 1 to 5pm, charging 2 DM ($1.20) for admission. In the Altstadt you can visit the house where the poet was born. It's at Bolkerstrasse 5 and is marked by a plaque.

TOURS

Rhine boats leave from the Rathausufer, on the periphery of Altstadt. As the most interesting jaunt, I recommend a trip to **Zons,** the only place on the lower Rhine that is still completely surrounded by walls and city towers, as in olden days. You can walk the ramparts, take in a tower or a windmill, and immerse yourself in a place that has been called the Rhenish Rothenburg.

Vessels depart only from April to September, Mon. to Sat. between 11am and 5pm, every hour on the hour, from a section of town called Benrath. The company's headquarters is in Zons (tel. 02106/4-21-49), and it will provide last-minute sailing schedules before your actual trip.

If time remains, I suggest a 12-minute S-Bahn train ride south of Düsseldorf to **Benrath Castle,** Benrather Schlossallee 104 (tel. 0211/899-61-72). A late baroque pleasure palace situated in a park, the castle and its original environment have been preserved unaltered. Planned and built between 1755 and 1770 by Nicholas de Pigage for Eleanor Palatine Carl Theodor, the château holds collections of precious marquetry furniture and Frankenthal porcelain. Visitors can also explore the park with its mirror lake and the English- and French-style gardens. Visiting hours are 10am to 5pm, with guided tours every 30 minutes; closed Mon. Admission is 2 DM ($1.20).

AFTER DARK

The place to go is the Altstadt. Between Königsallee and the Rhine River, this half square mile of narrow streets and alleyways is jam-packed with restaurants, discos, art galleries, boutiques, nightclubs, restaurants, and some 200 song-filled beer taverns. If Düsseldorfers are going to spend a night cruising the old town, they refer to the experience as *Altstadtbummel.*

Nightlife

A lot of beer is drunk every night in the Altstadt, and my favorite place is **Uerige Brauerei,** Bergerstrasse 1 (tel. 0211/84-455), with half a dozen hearty drinking rooms, often filled with young people. Nearly 10,000 mugs of Uerige are tossed across the counter every day. This unique beer can be purchased only at this brewery-operated tavern, and it costs 2.50 DM ($1.50) for a quarter liter. They also serve apple cider and food. The place is open from 10am to midnight except for four days a year, usually religious holidays.

In the other dozens of taverns, you can sample the leading beers of the city. I especially recommend that you try Schlösser and Frankenheim, two personal favorites.

Often, instead of going to a restaurant and spending a lot of marks, you can put together a decent meal right on the street (especially Flingerstrasse and Bölkerstrasse). Reibekuchen is a tasty potato pancake popular with Düsseldorfers. It's very fattening, filling, and good, and always inexpensive. Most Americans shun Blutwurst, a black (blood) pudding accompanied by raw onions. However, Bratwurst with one of those savory German mustards is delectable, as is Spanferkel Brötchen, a hefty slice of tender roast suckling pig, served on rye bread. In the winter, mussels are offered at several little *intime* restaurants (where you stand up to eat); sometimes they've been cooked in a Rhine-wine sauce.

On the nightlife circuit, **The Irish Pub** (also called Bei Fatty), Hunsrücken-strasse 13 (tel. 0211/13-31-81), is a sentimental favorite, housed in a building dating from 1648. Nowadays the alley out front is bombarded by disco music from every door, but this place tenaciously holds on to its Irish pub atmosphere, with the owner and most of the staff being Irish born and bred. It's a haven for anyone looking for the Bohemian auld lang syne of Düsseldorf artists, who made this their traditional dining and drinking spot. Artist-guests have contributed the paintings on the walls, and the decor is cluttered and charming, with gingham cloths, copper kettles and pots, and frosted lights shining softly on pewter plates. At a horseshoe-shaped bar, you can drink up, ordering anything from good beer to Irish coffee. A pint of Guinness costs 4.80 DM ($2.85). Hours are Mon. to Sat., 2:30pm to 3am; Sun., noon to 3am. There's often live entertainment.

Bei Tino, Königsallee (tel. 0211/32-64-63), in the heart of Düsseldorf, is the most preferred piano bar. The action spills out onto sidewalk tables in summer. It is open daily from noon to 3am, charging 8.50 DM ($5.05) for a drink.

Jerome's, Königsallee 60 (tel. 0211/32-85-64), is one of the best-liked cocktail bars in town and often fills up with a convivial crowd. The entrance is in the Kö-Galerie on Grunstrasse. Drinks cost from 8.50 DM ($5.05). Hours are 6pm to 1am Sun. to Fri., and Sat. from 10pm to 1am.

For the posh side of Düsseldorf nightlife, try some of the hotels, already described.

Cultural Entertainment

Deutsche Oper am Rhein, Heinrich-Heine-Allee 16a, is rated as one of the outstanding opera companies in Europe. The season usually closes the last week in June, reopening again by about mid-September. Telephone 0211/8-90-81 for more information.

You might also want to hear a concert by the **Düsseldorf Symphony Orches-**

tra, which performs in the Tonhalle, Ehrenhof 1 (tel. 0211/8-99-62). This first-class orchestra, among the top dozen or so in Germany, usually sells out.

There are also many cinemas in Düsseldorf. All foreign films are dubbed in German. Evening performances start at 8 or 8:30pm.

---

6. Koblenz

Just 55 miles southeast of Cologne, Koblenz has stood at the confluence of the Rhine and Mosel rivers for more than 2,000 years. Its strategic point in the mid-Rhine region has made the city a vital link in the international river trade routes of Europe. Visitors often find themselves here at either the start or finish of a steamer excursion through the Rhine Valley. Right in the heart of the wine country, Koblenz is surrounded by vine-covered hills dotted with castles and fortresses.

The town was heavily bombed during World War II, but many of the historic buildings have been restored. For the best overall view of the town, go to the point where the two rivers meet. This is called **Deutsches Eck** (corner of Germany). From the top of the base where a huge statue of Wilhelm I once stood, you can see the old town and across the Rhine to the Ehrenbreitstein Fortress.

The focal point of the old town is the **Liebfrauenkirche** (Church of Our Lady), a 13th-century Gothic basilica built on a Romanesque foundation. Of interest are the onion-shaped spires on the top of the church's twin towers. The early 18th-century **Rathaus** was formerly a Jesuit college. In the courtyard behind the hall is a fountain dedicated to the youth of Koblenz called *The Spitting Boy,* and that's just what he does. At the edge of the old town, near the Deutsches Eck, is Koblenz's oldest and most attractive church, **St. Castor's,** dating from 836. This twin-towered Romanesque basilica was the site of the Treaty of Verdun in the ninth century, dividing Charlemagne's empire.

The **Ehrenbreitstein Fortress,** across the Rhine from Koblenz, can be reached by chair lift, but if you have a fear of heights, you can drive via the Pfaffendorfer Bridge just south of the old town. The fortress was built on a rock, towering 400 feet above the Rhine. The present walls were built in the 19th century by the Prussians, on the site of the 10th-century fortress of the archbishops of Trier. It was the headquarters of the American Occupation Army following World War I. From the stone terrace you can see for miles up and down the Rhine, a view that includes not only Koblenz, but also several castles along the Rhine and the terraced vineyards of the region.

WHERE TO STAY

Expensive Hotels

Modern, glittering, and stylish, the **Scandic Crown Hotel,** Julius-Wegeler-Strasse 6, D-5400 Koblenz (tel. 0261/13-60), a Swedish-owned hotel, sits on a hillock at the edge of the Rhine. Opened in 1986, it easily qualifies as the newest, best, and most dramatic hotel in town. Its streamlined architecture is in contrast to the century-old trees and the ancient stones of the medieval town surrounding it. On the premises are two elegant restaurants, the more formal of which is reviewed separately. The hotel offers 167 comfortably furnished and well-insulated bedrooms, each with private bath, radio, air conditioning, and color TV with video, along with a minibar. Singles cost 190 DM ($112.80) daily, doubles 250 DM ($148.45), including a buffet breakfast, taxes, and service. On the premises is a Swedish sauna as well as a solarium and hot whirlpool. One of the city's loveliest riverside promenades lies just a short walk away.

Diehls, Am Rhein, Ehrenbreitstein, D-5400 Koblenz (tel. 0261/7-20-10), is right on the banks of the Rhine across the river from the town. All of its public rooms, lounges, dining rooms, and 68 bedrooms face the river directly. You can watch the sun set on the water from your bedroom. It's an old-style hotel, which often accommodates groups. Rooms are well furnished and contain color TVs; all have either private baths or showers and toilets. Another advantage, besides the magnificent views, is the sliding scale of room prices. Singles with showers or baths go for 90 DM ($53.45) to 148 DM ($87.90) daily. Doubles with showers or private baths range in price from 140 DM ($83.15) to 230 DM ($136.55). Tariffs quoted include a Continental breakfast, but for another 15 marks you'll be served either lunch or dinner.

Hotel Brenner, Rizzastrasse 20-22, D-5400 Koblenz (tel. 0261/3-20-60), close to the Kurfürstl Schloss (castle), and about five city blocks from either the Rhine or the Mosel, is a leading contender for top honors in Koblenz. The 25-room hotel might vaguely remind you of the famed institution of Baden-Baden with the same name. The owners offer four floors of gilt detailing on white walls, with lots of little tables and chairs. Everything looks Louis XIV. The garden retreat is a nice place in which to get back to nature. A single with shower or bath ranges from 100 DM ($59.40) to 145 DM ($86.10) daily, and a double costs 175 DM ($103.40) to 240 DM ($142.50). These tariffs include breakfast, service, and taxes. Each room has remote-control cable TV.

Moderately Priced Hotels

One of the few city hotels on the banks of the Rhine is the **Kleiner Riesen,** Rheinanlagen 18, D-5400 Koblenz (tel. 0261/3-20-77). In fact, its dining room terrace and most of its 27 bedrooms are close enough for waving at the boats as they go by. The hotel is a large, overgrown chalet, informal, with several living rooms and comfortable, clean bedrooms. A double with bath costs 150 DM ($89.05) daily; a single with bath, 80 DM ($47.50) to 100 DM ($59.40). Nicely situated away from the town traffic, it has a peaceful small-town quietness.

Hotel Höhmann, Bahnhofplatz 5, D-5400 Koblenz (tel. 0261/3-50-11), stands across from the main railway station, a symmetrical structure recently renovated inside and out. Travelers in the Mosel and Rhine regions stay in 41 rooms with comfortable beds, color TVs, baths or showers, toilets, and phones. Singles rent for 75 DM ($44.55) to 100 DM ($59.40) daily and doubles for 135 DM ($80.15) to 155 DM ($92.05). A family room sleeping four persons costs 185 DM ($109.85). All tariffs include a buffet breakfast, service, and taxes. Parking is provided for guests, and the hotel has an elevator. English is spoken here.

Budget Hotels

Trierer Hof, Dienhardplatz 1, D-5400 Koblenz (tel. 0261/3-10-60), a private hotel built in 1786 and converted into a Gasthof as early as 1789, was considered "revolutionary" at the time of its conversion. It is behind the Schloss in the midst of gardens and only a quarter of a mile from the Deutsches Eck, where the Rhine meets the Mosel. Most of the bedrooms and lounges are overscale, and the furnishings are simple and most adequate. Singles rent for 75 DM ($44.55) to 95 DM ($56.40) daily, and doubles cost 125 DM ($74.25) to 160 DM ($95); breakfast is included. On the premises is an independently run restaurant, Buffalo, an Argentine steakhouse.

Hotel Christ, Schützenstrasse 32, D-5400 Koblenz (tel. 0261/3-77-02), is a modest little inn that has been run by the same family for 60 years. Today Maria

Müller is in charge, and she does a fine job of offering homelike comfort. Life here is informal. Rooms are simple, clean, and comfortable. Singles cost 30 DM ($17.80) daily, doubles 60 DM ($35.65), including breakfast. The hotel rents three singles and six doubles, each with hot and cold running water. The showers and toilets are in the hallways.

Hotel Hamm, St.-Josef-Strasse 32, D-5400 Koblenz (tel. 0261/3-45-46), is a cozy, informal 29-room hotel run by the English-speaking Volker-Dick family. The public rooms are modern and the bedrooms comfortable. A single, depending on the plumbing, ranges from 70 DM ($41.55) to 85 DM ($50.45) daily, a double with shower or bath costing 120 DM ($71.25) to 145 DM ($86.10), all prices including a buffet breakfast. The Hamm lies near the railway station, a five-minute walk from the Rhine. It is closed from mid-December to mid-January.

Hotel Scholz, Moselweisserstrasse 121, D-5400 Koblenz (tel. 0261/40-80-21), is a personally run family hotel that has been under the same management for half a century. Only a five-minute bus ride from the town center, it offers 62 sparsely furnished units that contain showers, toilets, TVs, and phones. It makes for a comfortable, reasonably priced overnight stopover: singles rent for 70 DM ($41.55) daily, and doubles go for 120 DM ($71.25). Breakfast is also included.

Hotel Victoria, Stegemannstrasse 25, D-5400 Koblenz (tel. 0261/3-30-27), is set in the middle of the city within a three-story building dating from the 1960s. This is a clean and decent hotel without pretensions, each of its 27 bedrooms containing a private bath, toilet, and phone. There is an elevator on the premises. With breakfast included, singles range from 65 DM ($38.60) to 95 DM ($56.40) daily, with doubles costing 120 DM ($71.25) to 160 DM ($95). No meals other than breakfast are served, but a restaurant recommended by the hotel lies just two doors away.

WHERE TO DINE

In the previously recommended Scandic Crown Hotel, **Le Gourmet,** Julius-Wegeler-Strasse 6 (tel. 0261/13-60), is elegantly modern in both design and flavor, very much a statement of Scandinavia. It is also considered one of the leading restaurants of Koblenz. You dine on a wide flower-trimmed terrace in summer or else inside in a Nordic ambience of pastel colors and polished wood. Meals, served daily from noon to 3pm and 6 to 11pm, cost from 68 DM ($40.40). Typical dishes are beef filet, grilled veal steak, fresh herring from Holland, marinated salmon or fresh shrimp from a cold deli case, or sole strips in Riesling with truffles and carrot purée. Desserts are served from a well-stocked trolley.

Weinhaus Hubertus, Florinsmarkt 54 (tel. 0261/3-11-77), across from the Old Rathaus Museum, offers good meals in the old town. Dating from 1696, it looks like a timbered country inn, with boxes of red geraniums at the windows. The furnishings and the decor of the rooms are family style, providing a homelike atmosphere. It is the oldest wine tavern in town and offers you a choice of 100 wines, of which 30 can be served by the glass. The wine is accompanied by a choice of homemade dishes, beginning at 6.50 DM ($3.85) Meals cost from 15 DM ($8.90). The place is open from 4 to 11pm; closed Tues.

WINE TASTING

At the foot of the Pfaffendorfer Bridge, **Weindorf,** Julius-Wegeler-Strasse (tel. 0261/3-16-80), right on the Rhine, is the center for tasting the wines of the vineyards of the Mosel and Rhine regions. It's a timbered wine village where everyone gathers on festive evenings. In fair weather you'll prefer to do your sampling in the open beer garden or on the river-view terrace. Let someone else do the driving afterward. Meals, costing from 25 DM ($14.85), feature a hearty German cuisine, including such dishes as pork filet in a mushroom cream sauce and Sauerbraten. Perhaps you'd prefer something more continental—perhaps a rumpsteak Café de Paris. Weindorf is open daily from 10am to 2am. Live music is presented after 7pm.

A SIDE TRIP TO HÖHR-GRENZHAUSEN

Just 12 miles from Koblenz, in the Westerwald, lies this little town where pottery has been produced since the 16th century. The gray-bodied, salt-glazed ceramics for which the town is known are still hand-molded and some are fired in woodburning kilns, although most of the potters have changed to gas fires. The salt glazing of the products results in a strong, shiny finish on the pots and other items made here. To reach Höhr-Grenzhausen, take the no. 8 bus from Koblenz and change at Vallendar to the no. 7A bus.

At the **Keramik-Museum Westerwald,** Lindenstrasse 131 (tel. 02624/36-66), you can see examples of local pottery from the Roman era and the Middle Ages to the present day, as well as a display of ceramics made all over the world. The processing of the gray Westerwald clay and the glazing work are shown. The museum is open from 10am to 5pm; closed Mon. Admission is 3 DM ($1.80) for adults, 1 DM (60¢) for children, and 6 DM ($3.55) for families. Guided tours are given only in German, but some members of the museum staff can answer questions in English.

If you're here just for the day, a fine place to have lunch is the museum restaurant, where good, simple food is served on local ceramic dishes. For less than 15 DM ($8.90), you can have an assortment of cheese, sausages, and Westphalian ham, with black bread. The restaurant is open from 10am to 7pm; closed Mon.

The shops of several of the potters can be visited. Some follow time-honored methods of molding and firing, others make use of innovative processes and colors. **Otto Blum's,** Hermann-Geisenstrasse 64 (tel. 02624/71-63), is the only place where you can see a woodburning kiln still in use. The shop is open Mon. to Thurs. from 9am to noon and 1 to 5pm, on Fri. from 9am to noon. There are no guided tours except for groups that have made prior arrangements, but if you're there at the right time, no one seems to object if you tag along with a group.

Mühlendycks, Lindenstrasse 39 (tel. 02624/24-53), is open Mon. to Fri., 8 to 11:45am and 1 to 4:45pm; Sat., 9:30am to 2:30pm. You'll find many gift items here, and they'll ship things home for you.

Where to Stay and Dine

Kurhotel Heinz, Bergstrasse 77, D-5410 Hörh-Grenzhausen (tel. 02624/30-33). From certain perspectives the five stories of bay windows, terraces, balconies, and loggias make this 60-room hotel look almost like the stern of an ocean liner. The ensemble is capped by a red-tile roof whose many embellishments were completed around 1920. Peace and quiet are encouraged in this comfortable hotel with an adjacent spa facility. A buffet breakfast is included in the day rates of 65 DM ($38.60) to 115 DM ($68.30) for a single and 110 DM ($65.30) to 210 DM ($124.70) for a double, depending on the accommodation and the season. Most rooms have TVs, refrigerators, and private balconies. There are two restaurants on the premises, ranging in style from a country inn to a more formal dining room splashed with sunlight from the soaring windows. Meals cost 30 DM ($17.80) to 60 DM ($35.65). The apéritif bar serves drinks throughout the day.

A SIDE TRIP TO OBERWESEL

Hardly known to the average North American visitor, Oberwesel is a small village on the Rhine's left bank, about 26 miles south from Koblenz, or 45 minutes by train from Frankfurt. You can cross on the ferry at Kaub to Oberwesel. The town, dominated by Burg Schönburg, still boasts 18 watchtowers. While in the area, try to visit **Liebfrauenkirche** (Church of Our Lady), lying to the south of the village. The reddish church is Gothic, and is known for its altarpieces, including one from 1506, dedicated to St. Nicholas.

Where to Stay and Dine

Auf Schönburg, D-6532 Oberwesel (tel. 06744/70-27), is a 1,000-year-old castle where Wolfgang and Barbara Hüttl have restored rooms in the "romantik" German style and now shelter and feed paying guests. They have 19 double and three single rooms, all with baths or showers and toilets. A single rents for 85 DM ($50.45) to 200 DM ($118.75) daily, and a double goes for 135 DM ($80.15) to 260 DM ($154.40). Guests can relax, read, even enjoy coffee, tea, or a glass of wine in a small sitting room/library.

Three small restaurants seat about 30 diners each (closed on Mon.). The food is innovative and good, including such dishes as "pepper soup" (made with pink peppercorns) and a fresh soup of white mushrooms. Main dishes are likely to include veal steak flavored with whisky, or fresh salmon in a saffron sauce. For dessert you'll perhaps have plum sherbet with plum brandy. Their special before-dinner drink is a house cocktail, "Schönburg," which consists of four different liqueurs, campari, and lemon juice, filled with a dry Riesling Sekt. In addition to the à la carte menu, they offer two gourmet menus changing weekly, depending on what's fresh at the market. Five courses cost 50 DM ($29.70), and the seven-course repast goes for 89 DM ($52.85). Even if you don't stay here, you can stop in throughout the day, for breakfast, lunch, afternoon tea or coffee, or dinner. Lunch is served daily from noon to 2pm and dinner from 6:30 to 9pm. The Burghotel shuts down from December 1 to March 1.

A SIDE TRIP TO BACHARACH

From Koblenz, a journey of 31 miles will take you to the small town of Bacharach, that old wine town on the Rhine that still looks as if it basks in medieval romanticism. It's surrounded by vine slopes and steep slate rocks set against a backdrop of the typical Rhineland landscape. A highway bypass keeps all the unwelcome traffic noises away, and once inside the walls of Bacharach you can almost forget the 20th century.

The town is ideally situated for Rhine steamer excursions, as well as daily excursions by train with frequent departures to Koblenz, Mainz, and Wiesbaden. The Rhine trip from Koblenz is one of the most famous sections in the valley, known for its castles and the Lorelei Rock. Often visitors find that even in the height of the season they don't have to fight the crowds if they venture into Bacharach.

If you're driving, park your car outside the ramparts near the river and across from the landing dock. Bacharach is approached through a gateway, and it blooms best at a square known simply as the **Markt.** Here you'll see a fine collection of old houses built in the half-timbered style. You might also seek out the **Peterskirche,** which is open daily in season from 9am to 6pm (sometimes it closes earlier). Its Romanesque nave was one of the last known to have been erected in the country. Before leaving Bacharach, head for the antique fortress, **Burg Stahleck,** with its belvedere tower, which offers a panoramic sweep of the Rhine Valley.

Where to Stay and Dine

All accommodations in Bacharach are appropriately modest. The best is the **Altkölnischer Hof,** Blücherstrasse 2, D-6533 Bacharach (tel. 06743/13-39), a comfortable 22-room establishment in a picturesque half-timbered house. The kitchen is first-rate, and you may want to sample more than one bottle in the old Weinstube. You might also request Bitburger beer. The modestly furnished guest rooms are clean and reasonably priced, costing 50 DM ($29.70) to 70 DM ($41.55) daily for a single, 80 DM ($47.50) to 95 DM ($56.40) for a double. Of course, you'll want to take your meals here, with meals beginning at 28 DM ($16.65) and rising to 55 DM ($32.65) if you decide to get really extravagant. On Sat., music is played for dancing. The hotel is open from April to October.

---

7. Mainz

A 2,000-year-old city, once a powerful Episcopal see, Mainz had its origin in prehistoric times on the left bank of the Rhine across from the point where the Main River adds its waters to those of the great river of Germany. It is thought today that there may have been wine-producing vines in the area before the coming of the Romans in 38 B.C., although it was from that time that the regions of the Rheingau and Rheinhessen became widely known for fine viticulture. Mainz has retained its position as the wine center, with one of its top festive occasions being the annual Wine Fair in August and September of each year.

At the beginning of the Christian era, the settlement on the Rhine's left bank and the Roman fortifications opposite were connected by a bridge. Christianity came early to Mainz, which in the 8th century became a primary archbishopric. By the 15th century, church politics grew into a war between two rival archbishops. The city later became a military center, and target in several conflicts, being sometimes ruled by France (and called Mayence), sometimes by German states. Because of all these drastic changes (it was occupied by Allied troops after World War I, heavily bombed in World War II), Mainz never became the great commerce center its location would seem to assure. However, the Rhenish wine traffic and other trade activities have given it prosperity.

In festive Mainz, the most celebrated merrymaking is at the All Fools capers at Carnival each spring, broadcast throughout Germany like an annual Macy's parade. In June each year, the Gutenberg Festival sponsors a cultural season, a living memorial to the city's favorite son, the inventor of the movable-type printing press.

The city of Mainz sprawls over a large district, but the only part that interests most visitors is the old town, which is relatively compact and can be covered on foot. The heart of town is Marktplatz, which is dominated by the majestic Dom, or cathedral, and the sister square, Liebfrauen-Platz. From here you can branch out to explore satellite streets, which are about all that is left of the old town following heavy aerial bombardment. The most interesting streets and squares include Gutenbergplatz, Augustinerstrasse, Schillerplatz, and Ludwigsstrasse. Head east from the old town to reach the convention and concert center, the Rheingoldhalle. This area is also the home of the Hilton Hotel and the contemporary Rathaus, and is the departure point for vessels cruising the Rhine.

The Frankfurt Main International Airport is a 20-minute taxi ride from the center of the city.

WHERE TO STAY

Many people visit Mainz on a day trip from Frankfurt, 25 miles away. If you plan to stay over, however, be advised that reservations are needed during the spring and autumn festival seasons.

A Deluxe Hotel

Mainz Hilton, Rheinstrasse 68, D-6500 Mainz (tel. 06131/24-50 or toll free in the U.S. at 800/445-8667), is one of the most imaginatively designed and strikingly modern hotels in Germany, and certainly one of the most alluring along the Rhine Valley. It occupies two desirable plots of land near the center of town, a five-minute walk from the cathedral. Sheathed in reflective mirrors and soaring spans of steel, the hotel's twin sections are connected with a glass-sided covered walkway spanning the traffic below. There are enough bars, restaurants, nightlife possibilities, and health club facilities to amuse one for a week. Within each of its soaring yet still intimate meeting points, the hotel provides a lavish and elegant charm that is not lost on its up-market clientele. Within the labyrinthine interior are sun-flooded atriums with live plants, piano bars encrusted with polished mahogany and brass, and acres of marble flooring, along with 435 of the most plushly decorated bedrooms in the region. Depending on the size, singles range from 240 DM ($142.50) to 420 DM ($249.40) daily, doubles from 290 DM ($172.20) to 470 DM ($279.10). Children stay free in their parents' room. Each of the accommodations contains air conditioning, a minibar, color TV, direct-dial phone, fully equipped bath, and radio.

The Rheingrill restaurant, overlooking the flowing waters of its namesake, is a fine dining place. However, many visitors prefer either the French-inspired Bistro or, my personal favorite, the rustic Römische Weinstube. At night, one of the bars becomes a disco, open until very late. Jet lag can be worked off in the in-house sauna or in the carefully supervised health and exercise club.

Expensive Hotels
Hotel Mainzer Hof, Kaiserstrasse 98, D-6500 Mainz (tel. 06131/23-37-71), is six floors of modernity directly on the Rhine, almost at the point where some of the boats dock. It's a clean-cut, convenient stopover hotel on your journey down the Rhine. The 99 rooms were completely renovated in 1987 and equipped with showers or baths, direct-dial phones, TVs, radios, and minibars. The rate is 149 DM ($88.50) to 240 DM ($142.50) for a single, 190 DM ($112.80) to 380 DM ($225.65) for a double, breakfast included. The hotel has a restaurant open from 4pm to midnight.

Hotel Kurmainz, Flugplatzstrasse 44, D-6500 Mainz-Finthen (tel. 06131-491-0), is a modern 84-room hotel lying in the midst of orchards in the Rhine Valley, convenient for access to the nearby cities of Frankfurt and Wiesbaden, and only 15 minutes from the Frankfurt airport. The atmosphere is inviting; the bar has an open fireplace, and the atrium garden has a brook, pond, and exotic plants. Accommodations are comfortable, equipped with showers or baths, cable color TVs, direct-dial phones, minibars, and radios, as well as personal safes and hairdryers. Rates range from 125 DM ($74.25) to 185 DM ($109.85) daily for a single and from 160 DM ($95) to 300 DM ($178.15) for a double. The hotel also has a dinner restaurant. A wide range of sports facilities is available, including an indoor pool, sauna, steam bath, fitness center, and tennis court.

Moderately Priced Hotels
Europahotel, Kaiserstrasse 7, D-6500 Mainz (tel. 06131/63-50), is in the center near the railway station, its bright lights making it easy to find. Its bar and restaurants, as well as the Corona Classic Club, serve as attractive meeting places. The hotel offers 93 bedrooms, and you'll find all the up-to-date amenities here you're likely to need, including color TVs, videos, and phones. A single room ranges in price from 135 DM ($80.15) to 245 DM ($145.50) daily, a double from 262 DM ($155.60) to 362 DM ($214.95).

Hammer, Bahnhofplatz 6, D-6500 Mainz (tel. 06131/61-10-61), has been completely renewed, with a comfortable lobby and a breakfast room. The furnishings are modern, and the reception is bright. The 40 rooms are comfortable and of good size, all accommodations coming with private showers or baths, toilets, hairdryers, radios, color TVs, and minibars. The rates are 105 DM ($62.35) to 120

DM ($71.25) daily for a single, 150 DM ($89.05) to 180 DM ($106.90) for a double or twin. A buffet breakfast, taxes, and service are included in the tariffs. The Hammer has a sauna.

Central Hotel Eden, Bahnhofsplatz 8, D-6500 Mainz (tel. 06131/67-40-01), is housed in a very grand building with reddish neoclassical pediments on many of its windows, plus two modern floors added on top of the four original ones. Mainzers are fond of the café-restaurant on the ground floor, L'échalote, which has some of the best food in the city. The 60 bedrooms are high-ceilinged and comfortably appointed. Because of the thickness of the walls and the soundproof windows, you've got a better chance to catch up on your sleep. Singles rent for 106 DM ($62.95) to 120 DM ($71.25) daily, and doubles cost 140 DM ($83.15) to 210 DM ($124.70).

Novotel Mainz-Süd, Essenheimerstrasse 200, D-6500 Mainz (tel. 06131/3610-54). Its 121 well-planned rooms and easy access to the highways surrounding Mainz make it one of the best values for motorists in the region. Modern, angular, and efficient, this French chain–owned hotel is filled almost to capacity every night with business or vacation travelers who appreciate Novotel's standardized comfort and no-nonsense formula. It lies 3 miles northeast of the city center, near the Mainz-Lerchenberg exit from the Frankfurt–Wiesbaden Autobahn. Each room contains a phone, color TV, radio, bath, and enough bed space for three occupants. Singles cost 140 DM ($83.15) to 155 DM ($92.05) daily, with doubles going for 175 DM ($103.90) to 185 DM ($109.85). A good restaurant serves meals throughout the day. If you land at night, look for the illuminated sign in the company's trademark blue color to help guide you in from the Autobahn.

Budget Hotels

Near the university grounds, **Hotel am Römerwall,** Am Römerwall 53, D-6500 Mainz (tel. 06131/23-21-35), is two villas, pleasantly positioned in a garden. Here the accent is on homelike comfort, as reflected in the public living room and breakfast salon (the only meal served, incidentally). Each of the 51 bedrooms is comfortably appointed, and many have all-white furnishings and bright, contrasting fabrics. The price of a room depends on whether or not you have a private bath. Singles range from 60 DM ($35.65) to 120 DM ($71.25) daily, doubles from 90 DM ($53.45) to 140 DM ($83.15). Breakfast is included in all tariffs.

Schottenhot, Schottstrasse 6, D-6500 Mainz (tel. 06131/23-29-68), is nice and modern with a warm atmosphere. Off a busy avenue, the 38-room hotel is located on a dead-end street that leads to the railway station and transit pedestrian plaza. The comfortable rooms (with phones and TVs) have somewhat dark furnishings. Windows have been soundproofed. Singles with showers or baths cost 98 DM ($58.20) to 118 DM ($70.05) daily, and doubles with the same plumbing go for 145 DM ($86.10) to 165 DM ($98). On the premises is a small bar, and breakfast is the only meal served.

Hotel Mira, Bonifaziusstrasse 4, D-6500 Mainz (tel. 06131/61-30-87). The delicate pink of the hotel's facade is repeated in the pink tiles in the bathrooms inside. If you like pink (and many psychologists think it has a calming effect), you'll love it here. The Mira beckons warmly to tourists from its location near the Hauptbahnhof. Alfred Kohl is your host, providing maps (if available) and lots of useful information. He rents 16 singles and 26 doubles, some with showers or baths. Direct-dial phones and TVs are found in all units, and there is elevator service. A single begins at 55 DM ($32.65) daily, going up to 98 DM ($58.20), and a double costs 94 DM ($55.80) to 150 DM ($89.05), including a Continental breakfast.

Richter Eisenbahn, Alicenstrasse 6, D-6500 Mainz (tel. 06131/23-40-77), close to the train station, looks more like a pension than a 25-bedroom hotel. Accommodations are comfortable, and the prices are a good bargain. Bathless singles rent for 55 DM ($32.65) daily, singles with showers and toilets costing 60 DM

($35.65). Doubles cost 80 DM ($47.50) without baths, 85 DM ($50.45) with showers, and 95 DM ($56.40) with showers and toilets. Breakfast is included in the rates.

WHERE TO DINE

A good place to have a meal is **Drei Lilien,** Ballplatz 2 (tel. 06131/22-50-68). Head chef H. J. Stuhlmiller practices a form of cuisine moderne that he has dubbed *cuisine du marché.* Everything is cooked here with imagination and concern. Some of the chef's recipes were developed (with some foresight) as a result of what was at hand that day at the greengrocers. The decor of this wood-beamed, chandeliered eatery could be called "graciously rustic," the linens are impeccable, and the service is deferential. Try the grilled steak with wild trumpet mushrooms in a cognac sauce with grape leaves, or a delicately poached baby turbot in mushroom sauce. Table d'hôte dinners are offered for 70 DM ($41.55) and 100 DM ($59.40). À la carte costs 40 DM ($23.75) to 60 DM ($35.65). Drei Lilien is open from 6 to 10:30pm; closed Sun.

L'échalote, Bahnhofsplatz 8 (tel. 06131/61-43-31), on the ground floor of the Central Hotel Eden, has a vivid awning in front, shading the big windows from the public square near the train station. The head chefs direct a large staff to produce both modern and classic dishes. The soups are a delight, everything from lamb consommé to saffron soup, followed by, say, fish, which is brought in twice a week from Rungis, the centralized food market of Paris. Try, for example, the sautéed breast of Bresse hen with tomato noodles and baby vegetables. Fixed-price meals range from 55 DM ($32.65) to 75 DM ($44.55). Hours are 5 to 11pm; closed Sun.

Restaurant Walderdorff, Karmeliterplatz 4 (tel. 06131/22-25-15). Both its clientele and its cuisine change between lunch and dinner. At lunch, a less formal, bistro menu is offered, including such dishes as spinach salad with crabmeat, lamb chops in peppermint sauce, and apple strudel for dessert. In the evening, however, lights are dimmed, the place looks more formal, and the sienna walls take on a sophisticated and subdued kind of allure. Meals cost 35 DM ($20.80) to 75 DM ($44.55). If you're interested, ask about special vegetarian dishes. Lunch is served from 12:15 to 3pm, dinner from 6:30pm to midnight, closed Sun. and holidays.

Gebert's Weinstuben, Frauenlobstrasse 94 (tel. 06131/61-16-19), is a traditional Weinstube, housed in one of the oldest buildings of Mainz, with a decor that is almost spartan when compared to the opulence of some of the city's other restaurants. But decor is not the reason people come here, and they patronize it in great numbers, so you'll have to call to reserve one of the dozen or so tables. Once seated, you are treated to a traditional meal of game, fish, or regional specialties such as goose à l'orange. Meals cost 40 DM ($23.75) to 65 DM ($38.60), and they're served from 11:30am to 2pm and 6 to 10pm; closed Sat., for lunch on Sun., and from mid-July to mid-August.

Zum Augustiner, Augustinerstrasse 8 (tel. 06131/23-17-37), was a popular beerhall before the imaginative entrepreneur, Michael Müller, took charge. Today, all of Mainz knows that its fish (trucked in from Rungis) and its French vegetables are among the best in town. Go here for such dishes as breast of Bresse hen—either in raspberry vinegar or flamed in cognac—or the pork filet in puff pastry. Herr Müller is a master of the classic cuisine as well, using lots of truffles, cream, and champagne, enough to make Escoffier proud. A meal will cost from 40 DM ($23.75), but chances are you'll spend far more. Save room for one of the tempting desserts or pastries, made fresh daily. Hours are for dinner only, served from 6pm till closing; closed Sun.

Zum Löwen, Mainzerstrasse 2 (tel. 06131/4-36-05), in Consenheim. There's plenty to see in this suburb of Mainz besides this restaurant, but for delicious dishes both regional and modern, it makes an attractive stopping place. Hans and Gisela Klapp work to bring the best gastronomy to your table, with lobster cooked in many different ways. Or you may be tempted by their seasoned mixture of salmon and turbot in puff pastry, or their filet of veal with wild mushrooms and fresh plums. Many of the specialties change so frequently they aren't even on the menu. Fixed-price menus cost from 115 DM ($68.30). À la carte meals cost from 70 DM ($41.55). Zum Löwen is open for lunch from noon to 2pm and for dinner from 6 to 10pm; closed Sun. evenings and Mon. The annual closing is a variable two weeks in summer.

Löschs Weinstube, Jakobsbergstrasse 9 (tel. 06131/22-03-83), is an old-fashioned Weinstube, popular with generations of Mainzers and rich in tradition. Meals, costing 10 DM ($5.95) to 25 DM ($14.85), offer both hot and cold dishes, plus lots of Rhine wine. The daily changing bill of fare offers regional dishes and interesting salads. There are only 12 tables, but they seat some 85 guests who can visit any time from 4pm to 1am daily. Now that the Jakobsbergstrasse has been changed into a pedestrian mall, the Weinstube places six additional tables out front in summer.

Haus des Deutschen Weines, Gutenbergplatz 3 (tel. 06131/22-86-76), is a good wine restaurant. The shields outside represent the German wine districts, and the cellar inside stocks the finest bottles from the Rheingau. An easy walk from the Dom and the Gutenberg Museum, the House of German Wines makes a fine dining choice. The cuisine is essentially modern international and "new German." Game is featured in season. You can spend from 55 DM ($32.65) to 65 DM ($38.60) if you partake of the set menus. À la carte meals range from 38 DM ($22.55) to 70 DM ($41.55). Because the restaurant is affiliated with both the city of Mainz and the German Wine Institute, you can find a cross section of wines from the 11 leading wine regions of Germany. Hours are from 11:30am to 3pm and 5pm to midnight; closed Sun. and holidays.

THE SIGHTS

Above the roofs of the half-timbered houses in the old section of town rise the six towers of **St. Martin's Cathedral,** the most important Catholic cathedral in the country after Cologne. The Romanesque basilica, dating from A.D. 975, has been constantly rebuilt and restored, until its present form, dating mainly from the 13th and 14th centuries. Below the largest dome, a combination of Romanesque and baroque, is the transept, separating the west chancel from the nave and smaller east chancel. Many of the supporting pillars along the aisles of the nave are decorated with carved and painted statues of French and German saints. A collection of religious art is housed in the cathedral's **Diocesan Museum,** Domstrasse 3 (tel. 06131/25-33-44). Within it are exhibitions of reliquaries and medieval sculpture, including works by the Master of Naumburg. In the 1,000-year-old cathedral crypt is a contemporary gold reliquary of the saints of Mainz. Among the most impressive furnishings in the sanctuary are the rococo choir stalls and a pewter baptismal font from the early 14th century. The museum is open 9am to noon and 2 to 5pm; closed Sun. Entrance is free.

Gutenberg Museum, Liebfrauenplatz 5 (tel. 06131/12-26-40), opposite the east towers of the cathedral, is a unique memorial to the city's favorite son. In the modern display rooms, visitors can trace the history of printing from Gutenberg's hand press, on which he printed the 42-lined Bible from 1452 to 1455, to the most advanced typesetting processes. The collections cover the entire spectrum of the graphic arts as well as book production and printing, illustration, and binding in all countries, past and present. The most popular exhibit is a Gutenberg Bible. The admission-free museum is open Tues. to Sat. from 10am to 6pm, Sun. from 10am to 1pm; closed Mon.

Landesmuseum Mainz (Provincial Museum of the Central Rhineland), Grosse Bleiche 49-51 (tel. 06131/23-29-55), is worth a visit to get a pictorial history of Mainz and the middle Rhine, from prehistoric times to the present. The most impressive exhibits are the Roman marble head of the Emperor Augustus (or his nephew, Gaius Caesar), about A.D. 14, and the towering Column of Jupiter, erected in Mainz by the Romans in A.D. 67. Although the original is in the museum, you may, if you are pressed for time, see the true-to-life replica in front of the Parliament building. Also of interest is the gallery of the museum with paintings from the 15th through the 20th centuries. The Lapidarium shows one of the most important collections of Roman monuments in Europe. The museum is open Tues. to Sun. from 10am to 5pm; Fri. from 10am to 4pm; closed Mon. Admission is free.

---

8. Worms

This ancient city traces its beginnings back to the earliest civilizations. Before the Romans settled here, Germanic tribes had made Worms their capital. Here Siegfried began his legendary adventures, recorded in *The Nibelungenlied.* The town's most famous visitor, Martin Luther, arrived under less desirable circumstances. He was "invited" to appear before the Imperial Diet at Worms, and after refusing to retract his grievances against the Church of Rome, he was excommunicated. Now that the majority of Worms is Protestant, it has erected a huge monument to Luther and other giants of the Reformation.

Worms also has one of the oldest Jewish communities in Germany, with a synagogue dating back to the 11th century. The Hebrew cemetery is interesting, with hundreds of tombstones, some going back more than 800 years.

Towering physically and historically above all the other ancient buildings of the city is the majestic **St. Peter's Cathedral,** Lutherring 9 (tel. 06241/61-15), considered the purest Romanesque basilica in the Rhine Valley. The east choir, with a flat facade and semicircular interior, is the oldest section, dating from 1110. This was designed as the sanctuary, where the clergy performed the rites of the divine service. Lavishly decorated in baroque style during the 18th century by the famous architect Balthasar Neumann, the chancel glows with the gold and marble of the pillared enclosure for the high altar. This opulent work was so large that there was no place for a proper transept. In Gothic times the choir stalls had stood in the apse, but later they were built into the transept. The interior has a quiet elegance, with little decoration other than the rosette window and several memorial slabs and monuments to the dead buried beneath the cathedral. Between these two extremes, which symbolize the coordination of ecclesiastical and secular power, is the nave. A new organ built like a bird's nest has been placed where an organ was situated until its destruction in 1689. Well worth seeing is the highly decorated 14th- or 15th-century side Chapel of St. Nicholas, with its Gothic baptismal font and new stained-glass windows. The cathedral is open for visitors daily in summer from 8am to 6pm; in winter from 9am to 5pm.

WHERE TO STAY

The newest and most luxuriously appointed place to stay in Worms is the **Nibelungen Hotel,** Martinsgasse 8-16, D-6520 Worms (tel. 06241/69-77), in the center of town. It offers modern comfort behind a yellow and mustard-colored facade. Each of its 46 rooms has a bath with shower or tub, radio, phone, and minibar. The price for a single is 100 DM ($59.40) to 120 DM ($71.25) daily, rising to 150 DM ($89.05) to 180 DM ($106.90) in a twin, including a buffet breakfast.

Dom-Hotel, Am Obermarkt 10, D-6520 Worms (tel. 06241/69-13), is an all-purpose hotel, about a block from the cathedral. It's a postwar structure, recently renovated, built in a complex of shops and boutiques. The glass-walled bedrooms have an assortment of contemporary furnishings, and they offer adequate comfort. All units contain baths or showers, phones, TVs, and radios. Singles range from 79 DM ($46.90) to 100 DM ($59.40) daily, and doubles go for 115 DM ($68.30) to 160 DM ($95). The guest lounge is a good place for relaxation. In the wood-paneled dining room, a breakfast buffet is spread out in the morning, and later on, a French cuisine is served. Altogether, it's an ideal little hotel for the in-and-out traveler.

Central Hotel Worms, Kammererstrasse 5, D-6520 Worms (tel. 06241/64-58), was completely renovated in 1988 and is now one of the best of the small hotels of the city. Innkeeper Agnes Labidi rents 20 comfortably furnished bedrooms in her family-run hotel, each with private bath. A single ranges in price from 72 DM ($42.75) to 80 DM ($47.50) daily, a double going for 110 DM ($65.30) to 120 DM ($71.25). A good breakfast, as well as taxes, is included in the tariffs. The reception staff speaks English, and the hotel has an ideal central location, within walking distance of all the major historical monuments.

WHERE TO DINE
Despite the rustic beams of the ceiling and the massive stonework of the fireplace, **Rôtisserie Dubs,** Kirchstrasse 6, at Rheindürkheim (tel. 06242/20-23), has a feeling of elegant lightness. The decalorized cuisine adds to that impression. After traveling through France, the owners decided to feature such dishes as salmon in a champagne marinade, or a delicately seasoned pike-and-cabbage soup. A fixed-price meal will cost 65 DM ($38.60) to 110 DM ($65.30), and à la carte meals begin at 55 DM ($32.65). Service is from 11:30am to 2pm and 6 to 11pm; closed Tues. and for Sat. lunch.

Far less expensive, **Le Bistro Leger,** Siegfriedstrasse 2 (tel. 06241/46-27-7), is a stylish, nostalgically decorated bistro with a regional cuisine and a middle-bracket price structure. An outdoor terrace is much favored in warm weather. Wolfgang Dub is the congenial owner, and his personality infuses the place with a relaxed charm. Fresh ingredients go into the food; try, for example, veal cutlets prepared in the style of the Rhineland, a fresh filet, oysters in season, or roast beef. The well-chosen wine list is mainly French. Meals cost from 22 DM ($13.05) to 52 DM ($30.90), and hot food is served from noon to 2pm and 6pm to midnight; closed Sun.

---

9. The Rheingau

When God was looking for a place to set up Paradise, so goes the story, He once considered the sunny slopes between the Taunus Mountains and the Rhine. Today the Rheingau is the kingdom of another god, Bacchus, who reigns supreme here. Nearly every town and village from Wiesbaden to Assmannshausen, no matter how small, is a major wine-producer. The names suddenly seem familiar—Bingen, Johannisberg, Rüdesheim, Oestrich—because we have seen them on the labels of many favorite wines.

The Rheingau is also rich in old churches and castles, as well as landmarks. The **Niederwald Monument,** on a hill halfway between Rüdesheim and Assmannshausen—it can be reached by cable car from either town—is a huge statue of Germania, erected by Bismarck in 1883 to commemorate the reunification of Germany. Below it, on a small island at the bend of the Rhine, is the infamous Mäuseturm (Mouse Tower), where, according to legend, the harsh bishop of Mainz was devoured by a swarm of hungry mice. But the real attraction of the Rheingau is the cheerful character of the wine villages and their people.

RÜDESHEIM
With its old courtyards and winding alleyways lined with timbered houses, Rüdesheim is the epitome of the Rhine wine towns. The vineyards around the village date back to the Roman emperor Probus. Besides the full-bodied Riesling, brandy and champagne (Sekt) are also produced here. Rüdesheim is the scene of the

annual August wine festival, when the old taverns on the narrow Drosselgasse are filled with jovial tasters from all over the world. To prove how seriously Rüdesheimers take their wines, they have opened a wine museum in Bromserburg Castle. The **Rheingau-und Weinmuseum,** charging 2.50 DM ($1.50) for admission, is open daily, May to November, from 9am to noon and 2 to 6pm. It traces the history of the grape and has an exhibition of wine presses, glasses, goblets, and drinking utensils dating from Roman times to the present.

Where to Stay and Dine

Rüdesheimer Hof, Geisenheimerstrasse 1, D-6220 Rüdesheim (tel. 06722/ 20-11), is a village inn set back from the Rhine, with a side garden and terrace where wine tasters gather at rustic tables. You can dine here and spend the night. Most of the accommodations are roomy and comfortably furnished; all 42 rooms have showers and baths. Singles cost 65 DM ($38.60) to 85 DM ($50.45) daily, and doubles go for 90 DM ($53.45) to 130 DM ($77.20). The atmosphere is informal, and staying here is like sampling the pulse of a Rhine village—seeing the townspeople mingling with visitors, eating the regional food, and drinking the Rheingau wines. The inn opens in mid-February, closing in mid-November. If you're stopping by just to eat, you'll find set meals from 22 DM ($13.05) to 55 DM ($32.65). Guests dine at café tables placed under a willow tree. Food is served from 11:30am to 9:30pm.

Zum Bären, Schmidtstrasse 24-31, D-6220 Rüdesheim (tel. 06722/10-91), is a well-run hotel presided over by Karl-Heinz Willig and his family. The Willigs offers 26 comfortably furnished bedrooms with private baths, direct-dial phones, and TVs (on request). With a breakfast buffet included, singles range from 58 DM ($34.45) to 100 DM ($59.40) daily, with doubles costing 90 DM ($53.45) to 150 DM ($89.05). Guests pay a daily 20-DM ($11.90) per-person supplement for half board, which, considering the quality of the food, is good value. The restaurant offers good Rhineland cooking. Guests enjoy sitting on the cozy terrace and seem to like the central location. Meals costing 12 DM ($7.15) are served from noon to 2pm and 6 to 10pm; closed Tues. The restaurant is closed November to April. The hotel has a sauna.

Gasthof Krancher, Eibinger-Oberstrasse 4, D-6220 Rüdesheim (tel. 06722/ 27-62), has been in the Krancher family for four generations. The location is about a 10-minute walk from the town center, next to the inn's own vineyards. Naturally, the Kranchers make their own wines, and they'll gladly show you the cellar where they store bottles that have won gold and silver medals. The cuisine is first-class, and certainly the wines are. Everything is decorated in a regional motif. The two-building complex contains 100 beds. The cost is 40 DM ($23.75) to 50 DM ($29.70) per person nightly, including breakfast; all rooms have showers. For half-board, add another 20 DM ($11.90) to the rate quoted. From your bedroom window, you can look out at the vineyards. Perhaps you'll be there when the grapes are harvested in the autumn.

Hotel Garni Dries, Kaiserstrasse 1, D-6220 Rüdesheim (tel. 06722/24-20). In this wine-producing region of Germany, it seems appropriate for a tastefully decorated Weinstube to carve *In Vino Veritas* into one of the rustic beams. This, plus a sculpted ceiling and sea-green exterior balconies, identifies this cozy modern establishment, run by the Dries family. The hotel has its own swimming pool, along with a sun terrace decorated with flowerpots. Naturally there's a wide choice of local wines. Singles with showers and toilets rent for 67 DM ($39.80) daily, and doubles with showers and toilets cost 95 DM ($56.40), breakfast included. The hotel is open from April to November.

Hotel und Weinhaus Felsenkeller, Oberstrasse 39, D-6220 Rüdesheim (tel. 06722/20-94). The beautifully carved timbers on the facade of this popular guest house and Weinhaus suggest the kind of traditional aura you can expect inside. Since 1898 it's been run by the Rolz family. The establishment dates from 1613, and a

THE RHEINGAU □ 195

1982 addition was constructed in the half-timbered style of the building. A sampling of Rhine wine can be enjoyed in a room of vaulted ceilings stuccoed and muraled with vine leaves and pithy pieces of folk wisdom. In fair weather, guests are served on the terrace. Rooms, all with showers and toilets, are attractively modern and freshly painted, opening onto views of the vineyards surrounding the house. The hotel rents 60 rooms with showers and toilets, singles going for 70 DM ($41.55) to 110 DM ($65.30) daily, doubles for 120 DM ($71.25) to 160 DM ($95). Open Easter to October.

Hotel Rheinstein, Rheinstrasse 20, D-6220 Rüdesheim (tel. 06722/20-04). The elongated terrace facing the street is one of the most popular gathering places in Rüdesheim. Many locals drop in during the afternoon to enjoy the excellent cakes, all baked on the premises. Irene Gehrig has employed a helpful staff, and she offers 43 rooms with phones (nearly all with private baths or showers and toilets). Half board costs 64 DM ($38) to 85 DM ($50.45) per person daily. Some rooms have balconies with views of the Rhine. The hotel is open from April to mid-November.

A Hunting Lodge at Niederwald

Hotel Jagdschloss Niederwald, Auf dem Niederwald, D-6220 Rüdesheim (tel. 06722/10-04), a 52-room hotel, is perched high in the hills, 3 miles from the center of Rüdesheim. It's a world apart, attracting visitors for romantic weekends along with families on holiday. Part of the compound was the former hunting lodge of the dukes of Hesse; that tone is reflected in the entrance hall, with its hunting museum decor. A wide-view terrace has been enclosed, allowing for a panoramic sweep over the valley. Depending on the plumbing and room size (and the room's location), singles cost 135 DM ($80.15) to 165 DM ($98) daily, and doubles go for 198 DM ($117.55) to 240 DM ($142.50). Even more expensive suites are available. Half board costs an extra 48 DM ($28.50) daily per person. The management has added an indoor swimming pool, with a steam bath and solarium, plus two tennis courts.

After Dark

Rüdesheimer Schloss, Drosselgasse (tel. 06722/20-31), is one of the most colorful restaurants along the Rhine. The intricately carved timbers of this castle date from 1729. There is no cover charge for entrance here, where a live band often plays the Rüdesheimer Polonaise (conga!). The restaurant offers well-prepared traditional foods in a wide price range. Every vintage since 1929 is available, plus some older rare ones that include an 1893 Rheingau wine. Food service is from 11am until the small hours of the morning, anytime daily from March to November. Dishes are likely to include Sauerbraten or roast wild boar, perhaps stuffed suckling pig. A three-course "musical meal" with a small bottle of the local wine costs 40 DM ($23.75); with a large bottle, 50 DM ($29.70). Inexpensive lunches cost from 12 DM ($7.15) and dinner from 18 DM ($10.70). Heinrich and Susanne Breuer certainly run the liveliest place along the river, the revelry spilling into the garden in summer.

The establishment's wine cellars at Grabenstrasse 8 (tel. 06722/10-27), called **Georg Breuer,** have been recently renovated and include a modern vinotheque (wine shop) where all the estate-bottled wines can be tasted and purchased. The shop is open daily from March to November (9am to 6pm), and in winter if you call first. There are modern toilet facilities, a waiting room, and a cobblestoned courtyard.

ASSMANNSHAUSEN

At the northern edge of the Rheingau, this old village is built on the slopes of the east bank of the Rhine. The half-timbered houses and vineyards seem precariously perched on the steep hillsides, and the view of the Rhine Valley from here is awe-inspiring. Assmanshausen is known for its fine red burgundy-style wine.

Where to Stay and Dine

Krone Assmannshausen, Rheinstrasse 10, D-6220 Rüdesheim-Assmanns-hausen (tel. 06722/20-36), has a distinguished pedigree. Built on the banks of the Rhine, surrounded by lawns, gardens, and swimming pool, it traces its origins back 400 years. The inn is overscale, a great big gingerbread fantasy. A small second-floor lounge is virtually a museum, with framed letters and manuscripts of some of the more celebrated personages who have stayed here—Goethe, for one. There's a stack of 37 autograph books, signed by writers, painters, diplomats, and composers.

Your bedroom may be in a medieval building, a Renaissance structure, or a postwar house. The 62 bedrooms have an old-inn character, spacious with traditional furnishings. Singles range from 115 DM ($68.30) to 295 DM ($175.15) daily, with doubles costing 198 DM ($117.55) to 360 DM ($213.75). Even if you're not overnighting, you may want to stop to sample one of the finest meals you're likely to be served on the Rhine, costing 50 DM ($29.70) to 100 DM ($59.40). Specialties are homemade pâtés, including pâté of turbot and brook trout with a sorrel sauce; fresh salmon or eel from Lake Constance in a dill sauce; and saddle of venison in season. For dessert, try the Eisbecher Krone. The owners, the Hufnagel family, whose domaine is the famous Assmannshäuser Höllenberg Pinot Noir, maintains one of the finest assortments of Rhine wines in the world in the rock-hewn cellars of the inn.

Alte Bauernschänke-Nassauer Hof, Niederwaldstrasse 23, D-6220 Rüdesheim-Assmannshausen (tel. 06722/23-13), is owned by wine growers. They have completely renovated two of the oldest mansions of the town, turning them into a 56-room hotel and restaurant. The interior decor is luxurious, the comfort is fine, and the welcome is hearty. Near the church, the hotel lies about a quarter mile from the Rhine. Singles cost 75 DM ($44.55) to 80 DM ($47.50), with doubles going for 100 DM ($59.40) to 130 DM ($77.20). These prices include breakfast. The restaurant provides a folkloric experience, with musicians playing every night. A Gulasch soup, a peppersteak with fresh green beans and french fries, plus a half bottle of the growers' red wine, will cost a maximum of 50 DM ($29.70) per person. If you select from the menu less lavishly, you can get away for 25 DM ($14.85). Open April to October.

Unter den Linden, Rheinallee 1, D-6220 Rüdesheim-Assmannshausen (tel. 06722/22-88), is a converted Rhine-fronting villa, which places emphasis on its cuisine and terrace wine drinking. A building was added at the rear, offering units for overnight, but avoid the rear location because of heavy railroad traffic (the line runs 30 yards from your window, and a train passes by every three minutes). Up front, the dining room overflows onto part of an open terrace. In front is a wide terrace shaded by a grape arbor and linden trees. In summer revelers fill up every table. English is spoken, the food is good, and the wine is superb. All 28 bedrooms are pleasantly decorated and comfortable. A double costs 130 DM ($77.20) daily, increasing to 160 DM ($95) for a room with complete bath. A bathless single begins at 60 DM ($35.65), going up to 95 DM ($56.40) for a room with bath. A dish of the day is featured in the dining room. On one recent occasion I enjoyed filet of smoked Black Forest trout. Meals in the 28 DM ($16.65) to 70 DM ($41.55) range are offered. Open April to mid-November.

Schlön, Rheinuferstrasse 3, D-6220 Rüdesheim-Assmannshausen (tel. 06722/22-25), a family-run riverside hotel, offers 27 comfortable rooms, all with baths or showers, and a café-terrace fronting the river. Its original home was an olive-green baroque house; the building next door has been added on, painted harmoniously in the same color scheme. Most rooms have balconies facing the river. Singles range from 65 DM ($38.60) to 80 DM ($47.50) daily, while doubles go from 100 DM ($59.40) to 155 DM ($92.05). Rates include breakfast. A room with half board is priced at 85 DM ($50.45) to 115 DM ($68.30) per person per day. The hotel has an excellent restaurant, serving food daily from noon to 2pm and 6 to 9pm. It has had its own winery since 1752, and guests can visit the wine cellar. Open April to October.

Hotel-Café Post, Rheinuferstrasse 2, D-6220 Rüdesheim-Assmannshausen (tel. 06722/23-26), is a country-house type of establishment, with an inviting rustic ochre facade with dormers. This cozy place, known for its Rhine-fronting terrace, is run by the Hotger family, who fly a West German flag in front of their establishment every sunny day. They do everything they can to make you feel at home, and their 15 rooms provide a good resting place during the sojourn along the Rhineland. Single rooms cost 60 DM ($35.65) to 95 DM ($56.40) daily, and doubles go for 85 DM ($50.45) to 160 DM ($95). The Hotgers' kitchen is widely known for its good cooking, with meals costing 25 DM ($14.85) to 50 DM ($29.70). The place is open from March to mid-November.

Anker, Rheinuferstrasse 5-7, D-6220 Rüdesheim-Assmannshausen (tel. 06722/29-12), was already old when Bismarck stayed here in 1842. Constructed in baroque yellow stucco in 1660, the building served as a guesthouse for the passengers and crews of the horse teams that pulled the barges, Erie Canal style, along this section of the Rhine. Today it's a renovated 48-room hotel, with an arbor-covered Rhine terrace fronting the river. Many of the rooms have views of the Rhine, along with high ceilings and Oriental rugs. A double costs 108 DM ($64.15) to 148 DM ($87.90) daily, and singles range from 75 DM ($44.55) to 105 DM ($62.35). The restaurant is charmingly decorated with old porcelain, brass tankards, and copper pots, and serves meals that begin as low as 30 DM ($17.80) and climb to 60 DM ($35.65). The Anker is open from mid-March to mid-December.

Ewige Lampe und Haus Resi, Niederwaldstrasse 14, D-6220 Rüdesheim-Assmannshausen (tel. 06722/24-17). You'll find a lot to do in this wine-producing center. You're within a few miles of some historic vineyards, not to mention woodland trails through Rhenish forests. Engelbert and Renate Uri are your hosts, welcoming you to their cozy, tastefully furnished guesthouse. Many of their 24 rooms have wooden ceilings, some have colorfully tiled baths, and all of them are impeccably clean. The cost, depending on the room assigned, ranges from 50 DM ($29.70) to 65 DM ($38.60) daily for a single, from 90 DM ($53.45) to 120 DM ($71.25) for a double. A fortifying breakfast is often served on a sun terrace under parasols. Meals cost 14.50 DM ($8.60) to 28.50 DM ($16.90) per person.

SAMPLING THE HOSPITALITY OF THE RHEINGAU

Everywhere you turn in this vine-laden region, you come upon little village inns, or massive castles converted into hotels. Here are two of the most unusual and enjoyable.

Where to Stay and Dine

Hotel Schwan, Rheinallee 5-7, D-6227 Oestrich-Winkel (tel. 06723/30-01), is one of the most celebrated inns in Germany. You might spend the night in the favored tower room with its seven windows overlooking the Rhine, ascend the cantilevered wooden staircase built in 1628, or taste the Rheingau wine, Oestricher Lenchen, while sitting on a Rhine-fronting garden terrace. The innkeeping family, the Wencksterns, keep their 63-room Schwan preening proud and hospitable. This is an inn of Renaissance gables and a half-timbered facade. It opens onto the little front garden facing a boat landing dock from which Rhine cruises depart. The bedrooms have been brought up-to-date with modern plumbing and comfortable furnishings. Doubles with private baths, including taxes and service, go for 150 DM ($89.05) to 280 DM ($166.25) daily, and singles cost 90 DM ($53.45) to 170 DM ($100.95). Dining here is genuinely excellent, with meals in the 45 DM ($26.70) to 75 DM ($44.55) range. You'll also find a historical wine cellar here, with racks of rare vintages and huge wooden casks of "open wines." Open February to mid-December.

Gutsschänke Burg Schwarzenstein, D-6222 Geisenheim Johannisberg (tel. 06722/88-50), is a restaurant installed in a fort and surrounded by vineyards in this old monastery town. The establishment nestles in the ruins of a turreted tower, with dining tables on a 100-foot terrace overlooking the valley. The patio is covered with bearing grapes. For colder weather, there's an indoor dining room affording a panoramic view. Some people come here to sample the wine. The food is good, too, with meals priced from 25 DM ($14.85) to 60 DM ($35.65). Open in summer from 10am to midnight, closed Mon. Johannisberg is reached from Rüdesheim by taking the road to Winkel (from there, proceed on a northwestern route for approximately 1½ miles).

---

10. Speyer

As one of the oldest Rhine cities of the Holy Roman Empire, Speyer celebrated its 2,000th jubilee in 1990. It early became an important religious center, culminating in the Diet of Speyer, which in 1529 united the followers of Luther in a protest against the Church of Rome. Nothing recalls this medieval German empire as much as the **Domkapitel** (Imperial Cathedral), Domplatz 3 (tel. 06232/10-22-59), in Speyer, perhaps the greatest building of its time.

The Domkapitel, begun in the early 11th century, is the largest Romanesque edifice in Germany. Having weathered the damage of fires and wars, and after several restorations in former times, the cathedral was restored from 1957 to 1961 to its original shape. Only the huge dome over the transept has kept its curved sweep. Entering the church through the single west door set in a stepped arch, you are immediately caught up in the vastness of the proportions, as the whole length of the nave and east chancel opens up before you. Lit by the muted daylight from above, it contains the royal tombs of four emperors and four kings of the Holy Roman Empire, as well as a row of bishops' tombs. The cathedral is open April 1 to September 30, Mon. to Fri. from 9am to 7pm; Sat. from 9am to 4pm; Sun. from 1:30 to 4:30pm. In winter, hours are 9am to 5pm on weekdays; Sat., 9am to 4pm; and Sun., 1:30 to 4:30pm. Entrance to the crypt is free.

WHERE TO STAY

At the Rhine Bridge just outside the town, the **Rhein-Hotel Luxhof,** D-6832 Hockenheim (tel. 06205/35-81), is a hotel of unusual character. It's modern in style, with private bathrooms, but somehow the spirit of a rambling country inn has been retained. The dining rooms are charming and colorful. The 45 bedrooms are well designed and compact, often featuring small sitting areas that open onto tiny balconies. Singles cost 65 DM ($38.60) to 90 DM ($53.45) daily, doubles going for 98 DM ($59.20) to 150 DM ($89.05). A buffet breakfast is included. The hotel has a sauna, a solarium, and other fitness facilities.

A little hotel more like a guesthouse is the **Kurpfalz,** Mühlturmstrasse 5, D-6720 Speyer (tel. 06232/2-41-68), run by the Schimsheimer-Fuchs family, who speak English. The 10 rooms are comfortably furnished. A single with bath costs 90 DM ($53.45) to 120 DM ($71.25) daily, and a double rents for 130 DM ($77.20) to 160 DM ($95), with breakfast included.

Am Wartturm, Landwehrstrasse 30, D-6720 Speyer (tel. 06232/360-66), is a modern little guesthouse of 13 rooms, with parking for guests. Owner Herr Koithahn rents comfortable but simply furnished units, and will arrange for an evening meal if you request it. He charges 63 DM ($37.40) daily for a single and 102 DM ($60.55) for a double, both with shower and toilet.

Trutzpfaff, Webergasse 5, D-6720 Speyer (tel. 06232/7-83-99), is conveniently located near the cathedral. This family-run guesthouse offers personalized service from the English-speaking owner, Edgar Ulses, whose eight rooms are pleasantly and comfortably furnished. He charges from 59 DM ($35.05) daily for a single and from 89 DM ($52.85) for a double, with breakfast included.

Graf's Hotel Löwengarten, Schwerdstrasse 14, D-6720 Speyer (tel. 06323/7-10-51), lies several blocks from the cathedral. Karl-Heinz Graf is your host at this well-known hotel and restaurant. The Löwengarten has 40 rooms, all with showers, toilets, color TVs, and phones. A nourishing breakfast is included in the room tariffs: 80 DM ($47.50) to 135 DM ($80.16) daily for a single, 125 DM ($74.25) to 175 DM ($103.90) for a double.

WHERE TO DINE

In what used to be a bakery, the **Backmulde,** Karmeliterstrasse 11-13 (tel. 06232/7-15-77), is owned by Günter Schmidt, who has researched the centuries-old recipes of the Palatinate, added a modern touch, and come up with a combination that has made this the most important restaurant in Speyer. You can savor such unusual delicacies as a gratinée of oysters in a champagne sabayon, quail stuffed with well-seasoned sweetbreads, or roast baby lamb with freshly picked spinach. A menu of four courses costs 75 DM ($44.55), rising to 110 DM ($65.30) for six courses. Service is from 11:30am to 1:30pm and 6:30 to 9pm; closed Sun., Mon. for lunch, and for a three-week vacation in summer.

---

11. Idar-Oberstein

Idar-Oberstein, medieval twin cities, has long been considered the lapidary center of Europe, with many workshops, stores, and museums of rough and cut stones from all over the world. The location is 60 miles from Mainz. The **Deutsche Gemmologische Gesellschaft,** which is the principal German school for training gemologists, is there, and the city has a diamond and precious stones exchange, the only combined exchange in the world.

WHERE TO STAY

Rising 20 stories abruptly out of a surrounding forest, the **Merian,** Mainzerstrasse 34, D-6580 Idar-Oberstein (tel. 06781/40-10), is a steel-and-concrete box housing many visitors from the international gem-trading companies. The panoramic restaurant offers well-prepared meals in a warmly decorated ambience, while the breakfast buffet is served in a top-floor aerie with a panoramic view. The 106 rooms are freshly decorated in natural colors, and depending on the floor you're on, you might be able to see for miles around. Double rooms with baths cost 125 DM ($74.25) to 155 DM ($92.05) daily, and singles rent for 90 DM ($53.45) to 120 DM ($71.25).

Zum Schwan, Hauptstrasse 25, D-6580 Idar-Oberstein (tel. 06781/4-30-81), a 21-room hotel-restaurant in a building of classic architecture, offers a really personal atmosphere. Rooms are modern; most are quite spacious. A double without bath goes for 65 DM ($38.60) daily, increasing to 100 DM ($59.40) for a room with private plumbing. A single costs 33 DM ($19.60) without bath, going up to 65 DM ($38.60) for a room with bath. All rates include a big buffet breakfast.

WHERE TO DINE

Your best bet for dining is **Zum Schwan,** Hauptstrasse 25 (tel. 06781/4-30-81), previously recommended as a hotel. International cookery finds a place in this renowned diamond-trading town, and at this restaurant an open fireplace welcomes visitors on a nippy night to gutbürgerlich cookery and gemütlich charm. Regional dishes might include the chef's original recipe, an Idar-Obersteiner Spiessbraten (ask the waiter to explain it). Or you might partake of a filet of veal in a cognac cream sauce with green pepper and homemade Spätzle or lamb chops with baby cabbage leaves and a champagne mustard sauce. Fixed-price menus cost 32 DM ($19) to 60 DM ($35.65). A large à la carte menu is also available, costing from 40 DM ($23.75). Hours are 11am to 2pm and 6 to 10pm daily.

HEIDELBERG, STUTTGART, AND THE NECKAR VALLEY

Ancient castle ruins in the midst of thick woodlands, quiet university towns, busy manufacturing centers—all this truly belongs to the countryside of southwestern Germany, extending along the Neckar River from Heidelberg past medieval towns and modern cities as far as Tübingen. The Neckar flows between the Black Forest and the Schwäbische Alb; although the river is open to commercial shipping vessels as far as Stuttgart, much of the valley has remained unspoiled. This area has been the cradle of German royal families for centuries. The castles that lie around every bend in the river were once homes of the imperial families of Hohenstaufen and Hohenzollern. Many of the ruins were the summer palaces of kings and emperors. In the midst of all this royal splendor, many castles and country palaces offer bed and board to travelers.

1. Heidelberg

Summertime in Heidelberg, according to the song from the popular operetta *The Student Prince,* is a time for music and romance. Today it's also a time when droves of visitors invade this city on the Neckar—and with cause. Heidelberg is one of the few large German cities not leveled by the air raids of World War II, and many of its important buildings date from the latter part of the Middle Ages and the early Renaissance.

Heidelberg is, above all, a university town and has been since 1386. Students make up nearly 20% of the current population. The colorful atmosphere that university life imparts to the town is felt nowhere more than in the old student quarter, with its narrow streets and lively inns. This oldest university in Germany is officially named Ruprecht-Karl-University, honoring its founder, Elector Ruprecht I of the Palatinate, and the man who in 1803 made it the leading university in the state of

Baden, Margrave Karl Friedrich. The school was founded after the Great Schism of 1378, when conflicting claims to the papacy created unrest, and German teachers and students fled the Sorbonne in Paris. A papal bull from Urban VI in Rome authorized the founding of the University of Heidelberg.

The university grew rapidly. Monastic in character at first, it changed in the 16th century with the appointment of a married rector. The so-called Old University was built in the early 18th century, the New University constructed nearby in 1930–32. Funds for this structure came from many American sources, including Henry Ford. Today lecture halls, institutes, seminar buildings, and clinics are scattered all over town, but a new university quarter is being developed on the plain in the Neuenheim district, with multistory buildings and the most modern cancer research center in the Federal Republic. Seven university scientists have been recipients of Nobel Prizes in the fields of chemistry, physics, and medicine.

Modern Heidelberg is centered around Bismarck Square at the foot of the Theodor Heuss Brücke. The skyscrapers and shopping plazas contrast with the old town nearby. In the new city you will find many of the best hotels and restaurants. Across the Neckar are sports grounds, a zoo, and a large botanical garden. But before exploring the sights of Heidelberg, let's survey the range of accommodations and restaurants.

At **Tourist Information** at the main railway station (tel. 06221/2-13-41), you can get general information and help with room reservations if you need it.

ORIENTATION

The Neckar River forms the northern periphery of the monumental heart of Heidelberg, but wherever you go, Heidelberg Castle will be looming over you (locals refer to it as *das Schloss*). If you arrive by train, you'll be deposited at the Hauptbahnhof in the "west end," a modern sector of the city that will hardly live up to the image of romantic Heidelberg. However, don't despair. It opens onto a street, Kurfürstenanlage, that leads east to the old town. As you reach Adenauerplatz, you will be on the doorstep of the Altstadt.

If Heidelberg has a main street, it is the Hauptstrasse, where you'll find the city's major taverns, shops, and many, many restaurants. This street begins just north of Adenauerplatz on another square, Bismarckplatz, and stretches all the way to Karlsplatz, a long but interesting walk. The major bridge of town, the Theodor Heuss Brücke, was already mentioned, but in the heart of old town is the Alte Brücke, dating from the late 18th century. The more contemporary part of Heidelberg lies to the west of Bismarckplatz.

WHERE TO STAY

Expensive Hotels

Heidelberg's glamour hotel is **Der Europäische Hof-Hotel Europa,** Friedrich-Ebert-Anlage 1, D-6900 Heidelberg (tel. 06221/515-0 or toll free in the U.S. at 800/223-5652). Fronting the city park, this 150-room hotel is in the heart of the town, within walking distance of the castle, the university, and the old part of Heidelberg with its student inns. Its interior is like a gracious home, with antiques, crystal chandeliers, and Oriental rugs. The hotel has 50 units facing the quiet inside garden, some of them apartments with separate bedrooms and sitting rooms. The rooms are pleasantly traditional, done with rich taste. Each chamber is individually decorated and has a bath or shower, direct-dial telephone, radio, television, room safe, trouser press, and refrigerator. The rates depend on the season, the size of the room, and the location. Singles range from 219 DM ($130.65) to 259 DM ($154.40) daily, with doubles going from 280 DM ($166.25) to 480 DM ($285). The more expensive doubles contain alcoves. A buffet breakfast, service, and taxes are included in the rates. Meals are served in the Louis XVI restaurant, on the garden terrace (where windows can be lowered to floor level), or in the finely paneled Kurfürstenstube. Before dinner, guests congregate around the curved bar in the wood-paneled drinking lounge. An elegant shopping arcade, cafeteria Europ-Treff, a fitness center, swimming pool, massage room, and sun terrace, plus an underground parking garage, are on the premises.

Heidelberg Penta Hotel, Vangerowstrasse 16, D-6900 Heidelberg (tel. 06221/90-80), is an elegant new building on the river opposite the University Medical Research complex and just minutes from the city center, with easy access by bus or car. The 250 comfortable, air-conditioned rooms all have private baths, radios, color TVs, direct-dial phones, and minibars; most have views over the river or the hills. Singles rent for 190 DM ($112.80) to 210 DM ($124.70) daily and doubles for 235 DM ($135.55) to 255 DM ($151.40). All rates include service and taxes. The hotel's elegant Globetrotter Restaurant (open daily from 6:30am to 10pm), with terrace, has views over the gardens and river. It offers local and international specialties as well as health foods. The beer and wine pub, Pinte (from noon to 10pm), serves draft beer, wines, and light meals. The Lobby Bar is the ideal meeting place for relaxing over drinks. Among the amenities of the hotel are a health club with an indoor swimming pool, sauna, solarium, massage parlor, and exercise area, plus a hair and beauty salon, a boutique, and both underground and open-air car parking, as well as its own boat landing place.

Holiday Inn Crowne Plaza, Kurfürstenanlage 1, D-6900 Heidelberg (tel. 06221/91-70), which opened in 1988, quickly became one of the best-rated hotels in the city. In the center of Heidelberg, at Adenauerplatz, it is convenient for touring the major attractions. A first-class hotel with a number of facilities, the hotel offers 232 well-furnished bedrooms with private baths. Singles rent for 255 DM ($151.40) to 295 DM ($175.15) daily, with doubles going for 315 DM ($187.05) to 335 DM ($198.90). Its stylish restaurants include the Palatina and the less expensive Atrium. There is also a cozy cocktail bar. The hotel was designed with today's fitness-minded clientele in mind, and it contains a fitness center with an indoor swimming pool. There is also underground parking.

Prinzhotel Heidelberg, Neuenheimer Landstrasse 5, D-6900 Heidelberg (tel. 06221/4-03-20), in the town center and near the congress hall, is a first-class hotel owned and managed by the Kraft family. They offer 50 rooms and three penthouse suites that provide such amenities as private baths and toilets, direct-dial phones, minibars, TV/videos (with English programs), and safes. Singles cost 195 DM ($115.80) daily, doubles from 245 DM ($145.50). The hotel's Italian Ristorante Giardino is open from 10am to midnight; closed Tues. and in August. In the elegantly furnished room, with comfortable chairs and Murano glass chandeliers, guests enjoy fish, fowl, and meats artfully matched with superb Italian sauces, savory herbs, and spices revealing the culinary art of an Italian head chef. Meals cost from 65 DM ($38.60). Guests can also enjoy fine wines in the Winebar Chianti. Parking is available.

Hotel Hirschgasse, Hirschgasse 3, D-6900 Heidelberg (tel. 06221/4-99-21), is a historic guesthouse dating from 1472 that figured in the well-known love story of the poet Friedrich von Soest and the daughter of the Hirschgasse's innkeeper. Among its stellar lodgers have been the noted 18th-century German poet Hölderlin, Mark Twain, and Bismarck, the last honored with a suite named after him, including a Jacuzzi no less. The hotel's spacious Saal is still used by students for fencing. The Hirschgasse, nestled on the hillside of a historic lane adjoining Philosopher's Walk, is today a country home–style hotel, owned by the English-speaking Kraft family, who run the superb Prinzhotel Heidelberg (see above).

In 1988 its 42 bedrooms were reconstructed as 18 suites, decorated in Laura Ashley designs. Each has a salon and bedroom, a separate toilet, double wash basins, and a Jacuzzi. Especially for American guests there is cable TV news from home. Two persons, paying for all this luxury, are charged 330 DM ($195.95) daily in a junior suite, 450 DM ($267.20) in a senior suite, and 550 DM ($326.50) in an executive suite.

Regional, traditional, and modern cuisine is offered in the restaurant, Le Gourmet, which since 1472 has been attracting diners from Europe and abroad. It is open from 6pm to midnight, except Sun., charging from 65 DM ($38.60) per person for dinner. The Studentenstube keeps alive the atmosphere of the old students' fraternities.

Moderately Priced Hotels

A glorious old inn right out of the German Renaissance, **Zum Ritter,** Hauptstrasse 178, D-6900 Heidelberg (tel. 06221/2-42-72), is a well-preserved rarity. Built in 1592 by the Frenchman Charles Bélier, it is now listed among the major sightseeing attractions of this university town, having survived the destruction wrought by Louis XIV's troops in 1693. Deep in the heart of the student area of drinking houses and nightclubs, Zum Ritter holds its own. There are no public lounges; the 32 bedrooms play second fiddle to the fine restaurant downstairs. Singles rent for 110 DM ($65.30) to 185 DM ($109.85), with doubles costing 195 DM ($115.80) to 275 DM ($163.30).

Hotel Monpti, Friedrich-Ebert-Anlage 57, D-6900 Heidelberg (tel. 06221/2-34-83), is a small hotel with sophisticated charm, run on a personal basis and moderately priced. The owner, Peter Mack, was born in this stately little town house in 1939. After traveling extensively, especially in Spain, he returned to his native town, and converted his home into a super guesthouse, utilizing both his inherent and acquired tastes. Built in the neoclassical style, the Monpti is a charmer, painted an olive green with a distinctive architectural trim in white. Each bedroom has color and freshness. All of the practical items are behind doors, and your chamber is furnished like a little salon. All of the recently redecorated 14 double rooms have private showers and toilets, as well as phones and TVs. Two persons pay 130 DM ($77.20) to 160 DM ($95) daily, and one person is charged 115 DM ($68.30), including breakfast. There's a petite breakfast room where guests gather over morning coffee. The owner has transformed the lower level (it's built on a hillside) into the bodega Vinothek, where he, his wife, and friends gather in the evening to enjoy paella. Perhaps a Spanish guitarist will provide background music when you are there. The restaurant is open daily until 1am. Free parking is on the open terrace.

Holländer Hof, Neckarstaden 66, D-6900 Heidelberg (tel. 06221/1-20-91), in the heart of old Heidelberg, has an enviable position opening onto Alte Brücke. A pink-and-white building, it was one of the town's 12 guesthouses in medieval days. Rebuilt after a fire in 1693, it has hosted many celebrated visitors over the years. Today it offers 39 renovated and attractively furnished bedrooms, each with bath or shower, toilet, phone, and radio. There are six special rooms for people in wheelchairs. Singles range from 95 DM ($56.10) to 130 DM ($77.80) daily, doubles from 145 DM ($86.10) to 185 DM ($109.85). The Holländer Hof's restaurant, one of the finest in the Altstadt, offers a cuisine that ranges from home-style cookery to an international cuisine. Meals cost 35 DM ($20.80) to 65 DM ($38.60). Hours are 11am to 2pm and 6 to 10pm daily.

Acor, Friedrich-Ebert-Anlage 55, D-6900 Heidelberg (tel. 06221/2-20-44), is a recommendable 18-bedroom hotel that was converted from an old patrician house. An elevator has been installed and the furnishings updated. Most rooms are compact (although a few are large) and quite comfortable. Doubles with baths or showers are 165 DM ($98) to 210 DM ($124.70) daily. Singles with baths or showers cost 125 DM ($74.25) to 155 DM ($92.05). These tabs include a buffet breakfast, served in a little room overlooking a small rear garden. The street is busy with traffic, but soundproof windows have been installed.

Hotel Schönberger Hof, Untere Neckarstrasse 54, D-6900 Heidelberg (tel. 06221/2-26-15). Renovated in 1970, this baroque villa offers a hint of the grandeur of former times. It is attractively situated across from the Town Hall and

Montpellier Park, a short walk from the Neckar. The public rooms are rustically decorated, making use of original stonework and rough-hewn timbers. The 15 bedrooms have high ceilings and comfortable beds. A popular Weinstube fills the ground floor, where you'll probably want to stop in, if only for a beer. Singles rent for 80 DM ($47.50) to 110 DM ($65.30) daily, while doubles go for 160 DM ($95) to 180 DM ($106.90), including breakfast.

Parkhotel Atlantic, Schloss-Wolfsbrunnenweg 23, D-6900 Heidelberg (tel. 06221/2-45-45), a breakfast-only hotel, lies on the wooded outskirts of Heidelberg, near the Heidelberger Schloss. This rather grand hotel offers modern comfort in annexes built around the core of an older villa. The surrounding park is full of trees, and visitors are assured of calm and comfort. Often they take advantage of the many woodland trails extending through the Neckar Valley. The 23 rooms, decorated in circa-1965 modern, go for 100 DM ($59.40) to 140 DM ($83.15) daily for a single and 150 DM ($89.05) to 250 DM ($148.45) for a double, including breakfast.

Neckar-Hotel Heidelberg, Bismarckstrasse 19, D-6900 Heidelberg (tel. 06221/1-08-14), enjoys an enviable position, right on the Neckar River near the center of the university town. There is no garden, but a superb view. The facilities are substantial and comfortable, the 35 bedrooms fitted with Germanic-modern pieces. Doubles or twin-bedded rooms with baths or showers run from 140 DM ($83.15) to 180 DM ($106.90) daily. Singles, also with showers or baths, range from 100 DM ($59.40) to 140 DM ($83.15). These rates include breakfast, taxes, and service. Breakfast is the only meal served; parking is available in the tiny lot.

Hotel Vier Jahreszeiten, Haspelgasse 2, D-6900 Heidelberg (tel. 06221/2-41-64), lives up to its name and is a worthy choice in any of the "four seasons." The location is by the Old Bridge in the heart of Heidelberg, the starting point for many interesting walks. You can walk not only to the castle but to many old student inns. The 22-room hotel has been improved over the years, and rooms are comfortable if perhaps a bit dated. Depending on the plumbing, singles range from 60 DM ($35.65) to 140 DM ($83.15) daily, while doubles go for 105 DM ($62.35) to 190 DM ($112.80). These tariffs include breakfast. From the hotel there's good view over the Neckar.

Budget Hotels

In the heart of the city, **Hotel Anlage** Friedrich-Ebert-Anlage 32, D-6900 Heidelberg (tel. 06221/2-64-25), stands right on the street leading up to das Schloss. With its richly ornate facade, it occupies one wing of a lavishly built late 19th-century palace of orange brick and carved stone. Built in 1892, the structure has been well adapted to its present use as one of the best budget hotels in the city. It rents 20 cozy bedrooms, each with private shower or bath, toilet, direct-dial phone, and cable TV (with English programs). Singles cost 75 DM ($44.55) to 90 DM ($53.45) daily; doubles rent for 110 DM ($65.30) to 135 DM ($80.15). All tariffs include a plentiful breakfast, taxes, and service. The pleasant restaurant on the premises is reserved for guests.

Hotel Reichspost, Gaisbergstrasse 38, D-6900 Heidelberg (tel. 06221/2-22-52), is one of the better bargains of Heidelberg. A reliable budget hotel, it was built in 1954 on a quiet street. Simply furnished, it offers 28 comfortable rooms, some of which contain private baths. Singles cost 70 DM ($41.55) to 95 DM ($56.40) daily, and doubles go for 110 DM ($65.30) to 125 DM ($74.25). Breakfast, included in the rates, is the only meal served.

Hotel zum Pfalzgrafen, Kettengasse 21, D-6900 Heidelberg (tel. 06221/2-04-89), a simple town inn, has 28 good rooms. The hotel stands in the heart of old Heidelberg, only a 15-minute walk from most major sights. Parking is available, and there are also garages. The best rooms contain private showers, and these are priced accordingly. The bargains, however, are the rooms with hot and cold running water only. Showers are on the same floor. Doubles or twins without showers cost 80 DM

($47.50) daily; with showers, 125 DM ($74.25). Singles without showers are 55 DM ($32.65); with showers or bath, 90 DM ($53.95). All rates include service, taxes, and breakfast.

WHERE TO DINE

The Top Restaurants

The best dining spot in Heidelberg is the **Kurfürstenstube,** in Der Europäische Hof-Hotel Europa, Friedrich-Ebert-Anlage 1 (tel. 06221/515-0). Occupying a ground-floor wing of this outstanding hotel, the Weinstube is attractively decorated with provincial furnishings, pewter plates, and a stein collection. The menu is in English. Specialties include homemade goose liver pâté with apples, soup of Odenwald brook trout, consommé with green rye quenelles, slices of pike-perch fried in butter, filet of sole in Tokayer cream, saddle of venison with red-currant sauce, breast of duckling, and vegetables of the season. Rounding out the meal might be flamed pancakes with bananas and maple sauce. The wine list is very impressive indeed, and a complete meal ranges from 39 DM ($23.15) to 110 DM ($65.30). Hours are noon to 3pm and 6:30pm to midnight daily.

Simplicissimus, Ingrimstrasse 16, (tel. 06221/1-33-36), is elegant, ideal for a gourmet rendezvous for those tired of student drinking clubs. Cuisine moderne is prepared with consummate skill by the owner and perhaps the finest chef in Heidelberg, Herr Lummer. His restaurant is in the old town, and it's decorated simply but with taste and style, with white paneling, globe lights, and touches of crimson. *Gourmet* magazine said Herr Lummer "paints with food," and in so many ways he does. Not only are his platters delectable to the tastebuds, but their presentation seems equally important. The menu varies, but it is likely to include such fare as fresh mushrooms in a cream sauce with homemade noodles, crayfish with fresh melon and herb-flavored cream sauce, poached veal with exotic mushrooms and strips of quail, or monkfish with crayfish. A four-course set menu is offered for 65 DM ($38.60), an elaborate seven-course repast going for 98 DM ($58.20). You can also order à la carte, paying around 60 DM ($35.65) for the privilege. The restaurant is open from 6 to 11pm; closed Tues. Reservations are needed.

Zur Herrenmühle, Hauptstrasse 239 (tel. 06221/1-29-09). The house that contains this restaurant was originally built in the 17th century, as you'll quickly realize thanks to the thick walls, antique paneling, and frequently polished patinas. Maintained as a restaurant by the Ueberle family, the dining room prepares succulent versions of a classical French-inspired cuisine based on fresh ingredients and a rigorous culinary training. Open only in the evening, it has a sophisticated maître d' to add both glamour and an appropriate kind of theatricality. The restaurant charges from 75 DM ($44.55) for an à la carte dinner and from 55 DM ($32.65) to 95 DM ($56.40) for fixed-price meals. These might include such dishes as rack of lamb with herbs and homemade green noodles, cream of wild mushroom soup, filet of salmon with a saffron cream sauce and truffled rice, roast roebuck with a vinegar and honey sauce, and an array of desserts, perhaps a sorbet flavored with blood oranges and served with a parfait of mandarin oranges. Reservations are recommended for meals served nightly from 5:30pm to midnight.

Moderately Priced Restaurants

Kurpfälziches Wein Restaurant, Hauptstrasse 97 (tel. 06221/2-40-50), is a quiet culinary oasis in the precincts of the Kurpfälziches Museum. Housed in a baroque palace, the museum makes an interesting stopover before lunch. The restaurant's prices are moderate, the food good. You can order such dishes as rump steak Madagascar (with green pepper). Meals cost 35 DM ($20.80) to 70 DM ($41.55). From your table, you can enjoy the little garden and splashing fountain. Hours are 11am to midnight daily.

Zum Ritter, Hauptstrasse 178 (tel. 06221/2-42-72), is popular with both students and professors, for they know they can get not only good German cooking here, but delectable Dortmunder Actien-Brauerei beer as well. You dine either in the first-class Great Hall (the Rittersaal) or in the smaller Councillors' Chamber. I like the elegant larger room, with its sepia ceilings, wainscoting, and Oriental rugs. À la carte meals range in price from a low of 35 DM ($20.80) to a high of 75 DM ($44.55). The house specialty in season is saddle of venison for two. A good beginning might be game soup St. Hubertus with brandy foam, followed by crêpes Suzette for dessert. Open daily from noon to 2:30pm and 6 to 10:30pm.

Merian-Stuben, Neckarstadten 24 (tel. 06221/2-73-81), is housed in the Kongresshaus Stadthalle. One of the best restaurants in Heidelberg, it offers attentive service and good food, with complete dinners beginning at 30 DM ($17.80), ranging upward to 55 DM ($32.65). The menu is printed in English. You might begin with Alsatian snails cooked in a pan with onions, mushrooms, and fresh herbs, or frogs' legs sautéed in light garlic butter with glazed onions and tomatoes. For a fish selection, poached pike comes in a creamy mustard sauce, and you can also order pork filet à la Dijon (spit broiled, basted with a mustard sauce). For dessert a cherry-flavored ice cream is served with slivered chocolate and whipped cream. Lunch is served from 11am to 2pm and dinner from 6 to 10pm; closed Mon. and in January.

Budget Restaurants

Schönberger Hof, Untere Neckarstrasse 54 (tel. 06221/2-26-15). "Soothing" and "satisfying" best describe this gaily painted old German Weinstube, where Bavarian and French wines and hearty Germanic cookery prevail. It stands between Montpellier Park on the Neckar and the Stadthalle. The establishment is closed for two weeks in summer, but is otherwise open Mon. to Fri. from 6pm to midnight, with meals costing 42 DM ($24.95) to 66 DM ($39.20).

Konditorei-Café Schafheutle, Hauptstrasse 94 (tel. 06221/2-13-16). Rain need never ruin your summer afternoon outing in this partially roofed café-garden. A light meal, presented with attentive service, costs about 25 DM ($14.85), and there is a large choice of pastries. The café is open from 9am to 6:30pm (to 6pm on Sat. and 8:30pm on Thurs.); closed Sun. and holidays.

Student Drinking Clubs

Heidelberg's most famous and revered student tavern, **Zum Roter Ochsen** (Red Ox Inn), Hauptstrasse 217 (tel. 06221/2-09-77), opened in 1703. For six generations it's been in the Spengel family, who have welcomed everybody from Bismarck to Mark Twain. It seems that every student who has attended the university has left his mark on the walls—or at least his initials. Revelers sit at long oak tables under smoke-blackened ceilings. Distinguished patrons of yore have left mementos, often framed photographs of themselves. The series of rooms is arranged in horseshoe fashion; the "U" part has a pianist who sets the musical pace. As the evening progresses, the songs become more festive and vigorous. By midnight the sounds are heard blocks away. Motherly-looking waitresses bring in huge steins of beer and plates of food. A mug of beer costs from 5 DM ($2.95). Dishes include Gulasch soup, Sauerbraten Rhineland style, and veal steak Cordon Bleu. Meals cost 18 DM ($10.70) to 32 DM ($19). Service is from 5pm to midnight; closed Sun.

Zum Sepp'l, Hauptstrasse 213 (tel. 06221/2-30-85), next door to Roten Ochsen, is the second famous drinking club of Heidelberg. It is filled with photographs of former students at the university (hundreds have carved their initials), along with memorabilia that range from old Berlin street signs to Alabama license plates. The building itself dates from 1407. Lying right off Karlsplatz, it is open daily from 11am to midnight (to 1am on Sat.). You can order platters of food, such as farmers' sausages, and meals cost 7 DM ($4.15) to 18 DM ($10.70). When the university is closed, the activity here dies down considerably, except for merrymaking by tourists, but it remains a long-enduring favorite.

THE SIGHTS

All the important sights of Heidelberg lie on or near the south bank of the Neckar and you must cross the river (via the 18th-century Karl Theodore Bridge) for the best overall view. **Philosophen Weg** (Philosopher's Way), halfway up the mountain on the north bank, is best for viewing. And towering above the brown roofs of the town on the opposite bank is the rose-pink major attraction of Heidelberg, the castle.

Heidelberg Castle

In its magnificent setting of woodland and terraced gardens, the huge red-sandstone castle (tel. 06221/2-00-70) is reached from the town below by several routes. The quickest way is the two-minute cable-car ride from the platform near the Kormarkt (Grain Market). The round trip costs 4.50 DM ($2.65). You may also drive to the winding Neue Schlosstrasse, past the old houses perched on the hillside. This is also a walking route, rewarding because of the constantly changing view of the town and surrounding countryside. For a shorter walk, you may climb the steep Burgweg from the Kornmarkt, or take the more gradual walk from the Klingentor.

The castle is only a dignified ruin today; it was plundered and burned by the French in the latter part of the 17th century. Parts of the huge tower still lie in the moat where they fell after being blown up in 1693 at the command of Louis XIV. Lightning added to the destruction by striking the castle twice in the mid-18th century. Even in its deteriorated state, it's considered one of the finest Gothic-Renaissance castles in Germany.

Entering the castle walls at the main gate, you first come upon the huge **Gun Park** to your left, from which you can gaze down upon Heidelberg and the Neckar Valley. Straight ahead is the Thick Tower, or what remains of it after its 25-foot walls were blown up by the French. Leaving the Gun Park via Elizabeth's Gate, erected by Friedrich V in 1615 for his Scottish wife, Elizabeth Stuart, daughter of James I, you come to the Bridge House and the bridge crossing the site of the former moat.

Through the entrance tower lies the **castle courtyard,** the heart of the complex of structures. Surrounding it are buildings dating from the 13th to the 17th centuries. You'll notice that nature has done its best to repair the ravages by covering the gaping holes and roofless sections with ivy and shrubbery. Walking around the courtyard in a clockwise fashion, you come first to the Gothic **Ruprecht Building,** built about 1400. Adjacent is the **Library,** with a Gothic oriel window dating from the early 16th century. It once housed the library of Ludwig V.

The **Frauenzimmer** (Women's Rooms) was originally a three-story Gothic-Renaissance building housing the ladies of the court, but today only the ground level, the King's Hall, remains.

Along the north side of the courtyard stretches the stern palace of Friedrich IV, erected from 1601 to 1607. Less damaged than other parts of the castle, it has been almost completely restored, including the gallery of princes and kings of the German Empire from the time of Charlemagne. The palace has its own terrace, the Altan, which offers a splendid view of the plain of the Neckar. The ancient Bell Tower, at the northeast end of the Altan, dates from the early 1500s.

At the west end of the terrace, in the cellars of the castle, is the Wine Vat Building, built in the late 16th century and worth a visit for a look at the **Great Cask,** symbol of the abundant and exuberant life of the Rhineland-Palatinate. This huge barrel-like monstrosity, built in 1751, is capable of holding more than 55,000 gallons of wine.

On the east, connecting the palace of Friedrich IV to the **Ottheinrich Building,** itself an outstanding example of German Renaissance architecture, is the **Hall of Mirrors Building,** constructed in 1549—a Renaissance masterpiece. Only the shell of the original building remains, enough to give you an idea of its former glory, with its arcades and steep gables decorated with cherubs and sirens.

Next to Ottheinrich's palace is the Chemist's Tower, housing the **Pharmaceutical Museum.** Entrance fee: 1.50 DM (90¢). The museum, on the tower's ground floor, shows a chemist's shop with utensils and laboratory equipment from the 18th and 19th centuries. It is open during the usual castle visiting hours.

Returning to the Castle Gate, you will pass the old barracks for the soldiers of the garrison. Next to the barracks is the former well house, its roof supported by ancient Roman columns. Some of the household buildings, such as the bakery, kitchen, smithshop, and butchery nearby, have been restored.

In summer you can enjoy serenades and concerts in the large castle courtyard. But the biggest spectacle is the **castle illumination,** commemorating the battles of the 17th century. Several times throughout the summer, at dates rescheduled yearly, the castle is floodlit and fireworks are set off above it.

You can visit the castle grounds at any time during the day, free. If you wish to visit the interior of the castle, you must take one of the one-hour guided tours. The fee is 4 DM ($2.40). A visit to the Great Cask without the tour costs adults 1 DM (60¢), children .50 DM (30¢).

Other Sights

Back in the town itself, a tour of the main attractions begins with the **Marketplace** (Marktplatz) in front of the Rathaus. On market days the square is filled with stalls of fresh flowers, fish, and vegetables. At the opposite end of the square is the late Gothic **Church of the Holy Ghost,** built about 1400. For nearly 300 years the church was the burial place of the electors, but most of the graves were destroyed in the French invasion late in the 17th century. In 1706 a wall was erected, dividing the church, giving both Catholics and Protestants a portion in which to worship. The wall has since been removed and the church restored to its original plan.

Around the corner from the church is the famous old mansion, **Zum Ritter,** recommended in the hotel listings above. If you follow the Hauptstrasse past the hotel, you'll arrive at the **Kurpfälzisches Museum,** Hauptstrasse 97 (tel. 06221/5-85-21), the Museum of the Palatinate, housed in a baroque palace. The museum presents a large collection of paintings and sculptures from six centuries, among them the Riemenschneider Altar from Windsheim (1509) with Christ and the Twelve Apostles. There is also a cast of the jawbone of the Heidelberg Man, 500,000 years old; an archeological collection; examples of history and culture of the Palatinate; and paintings from the Romantic period. The museum is open from 10am to 5pm, on Thurs. to 9pm; closed Mon. Admission is 1 DM (60¢).

The Hauptstrasse also runs through the old student quarter of Heidelberg, with its inns. Of special interest is the **Karzer,** or Student Jail (tel. 06221/54-23-34), at Augustinergasse 2. The walls and even the ceilings of the prison are covered with graffiti and drawings, including portraits and silhouettes. The last prisoners were housed here in 1914. Visiting hours are 9am to 5pm; closed Sun. and holidays. Ring the caretaker's bell (same address) for admission, which is 1 DM (60¢) for adults, .70 DM (40¢) for students.

In the Environs

The Palatine electors in the 18th century journeyed to **Schwetzingen** (tel. 06202/811), 7 miles west of Heidelberg, which was their summer residence. Along this route came Voltaire and a host of other famous visitors.

Schwetzingen is home to the world-famous castle gardens, which are open to the public April to September, daily from 8am to 8pm (otherwise, from 9am to 5pm), charging an admission of 2 DM ($1.20). The gardens are laid out in the rococo style, adorned with ruins, temples, and sculpture that conjure up romantic images. A mosque suggests the charm of the Near East; watercourses, fountains, live animals, and flowerbeds complete the picture that the electors found "a paradise on earth." The best time to visit the gardens is late spring and early summer, when the lilacs and linden trees are in bloom.

The castle was formerly a low-lying fort surrounded by water. Later it became the hunting lodge and then the summer residence of Karl Theodor, the last Palatine elector. Productions are still staged at a rococo theater, and in the early summer of every year an international festival is held. Tours of the theater, costing 2 DM ($1.20), are possible at 11am, and at 4, 5, and 5:30pm. Tours are conducted daily from mid-June until mid-September.

Gourmets flock to Schwetzingen in the spring (mid-April to the end of June) to enjoy the celebrated asparagus grown here.

---

2. The Neckar Valley

Heidelberg is a good point from which to begin an exploration of the Neckar Valley. From Easter to the end of October, you can take one of the boat tours along the river as far as Neckarsteinach and back; a three-hour round trip costs 13 DM ($7.70) per person. You can order drinks or snacks on the boat. There are usually four or five round trips daily, and you need not return immediately on the same boat. That gives time to explore the various sights (four castles). Boats are operated by the **Rhein-Neckar-Fahrgastschiffahrt GMBH,** Stadthalle, Heidelberg (tel. 06221/2-01-81). Some of the people who take you on this pleasant trip may be descended from the Neckar fishermen who helped Mark Twain when he rafted down from Hirschhorn. The same families have been working the Neckar since the early 1600s.

The best way to get a close look at the many attractions along the banks of the Neckar is by car, leaving Heidelberg eastward along the right bank of the river.

HIRSCHHORN

Called the gem of the Neckar Valley, this medieval town still carries an aura of the past. It obtained its municipal rights in 1391. Overlooking the town and the Neckar from its fortified promontory is the 18th-century **Hirschhorn Castle.** The castle was erected on the site of an earlier Renaissance palace built by Ludwig von Hirschhorn in the late 16th century. The castle defenses are from the 14th century, and wall paintings from that period can be seen in the chapel. The castle is now a hotel and restaurant. For a view of the sharp bend of the Neckar below the town, climb to the top of the tower.

Where to Stay and Dine

Hotel Burg Hirschhorn, Auf Burg Hirschhorn, D-6932 Hirschhorn (tel. 0672/13-73), on Highway B37 (Heidelberg–Eberbach), provides an opportunity to stay in a hilltop castle. Accommodations are divided between a palace and a guest-house annex. The 25 double bedrooms are furnished in modern style, and each has a private bath or shower, phone, TV, river view, and a collection of good antiques. Central heating and an elevator have been installed. With breakfast included, the price is 100 DM ($59.40) to 125 DM ($74.25) daily for singles, 135 DM ($80.15) to 185 DM ($109.85) for doubles. The restaurant serves meals to nonresidents, but only if they phone in advance. Specialties include game of various kinds, smoked trout, and home-baked bread. The food is served in traditional ways. Food service is daily from noon to 2pm and 6 to 8 pm. A fixed-price meal costs 25 DM ($14.85), while an à la carte repast can run as high as 55 DM ($32.65). The hotel closes in December and January.

EBERBACH

Just 20 miles along the Neckar from Heidelberg is the ancient Imperial City of Eberbach, which traces its municipal rights back to 1227. Its castle is even older, dating from 1012. The fortress was destroyed in the 15th century, but its ivy-covered ruins attract many visitors today, as does the old Deutscher Hof, the medieval center of the town within the city walls.

Historical footnote: Queen Victoria was conceived at Eberbach, a momentous event commemorated by a plaque outside the home of her parents, Haus Thalheim.

Where to Stay and Dine

Hotel Kettenboot, Friedrichstrasse 1, D-6930 Eberbach (tel. 06271/24-70), is one of the better-known hotels in town—the kind of place where practically everybody has been for at least one meal. Its 16 bedrooms, comfortably and conservatively furnished, are priced at 45 DM ($26.70) to 65 DM ($38.60) daily for singles, 90 DM ($53.45) to 110 DM ($65.30) for doubles. The hotel's restaurant is a trustworthy place to get a well-cooked meal, with German, French, and international specialties costing 28 DM ($16.65) to 58 DM ($34.45). The restaurant is closed on Fri. and in the month of November.

Hotel Altes Badhaus, Am Lindenplatz 1, D-6930 Eberbach (tel. 06271/56-16), is one of the most interesting buildings in Eberbach. Its name, the Old Bath House, stems from its original function in the 16th century. The finest surviving example of its kind in southern Germany, it was painstakingly restored about 10 years ago and its beautiful vaulted ground floor is now a pleasant restaurant. Upstairs, gourmets can enjoy the creations of one of Germany's most distinguished chefs, Heinrich Goetzenberger. Meals cost 35 DM ($20.80) to 65 DM ($38.60). Twelve delightfully furnished singles, all with showers and toilets, rent for 98 DM ($58.20) daily; six comfortably furnished doubles go for 165 DM ($98) to 185 DM ($109.85), breakfast included. Two apartments for two persons each are priced at 195 DM ($115.80) to 265 DM ($157.35) daily.

Hotel zum Karpfen, Alter Markt 1, D-6930 Eberbach (tel. 06271/7-10-15), is one of the most colorful hotels in town. Authentic *sgraffito* (scratched on) paintings are to be found on its facade, depicting incidents from the history of Eberbach. Built more than two centuries ago near the river, the hotel still welcomes guests into its darkly paneled interior. It contains a full-fledged restaurant, where you can have well-prepared meals in an old-world setting, as well as an informal Weinstube, where tasty specialties are served in generous portions. The 34 comfortably furnished bedrooms rent for 40 DM ($23.75) to 100 DM ($59.40) daily for a single and 65 DM ($38.60) to 140 DM ($83.15) for a double, breakfast included.

Hotel Krone-Post, Hauptstrasse 1, D-6930 Eberbach (tel. 06271/20-13), was Eberbach's coach station in the horse-and-buggy days. It is one of the better-known hotels in the town. Its 44 bedrooms, comfortably and conservatively furnished, are priced at 65 DM ($38.60) to 135 DM ($80.15) daily for singles, 95 DM ($56.40) to 185 DM ($109.85) for doubles, breakfast included.

Haus Talblick, Gaisbergweg 5, D-6930 Eberbach-Brombach (tel. 06272/14-51). Anyone who admires 19th-century craftsmanship as well as a well-prepared cuisine will enjoy this attractive restaurant. In warm weather the outdoor terrace is popular. If you eat indoors, there's plenty to admire and appreciate. Reservations are a good idea, especially on busy weekends. Meals cost 32 DM ($19) to 65 DM ($38.60) and include fresh wild game and a full array of fish dishes. The availability of individual specialties changes with the supply of the ingredients in the local markets. You can choose from such dishes as calves' liver Berlin style with apples, bacon, and sautéed onions; grilled pheasant with pineapple; ragoût of venison with wild mushrooms, cranberries, and freshly made Spätzle. Dinner is served Fri. to Tues. from 5 to 9 pm. Sun. hours are noon to 2pm and 6 to 9 pm. Closed Wed. and Thurs. The restaurant also has five well-appointed double bedrooms to rent, charging 130 DM ($77.20) to 150 DM ($89.05) daily.

NECKARZIMMERN

In the Baden-Württemberg district, 15½ miles from Heilbronn, stands one of the best known places in the Neckartal or Neckar Valley.

It's **Burg Hornberg,** D-6951 Neckarzimmern (tel. 06261/40-64). The hotel is convenient if you'd like to stay outside Heidelberg or are passing by on your route from Heidelberg to Rothenburg.

In this hilltop castle, you climb into a great wooden antique bed and drop all your cares. Dating from the 11th century, the castle was once owned by Götz von Berlichingen (1480–1562), known as "Götz of the Iron Hand." Famed in his time as a redoutable warrior, he lost a hand in battle and had it replaced by an iron one. Hundreds of visitors pass through the hotel portion of the castle, but fortunately, the quarters for guests are private. The interior is handsome and colorful—somewhat like an inn, more informal than grandiose. The public rooms have beamed ceilings, thick walls, an antique tin collection, engravings and forge works, and a portrait of Götz himself.

The castle is moderately priced for an overnight stay, renting 27 bedrooms. Singles rent for 90 DM ($53.45) to 100 DM ($59.49) with shower. Doubles, depending on the plumbing, range from 140 DM ($83.15) to 160 DM ($95). In the old stables a restaurant, Im Alten Marstall, was built. Charcoal meats are a specialty of the Götzen Grill. Arrangements can be made for horseback riding, tennis, and swimming, within an area of 3 miles. You'll enjoy walks through hillside vineyards belonging to the castle. Best of all are the relaxing periods at the end of the day in front of an open fireplace. The hotel is open from March to November.

Meals cost from 40 DM ($23.75) if you're visiting just for the day.

HEILBRONN

The city on the Neckar, 33 miles north of Stuttgart, is an ancient town; documents show that a Villa Heilbrunna existed in 741. In 1371 the city was granted a free imperial city constitution by Emperor Karl IV. The town owes its name to a holy spring (Heiligbronn) that bubbled up from beneath the high altar at **St. Killan's Church,** the city's most important monument. In spite of its overlays of Gothic, it is regarded as the most important High Renaissance structure north of the Alps. The church was begun in 1020, completed in 1529, and destroyed in a 1944 air raid. It was rebuilt in the original style from 1954 to 1974. Its tower is nearly 210 feet high and is considered the earliest example of Renaissance architecture in Germany. Inside are many excellent original wood carvings, preserved during the war, including an elaborate choir and altar.

Opposite the church is the **Rathaus,** or Town Hall, which also forms a medley of Gothic and Renaissance architecture. On its balcony is an astronomical clock, going back to 1580. It was designed by the best-known horologist of the time, Isaak Habrecht, who created the famous clock inside the Cathedral at Strasbourg.

Heilbronn is the largest producer of wine in the Neckar, growing mainly Trollinger and Riesling grapes. The best Neckar wine grows in Heilbronn, or so goes an old German saying. The 550 acres of vineyards around the town yield about 5 million liters of wine annually. Every September a large arena around the Rathaus is converted into a **"wine village."** At various booths you can sample the vintage, often at bargain prices. Merriment and music fill the gap when one isn't drinking. Local food is sold as well, including Zwiebelkuchen (onion cake) and Dicker Hund, which has been compared to a "pork hamburger" (but you don't order it rare).

Centuries-old traditional festivals and fêtes take place here, including a **Volksfest** at the end of July and the beginning of August. There are stalls and sideshows, and the beer, naturally, flows freely.

The play, *Das Käthchen von Heilbronn* was written by Heinrich von Kleist in 1808, and performed for the first time in Vienna in 1810. It became so popular over the years that Käthchen is now the symbol of Heilbronn. Every two years a jury selects a "Käthchen," who represents the city at various functions. In addition, there are Käthchen dolls, a Käthchen Fountain, the Käthchen House, and even a Käthchen beer.

Regrettably, about 80% of Heilbronn was demolished in Allied wartime bombing raids, notably in December of 1944. But the people of the town rebuilt, reconstructing their landmark buildings in the old style, and today Heilbronn is a major commercial and cultural center of the Franconian region. In addition to that, the city definitely believes in "keeping fit" (perhaps to compensate for all that wine and beer drinking). Some 10,000 acres of wooded parkland surround the city, accessible by footpaths and nature trails.

WHERE TO STAY

Insel Hotel, Friedrich-Ebert-Brücke, D-7100 Heilbronn (tel. 07131/63-00), a modern hotel, is built on an island in the middle of the river, right in the heart of Heilbronn. Renovated in 1978, it now contains 120 rooms with 180 beds. Most of the bedrooms have balconies opening onto weeping willows and the hotel's park. The rooms are well designed and comfortable. All have private baths or showers, toilets, radios, and color TVs. A twin-bedded room ranges from 200 DM ($118.75) to 250 DM ($148.45) daily, a single from 140 DM ($83.15) to 190 DM ($112.80). All the tariffs include breakfast from a buffet that offers rolls, cheese, sausages, juices, cereals, and fruits. The front terrace is the beer and gossip center of town, a beehive of a place. Within, there's the cozy Swabian Restaurant, where you can have homemade Spätzle and other well-known specialties. The Insel also has a nightclub, an indoor swimming pool, a sauna, and a solarium.

Hotel Götz, Moltkestrasse 52, D-7100 Heilbronn (tel. 07131/15-50), is in a modern complex of business-related inner-city buildings. Many of the establishment's clients are connected with conventions and come here for annual meetings and policy discussions. There are 86 comfortable and well-designed accommodations, costing 128 DM ($76) to 158 DM ($93.80) for a single, 170 DM ($100.95) to 210 DM ($124.70) for a double, with breakfast included. Each room has a shower or bath, toilet, phone, TV, and radio. There's a plushly furnished dining room, as well as a Bierstube restaurant, on the premises.

WHERE TO DINE

Wirtshaus am Götzenturm, Allerheiligenstrasse 1 (tel. 07131/8-05-34). Its food is well prepared and reasonable in price, but many diners come as much for the charming antique-inspired decor as for the cuisine. By the light of oil-burning lamps, you'll appreciate the brightly polished copper pots, the small-paned windows, the time-blackened paneling, and the elaborate table settings. Full meals cost from 60 DM ($35.65), although a fixed-price menu begins at 40 DM ($23.75). Only dinner is served, from 6pm to midnight; closed Sun. The cuisine is an updated version of German cooking, along with a sophisticated cheese board and delectable desserts.

Ratskeller, Im Rathaus, Marktplatz 7 (tel. 07131/8-46-28), is one of your best bets for dining in Heilbronn. Though a true Ratskeller, unlike so many others, it's been given the modern treatment, with upholstered banquettes and wrought-iron grillwork. Tables are set on two levels. The prices are modest and the cuisine is regional. Typical main dishes include Gulasch, peppersteak with french fries and a salad, and grilled sole. There's an impressive wine list, but don't ignore the wine of the cellar. Meals cost 36 DM ($21.40) to 62 DM ($36.80). The restaurant is open from 8am to midnight; closed Sun.

---

3. Stuttgart

Unlike many large, prosperous industrial centers, Stuttgart is not a concrete city. On the contrary, within the city limits two-thirds of the land is devoted to parks, gardens, and woodlands. Yet Stuttgart is one of Germany's largest manufacturing cities, the home of Mercedes and Porsche automobiles, Zeiss optical equipment, and many other industrial concerns. As a city interested in export and trade, it is also the home of many international trade fairs and congresses. As a cultural center, it is without peer in southwestern Germany. The acclaimed Stuttgart Ballet performs throughout the world. Its State Opera and Philharmonic Orchestra are also highly regarded. In addition, Stuttgart has an abundance of theater groups, cultural festivals, and museums.

Stuttgart is the capital of the southwest German Federal State of Baden-Württemberg. The city produced the philosopher Hegel, who in turn inspired Marx and Engels. It also is the largest wine-growing city in Germany.

Its name comes from a stud farm owned by the Duke of Swabia, son of Emperor Otto the Great, and a horse can be seen today in the city's coat-of-arms. The name of the town first appears in a document from 1160. Stuttgart experienced major growth in the 13th century, and by 1428 it had become the official county capital and the residence of the counts of Württemberg. In 1803 Württemberg became an electorate; three years later, however, it was pronounced a kingdom. The city grew and prospered under the reign of Kaiser Wilhelm I (1816–64). At the turn of the 20th century, it had a population of 175,000. By the beginning of World War I, Stuttgart had reached out to embrace several districts, notably ancient Cannstatt, so that its land mass extended as far as the Neckar River.

In World War II it experienced the worst devastation in its history—53 bomb attacks leveled 60% of its buildings. Not one of its landmarks or historic structures came through intact.

Following a short period of French occupation, the Americans took over in July 1945. Stuttgart thus became the capital of the newly formed state of Baden-Württemberg (many still prefer to call it "Swabia"). Stuttgart's population today is about 560,000.

ORIENTATION

If you arrive by air, you'll land at the international airport 8 miles south of Stuttgart in the vicinity of Echterdingen. There is regularly scheduled bus service every 20 minutes or so from the airport to the Municipal Air Terminus. Buses depart from this terminal with the same frequency, heading for the airport.

Your arrival, however, is likely to be at the Hauptbahnhof, directly north of the historical core of Stuttgart. Around this postwar rail terminus are several hotels. Directly east of the rail center, which opens onto Arnulf-Klett-Platz, is the Schlossgarten, one of the vast parks of Stuttgart.

Running south, the historical Königstrasse is the main street of the city, filled with stores, shops, and restaurants. Along it are found such important sights as St. Eberhard's Cathedral and shop-lined Königsbau. It leads along the former town moat, which King Friedrich had built in 1806, into Schlossplatz (Castle Square), where Neues Schloss, the last castle of the Württemberg royals stands. Directly south of this square is another landmark square—the center of Stuttgart—Schillerplatz, and south of Schillerplatz is Marktplatz and the Rathaus. The home of Daimler-Benz, the oldest automobile factory in the world, is in the suburb of Untertürkheim, on the right bank of the Neckar River.

It's easy to discover the city, as a walking tour has been mapped out for you. Starting at the Hauptbahnhof, follow the yellow-and-black signs through the most important historical districts, as well as the Upper and Central Palace Gardens, going through the Lower Palace Garden as far as the Spa Hall at Bad Cannstatt. A free organized walking tour through historical Stuttgart leaves from the inner courtyard of the Old Castle on Schillerplatz on Saturday at 10am. The tour lasts until about 12:30pm.

Stuttgart and its environs are serviced by a streamlined bus and streetcar system. It also has a modern subway system in use, with more lines planned for the future. It's most economical to buy a 24-hour ticket, for 11 DM ($6.55), which allows visitors to travel on all city transportation facilities. Information about this ticket or information about sightseeing and hotels is available at **Touristik-Zentrum Verkehrsamts,** Klett-Passage (tel. 0711/222-8240).

WHERE TO STAY
No matter when you come to Stuttgart, you will probably find an international trade fair in progress, from the January glass and ceramics exposition to the December book exhibition (Stuttgart is also southern Germany's most important publishing center). Because of this, suitable accommodations may be difficult to find unless you reserve in advance.

Expensive Hotels
Steigenberger Hotel Graf Zeppelin, Arnulf-Klett-Platz 7, D-7000 Stuttgart (tel. 0711/29-98-81 or toll free in the U.S. at 800/882-4777), is the best hotel for those who want to wheel and deal with Stuttgart businesspeople. Although right at the railway station, it's not only attractive but possesses dignity and style. It has a sauna and an indoor swimming pool with a wood-paneled waterside lounge. The 280 soundproof bedrooms are colorfully decorated and come complete with baths or showers, plus direct-dial phones, color TVs, and minibars. Basic singles with showers begin at 239 DM ($141.90) daily, doubles go from 360 DM ($213.75) to 400 DM ($237.50) depending on the plumbing. A full American breakfast is included. Guests congregate in the Apéritif-Bar before making their way to the Restaurant Graf Zeppelin with its French cuisine; the Zeppelin-Stube, serving Swabian dishes; the Maukenescht (Swabian wine corner); or the ZEPP 7 (bistro-café). Later in the evening there is dancing in the Scotch-Club.

Hotel am Schlossgarten, Schillerstrasse 23, D-7000 Stuttgart (tel. 0711/20-26-0), is the tasteful bargain of the top contenders. Totally renovated in 1989, it's not splashy, but offers convenience and comfort. It stands 10 floors high on the railway station plaza. Most of its 126 bedrooms and apartments have their own baths, with showers or tubs. The rooms skirt the line between modern and traditional. Singles cost 215 DM ($127.65) to 255 DM ($151.40) daily, and doubles go for 320 DM ($190) to 380 DM ($225.65). Included in these rates is an American breakfast. The public rooms are consistently sedate, and the hotel bar is warm and cozy. Most intimate is the Zirbelstube, with knotty pine on the walls and ceiling and birch armchairs. You dine by candlelight in this tavern atmosphere. *Note:* There's a 400-car garage.

Park Hotel Stuttgart, Villastrasse 21, D-7000 Stuttgart (tel. 0711/28-01-61), is the choice for those who seek a first-class accommodation in a secluded and quiet area. It's out of the center, in the midst of the gardens of the Villa Berg, within walking distance of a mineral-water swimming pool surrounded by a park. Here the service is personalized, the decor handsome; for example, in the dining room, wood paneling and fabric screens provide semiprivacy, roses adorn the white tables, and glass-bowl droplights make a colorful setting. The 80 bedrooms are well designed, with a decidedly personal aura. Singles with showers or full baths go for 170 DM ($100.95) to 220 DM ($130.64) daily. Doubles with showers or baths range in price from 250 DM ($148.45) to 300 DM ($178.15). These rates include a buffet breakfast. If you arrive in time for dinner, there is a set meal for 40 DM ($23.75), besides many French and German specialties.

Hotel Royal, Sophienstrasse 35, D-7000 Stuttgart (tel. 0711/62-50-50), is centrally located, just a few paces from a major pedestrian walkway. An uneventful facade opens into a well-designed interior, with attractive geometric carpets whose design is repeated in the glass of some of the wall dividers. An octagonal-shaped bar could serve as a rendezvous point. The 100 rooms are warmly lit and comfortable. A single begins at a low of 195 DM ($115.80) daily, going up to 295 DM ($175.15); a double costs 265 DM ($157.35) to 390 DM ($231.60). The dining room serves good-quality meals.

Moderately Priced Hotels

Kronen Hotel, Kronenstrasse 48, D-7000 Stuttgart (tel. 0711/29-96-61), stands slightly beyond the city limits, with a view over the vineyards that are close to Stuttgart. This better-than-usual hotel offers spacious and elegant rooms furnished with upholstered armchairs in a variety of styles, along with Oriental rugs. The Kronen has 90 rooms, with different levels of plumbing, which naturally affect the room rate. Singles range from 100 DM ($59.40) to 140 DM ($83.15) daily, and doubles go from 135 DM ($80.15) to 280 DM ($166.25). The hotel has an interior patio, a sauna, a whirlpool, and solar facilities, plus an elevator designed to accommodate wheelchairs. Breakfast is the only meal served.

Rieker, Friedrichstrasse 3, D-7000 Stuttgart (tel. 0711/22-13-11), across the street from the Hauptbahnhof, is a well-furnished 63-room hotel. Its public rooms have lots of comfortably upholstered armchairs and Oriental rugs scattered over the parquet or terrazzo floors. Some of the virtually soundproof bedrooms are designed with sleeping alcoves and draw curtains. All accommodations have toilets and private baths (or showers), and many contain radios and TVs. You'll be only a one-minute walk from Stuttgart's Municipal Air Terminal, where buses leave frequently for Echterdingen Airport. The bilingual management charges 125 DM ($74.25) to 150 DM ($89.05) daily for a single and 168 DM ($99.75) to 180 DM ($106.90) for a double.

Hotel Ruff, Friedhofstrasse 21, D-7000 Stuttgart (tel. 0711/25-87-0). Some of the side benefits of this modern 85-room hotel include subtly lit tile bathrooms, an attractively tiled indoor pool with a sauna, and a manicured garden where a waiter will take your drink order. The service, much of which is performed by owner Jürgen Ruff, is helpful, and the dining room is an attractive place in which to eat. Singles, depending on whether or not there is a private bath, cost 109 DM ($64.70) to 127 DM ($75.40) daily, and doubles range from 152 DM ($90.25) to 180 DM ($106.90), all including breakfast, the only meal served.

Hotel Wartburg, Langestrasse 49, D-7000 Stuttgart (tel. 0711/20-45-0), lies one block off the main thoroughfare of the Theodor-Heuss-Strasse. This boxy 81-room hotel has balconies with flowerboxes and comfortable bedrooms decorated in earth tones. In the spacious lobby area, guests register for rooms that cost 120 DM ($71.25) to 185 DM ($109.85) daily for a single and 200 DM ($118.75) to 220 DM ($130.65) for a double.

Hotel Unger, Kronenstrasse 17, D-7000 Stuttgart (tel. 0711/20-99-0), lies about a block away from the main railway station. The renovated, fairly distinguished facade of this modern hotel welcomes visitors, and there is a helpful reception staff. All 80 rooms are soundproof and furnished with cable color TVs, radios, private baths or showers, and direct-dial phones. Single rooms cost 129 DM ($76.60) to 169 DM ($100.35) daily, and doubles go for 199 DM ($118.15) to 209 DM ($124.10). Rates include breakfast, service, and taxes. The hotel is within walking distance of the shopping center, Königstrasse. Only breakfast is served.

Budget Hotels

Mack and Pflieger, Kriegerstrasse 7 (tel. 0711/29-19-27), is a fairly modern little hotel on a hillside ledge, an eight-minute walk from the railway station. Home-like and cozy, it offers 85 up-to-date bedrooms that are small and basic, but quite adequate. Bathless singles cost 65 DM ($38.60) daily, those with showers and toilets going for 115 DM ($68.30). Bathless doubles rent for 130 DM ($77.20), those with showers and toilets for 175 DM ($103.90). Breakfast, service, and taxes are included in all the tariffs. There's a phone in each room, and the hotel has an elevator.

Hotel Wörtz-Zur Weinsteige, Hohenheimerstrasse 30, D-7000 Stuttgart (tel. 0711/24-06-81). The amber lights of a Weinstube welcome visitors to one of my favorite hotels in Stuttgart. Bedrooms are paneled and sometimes have massive hand-carved armoires; all rooms are soundproof and air-conditioned. Depending on the plumbing, singles range from 75 DM ($44.55) to 180 DM ($106.90) daily, doubles from 100 DM ($59.40) to 220 DM ($130.65). The Weinstube is perfect for relaxing with a beer or a glass of wine after a long trip. It evokes the feeling that you're in some remote corner of Swabia. The hotel is known for its garden terrace.

WHERE TO DINE

Alte Post, Friedrichstrasse 43 (tel. 0711/29-30-79), is a restaurant recommendable for both cuisine and high standard of service. Featuring an old tavern ambience, it provides the finest cuisine in Stuttgart. The hors d'oeuvres are superb, including goose liver parfait. Among fish dishes, I'd suggest the marvelous sole soufflé Alte Post. A special dish is saddle of deer Waidmannsheil with Spätzle. You can choose your dessert from the buffet. Luncheon menus cost 45 DM ($26.70) to 60 DM ($35.65), and an à la carte dinner could range from 65 DM ($38.60) to 100 DM ($59.40). Stuttgart is modern, but this mellow inn, with its antique interior, provides a comfortable link with the Germany of old. Closed from the end of July to mid-August.

Zeppelin-Stüble, Steigenberger Hotel Graf Zeppelin, Arnulf-Klett-Platz 7 (tel. 0711/29-98-81), is furnished with Swabian antiques and concentrates on such local specialties as Schwäbisches Vesper (a variety of Swabian cold meats), along with such classic local fare as Schwäbischer Rostbraten and Apfelküchle. In all, eight daily dishes are offered, with meals ranging from 18 DM ($10.70) to 55 DM ($32.65). Service is daily from 11am to midnight. And on the same premises you can patronize the elegantly appointed **Restaurant Graf Zeppelin,** where each dish is individually prepared from fresh ingredients, according to the season. Gourmets ask for lobsters and coquilles St-Jacques in puff pastry, veal liver in cassis sauce with leeks, or a Viennese Tafelspitz. Twice a week, duck, lamb, and fresh herbs are delivered direct from Paris markets. The cheese selection is stunning—40 different types (the oldest from 1891). The restaurant offers about 75 types of German wines. Meals cost 45 DM ($26.70) to 115 DM ($68.30). Hours are noon to 2:30pm and 6:30 to 10:30pm; closed Sun., for Sat. lunch, and public holidays. The elegant Italian-style Bistro Café ZEPP 7 offers fresh boiled lobster, broccoli quiche, and a variety of tortellini. The menu changes twice a month, and service is daily from 11am to midnight.

Fernsehturm Restaurant, Jahnstrasse 120, in the Degerloch suburb of Stuttgart (tel. 0711/24-61-04), is a tourist novelty that simultaneously offers good food and a panorama of Stuttgart. For 4 DM ($2.40), you'll be whisked to the top of the Television Tower to this skylit restaurant. The menu is à la carte, with most meals costing 28 DM ($16.65) to 70 DM ($41.55). Hours are 9am to midnight daily. On a higher level is a coffee shop, where you can order both lunch and bar snacks. At the bottom of the tower is the Landhaus restaurant, in a Black Forest motif, with a garden terrace, offering a set menu for only 12 DM ($7.15). It is open daily from 10am to 11:30pm. The tower is 10 minutes by car from the city center and the airport, up a steep, winding road. (For a more detailed description, refer to the sightseeing section, coming up).

Zur Weinsteige, Hohenheimerstrasse 30 (tel. 0711/24-53-96), in the Hotel Wörtz, was previously recommended as a hotel. The interior of this place might be called a celebration of German handcrafts. Everything looks handmade, from the hand-blown leaded glass in the small-paned windows to the carved columns and tables and chairs. International cuisine, with numerous regional specialties, is offered. In summer you'll be tempted to sit among the grape vines stretching over the sun terrace. Meals begin as low as 30 DM ($17.80), ranging upward to 78 DM ($46.30). The Weinstube is open from 7am to midnight, although warm food is available only from noon to 2pm and 6 to 10pm; closed Sat., Sun., and holidays.

Alter Simpl, Hohenheimerstrasse 64 (tel. 0711/24-08-21). Rustic and cozy warmth are the trademarks of this Germanic enclave of Gemütlichkeit. From the filtered light streaming in through the bull's-eye glass in the leaded windows to the sympathetic chatter of the other guests, this place has much charm. Your host, Jürgen Laustere, prepares predominantly Swabian specialties, with some light, modern entries. Because all the ingredients used are likely to be very fresh and expensive, the food is costly, ranging from 65 DM ($38.60) to 130 DM ($77.20), the latter a menu gastronomique of gourmet specialties. Hours are 6pm to 1am; closed Sat. and Sun.

Mövenpick Baron de la Mouette, Kleiner Schlossplatz 11 (tel. 0711/22-00-34), part of the Swiss chain, has a varied menu, including such specialties as fresh fish dishes, filet of rabbit with a chive-flavored mousseline, and Rösti (Swiss pan-fried potatoes). The food is consistently superior, the service professional. Dinners cost from 45 DM ($26.70) to 75 DM ($44.55). The restaurant serves daily from noon to 2:30pm and 6:30 to 10:30pm, and there's a café on the premises that opens for breakfast at 7:30am. Light café meals throughout the day cost from 25 DM ($14.85). There's also a pub. Even though it's part of a chain, there's nothing impersonal about this place.

Alte Kanzlei, Schillerplatz 5a (tel. 0711/29-44-57), is housed in the Old Chancellery in the center of Stuttgart. The structure was originally built by city fathers in 1533. Its warmly rustic interior, where the dining is decidedly informal, has been serving Swabian specialties for more than a century. One regional specialty is called Maultaschen, which is like a Stuttgarter ravioli stuffed with ham or spinach. You can order a tasty regional sausage, Saiten, and end your meal with Pilzkase, a blue-veined local cheese. You can also ask for some of the finest wines in Baden-Württemberg, including a pale rosé known as Schillerwein. Many diners ask for full-bodied red wines made from the Trollinger grape. Meals cost from 15 DM ($8.90), although tabs could run as high as 70 DM ($41.55), depending on what you order. The restaurant is open daily from 11am to midnight.

Dining in the Environs

Hotel Traube, Brabandtgasse 2, D-7000 Stuttgart 70-Plieningen (tel. 0711/45-48-33). An experienced mistress of her craft, the head chef of this venerable establishment (open since 1720) is Remy Recknagel. Her delectable concoctions could consist of Breton lobster, delicately seasoned Atlantic fish imported from France, fresh salads with wild mushrooms, or, in season, just about any variety of fresh game found in Germany. A grand menu costs about 105 DM ($62.35) at this cozy, paneled restaurant. Simpler meals are served for 22 DM ($13.05). The hotel is open on weekdays from 11am to midnight; closed Sat. and Sun. It also rents 22 comfortable rooms. Singles cost 75 DM ($44.55) to 165 DM ($98) daily, and doubles go for 200 DM ($118.75) to 250 DM ($148.45). The Traube is 8 miles south of the city center, five minutes on the Autobahn, and near the airport.

Gasthaus Lamm, Mühlstrasse 24 (tel. 0711/85-36-15), at Feuerbach, lies in a suburb of Stuttgart. A light, modern cuisine that looks westward to France is served, plus a few regional dishes. Try a clear truffled broth, dubbed "Paul Bocuse," a sweetbread soup flavored with cream and basil, or a filet of loup de mer (sea bass) in a saffron-flavored sauce. "Gala menus" range in price from a low of 65 DM ($38.60) to a high of 89 DM ($52.85). The restaurant has only seven tables, so reservations are imperative. Hours are Tues. to Fri. from noon to 2pm and 7 to 9pm; Sat. for dinner only; closed Sun. and Mon.

Öxle's Löwen, Veitstrasse 2 (tel. 0711/53-22-26), is at Muhlhausen, 6 miles from the city center. But the *neue deutsche Küche* of its chef and owner, Martin Öxle, is so celebrated that the world, including publishers and industrialists, beats a path to his door. In a simple setting, cuisine is king. The menu reflects time-tested dishes of the German repertoire as well as light, modern specialties made from very fresh ingredients. The creativity of the chef manifests itself in an array of game, shellfish, fish, and truffles, along with both red and white meats that his clients consume with much gusto. My most recent main course was a breast of pigeon with foie gras. Set meals range from 79 DM ($46.90) to 110 DM ($65.30). You can also order à la carte, with meals costing from 65 DM ($38.60). Hours are noon to 2:30pm, Tues. to Fri.; 6:30pm to midnight, Mon. to Sat.; closed Sun.

Relexa Waldhotel Schatten, Am Solitudering, D-7000 Stuttgart 80 (Büsnau) (tel. 0711/68-67-0), is a suburban hotel with a lot of admirers. The 110-seat Kaminhalle offers regional and international specialties, and in winter you can enjoy an open fireplace in the center of the room. Meals costing 35 DM ($20.80) to 65 DM ($38.60) are served daily from noon to 2:30pm and 6 to 11pm. You can also dine in the hotel's specialty restaurant, La Fenêtre (The Window), open for dinner only Tues. to Sat. from 6pm to 1am. In a room decorated in country provincial style, guests can enjoy French specialties, with meals costing from 70 DM ($41.55). The menu changes every week. Motorists may want to consider lodging here, making the hotel their base for exploring Stuttgart and its environs. Many of the hotel's 144 bedrooms are lacy and frilly, boudoir style, each containing a shower or bath, phone, minibar, radio, and color TV. Including a breakfast buffet, singles rent for 165 DM ($98) to 210 DM ($124.70) daily, with doubles costing 190 DM ($112.80) to 245 DM ($145.50). The hotel also has a fitness center with hot whirlpool and steam baths.

Hirsch-Weinstuben, Maierstrasse 9 (tel. 0711/71-13-75), in Möhringen, is attractively rustic, with a wooden ceiling and lots of hand-painted plates hanging on the walls. This popular restaurant run by Martin and Heiderose Frietsch, serves the kinds of Swabian specialties the local diners prefer. These are likely to include a ragoût of oxtail, Rostbraten with cabbage, and game dishes in season. Lighter dishes might include basil soup with quails' eggs and brains. Reservations are suggested, especially since the suburb of Möhringen is a few miles outside of Stuttgart. A set menu is offered for 40 DM ($23.75). À la carte costs from 30 DM ($17.80) to 50 DM ($29.70). Service is Tues. to Fri., noon to 2pm; Mon. to Sat., 6 to 10pm; closed Sun., and holidays. Also closed for three weeks at some point in summer.

THE SIGHTS

Many of the most remarkable structures in today's Stuttgart are of advanced technological design, created by such architects as Mies van der Rohe, Gropius, Scharoun, and Le Corbusier. The **Liederhalle,** constructed in 1956 of concrete, glass, and glazed brick, is fascinating inside and out. The hall contains three auditoriums so acoustically perfect that all can stage concerts at the same time and not disturb the others. Clustered around the Schillerplatz and the statue of that German poet and dramatist is the older section. The modern **Rathaus** faces the old Marktplatz, where flowers, fruits, and vegetables are still sold in open stalls.

For the best view of the city, you can climb to the top of the 1,680-foot **Birkenkopf** to the west of the city. The hill is composed of the debris of Stuttgart gathered after the air raids of World War II. The 20-minute walk to the top will be rewarded by a view of Stuttgart and the surrounding Swabian Hills, covered with vineyards and woods.

The **Television Tower** (Fernsehturm) (tel. 0711/24-61-04), south of the city (just off Route 3), offers an outstanding view of Stuttgart from a unique location. The 712-foot tower was considered an innovative design when it was constructed in 1956. You can take the elevator up 492 feet to the restaurant and observation platforms for 4 DM ($2.40). Hours are daily from 8am to 10:30pm.

Altes Schloss, the old castle facing Schillerplatz, is one of Stuttgart's oldest standing structures. The huge ducal palace was originally a moated castle built in the 13th century, but it was renovated in the 16th century into a more comfortable Renaissance style. It now houses the **Württembergisches Landesmuseum** (tel. 0711/279-34-00), which traces the art and culture of Swabia from the Stone Age to the present day. The most valuable items are displayed in the Dürnitzbau, including a survey of European handcrafts through the ages, the ducal art chamber, and the Crown Jewels. The museum houses a large collection of Swabian sculptures, and don't miss the exhibition of clocks, coins, and musical instruments. The world-famous treasures of the tomb of the Celtic prince of Hochdorf (circa A.D. 530) are here, as well as one of the biggest collections from the Merovingian period in the early Middle Ages. The museum is open from 10am to 5pm (on Thurs. to 7pm); closed Mon. Admission is free.

Neues Schloss (New Castle) at Schlossplatz, can be visited only by group tour. Constructed between 1746 and 1807, it was rebuilt beginning in 1958. Today it houses state government rooms.

The **State Gallery of Stuttgart,** Konrad-Adenauer-Strasse 30-32 (tel. 0711/ 212-50-50), is the city's finest art museum, exhibiting works spanning some 550 years. However, the best collection is from the 19th and 20th centuries, especially the works of the German expressionists—Kirchner, Barlach, and Beckmann—as well as representatives of the Bauhaus movement, Klee and Feininger. The largest collection of non-German painters is the group of works by French artists of the 19th and 20th centuries, including Manet, Cézanne, Gauguin, Renoir, Picasso, Braque, and Léger, and by the European and American avant-garde after World War II. The museum is open from 10am to 5pm (on Tues. and Thurs. to 8pm); closed Mon. Admission is free.

Major attractions outside of town include the **Wilhelma Zoo,** Neckartalstrasse, Stuttgart–Bad Cannstatt, one of the largest and most beautiful zoological and botanical gardens in Europe. Created in 1842 for King Wilhelm I of Württemberg as a Moorish garden, it contains more than 8,000 animals, along with important orchid cultures, an aquarium with a crocodile hall, and a famous coral fish collection. That's not all. Other attractions include a magnolia grove, an ape house, a camellia and azalea house, plus a restaurant and café terrace. Charging a 7-DM ($4.15) entrance fee, the zoo is open May 1 to August 31, daily from 8am to 6pm. It closes at either 4 or 5:30pm at other times of the year, depending on the season.

Porsche Museum, Porschestrasse 42, Stuttgart-Zuffenhausen, is a museum devoted to the world-famous manufacturer of racing and sports cars. Hours are Mon. to Fri. from 9am to noon and 1:30 to 4pm; admission free. Take S-Bahn no. 6 to Neuwirtshaus station. Free guided tours of the production lines are conducted. But you should phone for a reservation at 0711/827-56-85. Ferdinand Porsche, of Bohemia, founded the company after World War II and was the creator of the Volkswagen.

Daimler-Benz Museum, Mercedesstrasse 136, Stuttgart-Unterturkheim, a museum devoted to the oldest automobile factory in the world, was established to honor the invention of the motorcar by Carl Benz and Gottlieb Daimler. The two men, who worked separately, had their companies merged in 1926, but by then Daimler was dead and Benz had retired. To reach the plant, you take S-Bahn no. 1 to Neckarstadion. Head on foot to the entrance to the plant. You'll be taken on a special sealed bus to the museum (that way, you can't see out in case you should be an industrial spy). Nearly 75 historical vehicles are shown, including a Daimler Reitwagen from 1885, the first motor bicycle. You can also see the Daimler company's first Mercedes. The year was 1902. Both utility and luxury cars are displayed (one made for the royal family of Japan). Admission is free, and museum hours are Tues. to Sun. from 9am to 5pm.

AFTER DARK

The state theater, **Württembergische Staatstheater,** Oberer Schlossgarten (tel. 0711/2-03-20) is the leading cultural venue in Stuttgart. The theater consists of a Grosses Haus for opera and ballet, a Kleines House for theater, and the Kammertheater, which puts on experimental works. The theater is the home of the world-class **Stuttgart Ballet,** established by the choreographer John Cranko in the 1960s, and carried on today by its former prima ballerina Marcia Haydée. Tickets for events here can be purchased at the tourist office at Klett-Passage (tel. 0711/222-82-40), near the main railway station.

Classical and other concerts may be heard in the three halls of the **Liederhalle,**

Schlossstrasse (tel. 0711/29-94-71). If your German is good, there are a variety of theatrical offerings in the city. Consult the tourist office at Klett-Passage for information.

---

4. Tübingen

Often compared to Heidelberg, this quiet old university town on the upper Neckar has a look and personality all its own. The gabled medieval houses are crowded up against the ancient town wall at the bank of the river. In the summer the only movement to break this peaceful picture is that of the students poling gondolalike boats up and down the river. This far upstream, 25 miles south of Stuttgart, the Neckar is too shallow for commercial vessels, and Tübingen has been spared the industrial look of a trading community.

Progress has not passed the city by, however. In spite of its medieval look, it has a new residential and science suburb in the shadow of the Schoenbuch Forest north of the city, with medical facilities, research institutes, and lecture halls affiliated with the university. North of the Botanical Gardens stand the buildings of the old university, founded in 1477. The humanist Melanchthon taught here in the 16th century, and later on, Schiller, Hegel, and Hölderlin were students at the university. Most of the buildings are in a functional neoclassical design, but they fit right in with the old city around them.

A unique feature of Tübingen is the artificial island in the Neckar, with its promenade lined with plane trees. This street, known as **Platanenallee,** is always alive with summer strollers who cross from the main town via the wide Eberhardt Bridge. The island also offers the best view of the town, with its willows and houses reflected in the river. Towering above the roofs is the Renaissance castle, used by the university. Visitors to Tübingen should go to the castle, at least for the dramatic view from the terraces.

The narrow streets of the old town wind up and down the hillside, but they all seem to lead to the **Marktplatz** where festive markets are still held on Monday, Wednesday, and Friday. You'll feel like you're stepping into the past when you come upon the scene of country women selling their fruits and vegetables in the open square. In the center of all this activity stands the softly murmuring Renaissance fountain of the god Neptune. Facing the square is the Rathaus, dating from the 15th century, but with more recent additions, including the 19th-century painted designs on the facade overlooking the Marketplace.

On a hillside above the Marketplace stands **St. George's Church,** the former monastery church of the Stift, an Augustinian monastery. The monastery became a Protestant seminary in 1548 and its church the Collegiate Church. Worth seeing inside are the tombs of the dukes of Württemberg in the chancel and the French Gothic pulpit and rood screen, dating from the 15th century.

WHERE TO STAY

The university town's most prestigious hostelry, the **Krone Hotel,** Uhlandstrasse 1, D-7400 Tübingen (tel. 07071/3-10-36), is right off the river, in the heart of Tübingen. Dating from 1885, the hotel is both traditional and conservative. The interior has a homelike atmosphere with a liberal use of antiques or good reproductions. The 50 bedrooms are all personalized, with a well-planned arrangement of furniture. Many of the baths are decoratively tiled, with stall showers, and all rooms have private facilities. Singles cost 125 DM ($74.25) to 170 DM ($100.95) daily; doubles, 200 DM ($118.75) to 280 DM ($166.25). The owners, Karl and Erika Schlagenhauff, provide some of the best meals in town (recommendable even if you're not an overnighter). There are three dining rooms: the formal dining salon; the Uhlandstube, with an old-tavern atmosphere; and a country-style room, all served by one kitchen. The menu is international, typical dishes including filet of sole in butter, Wiener Schnitzel, and tournedos Rossini. Meals cost 38 DM ($22.55) to 75 DM ($44.55), and service is daily from noon to 2:15pm and 6 to 10:30pm.

Hotel Stadt Tübingen, Stuttgartnerstrasse 97, D-7400 Tübingen (tel. 07071/ 3-10-71), with shrubbery burgeoning on the balconies, looks almost like something you'd find in a subtropical climate. Nonetheless, the well-managed staff and the competent director convince you that the place is pure German, and generous doses of warm, up-to-date comfort are applied. The hotel was renovated in 1985, and a section was built around a sunny atrium full of plants. Each of the 56 accommodations includes a private bath, TV, phone, and minibar; a buffet breakfast is included in the rates. Single rooms rent for 90 DM ($53.45) to 120 DM ($71.25) daily, while doubles cost 140 DM ($83.15) to 210 DM ($124.70).

Hotel Hospiz, Neckarhalde 2, D-7400 Tübingen (tel. 07071/2-60-02), is comfortably furnished and subtly lit from the outside, its large windows overlooking the cobblestoned pavement in front. This is a delightfully old-fashioned 48-room hotel, with single rooms ranging from 55 DM ($32.65) to 110 DM ($65.30) daily and doubles from 135 DM ($80.15) to 160 DM ($95). All rooms have showers or baths, except six singles that share a shower on the same floor. The hotel opens onto a beautiful view of the old town and has an inviting and cozy Ratskeller. It's within walking distance of most of the major sights.

Hotel am Bad, Am Freibad 2, D-7400 Tübingen (tel. 07071/7-30-71). Lying in the center of one of Tübingen's well-maintained public parks, this 36-room hotel has the added advantage of containing an Olympic-size public swimming pool practically at its back door. Its rambling yellow exterior contrasts vividly with the masses of red flowers planted on the sun terrace. Inside, the comfortable rooms offer woodland calm not far from the city center. Singles cost anywhere from 68 DM ($40.40) to 95 DM ($56.40) daily, depending on the bath facilities, and doubles are 115 DM ($68.30) to 140 DM ($83.15); a buffet breakfast is included.

WHERE TO DINE

Outside of the hotel dining rooms, the **Restaurant Museum,** Wilhelmstrasse 3 (tel. 07071/2-28-28), is one of Tübingen's foremost eateries. The set lunches it serves for 20 DM ($11.85) to 32 DM ($19.00) are considered by many locals (including students) to be not only the best meals in town but the best value as well. À la carte dinners cost from 32 DM ($19). The restaurant is a pleasant place to dine on international specialties such as Marseille snail soup or a regional dish such as Swabian medallions of veal. It is open from 10am to midnight; closed Mon.

Landgasthof Rosenau, Beim Neuen Botanischen Garten (tel. 07071/6-64-66), near the Botanical Gardens, is like a roadhouse with a café-annex. The owner serves superb Swabian specialties along with modern cuisine. The typical regional fare is listed under the gutbürgerliche selections. Among these, for example, is a tasty and filling Swabian hot pot with Spätzle and fresh mushrooms. Under the section of the menu "reserved for gourmets," you might prefer veal steak with morels. Desserts are often elaborate concoctions. Prices range from 35 DM ($20.80) to 65 DM ($38.60) for a meal. The restaurant is open from noon to 2pm and 6 to 10 pm; closed Tues. In fair weather, guests can order drinks outside in the sun.

Alte Weinstube Göhner, Schmiedtorstrasse 5 (tel. 07071/228-70), is one of Tübingen's most reasonably priced restaurants and wine cellars. Here, in the heart of town, you will find students as well as local citizens. The owner offers local and regional specialties along with many kinds of wine. Full meals cost 12 DM ($7.15) to 25 DM ($14.85) and are served daily from 6pm to midnight.

The finest restaurant in the area is not in Tübingen but on the outskirts. It's the **Gasthof Waldhorn,** Schönbuchstrasse 49 (tel. 07071/6-12-70), at Tübingen-Bebenhausen, about 4 miles from the heart of the university town. Here Herr and Frau Schilling operate a restaurant decorated like a large farmhouse. They offer a light cuisine based on regional ingredients, backed up by an impressive wine list (many half-bottles). The menu changes daily, but is likely to include such dishes as trout terrine and wild venison with mushrooms, along with whatever vegetable is in season, perhaps fresh asparagus or forest mushrooms. The house dessert specialty is a soft cream concoction flavored with rose hips. Meals cost 52 DM ($30.90) to 82 DM ($48.70) and are served from noon to 2pm and 6:30 to 9 pm; closed Thurs. and for lunch Fri.). They shut down for three weeks sometime in summer.

5. Schwäbisch Hall

Technically, this medieval town is not in the Neckar Valley, but if you skip it in your travels through this region, you will have missed one of the treasures of southwestern Germany. Lying in the heart of the forests of the Schwäbische Alb, 40 miles east of Heilbronn, the town clings to the steep banks of the Kocher River, a tributary of the Neckar. The houses of the Altstadt are set on terraces built into the hillside, and from the opposite bank they appear to be arranged in steps, overlooking the old wooden bridges on the river.

The **Marktplatz** is possibly the most attractive market square in all of Germany. Flanking the square are fine timbered patrician houses, and at the lower end of the sloping square, stands the baroque Rathaus. In the center of the square is a 16th-century Gothic fountain, decorated with statues of St. Michael with St. George and Samson. Behind the fountain is a decorative wall holding the pillory where offenders in days gone by were left to be jeered at by the townspeople. Today the square is the scene of festive occasions, such as the annual Kuchenfest (Salt Maker's Festival), celebrating the ancient salt industry that grew up around the springs in Schwäbisch Hall.

On the northern side of the Marketplace, facing the Rathaus, are the imposing 54 large stone steps, delicately curved, leading up to **St. Michael's Cathedral.** The cathedral is a 15th-century Gothic Hallenkirche with a 12th-century tower. Many of the pews date from the 15th century, as does St. Michael's altarpiece in the side chapel. The church is open March to November, daily from 9am to noon and 1:30 to 5pm. Admission is 1 DM (60¢).

WHERE TO STAY AND DINE

Right on the Marketplace, the **Adelshof,** Am Markt 12, D-7170 Schwäbisch Hall (tel. 0791/61-81), is an attractive stone building, much of it dating from 1400. The 46-room hotel has been completely renewed, and its rooms are now of a good standard. A heated swimming pool is a further lure. Singles with toilets and showers cost 104 DM ($61.75) to 150 DM ($89.05) daily, and doubles go for 174 DM ($102.30) to 210 DM ($124.70), breakfast included. A sauna bath is extra. Downstairs, the restaurant serves some of the best food in town, with meals ranging in price from 35 DM ($20.80) to 75 DM ($44.55). Closed Mon.

Hotel Hohenlohe, Am Weilertor 14, D-7170 Schwäbisch Hall (tel. 0791/75-87-0), is a 96-room hotel built beside the Kocher River in the historic Freie Reichsstadt district. A good view unfolds from its several floors of bedrooms. The accomodations are comfortable and compact, with bright color accents, and all of them contain private baths. A single rents for 97 DM ($57.60) to 137 DM ($81.35) daily and a double for 168 DM ($99.75) to 196 DM ($116.40). These rates include breakfast on an open-view roof deck. The hotel's restaurant offers meals for 30 DM ($17.80) to 68 DM ($40.40), and there are also a cafeteria and a bar on the premises. Other facilities include an indoor and outdoor pool, a sauna, solarium, and massage parlor.

Hotel Simon, Schweickerweg 25, D-7170 Schwäbisch Hall (tel. 0791/30-76). The facade of this 17-room concrete hotel is relieved by the skillful use of planting and flowers. Ten minutes by car from the center of town, it has a public swimming pool within easy reach. All the well-furnished rooms have private toilets along with baths (or showers), costing 92 DM ($54.65) daily for a single, rising to 108 DM ($64.15) for a double, with breakfast included.

Hotel Garni Scholl, Klosterstrasse 3, D-7170 Schwäbisch Hall (tel. 0791/7-10-46), is beautifully located on the medieval square to the side of St. Michael's. This 32-room hotel is the union of two very old half-timbered houses, one pumpkin-colored, the other an olive green. You'll find plenty of visitors enjoying the café's sun terrace in front, overlooking the Marketplace. Doubles with showers and toilets rent for 105 DM ($62.35) daily, breakfast included, while singles on the same arrangement cost 72 DM ($42.75).

A Hotel in the Environs

About 17 miles from Schwäbisch Hall on the Hohenlohe plateau—named for one of the great German princely families of centuries past—stands the **Wald-und Schlosshotel Friedrichsruhe,** D-7111 Friedrichsruhe (tel. 07941/60-870). It's about 4 miles north of the little village of Ohringen. One of the two buildings comprising the hotel was built between 1712 and 1719 by Prince Johann Friedrich of the Ohringen branch of the Hohenlohe family. Constructed as a hunting lodge, the three-story edifice with a tile roof and baroque central gable was called Friedrichsruhe, or Friedrich's Refuge. A second building, added in 1953, about a three-minute walk from the original lodge, is modern inside—bedrooms with up-to-date conveniences, two restaurants, saunas, and a heated indoor swimming pool —but it was constructed to look old outside. There are also an outdoor pool and tennis courts.

Lothar Eiermann, who runs the hotel for its owner, the present Hohenlohe-Ohringen prince, welcomes guests to the 55 rooms of the three buildings. Singles cost 165 DM ($98) to 298 DM ($176.95) daily, and doubles go for 278 DM ($165.10) to 368 DM ($218.50). Herr Eiermann is a trained chef whose skills are evidenced by the food served. You can eat in the main dining room amid red walls, snow-white damask napery, and brass chandeliers, or in the less formal Stube, with a regional ambience produced by mounted antlers, carved-back chairs, and an old porcelain stove. Expect to pay 80 DM ($47.50) to 180 DM ($106.90) for a meal.

THE MOSEL VALLEY

Those returning from Germany singing the praises of the Rhine as the most scenic of German rivers have definitely not taken the short trip up the Mosel River. Weaving its snakelike path through the mountains west of the Rhineland, the Mosel (Moselle) encounters town after town whose sole purpose seems to be to beautify the banks of the river. Nearly every village and every hill has its own castle or fortress, surrounded by vineyards where green grapes are grown for the popular wines.

Many of the Mosel wines are superior to those of the Rhine Valley, and in spite of their lightness, they are rich and full-bodied. Mosel wines have the lowest alcoholic content, only about 9%, of any white wine in the world. Because of this, they are best enjoyed in their youth. The freshness of some vintages deteriorates with age.

The Mosel begins in the hills of France, and its most colorful portion is the last 120 miles before it flows into the Rhine at Koblenz. Along these banks, the visitor enjoys the lively landscapes, the legend-rich countryside, and, of course, the best wines. In recent years, locks have been built at strategic points along the river to enable vessels to sail the waters that once transported Roman ships. The locks have been incorporated into the landscape, and thus far have not hurt the appearance of the river.

If you enter Germany via France or Luxembourg, the Mosel is a good route by which to begin your tour of the German countryside. By following its path through the mountains, you'll first arrive at the major city of Trier.

1. Trier (Trèves)

As the Romans spread out over Europe, they established satellite capitals and imperial residences for ruling their distant colonies. Augusta Trevororum (Trier) eventually became known as Roma Secunda—the second Rome. For nearly five centuries, well into the Christian Era, Trier remained one of Europe's most powerful cities, politically, culturally, and religiously.

Officially founded by the Romans under Augustus in 16 B.C., Germany's oldest city actually dates back much further. In 2000 B.C., according to legend, the Assyrians established a colony here, and archeological findings indicate a pre-Roman (Celtic) civilization. The buildings and monuments still standing today, however, date from Roman and later periods.

Trier is an important gateway, lying on the western frontier of Germany, where the Ruwer and Saar rivers meet the Mosel. Just 6 miles from the Luxembourg border, it is the first major city on the Mosel—and one rich in art and tradition. It was an important market city by 958, a fact commemorated by the Market Cross placed on the old Hauptmarkt by the archbishop. Because of its location, it is one of Germany's largest exporters of wine. Karl Marx was born and grew up in Trier; his birthplace is now a museum (see below). As a young man, he traveled down the Mosel Valley and was shocked by the exploitation of the vineyard workers, wrote articles about such practices, and so began his career.

ORIENTATION

If you arrive by rail, you'll be deposited at the Hauptbahnhof, or rail terminus, opening onto Bahnhofplatz in the eastern part of town very near the old quarter. From here you can walk west (which is also the direction of the Mosel) along Theodor-Heuss-Allee to the major landmark of Trier, the Porta Nigra. From the Porta Nigra, you can take a pedestrians-only street, Simeonstrasse, which will deposit you at the Hauptmarkt, the major square of Trier. At this "living room of Trier," you'll be at several of the town's major attractions, including its Dom and Liebfrauenkirche. The city's two major bridges spanning the Mosel are the Römerbrücke (which still possesses its old Roman pilings) and the Kaiser-Wilhelm-Brücke (which crosses over an islet in the river known as Moselinsel).

WHERE TO STAY

Expensive Hotels

Across from the Roman ruins, the **Dorint Porta Nigra,** Porta-Nigra-Platz 1, D-5500 Trier (tel. 0651/2-70-10), offers a desirable accommodation that combines style, comfort, and position. It is a six-story 106-room building whose interior is decorated with primary colors and contemporary furnishings. The bedrooms usually have sitting areas; baths are ornately tiled. Rates depend on the view and size, with singles priced at 115 DM ($68.30) to 165 DM ($98) daily and doubles at 165 DM ($98) to 280 DM ($166.25). Guests enjoy drinks in the intimate bar before dining in the traditional restaurant. A café with an entire wall of glass provides a view of the Roman ruins. The hotel also houses a casino offering roulette and blackjack.

Europa Parkhotel, Kaiserstrasse 29, D-5500 Trier (tel. 0651/7-19-50). An unusual facade of curved concrete with soundproof windows greets visitors to this 85-room hotel. Bedrooms have all the conveniences of a first-class establishment. Singles rent for 138 DM ($81.95) to 178 DM ($105.70) daily, while doubles cost 195 DM ($115.80) to 270 DM ($160.35), breakfast included.

Scandic Crown Hotel, Zurmaienerstrasse 164, D-5500 Trier (tel. 0651/14-30), is one of the leading hotels in Trier. On the banks of the Mosel, it lies near the Autobahn exit labeled Trier-Nord-Verteilerkreis, some five minutes by car from the city center. A former Holiday Inn, it is a newly refurbished first-class hotel. It offers 216 comfortable and well-furnished bedrooms, most of which open onto views of the river. Each unit has a private bath, minibar, and multi-channel TV. Children under 16 can share their parents' room free. Otherwise, singles cost 170 DM ($100.95) daily, doubles are 220 DM ($130.65), and junior suites for two persons peak out at 260 DM ($154.40). The hotel offers two good restaurants, serving not only international and regional food but a Swedish cuisine as well, as befits the owners of the hotel. Other facilities include a swimming pool and sauna. There is also free parking. In the evening, guests relax in the bar with live piano music.

Moderately Priced Hotels

With a view over the city of Trier, the **Petrisberg,** Sickingenstrasse 11, D-5500 Trier (tel. 0651/4-11-81), is beautifully situated at a point where a forest, a vineyard, and a private park meet. This intelligently designed four-story 35-room hotel offers accommodations that contain almost one wall of glass, opening onto a refreshing view of the greenery outside. Furnishings include, for example, 7-foot armoires and reproductions of slant-topped antique desks. Singles go for 75 DM ($44.55) to 80 DM ($47.50) daily, and doubles rent for 115 DM ($68.30) to 130 DM ($77.20), depending on the plumbing. Breakfast is included, and some apartments, suitable for three persons, are available at 180 DM ($106.90) per night. The Weinstube on the ground floor is the gathering place for many residents who live nearby, particularly on weekends.

Villa Hügel, Bernhardstrasse 14, D-5500 Trier (tel. 0651/3-30-66). All the views from the windows of this lovely white house overlook either a private garden with old trees or the city of Trier. You can order food and beverages while sitting on a panoramic terrace. The sitting room/lobby area is decorated with masonry detailing and Oriental rugs, while the 26 bedrooms are spacious and high-ceilinged. The Schutt family, your hosts, rent singles for 75 DM ($44.55) to 110 DM ($65.30) daily and doubles for 105 DM ($62.35) to 140 DM ($83.15). All rooms contain baths, toilets, and phones, and a nourishing breakfast is included in the tariffs.

Altstadthotel, Porta-Nigra-Platz, D-5500 Trier (tel. 0651/4-80-42), is located in a refurbished and charming turn-of-the-century house with all modern conveniences (including elevator and parking lot), one block from the Porta Nigra, extending into a quiet side street. It offers 32 bedrooms, all containing baths, toilets, and phones, with a highly praised buffet-style breakfast included in the price. Singles range from 90 DM ($53.45) to 95 DM ($56.40) daily and doubles from 140 DM ($83.15) to 170 DM ($100.95).

Eurener Hof, Eurener Strasse 171, D-5500 Trier (tel. 0651/8-80-77), lies on the other side of the river, 10 minutes from downtown by car or 15 minutes by bus. It offers 61 bedrooms, all with baths, toilets, and phones. Singles range from 90 DM ($53.45) to 130 DM ($77.20) daily and doubles from 140 DM ($83.15) to 210 DM ($124.70). The Eurener Hof also offers one of the best restaurants in Trier; a swimming pool and sauna; and free parking.

Budget Hotels

If you're seeking a reasonably priced accommodation, **Hotel Monopol,** Bahnhofsplatz 7, D-5500 Trier (tel. 0651/7-47-55), across from the railway station, may fill the bill. Reached by elevator, its 35 rooms are both good-sized and well maintained. Singles range in price from 47 DM ($27.90) daily for a bathless room to 65 DM ($38.60) for a unit with a shower and toilet. Doubles cost 80 DM ($47.50) to 95 DM ($56.40), depending on the plumbing. The management has employed a helpful staff. The hotel is closed from Christmas to mid-February.

Hotel Kurfürst Balduin, Theodor-Heuss-Allee 22, D-5500 Trier (tel. 0651/2-56-10), lies only one block from the railway station. It is most convenient, yet far enough away to escape the noise coming from the station. The bedrooms have been remodeled, and each unit is neat, clean, and comfortable. The most expensive doubles (those with showers and toilets) range in price from 95 DM ($56.40) to 108 DM ($64.15) daily. Even cheaper doubles, containing only showers, cost 85 DM ($50.45) to 95 DM ($56.40). The bargain specials are the bathless doubles, costing 68 DM ($40.40) to 78 DM ($46.30). These tariffs include a Continental breakfast, service, and taxes. The innkeeper, Hella Schwarz, will give recommendations and directions for shops, restaurants, and sightseeing, and is in general a warm, friendly person. Readers have liked the old-fashioned charm of the hotel. Guests don't seem to mind the lack of an elevator, and often gather in the lounge–coffee room to watch television.

Deutschherrenhof, Deutschherrenstrasse 32, D-5500 Trier (tel. 0651/4-83-08), is identified by an elegantly discreet entrance. The 33 modern and comfortable bedrooms all have showers and toilets, TVs, and phones. Singles cost 65 DM ($38.60) to 85 DM ($50.45) daily, and doubles go from 100 DM ($59.40) to 120 DM ($71.25). The hotel, which stands in the middle of the town, has an attractive bar.

Kessler, Brückenstrasse 23, D-5500 Trier (tel. 0651/7-67-71), stands next to the Karl-Marx-Haus. Because of its position on an acute angle of a downtown street corner, this 21-room hotel has direct sunlight from three sides. It offers attractively maintained single rooms for 70 DM ($41.55) to 100 DM ($59.40) daily and doubles for 100 DM ($59.40) to 150 DM ($89.05), breakfast included. All the rooms have private showers and toilets. Guests gather in the evening in the hotel's cozy bar. The hotel is under the administration of Jörg Mueller, who speaks English and does everything he can to make your stay pleasant.

WHERE TO DINE

A preferred choice for dining is **Zum Domstein,** Hauptmarkt and Dom 5 (tel. 0651/7-44-90), overlooking the flower stands and the fountain on the Hauptmarkt. Opening onto an inner courtyard, it features an authentic local cuisine and sets a high culinary standard. The three dining rooms have a true gemütlich atmosphere, in the best German tavern tradition. English is spoken. For 9 DM ($5.35), you're given six different wines of the Mosel, Saar, and Ruwer regions, lined up so that you can drink them in proper order. In addition, 18 open wines and about 250 bottled ones are in the cellar awaiting your selection. The food is tempting; a typical offering is a platter of pike balls in a Riesling sauce with noodles. The restaurant opens daily at 9am, closing at midnight. Expect to spend from 25 DM ($14.85) to 55 DM ($32.65) to dine here. In winter you'll want to find a spot near the huge tile stove. You can also have a look at the **Römischer Weinkeller.** This room is in the area of the double cathedral (A.D. 326), excavated in 1970. Original Roman artifacts, many connected with food and cooking, decorate the cellar room. In the Römischer Weinkeller you are served dishes prepared according to recipes attributed to Marcus Gavius Apicius, said to have been the foremost chef at the court of the Roman emperor Tiberius. One food critic labeled this banquet "a curious mixture of flavors, unforeseen combinations, and sudden surprises."

Pfeffermühle, Zurlaubener Ufer 76 (tel. 0651/2-61-33), in Zurlauben. How do you make a restaurant successful in Trier? Siegbert and Angelika Walde use fresh ingredients, work long hours, and welcome diners to the bright, well-decorated dining room (with river view) where they are served a delectable French cuisine. Many critics consider this the best restaurant in Trier. Charging 60 DM ($35.65) to 85 DM ($50.45) for dinner, it's open from noon to 2pm and 6 to 10pm; closed Sun., holidays, and for three weeks from mid-July.

Lenz Weinstuben, Viehmarktplatz 4-5 (tel. 0651/4-53-10), near the city's newest Roman excavations, attracts clients familiar with quality meats. The maître d'hôtel encourages clients to order one of the excellent daily fixed-price specials, which vary, naturally, according to the season. Count on spending from 28 DM ($16.65) to 50 DM ($29.70). Everything served is wholeheartedly German, with such local specialties as Trierer meat pie or a medallion of lamb in white wine with onion and potato disks. Service is from 11am to 1am; closed Mon.

Brasserie, Fleischstrasse 12 (tel. 0651/7-52-31), is on the bottom floor of a beautifully maintained neoclassical house near the Hauptmarket. A pub-style restaurant, it serves the finest fish and wild-game dishes in its price range in Trier. Fixed-price menus cost 32 DM ($19) to 55 DM ($32.65). Everything is fresh here. Recipes feature international dishes at night, but at lunch there's a special emphasis on seasonal cookery. Try, for example, filet of doe in a wild mushroom cream sauce or marinated pork cooked by a special recipe. Food is served from 10:30am to 1am; closed Sun.

Brunnenhof im Simeonstift, in Simeonstift (tel. 0651/4-85-84), is nestled in historic ruins, occupying a portion of an old cloister and providing an excellent place to dine. In fair weather you may prefer to eat in the courtyard, where you can enjoy the splashing fountain and the pure line of the Romanesque arches. The food is somewhat standardized, but good. Set meals in the 35 DM ($20.80) range are offered daily from 11:30am to 2:30pm. The place is closed from January to mid-February.

THE SIGHTS

When the last Roman prefect departed from Trier in about 400, he left behind a vast collection of monuments to the centuries of Roman domination. The **Porta Nigra** (Black Gate) is the best-preserved Roman relic in Germany, the only survivor of the great wall that once surrounded Trier. The huge sandstone blocks, assembled without mortar, were held together with iron clamps, the marks of which can still be seen. From the outside of the gate, the structure appeared to be simply two arched entrances between rounded towers leading directly into the town, but intruders soon discovered that the arches opened into an inner courtyard where they were at the mercy of the town's protectors.

During the Middle Ages the Greek hermit Simeon, later canonized, chose the east tower as his retreat. After his death the archbishop turned the gate into a huge double church. When Napoleon came this way, however, he ordered all the architectural changes to be removed and the original Roman core restored. The Porta Nigra is open from 9am to 1pm and 2 to 6pm in summer (5pm in the off-season); closed Mon. Admission is 2 DM ($1.20).

The **Imperial Palace** district, stretching along the site of the former medieval wall of the city, begins with the huge Roman room known today as the **Basilica.** Although much of the original structure has been demolished, the huge hall that remains gives some idea of the grandeur of the original palace. Believed to be the throne room, the hall is 220 feet long, 90 feet wide, and 98 feet high. The two tiers of windows are arranged within high-rising arches in which fragments of some of the original wall paintings can be seen. The unique method of Roman central heating through a hollow floor was used to warm this hall from five large heating chambers outside the walls. Today the hall serves as the main Protestant church in the city.

Adjacent to the Basilica is the **Kurfürstliches Palais** (Electoral Palace), built in the 17th century as the residence for the archbishop-electors. Originally designed in the style of the German Renaissance, during remodeling in the 18th century it received a more rococo appearance in the wing facing the **Palace Gardens.** These formal gardens, full of ponds and flowers, are decorated with rococo statues.

The **Imperial Baths,** at the south end of the Palace Gardens, were erected in the early 4th century by Constantine I. Of the huge complex, more than 284 yards long, only the ruins of the hot baths remain. These baths were among the largest in the Roman Empire, and although never completed, were used in connection with the Imperial Palace, and built about the same time. Some older Roman baths, the Baths of St. Barbara, are on Südallee near the Roman bridge.

The **Amphitheater,** incorporated into the old Roman walls, is the oldest Roman construction in Trier, dating from A.D. 100. The stone seats, arranged in three circles separated by broad promenades, held at least 20,000 people.

St. Peter's Cathedral, north of the Palace Gardens and Basilica, stands above the former palace (4th century) of Empress Helena, mother of Constantine. This structure influenced the style adopted by the archbishop when he added the Romanesque facade in the 11th century. The Gothic and baroque additions in later centuries only helped to pull the ecclesiastical architecture into a timeless unity. The interior is also unique, combining baroque furnishings with the Gothic vaulting and archways. The treasury contains many important works of art, including the 10th-century St. Andrew's Altar, an unusual portable altar (if you could lift it) made of wood and covered with gold and ivory. But the most valuable treasure is the Holy Robe, alleged to be the seamless garment of Christ, brought to Trier by Empress Helena. The relic is so fragile that it was last displayed in 1959.

Liebfrauenkirche (Church of Our Lady), separated from the cathedral by a narrow passageway, is a parish church and is more pleasing aesthetically than its older sister. The first example of French Gothic in Germany, it was begun in 1235. The ground plan is in the shape of a Greek cross, creating a circular effect with all points equidistant from the central high altar. The structure is supported by 12 circular columns, rather than the typical open buttresses. The interior is bathed in sunlight, which streams through the high transoms. Although the restoration after the war changed some of the effect of the central construction, the edifice is still unique among German churches. Some of the important works of art have been placed in the Bishop's Museum; the sepulcher of Bishop Karl von Metternich is among the most interesting of those remaining. On the black marble sarcophagus is a sculptured likeness of the canon, who represented the archbishopric during the Thirty Years' War.

Rheinisches Landesmuseum, Ostallee 44 (tel. 0651/4-83-68), between the Imperial Baths and the audience hall (Basilica), at the edge of the Palace Gardens behind the medieval city wall, is one of the outstanding museums of Roman antiquities north of the Alps. Numerous reliefs from funerary monuments show daily life in Roman times. The museum's most popular exhibit is the *Mosel Ship,* a sculpture of a wine-bearing vessel crowning a big funerary monument of the third century A.D. Many ornamental and figurative mosaics and frescoes, ceramics, glassware (especially the great diatret-vessel), an outstanding numismatic collection, and prehistoric and medieval art and sculpture are also exhibited. The museum is open weekdays from 9:30am to 4pm; on Sat. to 1pm; Sun. from 9am to 1pm. Admission is free.

Bishop's Museum (Bischöfliches Museum), Windstrasse 8 (tel. 0651/710-52-55), also near the cathedral, contains valuable pieces of religious art from the Trier diocese. Among the most important is the ceiling painting from Constantine's palace, recently discovered under the cathedral. Also included are medieval sculptures and other works of art from the treasures of the churches of Trier. The museum is open Mon. to Sat. from 9am to 1pm and 2 to 5pm; Sun. from 1 to 5pm. Admission is 1 DM (60¢) for adults, .50 DM (30¢) for children.

Karl-Marx-Haus, Brückenstrasse 10 (tel. 0651/4-30-11), is the old burgher's house in which Marx was born in 1818. It has been made into a museum exhibiting his handwritten volumes of poetry, original letters, photographs with personal dedications, and first editions of such works as *Das Kapital.* The personal history of Marx is documented here as well as the development of socialism in the 19th century. The house contains one of the largest collections in the world of international editions of the *Communist Manifesto,* including rare first editions and printings that appeared before 1900. From April to October, the museum is open on Mon. from 1 to 6pm; Tues. to Sun. from 10am to 6pm. From November to March, it is open on Mon. from 3 to 6pm; Tues. to Sun. from 10am to 1pm and 3 to 6pm. Admission is 3 DM ($1.80) for adults, 2 DM ($1.20) for children under 15. At Simeonstrasse 8, there is a plaque stating that it was the residence of the Marx family from 1819. Karl lived here until he finished school in 1835.

Because of the importance of Trier as a wine export center, a visit to the huge wine vaults beneath the city is recommended. Tours of the vaults and special wine tastings (daily from 10am to 6pm) can be arranged through the **city tourist office** at An der Porta Nigra (tel. 0651/4-80-71). There you can also purchase a "Go-As-You-Please" ticket for one day, which is valid for use on all public transport in the central zone of Trier. The cost is 5 DM ($3). From May to October the tourist office offers a two-hour English-language tour Mon. to Fri., costing 7 DM ($4.15) per person.

In summer there are regular **cruises** and occasional excursions by boat starting from the city dock, Zurlauben. The boats go from Trier to Koblenz, a two-day tour, stopping at little Mosel villages along the way. The tourist office has all the details about these excursions, which fluctuate from season to season and vary widely in price.

2. Zell

This old town, stretching along the east bank of the Mosel, is best known for its excellent wine, Schwarze Katz (Black Cat). The grape is king here, as you'll realize if you come to Zell during the annual wine festival.

WHERE TO STAY AND DINE

If you're seeking accommodations, try the **Schloss Zell,** Schlosstrasse 8, D-5583 Zell (tel. 06542/40-84), one of the very special places in Germany. It is in-stalled in a 14th-century castlelike bastion, and is run by the Bohn family. Right in the heart of Zell, its twin domed towers are a village landmark. Because of high taxes and the ever-constant need for maintenance, the family now receives paying guests (try for the ornate bedroom used by Kaiser Maximilian, the last cavalier, in 1512, or the honeymooners' special in the tower). The salons and the drawing room are filled with antiques—a flamboyant use of gilt, ornate inlaid woods, stained glass, bronze, and crystal. Be sure to see the settee given to Josephine by Napoleon. Favored guests who stay more than one night are invited into the private drawing rooms, in them-selves museums of antiquity. For an accommodation here, you pay 75 DM ($44.55) to 110 DM ($65.30) daily per person, with breakfast included. Closed mid-December to mid-January.

Zur Post, Schlosstrasse 21, D-5583 Zell (tel. 06542/42-17). Painted a delight-ful shade of canary yellow, this beflowered hotel sits directly on the river. Its sun terrace is the kind of inviting space where you can catch up on your reading or gossip with a friend. The warmly decorated Weinstube is the kind of place where you'll meet a new one. The 16 rooms are carpeted, with French doors opening onto the balconies. All units have showers or baths. Singles cost 45 DM ($26.70) to 55 DM ($32.65) daily, and doubles go for 90 DM ($53.45) to 110 DM ($65.30). Meals are served daily except Monday, costing 22 DM ($13.05) to 45 DM ($26.70). The ho-tel is closed from February to mid-March.

Weinhaus Mayer, Balduinstrasse 15, D-5583 Zell (tel. 06542/45-30), is named after its founder. This balconied, five-story rustic hotel offers personalized comfort in 14 rooms, usually with a view over the Mosel. Singles rent for 50 DM ($29.70) daily, and doubles are priced at 90 DM ($53.95), with breakfast included. The hotel is open from April to November.

On the left bank of the Mosel, 5 miles from Zell and 20 from Cochem, stands the little wine village of **Alf.** The surroundings are idyllic, especially if you climb up to the Marienburg. From there, you get a fine view overlooking the Mosel and the vineyards of Zell.

3. Traben-Trarbach

Thanks to their central location on the Mosel, halfway between Koblenz and Trier, the twin cities of Traben and Trarbach have become the wine capitals of the Mosel Valley. The gardenlike promenades on both banks of the river are viewpoints for annual international speedboat and waterskiing competitions on the Mosel. The July wine festival attracts visitors from all over Europe to the old wine cellars and taverns of the towns. But behind all the bustle and activity, Traben-Trarbach is proud of its attractions, especially its thermal springs and health resort, **Bad Wildstein,** just south of town.

Above Trarbach, on the east bank of the river, stands the 14th-century **Grevenburg Castle,** which, with five other now-in-ruins castles in the vicinity, was the scene of hard-fought battles to gain control of this strategic spot on the Mosel. On the opposite bank, above Traben, are the ruins of **Mont Royal,** a fortress built in the late 17th century by the invading Louis XIV.

WHERE TO STAY AND DINE

If you plan to stay over, you might try **Rema Hotel Bellevue,** Am Moselufer, D-5580 Traben-Trarbach (tel. 06541/64-31), in Traben, a heavily Germanic 58-room structure right on the riverbank. It was created in an ornamental style about 1900 by the architect Moehring, with elaborate timberwork, a domed tower, a highly pitched roof, gables, and dormers. A special feature is the ivy-covered terrace, where you can dine. Inside, stained-glass windows are set in ecclesiastical frames, and overstuffed chairs are drawn up around Victorian fringed "parlor tables," resting under vaulted ceilings. The accommodations are warmly decorated. The managers charge 85 DM ($50.45) to 105 DM ($62.35) daily for singles. Doubles go for 140 DM ($83.15) to 220 DM ($130.65). All tariffs include breakfast and taxes. The hotel has been entirely renovated.

Hotel Krone, An der Mosel 93, D-5580 Traben-Trarbach (tel. 06541/63-63). Only a narrow country lane separates the sun terrace of this 22-room hotel from the waters of the Mosel. The architecture might be that of a ski chalet in Aspen, with big glass windows and a modern roofline above the flowers scattered across the balconies. The rooms are immaculately maintained, and all units contain private baths, minibars, radios, and TVs. Singles rent for 75 DM ($44.55) to 90 DM ($53.45) daily, and doubles cost 106 DM ($62.95) to 120 DM ($71.25). Meals cost 28 DM ($16.65) to 88 DM ($52.25). The restaurant is closed Mon.

Hotel-Restaurant Altes Gasthaus Moseltor, Moselstrasse 1, D-5580 Traben-Trarbach (tel. 06541/65-51), on the outskirts, is at Im Ortsteil Trarbach. The exterior of this four-story rectangular building, dating from 1838, is a masterpiece of fieldstone masonry from another era. Inside, a charming combination of new construction with antique elements from the original building creates a warm mixture of comfort and convenience. The Bauer family runs this 11-room hotel, renting singles for 50 DM ($29.70) to 80 DM ($47.50) daily and doubles for 80 DM ($47.50) to 130 DM ($77.20), including breakfast. The light cuisine is prepared by chef Ruth Bauer, whose reputation has spread to such a degree that German urbanites come here for a "gastronomic weekend." The restaurant is small—only 11 tables—with fixed-price menus costing 48 DM ($28.50) to 110 DM ($65.30). Hours are from noon to 2pm and 6 to 9pm; closed Tues. The hotel is open from January to December, but the restaurant is closed in February.

Bisenius, An der Mosel 56, D-5580 Traben-Trarbach (tel. 06541/68-10), is a 12-room family-run country-villa–style hotel, with balconies, flowers, a sun terrace with a view of the Mosel, and an indoor swimming pool. Breakfast only is served. All units have showers and toilets. Singles go for 65 DM ($38.60) to 88 DM ($52.25) daily and doubles for 120 DM ($71.25).

Zum Anker, Rissbacherstrasse 3, D-5580 Traben-Trarbach (tel. 06541/15-64), is a riverfront hotel efficiently run by the Ningel family. Many of their bedrooms have balconies facing the Mosel, and if yours doesn't, you can still enjoy a cup of coffee or a late-night beer at the café/sun terrace. All bedrooms have private baths. Prices, including breakfast, are 60 DM ($35.65) to 70 DM ($41.55) daily for singles, 85 DM ($50.45) to 105 DM ($62.35) for doubles, depending on the time of year. Even if you don't lodge here, you are invited to patronize the hotel's attractively rustic restaurant and Weinstube.

Central, Bahnstrasse 43, D-5580 Traben-Trarbach (tel. 06541/62-38), is an unembellished five-story, 34-room hotel with a gemütlich decor of bright fabrics and wooden ceilings. Centrally located, as its name implies, it charges 40 DM ($23.75) to 50 DM ($29.70) daily for singles, 74 DM ($43.95) to 84 DM ($49.90) for doubles, all with showers and toilets. Host Ernest Ochs has had an elevator installed in the hotel. Closed December 20 to January 10.

---

4. Bernkastel-Kues

Like Traben-Trarbach, this town is split into twin villages on opposite banks of the Mosel. In a valley of wine towns, Bernkastel stands out as the most colorful, with its old Marktplatz surrounded by half-timbered buildings in good condition, dating from as early as 1608. In the center of the square stands **St. Michael's Fountain** (17th century), which flows with wine during the annual September wine festival. Above the town stand the ruins of the 11th-century **Landshut Castle,** worth a visit for the view of the Mosel from the promontory on which it stands. During the wine festival the castle is illuminated by floodlights and fireworks.

WHERE TO STAY AND DINE

An orange gingerbread relic, the **Drei Könige** (Three Kings), Bahnhofstrasse 1, D-5550 Bernkastel-Kues (tel. 06531/20-35), stands on the banks of the Mosel at Orsteil Kues. Its architecture is characterized by gables, bay windows, and a timbered tower. There are 40 comfortable bedrooms, many of which contain private baths. To stay here costs 85 DM ($50.45) to 100 DM ($59.40) daily in a single, 125 DM ($74.25) to 150 DM ($89.05) in a double, depending on the accommodation you select. In the wine cellar you can sample Mosel wine. Open mid-March to mid-November.

Doctor Weinstuben, Hebegasse 5, D-5550 Bernkastel-Kues (tel. 06531/60-81). This intricately half-timbered building was the headquarters of the tax collector when it was constructed in 1652. Today it's perhaps the most visually interesting hotel in Bernkastel. Transformed into a tavern back in 1830, it still has many of its original woodcarvings, including an elaborate double balustrade (the motif in vines and fruits) leading to the upper floors. The 15 rooms are cozy, and doubles go for 100 DM ($59.40) to 130 DM ($77.20) daily, including breakfast. The Doctor serves some of the most savory viands in town. Fixed-price menus are offered at 32 DM ($19) to 68 DM ($40.40) and are available daily from noon to 2pm and 6 to 10pm. Closed Mon. in the off-season.

Römischer Kaiser, Markt 29, D-5550 Bernkastel-Kues (tel. 06531/30-38). The peach-colored facade of this 31-room hotel, covering the angle of two downtown streets, has a view of the Mosel from many of the upper windows. Public rooms are decorated almost like a private home, with paintings and Oriental rugs. Including breakfast, doubles go for 85 DM ($50.45) to 130 DM ($77.20) daily, depending on the plumbing, and singles cost 65 DM ($38.60) to 75 DM ($44.55). Many visitors come here just to dine, because the hotel is well known in the region for its gutbürgerlich cookery, using fresh ingredients if at all possible. Like any good restaurant along the Mosel, it features the wines of the region. A separate menu lists all the things anyone could possibly do with prawns. Meals cost 25 DM ($14.85) to 60 DM ($35.65); the place is open daily from 11am to 9:30pm. The restaurant closes annually in January and February.

Zur Post, Gestade 17, D-5550 Bernkastel-Kues (tel. 06531/20-22). Constructed in 1827 as a stopover point for men and their horses on the local postal routes, this 42-room hotel is today directed by Bernhard Rössling. He maintains the pastel-yellow and mustard-colored facade in good condition. A view of the interior will reveal an elegantly crafted stairwell flanked by half-timbered walls and a paneled, beamed dining room where excellent regional cookery is served with 100 varieties of Mosel wine. Single rooms go for 75 DM ($44.55) to 90 DM ($53.45) daily; doubles, depending on the plumbing, range from 110 DM ($65.30) to 140 DM ($83.15). The restaurant, open to the "public at large," serves daily from 11am to 2:30pm and 5:30 to 10:30pm. À la carte meals cost 30 DM ($17.80) to 65 DM ($38.60). Closed in January.

Hotel Burg Landshut, Gestade 11, D-5550 Bernkastel-Kues 11 (tel. 06531/30-19). The white neoclassical facade, with its triangular pediment and orderly windows, seems strangely out of place in this town of rustic dwellings. However, a tour of the 30-room hotel reveals painstakingly handcrafted herringbone floors and high-ceilinged bedrooms. Singles cost 50 DM ($29.70) to 100 DM ($59.40) daily, and doubles go for 85 DM ($50.45) to 150 DM ($89.05). Meals go for 28 DM ($16.65) to 65 DM ($38.60). The restaurant closes on Tuesday from November to April, and the entire hotel operation closes down in January and February.

Gasthof Moselblümchen, Schwanenstrasse 10, D-5550 Bernkastel-Kues (tel. 06531/23-35), lies on a narrow cobblestoned street for pedestrians only. Identified by a wrought-iron sign fastened to the corner of the building, the 22-room guest-house is within walking distance of everything in Bernkastel. Rooms here are clean and charmingly appointed. Visitors pay 40 DM ($23.75) to 60 DM ($35.65) daily for a single, 68 DM ($40.40) to 84 DM ($49.90) for a double. Breakfast is included in the tariffs, and it's also possible to order meals, at 20 DM ($11.90) to 55 DM ($32.65). The restaurant closes Monday in the off-season, and the whole guesthouse is closed from mid-February through March.

Rôtisserie Royale, Burgstrasse 19 (tel. 06531/65-72), is an embellished half-timbered house whose four narrow stories are sandwiched between its neighbors. In summer geraniums festoon the sills of leaded-glass windows, set on either side of the black-and-gilt hotel sign. Hugo König is the owner; he and his wife prepare an imaginative fixed-price menu that changes almost every day. Many of the specialties are grilled by Hugo himself at the charcoal grill, which occupies a corner of the dining room. You might enjoy such specialties as a terrine of pheasant in a madeira-flavored gelatin, a vol-au-vent of seafood with a lobster sauce, and tournedos "royale" with a fennel and tomato sauce. A fresh salad, cheeses, and freshly prepared raspberries might accompany your meal, which is likely to cost 45 DM ($26.70) to 70 DM ($41.55), with some wine included. Reservations are suggested. Only dinner is served, from 6pm to midnight (closed Mon.) for most of the year.

5. Beilstein

On the east bank of the Mosel, this ancient wine town has an unusual market-place hewn right into the rocky hillside. Above the town stands the former cloister church and the ruins of the 12th-century Metternich Castle.

WHERE TO STAY AND DINE

You can sample the wines that made Beilstein famous at its favorite inn, the picturesque **Haus Lipmann,** Moselstrasse 3, D-5591 Beilstein (tel. 02673/15-73). Time has been kind to this 1795 timbered inn in one of the oldest and most unspoiled villages along the Mosel. For six generations the same family has tended the vast riverside vineyards that have won them acclaim. Try either their Ellenzer Goldbäumchen or their Beilsteiner Schlossberg. The spots for drinking and dining are so tempting that it's difficult making a decision. Most popular in summer, however, is the vine-covered terrace, with a statue of Bacchus, overlooking the Mosel. Of course, there's the antiques-filled tavern or the wood-paneled Rittersaal, with its collection of old firearms and pewter. Candles are lit at night; in the cooler months, fires burn in either the tall walk-in fireplace or the tiny open hearth, with its copper kettle on a crane. Meals cost 25 DM ($14.85) to 60 DM ($35.65). Service is daily from noon to 2pm and 6 to 8pm. The Mosel eel in dill sauce is classic, but especially delectable is the fresh wild trout.

The five bedrooms in the main house have showers and toilets. Singles rent for 45 DM ($26.70) daily, and doubles go for 70 DM ($41.55) to 85 DM ($50.45). These rates include breakfast. The hotel closes from mid-November to mid-March. Activities get hectic at grape harvest time.

Klapperburg, Marktplatz 34, D-5591 Beilstein (tel. 02673/14-37), is built into the side of a hill. The masonry-and-stucco facade of this rustic hotel opens into a series of public rooms decorated with rows of antique kitchen utensils and more than 100 hand-operated coffee grinders. Overnight rates are attractively set at 40 DM ($23.75) to 55 DM ($32.65) daily for a single, 65 DM ($38.60) to 75 DM ($44.55) for a double, depending on the plumbing. If the Klapperburg is full, the same rates apply at another pension not far away. Called **Zur Guten Quelle,** it has the same ownership and houses guests in an attractive half-timbered structure.

Haus Burgfrieden, Im Mühlental 63, D-5591 Beilstein (tel. 02673/14-32). More a complex of buildings than a single hotel, this establishment has proved popular with locals and visitors alike for more than 25 years. The 38 comfortable rooms here rent for 40 DM ($23.75) to 60 DM ($35.65) daily for a single, 80 DM ($47.50) to 90 DM ($53.45) for a double, including breakfast. The hotel is open from April to October.

---

6. Cochem

In one of the best wine regions of the Mosel Valley, this medieval town is crowded against the left bank of the river by a huge vineyard-covered hill. The town is a typical wine village, with its tastings and festivals. But the biggest attraction is **Reichsburg Cochem** (tel. 02671/2-55), a huge castle at the top of the mound behind the town. Originally built in 1027, it was almost completely destroyed by the army of Louis XIV in 1689. It has since been restored after the original ground plans, and its medieval ramparts and turrets create a dramatic backdrop for the town. To reach the castle, follow the steep footpath from the center of town. The 15-minute walk is well worth it for the views of the town and the Mosel below. Although you can visit anytime, the interior of the castle is open daily from 9am to 5pm. Guided tours are conducted at regular intervals. Admission is 3.50 DM ($2.10) for adults, 1.50 DM (90¢) for children and students. It is open from mid-March to November.

WHERE TO STAY

Both a hotel and a wine restaurant, the **Alte Thorschenke,** Brückenstrasse 3, D-5590 Cochem (tel. 02671/70-59), is one of the oldest and best-known establishments along either side of the Mosel. The romantically conceived building, with its timbers and towers, was originally built in 1332. It became a hotel in 1960, when a modern wing was added, offering rooms with private baths. Most of the accommodations are reached via a cantilevered wooden staircase that has creaked for centuries —and probably will for a few more. Of course, there is an elevator in the rear if you want to make it easy on yourself. Depending on the plumbing, the rate for singles ranges from 65 DM ($38.60) to 115 DM ($68.30) daily; the rate for doubles, from 145 DM ($86.10) to 185 DM ($109.85). If you want a room with an old-fashioned four-poster bed, ask for the Himmelbetten (heaven beds). The hotel rents 35 bedrooms, mainly doubles. Not to be ignored are meals in the tavern, accompanied by Mosel wines. In summer, guests often take their lunch at one of the sidewalk tables. Meals range in price from 35 DM ($20.80) to 60 DM ($35.65). Closed January 5 to March 15.

The 500-year-old castle of Baron von Landenberg in Eller is about 4½ miles from Cochem. Guests of the hotel can visit the old cellars and enjoy tasting the wines.

Germania, Moselpromenade 1, D-5590 Cochem (tel. 02671/2-61), is a big, resort-style hotel, complete with dormers and balconies, as well as dining terraces surrounded by red geraniums. Best of all, it's right on the Mosel, with a view of Cochem Castle. The interior oozes with charm, leaning heavily on traditional wood paneling and provincial antiques. Part of the hotel dates back to 1749, but modernization has erased much antiquity. The 15 bedrooms all have baths or showers. There is only one single, costing 75 DM ($44.55) daily, and doubles rent for 120 DM ($71.25) to 180 DM ($106.90). Closed in January.

Burg Hotel, Moselpromenade 23, D-5590 Cochem (tel. 02671/71-17), is the happy domain of the Müller family, who offer guests a warm welcome. They have renovated the 50-room inn, providing private baths or showers and toilets, plus color TVs, for all the bedrooms. The furnishings are traditional, with a few antiques lending added style, and some rooms have balconies opening onto views of the Mosel. Singles rent for 45 DM ($26.70) to 65 DM ($38.60) daily and doubles for 80 DM ($47.50) to 140 DM ($83.15). In the restaurant, typical dishes include game fricassée with asparagus and rice; fresh trout meunière; and rumpsteak with mushrooms. A large selection of the best Mosel wines is available to accompany your meal. The hotel offers an indoor swimming pool, sauna, solarium, and TV room.

Lohspeicher, Obergasse 1, D-5590 Cochem (tel. 02671/39-76). A former warehouse for supplies for the local tannery, this generously proportioned 1832 building was constructed with lots of hand-hewn beams. Completely renovated in 1979, it's now a delightful hotel, serving excellent meals and offering lodging in eight well-furnished rooms. The charge for a single is 55 DM ($32.65) to 65 DM ($38.60) daily; for a double, 100 DM ($59.40) to 120 DM ($71.25). All tariffs include breakfast, service, and taxes. A gourmet meal, at what many consider the best table in town, costs 38 DM ($22.55) to 80 DM ($47.50). Specialties include onion or snail soup, followed by all kinds of fish and game dishes (try the filet of venison with wild mushrooms in a cream sauce). The restaurant is open from noon to 2pm and 6 to 11pm; closed Tues. The hotel closes in January and February.

Haus Erholung, Moselpromenade 65, D-5590 Cochem (tel. 02671/75-99). The restaurant of this 10-room pension is gaily decorated with hanging pink and white lamps and lots of green plants. The dormers and mansard roof of the house itself indicate that it was probably a private villa before the addition of the sun terrace. Many of the double rooms are sunny, with large windows exposing views of the countryside. Your hostess is Hildegunde Lehmann, who will indicate the direction of the sauna and swimming pool, and serve you the wholesome breakfast included in your room rate of 84 DM ($49.90) daily for a double with private toilet and shower. Overflow guests are housed in an annex, which opens onto a view of the river and castle. Open mid-March to mid-November.

Triton, Uferstrasse 10, D-5590 Cochem-Cond (tel. 02671/2-18), is the best hotel in Cochem-Cond. One of the finest things about this 18-room balconied hotel is the view of the baroque buildings and the fortified castle that you'll get from your river-view windows. Across the Mosel from the rest of Cochem, the hotel offers modern single rooms at 65 DM ($38.60) to 95 DM ($56.40) daily and doubles at 110 DM ($65.30) to 130 DM ($77.20), breakfast included. In keeping with the symbol of the hotel (Neptune's triton), the hotel also has an indoor swimming pool with a sauna, plus a waterside café–sun terrace built almost on the riverbank. The owner, Paul Thow, keeps his hotel open from mid-March to November 4.

Am Hafen, Uferstrasse 14, D-5590 Cochem-Cond (tel. 02671/84-74), is a riverside hotel operated by the Laux family, who offer 20 comfortable rooms priced at 70 DM ($41.55) to 110 DM ($65.30) daily for a double with shower and toilet, 40 DM ($23.75) to 70 DM ($41.55) for a single. The generously proportioned four-story building has terraces and a café on the ground floor. Meals cost 20 DM ($11.90) to 50 DM ($29.70). The hotel closes in January.

Am Rosenhügel, Valwigerstrasse 57, D-5590 Cochem-Cond (tel. 02671/13-96). The Goebel family are the hosts at this 23-room hotel, which has balconies and a sun terrace overlooking the Mosel. Some of the rooms offer spectacular views of the castle on the hill. Singles rent for 43 DM ($25.55) to 75 DM ($44.55) daily, and doubles cost 82 DM ($48.70) to 96 DM ($57), depending on the plumbing and the view. The place is closed in December and January.

Moselromantik Hotel-Café Thul, Brauselaystrasse 27, D-5590 Cochem-Cond (tel. 02671/71-34). Comfortably modern, this 24-room hotel offers clean rooms and Gemütlichkeit to guests who pay from 40 DM ($23.75) to 100 DM ($59.40) daily for a single, 70 DM ($41.55) to 120 DM ($71.25) for a double, breakfast included. The dining room serves good food in a comfortable setting, with meals costing 25 DM ($14.85) to 40 DM ($23.75). The establishment is open from March to November.

WHERE TO DINE

A hostelry with an illustrious tradition, the **Hotel Brixiade,** Uferstrasse 13, D-5590 Cochem-Cond (tel. 02671/30-15), seeks to maintain its position. The heyday of this hotel was in the period just preceding World War I, when it was a favorite of the poet Joseph von Lauff and of Kaiser Wilhelm II. Service is polite, and you can sit either in the Weinstube or on the garden terrace. A fixed-price menu begins at 25 DM ($14.85). Order Mosel wine here and you'll get the best of the region. The restaurant is open daily from 7am, and warm food is served from 11:30am to 2:30pm and 6 to 9:30pm. The hotel also rents 40 comfortably furnished rooms, charging 55 DM ($32.65) to 80 DM ($47.50) daily for singles, 80 DM ($47.50) to 110 DM ($65.30) for doubles.

Parkhotel Landenberg, Sehler Anlagen 1, D-5590 Cochem-Sehl (tel. 02671/71-10), offers a nice view to the Cochemer-Reichsburg and over the Mosel. The specialties of this area are venison, wild boar, and fish—to be enjoyed with a good bottle of white Mosel wine from the hotel's own cellar. Meal prices run from 20 DM ($11.90) to 60 DM ($35.65); serving hours are noon to 2pm and 6pm to 9pm daily. The 24 rooms in the hotel are comfortably furnished. Singles rent for 65 DM ($38.60) to 90 DM ($53.45) daily, doubles for 100 DM ($59.40) to 170 DM ($100.95). Facilities include a swimming pool, sauna, and solarium. The hotel closes in January.

Weissmühle 3, D-5590 Cochem (tel. 02671/89-55), is in Enterttal, an idyllic hamlet outside of Cochem. Before or after your meal, you'll enjoy a walk through the romantic little village. Many of the specialties on the menu are unique culinary inventions of the restaurant, and include a series of Wurst dishes, trout, or Spiessbraten grilled to perfection over an open fire. Meals are attractively priced from 32 DM ($19) to 65 DM ($38.60), and food is served daily from 10am to 9pm. Comfortably furnished rooms—36 in all—are rented. Singles cost 58 DM ($34.45) daily, while doubles go for 110 DM ($65.30) to 165 DM ($98).

---

7. Eltz Castle

This magnificent castle, **Burg Eltz** (tel. 02672/13-00), completely surrounded by woodlands, can be reached in about 40 minutes from **Moselkern,** or, more conveniently, in about 15 minutes if you arrive via **Münstermaifeld,** which has a remarkably beautiful Gothic abbey church, and **Wierschem.**

The castle is one of the few medieval castles in the Rhineland that is still intact. The original structure, built from the 12th to 17th centuries, has been preserved in all its glory—the romance of the Middle Ages really comes alive here. Completely surrounding a large inner court, the castle houses four separate residences, with original furnishings from the Gothic period, including some fine old paintings and tapestries. From April to November 1, the castle is open daily from 9am to 5:30pm (from 10am on Sun.). Admission is 5.50 DM ($3.25) for adults, 3.50 DM ($2.10) for children. A wine-tasting cellar and a treasury containing work by goldsmiths and silversmiths, armor, weapons, and other objects of value acquired by the family through the centuries, are open to the public at an extra charge. If you want to fortify yourself before the trek back to town, two small restaurants lie within the castle walls.

THE BLACK FOREST

When you visit the Schwarzwald, as this region in southwestern Germany is called, don't expect to come upon a little elf working on a cuckoo clock in his tiny gingerbread shop. What you will find, however, is nearly as exciting and altogether more enjoyable. The Schwarzwald covers a triangular section of the large province of Baden-Württemberg roughly 90 miles long and 25 miles wide. The pine- and birch-studded mountains are alive with fairy-tale villages, sophisticated spas, and modern ski resorts, but, sad to say, pollution now threatens one of the most beautiful parts of Germany. The peaks in the southern part of the forest reach as high as 5,000 feet, excellent for skiing in winter and hiking or mountain climbing in summer. The little lakes of Titisee and Schluchsee are popular for boating, swimming—and of course winter skating. Fish abound in the streams and lakes, and deer romp through the groves of pine.

Besides the cuckoo clock and the many toys manufactured in the Black Forest, this region is noted for another product—Kirschwasser, an unsweetened cherry brandy derived from the fruit of its black, twisted cherry trees. This, along with Black Forest bacon and provincial-style rye bread, constitutes a memorable meal.

The ideal way to explore the Schwarzwald is on foot, but time and energy would probably run out before the many scenic attractions did. So motoring is the best alternative. The roads through the forest are excellent, especially the **Schwarzwald Hochstrasse** (Black Forest High Road), the B500, running almost the entire length of the Black Forest region, some 100 miles, from Baden-Baden to Freudenstadt (40 miles), then resuming at Triberg and going on to Waldshut on the Rhine, where you can cross the border to Switzerland. This scenic route offers many opportunities to park your car and explore the countryside or to turn off on one of the side roads leading to hospitable villages, ancient castles, and rolling farmlands.

1. Baden-Baden

In the 19th century the nobility of Europe discovered Baden-Baden, where the bath-conscious Roman emperor Caracalla had taken the waters more than 1,500 years before. Most of the titles and crowns are merely dust collectors today, but the legacy left by these Romans and Romanovs has made the resort on the edge of the Black Forest the most elegant and sophisticated playground in Germany. The clientele may have changed, but Baden-Baden still evokes an aura of 19th-century privilege, combined today with the most up-to-date facilities.

Baden-Baden is the ideal choice for sports and outdoor enthusiasts who would like to settle in for a few days of golf, tennis, or horseback riding. Horse lovers will also enjoy the international racing season each August at Iffezheim Track. The surrounding countryside is good for hiking and mountain climbing. During the winter months Baden-Baden is still very active. As the gateway to the Black Forest, it is a convenient center for ski resorts—after a day on the slopes, you can return to a soothing swim in a thermal pool before a night out at the casino.

If you arrive in Baden-Baden by rail, you will be deposited north of the spa, at Baden-Oos, the main rail terminus. Regrettably, it's an expensive 20-minute taxi ride into the center. Once you arrive at your hotel, however—and assuming it's in the heart of town—you will find most of the spa's attractions within walking distance. As you leave the station, you ride along Rheinstrasse, which becomes Langestrasse and then Luisenstrasse as it stretches like a snake all the way to Leopoldsplatz. By the time you reach this square, you will have penetrated the heart of Baden-Baden.

From Leopoldsplatz, Sophienstrasse, a major artery of town, runs east to what is considered historic Baden-Baden. In and around the area north of Sophienstrasse are such attractions as the Neues Schloss, the Stiftskirche, and several baths, both ancient and modern. Back at Leopoldsplatz, you can take a bridge over the river which leads into Goetheplatz. From here it is but a short walk to the Kurhaus, the Spielbank, and the Trinkhalle.

South from here, Lichtentaler Allee is the major promenade boulevard of the spa. Lichtentaler Allee will take you to Lichtenthal, once a separate town, but now part of Baden-Baden. If you continue south, you can traverse the Schwarzwald Hochstrasse referred to in this chapter's introduction.

WHERE TO STAY

Deluxe Hotels

The Rolls-Royce of resort hotels in Baden-Baden is **Brenner's Park-Hotel & Spa,** An der Lichtentaler Allee, D-7570 Baden-Baden (tel. 07221/35-30). A distinguished hotel, it lies in a large private park facing the River Oos and Lichtentaler Allee. Some of its international habitués wouldn't dare let a year go by without making an appearance here for the cure. It's a glamorous place at which to stay. Celebrities who have patronized the waters here in the past have included Cornelius Vanderbilt and Igor Stravinsky. The 100 rooms offer good taste and comfort, with singles ranging in price from 240 DM ($142.50) to 430 DM ($255.35) daily and twins with baths from 290 DM ($172.20) to 1,290 DM ($766). The public rooms are fashionably conceived, each providing a rich background for the chic attire of guests. A pianist plays every afternoon in the lounge and in the evening at the Oleander-Piano-Bar for dancing. There is gourmet dining in the main restaurant or in the Schwarzwald-Stube.

The hotel, recognizing that people today are becoming health-conscious, has extensive health facilities. Adjoining the swimming pool in the basement are a sauna, solarium, and massage and fitness studio. The staff includes a well-equipped team of beauticians and masseurs. Other installations feature modern facilities for diagnosis and therapeutics. The staff can arrange golf, tennis, riding, climbing, and walking on marked footpaths and promenades.

Steigenberger Badischer Hof, Langestrasse 47, D-7570 Baden-Baden (tel. 07221/2-28-27 or toll free in the U.S. at 800/223-5652), with its colonnaded facade, is on a busy street in the center of town, but in the back you'll find an elegant garden with a wide balustraded terrace, flowerbeds, and a lawn around a stone fountain. Once a Capuchin monastery stood on this site, giving way to a spa hotel in 1809. Then the hotel began its career as a social center for famous personalities who spent "the season" there, taking the cure. One of its most distinguished guests, composer Carl Maria von Weber, wrote: "The beautiful dining room with its high ceiling, the tastefully decorated casino, and the fine stone-encased bathing facilities will make this guesthouse more and more popular with the years." And so they have. You'll look in amazement at the colonnaded, four-story-high hallway, with its great staircase and encircling balustraded balconies. Public rooms are attractive and old-world, and the 140 well-furnished bedrooms are priced according to size and view and according to season. Many rooms have private balconies. All the accommodations have private baths; those in the monastery building have thermal water piped into their baths. Singles range from 170 DM ($100.95) to 245 DM ($145.50) daily; doubles, from 260 DM ($154.40) to 420 DM ($249.40). A buffet breakfast is included. The hotel has a thermal-spring swimming pool, an open-air swimming pool, and a low-level garage. A magnificent park-restaurant is open in the monastery building, and next to it is a barroom connecting the two buildings.

Steigenberger Europäischer Hof, Kaiserallee 2, D-7570 Baden-Baden (tel. 07221/2-35-61 or toll free in the U.S. at 800/223-5652), stands opposite the Kurgarten and the casino, adjacent to the Oos River, which runs at the edge of the Kurpark. Actually, it's a pair of hotels joined together that were built during the period when spacious living facilities were considered important. Its colonnaded, classic central hallway is stunning, and many of its suites and bedrooms open off balconies. The hotel offers 140 well-furnished rooms equipped with radios, phones, and color TVs. The atmosphere is one of elegance. Single rooms with baths cost 170 DM ($100.95) to 270 DM ($160.35) daily, and doubles go for 255 DM ($151.40) to 435 DM ($258.30). All these tariffs include a large buffet breakfast. You may want to dine in the restaurant even if you're not a guest. It has been called "elegant and noble," and features a buffet set up in the middle of the high-ceilinged room. The chef specializes in French and Swiss dishes—meals cost 50 DM ($29.70) to 80 DM ($47.50)—and there is formal, old-world service, perhaps a lingering nostalgia for yesteryear. Windows overlooking a park sweep across one entire wall of the restaurant. Open daily from noon to 2pm and 6:45 to 10pm.

Schlosshotel Büherhöhe, Schwarzwald Hochstrasse 1, D-7580 Bühl 13 (tel. 07226/55-100), has long been one of the famous landmark hotels of the Black Forest. It opened in 1914 at the dawn of World War I—not a good time. However, its reopening following a massive restoration in the summer of 1988 was more auspicious. Towering majestically above Baden-Baden, the castle was originally built to honor Kaiser Wilhelm II. It was constructed on orders of "Generalin" Hertha Isenbarth, a native Scot and the wife of a Prussian Imperial officer who was ostracized by the society of her day.

Today, the complex embraces not only the Schlosshotel, but a spa clinic and the Plättig Hotel. The three separate buildings have a staff of 300 attending to the needs of clients on a 24-hour basis. The hotel has been fully converted to a world-class standard, the epitome of elegance and comfort, and it's filled with modern amenities, yet imbued with the most glamorous styling of yesterday. All rooms are beautifully fitted with superior carpeting and stylish furniture, including original oil paintings, cotton bedding, hairdryers, and electronic keys. In all, 90 bedrooms and suites are rented, with private baths, radios, color TVs, minibars, direct-dial phones, and private safes. Singles rent for 215 DM ($127.65) to 325 DM ($193) daily, with doubles costing 440 DM ($261.25) to 510 DM ($302.85), including breakfast, service, and taxes. Suites are more expensive, of course, and they are named after famous historical painters, with originals by the artist so honored.

The beauty farm on the premises offers an array of services, including fitness massages, shiatsu, mud packs, hayseed sacks, facial treatments, and many other treatments. Facilities include steam and sauna baths, hot whirlpools, Jacuzzi, underwater massages, and Kneipp applications. The swimming pool is also spectacular. The leisure and sports activities include angling, hunting, and riding. The Imperial Restaurant offers a refined Swabian and Alsatian-French cuisine, with a discriminating wine list. The elegantly appointed Schloss Restaurant features both national and regional dishes, with diet and calorie-conscious meals available upon advance order. There is also a piano bar with live music.

Expensive Hotels

A large modern hotel complex, **Der Quellenhof,** Sophienstrasse 27, D-7570 Baden-Baden (tel. 07221/2-21-34), could be your resting point in Baden-Baden, where your breakfast would be enjoyed in a room decorated with enlarged photographs of Baden-Baden and its royal patrons in the 19th century, and where dinner would be prolonged in the shelter of the all-wood walls of Im Süsses Löchel, the hotel's evening restaurant. Views of the spa's Wilhelminian architecture are generally spectacular from the balconies of the 51 soundproof bedrooms, which have all the modern conveniences. Singles rent for 145 DM ($86.10) to 165 DM ($98) daily, and doubles go for 194 DM ($115.20) to 230 DM ($136.55), with a buffet breakfast included.

Kurhotel Quisisana, Bismarckstrasse 21, D-7570 Baden-Baden (tel. 07221/34-46). Radiating from the core of a 19th-century villa, the annexes of this 55-room hotel contain some of the most up-to-date health facilities anywhere in the Black Forest. You can spend an early morning in group calisthenics, for example, followed by treatments with any one of a dozen different skin and muscle-toning techniques. An evening could be spent savoring the sophisticated cuisine available from the world-class kitchens before retiring to your spacious and well-appointed bedroom. One of the staff will direct you to the center of the spa, eight minutes away by foot. Rates go from 150 DM ($89.05) to 195 DM ($115.80) daily for a single and from 230 DM ($136.55) to 350 DM ($207.85) for a double, with breakfast included.

Der Kleine Prinz (The Little Prince), Lichtentalerstrasse 36, D-7570 Baden-Baden (tel. 07221/34-64), in a century-old baroque-style building is a small, cozy hotel run by Norbert and Edeltraut Rademacher, who know how to cater to American tastes. Norbert had 22 years of hotel experience in the United States at the Waldorf-Astoria and then at the New York Hilton. He and his wife have totally renovated and upgraded Der Kleine Prinz, offering 33 rooms with baths, cable color TVs (English TV), alarm radios, minibars, and hairdryers; some junior suites have whirlpool baths and video players. Each room has its own special feature—an open fireplace, a tower, a balcony. The furnishings are antiques or handmade of pine wood. Singles rent for 150 DM ($89.05) to 200 DM ($118.75) daily, doubles for 200 DM ($118.75) to 275 DM ($163.30), and junior suites for 350 DM ($207.85), with a buffet breakfast included. The small restaurant on the ground floor is also an elegant place for a four-course dinner, costing from 50 DM ($29.70), and you can have drinks at the adjacent lobby bar. Personalized service adds to the attractiveness of this intimate, immaculate little hotel.

Golf-Hotel, Fremersbergstrasse 113, D-7570 Baden-Baden (tel. 07221/2-36-91). Even if you don't play golf, you're still in luck if you choose this elegantly rambling 85-room hotel as your address in the Black Forest. You'll find, in addition to one of the finest golf courses in Germany, two swimming pools, a sauna, a gym, and tennis courts. The hotel offers a panoramic view of Baden-Baden and the Black Forest from nearly every room, as well as a dining room serving excellent meals. Singles rent for 130 DM ($77.20) to 170 DM ($100.95) daily; doubles cost 170 DM

($100.95) to 240 DM ($142.50). A buffet breakfast is included in the rates. Open April to October.

Holiday Inn Sporthotel, Falkenstrasse 2, D-7570 Baden-Baden (tel. 07221/21-90). Pleasantly situated in a forest, within five blocks of the casino, this hotel offers 121 comfortable rooms in a style you'd expect from a Holiday Inn, plus a moderately priced restaurant. Doubles cost 275 DM ($163.30) to 285 DM ($169.25) daily, while singles go for 190 DM ($112.80) to 230 DM ($136.55), including a rich buffet breakfast and unlimited use of the sauna and swimming pool. You can borrow a bicycle from the hotel's collection. Facial and body massages are available.

Bad-Hotel zum Hirsch, Hirschstrasse 1, D-7570 Baden-Baden (tel. 07221/2-38-96), beautiful and old-fashioned, had been operated by the same family since 1689. In 1982 the hotel was sold to the famed Steigenberger chain. It's a tranquil compound of several buildings, and throughout the centuries constant modernization has taken place. However, the antique furnishings have been retained, making the hotel a living museum of the fine period pieces. The formal dining room is dominated by crystal chandeliers and paneled walls; the Blauer Salon is equally attractive, with blue velvet provincial armchairs, and classic draperies; and there are several sitting and drawing rooms, each tastefully furnished. A breakfast terrace rests under an arbor, and an inner courtyard garden is an oasis. Each of the 58 interesting old-style bedrooms is individually furnished, as in a country home. Singles with baths cost 105 DM ($62.35) to 155 DM ($92.05) daily. Twin-bedded rooms with baths run 190 DM ($112.80) to 260 DM ($154.40). A buffet breakfast is included. All rooms have thermal water piped in. One of the special advantages of staying here: the abundant spa facilities at reasonable fees.

Holland Hotel Sophienpark, Sophienstrasse 14, D-7570 Baden-Baden (tel. 07221/3-56-0). Kings and princes, along with a well-known composer or two (among them Franz Liszt), have frequented this hotel during its 250-year history. Reopened in 1987 after a major renovation, it's now better than ever, with a fine restaurant. Its facade is chiseled sandstone carved into 19th-century baroque designs of shells and flowers, but its recent modernization has added glass and steel porticos. The 75 rooms, all with private baths, are stylishly furnished, often in pastels. Singles cost 120 DM ($71.25) to 245 DM ($145.50) daily; doubles, 190 DM ($112.80) to 260 DM ($154.40). Efficient English-speaking employees see to the needs of guests with professionalism and skill.

Moderately Priced and Budget Hotels

An inviting place to stay is **Haus Reichert,** Sophienstrasse 4, D-7570 Baden-Baden (tel. 07221/2-41-91). This five-floor 19th-century hotel has a round tower capped by a funnel-shaped "witch's cap." Inside, the rooms are high-ceilinged and comfortable, although practically none of the original furniture or detailing has survived the many renovations. Exercise equipment, a pool, and a sauna are all at your disposal here, along with a central location not far from the casino. Owned by the same family since 1860, the 42-room hotel charges 95 DM ($56.40) to 200 DM ($118.75) daily for a single and 150 DM ($80.05) to 300 DM ($178.15) for a double, breakfast included.

Sitting like a pleasant country inn on the old marketplace, **Hotel Am Markt,** Marktplatz 18, D-7570 Baden-Baden (tel. 07221/2-27-47), is far removed from the grander social life of Baden-Baden. It's in a gem of a location, with the quiet interrupted only by the chimes from the church across the square; a tiny terrace café in front has windowboxes of petunias. There is no lounge to speak of, but there is a tavern dining room with wooden dado, deep-set windows, and straight-back country armchairs—in all, a relaxed and informal atmosphere. Innkeeper Herr Bogner has 27 bedrooms with showers and toilets, each comfortably but simply furnished. A double costs 80 DM ($47.50) daily, a single 55 DM ($32.65), including breakfast.

Hotel-Restaurant zur Alten Laterne, Gernsbacherstrasse 10, D-7570 Baden-Baden (tel. 07221/27-13-18). The present owner maintains the 300-year-old facade of this attractive hotel in impeccable condition. In summer, masses of pink flowers add even more color to the already eye-stopping extravaganza of forest-green walls, crimson-colored shutters, and gilded embellishments. An awning shelters the sidewalk café, which offers meals and drinks to passersby. The establishment is the personal domain of Mike Brandau, who, in addition to his work as a restaurateur, maintains eight country-style bedrooms. Singles cost 65 DM ($38.60) to 90 DM ($53.45) daily, while doubles go for 120 DM ($71.25) to 160 DM ($95). The restaurant contains only 19 tables, at which visitors can enjoy the regional specialties that the kitchen prepares with gusto. Meals are served daily from 11am to 3pm and 5:30pm to midnight, costing about 30 DM ($17.80).

Bühlerhöhe Plättig-Hotel, Schwarzwald Hochstrasse 1, D-7580 Bühl 13 (tel. 07226/50-0), is a traditional Black Forest hotel with many comforts, including recently renovated interiors. It is part of the Schlosshotel Bühlerhöhe complex already recommended. Opened in the spring of 1988, it offers 58 handsomely furnished rooms and suites, each fully equipped with such modern amenities as radios, baths, color TVs, and direct-dial phones. Singles range in price from 95 DM ($56.40) to 105 DM ($62.35), with doubles costing 160 DM ($95) to 180 DM ($106.90), including breakfast, service, and taxes. Because of its out-of-town location, the hotel is suitable for motorists. One of the advantages of staying here is that guests are allowed to use the leisure and sporting facilities of the Schlosshotel. Facilities on the premises include a swimming pool, sauna, and solarium. The hotel's restaurant offers a traditional German cuisine, and you can also enjoy the rustically decorated Hubertus Stube, with its Black Forest specialties. In summer, pastry specialties from the hotel bakery are served on a terrace with a view.

WHERE TO DINE

Baden-Baden, as might be expected, offers a variety of good restaurants in all price ranges.

The Top Restaurants

Providing dining in the French manner, **Stahlbad,** Augustaplatz 2 (tel. 07221/2-45-69), is a luxury restaurant with a stunning decor. And what a production it is! Frau Elisabeth Schwank does the cooking, as she has for some 35 years, and her daughter, Frau Ursula Moench, welcomes you in the dining room. The atmosphere evokes a tavern: every square inch is covered with a collection of framed prints, copper cooking and serving equipment, antique pewter plates, mugs, and engravings. An open kitchen whets your appetite for the good food being prepared. Some of the specialties are peppersteak and venison steak (in hunting season), fresh fish, and lobster thermidor (priced according to weight and lethally expensive). The homemade fettuccine Alfredo with white truffles (in season) is as good as—or better—than any you'll have in Rome. Meals range from 65 DM ($38.60) to 110 DM ($65.30), and hours are 11:30am to 2:30pm and 6 to 10pm; closed Mon.

Schwarzwald-Stube, Brenner's Park Hotel, Schillerstrasse 6 (tel. 07221/35-30), it is generally conceded, serves the best food in Baden-Baden itself. At the corner of Lichtentaler Allee and Schillerstrasse, this is one of the renowned spa dining rooms of Europe, definitely worth its high price of 75 DM ($44.55) to 100 DM ($59.40) for a meal. The cuisine here reaches the peak of international standards, as does the service. Fish and crustaceans are the specialties, and many dishes emerge from the kitchen as spectacular events. Open daily from noon to 2pm and 6:30 to 11pm.

Moderately Priced Restaurants

At least among the young, **Oxmox,** Kaiserallee 4 (tel. 07221/2-99-00), is the most fashionable restaurant in Baden-Baden. Its bar, however, seems to do more business than the restaurant—a shame, really, since the food is among the best at the resort. The atmosphere has been described as 1920s nostalgia. This place was a former dining room of the czars, who stayed in Baden-Baden "taking the cure." A seven-course menu is featured for 84 DM ($49.90), but you can eat here à la carte for 58 DM ($34.45). You might begin with Baden-style snail soup and follow with filet of sole with lobster sauce or venison medallions with port-wine sauce and goose liver. Hours are 7pm to 1am; closed Sun. Closed mid-July to mid-August.

In the basement is one of the best nightclubs in Baden-Baden, **Griffin's Club,** Kaiserallee 4 (tel. 07221/2-43-40), open Wed. to Sun. from 10pm to 3am. It has a 15-year reputation as one of the best nightspots in southern Germany. You can swing to the music in the art nouveau atmosphere of the elegantly decorated club, or relax with a coffee in the attractive bistro. Drinks cost from 8 DM ($4.75).

Budget Restaurants

The spa's most popular summertime beer garden is the **Münchner Löwenbräu,** Gernsbacher 9 (tel. 07221/2-23-11), lying in the heart of the old town. It's also one of the best budget restaurants, and stays open all year, daily from 11am to 11pm. The terrace, beneath a copse of clipped and pruned linden trees, overflows in fair weather. If you climb a flight of stone steps at the rear, you'll be within the curved glass walls of the indoor dining room. Many kinds of German sausages are offered, along with an array of daily changing soup pots, Bavarian specialties, and a wide selection of cheeses. Regional devotees order pork knuckles fresh from "the pork knuckle grill." Regulars often ask for the "Löwenbräu platter of bites," which is one hearty plate filled with everything from black pudding to sliced pork. For dessert, I'd suggest the apple fritters. Meals cost from 32 DM ($19).

Zum Nest, Rettigstrasse (tel. 07221/2-30-76), near Leopoldsplatz, consistently serves the finest low-cost food in the old town. In a forestlike, wood-paneled room, waitresses in dirndls hurry about with platters filled with food and large mugs of beer. The menu is both regional and continental; you can enjoy artichokes with hollandaise, sole meunière, assorted roast meats with Spätzle. The Black Forest ham is always a good choice. Meals cost from 32 DM ($19) and are served from 11:30am to 2pm and 5 to 11pm; closed Thurs. The restaurant is closed from mid-January to February 8.

Dining at Neuweier

It's traditional for the people of Baden-Baden to visit the satellite resort of Neuweier, 6 miles to the southwest, to dine. Here are some suggestions.

Schloss Neuweier, Mauberbergstrasse 21 (tel. 07223/5-79-44), is a small 12th-century castle entirely surrounded by defensive water fortifications and vineyards belonging to the estate. Its restaurant is not large but offers impeccable service and a decor of tile walls hung with paintings of its former inhabitants. The house proudly produces its local wines, including an excellent Riesling, and practices international cookery with flair. Meals begin at 42 DM ($24.95), going up to 85 DM ($50.45). The dessert menu is wide-ranging and sinful. Hours are noon to 3pm and 6pm to 3am; closed Wed. and for lunch Tues. The staff takes a holiday for several weeks in winter.

Zum Alde Gott, Weinstrasse 10 (tel. 07223/55-13), is a very old wine cellar with a terrace restaurant, specializing in Badische foods. Wilfried Serr is one of the most distinguished chefs in the Baden-Baden area, drawing a clientele of devoted fans and new admirers every year. He is ably assisted by his wife, Ilse, who helps guide guests through the refined menu, which is likely to include everything from a carpaccio of lamb to a terrine of fresh plums. Wild game in season is a fine art here. Try also the Black Forest trout or the sea bass. There are only 12 tables, in soft green and white, and the ambience is bright and cheerful. The cost of a meal ranges from 68 DM ($40.40) to 95 DM ($56.40), and service is from noon to 3pm and 6 to 11pm; closed Thurs. and for lunch Fri.

Zur Traube, Mauerbergstrasse 107, D-7570 Baden-Baden–Neuweier (tel. 07223/5-72-16), is a restaurant with bedrooms. It features wines from the Black Forest and good, hearty Badische meals that range from 28 DM ($16.65) to 80 DM ($47.50), the latter for a gargantuan repast. The name of the restaurant means "bunch of grapes," and on a summer day guests drink a "lot from the vine," as they say here, and eat even more. The place is open from noon to 2pm and 6:30 to 9:30pm; closed Wed. For the 20 comfortably furnished rooms, each with bath or shower, TV, phone, and radio, charges range from 55 DM ($32.65) to 75 DM ($44.55) daily for a single and 100 DM ($59.40) to 160 DM ($95) for a double. Other facilities include a sauna, solarium, fitness studio, and whirlpool.

Dining at Varnhalt

In the same southwesterly direction from Baden-Baden, but only 4 miles from the center of the spa, Varnhalt is another dining goal.

Pospisil's Restaurant Merkurius, Klosterbergstrasse 2 (tel. 07223/54-74), is a family-run restaurant in a Landhaus-style building. This three-story modern structure has a brown roof and white stucco walls. Pavel Pospisil imports his produce and meats every day from culinary-conscious Strasbourg. The food is an unusual blend of Czech and French specialties wedded harmoniously to Black Forest dishes. You might opt for an eight-course "surprise menu," selected by the chef, who guarantees you a gastronomic thrill. The cost of such good food isn't low—from 100 DM ($59.40) to 135 DM ($80.15) for a meal. Hours are noon to 2pm and 7 to 10pm; closed Mon. and Sat. and for lunch Tues.

Gasthaus zum Adler, Klosterbergstrasse 15 (tel. 07221/5-72-41). Baden-Baden can be intimidatingly chic, so if you're in the mood for an informal, relaxed, and gemütlich experience, you'll appreciate the rusticity of this country inn where reasonably priced home-cookery costs from 30 DM ($17.80). If you order some of the most expensive specialties, you'll end up paying from 60 DM ($35.65). A choice of 12 daily specialties is offered, including fish and game (in season)—carp, roast hare or pheasant, possibly poached salmon or trout in Riesling. The house offers inexpensive wines. It's open from noon to 2:30pm and 6 to 9pm; closed Thurs. The inn also rents nine reasonably priced rooms, a single costing 60 DM ($35.65) daily, and a double with shower or private bath renting for 100 DM ($59.40). The Gasthaus closes annually from January 10 to February 9.

THE LEADING SPAS

Mark Twain, writing of his visit to Baden-Baden during a tour of Europe, didn't think much of the town, but he must have loved the baths: "I fully believe I left my rheumatism in Baden-Baden," he wrote.

It's likely that the waters that did Mark Twain so much good were those of the **Friedrichsbad,** also known as the Old Baths, Römerplatz 1 (tel. 07221/27-59-21), built 1869 to 1877 at the behest of Grand Duke Friedrich von Baden. Following the Roman-Irish method, it takes about two hours to have the complete bath program, which involves a shower; two saunas (from 130°F to 160°F) taken in a white-tile chamber whose vaulted ceiling is decorated with waterbirds; a brush massage soaping; thermal steam baths; and three freshwater baths ranging from warm to 60°. After a 30-minute period of rest and relaxation, wrapped in a sheet or blanket, you're supposed to be feeling somewhat rejuvenated. Other types of therapy, including massage, electrotherapy, and hydrotherapy, are also offered. Friedrichsbad is open Mon. to Sat. from 10am to 10pm. Admission is 32 DM ($19) per person.

The **Caracalla-Therme,** Römerplatz 11 (tel. 07221/27-59-40), have been made more visually pleasing by the addition of a round colonnaded extension with splashing and cascading pools. You can decide on your own bath system here, and medicinal treatment might include mudbaths, massages, whirlpools, and inhalation therapy. The slightly radioactive water, rich in sodium chloride, comes from the artesian wells 6,000 feet under the Florentiner Mountain. Its temperature is around

160°F. Bathers usually begin in cooler pools, working up to the warm water. The baths have a sauna area, with footbaths and sunbaths; sauna temperatures go from 185°F up to 200°F. You must wear bathing suits in the pools, but nudity is necessary in the saunas. The Caracalla Baths, open daily from 8am to 10pm, charge 15 DM ($8.90) per person for two hours of bathing. Also offered are group water gymnastics. The baths have a bar and a cafeteria.

Your hotel can give you full information on the facilities available at both the Friedrichsbad and the Caracalla.

THE SIGHTS

The center of Baden-Baden activity is **Lichtentaler Allee,** the park-promenade lining the bank of the Oosbach River (affectionately called the Oos—pronounced "ohs"), which runs through the center of town. As you stroll along this promenade, you'll be amazed at the variety not only of exotic shrubs and trees but of rhododendrons, azaleas, roses, and zinnias. At the north end of the park, on the banks of the stream, are the buildings of the Kurgarten, including the classical **Kurhaus.**

Behind its sparkling white columns and facade is the **Spielbank** (tel. 07221/210-60), the oldest casino in Germany, where for more than 200 years everyone from Dostoyevski's Alexei Ivanovich to the Prince of Wales has tested his or her luck at the roulette wheel or the baccarat table. Dostoyevski is supposed to have written *The Gambler* after he had lost his shirt, and almost his mind, at the gaming tables here (and in Wiesbaden).

The various rooms of the casino were designed more than 130 years ago in the style of an elegant French château, not unlike Versailles. In all this splendor, you can gamble year-round. The minimum stake is 5 DM ($2.95), but visitors are not obliged to play. The historic gaming rooms may be viewed daily from 10am to noon on a conducted tour costing 3 DM ($1.80). If visitors want to gamble later, a full day's ticket is available for 5 DM ($2.95). Jacket and tie are mandatory. To enter the casino during gambling hours, you must possess a valid passport or identification card and be at least 21 years of age.

Most of the older bathing establishments, including the Friedrichsbad and the Caracalla-Therme, are on the opposite side of the Oos, in the heart of the Altstadt. The spa gardens contain the **Pump Room** (Trinkhalle), Kaiserallee 3 (tel. 07221/27-52-77), where visitors can sip the water. Built in the 19th century, the loggia of the hall is decorated with frescoes depicting Black Forest legends. The springs of Baden-Baden have been recognized for more than 2,000 years, and their composition is almost the same today as when the Romans built their baths here in the 3rd century. Hours are 10am to 5:30pm daily. Admission is 2 DM ($1.20). The Pump Room is closed in winter.

Römanische Badruinen (Ruins of the Roman Baths), between Friedrichsbad and Caracalla-Therme (tel. 07221/27-59-36), is entered from Römerplatz. The old Roman baths were found in 1847 during the construction of the Friedrichsbad. The bathhouse was for the Roman soldiers. You can see a graphic example of hot-springs baths in ancient times. The restored ruins are open from 10am to noon and 1:30 to 4pm only from Good Friday until the end of October. Admission is 2 DM ($1.20).

Above Römerplatz stands the Renaissance castle, **Neues Schloss** (New Castle), Schlosstrasse (tel. 07221/2-55-93), the former residence of the margraves of Baden. The original building dating from 1437 was destroyed by a fire in 1689. The present structure, which is surrounded by a beautiful park, wasn't completed until 1847. The terraces offer an excellent view of the entire city. The castle houses the **Zähringer Museum,** containing historical rooms from the 19th century, when the castle was the summer residence of the grand dukes of Baden, as well as documents relating to the Grand Duchy of Baden. The castle is open Tues. to Sun. from 10am to 6pm, charging 2 DM ($1.20) admission.

Stiftskirche/Catholic Collegiate Church at Marktplatz, the Church of St. Peter and Paul, near the Roman baths, was a parish church as far back as 1245. It belonged to a collegiate order from 1452 to 1806. Badly damaged by fire in 1689, the church was rebuilt partly in the baroque style. Features of special interest are the 1467 late Gothic crucifix, the tombs of the margraves of Baden, a late Gothic tabernacle from around 1500, and modern stained-glass windows (1953–56), designed by Willy Oeser.

Sights in the Environs

On the fringe of Baden-Baden are some of the most interesting excursions in the Black Forest.

In the Lichtenthal quarter (once a separate town, referred to in the introductory section) stands **Brahmshaus,** Maximilianstrasse 85 (tel. 07225/7-11-72). The composer came here in 1865 and was to spend all his summer months until 1874 at this residence, working on the "Lichtentaler Symphony" (No. 1), among other works. The museum, containing much Brahms memorabilia, is open Mon., Wed., and Fri. from 3 to 5pm and on Sun. from 10am to 1pm, charging 1 DM (60¢) admission. Every two years in May, the Baden-Baden Brahms Days—a music festival with about eight concerts—are held. The next festival will be in 1991.

In the same neighborhood, you can visit the **Kloster Lichtenthal,** Hauptstrasse 40 (tel. 07221/7-23-32), a working nunnery since 1909, containing many works of art. This Cistercian convent was founded in 1245 by Irmingard, the margravine of Baden. You can visit the Gothic royal chapel containing the tombs of the margraves of Baden. The nuns also sell visitors a variety of liqueurs they make. The convent is open daily from 9am to noon and 2 to 5:30pm (Sun. from 3 to 5pm). Admission is 1.50 DM (90¢).

A notable landmark of Baden-Baden is **Merkur,** a mountain named for a sacrificial stone to the Roman god Mercury, which was discovered here. Until the 17th century, the mountain was known as Grosser Staufen. There are many paths with splendid views, and the Merkur Bergbahn, a mountain railway with a 54° slope, departs daily from 10am to 6pm, charging 5 DM ($2.95) for a round trip. At the station on top of Merkur are a restaurant, an observation tower, and a nature path. Lawns for sunbathing, with Kneipp facilities, are near the station.

Altes Schloss (tel. 07221/2-69-48) is an old castle with interesting ruins. From the 11th century to its destruction by fire late in the 16th century, it was known as Hohenbaden Castle, seat of the margraves of Baden. From the tower, there's a panoramic view of Baden-Baden and across the Rhine plain to the Vosges Mountains. Facilities are a terrace snackshop and parking area. The ruins can be visited (except Mon.) from 10am to 10pm free. To reach the castle, leave Baden-Baden by Zähringerstrasse and the Hohenbaden road north of the spa. You can return on the Gernsbach road. Allow about 1½ hours for this 8-mile jaunt.

A summer palace, **Schloss Favorite,** Rastatt-Niederbühl/Förch (tel. 07222/41-207), 3 miles southeast of Rastatt, was built in the baroque style in the early 18th century for Margravine Sibylla Augusts, the widow of "Türkenlouis" (Margrave Ludwig Wilhelm, so nicknamed because of his Turkish victories). It contains examples of the materials used at the time of its construction—stucco, wood, marble— and such arts-and-crafts techniques as mother-of-pearl inlaying, agate and ivory painting, lacquering, wax modeling, and pearl embroidery. There is also a famous porcelain collection. Concerts are given here, and there is a café. The scenic park has exotic trees and a Magdalene chapel. Guided tours are given from March to October. The palace is open from 9 to 11am and 2 to 5pm; closed Mon. Admission is 4 DM ($2.40).

A former knight's castle, **Yburg,** is a 4-mile run south from Baden-Baden, on the Yburg. Little is known about the origin of the castle, but it was mentioned in documents of 1245. Destroyed in the Peasants' War of 1525, it was restored by a margrave of Baden who appreciated the panoramic view of Baden-Baden, the vineyards, the Black Forest, the Rhine plain, and the Vosges Mountains. It can be visited free at any time during the day, and there is a castle restaurant for refreshments. You can climb the 110 steps to the tower, about a 15-minute trek. To reach the castle, take Fremersbergstrasse and Varnhalterstrasse (turn left at the bus stop near the Golf Hotel).

---

2. Badenweiler

Halfway between Freiburg and Basel, near the Swiss border, is the tiny spa of Badenweiler. The town authorities are so intent on keeping their community spotless that you will be required to park your car at the entrance. The designers of the Kurpark used the natural hillside setting to its best advantage by planting cypress and cedar trees in groves around the walks and buildings. The springs of the spa have been known since Roman times. The well-preserved Roman baths still stand today within the spa gardens.

In spite of its appearance of a sleepy German village, Badenweiler offers its visitors a wide range of entertainment and activity, from summer concerts in open-air pavilions to winter skiing.

The Badenweiler music festival is sponsored every year by the spa's leading hotel, Römerbad (see recommendation below). The festival, called **Römerbad Musiktage,** lasts from March 14 to 18 and November 7 to 11. It hosts classical concerts by composers from Wagner to contemporary ones. For information, contact the hotel directly.

About 12 miles south is **Schloss Bürgeln,** D-7846 Schliengen (tel. 7626/237). Built in 1764 by order of the abbot of St. Blasien, the castle sits on an extension of the Blauen, the southernmost reaches of the Black Forest. The castle offers a view of the surrounding countryside as far as the Swiss Alps. On a clear day you can see Basel and the bend in the Rhine as it flows into Switzerland. The gardens around the castle are a delight in summer. Guided tours are conducted through the baroque palace at regular intervals between 11am and 5pm except Tues. Admission for adults is 4 DM ($2.40); for children, 2 DM ($1.20).

WHERE TO STAY

Expensive Hotels

A stylish Victorian wedding cake, **Römerbad,** Schlossplatz 1, D-7847 Badenweiler (tel. 07632/7-00), is a distinguished 111-room hotel that has been family-owned since the early 19th century. Founded as a coaching inn in 1825, it is now run by Klaus Lauer and his mother, Elisabeth Fellman, who cater especially to the musicians who flock here annually for the musical festival. Over the years it's attracted everybody from Thomas Mann to Nietzsche to the Yale Alley Cats. It's a bone-white structure, with domes, balconies, a mansard roof, plus an open-air swimming pool set in a woodland amid lawns and flowerbeds. The interior has opera-house grandeur. The Römerbad bar is dominated by a large Warhol portrait of Goethe, and there's a stately dining room as well as an informal outdoor barbecue. The most recent addition is an enclosed swimming pool, with walls of glass allowing views of the neighboring park. In addition, there are numerous spa facilities and massage rooms. Rates, including Continental breakfast, are 190 DM ($112.80) to 310 DM ($184.10) daily for a single with bath, 290 DM ($172.20) to 370 DM ($219.70) for a double with similar plumbing. Two tennis courts with pro are reserved for guests.

Hotel Schwarzmatt, Schwarzmattstrasse 6, D-7847 Badenweiler (tel. 07632/60-42), is considered one of the leading hotels of Badenweiler, lying on the eastern fringes of the spa. With rows of flowerboxes along its balconies and surrounded by evergreens, this countryside hotel offers a relaxing atmosphere. It contains 45 comfortable accommodations, each with radio, private bath, phone, TV, and up-to-date furniture and amenities. Depending on the accommodation, singles range from 130 DM ($77.20) to 165 DM ($98) daily, with doubles going from 260 DM ($154.40) to 340 DM ($201.90), including breakfast.

Parkhotel Weisses Haus, Wilhelmstrasse 6, D-7847 Badenweiler (tel. 07632/50-41). A three-gabled white 19th-century house with awnings is the central building of this hotel complex, set on a forested hillside near Badenweiler. Guests take advantage of the sunny lawn to socialize in the chaise lounges. Attractively furnished singles rent for 100 DM ($59.40) to 110 DM ($65.30) daily, while doubles cost 220 DM ($130.65). The restaurant is reserved for hotel guests, who are received from March to mid-November.

Moderately Priced Hotels

An informal chalet building, the **Ritter,** Friedrichstrasse 2, D-7847 Badenweiler (tel. 07632/50-74), offers 60 accommodations. Its main building has traditional bedrooms with private baths; an annex contains modern apartments. Singles rent for 70 DM ($41.55) to 160 DM ($95) daily, doubles for 130 DM ($77.20) to 250 DM ($148.45). Rates include breakfast. The public rooms have a pleasant informality. At the swimming pool, one glass wall opens onto the lawn and woods. The hotel is just a short walk from the Kurpark and town social center.

Schlossberg, Schlossberg 3, D-7847 Badenweiler (tel. 07632/50-16), is a tastefully modern 28-room hotel that blends discreetly with the flowering trees and the landscaping around it. Guests enjoy the manicured garden near the sun terrace and the wrought-iron balconies attached to most rooms. Units are pleasantly furnished, costing 80 DM ($47.50) to 110 DM ($65.30) daily for a single and 140 DM ($83.15) to 175 DM ($103.90) for a double, breakfast included. Dinner is served only to guests. The management is helpful in directing you to interesting sights in the environs of Badenweiler. Closed mid-November to mid-February.

Romantik Hotel Sonne, Moltkestrasse 4, D-7847 Badenweiler (tel. 07632/75-08-0). The roof of this rambling 200-year-old building is covered in weathered terra-cotta tiles; the interior is warmly and comfortably furnished. The Fischer family runs this inviting complex, whose outdoor pool, surrounded by palms, suggests the Caribbean rather than the Schwarzwald. Singles go for 78 DM ($46.30) to 105 DM ($62.35) daily, and doubles cost 145 DM ($86.10) to 185 DM ($109.85), including breakfast. The 45 units contain toilets and either private showers or baths. The hotel is closed from mid-November to mid-February.

Hotel Post, Sophienstrasse 1, D-7847 Badenweiler (tel. 07632/50-51). This 60-room hotel has an ornamented facade and many modern additions and improvements inside. There's a tile swimming pool, a sauna, a sun terrace, a dining room with an arched wooden ceiling supported by ornate wooden columns, and an intimate Weinstube. Guests enjoy the hotel's proximity to many outdoor beauty spots. Overflow from the main building is directed to a guesthouse annex, the Gästehaus Grathwol, that has its own heated indoor swimming pool. All rooms have private baths. Singles rent for 70 DM ($41.55) to 110 DM ($65.30) daily, and doubles cost 130 DM ($77.20) to 200 DM ($118.75), including breakfast. The hotel is open from mid-February to November.

Budget Hotels

Most of the 14 rooms of the **Haus Christine,** Glasbachweg 1, D-7847 Badenweiler (tel. 07632/60-04), have their own balconies or sun terraces. Rooms are comfortable, with big windows to let in the light. Breakfast is included in the room price, which ranges from 55 DM ($32.65) to 75 DM ($44.55) per person daily.

WHERE TO DINE

A leading choice, **Restaurant Schwarzmatt,** Hotel Schwarzmatt, Schwarzmattstrasse 6 (tel. 07632/60-42), is in the previously recommended hotel. A comfortable restaurant, it extends onto an outdoor terrace in warm weather. You'll find many small dishes for small appetites, including an array of freshly baked pastries. Full meals include many traditional German selections, served daily from 11:30am to 1:45pm and 6 to 8:45pm. A more limited daily menu is served continuously from 8am to midnight. Full meals cost 50 DM ($29.70) to 90 DM ($53.45), depending on your tastes.

Romantik Hotel Sonne, Moltkestrasse 4 (tel. 07632/75-08-0), previously recommended, is a historic building dating from 1620 with a flower-filled courtyard. There is a high-ceilinged Weinstube, plus a wood-ceilinged restaurant that gives attentive service. Meals cost 38 DM ($22.55) to 65 DM ($38.60). The place is open from 11am to midnight; closed Wed. It closes from mid-November to mid-February.

Hotel Post, Sophienstrasse 1 (tel. 07632/50-51), is an economical Swiss-style restaurant. Meals cost 25 DM ($14.85). The house specialties are veal steak Badische and pigs' knuckles with Sauerkraut. Three versions of grilled filets are offered, including Indian style. Hours are 11am to 2pm and 6pm to midnight; closed Thursday and from November to mid-February. In addition to its restaurant, the Post rents 55 bedrooms, already recommended.

---

3. Freiburg im Breisgau

The largest city in the Black Forest region, Freiburg im Breisgau is often overlooked by visitors because this scenic and interesting city is off the beaten track. Its strategic location at the southern edge of the Black Forest brought the town under the rule of the Austrian Habsburgs in 1368, and it remained theirs for more than 400 years.

Approaching the city from the Rhine plain on the west, you will be faced with the town silhouetted against huge mountain peaks towering more than 3,000 feet. Within an hour you can reach most of these peaks by car, or in less time by funicular. Freiburg's situation is responsible for its remarkable climate. In early spring the town is usually bursting into bloom while the mountain peaks are still covered with snow. In the fall the smell of new wine fills the narrow streets while reports of snowfalls on the nearby peaks are already reaching the ears of the townsfolk. The reason for this unusual weather is that Freiburg lies in the path of warm air currents that come up from the Mediterranean through the Burgundy Gap, balanced by the winds from the Black Forest hillsides. The two forces join together to make Freiburg a year-round attraction and a sports center. The city is the home of a 400-year-old university, which has claimed among its faculty and alumni great scholars, scientists, and humanists such as Erasmus, Zasius, and Waldseemüller, the first geographer to put America on the map.

It's easy to get to this city via the efficient German Federal Railway, whose fastest trains stop at this junction en route to the Swiss Alps. Your arrival is likely to be at the Hauptbahnhof in the northwestern sector. This rail terminus opens onto Bismarckallee. The center of Freiburg is small enough to be explored on foot. If you head east on Eisenbahnstrasse, you will reach the heart of the Altstadt. Colombi Park will be on your left as you walk along. This street will become Rathausgasse, leading into Rathausplatz. From this square a small street with a big name, Franziskanerstrasse, leads to Kaiser-Joseph-Strasse, the largest commercial artery of the city. From here, take another small street, Münsterstrasse, to Münsterplatz and the famous cathedral, or Münster.

WHERE TO STAY

An Expensive Hotel

Snow-white walls and angular lines make the **Colombi Hotel,** Rotteckring 16, D-7800 Freiburg (tel. 0761/3-14-15), easy to spot in the downtown area. Despite its location, the rooms are quiet and peaceful. Many visitors are likely to be part of one of the business conferences that take place here, but the Colombi caters to independent travelers as well. This is the best hotel in town, and its restaurant (see below) is the most outstanding in Freiburg. The hotel's 96 accommodations, well furnished and comfortably appointed, cost 190 DM ($112.80) to 220 DM ($130.65) daily for a single and 275 DM ($163.30) to 300 DM ($178.15) for a double, including breakfast. There is a hairstylist on the premises.

Moderately Priced Hotels

Less than a block from the cathedral, **Novotel Freiburg,** Am Karlsplatz, D-7800 Freiburg (tel. 0761/3-12-95), offers 115 comfortable lodgings with modern amenities. Singles rent for 54 DM ($91.45) daily. Doubles cost 189 DM ($112.25). All tariffs include a buffet breakfast. Sports facilities include a tennis court, swimming pool, sauna, and nearby squash courts. The hotel's restaurant stays open to midnight.

Victoria, Eisenbahnstrasse 54, D-7800 Freiburg (tel. 0761/3-18-81), less than 400 feet from the Hauptbahnhof, is nevertheless peaceful, thanks to its frontage on Colombi Park. The facade is a symmetrical 19th-century rectangle, with big windows and dentil work as well as a wrought-iron balcony above the front door. The interior is lavishly paneled throughout the public rooms. Bedrooms are pleasantly furnished, costing anywhere from 130 DM ($77.20) daily for a single and 180 DM ($106.90) for a double, a buffet breakfast included. The hotel also has a good restaurant.

Zum Roten Bären, Oberlinden 12, D-7800 Freiburg (tel. 0761/3-69-13), is one of the oldest buildings in Freiburg, since parts of it date from 1120. A modern wing has been added, pleasantly blending in. The interior is delightfully decorated, emphasizing original construction elements along with scattered pieces of antique furniture. The 25 rooms are pleasantly styled and furnished, costing 190 DM ($112.80) to 210 DM ($124.70) daily for a double, 135 DM ($80.15) to 155 DM ($92.05) for a single, including breakfast. The restaurant serves traditional food and wines, with a high-standard menu. In summer you can stop by for a glass of wine or beer on the Weinstube's terrace.

Park Hotel Post, Eisenbahnstrasse 35, D-7800 Freiburg (tel. 0761/3-16-83). A marvelously baroque hotel, with an elaborate zinc cap on its octagonal turret, the 41-room Park Hotel Post is centrally located within walking distance of everything in Freiburg. The interior has been entirely renovated, with reliable modern comfort and up-to-date amenities as the emphasis. Breakfast, the only meal served, is included in the room price of 115 DM ($68.30) to 125 DM ($74.25) daily for a single, 165 DM ($98) to 185 DM ($109.85) for a double. All units have private toilets and showers or baths.

Central Hotel, Wasserstrasse 6, D-7800 Freiburg (tel. 0761/3-18-31), near the pedestrian zone, close to the cathedral, is a modern 49-bedroom hotel imaginatively designed with skylights, marble floors, and a pleasantly furnished lobby. Singles rent for 115 DM ($68.30) to 145 DM ($86.10) daily, and doubles cost 170 DM ($100.95) to 180 DM ($106.90). A buffet breakfast with a lavish choice of dishes is included in the rate. Drinks are offered until midnight in a cozy corner bar. There's parking in the basement.

Rappen, Münsterplatz 13, D-7800 Freiburg (tel. 0761/3-13-53), is a charming, typical Black Forest inn, with a wrought-iron hanging sign, little dormer windows in its steep roof, windowboxes, and shutters. Try to get a room overlooking the Gothic cathedral. There are three dining rooms, all with beamed ceilings, leaded-glass windows, and coach lanterns. The 12 rooms contain phones, color TVs, and minibars. Doubles with complete baths rent for 145 DM ($86.10) daily, and singles cost 130 DM ($77.20). Breakfast is included in the rates. You can dine on the sidewalk terrace or inside, the cuisine being recommendable for local dishes. Meals cost 26 DM ($15.45) to 60 DM ($35.65).

WHERE TO DINE

The most desirable restaurant in Freiburg, **Falken-und Zirbelstuben,** Colombi Hotel, Rotteckring 16 (tel. 0761/3-14-15), already recommended, gives guests special, personalized attention. You'll probably find your table discreetly separated from that of your neighbors by a leaded-glass and wood dividing wall. Accenting the room is a ceramic stove of white tiles. The chef de cuisine, Alfred Klink, prepares a light, modern cuisine. Dishes might include a terrine of turbot, chanterelles over a filet of venison, or an array of Atlantic fish dishes sumptuously prepared and impeccably served. Meals usually range from 80 DM ($47.50) to 145 DM ($86.10). The restaurant is open daily from noon to 3pm and 6pm to midnight.

Oberkirchs Weinstuben, Münsterplatz 22 (tel. 0761/3-10-11), is where you'll be saturated with old Freiburg and love it. The innkeeper provides excellent regional cooking and comfortable rooms. In the cellar are dozens of six-foot-high wooden kegs of various wines. The setting is pure picture postcard: on a colorful square, with step-gabled roofs, a wrought-iron sign hangs over the entrance, and tables are set out in front. The main Weinstube is old, with a monumental ceiling-high ceramic stove made with ornate decorative tiles. You get good old-fashioned food here—tasty soups, meat dishes, poultry—and plenty of everything. In season, you might try the young pheasant. Meals cost 30 DM ($17.80) to 62 DM ($36.80). Food is served daily. In the rear is a modern complex, fronting an open patio with a fish pond. The Weinstube also has 28 excellent rooms, most with private baths or showers. Depending on the plumbing, doubles cost 180 DM ($106.90) to 220 DM ($130.65) daily, and singles rent for 80 DM ($47.50) to 130 DM ($77.20), breakfast included.

Eichhalde, Stadtstrasse 91 (tel. 0761/5-48-17), is the most desirable French bistro in town. It is a comfortable, safe haven, enjoying a lot of neighborhood patronage (a long walk from the center). Set menus range from 60 DM ($35.65) to 90 DM ($53.45); the latter will make a gourmet's evening. The bill of fare is likely to include goose liver terrine with a gelée of port, sea bass in a thyme sauce, and a salad of turbot with a mustard sauce. Hours are noon to 3pm and 6pm to midnight; closed Tues., and Sat. for lunch.

Ratskeller, Am Münsterplatz 11 (tel. 0761/3-75-30). It's hard to improve upon a good thing, but that's what the directors of this municipal town hall cellar did when they renovated the old establishment in 1981. Now crowned with a modern adaptation of the traditional wooden ceiling, the place no longer radiates the medieval ambience of other Ratskellers, but attentive service and the elevated quality of the regional cookery make up for it. A three-course menu of the day costs between 24 DM ($14.25) and 40 DM ($23.75) at lunch, with a selection of fish or meat courses varied enough to please most diners. À la carte dinners go for 35 DM ($20.80) to 70 DM ($41.55). The cellar serves from noon to 2:30pm and 6pm to midnight; closed Mon.

Weinstube zur Traube, Schusterstrasse 17 (tel. 0761/3-21-90). If your grandmother of German extraction happens to be with you during this trip to Germany, she will love this 600-year-old Weinstube. The pewter and earthenware dinner services decorating the walls are art objects in their own right, and the ceramic stove is 300 years old. Cooking here is regional and well prepared, emphasizing game, meat, and fish. Complete meals are priced at 32 DM ($19) to 95 DM ($56.40). Hours are 11:30am to 2pm and 5 to 11pm; closed Sun. and from July 15 to 30.

Greiffenegg-Schlössle, Schlossbergring 3 (tel. 0761/3-27-28). The chef cooks up a storm, turning out regional and international dishes at this family restaurant. The most expensive fixed-price meal on the menu costs 65 DM ($38.60), although a selection of simpler meals is available, starting at 35 DM ($20.80). In summer, try for a seat on the terrace. The restaurant is open noon to 11pm; closed Mon. Closed in February.

On the Outskirts

Kühler Krug, Torplatz 1, at Günterstal (tel. 0761/2-91-03). Clients sit bistro style along a banquette here, except that instead of Gallic decor the furnishings are unmistakably Teutonic, with ceiling-level armoires, primitive Caucasian rugs, and rustic country chairs. The menu is international, with regional specialties offered when they become available in the marketplace. Your dinner could consist, for example, of a pâté of goose liver or standing rack of roast venison (served for two persons), or perhaps pheasant, hunter's style, in a mushroom sauce. The restaurant serves the most exceptional 29 DM ($17.20) menu I have eaten in the environs of Freiburg. But if you order à la carte, sampling some of the expensive specialties, your tab might run as high as 75 DM ($44.55). The restaurant's hours are 11:30am to 3pm and 5:30pm to midnight; closed Thurs., and Fri. until 6pm; also closed for three weeks in June. The inn also rents 9 bedrooms, costing 80 DM ($47.50) for a single and 110 DM ($65.30) to 120 DM ($71.25) for a double, including breakfast.

Schwärs Hotel Löwen, Kappelerstrasse 120, Freiburg-Littenweiler (tel. 0761/6-30-41), is just over a mile from the city center. Local residents have told me that the adroit service here comes "from the heart" of the concerned family that runs this place. The restaurant serves daily meals, ranging from a reasonable 25 DM ($14.85) to 60 DM ($35.65). The regional is emphasized, but international selections are also offered and are beautifully prepared. The restaurant is open daily from 11:30am to 2pm and 6 to 10pm. If you'd like to spend the night, the inn has 56 comfortably furnished bedrooms. Singles cost 44 DM ($26.15) to 106 DM ($62.95) daily, and doubles go for 74 DM ($43.95) to 170 DM ($100.95).

Gasthof Adler, Im Schulerdobel 3, Freiburg-Kappel (tel. 0761/6-54-13). This is a big, generous, gemütlich family-style place, where wine comes in pitchers and 10 hotel rooms are available for any patron who decides he or she needs to sleep over. There is a children's menu, along with an above-average list of international food items. A fixed-price meal ranges in price from 25 DM ($14.85) to 48 DM ($28.50). Service is from noon to 2pm and 6:30 to 9:30pm; closed Thurs. and for two weeks in summer. Those rooms I referred to cost 45 DM ($26.70) to 60 DM ($35.65) daily for a single, 70 DM ($41.55) to 80 DM ($47.50) for a double.

THE SIGHTS

A town of historical interest and significance—Marie Antoinette slept here on her way to marry Louis XVI—Freiburg offers a number of well-preserved monuments.

Freiburg Cathedral

Towering over Münsterplatz, where the busy weekly market is still carried on today, the cathedral is a grand sight with its unique spire of filigreelike stonework. The steeple sits on an octagonal belfry, whose historic bells include a five-ton wonder dating from 1258. Although construction on the church was begun in 1200 in Romanesque style, the builders had incorporated the style of every Gothic period— as well as a bit of the Renaissance—by the time it was completed in 1620. The overall look, however, is mainly Gothic, with heavy buttresses above the north and south walls, decorated with statues of biblical characters.

Entering the cathedral through the south door, you're in the transept facing an early 16th-century sculpture of the Adoration of the Christ Child by the Magi. Turning left into the nave, you'll see at the far end of the aisle, at the entrance to the tower, a 13th-century statue of the Virgin flanked by two adoring angels, a fine example of French Gothic art. Resting against one of the Renaissance pillars along the aisle is a carved 16th-century pulpit, with stairs winding around the curve of the column. The figures below the stairs are likenesses of the townspeople of the period, including the sculptor.

Of interest throughout the cathedral are the stained-glass windows, many of which are hundreds of years old. The oldest are the small round windows in the south transept, which date from the 13th century. Some of these, however, have been removed to the Augustinian Museum and replaced by more recent panels.

The vaulted chancel is the real treasure house of art within the cathedral. Most impressive is the painted altarpiece by Hans Baldung Grien, dating from 1516, above the high altar. If you follow the aisle around behind the choir, you can also see the reverse side of the work, depicting the Crucifixion. Each of the 12 chapels around the choir has its own important works of art, including the elaborate rococo font in the Stürzel Chapel and a 16th-century altarpiece by Sixt von Staufen in the Locher Chapel.

The cathedral can be visited at any time from 10am to 6pm. To climb the tower costs 1 DM (60¢); hours are Tues. to Sat. from 10am to 5pm, Sun. 1 to 5pm.

Around the Altstadt

Across Münsterplatz from the cathedral is the **Kaufhaus,** the most colorful building in Freiburg. The Gothic structure, with oriel windows at each end, was originally an ancient emporium to which a balcony was added in 1550. Above the massive supporting arches, the facade is decorated with the statues of four emperors of the Habsburg dynasty, all but one of whom visited Freiburg during their reigns. The red-painted building is still used as the town's official reception hall.

The **Rathaus,** on the attractively planted Rathausplatz just west of Münsterplatz, became a happy marriage of two 16th-century merchants' houses when an arcade was built between them in 1900. The Renaissance houses are in suitable condition, and among the decorations on the oriel windows and facades, the one most commented upon is the relief of *The Maiden and the Unicorn.*

The **Augustiner Museum,** Augustinoplatz (tel. 0761/216-3300), is housed in the former church and monastery of the Order of St. Augustine and contains the town's finest collection of art, including religious art spanning more than 1,000 years. Among the treasures are some of the original stained-glass windows from the cathedral and the most important part of its medieval gold and silver treasure, brought here for safekeeping. The best works, in the collection of medieval art, include the painting by Grünewald of *The Snow Miracle,* as well as works of Hans Baldung Grien (pupil of Albrecht Dürer). Besides, there is a rich collection of fine late-Gothic wooden sculpture. The museum also displays folk art from the Black Forest. It is open weekdays from 9:30am to 5pm; weekends from 10:30am to 5pm. Admission is free. Guided tours are conducted on Wed. at 6pm and on Thurs. at 4pm.

The modern art collection formerly housed in the Augustiner Museum is now at the **Museum für Neue Kunst,** Marienstrasse 10a (tel. 0761/216-36-71). Paintings and sculptures beginning with examples of German expressionism, Neue Sachlichkeit, and other classic modern works of art, especially by artists of southwest Germany, are displayed here. New tendencies and works done after World War II are also in the new museum. It's open weekdays from 9:30am to 5pm; weekends from 10:30am to 5pm. Admission is free.

AFTER DARK

Freiburg has a large cultural life centering around the **Städtischen Bühnen,** Bertoldstrasse 46 (tel. 3-48-74). The Freiburg Symphony plays at the theater for operas, operettas, and musical concerts. In the **Freiburger Stadthallen,** Schwarzwaldstrasse 80 (tel. 0761/7-10-20), both classical and rock concerts are presented, as well as all sorts of shows. Most of these are guest performances. There are many "off-Broadway" theaters, but you must know German to appreciate the presentations. Ask at the tourist office for details.

Weinstuben abound throughout the town, especially around the university area, where many bars and cafés cater to the students. Cabarets and some jazz clubs also exist. Ask the tourist office for details of what's going on.

STAYING IN HINTERZARTEN

Instead of stopping over in Freiburg, you might prefer to stay in Hinterzarten, less than 17 miles away.

Where to Stay and Dine

Parkhotel Adler, Adlerplatz 3, D-7824 Hinterzarten (tel. 07652/12-7-0), listed among the 195 "Leading Hotels of the World," is a historic gem in addition to being a fine 76-room hostelry. It can trace its history as far back as 1446, and has always been in the hands of the same family. Victor Riesterer represents the 15th generation of innkeepers at this hotel. It has attracted such prominent personages as Marie Antoinette, who spent a night at the then Zum Adler on her way from Austria to marry the Dauphin of France. Through the years, there have been many additions to the hotel, but it has been consistent in its high standards and courteous treatment of guests. You'll find the palatial lemon-and-white-painted structure in its own gardens a few steps from the onion dome of the village church.

The establishment has seven different bars and restaurants, which offer good drinks, good food, and good service. Clients who prefer apartment living opt for the nearby Adler Residenz. Live dance music is played every evening in one of the bars, and guests can divert themselves at the hotel's spa facilities. A full range of sports is offered, including indoor and outdoor tennis, as well as horseback riding. There is a hairdresser and a beauty parlor. Singles rent for 105 DM ($62.35) to 210 DM ($124.70), and doubles go for 210 DM ($124.70) to 420 DM ($249.40).

Sassenhof, Adlerweg 17, D-7824 Hinterzarten (tel. 07652/15-15). Set into an impeccably maintained lawn and garden, this stylish contemporary chalet is accented with plantings of geraniums. The hotel has an indoor swimming pool and a sauna, and in the vicinity there are many walking paths for nature-oriented visitors. Most clients check into one of the 21 well-furnished bedrooms, or else ask for a full apartment with a kitchen if they're interested in a self-catering holiday. Singles cost 65 DM ($38.60) to 130 DM ($77.20) daily, while doubles rent for 140 DM ($83.15) to 176 DM ($104.50), including breakfast, the only meal served.

---

4. Wildbad

This tiny town in the valley of the Enz River is one of the best-known spas in the Black Forest. Although not as elegant as nearby Baden-Baden, Wildbad lacks none of its important facilities and attracts visitors from all over Germany and Europe to its promenades and thermal springs. The river that flows through the town divides the colonnaded shopping streets and the spa center.

The thermal springs in the spa gardens are popular for both drinking and bathing. Among the many unusual baths is the **Graf-Eberhard Bath,** dating from the 19th century and decorated in a Moorish style, with sunken baths and tiles. In contrast, the **Kurhaus** has a terrace with glass walls opening onto lush greenery and thermal pools where you can bathe year-round.

One of the biggest attractions of Wildbad is its scenery. The paths and roads in the surrounding woodlands are always alive with strollers, the streams teeming with fish and fishermen. A cable railway runs from the town to the top of the

Sommerberg, a 1,000-foot peak overlooking Wildbad and visited by skiers and sightseers alike.

WHERE TO STAY

Expensive Hotels

The accommodations in the 98-room **Sommerberg Hotel,** Auf dem Sommerberg, D-7547 Wildbad (tel. 07081/17-40), almost 2 miles west of the center, are scattered over four balconied stories of glass and concrete, which curve in a gentle arc around a panoramic view of the surrounding forest. Many of the public rooms have sweeping expanses of glass; an appealing mixture of open fireplaces and conservatively modern furnishings offers dozens of places for relaxation. There's a hexagonal indoor swimming pool, whose large windows take in the outdoors, plus a well-trained staff willing to initiate you into the benefits of hydrotherapy. The Jägerstüble restaurant serves a mixture of modern cuisine and regional specialties. Singles cost 95 DM ($56.40) to 160 DM ($95) daily, while doubles go for 180 DM ($106.90) to 260 DM ($154.40), all tariffs including a buffet breakfast. A ski lift is a short walk from the hotel, which in winter attracts sports lovers.

Badhotel Wildbad, Am Kurplatz 5, D-7547 Wildbad (tel. 07081/17-60), was completely renovated in 1984 in an imaginative format, including views of a nearby stream, an array of painstakingly set mosaics, and an attractive integration of an old and a new building. The restaurant serves well-prepared dishes from the classic German repertoire. Both the forest and a heated indoor swimming pool are at hand. Single rooms cost 105 DM ($62.35) to 150 DM ($89.05) daily, doubles going for 200 DM ($118.75) to 220 DM ($130.65), including breakfast. A TV and radio are standard equipment in each of the 83 rooms, but private plumbing varies.

Moderately Priced Hotels

Right in the heart of everything, the **Kurhotel Post,** Am Kurplatz 2, D-7547 Wildbad (tel. 07081/16-11), is a beguiling 40-room inn. Its open dining terrace, with flowerboxes and plants, is suspended bridgelike across a river winding its way through the spa. The Post was once a humble guesthouse, but as the years passed by it was enlarged. In 1827 it became known as a gastronomic center, and in 1921 it came under the aegis of the Fritzsches, who provided plumbing for most of the bedrooms (more than a third have baths with either showers or tubs). Bathless singles cost 60 DM ($35.65) daily, the price rising to 90 DM ($53.45) for a room with bath. Doubles go for 110 DM ($65.30) to 135 DM ($80.15). If you can't dine on the terrace, there is a garden room with an informal atmosphere. In addition, an attractive tavernlike Weinstube grill also serves meals, offering vegetarian and light, modern specialties as well as regional dishes. Closed November 10 to December 20.

Hotel Bären, Am Kurplatz 4, D-7547 Wildbad (tel. 07081/16-81). The management tells me that there has been an inn of some sort here since the 16th century. With that tradition in mind, they have successfully re-created in a modern style the kind of wood-ceilinged Gemütlichkeit that has made the Black Forest so famous. The owners rent 44 well-furnished bedrooms, charging 55 DM ($32.65) to 90 DM ($53.45) daily for a single and 170 DM ($100.95) to 180 DM ($106.90) for a double. They also operate a good restaurant, with many vegetarian dishes.

Traube, König-Karl-Strasse 31, D-7547 Wildbad (tel. 07081/20-66). Owned and operated by the Wentz family for many years, this modern 38-room hotel has installed an attractive collection of reproduction furniture to create a warm ambience. The nicely decorated dining rooms serve well-prepared international and regional specialties. On a breakfast-only plan, singles rent for 67 DM ($39.80) to 85 DM ($50.45) daily, while doubles go for 126 DM ($74.80) to 150 DM ($89.05). Half-board plans are available for 90 DM ($53.45) to 120 DM ($71.25) per person daily.

A Budget Hotel

A chalet-style hotel, **Gästehaus Rothfuss,** Olgastrasse 47, D-7547 Wildbad (tel. 07081/1687), is built on the side of the hill, a virtual sun magnet. It's a steep walk from the center of town, and benches for resting are placed all along the way. Wide balconies surround the house, allowing private areas for sunbathing and breakfasts. The garden has abundant roses and geraniums, tended by Frau Richter. She and her husband, Wolfgang, keep a family staff busy seeing that everything is highly polished. The sitting room is personalized, cluttered, and intimate; the dining room has a woodland view. Prices for the 36 rooms are quite low. Singles with showers and toilets go for 48 DM ($28.50) daily, and doubles with the same plumbing cost 80 DM ($47.50) to 110 DM ($65.30). For the tariffs quoted, a breakfast is offered, usually featuring soft-boiled eggs, sausages, and cheese—the only meal served. There is free parking on the grounds, and in 1979 the hotel opened a medical treatment center, only a three-minute walk from the main building. Closed mid-November to December 20.

WHERE TO DINE

The most scenic spot for dining is the already recommended **Sommerberghotel,** Auf dem Sommerberg (tel. 07081/17-40), just under 2 miles from Wildbad's center. In its restaurant, Jägerstüble, the chef turns out a delectable modern cuisine. This is a special restaurant, seemingly unknown to most North Americans, attracting a largely German clientele. To dine here costs 45 DM ($26.70) to 75 DM ($44.55), and you can do so Wed. to Sun. from noon to 2pm and 6:30 to 9pm.

Hotel Birkenhof, Wildbaderstrasse 50, Wildbad-Calmbach (tel. 07081/64-87), is also on the outskirts of Calmbach, a distance of about 2 1/2 miles from Wildbad. For many years this gutbürgerlich (traditional) restaurant has been owned by the same family. The kitchen staff turns out tasty specialties, especially from Swabia. Fixed-price menus cost 25 DM ($14.85) to 55 DM ($32.65). Hours are from 11:30am to 2pm and 6 to 9pm; closed Tues. The hotel rents 12 comfortably furnished rooms costing 40 DM ($23.75) to 50 DM ($29.70) daily for singles, 75 DM ($44.55) to 90 DM ($53.45) for doubles. The hotel is closed from early January to late February.

---

5. Triberg

Deep in the heart of the Black Forest, Triberg claims to be the home of the cuckoo clock, and also has the highest waterfall in the country.

In the little shops you'll find woodcarvings, music boxes, and other traditional crafts. If you're determined to return from Germany with a cuckoo clock or some other Black Forest timepiece, you may want to visit the **Haus der 1000 Uhren** (House of 1,000 Clocks) (tel. 07722/10-85), at Triberg-Gemmelsbach, along the B33 between Triberg and Hornberg, open Mon. to Fri. from 9am to 5pm. You'll recognize it immediately, with its giant cuckoo clock and waterwheel in front of the house. A painter of clock faces, Josef Weisser, launched the business in 1824. He was the great-great-grandfather of the present owner. For many generations patrons have been flocking to this shop, with its special clocks and souvenirs. They ship to the United States and take all major credit cards.

WHERE TO STAY

Built in the early 1600s, the **Parkhotel Wehrle,** Marktplatz, D-7740 Triberg (tel. 07722/8-60-20), was acquired around 1730 by the family who has owned it ever since. Its lemon-yellow walls and gabled mansard roof occupy one of the most prominent street corners in town. The main house offers an old-world atmosphere, but forest-loving vacationers often request an accommodation in the chalet in a separate location near the woods. There, a swimming pool and breeze-filled balconies create a modern sylvan retreat. For either branch of this 56-room establishment, there is ample parking. Singles rent for 88 DM ($52.25) to 138 DM ($81.95) daily, and doubles cost 155 DM ($92.05) to 256 DM ($152).

Römischer Kaiser, Sommerauerstrasse 35, D-7740 Triberg-Nussbach (tel. 07722/44-18), just over a mile outside of Triberg, is a comfortable hotel that has been owned by several generations of the same family since 1840. The exterior is a charmingly preserved Black Forest hotel, with lots of exposed wood, and a restaurant that is recommended separately. There are 26 pleasantly furnished bedrooms. Singles cost 50 DM ($29.70) to 55 DM ($32.65) daily, while doubles go for 85 DM ($50.45) to 100 DM ($59.40), depending on the accommodation. The inn is closed from mid-November to mid-December.

WHERE TO DINE

At the previously recommended **Parkhotel Wehrle,** Marktplatz (tel. 07722/8-60-20), accompanied by the ticking of a stately grandfather clock, full meals are served to a clientele who relax in the cane-bottomed comfort of French-style armchairs. Some of the wild game specialties served here are prepared for two persons. There is also a selection of veal, fish, and regional specialties. If you like trout, it is prepared in about two dozen different ways. Meals range from 42 DM ($24.95) to 80 DM ($47.50), and are served daily from noon to 2pm and 7 to 10pm.

Römischer Kaiser, Sommerauerstrasse 35 (tel. 07722/44-18), along route B33, at Nussbach, was previously recommended as a hotel. Some guests consider one of the best views in the area is to be had from this restaurant—the mountains of distant Switzerland are visible on a clear day. However, it is the well-prepared modern cuisine that has made this restaurant so popular. Fresh fish is available throughout the year. Examples include lake trout served with a watercress mousse and wild salmon with a lobster cream sauce and fresh asparagus. Meals range from 30 DM ($17.80) to 55 DM ($32.65). Service is from noon to 1:30pm and 6 to 9pm; closed Wed. The establishment is closed from mid-November to mid-December.

THE SIGHTS

The **Wasserfall** (waterfall) is exceptional, but be prepared to walk an hour or so to reach it. You park your car in a designated area near the Gutach Bridge and walk along a marked trail daily anytime from 7am to 7pm in summer for a cost of 2 DM ($1.20). The Gutach Falls drop some 530 feet, spilling down in seven stages. At the bottom of the falls is a year-round café and restaurant serving the famed Black Forest cake for which, by then, you will have worked up an appetite.

The **Black Forest Museum** (Schwarzwald-Museum) of Triberg, Wallfahrtstrasse (tel. 07722/44-34), brings the olden days of the Black Forest vividly to life with displays of dresses, handcrafts, furnishings, bird music boxes, and, of course, exhibitions of clockmaking. You can also see a mineral exhibit of the area and examples of Black Forest woodworking. Children take delight in a model of the famed Schwarzwaldbahn railway, which really works. From May 1 to September 30, the museum is open daily from 9am to 6pm; from October 1 to April 30, hours are 10am to noon and 2 to 5pm. Admission is 3 DM ($1.80).

One of the most beautiful churches in the Black Forest, **Wallfahrtskirche Maria in der Tannen** (Church of Our Lady of the Fir Trees) is within easy reach. Built in the early years of the 18th century, it has superb baroque furnishings, including a remarkable pulpit.

After a visit here, you may want to drive to **Vogtsbauerhof,** a little village containing original Black Forest homes, some dating back as many as six centuries. In the museum you can see artifacts of the old way of life in the forest. In summer guides will demonstrate weaving on some of the looms and other skills. Visits are possible from April to the end of October, daily from 8:30am to 6pm for an admission of 3 DM ($1.80).

---

6. Freudenstadt

This sunny resort has no castle overshadowing it as many German villages do, but it does have the largest marketplace in Germany, laid out in the 16th century for a castle that was never built. History's loss is today's gain, because the market square that greets the visitor to Freudenstadt is a maze of lawns and pavement, broken by beds of flowers and kiosks. The buildings surrounding the square are mainly postwar, since the air raids of World War II almost completely destroyed the city. A few of the old Renaissance structures on the square have been reconstructed, up to their neat little archways and gabled roofs.

Originally founded by Protestants, the town takes pride in its **Stadtkirche,** dating from the 17th century. The unusual L-shaped architecture of the church brings the two main aisles together at right angles. Over the entrances stand identical towers, topped with rounded domes and narrow spires. The church's most important treasure is the reading desk from the 12th century. The desk is supported by carved and painted statues of the writers of the four Gospels.

Freudenstadt's attraction springs not from the town itself but from its ideal location in the midst of the best hiking and camping country in the Black Forest. Trails wind for hundreds of miles through the nearby hills, and in winter the snow-covered paths become ski trails.

WHERE TO STAY

An Expensive Hotel

Rising abruptly from the forest around it, the **Steigenberger Park-Hostellerie,** Karl-von-Hahn-Strasse 129, D-7290 Freudenstadt (tel. 0744/8-10-71), looks like a modern steel-and-glass cube. This well-directed chain hotel offers 134 comfortable rooms to guests, costing 180 DM ($106.90) to 250 DM ($148.45) daily for a double and 110 DM ($65.35) to 145 DM ($86.10) for a single, depending on season and room location. A variety of board plans are also offered, as well as a special gourmet program. The hotel has both the Zum Jagdhorn Restaurant and the Im Schnokeloch. I was impressed by the imaginative decor of the public rooms (there are a lot of them!) and by the size of the swimming pool. The comfortably carpeted bedrooms are upholstered in pleasing tones. The manager here will see that things run smoothly during your visit.

Moderately Priced Hotels

At least 50 years of ivy grows over the downtown **Luz Posthotel,** Stuttgarterstrasse 5, D-7290 Freudenstadt (tel. 07441/24-21), established in 1809. The dining room has Oriental rugs over the well-polished floors, while the 50 bedrooms are comfortably furnished. With breakfast, a single rents for 80 DM ($47.50) to 100 DM ($59.40) daily, and a double goes for 120 DM ($71.25) to 160 DM ($95). The sun terrace and café in front are popular with local residents.

Kurhotel Sonne am Kurpark, Turnhallestrasse 63, D-7290 Freudenstadt (tel. 07441/60-44). The streamlined electric candelabra lighting the path to this 45-room hotel promise an attractively imaginative interior, and that's just what you'll get at this family-franchised Ringhotel. Many of the ceilings are made of rustic wood paneling, with pink-and-mauve peacock designs set into panels in the dining room. The Espenlaub family charges 100 DM ($59.40) to 180 DM ($106.90) daily for a single, 175 DM ($103.90) to 245 DM ($145.50) for a double.

Hotel Bären, Langestrasse 33, D-7290 Freudenstadt (tel.07441/27-29). The pleasing proportions of this rustic country house right off Marktplatz promise a sympathetic visit. Indeed, the interior is warmly decorated—a mixture of white stucco and exposed beams—and the dining room serves a first-class cuisine. Singles with breakfast rent for 65 DM ($38.60) to 75 DM ($44.55) daily, while doubles run from 110 DM ($65.30) to 140 DM ($83.15). If the 15-room Hotel Bären is full, the management will direct you to their other establishment, the Landhaus Montigel, where rooms with breakfast are slightly less expensive.

Kur-und Sporthotel Eden, Im Nickentäle 5, D-7290 Freudenstadt (tel. 07441/70-37), is a 70-room complex of concrete, glass, and wood in a style reminiscent of an overblown chalet, but aesthetically pleasing nonetheless. You'll find a complete array of sports facilities here, including an indoor pool, a sauna, tennis, and golf. Prices, which include breakfast, range from 165 DM ($98) to 320 DM ($190) daily for a double, from 100 DM ($59.40) to 115 DM ($68.30) for a single. The hotel has full restaurant facilities.

Hotel Hohenried, Zeppelinstrasse 5, D-7290 Freudenstadt (tel. 07441/24-14), is a reconstructed chalet, with three floors of beflowered balconies and a modern annex stretching off to the side, only 15 minutes by foot from the center of town. The grounds contain a well-maintained lawn with trees. The 27 bedrooms are usually sunny and always well furnished. Singles cost 80 DM ($47.50) to 110 DM ($65.30) daily, and doubles go for 140 DM ($83.15) to 195 DM ($115.80). Facilities include an indoor swimming pool. A complete regime of beauty treatments is available from the licensed cosmetician. A gym session is supervised every morning, followed by a massage.

A Budget Hotel

A country house, **Landhaus Bukenberger,** Herrenfelderstrasse 65, D-7290 Freudenstadt (tel. 07441/27-71), has been owned by members of the congenial Bukenberger family since about 1900. Today its red-tile roof and steep gables shelter one of the most attractive and reasonably priced hotels in town. Guests climb to one of 14 bedrooms via a well-polished staircase. An array of paneled public rooms includes a TV salon, a comfortable breakfast room capped by an arched wooden ceiling, a formal dining room, and a country-rustic Weinstube. Singles cost 34 DM ($20.20) to 36 DM ($21.40) daily, and doubles go for 74 DM ($43.95) to 100 DM ($59.40), plus another 16 DM ($9.50) per person daily for half board.

WHERE TO DINE

A small inn directly on the marketplace is the **Ratskeller,** Marktplatz 8 (tel. 07441/26-93). The lower rooms are set back with three Romanesque colonnades, and the other levels have windows with shutters and windowboxes of red geraniums. The Ratskeller's manager disarmingly says, "We are a little house, but a fine house." The main dining room is traditional, with dark paneled walls and ceiling and tables arranged around a tile stove. Below is the antique wine cellar, all bricked, even its steep coved ceiling. The Ratskeller has a distinguished cuisine, with many international specialties. Try, for example, the sole meunière, medallions of veal, or tournedos sauté Tour d'Argent. Meals cost from 32 DM ($19) to 78 DM ($46.30). Open from noon to 2:30pm and 6 to 9:30pm; closed Tues.

Steigenberger Park-Hostellerie, Karl-von-Hahn-Strasse 129 (tel. 07441/8-10-71). The restaurant Im Schnokeloch, on the premises of the most prestigious hotel in Freudenstadt, serves a savory selection of grilled meats and Black Forest specialties such as trout in Riesling and wild game (in season). A complete meal here will cost 35 DM ($20.80) to 72 DM ($42.75). Service is daily from noon to 2pm and 6 to 9pm. Many of the guests at the restaurant are vacationing hikers who have spent the day traversing the myriad forest trails around the hotel.

Kurhotel Sonne am Kurpark, Turnhallestrasse 63 (tel. 07441/60-44). At this elegant Black Forest hotel, classic French cuisine in the grand style is served. Vegetarian dishes are also available. Everything is carefully organized and carried through under the direction of Elisabeth Espenlaub. Meals begin at 35 DM ($20.80), going up to 90 DM ($53.45) for a surprise banquet of eight courses. In this previously recommended hotel, the restaurant serves daily from noon to 2pm and 6 to 10pm. It's closed from December 1 to 26.

Hotel Schwarzwaldhof, Hohenriederstrasse 74 (tel. 07441/74-21). In wintertime a blazing fireplace welcomes guests to the dining room of this hotel. Its restaurant is known in the Black Forest as a "watering hole" for devotees of modern cuisine, which is reasonably priced for such a fine establishment. A dinner costs from 35 DM ($20.80), going up to 62 DM ($36.80) for the more elaborate specialties. You might try the suprême of capon or the veal in a saffron bouillon sauce. Vegetarian dishes are also offered. Service is daily from noon to 2pm and 6 to 9pm. The hotel also rents 40 of the best and most comfortable rooms in town. Singles cost 85 DM ($50.45) to 100 DM ($59.40) daily, and doubles rent for 145 DM ($86.10) to 195 DM ($115.80).

Weinstuben Bären, Langestrasse 33 (tel. 07441/27-29), is part of a hotel previously recommended. Catering to winter-sports enthusiasts and summer vacationers, this gemütlich hotel serves a cuisine in keeping with its decor. The restaurant prepares Swabian specialties, offering more than half a dozen fixed-price menus, ranging from 29 DM ($17.20) (which I found the best meal in Freudenstadt for the price) up to 65 DM ($38.60). Specialties include trout and game dishes, plus an array of Würste and a delightful Sauerbraten. The Weinstube's hours are 10am to midnight; closed Mon., Sun. after 3pm. It is also closed from January 10 to 30.

---

7. Titisee

After a brisk session of ice skating on the lake or cross-country skiing through the hills, you can return to your cozy inn in this tiny resort. The hospitality of Titisee knows no hour or season. This year-round resort on the banks of Lake Titisee, 20 miles southeast of Freiburg, is as popular for winter sleigh rides and skiing as it is for summer swimming, boating, fishing, and tennis. The surrounding mountains, including the **Feldberg,** the highest point in the Black Forest (5,000 feet), are ideal for hiking and climbing.

The town of Titisee is a well-staffed spa, with therapeutic thermal baths and various treatments for cardiac and vascular disorders, as well as for rheumatism and intestinal diseases. It has all the other activities of a resort town, too, including concerts in the open-air pavilion and various social events. At night a Bavarian marching band plays, its members going from one hotel to another.

Shoppers gravitate to the waterfront stores where they find good buys in Bavarian enamelware and Hummel figurines.

WHERE TO STAY

Expensive Hotels

As the most fashionable hotel in Titisee, **Treschers Schwarzwaldhotel am See,** Seestrasse 12, D-7820 Titisee-Neustadt (tel. 07651/81-11), gets "A" for position—in the heart of the village, right on the lakeside, with an unimpaired view. Most of its life centers around its waterside courtyard. Plants and garden furniture make for an easy life on the wide sun terrace. The dining room is provincial in style, the sun room a multitude of vines and plants (the latter is an ideal spot for breakfast). Also inviting is a rustic Weinstube for drinks before or after your meals. A large enclosed swimming-pool area has an all-glass wall on the lakeside, fitness equipment, and a beauty farm. The 86 rooms are wide-ranging, going from spacious to closet-sized. A single with shower in high season costs 140 DM ($83.15) daily, rising to 200 DM ($118.75) for a room with complete bath. A double with shower is 180 DM ($106.90), increasing to 280 DM ($166.25) for a room with complete bath in high season. Closed mid-November to the end of December.

Seehotel Wiesler, Strandbadstrasse 5, D-7820 Titisee (tel. 07651/83-30). Restful and well managed, this imposing 32-room chalet hotel rises from the lakeside at the foot of a hillock forested with pine trees. Most of the bedrooms are in an extension jutting from the main body of the building. There are a handful of conservatively decorated lounges, a small spa where massages can be requested, a sauna and a whirlpool, as well as a lakeside terrace doubling as a daytime café, and a wine cellar capped with a vaulted ceiling of well-aged brick. Each of the bedrooms has a balcony, comfortably modern furniture, and harmonious color schemes. Most (but not all) contain private baths. Depending on the plumbing, the Wiesler family charges 81 DM ($48.10) to 99 DM ($58.80) daily for a single and 172 DM ($102.15) for a double.

Kurhotel Brugger am See, Strandbadstrasse 14, D-7820 Titisee-Neustadt (tel. 07651/80-10), is one of the leading hotels around the waterfront. It's a modified chalet, with balconies and an all-window dining room. The café and Konditorei have open-beamed ceilings and country chairs. The interior is contemporary, done in harmonious colors. The 67 rooms are fair-sized. With a complete bath, a single ranges from 100 DM ($59.40) to 160 DM ($95) daily. For a double with bath, the charge goes from 150 DM ($89.05) to 260 DM ($154.40), depending on the quality of the room. On the premises are several cure baths and an indoor pool.

Moderately Priced Hotels

A country hotel popular in both winter and summer, **Parkhotel Waldeck,** Parkstrasse 6, D-7820 Titisee-Neustadt (tel. 07651/80-90), often draws an elegant crowd for the formal dinners the Franz family gives during the winter holidays. The exterior is sheltered against a pine-covered hillock, which attractively sets off the blunted ends of the gabled slate roof. The interior is richly decorated with Oriental rugs, hexagonal floor tiles, and a beamed and paneled wood ceiling. For activities, try the indoor pool or the miles of forest trails. There are 42 rooms. Singles cost 65 DM ($38.60) to 70 DM ($41.55) daily, breakfast included, while doubles go for 100 DM ($59.40) to 150 DM ($89.05). Don't be surprised if you meet the owners in the sauna—they have to relax too.

Romantik Hotel Adler/Post, Hauptstrasse 16, D-7820 Titisee-Neustadt (tel. 07651/50-66). Many residents of town praise this attractive restaurant and hotel, a historic coaching inn dating from 1576. In the subsequent centuries it was a relay station on the postal route between Innsbruck and Strasbourg. Today it is run by Werner Ketterer, whose great-great-grandfather purchased it. The building rises an imposing four stories from a street-corner location in the center of town. It has stone corner mullions, a red gabled roof, and sunflower-colored walls. The 32 bedrooms are usually furnished with hand-painted Schwarzwald-style furniture, as well as complete baths, phones, radios, and minibars. My favorite rooms are up under the eaves. With breakfast included, the rate ranges from 120 DM ($71.25) to 170 DM ($100.95) daily, based on double occupancy. Singles cost 70 DM ($41.55) to 100 DM ($59.40), depending on the plumbing and the season. There's an indoor swimming pool on the premises. Clients arriving by train should get off at the Neustadt/Schwarzwald train station instead of Titisee.

Budget Hotels

One of the pleasantest pension-hotels in the upper Black Forest region, **Rauchfang,** Bärenhofweg 2, D-7820 Titisee-Neustadt (tel. 07651/82-55), is a modern auberge, an authentic reproduction of a chalet, with masses of flowers on the wooden balconies. You'll find the interior of the public rooms covered in pine;

the 18 bedrooms can appear somewhat stark. The Edlefsens are your hosts here, and they charge from 56 DM ($33.25) to 80 DM ($47.50) daily for a single and 110 DM ($65.30) to 145 DM ($86.10) for a double, including breakfast. Guests can enjoy the indoor pool or the miles of forest walks stretching in all directions.

Rheinland, Jägerstrasse 25, D-7820 Titisee-Neustadt (tel. 07651/84-74), is pleasingly proportioned, with three well-constructed floors of oversize windows and wooden balconies. This recently built hotel is the property of the Kelletat family, who offer well-furnished rooms costing anywhere from 43 DM ($25.55) to 51 DM ($30.30) daily for a single and 100 DM ($59.40) to 110 DM ($65.30) for a double, breakfast included. The hotel has a sauna. The place closes from November 15 to the end of December.

WHERE TO DINE

A good place to take meals, **Treschers Schwarzwaldhotel am See,** Seestrasse 12 (tel. 07651/81-11), was previously recommended as the featured hotel of Titisee. Even if you're not staying there (and are on the board plan somewhere else), you might want to escape your hotel dining room for a meal here in a tranquil setting. The menu is written in three languages, reflecting the international cuisine available here. Many of the chef's specialties are regional and prepared from scratch. The carpeted dining room offers a panoramic view of the Titisee a few yards away. One of the most popular selections on the menu is a hunter's plate, a selection of game meats served with potato croquettes and cranberries, or a filet of venison with peaches and mashed potatoes. Meals range from 45 DM ($26.70) to 80 DM ($47.50). Hours are 7am (for the breakfast trade) to 11pm daily. The restaurant is closed from mid-November to the end of December.

Maritim Titisee Hotel, Seestrasse 16, Titisee-Neustadt (tel. 07651/80-80), stands near the Treschers Schwarzwald Hotel. Many guests consider the Titisee equally good, in both hotel amenities and food.Certainly it has an established restaurant, popular with both visitors and locals. The chef specializes in regional and French dishes against a backdrop of a Bavarian decor. A dinner here will cost 30 DM ($17.80) to 80 DM ($47.50). Clients can serve themselves from the elegant buffet set up most nights at one end of the restaurant. The establishment is attractively intimate, and hours are 12:30 to 2:30pm and 6:30 to 9:30pm daily. The hotel offers a total of 132 attractively furnished bedrooms, renting from 137 DM ($81.35) to 217 DM ($129.50) daily for singles, from 208 DM ($123.50) to 298 DM ($176.95) for doubles.

Romantik Hotel Adler-Post, Hauptstrasse 16 (tel. 07651/50-660), at Neustadt, in the environs, is one of the most famous establishments in the Black Forest. You'll find it crowded with local residents on holiday outings who savor the fresh trout, game dishes, and charcoal-grilled steaks, along with specialties of the season. You might begin with a truffled wild hare pâté, then follow with filet of trout in a Riesling cream sauce or any number of main dishes, including veal steak with fresh chanterelles. Game dishes are well chosen, including roast venison steak of hare with red cabbage. One section of the menu recognizes the needs of vegetarian guests. Meals cost 25 DM ($14.85) to 50 DM ($29.70). Hours are noon to 2pm and 6 to 9pm daily.

LAKE CONSTANCE

Even though three nations—Austria, Germany, and Switzerland—share the 162-mile shoreline of this large inland sea, the area around Lake Constance is united in a common cultural and historical heritage. The hillsides sloping down to the water's edge are covered with vineyards and orchards and dotted with colorful hamlets and busy tourist centers. The mild climate and plentiful sunshine make Lake Constance a vacation spot for lovers of sun and sand, as well as for sightseers and spahoppers. A well-organized network of cruise ships and ferries links every major center around the lake.

Lake Constance is divided into three lakes, although the name is frequently applied only to the largest of these, the **Bodensee**. The western end of the Bodensee separates into two distinct branches. One, the **Überlingersee**, is a long fjord; the other, the **Untersee**, is more irregular, jutting in and out of the marshlands and low-lying woodlands. It is connected to the larger lake by only a narrow channel of water —actually, the young Rhine, whose current flows right through the Bodensee. The blue Felchen, a pikelike fish found only in Lake Constance, furnishes the district with a renowned and tasty specialty.

Our exploration of Lake Constance begins with the city on the Rhine which bears the same name.

1. Constance (Konstanz)

Crowded against the shores of Lake Constance by the borders of Switzerland, this medieval town had nowhere to grow but northward across the river. The resort city lies on both banks of the infant Rhine as it begins its long journey from the Bodensee to the North Sea, a strategic position that made Constance the most important city on the lake. A Roman fortification was established here under Claudius in A.D. 41. In the 3rd century the fort was seized by the Germanic tribes, who later became Christianized and founded a bishop's see around A.D. 580. It was here that Emperor Frederick I Barbarossa made peace with the Lombard states in the 12th century.

The city's main early claim to fame is that it was the site of the Council of Constance, held here from 1414 to 1418. The council was convened to settle the claims of three rivals for the papacy, which it did by electing Pope Martin V. But its notorious act was to seize Jan Hus, the religious reformer from Prague, who, despite the promise of safe-conduct he had been given, was placed on trial for heresy and burned at the stake.

In 1531 Constance accepted the Reformation, was ceded to Austria after the defeat of the Protestant league it had supported, and remained Austrian territory until it was returned in 1805. Although Constance never regained the political and cultural status it had held in the early part of the 16th century, it is today still the economic and cultural center of the district.

Remains of the fortifications of the medieval town, on the left bank of the Rhine, are the Schnetz gate and a portion of the town wall with two towers.

WHERE TO STAY

An Expensive Hotel

Starting life as a Dominican monastery in the 13th century, the **Steigenberger Hotel Insel,** Auf der Insel 1, D-7750 Konstanz (tel. 07531/2-50-11), is now a first-class hotel. Its situation is prime for the area—on an island, with its own lakeside gardens and dock. The step-gabled building is white, with an inner Romanesque cloister. Its Seerestaurant has Windsor chairs, wood-paneled walls, and planters of flowers, not to mention ecclesiastical arches and pillars. The 100 well-coordinated bedrooms have patterned fabrics, and the furnishings are fine: most doubles have a living-room look with sofas, armchairs, and coffee tables. All rooms have their own baths. The cost ranges from 165 DM ($98) to 205 DM ($121.75) daily for a single and from 260 DM ($154.40) to 320 DM ($190) for a double. At twilight, guests gather at the intimate, clublike Zeppelin Bar, whose walls are cluttered with framed letters and documents. (The man who pioneered the airship also turned this abbey into a hotel.) A gemütlich spirit prevails in the Weinstube, with its knotty-pine bar, pine chairs and tables, parquet floors, ceramic collection, and decorative green-and-white eight-foot-high tile stove in the corner. Here guests order wine, beer, and light snacks.

Moderately Priced Hotels

Within view of the lake, the **Mago Hotel,** Bahnhofplatz 4, D-7750 Konstanz (tel. 07531/2-70-01), serving breakfast only, is just a two-minute walk from the Bahnhof. The entrance to this hotel is one of those elegantly and rigidly narrow archways with an ornate paneled and wrought-iron door set into it. The interior is boldly decorated, with modern chandeliers. The 31 rooms are sunny, comfortable, and warm, and come with plumbing, phones, TVs, and minibars (which you stock yourself). Singles go for 100 DM ($59.40) to 130 DM ($77.20) daily and doubles for 130 DM ($77.20) to 180 DM ($106.90), breakfast included. You're just a two-minute walk from the Bahnhof here, and within view of the lake.

Buchner Hof, Buchnerstrasse 6, D-7750 Konstanz (tel. 07531/5-10-35). A well-proportioned and pristine facade greets guests of this 13-room hotel in Petershausen, across the river from Constance. Nonetheless, you'll find the hotel a short walk from most points of interest. The hotel, incidentally, is named after the composer Hans Buchner, who became the organist of the town cathedral in 1510 and is said to have been one of the first musicians to arrange and catalogue the wealth of Gregorian chants he found in the region. Rooms are pleasantly and comfortably furnished, renting for 85 DM ($50.45) to 115 DM ($68.30) daily for a single and 120 DM ($71.25) to 180 DM ($106.90) for a double, including breakfast. The hotel has a sauna and a solarium.

Seeblick, Neuhauser Strasse 14, D-7750 Konstanz (tel. 07531/5-40-18). In summer you'll probably want to spend a lot of time beside the pool of this modern balconied hotel, with a low annex and a landscaped sun terrace. The hotel rents 85 comfortable rooms with breakfast included. Singles cost 100 DM ($59.40) to 120 DM ($71.25) daily, and doubles go for 165 DM ($98). The hotel also has a good restaurant, where meals cost 35 DM ($20.80) to 66 DM ($39.20).

Eden, Bahnhofstrasse 4, D-7750 Konstanz (tel. 07531/2-30-93), is close to the train station but still enjoys a quiet central location. This inconspicuous family-run guesthouse could be a comfortable lodging place during your holiday in Constance. Whether you prefer to stay at the hotel all day playing bridge, or go boating, the staff will do all they can to make your stay pleasant. They rent 18 cozy rooms for 68 DM ($40.40) to 118 DM ($70.05) daily for a single and 138 DM ($81.95) to 158 DM ($93.80) for a double, breakfast included.

Budget Hotels

The six-story **Hotel Deutsches Haus,** Markstatte 15, D-7750 Konstanz (tel. 07531/2-70-65), a breakfast-only hotel, offers 42 clean, quiet, comfortably furnished rooms behind a modern facade. Twin-bedded units rent for 120 DM ($71.25) to 140 DM ($83.15) daily, while singles go for 55 DM ($32.65) to 125 DM ($74.25), breakfast included. You might find some of the neighbors gossiping on the two wrought-iron benches in front of this hotel, and you might even find yourself joining them before the end of your stay.

Goldener Stern, Bodanplatz 1, D-7750 Konstanz (tel. 07531/2-52-28). The owner maintains an inviting atmosphere and tasteful decorations. The color of the dozens of healthy green plants is reflected in the pleasing tones of green throughout the Goldener Stern. The 20 rooms are comfortable and spotlessly maintained, costing 65 DM ($38.60) to 85 DM ($50.45) daily for a single and 110 DM ($65.30) to 140 DM ($83.15) for a double.

WHERE TO DINE

An outstanding choice for food, the best in Constance, the **Seehotel Siber,** Seestrasse 25, D-7750 Konstanz (tel. 07531/6-30-44), is run by Bertold Siber, a celebrated chef in the area. Earlier in his career Herr Siber studied with Paul Bocuse and Roger Verge, the famous French chefs. Today his establishment occupies an art nouveau–style villa near the casino, overlooking the lake, whose rich decor has been modernized. The cuisine is a conservative version of cuisine moderne. The menu changes daily, based on the seasonal availability of certain ingredients. Your meal might begin with a lobster terrine with butter and red basil, or freshly caught lake trout with an array of seasonings. You might also prefer, if featured, roast Barbary goose with a Beaujolais sauce or his stuffed turbot with lobster (served with freshly picked leaf lettuce). Most guests opt for one of three fixed-price menus, one of which is priced at 95 DM ($56.40). However, the tab could easily go as high as 140 DM ($83.15). The establishment opens daily at 11:30am and takes its last dinner order at 11pm.

Seehotel Siber is mostly acclaimed as a restaurant, but it is also a Relais & Châteaux hotel, renting 11 handsomely furnished rooms in a building adjacent to the restaurant. Singles rent for 170 DM ($100.95) to 240 DM ($142.58) daily and doubles for 250 DM ($148.45) to 300 DM ($178.15).

Casino Restaurant am See, Seestrasse 21 (tel. 07531/6-36-15). If you happen to have lost at roulette on one of your casino outings in Constance, you can revive your spirits (and drink a few too) on the lakeside terrace of this casino restaurant. The view is lovely, and the food first-rate. Meals cost 48 DM ($28.50) to 75 DM ($44.55). The restaurant offers a good choice of dishes, especially fresh fish. Everything is backed up by a good wine cellar. Open from 5:30pm to 2am; Sun. from 3pm to 2am.

Schwedenschenke, Mainau Island (tel. 07531/30-31-66). Local holiday-makers sometimes make a pilgrimage to this island in Lake Constance for a gourmet meal of regional and international food in a country villa housing an old-fashioned restaurant in a comfortable setting. Meals can easily run as high as 45 DM ($26.70), depending on what you order. Hours are 8:30am to midnight daily in summer. In winter, only dinner is served.

THE SIGHTS

The best way to see Constance is from the water. Several pleasure ships offer tours across the lake to Meersburg, or just along the shoreline of the city. Ferries to Meersburg leave every 15 minutes during daylight hours. From 10pm to 6am, service is curtailed to one ferry per hour. An average-size car costs 8.50 DM ($5.05) to transport, and each passenger is charged another 1.80 DM ($1.05). For more information, phone 07531/80-30. The water's edge is the most fascinating part of Constance, as the little inlets weave in and out of the land, around ancient buildings and the city gardens where concerts are presented outdoors during the summer.

Below the gardens is the **Council Building,** originally constructed as a storehouse in 1388, but used for many meetings during its early years; the most important was the Council of Constance. The hall was restored in 1911 and decorated with murals depicting the history of the town. On the harbor in front of the building is an obelisk erected in memory of Count Ferdinand Zeppelin, a citizen of Constance who invented the first dirigible airship in the late 19th century.

From the water you can also see the towers of the Romanesque **basilica** rising behind the city garden. Begun in 1052 on the foundation of an even older cathedral, the church took centuries to complete. The Neo-Gothic spire was added only in 1856. During the Council of Constance, the members of the synod met here. From the top of the tower, a view opens onto the lake and the city.

An Excursion to Mainau Island

Four miles north of Constance, in the arm of the Bodensee known as the Überlingersee, is the unusual island of Mainau, a tropical paradise. Here palms and orange trees grow in profusion and fragrant flowers bloom all year, practically in the shadow of the snow-covered Alps. In the center of this botanical oasis is an ancient castle, once a residence of the Knights of the Teutonic Order. Both the castle and the island are owned by the Swedish Count Lennart Bernadotte, but only the island with its gardens and parks can be visited by the public (open daily from 9am to 7pm). There are four restaurants on the island, but no hotel for overnight stays. You can get to Mainau either by tour boat from Constance or by walking across the small footbridge connecting the island to the mainland north of the city. Admission is 10 DM ($5.95) from March to October and 5 DM ($2.95) in winter. The island is open all year round, but the flower and garden season starts in March and goes until November.

---

2. Meersburg

Like the towns of the lake district of Italy, this village on the northern shores of Lake Constance cascades in terraces down the hillside until it touches the water. You can drive into town as far as the Neues Schloss, but it's best to leave your car at the northern edge and explore on foot. In the center, the streets become nothing but narrow promenades, and steps wander up and down the hillside.

The town turns south toward the sun. From the dock, both large and small boats set out for all kinds of trips on the water, and water sports are plentiful. As an added attraction, Meersburg has an open-air swimming pool.

The surrounding vineyards produce excellent wines, and on the second weekend in September wine growers around the lake come over to Meersburg for the Lake Constance Wine Festival.

One charming little detail of Meersburg is the presence of a night watchman who still makes his rounds, keeping alive an ancient tradition.

WHERE TO STAY

Moderately Priced Hotels

An 11-room chalet hotel, **Villa Bellevue,** Am Rosenhag 5, D-7738 Meersburg (tel. 07532/97-70), with balconies overlooking the lake, is directed by Fritz Brandner, whose generous spirit is reflected in the furnishings he has chosen. Every square foot is stuffed with Wilhelmian Gemütlichkeit, Oriental rugs, and heraldic emblems. In cool weather, there is often a fire burning in the sitting room. Single rooms go for 80 DM ($47.50) to 90 DM ($53.45) daily, while doubles rent for 150 DM ($89.05) to 196 DM ($116.90), including breakfast, the only meal served. The hotel is closed from the end of October until March.

Wilder Mann, Bismarckplatz 2, D-7758 Meersburg (tel. 07532/90-11). Built just beyond a stone embankment that defines the edge of the lake, the facade of this country baroque building is the backdrop for a painted illustration of a local version of the abominable snowman (*der wilde Mann*) contemplating whether he'll have a stag or a unicorn for supper. Even the roofline's step-gabled design evokes another era in building construction. Heinrich and Helen Sulger rent 33 bedrooms, charging 110 DM ($65.30) to 125 DM ($74.25) daily for singles, 140 DM ($83.15) to 250 DM ($148.45) for doubles, all with baths or showers and toilets. Tariffs include a buffet breakfast, service, and taxes. You can enjoy the view on a lakeside terrace, and later order a meal in the hotel's restaurant for 35 DM ($20.80) and up. The hotel is open from March to the end of November.

Terrassenhotel Weisshaar, Stefan-Lochner-Strasse 24, D-7758 Meersburg (tel. 07532/90-06). Separated from the lake by a few weeping willows and a slight elevation, the panoramic windows of this hotel with their awnings can be seen from far away. The establishment is proud of its genteel tradition and is acclaimed locally for its garden terrace, where guests flock from the first of March to October. Many come here just to dine and enjoy the view, with meals costing from 38 DM ($22.55). Service is from noon to 2pm and 6 to 10pm. The hotel rents 26 comfortably furnished bedrooms, with singles costing 60 DM ($35.65) to 115 DM ($68.30) daily and doubles going for 140 DM ($83.15) to 180 DM ($106.90).

Hotel 3 Stuben, Winzergasse 1-3, D-7758 Meersburg (tel. 07532/60-19), has an ambitious project of renovating the entire hotel, as it is one of the oldest structures in the downtown area and one of the very few that enjoys a landmark status. The rooms are being upgraded, modernized, and newly furnished and, the restaurant is being given a warmer ambience. Innkeeper Brigitte Drewing offers her guests reasonably priced rooms, which contain showers or complete baths, color TVs, and phones. This historic hotel is slated to reopen in the autumn of 1990, and its prices were unavailable at press time.

Weinstube Löwen, Markplatz 2, D-7558 Meersburg (tel. 07532/60-13), is an old inn right on the market square. Its raspberry-pink facade has green shutters, windowboxes filled with red geraniums, and vines reaching the upper windows under the steep roof. The Fischer family have updated its interior, especially the 21 bedrooms, which are almost all modernized. Each room has a bath of some sort. A single with shower rents for 80 DM ($47.50) to 110 DM ($65.30) daily; a double with shower costs 155 DM ($92.05). The family has been making everything homelike. The wood-paneled Weinstube, with a white ceramic stove in the corner, serves good food and drink.

Budget Hotels

Only a pedestrian walkway and an iron railing separate the **Seehotel zur Münz,** Seestrasse 7, D-7558 Meersburg (tel. 07532/90-90), from the tree-lined lakefront, a fact that brings a lot of business to the lakeside café and restaurant. The 14-room hotel is balconied, and has an ambience to make you forget the urban bustle. Bernd and Brigitte Knaus are your hosts, charging 74 DM ($43.95) daily for a single and 98 DM ($59.20) to 146 DM ($86.70) for a double, breakfast included. All units have showers and toilets.

Hotel zum Schiff, Bismarckplatz 5, D-7758 Meersburg (tel. 07532/60-25). This sprawling 35-room hotel, with a red-tile roof and a single square tower, has its sun terrace built directly on the water. The ambience is pleasant and the interior warm and comfortable. The owners' well-maintained bedrooms cost 55 DM ($32.65) to 75 DM ($44.55) daily for a single and 100 DM ($59.40) to 140 DM ($83.15) for a double. The hotel and its restaurant are open from April to mid-October.

Gasthof zum Bären, Marktplatz 11, D-7758 Meersburg (tel. 07532/60-44), is a picture-book inn right in the heart of the village. A five-story corner building with step gables, it has windowboxes overflowing with red geraniums, an ornately decorated corner tower with steeple, plus a tangle of purple wisteria crawling over most of the facade. The innkeepers are the English-speaking Gilowsky-Karrer family, who open their guesthouse from March to November. They treasure Zum Bären, which has been owned by their family since 1851. Today's Bären was built in 1605 on the foundations of a building dating from 1250 (the cellar of the original Bären is still there and can be seen). It is furnished with tavern pieces and alpine stools, all resting under beamed ceilings. The two dining rooms are colorful and the 16 bedrooms are most attractive. The cost for a single room is 53 DM ($31.45) daily, and a double with shower goes for 102 DM ($60.55) to 110 DM ($65.30). These tariffs include a Continental breakfast.

WHERE TO DINE

If you've come to Germany with images of a handcrafted Weinstube that radiates a gemütlich warmth, then the **Winzerstube zum Becher,** Höllgasse 4 (tel. 07532/90-09), is a place where you should dine. From a corner, a pea-green tile oven provides heat in winter. The chairs are not all that comfortable, but the rest of the beflowered, paneled, and happily cluttered room will guarantee you a pleasant evening. The specialty of the chef is an onion-flavored Swabian Rostbraten with Spätzle, along with a host of other regional specialties. A superb set dinner, costing 33 DM ($19.60), is offered, but you can spend far more ordering à la carte, perhaps as much as 65 DM ($38.60). The restaurant and Weinstube are open daily from 10am to 2pm and from 5pm to midnight. Hot meals are served from 11:30am to 2pm and 6 to 10pm. When meals are not served, the restaurant offers drinks (mostly wine) and snacks. The establishment is closed from mid-December to mid-January.

THE SIGHTS

Entering the town through the ancient **Obertor** (upper gate), you're at Marktplatz and facing the 16th-century **Rathaus** (Town Hall), containing a typical German Ratskeller. Leading off from this is Steigstrasse, the most interesting artery, passing between rows of half-timbered houses whose arcades serve as covered walkways above the street.

Nearby at Schlossplatz is the **Altes Schloss,** with its Dagobert's Tower dating from 628, the oldest German castle still standing. The town's most impressive monument is open March to October, daily from 9am to 6pm; and November to February, from 10:30am to 5pm. Admission is 5 DM ($2.95) for adults and 3 DM ($1.80) for children. Clubs, flails, armor, helmets, and axes—all the warlike relics of a bygone age are here, along with Gothic chests, Renaissance cupboards, and 28 fully furnished rooms, decorated with pieces from the various epochs. The bishops of Constance lived here until the 18th century, when they moved to Neues Schloss (see below). At that time, it would have been torn down if the Baron of Lassberg, thrilled with medieval romance, hadn't moved in and preserved it. He invited as a guest Annette von Droste-Hülshoff, his sister-in-law (1797–1848). She liked it a lot. As Germany's leading woman poet, she was instrumental in having the castle turned into a setting for artists and writers. Her luxuriantly furnished former chambers can be visited, as can the murky dungeons and the castle museum with its medieval jousting equipment. Adjoining is the Castle Mill (1620), with a 28-foot wooden waterwheel, the oldest of its kind in Germany.

You go from the medieval to the baroque when you enter **Neues Schloss,** Schlossplatz, which stands facing the Altes Schloss. The leading architect of the 18th century, Balthasar Neumann, was instrumental in some of the later castle's design. Elegant stucco moldings grace the ceilings and walls. Ceiling paintings and frescoes throughout were done by prominent artists and craftsmen of the day. Its hall of mirrors, the Speigelsaal, is the setting for an international music festival in summer. On the top floor is the **Dornier Museum,** tracing the history of Germany's aircraft and aerospace industries. Admission is 2.50 DM ($1.50) for adults and 1.25 DM (75¢) for children, and the museum is open from Easter to October, daily from 10am to 12:30pm and 1:30 to 5:30pm.

On the promenade below stands the **Great House,** dating from 1505 and housing ticket offices for the railway and steamer lines on Lake Constance. Regular ferry service to Constance leaves from the dock on the outskirts of town.

A 15-minute drive from Meersburg will take you to the famous **Wallfahrtskirche,** the pilgrimage basilica at Birnau, 3 miles southeast of Überlingen. It dates from the mid-18th century and was built in the rococo style, with rose, blue, and beige marble predominating. One statuette here is celebrated. The Germans call it a *Honigschlecker,* or "honey-taster"—it shows a baby sucking a finger as he's yanked out of a nest of bees. It's found to the right of the St. Bernard altarpiece. The 15th-century *Mother and Child* above the tabernacle on the main altar is an object of worship among the devout who flock here.

---

3. Lindau

Growing up where a Roman camp, the castrum Tiberii, once stood, Lindau dates back to the end of the 9th century. It developed into a central transit trade point between Bavaria and Switzerland. Its medieval status as a free imperial town was lost in 1804, when it became a part of Bavaria.

Its unique setting on an island at the eastern end of the Bodensee made Lindau such a tourist attraction that it outgrew its boundaries and spread to the shores of the mainland. It is today under landmark protection. The garden city, stretching for 5 miles along the shoreline, caters to your every whim, from bathing to baccarat. The island also offers a look into the past of a former free imperial town of the Holy Roman Empire.

Connected to the mainland by a road bridge and a causeway for walkers and trains, Lindau is easy to reach. It lies just at the edge of the Austrian frontier and is a transportation link between the western part of Lake Constance and the towns of Austria and Switzerland, which lie directly across the water.

At the harbor stand two lighthouses—one, called Mangturm, built in the 1200s, and the other constructed at the tip of a breakwater in 1856. Each tower is some 120 feet tall, and can be climbed by the hearty along narrow spiral staircases. The reward for those who make it to the top is a panoramic vista of the Alps, both Swiss and Austrian. One of the town's most interesting buildings is the Rathaus, dating from the 1400s. The frescoes on the building represent scenes from a session of the 1496 meeting of the Holy Roman Imperial Diet, whose members convened at Lindau. However, it is not just one building but the whole of Lindau that is of interest. You can wander at will through the maze of winding narrow streets and old houses that have stood the test of time.

WHERE TO STAY

A pair of hotels, under the same ownership and management, have taken over the best lakeside estate. They are right on the promenade facing the small harbor, with its monuments, stone sphinx, and lighthouse. The twosome is appropriate for two budget levels. The more expensive is the Bayerischer Hof, followed by the middle-income Reutemann und Seegarten. A family tree hanging in the Bayerischer Hof traces the lineage of the owners (the Spaeth family) back to the year 1660. The Reutemann and Seegarten have a special dining and dancing restaurant, Zum Lieben Augustin (closed in winter), a romantic tavern shared by both hotels. Tyrolean chairs and tables are set on two levels, and a small orchestra plays in the background.

A Deluxe Hotel

Hotel Bayerischer Hof, Seepromenade, D-8900 Lindau (tel. 08382/50-55), a 95-room hotel, is first-class in atmosphere and service. It rises stories high, one side facing the railway station plaza, the other the lake. Three-quarters of its rooms have a good view. The lesser chambers overlook a narrow thoroughfare. The dining room has dignity, with wide screened windows to allow a view for everyone. The lounge is luxuriously furnished and decorated. Singles with private baths cost 120 DM ($71.25) to 200 DM ($118.75) daily. Doubles with private baths are 190 DM ($112.80) to 352 DM ($209). Breakfast is included. Open Easter to October.

Moderately Priced Hotels

Hotel Reutemann und Seegarten, Seepromenade, D-8900 Lindau (tel. 08382/50-55), the same switchboard as the Bayerischer Hof), are two villas joined together to make one hotel, standing next door to the parent, the Bayerischer Hof. Each villa is different. The Reutemann section has its own waterfront garden, with outdoor furniture amid the lemon trees and wisteria vines. It is unself-consciously and traditionally furnished in fine style. Most rooms are large, and some have tile baths, along with heated towel racks, huge tubs, and endless hot water. The Reutemann has a glassed-in dining room, where good meals are served. The Seegarten has the more attractive facade. It's built like a Bavarian villa, with little flower-filled balconies and trailing vines. It too has an informal lakefront garden with flowerbeds and furniture for sunbathing. The public rooms are elegant, the 66 bedrooms spacious and handsome, especially the lake-view ones (at higher rates, naturally). Singles begin at 80 DM ($47.50) daily, climbing to 154 DM ($91.45). Doubles range in price from 125 DM ($74.25) to 262 DM ($155.60).

Right in the center of activity, the **Lindauer Hof,** Seepromenade, D-8990 Lindau (tel. 08382/40-64), is close to the boat docks and harbor, yet only a five-minute walk from the railway station plaza. An eye-catching shuttered and gabled building, it faces a square, with a second-floor water-view terrace. Here you can dine under a flourishing wisteria vine. The lounge has an attractive collection of Empire and Biedermeier furniture. The 23 bedrooms are nicely decorated, each in a unique fashion; try for one with a view of the plaza and lake. Singles range from 100 DM ($59.40) to 145 DM ($86.10) daily; doubles, from 140 DM ($83.15) to 195 DM ($115.80). Each room has a private bath or shower. Facilities include an indoor swimming pool and sauna. Open March 15 to mid-January.

Helvetia, Seepromenade, D-8990 Lindau (tel. 0832/40-02). In the evening the rows of lights below the eaves of this symmetrical building with striped sidewalk awnings give an effect like that of a carousel. The management tells me that a dye shop occupied the site of this hotel in the 12th century, but today the coloring vats have been replaced by barrels of beer and wine, which flow freely to the patrons of this establishment's busy sidewalk café. The interior has big windows and is warmly decorated, with hanging lamps and an open fireplace. Single rooms go for 95 DM ($56.40) to 140 DM ($83.15) daily, while double accommodations rent for 140 DM ($83.15) to 260 DM ($154.40). Breakfast is included, and you can also patronize the hotel's restaurant. The 50-room Helvetia is open from March to October.

Budget Hotels

Only a quarter mile from the lake, the **Insel-Hotel,** Maximilianstrasse 42, D-8990 Lindau (tel. 08382/50-17), is a completely renovated accommodation, with a small reception room, plus an elevator. The 28 upstairs rooms are furnished with modern pieces, and all have showers, toilets, TVs, and minibars. Singles rent for 78 DM ($46.30) to 98 DM ($58.20) daily and doubles for 130 DM ($77.20) to 136 DM ($80.75), with breakfast included in the prices. The breakfast room opens onto the traffic-free Maximilianstrasse (described under "The Sights").

Hotel-Pension Brugger, Bei der Heidenmauer 11, D-8990 Lindau (tel. 08382/60-86). Named after its owners, this 20-room breakfast-only hotel is pleasingly proportioned, with a gabled attic and expansive French doors that open onto the balconies in the back. Rooms are up-to-date, with toilets and showers and lots of light. With breakfast included in the price, a single rents for 65 DM ($38.60) to 75 DM ($44.55) daily, and a double costs 116 DM ($68.90) to 150 DM ($89.05). The same family owns an older building nearby where rates are slightly cheaper than those charged in the newer accommodations.

WHERE TO DINE

Some of the finest food on Lake Constance is provided at **Hoyerberg Schlössle,** Hoyerbergstrasse 64, at Lindau-Aeschach (tel. 08382/2-52-95). The location is in a building constructed as a private palace, then turned into an elegant bourgeois residence. Eventually the Schloss was purchased by the city of Lindau. Since 1979 the tenants have been a team of dedicated chefs who have come closer than anyone else to re-creating the ambience of the former Lustschloss. A beautifully decorated inner room with a view of the mountains and lake, or one of two terraces, could be your choice for sampling the delicacies produced by head chef Friedbert Lang. These include cream of scampi soup, Bodensee pike-perch stuffed with Champänerkraut, and Allgäuer roe saddle with small flour dumplings and French beans. A la carte meals cost from 60 DM ($35.65). A Hoyerbergschlössle menu is offered for 88 DM ($52.25) and a gourmet menu for 130 DM ($77.20). The café sections are open from 2 to 5pm, and warm food is served in the restaurant from noon to 2pm and 6 to 10:30pm; closed Mon. and during the month of February.

Bistro Beaujolais, Ludwigstrasse 7 (tel. 08382/64-49). Its style is that of a sophisticated but informal bistro and its walls are the same wine-red as the namesake of the place. Specialties include grilled scampi garnished with fresh melon, medallions of veal with fresh asparagus, lentil salad with fresh apples and alpine air-dried beef, zander from Lake Constance, and medallions of seawolf with spinach. You can also order a delectable bouillabaisse with a spicy garlic-flavored rouille. It is open from 11:30am to 2pm and 6 to 10:30pm; closed Mon. and for lunch on Tues. Meals cost from 60 DM ($35.65) if ordered à la carte or 59 DM ($35.05) to 89 DM ($52.85) on the fixed-price menus.

Spielbank Restaurant, Oskar-Groll-Anlage 2 (tel. 08382/52-00), is one of the most prestigious restaurants in Lindau, perfect for a celebration meal. It is, in reality, a pavilion right on the lake, with scenic views. You won't have to break the bank at the casino to dine here. For example, set lunches range from 35 DM ($20.80) up. In the evening, an à la carte dinner could cost as much as 75 DM ($44.55). The restaurant is open daily from noon to midnight.

Zum Sünfzen, Maximilianstrasse 1 (tel. 08382/58-65), is owned by the same family as the Insel-Hotel. In an old all-wood arched house/restaurant, with windows in the antique-glass style, it offers pleasant groups of tables covered with napkins. The food is good, the cost low. Dishes range from roast pork with vegetables to filet of venison. Meals begin at 25 DM ($14.85), climbing to 35 DM ($20.80). The restaurant is open daily from 11:30am to 10:30pm except from late January to the end of February.

THE SIGHTS

Whether you arrive at Lindau by boat or train, a tour of the Ferieninsel (Holiday Island) begins with the **old harbor,** seen from the lakeside promenade. The Mangturm, the old lighthouse, stands on the promenade as a reminder of the heavy fortifications that once surrounded the city. It also marks the point (now filled in) where Lindau was once divided into two islands. The entrance to the harbor is marked by two silhouettes, the 108-foot **New Lighthouse** (19th century) and the **Bavarian Lion,** standing guard as yachts and commercial ships pass by below. From the promenade, you can gaze out past these monuments over the water to the Alps on the opposite side of the lake.

In the center of the town, the **Hauptstrasse** is the main street of the Altstadt. The most easily recognized building is the **Altes Rathaus,** erected in 1422 on the site of a vineyard. The stepped gables are typical of the period, but the building's facade also combines many later styles of architecture. The interior, once used by the Imperial Diet as a council hall, is the town library.

Just north of the Hauptstrasse, with its half-timbered houses, is the town's most familiar landmark, the round **Diebsturm** (Thieves' Tower), with its turreted roof. Next to it is the oldest building in Lindau, **St. Peter's Church** (11th century), which houses a war memorial chapel. In the church is a group of frescoes painted by Hans Holbein the Elder.

Returning to the Hauptstrasse, which cuts through the exact center of the island, follow the street eastward to the **Haus zum Cavazzen** (tel. 08382/27-54-05), considered the handsomest patrician's house on Lake Constance. Rebuilt in 1730 in the style of a baroque country mansion, it houses the municipal art collections. Included are exhibits of sculpture and painting from the Gothic, Renaissance, and baroque periods. Some of the rooms are furnished with period pieces showing how wealthy citizens lived in the 18th and 19th centuries. The 18th-century murals on the facade have been restored. It is open Tues. to Sat. from 9am to noon and 2 to 5pm (on Sun. from 10am to noon only). It is closed Mon. and from January to March; admission is 3 DM ($1.80).

Passing across Marktplatz and by the Collegiate Church and St. Stephen's Church, both baroque, you come to the strange pile of rocks known as **Heathen's Wall,** dating from Roman times. Beyond this is the solitude of the **Stadtgarten** (Town Garden), which, although peaceful during the day, livens up at night when the wheels of the town's casino begin to whirl and spin.

THE ROMANTIC ROAD

1. BAD MERGENTHEIM
2. ROTHENBURG
3. DINKELSBÜHL
4. NÖRDLINGEN
5. AUGSBURG
6. FÜSSEN
7. THE ROYAL CASTLES

No area of Germany is more aptly named than this. Even if the road that runs through central Bavaria isn't romantic itself, the medieval villages and 2,000-year-old town through which it passes certainly are. The Romantische Strasse or Romantic Road stretches for 180 miles between the cities of Würzburg, in the north, and Füssen, in the foothills of the Bavarian Alps.

You may, if you wish, take a bus tour, accompanied by an English-speaking guide, which traverses the entire route each day. But the best way to see this stretch of Germany is by car, stopping whenever the mood suggests and then driving on through miles of vineyards and over streams until you arrive at the alpine passes in the south.

If you begin your tour of the scenic route at the north, you'll find yourself, after leaving the Franconian city of Würzburg, in Bad Mergentheim.

1. Bad Mergentheim

From the name you can guess that this little town along the northern stretches of the Romantic Road is a spa resort community, but that is only one of the faces of Bad Mergentheim. In fact, it was as recently as 1826 that the healing springs of the town were accidentally rediscovered (archeological evidence indicates that they had been known in the Bronze and Iron Ages). Bad Mergentheim, among its various treatments, offers a cure for obesity.

Perhaps a more pleasant cure than spa treatments for the overweight visitor would be a walking tour through the narrow, crooked streets to the old **Marktplatz** and the **Rathaus,** the town's major sightseeing attraction, and the **Mergentheim Palace** Deutschordensschloss, on the opposite bank of the Tauber from the spa facil-

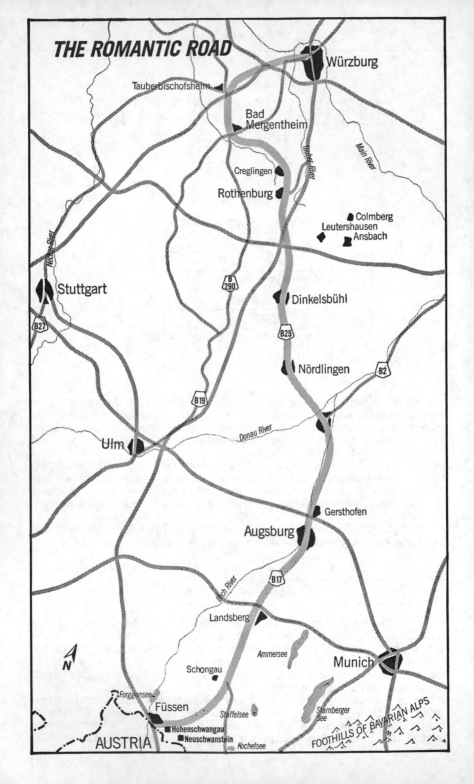

THE ROMANTIC ROAD

Würzburg

Tauberbischofsheim

Bad Mergentheim

Creglingen

Rothenburg

Colmberg
Leutershausen
Ansbach

Main River

Tauber River

Stuttgart

B 290

Dinkelsbühl

B25

Nördlingen

B2

B27

B19

Donau River

Ulm

Gersthofen

Augsburg

B17

Lech River

Landsberg

Ammersee

Schongau

Munich

Forggensee

Füssen

Staffelsee

Starnberger See

FOOTHILLS OF BAVARIAN ALPS

N

AUSTRIA

Hohenschwangau
Neuschwanstein

Kochelsee

ities. The palace was the seat of the Teutonic Knights from 1527 until their dispossession by Napoleon in 1809. During residence in this Renaissance castle, the order was a politically influential one, straying from its original purpose as a religious and military order founded during the Crusades. Especially interesting are the palace church, redesigned in the 18th century by Balthasar Neumann and François Cuvilliés in a rich baroque style with frescoes and rococo altars, and the museum. Tours are conducted on Sat., Sun., and holidays from 10am to noon and 2:30 to 5:30pm. Between March and October, there are also tours Tues. to Fri. from 2:30 to 5:30pm. Admission is 3 DM ($1.80). There are possibilities for excursions to Markelsheim for wine tasting or to see the *Stuppacher Madonna,* a beautiful medieval painting in Stuppach by Matthias Grünewald.

WHERE TO STAY

An Expensive Hotel

One of the best hotels at the spa, **Hotel Victoria,** Poststrasse 2, D-6990 Bad Mergentheim (tel. 07931/59-30), is a yellow-fronted 83-room building offering contemporary luxury combined with touches of traditional alpine rusticity. It sits in the historic heart of town, containing a mock half-timbered lobby whose terra-cotta tiles and wrought-iron lamps evoke a medieval Franconian marketplace. Except for two of its restaurants (recommended separately), the rest of the hotel is stylishly streamlined. Each of the beige- or pastel-colored rooms contains a private balcony, color TV, minibar, phone, private bath, and soundproof windows. With breakfast included, singles cost 85 DM ($50.45) to 125 DM ($74.25) daily, and doubles go for 150 DM ($89.05) to 180 DM ($106.90). A flowering garden provides a summer-only café. At night, a piano bar converts to a strobe-light disco. There is also a sauna, along with a fitness room and a heated rooftop swimming pool that can be closed to the elements or else opened to the summer sun.

A Moderately Priced Hotel

Bundschu, Cronbergstrasse 15, D-6990 Bad Mergentheim (tel. 07931/30-43), is perhaps even better known for its dining room than for its hotel facilities. Nevertheless, in its price range, it is also the best, offering 40 single rooms priced from 60 DM ($35.65) to 80 DM ($47.50) daily, and 20 doubles from 120 DM ($71.25) to 160 DM ($95). Accommodations have modern comforts, and the hotel places great importance on tranquility. It offers a swimming pool and a restaurant with both classical cuisine and regional dishes. Try, for example, grilled pig's liver with a leafy lettuce salad, venison with a ragoût of wild mushrooms, or stuffed breast of roast goose. Fixed-price menus cost 20 DM ($11.90) to 50 DM ($29.70). You can come here to dine even if you're not a guest, but you should make a reservation. Service is from 11:30am to 2pm and 6 to 9:30pm; closed Mon. and in February.

A Budget Hotel

An immaculate little hotel, **Garni am Markt,** Hans-Heinrich-Ehrler-Platz 40, D-6990 Bad Mergentheim (tel. 07931/61-01), far removed from the life of the typical spa hotel, sits right off Marktplatz. There are only 30 bedrooms, most of which have private baths with showers. The Scandinavian furnishings are restful to the eye and body. A bathless single costs 50 DM ($29.70) daily, rising to 70 DM ($41.55) with shower. A double with bath rents for 90 DM ($53.45) to 110 DM ($65.30). Closed mid-December through January.

WHERE TO DINE

A wood-paneled Weinstube, **Kettler's Altfränkische Weinstube,** Krumme Gasse 12 (tel. 07931/73-08), built in 1823, and doing a popular business ever since, the restaurant serves more than 120 kinds of wines, along with gutbürgerlich cooking, priced from 25 DM ($14.85) to 40 DM ($23.75) for a meal. Try those finger-size sausages, Nürberger Bratwürste, and study the large wine list. Service is from 2:30pm to midnight; closed Mon. and from Christmas to mid-January.

Zirbelstuben/Tiroler Stuben, Hotel Victoria, Poststrasse 2 (tel. 07931/59-30). The hotel that contains these two restaurants has gained an increasingly good reputation for its cuisine. The Tiroler Stuben is the less expensive and less formal of the two. Full meals, often consisting of South Tyrolean specialties, cost from 35 DM ($20.80), including a traditional array of roasts, grilled specialties, and highly caloric desserts. A highlight of the more formal Zirbelstuben is a five-course fixed-price gourmet meal costing 75 DM ($44.55) per person, but it requires at least two or more diners; otherwise, meals cost 45 DM ($26.70) to 70 DM ($41.55). Typical dishes include suprême of salmon in Noilly Prat with fresh mussels; sweetbreads with fresh shallots and herbs; river crabs in dill sauce; and Atlantic turbot with fennel. Both restaurants are open daily, but only the Zirbelstuben requires advance reservations. Meals are served from noon to 2pm and 6 to 11pm.

SOUTH TO CREGLINGEN AND DETWANG

As you continue on the Romantic Road towards Rothenburg, you will pass through some interesting medieval towns.

The **Herrgotts chapel** in Creglingen was an important place of pilgrimage in the 14th century, and contains one of the most important works of Tilman Riemenschneider, his altar dedicated to the Virgin Mary. There is also a unique museum in the town, the **Thimble Museum,** which exhibits more than 1,000 thimbles.

Detwang is dominated by the Romanesque **Church of St. Peter and St. Paul** where one of Riemenschneider's last works, the *Holy Cross Altar,* can be seen.

---

2. Rothenburg

Sometimes listed as Rothenburg-ob-der-Tauber, this city was first mentioned in written history in 804 as Rotinbure, a settlement on the Tauber River that grew to be a free imperial city, reaching the apex of its prosperity under Bürgermeister Heinrich Toppler, in the 14th century.

Admittedly, if you arrive at Rothenburg's Bahnhof (railway station) at the northeast corner of town, you may find it hard to believe that this is actually the finest medieval city in Europe. Contemporary life and industry have made an impact, and the first sight to greet your eyes as you leave the station are factories and office buildings. But don't be discouraged—inside those undamaged 13th-century city walls is a completely preserved medieval town, relatively untouched by the centuries that have passed by outside.

WHERE TO STAY

Expensive Hotels

The most celebrated inn on the Romantic Road, the **Eisenhut** (Iron Helmet), Herrengasse 3-5, D-8803 Rothenburg (tel. 09861/70-50), is perhaps the finest small hotel in Germany, attracting an international crowd. Four medieval patrician houses, dating from the 12th century, were joined to make this distinctive 80-room inn. It's a virtual museum of antiquity. Most impressive is the three-story galleried dining hall, with ornate classic wood paneling and balconies. There are additional places to dine as well, each richly decorated and furnished, although in sunny weather they're all deserted in favor of the multitiered flagstone terrace on the Tauber. Meals are à la carte, costing 50 DM ($29.70) to 80 DM ($47.50). The specialty of the house is filet of lamb with tarragon or pike dumplings in crayfish sauce. Service is daily from noon to 2pm and 6:30 to 9:30pm.

The main living room has a beamed ceiling, Oriental carpets, ecclesiastical sculpture, and a grandfather clock. The reception lounge continues the theme, with a wooden ceiling, wide staircase, and statuary. The rooms are individualized—no two are alike—your bedroom may contain handcarved and monumental pieces, or have a Hollywood touch with a tufted satin headboard. Because of the wide range of rooms, prices tend to be complicated. The highest rates are in effect from mid-April to October 31. At that time, singles with baths go for 160 DM ($95) to 170 DM ($100.95) daily, twins with baths for 225 DM ($133.60) to 300 DM ($178.15). All tariffs include breakfast. The Iron Helmet is easy to find, just across the street from the Rathaus. There is also a piano bar.

Hotel Tilman Riemenschneider, Georgengasse 11-13, D-8803 Rothenburg (tel. 09861/20-86). Named for the famous sculptor, its half-timbered facade rises directly above one of the most visited historic streets of Rothenburg. However, its rear courtyard offers a cool and calm geranium-bedecked oasis from the busy pedestrian traffic in front. One of the most prominent hotels in town, it contains alpine-inspired furniture (often painted in rustic floral motifs), stone floors, lots of mountain-style accessories, and an occasional porcelain stove set into a wall niche. Each of the 65 well-furnished, often stylish bedrooms contains a modernized private bath, and breakfast is included in the price. Depending on the accommodation, singles cost 100 DM ($59.40) to 140 DM ($83.15) daily, with doubles going for 140 DM ($83.15) to 220 DM ($130.65).

Goldener Hirsch, Untere Schmiedgasse 16-25, D-8803 Rothenburg (tel. 09861/708-0), is a first-class hotel, a remake of an inn that dated from 1600. In the heart of town, it's housed in a rustic building. The Blue Terrace, for dining, offers a panoramic view of the Tauber and the surrounding hills, or you may prefer to take your dinner in the blue-and-white Regency salon. So popular has this hostelry become that it's annexed another patrician house across the street. The 80 bedrooms are comfortable and homelike, showing a respect for traditional taste. Prices are based on the time of year and the type of bath you request. With baths or showers, singles cost 120 DM ($71.25) to 170 DM ($100.95) and doubles 190 DM ($112.80) to 280 DM ($166.25). Breakfast is included. The hotel is closed from mid-December through January.

Prinzhotel Rothenburg, An der Hofstatt 3, D-8803 Rothenburg (tel. 09861/60-51), is a 50-room first-class hotel. The owners follow the family tradition of providing guests with comfortable, well-furnished accommodations and excellent service. Rental units have direct-dial phones, radios, minibars, TVs on request, and bathrooms with hairdryers and toiletries. Charges are 170 DM ($100.95) daily for singles, 195 DM ($115.80) to 295 DM ($175.15) for doubles. Guests dine in the Kaminzimmer restaurant, where Franconian cuisine is included on the menu. An open fire in winter and a terrace for summer dining are inviting attributes, and you can take small meals in the Weinstube. This modern Prinzhotel is housed within a Franconian frame building with a handsome half-timbered facade.

Moderately Priced Hotels
Romantik Hotel Markusturm, Rödergasse 1, D-8803 Rothenburg (tel. 09861/23-70), belongs to the city's history. When it was built in 1264, one of Rothenburg's defensive walls was incorporated into the hotel building. Today that defense wall has been torn down, except for the section that is part of the hotel, which is still doing a lively business next to St. Mark's Tower. All the 24 rooms have private baths, and one has an antique bed that might be strong enough to support the entire hotel. Singles with breakfast go for 120 DM ($71.25) to 200 DM ($118.75) daily, and doubles cost 160 DM ($95) to 300 DM ($178.15). Closed from the second week in January to mid-February.

Hotel Merian, Ansbacherstrasse 42, D-8803 Rothenburg (tel. 09861/30-96), is a recently built hotel beside the old gates of the medieval town. Gisela Schmidt, the proprietor, sees to it that her hotel offers old-fashioned courtesy along with modern comfort and individual service. The 32 rooms and apartments are handsomely furnished, each having a shower and toilet, phone, alarm radio, minibar, hairdryer, and color TV on request. Singles cost 105 DM ($62.35) to 130 DM ($77.20) daily, while doubles go for 160 DM ($95) to 220 DM ($130.65). A buffet breakfast, service, and taxes are included in all rates. Guests can relax in the conservatory or the bar after a busy sightseeing day. The hotel is open from April to mid-December.

Mittermeier, Vorm Würzburger Tor 9, D-8803 Rothenburg (tel. 09861/50-41). Because of its long veranda, flanked by big trees, and its pleasing horizontal lines, the facade of this hotel could easily be found in the American Midwest. The interior is spaciously designed, with a freestanding fireplace in the sunny reception area, plus an indoor swimming pool that's quite beautiful, a solarium, and a sauna. The 21 rooms are contemporary and comfortable. Doubles rent for 140 DM ($83.15) to 190 DM ($112.80) daily, while singles cost 75 DM ($44.55) to 120 DM ($71.25), breakfast included. Closed January 7 to February 18.

Burg-Hotel, Klostergasse 1-3, D-8803 Rothenburg (tel. 09861/50-37), built on top of the old town wall, is a large, timbered 14-room hotel with a high-pitched roof, flower garden, windowboxes of geraniums, and a picket fence. The dining terrace provides a panoramic view of the Tauber River and the surrounding fields. The interior has been renovated by Gabrielle Berger, who has good, reliable taste. All the bedrooms, each with a tiled bathroom, are different: one has a four-poster bed of old oak, and others have swagged and draped beds; some are filled with antiques, and some have been done in sleek, contemporary style. Singles cost 135 DM ($80.15) to 160 DM ($95) daily, with doubles going for 180 DM ($106.90). An apartment for two rents for 270 DM ($160.35). Breakfast is served in an attractive room done in Louis XVI style, with a view.

Hotel Bären, Hofbronnengasse 9, D-8803 Rothenburg (tel. 09861/60-33), one of the leading old inns of town, dates back to 1577. Though modernized by the Müller family, it still has 15-inch oak beams and ornate wainscoting. The 35 rooms are all styled differently, with coordinated colors. For quiet moments, there is a reading and writing room with an open fireplace. Rates for a single with bath or shower run from 150 DM ($89.05) to 190 DM ($112.80) daily. For a twin with bath or shower, the price is 220 DM ($130.65) to 320 DM ($190). These rates include all taxes, a buffet breakfast, and the use of the indoor swimming pool. There's an extra charge for use of the sauna and solarium. The centrally located hotel has a spacious, elegant gourmet restaurant, Der Bärenwirt, as well as a cozy Bierstube outfitted with wooden beams and paneling, a tile stove, and an apéritif bar. Meals in the Bärenwirt cost 75 DM ($44.55) to 135 DM ($80.15). You can dine daily from 6 to 11pm. The "Bear" hibernates from November 1 to November 26 and January 4 to Easter.

Hotel Gasthof Glocke, Am Plönlein 1, D-8803 Rothenburg (tel. 09861/30-25). The designer of this comfortable hotel took pains to re-create a country-rustic decor. Most meals, drinks, and entertainment take place beneath heavily beamed ceilings and big windows framed with frilly curtains and well-polished paneling. The owners are justifiably proud of their restaurant—with its very complete wine cellar—where meals cost 25 DM ($14.85) to 60 DM ($35.65). It also rents 28 comfortably modern bedrooms, where singles cost 80 DM ($47.50) to 100 DM ($59.40) daily, and doubles go for 130 DM ($77.20) to 150 DM ($89.05), with breakfast included. Each accommodation contains its own bath, phone, radio, and often a private balcony.

Hotel Reichs-Küchenmeister, Kirchplatz 8, D-8803 Rothenburg (tel. 09861/24-06), is one of the oldest structures in Rothenburg. Built on different levels, it was once the seat of a chief steward for Rothenburg's nobility. Today you wander down the corridors to 30 nicely furnished bedrooms with regionally painted wooden furniture. Depending on the plumbing, singles cost 90 DM ($53.45) to 120 DM ($71.25) daily, and doubles go for 110 DM ($65.30) to 190 DM ($112.80). In the main restaurant the food is good, the choice wide. I recommend the Reichs-Küchen "master plate," including a choice of filet of pork, beef, and veal with fresh vegetables. In season, you may prefer a leg of roebuck with mushrooms, potatoes, and cranberries. You might also patronize the Weinstube, whose specialty is "steak from the hot stove." The hotel has a sauna, whirlpool, steam bath, and solarium for use of its guests.

Budget Inns and Guesthouses

One of the better little inns, **Gasthof Goldener Greifen,** Obere Schmiedgasse 5, D-8803 Rothenburg (tel. 09861/22-81), offers not only well-cooked meals at modest prices—from 18 DM ($10.70)—but also 21 comfortable bedrooms. Just off Marktplatz, in a patrician house, dating back to the 14th century, it stands next door to the prestigious Baumeisterhaus, recommended below. You can order your morning coffee in the garden amid roses and geraniums. The bedrooms are simple, but offer good comfort, eiderdowns, and hot and cold running water (10 contain private baths). Singles are 42 DM ($24.95) to 55 DM ($32.65) daily, and the rate for doubles is 84 DM ($49.90) to 95 DM ($56.40). The dining room is closed on Mon., and the whole operation shuts down from Christmas to the end of January.

Bayerischer Hof, Ansbacherstrasse 21, D-8803 Rothenburg (tel. 09861/34-57), a good and reasonably priced hotel, stands midway between the railway station and the medieval walled city. Willi and Katharina Schellhaas welcome guests, housing them in one of their nine clean and well-furnished accommodations. The hotel has been recently renovated, and its rooms have showers and toilets, plus TVs. Doubles rent for 95 DM ($56.40) to 120 DM ($71.25) daily, the charge being 65 DM ($38.60) for singles, including breakfast. The food is very good, with many international and Bavarian specialties.

WHERE TO DINE

Right off Marktplatz, the **Baumeisterhaus,** Obere Schmiedgasse 3 (tel. 09861/34-04), is housed in an ancient patrician residence. Built in 1596, it contains what is universally considered the most beautiful courtyard in Rothenburg (which, incidentally, can be visited only by guests). You must reserve well ahead in the day if you want a good table in the courtyard in the evening. The patio has colorful murals, serenely draped by vines. Try, for an appetizer, the soup of the day. Main dishes are well prepared and attractively served, and desserts are rich and luscious. Even though the cuisine is good, the prices are kept low: meals begin at 16.50 DM ($9.80), climbing to 38 DM ($22.55). The restaurant is open daily from 11am to 2:30pm and 5:30 to 9:30pm.

Ratsstube, Marktplatz 6 (tel. 09861/71-52), enjoys a position right on the square, one of the most photographed spots in Germany. The Ratsstube is a bustling center of activity throughout the day—a day that begins, incidentally, when practically every Rothenburger stops by for a cup of morning coffee, or perhaps a beer. Inside, a true tavern atmosphere prevails, with hardwood chairs and tables, vaulted ceilings, pierced copper lanterns, and decorative swords. On the à la carte menu are many regional dishes, including Sauerbraten, venison, and deer steak, all served with fresh vegetables and potatoes. Meals cost from 35 DM ($20.80), and are accompanied by the wines of Franconia. For dessert, you can order homemade Italian ice cream and a cup of espresso. The Ratsstube is open daily from 9am to 11pm, or even later in summer depending on business; closed for dinner Sun. If you arrive at 9am, the staff, if you wish, will serve you an American breakfast. Closed from January 7 to February 28.

Romantik Hotel Markusturm, Rödergasse 1 (tel. 09861/23-70). Decorated with hand-painted designs on the plaster walls, this old-fashioned establishment offers good Frankish wines and wholesome regional cookery. A quick inspection of the kitchens reveals about a dozen different aquariums, which are used to keep different species of fish alive until the last minute; they include trout, eel, carp, and sole. The restaurant, open daily from 11:30am to 2pm and 6 to 9:30pm, charges 32 DM ($19) to 68 DM ($40.40) for a complete meal. It is closed in February.

Goldener Hirsch, Untere Schmiedgasse 16 (tel. 09861/708-0), was previously recommended as one of the top hotels of Rothenburg. Its dining facilities have made it a preferred choice for many nonresidents. The cuisine is Frankish and international, and fixed-price meals cost 45 DM ($26.70) to 75 DM ($44.55). The menu changes every season as different produce becomes available. Open daily from noon to 2pm and 6 to 9pm. The inn is closed in December and January.

Hotel Gasthof Glocke, Am Plönlein 1 (tel. 09861/30-25), is a traditional hotel and guesthouse (previously recommended), serving regional specialties along with a vast collection of Frankish wines. Meals begin at 25 DM ($14.85), climbing to 60 DM ($35.65), with a heavy emphasis on seasonal dishes. Service is daily from 11am to 2pm and 6 to 9pm.

Tilman Riemenschneider, Georgengasse 11 (tel. 09861/20-86). A traditional old Weinstube, it's housed in one of the finest hotels in Rothenburg. The cook shows an elevated respect for old-fashioned regional cookery served with a rustic Gemütlichkeit. The well-prepared food is served in generous portions. You can have dinner for as little as 25 DM ($14.85), although some tabs climb to 60 DM ($35.65). Hours are 11am to 2:30pm and 6 to 9:30pm daily.

Reichs-Küchenmeister, Kirchplatz 8 (tel. 09861/20-46), might be called an old-fashioned entertainment complex. This hotel, previously recommended, offers a wide range of gastronomic choices that might include white herring with potatoes, carp au bleu, roast goose with potato dumplings and red cabbage, Bavarian liver dumplings with Sauerkraut and potatoes, and game stew with noodles and cranberries. You'll find a conservatively decorated Weinstube, a garden terrace, a Konditorei, and traditionally helpful service. A meal begins at 26 DM ($15.45), going up to 55 DM ($32.65). Open from 7am to midnight; closed Tues.

THE SIGHTS

The only way to see Rothenburg properly is to wander through the town on foot, beginning at the typical hub of any old German village, the **Rathaus.** Set on Marktplatz, Rothenburg's town hall consists of an older Gothic section from 1240 and a newer Renaissance structure facing the square. From the 165-foot tower of the Gothic hall you can get an overview of the town below. The belfry has quite a history. Fire destroyed the Gothic hall's twin (where the Renaissance hall now stands) in 1501. Prior to the fire, the tower had been used as a sentry's lookout post, but from that time on, it became a watchtower for fire. The guards had to ring the bell every quarter hour to show that they were wide awake and on the job. With an admission charge of 1.50 DM (90¢), the tower is open April to October, daily from 9:30am to 12:30pm and 1 to 5pm; in winter season, only on Sat. and Sun. from noon to 3pm.

The new Rathaus, built in 1572 to replace the portion destroyed in the fire, is decorated with intricate friezes, an oriel extending the full height of the building, and a large stone portico opening onto the square. The octagonal tower at the center of the side facing the square contains the grand staircase, leading to the upper hall. On the main floor is the large Court Room. Here an annual Whitsuntide festival, Der Meistertrunk, is held. In 1631 when the town was conquered by General Tilly, Bürgermeister Nusch saved the town from destruction by accepting the general's challenge to drink a tankard of wine in one draught. This sounds like a simple achievement until you see the actual tankard on display at the Reichstadtmuseum— it holds almost 3½ quarts (3¼ liters)! The Rathaus is open throughout the year:

Mon. to Fri. from 7am to 6pm and on Sat. and Sun. from 7am to 4pm. Entrance is free.

On the north side of Marktplatz, across from the Rathaus, is the former **Councillors' Drinking Hall** (1446), where only patrician families were allowed to drink. The most interesting feature of the tavern is the old clock on the facade facing the square. Daily at 11am and noon, and at 1, 2, 3, 8, and 10pm, the clock chimes and the windows on either side open to reveal Commander Tilly on the left standing in amazement while Bürgermeister Nusch downs the massive goblet of wine.

Leaving Marktplatz, walk north on the street that opens off the square between the Rathaus and the tavern. This will lead you to Klingengasse, a narrow old street that passes directly under **St. Jakobskirche** (Church of St. James), Klostergasse 15 (tel. 09861/30-57). A vertical Gothic edifice with three naves; the choir, dating from 1336, is the oldest section of the church. The altar was a gift of Bürgermeister Toppler, mayor during Rothenburg's most prosperous period; the fine painted-glass windows in the choir date from the same period. To the left is the tabernacle (1390–1400), which was recognized as a "free place" where condemned criminals could not be touched. The church's most important work is the Altar of the Holy Blood, created by Tilman Riemenschneider in 1504. A relic claimed to be the blood of Christ is kept in a piece of crystal in the Romanesque cross above the altarpiece. The most interesting work on the altar is a carving of the Last Supper in which all the figures were sculpted from three pieces of limetree. On the eastern side of the north nave are two more Riemenschneider altars. Hours are 9am to 5:30pm daily from the first of April until the end of October. From November until the end of March, the church is open only from 10am to noon and 2 to 4pm daily. Admission is only 2 DM ($1.20).

For a look at one of the old ramparts, follow Klingengasse northward, from the church to the **Klingentor,** its top portion adorned with four oriels and a ball lantern. You can wander along the covered ramparts of this portion of the wall, and to continue your tour of the town, walk on the wall west and south to the 13th-century Dominican nunnery, housing the **Reichsstadtmuseum,** Klosterhof 5 (tel. 09861/4-04-58), with the historical collection of Rothenburg. The cloisters are well preserved, and you can visit the convent hall, kitchen, and apothecary, and view the ancient frescoes and antiques. The museum collection includes period furniture and art from Rothenburg's more prosperous periods, plus the famous goblet that saved the town. Among the exhibits is the work of Martinus Schwartz, the 1494 *Rothenburg Passion* series, 12 pictures depicting scenes from the suffering of Christ. In the gallery you can also see the works of the English painter Arthur Wasse (1854–1930), whose pictures managed to capture the many moods of the city in a romantic way. The original glazed Elector's Tankard is displayed. There is a Jewish section with gravestones from the Middle Ages and some cult objects. You can also see the new section with archeological objects from prehistoric times up to the Middle Ages. The museum is open April to October, daily from 10am to 5pm; in winter, daily from 1 to 4pm. Admission is 2.50 DM ($1.50) for adults, 1.50 DM (90¢) for children.

From the museum it's just a short walk to **Herrngasse,** once the town's most exclusive street, which leads back to Marktplatz. Many of its half-timbered houses have been converted into shops. On one side of the street is the 13th-century Gothic **Franciscan Church,** with an unusual rood screen separating the east choir from the naves. The church is most notable for its numerous tombs, decorated with sculptures.

At the opposite end of Herrngasse from Marktplatz is the **Burgtor,** the tower that originally led to the Castle of the Hohenstaufen (destroyed in 1425). The tower once had a drawbridge, and although the moat and castle are both gone now, you can still see the holes where the ropes once raised and lowered the bridge and the huge hole, called the peat, through which hot oil or tar could be poured on an enemy.

The gardens where the castle once stood jut out from the rest of the town toward the Tauber River. Across the river from the Burggarten is the **Toppler Castle,** built in 1388 by the famous mayor, Toppler.

Take Burggasse for a short distance east and you'll come to the **Kriminal Museum** (Medieval Crime Museum), Burggasse 3 (tel. 09861/53-59), the only one of its kind in Europe. It's housed in a structure built in 1395 for the Order of the Johanniter, who cared for the sick. It was rebuilt in 1718 in the baroque style, the only edifice of this style still standing in Rothenburg. To give an insight into the life, laws, and punishments of medieval days, on four floors of the building the museum shows the legal history of seven centuries. You'll see chastity belts, women's shame masks, a shame flute for bad musicians, a cage for bakers who baked bread too small or too light, and other mementos of crime and punishment. The museum is open April to October, daily from 9:30am to 6pm; November to March, daily from 2 to 4pm. Admission is 3.50 DM ($2.10) for adults, 2 DM ($1.20) for children.

From here, it's just a few steps east to Schmiedgasse. Turn down this street and you'll arrive at the **Baumeisterhaus,** home of Leonard Weidmann, who built the Renaissance Rathaus. The facade is decorated with 14 carved stone figures representing the seven vices and virtues. The interior houses a restaurant, about which more later.

EXCURSIONS IN THE ENVIRONS

Using Rothenburg as your base, there are several interesting excursions that can be made from there.

Ansbach

This small Frankish town grew in prestige and influence under the Hohenzollerns, and under Frederick the Great the Ansbach-Bayreuth Dragoons won military fame throughout Europe.

The court life under the margraves, that held sway here in the 18th century was known for its brilliance and pomp, especially under the Margrave Wilhelm Friedrich. The seat of this splendor was the **Ansbach Residenz,** Promenade 27 (tel. 0981/31-86), at the edge of the town center, which dates from the 14th century. Gabrieli, architect to the Court of Vienna, later embellished it greatly in what is called the Franconian baroque style. Inside you can visit a porcelain gallery, with nearly 3,000 pieces, along with a dazzling salon of mirrors. In the red gallery you can stare eye-to-eye with the Hohenzollerns (at least their portraits), and you can also see the apartments once inhabited by the princes. Beautiful parks surround the castle. Summer visiting hours are from 9am to noon and 2 to 5pm (off-season from 10am to noon and 2 to 4pm); closed Mon. Admission is 3 DM ($1.80).

Afterward, save time for a visit to **St. Gumpert-Kirche,** right in the center of the Altstadt, a church that has a 15th-century Gothic chancel, but was much transformed over the centuries. In back of the main altar, a door to your left leads to the Schwanenritterordenkapelle, or Chapel of the Knights of the Order of the Swan.

What time remains should not be devoted to any more specific sights, but to the old town of Ansbach itself, which suffered no war damage. The town has many old structures, and as you walk along narrow lanes paved with cobblestones, you'll see a number of shops specializing in German handcrafts.

Ansbach is the site of a well-attended Bach festival, which takes place every other year.

WHERE TO STAY AND DINE My preferred choice in town is **Am Drechselsgarten,** Am Drechselsgarten 1, D-8800 Ansbach (tel. 0981/8-90-20). This cozy hotel has benefitted from an extensive renovation, which has made its 85 rooms even better than before. Each contains a private balcony, TV, radio, and phone, and many are filled with unusual, individually chosen furnishings. Guests find a pleasant dining room, a

Weinstube, and a morning buffet breakfast whose wake-up foods are included in the price of a hotel room. Singles rent for 115 DM ($68.30) to 150 DM ($89.05) daily, and doubles go for 145 DM ($86.10) to 220 DM ($130.65), depending on the accommodation and the season.

Der Platengarten, Promenade 30, D-8800 Ansbach (tel. 0981/56-11). You can leave your comfortable bedroom and find yourself in the mainstream of summer strollers, as this hotel is surrounded by the trees of one of the town's parks. French specialties are served in a stylish dining room, where meals range in price from 30 DM ($17.80) to 52 DM ($30.90). The dining room is closed on Sat. The 22 bedrooms cost 40 DM ($23.75) to 90 DM ($53.45) for a single and 70 DM ($41.55) to 170 DM ($100.95) for a double, including breakfast.

Leutershausen

About 10 miles east of Ansbach stands the old walled city of Leutershausen. It was rebuilt after World War II, having been damaged by U.S. Air Force incendiary bombs during a last-ditch stand there by fleeing SS troops.

The town is ancient, tracing its origin back to the year A.D. 1000 and the reign of Emperor Otto III. The gate tower contains a museum of local relics. Across from the new Rathaus, where the bürgermeisters meet, is the birthplace of the mother and maternal grandparents of Henry Kissinger, former secretary of state under President Richard Nixon. Kissinger's parents fled in the 1930s, but upon their triumphant return in 1976, they were honored by the town.

Another famous local son, Gustav Weisskopf, is credited by some with having flown in powered aircraft even before the Wright brothers took off at Kitty Hawk. A small museum in town named after him displays photographs of his early experiments in aviation.

Colmberg

Schloss Colmberg, D-8801 Colmberg (tel. 09803/615), is perhaps the most romantic stopover in the area, and in fact many couples come here to get married atop a medieval fortress. A hillside setting has been turned into a zoo, and the strutting peacocks are always a delight. The location of this castle, with its 12th-century stone walls, is some 4 miles from Leutershausen, in the direction of Rothenburg.

The castle rents 27 handsomely furnished bedrooms, costing 50 DM ($29.70) to 90 DM ($53.45) daily for a single and 95 DM ($56.40) to 150 DM ($89.05) for a double. The adjoining restaurant features wild-game dishes and local specialties, served in medieval and panoramic splendor guaranteed to evoke a nostalgia for the "good old days" of the Middle Ages. Full meals are served from 8am to midnight; closed Tues. The cost ranges from 25 DM ($14.85) to 40 DM ($23.75). Closed January and February.

---

3. Dinkelsbühl

Still surrounded by medieval walls and towers, this town is straight out of a story by the Brothers Grimm, even down to the gingerbread, which is one of its main products. Behind the ancient walls, originally built in the 10th century, is a dreamy village that seems to awaken only once a year for the **Kinderzeche** (Children's Festival), commemorating the saving of the village by its children. According to the story, they pleaded with conquering Swedish troops to leave their town without pillaging and destroying it, and got their wish. The pageant includes concerts given by the local boys' band dressed in historic military costumes.

In spite of the great hordes of tourists who come here, Dinkelsbühl retains its quiet, provincial attitude. The cobblestoned streets of the town are lined with fine 16th-century houses, many with carvings and paintings depicting biblical and mythological themes. In the center of the town is the late-Gothic **Georgenkirche** from 1450, containing a carved *Holy Cross Altar* from the same period. Many of the pillar sculptures were done by the pupils of the Gothic master TilmanRiemenschneider.

WHERE TO STAY AND DINE

An inviting place to stay is the **Eisenkrug,** Dr.-Martin-Luther-Strasse 1, D-8804 Dinkelsbühl (tel. 09851/60-17). The sienna walls of this centrally located 11-room hotel were originally built in 1620. Today the Eisenkrug's forest-green shutters are familiar to practically everyone in town, many of whom celebrate family occasions at its in-house restaurant. There's even a café with al fresco tables in warm weather. The stylish rooms are wallpapered with flowery prints and filled with engaging old furniture. With breakfast included, singles cost 85 DM ($50.45) daily, while doubles go for 120 DM ($71.25) to 140 DM ($83.15). Each unit contains a shower and toilet, phone, TV, and minibar. The main restaurant serves excellent food, as does the historic wine cellar.

Goldene Rose, Marktplatz 4, D-8804 Dinkelsbühl (tel. 09851/8-31), is a landmark in the heart of this village. Intricately timbered, it rises three stories high, with a steeply pitched roof and windowboxes overflowing with geraniums and petunias. It traces its history back to 1450. In the style of a country inn, the dining rooms are more important than the lounges. Adding to the ambience is a wealth of oak, antiques, and portraits of sovereigns (that's Queen Victoria at the bottom of the steps). The à la carte menu offers such tempting items as lobster and crab with dill and rumpsteak Goldene Rose. A good variety of tasty desserts includes fresh raspberries flambé. Meals cost 25 DM ($14.85) to 55 DM ($32.65). The 34 bedrooms are modernized, all with baths or showers, comfortable beds, phones, TVs, and minibars. Singles cost 65 DM ($38.60) to 85 DM ($50.45) daily, with doubles going for 89 DM ($52.85) to 150 DM ($89.05). All tariffs include breakfast.

Deutsches Haus, Weinmarkt 3, D-8804 Dinkelsbühl (tel. 09581/23-46), is behind a facade dating from 1440 and rich in painted designs and festive woodcarvings. In a niche on the second floor of the arched entrance is a 17th-century Madonna. Casually run, Deutsches Haus features a dining room with an elaborately decorated ceiling, inset niches with provincial scenic pictures and parquet floors. The 11 bedrooms are unique. You may find yourself in one with a ceramic stove or in another with a Biedermeier desk. A single costs 80 DM ($47.50) to 100 DM ($59.40) daily, depending on the plumbing. A double without bath rents for 130 DM ($77.20), one with bath for 170 DM ($100.95), breakfast included. Even if you're a nonresident, you may want to come here to dine in the Altdeutsches Restaurant, one of the finest in Dinkelsbühl. It is intimate, convivial, and an attractive rendezvous. À la carte meals cost 32 DM ($30.90) to 52 DM ($44.55). The restaurant serves Frankish and regional specialties daily from 8am to midnight. It's closed in February.

Blauer Hecht, Schweinemarkt 1, D-8804 Dinkelsbühl (tel. 09851/8-11), an elegant ocher building dating from the 17th century, has three hand-built stories of stucco, stone, and tile. Guests pay 75 DM ($44.55) to 95 DM ($56.40) daily for a single and 100 DM ($59.40) to 160 DM ($95) for a double. The 44 rooms are sunny, large, and comfortable—at least most of them—and they come in a variety of color schemes you may or may not love, according to your tastes. Closed Mon. and in February.

4. Nördlingen

One of the most irresistible medieval towns along the Romantic Road, Nördlingen is still completely encircled by the well-preserved city fortifications from the 14th and 15th centuries. You can walk around the town on the covered parapet, which passes 18 towers and fortified gates set into the walls.

At the center of the circular-shaped Altstadt within the walls is **Rübenmarkt**. If you stand in this square on market day, you will be swept into a world of the past—the country people have preserved many medieval customs and costumes here, which, along with the ancient houses, create a living medieval city. Around the square stand a number of buildings, including the Gothic **Rathaus**. A collection of antiquities is displayed in the **Reichsstadt Museum,** Vordere Gerbergasse, open from 10am to noon and 2 to 4pm. It is closed on Mon. and during December, January, and February. Admission is 2 DM ($1.20).

Georgenkirche, on the northern side of the square, is the town's most interesting sight, and one of its oldest buildings. The Gothic *Hallenkirche* is from the 15th century. The fan-vaulted interior is decorated with plaques and epitaphs commemorating the town's more illustrious residents of the 16th and 17th centuries. Although the original Gothic altarpiece by Friedrich Herlin (1470) has been placed in the Reichsstadt Museum, a portion of it, depicting the Crucifixion, remains in the church. Above the high altar today stands a more elaborate baroque altarpiece. The most prominent feature of the church, however, is the 295-foot French Gothic tower, called the "Daniel." At night the town watchman calls out from the steeple, his voice ringing through the streets of the town.

WHERE TO STAY AND DINE

In a bull's-eye position, next to the cathedral and the Rathaus, is the **Sonne,** Marktplatz 3, D-8860 Nördlingen (tel. 09081/50-67). It's practically heady from having entertained so many illustrious personalities since it opened as an inn in 1405. It has counted emperors, kings, and princes among its guests, including Frederick III, Maximilian I, and Charles V; even Goethe came this way. Also the American astronauts from *Apollo 14* and *Apollo 17* have stayed here. The Sonne is owned by the Madlener family, who perpetuate the tradition of hospitality. The interior has been completely modernized, providing tasteful accommodations with comfort. In a choice of dining rooms, you can order the soup of the day, main courses such as rumpsteak Mirabeau, and good, fattening German desserts. Meals range from 25 DM ($14.85) to 55 DM ($32.65). It's all quite casual; the waitresses even urge you to finish the food on your plate. The 34 well-planned bedrooms are on two price levels, depending on the plumbing you get. A bathless double goes for 70 DM ($41.55) daily, increasing to 120 DM ($71.25) for a room with private bath and toilet. A single costs 40 DM ($23.75) to 85 DM ($50.45). Breakfast, service, and taxes are included.

Am Ring, Bürgermeister-Reiger Strasse 14, D-8860 Nördlingen (tel. 09081/ 40-29), is a hotel with modern amenities. It should appeal especially to businesspeople, with its location near the Hauptbahnhof and its 39 dignified rooms decorated in a kind of executive modern style. Bedrooms, for the most part, are high-ceilinged, with tile baths and lots of light. The family owners rent singles for 60 DM ($35.65) to 75 DM ($44.55) daily, and doubles for 100 DM ($59.40) to 130 DM ($77.20), breakfast included. Closed mid-December to January 10.

Meyer's Keller, Marienhöhe 8 (tel. 09081/44-93). The conservatively modern decor seems a suitable setting for the restrained neue Küche of the talented chef and owner of this place, Joachim Kaiser. The cuisine changes according to the availability of ingredients and the inspiration of the chef; typical selections include a roulade of seawolf and salmon with baby spinach and wild rice, rack of Highland lamb with a truffle-dotted gratin of potatoes, breast of pheasant with a salad of wild lettuce, John Dory with a champagne-flavored tomato sauce, and an impressive array of European wines. Full à la carte meals begin at 50 DM ($29.70), although fixed-price menus start at 40 DM ($23.75) at lunch and at 70 DM ($41.55) at dinner. Meals, which require a reservation, are served from noon to 2pm and 6 to 10pm; closed Mon.

5. Augsburg

The 2,000 years that have gone into the creation of this, the largest city on the Romantic Road, also have made it one of the major sightseeing attractions in southern Germany. Little remains from its early Roman period (it was founded under Tiberius in 15 B.C.), but the wealth of art and architecture from the Renaissance is staggering in quantity and scope. Over the years Augsburg has been host to many distinguished visitors and has an array of famous native sons. These have ranged from Hans Holbein the Elder, Hans Holbein the Younger to Bertolt Brecht, whose Marxist proclivities infuriated the Augsburgers. It was to Augsburg that Martin Luther was summoned in 1518 to recant his 95 theses before a papal emissary.

An industrial center on the Frankfurt–Salzburg Autobahn, modern Augsburg is engaged in heavy engineering, textiles, tin, metal, chemical, and electrical industries, as well as the manufacturing of diesel engines, cars, airplanes, printing machinery, and shoes.

WHERE TO STAY

An Expensive Hotel

Rebuilt in a modern style in 1956, the **Steigenberger Drei Mohren Palasthotel,** Maximilianstrasse 40, D-8900 Augsburg (tel. 0821/51-00-31), was one of the most renowned hotels in Germany before its destruction in 1944 in an air raid. It had been a hotel since 1723, and was known to diplomats, composers, and artists; former guests include the Duke of Wellington, Mozart, Goethe, Mascagni, Paganini, and Franklin Roosevelt. The interior treatment of the "Three Moors" incorporates stylish contemporary pieces with traditional furnishings. For example, the drawing room contains a slatted natural-wood ceiling and wall, contrasting with a room-wide mural of Old Augsburg. In the formal dining room, international cuisine is offered. On the breakfast terrace, umbrellas and garden chairs are set in view of flowerbeds and three free-form splashing fountains. The 110 bedrooms are restrained and restful, handsomely proportioned. Singles go for 172 DM ($102.15) to 205 DM ($121.75) daily. Doubles with baths cost 270 DM ($160.35) to 320 DM ($190). Breakfast from the buffet is included.

A Moderately Priced Hotel

The high-rise **Holiday Inn–Augsburg,** Wittelsbacher Park, D-8900 Augsburg (tel. 0821/57-70-87), with 35 floors, is advertised as the tallest tower hotel in Europe. Students of architecture will see the similarity to Chicago's Marina City in the facade of this rounded and balconied concrete structure thrusting skyward. The hotel was totally renovated and newly furnished in late 1986, and offers comfortable, tasteful, and sunny rooms with rounded terraces, costing 192 DM ($114) daily for singles, 252 DM ($150.45) for doubles. Children up to 18 stay free in their parents' room. The hotel has a swimming pool, a sauna, a solarium, and a sun terrace, as well as ample free parking. On the 35th floor, you can dine in one of the two restaurants, La Fontaine and Le Bistro, or have a drink at the piano bar as you look over the housetops of Augsburg. The hotel is only 10 minutes from the heart of the city.

Budget Hotels

Offering 32 suitable rooms, the **Hotel Riegele,** Viktoriastrasse 4, D-8900 Augsburg (tel. 0821/3-90-39), is opposite the main railway station. Modern and efficient, it rents single rooms for 85 DM ($50.45) to 110 DM ($65.30) daily, doubles for 128 DM ($76) to 165 DM ($98). A copious buffet breakfast is included in the tariffs. The hotel's Riegele mit Bräustüberl, recommended separately, is popular with the people of Augsburg.

Dom Hotel, Frauentorstrasse 8, D-8900 Augsburg (tel. 0821/15-30-31). To arrive at this 44-room hotel, you can take trolley line no. 2 from the Hauptbahnhof, get off at Mozart House, and the hotel is 200 yards away. From your windows you'll have an interesting view of parts of the old city. You'll reach your room via a grand winding staircase with wrought-iron balustrades. Units have been renovated, and all contain private baths or showers and toilets. Singles range from 70 DM ($41.55) to 90 DM ($53.45) daily, and doubles rent for 95 DM ($56.40) to 140 DM ($83.15). Breakfast is included in all rents.

Hotel Fischertor, Pfärrle 14-16, D-8900 Augsburg (tel. 0821/15-60-51). Near the cathedral, this establishment is better known for its restaurant than for its rooms, which, admittedly, were added only in 1985 to the already successful restaurant. Each of the 21 well-furnished bedrooms contains a private bath, phone, TV, minibar, and comfortably modern furniture. Singles cost 75 DM ($44.55) to 100 DM ($59.40) daily, with doubles going for 110 DM ($65.30) to 140 DM ($83.15), breakfast included. You register in a contemporary reception area floored with a ruddy-hued stone.

Alpenhof, Donauwörther 233, D-8900 Augsburg-Oberhausen (tel. 0821/41-30-51), lies less than a mile off the Autobahn (take the Augsburg West exit), and as such might be ideal for motorists unwilling to negotiate the old streets of town. Quiet and peaceful, the hotel offers some 135 modernized bedrooms, each with radio, phone, TV, and other amenities. A generous breakfast buffet is included in the price of the well-furnished rooms, which cost 95 DM ($56.40) to 115 DM ($68.90) daily for a single and 130 DM ($77.20) to 250 DM ($148.45) for a double. There's a bar as well as a good restaurant on the premises, along with plenty of parking space.

Hotel Garni Weinberger, Bismarckstrasse 55, D-8901 Stadtbergen (tel. 0821/43-20-71), one of the least expensive and best budget accommodations in the area, lies about 2 miles from the heart of Augsburg, along the Augsburgerstrasse in the western sector. The owner rents 27 light and airy double rooms with complete private baths for 80 DM ($47.50) daily. Singles go for 40 DM ($23.75). The place is well patronized by Germans, who know a good bargain, and its café is one of the most popular in the area for small snacks.

WHERE TO DINE

In the heart of the historic section, **Zum Alten Fischertor,** Pfärrle 14 (tel. 0821/51-86-62), is the finest restaurant in Augsburg. Located near the cathedral, this charming, intimate 20-place restaurant offers a changing array of seasonal specialties. The cuisine is presented in unpretentious surroundings, waiters are attentive, and there is a superb collection of wines, more than 200 varieties. A typical meal might include goose liver terrine with mushrooms and cabbage, sole roulade with crêpes, turbot with chanterelles, or stuffed Bresse pigeon. Meals range from 75 DM ($44.55) to 125 DM ($74.25). Lunch is from 11:30am to 2pm and dinner from 6 to 11 pm Tues. to Sat. The kitchen takes a holiday from mid-August through September.

Welser Küche, Maximilianstrasse 83 (tel. 0821/3-39-30). Seven tables seat up to 80 guests here in long, informal rows. You just might be rubbing elbows with the Bürgermeister of Augsburg, or any of the local residents, because this is a historic place, having survived intact since the 15th and 16th centuries. A traditional menu of Schwäbish cookery is served nightly by *Knechte* and *Mägde,* (knaves and wenches) in 16th-century costumes. A 6- or 10-course menu, called a "Welser Feast," is served, costing 39.50 DM ($23.45) to 58.50 DM ($34.90). A dagger and fingers are used as utensils. Stone walls, knotty-pine paneling, and stucco arches frame the wooden tables with their earthenware pitchers, and the friendly hubbub of neighbors reminiscing about the old days. Many of the recipes served here were found in a cookbook that belonged to Freiin von Zinnenburg, the wife of the Habsburg Archduke Ferdinand II. Discovered in 1970, the cookbook serves as a culinary guide for some of the dishes. It takes about three hours to have an average meal here.

Guests are expected to arrive promptly at 7:30pm. Sometimes parties of two or four can be fitted in at the last minute, but reservations should be made as far in advance as possible.

Sieben-Schwaben-Stuben, Bürgermeister-Fischer-Strasse 12 (tel. 0821/31-45-63), specializes in Swabian dishes, and does so exceedingly well. This unusual restaurant has a high barrel-vaulted ceiling, with half-moon windows. Early in the history of this restaurant the owner conceived the idea of printing the establishment's menu in English, German, and French, and mailing it regularly to the best clients. Actually, prices vary according to the food served each day, and each day a different menu is written out. Meals range from 25 DM ($14.85) to 55 DM ($32.65). The restaurant is open daily from 11am to 1am.

Hotel Riegele mit Bräustüberl, Viktoriastrasse 4 (tel. 0821/3-90-39). The previously recommended hotel contains a restaurant with gutbürgerlich cookery and a cozy interior that evokes the Black Forest. Luring hungry diners here are traditional Bavarian and Swabian specialties, including country-style buffets, coupled with kind and attentive service, along with reasonable prices. You can try three different draft beers with the excellent cuisine. Angus steaks and fresh fish are also specialties. A la carte meals cost 25 DM ($14.85) to 55 DM ($32.65). The Stube is open daily from 9am to midnight.

Hotel Gregor Restaurant/Cheval Blanc, Landsberger Strasse 62, D-8900 Augsburg 21-Havnstetten (tel. 0821/8-00-50), lies 5 miles south of Augsburg, a rustic country restaurant that retains an antique flavor in spite of new construction. Swabian and Bavarian dishes are offered here, with some French classics. Soups are important, along with such rare treats as wild boar (in season). Meals in the highly rated Cheval Blanc cost 65 DM ($38.60) to 110 DM ($65.30) à la carte, with set menus ranging from 110 DM ($65.30) to 125 DM ($74.25). You can dine for less at the Lindenstube—25 DM ($14.85) and up. The restaurant is open Tues. to Sat. from 7 to 10pm; it's also possible to stay here in one of the 40 pleasantly furnished bedrooms. Singles cost 80 DM ($47.50) to 95 DM ($56.40) daily, while doubles go for 115 DM ($68.30) to 160 DM ($95), including breakfast.

Die Ecke, Elias-Holl-Platz 2 (tel. 0821/51-06-00). If you decide to dine here, your name can join a roster of distinguished clients. Since it was founded in the year Columbus sighted the New World, its guests have included Hans Holbein the Elder, Wolfgang Amadeus Mozart, and in more recent times, Rudolf Diesel of engine fame and Bertolt Brecht (Brecht, it is reported, often showed sharp-tongued irreverence, which tended to irritate the bourgeois diners of more conservative political leanings). The Weinstube ambience belies the sophisticated cuisine concocted by the chef. Both Gallic and Swabian cuisines are given modern touches, making for the kind of dining experience where reservations are imperative. À la carte repasts go for 35 DM ($20.80) to 75 DM ($44.55) on an average, and they are served daily from 11:30am to 2pm and 6pm to 1am. Your meal might include such elegant fare as breast of duckling, preceded by a pâté of pheasant, or perhaps a saddle of hare in tarragon sauce, or the filet of sole in Riesling sauce.

THE SIGHTS

Augsburg has been an important city throughout its history but during the 15th and 16th centuries it was the wealthiest city in Europe, mainly because of its textile industry and the political and financial power of its two banking families, the Welsers and the Fuggers. The Welsers, who once owned nearly all of Venezuela among other things, have long since faded from the minds of Augsburgers. But the founders of the powerful Fugger family have established themselves forever in the hearts of the townsfolk by an unusual legacy.

The **Fuggerei** is actually a miniature town, established in 1519 by the Fugger family to house the poorer of the townsfolk. A master mason fallen on hard times, Franz Mozart, once lived at Mittlere Gasse 14—he was the great-grandfather of Wolfgang Amadeus Mozart. The quarter consists of several streets lined with well-maintained Renaissance houses, as well as a church and administrative offices, all enclosed within its own walls. As the oldest social housing project in the world, it charges its tenants a rent of only 1.71 DM ($1) per year, a rate that has not changed in more than 450 years. But the tenants must pay the balance of their debt in an unusual form of payment—each night, when the gates of the Fuggerei are closed, they are obligated to pray for the souls of their patrons at the restored St. Marcus Church. Residents must be Roman Catholics. The Fugger family still owns the Fuggerei.

A house at Mittlere Gasse 13, next to the one once occupied by Mozart's ancestor, is now the Fuggerei's **museum,** open March to the end of October, daily from 9am to 6pm. The rough 16th- and 17th-century furniture, wood-paneled ceilings and walls, and cast-iron stove, as well as other objects of everyday life, show what it was like to live there in earlier times. Admission is 1 DM (60¢).

The **High Cathedral,** or Dom, of Augsburg has the distinction of containing the oldest stained-glass windows in the world. The Romanesque windows, from the 12th century, are younger than the cathedral itself, however, which was begun in 944 on the foundation walls of an early Christian baptismal church. The ruins of the original basilica are found in the crypt beneath the west chancel. Partially Gothicized in the 14th century, it stands on the edge of the park, which also fronts the Episcopal Palace, where the basic creed of the Lutheran Reformation was presented at the Diet of Augsburg in 1530. The cathedral remains the episcopal see of the Catholic bishop to this day. The 11th-century bronze doors, leading into the three-aisled nave, are adorned with bas reliefs of a mixture of biblical and mythological characters, including a scene of Adam and Eve. The interior of the cathedral, restored in 1934, contains side altars with altarpieces by Hans Holbein and Christoph Amberger. The windows in the south transept are the oldest, depicting prophets of the Old Testament in a severe, but colorful, Romanesque style. You reach the Dom by going up Hoher Weg.

The third most artistically significant church in Augsburg is **St. Anne's,** opening onto Annastrasse, a short walk from the Rathaus. Its most celebrated visitor was Martin Luther in 1518, who, it is said, did not put much faith in his imperial letter of safe conduct and slipped "out the back way" in the middle of the night. Still, his visit must have been powerful, because St. Anne's became Protestant some seven years afterward. Up to then, St. Anne's had formed part of a Carmelite monastery. It has rich decorations in both the flamboyant Gothic style and the rococo, the latter reflected in its richly adorned frescoes and stucco work. Dating from 1518 the Fuggerkapelle, or Fugger funeral chapel, is called the first example of the Italian Renaissance style that made its way into Germany from the south. Dürer designed two of the reliefs on the sepulcher. The church owns two works of art by Lucas Cranach the Elder, including a portrait of Luther. On the second floor, overlooking the cloisters, is a book-lined cell in which Luther found refuge.

From the cathedral, follow the Hoher Weg southward past the **Rathaus** built by Elias Holl in 1620. It was visited by Napoleon in 1805 and 1809. Regrettably, it was also visited by an air raid in 1944 (the flyers were trying to knock out a Diesel engine factory), leaving it gutted, a mere shell of a building that had once been known as a palatial eight-story monument to the glory of the Renaissance. The destruction left its celebrated "golden chamber" in shambles. Now, after much restoration and the spending of $6 million in funds raised by Augsburgers, the Rathaus can be visited by the public—daily from 10am to 6pm. Admission is free. In front of the Rathaus is the **Augustus fountain,** forged in bronze by the Dutch sculptor Hubert Gerhard in 1594 to commemorate the founding of Augsburg.

At this point, the main street of Augsburg's Altstadt begins. Extending southward from the Town Hall is the wide **Maximilianstrasse,** lined with old burghers' houses and studded with fountains by the Renaissance Dutch sculptor Adrien de Vries. Near the southern end of the street is the **Hercules Fountain,** and behind it, the most attractive church in Augsburg, the **Church of St. Ulrich and St. Afra,** which was constructed between 1476 and 1500 on the site of a Roman temple. As a tribute to the 1555 Peace of Augsburg, which recognized two denominations, the Catholics and the Lutherans, this church contains both a Catholic and a Protestant church within its walls. The church is 15th-century Gothic, but many of the furnishings, including the three altars representing the birth and resurrection of Christ and the baptism of the Church by the Holy Spirit, are done in the later baroque style. The large pulpit looks almost like a pagoda, with decorative angels dressed in Chinese red and gold. The crypt of the church contains the tombs of the Swabian saints, Ulrich and Afra. Ulrich was an Augsburg bishop who died in 973 and Afra was a young Roman woman who was sacrificed because she refused to recant her Christian beliefs. The lance and saddle of St. Ulrich are on display in the sacristy.

Schaezlerpalais, Maximilianstrasse 46 (tel. 0821/324-21-71), facing the Hercules Fountain, contains the city's art galleries—and what a collection is on display here. Constructed as a 60-room mansion between 1765 and 1770, it was willed to Augsburg after World War II. If only the works of artists who lived in Augsburg during the Renaissance were exhibited, it would be an imposing sight. (Regrettably, however, there is no painting by Titian in all the town, although he was here twice, in 1548 and again in 1551.) Works by local artists are displayed, including Hans Burgkmair and Hans Holbein the Elder (his even greater son, represented by a fine drawing, was born in a house nearby). Non-German European masters are represented by such greats as Rubens, Veronese, and Tiepolo. However, the larger number of paintings are by German artists of the Renaissance and baroque periods. One of the most famous of these is Dürer's portrait of Jakob Fugger the Rich, founder of the dynasty that once elected the heads of the Holy Roman Empire. Besides the art collections, the palace-gallery contains a rococo ballroom, with gilded and mirrored wall panels and a ceiling fresco of the *Four Continents.* Here Marie Antoinette danced the night away on April 28, 1770. The galleries are open from 10am to 5pm (in winter, from 10am to 4pm); closed Mon. Admission is 3 DM ($1.80).

The town's major collection of sculpture is displayed at the **Maximilianmuseum,** Philippine-Welser-Strasse 24 (tel. 0821/324-21-74, ext. 2171), together with works of art and highly important silver, as well as scientific instruments and ceramics. It is open May 1 to the end of September, from 10am to 5pm (in winter, until 4pm); closed Mon. Entrance fee is 3 DM ($1.80).

Roman figures, monuments, and sepulchral finds are found in the **Römisches Museum,** Dominikanergasse 15. The museum is housed in a former Dominican church. Seek out a gilded horse's head from the second century, all that remains of an equestrian statue of Roman emperor Marcus Aurelius. Open Tues. to Sun. from 10am to 4pm. Admission is free.

Augsburg is the native town of the Mozart family (see above). Leopold Mozart was born in Augsburg in 1719. He not only became the father of the world's greatest musical genius, but also founded the first violin school. The **Mozarthaus,** lying north of the Dom, is open from 10am to noon; closed Tues.; also open Mon., Wed., and Thurs. from 2 to 5pm, and Fri. from 2 to 4pm. It contains a 1785 pianoforte that was built by Johann Andreas Stein, an organ- and piano-maker whose instruments were not only eagerly sought by the young Mozart but by Beethoven. The magenta-colored house is at Frauentorstrasse 30; for information, call 0821/324-21-96. Admission is free.

6. Füssen

Depending on which direction you take, Füssen is the beginning or end of the Romantic Road. The town has a number of attractive buildings, including a 15th-century castle once used by the bishops of Augsburg as a summer palace. Füssen's popularity lies in its ideal location as a starting point for excursions into the surrounding countryside.

Besides being the terminus of the Romantic Road, Füssen is in the foothills of the Bavarian Alps, making it equally enjoyable for winter and summer vacationers. An added attraction to sightseers is its proximity to the royal castles of Neuschwanstein and Hohenschwangau.

Aside from the royal castles, a fascinating excursion from Füssen is to the **Wieskirche,** one of the most extravagant and flamboyant rococo buildings in the world, masterpiece of Dominikus Zimmermann, introduced in our survey of German art and architecture. On the slopes of the Ammergau Alps, lying between Ammer and Lech, the Wies Church is a world-class pilgrimage church, drawing visitors from all over the globe. The church, which in German means "in the meadows," was built to honor the memory of Jesus Scourged. With the help of his brother, Johann Baptist, Zimmermann worked on the building from 1746 to 1754. Around the choir the church has "upside down" arches, and its ceiling is richly frescoed. It was amazing that so much rich decoration could be crowded into such a small place. The great Zimmermann was so enchanted with his own creation that he constructed a small home in the vicinity of the church and there he spent the last decade of his life.

WHERE TO STAY

Moderately Priced Hotels

Hotel Christine, Weidachstrasse 31, D-8958 Füssen (tel. 08362/72-29), is one of the best choices. The long winter months are spent refurbishing the 15 rooms so that they'll be fresh and sparkling to greet spring visitors. Charges go from 80 DM ($47.50) to 130 DM ($77.20) for a single, from 130 DM ($77.20) to 160 DM ($95) for a double. Breakfast, included in the tariffs, is served on beautiful regional china as Mozart or some other classical composer is played in the background. Units contain showers or baths. The rooms are quite spacious, with balconies, and there are sitting areas in the lobby. The Christine is closed from mid-January to mid-February.

Fürstenhof, Kemptenerstrasse 23, D-8958 Fussen (tel. 08362/70-06), one of the town's two or three leading hotels, offers 15 well-furnished bedrooms. Here the ceilings are of massive exposed paneling, the full-grained beams set into the modern stucco with taste and craftsmanship. Singles go for 52 DM ($30.90) to 75 DM ($44.55) daily, and doubles cost 105 DM ($62.35), with showers and toilets. Each unit also has a phone and TV. Breakfast, included in the rates, is served by your hosts. The place is closed from November 24 through December.

Alpenblick, Uferstrasse 10, D-8958 Füssen (tel. 08362/5-05-70), is found at Hopfen am See, 3 miles from Füssen. It is an attractively designed mountain chalet whose encircling balconies are edged with borders of flowers. From the windows of many of the 46 bedrooms, guests can see the lake and the Alps. The premises are impeccably maintained in a rustic ambience of wood and hand-painted furniture. On a chilly evening you might seek out a quiet corner beside the open fireplace in the hotel bar. There's both an indoor and an outdoor swimming pool within walking distance, as well as a panoramic sun terrace where drinks and snacks are served to residents and roadside visitors as well. The comfortably furnished bedrooms rent for 115 DM ($68.30) daily for singles and 170 DM ($100.95) for doubles, depending on the room and the season. Each unit contains a TV, radio, and phone, and has its own balcony.

Budget Hotels

About 4 miles from Füssen lies **Gasthof Weissensee,** An dor B310, D-8958 ⁓üssen-Weissensee (tel. 08362/70-95), along the B310. The fish that your obliging hosts serve you during dinner might have been caught in the ice-blue waters of the nearby lake, whose far shore you can see from the dining room. The 22 paneled bedrooms have sliding glass doors opening onto a balcony overlooking the lake. Each accommodation contains a minibar stocked with beer, wine, and champagne. Breakfast is an appetizing and generous meal of cheese, marmalade, cold cuts, breads, pastries, eggs, and beverages served buffet style. Singles cost 65 DM ($38.60) to 85 DM ($50.45) daily and doubles 112 DM ($66.50) to 138 DM ($81.95). The hotel is open all year except from about the third week in November until just before Christmas.

Hotel-Gasthof zum Hechten, Ritterstrasse 6, D-8958 Füssen (tel. 08362/79-06). The Pfeiffers have maintained this impeccable 19-room guesthouse for generations. Its white-walled facade comes directly to the edge of the centrally located street where it sits. It is said to be one of the oldest guesthouses in town, but it has been unpretentiously and tastefully modernized into a functional format with its own kind of charm. It's laden with a conservative sense of peace and quiet. With breakfast included, bathless doubles rent for 70 DM ($41.55) daily, going up to 85 DM ($50.45) for rooms with baths. Bathless singles go for 40 DM ($23.75), rising to 50 DM ($29.70) for rooms with baths. Half board is another 15 DM ($8.90) per person daily.

Steig Mühle, Alte Steige 3, D-8958 Füssen-Weissensee (tel. 08362/73-73), is run by Josef and Guste Buhmann, who like it warm and cozy—almost a cliché of Bavarian charm. Theirs is a 10-room pension garni (serving breakfast only), which comes alive with the first breath of spring when the flowerboxes gracing this chaletlike hotel burst into bloom. Rooms open onto a view of the lake or mountains, and many have their own balconies and private baths or showers. Rooms are furnished in a neat, functional style, and are kept immaculately clean. Bathless singles cost 30 DM ($17.80) daily, those with showers, 35 DM ($20.80). Doubles with showers cost 66 DM ($39.20) to 70 DM ($41.55). The public rooms of the hotel are often paneled in wood and decorated with local artifacts of Bavaria. The Buhmanns are obliging hosts.

WHERE TO DINE

A conservatively flavorful blend of Swabian and Bavarian specialties is served to the loyal clients of **Zum Schwanen,** Brotmarkt 4 (tel. 08362/61-74), an attractively old-fashioned restaurant. The staff is amicable, and the ingredients strictly fresh. There are about half a dozen tables in the restaurant and another seven in an adjoining room, both pleasantly decorated. Fixed-price meals cost 18 DM ($10.70) to 30 DM ($17.80), and à la carte meals average up to 24 DM ($14.25). Food is served from noon to 2pm and 6 to 9pm; closed Mon. and on Sun. evening.

Fischerhütte, Uferstrasse 16, Hopfen am See (tel. 08362/71-03). To reach this restaurant, you have to drive 3 miles northwest of Füssen into the hamlet of Hopfen am See. There, at the edge of the lake, within sight of dramatic mountain scenery, lie four gracefully paneled old-fashioned and interconnected dining rooms. Each is laden with antiques and flowers and enjoys a view. A terrace in summer expands the dining area toward the great outdoors. As its name, Fisherman's Cottage, suggests, the establishment specializes in an array of seafood whose origins read a lot like an international atlas of the world: one half of an entire Alaskan salmon (for two); a garlicky version of French bouillabaisse; fresh alpine trout, prepared panfried or with aromatic herbs in the style of Provence; North Atlantic lobster; and grilled halibut. You can precede any of those dishes with a portion of lasagne. A limited array of meat dishes is also offered, as well as succulent desserts designed to make your gastronomic transition from sea back to land more palatable. Full meals cost 30 DM ($17.80) to 60 DM ($35.65). The place is open for hot meals from 11:30am to 2pm and 6 to 9:30pm; closed Thurs. It is closed mid-January to mid-February.

7. The Royal Castles

The 19th century saw a great classical revival in Germany, especially in Bavaria mainly because of the enthusiasm of the Bavarian kings for ancient art forms. Beginning with Ludwig I (1786–1868), who was responsible for many of the Greek-revival buildings in Munich, this royal house ran the gamut of ancient architecture in just three short decades. It culminated in the remarkable flights of fancy of Ludwig II, often called "Mad King Ludwig," who died under mysterious circumstances in 1886. In spite of his rather lonely life and controversial alliances, personal and political, he was a great patron of the arts.

Although the name "Royal Castles" is limited to the castles of **Hohenschwangau** (built by Ludwig's father, Maximilian II) and **Neuschwanstein,** the extravagant king was responsible for the creation of three magnificent castles. The remaining two, described in other parts of the book, are Linderhof (near Oberammergau) and Herrenchiemsee (Chiemsee). These pet projects were so close to the king's heart that when his ministers sought to check his extravagance, he became violent.

In 1868, after a visit to the great castle of Warburg, Ludwig wrote to his good friend, Richard Wagner: "I have the intention to rebuild the ancient castle ruins of Hohenschwangau . . . in the true style of the ancient German knight's castle." The following year, construction began on the first of a series of fantastic edifices, a series that stopped only with Ludwig's untimely death in 1886, only five days after he was deposed because of alleged insanity.

NEUSCHWANSTEIN CASTLE

Neuschwanstein was the fairy-tale castle of Ludwig II. Until the king's death, construction had taken 17 years. After his death, all work stopped, leaving a part of the interior not completed. In the years from 1884 to 1886, Ludwig lived in the rooms on and off for a total of only about six months.

Neuschwanstein was his most ambitious project, set in its isolated location atop a rock ledge high above the Pöllat Gorge. The ledge served as the foundation of the castle, and because of its unusual configuration, supported portions of the third floor as well as the first. This is obvious in the oddly shaped vestibule on the third floor, at the top of the main staircase of Untersberg marble. This hall, with its colorfully painted Romanesque vaults, is trapezoidal, the walls decorated with scenes from the primitive version of the Siegfried saga.

The doorway off the left side of the vestibule leads to the king's apartments. The study, like most of the rooms, is decorated with wall paintings showing scenes from the Nordic legends (which also inspired Wagner's operas). The theme of the study is the Tannhäuser saga, painted by J. Aigner. The only fabric in the room is hand-embroidered silk, used in the curtains and chair coverings, all designed with the gold-and-silver Bavarian coat-of-arms.

From the vestibule, you enter the throne room through the doorway at the opposite end. This hall, designed in a Byzantine style by J. Hofmann, was never completed. The floor of the hall is a mosaic design, depicting the animals of the world. The columns in the main hall are the deep copper red of porphyry. The circular apse where the king's throne was to have stood is reached by a stairway of white Carrara marble. The walls and ceiling are decorated with paintings of Christ in heaven looking down on the 12 Apostles and 6 canonized kings of Europe.

The king's bedroom is the most richly carved in the entire castle. It took 4½ years to complete this room alone, which, aside from the wall painting depicting the legend of Tristan and Isolde, is completely covered in oakwood carvings. The walls are decorated with panels carved to look like Gothic windows. In the center is a large wooden pillar completely encircled with gilded brass sconces. The bed, on its raised platform with its elaborately carved canopy, is the most ornate furnishing in the room. Through the balcony window you can see the 150-foot waterfall in the Pöllat Gorge, with the mountains in the distance.

Passing through the winter garden and a grotto with artificial stalactites, you come to the great parlor, whose theme is the Lohengrin saga, expressed in the paintings of Heckel and Hauschild. Note the heavy chandelier, holding 48 candles and studded with pieces of colored Bohemian glass.

The fourth floor of the castle is almost entirely given over to the Singer's Hall, the pride of Ludwig II and all of Bavaria. Modeled after the hall at Wartburg, where the legendary song contest of Tannhäuser was supposed to have occurred, this hall is decorated with marble columns and elaborately painted designs interspersed with frescoes depicting the life of Parsifal.

The castle can be visited year-round, and in September visitors have the additional treat of hearing Wagnerian concerts in the Singer's Hall. For information and reservations, contact the Verkehrsamt (tourist office) Schwangau, at the Rathaus (tel. 08362/8-10-51). The rooms are open April to September 30, daily from 9am to 5:30pm; in winter, from 10am to 4pm. Admission is 6 DM ($3.55).

Before returning down the slope, more energetic visitors can follow the winding path to the **Marienbrücke,** named for the mother of Ludwig II. This bridge crosses over the Pöllat Gorge at a height of 305 feet. From that vantage point you, like Ludwig, can stand and meditate on the glories of the castle and its surroundings.

To reach that magnificence, you must climb a steep hill—a 25-minute walk for the energetic, an eternity for anybody else. However, buses will take you to Marienbrücke for 3.50 DM ($2.10); the descent costs 2 DM ($1.20). Even so, you're not transported directly to the castle, but must add on a 10-minute hike to reach it. This footpath is very steep and not easy for elderly people to negotiate—or for anyone who has trouble walking up or down precipitous hills. The most romantic way to go is by carriage, costing 6 DM ($3.55) for the ascent, 3 DM ($1.80) for the descent. Some readers have objected to the buggy rides, though, complaining that too many people are crowded in. It should be pointed out, too, that the buggies don't bring you all the way to the top. As you get out, you're still faced with a steep uphill walk to the castle. The walk takes about 10 minutes. For information, phone 08362/8-10-35.

HOHENSCHWANGAU CASTLE

Not as glamorous or spectacular as Neuschwanstein, this Neo-Gothic castle nevertheless has a much richer history. The original structure dates back to the Knights of Schwangau of the 12th century. When the knights faded away, the castle began to do so too, helped along by the Napoleonic Wars. When Ludwig II's father, Crown Prince Maximilian (later King Maximilian II), saw the castle in 1832, he purchased it, and in four years had it completely restored. Ludwig II spent the first 17 years of his life here, and later received Richard Wagner in its chambers, although Wagner never visited Neuschwanstein on the hill above.

The rooms of Hohenschwangau are styled and furnished in a much heavier Gothic mode than those in the castle built by Ludwig. Many are typical of the halls of knights' castles of the Middle Ages in both England and Germany. There is no doubt that the style greatly influenced young Ludwig and encouraged the fanciful boyhood dreams that formed his later tastes and character. Unlike Neuschwanstein, however, this castle has a comfortable look about it, as if it actually were a home at one time, not just a museum. The small chapel, once a reception hall, is still the scene of Sunday mass. The suits of armor and the Gothic arches here set the stage for the rest of the room.

Among the most attractive chambers is the Hall of the Swan Knight, named for the wall paintings depicting the saga of Lohengrin—pre-Wagner and pre-Ludwig II.

Note the Gothic grillwork on the ceiling with the open spaces studded with stars. The furniture in the room once reserved for dining is a mixture of period Gothic, overdecorative gifts from admiring subjects, and cherry or maple Biedermeier pieces from the 19th century.

Probably the most authentically Gothic room is the Hall of Heroes. The paintings lining the walls depict the old German saga of Dietrich of Berne. On the long banquet table are centerpieces of hot-gilded bronze decorated with scenes from the Nibelungen saga.

From Ludwig's bedroom on the third floor the young king could keep an eye on his castle on the hillside above. As in other rooms, the ceiling of the bedroom was decorated with the typically Gothic stars—with one difference. Here they artificially lit up at night.

Nearby is the music room where Ludwig and Wagner spent long hours entertaining one another at the maple piano. The small chapel in the alcove off the music room was executed by Ludwig. The room also contains an exhibit of emotional letters sent by the king to Wagner, expressing his great admiration for him.

Hohenschwangau is open April to September 30, daily from 9am to 5:30pm; in winter, from 10am to 4pm. Admission is 7 DM ($4.15). Several parking lots nearby enable you to leave your car here while visiting both castles.

Where to Stay and Dine

Hotel Lisl und Jägerhaus, Neuschwansteinstrasse 1-3, D-8959 Hohenschwangau (tel. 08362/8-10-06), is a graciously styled villa with an annex across the street. It was seemingly made to order to provide views as well as comfort. Both houses sit in a narrow valley, surrounded by their own gardens. In the main house, two well-styled dining rooms serve good meals that average about 35 DM ($20.80). The restaurant features an international as well as local cuisine. If you're staying over, you'll find comfortably furnished and attractive bedrooms renting for widely varying prices. For a bathless single, the rate is 40 DM ($23.75) daily, rising to 100 DM ($59.40) for a room with bath. For a bathless double, the charge is 60 DM ($35.65), increasing to 240 DM ($142.50) for a room with complete bath. Forty-five rooms have baths, and another 11 are bathless.

Hotel Müller Hohenschwangau, Alpseestrasse 16, D-8959 Hohenschwangau (tel. 08362/8-10-56). The yellow walls, green shutters, and gabled alpine detailing of this hospitable inn are incentive enough for a stopover. However, its position near the foundation of Neuschwanstein Castle makes it even more alluring. An enlargement and an upgrading of the hotel in 1984 left its basic Bavarian lines intact, yet added extra modern conveniences. On the premises are a well-maintained restaurant lined with burnished pinewood; a more formal evening restaurant with views over a verdantly planted sun terrace; lots of rustic accessories; and 45 comfortable bedrooms, each with private bath, color TV or radio, and phone. Depending on the room assignment, singles cost 100 DM ($59.40) to 170 DM ($100.95) daily, and doubles go for 130 DM ($77.20) to 210 DM ($124.70), with breakfast included. Nature lovers usually enjoy the opportunity of hiking the short distance to nearby Hohenschwangau Castle as well.

THE BAVARIAN ALPS

If you walk into a rustic alpine inn along the German-Austrian frontier and ask the innkeeper if he's German, you'll most likely get the indignant response, "Of course not! I'm Bavarian." And he is undoubtedly right, because even though Bavaria is politically a part of Germany, many of its older folk can still remember the kingdom of Bavaria, which did not become part of the German Reich until 1918.

The huge province includes not only the Alps but Franconia, Lake Constance, and the capital city of Munich as well. However, we will take this opportunity to explore separately the mountains along the Austrian frontier, a world unto themselves. The hospitality of the people of this area is famous. The picture of the plump rosy-cheeked innkeeper with a constant smile on his face is no myth.

Many travelers think of the Alps as a winter vacationland, but you'll find that nearly all of the Bavarian resorts and villages boast year-round attractions.

1. Berchtesgaden

Ever since Ludwig I of Bavaria chose this resort as one of his favorite hideaways, the tourist business in Berchtesgaden has been booming. It is situated below the many summits of the Watzmann Mountain. According to legend, the peaks of the mountain were once a king and his family who were so evil that God punished them by turning them into rocks. The king has evidently not been completely silenced, however, because the Watzmann has been responsible for the deaths of several mountain climbers who have endeavored to scale the mile-high cliff on its eastern wall.

Many visitors who come here—or who don't—expect to see one of the favorite hangouts of Adolf Hitler, since the name of Berchtesgaden has been constantly linked with the Führer and the Nazi hierarchy. This is an erroneous impression.

Berchtesgaden is an old alpine village with ancient winding streets and a medieval marketplace and castle square. Hitler's playground in the Bavarian Alps was actually at Obersalzberg, on a wooded plateau about half a mile up the mountain from Berchtesgaden (see "Obersalzberg" below).

However, Hitler did spend some time in Berchtesgaden immediately following the defeat of his plot to seize power in the Munich "beerhall putsch" of 1923. After his jail term he was a guest of Dietrich Eckhart, founder of the Nazi party. The train runs to Berchtesgaden, still very much a quiet German town.

WHERE TO STAY

An Expensive Hotel

An ornate chalet inn on the upper fringes of Berchtesgaden, the **Geiger Hotel,** Berchtesgadenstrasse 111, D-8240 Berchtesgaden (tel. 08652/50-55), is a genuine antique. From its terraces (one with an open-air swimming pool), bedrooms, or breakfast rooms, one can enjoy fantastic views of the mountaintops. This remarkable retreat is owned by the Geiger family, who created the hotel more than a century ago.

Biedermeier enthusiasts will revel over the several sitting rooms completely furnished in that style. Any member of the Geiger family will give you the history of any of the furnishings, especially the painting in the paneled drawing room of *Silent Night* (it upset everyone by depicting Mary as awaiting the birth of Jesus on a Bavarian farm). Guests like to gather in the drawing room for after-dinner coffee and cognac in front of the fireplace. The Geiger's 49 comfortable bedrooms are also furnished with antiques, although the plumbing may strike you as having that same characteristic, too. Prices, including breakfast, are based on whatever bath facilities you request, plus your view—that is, if you have a balcony or not. Singles rent for 105 DM ($62.35) to 160 DM ($95) daily and doubles for 140 DM ($83.15) to 300 DM ($178.15). The hotel also has an indoor swimming pool. Dining is a true event here—be sure to try the alpine river trout. A la carte meals range from 45 DM ($26.70) to 72 DM ($42.75). And before you depart, have a drink of water from a fountain where Bach drank.

Moderately Priced Hotels

An old inn with modern extensions, the **Vier Jahreszeiten,** Maximilianstrasse 20, D-8240 Berchtesgaden (tel. 08652/50-26), has been in the hands of the Miller family since 1876. It's in the heart of the village and has a colorful and distinguished restaurant (see my dining recommendations). The inn has been remodeled and improved over the years and now brings a good level of comfort to its guests. Some of the newer units, furnished with many wooden pieces, resemble suites with their tiny sitting rooms and balconies. Depending on the plumbing, singles cost 78 DM ($46.30) to 120 DM ($71.25) daily, and doubles go for 130 DM ($77.20) to 200 DM ($118.75). In addition to the main dining room, there's a terrace for summer dining and viewing. The 65-room hotel has an indoor swimming pool, a sauna, and a solarium.

Wittelsbach, Maximilianstrasse 16, D-8240 Berchtesgaden (tel. 08652/50-61), has been stylishly modernized and now offers 29 well-furnished bedrooms in the heart of Berchtesgaden. It represents a combination of tradition and up-to-date comfort. The rooms and apartments are quiet and sunny, with showers or baths and toilets, minibars, and phones. Most have balconies with fine views of the mountains. Single rooms cost 60 DM ($35.65) to 90 DM ($53.45) daily, doubles from 150 DM ($89.05), triples from 160 DM ($95), and apartments for two persons from 300 DM ($178.15). The rates include a buffet breakfast, the only meal served. Closed mid-November to mid-December.

Demming, Sunklergässchen 2, D-8240 Berchtesgaden (tel. 08652/50-21), looks like a chalet, but on closer inspection the hotel is massive, with four floors of

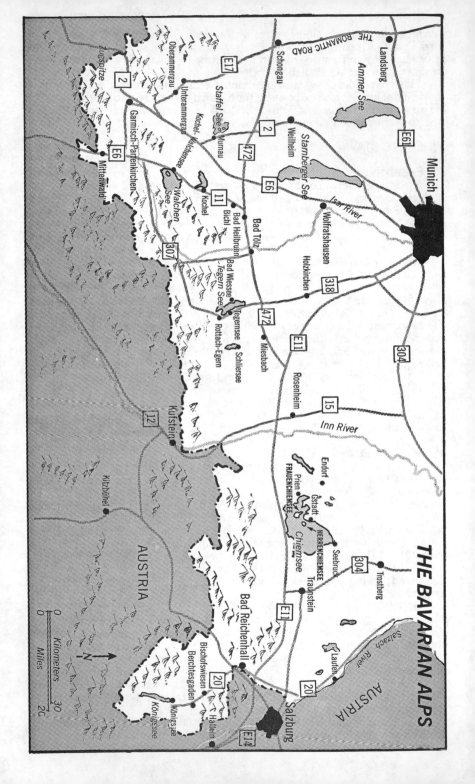

THE BAVARIAN ALPS

balconied rooms and an annex extending at right angles to the main building. The entire complex is nestled in a depression between two forested hills, which offer good views in both summer and winter. The 35 bedrooms are clean, comfortable, and furnished with reproduction alpine pieces. You may be interested in some of the artifacts in the reception area, among them two wine presses, their wooden screws somewhat weakened by time but still tinged with the color of the grape. All units have plumbing facilities, and a buffet breakfast is included in the tariffs, which are 80 DM ($47.50) to 95 DM ($56.40) daily for a single and 145 DM ($86.10) to 165 DM ($98) for a double. Guests have the use of an outdoor swimming pool. Closed November 20 through December.

Sporthotel Seimler, Maria am Berg 4, D-8240 Berchtesgaden (tel. 08652/ 60-50), lies about a mile outside of the center. You'll get the feeling of lots of light in this place, which is decorated in a traditional motif of paneling and beamed ceilings. Public rooms are spacious and airy. There's even a bowling alley if you're interested, along with a swimming pool; in the basement is a rustically decorated disco. The hotel is beautifully situated, with a view of the Alps from many of its 45 rooms, which rent for 104 DM ($61.75) to 125 DM ($74.25) daily for a double and 67 DM ($39.80) to 72 DM ($42.75) for a single, including breakfast. The Brandner family are your hosts. The hotel closes from mid-November to mid-December.

A Budget Hotel

On the square opposite the church, the **Watzmann,** Franziskanerplatz 2, D-8240 Berchtesgaden (tel. 08652/20-55), is a Bavarian country-town inn with 37 rooms. Everyone seems to stop by the wide front terrace day or night for a beer, coffee, or lunch. Inside, the Watzmann contains huge carved wooden pillars, oak ceilings, wrought-iron light fixtures, and a circular, antler-horn chandelier in the hunt dining room. Simply furnished bedrooms are kept immaculate; the beds are downy-soft. Bathless singles cost 40 DM ($23.75) daily, bathless doubles going for 73 DM ($43.35). With baths or showers and toilets, singles go for 65 DM ($38.60) and doubles for 118 DM ($70.05). The Piscantors do the innkeeping. The inn is closed from the first of November until just before Christmas.

WHERE TO DINE

In the Vier Jahreszeiten, recommended above, the **Hubertusstuben,** Maximilianstrasse 20 (tel. 08652/50-26), also directed by the Miller family, has one of the most elaborate menus in Berchtesgaden, and the wine list is also distinguished. Among the soups, a fresh fish soup is presented. Likely dishes are banana steak Bombay and deer steak with vegetables and homemade noodles (along with almond balls). For dessert, I'd suggest the apple fritters on walnut ice cream. Meals cost 25 DM ($14.85) to 58 DM ($34.45). The restaurant is open daily from 11:30am to 2pm and 5:30pm to 9:30pm.

Hotel Geiger, Berchtesgadenerstrasse 111 (tel. 08652/50-55), is a gabled, extravagantly ornate hotel that looks like what every tourist imagines a German hotel to be. It was previously recommended, but even if you don't stay there, you may want to visit for a meal. Its owner makes guests feel happy and well cared for in a cultivated atmosphere featuring good, hearty regional cookery along with international specialties, which range from 45 DM ($26.70) to 72 DM ($42.75) and are served daily from noon to 2pm and 6:30 to 9pm.

Demming-Restaurant Le Gourmet, Sunklergässchen 2 (tel. 08652/50-21), was previously recommended as a hotel, but it also houses one of the best restaurants in town. The copious proportions of what used to be a wealthy private house look out over a panoramic view of mountains and forests. Reservations are necessary for dining here, which many local residents regard as something of an event. Only fresh ingredients are used in the well-prepared dishes, including such hearty mountain fare as roast beef with chive sauce, plus an array of veal and fish dishes. À la carte meals cost 28 DM ($16.65) to 60 DM ($35.65). The restaurant is open daily from 6pm to midnight. Closed November 20 through December.

THE SIGHTS

Berchtesgaden grew up in the Middle Ages around the powerful Augustinian monastery, whose monks introduced the art of woodcarving for which the town is noted to this day. When the town became part of Bavaria in 1809, the abbey was secularized and eventually converted to a palace for the royal family of Wittelsbach. The **castle** has been turned into a museum, exhibiting the collections of furniture and art owned by the royal family. More interesting is the adjacent **Stiftskirche** (abbey church), from 1122. The church is mainly Romanesque, with Gothic additions. One of its ancient twin steeples was destroyed by lightning and rebuilt in 1866. The interior of the church contains many fine works of art, including the high altar with a painting by Zott dating from 1669. In the vestry is a small silver altar donated by Empress Maria Theresa of Austria.

Schlossplatz (Castle Square), partially enclosed by the castle and Stiftskirche, is the most attractive plaza in town. On the opposite side of the square from the church is a 16th-century arcade that leads to the **Marktplatz** with its typically alpine houses and a wooden fountain from 1677 (restored by Ludwig I in 1860). Some of the oldest inns and houses in Berchtesgaden line this square. Extending from the Marktplatz is the **Nonntal,** lined with more old houses, some of which have been built into the rocks of the Lockstein Mountain that towers above.

The **Salzbergwerk Berchtesgaden** (tel. 08652/60-02-0), at the eastern edge of town, are salt mines once owned by the Augustinian monastery. Operations began here in 1517. The mines contain two types of salt, one of which is suitable only for "salt licks" for cattle and other animals. The deposits are more than 990 feet thick and are still processed today from four galleries, or "hills." Visitors on guided tours enter the mine on a small wagonlike train after donning the protective costume of the miner. After nearly a half-mile ride, they leave the train and explore the rest of the mine on foot, sliding down a miner's slide, and enjoying a ride on the salt lake in a ferry. The highlight of the tour is the "chapel," a grotto containing unusually shaped salt formations illuminated to create an eerie effect. The best thing about the 1½-hour tour is that you can take it any time of the year, in any weather. From May 1 to October 15, hours are 8:30am to 5pm daily; off-season, Mon. to Sat. from 12:30 to 3:30pm The price of admission is 12.50 DM ($7.40) for adults and 6.50 DM ($3.85) for children.

THE ENVIRONS

Berchtesgaden is a center for excursions into the mountains and valleys that surround the town. Time may not permit you to take every excursion, but the two most popular sights make it well worth spending an extra night here.

Königssee

This "jewel in the necklace" of Berchtesgaden is one of the most scenic bodies of water in Europe. Its waters appear to be a dark green because of the steep mountains that jut upward from its shores. The northern edge of the lake borders enough low-lying land to contain a car park and a few charming inns and bathing facilities, but the rest of the lake is enclosed by mountains, making it impossible to walk along the shoreline. The only way to explore the waters, unless you're one of the mountain goats you may see on cliffs above, is by boat. **Electric motorboats**—no noisy gas-powered launches allowed—carry passengers on tours around the lake throughout the summer and occasionally even in winter. The favorite spot on the Königssee is the tiny peninsula on the western bank. It's the only flat area surrounding the lake, and was the site of a basilica as early as the 12th century. Today the Catholic **chapel of St. Bartholomew** is still used for services (except in winter). The clergy must arrive by boat since there is no other way to approach the peninsula. The adjacent buildings include a fisherman's house and a restaurant, where you can sample trout and salmon caught in the crisp, clean waters. At the southern end of the lake you come to the "Salet-Alm," where the tour boat makes a short stop near a thundering waterfall. If you follow the footpath up the hillside, you'll reach the summer pastures used by the cattle of Berchtesgaden Land.

Just over the hill is **Lake Obersee,** part of Königssee until an avalanche separated them eight centuries ago. If you prefer a shorter trip, you can take the boat as far as St. Bartholomew and back. To reach the lake from Berchtesgaden by car, follow the signs south from the town (only 3 miles). It's also a pleasant hour's walk, or a short ride by electric train or bus from the center of town.

For information about excursions, call 08652/40-27. An entire tour of Königssee requires about two hours. There are boats in summer every 15 minutes, so getting off one boat and climbing back aboard another is easy if you want to break up your tour. The important stops are at Salet and St. Bartholomew. A round-trip fare for a lake tour is 15 DM ($8.90) per person.

Obersalzberg

The drive from Berchtesgaden to Obersalzberg at 3,300 feet is along one of the most scenic routes in Bavaria. It was here that Hitler settled down in a rented cottage where he completed his book, *Mein Kampf.* After he came to power in 1933, he bought Haus Wachenfels and had it remodeled and turned into his Berghof, which became the center for holiday living for such Nazi bigwigs as Martin Bormann and Hermann Göring.

A major point of interest to visitors is the **Kehlstein,** or **"Eagle's Nest,"** which can be reached only by a thrilling bus ride up a 4½-mile-long mountain road, blasted out of solid rock and considered an outstanding feat of construction and engineering when it was begun in 1937, under the leadership of Bormann, who intended it as a 50th birthday gift for Hitler. The Eagle's Nest was not, as the name may suggest, a military installation. It was a site for relaxation, a tea house, and was not popular with Hitler, who reportedly visited it only two or three times. To reach the spot, you must enter a tunnel and take a 400-foot elevator ride through a shaft in the Kehlstein Mountain to its summit. The building, with solid granite walls and huge picture windows, houses a mountain restaurant. Called the Kehlsteinhaus, the restaurant is open from the end of May to the end of October (in good weather). Buses from the Hintereck parking lot in Obersalzberg run to the Eagle's Nest about every half hour. At the Eagle's Nest parking lot, you can purchase tickets for the elevator ride to enjoy the breathtaking view from the top, even if you don't patronize the restaurant. You can also explore the rooms of the original tea house, which include Eva Braun's living room.

Here you can observe the Obersalzberg area below, where Hitler's Berghof once stood, and nearby, the site of the house of Martin Bormann and the SS barracks. To the north you can see as far as Salzburg, Austria, and just below the mountain, to the west, Berchtesgaden, with its rivers dwindling off into threads in the distance.

For information about trips to Kehlstein call 08652/54-73. RVO buses (local buses based in Berchtesgaden) run from the Berchtesgaden Post Office to Obersalzberg-Hintereck, and from Hintereck special buses go to the Kehlstein car park. The return journey from Berchtesgaden to Obersalzberg costs 5.20 DM ($3.10). From Obersalzberg (Hintereck) to the Kehlstein car park is 14 DM ($8.30), and from the car park by elevator to Kehlsteinhaus (the summit) is 3 DM ($1.80). If you're hearty, you can also go from the car park on foot to Kehlsteinhaus in about half an hour. The Kehlstein line operates from mid-May to mid-October, during which there are full catering periods at Kehlsteinhaus. The Kehlstein road from Obersalzberg is closed to private vehicles.

Back at Obersalzberg, you can walk around the ruins of Hitler's famed Berghof. The Berghof was destroyed in 1952 by the Bavarian government authorities at the request of the U.S. Army. The only fully remaining structure from the Nazi compound is a guesthouse, which is behind the General Walker Hotel, used by U.S. troops stationed in the area. Wear good walking shoes and be prepared to run into some "Verboten!" signs.

The bunkers and air raid shelter were built by Hitler in 1943. The villas, pensions, and farms that had made this a favorite Bavarian holiday spot in pre-Hitler days were all confiscated to make way for the leaders of the Third Reich. Three thousand laborers completed the work in nine months, connecting all the major Nazi buildings of the Obersalzberg area to the underground rooms. Many readers have expressed their disappointment when reaching this site, apparently thinking they were going to be taken on a tour of Hitler's sumptuously decorated private apartments, which he shared with his mistress, Eva Braun. However, only a bunker is open for a visit, part of Hitler's air raid shelter system. The Americans didn't want a "monument" to Hitler—hence the destruction of the Berghof. Therefore go up the mountain for the magnificent view, not to see the faded retreat of the hierarchy of the Third Reich.

Obersalzberg is becoming an important health resort, with the ruins of Bormann's Gutshof being now the Skytop Lodge, a popular golfing center in summer and a ski site in winter.

WHERE TO STAY   In Obersalzberg, the **Hotel zum Türken,** D-8240 Berchtesgaden-Obersalzberg (tel. 08652/24-28), is legendary. It stands today in the alpine style, with terraces and views for everyone. On its facade is a large painted sign of "The Turk," and the foundation is stone, the windows framed in shutters. A large handmade sign is written across the hillside, with a rather ominous pronouncement, pointing the way to the "Bunker." The story goes that the original building here was erected by a veteran from the Turkish war. At the turn of the century it was acquired by Karl Schuster, who turned it into a well-known restaurant that drew many celebrities of the day, including Brahms and Crown Prince Wilhelm of Prussia. However, anti-Nazi remarks in the '30s led to trouble for Herr Schuster, who was arrested. In time, Bormann used the building as a Gestapo headquarters, a role that came to an end when Allied forces captured Obersalzberg. Air raids and looting in April of 1945 led to much destruction of the Türken. Many tourists erroneously think the Türken was Hitler's famed Berghof.

Herr Schuster's daughter, Therese Partner, was able to buy the ruin from the German government for a high price in 1949. She opened a café and then some bedrooms for overnight visitors. Today, 17 pleasantly furnished units are rented, costing 37 DM ($21.95) per person daily for a bathless room, 55 DM ($32.65) to 60 DM ($35.65) per person for a room with bath or shower and toilet. Breakfast is included in the tariffs. The Türken, now run by Frau Ingrid Scharfenberg, granddaughter of Karl Schuster, is closed on Tuesday.

---

2. Garmisch-Partenkirchen

The charm of the village that became Germany's top alpine resort is still there, even though Garmisch-Partenkirchen has grown into a big town. Even today you occasionally see country folk in their traditional costumes, and you may be held up in traffic while the cattle are led from their mountain grazing grounds down through the streets of town.

The symbol of the city's growth and modernity is the **Olympic Ice Stadium,** built for the Winter Olympics of 1936 and capable of holding nearly 12,000 people. On the slopes at the edge of town is the much larger **Ski Stadium,** with two ski jumps and a slalom course. In 1936 more than 100,000 people watched the events in this stadium. Today it is still an integral part of winter life in Garmisch: the World Cup Ski Jump is held here every year.

Garmisch-Partenkirchen is more a center for winter sports and for summer hiking and mountain climbing than for sightseeing. In addition, the town and its environs offer some of the most exciting views and colorful buildings in Bavaria. The pilgrimage chapel of **St. Anton,** on a pinewood path at the edge of Partenkirchen, is all pink and silver, inside and out. Its graceful lines are characteristic of the 18th century, when it was built. The adjoining monastery pays tribute to the local men who died in the two world wars. The strange memorial consists of a collection of hundreds of photographs of the local boys who never returned from the wars.

The Philosopher's Walk in the park surrounding the chapel is a delightful spot to wander, just to enjoy the views of the mountains around the low-lying town.

WHERE TO STAY

Expensive Hotels

The only deluxe hotel in the area, **Grand Hotel Sonnenbichl,** Burgstrasse 97, D-8100 Garmisch-Partenkirchen (tel. 08821/70-20), is on the hillside overlooking Garmisch-Partenkirchen, with views of the Wetterstein mountain range and the Zugspitze. The 90 rooms have all been renovated and offer all the modern amenities, including private baths, minibars, color TVs, videos, radio alarm clocks, and direct-dial phones. Doubles rent for 220 DM ($130.65) to 280 DM ($166.25) daily, and singles cost 135 DM ($80.15) to 200 DM ($118.75). The hotel boasts excellent food. You can have light, modern cuisine in the elegant gourmet restaurant, Blauer, or Bavarian specialties in the Zirbelstube. Afternoon coffee and fresh homemade cakes are served in the lobby or on the sunny terrace; cocktails are available in the Peacock Bar. A swimming pool, sauna, solarium, and fitness and massage rooms are here for the use of guests, and entertainment is offered on the premises.

Posthotel Partenkirchen, Ludwigstrasse 49, D-8100 Garmisch-Partenkirchen (tel. 08821/5-10-67), after many different stages in its development—it was once a posting inn—has emerged as one of the most prestigious hotels in town, especially when you consider the added asset of its unusually fine restaurant (refer to my dining suggestions). You feel apart from conventional hotel life here: it's old-world living, and the owners offer personalized service. The hotel's facade is studded with windowboxes of red geraniums, and around the front entrance are decorative murals and designs. Of the two dining rooms, the larger is known for its wooden beamed ceiling, wrought-iron chandeliers, and natural-wood chairs. Huge arches divide the room, making it more intimate. In the arched, rustic Weinlokal Barbarossa, there are nooks for quiet before- or after-dinner drinks. Musicians provide background music. The 61 U-shaped bedrooms are stylish, with antiques and hand-decorated or elaborately carved furnishings. Bedroom balconies are sun traps, overlooking a garden and parking for your car, and from them you'll have a view of the Alps. Singles with complete baths range in price from 95 DM ($56.40) to 185 DM ($109.85) daily, and doubles go for 165 DM ($98) to 235 DM ($139.55).

Alpina Hotel, Alpspitzstrasse 12, D-8100 Garmisch-Partenkirchen (tel. 08821/5-50-31), is a Bavarian hostelry where guests have all sorts of luxury facilities. It's a large chalet done in a tasteful manner. Only three minutes from the Hausberg ski lifts, it has its own covered swimming pool with a recreational terrace alongside, a garden with wide lawns and trees, and a large open patio with an open-air swimming pool and surrounding terrace for sunning. Its facade is graced with a wide overhanging roof and Tyrolean-style entranceway and windows. The open tavern dining room has two levels, and there is an extensive brick wine cellar, offering a wide and excellent choice. Each of the 35 bedrooms is personalized, with its own color scheme and restrained furnishings. Your room may have snow-white sofa, chairs, walls, lamps, and carpet, with original paintings as accents; or you may be assigned a room with sloped pine ceilings, a Spanish bedspread, and matching armchairs. Meals are served in the beamed, rustic dining room and on the sun terrace, both warmly accented. You pay 90 DM ($53.45) daily for a bathless single, 150 DM ($89.05) for a room with bath. Doubles cost 180 DM ($106.90) to 260 DM ($154.40).

Residence Hotel, Mittenwalder Strasse 2, D-8100 Garmisch-Partenkirchen (tel. 08821/75-61), a former Holiday Inn, offers 117 first-class bedrooms in a quiet park just 15 minutes from the railway station. The charge is 120 DM ($71.85) to 189 DM ($112.25) daily for a single, 150 DM ($89.05) to 243 DM ($144.30) for a double, with breakfast included. Children up to 16 stay free in their parents' rooms. The hotel has a swimming pool and all the accessories, such as a solarium and a sauna, as well as a tennis court. A good restaurant and an apéritif bar are on the premises.

Obermühle, Mühlstrasse 22, D-8100 Garmisch-Partenkirchen (tel. 08821/ 70-40). The Wolf family, the owners of this 93-room hotel, come from a 300-year-old line of hoteliers. Although their present building was constructed in 1969, they still maintain the traditional hospitality that has characterized their family for so long. Most of their rooms have balconies with views of the Alps. You'll also have access to the hotel's indoor pool, set below a wooden roof shaped like a modified Gothic arch (at least it's pointed). Nearby are miles of woodland trails crisscrossing through the nearby foothills. The garden and cozy Weinstube might be places you'll choose to wander through also. For singles, prices range from 110 DM ($65.30) to 195 DM ($115.80) daily, with doubles going for 200 DM ($118.75) to 300 DM ($178.15). Breakfast is included in the rates.

Reindl's Partenkircher Hof, Bahnhofstrasse 15, D-8100 Garmisch-Partenkirchen (tel. 08821/5-80-25), was opened in 1911, with guests from the aristocracy and the higher echelons of business patronizing it from the very first. A glittering array of celebrated people, ranging from the Rothschilds to American governors and senators (even General Haig and the German president), is included in the guestbook. Still maintaining the high levels of luxury and hospitality, the owners, Bruni and Karl Reindl, have kept this a special Bavarian retreat. There are annexes, the Wetterstein and the House Alspitz, both with balconies, and the main building has wraparound verandas, giving each room an unobstructed view of the mountains and the town. The 72 bedrooms have been redecorated and have private baths; many rooms have radios, color TVs, and safes. Rates vary according to the facilities and amenities. Singles cost 80 DM ($47.50) to 150 DM ($89.05) daily, and doubles go for 168 DM ($99.75) to 190 DM ($112.80). The place is also known for Reindl's much-honored restaurant, one of the best in Bavaria, recommended separately. The hotel's facilities include a covered swimming pool, sauna, sun room, and a beauty farm with a slimming gourmet menu. An open terrace for snacks, two attractive gardens, a large garage, and private parking are also provided.

Romantik-Hotel Clausing's Posthotel, Marienplatz 12, D-8100 Garmisch-Partenkirchen (tel. 08821/70-90), is all Bavarian, in a colorful way. In operation more than 350 years as a hotel, it offers village-center accommodations under delightful circumstances. Its elaborate pink facade is decorated with baroque statues, and a long awning shades sidewalk tables for refreshments and dining, from which you can look out across the central square. All the 31 bedrooms have baths or showers and toilets. Singles rent for 110 DM ($65.30) to 150 DM ($89.05) daily, doubles for 160 DM ($95) to 250 DM ($148.45).

Four eating places, each one open daily, are maintained by the hotel. From the roofed, glassed-in Boulevard-Terrasse, you can watch the world go by while you munch on homemade baked goods or order from the à la carte menu; open daily from 6:30am to 11pm, and piano music is played in the afternoon and evening. The elegance of Upper Bavaria surrounds you in the Klause and the Stüberl, open from 11:30am to 11pm, where you can order à la carte or else a special gourmet menu,

For typical Bavarian food, the Post-Hörndl and a beer garden are open from 11:30am to midnight, with live Bavarian entertainment in the evening.

Moderately Priced Hotels

Right in the hotel and shopping section, the **Garmischer Hof,** Bahnhofstrasse 52, D-8100 Garmisch-Partenkirchen (tel. 08821/5-10-91), couldn't be more dead center, but its encircling balconies and small rear garden where guests sunbathe give it a rural Bavarian character. The 43 bedrooms, all with baths or showers and toilets, are small but comfortable for sleeping. In high season, singles rent for 57 DM ($33.85) to 75 DM ($44.55) daily and doubles for 106 DM ($62.95) to 125 DM ($74.25). Prices include a buffet breakfast, the only meal served.

Vier Jahreszeiten Hotel, Bahnhofstrasse 23, D-8100 Garmisch-Partenkirchen (tel. 00821/5-80-84), is a 54-room hotel with a city touch, perfect for those who are not attracted to village quaintness. Actually, looking at its rather formal modern lounge and dining room, you would never think you were in the Garmisch area. There are numerous amenities: an elevator, balconies, phones, many private bathrooms with showers, and a cozy Bavarian beer cellar, the Bierstuben. Singles without baths are 55 DM ($32.65) daily; with baths, 85 DM ($50.45). Doubles without baths are 100 DM ($59.40); with private baths, 140 DM ($83.15). Off-season there is a 20% reduction (January 8 to 31, April 1 to May 30, and October 15 to December 15).

Boddenberg, Wildenauerstrasse 21, D-8100 Garmisch-Partenkirchen (tel. 08821/5-10-89), is a 24-room hotel run by the same family for 30 years. It can be recognized by its boxy shape, its balconies, and its location near the Olympic Ski Stadium ski jump. If you don't have a car, a bus caught at a nearby stop will take you quickly into town. The comfortable, sunny rooms, many of them with lots of wooden furniture and wood paneling, rent for 65 DM ($38.60) to 85 DM ($50.45) daily for a single and 120 DM ($71.25) to 170 DM ($100.95) for a double, all tariffs including a buffet breakfast. All units have showers or baths and toilets. Guests have unrestricted use of the heated open-air swimming pool. Closed mid-November to the end of December.

Wittelsbach, Von-Brug-Strasse 24, D-8100 Garmisch-Partenkirchen (tel. 08821/5-30-96). A rocky outcrop of the mountain chains Wetterstein and Zugspitze frames a visitor's view of the front of this fine hotel, with green-and-white verandas, and depending on the season, cascades of flowers or a covering of snow. The Obexer family manages this idyllic spot, maintaining the covered swimming pool in near-Olympic condition, overseeing the dining room's sumptuous buffets, and caring for the needs of clients who peacefully vow to return year after year. Doubles rent for 150 DM ($89.05) to 200 DM ($118.75) daily, depending on the season, while singles cost 105 DM ($62.35) to 170 DM ($100.95), breakfast included. The 60-room Wittelsbach closes from mid-October to mid-December.

Mercure-Königshof, St.-Martin-Strasse 4, D-8100 Garmisch-Partenkirchen (tel. 08821/72-70), is a holiday resort hotel with a lot of activity going on inside and out. The exterior is a massive rectangular solid broken by large windows and a triple-peaked roofline that evokes a chalet. The spectacular alpine backdrop helps with that impression, but so does the range of sports available. You'll find a sauna, a swimming pool, massage therapy, a collection of bars, boutiques, and nightclubs, plus a bowling alley and an underground garage for 50 cars. The dining room is large and sunny, with oversize windows and a view. The 82 bedrooms, spacious enough to feel comfortable in, cost 115 DM ($68.30) to 145 DM ($86.10) daily for a single and 130 DM ($77.20) to 235 DM ($139.55) for a double.

Budget Hotels and Guest Houses

The family-owned **Gasthof Fraundorfer,** Ludwigstrasse 34, D-8100 Garmisch-Partenkirchen (tel. 08821/21-76), is directly on the main street of the town, just a five-minute walk from the old church. Its original style has not been updated, and it retains the character of another day. Altogether there are three floors under a sloping roof, with a facade brightly decorated with windowboxes of red geraniums and decorative murals depicting a family feast. You'll be in the midst of village-center activities, near interesting shops and restaurants. The 33 bedrooms are pleasant, comfortable, and adequately furnished. Owners Josef and Bärbel Fraundorfer are proud of their country-style meals. In rooms with showers and toilets, rates range from 50 DM ($29.70) to 85 DM ($50.45) daily for a single and from 100 DM ($59.40) to 140 DM ($83.15) for a double, including a Continental breakfast. Except on Tues., when the inn is closed, there is an interesting Bavarian evening with yodeling and dancing. Dinner reservations are advisable. In addition, the owners also operate Gästehaus Barbara in back, with 20 more beds, the decor in a typical Bavarian style, including a *Himmelbett* ("heaven bed"). A double in their new house costs 120 DM ($71.25) a night.

Hotel Hilleprandt, Riffelstrasse 17, D-8100 Garmisch-Partenkirchen (tel. 08821/28-61). This cozy chalet is close to the Zugspitz rail station and the Olympic Ice Stadium. Its cutout wooden balconies, its attractive garden, and its backdrop of forest-covered mountains give the impression of an old-time alpine building. However, it was completely renovated in the 1970s into a streamlined format of modern comfort. Guests enjoy a fitness room, a sauna, a solarium, a pleasant breakfast room, and the personality of the accommodating owner, Klaus Hilleprandt. Each of the 17 comfortably furnished bedrooms contains a private balcony, private bath, phone, TV, and a collection of Bavarian folksy furniture. Singles rent for 68 DM ($40.40) to 90 DM ($53.45) daily, and doubles go for 100 DM ($59.40) to 130 DM ($77.20), including breakfast.

Zur Schönen Aussicht, Gsteigstrasse 36, D-8100 Garmisch-Partenkirchen (tel. 08821/24-74), is a beautiful, fairly new hotel above Garmisch-Partenkirchen, with a spectacular view of the mountains and the Olympic ski area from most bedrooms. Having a car would help, but the place can be reached by bus, plus a short walk from the bus line. Right across the road are the beginnings of several mountain paths. Prices are from 38 DM ($22.55) daily for a single, 68 DM ($40.40) for a double, and 88 DM ($52.25) for a double with bath and balcony. Breakfast is included in all the rates. Herr and Frau Maurer provide good food in their terrace restaurant.

Haus Lilly, Zugspitzstrasse 20a, D-8100 Garmisch-Partenkirchen (tel. 08821/5-26-00). Many visitors appreciate this spotlessly clean guesthouse lying near the rail station. It wins prizes for its copious breakfasts and the personality of its smiling owner, Maria Lechner, whose English is limited but whose hospitality is universal. Each of her clean and cozy bedrooms includes free access to a kitchen, so that in-house preparation of meals is an option for guests wanting to save money. Accommodations rent for 40 DM ($23.75) daily for singles, 75 DM ($44.55) for doubles, and 95 DM ($56.40) to 105 DM ($62.35) for three or four persons. Breakfast is included, offering a combination of cold cuts, rolls, cheese, eggs, pastries, and coffee, tea, or chocolate.

Gästehaus Trenkler, Kreuzstrasse 20, D-8100 Garmisch-Partenkirchen (tel. 08821/34-39), is in a central and quiet location. Frau Trenkler has made travelers feel comfortable and well cared for in her guesthouse for a number of years. She rents five double rooms with showers and toilets, and all others have hot and cold water. The price for a double is 60 DM ($35.65) to 75 DM ($44.55) daily, with breakfast included. Frau Trenkler gives guests a warm welcome.

Haus Erika, Wettersteinstrasse 45, D-8100 Garmisch-Partenkirchen (tel. 08821/48-09), a five-minute walk from the railway station, offers low-cost apartments with kitchens and showers, plus balconies opening onto beautiful mountain views. However, you must book for at least one week in peak season, two weeks off-season. Tariffs are 75 DM ($44.55) to 85 DM ($50.45) daily for an apartment for two persons, depending on the season. Apartments for four or five persons cost 130

DM ($77.20) to 140 DM ($83.15). The personable owner, Henriette Teufl, speaks English fluently.

WHERE TO DINE

One of the best places to eat in Partenkirchen is the **Reindl-Grill,** in the Partenkirchner Hof, Bahnhofstrasse 15 (tel. 08821/5-80-25). Many vacationing diners have memories of after dinner on its terrace in the warmth of a summer evening. Reindl's is a first-class restaurant in every sense of the word. The menu is composed according to the season, cooked as cuisine moderne as well as regional Bavarian dishes. The cuisine of France and a lot of the most famous French wines and champagnes, such as Romanée Conti, Château Lafitte Rothschild, and Château Petrus, are also represented. Karl Reindl apprenticed at the famous Walterspiel of Munich's Vier Jahreszeiten; he also worked in the kitchens of such places as Claridge's in London, Horcher's Madrid, Maxim's in Paris, Brenner's Spa in Baden-Baden, and Suvretta House in St. Moritz. The restaurant is known for honoring each "food season" in Europe. For example, if you are here in asparagus season in the spring, a special menu will be offered for your choice in sampling the dish in all the best-known varieties.

As a good opening to a fine repast, I suggest the scampi salad Walterspiel with fresh peaches, lemon, and tarragon or the homemade goose liver pâté with Riesling jelly. Or perhaps you'd prefer the lobster bisque with cognac. Among main dishes, I recommend coq au Riesling with noodles or veal roasted with Steinpilzen, a special mushroom from the Bavarian mountains. Among the fish dishes, try wild salmon with white and red wine and butter sauce or filets of sole Colbert with mushrooms and green pepper. For dessert, you can select a Grand Marnier sabayon with strawberry and vanilla ice cream or something more spectacular—a Salzburger Nockerl for two. Meals cost 35 DM ($20.80) to 70 DM ($47.55), with gourmet feasts (perhaps a lobster dinner) going higher, of course. Windows allow you to dine without street noises but with a view of the mountains. The restaurant is open daily from 11:30am to 2:30pm and 6pm to midnight. It's closed from mid-November to mid-December.

Posthotel Partenkirchen, Ludwigstrasse 49, Partenkirchen (tel. 08821/5-10-67), is renowned for its distinguished cuisine—in fact, its reputation is known throughout Bavaria. The interior dining rooms are rustic, with lots of mellow, old-fashioned atmosphere. You could imagine meeting Dürer here. Everything seems comfortably subdued, including the guests. Perhaps the best way to dine here is to order one of the set menus, costing 30 DM ($17.80) to 80 DM ($47.50). These table d'hôte selections change daily, depending on the availability of seasonal produce. The à la carte menu is long and extensive, featuring such products of the season as game in the autumn. Among the selections, ranging in price from 25 DM ($14.85) to 65 DM ($38.60), you can order soups such as fresh cauliflower, followed by such main dishes as Schnitzel Cordon Bleu or a mixed grill St. James. The Wiener Schnitzel served here with a large salad is the best I've had in the resort. Or you may prefer the entrecôte Café de Paris, another fine dish. Hours are daily from noon to 2pm and 6 to 9pm.

Obermühle, Mühlstrasse 22 (tel. 08821/70-40). The decor is not noteworthy, but there is an ambience radiating from the golden light of the hanging lamps. Part of a previously recommended hotel, the restaurant offers one of the finest 30-DM ($17.80) lunches at the resort, and you may want to stick to it since it's so good. The menu includes some delectable "fruits of the sea." If you're in the mood, you can request a special gourmet menu of seasonal specialties, which will cost a great deal more, perhaps 75 DM ($44.55). It will expand your culinary consciousness—and probably your waistline too. The restaurant serves daily from noon to 2pm and 6 to 10pm.

Alpenhof, Bahnhofstrasse 74, In der Spielbank (tel. 08821/5-90-55), is widely regarded as the finest restaurant in Garmisch outside the hotel dining rooms. In summer, try for an outside table. In winter, retreat to the cozy interior, which is flooded with sunlight from a greenhouse extension. Renate and Josef Huber offer a variety of Bavarian specialties, as well as trout "any way you want," salmon grilled with a mousseline sauce, and a ragoût of venison. An exceptional meal for 30 DM ($17.80)—perhaps the best for value at the resort—is presented daily. Some à la carte orders can climb as high as 65 DM ($38.60) or beyond. Hours are 11:30am to 2:30pm and 5:30 to 10pm daily.

Flösserstuben, Schmiedstrasse 2 (tel. 08821/28-88). Regardless of the season, a bit of the Bavarian Alps always seems to flower amid the wood-trimmed nostalgia of this intimate restaurant. It stands around the corner from the Goldener Engel Hotel, near the center of town. In the evening the weathered beams above the dining tables are likely to reverberate from the "evergreen" (folk) music a band is likely to be playing. You can select a seat at one of the colorful wooden tables or perhaps on one of the ox-yoke–inspired stools in front of the spliced saplings decorating the bar. A loyal crowd of local residents is attracted to the cuisine, which is not only German but Greek and international. Full meals cost 15 DM ($8.90) to 34 DM ($20.20). Hours are 11am to 2:30pm and 5 to 12:30pm daily.

Restaurant-Café Föhrenhof, Frickenstrasse 2 (tel. 08821/66-40) at Farchant. You'll find at the end of the 3-mile drive north from Garmisch to Farchant the best food in the area. It's presented in copious portions in an appetizing array of homemade specialties: Kellermeister toast, for example, is a juicy portion of rumpsteak along with bacon, mushrooms, hollandaise sauce, and salad. If you're in the mood for game (and it's in season), you might enjoy a filet of venison Hubertus with homemade Spätzle, cranberries, and salad. The restaurant thoughtfully provides a trio of children's specialties. Cheese might follow your main course, then a cream- or chocolate-covered portion of homemade ice cream. You might order a cup of Irish coffee. Full meals, costing around 40 DM ($23.75), are served daily from 11am to 3pm and 5:30 to 9pm.

SIGHTS AND EXCURSIONS

From Garmisch-Partenkirchen, you can see the tallest peak of them all, the **Zugspitze,** at the frontier of Austria and Germany, the highest mountain in Germany, its summit towering more than 9,700 feet above sea level. Its slopes for skiers begin at the **Hotel Schneefernerhaus** at a height of 8,700 feet. For a spectacular view of both the Bavarian and Tyrolean (Austrian) Alps, go all the way to the peak. To get to the Zugspitze summit, you have a variety of transportation choices. I will concentrate only on those from the German side, but there are also means of access from the Austrian side.

From Garmisch, drive to Eibsee, a small lake at the foot of the mountain, and then take the underground railway leading up to the hotel. From the hotel you board the short cable-car lift to the peak. Or you may take the one-hour train ride from Garmisch, which merges with the underground railway. An alternative route is the funicular from Eibsee directly to the summit.

The cogwheel train to the Schneefernerhaus Hotel at the Zugspitzplatt leaves Garmish every hour between 7:35am and 3:35pm. The travel time from Garmisch is 75 minutes. The Eibsee cable car (Eibsee-Seilbahn) leaves from Eibsee directly, going to the Zugspitze summit at nearly 10,000 feet. It runs at least every half hour from 8:15am to 5:45pm (in July and August till 6:15pm), a 10-minute ride.

The cable car to the Zugspitze summit (Gipfelseilbahn) departs from Schneefernerhaus to the Zugspitze summit at least every half hour during the operating hours of the cogwheel train and the Eibsee cable car, the latter a four-minute ride.

The Zugspitze summit and return or the Zugspitze round trip is 43 DM ($25.55) in winter, 50 DM ($29.70) in summer.

The **Alpspitz** region can also be explored. It's a paradise for hikers and nature lovers in general. From early spring until late fall its meadows and flowers are a delight, and its rocks evoke a prehistoric world. At altitudes of 4,600 to 6,300 feet, the

Alps present themselves in a storybook fantasy. Those who want to explore the northern foot of the Alpspitz can take the Alpspitz round trip by going up with the Osterfelder cable car, over the Hochalm, and back down with the Kreuzeck or Hausberg cable car, allowing time in between for hikes lasting from half an hour to an hour and a half. Snacks are served at the top station of the Osterfelder cable car or at the more rustic Hochalm Chalet.

The Osterfelder cable car to Osterfelderkopf, at a height of 6,300 feet, runs at least every hour from 8am to 5pm, a nine-minute ride. The round-trip cost is 26 DM ($15.45) for adults, 17 DM ($10.10) for children 4 to 14.

The Hochalm cable car from the Hochalm to Osterfelderkopf runs at least every hour during the operating hours of the Osterfelder cable car, a four-minute ride. A single ride costs adults 6 DM ($3.55); children, 4 DM ($2.40).

The Alpspitz round trip with the Osterfelder cable car, the Hochalm cable car, and the Kruezcek or Kreuzwankl/Hausberg cable car is 36 DM ($21.40) for adults and 24 DM ($14.25) for children.

These fares and times of departure can fluctuate from season to season. Therefore, for the latest details, check with the tourist office, **Kurverwaltung,** Bahnhofstrasse 34 (tel. 08821/25-70), open Monday to Saturday from 8am to 6pm and on Sunday from 10am to noon only.

From Garmisch-Partenkirchen, many other peaks of the Witterstein range are accessible as well, via the 10 funiculars ascending from the borders of the town. From the top of the **Wank** (5,850 feet) to the east, you get the best view of the plateau on which the twin villages of Garmisch and Partenkirchen have grown up. This summit is also a favorite with the patrons of Garmisch's spa facilities, because the plentiful sunshine makes it ideal for the *Liegekur* (deck-chair cure).

Another excursion from the town is a hike through the **Partnachklamm Gorge,** lying between the Graseck and Hausberg peaks. After taking the cable car to the first station on the Graseck route, follow the paths along the sides of the slope to the right and trail the river as it cascades over the rocks. The path circles around by crossing the gorge, and returns you to the point where you entered. Many readers have found this one of their most memorable sightseeing adventures in Bavaria. The experience of walking along a rocky ledge just above the rushing river and often behind small waterfalls, while looking up at 1,200 feet of rocky cliffs, always fills me with awe.

THE CASINO
You can play roulette, baccarat, or blackjack, or have fun with 70 slot machines and automatic roulette machines, at the **Spielbank Garmisch-Partenkirchen,** Bahnhofstrasse 74 (tel. 08821/5-30-99), open daily from 3pm to 2am.

ON THE OUTSKIRTS OF MURNAU
A deluxe hotel and restaurant, the **Alpenhof Murnau,** Ramsachstrasse 8, D-8110 Murnau am Staffelsee (tel. 08841/10-45), lies halfway between Munich and Innsbruck, off the Autobahn Garmisch to Murnau, some 9 miles north of the Autobahn's end. Set in hilly terrain, the hotel lies in a large, pasturelike park. It's built in a chalet style with a widely spread, overhanging roof. Bowers of red geraniums are placed at the windows in summer. Its bedrooms are built like a motel-style Spanish hacienda, forming a courtyard. Each unit has a generous covered balcony, and the view from every room is beautiful and restful. The Alpenhof is a member of *Relais & Châteaux,* which means that it pampers its guests. The 48 rooms are individualized, some with modern canopy beds, Oriental rugs, and spacious bedroom–sitting room combination areas. Singles range from 130 DM ($77.20) to 245 DM ($145.50) daily, doubles from 175 DM ($103.90) to 420 DM ($249.40).

The restaurant is the best in the area. The cuisine is inspired, and the service is attentive, informal yet courteous. The dining room, in a stylized chalet decor, has white plaster walls, a decorative wood-beamed ceiling, and highback Windsor chairs. Adjoining is a Weinstube created in an idealized tavern style, reminiscent of Spanish paradors. You can order a gourmet menu at 125 DM ($74.25) or make selections from the à la carte menu, where meals cost 52 DM ($30.90) and up. I'd recommend the chef's specialty, a soup of mussels. For a main course, I'd suggest the veal fricassée or the *Lammsattel fines herbes* with gratin dauphinoise. For dessert, the specialty is soufflé glacé Grand Marnier. The dining room is open daily from noon to 2pm and 6:30 to 10:30pm.

The Alpenhof Murnau can be used as a break on the trip from Munich to Austria. In fact, it's possible to check in after a transatlantic flight from North America. Just pick up a rental car at the airport, get on the Autobahn, and before you know it you're enveloped in peace and beauty. Have a swim in the garden pool, an exquisite lunch, and a nap on your balcony with its view of the Alps.

3. Chiemsee

Known as the "Bavarian Sea," Chiemsee is one of the most beautiful lakes in the Bavarian Alps, in a serene landscape. In the south, the mountains reach almost to the water. Many resorts line the shores of the large lake, but the main attractions of Chiemsee are on its two islands, Herrenchiemsee and Frauenchiemsee.

From the liveliest resort, **Prien,** on the west shore, you can reach either or both of the islands via the lake steamers that make regular trips throughout the spring and summer. The round-trip fare is 13 DM ($7.70) for 2½ hours. The steamers, operated by **Chiemsee-Schiffahrt Ludwig Fessler,** D-8210 Prien am Chiemsee, Postfach 1162 (tel. 08051/60-90), make round trips covering the entire lake. Connections are made from Gstadt, Seebruck, Chieming, Übersee/Feldwies, and Bernau/Felden. Large parking areas are found in Prien/Stock (harbor) and in all the villages around the lake. Boats leave Prien/Stock about every 20 minutes for Herrenchiemsee (castle of Ludwig II) at the island of Herreninsel from June to September 23 between 9am and 4:30pm. The last return is at 7:25pm.

There is also bus service from the harbor to the DB-station in Prien (Chiemsee-Schiffahrt) and around the lake by RVO. In summer (May to September), guests can enjoy the famous "Chiemseebahn," the last steam-tramway in the world, operating since 1887

WHERE TO STAY

The best place to stay on the lake is **Yachthotel Chiemsee,** Harrasser Strasse 49, D-8210 Prien am Chiemsee (tel. 08051/69-60), on the western shore of the "Bavarian Sea." Launched in 1989, the hotel offers 97 attractively furnished bedrooms, all with private bath or showers, king-size beds, radios, color TVs, direct-dial phones, minibars, and balconies or terraces opening onto the water. Singles cost 145 DM ($86.10) to 195 DM ($115.80) daily, and doubles go for 185 DM ($109.85) to 235 DM ($139.55). The hotel has such facilities as a sauna, a solarium, a health and fitness center, an outdoor whirlpool, and an indoor swimming pool. In addition, it offers four restaurants that provide the best views along the lake; the main restaurant extends over a lakeside terrace and the marina. Meals range in price from 45 DM ($26.70) to 82 DM ($48.70). The hotel also offers a full array of sporting activities, including sailing, rowing, tennis, riding, and golf (nearby), as well as horse-drawn carriage trips. In winter, the hotel's bus service brings you to the slopes in 10 minutes. There's even a spa department, plus a beauty care center.

The Estermann family will welcome you to the **Bayerischer Hof,** Bernauerstrasse 3, D-8210 Prien am Chiemsee (tel. 08051/10-95). The decorator must have applied extraordinary care to produce rustic touches that at times create the illusion that this relatively severe modern hotel is indeed older and more mellow than it is. Of particular note is the painted ceiling in the dining room. The rest of the

48-room hotel is more streamlined—modern, efficient, and quite appealing. The charges are 65 DM ($38.60) daily for a single, 120 DM ($73.05) for a double. Closed mid-November to early December.

Reinhart, Seestrasse 117, D-8210 Prien am Chiemsee (tel. 08051/10-45). This 24-room hotel and restaurant borders on the lake, offering three well-appointed floors. You'll find a heated indoor swimming pool, a family-run sauna, and a series of public rooms beautifully decorated with Oriental rugs, warm colors, and chalet chairs. Double rooms with baths or showers cost 130 DM ($77.20) to 180 DM ($106.90) daily, while singles with the same appointments rent for 65 DM ($38.60) to 80 DM ($47.50). A breakfast buffet comes with a generous portion of yogurt, cheese, and cold cuts. There is access to a nearby golf course. The hotel is closed in November and from January 8 to mid-April.

FRAUENCHIEMSEE

Frauenchiemsee, also called Fraueninsel, is the smaller of the two islands. Along its sandy shore stands a fishing village whose 60 boats drag the lake for its pike and salmon. At the festival of Corpus Christi these boats are covered with flowers and streamers, the fishermen are outfitted in Bavarian garb, the young women of the village are dressed as brides as the boats circle the island, stopping at each corner to sing the Gospels. The island is also the home of a Benedictine nunnery, founded in 782. The convent is known for a product called Kloster Likör—literally translated, that's "cloister liqueur." Sold by nuns in black cowls with white-winged headgarb, it's supposed to be an "agreeable stomach elixir."

HERRENCHIEMSEE

Herrenchiemsee, also called Herreninsel, is the most popular tourist attraction on the lake because of the fantastic castle, **Neues Schloss,** begun by Ludwig II in 1878. Although never completed because of the king's death in 1886, the castle was to have been a replica of the grand palace of Versailles, which Ludwig so greatly admired. A German journalist once wrote: "The Palace, a monument to uncreative megalomania and as superfluous as the artificial castle ruins of the 19th century, is an imposing postlude of feudal architectural grandeur nonetheless." One of the architects of Herrenchiemsee was Julius Hofmann, whom the king had also employed for the construction of his fantastic alpine castle, Neuschwanstein. When the work was halted in 1886, only the center of the enormous palace had been completed. Surrounded by woodlands of beech and fir, the palace and its formal gardens remain one of the most fascinating of Ludwig's adventures, in spite of their unfinished state.

The entrance to the palace is lit by a huge skylight over the sumptuously decorated state staircase. Frescoes depicting the four states of man's existence are alternated with Greek and Roman statues set in niches on the staircase and in the gallery above. The vestibule is adorned with a pair of enameled peacocks, the favorite bird of Louis XIV.

The **State Bedroom** is brilliant to the point of gaudiness, as practically every inch of the room is gilt. On the dais, instead of a throne, stands the richly decorated state bed, its purple velvet draperies weighing more than 300 pounds. Separating the dais from the rest of the room is a carved wooden balustrade covered with gold leaf. On the ceiling is a huge fresco depicting the descent of Apollo, surrounded by the other gods of Olympus. The sun god's features bear a strong resemblance to those of Louis XIV.

The **Great Hall of Mirrors** is unquestionably the most splendid hall in the palace, and probably the most authentic replica of Versailles. The 17 door panels contain enormous mirrors reflecting the 33 crystal chandeliers and the 44 gilded candelabra. The vaulted ceiling is covered with 25 paintings depicting the life of Louis XIV. At the entrance to what would have been the private apartments of the king (Ludwig spent less than three weeks in the palace) is a smaller hall of mirrors, with mirrored panels set into the marble walls.

The **Dining Room** is a popular attraction for visitors because of the table nick-named "the little table that lays itself." A mechanism in the floor permitted the table to go down to the room below to be cleaned and relaid between each course. Over the table hangs the largest porcelain chandelier in the world, produced by Meissen, the most valuable single item in the whole palace.

The **Royal Bedroom** is the only room in the palace to make use of rich solid colors on the walls. Set in gilded panels, royal-blue silk—which matches the fabric of the draperies and canopy over the bed—offsets the gilded ceiling and furnishings of the room. Separating the bed from the rest of the room is a gilded balustrade like that in the throne room.

You can visit Herrenchiemsee at any time of the year. In summer, April to September 30, tour hours are daily from 9am to 5pm; in winter, from 10am to 4pm. Admission (in addition to the round-trip boat fare) is 5 DM ($2.95) for adults. Students and children pay 2.50 DM ($1.50).

---

4. Oberammergau

If you were an actor in this alpine village, you'd be wise to find another trade to occupy you since the only theatrical production presented here is the world-famous Passion Play, with performances generally 10 years apart. Surely the world's longest running show (in more ways than one), it began in 1634 as the result of a vow taken by the town's citizens after they were spared from the devastating plague of 1633. Lasting about eight hours, the play is divided into episodes, each of which is introduced by an Old Testament tableau connecting the incidents of Christ's suffering to the predictions of the great Prophets.

A visit to Oberammergau is ideal in summer or winter. It stands in a wide valley surrounded by forests and mountains, as well as sunny slopes and green meadows. It has long been known for the skill of its woodcarvers. Here in this village right under the Kofel are farms still intact, as well as first-class hotels, cozy inns, and family boarding houses.

A wide variety of sports activities is offered. Numerous hiking trails lead through the mountains around Oberammergau to hikers' inns such as the Kolbenalm or the Romanshöhe. You can, however, simply go up to the mountain tops on the Laber cable railway or the Kolben chairlift. Not only hikers have a good time in Oberammergau, but also tennis buffs, minigolf players, cyclists, swimmers, hang-gliding enthusiasts, and canoeists. A visit to the recreation center, Wellenberg, is always a special experience. This large alpine swimming complex with its open-air pools, hot water and fountains, sauna, solarium, and restaurant is said to be one of the most beautiful recreation centers in the Alps.

In Oberammergau, it is worth seeing the Passion Play Theater, the local museum, and Pilate House, where you can watch local artists at work, including woodcarvers, sculptors, painters, and potters. The Ammer Valley, of which Oberammergau lies in the center, is a treasure trove for explorers, who use it as a base for visiting such attractions as Linderhof Castle, the Benedictine monastery at Ettal, or Neuschwanstein Castle or Hohenschwangau.

WHERE TO STAY

A Deluxe Inn

Seasoned travelers who have made pilgrimages to the Passion Play in Oberammergau will recognize the name of the **Alois Lang,** St.-Lukas-Strasse 15, D-8103

Oberammergau (tel. 08822/10-01). It was in 1929 that handsome, long-haired Alois Lang was elected by the village to play the role of Christ in the pageant. Long ago the custom originated of the players having as paying guests in their homes visitors who came to see the now-famous production. Within walking distance of the village center, this inn on the site of Alois's rustic home, run by the Lang family, was built chalet style, with long bedroom extensions. The accommodations are modern Bavarian, the beds are soft, and all is kept immaculate. Meals are elaborate, including sophisticated international specialties in addition to local dishes. You may want to dine in the inner tavern, or on the open sun terrace, where you can enjoy a view of the mountains. All 43 rooms have private baths. For a single, the rate ranges from 90 DM ($53.45) to 120 DM ($71.25) daily; for a twin-bedded room, from 160 DM ($95) to 200 DM ($118.75). The inn has a sauna, a fitness center, and the biggest private-hotel park in the whole area.

Moderately Priced Hotels

An overgrown Bavarian chalet, the **Wolf Restaurant-Hotel,** Dorfstrasse 1, D-8103 Oberammergau (tel. 08822/30-71), is right in the heart of village life. Its facade is consistent with others in the area: an encircling balcony, heavy timbering, and windowboxes spilling cascades of red and pink geraniums. Inside it has some of the local flavor, although certain concessions have been made: an elevator, conservative bedroom furnishings, a dining hall with zigzag paneled ceiling, and spoke chairs. The Keller is a regional rustic place for beer drinking as well as light meals. Only five singles are available, renting for 65 DM ($38.60) to 80 DM ($47.50) daily. Doubles cost 100 DM ($59.40) to 160 DM ($95). All 32 accommodations contain private baths or showers. Dining here can be both economical and gracious, with menus ranging from 25 DM ($14.85) to 50 DM ($29.70). There's always a freshly made soup of the day, followed by a main course such as Wiener Schnitzel or roast pork with dumplings and cabbage. The helpings are generous.

Alte Post, Dorfstrasse 19, D-8103 Oberammergau (tel. 08822/10-91), is a provincial inn right in the heart of the village, with lots of Bavarian character. Built in chalet style—wide, overhanging roof, green shuttered windows painted with decorative trim, a large carved crucifix on the facade, and tables set on a sidewalk under a long awning—it's the social hub of the village. The interior has storybook charm, with a ceiling-high green ceramic stove, alpine chairs, and shelves of pewter plates. The 32 rustic bedrooms have wood-beamed ceilings, wide beds with giant posts, and (from most rooms) views. Bathless singles rent for 45 DM ($26.70) daily, singles with bath costing 80 DM ($47.50). Doubles go for 90 DM ($53.45) without bath, for 110 DM ($65.30) with baths. Breakfast is included. The main dining room is equally rustic, with a collection of hunting memorabilia, and there is an intimate drinking bar. The restaurant provides excellent dishes. On the à la carte menu, meals average 22 DM ($13.05) to 40 DM ($23.75). Closed mid-October to Christmas.

Hotel Schilcherhof, Bahnhofstrasse 17, D-8103 Oberammergau (tel. 08822/47-40), is an enlarged chalet with surrounding gardens and a modern wing that provides excellent rooms. There's even a small group of apartments. In summer, the terrace overflows with festive living and lots of beer. Five minutes away lies the Passion Theater; also nearby is the Ammer River, which flows through the village. In the high season it's not easy to get a room here unless you make reservations well in advance. Singles cost 48 DM ($28.50) to 68 DM ($40.40) daily, and doubles go for 80 DM ($47.50) to 100 DM ($59.40). Tariffs include breakfast. Although the house is built in the old style, with wooden front balconies and tiers of flowerboxes, it has a fresh, new look to it. The 26-room hotel is closed from November 20 to Christmas.

Parkhotel Sonnenhof, König-Ludwig-Strasse 12, D-8103 Oberammergau (tel. 08822/107-11), is surrounded by conifers bigger than the hotel itself. The

four-story chalet with weathered balconies offers 66 comfortable, attractively furnished rooms with up-to-date baths. Singles cost 95 DM ($56.40) to 130 DM
($77.80) daily, with doubles renting for 140 DM ($83.15) to 200 DM ($118.75).
You can enjoy your meal in a paneled dining room with decorative stucco arches.

Hotel Restaurant Böld, König-Ludwig-Strasse 10, D-8103 Oberammergau
(tel. 08822/302-11). Only a stone's throw from the river, this well-designed 58-
room chalet hotel offers comfortable public rooms in its central core and well-
furnished bedrooms in its contemporary annex. The prices are 93 DM ($55.20) to
119 DM ($70.65) daily for singles, 148 DM ($87.90) to 168 DM ($99.75) for dou-
bles. The Böld could serve as an attractive base for either your summer or your
winter sports program, which might include skiing, minigolf, tennis, or just a peaceful walk in the country. A sauna is offered for guests' relaxation, as are a fitness room
and whirlpool. The restaurant features an international and a regional cuisine. In the
cellar bar you'll find a peaceful atmosphere, plus well-prepared cocktails and attentive service. Raimund Hans and his family are the hosts.

Turmwirt, Ettalerstrasse 2, D-8103 Oberammergau (tel. 08822/30-91), is a
cozy 22-room hotel in the Bavarian style, many of its rooms containing private balconies opening onto views of the mountains. A lodging house stood on this spot in
1742, and the present building was constructed in 1889. It has received many altera-
tions and renovations over the past few decades. It's an intricately painted, green-
shuttered country house, with hints of baroque embellishments on the doors and
window frames. The homey interior is well maintained, with chintz-covered armchairs, wooden banquettes, Oriental rugs, beamed ceilings, and handcrafted
cubbyholes with tables and chairs. Including a buffet breakfast, doubles with private
baths rent for 110 DM ($65.30) to 150 DM ($89.05) daily, while singles go for 75
DM ($44.55) to 95 DM ($56.40). Rooms contain color TVs. The owners are three
generations of the Glas family. The center of town is an invigorating five-minute
walk from the hotel.

Friedenshöhe, König-Ludwig-Strasse 31, D-8103 Oberammergau (tel.
08822/5-98), is set in an alpine meadow with huge conifers towering over parts of
it. From the compact core, which at one time might have been a private home, there
sprawl two modern wings decorated in rural Gemütlichkeit. You'll find villagers taking morning coffee on the terrace. The owners see that everyone gets attentive
service. Singles rent for 50 DM ($29.70) to 95 DM ($56.40) daily, while doubles
cost 98 DM ($58.20) to 150 DM ($89.05), depending on the season. All 11 units
have balconies, phones, toilets, and baths or showers. Breakfast is included in the
prices. The hotel is closed from late October to December 20.

Wittelsbach, Dorfstrasse 21, D-8103 Oberammergau (tel. 08822/10-11).
Elisabeth and Julius Streibl own this place, which sprawls over a village street corner.
It has light-brown shutters, a red roof with ice catchers on the edges, prominent gables, and yards of balconies with flowers virtually spilling over the edges. The
Streibls offer 48 bedrooms that are clean, sunny, and cozy. All are recently renovated
and contain private baths or showers and toilets. Singles rent for 65 DM ($38.60) to
75 DM ($44.55) daily, and doubles cost 100 DM ($59.40) to 120 DM ($71.25),
including a buffet breakfast. Half board costs another 20 DM ($11.90) per person
daily. Regardless of the season, the dining room has a kind of "après-ski" ambience
where diners feel relaxed and low-key as they linger over drinks. The hotel is closed
from late October until just before Christmas.

A Budget Hotel

ABC Hotel, Ludwig-Lang-Strasse 21, D-8103 Oberammergau (tel. 08822/45-
50), is a cozy family chalet hotel. All bedrooms have showers/baths and toilets;
those on the second and third floors have balconies. Singles are priced at 50 DM
($29.70) daily, doubles at 100 DM ($59.40). A good breakfast is included. The
owners also rent apartments, housing from two to eight persons and costing 75 DM
($44.55) to 140 DM ($83.15) daily, with linens and cooking facilities available. The

ABC Hotel and the apartments are on 60,000 square feet of land in quiet surroundings within a 10-minute walk of the village center.

THE SIGHTS

If you visit Oberammergau in an "off" year, you can still see the **Passionspielhaus,** the modern theater at the edge of town. The roofed auditorium holds only 4,700 spectators, but the open-air stage is a wonder of engineering, with a curtained center stage flanked by gates opening onto the so-called streets of Jerusalem. The theater and production methods are of today, but the spirit of the play is marked by the medieval tradition of involving the entire community in its production. The 124 speaking parts are taken by amateur actors from the surrounding villages. The balance of the community seems to be included in the crowd scenes. The impressive array of scenery, props, and costumes is open to the public daily from 10am to noon and 1:30 to 4:30pm. Admission is 4 DM ($2.40).

Aside from the actors, Oberammergau's most respected citizens include another unusual group, the woodcarvers, many of whom have been trained in the woodcarvers' school in the village. You'll see many examples of this art form throughout the town, on the painted cottages and inns, in the churchyard, and in the **Heimatmuseum,** Dorfstrasse, which has a notable collection of Christmas crèches, all hand-carved and -painted, from the 18th through the 20th centuries. It is open May 10 to October 15, Tues. to Sat. from 2 to 5pm. Admission is 2.50 DM ($1.50). Also worth seeing on a walk through the village are the houses painted with frescoes by Franz Zwink (18th century) and named after fairy-tale characters, such as the "Hansel and Gretel House" and the "Little Red Riding Hood House."

SIGHTS IN THE ENVIRONS

Outside Oberammergau can be seen King Ludwig's creation, Schloss Linderhof, as well as Ettal Abbey.

Schloss Linderhof

Eight miles west of the village, until the late 19th century, stood a modest hunting lodge on a large piece of land owned by the Bavarian royal family. In 1869 "Mad Ludwig" struck again, this time creating in the Ammergau Mountains a French rococo palace. Unlike Ludwig's palace at Chiemsee, the Linderhof was not meant to be a copy of any other structure. And unlike his castle at Neuschwanstein, its concentration of fanciful projects and designs was not limited to the interior of the palace. In fact, the gardens and smaller buildings at Linderhof are, if anything, more elaborate than the two-story main structure.

As you stand on the steps in front of the castle's white stone facade, you'll note that the ground floor is rather plain while the upper story is adorned with relief columns altered with niches occupied by statues of mythological figures. In the center, over the three arched portals, is a large statue of Victory. Towering above the gable with its oval windows is a huge statue of Atlas supporting a world that seems just a bit too much even for him.

The most interesting rooms inside the palace are on the second floor, where ceilings are much higher because of the unusual roof plan. Ascending the winged staircase of Carrara marble, you'll find yourself at the West Gobelin Room (Music Room), with carved and gilded paneling and richly colored tapestries. This leads directly into the **Hall of Mirrors.** The mirrors are set in white-and-gold panels, decorated with gilded woodcarvings. The ceiling of this room is festooned with frescoes depicting mythological scenes, including *The Birth of Venus* and *The Judgment of Paris.*

The two side rooms are oval in design, each having a smaller, horseshoe-shaped anteroom. The eastern room is the **dining room,** mirrored and decorated with marble fireplaces, mythological sculptures, and an elaborately carved and gilded sideboard. The table, like that at Chiemsee, could be raised and lowered through the floor to permit the servants in the room below to reset the various courses without intruding on the shy king's privacy.

The **king's bedchamber** is the largest room in the palace, and placed in the back, overlooking the Fountain of Neptune and the cascades in the gardens. In the tradition of Louis XIV, who often received visitors in his bedchamber, the king's bed is closed off by a carved and gilded balustrade.

In the popular style of the previous century, Ludwig laid out the gardens in formal parterres with geometrical shapes, baroque sculptures, and elegant fountains. The front of the palace opens onto a large pool with a piece of gilded statuary in its center, from which a jet of water sprays 105 feet into the air.

The steep slopes behind the palace lent themselves well to the arrangement of a long cascade, made up of 32 marble steps and adorned with vases and cherubs. At the base of the cascade is the Fountain of Neptune, surrounded by a bed of flowers. Around these formal terrace and garden designs is the large English Garden, merging almost imperceptibly into the thick forests of the Ammergau.

The park also contains several other small but fascinating buildings, including the **Moorish Kiosk,** where Ludwig often spent hours smoking chibouk and dreaming of himself as an Oriental prince. The **magic grotto** is unique, built of artificial rock, with stalagmites and stalactites dividing the cavelike room into three chambers. One wall of the grotto is painted with a scene of the Venus Mountain from *Tannhäuser.* The main chamber is occupied by an artificial lake illuminated from below, and in Ludwig's time it had an artificial current produced by 24 dynamo engines. A shell-shaped boat, completely gilded, is tied to a platform called the Lorelei Rock.

The fantasy and grandeur of Linderhof (tel. 08822/5-12) is open to the public throughout the year and makes a day trip from Munich, as well as Oberammergau. From April to September 30, hours are 9am to 12:15pm and 12:45 to 5:30pm daily. From October to March 31, the grotto and Moorish Kiosk are closed, but the castle is open from 10am to 12:15pm and 12:45 to 4pm. Admission is 6 DM ($3.55) in summer, 4 DM ($2.40) in winter.

A short drive from Oberammergau leads to:

Ettal Abbey

In a valley sheltered by the steep hills of the Ammergau, Ettal Abbey was founded by Emperor Ludwig the Bavarian in 1330. Monks, knights, and their ladies shared the honor of guarding the statue of the Virgin, attributed to Giovanni Pisano. In the 18th century, the golden age of the abbey, there were about 70,000 pilgrims every year. The Minster of Our Lady in Ettal is one of the finest examples of Bavarian rococo architecture in existence. Around the polygonal core of the church is a two-story gallery. An impressive baroque facade was built from a plan based on designs of Enrico Zuccali. Inside, visitors stand under a vast dome, admiring the fresco painted by Joh. Jacob Zeiller in the summers of 1751 and 1752.

5. Mittenwald

Seeming straight out of *The Sound of Music,* the year-round resort of Mittenwald lies in a pass in the Karwendel Range through which heavy commercial traffic once passed. The roads to the village are kept busy today as well, but the traffic now is mainly tourists who flock here with cameras and walking shoes.

Before setting out for the 80-some miles of paths winding up and down the mountains around the village, you will want to take a look at the old market town. Especially noteworthy and photogenic are the painted Bavarian houses with their overhanging eaves. Even the tower of the baroque church is covered with frescoes. On the square stands a monument to Mathias Klotz, who introduced the town's major industry, violin making, to Mittenwald in 1684. The town's museum, with a workshop, has exhibits devoted to violins and other stringed instruments, from their conception through the various stages of their evolution. The **Geigenbau- und Heimatmuseum,** Obermarkt 4 (tel. 8823/85-61), is open Mon. to Fri. from 10 to 11:45am and 2 to 4:45pm, on Sat. and Sun. from 10 to 11:45am, charging an admission of 2 DM ($1.20).

Mittenwald also has good spa facilities, in large gardens landscaped with tree-lined streams and trout pools. Concerts are given during the summer in the music pavilion.

On daily excursions into the countryside, you are constantly exposed to changes in the scenery of the Wetterstein and Karwendel ranges. Besides hiking through the hills on your own, you can take part in mountain-climbing expeditions, trips by horse and carriage, or coach tours from Mittenwald to the nearby villages of Bavaria. In the evening you are treated to typical Bavarian entertainment, often consisting of folk dancing or singing, zither playing, and yodeling, but you also have your choice of spa concerts, dance bands, cinemas, discos, and bars.

WHERE TO STAY

A particularly inviting place to stay is the **Alpenrose,** Obermarkt 1 D-8102 Mittenwald (tel. 08823/50-55), which has about everything one could hope for in an alpine village inn. It's in the center of the village, at the foot of a rugged mountain. The facade of the hotel is covered with decorative designs, with windowboxes holding flowering vines. The basic structure of the inn is 14th century, although refinements, additions, and improvements have been made over the years. The present inn is comfortable, with suitable plumbing facilities. Its tavern room, overlooking the street, has many ingratiating features, including coved ceilings (one decoratively painted), handmade chairs, flagstone floors, and a square tile stove in the center. In the Josefkeller, beer is served in giant steins and in the evening musicians gather to entertain guests. The dining room provides many excellent meals, including Bavarian specialties. Just as winning as the public rooms are the 10 decoratively painted bedrooms. For singles, the rate is 78 DM ($46.30) to 90 DM ($53.45) daily, with doubles renting for 140 DM ($83.15) to 172 DM ($102.15); these tariffs include breakfast.

Berghotel Latscheneck, Kaffeefeld 1, D-8102 Mittenwald (tel. 08823/14-19). Set against a craggy backdrop of rock and forest, this 14-room chalet is ringed with green shutters, wraparound balconies, and a flagstone-covered sun terrace. Guests are never far from a vista, since large expanses of the exterior walls are devoted to rows of weatherproof windows that flood the wood-trimmed interior with sunlight. During chilly weather an open fireplace is likely to illuminate the knickknack-covered walls of the eating areas. The Kaizik family are the owners of this place, which you'll find in a forest a short walk above the center of town. The Kranzberg ski lift is nearby, making the place attractive to skiers. A covered swimming pool and a sauna can provide a relaxing prelude before a well-prepared dinner. The hotel's restaurant is open only to guests, and the establishment is closed from the end of October to mid-December and in April. Booking is possible only on half-board terms, costing 210 DM ($124.70) to 230 DM ($136.55) per person daily.

Rieger Hotel, Dekan-Karl-Platz 28, D-8102 Mittenwald (tel. 08823/50-71), is an attractive Bavarian hotel, whether snow is piled up outside or the windowboxes are cascading with petunias. The living room has a beamed ceiling, wide arches, and a three-sided open fireplace. Another attractive feature is the indoor swimming pool with a picture-window wall. Add to this a room for sauna and massages (segregated except on Mon., family time, when both sexes join the crowd). Prices are modest for room and breakfast buffet only. Singles begin at 66 DM ($39.20) daily, climbing to 81 DM ($48.10), and doubles cost 106 DM ($62.95) to 192 DM ($114). Fashionably decorated, the 50 bedrooms are pleasant and comfortable. The dining room has a view of the Alps.

Hotel Post, Obermarkt 9, D-8102 Mittenwald (tel. 08823/10-94), is one of the more seasoned, established chalet hotels. Dating from 1632, it captures much of the charm required for a successful inn (the competition is high). It's delightful to have breakfast here on the sun terrace (or on a balcony), with a view of the Alps. Although the lobby is basic and simple Bavarian, the tavern and three restaurants go all-out with mountain-chalet decor—black-and-white beams, a collection of deer antlers, and wood paneling. The 95 bedrooms are furnished in a standard way, and all have showers/baths and toilets. Singles are priced at 55 DM ($32.65) to 100 DM ($59.40) daily, and doubles cost 100 DM ($59.40) to 260 DM ($154.40). A buffet breakfast is included. The hotel has an indoor swimming pool, massage facilities, and a sauna.

Gästehaus Sonnenbichl, Klausnerweg 32, D-8102 Mittenwald (tel. 08823/ 50-41). Set into a hillside, this adaptation of a chalet is an inviting choice. From the balconies there's a view of the village set against a backdrop of the Alps. All 20 rooms contain private baths (or showers) and are freshly decorated in vivid natural colors, with impeccably clean sheets and furnishings. The guesthouse is often completely booked, so reservations are a good idea. Single rooms rent for 58 DM ($34.45) to 80 DM ($47.50) daily, while doubles cost 90 DM ($53.45) to 120 DM ($71.25), depending on the season. Breakfast is included. Closed November 15 through December.

Gästehaus Franziska, Innsbruckerstrasse 24, D-8102 Mittenwald (tel. 08823/50-51). When Olaf Grothe built this guesthouse, he named it after the most important person in his life, his wife, Franziska. Both have labored to make it the most personalized guesthouse in town, by furnishing it tastefully and by giving their sympathetic attention to the needs of their guests. Although the building is relatively new, there is nonetheless an old-fashioned green-tile oven against a wall of one of the wood-paneled public rooms. Singles with shower go for 45 DM ($26.70) to 90 DM ($53.45) daily, while doubles cost 85 DM ($50.45) to 150 DM ($89.05), depending on the accessories (balconies, private baths) and the season. The place is closed from early November to the second week in December.

WHERE TO DINE

Housed in a modern chalet hotel on the outskirts of town, the **Restaurant Arnspitze,** Innsbruckerstrasse 68 (tel. 08823/24-25), is the finest dining room in Mittenwald. The restaurant is decorated in the old style with alpine features; the cookery is honest and good—solid, satisfying, and wholesome. You might order sole with homemade noodles or veal steak in a creamy smooth sauce, topped by the dessert specialty, Guglhupf-parfait Wipfelder. For a meal composed of soup or hors d'oeuvres, a main dish with vegetables, plus a dessert, you are likely to pay anywhere from 35 DM ($20.80) to 65 DM ($38.60). Hours are noon to 2:30pm and 6 to 9pm; closed for lunch Tues. and Wed. The restaurant shuts down from October 20 to December 20.

---

6. Starnberger See

Less than 20 miles southwest of Munich, this large lake is a favorite with Münchners on holiday. From the water—steamer cruises are frequent on the lake in summer—you can observe the change in terrain from the low-lying marshlands on the north to the alpine ranges towering above the lake in the south. Around the 40-mile shoreline you can see no fewer than six castles, including the Schloss Berg, where Ludwig II was sent after he was certified insane in 1886.

It was in the Starnberger See that Ludwig was drowned, along with his doctor, just a few days after he was deposed. The mysterious circumstances of his death have never been explained, and many historians have suggested that he was murdered. A cross on the water marks the spot where his body was found. A Votivkapelle (a memorial chapel to Ludwig) is on the shore above the cross. It is reached by walking up the hill from the village of Berg, into the Hofgarten and along the wall of the Schloss Berg (no connection with the hotel of the same name recommended below), which lies 3 miles southeast of Starnberg and is not open to the public.

WHERE TO STAY AND DINE

Named for the castle but with no connection to it is the **Strandhotel Schloss Berg,** Seestrasse 11, D-8137 Berg (tel. 08151/5-01-06). In summer, residents from the surrounding hamlets come here for the daily dance music accompanying the sunshine and beer on the outdoor terrace. Many of the 22 comfortably modernized bedrooms offer lake views, and they cost 65 DM ($38.60) to 170 DM ($100.95) daily for singles and 120 DM ($71.25) to 180 DM ($106.90) for doubles. Meals in the well-appointed dining room cost 32 DM ($19) to 75 DM ($44.55). You can also order a light snack in the café. Tennis lovers can arrange a game nearby, and boats can be rented at a nearby marina.

Dorint-Seehotel Leoni, Assenbucher Strasse 44, D-8137 Berg (tel. 08151/50-60). Its many balconies look out over the lakeside, where sailboats and bathers make the most of the clear waters of the lake, less than a mile from the center. On sunny days the colorful awnings shield sun-sensitive visitors from the reflected glare of the water, which laps almost to the foundations of the terraces in front. There's a Biergarten near the boat docks, along with a café, an accommodating bar, and a panoramic dining room serving a well-prepared cuisine. Each of the 72 bedrooms contains a private balcony, phone, TV, radio, and minibar. Singles cost 125 DM ($74.25) to 160 DM ($95) daily, with doubles going for 185 DM ($109.85) to 230 DM ($136.55).

---

7. Tegernsee

Lying 30 miles southeast of Munich, this alpine lake and the resort town on its eastern shore have the same name. Although small, this is one of the loveliest of the Bavarian lakes, with huge peaks seemingly rising right out of the water. The lake and its string of resort towns (the finest, I think, is Rottach-Egern) are popular year-round. Because of the size of the lake, it freezes over early in winter, making it an attraction for skaters.

In the town of Tegernsee, the two major sights span some 12 centuries. The oldest of these is the Benedictine monastery, turned into a castle and village church. The other attraction is a contemporary church, one of the finest examples of German architecture, designed by Olaf Gulbransson of Munich.

WHERE TO STAY AND DINE

Bachmair Hotel am See, Seestrasse 47, D-8183 Rottach-Egern (tel. 08022/27-20), dating from 1826, is the most attractive all-around resort establishment in the entire area. A world unto itself, with every conceivable recreational facility at your disposal, it is rich in the Bavarian spirit. The complex of nine buildings is on the lake, surrounded by lawns and parkland, with wide terraces under linden trees, umbrellaed tables, and a covered garden room with wall-to-wall windows, white wrought-iron furniture, and garlands of vines trailing over the ceiling. Outdoors is a large free-form swimming pool, edged by lawns for sunbathing, and there's also a beautiful covered pool where you can swim in any weather, enjoying the view of snow-capped mountains. Extensive buildings house facilities for the cure—saunas, special baths, and massage rooms. Additional attractions are a nightclub, minigolf, skiing, boating and water sports, bowling, ice skating, and shuffleboard on ice during the winter months.

The Bachmair's interior is stylized rustic, but done with sophistication. Baroque gilt carvings, ecclesiastical paintings, and country-style furniture are mixed with antiques and reproductions, including Louis XV, Directoire, and Biedermeier. Each of the many sitting rooms, lounges, cafés, and restaurants has its own particular style. In the evening the Bavarian beerhall has local dances, yodeling, and zither playing, as well as conventional music. The 306 bedrooms, again featuring an eclectic combination of furnishings, are often dramatically conceived. All rooms have private baths. Guests book in here on half-board terms: 175 DM ($103.90) to 260 DM ($154.40) for a single and 280 DM ($166.25) to 420 DM ($249.40) for a double.

Seehotel Überfahrt, Überfahrtstrasse 7, D-8183 Rottach-Egern (tel. 08022/66-90), is a 115-room chalet resort facing the lake and surrounded by a view of the Alps. It is in fact more than a resort, also having fine modern spa facilities. The facade is characterized by balconies (big enough for sunbathing and breakfast) and windowboxes with profusions of flowers. The attractive interior, upper-level rustic, boasts stylish comfort. The living room has clusters of armchairs and sofas placed to allow a view of the lake through roomwide windows. For dining, you can use the room with booths set against picture windows, or choose a more formal room with a stage and a dance floor for weekend entertainment. The tavern, with pine stools, a slat-wood ceiling, and farm artifacts, is popular in the evening. Bedrooms show a decorator's flair. Some have terraces, some balconies, others sitting-room areas. According to the size and exposure of your room, you pay the following: singles with shower/bath rent for 150 DM ($89.05) daily, peaking at 220 DM ($130.65) for rooms with complete baths and views of the lake. Again, depending on the view and the plumbing, doubles range in price from 220 DM ($130.65) to 280 DM ($166.25). Use of the indoor swimming pool and parking space is free to guests.

Hotel Franzen and **Pfeffermühle,** Karl-Theodor-Strasse 20, D-8183 Rottach-Egern (tel. 08022/60-87). The outside of the building looks like lots of other chalet hotels in Bavaria, except the detailing is a little more elaborate, the flowers a little fresher. Inside, however, you'll encounter public rooms that are beautifully decorated with warmly patterned carpeting and a profusion of provincial antiques. The whole effect is pleasing. Some of the 14 bedrooms are furnished with painted country baroque armoires and headboards, and others with grained late-19th-century pieces. Singles cost 95 DM ($56.40) to 140 DM ($83.15) daily, and doubles rent for 140 DM ($83.15) to 205 DM ($121.75). Units are equipped with private showers or baths and balconies, and all rates include a buffet breakfast. The Pfeffermühle restaurant on the premises attracts a large following with its meals, which range in price from 38 DM ($22.55) to 62 DM ($36.80). In the grill corner of the restaurant, guests broil their own steaks and vegetables on individual grills built into the specially constructed wooden tables. The owners of this hotel and their manager speak English. *Pfeffermühle* is the German word for "peppermill."

Gästehaus Maier-Kirschner, Seestrasse 23, D-8183 Rottach-Egern (tel. 08022/6-71-10). For anyone who ever dreamed of making an entrance on an elegantly carved marble staircase, this is the place to do it. That, of course, would take place in the central hall of this lakeside hotel. The preambles to that entrance would be in the paneled and rustically decorated public rooms, all of which invite guests to linger over their newspaper or coffee. The 30 bedrooms, for the most part, are furnished with voluptuously carved neobaroque headboards, and feature comfortable armchairs. Singles rent for 75 DM ($44.55) to 85 DM ($50.45) daily, while doubles cost 130 DM ($77.20) to 150 DM ($89.05), breakfast included.

Gasthof zur Post, Nördliche Hauptstrasse 17, D-8183 Rottach-Egern (tel. 08022/2-60-85). Four stories of elaborate decoration and flowered balconies contribute to the facade of this chalet in the heart of the resort. The interior is beautifully crafted, with a soft patina glowing from the crossbeams and diagonal supports of the wooden ceilings, found in many forms throughout the public rooms. The 45 bedrooms are furnished with large armoires made of natural-grained white pine. Some of the windows are a little undersized, but the accommodations are clean and comfortable, each with private bath. Charges, on the breakfast-only plan, range from 80 DM ($47.50) daily for a single, from 110 DM ($65.30) to 155 DM ($92.05) for a double. Zur Post also operates a restaurant.

FRANCONIA AND THE GERMAN DANUBE

The Renaissance swept across Germany, but it seemed to concentrate its full forces on the part of northern Bavaria that had once been a Frankish kingdom. In spite of history's tendency to destroy the past through progress and war, Franconia still holds some of Germany's greatest medieval and Renaissance treasures. From its feudal cities sprang some of the greatest artists the world has seen—Albrecht Dürer, Lucas Cranach, Veit Stoss, Adam Krafft, and many others. As a center for cultural events, Franconia draws music lovers from all over to its annual Mozart Festival in Würzburg and Wagner Festival in Bayreuth.

The hillsides of Franconia are dotted with well-preserved medieval castles, monasteries, and churches. Part of the architecture of the region owes its beauty to the limestone range along the southern edge of the province. And between these hills and the edge of the Bavarian Forest is Germany's "other" river, the young Danube. It gradually builds up its force from the many smaller streams flowing out of the Alps and Swabian Jura until by the time it reaches the Austrian border at Passau, it is powerful enough to carry commercial ships and barges. Although not as important to the German economy as the Rhine, the Danube was responsible for the growth of several influential centers in centuries past.

1. Ulm

First mentioned in 854, Ulm became a town in 1027 and was soon the leading settlement in the Duchy of Swabia. It became a free imperial town in 1155, with increasing trade and commerce. It is situated at a strategic spot on the Danube, between the points where the young stream is joined by the Ilier River above and the Blau River below, making it a navigable waterway. Ulm's importance as a commercial terminal river port has made it a prosperous city ever since the Middle Ages.

Students of music and literature are interested in Ulm as the place where the Meistersinger tradition survived the longest. The city's most famous son is Albert Einstein.

WHERE TO STAY

Expensive Hotels

Neu-Ulm Mövenpick-Hotel, Silcherstrasse 40, D-7910 Neu Ulm. This hotel was the first member of the Swiss-owned Mövenpick chain to be built in Germany, in 1980. The hotel contains a pub and a restaurant known for its salad buffet, and 132 comfortable standardized bedrooms. Each of these has a phone, radio, TV, private bath, and minibar. Because of the hotel's location beside the Danube, many rooms have views of the river. Singles cost between 165 DM ($98) and 205 DM ($121.75) daily, doubles between 205 DM ($121.75) and 245 DM ($145.50), with a buffet breakfast included. On the premises are a Swiss-inspired restaurant designed in the Mövenpick chain formula, a café, and a pub.

Hotel Neuthor, Neuer Graben 23, D-7900 Ulm (tel. 0731/1-51-60). In the center of town, this 85-room hotel blends harmoniously into the old city, yet has a modern interior. The lobby has Oriental rugs, gray marble floors, and hospitable leather armchairs. Bedrooms, all with baths or showers and toilets, cost 105 DM ($62.35) to 112 DM ($66.50) daily for singles and 138 DM ($81.95) to 155 DM ($92.05) for doubles, all tariffs including breakfast.

Moderately Priced Hotels

Less than three blocks from both the railway station and the cathedral, the **Hotel Stern,** Sterngasse 17, D-7900 Ulm (tel. 0731/6-30-91), is a modern establishment with a cheerful facade. Bigger than it looks from the outside, the hotel offers 62 bedrooms with baths. There is also an elevator, plus a sauna. Comfortably furnished singles rent for 92 DM ($54.65) to 110 DM ($65.30) daily, while doubles cost 130 DM ($77.20) to 170 DM ($100.95), a filling buffet breakfast included.

Hotel Engel, Loherstrasse 35, D-7900 Ulm (tel. 0731/6-08-84). Completely overhauled and renovated, this older guesthouse contains 41 accommodations, each of which has a phone, radio, TV, and rustic furniture of light-grained wood. A buffet breakfast is included with the price of the room, which ranges from 80 DM ($47.50) to 88 DM ($52.25) daily for a single and from 110 DM ($65.30) to 130 DM ($77.20) for a double. Much of the establishment's business comes from its informal restaurant, which serves Teutonic specialties. Fixed-price menus cost 15 DM ($8.90) to 60 DM ($35.65), and are served daily from 11am to 11pm. The pub-style bar is open from 3pm to about 1am; closed Sun.

Hotel und Rasthaus Seligweiler, D-7900 Ulm-Seligweiler, Autobahn–Ausfahrt Ulm–Ost (tel. 0731/2-05-40). From across the meadow, the first thing you'll see is the gold lettering of the word "Hotel" splashed across the top floor of this 118-room establishment. All accommodations have modern baths, air conditioning, and soundproof windows and walls. There is also a swimming pool equipped with whirlpool jets, plus three bowling alleys. The hotel, suitable for motorists, lies about 5 miles (a six-minute car ride) from the center of Ulm. Singles with breakfast go for 65 DM ($38.60) to 75 DM ($44.55) daily, while doubles run from 95 DM ($56.40) to 128 DM ($76).

Budget Hotels

Right beside the cathedral, the **Ulmer Spatz,** Münsterplatz 27, D-7900 Ulm (tel. 0731/6-80-81), is a corner stucco hotel-and-restaurant combination, with most of its bedrooms overlooking the cathedral tower. The little Weinstube serves tasty meals in a mellowed setting of wood paneling. The bedrooms are fairly priced. Singles cost 58 DM ($34.45) to 85 DM ($50.45) daily, and doubles go for 100 DM ($59.40) to 125 DM ($74.25). Set meals cost 25 DM ($14.85) to 50 DM ($29.70), and the à la carte menu has good main dishes, such as roast pork Schwäbisch.

Goldenes Rad, Neuestrasse 65, D-7900 Ulm (tel. 0731/6-70-48). Because of its location directly on Münsterplatz, you'll have a view of the cathedral from many of the soundproof windows of this 1960s hotel. The 17 rooms are clean and hospitable, with color-coordinated wallpaper and curtains along with colored-tile baths. Singles range in price from 80 DM ($47.50) to 120 DM ($71.25) daily, while doubles cost 140 DM ($83.15) to 180 DM ($106.90), breakfast included.

WHERE TO DINE

In a central spot, close to the cathedral, the **Ratskeller,** Marktplatz 1 (tel. 0731/6-07-22), offers dining on almost any budget level, featuring varied menus in a restful atmosphere. It's fairly recently renovated, with comfortable leather chairs. There is no mad rush here—just dignified dining with self-service. Set meals range from 16 DM ($9.50) to 40 DM ($23.75). You can order a Wiener Schnitzel, which is very good here. Wines are inexpensively priced, and desserts are excellent. The Ratskeller is open Mon. to Sat. from 11am to midnight; Sun. from 11am to 2pm.

Zum Pflugmerzler, Pfluggasse 6 (tel. 0731/6-80-61). Intimate, and open later than most restaurants in Ulm, this place might be perfect for an after-concert supper in an old-world setting. The kitchen turns out a variety of Swabian, Bavarian, and international meat and fish dishes, offering an exceptional set meal at 39 DM ($23.15), one of the best in town for value and taste. Hours are noon to 2pm and 5pm to midnight.

Zur Forelle, Fischergasse 25 (tel. 0731/6-39-24). With only 10 tables, owners Renate and Guido Heer have created a sympathetic and cozy environment where Swabian specialties and cuisine moderne share equal billing. They offer such fare as homemade parfait of eel, lobster, goose, and stag, or perhaps filet of trout (forelle) in a puff pastry with mushrooms and slices of smoked ham. Dinners cost 38 DM ($22.55) to 70 DM ($41.55). The place is open from 10am to 2pm and 5pm to midnight; closed Sun.

THE SIGHTS

If you approach the town from the Stuttgart–Munich Autobahn, you'll miss the best view. So sometime during your visit, cross the Danube into Neu Ulm for a look at the gables and turrets of the Altstadt lining the north bank of the river. Here is the **Fishermen's Quarter,** with its little medieval houses and tree-shaded squares. Nearby are the more elaborate Renaissance patrician houses and the Gothic-Renaissance Town Hall.

Ulm Cathedral (Münster)

The spirit of the whole town is dominated by its major attraction. Before you even reach the city, you'll recognize the skyline of Ulm by its towering cathedral (tel. 0731/15-11-37). Its steeple at 530 feet is the tallest in the world, and the Münster is second only to the Cologne Cathedral among the huge Gothic structures of Christendom. Without the pews, the nave of the church could hold nearly 20,000 people, more than twice the population of Ulm at the time the cathedral was built in 1377. When Ulm joined the Protestant movement in 1531, work on the building was suspended, not to be resumed until 1844 and lasting until 1890. Miraculously, the cathedral escaped serious damage during the air raids of World War II.

The exterior is almost pure German Gothic, even though bricks were often used in the walls along with the more typical stone blocks. The unique feature of Ulm's Münster, however, is that the architects placed as much emphasis on horizontal lines as the Gothic style usually places on the vertical. Before entering, stop to admire the main porch, whose three massive arches lead to two Renaissance doors. This section dates from the 14th and 15th centuries and contains a wealth of statues and reliefs.

On the inside, you can climb the tower as far as the third gallery (all 768 steps), where you can look out on the town and surrounding countryside over the Danube plain as far as the Alps.

The five aisles of the cathedral lead directly from the hall below the tower through the nave to the east chancel. The conspicuous absence of a transept heightens the emphasis on the chancel and also increases the length of the nave. Each of the five aisles is enclosed by huge pillars towering into steep arches. Above them, the ceiling is swept into net-vaults so high that many of Germany's church steeples could sit comfortably beneath them. The nave is so large that, even with the pews, it can accommodate more than 11,000 people at one service.

Up the central aisle toward the chancel, you come to the 15th-century pulpit. Above the canopy is a second pulpit, symbolizing the Holy Spirit. Just to the left is a handsomely decorated tabernacle, containing the elements of the Eucharist. The wood panels, carved with figures, date from the years 1469–74.

The chancel is entered through baroque iron gates set in the "triumph arch." Above the arch is a fresco depicting the Day of Judgment (1471). The other treasures are diminished by the grand choir stalls carved by Jörg Syrlin the Elder between 1469 and 1474. The 89 seats of dark oak are divided into sections, marked by busts of biblical and heathen characters. The stalls on the north side of the chancel are adorned with figures of men; those on the south, of women. The panels behind the stalls are decorated with elaborate tracery, containing figures from the Old and New Testaments, as well as several saints.

The most attractive stained-glass windows of the chancel are in the little Besserer Chapel, on the south side behind the women's choir. The five windows in this room are from the 15th century and depict scenes from the Old and New Testaments. The main south window, from the same period, represents the Day of Judgment in striking colors and figures. Although most of the windows in the side aisles of the nave were destroyed in the war, the tall Gothic windows behind the chancel were preserved.

The Ulm Cathedral is open daily, except during services on Sunday mornings. From October through February, the hours are 9am to 4:45pm; in March, to 5:45pm; in April, to 6:45pm. In May, hours begin at 8am, and in the busy months of July and August, the cathedral remains open until 7:45pm. A ticket to the tower costs 2 DM ($1.20).

The **Rathaus** was built in 1370 as a warehouse, but it has been the town hall since 1419. A Gothic and Renaissance building, it has ornate murals dating from the mid-16th century and allegorical decorations. On the south gable are the coats-of-arms of the cities and countries with which Ulm is linked by trade and commerce. On the east gable is the astronomical clock dating from 1520. Above the interior staircase is a replica of the flying machine constructed by A. L. Berblinger, "the tailor of Ulm." In 1811 he was the first man (or one of the first) to make a serious attempt to fly.

The **Ulm Museum,** Marktplatz 9 (tel. 0731/161-43-12), in the vicinity of the cathedral, contains an important collection of the arts and crafts produced in Ulm and Upper Swabia from medieval times onward. There are also successive exhibitions of both ancient and modern art, including those of the masters of Ulm. It also has exhibits from the prehistory of the region. Open from 10am to 5pm (on Thurs. to 8pm); closed Mon.

---

2. Aschaffenburg

Originally a Roman settlement on the right bank of the Main River, Aschaffenburg, fortified in the early 13th century, was the site of important meetings in the Middle Ages, including a synod and an imperial diet at which the Aschaffenburg Concordat was decided. Just 26 miles southeast of Frankfurt, it was extensively damaged in World War II.

Industrial growth in recent years has not destroyed the pastoral illusion created by the parks and shady lanes in and around this city, the gateway to the streams and woodlands of the Spessart Hills. With 250 garment manufacturers in the city, it has become the production center for men's clothing in West Germany. Yet it has remained a peaceful, provincial town, where weekly fairs are held on the square and seafood is sold directly from the buckets of the fishermen along the banks of the river. The traditional shopping streets are in a pedestrian zone, made peaceful by lamps, fountains, and flowers. You are invited to stroll and to chat, as you look into store windows.

WHERE TO STAY

An Expensive Hotel
Romantik Hotel Post, Goldbacherstrasse 19, D-8750 Aschaffenburg (tel. 06021/2-13-33), close to the heart of the town, provides comfortable accommodations and some of the best food in Aschaffenburg. Its exterior may be conventional, but there is drama inside. The focus of attention is the dining room, a stylized version of an old posting inn, including an original mail coach, timbering on the walls and ceiling, leaded-glass windows, and tavern chairs. A miniature sitting room is almost New England in character, with natural pine chairs, café curtains, and hanging oil lamps, plus lots of decorative copper. All 71 rooms have baths or showers. Singles with showers start at 85 DM ($50.45) daily, peaking at 110 DM ($65.30) for rooms with private bath. Doubles cost 170 DM ($100.95) to 200 DM ($118.75). Each unit is uniquely furnished.

Moderately Priced and Budget Hotels
At the edge of town, the **Wilder Mann,** Löherstrasse 51, D-8750 Aschaffenburg (tel. 06021/2-15-55), is a stylized, overgrown inn with a modern interior. The namesake of the inn (wild man) is pictured on the wrought-iron-sculpture sign on the facade. A treasured possession of the 60-room hotel, which has existed in one form or another since 1558, is a fine baroque carved wood statue of the Madonna and Child. The breakfast room is decorated with bentwood chairs and bronze chandeliers. Depending on the plumbing, singles cost 75 DM ($44.55) to 95 DM ($56.40) daily, and doubles go for 130 DM ($77.20) to 190 DM ($112.80).

Aschaffenburger Hof, Weissenburgerstrasse 20, D-8750 Aschaffenburg (tel. 06021/2-14-41), is housed in a tall yellow building with a single balcony on each floor. This 65-room establishment offers the kind of thoughtful details that turn a good hotel into an exceptional one. Popular in town, the place is used for meetings by members of the local Rotary Club, who enjoy the fresh food of its modern cuisine. Rooms are pleasantly and comfortably furnished, costing 88 DM ($52.25) to 128 DM ($76) daily for a single and 148 DM ($87.90) to 188 DM ($111.65) for a double, breakfast included. The hotel is 40 minutes' drive from Frankfurt on the Autobahn. Turn off at the Aschaffenburg–Ost exit.

Hotel-Restaurant Schönbusch, Kleine Schönbuschallee 1, D-8750 Aschaffenburg (tel. 06021/8-00-05), dates back to 1783, when food and drink were first sold here. The building that houses the establishment was at one time the living quarters of the court gardener, a high court official with eight personal servants at his disposal. It was among the first buildings erected after Schönbusch Park (see "The Sights," below) was planned. The Bischofszimmer, the largest room in the house and now the main dining room, once served as the gardener's living room. The garden room provides direct access to the garden and a view of a two-centuries-old red beech planted by the Princess of Bavaria. You can walk in the park with its very old and rare trees, taking a look at the Lustschlosschen, where King Ludwig I of Bavaria entertained his mistress, the notorious Lola Montez. The hotel rents 10 comfortable bedrooms, each with shower, toilet, phone, and TV. Singles cost from 85 DM ($50.45), doubles going for 135 DM ($80.15) to 150 DM ($89.05), including breakfast.

Syndikus, Löherstrasse 35, D-8750 Aschaffenburg (tel. 06021/2-35-88). An unpretentious three-story facade with a vertical sign announcing "Hotel" greets visitors to this modern but traditional hostelry a few blocks from the basilica. The bar area is rustically decorated with timbered ceilings, wheel chandeliers, and old pieces of salt-glazed pottery and pewter. All 19 bedrooms have large baths, up-to-date fixtures, and wooden ceilings. Doubles rent for 110 DM ($65.30) to 180 DM ($106.90) daily, while singles cost 75 DM ($44.55) to 140 DM ($83.15).

WHERE TO DINE

Good service and traditional cookery are the hallmarks of the limited-menu restaurant at the previously recommended **Syndikus,** Löherstrasse 35 (tel. 06021/2-35-88), which serves two versions of a table d'hôte menu daily. The emphasis is on fresh fish and shellfish. The capable chef uses only the freshest of ingredients, and the choice of menus is determined by what's in season and what's currently contained in the enormous saltwater aquarium. Specialties include fresh crayfish grilled in an envelope of bacon, goose liver pâté, or a rack of lamb with fresh baby cabbage. Meal prices range from 38 DM ($22.55) to 75 DM ($44.55). Open from 5pm to 1am; closed Sun. and the month of August. There's also a bar.

Romantik Hotel Post, Goldbacherstrasse 19-21 (tel. 06021/2-13-33). Dining here ranks as a special event for the townspeople. The restaurant is architecturally divided into several sections by low wooden partitions. The most noticeable part of the decor: the original post coach that once made the frequent run through Bavaria in 1880 and that now sits like a museum piece in one corner of the 50-table restaurant. The menu is long, with more than 70 items. Though many international dishes are served, the cook concentrates on regional dishes such as pork tongue, Swabian style, and beef consommé with liver dumplings. In season, quail, venison, and stag are featured. Diet and vegetarian meals are also offered. Meals range in price from 50 DM ($29.70) to 80 DM ($47.50), if you're being extravagant. Service is daily from 6am to midnight.

Wilder Mann, Löherstrasse 51 (tel. 06021/2-15-55), which was previously recommended as a hotel, also serves good food. Traditional in cookery, it specializes in trout along with wild game. You face a choice of 12 main courses. The restaurant opens early every day, serving breakfast from 9am until the' last dinner orders are taken at midnight. The dessert table holds a cornucopia of breadstuffs and desserts. To have dinner here will cost 28 DM ($16.65) to 55 DM ($32.65). Closed around Christmas, reopening after the first week in January.

Aschaffenburger Hof, Weissenburgerstrasse 20 (tel. 06021/2-14-41), is a previously recommended modern hotel with a restaurant popular with locals, who concentrate on the good, honest, gutbürgerlich food. Lunch, featuring a large salad buffet and whole-grain rolls, costs from 30 DM ($17.80). The dinner menu offers at least 10 main courses, complete meals beginning at 65 DM ($38.60). The emphasis is on natural ingredients, and diet and vegetarian dishes are also available. The restaurant is open daily from noon to 2pm and 6 to 10pm.

Schlossweinstuben, Schloss Johannisburg (tel. 06021/1-24-40). One of the most alluring corners of this historic castle is its popular wine cellar. You'll find a wide variety of German wines to complement anything that might strike your fancy among the conservative but well-prepared menu items. A meal might begin with liver noodle soup, then follow with a game specialty (depending on the season and availability, of course). A list of very fresh fish is likely to include trout and pike, as well as several Frankish specialties. Several fixed-price meals are offered. Count on spending from 18 DM ($10.70) to 35 DM ($20.80). The Weinstube is open daily from 11am to midnight; closed Mon.

THE SIGHTS

The favorite park in Aschaffenburg is **Schönbusch Park,** where you can ramble along shaded paths through groves of old trees. It is across the Main (2 miles on foot or by car), a marvel of planning, using the natural surroundings as a setting for formal 18th-century gardens, wandering lanes, temples, and gazebos. At the edge of the mirror-smooth lake is a small neoclassic castle, really a country house, once used by the electors of Mainz. The house is open from April 1 to September 30, daily from 8am to 1pm and 2 to 5pm, charging 1.50 DM (90¢) for admission. In summer it's possible to rent small boats to go on the lake, and the café-restaurant is open each day from 8am to 8pm.

The most impressive castle in Aschaffenburg is the huge Renaissance **Schloss Johannisburg,** Schlossplatz 4 (tel. 06021/2-24-17), reflected in the waters of the Main. Erected from 1605–14 it replace an earlier structure, and became the residence of the rulers of the town, the prince-electors of Mainz. The red sandstone castle is almost perfectly symmetrical, with four massive lantern towers surrounding an inner courtyard. From April through September, the castle is open from 9am to noon and 1 to 5pm; off-season, it is open from 9am to noon and 1 to 4pm; closed Mon. Admission is 3 DM ($1.80). A few treasures remain. From the gardens of the castle you reach the **Pompeianum,** built by Bavaria's King Ludwig I as a replica of the Castor and Pollux palace discovered among the ruins of Pompeii.

The abbey **Church of Sts. Peter and Alexander** (Stiftskirche) has stood on its hill overlooking the town for 1,000 years. Its architecture has changed over the centuries, however, as it was remodeled and reconstructed, until today it stands as a combination of Romanesque, Gothic, and baroque. Its most precious treasure is the painted retable, *The Lamentation of Christ,* by the court painter Grünewald. The interior is decorated with several paintings of the school of Lucas Cranach, as well as a marble-alabaster pulpit by Hans Juncker. One of the oldest pieces is a Roman-style crucifix from 980. Adjacent to the north side of the church is a Romanesque cloister from the 13th century. The church is open to the public from 9am to 8pm (closes at 5pm in winter). To view the treasury and the cloister, you must request admission through the sacristan at Stiftsgasse 1. The charge is 1 DM (60¢).

---

3. Bamberg

A living piece of history, Bamberg is set in the rolling Franconian hills, by the estuary of the Regnitz River, where it flows into the Main. The architecture of the town shows evidence of 1,000 years of building, with styles ranging from Romanesque to Gothic, Renaissance to baroque up to the eclecticism of the 19th century. It has narrow cobblestoned streets, ornate mansions and palaces, and impressive churches.

Bamberg today is actually two towns divided by the river: the ecclesiastical town of the prince-bishopric, of which Bamberg was the capital for 800 years, and the secular town of the world of business and commerce, directed by the burghers. First noted in history as the residence of a count in 902, a century later Bamberg became the capital of the German empire, established by the Holy Roman Emperor Henry II and his wife, who were later recognized as saints.

Today Bamberg and beer go together like barley and hops. It's been called "a beer drinker's Eden," outranking Munich in the number of breweries concentrated within its city limits. The average Bamberger drinks 50 gallons of beer a year, making the rest of the German people look like teetotalers by comparison. Many brew fanciers journey all the way to Bamberg just to sample Rauchbier, a smoked beer first brewed in 1536.

WHERE TO STAY

Expensive Hotels

Such a grand-looking hotel as the **National,** Luitpoldstrasse 37, D-8600 Bamberg (tel. 0951/2-41-12), could as easily be found in Paris as in Bamberg. With its black mansard roof, iron balconies, and baroque and classical detailing, you'll quickly understand why. Public rooms are appropriately opulent, and the bedrooms are whimsically decorated in light-colored floral prints. Singles rent for 85 DM ($50.45) to 135 DM ($80.15) daily, and doubles cost 126 DM ($74.80) to 180 DM ($106.90). All units have showers or baths and toilets, and a buffet breakfast is included in the rates.

Bamberger Hof Bellevue, Schönleinsplatz 4, D-8600 Bamberg (tel. 0951/2-22-16), a great old palace of stone, crowned by a tower and facing a little park, was renovated in 1984 with the old style retained. All 48 comfortably furnished bedrooms have private baths or showers, toilets, TVs, radios, minibars, and phones. Try to get one of the bedrooms that is large enough to contain several sitting areas. Prices depend on placement and size: doubles range in price from 150 DM ($89.05) to 220 DM ($130.65) daily, and singles run from 105 DM ($62.35) to 155 DM ($92.05). All tariffs include a large buffet breakfast. In the hotel's first-class restaurant, the service is helpful and attentive. Set meals start at 38 DM ($22.55).

Moderately Priced Hotels

The owners of the symmetrical confection that is the **Barock Hotel am Dom,** Vorderer Bach 4, D-8600 Bamberg (tel. 0951/5-40-31), have retained every detail of the original ornamented facade and renovated key areas of the interior. The result is a winning combination of baroque elements in a well-lit modernized building. Singles with showers and toilets rent for 67 DM ($39.80) daily. Doubles go from 100 DM ($59.40) to 125 DM ($74.25), depending on whether they are equipped with showers or baths. All rooms are equipped with radios and most have TVs. Tariffs include service and a nourishing breakfast of everything you might expect, plus Wurst and cheese. The breakfast room is in the old cellar, where the management has set up tables with colorful napery under the plastered stone vaulting, added a new floor, new lighting, fresh paint, and *violà!* They've created about the most unusual breakfast room in Bamberg.

Hotel Brudermühle, Schranne 1, D-8600 Bamberg (tel. 0951/5-40-91). My favorite ornament on the facade of this white–and–terra-cotta building is a corner statue of a saint being protected by two cherubs. I can't guess the age of the statue, but the building itself dates from 1314 when it was constructed as a mill powered by the Regnitz River. The hotel couldn't be more centrally located, within a few blocks of the cathedral. Rooms are attractively furnished and immaculately kept. Singles cost 75 DM ($44.55) to 85 DM ($50.45) daily, with doubles going for 120 DM ($71.25). Breakfast is included. All 16 accommodations have showers, toilets, radios, and phones.

Hotel Altenburgblick, 59 Panzerleite, D-8600 Bamberg (tel. 0951/5-40-23). Surrounded by majestic deciduous trees, which don't interrupt the fine view from the balconied windows, this modern 46-room hotel charges 60 DM ($35.65) to 80 DM ($47.50) daily for a single and 120 DM ($71.25) for a double. Rooms are comfortably appointed and well maintained, with carpeting and lots of light. All units have private baths.

Romantik Hotel-Weinhaus Messerschmitt, Langestrasse 41, D-8600 Bamberg (tel. 0951/2-78-66), mainly visited because of its restaurant, also rents rooms, 14 in all. The exterior is a gabled expanse of pale blue and yellow, with baroque patterns carved into the window frames. Inside, dozens of windows, paneling, ceramic ovens, and antiques make a mellow decor. Many of the beds upstairs have meticulously crafted headboards. Single rooms cost 63 DM ($37.40) to 95 DM ($56.40); doubles, 169 DM ($100.35) to 185 DM ($109.85). Breakfast is included. Otto Pschorn is in charge of this complex and does everything he can, with the assistance of his staff, to be helpful.

Gästehaus Steinmühle, Obere Mühlbrücke 5, D-8600 Bamberg (tel. 0951/5-40-74), is one of the little gems of Bamberg, its facade dating from 1855. It was turned into a 21-room guesthouse in 1984. The owners are Victor and Maria Orsenne, who also operate the most prestigious restaurant in town, the Böttingerhaus (see below). The rooms of the hotel are located just around the corner ("38 meters away") from the restaurant. Singles rent for 110 DM ($65.30) daily, with doubles costing 180 DM ($106.90). Some of the rooms overlook the Regnitz River, and free parking is available.

Right next door to the Steinmühle, Herr and Frau Orsenne have also opened **Molitor Haus,** Obere Mühlbrücke 7 (tel. 0951/5-40-74), which was built in 1744. It was also beautifully restored and turned into an inn with 10 elegant rooms, quite in the style of the Steinmühle. One accommodation is suitable for a disabled person in a wheelchair. Including garage fee and breakfast, room rates are 180 DM ($106.90) daily for a double or twin and 110 DM ($65.30) for a single.

Budget Hotels

One of the most reasonably priced hotels in Bamberg is **Die Alte Post,** Heiliggrabstrasse 1, D-8600 Bamberg (tel. 0951/2-78-48), dating from 1920. The helpful hosts do much to make a guest's stay comfortable in one of the well-maintained units. Each of the rooms in this 70-bed hotel has a shower, toilet, phone, and TV. Double rooms cost 110 DM ($65.30) to 130 DM ($77.20) daily, and singles run 70 DM ($41.55) to 80 DM ($47.50). For the price quoted, you're given a good breakfast with orange juice, fresh cheese, and sausage. There's also a restaurant on the premises, as well as a sauna, fitness room, and solarium for guests only.

Hotel Garni Graupner, Langestrasse 5, D-8600 Bamberg (tel. 0951/2-60-56). Many residents of town know this establishment by its big-windowed café and pastry shop occupying the ground floor. Much renovated, rebuilt, and overhauled over the years, it has a very long tradition (since the 14th century) of accepting overnight guests. The café is open daily from 8am to 7pm. You can usually get a room here. Each of the 30 accommodations contains a phone, while many have private baths and views over the old city. Depending on the plumbing, singles in the main hotel cost 40 DM ($23.75) to 70 DM ($41.55) daily, while doubles go for 70 DM ($41.55) to 100 DM ($59.40), with breakfast included. If the main hotel is full, guests are directed to a guesthouse at **Kapellenstrasse 21a,** about eight blocks away across the canal. Constructed in the late 1960s, it offers 10 comfortably modern rooms for the same price charged in the main hotel. The same family also owns a rose-garden café, a stone's throw from the cathedral.

WHERE TO DINE

On a secluded street near the river, the **Würzburger Weinstube,** Zinkenwörth 6 (tel. 0951/2-26-67), is an old, attractive half-timbered inn with a courtyard in front for warm-weather dining. The bottled wines available from the owner, Hans Krebs, will keep you smiling, but don't hesitate to drink the open wine of the house. The set meal at 35 DM ($20.80) is one of the outstanding values in the city. On the à la carte listing you'll find rainbow trout from nearby streams and tenderloin of pork cooked in a cream sauce. If you order à la carte, you can spend as much as 60 DM ($35.65). The Weinstube serves food from 11:30am to 2pm and 6 to 9:30pm; closed Wed., for dinner on Tues. and from the end of August to mid-September.

Romantik Restaurant-Weinhaus Messerschmitt, Langestrasse 41 (tel. 0951/2-78-66), comfortable and pleasant, serves mainly Franconian specialties. The restaurant is 160 years old, and the sixth generation of the same family runs it. It's known through Bamberg for its "Romantik-Menu," a complete meal costing 52 DM ($30.90) to 72 DM ($42.75). The dishes offered depend on seasonal shopping; in spring you get fresh white asparagus. Freshwater fish are kept in an aquarium. Game is another specialty, and the veal and lamb dishes are prepared with exquisite care. The Weinhaus is open daily from 9am to 11pm.

Böttingerhaus, Judenstrsse 14 (tel. 0951/5-40-74), is a most elegant dining choice. The baroque ornamentation of this restaurant's facade stands in sharp contrast to the deliciously light-textured cuisine served. Visitors are amply rewarded after climbing the flight of steps leading to the dining room, where the Orsenne family, Victor and Maria, maintain a daytime coffeehouse as well as an evening restaurant. Specialties include veal Gulasch, mussels in a saffron-flavored sauce, and an array of such mouthwatering desserts as raspberry charlotte. You can order pastry and coffee throughout the day. Lunch is often served on the garden terrace, and steaks are prepared in the grill over an open flame. Full meals cost 65 DM ($38.60) to 120 DM ($71.25), with a set lunch menu going for 35 DM ($20.80). Meals are served daily from noon to 2pm and 7 to 10pm. In the rustic wine cellar you can enjoy a steak or salad while you drink local, Rhine, or Mosel wine served by the glass. The wine cellar is open from 6pm to midnight; closed Sun. There's live entertainment on Saturday.

Historischer Brauereiausschank Schlenkerla, Dominikanerstrasse 6 (tel. 0951/5-60-60). Clients sit here much as they did in 1678, when the brewery (which is what this used to be) was established. The decor is rustic, with long wooden tables and smallish chairs. The price is right and the gemütlich atmosphere genuine. Wholesome German food is served, costing 12 DM ($7.15) to 25 DM ($14.85) for a meal. It is open from 9:30am to 11pm; closed Tues. It closes for about two weeks in January.

THE SIGHTS

Handsomely positioned on seven hills, Bamberg is a cathedral city, just 39 miles north of Nürnberg. Though not large in size, it is considered the leading medieval city of Germany, a powerful ecclesiastical center whose roots go back 1,000 years. It suffered relatively little damage in World War II.

Domplatz (Cathedral Square) is dominated by the **Alte Hofhaltung,** the Renaissance imperial and episcopal palace, with a courtyard surrounded by late-Gothic framework buildings. Within the palace are the remains of the original Diet hall, built in the 11th century. Opposite is the 17th-century **Neue Residenz** (tel. 0951/5-63-51), the much larger palace of the prince-bishops, showing both Renaissance and baroque influence. It is open daily between April 1 and September 30 from 9am to noon and 1:30 to 5pm (closes at 4pm the rest of the year). Admission is 2.50 DM ($1.50).

On Domplatz sits the **Kaiserdorn** (Imperial Cathedral), begun in 1237 in a Romanesque and early-Gothic style. Resting on a hillside, the cathedral is a basilica with a double chancel, the eastern one raised on a terrace to compensate for the slope. The massive towers at the four corners of the church dominate the skyline of the city. The interior of the cathedral contains some of the most noted religious art in Christendom. The best-known is the *Bamberger Reiter,* an equestrian statue from the 13th century representing the idealized Christian king of the Middle Ages. Among the many tombs is that of Emperor Heinrich II, who erected the original cathedral. Tilman Riemenschneider labored more than a decade over this masterpiece and the one devoted to the emperor's wife, Kunigunde, who was suspected of adultery—a fact actually commemorated in one of the scenes on the tomb. The only papal tomb in Germany—in fact, the only one north of the Alps—contains the remains of Pope Clement II, who died in 1047; he is buried in the west chancel. The cathedral may be visited at any time during daylight hours, except between noon and 2pm (and during services, of course). The Cathedral Treasury, a rich collection, may be seen in the **Diözesenmuseum,** Kapitelshaus, Domplatz 5 (tel. 0951/50-21). It can be visited April to November, Tues. to Sun. from 10am to 5pm; closed Mon. Admission is 2 DM ($1.20).

Among the other places of interest is the **Altes Rathaus,** considered the strangest town hall in Germany. Determined not to play favorites between the ecclesiastical and secular sections of the city, the town authorities built this Gothic structure (with more recent rococo overtones) on its own little island in the middle of the Regnitz River—halfway between the two factions—a true middle-of-the-road (or river) political stand. From the island you get the best view of the old fishermen's houses along the river in the section called **"Little Venice."**

E.T.A. Hoffmann Haus, Schillerplatz 26, was the home of the writer, poet, and critic from 1809 to 1813. The little narrow-fronted house is filled with mementos and memorabilia of the storyteller whose strange tales formed the basis of Offenbach's famous opera, *The Tales of Hoffmann.* For an appointment to see the house, phone Dr. Wirth at 0951/18-80.

Excursions in the Environs

The most interesting excursion from Bamberg is to **Schloss Weissenstein** (also called Pommersfelden Castle) at Pommersfelden (tel. 09548/203), lying about 13 miles from the heart of Bamberg, and reached by taking the Würzburg highway. After some 5 miles, take a left-hand turn onto Route 22 heading toward Oberndorf. Signs point the way.

Considered a treasure of the secular baroque, one of the finest examples in the country, the castle was built between 1711 and 1718. One of its most stunning architectural achievements is called "the well," a spectacular three-story staircase; above, Apollo's chariot races across the ceiling. A ground-floor room with elaborate shell decorations has the kind of grotto effect popular in the eighteenth century. A detailed tour takes in the apartment of the bishops of Bamberg, along with a picture gallery and a hall of mirrors. From April 1 to October 31, guided tours go daily through the castle from 9am to noon and 2 to 5pm. A 30-minute tour costs 4 DM ($2.40), an hour's trip going for 6 DM ($3.55).

A gem of the rococo, the pilgrimage **Vierzehnheiligen Church** lies to the northeast of Bamberg. In the mid-15th century a herdsman reportedly saw visions of the "Fourteen Saints of Intercession," the last of which was identified as being the Christ Child. Over the years thousands of pilgrims were attracted to a chapel on the site, which eventually gave way to the sumptuous rococo church constructed in 1743 by Balthasar Neumann.

The building proves that Neumann was indeed a master of baroque architecture. Of ocher-colored stone, the church is characterized by its domed towers. Inside, in addition to enjoying the elaborate but also subtle decoration, seek out the Nothelfer Altar, dating from 1764. The altar, a rococo pyramid, stands on the spot where the alleged visions were said to have taken place. The saints of the intercession are depicted, including St. Acacius, in the "agony of death."

After viewing Vierzehnheiligen, it is but a short distance to **Banz Abbey** (tel. 09573/73-11), which lies 19 miles north of Bamberg. This baroque church, celebrated for its astonishing beauty, was built on the opposite slope from Vierzehnheiligen on what is called "the holy mountain of Franconia." This cluster of baroque buildings, part of which now house a colony of Germany's senior citizens, was constructed between 1698 and 1772. The Klosterkirche, or abbey church, finished in 1719 and designed by Johann Dientzenhofer, is open to the public daily from 8:30 to 11:30am and 1 to 5:30pm. In winter it closes at 4:30pm and on Sun. and holidays it opens at 10am. One of the statues decorating the front of the abbey depicts St. Denis, of whom the Franks had made a cult figure in the Middle Ages. From the terrace you'll have a stunning panoramic sweep of the Main Valley and the just-visited Vierzehnheiligen Church.

4. Coburg

This town, about 30 miles north of Bamberg near the East German border, is forever linked to the Saxe-Coburgs. In their day they were called a "royal stud farm," as they provided queens, kings, and consorts for the ruling families of Europe, including those of England, Portugal, Bulgaria, and Belgium. At the zenith of their power they were said to "rule over half the globe." One of the most notable members of this family was Prince Albert, Queen Victoria's "beloved Albert." The queen herself was descended from this same aristocratic family.

A possession of Emperor Otto II in the 11th century, the settlement on the left bank of the Itz River grew and prospered because the fortified castle was on the busy trade route connecting Augsburg and Nürnberg to Hamburg. Coburg was owned by the margraves of Meissen from 1343 to 1918, and it was this branch of the Wettin family that took the title of Dukes of Saxe-Coburg-Gotha in 1826, becoming progenitors of European royalty.

WHERE TO STAY

The leading choice in town is the **Blankenburg Hotel,** Rosenauerstrasse 30, D-8630 Coburg (tel. 09561/7-50-05). Its location a few steps from both an indoor and outdoor swimming pool, as well as the comfortably solid nature of its furnishings, makes this 36-room establishment suitable for a family vacation. This rambling and cozy hotel has a policy of allowing children under 16 to stay free in their parents' bedroom. Each accommodation contains a phone and radio, and the majority offer private baths and color TVs. Except for fair periods in May and November, a single costs 79 DM ($46.90) to 99 DM ($59.80) daily, a double 120 DM ($71.25) to 142 DM ($84.30), with a buffet breakfast included. The Blankenburg's restaurant is recommended separately.

If you're looking for a location central to everything in town, consider the **Goldene Traube,** Am Viktoriabrunnen 2, D-8630 Coburg (tel. 09561/98-33), a bay-windowed, white-walled 83-room hotel whose facade is partially screened in summer with awnings. Breakfasts are served from an amply stocked buffet, and evening meals are well prepared, generous, and reasonably priced, ranging from 25 DM ($14.85) to 55 DM ($32.65). Singles cost 50 DM ($29.70) to 95 DM ($56.40) daily, the latter price for rooms with private baths. Likewise, doubles run from a low of 120 DM ($71.25) to a high of 180 DM ($106.90), including breakfast.

WHERE TO DINE

Knowledgeable diners from the region make special efforts to eat at the Blankenburg Hotel's restaurant, **Kräutergarten** (herb garden), Rosenauerstrasse 30 (tel. 09561/7-50-05). The walls of the comfortably cluttered dining room are crafted from light-colored pinewood and covered with herb-related artifacts and paintings. An open fireplace adds warmth to cold-weather meals. As would be expected from an establishment that celebrates and pays homage to herbs and seasonings, aromas from the bustling kitchen play a vital part in the presentation of food. You can order a French-inspired truffle soup, marinated salmon with a pike-flavored mousse covered with a saffron sauce, or a zander filet with herb sauce. A gourmet fixed-price meal costs 85 DM ($50.45), while an à la carte dinner goes for about 70 DM ($41.55). Meals are served with advance reservations from noon to 2pm and 6:30 to 11pm; closed Sun.

In a residential neighborhood on the town's outskirts, **Coburger Tor-Restaurant Schaller,** Ketschendorferstrasse 22, D-8630 Coburg (tel. 09561/2-50-74), is a plushly elegant restaurant in a medium-size hotel. Comfortable banquettes and hanging lamps typify the decor. The gourmet cuisine is the personal fiefdom of chef Ulrich Schaller. Menu specialties depend on fresh ingredients, and their availability changes with the seasons. Examples include an array of homemade terrines, several kinds of fish in puff pastry, and wild game with seasonal mushrooms. It would be unfortunate to miss one of the establishment's desserts, since much of the effort of the chef is devoted to his pastry trolley. Have you ever enjoyed three flavors of chocolate mousse, all served on the same platter? Fixed-price lunches cost 34 DM ($20.20). Many evening diners choose the six-course fixed-price meal, costing 78 DM ($46.30). The restaurant is open from 11am to 2pm and 5:30 to 10pm; closed for dinner on Fri. and at lunch on Sat. Reservations are important. Closed for two weeks in January and about 10 days in midsummer. Single rooms in the adjoining 17-room hotel cost 60 DM ($35.65) to 95 DM ($56.40) daily, with doubles going for 100 DM ($59.40) to 150 DM ($89.05).

Künstler-Klause, Theaterplatz 4 (tel. 09561/7-52-61). If you plan on an evening at the theater, you'll find both the performers and members of the audience at this stylish bistro a few steps from the stage. If the culinary tastes of your companions range from cuisine moderne to classic German specialties, the accommodating chefs are happy to provide. One of the evening fixed-price meals, ranging from 35 DM ($20.80) to 100 DM ($59.40), might include lobster with mango, medallions of venison with potato puffs, an internationally derived cheese platter, or a Campari parfait with amaretto mousse. Noonday meals cost 25 DM ($14.85) to 40 DM ($23.75). A la carte meals cost from 50 DM ($29.70). Reservations are important, as there are only about 10 tables. Lunch is offered Mon. to Fri. from 10:30am to 2pm, and dinner Mon. to Sat. from 6pm to 1am.

THE SIGHTS

In the **Market Square** (Marktplatz) visitors can compare the statue of Prince Albert here with the famous one in London. On the square is the **Stadthaus,** in Renaissance style, and the **Rathaus,** which was first constructed in the 1500s but later reconstructed, with its Great Hall remaining intact during the rebuilding. The greatest Renaissance structure, however, is the **Gymnasium Casimirianum,** or Casimir School. Built in 1605, it is considered the most important secular Renaissance building in town. It faces the Church of St. Maurice.

One can also visit **Ehrenburg Castle,** which in 1547 was converted into a ducal residence from a religious house that had been secularized during the Reformation. A Renaissance structure, it saw much rebuilding in the 19th century. Visitors can wander through the classical throne room, inspect the Hall of the Giants, and admire the Gobelin salon with its many tapestries. The baroque chapel is also of interest. From April to the end of September, tours are given at 10 and 11am, and again at 1:30, 2:30, 3:30, and 4:30pm; closed Mon. From October to the end of March, the hours are the same except that there is no 4:30pm tour. Admission is 2.50 DM ($1.50).

Seen from a great distance, the **Veste** is one of the largest fortresses in Germany. Originally dating from the early Middle Ages, it has a double ring of heavily fortified walls from the late 16th century. Martin Luther stayed here in 1530. With its high roofs and dormers, it is an impressive sight, and the government has filled it with museums that will take several hours to explore. The **Kunstsammlungen der Veste Coburg** (tel. 09561/9-50-55) are internationally known for their collections of arms and armor, glass, and graphics. There is also a fine collection of sculpture and painting from the 16th and 17th centuries, as well as decorative arts from the Middle Ages to the present day. From April 1 to October 31, the hours are 9:30am to 1pm and 2 to 5pm; in winter, 2 to 5pm only; closed Mon. Admission is 2.50 DM ($1.50). The **Fürstenbau**, or Palace of the Princes (tel. 09561/9-20-88), used to be at times the residence of the dukes of Saxe-Coburg. It is open April 1 to the end of November from 9:30 to noon and 2 to 4pm; closed Mon.; in winter, from 2 to 4pm only. Admission is 3.50 DM ($2.10).

A newly opened branch museum of the Kunstsammlungen der Veste Coburg at nearby Rodental is the **Museum of Modern Glass,** the first museum of its kind in Germany. Opening hours and admission prices are the same as those of the Kunstsammlungen. It is in a beautifully landscaped English garden and close to a small castle built in Neo-Gothic style, where Prince Albert, later Prince Consort of Queen Victoria, was born.

Between the fortress and the Ehrenburg Castle is the Hofgarten, where you will find the **Naturwissenschaftliches Museum** (Natural History Museum) (tel. 09561/7-50-68), open daily from 9am to 6pm (to 5pm in winter), charging an admission of 2 DM ($1.20). Its bird collection, with some 9,000 specimens, is reputed to be one of the biggest on the continent. The museum also has an impressive display of all earth sciences (minerals, rocks, and fossils), an exhibit based on the biological and cultural evolution of man, and a collection of shells from all over the world, some 50,000 specimens.

---

5. Nürnberg (Nuremberg)

When this, the largest city in Franconia, celebrated its 900th birthday in 1950, the scars of World War II were still fresh in its memory. It was once considered the ideal of medieval splendor, but that legacy was lost in the ashes of World War II. With the exception of Dresden, no other German city suffered such devastation in a single air raid as did Nürnberg. On the night of January 2, 1945, 525 British Lancaster bombers rained fire and destruction on the city considered the ideological epicenter of the Third Reich. Many of the most important buildings have been restored, or reconstructed.

Visitors in Nürnberg today can see not only the ruins of the ramparts that once surrounded the city, but also the **Justice Palace,** where the War Crimes Tribunal sat in 1946. You can also visit the Zeppelinfeld arena, the huge amphitheater where Hitler staged those dramatic rallies in which a million troops could be reviewed. Hitler's architect, Albert Speer, constructed what has been called a "concrete mecca," but today the grounds have been turned into a park with apartment blocks, a trade fair, and a concert hall. Speer's Congress Hall, larger than the Colosseum in Rome, is today a recording studio and warehouse.

Centuries of art and architecture went to make Nürnberg a little treasure chest of Germany. Some of the most important churches in Germany are here. Always an important trade center, Nürnberg today is a notable industrial city. It is still associated with its traditional gingerbread products and handmade toys. The first pocket watches, the Nürnberg eggs, were made here in the 16th century.

ORIENTATION

Your arrival is likely to be on the southern fringe at the Hauptbahnhof, or railway terminus, which is also the district for most of the major hotels of the city. Opening onto Bahnhofplatz, the rail center lies on the threshold of the old town.

From this rail square, you can take Königstrasse right into the historical section of Nürnberg.

This historical core can be covered easily on foot—in fact, that is about the only way to explore it. Along the way, you'll pass many pedestrians-only shopping streets. Eventually, you'll reach a pair of bridges spanning the Pegnitz River. Take either of them and continue north until you reach Hauptmarkt, which is the principal plaza of Nürnberg. This is a popular center for tourists, and many cafés are found here. You can continue north from here, going along Winklerstrasse, bypassing the huge Altes Rathaus, or Old Town Hall. You'll also see St. Sebald's Church, opening onto Sebalderplatz (but more about that later). When you reach Albrecht-Dürer-Platz, continue up to no. 39 if you wish to visit the house of this great artist. Or else go up Burgstrasse until you reach the Kaiserburg.

WHERE TO STAY

Expensive Hotels

Built in 1986, the most stylish and sought-after hotel in the city is the **Maritim,** Frauentorgraben 11, D-8500 Nürnberg 70 (tel. 0911/2-36-30). It's set near the railroad station, just across a busy traffic artery from the southern edge of Nürnberg's medieval fortifications. It offers 316 attractively furnished bedrooms, each with a private bath, color TV, phone, and radio, with a buffet breakfast included. Singles rent for 185 DM ($109.85) to 325 DM ($193) daily, doubles for 238 DM ($141.30) to 398 DM ($236.35). Hotel guests can spend time in the elegant lobby-level bar, in the indoor pool, or in the sauna and the steam bath. There are two well-run restaurants on the premises, along with a comfortable lobby decorated a bit like a London private club, with checkerboard floors of white and russet marble, leather couches, and mahogany paneling.

Across from the railroad station, the **Grand Hotel,** Bahnhofstrasse 1, D-8500 Nürnberg 1 (tel. 0911/23-22-0), is a solid six-story blockbuster, built "when hotels were really hotels"—that is, before World War I. To ensure quiet in this busy location, all rooms have soundproof windows. The restaurant provides dignified dining, and the cuisine is international-Germanic. The best beers and wines by the glass are served in a cozy pub along with local specialties and light snacks. The Grand Hotel's 185 bedrooms are spacious, with private baths and showers. Most of the double rooms are twin-bedded. Singles with baths cost 180 DM ($106.90) to 245 DM ($145.50) daily, twins with baths going for 220 DM ($130.65) to 275 DM ($163.30).

Carlton Hotel Nürnberg, Eilgustrasse 13-15, D-8500 Nürnberg 1 (tel. 0911/2-00-30), a first-class hotel considered by some the best in Nürnberg, stands on a quiet street a block from the railway station. Though the Carlton has a well-known restaurant, the Zirbelstube, many prefer to have luncheon on the outdoor stone terrace with its umbrella-shaded tables and flower garden. All the 130 bedrooms have private baths or showers, color TVs, minibars, radios, and phones. Some doubles have a pair of L-shaped sofas with coffee tables so they can serve as combined living-sleeping rooms. Rates are based on the size of the accommodation. A single with shower costs 143 DM ($84.90) to 159 DM ($94.40) daily, peaking at 185 DM ($109.85) for a room with full bath and toilet. A double with shower costs 188 DM ($111.65) to 240 DM ($142.50), increasing to 330 DM ($195.95) to 500 DM ($296.90) for two in an apartment with bath or shower and toilet.

Atrium Hotel, Münchenerstrasse 25, D-5800 Nürnberg 50 (tel. 0911/4-74-80). Whoever designed this 200-room hotel was concerned with the distribution of natural light, and did everything possible to pierce windows through to the greenery beyond the walls. One of the newest hotels in Nürnberg, looking like a four-story collection of concrete cubes set up on stilts, it is set in a landscaped park on a manicured lawn five minutes by car from the city center. Rooms are spacious, with all the

NÜRNBERG

KEY TO NUMBERED SIGHTS:

1. Kaiserburg
2. Albrecht-Dürer-Haus
3. Fembohaus
4. St. Sebald's Church
5. Town Hall
6. "Beautiful Fountain"
7. Holy Ghost Hospital
8. University
9. Gewerbemuseum
10. Nassauer Haus
11. St. Lorenz Church
12. Germanic National Museum
13. Oper
14. Transport Museum
15. Schauspielhaus

conveniences you'd expect. The single rooms come with double beds big enough to sleep two persons and cost 160 DM ($95) to 295 DM ($175.15) daily for one. The regular doubles (where children under 12 can stay free) go for 215 DM ($127.65) to 350 DM ($207.85). Breakfast is included, along with the use of an indoor pool. The hotel accommodates handicapped clients in three specially designed rooms, and is directly connected to the Meistersingerhalle, used by Nürnbergers for concerts and conventions.

Dürer-Hotel, Neutormauer 32, D-8500 Nürnberg 1 (tel. 0911/20-80-91), opened in 1989 and quickly became one of the best first-class hotels in the city. It stands beside the birthplace of this world-famous artist, from whom it takes its name, right under the castle and near all the major sightseeing attractions. The hotel offers 105 comfortably appointed bedrooms, many having quite a bit of character. Each is equipped with private bath, TV, phone, and minibar. Charges range from 135 DM ($80.15) to 170 DM ($100.95) daily for a single and 170 DM ($100.95) to 250 DM ($148.45) for a double. The Dürer offers a Bistro Bar, a fitness center, and a garage, but it is a hotel garni, meaning it serves only breakfast. However, you'll be a short walk from many of the city's leading restaurants. The ambience of the hotel is one of cozy antique charm, combined with modern amenities.

Moderately Priced Hotels

Directly across from the south entrance of the railroad station, **Loew's Hotel Merkur,** Pillenreutherstrasse 1, D-8500 Nürnberg 40 (tel. 0911/44-02-91), is a three-minute walk from the old city. Behind the neobaroque facade of this family-run hotel are 150 comfortable rooms with private baths. Most units are large and high-ceilinged, with either plush carpeting or well-chosen Oriental rugs. The hotel charges 135 DM ($80.15) to 280 DM ($166.25) daily for a double, 90 DM ($53.45) to 160 DM ($95) for a single, including private bath, TV, minibar, and breakfast. The hotel also has an indoor swimming pool, a sauna, and a solarium.

Deutscher Hof, Frauentorgraben 29, D-8500 Nürnberg 70 (tel. 0911/20-38-21). Just two blocks from the railroad station, this is probably one of the most imaginatively decorated modern hotels in Nürnberg, making a bold, rustic statement by the use of plaids, full-grained paneling, and sophisticated lighting. The 50 bedrooms are spacious, bright, clean. Breakfast is included in the rates, which are 100 DM ($59.40) to 120 DM ($71.25) daily for a single and 160 DM ($95) to 180 DM ($106.90) for a double.

Reichshof, Johannesgasse 16, D-8500 Nürnberg 1 (tel. 0911/20-37-17). Two blocks from the Lorenzkirche, one of the landmark churches of Nürnberg, this 52-room hotel offers quiet and well-appointed rooms, usually soundproof. Singles cost 65 DM ($38.60) to 125 DM ($74.25) daily, depending on the plumbing, and doubles anywhere from 110 DM ($65.30) to 180 DM ($106.90). Since 1914 the Reichshof has been in the hands of the same family, and has always been known as a hotel of high standard and solid character.

Victoria, Königstrasse 80, D-8500 Nürnberg 1 (tel. 0911/20-38-01). Not far from the Lorenzkirche, the entrance to this 59-room hotel is identified by restrained carving on the sandstone facade, which dates from the 19th century. In 1976 the Victoria was completely renovated and equipped with soundproof windows and doors, direct-dial phones, private baths (or showers), and toilets in all units. The interior is modernized, but still has an elegantly curved staircase leading to bright rooms on the second floor. Singles rent for 75 DM ($44.55) to 85 DM ($50.45) daily, and doubles cost 120 DM ($71.25) to 140 DM ($83.15), with a buffet breakfast included.

Weinhaus Steichele, Knorrstrasse 2, D-8500 Nürnberg 1 (tel. 0911/20-43-78). The overflow from the original building spills into a modern annex next door that blends harmoniously with the more antique structure. The central core is a beautifully balanced and handcrafted building of heavy stone blocks with a curved sloping roofline that supports a half-timbered gable. The 32 rooms have a bright, big-windowed feeling. Singles rent for 70 DM ($41.55) to 85 DM ($50.45) daily, and doubles range from 110 DM ($65.30) to 140 DM ($83.15). Breakfast is included in all these rates.

Drei Linden, Aüssere-Suizbacher-Strasse 1, D-8500 Nürnberg 20 (tel. 0911/ 53-32-33). The 100th anniversary of this renovated guesthouse was celebrated in 1977 by the third generation of the Zeuner family. You'll find big-windowed comfort in the 28 rooms, all with private baths. The public rooms are attractively decorated in a modern style. Including breakfast, a single costs 95 DM ($56.40) to 110 DM ($65.30) daily, and a double goes for 140 DM ($83.15) to 170 DM ($100.95).

Burghotel–Grosses Haus, Lammsgasse 3, D-8500 Nürnberg 1 (tel. 0911/ 20-44-14). This unusual hotel offers, among other attractions, the luxury of a heated indoor swimming pool opening onto a tile bar area furnished with plants, antiques, and bar stools, where you can sip your favorite drink and pretend you're in the Caribbean. Even better, your door will practically open into one of the most historic parts of the old city of Nürnberg. Carefully chosen colors augment the 46 bedrooms, which rent for 100 DM ($59.40) to 135 DM ($80.15) daily for a single and 140 DM ($83.15) to 250 DM ($148.45) for a double, breakfast included.

Novotel Nürnberg-Süd, Münchenerstrasse 340, D-8500 Nürnberg 50 (tel. 0911/8-12-60), offers 117 comfortable and spacious rooms, each with bath and shower, extrawide bed, toilet, phone, radio, color TV, alarm clock, and minibar. The rooms, quietly positioned in the gardens, are fully air-conditioned and soundproofed. The cost is 175 DM ($103.90) to 195 DM ($115.80) daily for a double room. Singles rent for 140 DM ($83.15) to 160 DM ($95). The restaurant starts serving breakfast at 6am and closes at midnight. It will provide special menus for children. Recreational facilities include a children's playground, a heated outdoor swimming pool, and a big sun terrace, along with a sauna and solarium. The hotel is easily reached from all motorways, and an underground train will take you into the heart of Nürnberg in about five minutes. Parking is provided free.

Hotel am Sterntor, Tafelhofstrasse 8-14, D-8500 Nürnberg 70 (tel. 0911/23-58-1), is one of the railway station hotels that has been reconstructed and freshly decorated. Most important, it's not too noisy. The front lobby, with its contemporary elegance, sets the example for the 116 nicely furnished bedrooms, all with TVs and private baths or showers. Singles rent for 90 DM ($53.45) to 120 DM ($71.25), with doubles costing 140 DM ($83.15) to 180 DM ($106.90).

Budget Hotels

Erected in 1889, the **Deutscher Kaiser,** Königstrasse 55, D-8500 Nürnberg 1 (tel. 0911/20-33-41), has one of the most attractive old-world exteriors of any of the Nürnberg hostelries. At the top of a vehicle-free pedestrian mall, it is built of gray stone, with steep gables and a highly pitched roof studded with dormers. Three Romanesque-style arches lead into the main lobby. As for the dining room, it is rather simple, but fresh and clean; the 51 bedrooms have matching modern decor. The general effect is one of comfort in immaculate surroundings. Bathless doubles are 86 DM ($51.05) daily; with showers or baths, they are 101 DM ($59.95). Singles with hot and cold running water cost 48 DM ($28.50); singles with baths, 70 DM ($41.55). The Deutscher Kaiser, which has been owned and managed by the same family for more than 80 years, is crowded during December and February, when German tourists reserve ahead. They know this one's a good bargain. Parking is available. In the basement is one of the Wienerwald restaurants.

Drei Raben, Königstrasse 63, D-8500 Nürnberg 1 (tel. 0911/20-45-083), offering comfortable beds in clean rooms is a good place to consider. Owned and operated by Herr and Frau Werner Deibel, this modest little establishment stands one block from the station. A three-passenger elevator takes you upstairs to the bedrooms, all 31 of which have baths or showers, toilets, color TVs, radio/alarms, minibars, and direct-dial phones. Singles rent for 95 DM ($56.40) to 115 DM

($68.30) daily, while doubles go for 130 DM ($77.20) to 160 DM ($95); breakfast is included in the tariffs. English is spoken. About 60 yards from the hotel is a parking lot.

City Hotel, Königstrasse 25-27, D-8500 Nürnberg 1 (tel. 0911/22-56-38), is one of the best budget hotels in the city. The location is on the third, fourth, and fifth floors of an old-fashioned building a few steps from Lorenzkirche on a wide pedestrian thoroughfare in the historic center. Take a cramped elevator upstairs to the third-floor reception area, where the efficient owner, Frau Eleonore Pache, will show you one of her 21 simple but immaculate bedrooms. Each unit contains a private bath and functional furnishings. With breakfast included, singles cost 85 DM ($50.45) daily, doubles 140 DM ($83.15). The hotel is open all year except for a two-week vacation beginning at Christmas. If you go by U-Bahn, get off at the Lorenzkirche stop.

WHERE TO DINE

The Top Restaurants
The number-one restaurant in Nürnberg, **Essigbrätlein,** Weinmarkt 7 (tel. 0911/22-51-31), is also one of the outstanding gourmet eating places in Germany. The house dates back to 1550, when it was mentioned for the first time in a chronicle of the city. The oldest original restaurant in Nürnberg, it was a favorite meeting place of wine merchants. At the entrance level there is room for only 25 diners. Up a flight is a library and cocktail lounge with a private gastronomic museum. In summer a small garden restaurant is opened. The kitchen harmoniously blends local fare with exciting cuisine moderne offerings. Everything is cooked to order, and only the best and freshest produce from the market is used. A gourmet meal is likely to cost 70 DM ($41.55) to 90 DM ($53.45), including many small courses. The hosts serve from 7pm to midnight; closed Mon. Reservations are imperative.

Goldenes Posthorn, Glöckleingasse 2 (tel. 0911/22-51-53), is lodged in a building whose history goes back to 1498. A drinking glass used by Albrecht Dürer and a playing card belonging to Hans Sachs from about 1560 are among the mementos here. However, the present structure was rebuilt in 1960. Once one of Germany's most famous restaurants, it offers a modern Franconian cuisine based on products of the region. Two special set menus are offered: a four-course house menu at 56 DM ($33.25) and a five-course Franconian menu for even less, 52 DM ($30.90). Regular meals range in price from 45 DM ($26.70) to 76 DM ($45.15). There are fine wines dating back to 1889. The restaurant is open daily from 11am to 2:30pm and 6 to 11:30pm.

Die Entenstub'n, Guntersbühlerstrasse 145 (tel. 0911/59-80-413), is considered by some food critics as the best dining spot in Nürnberg. Other restaurants may be better established, but this small and well-decorated place is more in tune with cuisine moderne and sophisticated upscale versions of experimental dishes. It is tastefully appointed with light-grained paneling and depictions of geese, the establishment's namesake. Reservations are absolutely necessary. Your main course might be marinated lettuce with strips of braised chicken, carpaccio of beef in a truffle-flavored oil, or medallions of seawolf in a champagne sauce; among the succulent desserts, you might enjoy the hazelnut torte with fresh fruit. Fixed-price meals cost from 50 DM ($29.70) at lunch and range from 75 DM ($44.55) to 95 DM ($56.40) in the evening. A la carte meals go from 45 DM ($26.70) to 85 DM ($50.45). The establishment's hours are noon to 2pm, Tues. to Fri. and Sun.; 6:30 to 10pm, Tues. to Sat.

Moderately Priced Restaurants
Lying conveniently between the Albrecht Dürer House and the Kaiserburg, **Zum Waffenschmied,** Obere Schmiedgasse 22 (tel. 0911/22-58-59), is attractively

decorated with naturally aged paneling, mustard-colored walls, and bright napery. This restaurant serves traditional Franconian food to the dozens of local Nürnbergers who show up regularly. The chef can cook an entire roast pig as easily as he can concoct Norwegian trout served with a sauce of wild mushrooms and cream, roast Aberdeen steer, Bresse hen with fresh vegetables, or a rack of lamb with rosemary. Food is served daily from 11am to midnight, and a complete meal costs 35 DM ($20.80) to 58 DM ($34.45).

Nassauer Keller, Karolinenstrasse 2-4 (tel. 0911/22-59-67), occupies the cellar of one of the most romantic buildings in Nürnberg, opposite the Lorenzkirche. It features an original cuisine, specializing in trout and game in season. Main dishes include Wiener Schnitzel Cordon Bleu or filet of venison with mushrooms and cranberries. Meals range from 15 DM ($8.90) to 35 DM ($20.80). Hours are noon to 2:30pm and 6 to 10:30pm daily.

Budget Restaurants

Bimbala voy Laff, Bergstrasse 24-26 (tel. 0911/22-59-41), standing next to the Imperial Castle, is a good place to go for meals at reasonable prices. It is a charming old Franconian restaurant, serving such local specialties as potato pancakes, Nürnberg sausages, and homemade cheese. For my money, it has the best beer in town: Arnold Bier Pils and Dunkel fresh from the barrel. Expect to spend anywhere from 25 DM ($14.85) for a meal. The owner, Werner Becker, will entertain you with his guitar and by singing folk songs. The establishment is open from 11:30am to 2:30pm and 6pm to midnight; closed Sun. and for lunch Mon.

Weinhaus Steichele, Knorrstrasse 2 (tel. 0911/20-43-78), was previously recommended as a hotel. But it also has the finest and tastiest 26-DM ($15.45) set dinner in Nürnberg. It has walls covered with polished copper pots, antique display cases lit from within, and hanging chandeliers that are carved into double-tailed sea monsters, salty mariners, and mythical beasts. The Franconian specialties are a delight, backed up by a superb wine list. Hours are noon to 2:30pm and 6 to 10:30pm daily.

Böhms Herrenkeller, Theatergasse 19 (tel. 0911/22-44-65). Parts of this Weinstube date from 1489, with later additions completed in 1948. You'll get a feeling of history here as you sample the well-rounded collection of wines and the straightforward gutbürgerlich cookery. A fixed-price menu begins at 22 DM ($13.05), going up to 55 DM ($32.65). The kitchen is open from 11:30 to 2pm and 5:30 to 10pm, although drinks and cold plates are served until midnight; closed Sun. in summer, and for dinner Sun. in winter.

Heilig-Geist-Spital, Spitalgasse 12 (tel. 0911/22-17-61), an old tavern entered through an arcade near the river, is Nürnberg's largest historical winehouse. Carp is a specialty, priced according to weight. The wine is abundant and excellent, with more than 100 different vintages to go with the typically Franconian specialties. Main dishes are hearty and filling, and not too expensive. In season you can order a leg of venison with noodles and berries. Meals cost 28 DM ($16.65) to 60 DM ($35.65) and can be ordered daily from 11am to midnight.

Historische Bratwurst-Glöcklein, Im Handwerkerhof (tel. 0911/22-76-25), lies in the "village" of craftspeople. If you want to try Bratwurst in all its variations before leaving Nürnberg, this is the place to do it. The kitchen prepares a six-course meal of Bratwurst as a main course, with traditional side dishes, for a low price of 15 DM ($8.90). It's served on a tin plate. Since beer goes perfectly with Wurst, you'll enjoy sampling some of the brews on tap here while admiring the craftsmanship of the room around you, which dates from the Middle Ages. More expensive fixed-price meals are available as well, costing from 25 DM ($14.85). Be careful that you don't spend your entire afternoon on the sun terrace here—it's that tempting. Open from 10:30am to 9pm; closed Sun.

Bratwurst-Häusle, Rathausplatz 1 (tel. 0911/22-76-95). Because it's opposite the Rathaus, you might want to visit this sausage restaurant on a luncheon stopover as you explore historic Nürnberg. In winter you'll find an open hearth to warm you from the Franconian snows, and in summer, a refreshingly cool retreat from the heat. Fixed-price menus here begin at only 15 DM ($8.90), going up to 25 DM ($14.85), including a host of regional specialties; most diners, though, prefer a platter of Bratwurst and beer, especially the large student clientele. Open from 10am to 10pm; closed Sun.

Dining in the Environs

With one or two exceptions, you get your best food not within the city center of Nürnburg but in one of the rapidly developing suburbs.

Romantik-Restaurant Rottner, Winterstrasse 15 (tel. 0911/61-20-32), at Grossreuth bei Schweinau, lies just a few miles west of the city center. This half-timbered house with a garden terrace has green and red shutters and a chevron design carved into the door. It's one of the area's most popular and idyllic dining locales. Regional cookery is featured here, and specialties include wild game in season, all kinds of local fish (with other seafood flown in from the Mediterranean), and asparagus in the spring. Fixed-price menus, served in an ambience of wood paneling, cost 45 DM ($26.70) to 95 DM ($56.40), the latter for a gourmet repast. Hours are 10am to 1am; closed Sun. and for lunch Sat.

Gasthof Bammes, Bucher Hauptstrasse 63 (tel. 0911/38-13-03), at Nürnberg 90-Buch, near the airport. This honest and straightforward establishment is decorated in rustic colors and lots of wood paneling. Noonday meals are traditionally gutbürgerlich, although the chefs take some imaginative risks at night by combining fresh produce with low-calorie ingredients. Sample dishes might include trout, mussels with wild rice, a gratinée of pike, among other specialties. Your bill is likely to run from 50 DM ($29.70) to 98 DM ($58.20). The kitchen is open from 11:30am to 2pm and 6 to 10pm; however, you can drink anytime from 11am to 10pm; closed Sun.

Alte Post, Kraftshofer Hauptstrasse 164 (tel. 0911/30-58-63), at Kraftshof. If you're lucky enough to visit in summer, you'll find masses of flowers in vases enhancing the traditional wood-paneled decor of this gemütlich restaurant, which serves specialties from the Franconian region "just like grandmother made." These might include Bratwurst in vinegar with onions, a "farmer's plate," or an assortment of sausages and meats sautéed together. Try, for example, a whole leg of veal with noodles and a salad, asparagus (in spring), carp, or venison. Service is polite, and the food is moderately priced, with meals beginning at 32 DM ($19), although you could spend far more, of course. Hours are 11am to 2pm and 5pm to midnight daily.

THE SIGHTS

During the 15th and 16th centuries Nürnberg had a flowering of culture that made it the center of the German Renaissance, bringing together Italian Renaissance and German Gothic traditions. In the artists' workshops were found such talents as Albrecht Dürer, the greatest of the artists, Veit Stoss, Peter Vischer, Adam Kraft, and Michael Wolgemut. Koberger set up his printing press here, and Regiomontanus his astronomical observatory. The guilds of the Meistersingers, composed of prosperous artisans, flourished; Wagner made their most famous member, Hans Sachs, the hero of his opera, *Die Meistersinger von Nürnberg*.

Nearly all the attractions of the city are within the medieval fortifications, parts of whose walls still remain. Between the main wall (with rampart walks), and the secondary wall once ran the waters of a protective moat. Set at the "corners" of the old town are the massive stone towers of the city gates. Four major gateway towers are intact, and the remains of dozens of others still exist along the ramparts. Crowning the northern periphery of the Altstadt is the Kaiserburg (Imperial Castle).

The **Helig-Geist-Spital** (Holy Ghost Hospital) was established as early as 1331. The building is supported on arches that span one branch of the Pegnitz River.

Possibly the best example of Nürnberg's passion for beauty is the **"Beautiful Fountain"** on the Marktplatz. The stone pyramid, 60 feet high, dates from 1396 and is adorned with 30 figures arranged in four tiers. Within it is enclosed the symbol of Nürnberg, the journeyman's ring.

The town's most popular shrine is the **Albrecht Dürer House,** Am Tiergartnertor, Albrecht-Dürer-Strasse 39 (tel. 0911/16-22-71), just up the cobblestoned Burgstrasse from the Dürer Monument and St. Sebald's Church. It was the home of the greatest German Renaissance artist during the last 19 years of his life. Aside from the historical and artistic contents inside, the house is well worth the short walk up the hill. Typical of the half-timbered burghers' houses of the 15th century, the structure is the only completely preserved Gothic house in Nürnberg. The first floors are sandstone, surmounted by two half-timbered stories and a gabled roof with a view of the town below. Dürer bought this house near the medieval city walls in 1509 and painted many of his masterpieces here before his death in 1528. The building houses a museum devoted to the life and works of the multifaceted individual who helped establish Nürnberg as a flourishing cultural center. Many of the rooms are furnished with important historical pieces and contain original etchings and woodcuts, plus copies of Dürer's paintings. The house is closed Mon., but seasonal times of opening vary. From November through February, hours are 1 to 5pm, Tues. to Fri. (Wed. to 9pm); 10am to 5pm, Sat. and Sun. From March through October, hours are 10am to 5pm daily (Wed. to 9pm). Admission is 3 DM ($1.80) for adults, 1 DM (60¢) for children.

St. Lorenz Church (Lorenzkirche), Lorenzer Platz (tel. 0911/20-92-87), across the Pegnitz River, is the largest and stateliest church in Nürnberg. Begun in 1270, it took more than 200 years to complete, but the final result is one of Gothic purity, inside and out. The twin towers flank the west portal, with its profusion of sculptures depicting the whole theme of Redemption, from Adam and Eve through the Last Judgment. Upon entering the church, you can appreciate the color and detail in the stained-glass rosette above the portal. The interior is defined by pillars that soar upward to become lost in the vaulting shafts above the nave. Each pillar is adorned with sculptures carrying on the theme introduced at the entrance. The oldest of these works is *Mary with Child,* created about 1285. The continuing theme of the sculptures urges you forward toward the single east choir, the last portion of the church to be completed (1477). *The Angelic Salutation* (1519) was carved in linden wood by Veit Stoss and suspended from the roof of the church just behind the Madonna Chandelier. To the left of the altar is the Gothic Tabernacle, hewn from stone by Adam Kraft (1496), its upthrusting turret repeating the vertical emphasis of the church. Above the high altar is another masterpiece by Veit Stoss, a carved crucifix.

The church is filled with woodcarvings, paintings, and reliefs, seemingly utilizing every artists' workshop that flourished in Nürnberg during the Renaissance. Among these are the painted panels at the beginning of the choir by Michael Wolgemut, Dürer's teacher. In the first chapel on the left off the nave is a sandstone relief of the three saints, Barbara, Catharine, and Agnes (1420). Halfway up the right side is another sandstone relief by Adam Kraft, this one depicting the strangulation of St. Beatrice. The beauty of the church is heightened by the well-preserved stained and painted glass, much of it dating from pre-Dürer Nürnberg. The church can be viewed Mon. to Sat. from 9am to 5pm (Sun. from 2 to 4pm).

St. Sebald's Church, Sebalder Platz, consecrated in 1273, is a fine example of the 13th century transition from Romanesque to German Gothic. The nave and west choir are late Romanesque, with a narrow chancel containing a simple altar and an ancient bronze baptismal font. The larger east choir, consecrated in 1379, is pure Gothic, and contains the most important treasures of the church. Between the two east pillars is a huge 16th-century Crucifixion group dominated by a life-size crucifix by Veit Stoss. Just behind the altar is the elaborate shrine of St. Sebald, whose remains are encased in a monument cast in brass by Peter Vischer in 1519. The nave of the church also holds several important works of art, including 14th-century statues of St. Catherine and St. Sebald and a Madonna with a Halo (1440). On the outside wall of the east choir is the tomb of the Schreyer-Landauer family, decorated with scenes of the Passion and Resurrection of Christ. The church is open April to September, daily from 9am to 6pm; October to March, daily from 10am to noon and 2 to 4pm.

The **Kaiserburg** (Imperial Castle), on Burgstrasse (tel. 0911/22-57-26), looms above the city from its hilltop at the northern edge of the old town. For more than 500 years, from 1050 to 1571, it was the official residence of the German kings and emperors, including Frederick Barbarossa, the zealous Crusader who entertained such exotic guests as the emperor of Byzantium and the sultan of Tyre within its walls. The castle is divided into three complexes of buildings, indicating its main periods of architecture and history: the **Imperial Castle,** the **Burgraves' Castle,** and the **Municipal Buildings of the Free City.**

The oldest portion of the complex is the Pentagonal Tower (1050). It probably dates from the previous palace of the Salian Kings, over which the Burgraves' Castle was constructed. Although the Burgraves' Castle has been in ruins since it was destroyed by fire in 1420, it offers the visitor an interesting look into the layout of a feudal castle. The heavy ramparts with the parapet walks and secret passages were used by the watchmen and guards who protected not only the burgraves but also the emperors, who lived in the inner core of the castle complex.

The Imperial Castle, grouped around the Inner Court within the ramparts of the Burgraves' Castle, was the residence of the kings and emperors of Germany. Most of the buildings were constructed during the 12th century, centering around the once-magnificent Palas built by Konrad III in 1138. The great Knights' Hall on the ground floor and the Imperial Hall on the floor above look much as they did when King Frederick III rebuilt them in the 15th century, with heavy oak beams and painted ceilings. The rooms are decorated with period Gothic furnishings. Adjoining the Palas is the **Imperial Chapel,** the most important building in the castle complex. It consists of two chapels, one above the other in cross section, but united at the center by an open bay. Thus the emperor could worship with his court in the upper chapel to the same liturgy as the lesser members of his retinue in the lower chapel.

The third set of buildings on the Castle Hill, built outside the Burgraves' Castle, was erected by the council of Nürnberg in the 14th and 15th centuries when it took over the responsibility of protecting the emperor. This section includes the Imperial Stables, now housing a youth hostel, the massive bastions of the fortress, and the Castle Gardens.

From April to September, the castle is open daily from 9am to noon and 12:45 to 5pm; from October to March, daily from 9:30am to noon and 12:45 to 4pm. Admission for all parts of the castle is 3 DM ($1.80) for adults, 2 DM ($1.20) for children. Even more impressive than the fortress, however, is the view of the roofs and towers of Nürnberg from its terraces.

The **Germanic National Museum** (Germanisches Nationalmuseum), Kornmarkt (tel. 0911/1-33-10), the most comprehensive collection of German art and culture, is just inside the south section of the medieval city walls (near the main railway station). Its setting, incorporating the buildings of the former Carthusian monastery into its complex, covers the entire spectrum of German craftsmanship and fine arts from their beginnings to the 20th century. The pre- and early historical section contains finds from the Stone Age to the burial sites of the Merovingians. The extensive painting and sculpture sections include works by two of the city's most important artists, Albrecht Dürer and Veit Stoss. The demonstrations of the boundless variety and richness of German handcrafts play a major role in the museum's orientation toward cultural history. In this area, medieval bronze casting and tapestries, works of goldsmithery, scientific instruments, costumes, arms, armor, and toys are well represented. During the last few years the folk art section and the section devoted to historical musical instruments have been greatly expanded. The

Print Room and the Numismatic Collection are among the most comprehensive of the German-speaking world. Many original parchment documents from important families are housed in the Archive. The active and broad-based scholarly programs of the museum would not be possible without its library of more than 500,000 volumes, including manuscripts, incunabula, engraved and illustrated works. Hours are 10am to 5pm on Tues., Fri., Sat., and Sun.; additional hours, 8pm to 9:30pm Thurs. Admission is 4 DM ($2.40) for adults, 1.50 DM (90¢) for students. No one pays admission on Sun. or public holidays.

Tucher Castle (Tucherschlösschen), Hirschelgasse 9 (tel. 0911/16-22-71), was the summer residence of Nürnberg's most famous and still existing patrician family, the Tuchers, known for beer. The structure was built in 1534 by Peter Flötner, and it contains a small but precious collection of artworks commissioned by the Tuchers since the days of the Renaissance. Tours Mon. to Thurs. are at 2, 3, and 4pm; Fri. at 9, 10, and 11am; and Sun. at 10 and 11am. Closed Sat. The entrance fee is 1.50 DM (90¢).

Spielzeugmuseum (Toy Museum), Karlstrasse 13 (tel. 0911/16-31-64). Nürnberg is recognized as the toy capital of the world. It is only fitting that the city devote a museum to this industry, containing toys made not only in Nürnberg but around the world. Some date from medieval times. The collection of old dollhouses is vastly amusing, as is a mechanical ferris wheel. Toys, both hand- and machine-made, fill three floors. You'll often see adults (without children) enjoying this museum. Hours are 10am to 5pm Tues. to Sun.; until 9pm on Wed.; closed Mon. Charging an admission of 2 DM ($1.20), the museum occupies a restored Renaissance house.

Entering the **Handwerker Hof** (Artisans' Courtyard), Königstor from Königstrasse, is like a walk back into the past where you find yourself in a land of half-timbered houses. Craftspeople can be seen at work making handcrafts, which you can purchase as souvenirs. You can also eat many local specialties such as small pork sausages, Röstbratwurst, which the law says must be served the same day they are made. The Artisans' Courtyard is open March 20 to December 23, closed Sun. and public holidays. Craft shops are open from 10am to 6:30pm, restaurants from 10:30am to 10pm. During Christkindlesmarkt (in Advent), the entire establishment is open daily from 10am to 6:30pm.

Lochgefängnis (tel. 0911/16-26-90), under the Altes Rathaus (Old Town Hall), is a medieval prison with the original cells and torture chamber. This gruesome attraction is open from May 2 until the 30th of September, Mon. through Fri. from 10am to 4pm; Sat. and Sun. from 10am to 1pm. Admission is 3 DM ($1.80).

The oldest transport museum in Germany, the **Verkehrsmuseum,** Lessingstrasse 6 (tel. 0911/219-24-28), lies just outside the city wall. Its major exhibit is a reconstruction of the famous train that ran between Nürnberg and Fürth in 1835. Philatelists will be delighted to know (if they don't already) that the museum has one of the largest postage stamp collections anywhere. You can also see stagecoaches and early railroad cars. Open daily from 9:30am to 5pm. Admission is 4 DM ($2.40) for adults, 2 DM ($1.20) for children.

---

6. Würzburg

For the German, the south begins at Würzburg, one of the loveliest baroque cities in all the country. It has been called a "baroque jewel box." Würzburg is the starting point for the Romantic Road, and is also at the junction of the most important motorways in Germany. The location is only 60 miles from Frankfurt.

Remaining faithful to the Catholic Church throughout the Reformation, this city on the Main has been called "the town of Madonnas" because of the more than 100 statues of its patron saint that adorn the housefronts. The best-known of these statues is the *Patrona Franconiae,* a baroque Madonna that stands among other Franconian saints along the buttresses of the 15th-century Alte Mainbrücke, Germany's second-oldest stone bridge.

On March 16, 1945, Würzburg was shattered by one bombing raid in 20 minutes. In a miraculous rebuilding program, every major structure has been restored.

WHERE TO STAY

Expensive Hotels

The leading choice in the city is the **Hotel Maritim,** Pleichertorstrasse 5, D-8700 Würzburg (tel. 0931/30-53-0). Known throughout the region as a convention center, this riverside hotel was built with views over the Main in 1984. Modern and imposingly proportioned, its yellow facade is topped by a baroque-style mansard roof. It has an assortment of bars, restaurants, and discos. Each of the 293 well-upholstered bedrooms contains a private bath, color TV, phone, radio, and minibar. Singles cost 219 DM ($130.05) to 265 DM ($157.35) daily, doubles 276 DM ($163.90) to 326 DM ($193.60), with a buffet breakfast.

A comfortable Weinstube and a café are on the premises, but the establishment's gourmet citadel is the Palais Restaurant. Shining crystal and carefully crafted paneling, with an amber glow from the lamps, combine to create the most elegant restaurant in town. Lunch is daily from noon to 2:30pm and dinner from 6:30 to 11pm. Both fixed-price and à la carte meals begin at 62 DM ($36.80). The menu changes frequently, but typical dishes might include rabbit filet with figs, marinated salmon with coriander, or breast of goose in an orange and mustard sauce, followed by a mango dessert prepared three different ways. Reservations are necessary.

Unique and impressive, the **Hotel Rebstock,** Neubaustrasse 7, D-8700 Würzburg (tel. 0931/30-93-0), is housed in a palace and decorated with style. Through a classical doorway, you enter a wide foyer with carved wooden doors and an old Spanish sea chest. A red carpet guides the way to the reception area. The interior is splashy in a tasteful way; contemporary furnishings have been well coordinated with the old. The main parquet-floor restaurant has been entirely redecorated, with the hand-painted wooden ceiling indirectly lighted. Gourmet cuisine is served. The Fränkische Weinstube comes with oak beams, stark-white walls, and a gilded baroque painting along with a carved Madonna. Here, guests gather for local wine.

The 81 bedrooms are equipped with wall-to-wall draperies and matching sofas, TVs, minibars, hairdryers, phones, and coffee tables. Baths are tiled. Singles cost 125 DM ($74.25) to 198 DM ($117.55) daily, and twin-bedded rooms go for 238 DM ($141.30) to 299 DM ($177.55). A buffet breakfast is included in the rates. An architectural feature of the hotel is a winter garden with a fountain, chimney, and bar, replacing an old courtyard.

Moderately Priced Hotels

A family-run hotel, the **Amberger,** Ludwigstrasse 17, D-8700 Würzburg (tel. 0931/5-01-79), is close to the center of town, near the Berlinger Ring. The exterior color scheme is cream and coffee, and the comfortable public rooms inside are high-ceilinged, with wood moldings. The 15 bedrooms on the upper floors usually have one inwardly sloping wall. All have modern tile baths. The hotel is named after the family who own it. They charge 115 DM ($68.30) to 140 DM ($83.15) daily for a single and 140 DM ($83.15) to 210 DM ($124.70) for a double, breakfast included.

Hotel und Weinrestaurant Schloss Steinburg, Auf dem Steinberg, D-8700 Würzburg (tel. 0931/9-30-61). Amid a cluster of trees, this turreted castle and its outbuildings sprawl high on a hill overlooking Würzburg, about 2 miles away. From the sun terrace, guests appreciate the view of the Main River, the acres of vineyards surrounding the property, and the web of rail lines that carry cargo far into the distance. The foundations of this castle date from the 13th century, but what you see was largely rebuilt around 1900. The 50 comfortable bedrooms sometimes have parquet floors and a country nostalgia. With breakfast included, the rate for singles ranges from 95 DM ($56.40) to 110 DM ($65.30) daily, while doubles go for 155 DM ($92.05) to 170 DM ($100.95). The hotel has an indoor swimming pool and a sauna.

Schönleber, Theaterstrasse 5, D-8700 Würzburg (tel. 0931/1-20-68). Thirty-four rooms lie behind the salmon-colored facade of this family hotel in the central part of historic Würzburg. The ground floor is rented to boutiques, which monopolize the two enormous arched windows facing the sidewalk. The upper floors offer smallish but comfortable rooms with a variety of plumbing options. Singles rent for 48 DM ($28.50) to 85 DM ($50.45) daily, while doubles cost 80 DM ($47.50) to 130 DM ($77.20).

Walfisch, Am Pleidenturm 5, D-8700 Würzburg (tel. 0931/5-00-55). The logo of this appealing 41-room hotel is a smiling whale with a laughing cherub on its back. The cherub is holding a bunch of grapes, an appropriate reminder that the Weinstube here serves a good selection of wines and generous portions of traditional Germanic food in its timbered modern dining room. From the windows of your bedroom you'll be able to gaze across the Main River as far as Marienberg Castle high on the opposite hill. Small, cozy singles rent for 120 DM ($71.25) to 150 DM ($89.05) daily, and doubles cost 160 DM ($95) to 240 DM ($142.50), breakfast included.

Würzburger Hof, Barbarossaplatz 2, D-8700 Würzburg (tel. 0931/5-38-14), lies in the center of town, a five-minute walk from the central station. You'll recognize it by the gabled roofline, which gracefully curves inward, and the enormous half-round windows on the ground floor. You'll move from the austere lobby area, the floor of which is covered with blue tiles, to one of the 36 high-ceilinged bedrooms, all with baths and TVs. Some of these units are carpeted; many are decorated with garlands of fruit and flowers. Single rooms rent for 55 DM ($32.65) to 120 DM ($71.25) daily, while doubles cost 150 DM ($89.05) to 210 DM ($124.70), breakfast included. The Heinen family are your hosts.

Franziskaner, Franziskanerplatz 2, D-8700 Würzburg (tel. 0931/1-50-01), sleek and internationally modern, has an illuminated sign in blue neon identifying the sidewalk parapet leading to the door of your waiting car. However, even if you're on foot, you'll still receive a hearty welcome from the staff, who will charge you 48 DM ($28.50) to 90 DM ($53.45) daily for a single and 85 DM ($50.45) to 132 DM ($78.40) for a double, breakfast included. The hotel offers 47 bedrooms. The lobby has attractive black panels surrounded with natural wood, while the dining room has fine large windows looking out to the greenery beyond.

Central, Koellikerstrasse 1, D-8700 Würzburg (tel. 0931/5-69-52), five minutes from the rail station, is aptly named. It stands across the street from the Juliusspital. Although it presents an undistinguished facade to the street, it nonetheless offers 23 quiet, clean, and comfortable rooms to visitors, charging 65 DM ($38.60) to 75 DM ($44.55) daily for a single and 97 DM ($57.60) to 120 DM ($71.25) for a double. Rooms have soundproof windows, and are pleasantly decorated with neutral colors and angular wooden furniture. The owners are helpful.

Bahnhof Hotel Excelsior, Haugerring 23, D-8700 Würzburg (tel. 0931/5-04-84).
The central core of this imposing hotel with its five-story classical facade is a garden courtyard awash with potted shrubs and flowers, visible through the fan-shaped windows of the attractive breakfast room. Each of the 52 comfortable bedrooms is differently designed, and some of them are accessible via a labyrinthine series of upper hallways. Most rooms contain private baths, phones, minibars, and TVs. Singles range from 50 DM ($29.70) to 90 DM ($53.45) daily, while doubles cost 90 DM ($53.45) to 200 DM ($118.75), including a buffet breakfast. The management and staff are helpful, and the hotel is near the railway station.

Hotel Alter Kranen, Kärrnergasse 11, D-8700 Würzburg (tel. 0931/5-00-39), occupies one of a long row of five-story houses on the quay next to the river. Its yellow facade is highlighted with country-style stencils. Inside you'll find a warm, contemporary environment with thick upholstery and gleaming exposed wood. Each accommodation has a private bath, radio, TV connection, and direct-dial phone. With breakfast included, singles cost 70 DM ($41.55) to 100 DM ($59.40) daily, and doubles go for 100 DM ($59.40) to 120 DM ($71.25). This hotel appreciates advance reservations.

Budget Hotels

If you want the good simple life, **Gasthof Greifenstein,** Hafnergasse 1, D-8700 Würzburg (tel. 0931/5-16-65), is recommendable. Easy to spot, with its shutters and windowboxes dripping with bright geraniums, it's a true tavern, abounding in village atmosphere, just off the Marienkapelle with its food market. The dining room is center stage, and the 42 upper-floor bedrooms have a private entrance. All rooms have basins with hot and cold running water, and some contain private baths. According to room size and location, singles cost 85 DM ($50.45) to 95 DM ($56.40) daily, with doubles going for 140 DM ($83.15) to 165 DM ($98). For a hearty Germanic cuisine, the restaurant is economical. An underground parking garage provides space for the cars of hotel guests. A city parking space is also nearby.

St. Josef, Semmelstrasse 28, D-8700 Würzburg (tel. 0931/308-68-0), has long been recognized as one of the best of the budget accommodations in the Altstadt. Its owner, Karl Siedler, has been successful in bringing it up-to-date. All of its 30 pleasantly and comfortably furnished bedrooms contain private baths or showers and toilets. Singles begin at a low of 65 DM ($38.60) daily, climbing to 80 DM ($47.50), and doubles go for 110 DM ($65.30) to 140 DM ($83.15), with a buffet breakfast included. The rooms are well maintained. Since breakfast is the only meal offered, you'll be directed to the many Weinstuben in the area, or you can pick a dining choice from the reviews coming up. If you're driving, you can park in a garage nearby, but it'll cost you. Fresh flowers add a personalized touch to this well-run establishment.

WHERE TO DINE

The town has numberous Weinstuben, where most of the nightlife occurs. Try a local specialty, Zwiebelkuchen, which is like a quiche Lorraine, and also look for a fish specialty, Meefischle. The white Franconian wines go well with the local sausages.

Wein-und-Fischhaus Schiffbäuerin, Katzengasse 7 (tel. 0931/4-24-87), is one of the best restaurants in the region. A combined winehouse and fish restaurant, it is across the river in an old half-timbered building on a narrow street, about one minute from the old bridge. The house specializes in pike, carp, char, tench, trout, wels, and eel (blue grilled or frite). Most of these dishes are priced per 100 grams. Soup specialties are fish, snail, lobster, and french onion. Food is served from 11am to 2:30pm and 5:30pm to 9:30pm: closed Mon. and Sun. for dinner. It closes from mid-July to mid-August. Meals cost 23 DM ($13.65) to 35 DM ($20.80).

Ratskeller Würzburg, Langgasse 1 (tel. 0931/1-30-21), is not only an interesting place to visit, but it also serves tasty Franconian specialties at reasonable prices. Country cookery is an art here. The English-speaking hosts will help you with menu selections, which, in season, might be game. They also specialize in the local beer and Franconian white wines. Meals range in price from 20 DM ($11.90) to 35 DM ($20.80). Lunches are served daily from 11:30am to 2:30pm and dinners from 5:30 to 11pm. The place is closed from mid-January until after the first week in February. The cellar is part of the Town Hall in downtown Würzburg, near the old stone bridge.

Bürgerspital-Weinstuben, Theaterstrasse 19 (tel. 0931/1-38-61), near the

Stadtheater, is a high-ceilinged restaurant wide and long enough for echoes to reverberate when it's empty, which it almost never is. The floors are gleaming blond wood, and the arched plasterwork on the ceiling is painted a clear white. The overall effect is lovely, and the diners chattering intimately together certainly give the impression of a fun time in Old Würzburg. Wines here are superb, and the chef specializes in typically Franconian dishes, a meal starting at a modest 22 DM ($13.05) and going up to 40 DM ($23.75). Hours are 9am to midnight; closed Tues. The place is closed mid-July to mid-August.

Weinstuben Juliusspital, Juliuspromenade 19 (tel. 0931/5-40-80), is one of the best known of the Franconian wine taverns of Würzburg. It is traditionally decorated with paneling and the beamed ceiling you've come to expect. The place is distinguished by the wide range of its regional dishes. A good meal can be ordered here for 20 DM ($11.90), and even if you're being extravagant, it's unlikely that you'll spend more than 35 DM ($20.80). The restaurant is a top address for wine lovers. You can taste a whole range of characteristic Franconian vintages. Service is polite and efficient, and they are open from 10am to midnight, closed Wed. and in February, when the staff takes a much-needed break.

Backöfele, Ursulinergasse 2 (tel. 0931/5-90-59). There has been a tavern at this address for the past 500 years, and since it's a short walk to both the Residenz and the Rathaus, you'll probably include it for at least one of your meals in Würzburg. Even the locals don't really know whether to call it a beerhall, a wine cellar, or a restaurant. The family owners don't worry about the label. All that matters to them is that traditional Franconian food is served, that it's well prepared, and that it's dished up in copious quantities. A fixed menu of the day will cost 18 DM ($10.70) to 30 DM ($17.80). Food is offered daily from 6:30 to 11pm.

Mühlenhof-Daxbaude, Frankenstrasse 205 (tel. 0931/2-10-01), on the outskirts at Versbach, is so ancient that historians have traced the names of other Weinstuben that have stood on this site since the Middle Ages. (They've already counted three.) Meals, beginning at 35 DM ($20.80), are offered in the paneled and beamed dining room. The cuisine usually consists of traditional Franconian specialties, including game, veal, pork, and fish. Open from 11:45am to 2:45pm and 6 to 10pm; closed Mon.

Zur Stadt Mainz, Semmelstrasse 39, D-8700 Würzburg (tel. 0931/5-31-55). Since the facade of this 500-year-old guesthouse looks like an elaborately iced wedding cake, the owners probably decided that a sign wasn't necessary: all that identifies this establishment is a discreet "39" and a red-and-white heraldic shield over the street. Since 1430 local residents have come here to savor such delights as the legendary oxtail stew or roasted spareribs. They offer the best table d'hôte meal in town, costing 26 DM ($15.45). The restaurant is open from 6:30am to midnight; closed Mon., for dinner Sun., and holidays; it also shuts down from December 20 to January 20. The Stadt Mainz offers some of the best bargain accommodations in Würzburg, with 15 newly renovated rooms with showers and toilets costing 120 DM ($71.25) for a single and 180 DM ($106.90) for a double per night. The price includes breakfast (buffet style).

Weinhaus zum Stachel, Gressengasse 1 (tel. 0931/5-27-70). There are dozens of winehouses in Würzburg—many with integrity and character—but none is as old as this one, constructed in 1413. The seats and walls have been burnished by the homespun clothing of the hundreds of drinkers and diners who have sated their appetites here for the past 500 years on the conservative Franconian cookery. Meals, costing 28 DM ($16.65) to 55 DM ($32.65), are served from 4pm to midnight; closed Sun., and from mid-August to mid-September. The portions are copious. In summer you can sit in a vine-draped outdoor courtyard.

THE SIGHTS

Much of the original splendor of the city was due to the efforts of one man—Balthasar Neumann (1687–1753), the greatest master of the German baroque. His major accomplishment as court architect to the prince-bishop of Würzburg was the Residenz.

The Residenz

Begun in 1720 to satisfy Prince-Bishop Johann Philipp Franz von Schönborn's passion for elegance and splendor, this palace at Residenzplatz is the last and finest of a long line of baroque castles built in Bavaria in the 17th and 18th centuries. The great horseshoe-shaped edifice was completed within 24 years, the joint effort of the best Viennese, French, and German architects working under the leadership of Neumann. Because it was built in such a short time, the castle shows a unity of purpose and design not usually evident in buildings of such size.

Leading upward from the vestibule at the center of the castle is the **Treppenhaus** (staircase), standing detached in the lower hall and branching into twin stairways at a landing halfway to the second floor. This masterful creation by Neumann is the largest staircase in German baroque art. The high, rounded ceiling above it is decorated with a huge fresco by Tiepolo. At the center, Apollo is seen ascending to the zenith of the vault. The surrounding themes represent the four corners of the world, the seasons, and the signs of the zodiac. The illusion of the painting is so thorough that it appears to be overflowing onto the walls of the upper hall.

At the top of the staircase you enter the White Hall, where absence of color provides the ideal transition between the elaborate staircase and the connecting **Imperial Hall** (Kaisersaal), culmination of the splendor of the entire castle. Based on Neumann's design, Tiepolo worked on this room in conjunction with the accomplished sculptor and stucco artist Antonio Bossi. The walls of the hall are adorned with three-quarter marble pillars with gilded capitals. In the niches between the columns are original sculptures of Poseidon, Juno, Flora, and Apollo by Bossi. The highlight of the hall, however, is in the graceful combination of the white and gold stucco work, and the brilliantly colored paintings on the upper walls and ceiling. The work is so well done that it is difficult to tell where the paintings leave off and the relief work begins. On the flat part of the ceiling Tiepolo has depicted an allegorical scene of Apollo escorting the bride of Frederick Barbarossa to the emperor. The paintings between the upper, rounded windows glamorize important incidents in the history of Würzburg.

The other important attraction in the Residenz is the **Court Chapel,** in the southwest section. Neumann placed the window arches at oblique angles to coordinate the windows with the oval sections, thus creating a muted effect. The rectangular room is divided into five oval sections, three with domed ceilings. Colored marble columns define the sections, their gilded capitals enriching the ceiling frescoes by Byss. Bossi trimmed the vaulting and arches with intricate gilded stucco work. At the side altars, Tiepolo painted two important works—*The Fall of the Angels* on the left and *The Assumption of the Virgin* on the right.

The **Court Gardens,** at the south and east sides of the Residenz, are entered through the gate next to the Court Chapel. The terraces are connected by walks and stairways and end in a large orangerie on the south side. The various gardens are laid out in geometric designs and studded with little statues by Johann Peter Wagner, plus several fountains spouting from sunken parterres.

In the 1945 bombings the roofs of such buildings as the Imperial Hall were pierced. Rain could easily have damaged the magnificent Tiepolo ceiling. And it would have had not Lt. John D. Skilton, a U.S. Army officer, intervened. He arranged for lumber to be shipped down the Main, and at Heidingsfeld he set up a sawmill, which turned out the planking needed to cover the roofs. The lieutenant also personally financed the whole operation, and anyone who goes to Würzburg today can be grateful for his foresight and generosity.

From April through September you can visit the Residenz from 9am to 5pm. During the winter, hours are reduced to 10am to 4pm; closed Mon. all year.

Admission is 3.50 DM ($2.05). During the summer the Mozart Festival is held in the upper halls. (For information, phone 0931/37-33-6).

The Marienberg Fortress

The Marienberg Fortress (tel. 0931/4-41-58), over the stone bridge from the Altstadt, was the residence of the prince-bishops from 1253 to 1720, when transition was made to the more elegant Residenz. Although portions of the stronghold have been restored, the combination of age and wartime destruction has taken a serious toll on its thick walls and once-impenetrable ramparts. But what remains is worth a visit. One of the oldest churches in Germany, the **Marienkirche,** from the 8th century, stands within its walls.

In the former arsenal and Echter bulwark, to the right of the first courtyard, is the **Main-Franconian Museum,** housed here since 1946. A treasure house, the museum contains a history of Würzburg in art, from marble epitaphs of the prince-bishops to a carved wood model of the town in 1525. Works by the greatest artists engaged by patrons of Würzburg art are included here—a well-known collection of sculptures by Tilman Riemenschneider, including his *Adam and Eve,* paintings by Tiepolo, sculptures by Peter Wagner, and sandstone figures from the rococo gardens of the prince-bishops' summer palace. A further tribute to one of the few industries of the city, that of winemaking, is paid in the presshouse, the former vaults of the fortress. A look at historic casks and carved cask bases and a large collection of glasses and goblets concludes the museum and castle tour. The fortress is open from 9am to 5pm (from 10am to 4pm in winter); closed Mon. Admission is 1.50 DM (90¢). The museum, entered separately, is open daily from 10am to 5pm (from 10am to 4pm in winter). The charge here is 2.50 DM ($1.50).

Other Sights

The **Cathedral of St. Kilian** (Dom), at the end of Schönbornstrasse, was begun in 1045, and it ranks as the fourth-largest Romanesque church in Germany. The east towers date from 1237, and the interior was adorned with high-baroque stucco work after 1700. The Dom is dedicated to St. Kilian, an Irish missionary to Franconia in the 7th century. Destroyed in the early spring bombings of 1945, the Dom has been rebuilt. The baroque stucco work in the cross aisle and the choir has been preserved. The imposing row of bishops' tombs begins with that of Gottfried von Spitzenberg (circa 1190). Look for such Franconian works of art as tombstones by Riemenschneider.

Few visitors leave Würzburg without making the drive up to the baroque hilltop church, the bulb-topped **Käppele.** Often visited by pilgrims, this church was erected by Neumann in the mid-18th century. It has splendid interior stucco work by J. M. Feichtmayr, along with frescoes by Matthäus Günther. Visitors come here not only to see the church but also to enjoy the view over Würzburg, the vine-covered hills, and, in the far distance, the Marienberg Fortress.

The most interesting excursion in the area is to **Veitschöchheim** (tel. 0931/5-56-33), a distance of about 5 miles. You can take a Main River excursion (about 30 minutes) to this summer retreat of the prince-archbishops of the 18th century. The park is a rococo jewel box. The Parnassus group, carved in the mid-18th century and standing in the center of the lake, depicts Apollo and the Muses. It is open April to September, from 9am to noon and 1 to 5pm; closed Mon. Admission is 2.50 DM ($1.50).

---

7. Bayreuth

Lying in a wide valley on the upper basin of the Rose (Red) Main River, Bayreuth is capital of the government district of Upper Franconia, its claim to fame being that it is the site of the **Richard Wagner Festival.** Because of its location on a major trade route, it was early given the protection of a fortified castle, belonging to the counts of Andechs-Meranien. The town became the property of the Hohenzollerns in medieval times, and grew into one of the leading centers of that part of Germany.

By the 18th century, art and architecture became important in Bayreuth, with construction of many fine baroque buildings. One of the more notable of these is the baroque opera house (see below).

If you arrive in this city on the Main during the late summer months, you may think the whole town has turned out to pay homage to the great opera composer who lived here (and was buried here following his death in Venice). Indeed, for five weeks each year, everything else in Bayreuth centers around the festival.

Warning: During the five weeks of the festival—from mid-July until the end of August—hotelkeepers raise their rates quite a bit. Always firmly establish the rate before booking a room, and make reservations far in advance; otherwise, you may have to stay in a neighboring city and commute to Bayreuth.

WHERE TO STAY

Expensive Hotels
The leading Bayreuth hotel is the **Bayerischer Hof,** Bahnhofstrasse 14, D-8580 Bayreuth (tel. 0921/2-20-81), near the railway station, with a small garden of weeping willows and an indoor swimming pool. An elevator takes you to a roof-garden restaurant overlooking the Festspielhaus and the environs of Bayreuth. All in all, "The Hof" is a substantial hotel, combining contemporary furnishings with traditional. Some bedrooms have French pieces; others are Nordic modern in design. Singles cost 70 DM ($41.55) to 130 DM ($77.20) daily, and doubles go for 130 DM ($77.20) to 240 DM ($142.50), all with showers or baths and with breakfast included. The Bayerischer Hof also has a bar, a sauna, a solarium, and a fitness center.

Hotel Königshof, Bahnhofstrasse 23, D-8580 Bayreuth (tel. 0921/2-40-94). The stylish opulence of this hotel's gilded, paneled, and rococo interior hints at the kind of grandeur that might have appealed to Frederick the Great. In the establishment's formal dining room, the Königsstuben, where crystal chandeliers and gilt trim complement the well-prepared meals and elaborate desserts, fixed-price meals cost 40 DM ($23.75) to 72 DM ($42.75), depending on seasonal availability of ingredients. Reservations are suggested. Each of the 37 bedrooms is individually decorated, sometimes with antique furniture and a scattering of fine carpets. A buffet breakfast is included in the room prices: 65 DM ($38.60) to 110 DM ($65.30) daily for a single and 110 DM ($65.30) to 250 DM ($148.45) for a double.

A Moderately Priced Hotel
Waldhotel Stein, Richtung Eremitage, D-8580 Seulbitz bei Bayreuth (tel. 0921/90-01), sits in the woodlands above Bayreuth, benefiting from a view of the town and Festspielhaus. With white exterior walls and 48 accommodations, the hotel rents both traditional bedrooms as well as a handful of bungalows. The bedrooms are modern, comfortable, and filled with conservative furnishings. Singles cost 60 DM ($35.60) to 150 DM ($89.05) daily, with doubles going for 95 DM ($56.40) to 280 DM ($166.25). The hotel contains an indoor swimming pool and a sauna. No guests are received from mid-December to mid-January.

Budget Hotels
With a rear garden opening onto the castle grounds, **Am Hofgarten,** Lisztstrasse 6, D-8580 Bayreuth (tel. 0921/6-90-06), is a private home on a residential street. From some of the windows you see Richard Wagner's former home as well as the former home of Franz Liszt. Ingeniously rebuilt, the hotel provides per-

sonalized accommodations at attractive prices. The Bauernstube (for drinks) has a country theme; the dining room is pine-paneled, with a trio of picture windows. Best of all is the garden in the back, with its little terrace lawn and flowerbeds. The 17 small bedrooms are decorated attractively in individual styles. Bathless singles start as low as 60 DM ($35.65) daily. With bath or shower, a single rents for 100 DM ($59.40). Bathless doubles run 110 DM ($65.30), rising to 155 DM ($92.05) for rooms with baths. Breakfast is included. The English-speaking staff will help you find your way around the town. A plaque on the house opposite Am Hofgarten says that Franz Liszt lived there.

Goldener Anker, Opernstrasse 6, D-8580 Bayreuth (tel. 0921/6-50-51), is the unquestioned choice for opera enthusiasts. Next door to the Festspielhaus, it has been *the* hotel for distinguished composers, singers, operatic stars, and conductors for more than 200 years. Framed photographs on the time-seasoned oak-paneled walls are museum treasures. The guestbook includes signatures of such writers and artists as Richard Strauss, Elisabeth Schwarzkopf, Arturo Toscanini, Thomas Mann, Fritz Kreisler, Bruno Walter, William Saroyan, Lauritz Melchior, and Patrice Chéreau. The inn is furnished with fine antiques and Oriental rugs. Of the 32 individually designed bedrooms, 28 have private baths. Singles without baths rent for 65 DM ($38.60) daily, singles with baths going for 85 DM ($50.45). Doubles cost 90 DM ($53.45) without baths, 130 DM ($77.20) to 150 DM ($89.05) with baths. Tariffs include breakfast, taxes, and service.

Brauerei-Gasthof Goldener Löwe, Kulmbacher Strasse 30, D-8580 Bayreuth (tel. 0921/4-10-46). Its facade set off by windowboxes loaded with flame-red geraniums, this is an unpretentious, well-managed guesthouse containing 11 pine-trimmed bedrooms and a series of dining rooms devoted to the consumption of conservative and flavorful German food. Bedrooms have a Bavarian theme of checker-patterned down comforters and light-grained pinewood trim, as well as showers, toilets, and phones. Singles rent for between 50 DM ($29.70) and 60 DM ($35.65) daily; doubles, for between 80 DM ($47.50) and 100 DM ($59.40).

Gasthof Spiegelmühle Hotel, Kulmbacher Strasse 28, D-8580 Bayreuth (tel. 0921/4-10-91). Its original namesake was built in 1555 as part of a working mill, although the stone walls and tile roof of this country-baroque building were completed about 1796. The high-ceilinged interior, which once ground grain into flour, has been transformed and upgraded into a stylish hotel whose 13 bedrooms are usually booked far in advance during festival season. There's a bar, plus a breakfast room and a Bierstube/Biergarten, serving traditional and flavorful food. Each bedroom contains a shower or bath and toilet, phone, and TV, and there's adequate parking on the premises. Single rooms rent for between 50 DM ($29.70) and 70 DM ($41.55) daily; doubles, for between 85 DM ($50.45) and 110 DM ($65.30). Breakfast is included.

WHERE TO DINE

Cuvee, Markgrafenallee 15 (tel. 0921/2-34-220), serves a modern interpretation of regional and nouvelle cuisine, using tasty and fresh ingredients. In fact, owner Wolfgang Hauenstein operates the finest restaurant within the city limits. Try, if featured, home-marinated salmon with caviar and quail eggs, avocado mousse with fresh shrimp and curly-leaf-lettuce salad, or one of the different dessert parfaits. In addition to a good selection of reds and whites, the wine list has 14 different kinds of champagne. Meals range from 50 DM ($29.70) to 72 DM ($42.75). Open from 12:30 to 2pm and 7 to 9:30pm; closed Mon. Reservations are necessary.

Schloss Thiergarten, Oberthiergartener Strasse 36, D-8580 Bayreuth (tel. 0920/9-13-14). 3½ miles south of Bayreuth, this building with its hexagonal baroque tower was built as a private hunting lodge. Some of its original embellishments are still in place. There are two different dining rooms, the Kamlin (meaning "fireplace") and the Venezianischer salon, whose Venetian chandelier is 300 years old. The food derives from the culinary traditions of France, Italy, and Germany, and might include such choices as lobster risotto with basil, stuffed halibut with caviar sauce and kohlrabi noodles, and terrine of sweetbreads. There is an impressive wine list, and wines are stored in very old cellars with vaulted brick ceilings. Fixed-price meals cost 70 DM ($41.55) to 110 DM ($65.30), and à la carte dinners range from 50 DM ($29.70) to 80 DM ($47.50). Hours are noon to 2:30pm and 7 to 10:30pm; closed Mon. and for dinner Sun.; and from mid-February to mid-March.

The establishment is also a cozy hotel with eight large bedrooms boasting all the modern accoutrements. Singles range from 100 DM ($59.40) to 110 DM ($65.30), doubles from 180 DM ($106.90) to 220 DM ($130.65).

An appealing restaurant, **Annecy,** Gabelsbergerstrasse 11 (tel. 0921/2-62-79), offers French specialties and French wines. There is a choice of about a dozen main dishes every day, with three fixed-price menus ranging from 35 DM ($20.80) to 85 DM ($50.45). The food is good, the service attentive, and hours are 6pm to midnight; closed Sun.

Hotel Bayerischer Hof, Bahnhofstrasse 14 (tel. 0921/2-20-81), already recommended as a hotel, is the major place to eat in town, offering you a selection of dining spots, with both French and international cooking. The Hans Sachs Stube, an air-conditioned replica of an old inn, has walls covered with pictures of famous singers who have performed in Bayreuth. The kitchen also offers nine daily Franconian specialties. À la carte meals are in the 35 DM ($20.80) to 65 DM ($38.60) bracket. Only dinner is served, from 6 to 11pm; closed Sun.

Braunbierhaus, Kanzleistrasse 15 (tel. 0921/6-96-77), is the oldest house in Bayreuth, built in 1430 but with foundations that date back to the 13th century. It offers inexpensive and down-to-earth food as well as a special kind of beer. The specialty of the kitchen is a Holzfallersteak, which means "wood cutter's steak"; served with hash-brown potatoes and a fresh salad, it costs from 16 DM ($9.50). Service is daily from 11am to 2pm and 6 to 10pm.

THE SIGHTS

The operas of Wagner are dispensed like a musical Eucharist from the **Festspielhaus,** on Schulstrasse at the northern edge of town. Pilgrims from all over the world gather here for performances. The theater, designed by the composer himself, is the perfect setting for his operas. Although the opera house is not a beautiful building, it is an ideal Wagnerian theater, with a huge stage capable of swallowing up Valhalla, and excellent, beautifully balanced acoustics throughout the auditorium; because of the design, the orchestra never overwhelms the singers. When the festival was opened here in 1876 with the epic *Ring* cycle, it was so well received that the annual tradition has been carried on for most of the 20th century. When the composer died in Venice, his wife, Cosima, daughter of Franz Liszt (who also is buried in Bayreuth), took over. Today, Wagner's grandson Wolfgang produces the operas, with exciting staging and the best musicians and singers from all over the world. Guided tours (in German only, but with English leaflets available) are conducted from April 1 to October 31 at 10, 10:45, and 11:30am; again at 1:30, 2:15, and 3pm. Closed Monday. Tours might not be possible during rehearsals and at festival time, and there are no tours in November. The price is 2 DM ($1.20). *Note:* Tickets to the festival operas are extremely hard to get, and usually must be booked through a festival package tour.

Markgräfliches Opernhaus, on Opernstrasse, is considered the only authentic as well as the finest baroque theater in Germany. It is still in its original condition. Behind its weathered wooden doors is a world of gilded canopies and columns, ornate sconces, and chandeliers. The house was built under the auspices of the Margravine Wilhelmine, who was known for her taste and her cultivation of the arts. The theater was formally opened by her brother, Frederick the Great in 1748; up until that time, operas (notably those of Telemann) had been performed in the court theater. Today the opera house, which seats only 520 people, is used for Bayreuth's "second" festival—the **Franconian Weeks' Festival,** usually held late in May. Concerts are also given during the summer. You may visit the opera house from April to September from 9 to 11:30am and 1:30 to 4:30pm; from October to March from 10 to 11:30am and 1:30 to 3pm. Guided tours, in German only, are conducted every day except Mon. for 2 DM ($1.20).

The well-preserved **Neues Schloss** (New Palace), Ludwigstrasse 21, in the center of town one block from the Markgräfliches Operahaus, also shows the influence and enlightened taste of the talented and cultured Wilhelmine. Dating from the mid-18th century, when fire nearly destroyed the old palace, it was built in baroque style (with a definite French touch). The apartments of Wilhelmine and her husband, Margrave Friedrich, are decorated in a late rococo style, with period furnishings. Guided tours, in German with English leaflets available, cost 2 DM ($1.20). Open April 1 to September 30, daily from 10 to 11:20am and 1:30 to 4:30pm. From October to March 31, tours are daily from 10 to 11:20am and 1:30 to 2:50pm.

The margraves of Bayreuth also had a pleasure palace outside the city, the **Schloss Eremitage** (Hermitage), just 3 miles northeast of Bayreuth, reached via a road lined with chestnut trees planted in honor of Frederick the Great. Bus no. 22 runs every 20 minutes during the day. This summer palace was built in 1718 as a retreat by Margrave Georg Wilhelm. The structure almost looks as if it had been hewn out of a rock, but the interior again felt the touch of Margravine Wilhelmine. Seek out the Japanese salon and the rococo music room. The castle is set in a park, full of formal as well as English-style gardens. The palace is open from 9 to 11:30am and 1 to 4:30pm (in winter, from 10 to 11:30am and 1 to 2:30pm); closed Mon. Admission is 2 DM ($1.20). Call 0921/9-25-61 for information. In the gardens, which never close and can be entered at any time, you can see the New Palace of the Hermitage, built around 1750. Its columns are covered with polychrome pebbles in mosaic style, a unique structural element in German architecture. A part of the palace becomes a café in summer, and painting exhibitions are put on here.

The **Richard Wagner Museum** (Wahnfried), Richard-Wagner-Strasse 48. Wagner lived here starting in 1874, and the house remained in his family until as late as 1966. Only the front of the original wahnfried—which means "supreme peace" —remains intact. Wagner's life comes alive, as music fans view a wide range of memorabilia, including manuscripts, pianos, furnishings, artifacts, even a death mask. The museum is open daily from 9am to 5pm, charging 2.50 DM ($1.50) for admission, a price raised to 3.50 DM ($2.10) at festival time. If you walk to the end of the garden, fronting the rotunda, you'll see the graves of the composer and his wife, Cosima, who was the daughter of Franz Liszt. Liszt himself was buried in the town cemetery.

Germany's Oldest Castle

A fairy-tale castle owned by the State of Bavaria, **Burghotel auf Burg Lauenstein,** Burgstrasse 4, D-8642 Lauenstein im Frankenwald (tel. 09263/2-56), at Lauenstein near Ludwigstadt, is the oldest castle in Germany, dating back to 915, when it was built as a sprawling fortress. Approached by a narrow and winding road, it stands like a crown on the mountain, often veiled by clouds. The location near the East German border is secluded, although the castle lies only 47 miles north of Bayreuth and 18½ miles from Kronach. It has a central core with stone towers, turrets, and a narrow moat. The hotel is in the manor house, which partially encircles the castle; it has recently been modernized, turning it into a simple yet comfortable hotel.

Its 21 bedrooms vary in size and character, and all have good views. Several of the accommodations contain private baths, while others share tower bathrooms with monumental tubs. Bathless singles cost 35 DM ($20.80), rising to 51 DM ($30.30) for rooms with showers. Bathless doubles are tabbed at 60 DM ($35.65), doubles with showers costing 90 DM ($53.45). Breakfast is included in the prices. Full meals are regional and well prepared, costing 20 DM ($11.90) to 45 DM

($26.70). Lunch is served daily from noon to 2pm, dinner from 6 to 9pm. There is no grand hall or lounge with suits of armor, but there is a dining room with mountain-style furnishings. Weather permitting, meals are served on a covered veranda with a panoramic view of the neighboring Franconian woods. The castle shuts down in February.

---

8. Regensburg

Called Ratisbon by the English and Ratisbonne by the French, Regensburg started life as a Celtic settlement, Radespona, about 500 B.C. The Romans took it over, renamed it Castra Regina, and made it the center of their power on the upper Danube. The Regen River, from which it takes its name, flows into the Danube at this point. The town, dating from the 7th century, was the center from which Christianity spread over southern Germany, as well as a commercial city.

The Regensburg of today looks just as many visitors expect a German city to appear. The architecture that remains from its 2,000 years of history testifies to its past grandeur, which, by the beginning of the Gothic era, had already reached its peak. Fortunately, the wars of this century did not touch Regensburg, and its buildings and towers offer an unspoiled glimpse into history. Many of its ancient structures are not just museum pieces, but are in active use today. The best example of this is the **Stone Bridge,** built in 1146 on 16 huge arches, in continuous service for more than 800 years.

WHERE TO STAY

Expensive Hotels
The next best thing to staying in one of Ludwig's palaces is to anchor into the 52-room **Parkhotel Maximilian,** Maximilianstrasse 28, D-8400 Regensburg (tel. 0941/56-10-11), an exquisitely renovated neorococo building whose facade and public rooms have been classified as a public monument. The day café inside is a Bavarian fantasy in soft colors, crystal chandeliers, and elaborate plaster detailing, sometimes illuminated with gilt paint. The main salon, with a ceiling that is supported by columns of polished red stone, continues the elegant theme of 18th-century opulence coupled with 20th-century convenience. Facilities include an Italian restaurant and a coffee shop. Rooms are attractively furnished (with modern plumbing) and cost 157 DM ($93.25) daily for a single and from 197 DM ($117) for a double, including breakfast.

Avia Hotel, Frankenstrasse 1, D-8400 Regensburg (tel. 0941/43-00). The 80-room Avia is one of the city's best modern hotels, composed of at least three architectural units. The Avia offers rooms with comfortable beds, Oriental rugs, up-to-date plumbing, and views over a manicured garden. Singles go for 136 DM ($80.75) to 162 DM ($96.20) daily, and doubles cost 99 DM ($58.80) to 124 DM ($73.65). This hotel is popular with businesspeople.

Moderately Priced Hotels
Constructed as an ecclesiastical academy by the bishops of Regensburg in 1810, **Bischofshof am Dom,** Krautermarkt 3, D-8400 Regensburg (tel. 0941/5-90-86), is now a 62-room hotel that blends the 19th-century monastic with the modern secular. The vaulted ceiling in the dining room is supported by a single massive Romanesque column. The Weinstube has a green tile oven. Behind the hotel is one

of Regensburg's most popular sun terraces. Bedrooms are comfortable and attractively furnished, costing 65 DM ($38.60) to 95 DM ($56.40) daily for a single and 100 DM ($59.40) to 198 DM ($117.55) for a double, including breakfast.

St. Georg, Karl-Stieler-Strasse 8, D-8400 Regensburg (tel. 0941/9-70-66). Slightly outside the city limits, this hotel lies between the Autobahn and the historic center. You'll find this a family-run hotel of 67 rooms, where guests lodge in parts of a connected compound (its various elements probably erected in different eras). The interior is decorated in a no-nonsense functional way; shallow half timbers are visible through the distressed stucco wall of the dining room. Singles go for 65 DM ($38.60) to 95 DM ($56.40), doubles for 140 DM ($83.15) to 198 DM ($117.55), breakfast included.

Kaiserhof am Dom, Kramgasse 10, D-8400 Regensburg (tel. 0941/5-40-27), is housed in an old building with deep windows set at irregular intervals below the gabled roof with iron ice-catchers. The interior is nothing short of elegant, with a beamed ceiling in the dining room and fieldstone masonry in the Weinkeller. From the sun terrace and from many of the hotel's windows you'll have a view of the cathedral. The 31 rooms, all of which contain showers and toilets, are soothingly lit and decorated in good taste. Including breakfast, rates are 120 DM ($71.25) daily for a double and 68 DM ($40.40) to 88 DM ($52.25) for a single. My favorite spot is the reading room, which has carved sandstone ribs supporting the plaster vaulted ceiling. The restaurant has earned more than a dozen gold medals. The owners have patented their special recipe for herb and cream sauce, which, if you ask for it, will be served with dozens of specialties from all over Germany. Meals range in price from 25 DM ($14.85) to 60 DM ($35.65), and service is daily from 10am to midnight.

Karmeliten, Dachauplatz 1, D-8400 Regensburg (tel. 0941/5-43-08), is a 77-room hotel with 125 years of tradition, yet with a young, modern look. It's set on a square about three blocks from the river and a four-minute walk from the Dom, reached via an open-air fruit and vegetable market. The bedrooms, the public lounges, and the breakfast rooms are in a family style. The restaurant, open daily from 6pm to midnight and located in the 16th-century monastery cellars of the house, serves Spanish and German specialties. Set meals range in price from 30 DM ($17.80) to 50 DM ($29.70), and extensive à la carte listings are offered as well. Bathless singles cost 60 DM ($35.65) daily, and those with baths rent for 98 DM ($58.20) to 120 DM ($71.25). Doubles cost 95 DM ($56.40) to 180 DM ($106.90) for a suite. Rates include breakfast, service, and taxes. Closed from just before Christmas to the third week of January.

A Budget Hotel

On a street corner at the eastern edge of Regensburg, the **Straubinger Hof,** Adolf-Schmetzer-Strasse 33, D-8400 Regensburg (tel. 0941/79-83-55), is an attractive, unpretentious hotel that has been run by the same family for more than 60 years. The 64 rooms are perfectly satisfactory, with lots of sunlight, unadorned wood-grained armoires, and pleasing color schemes. The more expensive units have self-contained baths, while the cheaper ones have only sinks. Singles rent for 54 DM ($32.05) to 85 DM ($50.45) daily, while doubles cost 125 DM ($74.25) to 140 DM ($83.15). Breakfast is included in the room price. Inexpensive and satisfying lunches and dinners are also served in the dining room.

WHERE TO DINE

The leading dining choice for Regensburg is **Zum Krebs,** Krebsgasse 6 (tel. 0941/5-58-03), contained within a historic house a few blocks from the Rathaus (Town Hall). Elegantly understated in decor, it is operated by chef Christian Gautsch and his wife, Annette, the hostess. Representative menu items include mousse of home-smoked freshwater eel (served with caviar), freshwater fish from the Danube, mussel soup flavored with saffron, and rack of hare with a sauce made of wild mushrooms. A dessert specialty is likely to be freshly made crêpes filled with homemade chocolate ice cream and garnished with strawberry liqueur. The Gautsches charge 75 DM ($44.55) to 100 DM ($59.40) for an à la carte dinner. They also offer a three-course fixed-price lunch for 40 DM ($23.75) and a five-course set dinner for 98 DM ($58.20). Reservations are necessary. Service is Mon. to Sat. from 6pm to midnight.

Traditional and unspoiled—that describes the **Ratskeller,** Rathausplatz 1 (tel. 0941/5-17-77). Here you get some of the best meals for your money in Regensburg. Just five minutes from the Dom, this comfortable middle-class establishment consists of two dining rooms, with vaulted ceilings, paneled walls, and painted crests. The cooking is good, in the Germanic tradition, although internationally inspired offerings are introduced to add variety and flair. The best buy is the set luncheon, ranging in price from 28 DM ($16.65). If you order à la carte, you will rarely pay as much as 55 DM ($32.65). Good, hearty Franconian soups are made here, followed by such offerings as Schnitzel Cordon Bleu or perhaps, as an exotic touch, an Indonesian nasigoreng. The cellar is open from 10:30am to 3pm and 5:30pm to midnight; 10:30am to 3pm, Sun.; closed Mon.

Historische Wurstküche, Thundorferstrasse 3 (tel. 0941/5-90-98). The owners will tell you that this is one of the oldest Bratwurst-Stuben in Europe, and considering the age of Regensburg, that's not too far-fetched. Much of the decor is original, so dining here might be somewhat of a lesson in social history. Only pork sausages are served, and they cost 1.30 DM (80¢) each. A generous helping of Sauerkraut comes with it, and a large beer costs from 3.50 DM ($2.10). The kitchen is open daily from 8am to 7pm.

For more elegant dining, call for a table at **Gänsbauer,** Keplerstrasse 10 (tel. 0941/5-78-58), which in my opinion is one of the best restaurants in the city. The setting is mellow and old-fashioned, with provincial artifacts and wood paneling, but the cuisine is strictly *neue Küche,* or modern cuisine. Here, well-known Bavarian dishes are given a lighter, fancier touch, and only the freshest ingredients are used. My recently sampled baby turbot in a Pernod sauce was superb in every way. Desserts are often exotic. Meals range in price from 50 DM ($29.70) to 75 DM ($44.55). Only dinner is served, and it's offered Tues. to Sat. from 6pm to 1am.

THE SIGHTS

Regensburg is a city of churches—and for good reason. When Christianity was introduced into Germany, this city became the focal point from which the religion spread throughout the country and even into Central Europe via the Danube. The most majestic of these churches is the towering **St. Peter's Cathedral,** on Domplatz. Begun in the 13th century on the site of an earlier Carolingian church, it was inspired by the French Gothic style. Because of its construction of easily corroded limestone and green sandstone, the edifice is constantly being restored. The massive spires of the two western towers, only added in the mid-19th century, were almost completely replaced in 1955 with a more durable material. Most impressive are the well-preserved stained-glass windows in the high choir (14th century) and south transept (13th century). Most of the pillar sculptures on the aisles of the nave were made in the cathedral workshop in the mid-14th century. The two little sculptures in the niches on opposite sides of the main entrance (inside the cathedral) are called "The Devil" and "The Devil's Grandmother" by the townsfolk. The cathedral is home of a famous boys' choir.

You can also visit the treasures of the cathedral, the **Domschatzmuseum,** Krautermarkt 3 (tel. 0941/5-10-68), which shows goldsmiths' works and splendid textiles from the 11th to the 20th centuries. Entrance is through a portal at the northern nave in the cathedral. It is open April to October, Tues. to Sat. from 10am to 5pm; Sun. from noon to 5pm; closed Mon. During the winter months it is generally open only on Fri. and Sat. from 10am to 4pm; Sun. from noon to 4pm. It's closed in November. The charge is 2 DM ($1.20).

The permanent collection of the **Diözesanmuseum St. Ulrich** is on exhibition in the former Church of St. Ulrich, an early Gothic building to the side of the cathedral, Domplatz 2 (tel. 0941/5-10-68). Sculptures, paintings, and goldsmiths' works form a representative selection of religious art in the diocese from the 11th to the 20th centuries. Of particular interest are various works on loan from the monastic foundations of the diocese. The museum is open April to October, from 10am to 5pm; closed Mon. Admission is 2 DM ($1.20).

Crossing the cathedral garden, you enter the **Cloister,** with its Romanesque All Saints' Chapel and St. Stephen's Church. The ancient frescoes on the walls of the chapel depict liturgical scenes from All Saints' Day. The 11th-century Ottonian church of St. Stephen contains an altar made of a hollowed limestone rock with openings connecting to a martyr's tomb. Although the cathedral is open during the day, you may visit the Cloister and St. Stephen's Church only with the regular guides. Visiting hours are daily from mid-May until the end of September at 10 and 11am and 2pm. From October to March, tours are at 11am. From April to mid-May, tours leave at 11am and 2pm. The charge is 2.50 DM ($1.50).

Among the remnants of the Roman occupation of Regensburg, the ancient **Porta Praetoria,** behind the cathedral, is the most impressive, with its huge stones piled in the form of an arched gateway. Through the grille beside the eastern tower you can see the original level of the Roman street nearly 10 feet below (which is why you often step down into the churches of Regensburg).

Of the four **Museen der Stadt Regensburg,** the most important is **Kunst-und-Kulturgeschichtliche Sammlungen,** Dachauplatz 2-4. This is not only the main museum of the city, but one of the most notable in eastern Bavaria. Its displays show major developments in the history of the region from the earliest days up to the present. You'll see, for example, relics of the Roman period, including a stone tablet marking the establishment of a garrison at Regensburg in the 2nd century. You'll also view a stone altar to the Roman god Mercury, as well as several Christian tombstones. The museum is open from 10am to 4pm; closed Mon. Admission is 2 DM ($1.20).

No town hall in Germany has been preserved better than Regensburg's **Altes Rathaus,** Kohlenmarkt (tel. 0941/507-21-49). The Gothic structure, begun in the 13th century, contains a **Reichssaal** (Imperial Diet Hall), where the Perpetual Diet sat from 1663 to 1806. In the basement of the Town Hall are the dungeons, with the torture chamber preserved in its original setting. The Altes Rathaus is open daily. Guided tours are conducted Mon. to Sat. from 9:30am to 4pm, costing 3 DM ($1.80).

In the environs, the 13th-century **Castle Wolfsegg** lies 9½ miles to the north of Regensburg. This castle retains its original structure, with modifications from later times. Reopened in 1989, a museum inside contains a permanent collection illustrating daily life from the Middle Ages. It is open from May 1 to September 30, from 10am to 4pm; closed Mon. Entrance is 3 DM ($1.80).

Attractions in the Environs

A perfect copy of the Parthenon, **Valhalla** was built in 1842 on orders of Ludwig I. It rises from a hill called Breuberg near the village of Donaustauf, 6 miles down the river from Regensburg. Conceived as a memorial to honor Teutonic art and achievement, it commemorates either in plaques or busts, nearly 200 outstanding Germans in many fields, including science, art, music, politics, and writing. Some one million visitors a year pour through its doors, which are open daily from 9am to 6pm from April to October, and from 10am to noon and 1 to 4pm in the off-season. Admission is 2 DM ($1.20). Some of those honored may not, in the strictest sense, be German at all, including Peter Paul Rubens and Maria Theresa of Austria, but they are honored nevertheless, as are a host of others. The memorial to Franz Joseph Haydn has the misspelling "Heyden," forever chiseled in marble. The Bavarian ministry of culture continues to add names to the hall of fame.

If you head up instead of down the river, you will reach **Befreiungshalle,** some

15 miles from Regensburg. This "Liberation Hall" stands on a mountain overlooking the Danube town of Kelheim. It is open daily from 8am to 6pm from April to September, but only from 9am to noon and 1 to 4pm in winter, charging an admission of 2 DM ($1.20). In summer, ask at the tourist office in Regensburg about the excursion steamer you can take to reach this attraction. You can also drive there. Also ordered by Ludwig I, this monument was finished in 1863, but by then he'd been forced to abdicate. However, this Greco-Roman temple remains as an enduring monument to his tastes. It was consecrated on the 50th anniversary of the Battle of Leipzig (sometimes called "The Battle of Nations," in which Prussia, Russia, and Austria brought a major defeat to Napoleon). The heroes of the battle are honored by plaques imbedded in sculptures of goddesses and Valkyries. Go here more for the scenic value of the attraction and the trip rather than to view a great statement in art and architecture.

---

9. Passau

An episcopal see of Germany, Passau lies close to the Austrian border. A Celtic settlement stood here, and the Romans also established a colony in the area. A bishopric founded here by St. Boniface held extensive power. It included most of the archduchy of Austria, as well as much of Bavaria.

One reason for visiting this *Dreiflüssestadt* (town of three rivers) on the Austrian frontier is to take one of the numerous boat tours along the Danube and its tributaries, the Inn and Ilz rivers, which join the Danube at Passau. The trips range from a one-hour three-river tour to a steamer cruise downriver to Vienna. If you hold a Eurailpass, you can travel free on the **Erste Donau Dampfschiffahrts steamer,** which makes the run between Passau and Vienna (your auto can't be carried). Food and drink are served on board. In Passau, call 0851/33-0-35 for information.

WHERE TO STAY

When it opened in 1988, the **Holiday Inn,** Bahnhofstrasse 24, D-8390 Passau (tel. 0851/59-00-0), immediately became the most stylish—and the best—hotel in Passau. Carefully integrated within the city's largest shopping center, it contains a good restaurant serving both international and regional specialties. Its 132 bedrooms have all the up-to-date amenities. With a buffet breakfast included, singles cost 125 DM ($74.25) to 140 DM ($83.15) daily, with doubles ranging from 165 DM ($98) to 175 DM ($103.90).

Passauer Wolf, Rindermarkt 6, D-8390 Passau (tel. 0851/3-40-46), on the banks of the Danube, is a hotel with an elegantly crafted baroque facade. Inside are 40 modern and comfortable bedrooms with up-to-date plumbing, radios, TVs, phones, and minibars. Singles cost 90 DM ($53.45) to 140 DM ($83.15) daily, while doubles go for 140 DM ($83.15) to 210 DM ($124.70), with breakfast included. Service is friendly. The hotel has one of the most distinguished restaurants in town, and you may want to make it your dining choice even if you're not staying there. Classic dishes and regional specialties range from 35 DM ($20.80) to 65 DM ($38.60). Open 11:30am to 2pm and 6 to 11pm (closed for Sun. dinner).

Hotel König, Untere Douaulände 1, D-8390 Passau (tel. 0851/3-50-28), is a good choice for a stopover in Passau. At the edge of the Danube, it stands behind massive stucco-covered buttresses and a salmon-colored facade accented in summer with flowering windowboxes. The location is between the city's pedestrian shopping zone and the old city at the edge of a spit of land separating the Danube and Inn rivers. Despite its fortresslike facade, it has an interior that is comfortably up-to-date. Each of the 39 well-scrubbed bedrooms has pinewood accents, a TV set, and a private bath. The owners charge 68 DM ($40.40) to 85 DM ($50.45) daily for a single and 120 DM ($71.25) to 150 DM ($89.05) for a double, including breakfast.

Weisser Hase, Ludwigstrasse 23, D-8390 Passau (tel. 0851/3-40-66), has been completely rebuilt. One would never know that it traces its history back to 1512. The only clue would be a pair of antique family portraits hanging over a tufted Victorian sofa in a little salon. The Weisser Hase is in the heart of Passau, off Ludwigsplatz, halfway between the Dom and the railway station. It straddles the peninsula, between the Danube and the Inn rivers. The Weinstube has a Bavarian-Austrian decor, with much woodcarving and provincial chairs. The 117 accommodations are clean and comfortable, with modern furnishings. Bathless singles range in price from 45 DM ($26.70) daily; bathless doubles go for 70 DM ($41.55). Singles with baths or showers cost 90 DM ($53.40) to 100 DM ($59.40), while doubles with private baths or showers are 150 DM ($89.05), breakfast included.

Altstadt-Hotel Laubenwirt, Braugasse 27-29, D-8390 Passau (tel. 0851/3-34-51). The waters of the Danube, the Ilz, and the Inn converge at a point a few steps from the foundations of this 40-room hotel. It's built in two interconnected sections, each of which merges tastefully with the surrounding buildings. Inside, guests find a well-maintained and plushly upholstered environment. Each comfortably furnished bedroom has a private bath, phone, and TV connection. Singles cost 65 DM ($38.60) to 80 DM ($47.50) daily, while doubles go for 120 DM ($71.25) to 140 DM ($83.15). The in-house pub is a popular gathering spot for locals, and the hotel also has two restaurants. Motorists can use the underground garage.

Schloss Ort, Ort 11, Am Dreiflusseck, D-8390 Passau (tel. 0851/3-40-72), is a reconstruction of a 1250 castle, standing right on the banks of the Inn River, rising five stories directly from the water's edge. The most dramatic feature of the 36 bedrooms is their view of where the town's rivers converge. All rooms are modern. Singles with showers (no toilets) cost 55 DM ($32.65) daily, rising to 70 DM ($41.55) for rooms with both showers and toilets. Doubles with showers (no toilets) rent for 85 DM ($50.45), going up to 98 DM ($58.20) to 120 DM ($71.25) for rooms with more elaborate plumbing. Your morning meal is best taken on the open terrace overlooking the Inn River. Riverboat excursions begin at the dock right at the foot of the castle. Closed January and February.

WHERE TO DINE

A little inn born in 1358, **Heilig-Geist-Stift-Schenke,** Heiliggeistgasse 4 (tel. 0851/26-07), is easily found, across from the Weisser Hase, previously recommended. Many good, low-cost regional dishes emerge from its ancient kitchen, including Serbian bean soup, sirloin steak, and grilled pork cutlet. The Passauer Schlosserbaum is definitely worth sampling for dessert. Meals range in price from 25 DM ($14.85) to 50 DM ($29.70), and hours are 11am to 1am; closed Wed. and in January.

THE SIGHTS

The Altstadt is built on a rocky spur of land formed by the confluence of the Inn and Danube, 75 miles downstream from Regensburg. To best appreciate its setting, cross the Danube to the **Veste Oberhaus,** a medieval episcopal fortress towering over the town and the river. Note how many of the houses are joined together by arches, giving them a unity of appearance. As you view the town, you can sense in its architecture that it is more closely allied to northern Italy and the Tyrolean Alps than to its sister cities to the north. Veste Oberhaus houses a museum of regional history going back to Roman times. It is open mid-March to the end of October, Tues. to Sun. from 9am to 5pm, charging an admission of 3 DM ($1.80).

Dominating the scene are the twin towers of the **Dom** (St. Stephen's Cathedral), on the Domplatz. The original Gothic plan of the church is still obvious in spite of its 17th-century reconstruction in grand baroque style. Its most unusual feature is the octagonal dome over the intersection of the nave and transept. The interior of the catheral is mainly Italian baroque—almost gaudy, with its many decorations and paintings. Of particular interest is the east wing, which remains from the Gothic period. The cathedral's newest addition is a huge organ, possibly the largest in the world, built in 1928 and placed in an 18th-century casing. Concerts are given every day at noon in summer.

Below the cathedral, on the bank of the Danube, is the attractive Marktplatz with its **Rathaus.** Dating from the 13th century, Passau's Town Hall has a facade decorated with painted murals depicting the history of the town. Inside, the huge Knights' Hall contains two large 19th-century frescoes illustrating incidents from the German epic, the legend of the Niebelungen.

LOWER SAXONY AND NORTH HESSE

The wide expanse between Frankfurt and Hamburg is probably Germany's most neglected tourist area, and yet it holds some of the most pleasant surprises for sightseeing. Some of the best-preserved medieval timbered towns stand in the flatlands and rolling hills of Lower Saxony and North Hesse, as well as many of the major spas.

Extending from the Netherlands to the East German border, this area includes a wide variety in its landscape, from the busy port of Bremen to the isolation of the Lüneburg Heath. It contains one of Germany's best winter resort areas, the **Harz Mountains.** These mountains and the flatlands around the Weser River nearby gave rise to some of the most familiar legends and fairy tales in Western literature.

THE FAIRY-TALE ROAD
This is the trail of the Brothers Grimm and the Germany made immortal in their fascinating collection, published in the early 19th century, of legends, myths, and fables. Today you can follow the Fairy-Tale Road, a 270-mile journey from Bremen, where the town musicians are memorialized, to the town of Hanau near Frankfurt, where the brothers were born. The route goes through some of the pretti-

est medieval villages in the country, listed on the German Tourist Office's maps of the road and its important sights. At some of the towns along the road, marionette shows (in German, but universal in appeal) are given in summer, and there are museums keeping the legends alive, such as the one in Ziegenhain in the Schwalm Valley, where costumes that might have been worn by Little Red Riding Hood and her grandmother can be seen.

The characters in the stories by the Brothers Grimm come to life along the road —Rapunzel, Snow White and the Seven Dwarfs, the Goose Girl, Sleeping Beauty, Rumpelstiltzkin, and Hansel and Gretel. It was along here that they killed the goose that laid the golden eggs, the two cruel brothers were turned into two black stones, and the Pied Piper played his merry tune that was the lure of rats and children in Hameln. For information on the Fairy-Tale Road, write or call the **German Tourist Office,** 747 Third Ave., New York, NY 10017 (tel. 212/308-30-00).

---

1. Bremen

Whether you arrive at "this ancient town by the gray river" by land, sea, or air, you are instantly aware that Bremen is closely tied to the sea. The sights and smells of coffee, cocoa, tropical fruit, lumber, and tobacco give this port city an international flavor. In the days of the transatlantic ocean crossing, most travelers disembarked at Bremerhaven, Bremen's sister port 40 miles up the Weser River. Many visitors rush immediately off in all directions from the port, ignoring the treasure right under their noses—Bremen, second only to Hamburg among German ports.

Growing from a little fishermen's settlement on a sandy slope on the right bank of the river, Germany's oldest coastal city was already a significant port when it was made an episcopal see in 787. In the 11th century, under the progressive influence of Archbishop Adalbert, Bremen became known as the "Rome of the North." During the Middle Ages it was one of the strongest members of the Hanseatic League and remains one of Europe's most important port cities.

Today, Bremen is not just a city. Together with Bremerhaven, it comprises the smallest of West Germany's 10 federal *Lands,* or states.

GETTING AROUND

A single ticket, good for one ride on Bremen's network of **trams,** costs 2.50 DM ($1.50). Most visitors, however, prefer to invest in a strip of 10 tram tickets, which are sold as a unit to adults for 22 DM ($13.05), to children for 9 DM ($5.35). If you prefer to travel by taxi, the meter begins at 3.60 DM ($2.15).

Sightseeing tours of the city, in both English and German, depart from the central railway station, costing 12 DM ($7.15) for adults and 6 DM ($3.55) for children. From the beginning of May until the end of October, they leave at 10:30am from Mon. to Sun. From November to April, they leave at 10:30am on Sun. Tickets must be obtained at the tourist information kiosk, **Verkehrsverein** (tel. 0421/30-80-00), opposite the central railway station. Open Mon. to Fri. from 8am to 8pm, on Sat. to 6pm, and on Sun. from 9:30am to 3:30pm.

You can also ask the tourist office about trips around the harbor, departing from the Martini Church jetty (a three-minute walk from Marktplatz along Böttcherstrasse), lasting 1¼ hours. From the end of March until the end of October, they leave at 10 and 11:30am, and at 1:30, 3:15, and 4:40pm. The cost is 10 DM ($5.95) for adults, 5.50 DM ($3.25) for children.

WHERE TO STAY

Before we explore the impressive array of sights, let's see what Bremen holds in the way of accommodations.

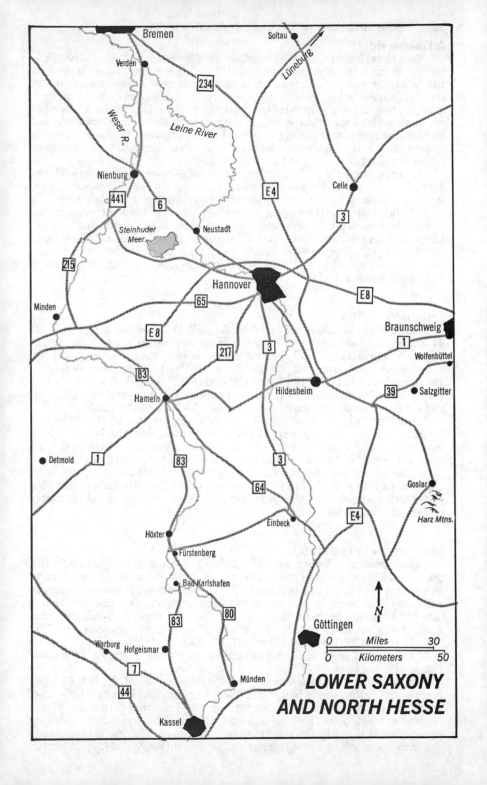

LOWER SAXONY
AND NORTH HESSE

A Deluxe Hotel

Park Hotel Bremen, Im Bürgerpark, D-2800 Bremen (tel. 0421/3-40-80), is without question the most outstanding and charming hotel in Bremen. It occupies an enviable site, a park whose meandering lakes, exotic trees, and zoo are the pride of the city. Despite the hundreds of century-old beeches, oaks, and lindens surrounding it, the hotel is just a short ride from the center of town. Designed in a stately but modernistic Hanseatic style, the Park sits behind a large, symmetrical reflecting pool that has a stream of water arcing into the sky. Its terra-cotta dome and its evenly proportioned side wings were rebuilt in 1955 to emulate a turn-of-the-century pleasure pavilion.

An imposing series of dignified public rooms—many designed around oval floor plans—includes a bar and three restaurants, one of which occupies an elegant terrace overlooking the colonies of ducks and songbirds in or around the lake.

The hotel offers 150 bedrooms, each stylishly decorated with soft pastel colors, summer-inspired furniture, and large-dimensioned windows overlooking the park. Each contains a private bath, radio, color TV, hairdryer, and minibar. Affiliated with the "Leading Hotels of the World" and the Steigenberger reservations network, the hotel charges from 260 DM ($154.40) daily for a single, 380 DM ($225.65) to 450 DM ($267.20) for a double.

Expensive Hotels

Hotel Mercure Columbus, Bahnhofsplatz 5-7, D-2800 Bremen (tel. 0421/1-41-61), sits behind a glistening white facade across from the ornate brickwork of Bremen's railway station. Its 151 rooms offer a well-scrubbed, no-nonsense decor, and come with fully equipped private baths, color TVs, phones, and minibars. Singles range from 170 DM ($100.30) to 180 DM ($106) daily; doubles are 220 DM ($129.80) to 260 DM ($153.40). On the premises are a multilevel car park, a bar, and a good restaurant offering meals for 15 DM ($8.90) to 45 DM ($26.70).

Hotel zur Post, Bahnhofsplatz 11, D-2800 Bremen (tel. 0421/3-05-90), a longtime favorite, offers top-notch facilities and comfort, as well as Bremen's leading restaurant, L'Orchidée. The present structure has had four ancestors, the first built in 1889. The latest renovation has created 211 up-to-date accommodations. Singles with baths or showers cost 150 DM ($89.05) to 190 DM ($112.80) daily, and doubles with baths are 185 DM ($109.85) to 280 DM ($166.25). It's an ideal choice for train passengers, who can refresh themselves after their journey in the hotel's tropical fitness club.

Moderately Priced Hotels

Überseehotel, Wachtstrasse 27, D-2800 Bremen (tel. 0421/3-60-10), doesn't look like a hotel, but it is—and a practical and efficient one at that. It occupies the top four floors of a business building a short block from the city center. Adjoining Böttcherstrasse, it is a satisfactory combination of the new and the old. The 126 bedrooms are both efficient and immaculate, many with sofas as well as desks. All rooms are equipped with baths or shower, toilets, minibars, and cable TVs. The cost is 100 DM ($59.40) to 140 DM ($83.15) daily for a single, 140 DM ($83.15) to 180 DM ($106.90) for a double, all tariffs including a big buffet breakfast, service, and taxes.

Bremer Haus, Löningstrasse 16, D-2800 Bremen (tel. 0421/3-29-40). This hotel is one of a long row of buildings a few blocks from the Hauptbahnhof—all of which are painted white, which accentuates the low relief of the arched and ornamented windows. The hotel is identified by a double staircase welcoming guests from the sidewalk. Once inside, those guests find modern public rooms and a sun terrace overlooking a flowering garden. Singles rent for 98 DM ($58.20) to 105

DM ($62.35) daily, while doubles cost 135 DM ($80.15) to 155 DM ($92.05). All 76 units have baths or showers and toilets, and contain functional chairs, tables, and headboards. Breakfast is included in the rates.

Hotel Munte, Am Stadtwald, D-2800 Bremen (tel. 0421/21-20-63). You'll think you're in the country here, because this brick hotel fronts directly onto one of Bremen's biggest parks, the Bürgerpark (an invigorating walk through the park will eventually lead to the Town Hall). Inside the hotel, you'll find a wood-ceilinged swimming pool with a sauna and massage table, a sympathetic Weinstube (the Fox), a sunny dining room with a panoramic view of the woods, and 123 clean and comfortable bedrooms decorated with woodland colors. Singles rent for 120 DM ($71.25) on the ground floor, 180 DM ($106.90) on the upper floors; and doubles cost 150 DM ($89.05) on the ground floor, 210 DM ($124.70) on the upper floors. All units contain private baths and come with a big breakfast.

A Budget Hotel

Residence, Hohenlohestrasse 42, D-2800 Bremen (tel. 0421/34-10-20). Advertised as a hotel with a Flemish ambience, the Residence has public rooms that are elegantly high-ceilinged, with polished and crisscrossed timbers supporting the chandeliered ceiling of the main salon. You'll find both a sunny breakfast room and a Nordic sauna on the premises. Singles rent for 45 DM ($26.70) to 75 DM ($44.55) daily, doubles for 80 DM ($47.50) to 110 DM ($65.30). Not all of the 40 units contain private baths, however. Herman and Brigitte Straten, your hosts, are fluent in English.

WHERE TO DINE

As a seaport, Bremen has developed its own style of cooking, concentrating much of its effort, naturally, on seafood from Scandinavia and the North Sea.

L'Orchidée (Hotel zur Post), Bahnhofsplatz 11 (tel. 0421/30-59-888). Set on the sixth floor of this previously recommended hotel, it has an elegantly sophisticated gold, cream, and black decor to go with the candles, silverware, and fine porcelain. The chef offers two menus for 70 DM ($41.55) and 95 DM ($56.40). Try the terrine of zander and salmon, halibut with two paprika-based sauces, salmon-cream soup, breast of goose, and a dessert specialty of fruitcake parfait with a red-wine and orange sauce. The wine list is very extensive. Meals cost 70 DM ($41.55) to 90 DM ($53.45). The restaurant is open from 6:30pm to 10pm daily.

Meierei im Bürgerpark, Im Bürgerpark (tel. 0421/340-86-19). Set in the center of a city park, this charming and lovely restaurant is managed by the previously recommended Park Hotel. Many residents of Bremen combine a meal within its elegant walls with a promenade in the park, which has dozens of paths and arched bridges. The restaurant occupies what was originally a local aristocrat's summer house. Sheathed in lacy gingerbread, it is ringed with ornate verandas and contains four dining rooms furnished in a Hanseatic style. Typical menu items include fish consommé with scallops and saffron, fried breast of duck filled with herbs, sautéed squab with a forest mushroom risotto, and medallions of monkfish with orange butter and basil sauce. Meals cost 55 DM ($32.65) to 75 DM ($44.55) or even higher, depending on what you order. Coffee and pastries are served every afternoon, but daily full meal service is only from noon to 2:30pm and 6 to 10pm. Reservations are necessary.

Deutsches Haus-Ratsstuben, Am Markt 1 (tel. 0421/32-90-920), combines pure local color with some of the best food in town. The high-gabled, six-story patrician building sits on the Marketplace (Marktplatz) opposite the Ratskeller. You dine on either of two levels, including the second-floor Ratsstuben. If the time is right, you may catch a festive group singing, especially on Sunday night. The food is excellent, from the mock turtle soup to the creamy desserts. Meat dishes are usually fine. For seafood, try the sole meunière, priced according to weight. Meals range from 35 DM ($20.80) to 60 DM ($35.65). Service is daily from noon to 10pm. This restaurant is highly recommended for cuisine, atmosphere, and location.

Ratskeller, Am Markt, in the 500-year-old Rathaus (tel. 0421/329-09-10), is one of Germany's most celebrated dining halls—and certainly one of the best. The wine list is outstanding, probably the longest list of German vintages in the world. Some of the decorative kegs have actually contained wine for nearly 200 years. It's traditional for friends to gather in the evening over a good bottle of Mosel or Rhine wine. Beer is not served in the Ratskeller. The starred items on the menu are available at night only. You may prefer the Hubertus Topf or the game ragoût with orange and vegetables. If you order dinner à la carte, expect to spend from 35 DM ($20.80) to 60 DM ($35.65). Hours are 10am to midnight daily.

Alte Gilde, Ansgaritorstrasse 24 (tel. 0421/17-17-12), is housed in one of the most ornately decorated houses in Bremen. In spite of the new buildings surrounding it, the 17th-century structure, with its gilt gargoyles and sea serpents, clings tenaciously to the past. The restaurant (entrance on Hutfilterstrasse) is in the vaulted cellar. The chef prepares many fresh fish dishes, or you might try the pork steak à la Kempinski, with poached eggs and béarnaise sauce. It costs 35 DM ($20.80) to 60 DM ($35.65) to dine here à la carte. Set lunches cost 15 DM ($8.90) to 25 DM ($14.85). Hours are 11am to 11pm Mon. to Sat., 11am to 3pm on Sun.

Grashoff's Bistro & Weinbar, Contrescarpe 80, Hillmann-Passage (tel. 0421/ 1-47-40), is an intimate French restaurant serving many delicacies produced from ingredients imported every day from Paris. Two men, Rüdiger Konig and Jürgen Schmidt, are responsible for the good food prepared here. Their favorite dishes include roast beef Italian style, fresh she-crab soup, a gratinée of spinach with mushrooms, filet of turbot in a champagne sauce, and goose à l'orange. The hosts' attention to the wine list is also conscientious, and the walls are covered with shelves containing practically every known variety of liquor or liqueur. À la carte meals range from 65 DM ($38.60) to 88 DM ($52.25), and are served from noon till 6pm. The gentlemen, after all that work, want the evening off. You can sit at the bar, sampling "one of everything," from 10am to 6:30pm (to 2pm on Sat.); closed Sun.

Restaurant Flett, Böttcherstrasse 3 (tel. 0421/32-09-95), basks in the amber tones of the stained-glass windows that serve as this restaurant's room dividers. Clients seat themselves on modified Windsor chairs set on Oriental carpets before beginning full meals costing 35 DM ($20.80) to 60 DM ($35.65). Fresh seafood is a specialty of the house, and you can also order a full array of classic German dishes. Meals are served from noon to 3pm and 6 to 11pm; closed Sun.

Comturei, Ostertorstrasse 31 (tel. 0421/32-50-50). If ever a restaurant in Europe should harbor a resident ghost, this one should. The building itself goes back to the 13th century, when it was a church. Then it was the headquarters of a branch of German knighthood, where new members were initiated; later it was a city mint. The feasts of the knights of yesterday can be repeated, however, in the restaurant of today. Traditional Bremen cuisine—sometimes jazzed up with modern cooking— is offered here, including crab, trout, halibut, and marinated herring, all delectably seasoned and beautifully served. Other dishes include Bratwurst and roast goose. Menus are set at 40 DM ($23.75) and 60 DM ($35.65), and main dishes à la carte begin at 15 DM ($8.90). The restaurant serves from noon to 3pm and 5pm to midnight; closed Sun.

Becks in'n Snoor, Schnoor 35-36 (tel. 0421/32-31-30), stands in one of the oldest sections of the Hanseatic city. You'll be escorted to whichever of three rooms you'll feel most comfortable in. The Unner Deck is the bar area. De Schinken-Deel is the less formal of the two restaurants, specializing in ham and Wurst, along with North Atlantic fish and cold fish salads of all kinds. Finally, De Goode Stuub serves North Germanic specialties in a more elaborate format, tantalizingly prepared.

You'll probably wash everything down with copious quantities of the dark beer produced in Bremen. Fixed-price meals in either restaurant cost 25 DM ($14.85) to 45 DM ($26.70), with an ever-changing list of daily specials, which might include crab and eel along with ham prepared in no fewer than 10 different ways. The restaurant serves daily from 11am to midnight, although the bar (opening at 6pm) serves drinks until 2am.

La Villa, Goetheplatz 4 (tel. 0421/32-79-63), is an attractively contemporary restaurant whose specialty is hearty Italian food. There's a flower-dotted garden terrace, ideal for conjuring up images of Italy in springtime. You can order any of the typical dishes, including pasta, veal, and fish. Interesting dishes include a ragoût of snails and a paper-thin carpaccio with forest-fresh mushrooms. Full meals, ranging from 42 DM ($24.95) to 65 DM ($38.60), are served from noon to 2:30pm and 6pm to midnight. The restaurant is closed Sat. night and all day Sun.

THE SIGHTS

The most practical way to see Bremen is on foot. If you don't like to explore on your own, guides are available for walking tours, as well as motorcoach tours.

The Major Sights

The main sights center around **Marktplatz,** the "parlor" of Bremen life for more than 1,000 years. The 30-foot statue of the city's protector, **Roland,** nephew of Charlemagne, erected in 1404, still stands today, his sword raised toward the cathedral, symbolizing Bremen's declaration of freedom from the Church. Shortly after the statue was put up, Bremen became Germany's first Protestant state. Local legend has it that so long as the statue of Roland stands in the Marketplace, Bremen will survive as a free city. During World War II, when this area was hard hit by Allied bombs, extensive measures were taken with bomb-proof concrete and mountains of sandbags to protect the image.

The **Rathaus** (Town Hall) has stood for some 560 years on Marktplatz and has seen several periods of transformation. The original Gothic foundations remain basically unchanged, but the upper section reflects the 17th-century Weser Renaissance style in the facade; the tall windows alternate with relief statues of Charlemagne and the electors of the Holy Roman Empire. The Upper Hall, part of the original structure, contains a beautifully carved oak staircase dating from the early 17th century and a mural (1537) depicting *The Judgment of Solomon* and typifying the hall's original character as a council chamber and courtroom. In the Lower Hall are oak pillars and beams supporting the building, and below, the historic wine cellar, the previously recommended "good Ratskeller of Bremen." At the west end of the Rathaus is one of the most recent additions, a sculpture of Bremen's visitors from the land of Grimm—the Bremen Town Musicians. The donkey, dog, cat, and cock are stacked, pyramid style, in a constant pose for the ever-present cameras. For tours of the Town Hall, inquire at the information booth at the **New Town Hall** (entrance opposite the cathedral). When there is no session of the city fathers, tours generally depart at 10am, 11am, and noon. Closed Sat. and Sun.

Dom St. Petri (St. Peter's Cathedral) is set back from the square, but towers majestically over all the other buildings in the **Altstadt.** Originally designed in 1043 as the archbishop's church, it was rebuilt in the 16th and 19th centuries. Dating from the early church, however, is the Romanesque west crypt, containing the tomb of Adalbert and an organ on which Bach once played. Another crypt, from the same period, houses a bronze baptismal font, a fine example of 12th-century workmanship. There is a collection of mummies in the chapel in the cathedral cellar. The cellar and tower are open May to October from 9am to noon and 2 to 5pm (closed Sat. afternoon, Sun., and holidays). Admission is 2 DM ($1.20). It costs 1 DM (60¢) to climb the tower.

You can also visit the **Dom Museum,** which is entered through the church. It is open all year, charging an entrance fee of 2 DM ($1.20). Its hours are those of the cellar and tower in summer, but unlike the other two sights, it remains open in winter as well: Mon. to Fri. from 1 to 5pm, on Sat. from 10am to noon, and on Sun. from 2 to 5pm.

Across the square from the Rathaus stands another example of a happy merger of Gothic and Renaissance architecture, the **Schütting,** a 16th-century guildhall used by the Chamber of Commerce. In direct contrast to these ancient masterpieces is the **Haus der Bürgerschaft,** home of Bremen's Parliament, constructed in 1966. The structure was scaled down to fit in with its surroundings. Even though the architecture is a maze of glass, concrete, and steel, it does not look entirely out of place.

Other Sights

Böttcherstrasse, running from Marktplatz to the Weser River, is a brick-paved reproduction of a medieval alley, complete with shops, restaurants, museum, and galleries. The street was the brainchild of a wealthy Bremen merchant, Ludwig Roselius, and designed to present a picture of Bremen life, past and present. Dedicated in 1926 and rebuilt after World War II, the artery is one of Bremen's biggest attractions. Try to visit daily around noon, 3pm, or 6pm, when the Meissen bells strung between two gables set up a chorus of chimes for a full 15 minutes. Besides the fine handcraft and pottery shops, the street also contains buildings of historical significance.

The **Paula-Becker-Modersohn House,** Böttcherstrasse 8, is dedicated to Bremen's most outstanding contemporary painter and contains many of her best works, including several self-portraits and some still lifes. Next door, the **Roselius House,** at no. 6 (tel. 0421/32-19-11), is a 16th-century merchant's house containing Roselius's collection of medieval objets d'art and furniture. The two houses are open Mon. to Thurs. from 10am to 4pm, on Sat. and Sun. from 11am to 4pm. Closed Fri. Admission is 2.50 DM ($1.50).

The **Schnoor,** the old quarter of Bremen, has undergone restoration by the custodian of ancient monuments. The cottages of this east-end district, once the homes of simple fishermen, have been rented to artists and artisans in an effort to revive many old arts and crafts. Sightseers visit not only for the atmosphere but for the unusual restaurants, shops, and art galleries.

The **Rampart Walk** is a green park where the ramparts protecting the Hanseatic city used to stand. The gardens divide the Altstadt from the newer extensions of the city. Extending along the canal (once Bremen's crown-shaped moat), the park is a peaceful promenade just a few short blocks from Marktplatz. Its major attraction is an ancient windmill, still functioning.

---

2. Hannover

Every student of English history is aware of the role that the House of Hannover played in the history of Great Britain. For more than 100 years, until Victoria split the alliance, Britain and Hannover were ruled simultaneously by German monarchs, some of whom preferred to live in their native state (much to the annoyance of the British).

The city of Hannover today has lost much of its political influence, although it is the capital of the province of Lower Saxony. It has instead become one of Germany's hubs of industry, transportation, and commerce. The annual industry trade fair is a magnet. Held the last 10 days in April, the Hannover Fair has grown to be the largest trade fair in the world. Producers and buyers from around the globe meet en masse. Thanks to its central location in West Germany, the city has become a major railway terminus. Its international airport is a convenient shuttle point for flights to Berlin.

The Green Metropolis is a masterpiece of advanced planning, combining parks and tree-lined streets with bold and imaginative solutions to a large city's traffic problems.

ORIENTATION

If you arrive by train, you'll be delivered near the historic core of Hannover. The rail terminus is right at the heartbeat Ernst-August-Platz, a beehive center of life in the city. From here, you can walk down the pedestrians-only Bahnhofstrasse, one of the most modern and sophisticated shopping malls in Germany. It was built on two levels. At the end of the street is the Kröpcke, which has been called "the living room" of Hannover. Running in both directions from this square, Georgstrasse leads to the Staatstheater (actually on the Rathenauplatz) along with many popular cafés and restaurants.

Bahnhofstrasse becomes Karmarschstrasse, which will lead eventually to a major artery, Friedrichswall, which heads west to a major square, Friedenrikenplatz. The Altes Rathaus is north of the street, and the more modern Rathaus south of the street. The new city hall opens onto Maschpark with its lake and museums. The major attraction of Hannover, the Herrenhauser Gärten (more about this later), lies in the northwest part of the city.

WHERE TO STAY

Hannover is a businessperson's city, and the hotel accommodations reflect this in the superabundance of deluxe and first-class hotels, which are big on comfort but short on romantic architecture.

A Deluxe Hotel

Maritim Hotel, Hildesheimerstrasse 34-40, D-3000 Hannover (tel. 0511/1-65-31). One of the city's best hotels was built in an ideal location in 1984: the casino, the old city, and the commercial center are all nearby. An oasis of greenery separates the awnings of the front portico from the street. On the premises is a plant-filled restaurant serving a superb international cuisine, staffed by a polite, uniformed crew of well-trained personnel. The hotel also has a café, a bar, and 293 well-furnished, up-to-date bedrooms, each air-conditioned and containing a private bath, phone, radio, TV, and minibar. Many of the accommodations have narrow private terraces. Singles cost 209 DM ($124.10) to 339 DM ($201.35) daily, while doubles rent for 288 DM ($171) to 478 DM ($283.85), all tariffs including a buffet breakfast. The Maritim is a mile from the city center and has its own sauna, solarium, indoor swimming pool, and health facilities.

Expensive Hotels

Kastens Hotel Luisenhof, Luisenstrasse 2, D-3000 Hannover (tel. 0511/1-24-40). Many frequent travelers to Hannover consider this the leading and most traditional hotel in town. It is part of the Steigenberger reservations network, and its stately glass-and-stone facade is just minutes from the main rail station in the center of the city. Owned by descendants of Heinrich Kasten, who originally established it in 1856, the hotel has benefited from a series of modernizations that have enhanced comfort while maintaining conservative good taste. The English-speaking staff makes overseas visitors welcome. The lobby-level grill room serves food that is superlative by any standard; a few steps away, a cozy modern pub offers drinks and salads. The 160 carefully renovated bedrooms are stylishly furnished, each with a minibar, radio, color TV, private bath, and phone. Depending on the accommodation and its facilities, singles range from 175 DM ($103.90) to 319 DM ($189.45) daily, and twins or doubles cost 208 DM ($123.50) to 498 DM ($295.70), with a buffet breakfast included. There are parking facilities for 120 cars.

Schewizerhof Hannover, Hinüberstrasse 6, D-3000 Hannover (tel. 0511/3-49-50). Built in 1984, this 115-room hotel is one of the most imaginatively designed in the city. It sits on a quiet street in the central business district, behind a red-brick facade whose angular lines were inspired by medieval Hanseatic models. Any parallels to the past, however, are pleasingly updated by the use of such touches as illuminated plexiglass columns, sweeping expanses of russet-colored marble, and color-coordinated accents of gleaming brass and light-grained wood. It serves an affluent and conservative clientele, often attracting visiting celebrities. Rates are 210 DM ($124.70) to 285 DM ($169.25) daily for a single, 285 DM ($169.25) to 345 DM ($204.85) for a double. Clients arriving at the airport can be met with a car if arrangements are made in advance.

On the lobby level, the Schu's Restaurant is one of the most stylish—and one of the best—in the city. It is open daily from noon to 2:30pm and 6pm to midnight. The kitchen prepares such classical and cuisine moderne specialties as lobster salad with green and white asparagus, monkfish medallions with thyme-flavored butter and stuffed zucchini, and calves' kidneys and sweetbreads in a red-currant sauce. Fixed-priced and à la carte meals range from 82 DM ($48.70) to 110 DM ($65.30). Reservations are important.

Congress Hotel am Stadtpark, Clausewitzstrasse 6, D-3000 Hannover (tel. 0511/2-80-50), stands next to the Rathaus, near the main railway station. This upper-bracket hotel contains 252 rooms and suites, along with an array of facilities that includes hairdressers, an indoor pool, a sauna, massage facilities, and a bicycle-rental center. Completely modern, the hotel is made up of three wings arranged at equal distances around a central core that rises high into the Hannoverian skies. Singles rent for 136 DM ($80.75) to 288 DM ($171) daily, while doubles cost 238 DM ($141.30) to 248 DM ($147.25), including a buffet breakfast. The Bristol Grill is one of the best places to eat in Hannover, charging 35 DM ($20.80) to 85 DM ($50.45) for a meal.

Queens Hotel am Tiergarten, Tiergartenstrasse 117, D-3000 Hannover (tel. 0511/51-03-0), in the suburb of Kirchrode, is an excellent choice, about 4 miles from the town center. The 108 modern rooms, renovated in 1988, are decorated in pastel colors and contain private baths or showers, minibars, color TVs, trouser presses, radios, direct-dial phones, and tea/coffee makers. A double room rents for 252 DM ($149.65) to 330 DM ($195.95) daily and a single for 200 DM ($118.75) to 235 DM ($139.55). Weekend arrangements are often cheaper if you inquire. The hotel, set in a 240-acre deer park where guests can relax, is easily reached from the Hannover-Anderten exit of the Hamburg–Kassel motorway, just a mile away.

Grand Hotel Mussmann, Ernst-August-Platz 7, D-3000 Hannover (tel. 0511/32-79-71), stands right in the heart of Hannover, opposite the air terminal and the railroad station. A pleasant, top-rate establishment, it offers 100 comfortable and soundproof rooms, all with phones, TVs, radios, hairdryers, and large bathrooms, some with windows. Singles cost 148 DM ($87.90) to 358 DM ($212.60) daily, and doubles go for 188 DM ($111.65) to 398 DM ($236.35). All tariffs include a buffet breakfast. Everything about this place is efficient, modern, and well run.

Moderately Priced and Budget Hotels

Hotel am Leineschloss, Am Markte 12, D-3000 Hannover (tel. 0511/32-71-45), across from the Rathaus, is a surprise discovery—one of the best values in Hannover. It's the preferred hotel for those who want to be in the heart of the old section, yet it's quiet despite its central location. The 81 generously sized rooms, with their bright colors, are housed in an advanced-design structure. Most units have sitting areas big enough for a leisurely breakfast. Every room has either a bath or shower as well as toilet. Singles with showers rent for 55 DM ($32.65) to 250 DM

($148.45) daily and doubles with baths for 210 DM ($124.70) to 305 DM ($181.10). The good comfort and individual service may make you want to prolong your stay. There is a garage, or you can park in the space in front of the hotel. The only meal served is a buffet breakfast, included in the rates.

Thüringer Hof, Osterstrasse 37, D-3000 Hannover (tel. 0511/32-64-37), lies just a few blocks from the railway station. It presents a somewhat grim facade of white brick and unadorned windows to passersby. However, all those windows open into 55 sunny bedrooms, all of which have private baths, wallpaper, patterned rugs, and reproductions of 19th-century furniture. The lobby area boasts a magnificent red Oriental rug, which is reflected in the polished paneling on the walls. Singles rent for 85 DM ($50.45) to 190 DM ($112.80) daily, while doubles cost 150 DM ($89.05) to 200 DM ($118.75), with breakfast included.

Hotel Königshof, Königstrasse 12, D-3000 Hannover (tel. 0511/31-20-71). Both the skylights and the modernized crenellations on this hotel's mansard-style roof make it look like an updated version of a feudal fortress. The 84-room hotel was built in 1984 above a glass-and-steel shopping arcade in the center of town. Upstairs, each of the plushly carpeted accommodations has an eye-stopping white- and turquoise-colored tile bath. The couch in each of the rooms converts to a bed, permitting visitors under 16 to pay half price when accompanied by their parents. The owners have installed a pair of bars on the premises. They charge 145 DM ($86.10) to 290 DM ($172.20) daily for a single and 180 DM ($106.90) to 380 DM ($225.65) for a double, with breakfast included. An Italian and Austrian-Heurigen restaurant, under separate management, is on the premises.

Loccumer Hof, Kurt-Schumacher-Strasse 16, D-3000 Hannover (tel. 0511/32-60-51), a short walk from the station, is one of the best economy finds in the city. The rates are reasonable, considering the general comfort and amenities offered. The 70 utilitarian rooms are small, service and frills minimal, but the hotel makes a good stopover. With private bath, phone, TV, and minibar, a single costs 105 DM ($62.35) daily, and a double goes for 140 DM ($83.15) to 160 DM ($95). Prices include service, taxes, and buffet breakfast. The standard fare in the hotel's dining room is quite good. Prices are raised during the Hannover fairs.

Am Rathaus, Friedrichswall 21, D-3000 Hannover (tel. 0511/32-62-68), is a hotel directly facing the Rathaus. It offers a good choice of small, comfortable rooms, well furnished with oak pieces. The 47-room hotel is immaculately kept as well. The reception is tiny, but the welcome is big. An elevator takes you to one of the guest bedrooms, all of which have private baths or showers. The price for a single runs from 110 DM ($65.30) to 220 DM ($130.65) daily, a double costing 160 DM ($95) to 300 DM ($178.15).

Hotel am Funkturm, Hallerstrasse 34, D-3000 Hannover (tel. 0511/31-70-33), is a 45-room hotel in the city center—and one of the best accommodations for value in Hannover, if you can get in. The bedrooms, with private marble-floored baths, have antiques scattered throughout. Singles rent for 88 DM ($52.25) to 198 DM ($117.55) daily and doubles for 158 DM ($93.80) to 296 DM ($175.75), with breakfast included. An Italian restaurant, Milano, is under separate management.

A Country Retreat Within the City

Georgenhof Stern's Restaurant, Herrenhäuser Kirchweg 20, D-3000 Hannover (tel. 0511/70-22-44), is a country inn within a private park near the Herrenhausen Gardens. The 13-room hotel is the quietest, most secluded retreat in Hannover. Singles range from 105 DM ($62.35) to 220 DM ($130.65) daily, depending on the plumbing, and doubles cost 180 DM ($106.90) to 290 DM ($172.20). The accommodations are clean and pleasant, furnished with a mixture of antiques and traditional furniture, often hand-painted pieces. The restaurant is among the finest in Hannover, and you may want to call for a table reservation even if you're not staying there. All selections are à la carte and rather expensive, but well worth the price. A selection of international dishes is featured, including Valencian paella. Seafood and fresh fish, prepared in the cuisine moderne style, will tempt the diner, as will the game dishes. A dinner costs 75 DM ($44.55) to 110 DM ($65.30). Hours are noon to 3pm and 6 to 11pm daily. In summer, tables are set out on the terrace, overlooking a restful garden and pond. The Georgenhof is highly recommended for both food and lodging.

WHERE TO DINE

Besides the fine food served in many hotel dining rooms and restaurants, such as the Kastens and the Georgenhof, Hannover offers a wide variety of cuisine. You can find anything from a hamburger to chop suey to cuisine moderne.

Witten's Hop, Gernsstrasse 4 (tel. 0511/64-88-44), on the outskirts at Hannover 51-Bothfeld. Three hundred years ago this served as a prosperous farmer's home, as evidenced today by the hand-hewn ceiling timbers and the glowing patina of the antiques in this upper-level restaurant. Specialties are pâté of calves' sweetbreads, goose liver, and black truffles, fresh salads with poultry of Lower Saxony or seafood, cassolette of lobster, and dorade royale. The owner, Andreas Lüssenhop, is an unabashed Francophile (he spent a lot of time in Alsace) when it comes to cuisine. Meals cost 78 DM ($46.30) to 110 DM ($65.30). The wine list contains about 450 great and famous wines from the best vineyards of France, Italy, Spain, and Germany. The place is filled with classical music, masses of flowers, and candlelight. The restaurant is open Mon. to Sat. from 6pm till "closing." Open Sun. and holidays for lunch from noon to 2pm, reopening for dinner at 7pm.

Wichmann, Hildesheimerstrasse 230, at Hannover 81-Döhren (tel. 0511/83-16-71), on the eastern edge of Hannover. A family-owned establishment, this white-walled, shuttered inn, with slate walks and carefully tended flowerbeds, is an oasis of comfort. Guests have a choice of five rooms in which to dine. Cooking is gutbürgerlich—wholesome, hearty—one of the best samplings of such specialties as fish terrine, rack of lamb, homemade noodles, and an array of wines and cheeses from all over Germany. A full meal here averages 58 DM ($34.45) to 90 DM ($53.45). The place is open Tues. to Sat. from noon to 3pm and 6pm to midnight; closed holidays.

Steuerndieb, Steuerndieb 1 (tel. 0511/69-50-99), is a rustic restaurant on the edge of a public forest to the east of Hannover, serving excellent food. Many of the specialties are cooked over an open fire, and some of the chef's dishes enjoy quite a reputation. The house specialties are roasts of lamb, beef, pork, rabbit, and venison in orange or green-pepper sauce, plus selected fresh vegetables, fruits, and salads with special dressings. A set lunch is offered for 25 DM ($14.85), whereas à la carte dinners range from 40 DM ($23.75) to 65 DM ($38.60). The restaurant serves Mon. to Sat. from 11am to 11pm; Sun. to 6pm.

Hindenburg Klassik, Gneisenaustrasse 55 (tel. 0511/85-85-88). The decor of this restaurant runs a fine line between the classic and the modern. The Oriental rugs are intricate and well chosen, and the walls look like some extension of an art gallery. The wooden chairs are elegantly upholstered in white. The owners call their menu modern Italian, and this means impeccably fresh ingredients (fish from all the European seas is a specialty), served with unusual variations. Whoever created the dessert menu, I suspect, must have foraged through the tropics to discover the unusual fruits that the chef uses so lavishly. Meals cost 35 DM ($20.80) to 70 DM ($41.55) but could range far higher, of course. There's a good choice of wines from the best Italian vineyards. The restaurant is open from noon to 3pm and 6pm to 2am, although the kitchen closes at 11:30pm; closed Sun., and for three weeks in summer, for two weeks around Christmas. Always call ahead for a reservation.

Mövenpick Café Kröpcke–Baron de la Mouette, Georgstrasse 35 (tel. 0511/32-62-85), offers some delectable Swiss specialties. I recently enjoyed Zürcher Geschnetzeltes with Rösti (sliced veal in white-wine crème sauce with Swiss Rösti potatoes). Desserts are so elaborate you'll think you're in Vienna. It's cheaper to dine in the café, where a meal begins at 28 DM ($16.65). In the Baron, expect to spend from 42 DM ($24.95) to 63 DM ($38.60). Open daily from 8am to midnight.

Bakkarat im Casino am Maschsee, Arthur-Menge-Ufer 3 (tel. 0511/80-10-20). This elegant second-floor restaurant sits at the end of the squared-off lines of the Maschsee, with direct access to the fashionable casino of Hannover. The decor is restrained and the service excellent. You'll find that the fish selections include the freshest available at the market that day, including Norwegian salmon and trout. Set menus range from 55 DM ($32.65) to 65 DM ($38.60), with à la carte meals costing 40 DM ($23.75) to 75 DM ($44.55). You can always have a drink here, but warm food is served daily from noon to 2:30pm and 6pm to midnight.

Clichy, Weissekreuzstrasse 31 (tel. 0511/31-24-47). If you befriend a native of Hannover, he or she might confide one of the city's better-kept secrets: the address of this elegantly decorated restaurant a few blocks northeast of the Hauptbahnhof. You'll see lots of gold and cream, with an appealing combination of art nouveau and art deco (unfortunately, none of the sculpture is for sale). The cuisine is a sophisticated cuisine moderne. Meals, ranging in price from 55 DM ($32.65) to 124 DM ($73.65)—the latter the price of "the great menu"—could include a pâté of goose liver in port, a fricassée of shellfish in a champagne sauce, Barbary goose in cognac, and seawolf in a Pernod sabayon. Owner and chef Ekkehard Reimann opens his establishment from noon to 3pm and 6:30pm to midnight; closed for lunch Sat.

Alte Mühle, Hermann-Löns-Park 3, Hannover 71-Kleefeld (tel. 0511/55-94-80). This half-timbered building on the outskirts of the city has gained many additions since its construction as a mill back in the 16th century. It sits today in a manicured park; greatly modernized, it's like the clubhouse of an elegant country club. Wild game is a specialty in season, and a number of regional specialties are prepared with flair and beautifully served. A set lunch goes for 28 DM ($16.65), with à la carte dinners ranging from 50 DM ($29.70) to 75 DM ($44.55). The Alte Mühle is open from 10am to 11pm; closed Thurs.

Altdeutsche Bierstube, Lärchenstrasse 4 (tel. 0511/34-49-21), is pleasantly decorated and old-fashioned, a Bierstube with many of the original elements left over from generations ago. The unpretentious food is hearty, wholesome, and filling, with the regular fare augmented by seasonal specialties. The place is open from midmorning until midnight for drinks, and hot food is served from 11:30am to 2:30pm and 5pm to 11pm; closed Sun. and holidays. Meals range from 35 DM ($20.80) to 55 DM ($32.65).

Ratskeller, in the historic Altes Rathaus, Schmiedestrasse 1 (tel. 0511/1-53-63), as in most German cities, is one of the most popular dining spots for townspeople and visitors alike. Patrons dine in two rooms at tables set under vaulted brick arches. The lunches are among the best bargains in town. From noon to 3pm, a complete luncheon, including soup, main course, and dessert, ranges from 25 DM ($14.85) to 65 DM ($38.60). Service is from noon to midnight; closed Sun.

THE SIGHTS

No matter where you go in Hannover, you will not be far from a park or garden. But if you have time to explore only one of these, it might be the **Herrenhäuser Gärten** (Royal Gardens of Herrenhausen), Herrenhäuser Strasse 4, the only surviving example of Dutch/Low German early baroque-style gardening. Designers from France, the Netherlands, England, and Italy, as well as Germany, worked together to create this masterpiece of living art. The **Grosse Garten,** from 1666, is the largest, consisting of a rectangle surrounded by a moat. Within the maze of walks and trees are examples of French baroque, rococo, and Low German rose and flower gardens. The Grosse Garten also contains the highest fountain in Europe, shooting jets of water 270 feet into the air, and the world's only existing baroque hedge-theater (1692), where Shakespeare, Molière, and Brecht are still performed today, along with ballets and jazz concerts. The smaller 17th-century **Berggarten,** across the Herrenhäuser Strasse from the Grosse Garten, is a botanical garden with several houses containing rare orchids and other tropical flowers. The gardens are open daily from 8am to 8pm in summer, to 4:30pm in winter. The Grosse Garten is illuminated on Wed., Fri., Sat., and Sun. after dusk from May to the end of September. The ornamental fountains play from May to September, Mon. to Fri. from 11am to noon and 3 to 5pm; Sat., Sun., and holidays from 10am to noon and 3 to 6pm. Admission to the gardens is free except during illuminations and other events in the Grosse Garten.

Information about the gardens and other attractions is available at the **Verkehrsbüro Hannover,** Ernst-August-Platz 8 (tel. 0511/1-68-23-19).

The **Market Church,** on the Market Square, is one of Hannover's oldest structures, built in the mid-14th century. Its Gothic brick basilica houses several religious works, including a 15th-century carved altarpiece and a bronze baptismal font. The **Altes Rathaus,** facing the square, is from 1425. Badly damaged during the war, it has been restored and houses a museum and the civic archives.

The "new" **Rathaus** is a large structure built between 1901 and 1913 on 6,026 beech piles. The building is attractive because of its location in the Maschpark, reflected in a small lake, just a short distance from the extensive man-made Maschsee, frequented by Hannoverians for its beach, boating, and restaurants. It supports the only inclined elevator in Europe other than the one at the Eiffel Tower, which takes visitors up to the 330-foot-high dome. In the dome hall, four different models depict Hannover's history from 1689 to today. The elevator makes the trip up hourly from 10am to 1:30pm and 5pm daily, April to October, costing 2 DM ($1.20) for adults, 1 DM (60¢) for children. Sat., Sun., and bank holidays, the Rathaus opens at 10am.

Kestner-Museum, Trammplatz 3 (tel. 0511/168-27-30), next to the City Hall, contains treasures representing 6,000 years of history. Its four departments (Egyptian Art, Greek and Roman Art, Decorative Art, and Numismatics) show objects of the finest quality. The museum is open Tues., Thurs., and Fri., from 10am to 4pm; Wed. from 10am to 8pm; and Sat. and Sun. from 10am to 6pm. Admission is free.

The **Niedersächsisches Landesmuseum** (Lower Saxony State Museum), Am Maschpark 5 (tel. 0511/88-30-51), is one of the most important regional museums in Germany, its valuable collections dating back for centuries. Lying near the Maschpark, it offers four exhibit areas, including a department of ethnology, another devoted to biology, one centering on prehistoric times, and finally, a gallery of painting and sculpture. Housed in a Neo-Renaissance–style building, the museum opened in 1902 and has been enthralling visitors since then. An aquarium was added in 1984. You can wander in a world of exotic fish, amphibians, and reptiles. The prehistoric collection displays objects that date back 200,000 years, and contains a rich assortment of bronze vessels, stone utensils, jewelry, coins, and earthenware.

The gallery of art is exceptional, a treasure house that spans seven centuries. Included in the exhibits are celebrated winged altarpieces, including the *Passion Altar* dating from 1390–1400 (the work of Meister Bertram von Minden). You'll see paintings by Rembrandt, Van Dyck, Rubens (see his *Madonna*), and such works as the *Four Times of Day* series by Caspar David Friedrich. Many German and Italian primitives, along with 17th-century Dutch paintings, are on display. The museum is particularly rich in 19th-century German Impressionist paintings. It is open Tues. to Sun. from 10am to 5pm; Thurs. from 10am to 7pm. Admission is free.

An Excursion from Hannover

The beer capital of medieval Germany, Einbeck, where bock beer was born, is about 40 miles south of Hannover. The leading bock beer producer, and the only brewery in Einbeck, is the **Einbecker Brauhaus AG,** Papenstrasse 4-7 (tel. 05561/79-70). In the 14th century, more than 600 private homes brewed a heavy bock in Einbeck. After most of the houses were destroyed by fire in the mid-17th century, the brewing was taken over by a central brewery, which in turn burned. Two firms took over, and in 1920 the two merged and became the Einbecker Brauhaus of today. A tour of the brewery includes a slide show tracing the history of bock beer (in German) and the process that is required for the brewing, as well as a chance to sample the product. On the day you are there, you may be given pilsener rather than bock beer to taste, but three bocks are made, so the chance that you'll taste one of them is good. The tours are given Mon. to Fri. at 2:30pm, and you should reserve in advance at the address given above.

Free tours of the town of Einbeck in English are available on Thurs. afternoon from July to September. You can see the architecture that grew up around the beer business of the Middle Ages. For information, get in touch with the **Foreign Tourist Office,** Postfach 126 (tel. 05561/31-61-21).

---

3. Celle

The well-preserved town of Celle stands at the edge of a silent expanse of moorland, looking like something out of a picture book. Its ancient half-timbered houses were spared in the air raids of the war, and the legends carved on their beams seem to live on today. Most of the houses date from the 16th and 17th centuries—the oldest was built in 1526—but they are in such good condition that they could have been built in this century.

One of the landmarks of the town is the **Palace of the Dukes of Brunswick and Lüneburg,** a square Renaissance castle with towers at each corner. The palace's bizarre 16th-century Renaissance chapel was designed by Martin de Vos, with galleries and elaborate ornamentation. But the pride of the castle, and of the town, is its **baroque theater,** the oldest in Germany (1674) and still in regular use today. The Ducal Palace is open for guided tours only, at 10 and 11am, noon, and 2, 3, and 4pm; closed Sat. afternoon. Admission is 2 DM ($1.20).

For a picture of life as lived from the 16th to the 20th centuries in Celle, visit the **Bomann Museum,** Schlossplatz 7 (tel. 0541/12-372), one of Germany's finest regional museums, with extensive exhibits illustrating the life in the country and in the town. Included is a complete 16th-century farmhouse, as well as rooms from old cottages, period costumes, and Hannoverian uniforms from 1803 to 1866. In the portrait gallery of Brunswick-Lüneburg dukes, you can see pictures of the electors, later kings of England and Hannover. From April to October, it is open daily from 10am to 5pm. From November to March, it is open Mon. to Sat. from 10am to 5pm; Sun. and holidays from 10am to 1pm. Admission is 1 DM (60¢).

WHERE TO STAY

If you're stopping over, either for lodgings or meals, you might consider one of the following.

Expensive Hotels

Fürstenhof Celle–Restaurant Endtenfang, Hannoverschestrasse 55, D-3100 Celle (tel. 05141/20-10), far superior to any other accommodation, is surprisingly sophisticated for such a provincial town. Standing at the edge of Celle, it is a small-scale 17th-century manor house flanked with timbered wings that contain beauty parlors, shops, and a Bierstube. The brick courtyard in front of the salmon-colored mansion is shaded by a towering chestnut tree. The hotel's interior has formal neoclassical paneling and a collection of antiques. A modern annex beyond the rear courtyard contrasts with the main building in its use of refreshing colors in the rooms and apartments. On the lower level is a tile swimming pool. All 75 rooms have toilet facilities, and depending on whether you prefer bath or shower, the price of a single room ranges from 110 DM ($65.30) to 200 DM ($118.75) daily. Doubles go from 185 DM ($109.85) to 380 DM ($225.65), which includes breakfast, use of the hotel's indoor swimming pool, service, and taxes. All the doubles have been refurnished, and further amenities include color TV sets and minibars. The hotel also has a sauna and massage rooms for guests.

Fürstenhof's restaurant, Endtenfang, warmly formal, is considered one of the best in Lower Saxony. An elegant dining room decorated with painted tapestries, it is known for its ducal duck, after an old recipe from the court of Celle. The barroom is in the ancient vaults of the mansion. Fine food and wine are the order of the day, with meals costing 70 DM ($41.55) to 105 DM ($62.35). The beer tavern, Kutscherstube, built into the old coach house, is more informal, with its old wooden tables and farm artifacts. Here, meals range from 35 DM ($20.80) to 60 DM ($35.65).

Moderately Priced Hotels

Hotel Cellar Hof, Stechbahn 11, D-3100 Celle (tel. 05141/2-80-61), is on the street where tournaments were once held. Considering the old-world architecture of the hotel and its neighboring timbered houses, the interior furnishings are incongruously modern, but quite pleasing. The Celler Hof's advertisement of *"internationaler Komfort"* holds true for all the 60 guest rooms. With bath or shower, the price for a single is 89 DM ($52.85) to 148 DM ($87.90) daily; for a double, 138 DM ($81.95) to 189 DM ($112.25).

Borchers, Schuhstrasse 52, D-3100 Celle (tel. 05141/70-61), a half-timbered family-run establishment, lies about 90 yards from the Rathaus. Guests here benefit from the gravel-slabbed sun terrace, and from 19 big-windowed, tastefully furnished bedrooms that cost 95 DM ($56.40) to 145 DM ($86.10) daily for a single and 130 DM ($77.20) to 195 DM ($115.80) for a double, including breakfast.

Hotel Schifferkrug, Speicherstrasse 9, D-3100 Celle (tel. 05141/70-15). The brick and timber walls of this comfortable hotel have witnessed more than three centuries of innkeeping tradition. The very clean bedrooms have lace curtains and eiderdowns. There are only about a dozen rooms, most of which are doubles. The few singles rent for 70 DM ($41.55) to 80 DM ($47.50) daily, while doubles range from 100 DM ($59.40) to 150 DM ($89.05), including a buffet breakfast. The doubles contain phones, TVs, and radios. There's a bar on the premises, along with a rustic Weinstube and a more formal restaurant with a conservative but tasty German menu.

WHERE TO DINE

I always enjoy taking a meal at the **Historischer Ratskeller,** Markt 14 (tel. 05141/2-90-99), a plusher version of the typical German town hall dining room. The food, as well, is superior to the usual Ratskeller fare. The attentive waiters are constantly passing by, carrying silver platters heaped with spicy, flavorful dishes. Complete lunches, including soup and dessert, are priced from 36 DM ($21.40). At night, the à la carte menu is varied, with meals costing as much as 38 DM ($22.55) to 68 DM ($40.40). Hours are 10am to midnight; closed Tues.

Städische Union Celle, Thaerplatz 1 (tel. 05141/60-96). The view from the terrace of this attractively art nouveau restaurant encompasses the walls of the town castle. The cuisine is imaginatively contrived from fresh ingredients to create frequently changing daily seasonal specialties. Your meal might include a terrine of trout, a three-fish platter of local grilled delicacies swimming in an aromatic dill-flavored sauce, and a delectably tempting dessert awash in pungently textured flavors. Fixed-price menus range from 35 DM ($20.80) to 60 DM ($35.65), and are served from noon to 11pm; closed Mon.

Hotel Celler Tor, Cellerstrasse 13, D-3100 Celle–Gross Hehien (tel. 05141/5-10-11), is about 2 miles outside of town. You'd never guess that this hotel with a gabled red-tile roof and banks of geraniums is a secret haven for a Brazilian and Javanese restaurant—but that's exactly what it is. You can get some good shrimp and rice dishes here. Chef Horst Niebuhr also knows how to prepare gutbürgerlich specialties, including wild game in season, perhaps a ragoût of stag with mushrooms. Fixed-price menus begin at a reasonable 32 DM ($19), going up to 60 DM ($35.65). Service is from 6am to 1am; closed Sun. for dinner. Celler Tor has 64 of the most desirable and comfortable bedrooms in the area, costing 89 DM ($52.85) to 149 DM ($88.50) daily for a single and 154 DM ($91.45) to 235 DM ($139.55) for a double. A new section of the hotel contains a saltwater indoor pool, massage facilities, a sauna, a solarium, and a workout room.

---

4. Lüneburg and the Heath

Motorists driving south from Scandinavia through the Baltic port of Lübeck often find themselves on the Old Salt Road leading to the Hanseatic city of Lüneburg. The road was so named because it was the route by which the heavy salt deposits of Lüneburg were delivered to the countries of Scandinavia during the Middle Ages. Most of the buildings of the Salt City are from its most prosperous period, the 15th and 16th centuries. Although the medieval brick buildings are the most prevalent, seven centuries of architecture are represented in this 1,000-year-old city. The rising gables of the once-patrician houses range from Gothic to Renaissance to baroque.

The **Rathaus,** reached along Auf der Meere, is a perfect example of several trends in architecture and design. You'll enter through a Gothic doorway into a Renaissance hall. The Great Council Room is its most outstanding feature, with sculptures and bas-reliefs by Albert von Soest (1566–84). From the painted beamed ceiling in the Fürstensaal, chandeliers made of antlers hang down. From May to October, guided tours are conducted at 10am, 11am, noon, 2pm, and 3pm from Tues. to Fri.; 10am, 11am, 2pm, and 3pm on Sat. and Sun. In winter, there are tours also from Tues. to Sun. No tours are conducted on Mon. The cost is 5 DM ($2.95). For information, phone 04131/30-92-30.

Because of its heavy salt deposits, Lüneburg remains a spa even today. In the **Kurpark** is a bathing house where visitors take brine mud baths. In the spa gardens there are also indoor swimming pools, sauna baths, and tennis courts.

Lüneburg is the ideal starting point for excursions into the **Lüneburg Heath.** The soil of the heath is sandy and is mainly covered with brush and heather, although there are a few oak and beech forests in the northern valleys. The heath covers nearly 300 square miles and includes many beauty spots for the outdoors person. The **Wilsede National Park** is a 100-square-mile sanctuary for plants and wildlife, and for people as well. Strict laws enforce the maintaining of the thatched houses and rural atmosphere. The heath is beautiful in late summer and early autumn, when the heather turns shades of deep purple. The pastoral scene of shepherds, sheep, and undulating hills is peaceful.

WHERE TO STAY

You may wish to spend the night in Lüneburg or at least have a meal before continuing to Hamburg, Hannover, or some other destination.

Moderately Priced and Budget Hotels

Residenz, Münstermannskamp 8, D-2120 Lüneburg (tel. 04131/4-50-47). The buff-and-brown units of this tasteful 35-room hotel are so separated from one another that the place will remind you of an apartment building. Since the establishment is right inside the city's Kurpark, you'll get enough shade to pretend you're in a forest. Inside, you'll find an inviting bar and an up-to-date restaurant, serving both international and regional specialties. Rooms are elegant and comfortable, and have tile baths with lots of mirrors. Everything is designed to make for a good stay. Singles rent for 95 DM ($56.40) to 105 DM ($62.35) daily, while doubles cost from 150 DM ($89.05). Breakfast is included.

Wellenkamp's Hotel, Am Sande 9, D-2120 Lüneburg (tel. 04131/4-30-26). A building so unusual could only have been designed for public use, and in fact, this 45-room hotel used to be a post office. The reddish brick exterior is in a style that could be described as 19th-century neofortification. One of the public rooms is entirely furnished in vintage Biedermeier. Bedrooms are usually sunny, modern, and comfortable. Singles with modern plumbing go for 52 DM ($30.90) to 90 DM ($53.45) daily, doubles for 90 DM ($53.45) to 150 DM ($89.05). Today the bins in the cellar that once held coal contain some of the finest wines in the region, attracting locals from far and wide. The restaurant also offers a delectable cuisine, meals beginning at 42 DM ($24.95).

Bremer Hof, Lünerstrasse 13, D-2120 Lüneburg (tel. 04131/3-60-77). The logo of this hotel is an illustration of the animals of Bremen, who, with their noise, frightened away the robbers. The facade of this family-run hotel looks like something straight out of the 16th century. You'll be only two minutes on foot from Marktplatz, and your room will be modern, up-to-date, and sunny. Charges are 43 DM ($25.55) to 110 DM ($65.30) daily for a single, 68 DM ($40.40) to 170 DM ($100.95) for a double. Host Albert Brakel's family has owned this place since 1889.

WHERE TO DINE

A good choice for lunch, dinner, or in between is the **Ratskeller,** Marktplatz 1 (tel. 04131/3-17-57). Right on the Marktplatz, the town's dining hall offers a varied menu, including game and regional specialties served according to the season. You can always count on good homestyle cooking in a pleasant setting, backed up by a fine wine list. The cheapest meal costs about 28 DM ($16.65), but your tab might climb to 60 DM ($35.65) if you order some of the specialties. The cellar is open from 11am to 11pm; closed Wed.

5. Braunschweig (Brunswick)

Between the Harz Mountains and Lüneburg Heath, Braunschweig (Brunswick in English) is the second-largest town in Lower Saxony. Henry the Lion fortified and improved the town, making it his residence. Brunswick was one of the chief cities of the Hanseatic League.

Up until 1918 the city was a German duchy. Brunswick was virtually destroyed in World War II, but it has been rebuilt. The "isles of tradition"—that is, the castle square and the old town market—were restored authentically.

Brunswick is a main stopover on the Hannover–Berlin route. Motorists nearing the East German border in the late afternoon or early evening might want to stop at Brunswick to spend the night before crossing over.

WHERE TO STAY

Expensive Hotels

Ritter St. George, Alte Knochenhauerstrasse 13, D-3300 Braunschweig (tel. 0531/1-30-39). The elaborately half-timbered medieval building that contains this hotel and restaurant was built in the 14th century—some of the original oaken beams are still in place. For many years, it was a brewery and later a guesthouse. It was transformed into the elegant restaurant-hotel you see today—the best in town —in 1985.

The hotel contains 22 bedrooms, some accented with antiques, others more modern and streamlined. Regardless of style, each has a private bath, radio, phone, minibar, and TV. Singles cost 105 DM ($62.35) to 175 DM ($103.90) daily; doubles, 155 DM ($92.05) to 260 DM ($154.40).

The restaurant is a long, narrow room with a very high ceiling, elaborate painted baroque designs, and a suit of polished ceremonial armor overseeing the elaborate table settings. Try essence of lamb with herbs or roast goose with gratinéed kohlrabi and potatoes, and for dessert, cranberry parfait with enriched cream. Vegetarian specialties are also available, including stuffed peppers with saffron-flavored risotto. Meals cost 50 DM ($29.70) to 90 DM ($53.45). This very elegant restaurant is not to be confused with the less formal Restaurant Altes Haus, under the same management, in a second very old house next door to the hotel.

Mercure Atrium, Berliner Platz 3, D-3300 Braunschweig (tel. 0531/7-00-80). A pedestrian bridge over the road separates the hotel from the Hauptbahnhof. The atrium in the center (hence the name) shelters a three-tiered lit fountain, surrounded by a landscaped collection of flowering shrubs. Most of the activity of the hotel, built in 1976, centers around this central courtyard. The 130 rooms are spacious and handsome, with all the modern conveniences. Singles cost 143 DM ($84.90) to 182 DM ($108.05) daily, and doubles go for 189 DM ($112.25) to 289 DM ($171.60), including breakfast. Children can stay free in their parents' room. The hotel has a restaurant, Petit Mercure, serving an international and regional cuisine.

Mövenpick Hotel, Joddenstrasse 3, D-3300 Braunschweig (tel. 0531/4-81-70). Although the hotel was built during the past decade, its brick facade and three-story elevation fit gracefully into the neighborhood of medieval buildings surrounding it. It contains 132 accommodations (of which 20 are suites or apartments), all of which have extra-wide beds, minibars, color TVs, phones, and private baths with hairdryers. Single rooms cost 190 DM ($112.80) to 200 DM ($118.75) daily, and doubles go for 245 DM ($145.50) to 255 DM ($151.40), with a buffet breakfast included. On the premises are an indoor swimming pool, a piano-pub, a wine-and-gourmet food shop, a large Swiss-style restaurant with a tempting salad bar, and a German Bierstube.

Moderately Priced Hotels

With a pleasingly symmetrical facade, **Deutsches Haus,** Burgplatz 1, D-3300 Braunschweig (tel. 0531/4-44-22), opens onto views of the cathedral from many of its rooms. The pink-and-brown brick fronting is attractively embellished with an arched portico (the columns and arches of which are repeated on the interior stairwells), Renaissance-style bay windows, and stone corner mullions. The interior is high-ceilinged, richly appointed, and detailed as only a 19th-century building can be. The 84 bedrooms, stripped of their former embellishments, have patterned modern wallpaper and carpeting. They are clean, comfortable, and spacious, for the most part. Singles rent for 90 DM ($53.45) to 165 DM ($98) daily, while doubles cost 130 DM ($77.20) to 215 DM ($127.65). All units contain showers or baths and come with breakfast.

Fürstenhof, Campestrasse 12, D-3300 Braunschweig (tel. 0531/79-10-61). The swimming pool of this family-run hotel is guarded at the edges by two cement statues of hobgoblins; the rest of this comfortable establishment is cozily decorated with Oriental rugs, hanging lamps, and warm colors. The 44 bedrooms have their own baths (or showers) and cost 80 DM ($47.50) to 90 DM ($53.45) daily for a single and 130 DM ($77.20) to 160 DM ($95) for a double, including breakfast.

Lessing-Hof mit Gästehaus, Okerstrasse 13, D-3300 Braunschweig (tel.

0531/4-54-55), consists of two guesthouses across the street from each another a few blocks from the Andreas-Kirche in the center of Brunswick. The 42 rooms of the two establishments are clean and comfortable, and a restaurant on the premises serves unpretentious food from 5:30 to 11:30pm. Mon. to Sat. Single rooms in either hotel, depending on the plumbing, range from 90 DM ($53.45) to 130 DM ($77.20) daily and include breakfast.

A Budget Hotel

A substantial corner hotel with a modern Germanic look, **Frühlings Hotel,** Bankplatz 7, D-3300 Braunschweig (tel. 0531/4-93-17), may not win style awards, but it does excel at comfort. There is a respectable dining room, plus a cozy bar and lounge. All of its 66 adequately furnished bedrooms have private baths, phones, and TVs. Singles cost 75 DM ($44.25) to 125 DM ($73.75), doubles from 115 DM ($57.50) to 175 DM ($103.25). Breakfast, taxes, and service are included.

WHERE TO DINE

Gewandhauskeller, Altstadmarkt 1 (tel. 0531/4-44-41), on the most beautiful square in Brunswick, is a stone-vaulted building dating from 1352. Once a guildhouse for clothmakers, it later acquired an elegant Renaissance facade. Its fine wines are kept in a 1,000-year-old cellar, with Rhine and Mosel vintages a specialty. Well-prepared international dishes are served, including such dishes as tournedos Monte Carlo and sole Ceylon. Meals range from 35 DM ($20.80) to 70 DM ($41.55), and hours are 11am to midnight; closed Sun.

Haus zur Hanse, Güldenstrasse 7 (tel. 0531/4-61-54), is another historic restaurant. Built in 1567, it lies behind a half-timbered structure with the most interesting facade in Brunswick. Plan to make an evening of it. I'd recommend warm salad with Barberie-duck, followed by mushrooms with fresh herbs, and veal steaks in Armagnac with young spinach. Another specialty is king-size prawns in walnut oil. Meals begin at 38 DM ($22.55), climbing to 75 DM ($44.55). Hours are 11am to 3pm and 5pm to midnight daily.

Hotel Deutsches Haus, Burgplatz 1 (tel. 0531/4-44-22). The location of this restaurant, in a previously recommended hotel, might suit anyone making a tour of the city, as it stands next door to the cathedral. And because it has specialties from practically every region of the country, the menu might be called "PanGermanic." Also featured is a series of Dutch specialties. The restaurant is open daily from 6am to 1am, charging 30 DM ($17.80) to 70 DM ($41.55) for a satisfying meal.

THE SIGHTS

The castle square of **Burgplatz** is in the Romanesque style. In the center is a lion monument, **Löwendenkmal,** the emblem of Brunswick. The sculpture was erected by Henry the Lion in 1166.

Dominating the square is the cathedral of Brunswick, **St. Blasius,** from 1173. The crypt contains the tombs of the Dom's founder, Henry the Lion, and his consort, Matilda of England. Emperor Otto IV is also entombed here, as are the Guelphs of the Brunswick line from 1681. The most outstanding artwork is a triumphal cross carved by Master Imerward in the mid-12th century. Visiting hours are 10am to 1pm and 3 to 5pm daily.

The **Burg Dankwarderode,** also at Burgplatz, a 19th-century reconstruction of the 12th-century palace of Henry the Lion, houses part of an important collection of medieval art of the **Herzog Anton Ulrich-Museum,** Museumstrasse 1 (tel. 0531/484-24-00), founded in 1754 by Carl I, Duke of Braunschweig. This neoclassical building, designed in 1887, has on its first floor an art library with engravings, etchings, and drawings by Cranach, Dürer, Holbein, Rembrandt, and Rubens, plus prints from the 15th century to the 20th century. On the second floor, the picture gallery has paintings by Cranach, Van Dyck, Tintoretto, Rubens, Rembrandt, Vermeer, Holbein, Palma Vecchio, and a noble self-portrait by Giorgione. An antiques collection containing the Mantuan Onyx Vase, together with a large collection of minor Renaissance and baroque artworks, is on the third floor. Hours are 10am to 5pm Tues. to Sun.; 10am to 8pm Wed.; closed Mon. Admission is free.

At **Altstadtmarkt** is the old **Town Hall,** a gem of Gothic architecture from the 13th century. From there you can walk to the **Gewandhaus,** the cloth merchant's hall, characterized by its richly ornamented Renaissance facade. Nearby, at the far end of Altstadtmarkt, is **St. Martini,** dating from 1180. Originally a Romanesque basilica, it was enlarged in the 13th century in the Gothic style. Its Annenkapelle, from 1434, is the first chapel in the south aisle. The church is open from 10:30am to 12:30pm; closed Mon.

---

6. Hildesheim

Just 15 miles southeast of Hannover on the Innerste River, at the northern foot of the Harz Mountains, the town of Hildesheim basks in the glory of its more than 1,150 years. It was considered the capital of Ottonian Romanesque art, but many of its treasures were lost to Allied bombing missions in the spring of 1945. The history of the community is closely tied to a romantic tale about the rose tree, still flourishing today, which supposedly marked the spot for the founding of the seat of the bishopric. As with most episcopal sees, Hildesheim became a free city and prospered not only as a religious center, but as a center for art and industry as well.

WHERE TO STAY

The best place is the **Forte Hotel,** Am Markt 5, D-3200 Hildesheim (tel. 05121/30-00), which opened in 1988. It is a complete restoration of a 14th-century building at the edge of the marketplace in old Hildesheim, a marvel of Hanseatic architecture, pierced with dozens of windows and capped with a double row of dormers. Managed by a British company, Trusthouse Forte, it offers 109 modern bedrooms. Singles range from 154 DM ($91.45) to 216 DM ($128.25) daily, with doubles costing 209 DM ($124.10) to 288 DM ($171). There are two restaurants on the premises, plus a fitness center with an indoor pool, a sauna, and a solarium.

An inviting accommodation is **Gollart's Hotel Deutsches Haus,** Carl-Peters-Strasse 5, D-3200 Hildesheim (tel. 05121/1-59-71), a few blocks from the Hauptbahnhof. The tasteful modern exterior of the seven-floor building is constructed of polished concrete and darkly enameled aluminum. Inside, there are a rustic Bierstube and a swimming pool almost 40 feet long. All of the 45 comfortable bedrooms have baths, color TVs, phones, and radios. They rent for 80 DM ($47.50) to 115 DM ($68.30) daily for a single and 120 DM ($71.25) to 140 DM ($83.15) for a double. You'll be able to release the tension of traveling in the hotel's fitness room, followed by a session in a sauna.

Bürgermeisterkapelle, Rathausstrasse 8, D-3200 Hildesheim (tel. 05121/1-40-21). You can identify this establishment by the vertical sign that says "Hotel." Clean, comfortable, and sunny, it has some units snuggled under the eaves near the triangular window just under the roofline. All 40 rooms have private showers or baths, as well as TVs and phones. Singles rent for 80 DM ($47.50) to 85 DM ($50.45) daily, and doubles cost 120 DM ($71.25) to 140 DM ($83.15), with a rich buffet breakfast included.

Hotel Schweizerhof, Hindenburgplatz 6, D-3200 Hildesheim (tel. 05121/3-90-81). Conveniently located in the center of the historic district, this 52-room hotel was tastefully renovated in 1985. Guests appreciate the parking garage and cozy second-floor restaurant, Tessiner Stube. As the name of the hotel implies, specialties in the restaurant are Swiss-inspired. Each of the well-furnished bedrooms contains a phone, TV, and radio. Singles cost 110 DM ($65.30) to 140 DM ($83.15) daily, and doubles go for 150 DM ($89.05) to 180 DM ($106.90), with a buffet breakfast included.

WHERE TO DINE

An attractive dining room, **Der Ratskeller,** Markt 1 (tel. 05121/1-44-41), is under a vaulted ceiling in the cellar of the old Rathaus. Every attempt has been made to create a cozy atmosphere. Main courses are reasonably priced and consist of both regional and international specialties. Dinners begin at 29 DM ($17.20), going up to 65 DM ($38.60). With every meal, you have a selection from 40 freshly prepared salads. Lunch, costing from 12 DM ($7.15), includes soup, salad, and a main course. Some 30 open wines are featured and sold by the glass. Hours are 11am to 3pm and 6pm to 11pm daily.

Romantik-Restaurant Kupferschmiede, Steinberg 6 (tel. 05121/26-30-25), stands outside town some 3½ miles, at Ausserhalb. Built at least a century ago as a rendezvous for gourmets, this family-run establishment still serves that purpose for the hundreds of locals who prefer it to any other eatery. Owner Wolfgang Bleckmann encourages his staff to prepare an original interpretation of cuisine moderne, with such specialties as loup de mer (sea bass) in a basil sauce or, according to the preference of a client, in puff pastry. Or perhaps you might be offered breast of Barbary goose in a peppermint sauce, or a gratinée of baby piglet in a spicy ratatouille. The desserts run the gamut from modern to traditional Germanic sumptuous. Fixed-price meals cost 44 DM ($26.15) to 99 DM ($58.80). The restaurant is open from noon to 2pm and 6:30 to 9:30pm; closed Sun.

THE SIGHTS

Some of the original ramparts, built by the bishop about A.D. 1000, are still standing. The streets are lined with houses with overhanging upper stories and elaborately adorned wooden facades. Life centers around the heartbeat **Marktplatz** with its 15th-century **Rathaus** (tel. 05121/30-11), containing frescoes illustrating the history of Hildesheim. It is open daily from 9am to 4pm. Another notable building is the **Knochenhaueramtshaus,** or butchers' guildhall, built in 1529 but severely damaged in 1945 air raids. It was rebuilt in 1989, and some critics of architecture have called it "the most beautiful half-timbered house in the world."

The chief attraction, however, is the **Dom** (tel. 05121/3-20-21), which, although badly bombed, has been restored. It is reached via Burgstrasse. The present structure, built in the 11th century, occupies the site of an earlier, 9th-century building. The basilica is Romanesque in design, but the side chapels are Gothic and the dome neoclassical. The 11th-century bronze bas-relief doors were turned out by local artisans under St. Bernward, bishop of Hildesheim. The cathedral also contains a treasury full of valuable works, including an intricately designed bishop's staff. Within the church are also many works of art, and last but not least, the Romanesque cloister at the end of the cathedral houses the town's most valuable possession, the ancient rose tree.

The **Pelizaeus-Museum,** Am Steine 1-2 (tel. 05121/1-59-79), is an important collection of ancient Egyptian culture. In 1987 the first part of a new installation of the galleries (statues, reliefs, and a tomb-chapel dating from the time of the great pyramids) was reopened. The museum is open from 10am to 4:30pm; closed Mon. Admission is 3 DM ($1.80). The charge may be altered during special exhibitions in summer.

Other than the Dom, the most remarkable ecclesiastical building in Hildesheim is **St. Michaelis Kirche,** a 10-minute walk west of Marktplatz, which was first constructed in the early part of the 11th century. Gutted in 1945, it has since been rebuilt in the early Romanesque Ottonian style, as was typical of the region. The decor and architectural plans of old Saxony were respected here, and today you can see two apses and a nave with a restored painted ceiling that was originally done in the 1200s. In the transept you will see two-tiered galleries in the Romanesque style. An "angel screen," seen to the right of the west chancel, is what remains of the church's original embellishments.

---

7. Minden

Also in the *Land* of North Rhine–Westphalia, Minden is just 44 miles from Hannover, so it's included in this chapter for convenient touring purposes. On the left bank of the Weser, the old Hanseatic city made its mark in history as the site of the Battle of Minden, fought in 1759, at which time the British infantry defeated the French cavalry in the Seven Years' War.

Minden's best-known building is its **Dom,** dominating the Altstadt, or old town. Characterized by a Romanesque facade, the Dom has somewhat the look of a fortress. Inside, its most valued art treasure is a Romanesque crucifix from the 11th century.

The **Mittellandkanal** in the northern part of the city merits a visit too. It crosses the Weser by means of a 1,200-foot-long bridge, allowing the canal to go from the Münster to Hannover without benefit of locks.

In the environs, **Porta Westfalica** (Westphalian Gap) is a natural geological attraction. From either the Bismarck Tower or the monument to Kaiser Wilhelm across the river, there is a panoramic view of the Weser as it enters the plains of North Germany. The location of what is a holiday resort and spa today is 5½ miles downstream and reached by train.

WHERE TO STAY

In a quiet wooded area a few miles from the center of town, the **Hotel Exquisit** and **Gaststätte zum Bären,** In den Bärenkämpen 2a, D-4950 Minden (tel. 0571/4-30-55), form a unified complex. Tennis lovers will enjoy the use of three illuminated indoor courts about a mile from the hotel, and after the match they can relax in the hotel pool and sauna. The 45 rooms are clean and unpretentious, costing 115 DM ($68.30) to 195 DM ($115.80) daily for a double and 75 DM ($44.55) to 100 DM ($59.40) for a single. The more expensive accommodations are in the main house, and the cheapest rooms, which are still most satisfactory, are in the guesthouse across the street. All units are furnished with showers, and toilets; breakfast is included in the rates.

Kruses Park Hotel, Marienstrasse 108, D-4950 Minden (tel. 0571/4-60-33). My favorite part of this gemütlich 34-room hotel is the covered terrace where meals and drinks are served until late at night in summer. In any season, however, you are given a gracious reception by your host, Horst Kruse. Rooms are spacious and decorated in pleasing shades of light colors. Since the establishment is part of the Ringhotel chain, you can be assured of better-than-average quality. Accommodations rent for 83 DM ($49.30) to 97 DM ($57.60) daily for a single (with a wide range of plumbing possibilities) and 130 DM ($77.20) to 146 DM ($86.70) for a double. The hotel lies at the northern edge of the city, and many residents of the town come to the restaurant/Konditorei for its gutbürgerlich and international specialties. Something you might want to try is a combination of ham, pickles, and cranberries, seasoned in "a secret way" known only to the chefs. Meals cost 28 DM ($16.65) to 50 DM ($29.70). The two-part restaurant, comprising the Blue Salon and the Hunter's Lodge, is open daily from noon to 3pm and 6 to 10pm.

Hotel Kronprinz, Friedrich-Wilhelm-Strasse 1-3, D-4950 Minden (tel. 0571/

310-05), lies conveniently close to the main train station, near the center of town. You'll register in a narrow, marble-floored lobby before being escorted to one of 22 modern and fully carpeted bedrooms. Each of these contains a private bath, phone, color TV, radio, and minibar, and each is small but comfortable. With breakfast included, singles cost 55 DM ($32.65) to 95 DM ($56.40) daily; doubles, 120 DM ($71.25) to 140 DM ($83.15). Motorists appreciate the in-house garage.

Silke, Fischerglacis 21, D-4950 Minden (tel. 0571/2-37-36), is a modern 21-room hotel raised on concrete stilts above a well-tended lawn with potted geraniums. Rooms are bright, big-windowed, and sunny; they cost from 150 DM ($89.05) daily for a single, from 170 DM ($100.95) for a double, and contain private showers and toilets. The hotel's location, somewhat isolated from downtown, should appeal to those seeking tranquility.

Hotel Bad Minden, Portastrasse 36, D-4950 Minden (tel. 0571/5-10-49). This comfortably furnished 31-room hotel with its low-slung brick facade is in one of the town's most spacious public parks. The trees extend right up to the blue neon sign and the sweeping modern portico of the reception area. The hotel's kitchen turns out a well-prepared cuisine, and facilities include massage, sauna, and hydrotherapy treatments. Accommodations are sunny, spacious, clean, and generally pleasant; singles cost 85 DM ($50.45) to 190 DM ($112.80) daily, and doubles go for 135 DM ($80.15) to 248 DM ($147.25). All rooms contain private baths, TVs, and minibars.

WHERE TO DINE

Gasthaus Alt-Minden, Hahlerstrasse 38 (tel. 0571/2-22-08), has been going strong since 1950. This is one of those comfortably cluttered restaurants where the chef will probably come out to inquire about his customers' satisfaction. The restaurant serves such specialties as flambé meats, fresh trout from its aquarium, marinated snails, and wild game dishes grilled over an open fire. Klaus Kothe is owner and chef, offering meals that range in price from 30 DM ($17.80) to 55 DM ($32.65). The restaurant is open Mon., Wed. to Fri., and Sun. from noon to 2:30pm and 5:30pm to 1am; Tues. and Sat. from 6pm to 1am.

---

8. Detmold

Detmold was the capital of Lippe, a former *Land* of the German Reich. After World War II it was incorporated into North Rhine–Westphalia and is included in this chapter for convenient touring purposes. Until 1918 Detmold was the center of the family of Prince Bernard of Holland.

About 10 miles from Bad Pyrmont, Detmold is a center for many tours. Following are several examples: **Teutoburger Forest,** where visitors travel a distance of 4 miles to the **Hermannsdenkmal** (Arminius Monument), commemorating the victory of native tribes against the Roman legions in A.D. 9. With the dawn of German nationalism, the monument was completed in 1875. Armed with a sword, the copper statue of the hero Arminius stands more than 50 feet high. In summer you can visit daily from 8am to 6pm, providing you don't mind climbing 75 steps for a panoramic view. Admission is 1 DM (60¢).

Another 3 miles and you're at **Externsteine,** the collection of limestone rocks (known in English as the Extern Stones). Beside a lake, this was a place of pagan worship, turned into a pilgrimage site for Christians in the Middle Ages. A remarkable bas-relief, *The Descent from the Cross,* was carved into the rock in the 12th century.

Back in Detmold, you can visit the **Detmold Schloss** a Renaissance building from the 16th century, with interior decoration from the 18th and 19th centuries. The front wing of the inner courtyard is exceptional, in the Weser Renaissance style.

Tapestries of the 17th century, most of them woven in Belgium, were based on cartoons by Rubens and Le Brun. Hours are 9:30am to noon and 2 to 5pm daily, April 1 to October 31. From November 1 to March 31, guided tours are at 10 and 11am and at 2, 3, and 4pm. Admission is 4 DM ($2.40).

FOOD AND LODGING

A hostelry since the 16th century, **Detmolder Hof,** Langestrasse 19, D-4930 Detmold (tel. 05231/2-82-44), has a handsome landmark gable. Tradition still prevails, as reflected by the sumptuous hall, with its marble and luxurious carpeting, and the deluxe dining room. The 39 large bedrooms, all with baths, are also tastefully furnished. With all of this, the cost is still not exorbitant: singles run 85 DM ($50.45) to 100 DM ($59.40) daily; doubles, 130 DM ($77.20) to 230 DM ($136.55). Breakfast is included. The culinary reputation is high, and the wine cellar is excellent.

Hotel Lippischer Hof and **Restaurant Le Gourmet,** Allee 2, D-4930 Detmold (tel. 05231/3-10-41). This elegantly decorated restaurant in a hotel dating from 1724 (one of Detmold's most historic houses) serves a light cuisine featuring such specialties as green dill soup with fresh lobster, or pike presented in unusual and imaginative ways. À la carte meals range in price from 45 DM ($26.70) to 80 DM ($47.50), with set luncheon meals costing 20 DM ($11.90) to 35 DM ($20.80). Food is offered daily from noon to 2pm and 6pm to midnight. The garden terrace welcomes you in summer with its masses of flowers. The 24 accommodations are attractively and comfortably furnished, among the best in town. Singles range in price from 75 DM ($44.55) to 90 DM ($53.45) daily, while doubles cost 120 DM ($71.25) to 170 DM ($100.95).

Hirschsprung, Paderbornerstrasse 212, D-4930 Detmold-Berlebeck (tel. 05231/49-11), lies in a suburb a few miles from the center of Detmold. You'll find an elegantly decorated restaurant that looks somewhat like a wealthy gentleman's private hunting lodge. The cuisine is an assemblage of regional specialties with an emphasis on game. Dinners cost 45 DM ($26.70) to 75 DM ($44.55), and children's menus are also available. Lunch is served from noon to 2pm and 6 to 10pm; closed Thurs. in winter. You'd be wise to phone ahead, as there are only 11 tables. The inn also has 10 comfortably and pleasantly furnished bedrooms, costing 65 DM ($38.60) to 95 DM ($56.40) daily for a single, 100 DM ($59.40) to 180 DM ($106.90) for a double.

Falkenberger Hof, Am Krugplatz 14, Heiligenkirchen (tel. 05231/4-74-47). Both the restaurant and its owner-chef have had many years of experience feeding large groups of people. The restaurant has a 200-year-old history. Typical dishes are filets of grilled carp with cabbage hollandaise and fresh mushrooms, fresh green eel in dill sauce, pike in a cabbage cream sauce, and as a change of pace, marinated filet of wild boar Russian style, served with applesauce, rosemary, baby cabbage, and mushrooms. Try to get a seat in one of the intimate niches below the balcony. Meals are modest in price: 30 DM ($17.80) to 45 DM ($26.70). They're served from 10am to 2:30pm and 5 to 10:30pm; closed Mon. The restaurant is closed for parts of February and March.

9. Hameln

Halfway from Hannover to Bad Pyrmont or Detmold in Lower Saxony lies Hameln (Hamelin in English), best known for the folktale about that famous ratcatcher the Pied Piper, immortalized by both Goethe and Robert Browning.

The legend is that in 1284 the town was infested by rats. There appeared a piper who, for a fee, offered to lure the vermin into the Weser River. The ratcatcher kept his bargain; the stingy denizens of Hameln did not, claiming he was a sorcerer. He reappeared the next Sunday and played a tune that lured all the children, except one lame boy, into a mysterious door in a hill. The children and the Pied Piper were never heard from again. There is some historical basis for the story, inasmuch as there was a departure from Hameln by its children several centuries ago, for a reason no one is sure of today. The story is retold every summer Sunday at noon in a special performance at the **Hochzeitshaus** (Wedding House) on Osterstrasse. In the shops of the town, you can buy rats made of every conceivable material, even candy.

Hameln traces its history back to the 11th century. Among its most interesting buildings is the **Münster,** dedicated to St. Boniface and built in the Gothic style; overlooking the Weser River, it lies at the end of Backerstrasse. Other attractions include the **Rattenfängerhaus** (Ratcatcher's House), on Osterstrasse, with frescoes illustrating the Pied Piper legend; and the already mentioned Hochzeitshaus, with its trio of attractive gables. The finest houses in the town are built in what is known as the Weser Renaissance style, from the late 16th century. You can admire these nicely sculpted houses as you stroll along pedestrians-only streets.

WHERE TO STAY

In the center of this historic town, **Zur Krone,** Osterstrasse 30, D-3250 Hameln (tel. 05151/74-11), an old house with antique furniture, is both comfortable and clean. The dining rooms are small but numerous. Singles with bath cost 90 DM ($53.45) to 180 DM ($106.90) daily, and doubles with showers or tubs rent for 160 DM ($95) to 240 DM ($142.50). The 34-room hotel has a garage.

Dorint Hotel Hameln, 164er Ring 3, D-3250 Hameln (tel. 05151/79-20), stands in a park with lots of trees, but is within walking distance of the heart of the old city. This comfortable 103-room hotel rises like a futuristic collection of building blocks, its oversize glass walls aimed toward the sunlight. All units contain private baths or showers, and guests have access to a pool, sauna, solarium, and massage facilities. Singles, with breakfast included, rent for 132 DM ($78.40) to 165 DM ($98) daily, while doubles cost 185 DM ($109.85) to 248 DM ($147.25).

Hotel zur Börse, Osterstrasse 41a, D-3250 Hameln (tel. 05151/70-80), lies within the walls of the old city. This balconied 34-room hotel can be identified by the four peaks of the modern roofline and by the parasols set up on the garden terrace. The interior is refreshingly uncluttered. Rooms are spacious and sunny, all with showers and toilets. The charge is 55 DM ($32.65) to 92 DM ($54.65) daily for a single, 102 DM ($60.57) for a twin-bedded room. The hotel has an elevator, a restaurant, and parking facilities.

Weisses Haus, D-3253 Hesse-Oldendorf (tel. 05152/85-22), about 3 miles northwest of Hameln, is a small country hotel operated by Herr and Frau Bromund, who are aided by their son and his wife. Their 12-room hotel enjoys a bucolic setting and is built in a classic style, with stone, timbers, and tiles. It is really an old estate, with a large park and many trees, lying on one of the Süntel hills at the edge of the Hameln forest. The estate is in harmony with the landscape, and offers a splendid view over the village of Fischbeck, with its old Romanesque church founded in 855. Paths, starting at the door to the hotel, invite you to spend hours wandering through the landscape. The rooms are comfortable, with phones and private baths and showers. Each room has been decorated with a different color, adding a personal note. Singles range from 60 DM ($35.65) to 65 DM ($38.60) daily, while doubles cost 90 DM ($53.45) to 105 DM ($62.35). English is spoken, and the cooking at the hotel is especially good, including game dishes in season.

Komfort-Hotel Garni Christinenhof, Alte Marktstrasse 18, D-3250 Hameln (tel. 05151/71-68), occupies a 300-year-old half-timbered building whose gabled windows overlook a cobblestoned street in the middle of the old town. Despite its antique facade, much of its interior is streamlined and modern, with many conveniences. There's a swimming pool beneath the vaulted stone ceiling of the old cellar, plus a sauna, a solarium, and a series of conference rooms. Each of the 18 bedrooms contains a phone, radio, minibar, cable-connected color TV, and a tile-covered private bath. Singles cost from 80 DM ($52.85) to 100 DM ($59.40) daily; doubles, 138 DM ($81.95).

WHERE TO DINE

Dating from 1603, the **Rattenfängerhaus,** Osterstrasse 28 (tel. 05151/38-88), is the Renaissance building referred to earlier as the Ratcatcher's House. The outside is well preserved, and inside are small wood windows, antiques, and pictures. It's practically like eating in a museum. The house specialty is rumpsteak Madagascar with green pepper, potato croquettes, and green beans. Another specialty is Rattenschwänze Balireis with salad and a "mousecatcher" plate, a pork filet. Menus range in price from 28 DM ($16.65) to 60 DM ($35.65), and à la carte costs 30 DM ($17.80) to 55 DM ($32.65). Meals are served from 11am to 2:30pm and 6 to 9pm; closed Tues.

Klütturm, Auf dem Klütberg (tel. 05151/6-16-44). Although lovely, the traditional decor of this restaurant takes second place to its panoramic view of the old city. Meals are traditional German, costing 55 DM ($32.65) to 85 DM ($50.45), with special care lavished on the dessert wagon, whose confections are changed every day. In season the cook will prepare game dishes, and throughout the year rack of baby lamb with fresh vegetables or perhaps entrecôte of beef with escargots. Hot food is served only from noon to 2:30pm and 6 to 9pm; closed Tues. and in January.

---

10. Upper Weser Valley

Running for 273 miles, the Weser River winds through Germany's "fairy-tale country." Sleeping Beauty, the characters in Grimms' **Fairy Tales,** and the tall tales of Baron Münchausen were created here.

This most interesting day tour traditionally begins at Münden. At this point the Fulda and Werra rivers meet. Many end their jaunt in the Pied Piper town of Hameln in the north. The most romantic way to see the river is on a paddle-steamer in summer.

MÜNDEN

In the center of town are 700 half-timbered houses built in many styles. At the confluence of the Werra and Fulda rivers, the Weserstein (Weserstone) commemorates the joining. In the medieval town you can park your car and begin your exploration of Münden by going inside **St. Blaise's Church,** which is located between the Markt and Kirchplatz. In the nave is the tomb of William of Brunswick, who died in 1503. With its trio of gables, the **Rathaus,** next door, is also interesting. The facade is a good example of the style known as Weser Renaissance. From here you can branch out and tour the already-mentioned medieval houses. Also in Münden is the tombstone of the much-maligned Doctor Eisenbart, who is honored every year at a folk festival.

Where to Stay and Dine

Berghotel Eberburg, Tillyschanzenweg 14, D-3510 Münden (tel. 05541/50-88). This is an attractively decorated 27-room guesthouse set in a forest not far from the center of town. You won't be alone if you choose to dine on the sun terrace or inside the restaurant, because many locals from the city do just that. Attractively styled and comfortably furnished singles rent for 45 DM ($26.70) to 70 DM ($41.55) daily, while doubles cost 80 DM ($47.50) to 120 DM ($71.25), including a generous buffet breakfast. À la carte meals go for 38 DM ($22.55) to 50 DM ($29.70).

Jagdhaus Heede, Hermannshägerstrasse 81, D-3510 Münden (tel. 05541/23-95). Thanks to its location inside the town's nature preserve, this 18-room hotel offers peaceful accommodations. It originated as a conservatively designed house, but over the years the owners added a sprawling three-story modern wing filled with sun-washed bedrooms and lots of comfort. Each of the accommodations contains a private balcony, phone, and a view of the forest. The hotel charges 48 DM ($28.50) to 60 DM ($35.65) daily for a single, 84 DM ($49.90) to 94 DM ($55.80) for a double. There's a café-style sun terrace on the premises, as well as a children's playground. In the dining room a conservative German cuisine is prepared with flavor and served in generous portions. The hotel is closed in November.

Ratskeller, Am Markt 3 (tel. 05541/10-00). The Rathaus of Münden, dating from 1605, is one of the best examples of a Renaissance public building north of the Alps. Its Keller is no less an architectural curiosity. Much of the original decor is still intact, although new kitchens have been added. Typical dishes are veal chops in a mustard madeira sauce, breast of goose with red cranberries, and rack of lamb provençal cooked with lots of garlic and fresh beans. The Ratskeller has a seawater basin with lobsters, oysters, and crayfish. Meals cost 32 DM ($19) to 55 DM ($32.65). Food is served from 11am to 2:30pm and 6 to 10:30pm; closed Mon.

After leaving Münden, you have to detour west of the river at a marked turnoff to reach our next stop.

HOFGEISMAR-SABABURG

In Hesse, visit **Schloss Sababurg,** 8½ miles north of Kassel, which you come upon after driving through the magnificent Forest of Reinhard, one of the largest forest areas in Germany. This is where Sleeping Beauty, in the fairy tale by the Brothers Grimm, allegedly slept for 100 years. You can almost believe it when you see the Italianate turrets of the castle, which stands in a zoological park. The castle has had a long and turbulent history since it was first built in 1334 by the archbishop of Mainz. It eventually fell to ruin, but between 1490 and 1492, Count Wilhelm I constructed a hunting lodge on the ruins, and in time it became known for its banquets of the hunt. Count Wilhelm had a zoological garden laid out on the 500-acre estate, and it is claimed to be the oldest zoological garden in the world. Troops plundered the castle during the Thirty Years' War, and the French caused further damage during the Seven Years' War. Friedrich II turned the castle back into a hunting lodge in 1765, but that, too, was allowed to deteriorate.

Since 1971, the zoological gardens have been restored, with a forest preserve that is a home for rare animals, including bison and reindeer, as well as a hunting museum. To the west of the castle lie 70 acres of forest, untouched for more than a century. The wilderness of ancient oak and beech trees, along with tall ferns, adds to the fairy-tale atmosphere of the area. In the castle courtyard, where sweet-smelling briar roses still bloom, you almost expect to see the prince coming to find Sleeping Beauty and awaken her with a kiss.

In summer you usually have to park down below and walk up to the castle, as the limited parking space at the top is almost always filled.

Where to Stay and Dine

Dornröschenschloss Sababurg, D-3520 Hofgeismar-Sababurg (tel. 05678/10-52), in a section of the old castle, is a hotel and restaurant retaining the magic of the past, with bedrooms furnished in period style, with such names as "Das Einhorn" (The Unicorn) and "In der Wilden Sau" (The Wild Sow). All 19 of the units, however, have such modern amenities as baths, phones, and radios. Singles rent for 95 DM ($56.40) to 160 DM ($95) daily, doubles for 178 DM ($105.70) to 240 DM ($142.50), all with breakfast included.

In the restaurant you can dine at tables with spectacular views over the ancient game park, enjoying game dishes from the forest and fish from the clear mountain streams. Meals cost 40 DM ($23.75) to 70 DM ($41.55). Summer barbecue evenings are held in the torchlit ruined part of the castle, and fairy-tale feasts are sometimes offered in the banqueting hall, with Sleeping Beauty and the Brothers

Grimm welcoming you. In summer, theater and concerts are also presented in the ruined castle section. The hotel and restaurant are closed in January and February. Lunch is served daily from noon to 2pm and dinner from 6:30pm to 9pm.

Again, you have to traverse the Reinhardswald, an oak forest, to reach the main route along the Weser.

BAD KARLSHAFEN

This baroque town founded in 1699 by the Huguenots lies at the confluence of the Diemel and the Weser. In the town is one of the most interesting stopovers for both food and lodging along the Weser River, previewed below.

Where to Stay and Dine

Hotel zum Schwan, Conradistrasse 3, D-3522 Bad Karlshafen (tel. 05672/ 10-44), is an elegant although miniature 32-room spa hotel situated beside the main bathhouse and opposite the town pond, on which swans float. Built in 1765, it has the baroque facade of a small palace, with an entrance terrace overlooking the river. Life is informal here, even if the rococo dining salon is rather grand, with its paneled walls and monumental ceramic stove. The living room is modern, and in the rear you'll find an attractive courtyard garden. Breakfast is served in a period-piece room, with beaded hanging lampshades and lace curtains. Singles rent for 75 DM ($44.55) to 100 DM ($59.40) daily and doubles for 130 DM ($77.20) to 170 DM ($100.95), all tariffs including breakfast. English is spoken. Closed January 15 through February.

Continue north along the river, and you will pass **Fürstenburg** where, on a hill overlooking the right bank, a castle-factory has been making a famous porcelain since 1747.

HÖXTER

This town, the easternmost in Westphalia, is filled with Renaissance and baroque buildings. The most visited, called **Dechanei,** or the deanery, stands to the right of St. Nicholas's Church; to reach it, walk down Marktstrasse. It has twin gables and dates from 1561. A walk on Westerbachstrasse reveals many half-timbered medieval buildings. The 11th-century **Kilianikirche** contains an outstanding Renaissance pulpit decorated with motifs in alabaster. The red sandstone twin towers of this church dominate the center of Höxter.

Take the Corveyer Allee from Höxter for about 2 miles to **Corvey,** one of the oldest Benedictine abbeys in Germany, planned by Charlemagne and constructed by his son, Ludwig the Pious, in 822. In the 9th and 10th centuries, the abbey was one of the most important cultural centers of North Germany. During the Thirty Years' War, most of Corvey was destroyed, the only section remaining being the west facade of the church with its two spires. It was rebuilt about 1730 in its present form, together with the monastery and farm buildings. The abbot's palace and the monastery property became the castle of the Landgrave of Hessia-Rotenburg in 1820 and are still owned by that family. Guided tours take visitors through the library and imperial halls. You're invited to visit the second floor with its exhibitions on folklore, prehistoric times, and natural sciences. The abbey is open April to the end of October, daily from 9am to 5pm. Admission is 4 DM ($2.40).

You can also dine within the castle precincts at **Schloss-Restaurant,** Schloss Corvey (tel. 05271/83-23). In summer, ask for a table on the garden terrace. This restaurant is installed in the former living quarters of the castle. It's surrounded on two sides by well-trimmed linden trees. The great hall is used mainly for special events, and the tavern dining room offers luncheons and dinners with a fairly large international repertoire of dishes. The waiters are cordial, and the food is well prepared. The restaurant, really a Weinstube, is open only from March to December. Hours are 8:30am to 10pm; closed Mon. The least expensive meal here will cost about 20 DM ($11.90), but it's also possible to spend 60 DM ($35.65).

BODENWERDER

Thirteen miles south of the Pied Piper's Hameln lived Baron Münchausen and his son. The Münchausen name has gone down in literary history. A hunting lodge owned by the baron is a pilgrimage site for dreamy souls. Münchausen's renowned narrative about his "travels and campaigns" in Russia was translated into many languages. The original author was Rudolf Erich Raspe, who apparently became acquainted with Freiherr von Münchausen upon his retirement in 1760 from Russian service against the Turks. He was widely known for his tall tales about his prowess as a sportsman and a soldier. Many of the stories for which Münchausen is celebrated were actually inspired by other tellers of tall tales and were included in subsequent editions.

Where to Stay and Dine

Deutsches Haus, Münchhausenplatz 4, D-3452 Bodenwerder (tel. 05533/39-25). Its location on one of the town's most prominent squares makes this modern hotel easy to find. Its 39 bedrooms are clean and styled for up-to-date comfort, with a buffet breakfast included in the price of the room. The bedrooms cost 45 DM ($26.70) to 65 DM ($38.60) daily for a single and 65 DM ($38.60) to 110 DM ($65.30) for a double. All accommodations have phones and radios, while the doubles contain TVs. An in-house restaurant provides tasty and generous meals. A public swimming pool and options for various promenades are all within walking distance.

---

11. Goslar

In spite of the progress and growth of Goslar, the old portion of the town looks just as it did hundreds of years ago. This ancient Hanseatic town lies at the foot of the Harz Mountains. Goslar owed its early prosperity to the mines in the Harz Mountains, from which silver was drawn as early as 968. The town still works the lead and ore mines in nearby Rammelsberg. The 600-year-old streets are in use today and the carved, half-timbered houses are more than just monuments to the past: many are still used as homes or offices.

Incidentally, for hikers and other outdoor enthusiasts, Goslar is a suitable starting point for day trips and excursions into the Harz Mountains, where some of Germany's best skiing resorts and several spas are found.

For the demonology expert, the Harz region is rich in tales of witchcraft and other folklore. Walpurgis Eve (Witches' Sabbath) is still celebrated in the hills each year.

WHERE TO STAY

Right in the heart of town, the **Kaiserworth,** Markt 3, D-3380 Goslar (tel. 05321/2-11-11), is a big old-fashioned hotel. The building dates from 1494 and is considered a sightseeing attraction. Below the eaves are carved baroque statues of the German emperors. The hotel's exterior is Gothic, with an arched arcade across the front of the structure, topped by a turreted oriel window facing Marktplatz. The 56 rooms are large; in fact, the corner rooms are big enough to be suites. Room 110 (a corner room) offers the best view of the 6 o'clock concert by the clock on the square. The rooms are designed with an accent on comfort. With bath, the price is 95 DM ($56.40) to 120 DM ($71.25) daily for a single and 140 DM ($83.15) to 180 DM ($106.90) for a double. On the ground floor the hotel has a sedate, wood-paneled breakfast room and a vaulted-ceilinged dining room, Die Worth. Step through a 1,000-year-old cistern and you are in the cellar restaurant, the Dukatenkeller, with its stone pillars and ecclesiastical chairs. The hotel is closed from November to mid-December.

Der Achtermann, Rosentorstrasse 20, D-3380 Goslar (tel. 05321/2-10-01), was completely gutted and has been restored. The reputation of this historic structure has spread throughout the Harz region. The 155 rooms are completely modernized, each with private bath, TV, and radio. Singles cost 90 DM ($53.45) to 175 DM ($103.90) daily, and doubles go for 165 DM ($98) to 300 DM ($178.15). In addition to the major dining room, the hotel has an intimate bar and a Bierstube. The latter is housed in the circular medieval tower for which the hotel is named.

Hotel-Restaurant das Brusttuch, Hoherweg 1, D-3380 Goslar (tel. 05321/2-10-81), sits like a dunce cap on a narrow street corner in the old city, with a sharply peaked roof rising as high as the main body of the building itself. The ground floor is made of rough-hewn stone; a half-timbered second story is gaily decorated with sea dragons, nymphs, and flowers. Inside is an elaborately decorated restaurant/wine cellar, with so many unusual artifacts below the soaring ceiling that it's difficult to concentrate on the menu. Aside from the restaurant, you'll find 13 rooms with modern baths renting for 85 DM ($50.45) to 135 DM ($80.15) daily for a single and 140 DM ($83.15) to 195 DM ($115.80) for a double, including breakfast.

Schwarzer Adler, Rosentorstrasse 25, D-3380 Goslar (tel. 05321/2-40-01). Wolfgang Schmidt is your gracious host at this modern 27-room hotel, which benefits from a long tradition of good food, hospitality, and comfort. Singles rent for 80 DM ($47.50) to 90 DM ($53.45) daily, while doubles cost 110 DM ($65.30) to 130 DM.

Goldene Krone, Breitestrasse 46, D-3380 Goslar (tel. 05321/2-27-92), near the Breites Tor (Wide Gate), is a village inn complete with a friendly innkeeper and his wife, Herr and Frau Fehrenbach, who attend to the rooms and the meals. If you enjoy local color, this 25-room hostelry is a real find. Singles without baths rent for 45 DM ($26.70) daily, 60 DM ($35.65) for rooms with bath. Doubles without baths cost 70 DM ($41.55), those with showers 125 DM ($74.25). Breakfast and taxes are included. The rooms are simple but homelike and clean. The food and drink available are good and inexpensive.

Dorint-Harzhotel Kreuzeck, Am Kreuzeck 1-4, D-3380 Goslar 2-Hahnenklee (tel. 05325/7-41), about 9 miles from Goslar, is a well-rated hotel set directly on a small lake in an area with beautiful mountain scenery. The only noise might be the roar of a big stag in the distance. The 105-room hotel offers comfort, country hospitality, and exceptional food, and you may want to drive here for a meal even if you can't stay (see "Where to Dine"). In winter, numerous ski lifts are in the vicinity, as well as an 18½-mile cross-country ski course. Ice-skating rinks are also nearby. In a horse-drawn sleigh, guests can enjoy an old-fashioned ride. In summer, sports include sailing, windsurfing, hiking, tennis, and bicycle riding. Rooms are comfortably furnished with a number of amenities. Singles rent for 119 DM ($70.65) to 139 DM ($82.55) daily, with twin-bed accommodations going for 185 DM ($109.85) to 205 DM ($121.75). If you're driving, take the highway A7 (marked Flensburg–Hamburg–Hannover), exiting at Seesen.

WHERE TO DINE

The most rustic and also the most attractive dining room in Goslar is **Die Worth,** Markt 3 (tel. 05321/2-11-11). Right in the heart of town, in the previously recommended Kaiserworth, the restaurant is a Gothic stone crypt with vaulted ceilings and arches, stained-glass windows, wrought-iron lanterns, and trestle tables. The food is good, and the portions are hearty. In season, roast game is featured with wild mushrooms, mashed apples, and berries, or else try the Tafelspitz or the rumpsteak. A set lunch goes for 30 DM ($17.80), and dinners can cost up to 62 DM ($36.80). Hours are noon to 2:30pm and 6 to 9:30pm daily. Closed November to mid-December.

La Romantica, Mauerstrasse 4 (tel. 05321/4-02-07), is one of the most popular dining rooms in town. Its decor is undeniably Italian, similar to something you'd find much farther south, and its sophisticated kitchen offers the expected Italian specialties, but with a modern flair. Seasonal specialties change with the availability of fare. Meals cost 45 DM ($26.70) to 65 DM ($38.60) and are served from noon to 2pm and 6 to 11pm daily. Closed from mid-July to mid-August. Reservations are essential.

Harzhotel Bären, Krugwiese 11a (tel. 05321/78-20). Music and dancing often accompany a meal at this modern hotel-restaurant frequented by partying locals. The comfortably rustic Bierstube could provide a suitable spot for a beer or some Schnapps before moving into the main restaurant, where meals cost anywhere from 28 DM ($16.65) to 50 DM ($29.70). Specialties of the house include grilled goose, roast piglet, or a shank of either pork or veal. They also serve "Kentucky ham" with buttered corn. Service is daily from noon to 11pm.

Goldene Krone, Breitestrasse 46 (tel. 05321/2-27-92). Everyone in town seemingly knows about this historic Weinstube on the eastern edge of Goslar, which features an international menu with meals costing 25 DM ($14.85) to 45 DM ($26.70). It's open from 7am to midnight; closed Wed. Hot food is offered only from 11am to 2pm and 6 to 9pm. The decor is rustic and cozy, and you'll surely feel at home with the polite service.

Dorint-Harzhotel Kreuzeck, Am Kruezeck 1-4, Hahnenklee (tel. 05321/7-41), lies in a wooded area south of Goslar. This rustic villa serves a cuisine moderne in its restaurant, Bergkanne, with meals costing 40 DM ($23.75) to 75 DM ($44.55). All the products used are the freshest available, and many are imported directly from France. Some of the specialties include filet of turbot with fresh mushrooms, juicy steaks poached in butter, and sautéed medallions of Charmoise lamb with fresh vegetables and potatoes dauphinoise. Music and dancing often accompany the meal, which could be capped with a tempting array of fresh sorbets. The restaurant is open daily from noon to 2:30pm and 6 to 11pm.

THE SIGHTS

To best explore this 1,000-year-old town, park your car, put on a pair of comfortable shoes, and set out on foot through the one-square-kilometer Altstadt. That way you won't miss any of the numerous attractions that await you, beginning with the **Rathaus** (Town Hall) on Marktplatz (tel. 05321/70-42-26), one of the oldest and most impressive town halls in Germany. Begun in the 12th century, the main section was not constructed until 1450. This part of the structure consists of an open portico with Gothic crossvaulting, topped by the burghers' hall. The open arcade on the ground level was used for centuries as a market by the townspeople. The open gallery on the second floor was closed up with stained-glass windows in the 17th century. In the early 1500s the original assembly hall in the Rathaus was turned into a **Hall of Homage** and lavishly decorated with a cycle of 55 paintings called *The Incarnation of God in Jesus Christ.* The paintings, which cover the walls and ceilings of the room, include not only works depicting the life of Christ, but those dealing with other biblical characters as well. Many of the faces are actually the portraits of townspeople of the period. It is open June to September, daily from 10am to 5pm; and October to May, daily from 10am to 4pm. Admission is 2 DM ($1.20).

Marktplatz, in front of the Rathaus, was for a long time the town's hub of activity. In the center of the large square is a 13th-century fountain with two bronze basins and the German Imperial Eagle at the top. Townspeople and visitors alike gather in the square at 6pm each evening to hear the clock concert and to watch the parade, including the zinc miners returning home from the Rammelsberg mines.

The churches of Goslar provide a look into the architectural history of the area. Many of the oldest churches—five had already been built by 1200—have been expanded and altered from their original Romanesque style to their current Gothic appearance. The Romanesque **Marktkirche,** just behind the Rathaus, still has its 700-year-old stained-glass windows and a 16th-century bronze baptismal font. From Marktplatz, take Rosentorstrasse northward to reach the **Jakobikirche,** which dates from the 11th century. It has been transformed into a Gothic masterpiece, complete with baroque altars. The church contains a *Pietà* by Hans Witten (1520). Farther down the street, the **Neuwerkkirche** has retained its purely Romanesque basilica, and its well-preserved sanctuary contains a richly decorated choir and stucco reliefs. Standing in a garden, it was originally constructed as a Cistercian convent in the late 1100s.

The **Frankenberg Kirche,** on Bergstrasse, is from the 12th century, but was completely remodeled in the 1700s. Over the elaborate baroque pulpit and altars hangs the intricately carved "Nun's Choir Gallery," bedecked with gilded saints and symbols.

One of the reminders that Goslar was once a free Imperial and Hanseatic city is the **Breites Tor** (Wide Gate), a fortress with 23-foot-thick walls and ramparts stretching to Kaiserplatz, a palatinate of the emperor (tel. 05321/70-43-58). Rebuilt in the 19th century along the lines of its 11th-century original is a Romanesque hall. Within its walls is the 12th-century twin-storied chapel of St. Ulrich, containing the sarcophagus of Emperor Henry III. From May 1 until the end of September, it's open daily from 9:30am to 5pm; in March, April, and October, from 10am to 4pm; and from November to February, from 10am to 3pm. Admission is 2.50 DM ($1.50). To reach it, head down Peterstrasse.

For a quick and less exhausting look at the history of Goslar, visit the **Civic Museum** (Goslarer Museum), at the corner of Abzuchtstrasse and Königstrasse (tel. 05321/70-43-59), which has displays of the early town, its modes of architecture, and several relics of the past. The museum also contains an exhibition of 1,000 years of mining, including a large geological collection from the Harz Mountains. The Civic Museum is open June to September, daily from 10am to 5pm (Sun. from 10am to 4pm); the rest of the year, from 10am to 4pm (Sun. from November to May, from 10am to 1pm). Admission is 2.50 DM ($1.50).

---

12. Göttingen

Göttingen was pronounced "famed for its sausages and university" by Heinrich Heine. The university in this Gothic town is one of the most respected and one of the oldest in Germany, and it suffered little damage during World War II.

Medieval romanticism and the vivacity of student life, particularly as lived in the numerous taverns, make Göttingen worth a day's visit. By making a slight detour, you can explore the university town before dipping into the fairy-tale country of the Upper Weser Valley. Göttingen is halfway between Bonn and Berlin.

In 1737 George II, king of England and elector of Hannover, opened the Georgia Augusta University, and in time Göttingen became the most popular university town in Europe. The university granted absolute freedom in doctrine and research. It was the first university to admit women and Jewish students.

The **Altes Rathaus,** begun in 1369, wasn't completed until 1443. **Marktplatz** is the most interesting section of Göttingen: here the Goose Girl is immortalized in bronze in front of the Altes Rathaus. A tradition has grown up that every male student must implant a kiss on her lips when he attains his degree.

In the center of Göttingen you can wander down narrow streets, looking at wide-eaved, half-timbered houses. Some of the facades are carved and painted.

A visit to Göttingen is traditionally capped by going to one of the student taverns, such as **Zum Altdeutschen,** Prinzenstrasse 16 (tel. 0551/5-65-45), or **Trou,** Burgstrasse 20 (in the cellar) (tel. 0551/4-39-71).

WHERE TO STAY

Housed in a grand building that reminds me of a Tuscan villa, **Gebhards Hotel,** Goethe-Allee 22, D-3400 Göttingen (tel. 0551/4-96-80), stands in front of the station. This comfortable hotel has a modern balconied annex built onto the back. The renovated interior offers high-ceilinged public rooms, a pleasant bar area, a swimming pool, and several restaurants. Singles go for 110 DM ($65.30) to 180 DM ($106.90), while doubles rent for 180 DM ($106.90) to 290 DM ($172.20). The cheapest double has a toilet and shower; the most expensive is an apartment with a complete private bath. All rooms are furnished with TVs. The attached restaurant has gained fame as a place where a king of Denmark and a few German presidents have dined. The menu is likely to feature homemade pâtés in aspic, fresh fish and fresh fish terrines, turbot poached in cider, medallions of quail, and Swabian pork with apple compote. Meals range from 25 DM ($14.85) to 75 DM ($44.55), and are served daily from noon to 2:30pm and 6pm to midnight.

Central Hotel, Judenstrasse 12, D-3400 Göttingen (tel. 0551/5-71-57). Although this quiet hotel is centrally located, as its name indicates, on a pedestrian walkway near the university, its best feature is the imaginative care the designers have used to decorate the 45 bedrooms. One is flamboyantly wallpapered and curtained in vivid yellow and white tones, while another seems to be covered in pink silk. All bedrooms contain private baths, color TVs, and phones, renting for 75 DM ($44.55) to 110 DM ($65.30) daily for a single and 140 DM ($83.15) to 170 DM ($100.95) for a double, with breakfast included.

Eden-Hotel, Reinhauser Landstrasse 22a, D-3400 Göttingen (tel. 0551/7-60-07), is centrally located near the new Rathaus. All its 62 comfortable rooms contain private baths or showers. Singles cost 80 DM ($47.50) to 120 DM ($71.25) daily, and doubles run from 115 DM ($68.30) to 180 DM ($106.90). Breakfast is included.

WHERE TO DINE

Dating from 1503, in a black-and-white timbered corner building, **Junkernschänke,** Barfüsserstrasse 5 (tel. 0551/5-73-20), is a traditional restaurant steeped in ancient traditions. Inside the atmospheric hostelry are three dining rooms with beamed ceilings and wood carvings. Set dinners cost 25 DM ($14.85) to 70 DM ($41.55). Food is served from noon to 2:30pm and 6 to 10:30pm; closed Mon.

Zum Schwarzen Bären, Kurze Strasse 12 (tel. 0551/5-82-84), a fine restaurant, is also housed in a black-and-white timbered circa-1500 building. It still has the original stained-glass leaded windows. The facade has name plates of well-known guests. Inside, the ambience is tavern style, with a ceramic stove in the corner and dining rooms with intimate booths. The innkeeper suggests brook trout from the Harz Mountains or Bear's Pan (various filets with Spätzle). The restaurant serves complete meals for 20 DM ($11.90) to 65 DM ($38.60). Hours are noon to 2pm and 6 to 10pm; closed Mon.

Ratskeller, Markt 9 (tel. 0551/5-64-33). This 600-year-old restaurant lies in the historic cellar of the Old Town Hall. The specialties of the Ratskeller include Old German Farmer's Plate (chicken breast and pork steak with fried potatoes and roasted onions) or fresh trout au bleu with parsley potatoes. Meals cost 20 DM ($11.90) to 50 DM ($29.70), and hours are noon to 2pm and 6 to 9:30pm daily.

13. Kassel

Much of Kassel's 1,000-year history went down in ruins in World War II, but the city that rose from the rubble holds its own culturally and industrially. Known as a city of gardens, Kassel has been designed with traffic-free promenades and pedestrian tunnels. Public parks and sports grounds offer residents and visitors relaxation and entertainment.

The town was first mentioned in written records in A.D. 913 as Chassala or Chassela. In medieval times it was usually spelled Castle and was a stronghold of Franconian kings.

Culturally, Kassel has earned fame as the home of the **Dokumenta,** possibly the world's most important international art exhibition. Its **State Theater** sets the stage for operatic and dramatic productions. Long a center for drama and the arts, Kassel also boasts the **Ottoneum,** Steinweg 2, the oldest permanent theater building in Germany (1604), housing the **Natural Science Museum,** which is open Tues. to Fri. from 10am to 4:30pm and on Sat. and Sun. from 10am to 1pm. Admission is free.

Kassel is considered the center of the Fairy-Tale Road, because of the long stay of Jacob and Wilhelm Grimm in this area.

WHERE TO STAY

In Kassel, you have a choice of living in fine hotels within the city proper or in comfort on the outskirts.

Schloss Hotel Wilhelmshöhe, Schlosspark 2, D-3500 Kassel-Wilhelmshöhe (tel. 0561/3-08-80), is misnamed. It's not an old castle at all, but completely modern in the tradition of an American motel. Built directly across the street from the palace, and next to what were once the imperial stables, the 105-room hotel has many private terraces with views of the rolling castle park and its buildings. There are also a swimming pool and a bowling alley. The bedrooms are comfortable and decorated in a bright, airy style. The rooms are of a high standard and equipped with baths or showers, toilets, phones, radios, color TVs, and minibars. Single rooms cost 140 DM ($83.15) daily. Doubles go for 190 DM ($112.80), including a buffet breakfast. Adjoining the hotel is an excellent restaurant-café. In fair weather you can dine at a café table on the terrace, listening to band music and enjoying the panorama of Kassel.

Dorint Hotel Reiss, Werner-Hilpert-Strasse 24, Am Hauptbahnhof, D-3500 Kassel (tel. 0561/7-88-30), stands close to the railway station. This 102-room hotel welcomes guests with its comfortable, clean rooms. Windows are soundproof. Singles with baths cost 125 DM ($74.25). Doubles, each with private bath, range from 160 DM ($95) to 180 DM ($106.90). Breakfast is included in the room price. The restaurant serves international foods; these might include broiled steaks and sautéed meats of all kinds, each delicately seasoned and properly cooked. The restaurant is open daily from noon to 2pm and 6 to 9pm, charging 35 DM ($20.80) to 65 DM ($38.60) for an average meal.

Hotel Domus, Ezbergerstrasse 1-5, D-3500 Kassel (tel. 0561/10-23-85), was built about 1900. This four-story brick hotel near the Hauptbahnhof was the former headquarters for a trading house until it became one of the most popular hotels in Kassel. The canopy over the entrance is crafted from an art nouveau metal frame with glass insets (a style repeated in the hanging lamps throughout the hotel). The 51 bedrooms are sunny and tastefully decorated, with graceful curves in the woodworking of the furniture and doorways. Singles cost 105 DM ($62.35) to 115 DM ($68.30) daily, while doubles rent for 160 DM ($95) to 170 DM ($100.95). Breakfast is included, and all units contain private baths.

Schweizer Hof, Wilhelmshöher Allee 288, D-3500 Kassel-Wilhelmshöhe (tel. 0561/3-40-48). The Bierstube-restaurant attached to this 46-room hotel is rustically decorated, while the rest of the establishment is as modern and efficient as a Swiss watch. All units contain private baths, radios, phones, and TVs. Guests have free access to the bowling alley, a bar area tiled in black, and a heated swimming pool landscaped with a slate-covered island connected by a bridge to the mainland. Singles rent for 85 DM ($50.45) to 110 DM ($65.30) daily, while doubles go for 130 DM ($77.20) to 180 DM ($106.90).

Hotel Seidel, Holländischestrasse 70, D-3500 Kassel (tel. 0561/8-60-47), is comfortably perched in the center of town on a tree-lined street with a popular bar and café on the ground floor. This five-story 40-room hotel offers clean, sunny rooms to guests, charging them 72 DM ($42.75) to 85 DM ($50.45) daily for a single and 104 DM ($61.75) to 115 DM ($68.30) for a double. Accommodations contain radios, color TVs, and direct dial phones, and minibars. Only breakfast is served.

WHERE TO DINE

Seemingly everyone's favorite place for dining is the **Ratskeller,** Obere Königstrasse 8 (tel. 0561/1-59-28). The attractive, semirustic atmosphere makes people forget their troubles and helps them relax and enjoy their meals. The Ratskeller serves both international specialties and regional dishes such as Ratsherrentopf and Altdeutsches Schnitzel. Among international dishes you will find medallions of turkey fried in egg and cheese, garnished with tomatoes and served with macaroni and green salad; medallions of pork Alsatian style; and pork steak in spicy beer sauce with bacon, onions, sausages, and green beans. At lunchtime there is a special menu prepared for clients in a hurry. The extraordinary ice-cream menu is well known. Meals begin at 30 DM ($17.80), going up to 60 DM ($35.65). Hours are 11am to 11:30pm daily.

Restaurant Au-Garden, Karlsaue Auedamm (tel. 0561/1-87-03), is a modern pavilion open daily from 11am to midnight. It is actually a garden within a garden, lying in the Karlsaue, a huge park first landscaped in the 18th century. Beautifully situated, the restaurant offers 120 seats indoors or in fair weather 140 seats outside. The setting is romantic: a lake filled with sprinklers. Menu prices range from 15 DM ($8.90) to 45 DM ($26.70). You can order from the "market square buffet," or perhaps you'll be there when the chef features a Mediterranean night with Spanish paella. Live piano music is played at certain times.

Hotel Gude-Restaurant Pfeffermühle, Frankfurterstrasse 229, D-3500 Kassel-Niederzwehren (tel. 0561/4-80-50). There are so many comfortably intimate cubbyholes within this establishment that choosing one is a minor accomplishment. A walk-in grill is ringed with a large stone mantelpiece; from a vantage point nearby, a uniformed chef prepares succulent roasts and grills. A specialty of the house is rumpsteak Strindberg, served with a mustard sauce and lightly glazed onions. Full meals cost 30 DM ($17.80) to 50 DM ($29.70). They are served daily from 11am to 2pm and 5pm to 1am. Sixty-five comfortable rooms, some of them decorated in alpine style with painted furniture and flowery wallpaper, are rented to overnight guests. These cost 140 DM ($83.15) to 170 DM ($100.95) for a double, with breakfast included. On the premises are a fitness center, an indoor swimming pool, and hydrotherapy facilities.

THE SIGHTS

Visitors to Kassel are drawn here for a variety of reasons—for the art exhibitions, for trade conferences, or for the theatrical productions.

Schloss Wilhelmshöhe

Built on a small wooded slope where a monastery once stood, this 18th-century classic castle was the summer residence of the Landgraves and electors of Hessen-Cassel. For seven years it became the residence of Napoleon's brother, the king of Westphalia, and later became the summer palace of Kaiser Wilhelm II. This is richly and lavishly furnished with good period pieces, and art lovers go to Kassel just to see the fine collection of Dutch, Flemish, Italian, and German old masters in the castle. There is an important Rembrandt collection. Though some attributed works have been revealed to be "school of Rembrandt," the collection nevertheless does contain many great works by the Dutch Master, including *Jacob Blessing His Grandchildren.* There are also works by Dürer, Lucas Cranach, Rubens, Van Dyck, and Frans Hals, as well as Titian, Piazzetta, Jan Liss, and others. In addition to the picture gallery, the castle also houses a collection of Greek and Roman sculpture, gold, and pottery.

Also interesting is the huge **castle park,** unique in Europe because of its layout across the slopes of Habichtwald. The crowning feature of the park is the massive **Hercules Monument,** constructed in the early 18th century to a height of 250 feet. From the foot of the monument, a series of waterfalls cascades down the slope of the 800-foot hill. The park also contains the **Löwenburg Castle,** a romantic imitation of a ruined English castle, built at the same time as the Wilhelmshöhe. The park and castles are open from 10am to 5pm (slightly shorter hours in winter); closed Mon. Admission to Schloss Wilhelmshöhe, Löwenburg Castle, and the Hercules Monument is 2 DM ($1.20) each. The castle grounds are open free to the public during the same hours indicated above.

Other Sights

The Waldeck Region, the Reinhards Forest, and Kassel were responsible for the birth of many legends and tales about witches, sleeping princesses, strange beasts, and magic spells. These tales had a profound influence on the Brothers Grimm, who lived in Kassel from 1798 to 1830. The **Brüder Grimm-Museum,** Schöne Aussicht 2 (tel. 0561/77-48-66), contains letters, portraits, and mementos of the famous brothers and their relatives. The most interesting exhibit is a collection of editions of their fairy tales from the first copy to the present day. Admission to the museum is free. It's open daily from 10am to 5pm.

Nearby is Kassel's second-largest park, the **Karlsaue,** extending along the bank of the Fulda River. The park contains the orangerie, flanked by the **Marble Pavilion,** worth a visit to look at the 12 statues of mythological characters.

The **Hessisches Landesmuseum,** Brüder-Grimm-Platz 5 (tel. 0561/78-00-36), and **Neue Galerie,** Schöne Aussicht 1 (tel. 0561/1-52-66), contain exhibits of interest. In the former, there are four departments: prehistory; Hessian folk art; European arts and crafts, including French and Germanic art nouveau, armoires, glassware, and medieval triptychs and sculptures; and for the science buff, there is the astronomy and physics collection, containing priceless scientific instruments dating as far back as Copernicus. Displayed is the first solidly constructed observatory in Europe, dating from 1560.

The New Gallery, on the green terrace high above the River Fulda, houses German and international paintings, sculptures, and objects from 1750 to today. There are many works of the Tischbein family and the elder Kassel school. Modern artists such as Lovis Corinth, Max Ernst, Paul Klee, Ernst Ludwig Kirchner, Joseph Beuys, Richard Hamilton, Claes Oldenburg, A. R. Penck, G. Baselitz, G. Richter, and M. Merz are also represented.

Admission to the Landesmuseum and the gallery is free. They are open from 10am to 5pm; closed Mon.

LIVING IN A CASTLE

The von Stockhausen family invites paying guests to their **Burg Hotel,** Trendelburg, D-3526 Trendelburg (tel. 05675/10-21), 21 miles from Kassel, from mid-February to December. Some of the trees that grow within the 15-foot-thick stone walls of this brooding medieval fortress are ancient in their own right. The fortress was built seven centuries ago on a hillock overlooking the surrounding countryside. The owners have added tennis courts and a swimming pool, but there's still plenty on hand to impart a feeling of medieval history. Access to the stone-floored courtyard takes you over a dried-out moat beneath narrow overhead slits from which an earlier generation of inhabitants poured boiling oil onto unwelcome guests. Visitors can explore the building's myriad passageways, as well as the array of stone and wooden staircases. Some of these lead into mysterious corners and baronial halls, many of which are furnished with antique halberds, swords, and oversize armoires.

Some of the 23 bedrooms contain four-poster beds, perfect for sleeping away the aches left over from an afternoon of horseback riding (there's a stable nearby). Most of the well-furnished rooms contain private baths. The accommodations in the main house are supplemented by a handful of units in an outlying building. Each contains a phone, radio, and minibar, and costs 120 DM ($71.25) daily for a single and 180 DM ($106.90) for a double. Meals in the dining room cost 35 DM ($20.80) to 72 DM ($42.75).

HAMBURG

Hamburg has many faces. A trip through the canals makes you realize why it has been called "the Venice of the North." A walk down the neon-lit Reeperbahn at night assures you that it is the "wickedest city in Europe." A ride around the Alster Lake in the center of the city reveals the elegance of its finest parks and buildings. A view from the old tower of the baroque church of St. Michael opens on the steel-and-glass buildings of modern Hamburg. A Sunday-morning visit to the Altona fish market gives you a good look at early shoppers mingling with the late-nighters from the Reeperbahn.

Above all, Hamburg has a unique and versatile personality. It's a flexible city—it has had to be to recover from the many disasters during its 1,100-year history. Not the least of these was the almost total destruction of this North Sea port during World War II. But the industrious Hamburgers seized this as an opportunity to re-build a larger and more beautiful city, with huge parks, impressive buildings, and cultural institutions.

1. Orientation

Hamburg was subject to several severe bombings in the summer of 1943, and more than half the city, including 295,000 houses, was completely destroyed. Instead of restoring the demolished buildings, the city fathers decided on a creative plan of action, and today Hamburg is Germany's showplace of modern architecture. Many historic structures stand today, side by side with towering steel-and-glass buildings. The 4½ square miles of parks and gardens are a vital part of the city. Hamburgers are proud of their 22 square miles of rivers and lakes as well.

The **Alster** is the perfect starting point for a pleasurable exploration of Hamburg. This lake, rimmed by the city's most significant buildings, sparkles with the white sails of small boats and ripples with the movement of motor launches. The lake is divided by the Lombard and John F. Kennedy Bridges into the **Binnenalster** (Inner Alster) and the larger **Aussenalster** (Outer Alster). The Binnenalster is flanked on the south and west by the **Jungfernstieg,** one of Europe's best-known streets and Hamburg's most vital artery, and also its best shopping district. For land-lubbers, the best view of the Alster is from this "maiden's path."

The **Port of Hamburg** is the world's fifth-largest harbor, stretching for nearly 25 miles along the Elbe River. More than 1,500 ships call at this important port each month, connecting it with 1,000 other cities throughout the world. Since 1189 the stretch of water has been one of the busiest centers for trade on the continent, making Hamburg one of Germany's wealthiest cities.

From the Hauptbahnhof, the rail terminus (one of the most important in the Federal Republic) on the eastern fringe of the heart of town in the vicinity of the Binnenalster, two major shopping streets fan out in a southwesterly direction, toward St. Petri Church and the Rathaus. They are Spitalerstrasse (reserved for pedestrians) and Mönckebergstrasse, paralleling it to the south. These streets contain some of the city's finest stores. Stay on Mönckebergstrasse to reach Rathausmarkt, which is dominated by the Rathaus, a Renaissance-style palace.

The center of Hamburg offers opportunities for walking, and often you can combine a stroll along a scenic boulevard with visits to stores and shops (more about that later). For example, the eastern shoreline of the Binnenalster opens onto Ballindamm, which contains many elegant stores. At the foot of this lake is the Jungfernstieg, already mentioned, but along its western shoreline is yet another main artery, the Neuer Jungfernstieg. At the intersection of the Jungfernstieg and Neuer Jungfernstieg is one of the more fascinating streets of Hamburg, the **Colonnaden,** which is a colonnade of shops and cafés. In this neighborhood stands the **Hamburgische Staatsoper** (at Dammtorstrasse 28), the famous opera house.

The city is not so compact, however, that it can be easily covered on foot. Many sections of interest are far apart, and you'll have to depend on public transportation or a taxi to reach them. For example, the infamous Reeperbahn, with its many erotic performances, lies on the western fringe, the St. Pauli district.

AIRPORT SERVICE

Fuhlsbüttel, Paul-Bämer-Platz 1-3 (tel. 040/508-0), is a straight run by bus no. 110, the HVV Airport Express, from the Ohlsdorf U- or S-Bahn station. The bus runs every 10 minutes and charges the regular fare. A special airport coach goes from the main station, stopping at coach station ZOB, the Reichshof, the Atlantic and Hamburg Plaza hotels, and the fairgrounds and exhibition center. You can watch planes from an observation platform, and at 10am, noon, and at 2 and 4pm, a scale model of air traffic handling and a film are shown.

Air taxi service can be arranged at Katnerweg 43 (tel. 040/640-10-81).

AirLift Service is offered at the airport, Building 175, Room 2009 (tel. 040/508-21-51).

GETTING AROUND HAMBURG

A word to the wise—park your car and use the public transportation in this busy and, at times, frantic city.

Public Transportation

Hamburg's **U-Bahn** is one of the best subway systems in Germany, serving the entire downtown area and connecting with the **S-Bahn's** surface trains in the suburbs. This train network is the fastest means of getting around, but if you refuse to go underground, the buses offer a good alternative. The advantage of surface travel, of course, is that you get to see more of the city. Fares range between 2 DM ($1.20) and 5.10 DM ($3.05), depending on the distance traveled.

You buy your ticket from the driver or from slot machines at stops and stations.

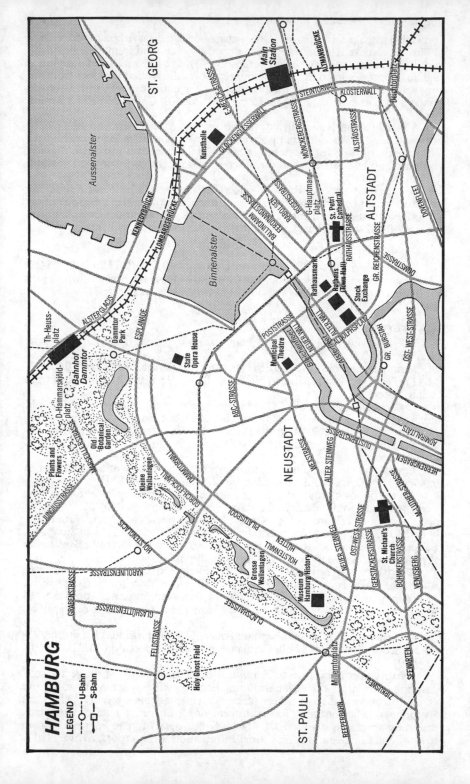

If you plan to make a day of it, you can purchase one of the day tickets and travel on it as often as you like. The **9am City Rover** is a day ticket, valid from 9am weekdays, and all day on Sat., Sun., and holidays. Costing 7 DM ($4.15), it's good until late at night in fare zones 1 and 2. The **24-Hour Rover** is valid around the clock from the time stamped on it. It can be used throughout the entire network of Hamburg's public transport system, and costs 12.50 DM ($7.40). Children under 12 travel free.

A **Family Rover** is also offered, valid from 9am Mon. to Fri. and all day Sat., Sun., and holidays, good for transportation for up to four adults and three children. There are two versions of this ticket: one is good for fare zones 1 and 2 in the city, costing 10.50 DM ($6.25); and the other is valid for the entire network, costing 14.50 DM ($8.60).

You can reserve your tickets in advance. (Day tickets are valid from the time they are actually issued.) Ask for tourist tickets at Tourist Information in the main railway station. For further information as to the transport services, fares, and special offers, phone 040/32-29-11 from 7am to 8pm.

Taxicabs

Taxis are available at all hours by telephoning 040/44-10-11 or 040/68-20-01. For a taxi for the disabled, phone 040/410-54-58. A taxi from the airport into the center costs about 25 DM ($14.85). In town, taxi meters start at 3 DM ($1.80).

FAST FACTS

The following information may help you make your visit to Hamburg more pleasant.

American Express: The office in Hamburg is at Rathausmarkt 5 (tel. 040/33-11-41). The office is open Mon. to Fri. from 10am to 1pm and 2 to 5pm; Sat. from 9am to noon.

Churches: Services in all of Hamburg's Protestant churches are generally held Sun. at 10am; St. Michaelis, St. Petri, and St. Jacobi also have services Sun. at 6pm. The English Church of St. Thomas à Becket is at Zeughausmarkt (tel. 040/31-28-05). A Lutheran service in English is held the first Sun. in the month at 6pm at St. Petri, Speersort 10.

Consulates: In case you lose your passport, or have some other needs, get in touch with the **U.S. Consulate** at Alsterufer 27 (tel. 040/44-10-61).

Currency exchange: You can exchange your currency at the Deutsche Verkehrs-Kredit-Bank branch at the main railway station (tel. 040/30-80-04-75), open daily from 7:30am to 10pm, as well as at its branch at Altona Station (tel. 040/340-37-70), open Mon. to Sat. from 7:30am to 1pm and 1:45 to 8pm; Sun. and public holidays from 10am to 1pm and 1:45 to 6pm. The Deutsche Bank has an airport branch, open daily from 6:30am to 10:30pm.

Drugstores: Pharmacies that stock foreign drugs are **Internationale Apotheke,** Ballindamm 39 (tel. 040/33-53-33), open Mon. to Fri. from 8:30am to 6:30pm; and Sat. from 9am to 2pm. **Roth's Alte Englishe Apotheke,** 48 Jungfernstieg (tel. 040/34-39-06), is open Mon. to Fri. from 8am to 6:30pm; Sat. from 9am to 1pm.

Emergencies: Phone numbers are: Police, 110; fire brigade, 112; doctor, 22-80-22; dentist, 040/468-32-60; German Automobile Association (ADAC), 040/23-99-9.

Information: For visitors to Hamburg, information is offered at several places, covering different types of data, including hotel bookings, port information, and general matters such as tour tickets, planned events, and guide services. Offices are: **Fremdenverkehrszentrale** (Tourist Information), Bierberhaus, Hachmannplatz, near the main railway station (tel. 040/24-87-00), open Mon. to Fri. from 7:30am to 6pm, Sat. from 8am to 3pm; Tourist Information at the **airport,** Arrival Hall D (tel. 040/300-51-240), open daily from 8am to 11pm; Tourist Information, **main railway station,** Kirchenallee exit (tel. 040/24-87-02-30), open daily from 7am to 11pm; **Port Information,** St. Pauli Landungsbrucken (tel. 040/31-97-77), open daily from 9am to 6pm; and Hamburg information in the **city center,** Hanse Viertel shopping mall: entrance Poststrasse (tel. 040/32-47-58), open Mon. to Fri. and the first Sat. in each month from 9am to 6pm (other Sat. from 9am to 2pm).

Lost property: Municipal and S- and U-Bahn lost property offices are at Bäckerbrietergang 73 (tel. 040/35-18-51), open Mon. and Thurs. from 8am to 3:30pm; Tues., Wed., and Fri. from 8am to noon. Railway lost property offices are at Stresemann 114 (tel. 040/39-18-55-89), open Mon. to Fri. from 7:30am to 3pm.

Swimming: Hamburg has 20 indoor and 20 outdoor swimming pools. For information, phone 040/33-97-01.

---

2. Where to Stay

With thousands of hotel beds in Hamburg, the visitor has a wide selection of accommodations to choose from, ranging from luxurious living overlooking the Alster, to clean boarding houses in the suburbs. Hamburg is an expensive city, and you'll find an abundance of first-class hotels, but a limited number of budget accommodations, especially in the city proper. During a busy convention period, you may have trouble finding a room on your own. The airport, railway station, and Bieberhaus tourist information offices have hotel booking desks. This assistance is also offered at the airport in Arrival Hall A, at Am Lehmsaal Autobahn services (Autobahn A7, northbound side), and Buddikate Autobahn services (Autobahn A1, southbound side, exit Fehmarn, Lübeck). However, if you reserve in advance, there are excellent choices available.

DELUXE HOTELS

One of the leading hotels in the world, and some say the finest in Germany, **Vier Jahreszeiten** (Four Seasons), Neuer Jungfernstieg 9, D-2000 Hamburg 36 (tel. 040/3-49-40), is a warm, mellow establishment founded in 1897 by Friedrich Haerlin and still a family business. Its position is ideal, right on the Binnenalster. Built in the baronial style, with rich wood paneling, it evokes a memory of the grand Edwardian hotels. No two of the bedrooms alike, they are immaculately kept, and despite the large size of the hotel (172 rooms), personal service is a hallmark. Single rooms with baths range from 275 DM ($163.30) to 355 DM ($210.80) daily, and double rooms with baths go from 375 DM ($222.70) to 445 DM ($264.25). The inclusive prices vary with the view and size of accommodations. All rooms contain color TVs and direct-dial phones.

The hotel's dining room, Haerlin, bedecked with old tapestries, gold-framed mirrors, and four Dionysian porcelain cherubs, is an attractive setting for the excellent international cuisine. There's also an informal Grill Room where meats are roasted on spits along one wall. The tea room, the two-level Condi (Hamburg's answer to Demel's of Vienna), is a favorite rendezvous point. International bands play in the hotel's own nightclub. Garage and parking facilities are available for guests. There are also a cocktail bar, a wine shop, and a confectioner's shop selling the chef's own pastry.

Atlantic Hotel Kempinski, An der Alster 72, D-2000 Hamburg 1 (tel. 040/2-88-80). This sumptuous hotel was one of the few buildings in its neighborhood to escape the bombs of World War II. Today, it's classified as one of the grandest hotels in the country. It occupies an enviable position near the Aussenalster in a central location filled with trees and imposing villas. Considered the flagship of the

Kempinski hotel chain, it boasts a turn-of-the-century maritime theme of Ionic columns with touches of Atlantic blue and glistening white, with detailing that might have been designed into an oceangoing yacht. These include sumptuous proportions and regal furnishings, a soaring stairwell, and a baronial lobby.

The hotel's 256 rooms and 13 luxurious suites have hosted an array of luminaries from around the world. Singles range from 270 DM ($160.35) to 330 DM ($195.95) daily and doubles from 310 DM ($184.10) to 350 DM ($207.85). The hotel provides all the services a tourist or business visitor could want, including a beautifully maintained chlorine-free indoor swimming pool and sauna. The elegance of the Atrium Bar opens onto a neoclassical fountain. The least expensive place to dine is the pub-style restaurant, Atlantic Mühle. However, the best news of the "White Castle" on the lake is saved for last: it's the Atlantic Grill, one of the finest dining rooms in North Germany. Some 55 cooks prepare a cuisine that attracts discriminating gourmets. In a stylishly sophisticated atmosphere, a modern haute cuisine is matched by a superb wine list. Meals average 68 DM ($40.40) to 110 DM ($65.30) and are served daily from noon to 3pm and 6pm to midnight.

EXPENSIVE HOTELS

A 19th-century building with 20th-century comfort is **Ramada Renaissance,** Grosse Bleichen, D-2000 Hamburg 36 (tel. 040/34-91-80). You enter a glass-and-hardwood empire of subtle lighting and comfort. From the elegant lobby to the carpeted bar area, where the primary impact is one of warm brass and polished wood, you'll be fêted by an army of waiters and serenaded by a resident pianist. Accommodations range from a well-appointed double-bedded room to a sumptuously upholstered series of suites. Singles rent for 310 DM ($184.10) to 425 DM ($252.35) daily, and doubles go for 385 DM ($228.60) to 500 DM ($296.90). Substantial reductions are sometimes granted for weekend visits. You can relax in the whirlpool or sauna before drinks in the lounge bar and dinner at the Noblesse restaurant. The 211-room hotel was built into the facade of a historic building, and the entire complex was designed with connections to the Hanse Viertel Galerie Passage, Europe's longest shopping arcade (see "Shopping").

Hamburg Marriott Hotel, ABC-Strasse 52, D-2000 Hamburg 36 (tel. 040/35-05-0), is one of the newest hotels to open in Hamburg, inaugurating its services in 1988. Built on the site of the old Gänsemarkt, where in the Middle Ages geese were sold, it stands near the Hanse Viertel shopping complex. The area surrounding the Marriott has become one of the most fashionable in Hamburg, with boutiques, wine bars, shops, and restaurants. Traditional in styling, the hotel offers 278 bedrooms with private baths floored with marble tile and sinks topped with a slab of polished granite, two phones, color TVs, minibars, and 24-hour room service. Depending on the accommodations, singles or doubles range from 290 DM ($172.20) to 380 DM ($225.65) daily. The less expensive price is for the standard rooms, and the more expensive tariff is charged for studios. Suites, and lavish ones they are, are even more expensive, of course.

The hotel also contains a modern indoor swimming pool along with a health club with exercise weights and a sauna. Many thoughtful guest services are provided, including babysitting, same-day dry cleaning and laundry (but not on weekends), a garage, and an ice machine on every floor. Guests enjoy music in the lobby-level piano bar (live music begins at 5pm), before retreating to the Sea Grill Restaurant, where, as befits Marriott's location in Hamburg, seafood specialties are served. Full meals, costing from 70 DM ($41.55), are served daily from noon to 3pm and 6pm to midnight.

SAS Hamburg Plaza, Marseillerstrasse 2, D-2000 Hamburg 36 (tel. 040/35-02-0), in Planten un Blomen Park, looks like a collection of narrow black lines banded vertically together and gives an impression of real architectural interest. Opened in 1973 and renovated in 1989, this high-rise offers 564 beautifully appointed rooms, many with handsomely paneled walls; all units come with baths, individually controlled air conditioning, color TVs, radios, and direct-dial phones. Singles rent for 225 DM ($133.60) to 310 DM ($184.10) daily, while doubles cost 275 DM ($163.30) to 360 DM ($213.75). Substantial weekend discounts are likely to be offered. The hotel stands near the international railway station, Dammtor, a 20-minute taxi ride from the airport. The disco, Blauer Satellit, on the 26th floor, offers a view over Hamburg and its harbor. The hotel has both a gourmet restaurant and a coffee shop. On the premises are a heated pool, sauna, solarium, and fitness studio.

Still steeped in Hanseatic flair and tradition, **Maritim Hotel Reichshof,** Kirchenallee 34-36, D-2000 Hamburg 1 (tel. 040/23-84-30), was built in 1910 across from the ornate spire of the Hamburg railway station. At that time, this was the most desirable location in town for a hotel, its accommodations going for 3.50 DM ($2.10) a night, regardless of the room category. Noteworthy for being the largest hotel in Europe, the Reichshof had a lobby known even then as a landmark in art deco styling.

In World War II, multiple fire bombings destroyed most of the upper floors, but the lobby with its gilded pilasters and marble sheathing was left intact. A complete renovation has substantially upgraded the hotel; renewed bedchambers are modern, and filled with reproductions of art nouveau furniture. All contain minibars, color TVs with in-house movies, and tiled private baths. The hotel is today a favorite with business travelers; consequently, it has a large number of singles (in fact, more than half of its rooms are classified as singles). They range from 185 DM ($109.85) to 285 DM ($169.25) daily, with doubles costing 250 DM ($148.45) to 370 DM ($219.70). Apartments and studios are also rented.

The hotel's restaurant, one of the finest in the heart of town, is recommended separately. Located next door to the Schauspielhaus, the Reichshof is only a few minutes from the Alster and the Elbe.

Aussen Alster Hotel, Schmilinskystrasse 11, D-2000 Hamburg 1 (tel. 040/ 24-15-57), small and exclusive, attracts actors, advertising directors, executives, writers, and artists. Its stylish, ultramodern interior was designed by one of Germany's most famous architects. This 27-room hotel sits on a quiet residential street, about a five-minute walk from the railway station and a three-minute walk from the Alster. Its 19th-century facade is painted milk white, capped with an Italianate-inspired frieze. Intimate, charming, and managed with panache, the hotel is owned and operated by Hamburg film producer Klaus Feddermann and his partner Burkhard Stoelck. The lobby walls exhibit works of a number of European artists. There's a garden in back, as well as a sauna and an Italian restaurant. Rooms are white-walled, angular, and consciously simple except for the modern art decorating their walls. They cost 150 DM ($89.05) to 185 DM ($109.85) daily for a single and 190 DM ($112.80) to 250 DM ($148.45) for a double, with breakfast, taxes, and service included.

Hotel Berlin, Borgfelderstrasse 1-9, D-2000 Hamburg 26 (tel. 040/25-16-40), at a busy intersection about half a mile from the main railway station, is a convenient accommodation, particularly for motorists. Its handsome bedrooms—93 in all—have extra-wide beds, minibars, color TVs, radios, direct-dial phones, baths and showers, toilets, hairdryers, and double-glazed windows. Special pleasure is added by the small basket of fruit in your room on your arrival, a morning newspaper at breakfast, and a bedtime candy treat. Singles cost 115 DM ($68.30) to 145 DM ($86.10) daily, depending on the size, the price of doubles being 160 DM ($95) to 190 DM ($112.80). Children under 18 can sleep in their parents' rooms free. À la carte meals are served in the Brasserie daily from noon to 3pm and 6 to 10pm. The hotel has a bar, a car park, and an underground garage.

Garden Hotel Poseldorf, Magdalenenstrasse 60, D-2000 Hamburg 13 (tel. 040/44-99-59), has had a long history, dating from 1791. Over the years it has entertained many luminaries, including King Christian VIII of Denmark in 1824. The location, however, isn't for everyone. It stands in the Hamburg-Harvestehude district, about a mile from the historic heart of town and some 6 miles from the Hamburg airport. On the western sector of the Outer Alster Lake, it attracts many visitors from the publishing industry. An opulent display of potted plants lends justification to the name of "garden" hotel. Modern art and well-chosen antiques add to the sophisticated comfort of the rooms, 73 in all, ranging from 155 DM ($92.05) to 255 DM ($151.40) daily for a single, 270 DM ($160.35) to 380 DM ($225.64) for a double. The hotel, which serves breakfast only, has a bar adjoining the winter garden.

Europäischer Hof, Kirchenallee 45, D-2000 Hamburg 1 (tel. 040/24-82-48), established in 1925 and still directed by the Berk family, is the largest privately owned hotel in Hamburg. All 320 rooms are equipped with baths or showers, cable color TVs, minibars, and direct-dial phones. Singles cost 130 DM ($77.20) to 210 DM ($124.70) daily, with doubles going for 160 DM ($95) to 260 DM ($154.40), including service and taxes. In the city center, the hotel stands across from the main station and is protected from noise by soundproof windows. A trio of restaurants awaits visitors, including the Hamburger Restaurant, the Bürgerstuben, and the Jägerstuble, serving both an international and regional cuisine. A garage is connected directly to the hotel, which also has a sports and leisure center.

Prem Hotel, An der Alster 9, D-2000 Hamburg 1 (tel. 040/24-54-54), is an elderly house in a beautiful situation. An attractive and sophisticated clientele makes this "white house on the Alster" its home in Hamburg during frequent trips to the city. Originally a mansion, the hotel has been in the possession of the Prem family since it was first established in 1912. The glistening white facade overlooks the lake, and the rear faces a quiet garden with umbrella-covered tables. The reception salons are dignified and show off a personalized collection of French antiques and reproductions. A beautiful Gobelin tapestry hangs in the lobby, and, most of the 52 bedrooms are furnished with white-and-gold Louis XV–style pieces. Singles are priced at 185 DM ($109.85) to 305 DM ($181.10) daily, and doubles rent for 270 DM ($106.35) to 340 DM ($201.90). The garden-facing accommodations are much quieter than the front rooms on the Alster. You can enjoy breakfast in the white-and-gold dining room jutting out into the garden. The restaurant also serves well-prepared lunches and dinners.

MODERATELY PRICED HOTELS

Seven floors of modern architectural design greet visitors to the **Ambassador,** Heidenkampsweg 34, D-2000 Hamburg 1 (tel. 040/23-00-02), a 124-room hotel affiliated with Best Western. The bar, restaurant, swimming pool, and bedrooms are all attractive and pleasant places to spend time in, and the management blends chain-hotel efficiency with personal service. Singles range in price from 105 DM ($62.35) to 165 DM ($98) daily, while doubles cost 185 DM ($109.85) to 260 DM ($154.40), breakfast included.

Hotel Bellevue, An der Alster 14, D-2000 Hamburg 1 (tel. 040/24-80-11), just a short ride from the central station, faces the Alster. The 80-room building has been considerably updated. Though some of the larger rooms contain traditional furnishings, the newer singles are modern, often in the Scandinavian style. All rooms contain direct-dial phones, color TVs, and minibars. The front windows open onto the lake, but the back rooms are quieter. Singles with private baths go for 130 DM ($77.20) to 160 DM ($95), and doubles with baths or showers cost 185 DM ($109.85) to 210 DM ($124.70); prices include service and taxes, plus a buffet breakfast. The Alster Room on the ground floor serves as a breakfast room, and you can enjoy international cuisine as well as regional specialties in the cozy Pilsner Urquell Stuben. Live organ music is played in the INA bar after 8pm. Guests may leave their cars in the hotel parking lot or in the underground garage. Many theatrical celebrities make this their Hamburg choice.

Alster-Hof, Esplanade 12, D-2000 Hamburg 36 (tel. 040/35-00-70), is a serviceable 120-room hotel on a quiet street near the Binnenalster. Bathless singles rent for 120 DM ($71.25) daily; with showers and toilets, the price goes up to 150 DM ($89.05). Doubles cost 180 DM ($106.90) to 210 DM ($124.70), depending on plumbing and location. One of the better-known middle-bracket hotels of Hamburg, the Alster-Hof is well recommended.

Fürst Bismarck, Kirchenallee 49, D-2000 Hamburg 1 (tel. 040/280-10-91). This building looks best when approached through one of Hamburg's frequent mists, when it rises abruptly from a narrow corner lot in all its black, white, and gilded splendor. The interior has been carefully renovated to keep the personalized feeling of being in a special place. The 59 rooms rent for 155 DM ($92.05) daily for a double with shower and toilet, dropping to 100 DM ($59.40) to 125 DM ($74.25) for a single.

Hafen Hamburg, Seewartenstrasse 9, D-2000 Hamburg 1 (tel. 040/31-11-30). Constructed in the Wilhelmian style, this Hamburg landmark offers splendid views of the river and harbor traffic. The grand staircase is an elaborately twisting wrought-iron fantasy "like they'll never make again," and the 252 rooms are unusually spacious. Singles go for 105 DM ($62.35) to 145 DM ($86.10) daily, while doubles rent for 140 DM ($83.15) to 180 DM ($106.90), breakfast included. If you can afford it, take the more expensive harbor-view rooms.

St. Raphael, Adenauerallee 41, D-2000 Hamburg 1 (tel. 040/24-82-00). This well-administered hotel on the famous Adenauerallee is constructed of white brick, with modern soundproof windows to guarantee a good night's sleep. The interior has the kind of simplicity that soothes and relaxes you after a decadent night on the Reeperbahn. Hans Gerst is the manager here, and he charges 150 DM ($89.05) to 170 DM ($100.95) daily for a single and 170 DM ($100.95) to 190 DM ($112.80) for a double. The hotel has recently been completely redecorated, all rooms featuring showers or baths, radios, TVs, in-house movies in English, minibars, hairdryers, electric trouser presses. A buffet breakfast is included in the rates. The hotel has a fitness center with a sauna, a solarium, and a Jacuzzi, plus a sweeping view over Hamburg and its port.

Hotel Norge, Schäferkampsalle 49, D-2000 Hamburg 36 (tel. 040/44-11-50), lies away from the center in the Eimsbüttel district. It offers you Norwegian hospitality and a "Gateway to Scandinavia" from the Continent. The hotel is modern and undistinguished on the outside, but warms considerably in its interior. Its Kon Tiki Grill merits a separate recommendation (see below). The 90 rooms are compact, but have all the conveniences: showers, direct-dial phones, trouser presses, videos, minibars, and cable TVs. Single rates are 150 DM ($89.05) daily, with doubles costing 175 DM ($103.90). Facilities include a pool, sauna, and massage service.

BUDGET HOTELS

A 23-room family-style hostelry, the **Wedina Hotel,** Gurlittstrasse 23, D-2000 Hamburg 1 (tel. 040/24-30-11), is just a minute from the lake and a five-minute walk from the railway station. Most of the bedrooms open onto a small, informal rear garden. It's a pleasant, quiet retreat, owned and run by an English-speaking family. Bathless singles rent for 65 DM ($38.60) to 70 DM ($41.55) daily. With bath or shower, the price for a single is 90 DM ($53.45) to 95 DM ($56.40); for a double, 115 DM ($68.30) to 135 DM ($80.15). Breakfast, service, and taxes are included, and these tariffs also cover the use of a swimming pool. No parking facilities are available other than metered spaces in front of the hotel.

Hotel Pension am Dammtor, Schülterstrasse 2, D-2000 Hamburg 13 (tel. 040/510-63-00), was originally built as a private villa, its yellow stone walls rising four imposing stories above a small but heavily forested plot of linden trees. It lies within a 10-minute walk north of the center of Hamburg, near the television tower and the residential neighborhood of Dammtor. Owned and operated by the Hamann family (Erika and Hans), the place contains 42 clean and decent rooms, most (but not all) of which contain private baths. With breakfast included, and depending on the plumbing, singles range from 55 DM ($32.65) to 85 DM ($50.45), with doubles renting for 75 DM ($44.55) to 120 DM ($71.25). Other than breakfast, no meals are served, but a wide selection of Greek, Yugoslav, Turkish, French, and German restaurants are in the neighborhood. U-Bahn and S-Bahn stops are Dammtor. The university is within close walking distance.

Süderelbe, Grosser Schippsee 29, D-2000 Hamburg 90 (tel. 040/77-32-14). Only breakfast is served in this modern hotel, which was built next to one of Hamburg's outlying parking garages. The hotel is in the Harburg district, away from the center of town. Many guests save money by staying here and reaching the heart of Hamburg by public transportation. Each of the 21 quiet, pleasant bedrooms is filled with a collection of comfortable contemporary furniture and contains a private bath, phone, and radio. Rooms cost 95 DM ($56.40) daily for a single and 120 DM ($71.25) to 130 DM ($77.20) for a double.

---

3. Where to Dine

Hamburg life is tied to the sea, and nothing reflects this more than the cuisine. Lobster from Helgoland, shrimp from Büsum, turbot, plaice, and sole from the North Sea, and fresh oysters in huge quantities, make up the Hamburger's diet. Of course, there's also the traditional meat dish, Hamburger steak, called Stubenküchen, and the favorite sailor's dish, Labskaus, made with cured meat, potatoes, herring, and Gherkins. The eel soup is probably the best known of all Hamburg's typical dishes. Sweet-and-sour eel soup is said to contain more than 75 different ingredients. The cuisine of Hamburg was commented upon by Heinrich Heine, who knew the city in his youth. He called it "the best Republic: Its manners are from England and its food is from Heaven."

THE TOP RESTAURANTS

North of the city center, at Eppendorf, is **Le Canard,** Martinistrasse 11 (tel. 040/880-50-57), whose haute cuisine has given it the reputation of one of the best restaurants in Germany. Virtually every major restaurant critic in the Federal Republic has lauded the unusual cuisine moderne of its imaginative owner-chef, Josef Viehhauser. You'll dine amid an unpretentious decor of flowers, framed lithographs, and contemporary accents, made more alluring by the softly discreet lighting. Meals are culinary events. Your elegant repast might include a set of seasonally adjusted dishes, including medallions of lobster garnished with mussels and leaf spinach, a suprême of sea bass with an herb-flavored sabayon, or Barbary duckling stuffed with goose liver. For dessert you are faced with a wide choice, including a melon-flavored cake garnished with strawberry cream or a mocha-flavored parfait with mango segments. A fixed-price "quick lunch" can cost as little as 60 DM ($35.65), but be prepared to pay between 100 DM ($59.40) and 125 DM ($74.25) in the evening. Hours for lunch begin at noon; for dinner from 6pm to 11pm; closed Sun. Advance reservations are essential.

Landhaus Scherrer, Elbchaussee 130 (tel. 040/880-13-25), was a brewery in its previous incarnation, but that is all gone now. The Landhaus is a citadel of gastronomy on the Elbe River at Altona outside the heart of Hamburg. It has gained a reputation for correct service and imaginatively prepared food in an amiable and genteel setting. Specialties are fresh fish and shellfish, excellent meats, and mushrooms imported from Morocco. An unusual variation might be roast goose with rhubarb in a cassis sauce. Dessert might be a praline cream or one of 30 types of pastries loading down the sweets trolley. Meals begin at 60 DM ($35.65), going up to 145 DM ($86.10) for a special menu. Service is from noon to midnight; closed Sun. Because of the restaurant's location in a country house surrounded by trees, it's also popular with local residents for wedding receptions.

One of Hamburg's leading restaurants is **Peter Lembcke,** Holzdamm 49 (tel. 040/24-32-90), in an unprepossessing location on the second floor of an old town house. It attracts a widely diverse clientele, from sculptors to bankers. The good-hearted, helter-skelter service adds to the charm, but the food is the real attraction here. Lembcke specializes in the cuisine of northern Germany, including the most local dish of all, Labskaus. A house specialty that attracts a loyal following of gourmets is the eel soup, with dill and fruit swimming in the broth. Possibly a more appealing dish to the foreign palate is the house bouillabaisse. Besides the best Kalbs filet, the restaurant serves excellent steaks. Dinner ranges in price from 50 DM ($29.70) to 85 DM ($50.45). Meals are served from noon to 11pm; closed Sun. Lembcke's is invariably crowded, and late arrivals without reservations must wait it out in the foyer, so phone ahead.

W. Schumann's Austernkeller, Jungfernstieg 34 (tel. 040/34-62-65), is admittedly one of the most expensive restaurants in the city, but this one is really worth it. You'll pay dearly for a dozen oysters at this "oyster cellar," but what a treat for those who can afford it. Available September through April, the oysters are selected by the chef as if he were buying pearls. To enter this belle-époque restaurant, founded in 1884, is to be instantly transported back into the grand, elegant world of the Kaisers. You can dine "in state" in one of the tiny private dining salons, each one decorated differently, from intimate rustic to Empire, with silk damask wall coverings, paneled dadoes, doors with large brass handles, and gilt mirrors. There are even a few Biedermeier salons. The restaurant, suitably situated in the Heinrich Heine House, has been in the same family for about a century. The best of fresh fish is served, and the chef knows how to prepare a platter just right. Meals begin at 55 DM ($32.65), but could easily go up to 130 DM ($77.20). Hours are noon to 3pm and 6 to 11pm; closed Sun.

Fischereihafen Restaurant, Grosse Elbstrasse 143 (tel. 040/38-18-16), established some 35 years ago, is considered the best seafood restaurant in Hamburg. Every day the staff buys only the freshest of fish and shellfish at the Hamburg auction hall. The menu is changed daily depending on what "fruits of the sea" are available. On the second floor, the place is said to be filled with "fish and VIPs"—the latter including the likes of Helmut Kohl or Tina Turner. The former is likely to include an appetizer of filet of sole and lobster à la nage, or perhaps a plate of fresh oysters. You can then peruse the rest of Neptune's creations, including the house special, turbot with salmon mousse that has been dotted with truffles. Meals cost 40 DM ($23.75) to 95 DM ($56.40) and are served daily from 11:30am to 10:30pm. Picture windows open onto a view of the Elbe. The restaurant is a 10-minute taxi ride from the wharf area of Landungsbrücken.

Mühlenkamper Fährhaus, Hans-Henny-Jahnn-Weg 1 (tel. 040/220-69-34), in the Hamburg-Uhlenhorst district, near the Alster Fleet, has been a Hamburg landmark for some 50 years. A favorite rendezvous of the city's most discerning diners, it has a menu that is a virtual encyclopedia of German, French, and international food; overall, the cuisine reflects a light touch, based on North German ingredients. For example, you might enjoy an eel in dill jelly. The chef will also prepare game specialties, even diet dishes as per your desire. In my opinion, however, he excels in such classics as goose liver with truffles. Three hundred varieties of wine are available. A fixed-price meal, and it's a honey, is offered for 70 DM ($41.55). However, you can dine for less, about 50 DM ($29.70), if you are modest in your selections. The family owners keep the place open from noon to 11pm; closed for Sat. dinner and Sun. Reservations are essential, as this place is a celebrity favorite.

MODERATELY PRICED RESTAURANTS

The city takes pride in the distinguished **Ratsweinkeller Hamburg,** Grosse Johannisstrasse 2 (tel. 040/36-41-53), in business since 1896. The theme is suggested at the entrance, where you'll find a stone statue of Bacchus. The main dining hall has high vaulted ceilings, wood-paneled columns, and medieval scenes depicted on the three large stained-glass windows. One excellent dish is the halibut steak in a curry sauce. The fresh sole bonne femme is heavenly and served in large portions, and try the Hamburg crab soup. Meals begin at 35 DM ($20.80), going up to 80 DM ($47.50) and beyond. Listen for the great-grandfather clock to chime the quarter hour, resounding throughout the chambers. They serve from 10am to 11pm; closed Sun. and holidays.

Classic-Restaurant, Maritim Hotel Reichshof, Kirchenallee 34-36 (tel. 040/24-83-30), is in the vicinity of Hamburg's railway station. For traditionalists who gravitate to a lavish belle-époque style, this previously recommended hotel is a local landmark. The dining room was designed to resemble the dining room on a favorite transatlantic steamer, *Cap Polonia*. Today, its translucent marble lighting fixtures and carved wooden cherub heads and art deco glamour make it one of Hamburg's favorite places for a before- or after-theater supper. Two of the city's major theaters are just a short walk from the hotel.

During the day, guests enjoy tea in the lounge, a popular meeting place, and in the evening they can relax over a pre-dinner drink in the bar. The Piano Bar, richly decorated with paneling and leather upholstery, offers live music every night (except Sun.) from 8pm to 2am. The bar is open daily from 5pm to as late as 5am, depending on business, and the restaurant serves from noon to 3pm and 6pm to midnight; closed Sun.

Always look for a page on the menu outlining the specials of the day, which you can often order for as little as 30 DM ($17.80). Otherwise, you can select from an extensive à la carte menu, beginning with anything from fresh lobster to Beluga caviar. A local favorite is smoked eel with scrambled eggs. Rich soups are always available, as is a wide selection of fish, including North Sea turbot prepared in several ways. You can also enjoy a number of beef dishes, or what Germans call *traditionelle Gerichte* (popular dishes), such as veal Züricher style or fried calves' liver with onions, apple slices, and mashed potatoes. Desserts are homemade, ranging from peach Melba to crêpes Reichshof. À la carte dinners cost from 45 DM ($26.70).

Alsterpavillon, Am Jungfernstieg 54 (tel. 040/34-50-52), is a pavilion built right on the Binnenalster. Café tables are placed outside in summer, when the lake takes on a festive air. The food isn't ignored, however, just because of the scenic location: the sole meunière in chive butter is a superb selection, and other specialties include Strasbourg Sauerkraut with pork. A good beginning for any meal is Matjes herring. Set lunches are served daily from 35 DM ($20.80); an average à la carte meal will cost from 50 DM ($29.70). Food is served daily from 11am to 8pm. The Alsterpavillon has been in business for almost two centuries, albeit with intermittent closings and reopenings. Heinrich Heine was a regular customer, perhaps thinking romantic and poetic thoughts as he watched the world go by.

Petit Délice, Grosse Bleichen 21 (tel. 040/34-34-70), is part of the rapidly emerging "new Hamburg," a restaurant movement characterized by a light minimalist decor, Neue Küche, and small, intimate tables. The location of this 10-table modern bistro is at the rear of In der Galleria, a stylish shopping complex in the center of the city. The menu is based on seasonal shopping and therefore changes frequently. Many models who visit the place begin with a fresh garden salad, made with a number of different types of crisp lettuce. You might ask for dandelion greens with braised goose liver, which could be followed with a perfectly flavored lamb platter (cooked pink) served with ratatouille and crisply cooked vegetables. The menu is wisely limited, and everything is prepared to order. It's not inexpensive either, with meals costing 60 DM ($35.65) and up. Service is from noon to 3pm and 6 to 11pm; closed Sun. Because of the limited space, reservations are necessary.

il ristorante, Grosse Bleichen 16 (tel. 040/34-33-35), is perhaps the most fashionable Italian restaurant in Hamburg. In the heart of town, in a very modern building, it is luxurious and rather formal. You reach it by going up a metal stairwell, exposed by glass to the street, one level below. There, at the top, amid seasonal flowering shrubs, you can enjoy the ambience, the formal service, and the high-quality meals, which make use of very fresh ingredients. Typical dishes are likely to include crayfish in a saffron sauce, marinated salmon with a green asparagus mousse, and a cream of carrot and celery soup that is perfectly done. A set meal costs 80 DM ($47.50). However, you can get by on the à la carte menu for about 40 DM ($23.75) and up. Hours are daily from noon to midnight. Reservations are needed.

Restaurant im Finnlandhaus, Esplanade 41 (tel. 040/34-41-33), is a panoramic restaurant close to the heart of the city. The setting is Finnish, with warm autumnal colors and stylish molded armchairs, and the cuisine is Finnish as well, along with international recipes. It's a chic place to dine, in the modern glass Finland House near the Binnenalster. Take the elevator to the top, where the restaurant opens on three sides to spectacular views of the city. On the à la carte menu, a good beginning is the Brazil avocado with crabmeat. Specialties include Finnish salmon soup, cured salmon, and moose prepared several different ways. Meals cost 45 DM ($26.70) to 80 DM ($47.50). The kitchen is open Mon. to Fri. from noon to 10pm and on Sun. from 11:30am to 3pm, when a good Finnish buffet is served. Closed Sat. and for dinner Sun.

Fernsehturm Hamburg Restaurant, Lagerstrasse 2-8 (tel. 040/43-80-24), serves food as good as the view you get while you dine about halfway up Hamburg's 900-foot Television Tower (in the suburb of Rotherbaum) and the fully air-conditioned room revolves (one complete turn each hour). One of Hamburg's best-known chefs is in charge, and English-speaking waiters are available. Meals range from 27 DM ($16.05) to 75 DM ($44.55). During the afternoon, you can have coffee and cake. Visitors must have a 5-DM ($2.95) ticket to ascend the tower.

Alte Mühle, Alte Mühle 34, in Bergstedt (tel. 040/6-04-91-71), is a restaurant in a residential quarter, near a waterfall with an old mill. Home-style German fare is featured, including pigs' trotters with Sauerkraut and potatoes. Many Hamburgers make the journey here just to enjoy the fresh carp with melted butter, horseradish, and potatoes. However, the chef delivers his peak performance when he serves venison with red cabbage. An average meal will cost 30 DM ($17.80) to 60 DM ($35.65). The old mill is open for dining from 11am to 10pm; closed Wed. After a satisfying meal, you can take a walk through the pond-filled woods and watch the horses nearby.

Alsterpark, Brombeerweg 12c (tel. 040/59-65-34), is a restaurant with elegantly set tables with masses of flowers, run by Jaap Niermeijer. It's a gemütlich place near where the Alster River leads into the Alstersee. Summertime patrons prefer to sit on the terrace, but the interior is decorated with taste and flair. Weekly specials change frequently. A six-course fixed-price meal is offered for 50 DM ($29.70), an eight-course meal going for 75 DM ($44.55). The cuisine is a mixture of classical French and modern, including such specialties as breast of hen sautéed with green peppercorns, pike mousse in fresh crab sauce, and rack of wild hare. The restaurant is open from noon to 2:30pm and 6 to 9:30pm; closed Sat. and closed for a few weeks' vacation (the exact dates change yearly).

Deichgraf, Deichstrasse 23 (tel. 040/36-42-08), is an elegant restaurant with an unusual collection of antiques, one of which is a four-foot model of a many-sailed schooner. You'll recognize the building by its five-story town-house structure sandwiched into a centrally located city block. Featured are such northern German specialties as salmon in a mustard-flavored dill sauce and fresh seasonal lobster prepared in any number of ways. You can also order several kinds of fondue here. Many of the shellfish specialties are sold by weight. You can get a filling meal for about 50 DM ($29.70), but your tab will run far more, of course, if you order lobster. The establishment is open from 11am to 11pm; Sat. from 6 to 11pm; closed Sun. and public holidays. The restaurant is dedicated to the man who was responsible for the area's dikes and the thousands of men who have maintained them, preventing parts of the city from being flooded on many occasions.

Old Commercial Room, Englische Planke 10 (tel. 040/36-63-19), founded in 1643, is so tied into maritime life in Hamburg that many residents consider it the premier sailor's stopover. It is, in my opinion, the best place in town to order Labskaus, prepared with devotion by the chef of the restaurant. Labskaus is actually a kind of North Sea hash, a mixture of beer, onions, pickles, and beets. If you order a plate of it, you're given a numbered certificate proclaiming you as a genuine Labskaus-eater. You can also order many other traditional North German dishes. Fixed-price meals cost from 48 DM ($28.50). Located at the foot of St. Michaelis Church, the sailors' church, the establishment is open daily from 11am to 1am. Its name, along with that of the street, Englische Planke, speaks of the historic mercantile links between Hamburg and England.

BUDGET RESTAURANTS

The oldest vegetarian restaurant in the world—and certainly the best known —**Vegetarische Gästatte,** Neuerwall 13 (tel. 040/34-47-03), makes a refreshing change of pace. The second-floor restaurant, which has been around since 1892, consists of three generous rooms, one of them in terrace style with surrounding windows. Yogurt fans will find the product here among the best. Meals cost 12 DM ($7.15) to 25 DM ($14.85). Get your check as you enter. The restaurant is open Mon. to Fri. from 11:30am to 7:30pm; Sat. from 11:30am to 5pm; Sun. from noon to 5pm.

Destille, Brockestrasse 1 (tel. 040/280-33-54), is sheltered within one of Hamburg's museums, Das Museum für Kunst und Gewerbe. This art nouveau restaurant has been called a rendezvous point for entrepreneurs, art dealers, and minor celebrities. The food is uncompromisingly good, including an array of salads, cold marinated meats, and an enormous cheese board. Every day at lunch a portion of the steaming "hot pot" will cost a reasonable 9 DM ($5.35). An enormous salad plate can make your lunch at 21 DM ($12.45), or for 25 DM ($14.85) you can have a meal large enough to sate your appetite for hours. The place is open daily from 10am to 5pm; closed Mon.

Hotel Norge with **Kon-Tiki Grill,** Schäferkampsallee 49 (tel. 040/44-11-50), lies outside the center, in the Eimsbüttel district. Scandinavian specialties are featured at this hotel dining room with a modern decor. The Kon-Tiki buffet is something you'd otherwise have to go to Oslo for, and the other specialties include fish, meats, and both hot and cold vegetable dishes. A fixed-price meal begins at 30 DM ($17.80), but you can spend far more, of course, unless you're careful. Open from noon to 3pm and 6 to 11pm.

Flic Flac Bistro, Blankeneser Landstrasse 29 (tel. 040/86-53-45), is an attractive bistro awash with unusual lithographs and fresh flowers—the personal statement, in fact, of its owner, Iris Seybold. After it opened a few years ago, its garden terrace quickly became popular with a young professional crowd. Menu items include a full repertoire of French and German cuisine moderne, with an emphasis on fresh vegetables and light-textured sauces. Only dinner is served. Full meals begin as low as 35 DM ($20.80) but could go as high as 55 DM ($32.65). Hours are from 6pm to around midnight; closed Mon. The annual closing stretches from mid-March to mid-April.

Fischerhaus, Fischmarkt 14 (tel. 040/31-40-53), is a classic Hamburg seafood restaurant, and also most reasonable in price, with meals costing from 35 DM ($20.80). The German home cooking served here daily from 11am to midnight has been called "down to earth"; everything from Hamburger eel soup to Helgoland crab soup to sole meunière, from lake trout to tuna steak with onions and spices, is offered. Seasonal specialties include steamed fresh carp with creamed horseradish, butter sauce, and boiled potatoes, and fresh mussels in white wine sauce with leeks, onions, and garlic. You get no culinary surprises here, but few disappointments either. Tables are often shared, and the atmosphere is rustic and informal, just the way the long line of habitués wants to keep it.

Zum Wattkorn, Tangstedter Landstrasse 230 (tel. 040/520-37-97). Austrian cuisine is served in generous portions in the popular Biergarten of this old-fashioned guesthouse. It's situated outside the commercial core of the city in a green oasis of nesting birds and flowering plants. The menu, which changes each week, makes good use of seasonally available fruits and vegetables. Fixed-price meals begin at 28 DM ($16.65), going up to 55 DM ($32.65). Hours are from noon to 2:30pm and 6 to 9pm; closed Mon. A handful of bedrooms are also available.

Nikolaikeller, Cremon 36 (tel. 040/36-61-13). You can see the sprawling maritime facilities of Hamburg from the windows of this place, filled with a no-nonsense crowd of local businesspeople and workers. The menu includes more than two dozen varieties of herring, including all traditional preparations. Ample quantities of local beer are provided in oversize mugs. Full meals begin at a low of 20 DM ($11.90) and are served from noon to midnight; closed Sun. and annually in July.

Restaurant Cuneo, Davidstrasse 11 (tel. 040/31-25-80), is in the St. Pauli neighborhood, a place for good Italian food at reasonable prices. If you're in the area for fun at night, and want reliable cookery, then head here. Behind an unprepossessing facade, it opens onto crowded rooms that look like an art director's concept of what a Greenwich Village eatery might have been like in the 1930s. People from all walks of life crowd into this place, which is usually filled to overflowing every evening. Grilled fish is one of the most expensive items on the menu, but you can also order pizza, carpaccio, spaghetti with pesto, gnocchi with Gorgonzola, and Venetian-style liver. Meals, costing from 40 DM ($23.75), are served nightly from 7pm to 1am.

DINING IN THE ENVIRONS

Sagebiels Fährhaus, Blankeneser Hauptstrasse 107 (tel. 040/86-15-14), in an old house on a terrace above the Elbe River in Blankenese, has a clear view of ships going up and down the stream. Kaiser Wilhelm once celebrated his birthday here. In the glassed-in dining room, you can enjoy traditional German food, served attractively and capably. Try to get a seat on the garden terrace if the weather is fine. Meals cost 40 DM ($23.75) to 80 DM ($47.50), and hours are noon to 11pm. In the off-season, the restaurant is closed on Mon. Blankenese is 10 miles from the heart of Hamburg.

---

4. The Sights

Before you tour the city, you can get a good overall view from the tower of the **Hauptkirche St. Michaelis,** Kravenkamp 4c (Michaeliskirchplatz), Hamburg's favorite landmark. It is considered the finest baroque church in North Germany. The view from the top of the hammered copper tower is magnificent. Church and tower are open Mon. to Sat. from 9am to 5:30pm; Sun. from 11:30am to 5:30pm (in winter, from 10am to 4pm; Sun. 11:30am to 4pm). Take the elevator or climb the 449 steps.

The Altstadt actually has little left of the old architecture, but there are a few sights among the canals (fleets) that run through this section from the Alster to the Elbe. The largest of the older buildings is the **Rathaus** (tel. 040/36-81-20-62), which is modern compared with many of Germany's town halls. Hamburg's Rathaus is a Renaissance-style structure built in the late 19th century on a foundation of 4,000 oak piles. With a sumptuous 647-room interior, this seat of the senate and the city council can be visited on guided tours, costing 1 DM (60¢). Tours in English are given Mon. to Thurs., hourly from 10:15am to 3:15pm; Fri., Sat., and Sun. from 10:15am to 1:15pm. No guided tours are given during official functions. The Rathaus's 160-foot clock tower overlooks the **Rathausmarkt** and the **Alster Fleet,** the city's largest canal. A visit to the Rathaus can be combined with a stop at the **Hamburg Stock Exchange** on Adolphsplatz (tel. 040/36-74-44), which is back-to-back with the Rathaus. Guided tours are provided Mon. to Fri. at 11:15am.

A few blocks away is **St. Petri Church,** Mönckeberstrasse (tel. 040/32-44-38), built in the 12th century and renovated in 1842. The lionhead knocker on the main door is the oldest piece of art in Hamburg, dating from 1342. The nearby 14th-century church of **St. Jacobi,** Jacobikirchhof an der Steinstrasse (tel. 040/32-77-44), was destroyed during World War II, but its tower and the Arp-Schnittger organ were rebuilt.

Hamburg's highest structure is the 900-foot **Heinrich-Hertz-Turm,** (the television tower), Lagerstrasse 2-8 (tel. 040/43-80-24). Visitors can climb to the observation platform, at 425 feet, where there's a restaurant, open daily from 9am to 11pm in summer; from 10am to 10pm in winter, already recommended. To go up in the tower by elevator costs 5 DM ($2.95).

The **Museum of Hamburg History** (Museum für Hamburgische Geschichte), Holstenwall 24, contains the **Historic Emigration Office** (tel. 040/349-12-23-60), which allows you to trace your roots if your ancestors came through Hamburg. The Hamburg Association for the Protection of Emigrants was founded in 1850 to protect the city's migrant guests from many countries. Ships' agents were required to give the authorities complete lists of all passengers, with names, sexes, ages, occupations, and places of origin. The Emigrant Lists, a treasure of America's heritage, survive intact, so if your ancestors include persons from Germany, Russia, Poland, or other Eastern European countries, you can have their names looked for. This service costs $30 for each year covered in the research, whether the name you want is found or not. The office is open Tues. to Sat. from 10am to 1pm and 2 to 5pm. The museum also has displays on local history. It is open from 10am to 5pm; closed Mon. Admission to the museum is 3 DM ($1.80) for adults, 70 DM (40¢) for children. A family ticket for parents and children costs 5 DM ($2.95).

Hamburger Kunsthalle, Glockengiesserwall 1 (tel. 040/24-86-1), is the leading art museum in northern Germany. One of the most outstanding works is the altarpiece painted for the St. Petri Church in 1379 by Master Bertram, Hamburg's first painter known by name, and the leading master of 14th-century Germany. The 24 scenes on the wing-panels are a free adaptation of the medieval text "The Mirror of Human Salvation," and depict the story of mankind from the Creation to the Flight into Egypt. Particularly interesting is the panel showing the creation of the animals, in which a primitive Christ-like figure is surrounded by the animals of His creation, from the fish of the sea to the fowl of the air. As a sardonic note, or possibly prophetic, one little fox is already chewing the neck of the lamb next to it. In the center panel of the Crucifixion, Master Bertram has depicted prophets, apostles, and saints; in a band above, more prophets appear in medallions. The wise and foolish virgins are lined up above the center shrine.

The museum also contains works by Master Francke, a Dominican monk, including the altar of St. Thomas of Canterbury (1424) with the first representation of the murder in the cathedral. There is a remarkable collection of Dutch and local paintings of the 17th century. Van Dyck, Rembrandt, Claude Lorrain, Ruisdael, Tiepolo, Goya, Boucher, and Fragonard are well represented, as is the German school, particularly by Mengs, Denner, and Tischbein. Emphasis is laid on 19th-century art, beginning with Wilson, Reynolds, and Fuseli. Friedrich's landscapes and Runge's visions are hardly to be seen better anywhere else where work of the Romantic Movement is to be viewed. The Nazarenes (Overbeck, Cornelius) are followed by the British Pre-Raphaelites (Rossetti, Burne-Jones, Dyce). Later trends are represented by Meissonier, Corot, Daubigny, Courbet, von Marées, Menzel, Leibl, Böcklin, Feuerbach, Liebermann, and Corinth. Notable works by French impressionists are the *Nana* by Manet and paintings by Degas, Monet, and Renoir. Twentieth-century artists are represented by Munch, Kirchner, Dix, Beckmann, Kandinsky, Klee (*Golden Fish* and *Revolution of the Viaduct*), and Ernst. Sculpture of the 19th and 20th centuries—by Rodin, Maillol, Matisse, Barlach, Marini, Moore, Calder, Segal, Luginbuehl, and Nachi—is also shown. Hours are Tues. to Sun. from 10am to 5pm. In addition, seven or eight exhibitions are staged every year, some of international prominence. Admission is 3 DM ($1.80).

Carl Hagenbeck's Tierpark, at Stellingen (tel. 040/540-00-10), in the north-west suburbs, was the first of its kind. This zoo was founded in 1848 and today has about 2,100 animals. The unfenced paddocks and the well-tended landscaped park are world-famous. There are sea lion, dolphin, and troparium shows, rides on ele-phants and camels, a train ride through fairyland, and a spacious children's playground. The zoo is open daily from 8am to 6pm. Admission is 14 DM ($8.30) for adults, 7 DM ($4.15) for children. The U-Bahn takes you to the Tierpark from the main station in Hamburg almost directly to the entrance, with its bronze ele-phants, in about 20 minutes.

A SIDE TRIP TO WILLKOMM-HÖFT

By car you leave the center of Hamburg via Elbchaussee or Osdorfer Landstrasse, heading for Wedel, the trip taking about half an hour. From there you can follow the signs to Willkomm-Höft, or Welcome Point. Ships of various nations go past this point, and from sunrise to sunset (8am to 8pm in summer), they're wel-comed in their own language, as well as German, and their national anthem is played as a salute. You can also reach the point by taking the S-Bahn up to Wedel. A bus will take you from the station, or you can enjoy the 15-minute walk. In summer the best way to go is to take a **Hadag** riverboat, leaving from St. Pauli Landungsbrücken in Hamburg, the ferry taking more than an hour.

The station was founded in the late spring of 1952. It is at this point that the sailor first catches sight of the soaring cranes and slipways of the Port of Hamburg. As a vessel comes in, you'll see the Hamburg flag on a 130-foot-high mast lowered in salute. The ship replies by dipping her own flag. More than 50 arriving ships, and as many departing ones, pass Welcome Point within 24 hours.

If you're planning a visit there, you can have lunch at **Schulauer Fährhaus,** Parnasstrasse 29 (tel. 040/38-30-94), in Wedel. Attractively situated on the wide lower Elbe, the place is run by the sons of Otto Friedrich Behnke, who founded Wel-come Point. The restaurant has a large enclosed veranda, a big open veranda, and a spacious tea garden. Guests are welcomed for breakfast, lunch, tea, or dinner. Fish dishes are a specialty of the kitchen, and seasonal German specialties are offered as well. For example, I recently enjoyed a tasty platter of Sauerbraten. The wine list is modest but interesting. The restaurant has its own bakery, turning out a tempting array of goodies. Meals cost from 32 DM ($19) to 75 DM ($44.55). Hours April to October, are 9am to 9pm; November to March, 10am to 7pm; closed Mon. all year.

In the cellars of the Schulauer Fährhaus is the **Buddelschiff-Museum,** where more than 150 little vessels are carefully preserved in bottles. The museum is open daily from 10am to 6pm. Admission is 2.50 DM ($1.50) for adults, 1.50 DM (90¢) for children.

BOAT TOURS

You can tour Hamburg by water, on both the Inner and the Outer Alster, exper-iencing all the charm of the Alsterpark, the villas, and the sailing boats set against the panorama of towers and church spires. **ATG-Alster Touristik,** Am Anleger Jungfernstieg (tel. 040/341-14-541), has daily departures every 40 minutes from 10am to 5:15pm, with trips lasting about two hours. The ships leave from the Jungfernstieg quayside. Cassettes with a description of the tour in English, plus a brochure in four languages, are available from the captain. Trips cost 15 DM ($8.90) for adults, 7 DM ($4.15) for children. Other, longer tours are also offered.

BG Travel Agency, Von-Eicken-Strasse 13a (tel. 040/56-45-23), offers one-hour trips in a comfortable, heated pleasure boat with a commentary in English. The tours leave from Landungsbrücken pier no. 1. You see modern, high-capacity cargo terminals, locks and canals, shipyards and docks, the famous old red-brick ware-house complex (Speicherstadt), and many ships. The tours leave at 11:15am from March to November. The fare for adults is 14 DM ($8.30), half price for children.

5. Shopping

A stroll through the city center is like taking a look at one large international shop window. Hamburg is a city of merchants. In general, stores are open Mon. to Fri. from 9am to 6:30pm (Sat. from 9am to 2pm). Unfortunately, the interesting shops are not concentrated in just one location. Two of the oldest and most important shopping streets, **Grosse Bleichen** and **Neuer Wall,** run parallel to the canals, connected transversely by Jungfernstieg and Ufer Strasse on the Binnenalster.

Hamburg is a city of shopping malls, with nine major ones. Even on the grayest, rainiest day in winter, you can shop in Hamburg in relative comfort. The glass-roofed **Hanse Viertel Galerie Passage** is some 220 yards long. Among its stylish and desirable stores, you'll find a sunken Mövenpick Restaurant set within a garden-style interior and illuminated from above by a huge circular skylight. There is also a scattering of cafés, even a stand-up seafood bar where glasses of beer or Sekt are served at tiny tables.

Mönckebergstrasse, a street connecting the main station with the Town Hall, is the city's traditional shopping district, with big department stores such as **Kaufhof,** Mönckebergstrasse 3 (tel. 040/32-14-51), and **Horton,** Mönckebergstrasse 1 (tel. 040/32-81-21). The Mö, as it's called, also has elegant boutiques.

If you walk down Bergstrasse to the second part of the city center, you pass along the **Jungfernstieg,** with tourist boats of the Alster Fleet on the right and a teeming street for shopping on the other side. About a block farther along you come to the **Hamburger Hof,** the elegant entrance to one of the most attractive chains of shopping galleries in Europe, with escalators carrying shoppers to upstairs boutiques.

At the end of the Jungfernstieg, you can cross Gänsemarkt to **Gänsemarkt Passage,** another shopping gallery, with stores on three levels.

An up-market shopping area of the city is **Eppendorf,** Hamburg's oldest village, first mentioned in written history in 1140. Many prosperous avant-garde Hamburgers live in the stately 19th-century homes and apartments of the city village. The shopping area, from Klosterstern to Eppendorfer Markt, has exclusive boutiques selling fashions from Paris, Milan, and New York, colorful shops with odds and ends for your home, antiques shops, and places where you can not only make purchases but watch goldsmiths, hatmakers, potters, and weavers at work.

The Hamburg fish market, **Fischmarkt,** between Hexenberg and Grosse Elbstrasse, is held every Sunday beginning at 6am. Not just fish but everything movable is bought and sold at this traditional market, in existence since 1703. Flowers, fruit, vegetables, plants, and pets are for sale. Fresh fish, such as eels, plaice, and cod, direct from the trawlers, is just an incidental item nowadays. The nearby taverns are open to serve Fischmarkt visitors and vendors.

Specific shops worth recommending include the following:

For high-fashion men's clothing, go to **Theo Wormland,** Jungfernstieg 4 (tel. 040/32-62-79).

For women's fashions, patronize **Penndorf Das Hamburger Modehaus,** Mönckebergstrasse 10 (tel. 040/32-29-01), a stylish fashion shop.

One of the city's leading hairdressers is **Marlies Möller.** This *Frisiersalon* is at Tesdorpfstrasse 20 (tel. 040/44-40-01). Perfumes and cosmetics are also sold here.

One of the leading jewelry stores of Hamburg is **Brahmfeld & Gutruf,** Jungfernstieg 12 (tel. 040/34-61-03).

One of the best collections of children's clothing is found at **Hamburger Kinderstube,** Jungfernstieg 34 (tel. 040/34-66-46).

A wide selection of books, including novels and travel maps and other aids, is found at **Thalia.** Hermannstrasse 18-20 (tel. 040/300-50-50).

For an impressive array of glassware and porcelain, head for **E. B. Lattorff,** Dammtorstrasse 35 (tel. 040/350-90-90).

Shoes, well made and fashionably styled, are sold to both men and women at **Prange Schuhhaus,** Jungfernstieg 38 (tel. 040/34-31-51).

---

6. After Dark

From the most prestigious cultural events, including opera, classical music, and theatrical presentations, to some of the most sleazy erotic performances in Europe, Hamburg offers an unequaled diversity of nightlife.

CULTURAL ENTERTAINMENT

Hamburg is the cultural center of northern Germany. Its state opera, **Staatsoper,** Dammtorstrasse 28 (tel. 040/35-17-21), is known throughout the world, with an international repertoire of operas and ballet presented during its season. The opera house is also one of the most modern in design and in stage facilities.

The city's three symphony orchestras and several chamber groups, known for recordings, give frequent concerts throughout the year. At the **Musikhalle,** Karl-Muck-Platz (tel. 040/34-69-20), you can hear performances of the Hamburg Philharmonic, the Hamburg Symphony, and the NDR Symphony. The Monteverdi-Chor is famous for interpretations of baroque and Renaissance music. There are also many musical performances in the churches, especially at Easter and Christmas.

Hamburg is blessed with more than 15 theaters, but for most of these a good knowledge of German is necessary. Plays in English, however, are presented at the **English Theater,** Lerchenfeld 14 (tel. 040/22-55-43).

If you do speak German, then you may want to attend a performance at the **Deutsches Schauspielhaus,** Kirchenallee 39 (tel. 040/24-86-10). It is recognized as one of the outstanding theaters in the German-speaking world, performing both the classics and the avant-garde.

Some of the greatest stars of the German-speaking stage perform at the **Thalia Theater,** Raboisen 67 (tel. 040/32-81-40).

And for children, where language is often not a problem, there is the **Theater für Kinder,** Max-Brauer-Allee 76 (tel. 040/38-25-38).

Hansa Theater, Steindamm 7 (tel. 040/24-14-14), is a North German variety show that claims it's intelligible to all foreigners. The humor is so broad that that's surely true. Each show includes 11 to 14 international attractions, such as acrobatic acts, clowns, dancers, magicians pulling rabbits out of hats, and aerialists balancing on wires above the stage. Each show usually has about 40 performers. There are special tables for smoking and drinking. Two shows are performed daily, one at 4pm and another at 8pm. If you go to the 8pm show, you're out by 11pm. On Sun. the first show starts at 3pm and the second at 7pm. Prices range from 15 DM ($8.90) to 21 DM ($12.45) for the afternoon show, increasing to 21 DM ($12.45) to 26 DM ($15.45) on Sat. and Sun. For the night show, tickets range from 23 DM ($13.65) to 29 DM ($17.20), going up to 29 DM ($17.20) to 35 DM ($20.80) on Sat. The season is from September 1 to June 30.

JAZZ

Hamburg has become firmly established as the number-one jazz city in Germany. Stars in the music field also make appearances here.

A good spot I'm fond of is **Dennis' Swing Club,** Papenhuderstrasse 25 (tel. 040/229-91-92), in the district north of the center of town called Uhlenhorst. It's a completely informal atmosphere for jazz, and it's operated by Dennis Busby, who is not only the owner and manager but the piano player and bartender as well. He's been an accompanist to some of the finest Stateside jazz talents, and old friends who remember him from those days are always passing through Hamburg. Dennis came to Hamburg from Louisiana many years ago. Beer costs 5 DM ($2.95) to 6 DM ($3.55), with whisky beginning at 6 DM ($3.55). The door charge ranges from 5 DM ($2.95) to 30 DM ($17.80), depending on who is appearing. The small, intimate, charming bar is open daily from 8pm to 4am, depending on business.

Cotton Club, Grossmarkt 50 (tel. 040/34-38-78), is legendary. One of the oldest (almost 30 years) and the best established of the Hamburg jazz clubs, it has a motto: *Wo Jazz noch Jazz ist* (Where jazz is still jazz). Jazz bands come here from throughout Europe and the United States. Beer costs about 5 DM ($2.95) per glass, and a small carafe of wine is available for about 6 DM ($3.55). It's open daily from 8pm to 1am.

ROCK

For one of the best rock programs in Germany, go to the **Markthalle,** Kosterwall 9-21, near the Hauptbanhof (tel. 040/33-94-91). It often provides a forum for up-and-coming English groups who like to play here. It's a series of boutiques and dining areas set in a marketplace. For an admission fee ranging from 15 DM ($8.90) to 20 DM ($11.90), you are admitted to the performing area, which is an indoor amphitheater with a stage and a large central section. You can listen to the artists in concert fashion or else view them in theater-in-the-round style. Seats are really backless benches. You're allowed to bring beer or other drinks into the hall as you listen to the music. Hours vary from night to night, depending on the program.

Logo, Grindelallee 5 (tel. 040/410-56-58), near the university, is one of the most popular clubs for young college-age visitors to meet their Hamburg contemporaries. It's a small, informal place that often features rock bands, and sometimes well-known singers appear here in concert. Audiences often sit on the floor. Entrance fees range from 10 DM ($5.95) to 20 DM ($11.90), with beer costing from 5 DM ($2.95). It's open from 8pm to 2am; closed Sun.

Fabrik, Barnerstrasse 36 (tel. 040/39-15-63), five minutes from Bahnhof Altona, is a cultural center, along the same style as Markthalle. Originally it was an old ammunition depot (circa 1830), until it was burned down. It was rebuilt in the same style. The entrance fee ranges from 5 DM ($2.95) to 18 DM ($10.70), and beer and snacks cost 5 DM ($2.95) to 10 DM ($5.95). Children often come here in the afternoon with their parents (hours then are noon to 6pm). After 7:30pm and until midnight (later on Sat. and Sun.) it's a nightclub, offering a mixed program (rock, perhaps classical). The club is in a district peopled, in part, by the Turkish and Greek workers who flood into Hamburg.

THE "INFAMOUS" REEPERBAHN

For the true nightlife of Hamburg, you have to go where the action is, on the Reeperbahn in the St. Pauli quarter of the city. The hottest spots are on a tawdry little side street called Grosse Freiheit, meaning Great Freedom. St. Pauli is the sailors' quarter. *Warning:* Be on guard, the area can be dangerous. This section is *not* for women traveling alone.

The streets are lined with pornography shops, interspersed with clubs with names such as Las Vegas and San Francisco. Be aware that German law requires restaurants and nightclubs to display their price list. Know the cost of your drinks before ordering. If the management refuses to give you a price list, get up and leave.

The **Colibri,** Grosse Freiheit 34 (tel. 040/31-32-33), is not for prudes. Its shows, depicting the most lurid forms of sexual intercourse between man, woman, beast, or whatever, are among the most erotic you'll see in Germany, but this is the main attraction of Reeperbahn nightlife. You'll pay 15 DM ($8.90) for beer, plus 5 DM ($2.95) to enter. But don't expect to make one beer last for the whole show.

Minimum consumption is 20 DM ($11.90). The shows are long, seemingly endless, and 80 attractions are advertised each night. Go between 8pm and 4am nightly.

The farmer from the environs, in the old seaport without his wife, wants to go on a **"Safari."** That's the name of a club at Grosse Freiheit 24 (tel. 040/31-54-00). This is what is known as a *Kabarett d'amour.* It offers live sex on the stage, in some actions and forms perhaps unfamiliar to you. Minimum consumption is 20 DM ($11.90), entrance is 5 DM ($2.95), and beer costs from 15 DM ($8.90). It's open nightly from 8pm to 4am.

Other clubs on the same street impose about the same prices, but you should always exercise caution. Stick to beer. Avoid ordering whisky or, especially, "champagne."

Another major tourist attraction is not in a club at all, but a street. It's the famous **Herbertstrasse,** which every sailor in town visits when he's in port. For years it's been celebrated as the "street of harlots." These working girls sit in windows on this little alleyway, hustling men to come inside. Naturally, the windows are lit in red. When the curtains are closed, the occupant of the cage is "engaged." Exhibitions and "special requests" are catered to in the second and third stories of these little houses. *Warning:* Women tourists walking down this street can be harassed.

MALE STRIPTEASE

It's usually closed in summer, but **Crazy Boys,** Pulverteich 12 (tel. 040/24-62-85), is one of the most popular clubs in Hamburg. Every Wednesday night this amusing but risqué cabaret is reserved for women only for the kind of male strip show that has made TV talk shows in America. The rest of the week, the cabaret caters to a predominantly gay male clientele, but not exclusively, as many men take their wives or women friends here as well. Entrance costs 15 DM ($8.90) per person, with the first drink also costing 15 DM ($8.90). Open Mon. to Fri. from 4pm to 4am; Sat. and Sun. from 7pm to 6am. However, shows begin about 10pm, midnight, and 2am. There's an additional show at 4am on Fri. and Sat.; Wed. and Sun. there's also a show at 3:30am but only for women. The actors are often attractive, well-proportioned young men who perform strip shows, sketches, songs, or whatever. Costumes range from "unusual fantasy" to suits "worn only by Adam."

DRAG SHOWS

The best-known drag show, **Pulverfass,** Pulverteich 12 (tel. 040/24-97-91), is usually featured on the "Hamburg by Night" tours. This place is not for the timid. The shows can get downright vulgar, which you'll hear if you know German. Female impersonators from all over Europe appear here, and you can order steaks if you're hungry. The entrance fee is 15 DM ($8.90) to 20 DM ($11.90), and your first drink goes for 15 DM ($8.90). Three shows are presented nightly, usually at 8:30pm, 11:15pm, and 2am.

DISCO

One of the best is **Chesa,** Beim Schlump 15 (tel. 040/45-88-11), which draws an over-25 crowd. The cookery is good in case you're hungry, full meals costing 28 DM ($16.65) to 55 DM ($32.65), although the main focus of the place is on dancing and conviviality. A glass of beer costs around 10 DM ($5.95). This isn't a place for teenagers. Open nightly from 9pm to 4am.

The discotheque **After Shave,** Spielbudenplatz 7 (tel. 040/319-32-15), features not only funk and soul but also jazz and fusion. It's a place for dancing as well as for meeting people and draws a crowd in the 20-to-30 age group. The location is near Hamburg's famous Reeperbahn, but that's not why one goes to After Shave. The music is wide-ranging, featuring the latest imports but no hard rock or heavy metal. A bottle of beer costs from 6 DM ($3.55). Hours are Sun., Wed., and Thurs. from 10pm to 4am; Fri. and Sat. from 10pm to 6am; closed Mon. On Tues. jazz and fusion are featured exclusively from 11pm to 2am.

GAY HAMBURG

Hamburg, like Berlin, is one of the major gay havens of Europe. Some gay places have a mixed clientele: the famous **Spundloch,** Paulinenstrasse 19 (tel. 040/ 31-07-98), for example, is sometimes patronized by heterosexual couples, perhaps curiosity seekers. Its elegant bar and disco draw a youngish crowd. Beer costs around 5 DM ($2.95). Open from 8pm to 4am (to 6am on Sat.); closed Mon.

The **Pit Club-Saloon/Tom's Bar,** Pulverteich 17 (tel. 040/24-33-80), is a combination leather bar and gay disco near the railway station. No entrance fee is charged, but the cost is 6 DM ($3.55) for a beer. It is open nightly from 9pm to at least 4am.

FOR DANCING

A place to spend a Bavarian night in Hamburg is **Bayrisch Zell,** Reeperbahn 110 (tel. 040/31-42-81). It may be on the Reeperbahn, but you could take your great-aunt there, especially if she likes to dance the polka. Clearly an imitation of Munich's famed Hofbräuhaus, Bayrisch Zell attracts couples young and old, and it has plenty of seats for all of them, 1,200 in all. One of the most popular places in the St. Pauli district, it has good cookery, with meals costing from 30 DM ($17.80) and beer from 6.50 DM ($3.85). If you see someone whom you find attractive, you can ring him or her from your table—that's what those phones are for. Hours are 7pm to 4am daily.

Zillertal, Spielbudenplatz 27 (tel. 040/31-46-03), off the Reeperbahn, is much the same thing as Bayrisch Zell, and it can also seat some 1,200 revelers on a busy night. It's open Mon. to Fri. from 7pm to 2am and on Sat. and Sun. until 4am. Here you can order a meal for 30 DM ($17.80), and you'll pay another 1 DM (60¢) to enter. King George once visited here, a fact the management has never forgotten. It's very touristy, and a lot of fun if you're in the mood. Locally it's known as the "Bavarian Embassy" and has been an enduring Hamburg tradition, since it existed before the war.

Café Keese, Reeperbahn 19-21 (tel. 040/31-08-05), features a "Ball Paradox." That means the women can choose the men as dance partners. The doorman tries to keep out hustlers. Actually, the place is legitimate, even though it wouldn't let Jayne Mansfield in back in the 1950s (she refused to surrender her fur coat at the door). Live bands entertain, and women go there to look for a man. Sandwiches cost around 9 DM ($5.35), with beer going for 7.50 DM ($4.45). The café is open daily from 8pm to 4am.

WINE DRINKING

One of Hamburg's most venerated winehouses is **Schwenders,** Grossneumarkt 1 (tel. 040/34-54-23). In modern times it has been spruced up, and is now as good as ever. The namesake Schwenders came from Vienna, bringing their style and charm to this old Hanseatic city. Apparently they made a lasting impression, as the place today often attracts some 400 or more patrons, even though there is room for only 200 to sit down to drink and be entertained in a belle-époque setting filled with nooks and crannies. The music presented might be derived from anything from a Viennese operetta to cabaret, sometimes performed by local, amateur, or temporarily out-of-work musicians. Entrance is free, but beer costs from 5 DM ($2.95), with a bottle of wine beginning at 25 DM ($14.85). Deli cold cuts and excellent cheese will do if you want something to eat with your drinks. Open Mon. to Thurs. from 4pm to 2am; Fri. and Sat. from 4pm to either 3am or 4am; Sun. from 5pm to midnight.

GAMBLING

You can play roulette, baccarat, and blackjack at the **Spielbank Hamburg,** the casino in the Hotel Inter-Continental, Fontenay 10 (tel. 040/44-70-44). All games are played according to international rules. The minimum stake for roulette is 5 DM ($2.95), 10 DM ($5.95) for blackjack. Admission to the casino is 5 DM ($2.95). It's open daily from 3pm to 3am. Minimum age for play is 18, and a passport is required for foreign visitors. You can reach the hotel by driving along Fontenay, and there's also an entrance in Badestrasse.

AN ELEGANT BAR

Perhaps the most elegant bar in Hamburg is the **Simbari,** in the already recommended deluxe hotel, Vier Jahreszeiten, Neuer Jungfernstieg 9-14 (tel. 040/3-49-41). It's tiny, intimate, cozy, and select in its clientele. You can sit downstairs or else retreat up the steps to a little nook. The overall atmosphere is like a conservative gentleman's club in London. Drinks cost from 15 DM ($8.90) and are served daily from 11am to 2am. The bar is named for the contemporary pictures and posters of circus performer Nicola Simbari.

A NIGHTCLUB

The rendezvous of haute Hamburgers, along with the most elegant visitors, is **Die Insel,** Alsterufer 35 (tel. 040/410-69-55). In the vicinity of the Kennedy-Brücke, opening onto Aussenalster, this is a three-floor town house with a diversity of food, entertainment, and amusement. Around its champagne bar, you'll find members of the German arts and media worlds. It's especially popular as an après-concert rendezvous. Hours are 8pm to 4am daily. The decor is sumptuous, with an effective use of chrome, spots, marble, and leather. In winter an open fireplace casts a mellow glow. You can dine elegantly here, but are likely to spend from 85 DM ($50.45) for a meal. Hours are 8pm to 2am. There's a men's bar on the first floor, as well as a disco with a round dance floor. Drinks cost from 15 DM ($8.90), and the place is modern, beautiful, up-to-date, and popular with young singles.

SCHLESWIG-HOLSTEIN

1. LÜBECK
2. KIEL
3. SCHLESWIG
4. WESTERLAND (SYLT)
5. HELGOLAND

You walk along the dunes and hear the roaring waves breaking fiercely on the rocks. Or perhaps you lie on a tranquil beach while tiny waves lap at your feet. Sounds inconsistent, doesn't it? Not in Schleswig-Holstein. This northernmost province of Germany borders both the turbulent, chilly North Sea and the smooth, gentle Baltic. And between these two bodies of water are rolling groves and meadows, lakes and ponds, and little fishing villages with thatched cottages. Fashionable seaside resorts line the North and Baltic seas. Even in the coldest weather you can swim in heated seawater at the resorts of Westerland and Helgoland. In Kiel you can wander around the harbor and explore Schleswig with its Viking ghosts.

But let's begin our tour of Germany's north country with a visit to the Queen of the Hanseatic Cities, Lübeck.

1. Lübeck

It is said that nothing testifies to the wealth of an old European city as much as the size and number of its church spires. If this is so, Lübeck is rich indeed, for no fewer than seven towering steeples make up the skyline of this Hanseatic city. It has prospered since it was made a Free Imperial City in 1226 by Emperor Frederick II. Lübeck held this position for 711 years, until 1937. In addition, it was the capital and Queen City of the Hanseatic League for centuries, and retains the title even though the economic and political importance of the league dissolved with its last meeting in 1630.

Lübeck is a city of high-gabled houses, massive gates, and strong towers. The Hanseatic merchants decorated their churches with art treasures and gilded their spires to show off their wealth. Many of these survivors of nearly 900 years of history stand side by side today with postwar housing developments, and the neon lights of the business district shine out on the streets and narrow passageways of bygone days.

Lübeck has two famous sons: Thomas Mann and Willy Brandt. As a young man, Brandt, who was later the West German chancellor and 1971 Nobel Peace Prize winner, opposed the Nazis so stubbornly he fled his hometown on a boat to

Norway. Mann won a Nobel Prize in 1929 for literature. His novel *Buddenbrooks* was set in his hometown and had catapulted the 27-year-old author to international fame in 1902.

The city is the capital of marzipan. According to legend, Lübeckers, riding out a long siege, ran out of flour and started grinding up almonds to make bread. So delighted were they with the results, they've been doing it ever since. To sample marzipan on home turf, go to the Niederegger shop across from the Rathaus.

WHERE TO STAY

Mövenpick-Hotel Lysia, Auf der Wallhalbinsel 3, D-2400 Lübeck (tel. 0451/1-50-40), stands in a garden setting opening onto a canal. The 197-room Lysia is right at the entrance to old Lübeck. Its rooms are colorful and compact, almost motellike. The desirable accommodations are in back—the front bedrooms open onto railway tracks. A single with shower and toilet ranges in price from 135 DM ($80.15) to 165 DM ($98) daily. A twin-bedded room with shower or tub and toilet is in the 165 DM ($98) to 195 DM ($115.80) bracket. On the premises is a Café-Konditorei, plus a Bierstube. Tables outside are hedged in by boxes of geraniums. The Mövenpick Restaurant serves tasty specialties, with meals costing 35 DM ($20.80) to 60 DM ($35.65).

Kaiserhof, Kronsforder Allee 13, D-2400 Lübeck (tel. 0451/7-91-011), a successful remodeling of a patrician town house into a 70-room hotel, stands outside the center on a tree-lined boulevard. The owner has created a fashionable homelike environment, with every room uniquely furnished and having a private shower or bath. The rate for singles, depending on the placement of the room, ranges from 98 DM ($58.20) to 150 DM ($89.05) daily. A double costs 135 DM ($80.15) to 185 DM ($109.85). An elevator takes guests to all floors. An elaborate and authentic Scandinavian sauna opens off the rear garden, and a large swimming pool, a Roman vaporbath, a fitness center, and a solar studio are also available free for the use of guests.

One of the best moderately priced hotels is the **Jensen,** An der Obertrave 4-5, D-2400 Lübeck (tel. 0451/7-16-46). Right on a canal, near Holstentor, it offers fine views from its bedroom windows of the Hanseatic brick architecture across the canal. The 94 rooms are modestly furnished in modern style. For a double with bath, two persons pay 140 DM ($83.15) to 170 DM ($100.95) daily. Singles cost 90 DM ($53.45) with shower to 120 DM ($71.25) with bath. Breakfast is served in a room with picture windows overlooking the old canal, a delightful way to begin your day. Either lunch or dinner is good in the warmly decorated tavern-style restaurant. Meals cost 30 DM ($17.80) to 60 DM ($35.65).

Hotel Excelsior, Hansestrasse 3, D-2400 Lübeck (tel. 0451/8-80-90), in a symmetrical baroque building with splendid proportions, has an entirely renovated and modernized interior. The 70-room hotel is comfortable and clean, all rooms having showers or baths, toilets, phones, and radios; some have minibars and TVs. Singles with showers and toilets rent for 75 DM ($44.55) to 130 DM ($77.20) daily, while doubles go for 99 DM ($58.80) to 170 DM ($100.95), all with a buffet breakfast included. The Excelsior is near Lindenplatz.

WHERE TO DINE

A classic example of Hanseatic architecture on a medieval street, **Das Schabbelhaus,** Mengstrasse 48-52 (tel. 0451/7-50-51), is installed in two patrician buildings dating from the 16th and 17th centuries. In the restaurant, ceiling-high studio windows overlook the small gardens; a pair of 15-foot-high armoires hold the restaurant's linen and glassware. The fare includes such tempting items as Lübecker crab soup, fresh items from the sea, and steaks. Meals begin at 48 DM ($28.50), going up to 85 DM ($50.45) for the most elaborate specialties. Hours are noon to 3pm and 6 to 11pm daily; closed Sun. A wooden staircase and balcony lead to two rooms devoted to memorabilia of Thomas Mann.

Haus der Schiffergesellschaft, Breitestrasse 2 (tel. 0451/7-67-76), opposite the Church of St. Jakobi, basks in the Hanseatic tradition. Memorabilia such as ship models hang from the ceiling and decorate the walls. Dining in this mellowed Baltic atmosphere is like entering a museum of Hanseatic architecture. The restaurant was once patronized exclusively by sailors and other men of the sea; today good food (and large portions) is served on scrubbed-oak plank tables as you sit in a carved high-backed wooden booth, showing coats-of-arms of Baltic merchants. Often you must share a table here. Meals, including soup and dessert, cost 40 DM ($23.75) to 100 DM ($59.40). The most expensive price includes such elaborate dishes as sole meunière (one pound) with a salad. You should have a drink in the cocktail bar of the historical Gotteskeller, open 6pm to 2am; closed Sun. The restaurant is open from 10am to 1am; closed Mon.

Stadtrestaurant, Am Bahnhof 2-4 (tel. 0451/8-40-44). Close to everything in the heart of town, the enormous expanse of this elegant dining room on the first floor of the railway station offers well-prepared meals to travelers. The rooms are furnished in Venetian, Empire, baroque, and English styles. Some critics consider it the best restaurant in Lübeck. Under the same roof you'll also find a café and several private salons, usually for conferences. Specialties include an assortment of fish à la maison, with dishes such as turbot and salmon, or stuffed breast of veal Old Lübeck style. In season, the chef offers escalopes of deer with apples and cherries, cream sauce flavored with rum, beans, and potato croquettes. Meals range in price from 28 DM ($16.65) to 65 DM ($38.60) and are served daily from 10:30am to 11pm. Parking is available in front of the station.

L'Étoile, Grosse Petersgrube 8 (tel. 0451/7-64-40). After years of experience in another restaurant, Michael and Margitta Schunzel decided to open their own establishment inside their art nouveau home. Regular French food is served in a bistro section and cuisine moderne cooking in a restaurant. The menu changes daily. Fixed-price lunches are offered for 25 DM ($14.85) and 37.50 DM ($22.25), and set dinners cost 55 DM ($32.65) to 85 DM ($50.45). They serve Italian-style carpaccio, Barbary duckling, and other foods from France such as fresh goose liver. Lunch is daily from noon to 3pm and dinner from 6 to 10:30pm.

Lübecker Hanse, Am Kolk 3 (tel. 0451/7-80-54), is one of the most expensive restaurants of Lübeck, but many locals swear by it. The exterior is authentically weathered, and dark paneling graces much of the interior. French food, regional meals, and lots of fresh seafood are offered, and there's also an elaborate salad buffet that is most popular. Specialties of the chef include a seafood terrine, bouillabaisse, wild game, and a never-ending series of plats du jour. Meals begin at 40 DM ($23.75) but could climb to 70 DM ($41.55) if you order the more expensive specialties. They serve from 11:30am to 2:30pm and 6 to 11:30pm; closed Sun.

Historische Weinstuben, Heiligen-Geist-Hospital, Koberg 8 (tel. 0451/7-62-34). In the basement of one of Lübeck's monuments (Holy Ghost Hospital), you'll find this first-class restaurant and 12th-century wine cellar. Specialties are likely to include half a dozen snails prepared Alsace style, followed by roast curried prawns Bombay style in a sauce of mustard and fresh fruits. Full meals here average about 50 DM ($29.70), but perhaps you'll do it for less. Service is from noon to 3pm and 5pm to 1am; closed Tues.

Ratskeller, Am Markt 13 (tel. 0451/7-20-44), is the dining cellar of the Town Hall. Make your way through the flower vendors on the square outside to enjoy the offerings of the ambitious chef, whose high standards and excellent food are the order of the day. The menu is backed up by a good wine list. As befits a seaport, fish is the house specialty. Wide-ranging delicacies are offered, including some high-priced lobster and caviar. Vegetarian recipes are also on the menu. Depending on your selection, expect to spend 25 DM ($14.85) to 65 DM ($38.60) for a meal. The cellar is open daily from 10am to 1am.

J. G. Niederegger, Breitestrasse 89 (tel. 0451/7-10-36), sells that "sweetest of all sweetmeats," the famous Lübeck marzipan. If you've had lunch, I suggest that you skip dessert at the restaurant and head for this pastry shop, dating from 1806. It's right across from the main entrance to the Town Hall. On the ground floor you can purchase pastries to savor later, or you can go upstairs to a pleasant café where you can order dessert and excellently brewed coffee (the best in Lübeck). Ask for their pastry specialty, a nut Torte resting under a huge slab of fresh marzipan. Then swear off pastries for life! Go between 10am and 5:30pm; closed Sun.

THE SIGHTS

The Altstadt of Lübeck is surrounded by the Trave River and its connecting canals, giving it an islandlike appearance. It suffered heavily during World War II— it is estimated that one-fifth of the city was leveled. Today most of the damaged buildings have been restored or reconstructed, and Lübeck still offers a wealth of historic attractions.

Just across the south bridge from the Altstadt, the **Holstentor** (Holsten Gate) is the first thing to greet visitors emerging from the railway station. At one time it was the main town entrance, built in the 15th century as much to awe visitors with the power and prestige of Lübeck as to defend it against intruders. To the outside world the towers look simple and defiant, rather like part of a great palace. But on the city side they contain a wealth of decoration, with windows, arcades, and rich terra-cotta friezes. Within the gate is the municipal museum, **Museum im Holstentor** (tel. 0451/12-241-29), housing a model of Lübeck as it appeared in the mid-17th century. It is open from 10am to 5pm (to 4pm off-season); closed Mon. Admission is 3 DM ($1.80).

The **Salt Lofts,** if viewed from the river side near the Holstentor, are among the most attractive buildings in Lübeck. Dating from as early as the 16th century, they were once used to store salt brought here from Lüneburg before it was exported to Scandinavia. Each of the six buildings is slightly different, reflecting several trends in Renaissance gabled architecture.

The **Rathaus** traces its origins back to 1230. It has been rebuilt several times, but there are remains of the original structure in the vaulting and Romanesque pillars in the cellar and the Gothic south wall. The towering walls have been made with open-air medallions to relieve the pressure on the Gothic-arcaded ground floor and foundations.

It is estimated that within an area of 2 square miles around the city hall stand 1,000 medieval houses. Nearby is **Petersgrube,** the finest street in Lübeck, lined with some of the best-restored structures in Europe; one is from as early as 1363.

Two patrician houses, **Dragerhaus** and **Behnhaus,** have been converted to museums. Both entered on Breitestrasse, north of Glockengiesser Strasse, they were constructed in a long, narrow fashion to avoid a heavy tax that was based on frontage. The Behnhaus displays a collection of paintings, some by Kirchner and Edvard Munch. Thomas Mann buffs, however, gravitate to Dragerhaus, a branch of the Museum for Art and Cultural History. The drawing aspect of this museum is the section that highlights the lives of the city's two great literary giants, Thomas Mann and his brother, Heinrich. Thomas Mann, of course, was the author of such world classics as *Death in Venice* and *The Magic Mountain,* the latter perhaps his best-known work. Less well known, Heinrich is remembered today for *Professor Unrat,* better known in its movie version, *Der Blaue Engel (The Blue Angel),* which brought Marlene Dietrich international stardom. The museum displays a model of the house in which the Thomas Mann novel *Buddenbrooks* was set. The museum also contains antique furniture and porcelain. Hours are 10am to 5pm from Tues. to Sun., and entrance is 2 DM ($1.20).

St. Mary's Church (Marienkirche), across the Marktplatz from the Rathaus, is the most outstanding church in Lübeck, possibly in northern Germany. Built on the highest point in the Altstadt, it has flying buttresses and towering windows that leave the rest of the city's rooftops at its feet. St. Mary's is undoubtedly a fine example of a Gothic brick church, and one of the largest of its kind in the world. Some of its greatest art treasures were destroyed in 1942, but after the fire was put out, the original painted decoration on the walls and clerestory was discovered. The original bells fell in a World War II air raid and embedded themselves in the floor of the church, where they remain to this day. Organ concerts take place during the summer months, carrying on the tradition established by St. Mary's best-known organist, Dietrich Buxtehude (1668–1707).

Many of the art treasures of old Lübeck have been preserved in **St. Anne's Museum** (tel. 0451/12-241-37), a former convent built in 1502. The museum is devoted mainly to religious works and statues, many of which were removed from the bombed churches of the city. A major art treasure here is Memling's 1491 *Passion Altarpiece*. The museum is open from 10am to 5pm (to 4pm off-season); closed Mon. Admission is 3 DM ($1.80).

The house where the grandparents of Thomas Mann lived is at Mengstrasse 4, close to the Marienkirche. Called **Buddensbrookhaus,** it is a big, solid stone structure with a gabled roof and recessed doorway. Above a leaded-glass fan over the heavy double doors is the date 1758. This is the house Mann described as the home of the family in *Buddenbrooks*. It is a bank building today.

The **Seamen's Guild House** (Haus der Schiffergesellschaft) is one of the last of the elaborate guild houses of Hanseatic Lübeck, built in 1535 in Renaissance style, with stepped gables and High Gothic blind windows. It's worth seeing just for the medieval furnishings and beamed ceilings in the main hall, now a restaurant (see my recommendation above). A walk through the old streets of Lübeck reveals a continuing use of brick as the local building material (the city insisted on this after fires in the 13th century). The effect is one of unity among all the houses, churches, shops, and guildhalls.

You can take an excursion boat around **Lübeck Harbor,** departing from Trave Landing, right in front of the hotel Jensen. In season, departures are every half hour, anytime between 10am and 6pm.

2. Kiel

Even the name of this port and fishing city—it means "haven for ships" in old Anglo-Saxon—shows the importance of the sea to the growth and prosperity of Kiel. The perfect natural harbor at the end of the 7-mile-long extension of the Baltic Sea made Kiel a center for commerce with other northern European countries. The opening of the Kiel Canal in 1895 connected the Baltic Sea with the North Sea and western trade.

Kiel Week, held each June, is a further example of the port's close ties with the sea. This week of special events, held each summer for the past 85 years, includes a spectacular regatta in which hundreds of yachts race on the waters of the Roadstead. In 1972 the Olympic yacht races were held on the waters at Schilksee. Stretches of sandy beaches in the nearby resorts make the port a Baltic vacation spot as well.

Although Kiel is nearly 1,000 years old, there is little in the way of streets or building to make the casual visitor believe that the town ever was anything other than a modern city. Almost all its buildings were destroyed in World War II, and in their place is an admirable example of modern town planning. Kielers are proud of their broad streets, spacious squares, and green parks in the heart of town.

WHERE TO STAY

Rated "superior first class," the **Maritim-Bellevue,** Bismarckallee 2, D-2300 Kiel (tel. 0431/3-89-40), built in 1972, is a convention hotel opening onto the shore promenade of the Baltic, a few steps from the Düsternbrooker Seebad and the Kieler Yacht Club's marina (a 10-minute drive to Olympic Harbor). This well-appointed hotel offers 89 attractively styled and well-furnished bedrooms, many of them with good views of the sea, all with baths, balconies, radios, and TVs. Singles begin at 149 DM ($88.50) daily, rising to 249 DM ($147.85) for the most superior units; doubles, likewise, range from 268 DM ($159.15) to 378 DM ($224.45), the latter for the luxurious corner accommodations. All tariffs include a buffet breakfast. You'll have access to the hotel's swimming pool, sauna, fitness room, solarium, bar, restaurant, and nightclub.

Hotel Conti-Hansa, Schlossgarten 7, D-2300 Kiel (tel. 0431/5-11-50), is only a three-minute walk from the pedestrian shopping area. Half of the 164 bedrooms overlook the Oslo Kai; the other half, the Palace Park with its pond, the Kleine Kiel. Each unit contains bath/shower, toilet, color TV, radio, direct-dial phone, trouser press, hairdryer, and minibar. Singles cost 165 DM ($98) to 235 DM ($139.55) daily, and doubles go for 210 DM ($124.70) to 285 DM ($169.25). You can choose between two dining rooms: the international Hansa-Pavillon and the well-known evening restaurant, Fayence.

Hotel Kieler Yacht-Club, Hindenburgufer 70, D-2300 Kiel (tel. 0431/8-50-55), is exactly what its name implies—a yacht club with unusually fine guest facilities. It's an old classical building, standing back from the harbor, with an adjoining motel annex of contemporary design. It's the most spirited accommodation in Kiel. In all, the hotel rents 60 bedrooms. Prices are lower in the older portion, which also has the more spacious rooms; newer rooms are designed yacht-cabin style. In the old building, doubles with baths are 140 DM ($83.15) daily, increasing to 195 DM ($115.80) in the annex. Singles with baths are 105 DM ($62.35) in the old part, 135 DM ($80.15) in the new. All tariffs include breakfast and service. There is a multitiered restaurant where the tables are staggered to provide the best views. The Mastenkeller in the basement is for beer drinking. *Note:* Front rooms with water views are preferred, although the accommodations in the back open onto greenery. On the water side, sidewalk tables and chairs are placed on terraces surrounded by planters of roses.

Hotel Astor, Holstenplatz 1, D-2300 Kiel (tel. 0431/9-30-17), is within a short walk of both the ferryboat station and the Hauptbahnhof. The hotel shares a modern office building with several corporations. All 60 well-appointed bedrooms have toilets and showers or baths. Singles cost 65 DM ($38.60) to 100 DM ($59.40) daily, while doubles rent for 130 DM ($77.20) to 150 DM ($89.05). The hotel restaurant, considered one of the best in Kiel, serves an international array of food, a fixed-price meal beginning at 28 DM ($16.65). The restaurant is open from 7am to 11pm; closed Sun. It's decorated with Scandinavian furnishings, offering an impressive view from its big windows. A small bar on the 10th floor, run by one of Germany's best barmen, is the "in" place to go.

Hotel Wiking, Schützenwall 1-3, D-2300 Kiel (tel. 0431/67-30-51), has a name that always reminds me of how far north I am, and how close to the Scandinavian countries. The dark facade of this modern 42-room hotel is ornamented with heavy walled balconies, painted a vividly contrasting white. In the center of Kiel, the Wiking offers sunny bedrooms and prices that vary according to the season. Singles rent for 78 DM ($46.30) to 110 DM ($65.30) daily, doubles for 115 DM ($68.30) to 160 DM ($95), including breakfast. The restaurant and breakfast rooms are especially attractive, with a warm Nordic ambience.

WHERE TO DINE

One of the finest restaurants in Kiel, **Restaurant im Schloss,** Wall 80 (tel. 0431/9-11-58), is also the most elegant, the most expensive, and the most formal. The service is superb, as are the food and choice of wine. It's a modern restaurant, across from the embarkation point for boats to Scandinavian countries. In a stone building overlooking the harbor, the Schloss looks like a museum set in a park. If you reserve, you can get one of the window tables opening onto the water. Set meals are offered for 45 DM ($26.70), but tabs can run as high as 75 DM ($44.55). The staff here keeps a long day: from 9am to midnight. However, the kitchen's got to take a break sometime—closed for Sun. dinner and Mon. lunch.

Kieler Yacht-Club, Hindenburgufer 70 (tel. 0431/8-50-55), is found in this previously recommended hotel. The bar is a sophisticated hangout that attracts the yachting set from Newport to St. Tropez. The food is good and attractively served. The specialty, naturally, is seafood, with meals beginning at 25 DM ($14.85) and going up to 80 DM ($47.50). The decor, predictably, has a nautical flavor. Hours are daily from noon to 2:30pm and 6 to 10pm.

Restaurant Fayence, Hotel Conti-Hansa, Schlossgarten 7 (tel. 0431/5-11-50), is one of Kiel's most elegant restaurants. Sheltered in the previously recommended hotel, it has a striking, opulent decor of royal blue and polished brass. In this stimulating ambience, the table settings reflect high taste and style. You might begin with a mussel-and-spinach salad, perhaps cream of wild-mushroom soup, then follow with a main course such as salmon in a Riesling sauce or else a roulade of calves' liver stuffed with wild mushrooms and a julienne of vegetables with a wild-berry sauce. To the chef, the way food looks is almost as important as the way it tastes. You can order a five-course set meal at 80 DM ($47.50); otherwise, à la carte orders average about 45 DM ($26.70). Hours are 6pm to 1am; closed Sun. Reservations are important.

Claudio's Ristorante, Königsweg 46 (tel. 0431/67-68-67), is considered one of the most attractive restaurants in town. Chef Claudio Berlese prepares all kinds of light-textured Italian dishes for his highly responsive clientele. Specialties are concocted from the day's inventory of lobster, mussels, oysters, game fowl, and fresh vegetables. You might enjoy eggplant stuffed with mozzarella and tomatoes, spaghetti with mussels, or oven-cooked salmon with fresh basil. The choice of wines is appropriately tempting. Fixed price meals cost 70 DM ($41.55) to 90 DM ($53.45). The country-modern establishment is open only for dinner, beginning at 7pm; last orders taken at midnight; closed Sun.

THE SIGHTS

Most of the attractions of Kiel center in and around the harbor. For the best overall look at the city and the Roadstead, go to the top of the Town Hall's 350-foot tower. Guided tours are daily at 10:30 and 11:30am from May to mid-October. For a closer view, wander the **Hindenburg Embankment** (Hindenburgufer) stretching for 2 miles along the west side of the fjord, opposite the shipyards. It's also one of the best spots from which to watch the regatta.

The **Sea Fish Market,** on the east bank of the fjord, is one of the largest in the world, and a fascinating place to visit, if the smell doesn't turn you off. You'll see a wide variety of sea life here.

If you have the time, take a short steamer trip to one of the nearby Baltic towns, such as Laboe with its sandy beach. Steamers and ferries also connect Kiel with Baltic ports in Denmark, Norway, and Sweden.

In the environs, the **Schleswig-Holstein Open-Air Museum (Freilicht-museum)** (tel. 0431/6-55-55), lies 4 miles outside Kiel. Take the B4 highway to Neumünster. Farms and rustic country homes, dating from the 16th to the 19th centuries, have been assembled here in a sylvan setting. Local craftspeople operate the shops, and working animals have been brought in. A half-timbered inn serves tasty lunches. The park is open from April 1 to mid-November, Tues. to Sat. from 9am to 5pm and on Sun. from 10am to 6pm. In the off-season it's open only on Sun. from 10am to dusk. It's always closed on Mon., and admission is 5 DM ($2.95).

Kiel is the center of the Schleswig-Holstein Music Festival, with performances by musicians such as Leonard Bernstein, between the end of June and August every year. For more information contact Tourist Information Kiel, Sophienblatt 30, D-2300 Kiel 1 (tel. 0431/62230).

3. Schleswig

This one-time Viking stronghold on the Schlei (an arm of the Baltic Sea) is Schleswig-Holstein's oldest town, and it is steeped in all the myths and legends that go with such a long history. Even the seagulls, whose eggs are a delicacy here, have a legend of their own. According to tradition, the birds nesting on Seagull Island in the middle of the Schlei are actually the fellow conspirators of Duke Abel, who in 1250 murdered his own brother, King Eric. The crime was discovered when the king's body, weighted with chains, washed ashore from the Schlei. The duke went mad, and eventually died and was impaled and buried in the Tiergarten. But his followers, according to the story, became seagulls, doomed to nest forever on Seagull Island.

Fortunately, legends are not the only survivors in this ancient city. The bombing raids of World War II did not touch Schleswig, and it stands today a witness to 1,200 years of history.

WHERE TO STAY

Strandhalle, Strandweg 2, D-2380 Schleswig (tel. 04621/2-20-21), has been a family-run business since 1905. Actually it's more of a holiday resort—right on the water, with its own rowboats, a swimming pool in a beautiful garden, and its own natatorium with steam bath. The owners offer an informal atmosphere in 28 comfortable rooms. You should ask for one opening onto the water, with a view of the yacht harbor. Bathless singles range in price from 41.50 DM ($24.65) daily; with showers, from 93 DM ($55.20). Doubles with showers or complete baths and toilets cost 100 DM ($59.40) to 150 DM ($89.05). Meals cost 28 DM ($16.65) to 60 DM ($35.65). The wine list contains more than 250 different wines. You can take a cool dip in the pool, or bake out in the sauna.

Waldhotel am Schloss Gottorf, An der Stampfmühle 1, D-2380 Schleswig (tel. 04621/2-32-88), is a brick mansion lodged on a grassy plateau surrounded by a park and pine trees. It's on the outskirts of Schleswig, en route to the castle, and approached by a winding driveway. A secluded holiday retreat, it's a fine bargain. There are no lounges to speak of, but the emphasis is placed on the sunny dining room and the comfortable bedrooms (large enough to have breakfast in, unless you prefer your morning coffee on the front terrace). Only two singles are rented, costing 62 DM ($36.80) daily. The eight doubles rent for 105 DM ($62.35). All prices include breakfast.

Hotel Waldschlösschen, Kolonnenweg 152, D-2380 Schleswig-Pulverholz (tel. 04621/38-32-83), a mile to the southwest. This elegant country hotel is equipped with every convenience to make your stay here interesting and comfortable. You'll notice a rock garden, a gabled house, an elongated annex, and lots of green trees before you enter the public rooms, which are intimately lit and decorated with tasteful carpeting, warm brick detailing, and wood paneling. The swimming pool is centrally heated year-round, and there is a bowling alley. The carpeted bedrooms, with private baths, are completely satisfactory in every way. The English-speaking owner charges 115 DM ($68.30) to 150 DM ($89.05) daily for one of the 60 double rooms, 75 DM ($44.55) to 180 DM ($106.90) for one of the 20 singles. Each of the units has a private bath and phone.

Hotel and Restaurant Skandia, Lollfuss 89, D-2380 Schleswig (tel. 04621/2-41-90), in the center of town, is a modern 26-bedroom building without much external adornment other than pleasing proportions. Inside, however, you'll find a collection of banqueting halls and high-ceilinged public rooms, along with small bedrooms decorated with modern wood-grained pieces. All units have tile baths,

TVs, radios, and phones. With breakfast, the rate is 50 DM ($29.70) daily for a single and 90 DM ($53.45) for a double. The hotel has an excellent kitchen, turning out North German specialties, with meals costing 25 DM ($14.85).

WHERE TO DINE

A fine choice for dining, **Schloss Keller,** Schloss Gottorf, An der Stampfmühle 1 (tel. 04621/2-32-88), is on the lower level of the previously recommended castle. There's also a café for light snacks and refreshments. Meals in the pleasant restaurant (which include soup of the day) cost 25 DM ($14.85) to 50 DM ($29.70). The cuisine is typically and reliably Germanic, with dishes such as Wiener Schnitzel, rumpsteak, and sole. Open daily from 11:30am to 2:30pm and 6 to 10pm.

Olschewski's Hafenstrasse 40 (tel. 04621/2-55-77). In the center of town, close to the waterfront, this cozy and well-managed restaurant expanded from the white-walled private house that originally contained it. You can dine within a glass-sided modern extension jutting off to one side, or within the comfortably unpretentious dining room with views of the Schlei (the harbor of Schleswig). You can order very fresh salads in almost any season, cream of fresh tomato soup, fresh salmon with a tangy cream-base or a Riesling sauce, filet of sole with a saffron sauce and an herb-flavored mousse, filet of lamb with rosemary, or roast goose. Fixed-price meals cost 55 DM ($32.65) to 80 DM ($47.50); à la carte dinners, 30 DM ($17.80) to 65 DM ($38.60). Hours are from 11:30am to 2:30pm and 5:30pm to midnight; closed Tues.

THE SIGHTS

A tour of the attractions usually begins in the Altstadt, with a visit to the jewel of Schleswig, **St. Peter's Cathedral,** Norderdomstrasse, a brick Romanesque-Gothic hall-church begun in the 12th century. The towering spire makes the rest of the Altstadt seem like so many dollhouses by comparison. Inside is the outstanding 16th-century *Bordesholm Altarpiece,* a powerful work carved in oak by Hans Brüggemann for the convent at Bordesholm. It was brought to the cathedral in 1666. Its elaborately carved Gothic panels contain nearly 400 figures. The cathedral and cloisters also contain art treasures, including the *Blue Madonna* by J. Ovens and 13th-century frescoes. From May to September, the cathedral is open daily from 9am to 5pm, Fri. from 9am to 3pm. From April to October, it is open Mon. to Thurs. and on Sat. from 10am to 4pm; Fri. from 10am to 3pm, and on Sun. from 1 to 4pm.

Schloss Gottorf lies on a small island in the Burgsee, a bay at the west end of the Schlei. A dam and a bridge connect the island with the town. As you walk around the harbor, the panorama of the Alstadt and the widening bay opens up behind you. The castle is the largest in Schleswig-Holstein. The foundations date from the original 13th-century ducal palace, and the present structure was built mainly in the 16th and 17th centuries, and reconditioned since 1948 to house two museums and the State Archives.

The **Provincial Museum of Archeology** (tel. 04621/81-33-00) is one of the two museums housed in Schloss Gottorf. Contained in a separate building is the most remarkable exhibit, the Nydam Boat, a 4th-century ship found in the Nydam marshes in 1863. In glass cases in the same room are artifacts and weapons found with the ship and corpses found preserved in the moor, all adding up to the major archeological finds in northern Germany. Admission is 3 DM ($1.80) for adults, 1.50 DM (90¢) for children.

About 1½ miles from Schleswig at Haithabu is a **Viking Museum,** opened in 1985, containing the results of archeological excavations of the Viking-age town of Haithabu. Shown are all aspects of daily life, including a Viking longship. The museum is open April to the end of October, daily from 9am to 6pm. From November to March, it's open Tues. to Fri. from 9am to 5pm; Sat. and Sun. from 10am to 6pm. Admission is 3 DM ($1.80). In summer you can reach the site by boat, a 20-minute scenic ride. Departures are from Stadthafen, the town quay in Schleswig, south of the cathedral. After you dock, it's a 10-minute walk to the museum.

The **Schleswig-Holstein State Museum** (tel. 04621/81-32-22), also housed in the castle, contains an exceptional collection of fine and applied arts from medieval times to the 20th century (paintings, sculptures, furniture, textiles, weapons). Outstanding are the late Gothic King's Hall, the 17th-century ducal living rooms with rich stucco ceilings, and the Renaissance chapel with a private pew for the ducal family decorated with intricate and elaborate carvings and inlays. Two separate buildings east of the castle contain the collections of contemporary art in Schleswig-Holstein, including outstanding works of German expressionism and modern sculpture, plus the ethnological collection with its extensive displays of implements and tools representing the rural life of farmers, artisans, and fishermen in Schleswig-Holstein.

From April to October, they are open Tues. to Sun. from 9am to 5pm; Mon., only the Nydamhalle and the Middle Ages collection are open to the public. From November to March, the museums are open Tues. to Sun. from 9:30am to 4pm; closed Mon. The 3-DM ($1.80) ticket admits you to both museums.

---

4. Westerland (Sylt)

The long, narrow island of Sylt and its capital, Westerland, form the northernmost point of West Germany. Pronounced "zoolt," Sylt lies in the North Sea off the coasts of Denmark and Schleswig-Holstein. In land area, the island is about 36 square miles, its west coast a stretch of beach some 24 miles long. The "Watt" is the name given to the eastern coast, facing the mainland. Pounding winter storms seem to take more and more of the coastline each year, and there are those who think that Sylt will just one day disappear back into the sea.

People come here to breathe the iodine-rich air and enjoy a climate the Germans call *Reizklima*. Temperatures in midsummer are usually in the low 70s, but rain can come at any minute. This has given rise to the Sylt "mink," or yellow oilskin, which chic visitors wear to protect themselves from the elements. Once it was an island of seafaring folk who earned their living the hard way by fishing for herring. Later they turned to whaling. But in the postwar era, Sylt became known as "the St. Tropez of the north," attracting such headliners as Peter Ustinov, Gunther Sachs, Lilli Palmer, and Curt Jurgens. It is now the most exclusive resort in West Germany, its hotel prices reflecting its lofty status.

The basic therapy here is sunshine, pure air, and seawater, but in recent years mud baths have also become a method of treatment. The spa has facilities for the treatment of everything from heart disease to skin irritations.

Some of the more remote sections of the dunes have been turned into nudist beaches for purists in the art of sunshine therapy. In addition to bathing, there are facilities in and around Westerland for horseback riding, along with surf, golf, and tennis, as well as more sedentary entertainment such as the theater and concerts.

When the sunlight begins to fade at the end of each day, the casino (Spielbank) becomes the center of activity. In the center of town, it is in the same building as the Rathaus. All major games are played here: baccarat, roulette, and blackjack. The Casino bar serves the best drinks in town and is open daily from 5pm.

The only link between the mainland and Sylt, other than car-ferry, is the causeway running from the town of Niebüll. However, this causeway is only a railroad track, so if you wish to bring your car to the island, you'll have to load it on the train at Niebüll for the long slow ride. No advance booking is necessary. You just arrive and take your chances. Passengers are carried free.

The other way to go is by car-ferry between Havneby on the Danish island of Römö, which can be reached by highway from West Germany, and List, at the northern tip of Sylt. There are at least a dozen crossings in summer, with a much-reduced schedule in winter. Unlike the railway, the car-ferries accept reservations. Call Havneby in Denmark (00454/75-53-03); or in West Germany, the Haus der Reise, Grosse Bergstrasse 154 in Hamburg (040/38-18-21). In List itself, you can dial 04652/475.

WHERE TO STAY

Most hotels are found at Westerland, but scattered accommodations lie at other spots on the island, including Sylt Ost, Kampen, and Wenningstedt.

A Deluxe Hotel

Stadt Hamburg, Strandstrasse 2, D-2280 Westerland/Sylt (tel. 04651/85-80), the superior hotel on the island, is more like a well-appointed country home than a hotel, its gleaming white entrance reached through a white picket fence with street lanterns. It's built close to the street, next to the Casino, and its rear windows overlook a well-kept lawn. The bright and cheerful interior has country-estate furnishings, including wing chairs and floral-covered armchairs. Each of the 75 bedrooms is individually furnished, with homelike touches. In high season, singles with showers or tubs rent for 142 DM ($84.30) to 178 DM ($105.70) daily, and doubles with similar facilities cost 162 DM ($96.20) to 320 DM ($190). You'll want to take your morning meal in the breakfast room, with its blue-and-white ceramic stove. Guests gather on cooler evenings around the open fireplace. The hotel's restaurant serves some of the best cookery at the resort (see below).

Moderately Priced Hotels

Wünschmann Hotel, Andreas-Dirks-Strasse 4, D-2280 Westerland/Sylt (tel. 04651/50-25), is the second choice for accommodations. This 33-room hotel may be in the core of a plaza of modern buildings (with more than two dozen boutiques), but its inner aura is one of comfortable old-world tranquility. Food is offered in a woodsy and informal dining room, a pleasant place. The one-of-a-kind bedrooms are cheerful, all with strong colors, and they have private showers or baths. The high-season rates are as follows: singles range from 130 DM ($77.20) to 220 DM ($130.65) daily; doubles, from 200 DM ($118.75) to 335 DM ($198.90). Breakfast is included, as are taxes and service. The hotel is in the heart of the tourist belt of Westerland, yet only minutes from the sand dunes. Closed mid-January to March and mid-November to mid-December.

Dünenburg, Elisabethstrasse 9, D-2280 Westerland/Sylt (tel. 04651/60-06), is a standard modern hotel, set a block from the town center and beach. All its 38 front bedrooms face the water and have balconies (the higher up you go, the better the accommodation). Every bedroom is immaculate, comfortable, nicely furnished, and each has its own shower and toilet, color TV, and minibar. High-season rates are charged from June 1 to September 30. Singles with showers and toilets range in price from 110 DM ($65.30) to 150 DM ($89.05) daily; doubles with baths and balconies, from 180 DM ($106.90) to 260 DM ($154.40).

Vier Jahreszeiten, Johann-Möller-Strasse 40, D-2280 Westerland/Sylt (tel. 04651/2-30-28), resembles an informal country inn. Although practically in the sand dunes, it is still near the heart of resort activity, about a five-minute walk from the Casino and the swimming pool. It's easy to spot: bone-white walls and a red-tile roof. Most of its 26 bedrooms embrace the sea, and the lifestyle here is informal. In high season, depending on the plumbing, the hotel charges 85 DM ($50.45) to 130 DM ($77.20) daily for a single room and from 190 DM ($112.80) for a double, although some suitelike accommodations could cost as much as 210 DM ($124.70).

Hotel Roth, Strandstrasse 31, D-2280 Westerland/Sylt (tel. 04651/50-91), stands at the edge of the sea. This modern balconied 55-room hotel would look as much at home in southern Florida as it does in northern Germany. Rates are complicated and depend on the season. They begin at 108 DM ($64.15) for the most modest off-season single, climbing to 160 DM ($95) at the peak of the season. Off-season, you can stay here in a small, simple double for 160 DM ($95); however, for the best double room at the height of the summer season you might pay as much as 300 DM ($178.15).

Hotel Miramar, Friedrichstrasse 43, D-2280 Westerland/Sylt (tel. 04651/85-50). The 86-room hotel sits on a bluff just above the beach, surrounded by an arched veranda. Its public rooms are graced with enormous arched windows with views of the sea beyond. The comfortable sitting salon, my favorite room, is illuminated from above by an octagonal light, a detail left over from the building's 1903 construction. Regardless of the season, you'll be able to go swimming—in winter in the sunny indoor pool near the sauna and fitness room. The high-ceilinged bedrooms, all of which contain baths, toilets, phones, and TVs, cost 95 DM ($56.40) to 340 DM ($201.90) daily for a single and 170 DM ($100.95) to 440 DM ($261.25) for a double. Keep in mind that the wide price differences are caused by the fact that Sylt hotels double or triple their rates in the peak weeks of July and August. Breakfast is included in the tariffs.

Hotel Hanseat, Maybachstrasse 1, D-2280 Westerland/Sylt (tel. 04651/2-30-23), is centrally located in the middle of town on a pedestrian walkway. The owner of this family-run establishment offers spacious, light-colored public rooms and 21 clean, comfortable bedrooms. Singles rent for 110 DM ($65.30) to 160 DM ($95) daily, and doubles go for 220 DM ($130.65) to 260 DM ($154.40), depending on the season. Units are equipped with TVs, baths or showers, toilets, and phones.

WHERE TO DINE

The most elegant dining on the island is at **Jörg Müller,** Süderstrasse 8 (tel. 04651/2-77-88). The brick building that contains this restaurant is almost a landmark in itself, thanks to its thatched roof, steep gables, and Frisian architecture. Since the culinary star of Sylt, Jörg Müller, took over the premises in 1988, its fame has eclipsed that of every competitor. Menu items change with the seasons, and include a blend of cuisine moderne with imaginative variations of French recipes. These might include a lobster salad with herb-flavored vinaigrette sauce, a palate-cleanser of yogurt sorbet with a clear-colored liqueur distilled from essence of raspberries, sliced and braised goose liver with segments of glazed apples, a salad of veal's head with an herb-flavored vinaigrette, or roast salt-marsh lamb flavored with herbs and served with a ratatouille-flavored cream sauce. You can also enjoy local oysters with a compote of red shallots and champagne sauce or halibut baked in fennel. For dessert, you might order a compote of fresh fruits with pistachio nuts or a feuilleté of chocolate served with both a light and a dark chocolate mousse. Set menus cost 68 DM ($40.40) to 150 DM ($89.05), with à la carte meals ranging from 60 DM ($35.65) to 125 DM ($74.25). Meals are served daily from 11:30am to 2pm and 6 to 10pm; closed for vacation from mid-January to mid-February. Reservations are absolutely necessary. Most visitors arrive here on foot, since the place lies only a five-minute walk from the center.

Top-rate cuisine is offered in an attractive setting at **Stadt Hamburg Stuben,** Strandstrasse 2 (tel. 04651/85-80). Even if you aren't a guest at the hotel, you're welcome to drop in either for lunch or dinner. The menu is so wide-ranging it makes selection difficult, but among the à la carte listings, the smoothest beginning is the cream of lobster soup. There are many seafood specialties, such as pan-fried fresh North Sea plaice and turbot medallions in saffron sauce with zucchini. Other good dishes are the rack of lamb (raised on the salty grasslands of the island) and a dessert, homemade Rote Grütze—different kinds of berries and cherries topped with vanilla ice cream. Meals start modestly at 35 DM ($20.80), going up to 130 DM ($77.20); à la carte orders range from 40 DM ($23.75) to 85 DM ($50.45). Meals are served daily from noon to 2pm and 6 to 10pm.

Hardy auf Sylt, Norderstrasse 65 (tel. 04651/2-27-75), is a round, thatched restaurant with a nostalgic interior, run by French gastronomer André Speisser. The decor features furniture dating back to about 1890. Finely worked columns and an intricate veneer adorn the dining area, and there are some imposing old oil portraits. Beautiful glass lamps and skillfully wrought candlesticks combine to create a relaxed, intimate dinner, with candlelight, soft music, the best of wines, and good food. The recipes are both international and regional. There is also a fine selection of French and German wines. A full meal costs 40 DM ($23.75) to 65 DM ($38.60). Service is daily from 6pm to midnight. The restaurant is open from March to the end of October and from Christmas to mid-January.

Alte Friesenstube, Gaadt 4 (tel. 04651/12-28). The thatched building housing this Stube was first constructed in 1648. The restaurant serves northern German and Frisian specialties in a warmly old-fashioned kind of style. The menus are written on the wall in a dialect of low German, but someone will gladly assist you in deciphering some of the specialties, which include an array of regional pork, fish, and beef dishes. The establishment is open for dinner only, which begins at 6 and lasts until 10pm; closed Mon. Full dinners cost 38 DM ($22.55) to 70 DM ($41.55).

Das Kleine Restaurant, Strandstrasse 8 (tel. 04651/2-29-70), is chic and hip, a social rendezvous of the monied set who like to be seen at the right places, but also demand some of the best food available on the island, which they find here. Cuisine moderne has taken hold here in the specialties concocted by the chef: mousse of coquilles St-Jacques, goose liver pâté in port wine and vinegar garnished with red onions, and breast of Bresse hen stuffed with scampi mousse. Meals cost 60 DM ($35.65) to 90 DM ($53.45) and are served from 6pm to 1am; closed Sun.

5. Helgoland

Helgoland (also Heligoland) lies about 42 miles from the mouth of the Elbe River. It can be visited on a day trip, or else you can stay at one of its modern hotels or find bed-and-breakfast accommodations among the islanders.

Tourist officials are fond of pointing out that Helgoland attracts more summer visitors than, say, Capri. But don't get the wrong idea. Most of its visitors, nearly all of whom are German, flock to Helgoland because of its status as a duty-free haven. Cigarettes, whisky, and such staples are sold at about half the price charged on the mainland. Many visitors from Hamburg call a visit here a *Butter Fahrt,* meaning "butter ride," as they're allowed to take back 5 kilos of butter. Some try to get away with more, but visitors are subjected to random inspection by Customs officials.

It takes about two hours to cross the sea to Helgoland, where some 2,700 persons live. Excursion ships arrive en masse, especially in the summer months, but these vessels can't dock. Passengers are transferred to a flotilla of small boats, piloted by Frisian sailors, for the ride into town. One way to reach this traffic-free island is to take a train to Cuxhaven, where you can board a ship to Helgoland.

Helgoland is ancient, its origins going back to the 8th century, when it was an ecclesiastical center. In fact, its name means "holy land," from the German *heiliges Land.* In time it became a haven for smugglers, attracting pirates who menaced North Sea shipping. Over the years it has been ruled by Britain and Denmark, as well as Germany, because of its strategic position. In 1890 Kaiser Wilhelm II wanted Helgoland back so badly that he gave up Zanzibar in East Africa to gain Helgoland's release from British forces. Even before Victoria became queen of England, Helgoland had been turned into a spa, attracting artists and writers, and later wealthy visitors who gambled at the casino and attended summer theater after feasting on a supper of Helgoland lobster (which is quite expensive and much rarer these days).

Helgoland had a more ominous role to play in both world wars, when it was turned into a submarine base. Britain reclaimed the island at the end of World War II and attempted to blow it up, not wanting it to become another base in the event of some future war with Germany, but the sandstone island resisted the attempts. In 1952 the island was returned to West Germany. The population, which had fled to the mainland in the closing months of World War II, began to drift back. It's possible to go on a tour of the bunkers and underground tunnels where Helgolanders took shelter during bombing attacks. Therefore, don't come here looking for quaint Hansel and Gretel architecture. Every building, including the pastel-washed homes of the islanders, is new.

After landing at the pier, you can stroll along the main street of town, Lung Wai, or "long way." Actually it's not all that long, and the street is flanked with shops hawking duty-free wares for day-trippers. The town is made up of two parts, Oberland and Unterland. You can walk a stairway of 180 steps or take an elevator to the upper level. The scenic walk around the island passes the bird rocks, tall red cliffs, and North Sea scenery. At some point you can take a ferryboat over to Dune, the sister island of Helgoland. These islands were joined until a storm in the 18th century split them apart. Many come here for the beaches, where hooded wicker chairs, so typical of North Sea resorts, can be rented. Others seek out the beaches reserved for nudists. You can also visit an aquarium on the island, filled with North Sea fauna.

WHERE TO STAY AND DINE

A good accommodation choice is **Hanseat,** Südstrand 21, D-2192 Helgoland (tel. 04725/663). Many of this hotel's 22 accommodations are individually decorated, and each has its own private balcony and TV. There is easy access to an indoor swimming pool a short distance from the hotel. It's closed every year between November and February, but open otherwise, charging 60 DM ($35.65) to 80 DM ($47.50) daily for a single and 100 DM ($59.40) to 150 DM ($89.05) for a double. A generous breakfast, included in the price, is served.

Hotel Helgoland, Südstrand 16, D-2192 Helgoland (tel. 04725/220), is a first-class hotel that has been totally reconstructed. All 14 rooms have modern furniture. The charge for single rooms with showers, toilets, sea views, and balconies, plus buffet breakfast, is 65 DM ($38.60) to 80 DM ($47.50) daily. Doubles with the same amenities rent for 130 DM ($77.20) to 160 DM ($95). Owners Bärbel and Gerald Labes welcome visitors and grant them reductions from October to the end of April.

Haus Hilligenlei, Kurpromenade 36, D-2192 Helgoland (tel. 04725/77-33). Its simple, boxy design is accented with horizontal rows of recessed loggias and jutting balconies, most of which offer a view of the sandy shoreline. This is a well-scrubbed and unpretentious hotel, where each of the 32 comfortably modern bedrooms has summer-inspired furnishings, a phone, and a private bath. Singles go from 75 DM ($44.55) to 85 DM ($50.45) daily, doubles from 130 DM ($77.20) to 138 DM ($81.95), with a buffet breakfast included. The hotel is in Unterland.

Hotel Pension Mailänder, Am Falm 313, D-2192 Helgoland (tel. 04725/566). Set on the flat sandy stretches of Oberland, this flat-roofed hotel benefits from rambling rows of second-floor windows, which permit a maximum amount of northern sunlight into the 28 simple but comfortable bedrooms. Most have balconies, private baths, phones, and views over the barren landscape outside. The restaurant is open only to hotel guests, most of whom elect for the half- or full-board plan. Singles cost 41 DM ($24.35) to 90 DM ($53.45) daily, and doubles go for 82 DM ($48.70) to 132 DM ($78.40). The hotel is closed from November 16 through December.

WEST BERLIN

If you were one of the pilots bringing supplies to the people of Berlin in the great airlift of 1948 and 1949, you wouldn't recognize the city today. It was Hitler's capital, of course, and because of that dubious distinction it was bombed out of existence. The same optimistic spirit and strength of will that caused the remarkable Berliners to survive the destruction of the war and the postwar Soviet blockade of the city have caused the creation of a new West Berlin, a metropolis unequaled in Germany. Structures of steel and glass now tower over streets where in 1945 only piles of rubble lay. Parks that were once reduced to muddy swamplands are again lush forests and gardens.

The tragedy of the city is that in the postwar years it was not one Berlin, but two. Families and friends were divided by the concrete barrier, the Berlin Wall, a graffiti-covered monument dismantled in 1990 and sold for souvenirs. Even before that, beginning in 1989, West Berlin ceased to be the lonely "outpost" it had been for decades, surrounded by a Communist-controlled East Germany and literally encircled by an almost astonishing array of Soviet divisions.

Today, both West and East Berliners wander back and forth from one city to the other, as if indeed it were one city. And it may well be one city again, or even regain its status as the capital of Germany, but as of this writing, only those with crystal balls know such things.

From a legal standpoint, in the beginning of 1990, West Berlin was still occupied by the victorious Allies of World War II—the United States, Great Britain, and France. However, those Allies long ago granted West Berlin the right to elect its own mayor and send members to the West German Parliament in Bonn, where for decades they were nonvoting delegates. How long this occupied status will last depends on a number of factors.

Even if Berlin were to become whole overnight, a walk between East and West —at least for the foreseeable future—would still be a study in contrasts. History may move rapidly, but it cannot transform the city into one Berlin—except politically—overnight. That may take years.

But as both East and West Berlin move into the 1990s, they face a bright future for the first time in decades: a megalopolis of some 3 million citizens waiting to reclaim its stellar position as one of the great capitals of European industry and culture.

During these fast-moving times, the tourist rush to Berlin is inevitable. Visitors from around the world want to be there—to see for themselves what is happening as history is being written before their very eyes.

1. Berlin—Past and Present

Berlin, which for so many centuries has stood at the crossroads of history, is the object of world attention today. It's found a new popularity, and hotel reservations are harder to come by than in previous years.

Some want to come and see the "new Berlin," a long-divided city in search of another identity. Both East and West Berliners, as mentioned, now freely cross from one city to the other. Not so for foreign visitors. They—at least as of this writing—must still go through border formalities.

WHAT IT WAS

The year 1987 marked the 750th anniversary of Berlin. These dynamic seven and a half centuries saw Berlin go through many eras, climaxing in its most famous role—capital of Hitler's Third Reich, a position of dubious distinction that caused it to be reduced to rubble. It rose again, only to face another dubious distinction—its role as front-line "battleground" in the Cold War from 1945 to 1990. And regardless of the "global warming" of the Cold War, that role lingers on even today.

Actually—and rather amazing for a capital of Europe (or former capital, as the case may be)—Berlin only became a metropolis on October 1, 1920, in the aftermath of World War I. Though facing defeat and ruin, it ushered in what is now nostalgically called the Golden Twenties, the heyday of café, cabaret, and boulevard life—to some, a halycon time "between the wars." It was in 1920 that seven cities, 27 old baronial estates, and 59 townships joined to form one Berlin, a measure decreed by the Prussian government.

Before, in its earliest recorded history, it had been twin cities: the older Cölln and the slightly younger Berlin. Both towns developed from merchant settlements. The first mention of Cölln was in 1237, the first mention of Berlin in 1244. These towns on the River Spree, always closely linked economically, decided to unite as one city in 1307 and surrounded themselves with fortifications. At the crossroads of trade routes of the Middle Ages, they soon flourished. Distant Berlin was viewed almost as "part of Asia" by the rest of Germany, and the relatively remote city played little part in the latter's rich cultural and economic life.

At the beginning of the 1400s, the Hohenzollerns came to power, and were to be supreme rulers for five centuries. They made Berlin their seat of power. Hard times were to come. The ravages of the Thirty Years' War (1618–48), along with a series of epidemics, reduced the population to 6,000.

The Great Elector, Frederick William, who reigned from 1640 to 1688, invited the Protestant Huguenots fleeing religious persecution in France to Berlin. After the revocation of the Edict of Nantes in 1685, some 6,000 of them arrived, bringing about an economic revitalization of the stagnant Berlin economy. They eventually introduced several industries, including paper mills, glassworks, silk mills, and even the cultivation of tobacco. In the years that followed, the city became a new home to other Protestants, such as those from Switzerland and Bohemia, who were also fleeing religious persecution. The elector also invited wealthy Austrian Jews who had been expelled from their country to settle in Berlin.

In the meantime, the Hohenzollerns continued to grow in power and possessions, extending their lands to the Russian frontier. Frederick I was crowned "king in Prussia" (as opposed to "of") in 1701. He merged five towns and formed a royal residence, making Berlin the capital in 1709.

Frederick the Great (1712–86) came to the throne in 1740. The "Soldier King" presided over the Silesian Wars, the Seven Years' War, the partition of Poland, the split with the Habsburgs, but he also ruled over a period of enlightenment as well. During the 1700s, in fact, Berlin developed as an important city of commerce and culture.

In 1806 Napoleon's troops occupied Berlin, the emperor entering through the Brandenburger Tor, beginning nearly a decade of rule from Paris. This led to the war of liberation of 1813–15. But the peace as promised by the Congress of Vienna in 1815 did not bring the new freedom expected. Following the repression of Frederick William III (1797–1840), the year 1848 brought revolution to the streets. But the rebellion was crushed.

In 1871 Otto von Bismarck, the Prussian prime minister, united Germany with "iron and blood." Bismarck (1815–98) became the "Iron Chancellor" until he was dismissed in 1890.

Berlin continued to grow through all these changes and upheavals. In 1906 its population was reported at 2 million.

World War I arrived in Berlin in 1914, with its dire, dark consequences. Following Germany's defeat and the abdication of the Kaiser in November 1918, the first democratic republic was proclaimed in Germany. It was called the Weimar Republic, but in spite of its name, Berlin was still the capital.

By 1920 Berlin had emerged as the largest industrial power on the Continent, the nerve center of a vast rail network, the home of the German press, and a cultural and intellectual center that drew such names as Bertolt Brecht (*The Threepenny Opera*). But it was also a time of turmoil and brawls between, among others, Communists and Nazis.

On January 30, 1933, President von Hindenburg appointed Adolf Hitler chancellor of Germany. The Reichstag (parliament building) was mysteriously burned on February 27, 1933. A reign of terror ensued, culminating in the events of November 9, 1938, as Nazi hooligans set fire to synagogues and destroyed the shops of Jewish merchants. Berlin had the infamous distinction of leading Nazi Germany into World War II, a tragic military blunder that would rain Allied destruction on the city, culminating in German surrender on May 8, 1945.

Berlin had been virtually destroyed, with some 80,000 dead (no one knows just how many). The city had been reduced to rubble. The "Thousand-Year Reich" hadn't made it. Berlin, no longer the capital of Germany, was divided into four zones of occupation: Soviet, U.S., British, and French.

On June 24, 1948, Stalin launched the Berlin blockade, closing roads, rails, and waterways to the west, "trapping" 2 ½ million West Berliners without food supplies or electricity. The policy was to use mass starvation to bring about a political takeover and occupation.

On June 25, an American transport plane carrying 3 tons of freight landed at Tempelhof Airport in Berlin. The Berlin airlift had begun. Bowing to its success, the Soviet Union lifted the blockade on May 12, 1949. West Berlin further lost status on September 7, 1949, when the Federal Republic of Germany made Bonn its provisional capital. More than ever, West Berlin felt cut off from the rest of Germany. East Berlin was named capital of the German Democratic Republic on October 9, 1949.

On June 17, 1953, the East German government, aided by Soviet troops, repressed an uprising in East Berlin. In 1958 the Soviet Union demanded that West Berlin be turned into "a free and demilitarized city." The demand was not heeded, and by 1959 Krushchev had dropped the ultimatum.

On August 13, 1961, the East German government launched construction on the Berlin Wall to stop the flow of its citizens to the West. At first a barbed-wire barrier, it was turned into a heavily guarded concrete wall. Two years later, on June 26,

1963, near the end of his life, President John F. Kennedy arrived to deliver his now famous "I am a Berliner" line at Schöneberg Town Hall.

In 1972 West Berliners were allowed to visit East Germany and, a decade later, Berlin saw the historic visit of another American president, Ronald Reagan. In 1986 cultural contacts between East and West Germany were established, just in time for the 1987 celebration of the 750th anniversary of the two cities (or one city, as the case may be).

Nothing had prepared the world for the sudden events of 1989 and 1990 that led to the dismantling of the Berlin Wall and the prospect of reunification.

WHAT IT IS TODAY

Following its partition at the end of World War II, Berlin has forged a new identity. In spite of its "quadripartite status," it has become a vibrant, self-critical city, always receptive to new ideas and change.

It has now taken on the role of a major economic and cultural center, and it is one of Germany's largest university cities, a leader in development and research. It's also a popular destination for tourists and, because of its excellent facilities, is one of Europe's favored sites for trade fairs, congresses, and conventions, attracting 6 million visitors a year.

The panoramic view Berlin visitors see as they arrive at Tegel Airport is splendid. Few metropolitan areas in the world are blessed with so many lakes, woodlands, and parks, covering about a third of the city's area. Visitors who arrive for the first time are astonished to learn that small farms with fields and meadows still exist.

Berlin is subdivided into 12 boroughs of town-size dimensions, each independently administered from its town hall. Each borough has a character of its own, with marketplaces, shopping areas, and service centers. Here and there throughout the city are "villages," with their own warmth and atmosphere.

Cultural events of international importance define Berlin as a metropolis. These include opera premieres and other theatrical events; music festivals such as Berlin Bach Days, the Berlin Festival, and the Berlin Jazz Festival; and the International Berlin Film Festival.

One can dine to the midnight chimes, breakfast outdoors to the beat of a jazz band, join the strollers along the Kurfürstendamm. Berlin is lively around the clock, with various attractions to suit every taste.

2. Orientation

The center of West Berlin activity is the 2½-mile-long street named the **Kurfürstendamm,** but called the Ku'damm by Berliners, who seem to have a habit of irreverently renaming every street and building in the city. Along this wide boulevard you'll find the best hotels, restaurants, theaters, cafés, nightclubs, shops, and department stores. As the showcase of West Berlin, it is the most elegant and fashionable spot in the city, but like the paradox that is West Berlin itself, the Ku'damm combines chic with sleaze. Some visitors walk the entire length of this street, whereas others, not so hale and hearty, give up (as Berliners often do) and head for one of the popular cafés lining the boulevard for a drink or a cup of coffee.

Berlin today is an almost completely modern city risen from the ashes. Regrettably, it is hardly the architectural gem that old-time visitors remember from the pre-Nazi era. It was not rebuilt with the same kind of care that was lavished on such West German cities as Cologne. Parts of it are architecturally tawdry and uninteresting. Berlin is rich in other attractions, including great museums, but I suspect it is the city's tremendous vitality that attracts so many visitors.

North of the Ku'damm is the huge **Tiergarten,** the city's largest park. The Tiergarten is crossed by Strasse des 17 Juni, which leads to the famed **Brandenburg**

Gate (just north of here is the **Reichstag**). In the distance, the Brandenburg Gate opens onto **Unter den Linden,** the main street of East Berlin. On the southwestern fringe of the Tiergarten is the **Berlin Zoo,** which we'll visit later.

Since Berlin is so spread out (many lakes and pleasure areas are included within its boundaries), you will need to depend on public transportation.

If you fly into West Berlin, you'll land at Flughafen Tegel, which is slightly northwest of the city center, but only a short taxi or bus ride away. From the Ku'damm you can take Hardenbergstrasse, crossing Bismarckstrasse and traversing Otto-Suhr-Allee, which will lead to the Schloss Charlottenburg and Museums, one of your major sightseeing goals. The Dahlem Museums are on the southwestern fringe, often reached by going along the Hohenzollerndamm.

GETTING TO BERLIN

You can reach West Berlin from West Germany or other points in Western Europe by air, by car, or by train.

By Air

Many leading European and American airlines make regular flights into West Berlin from the West. One of the by-products of the international agreements that ended World War II was that the West German national airline, Lufthansa, could not fly over East German air space for flights to Berlin. That effectively blocked Lufthansa's ability to participate in the lucrative market between West Berlin and West Germany. Other airlines, such as Pan American, Air France, British Airways, and Trans World Airlines, filled in the gap.

However, in 1988 a loophole was discovered in the agreements, and this sparked the establishment of a new airline, **EuroBerlin France,** in which Lufthansa owns a minority (49%) interest. EuroBerlin, whose corporate colors are blue, white, and red, serves West Berlin several times a day from Frankfurt, Stuttgart, Munich, and Cologne. It flies B-737-300s at prices competitive with those fares charged by the more established airlines. Its support services, such as engineering and maintenance, depend on the experience of its two parents, Air France and Lufthansa. However, agreements regarding Lufthansa could undergo significant changes in the future, so check with a travel agent before booking your flight.

Pan American offers nonstop flights into West Berlin from Frankfurt, Munich, Hamburg, and Zurich. It also has nonstop flights from New York to West Berlin five times a week. **British Airways** flies from Hannover and London, and **Air France** flies from Paris via Düsseldorf. A typical one-way fare from Frankfurt to West Berlin is 211 DM ($125.30), which is subject to change, of course. This fare or similar fares apply year-round.

Certain promotional fares are offered (ask a travel agent). For example, Pan American will fly passengers under 25 years of age in both directions for a round-trip fare of 306 DM ($181.70). If you're a student with a student ID, you can purchase a one-way passage for 153 DM ($90.85), providing you're under 26. Standby tickets technically are available, but they apply only during such high-volume seasons as Easter, Christmas, and midsummer, which almost guarantees that none will be available.

By Car

West Berlin is also accessible by car, bus, and train. There are three major points of entry for motorists traveling from West Germany to West Berlin. The shorter route (approximately two hours) leads from the border town of Helmstedt, east of Hannover. You can also go east from Frankfurt in the direction of Bad Herzfeld

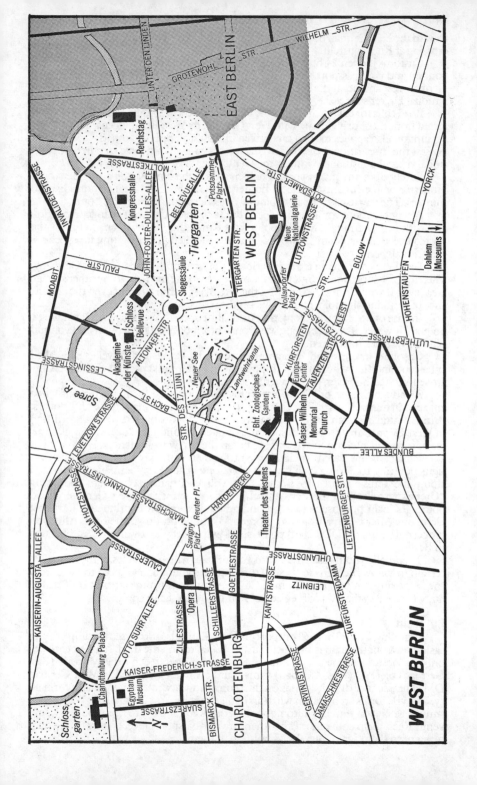

toward the East German border. Finally, another Autobahn north of Nürnberg has a crossing at Rudolphstein.

Customs is open 24 hours a day. You must carry the proper traveling papers for your car and your passport, of course; you'll have to cross the West German and East German checkpoints at the border. If you're the driver, you should possess an International Driver's License.

Road tolls for driving in Deutsche Demokratische Republik (DDR) are not collected from those driving cars with West German or West Berlin license plates. This exemption also applies to such cars driven into East Berlin on a one-day visa. If you possess the International Green Card insurance, you will not need to purchase additional vehicular insurance while in the DDR.

Rarely does any guard speak English, although some words are understood. Under favorable circumstances, all border formalities need take no more than 20 minutes. The trip itself from any point in West Germany is about 2½ hours.

Along the route you'll notice speed limits posted. They can change frequently and with little warning. Fleets of police cars patrol the Autobahnen, so follow the posted speed limits. Many police hide out in concealed places waiting for speeders. Occasionally cars are stopped.

Drinking and driving is a very serious offense in both East and West Germany. Therefore, be sure to keep any alcoholic beverages in the trunk or some other storage area (even if you're only transporting them to West Berlin). Avoid even the appearance of drinking alcohol while driving on the roads.

In case of breakdowns along the Autobahnen, call boxes are placed at strategic points. However, if you are a long way from a box, police cars will often find you and send a tow truck if required.

Gasoline stations and restaurants intended for Western travelers are called Inter-tank and Inter-shop. When stopping at the Inter-tank, bear in mind that many are self-service; however, others are full-serve.

Although the use of West German marks is preferred for many reasons when engaged in transactions in East Germany, in a pinch you can instead use U.S. dollars, British pounds, French francs, or whatever. You will probably receive change (if any) in West German marks. Not all stations are open around the clock, so pay close attention to your fuel supply. It's wise to begin the trip with a full tank.

Persons using the West German Autobahnen must keep their eyes open for signs pointing to Berlin or, in their absence, one of the East German cities located along the transit routes to Berlin. You will eventually see a sign indicating "Grenzkontrollstelle" (border control point), which is the West German checkpoint. Its main purpose is to assist and advise before you continue on into East Germany. After being allowed to proceed, continue on down the road. After you proceed through the DDR checkpoint, signs will direct you toward the Autobahnen to Berlin.

Eventually you'll reach the Berlin Ring Road, which encircles both Berlins. Be certain to follow the signs to West Berlin, if that is your goal. Proceed to the border check, passing through East German Customs once again and across into West Berlin, where the traffic laws of the Federal Republic once again apply.

By Train

Traveling by air to Tegel Airport in West Berlin is of course the simplest and easiest way, but the train isn't much harder. When taking the train, remember to pay only in Western money. The dining car may be operated by the Mitropa (East German) or DSG (West German) firms, but payment is required in West German DM. The issuance of transit visas on the train is now not much more than a formality. The visa forms aren't taken when arriving either in West Germany or West Berlin (unlike when you travel by automobile). Perhaps you'll want to keep yours as a souvenir. Keep them someplace other than in your passport since, chances are, you'll never need them again. But always hold on to them.

The rail trip from Frankfurt to West Berlin should take seven hours (sometimes a little more). Round-trip fares are sold for 338 DM ($200.70) in first class, 225 DM ($133.60) in second class. Rail fares from Hamburg to West Berlin are 190 DM ($112.80) round trip in first class, 126 DM ($74.80) in second class. This trip requires about three hours in each direction. Of course, these are independent fares. You may find it much cheaper, if you're traveling all over Germany, to purchase one of the GermanRail passes previously reviewed.

Eurailpass and GermanRail Tourist Cards are not valid for those sections of any transit that crosses over East German territory, although this may be subject to change in the future. These passes, however, are valid for transit over West German railroad lines up to the actual frontier of East Germany. Holders of these two cards, therefore, can benefit from reduced fares (but not free passage) if they purchase their tickets to West Berlin within West Germany at any office of GermanRail or at any authorized travel agency. Show your Eurailpass or your GermanRailpass. The most popular routing, for example, is from Frankfurt to the border town of Gerstungen. From Gerstungen to the city limits of West Berlin, you must pay a first-class fare of 111 DM ($65.90) one way, 222 DM ($130.65) round trip. If your trip originates in Hamburg, your rail pass will carry you only as far as the border town of Buchen. The fare through the DDR between Buchen and the city limits of West Berlin is 75 DM ($44.55) in first class one way or 152 DM ($90.25) round trip. In second class, you pay 50 DM ($29.70) one way or 101 DM ($59.95) round trip.

As East and West Germany move toward reunification, the information in this section may change. Consult the German tourist information offices about changing travel conditions to Berlin and East Germany.

TRANSPORTATION IN THE CITY

The bus and subway (underground lines) of West Berlin are operated by an efficient organization known as the **Berliner Verkehrs-Betriebe (BVG)**, Potsdamerstrasse 188 (tel. 030/2-56-1).

Tegel Airport lies within the city limits, about 5 miles to the north of West Berlin. Economically, this is a great boon to the visitor, since public transportation is convenient to all points. Downtown connections are possible by bus, taxi, and U-Bahn. A 30-minute bus ride costs 2.70 DM ($1.60), whereas a combination bus and U-Bahn connection, taking about 20 minutes to reach the center, costs the same. A taxi, on the other hand—a ride lasting about 20 minutes—ranges upward in price from 20 DM ($11.90). No porters are available to handle your luggage, but pushcarts are free. There's an airport Novotel with a connecting shuttle, if you have to spend the night to catch an early flight. For information about Flughafen Tegel (D-Berlin 51), call the information office at 030/41-23-07.

It is unlikely that you will land at the famed **Tempelhof Airport**, remembered chiefly in the West for the days of the Berlin airlift of 1948. It's still there; a newly established and privately owned airline, Tempelhof Airlines, flies in here from Hamburg and from the West German cities of Paderborn and Dortmund.

If you should land at Schönefeld Airport in the DDR, just outside the city limits of East Berlin, there is a bus service available between that airport and the Funkturm in West Berlin. The cost is 2.70 DM ($1.60) to the Funkturm (Radio Tower). Once there, you can take another bus to Schönefeld. The second bus costs 7 DM ($4.15), and runs every hour on the hour from 6am to 10pm. For information at Schönefeld Airport (when dialing from West Berlin), call 00372/672-4031).

The Berlin transportation system consists of **buses,** the **U-Bahn** (underground), and the **S-Bahn** (surface trains). Fares for the U-Bahn, S-Bahn, and buses, which operate only from about 4:30am to 12:30am daily (except for a few additional night buses), cost 2.70 DM ($1.60) for a single fare.

Both the U-Bahn and S-Bahn run in both West and East Berlin. One U-Bahn line and one S-Bahn line have been established for frontier crossings, and the station for travel between West and East Germany is the Bahnhof Friedrichstrasse. An additional S-Bahn line stops at Friedrichstrasse, the so-called partly underground Nordsüdbahn, which travels between the northern and southern parts of West Berlin. They all use the same border-crossing point (Grenzübergangstelle). On another U-Bahn line, going through East Berlin (U8), one of the East Berlin stations—Jannowitzbrucke—has been reopened for passenger service. It is said that other East Berlin stations will follow. Currently, Jannowitzbrücke is only a border-crossing point for West German citizens.

In 1984 the Berlin Tourist Information Office (BVG) took over the running of the S-Bahn train system in West Berlin. For some visitors to West Berlin, the location of certain S-Bahn stations may make its use more convenient than the U-Bahn or a bus. Under the operation of the BVG the service has been extended and former lines reopened.

The train station for West Berlin is known as the **Bahnhof Zoologischer Garten** (called Bahnhof Zoo for short). It lies near the zoo (also the Kurfürstendamm). Trains to West Berlin, of course, run through East Germany. For information about the train schedules or whatever, call 030/19-419.

A special service to tourists is the **Berlin Ticket,** a ticket good for unlimited travel on the U-Bahn, S-Bahn, and buses. This ticket can be purchased at the BVG information booth across from the Bahnhof in front of the zoo. The ticket, with a 24-hour validity, costs 9 DM ($5.35) and is also good for ferryboats on Wannsee Lake. At the booth, you can also purchase a **Sammelkarte,** which is valid for five rides, costing 11.50 DM ($6.85), good for two hours of transport in all directions. You are allowed to switch from underground to bus and S-Bahn. Keep your ticket to the end of your journey; otherwise, you may be subject to a fine of 40 DM ($23.75).

Special **excursion buses,** marked with a small triangular symbol, provide fast and convenient access from the center of the city (the Zoo Railway Station) to the recreation areas at Schildhorn, the Grunewald Tower, and Pfaueninsel, from Wannsee station to Pfaueninsel and the S-Bahn station at Nikolaussee to Wannsee Beach during the summer months only.

Taxis are readily available throughout Berlin, and can be either hailed on the street or called at 030/69-02. The average fare is about 15 DM ($8.90), and the meter drops to 3.40 DM ($2) before you've gone even a foot. You are usually charged 1 DM (60¢) for each suitcase.

FAST FACTS

"Fast Facts for West Germany," in Chapter II, are of course applicable to West Berlin. However, some data specifically for this city may be of help to visitors.

American Express: The offices of American Express are at Kurfürstendamm 11 (tel. 030/882-75-75), a second-floor location. They are open Mon. to Fri. from 9am to 5:30pm (on Sat., only from 9am to noon). If you have mail sent here and don't possess an American Express card or traveler's checks, you must pay 2 DM ($1.20) just to inquire if you have any mail.

Consulates: The U.S. Consulate is at Tempelhofer Damm 7 (tel. 030/832-40-87), and is open Mon. to Fri. from 8:30am to 1pm. The Canadian Consulate is on the 12th floor of the Europa-Center (tel. 030/261-11-61), open Mon. to Fri. from 9am to noon. The British Consulate, Uhlandstrasse 7–8 (tel. 030/309-52-93), is open Mon. to Fri. from 9am to noon and 2 to 4pm. However, for visas, go only in the morning.

Currency exchange: There is a facility for exchanging currency at the Bahnhof Zoo, open Mon. to Sat. from 8am to 9pm, on Sun. from 10am to 6pm.

Drugstore: If you need a pharmacy (Apotheke) at night, go to one on any corner. There you'll find a sign in the window giving the address of the nearest drugstore open at night. This is required by law.

Information: For tourist information and possibly hotel bookings, head for the Berlin Tourist Information Office, Europa-Center (on the Budapesterstrasse side) (tel. 030/262-60-31). It's open daily from 7:30am to 10:30pm. There's a branch office in the main lobby of Tegel Airport (tel. 030/41-01-31-45), which is open daily from 8am to 11pm. Another office is at the border-crossing point, Grenzkontrollpunkt Dreilinden (tel. 030/803-90-57), open daily from 8am to 11pm. There is also a hotel-booking office at the main railway station (tel. 030/313-90-63).

Medical care: In a medical emergency, telephone 030/25-85.

Post office: The post office is open 24 hours a day at the main rail terminal, the Bahnhof Zoo. If you have mail sent there, have it marked "poste restante." You can also make long-distance telephone calls at night.

---

3. Where to Stay

The days of *Grand Hotel,* when the lives of gamblers, ballerinas, noblemen, and stenographers became intertwined behind those revolving doors, are no more. The prewar ideal of luxury has been replaced by modern comfort and convenience. In many of Berlin's newest hotels, electric eyes and pushbuttons have made doormen and elevator operators obsolete. If you're still looking for that personal touch, Berlin has that too, in the many small hotels and pensions in the vicinity of the Ku'damm.

Berlin is the scene of frequent international trade fairs, conferences, and festivals, and during these times there are unlikely to be any vacancies in the city. Elsewhere in West Germany, travelers can simply go to another town to find accommodations, but because of the location of West Berlin, there's nowhere else to go, and East Berlin has severely limited accommodations. It's always wise to make reservations in advance, especially at the deluxe and first-class hotels. When there are no special events, you should have no problem finding accommodations to suit both your taste and your pocketbook. I'll survey some of the best choices in all price categories below.

ON OR OFF THE KURFÜRSTENDAMM
Here are the most central hotels in Berlin, in all price ranges.

Deluxe Hotels
Hotel Bristol Kempinski Berlin, Kurfürstendamm 27, D-1000 Berlin 15 (tel. 030/88-43-40), is a legend in Berlin. A century ago Kempinski was the name of one of the most renowned restaurants in Germany. In 1952 it rose out of the debris of World War II to become a landmark hotel, enjoying a position in West Berlin similar to that of the Waldorf-Astoria in New York. Businesspeople who want to conclude international deals select the Kempinski as their base of operation, knowing they will be assured of a dignified ambience, attentive service, and a setting in the center of the city. The lobby sets the relaxed mood, with its fine and comfortable groupings of furniture. A high-level cuisine is served in the Restaurant Kempinski, which opens onto a Kurfürstendamm terrace. Other discriminating diners prefer the Kempinski Grill, one of the finest in West Berlin, for lunch, dinner, or late-night supper. It's open from noon to 3pm and 6pm to 2am; closed Sun. The Bristol Bar is low-key, with patent-leather chairs and a pianist playing soft background music. An outstanding feature is the Kempinski Pool, a recreation center with an inside swimming pool (24 by 48 feet), a sauna, massage facilities, a solarium, a fitness center, and a pool bar. The bedrooms—315 in all, with marble bathrooms, full air conditioning, col-

or TVs, direct-dial phones, and fully stocked minibars—match the public rooms in taste. The accommodations are richly carpeted, the furnishings a selection of antique reproductions combined with modern. A single room with complete bath ranges in price from 330 DM ($195.95) to 380 DM ($225.65) daily; a double with complete bath ranges from 380 DM ($225.65) to 430 DM ($255.35). If you'd like to experience an added touch of class, try the Kempinski Luxury Limousine Service. You can use it for transportation from and to the airport, or for a sightseeing tour, and you'll be riding in an old-fashioned, chauffeur-driven Daimler limousine.

Hotel Steigenberger Berlin, Los-Angeles-Platz 1, D-1000 Berlin 30 (tel. 030/2-10-80 or toll free in the U.S. at 800/223-5652). No expense seems to have been spared during the 1981 construction of this excellent choice among the expensive modern hostelries of Berlin. The facade boasts a double level of panoramic windows on the ground floor, overlooking the landscaped expanse of the front garden, and the reception and the second-floor sitting areas make extravagant use of a well-decorated space. All 400 bedrooms have modern conveniences, and are handsomely appointed in warm, subdued colors. A kind of lemon light often suffuses the glass, marble, chrome, and plush upholstery. Singles rent for 195 DM ($115.80) to 350 DM ($207.85) daily, while doubles cost 260 DM ($154.40) to 420 DM ($249.40). The hotel's dining room, one of Berlin's best, offers both classical and modern cuisines. Fixed-price menus in the evening range from 85 DM ($50.45) to 105 DM ($62.35). It is open Tues. to Sun. from 6pm to midnight. You'll be able to relax under the wood-ribbed dome of the swimming pool before entering the mixed sauna, where au naturel seems to be the native dress.

Grand Hotel Esplanade, Lützowufer 15, D-1000 Berlin 30 (tel. 030/26-10-11), is the most dramatic and sophisticated modern hotel in Berlin, located within a 10-minute drive of the commercial center. Set beside a canal, which the city of Berlin commissioned in the 19th century as a public-works project for the city's unemployed, the Esplanade was opened in 1988. The disembarkation zone for cars and taxis is enclosed with a cascade of water that flows gracefully down a massive concrete screen. The hotel's public rooms incorporate many of the design concepts you'd expect in a museum of ultramodern art, with even a hint of influence from such pop masters as Andy Warhol.

Each of the 369 well-furnished accommodations contains air conditioning, full bath, cable TV, video, minibar, phone, and sound insulation. Single rooms range from 240 DM ($142.50) to 260 DM ($154.40) daily, doubles from 285 DM ($169.25) to 305 DM ($181.10). Suites begin at 445 DM ($264.25) for two. There's a beer-restaurant with a neon-encrusted Würlitzer jukebox (the *Eck-Kneipe*), and a gourmet restaurant devoted to cuisine moderne and modern decor called the Harlekin. Within the hotel are a triangular-shaped swimming pool, a whirlpool, and a sauna.

Expensive Hotels

Savoy Hotel, Fasanenstrasse 9–10, D-1000 Berlin 12 (tel. 030/311-03-0), is one of the leading hotels of Berlin. After funds were lavishly spent on a total and stylish rehabilitation, it is now ranked as a hotel equal to its long history and fame. Built in 1929, it was the first hotel in the city to have a private bath connected to each bedroom, a revolutionary idea in its day. Over the years, it has attracted some of the most illustrious people of Berlin, as well as a long list of celebrated foreigners, often musicians and artists.

The Savoy offers 130 elegantly furnished bedrooms that can be rented either as singles or doubles. It is classified as a first-class hotel only because of its lack of a swimming pool, for which clients would pay higher room rates. Therefore, this remains a first-class hotel with deluxe rooms, beautifully furnished in muted colors with many extra amenities. Singles rent for 195 DM ($115.80) to 240 DM ($142.50) daily, with doubles costing 280 DM ($166.25) to 420 DM ($249.40). Breakfast, a copious buffet in the street-level restaurant, can be served on a sixth floor terrace in warm weather. Both the Savoy's restaurant, Belle Époque, and its bar will be recommended separately. Smoothly overseeing the operation is the hotel's outstanding director, Hans Eilers, who has employed a thoughtful, concerned staff. Bodo Wulfert, the reservations director, is a cordial, gracious hotelier of much charm. The hotel is one of the founding members of the worldwide Steigenberger Reservations System.

Hotel Mondial, Kurfürstendamm 47, D-1000 Berlin 15 (tel. 030/88-41-10), is one of the finest hotels—other than the Kempinski and Steigenberger—in this area of the city, considered "the best part" of the Kurfürstendamm. It is located near the Theater am Kurfürstendamm and the Komödie. Contemporary comfort and service are provided, with welcoming public rooms and comfortable accommodations. There are 75 spacious and attractively furnished bedrooms, some air conditioned, with double-glazed windows, all with private baths (or showers), color TVs, radios, minibars, and direct-dial phones. Singles rent for 170 DM ($100.95) to 300 DM ($178.15) and doubles for 220 DM ($130.65) to 360 DM ($213.75). Included in the prices is a buffet breakfast. The Mondial has facilities for handicapped persons, including 22 rooms suitable for wheelchairs. There are no steps leading to the rooms, so that the disabled can move freely, and elevators, bathroom wash basins, and furniture have been especially adapted. Other facilities include indoor parking for 35 cars and an indoor swimming pool, along with a Jacuzzi and solarium. Dining is in the 120-seat Kräutergarten, which offers both international and regional dishes, along with fish specialties.

Arosa Parkschloss Hotel, Lietzenburgerstrasse 79–81, D-1000 Berlin 15 (tel. 030/88-00-50), has a deceivingly austere facade, giving no clue as to the charm, style, and flair within. It's strongly recommended for many reasons, but especially because it opens onto a rear courtyard and garden with a good-sized open-air swimming pool and terrace for relaxation, refreshments, and good summer food. On the premises are two restaurants, Schneider's Fass and Schneider's Restaurant, as well as Schneider's Bar. The "Fass" has a rough wooden ceiling, heavy beams, alpine chairs, and pine tables, not to mention excellent provincial cuisine. The 90 bedrooms are skillfully styled as well, with cable TVs and showers. Singles rent for 153 DM ($90.85) to 213 DM ($126.50) daily, and doubles/twins run 226 DM ($134.20) to 286 DM ($169.80). All rates include a buffet breakfast, free use of the outdoor pool, and taxes.

Moderately Priced Hotels

Hotel am Zoo, Kurfürstendamm 25, D-1000 Berlin 15 (tel. 030/88-30-91), sits snugly on the main street of Berlin. Substantial and well maintained, it was built as a private home in 1900. The 135 rooms are well furnished, clean, and comfortable; all units now have private baths. Singles cost 170 DM ($100.95) daily, and doubles go for 200 DM ($118.75). Breakfast is included. There are three different kinds of rooms: those facing the Ku'damm have triple-glazing on the windows, but can still be noisy; rooms facing the inner courtyard are quieter, yet get much less light; and those opening onto a parking area are sunny and moderately quiet, but with an uninspired view. Incidentally, on his visit to Berlin in the 1930s, author Thomas Wolfe stayed here.

Hotel Meineke, Meinekestrasse 10, D-1000 Berlin 15 (tel. 030/88-28-11), could become your pied-à-terre while in Berlin. Although greatly remodeled, this 58-room hotel was around before the war—World War I, that is. In an apartment house on a quiet street, it caters mainly to the increasing number of foreign visitors to Berlin, and you're likely to see French and Japanese, as well as Americans and Canadians. Bedrooms are simply furnished and comfortable. All except six contain private baths or showers. Singles with baths or showers cost 115 DM ($68.30) to 130 DM ($77.20) daily, and doubles rent for 170 DM ($100.95) to 190 DM ($112.80). Without bath, a single is priced at 75 DM ($44.55), a double at 120 DM ($71.25).

Very similar in character, the **Domus Berlin,** Uhlandstrasse 49, D-1000 Berlin 15 (tel. 030/88-20-41), lies on a relatively quiet side street off the heartbeat Kurfürstendamm. Generally improved in recent years, it offers 73 rooms that are adequate in size and fairly comfortable, with baths that have been modernized. The hotel is run with notable concern for personalized service. You'll pay 98 DM ($58.20) daily for a single, 146 DM ($86.70) for a double. These tariffs include a buffet breakfast and taxes. On the ground level is a bustling little brasserie-restaurant, where the action overflows onto a sidewalk café.

Hotel Bremen, Bleibtreustrasse 25, D-1000 Berlin 15 (tel. 030/881-40-76), is a first-rate hotel garni that also offers very good service. Completely renovated, it is now more inviting than ever. Its 53 bedrooms offer cable TVs, phones, hairdryers, minibars, private baths (with showers and toilets), among other amenities. Rooms are well-furnished and comfortable, costing 190 DM ($112.80) daily for a single, 230 DM ($136.55) for a studio for two or 250 DM ($148.45) for a twin. Some suites are more expensive, of course. The hotel grants reductions to winter visitors. All tariffs include service, taxes, and a big buffet breakfast. You'll be in the center of the Kurfürstendamm if you stay here, a heartbeat location that pleases many visitors.

Hotel Kurfürstendamm am Adenauerplatz, Kurfürstendamm 68, D-1000 Berlin 15 (tel. 030/88-28-41), was opened in 1981 as a 35-room hotel. Its public rooms look distinguished and inviting. In the dining room, where only breakfast is served, the light from the double-tiered windows is bordered by draperies that frame the view of the street beyond. You'll be close to everything here, and your room will be comfortable and well furnished. Singles rent for 80 DM ($47.50) to 108 DM ($64.15) daily, while doubles cost 158 DM ($93.80), including breakfast. The staff here is alert and helpful.

Hotel Kronprinz Berlin, Kronprinzendamm 1, D-1000 Berlin 31 (tel. 030/89-60-30). The facade of this place has remained virtually unchanged since it was constructed in 1894. The owners have renovated the interior into a kind of art deco severity, which doesn't detract from the comfort of the well-appointed bedrooms. Many of the guests congregate in the cozy in-house bar before heading to their various nighttime obligations. The 53 bedrooms are each suitable for two persons, who pay 160 DM ($95) to 180 DM ($106.90). If a single person wants to rent one of the doubles, the charge drops to 110 DM ($65.30) to 125 DM ($74.25). A buffet breakfast is included in the price. Each accommodation contains a private shower and toilet, balcony, radio, phone, color TV, and minibar. In summer, hotel guests and Berliners gather in the garden under the chestnut trees for draft beer and wine.

Hotel Residenz Berlin, Meinekestrasse 9, D-1000 Berlin 15 (tel. 030/88-28-91). Its neobaroque facade and ornate balconies were originally built in 1910 as part of a large and impressive private house. Surviving the war and countless political and financial disasters, it was transformed into an 80-room hotel in 1980. Tastefully up-graded and completely renovated, it contains a comfortably informal pub-style bar and a well-respected restaurant, Grand-Cru, whose frescoed ceiling and art nouveau setting contribute to elegant meals. Each bedroom contains a private bath or show-er, toilet, color TV, radio, minibar, and phone. With a buffet breakfast included, single rooms cost 148 DM ($87.90) daily, doubles 186 DM ($110.45). Apart-ments for two begin at 216 DM ($128.25), with taxes and service included. The hotel lies on one of the residential streets radiating off from the heavily congested inner-city core that includes the Kaiser Wilhelm Memorial Church and the Europa-Center.

Astoria, Fasanenstrasse 2, D-1000 Berlin 12 (tel. 030/312-40-67). The exteri-or of this rebuilt, modernized hotel, just off the Kurfürstendamm and near the Bahnhof Zoo, resembles that of a town house. You can stay here for a moderate amount of money in a rather expensive section of Berlin. The hotel rents a total of 33 bedrooms, all but 3 of which contain private baths or showers. Rooms cost 142 DM ($84.30) for a single and 196 DM ($116.40) for a double, breakfast included. With-out bath, a single is 78 DM ($46.30), a double 99 DM ($58.80). A buffet breakfast is included in the rates. The bedrooms contain all the necessary comforts. The miniature dining room is restrained, with wood paneling and bright walls and chairs.

Hotel Askansicher Hof, Kurfürstendamm 25, D-1000 Berlin 15 (tel. 030/881-80-33). Despite the no-nonsense postwar modernization of its smooth stucco facade, this building was originally constructed in 1900. Transformed into a 20-room hotel in 1925, it has thrived in recent years as more and more visitors make it their temporary home in Berlin. It lies on the corner of the Kurfürstendamm, within a busy neighborhood loaded with bars and restaurants. Clients take an elevator or a staircase one floor above street level to reach the hotel reception area. Many of the elaborate stained-glass windows of the hotel's original construction, as well as some of the art deco and Jugenstil (art nouveau) furniture, are still in place. Fourteen of the bedrooms contain private baths and toilets. The remaining six rooms have showers, but toilets are in the communal hallways. No meals are served other than breakfast, which is included in the room rates of between 95 DM ($56.40) and 135 DM ($80.15) daily for a single and between 145 DM ($86.10) and 175 DM ($103.90) for a double.

Hotel Ahorn Berlin, Schlüterstrasse 40, D-1000 Berlin 15 (tel. 030/881-43-44). Conveniently located near a corner of the Kurfürstendamm, within a neighborhood liberally sprinkled with *Kneipen* (bars) and restaurants, this is a simple but very clean and cost-conscious hotel. Built in the 1970s, with few frills or architectural embellishments, it contains 26 rooms; each has private bath, wall-to-wall carpeting, color TV, phone, minibar, and radio. Depending on the accommodation, singles range from 100 DM ($59.40) to 120 DM ($71.25) daily, and doubles cost 155 DM ($92.05). Between November and March, these prices are reduced by 10%. Some of the doubles contain compact kitchenettes, which are unlocked for a supplement of 5 DM ($2.95) per day. The staff is polite and helpful.

Hotel Lenz, Xantenerstrasse 8, D-1000 Berlin 15 (tel. 030/881-51-58), is in a building originally constructed as a private house just before World War I. It lies on a residential street a few blocks from the Kurfürstendamm, a short distance from the stopping point for the express bus from West Berlin's Tegel Airport. Operated by English-speaking John Foss and his wife, Karla Schroter, it contains a small but convivial pub-style bar where cold snacks are served, as well as a separate breakfast room. The high-ceilinged bedrooms, 28 in all, have private baths, sofas, phones, and color TVs. Depending on the accommodation and the season, single rooms cost 110 DM ($65.30) to 125 DM ($74.25) daily, doubles 150 DM ($89.05) to 175 DM ($103.90), with breakfast, service, and taxes included.

Budget Hotels

Hotel Artemesia, Brandenburgischestrasse 18, D-1000 Berlin 31 (tel. 030/87-89-05). Conceived and designed as a hotel for women only, this establishment occupies the fourth and fifth floors of a residential building near the Kurfürstendamm. You'll take an elevator from the building's lobby to reach the 10-room hotel, whose interior has been modernized and set with recessed lighting. In cold weather, a fire sometimes burns in one of the sitting rooms. You'll usually find a temporary exhibition of art within the public rooms, which are occasionally rented for women's conferences and consciousness-raising sessions. On the premises is a rooftop terrace where breakfast is served on summer mornings, plus a bar.

Each of the bedrooms is named after (and dedicated to) the memory of a woman who influenced the quality of life in Europe, either in science or art. Bedrooms are outfitted in shades of white, pink, and turquoise. Each contains a private bathroom, writing desk, hairdryer, and telephone. With breakfast included, single rooms range from 95 DM ($56.40) to 105 DM ($62.35), double rooms from 120 DM ($71.25) to 150 DM ($89.05). Children under 6 sharing a room with their mothers stay free. Children and adolescents from 6 to 12 receive a 50% discount.

Bogotá, Schlüterstrasse 45, D-1000 Berlin 15 (tel. 030/881-50-01). Although you're just off the Kurfürstendamm, when you walk into the Bogotá you'll think you're in a small town on the northern coast of Spain. When you hear Spanish spoken, your impression will be confirmed. The lobby is Iberian in character, with a high beamed ceiling, an open wooden staircase leading through an arch to the bedrooms, a wooden balcony, and a heavy bronze chandelier. There are 130 rooms, 80 with private baths or showers. With bath, singles cost 85 DM ($50.45) daily, with doubles going for 145 DM ($86.10). There are 10 rooms with showers but no toilets, whereas others have only hot and cold running water. Ask for one with a shower, since the price is the same in both a single, at 67 DM ($39.80), and a double, at 110 DM ($65.30).

Cortina, Kantstrasse 140, D-1000 Berlin 12 (tel. 030/313-90-59), is a modest, well-maintained 20-room pension just off the Kurfürstendamm. Its prices won't break the bank. Bathless singles cost 46 DM ($27.30) daily; doubles, 76 DM ($45.15); and triples, 99 DM ($58.80). Rates include use of the corridor bath, as well as a Continental breakfast. Every room has hot and cold running water, as well as a phone, and many doubles have a little sitting area where you can take your morning meal. It's not a fancy place, yet there's a pleasant feeling of roominess and cleanliness. An English-speaking management helps out too.

Hotel Crystal, Kantstrasse 144, D-1000 Berlin 12 (tel. 030/312-90-47), is set a few paces from the manicured garden of the well-located Savignyplatz, a short walk from the Kurfürstendamm. This decent, well-scrubbed, and respectable hotel offers cost-conscious and comfortable accommodations, providing a safe haven in West Berlin. There are 33 uncluttered rooms, most (but not all) of which contain private baths and toilets. With a Continental breakfast included, singles range from 65 DM ($38.60) to 80 DM ($47.50) daily, and doubles cost 100 DM ($59.40) to 120 DM ($71.25), depending on the plumbing. In contrast to the building's angular modern facade, a warmly and traditionally decorated Teutonic Stube lies a few paces from the reception area. Open only to residents, it serves an occasional drink but no food, as breakfast is the only meal offered here. However, at the doorstep are numerous moderately priced cafés and restaurants.

NEAR THE MEMORIAL CHURCH AND ZOO

The bomb-flattened area between the Memorial Church and zoo has become the major hotel belt of Berlin. The Kurfürstendamm changes character at the church and becomes less a promenade shopping street and more an avenue of first-class hotels. It is the most prestigious place in Berlin to stay.

Expensive Hotels

Hotel Palace Berlin, Im Europa-Center, Budapesterstrasse 42, D-1000 Berlin 30 (tel. 030/25-49-70), is a hotel in the heart of downtown Berlin next to the Memorial Church, lying between the Kurfürstendamm and Tauentzienstrasse shopping district. The hotel offers 258 well-furnished rooms and suites, each soundproofed and air conditioned and each containing a private bath, shower, minibar, cable TV, radio, and direct-dial phone. In 1989 the Palace added its Casino Wing. Each unit in the new wing has about 376 square feet and is beautifully appointed, with individually controlled air conditioning, cable TV with 25 channels, direct-dial phone, minibar, and trouser press. The marble bathrooms offer such amenities as separate bathtubs and showers, cosmetic mirrors, even direct-dial phones and radios. Singles cost 220 DM ($130.65) to 340 DM ($201.90) daily, with doubles going for 260 DM ($154.40) to 400 DM ($237.50).

Four restaurants on the premises offer a large selection of international, German, and typically Berliner dishes. The buffet breakfast and lunch are in the main restaurant on the second floor with its view of Elephant Gate, the entrance to the Zoological Garden. A small restaurant, La Réserve, is the hotel's gourmet dining room, and in the adjacent Europa-Center, you can dine inexpensively at Alt-Nürnberg (recommended separately). At the café-restaurant, Tiffany's, you can enjoy homemade tarts and pastries, along with various ice creams. Next to the Palace is the Thermen am Europa-Center, a large health club with several facilities, including both an indoor and outdoor swimming pool and sauna. Admission is free to hotel guests.

Hotel Ambassador Berlin, Bayreutherstrasse 42–43, D-1000 Berlin 30 (tel. 030/21-90-20), is an upper-grade 200-room hotel whose dining rooms and lounges are among the best conceived and designed of any Berlin hotel in this price range. One of the best places for fish dishes in town is the Conti-Fischstuben, whose walls are decorated with lobsters, crayfish, and crabs fashioned from brass. Mirrors and lamps contribute to the harmony of this restaurant. One glass wall opens onto a maritime garden. The bar is also attractive, and in the Schöneberger Krug tasty international and Berlin dishes are served. A lively crowd is drawn to the heated tropical pool on the eighth floor and the sun lounge on the roof. Bedrooms are excellent and well planned, each with a shower or private bath, radio, color TV, minibar, and international direct-dial phone. A single costs 188 DM ($111.65) to 238 DM ($141.30), and a twin-bedded room goes for 248 DM ($147.25) to 288 DM ($171).

Berlin Excelsior, Hardenbergstrasse 14, D-1000 Berlin 12 (tel. 030/3-19-93). The name of the hotel is elaborately set into gray tiles near the entrance of this modern establishment, a few blocks from the main railway station. The reception area and the high-ceilinged bar give the feeling of almost unlimited space, with modern partitions crafted of valuable hardwoods; patterned carpeting muffles the footsteps of the hundreds of international guests who stay here every year. Even though one wing of this 320-room hotel faces the Kurfürstendamm, your sleep will be aided by the soundproof windows. All units have private baths tiled in dark colors, and a collection of electronic devices diverse enough to keep anyone happy. Rooms are well furnished and attractively styled, costing 175 DM ($103.90) to 238 DM ($141.30) daily for a single and 245 DM ($145.50) to 318 DM ($188.80) for a double, including a buffet breakfast. The Peacock Restaurant, with elaborate representations of that bird in brilliant blues and greens, serves world-class meals in an aura of intimate simplicity. A second restaurant, the Store House Grill, offers meals from its lava-stone grill and a superb choice of fresh salads in a Mississippi-style atmosphere.

Berlin Penta Hotel, Nürnbergerstrasse 65, D-1000 Berlin 30 (tel. 030/21-00-70), stands in the heart of the city, an excellent chain-run hotel with 425 air-conditioned and soundproofed rooms, each with private bath, radio, color TV, in-house movies, direct-dial phone, and minibar. Singles rent for 200 DM ($118.75) daily, doubles for 240 DM ($142.50), and triples for 280 DM ($166.25). These rates include service charge, taxes, and free use of the indoor pool. An opulent buffet breakfast costs extra. Special bedrooms are available for nonsmokers and the disabled. The Globetrotter Restaurant offers elegant dining, whereas the Follow Me Bar and the cozy Pinte Bierstube with its Pintengartchen are relaxing places for a drink. Leisure facilities include a swimming pool, sauna, solarium, and massage service, along with a hairstylist, boutique, and parking garage.

Schweizerhof, Budapesterstrasse 21–31, D-1000 Berlin 30 (tel. 030/2-69-61), has brought honors and success to its Swiss owners. Built in a fashionable and convenient section, close to the Memorial Church and opposite the Zoo, it's clearly a winner in every department. The service, the amenities, and the comfort are first-class. However, the overall effect is not one of lavishness—rather, dignified restraint. Increased patronage has led to a whole new wing of streamlined bedrooms, both substantial and comfortable. An Olympic-size swimming pool, even a whirlpool, suggests that the Schweizerhof is one of the leading first-class hotels of Berlin. It's also the largest hotel in its class—430 rooms. Singles range from 195 DM ($115.80) to 380 DM ($225.65) daily and doubles from 245 DM ($145.50) to 430 DM ($255.35). The Schweizerhof Grill, offering a Helvetian and international cuisine, backed by Swiss wines, is recommendable. You can also dine in the Zunft-

Stube and the Schützen-Stübli, after having a before-dinner drink in the Lobby Bar. For small snacks in a cozy atmosphere, there's the Fassbier-Stübli, where good draft beer is served.

Hotel Berlin, Lützowplatz 17, D-1000 Berlin 30 (tel. 030/1-60-50), is a true international hotel, built in angular modern style, with its own grounds and gardens. Each of the 537 rooms is well furnished and comfortable. This chain hotel is noted primarily for its Berlin-Grill, considered one of the finest dining rooms in the city. Accommodations are rather cozy, with TVs, phones, baths or showers, and toilets. Singles go for 180 DM ($106.90) to 325 DM ($193) daily, and doubles cost 195 DM ($115.80) to 450 DM ($267.20). All rates include a buffet breakfast. The Hotel Berlin has an annex, Kurfürstenflügel, that contains a beauty shop, fitness room, steam bath, sauna, solarium, souvenir shop, and library.

Hotel President Berlin, An der Urania 16–18, D-1000 Berlin 30 (tel. 030/21-90-30), a Best Western hotel, offers four-star comfort at a moderate price in a prestigious central address. Most of the major sights of Berlin are within easy access, and the main shopping centers, the Kurfürstendamm, the Europa Center, and KaDeWe (the leading department store), are only a few minutes' walk away. Together with its unique atmosphere, this favorite choice offers all the facilities you'd expect of a modern first-class hotel. It rents 132 well-furnished bedrooms and suites, most of which contain air conditioning and are equipped with electronic security locks, color TVs, hairdryers, direct-dial phones, and minibars. Singles range from 172 DM ($102.15) to 235 DM ($139.55) daily, with doubles costing 198 DM ($117.55) to 275 DM ($163.30). The President's major restaurant, Die Saison, lives up to its name by offering a menu of seasonal specialties. Other facilities include a fitness center with a sauna and a steam bath, and the hotel also has its own car park.

Sylter Hof, Kurfürstenstrasse 116, D-1000 Berlin 30 (tel. 030/2-12-00), offers rich trappings at moderate prices. The main lounges are warmly decorated in an old-world style, with chandeliers, Louis XV–style and provincial chairs, and such antiques as an armoire and a grandfather clock. The bar-lounge serves drinks to guests seated in velvet armchairs nestling on Persian rugs. The dining room is more conservative. Although small, the 154 bedrooms are warmly appointed, with compact, traditional furnishings, plus private tile baths. Singles rent for 170 DM ($100.95) daily; doubles, for 250 DM ($148.45). Garage parking is available.

Moderately Priced Hotels

Hamburg, Landgrafenstrasse 4, D-1000 Berlin 30 (tel. 030/26-91-61), is one of Berlin's newer streamlined hotels, renovated in 1987 and offering 240 up-to-date accommodations at reasonable prices. The Hamburg, with its metallic-appearing facade of glass, is a five-minute walk from the Kurfürstendamm. Each bedroom contains its own tile bath and shower, phone, radio, and color TV; the decor of the rooms satisfactorily combines a Germanic modern approach with wall-wide draperies and comfortably upholstered armchairs. Singles are 159 DM ($94.40) to 179 DM ($106.30) daily; doubles, 188 DM ($111.65) to 235 DM ($139.55). A buffet breakfast is included in the tariffs. Facilities include a cocktail lounge, where the bartender offers fresh draft beer and prides himself on international brews. Best of all is the living room, with its clusters of deep, well-styled, velvet-upholstered armchairs arranged around tables, and its marble fireplace with an art deco look.

Hotel Remter, Marburgerstrasse 17, D-1000 Berlin 30 (tel. 030/24-60-61). An awning extends over the sidewalk in front of this saffron-colored building, only two blocks from the Kaiser Wilhelm Memorial Church. Each of the hotel's 34 bedrooms has a color TV, radio, safe, private bath or shower, and phone. Prices range from 102 DM ($60.55) to 115 DM ($68.30) daily for a single and from 150 DM ($89.05) to 170 DM ($100.95) for a double, with a buffet breakfast included. The interior is clean and comfortable, decorated in a sort of Berlin-airlift modern style (such as unframed hexagonal mirrors in the dining room). An elevator and free parking contribute to guests' comfort.

SOUTH OF THE KURFÜRSTENDAMM
This area has no special geographical boundaries except for its northern border. Only a few hotels are in this area, as it's mostly a residential and shopping section.

A Moderately Priced Hotel
Alsterhof Ringhotel Berlin, Augsburgerstrasse 5, D-1000 Berlin 30 (tel. 030/ 21-99-60), is a relatively unknown hotel but an excellent buy. Built in two different sections—one in the late 1960s, the other in the mid-1980s—the seven-story hotel is set back from the street. The lounges and reception area have walls of glass. There is a restaurant with bar. Each of the 144 bedchambers has its own private bath, radio, TV, minibar, and telephone, and is furnished with fine-grained wooden pieces. Many contain a sitting area as well. Singles range from 129 DM ($76.60) to 191 DM ($113.40) daily, with doubles costing 198 DM ($117.55) to 248 DM ($147.25).

A Budget Hotel
Dom Hotel, Hohenzollerndamm 33, D-1000 Berlin (tel. 030/87-97-80). In a 19th-century building with an absolute minimum lobby, this hotel provides good sleeping rooms at quite economical rates. Of the 40 adequate units, 20 come with private toilets and showers, and 20 come with showers only. With showers and toilets, singles rent for 85 DM ($50.45), with doubles costing 115 DM ($68.30). Rooms with showers but no toilets cost 70 DM ($41.55) for a single and 95 DM ($56.40) for a double. Meals are served in the restaurant, Dom Klause. The hotel, rising four stories, lies about a 10-minute walk from Adenauerplatz, or you can take the U-Bahn to Fehrbellinerplatz.

IN GREATER CHARLOTTENBURG
This is an area combining private residences, apartment houses, and hotels, about a 5- to 10-minute taxi drive from the Memorial Church and the Kurfürstendamm. On its main artery, Bismarckstrasse, stand the Deutsche Oper and the Schiller Theater. Actually, Charlottenburg embraces all the hotels we've considered so far. But because the entire district is so large (12 square miles), we've broken it up into the most central accommodations (see above) and those farther afield (see below). It's an area with many sightseeing attractions, including the Funkturm (the Radio Tower) and, even more distantly located, Olympic Park.

Expensive Hotels
Seehof, Lietzensee Ufer 11, D-1000 Berlin 19 (tel. 030/32-00-20), is one of the most attractive and enjoyable hotels in Berlin. It's comparatively unknown, lying in the residential section of Charlottenburg, yet it's only five minutes from the center by taxi and within walking distance of the Funkturm and surrounding fairgrounds, as well as the International Congress Center (ICC). The hotel borders Lake Lietzensee and its beautiful park. The Seehof's blue-and-white checkerboard facade opens onto a tree-shaded street. On the waterside stone terrace in the rear, you can have refreshments, sunbathe, or take your lunch and dinner. You start your day here with a swim in the glassed-in pool, then order breakfast at one of the garden tables.

There are two tastefully designed private rooms overlooking the lake, one with its 200-year-old Gobelin, the other with its natural stone wall, planter, and window wall. The main dining room, Restaurant "au Lac," is seductively designed; a pianist plays soft background music. Drinks are available in the rustic tavern bar. The bedrooms, all overlooking the lake and park, are provided with private bathrooms, color TVs, minibar, and direct-dial phones. They have armchairs and cocktail tables for relaxation, plus a desk if you need to do a little work. Singles with showers or baths cost 150 DM ($89.05) to 210 DM ($124.70) daily, doubles with baths ranging from 250 DM ($148.45) to 280 DM ($166.25), including a copious buffet breakfast.

Moderately Priced Hotels

Hotel Ibis Berlin, Messedamm 10, D-1000 Berlin 19 (tel. 030/30-39-30), built in 1966, stands halfway between the Olympia Stadium and the Europa-Center, and adjacent to the Berlin Exhibition Grounds and the International Congress Center, at the end of the Federal and Berlin City Highways. Its features are attractive and winning. Besides full baths, its 191 bedrooms have wall-wide glass windows, radios, phones, desks, and armchairs. Single rooms cost 120 DM ($71.25) daily; doubles, 162 DM ($96.20). Breakfast is included. There's an intimate wood-paneled bar and cocktail lounge, but the hotel doesn't manage its own restaurant. (However, there are three restaurants nearby: a German one, a Chinese one, and a steakhouse.) The Ibis is a leader in the moderately priced field. To reach the hotel, which lies five underground (U-Bahn) stops from the Europa-Center, take the subway to Kaiserdamm.

Hotel am Studio, Kaiserdamm 80, D-1000 Berlin 19 (tel. 030/30-20-81), is recommended to those seeking a bright and cheery accommodation at lower-than-usual prices. This marble-and-glass structure stands in the Charlottenburg district, near the Olympic Stadium and next to the Radio and Television Center. The 78 bedrooms are pleasantly decorated and comfortable, and all but 5 contain private baths. These few bathless rooms, under the eaves, cost 75 DM ($44.55) a night, single or double; other rooms rent for 115 DM ($68.30) for a single and 145 DM ($86.10) for a double, including breakfast. The hotel was built in the 1960s and has minibars, TVs, and phones in its rooms. Take the U-Bahn to either Kaiserdamm or Theodor-Heusse-Platz.

Kanthotel, Kantstrasse 111, D-1000 Berlin 12 (tel. 030/32-30-26), has architecture that looks vaguely like something out of the Bauhaus. The interior is spacious, high-ceilinged, and modern, with up-to-date bathrooms and color TVs in all of its 55 units. Singles rent for 144 DM ($65.50), with doubles going for 184 DM ($109.25), including breakfast. The hotel has no bar or restaurant, but it lies in a neighborhood peppered with them. Take the U-Bahn to Wilmersdorferstrasse.

A Budget Hotel

Econtel Berlin, Sömmeringstrasse 24–26, D-1000 Berlin 10 (tel. 030/34-40-01), has been luring economy-minded visitors to West Berlin since its opening in 1984. It calls itself an "international economy hotel," and lives up to its self-billing. A total of 205 rooms are offered, including 110 twin-bedded ones and dozens containing three or four beds; the most expensive units are 10 "business class" rooms. Prices are reasonable, with singles costing from 119 DM ($70.65) daily, doubles going for 138 DM ($81.95), three-bedded units renting for 153 DM ($90.85), and four-bedded accommodations peaking at 176 DM ($104.50). Children up to 12 years sharing a room with their parents pay only for breakfast.

The rooms are simply but comfortably furnished with modern functional pieces. Each unit is fully equipped with shower, toilet, radio, and direct-dial phone. On the premises is a snack restaurant, seating 200, as well as a lobby with a beer bar. There is a spacious underground car park. The location is near the bank of the Spree River and Charlottenburg Palace. Tegel Airport is 3 miles away, and the hotel can be reached via the city motorway, Stadtring Nord, exiting at Spandauer Damm. The nearest underground station is Mierendorffplatz. It's ideal for those who don't mind being lodged away from the center, and paying less in return for the trouble of getting there.

IN KREUZBERG

Near the Tiergarten stands a modern hotel that is just five minutes by taxi, or 15 minutes by bus, from the heart of Berlin.

A Moderately Priced Hotel

Hervis Hotel International, Stresemannstrasse 97, D-1000 Berlin 61 (tel. 030/261-14-44), made its debut in 1968. The rear of this hotel, which overlooks a lawn, looks somewhat like a U-shaped condo in Florida. You'll be able to see the Brandenburg Gate from many of the private rooms, and from the top floors you can glimpse East Berlin. The hotel is within walking distance of the Nationalgalerie and the Philharmonie, and stands across the street from the Martin Gropius building (the former arts and crafts museum). All 70 bedrooms are sunny and spacious, and decorated with steel-and-wood contemporary furnishings along with patterned wall-to-wall carpeting. Including a buffet breakfast, singles rent for 115 DM ($68.30) to 135 DM ($80.15) daily, while doubles cost 160 DM ($95) to 205 DM ($121.75). All units contain showers or baths along with toilets, color TVs, radios, and minibars. To reach the hotel, take the U-Bahn to Möckern Brücke or the S-Bahn to Anhalter Bahnhof.

IN GRÜNEWALD

The "Green Forest" of Berlin is the most desirable residential section of the city, with tree-shaded streets and many town houses that were spared the destruction of war. It's ideal for a peaceful night's sleep.

A Moderately Priced Hotel

Schlosshotel Gehrhus, Brahmsstrasse 4–10, D-1000 Berlin 33 (tel. 030/826-20-81), offers a rare opportunity to live in an Italian Renaissance–style palace. Created in 1912 by Dr. Pannwitz, personal attorney to Kaiser Wilhelm II, who was the hotel's first guest, the palace was built as a showcase to house the attorney's outstanding art and china collection. It miraculously escaped destruction in World War II. Today the villa is owned by Regine Gehrhus. On a shady street—it is reached via a formal driveway—it is a 15-minute taxi ride from the center. Surrounding the estate are tranquil parklike gardens. Inside, the architectural grandeur remains the same. Gilt is used flamboyantly. The two-story grand hall contains an elaborate staircase and minstrel gallery. Glittering chandeliers glow in the French-style salons, with their brocaded walls. The 33 bedrooms vary greatly, ranging from grand to average. A bathless single costs 75 DM ($44.55), one with bath going for 90 DM ($53.45). Bathless doubles rent for 120 DM ($71.25), doubles with baths going for 165 DM ($98) to 205 DM ($121.75). Suites for two persons are priced at 230 DM ($136.55) to 395 DM ($234.55). Even though they're not guests of the hotel, many tradition-minded Berliners come here just to have coffee or tea—perhaps a nostalgic reminder of the past. Others use the Gehrhus for fashionable weddings, receptions, and cocktail parties.

SPANDAU

Spandau, famous for the prison that once housed Rudolf Hess and for its citadel, is not thought of as a hotel district, but there are some accommodations. It is the only part of Greater Berlin on the west bank of the Havel, sharing a 20-mile border with the district of Potsdam in East Germany. In the Kladow district, where the following hotel lies, the German Overseas Development Agency trains volunteers for work in the Third World.

A Budget Hotel

In the suburbs of West Berlin at Kladow, **Havelhaus,** Imchenallee 33–35, D-1000 Berlin 22 (tel. 030/365-58-00), lies on the Havel River south of Spandau, about a 22-minute ride from the center. Built in 1910 as a boat factory, in the mid-

1960s it was transformed into a cost-conscious hotel. It has its own bathing beach in summer, but may shut down for a monthlong holiday right in the peak of the season (always call before heading out here). At times it's possible to rent a boat for a little cruise on the river. A tranquil choice, Havelhaus offers 25 clean but small units, each with hot and cold running water. The price is right: from 45 DM ($26.70) daily for a single to 70 DM ($41.55) for a double.

SCHÖNEBERG

In the general vicinity of Schöneberg—the area where 400,000 Berliners turned out in 1963 to cheer President Kennedy—there is one recommendation.

A Budget Hotel

Hotel-Pension Dittberner, Wielandstrasse 25, D-1000 Berlin 15 (tel. 030/881-64-84), is in a building (originally constructed around 1910) that contains an art gallery, a handful of private apartments, and another inexpensive pension. To reach the Dittberner, take an elevator from the building's street level to the third floor. There, owner Frau Ally Lange rents 20 simple but clean bedrooms, only seven of which contain private baths or showers and toilets. The rest have communal facilities off the hallways. Depending on the plumbing and the accommodation, singles range from 65 DM ($38.60) to 70 DM ($41.55) daily; doubles, from 102 DM ($50.55) to 130 DM ($77.20), with breakfast included. An extra bed can be arranged in any room for an additional 30 DM ($17.80) per night.

---

4. Where to Dine

If it's true that optimism and appetite go hand in hand, the West Berliners must be among the most optimistic people in Europe. In breads alone, the visitor is likely to be tempted by a dozen varieties, including Brötchen, Mohnbrötchen, Milchbrötchen (all types of rolls), Graubrot (rye), Pumpernickel, and several others. If you're interested in local food, these breads go equally well with the Berliner Schlachteplatte (cold plate) or pigs' trotters cooked with sauerkraut and pea purée.

But Berlin does not limit itself to German cuisine—the cuisine of nearly every major nation on the globe is represented here. Only the thickness (or thinness) of your wallet and the flexibility of your tastebuds need determine your choices. And don't think that an excellent dinner in Berlin has to be expensive. On the contrary, as you'll see in the recommendations below, you can have a memorable dinner in an unheralded wine restaurant or sidewalk café.

THE TOP RESTAURANTS

One of Berlin's leading candidates for in-depth preparation of haute cuisine is the **Berlin-Grill,** Hotel Berlin, Kurfürstenstrasse 62 (tel. 030/2605-25-62). You feel absolutely coddled here as a train of serving carts with your choices is brought to your chair. If finger food is served, it is followed by hot, scented towels. Everything is top-grade. In the illustrated bilingual menu—the cuisine is German-international —you'll find weekly and seasonal specialties. Many of the soups are prepared and served right at your table, including consommé of lobster with parfait of turbot. A favorite appetizer is the fresh salad made with Canadian king crab and served with an aged-sherry dressing. In season, the chef might offer filet of venison with homemade noodles, fresh cranberries, and exotic mushrooms. Sometimes an array of fresh fish is wheeled to your table so that you can make a selection. A set dinner costs 79 DM ($46.90) for five courses and 96 DM ($57) for six courses, whereas regular à la carte dinners range from 80 DM ($47.50) to 120 DM ($71.25). The grill is open from 6pm to 1am; closed Sun.

Rockendorf's Restaurant, Düsterhauptstrasse 1 (tel. 030/402-30-99), occupies the primary position in a 19th-century art nouveau villa near the Englischer Garten in north Berlin, a 20-minute taxi ride from the center. The chef, Siegfried Rockendorf, whose name graces this elegant restaurant, often sticks to the classical French cuisine, which he prepares beautifully. However, he frequently extends his creativity to cuisine moderne, concocting some strikingly original dishes. Perhaps you'll try his fresh jellied aspic with cucumber sauce; perhaps filet of turbot in a Ricard sauce, or goosemeat pâté in sauterne with cranberries. Ever had a fennel soufflé? Other lures are the saffron fish soup and venison Colbert flavored with vanilla. The innovative thinking of Herr Rockendorf also goes to the borders of China, with his bouillon of wild quail, served with breast of quail over fresh quail eggs. The furnishings of this restaurant are restrained. Fixed-price menus are featured, including three different choices at lunch: three courses for 85 DM ($50.45), four courses for 98 DM ($58.20), and six courses for 155 DM ($92.05). In the evening, a six-course dinner goes for 155 DM ($92.05), a nine-course repast for 190 DM ($112.80). Rockendorf's is open Tues. to Sat. from noon to 2pm and 7 to 9:30pm; closed Sun., Mon., and holidays.

Bamberger Reiter, Regensburgerstrasse 7 (tel. 030/24-42-82), is acknowledged by some critics as the city's best restaurant, serving French, German, and Austrian dishes. Don't judge it by its location in an undistinguished 19th-century apartment house. Excellent in its forthright approach to fresh ingredients, and meticulous in its preparation and service, the restaurant enjoys a loyal following among the business elite of Berlin. The decor evokes old Germany, with lots of exposed wood, mirrors, and fresh flowers. The Raneburger family, Doris and Franz, are your unpretentious hosts. Two set menus are offered: one for 96 DM ($57), another for 135 DM ($80.15). Otherwise, à la carte orders range from 80 DM ($47.50) to 110 DM ($59.40). Only dinner is served, nightly from 7 to 10pm, and reservations are absolutely necessary.

Don't even attempt to guess what's on the menu the night of your arrival. It might be strips of sautéed pigeon breast with fresh melon, filet of John Dory sautéed with herbs in a casserole, a mousse of calf's sweetbreads, or a ragoût of shellfish with baby vegetables. The wine list, supervised by Doris herself, is enormous, containing around 20 varieties of champagne alone.

hemingway's, Hagenstrasse 18 (tel. 030/825-45-71). West Berlin seems an unlikely setting in which to open a restaurant honoring Papa, but this one works. It even catches the author's informality by spelling his name with a small *h*. In fact, the man himself might feel at home here, as it is vaguely neocolonial, somewhat like an elegant old-style Cuban hacienda, with lots of latticework and white wicker. A meeting place for gourmets, where reservations are essential, it is five minutes away from the center.

A classic international and cuisine moderne menu is presented. There's a limited selection of high-quality meat dishes, as the chefs seem to feel more at home with Neptune's children. You might select turbot and salmon with two kinds of caviar, or an orange-flavored carpaccio of salmon with hollandaise sauce. Perhaps the pheasant terrine will interest you, followed by filet of beef charolais in a blue-cheese sauce. Everything is fresh here. For example, in season fresh asparagus is prominently featured, and in summer fresh berries make up the most tempting desserts. Perhaps they'll appear in a raspberry parfait or as fresh strawberries with a Grand Marnier sauce. The wine list is well chosen and exclusive. A set three-course menu at lunch costs 45 DM ($26.70), whereas set dinners go for 75 DM ($44.55) and 115 DM ($68.30). À la carte meals range from 65 DM ($38.60) to 80 DM ($47.50). The place is open daily, offering lunch from noon to 3pm and dinner from 7pm to midnight, although guests often linger until 2am.

OTHER LEADING RESTAURANTS

For fine Italian food, **Da Antonio,** Rankestrasse 26 (tel. 030/24-72-50), is one of the most outstanding restaurants in the Wilmersdorf section. This was the site for many years of the famous Restaurant "R." Here two Italians, Antonio Capíraso and Ciro Ambrosio, operate Da Antonio, offering a full repertoire of dishes from both northern and southern Italy. "All you need is to taste the food and then you'll fall in love with it," the owners promise. You can begin with a trio of pastas served as an appetizer, including fettuccine with wild mushrooms in a mustard sauce, ravioli stuffed with fresh pesto, and green noodles with pink salmon. For your main course, you might select spicy rack of lamb cooked pink and sliced at your table with great ritual, or else baby halibut in a white mustard sauce. For dessert, chocolate lovers may gravitate to the Schwarzem Dessertteller, a platter that includes parfaits, creams, and dark mousses. A four-course meal costs 65 DM ($38.60), the cost rising to 90 DM ($53.45) for a "surprise menu." À la carte dinners cost 40 DM ($23.75) to 100 DM ($59.40). Lunch is served from noon to 3pm and dinner from 6:30pm to midnight; closed Sun.

Ristorante Anselmo, Damaschkestrasse 17 (tel. 030/323-30-94), is a modern restaurant, seating diners at 14 tables in a setting that might be called futuristic chic. People go here for good Italian food, expensively priced at 60 DM ($35.65) to 90 DM ($53.45) for dinner. The decor of pin lights, magenta walls, lots of chrome and light, along with stark tables and chairs, draws many theatrical personalities. The owner, Anselmo Bufacchi, who has spent long years in Germany, freely gives advice on the available selections in his kitchen. For a typically Italian beginning, try any of the pasta dishes, which are homemade. Among main-dish selections are saltimbocca alla romana, perfectly seasoned lamb chops, and scampi alla mozzarella. The carpaccio is also excellent, and you might top your meal with a zabaglione. The restaurant serves from noon to midnight; closed Mon. In fair weather, there is open-air dining on a terrace.

Belle Epoque, Savoy Hotel, Fasanenstrasse 9–10 (tel. 030/311-03-0), is one of the finest hotel dining rooms in Berlin. On the ground floor of this previously recommended first-class hotel, the Belle Époque lives up to its name with a turn-of-the-century ambience of champagne, white colors, and crystal chandeliers—all in a Berlin landmark that survived World War II bombs. Everything is prepared to order. Only the finest and freshest ingredients are used. Watch for the weekly specials, as they tend to follow seasonal changes in the market. For example, when spring asparagus comes in, it appears on the menu in many variations. Or from September to December, you are likely to be treated to game specialties, including pheasant or deer. One week will be devoted to the Hungarian cuisine, another week perhaps to the table of Norway.

The chefs are also aware of calorie-conscious patrons, and many dishes reflect a lighthearted approach. Typical menu selections are likely to include such dishes as king prawns provençal style, with mushroom rice and chicory salad; tender pot-roasted chicken with mushrooms; and medallions of venison with chanterelles. One salad recently enjoyed was made with forest mushrooms, avocado, and grapefruit sections. Several dishes are served flambé style, including luscious crêpes Suzette with walnut ice cream. Service is daily from noon to 3pm and 6 to 11:30pm, which makes an after-theater dinner a good idea. Meals cost from 50 DM ($29.70).

Conti-Fischstuben, Bayreutherstrasse 42, in Hotel Ambassador Berlin (tel. 030/21-90-20). In spite of its name, this is a hotel restaurant that specializes not only in fish but also in meat. Gastronomic highlights are offered in a modern and elegant atmosphere. The walls are decorated with lobsters, crayfish, and crabs made of brass. Valuable mirrors and lamps contribute to the harmony of this first-rate restaurant. Fresh fish are selected every day from the market, and they are superb and delicately seasoned. You face a staggering choice of wines from all over Europe. The restaurant charges 60 DM ($35.65) to 90 DM ($53.45) for a complete menu with up to seven courses. Service is from 6pm to midnight; closed Sun.

Carmer's, Carmerstrasse 2 (tel. 030/312-31-15). You might find either Tom Jones or Engelbert Humperdinck dining at this stylish restaurant. It sits on a quiet residential street off Steinplatz, not far from the Kurfürstendamm, behind an ornate facade that might have been removed from an elegant section of Paris. The menu changes every week, but typical items are likely to include chicken terrine, a ragoût of quail with wild mushrooms, and medallions of seawolf flavored with saffron. Full meals, costing 70 DM ($41.55), are served nightly from 7pm to 1am. You might begin or end a meal with a glass of vintage wine from the piano bar next door (it's under the same management), called Chez Alex. It sells European wines by the glass at 10 DM ($5.95). The piano bar is open from 10pm to 5 or 6am.

MODERATELY PRICED RESTAURANTS

In this category West Berlin has dozens of dining spots. Here are some of the best choices.

Alt-Luxemburg, Pestalozzistrasse 70 (tel. 030/323-87-30). Its dark paneling, evenly spaced mirrors, antique chandeliers, and old-fashioned chairs create the kind of ambience you might have expected to find in the early 1900s. Despite the decor, the food here is very tuned in to the new style of Teutonic cuisine. The place is owned and operated by one of Berlin's most highly respected chefs, Karl Wannemacher. Menu choices are not as chillingly expensive as you might expect. Full meals begin at 65 DM ($38.60), although your tab could run as high as 85 DM ($50.45). Dishes depend on the season. Examples include a terrine of cauliflower garnished with rondelles of fresh lobster, fresh tomato salad with quail eggs, breast of goose with a honey sauce, rack of lamb with green beans and lentils, plus an array of wines. No meals are served at lunch. Dinner is offered Tues. to Sat. from 6:30 to 11:30pm. Annual closing is for two weeks in January and for three weeks some time in midsummer. Reservations are necessary.

Kopenhagen, Kurfürstendamm 203 (tel. 030/883-25-03). The Danes are among the finest cooks in Europe. Just ask them! Their most famous specialty is smørrebrød (literally, bread and butter), on which they are likely to pile everything from a slice of Danish cheese to steak tartare crowned by a raw egg. These open-face sandwiches, when prepared correctly, are a delight. More than a quarter of a century ago, Copenhagen invaded Berlin (not the other way around). The restaurant operates out of a long, narrow, bistro-style room, with a glass-enclosed entrance overlooking the Ku'damm. The selection of smørrebrød is so huge that you may spend half your lunchtime deciding what to order. I favor the marinated herring and roast beef with rémoulade sauce; however, the liver pâté is heartily recommended as well. A special smørrebrød is the aquavit cream cheese. Naturally, you'll want to accompany your meal with a Danish Carlsberg beer. Hot main dishes, Danish style, are featured as well, including lobster soup. A good main course is game pie with Cumberland sauce and a Waldorf salad. A dinner will cost 40 DM ($23.75) to 55 DM ($32.65). Kopenhagen is open from 11:30am to 1am.

Zlata Práha, Meinekestrasse 4 (tel. 030/881-97-50), serves the best Eastern European cuisine of any restaurant in Berlin. Hungarian, Bulgarian, and Austrian wines are featured. However, the pièce de résistance is the special tap-drawn beer, Pilsner Urquell das Echte. Actually, if your palate isn't Slavic, you may want to steer clear of this brew; otherwise, it makes the perfect drink for toasting your Czech friends at the next table. Most of the food seems inspired by the Prague kitchen. Although many of the dishes may be unfamiliar to you, you'll recognize the Balkan salad and the bean soup. Among the main-dish specialties are the paprika Schnitzel and the Sauerbraten. Few can resist the Topfer Strudel. Meals cost 30 DM ($17.80) to 55 DM ($32.65). Go between noon and midnight; closed Sun.

Restaurant Kamin-Stuben, Fasanenstrasse 15 (tel. 030/883-72-63). Part of its allure comes from the contrast between its warmly unpretentious wood-sheathed Gemütlichkeit and its enviable position between two of West Berlin's most sophisticated hotels, the Savoy and the Kempinski. Its name is derived from the wood-burning stove (Kamin) that occupies one corner of its floor space. There's a long bar, an almost constant background of American rock and roll music from the 1950s, and a handful of long tables that you might find yourself sharing with other occupants. Because of its late closing (hours are 6pm to 3am; closed Mon.), it attracts many posttheater clients. Set menus cost 25 DM ($14.85) to 85 DM ($50.45). The owners are Peter Prochnow, who handles the order-taking, the seating, and the bar, and his blond wife, Katja, who bustles from the kitchen bearing steaming platters of delicious food. The menu lists homemade soup, fresh and varied salads, and different versions of German-derived beef and pork.

Marjellchen, Mommsenstrasse 9 (tel. 030/883-26-76), is the only restaurant in West Berlin specializing in the cuisine of Germany's long-lost province of East Prussia. Deriving its unusual name from an East Prussian word meaning "young girl," the establishment divides its space among three rooms, the first of which has a Kneipe-style bar dominating it, plus a series of turn-of-the-century photographs of historic buildings in cities that now lie within Poland and the USSR.

Ramona Azzaro, whose father was Italian and whose East Prussian mother taught her many of the region's most famous recipes, is the creative force here. Amid a Bismarckian ambience of still-life paintings, vested waiters, and oil lamps, you can enjoy a savory version of red-beet soup with strips of beef, falsch Gänsebraten (pork spare ribs stuffed with prunes and bread crumbs "as if the cook had prepared a goose"), marinated elk, marinated eel, zander salad, East Prussian potato soup with crabmeat and bacon, and Mecklenburger Kummelfleisch (lamb with chives and onions). Meals cost 35 DM ($20.80) to 65 DM ($38.60). The place is open nightly from 5pm to 1am.

Bacco, Marburgerstrasse 5 (tel. 030/211-86-87), is small and Tuscan, lying near Europa-Center. Owner and head chef Massimo Manozzi practices a classical Italian cuisine. Fish comes from Rungis, the market outside Paris, where he flies three times weekly to buy only the freshest ingredients. A house specialty is the piccata, three little veal steaks with artichokes, mushrooms, tomatoes, and an aromatic pepper-flavored wine sauce. You get good service *con brio* (with flair). Meals cost 30 DM ($17.80) to 70 DM ($41.55), and they're served from noon to 3pm and 6pm to midnight. Bacco is closed Sun. at lunchtime and all day Sun. in July and August.

Kamper's, Mommsenstrasse 42 (tel. 030/323-79-25), offers a French cuisine with both contemporary dishes and those from the classical repertoire. Fish and shellfish are the specialties. The chef also prepares Historical Berliner menus. The place has a warm, rustic Gemütlichkeit. Featured in the center of the room are two large millstones that now serve as tables for hors d'oeuvres display. A daily fixed-price menu, ranging from three to seven courses, is available for 60 DM ($35.65) to 140 DM ($83.15). Two other menus are presented, one a standardized à la carte listing, another enumerating the specialties of the day. Before dinner you might enjoy a drink in the apéritif bar. Hours are 7pm to midnight; closed Thurs. and holidays.

Paris Bar, Kantstrasse 152 (tel. 030/313-80-52), is one of the most fashionable French bistros in the city. It enjoys the patronage of film and media personalities. One of its attractions is its long hours, nonstop from noon to 1am, except Sun. Near the heart of the city, it is decorated in a classic bistro format. The food is invariably fresh and often well prepared (there are good days and bad ones). You might begin with one of the terrines and then order a grilled steak or some grilled fish, perhaps oysters if you feel like it, finishing off with a classic chocolate mousse. Meals cost 40 DM ($23.75) to 80 DM ($47.50).

Estiatorio (also called Fofi), Fasanenstrasse 70 (tel. 030/881-87-85), is decidedly chic. In summer the doors open up and the action spills onto the sidewalk. Otherwise, on a winter's night, you are likely to see some of the more dazzling Berlin personalities around the metal bar, admiring or disapproving of the latest exhibition of contemporary art. John le Carré used it as a setting for *The Little Drummer Girl.* Estiatorio, the name on the door, means bistro in Greek, but all the habitués call the place Fofi, named after its owner. You might begin with a selection of Greek hors d'oeuvres and then go on to the grilled scampi. Lamb is also imaginatively prepared. The Greek-inspired cuisine costs from 50 DM ($29.70) and is served nightly from 7pm to 1am. There's more glitz and glitter the later you go.

Ponte Vecchio, Spielhagenstrasse 3 (tel. 030/342-19-99). Relatively expensive, filled with Italian charm and Tuscan flavors, this Italian restaurant promotes its cuisine to an appreciative crowd of Berliners, some of whom consider it their preferred restaurant. Meals are served only at dinner, which is offered from 6pm to 1am; closed Tues. Full meals cost from 55 DM ($32.65), but could go as high as 75 DM ($44.55). Typical dishes are likely to include carpaccio with fresh mozzarella and ripe tomatoes, many variations of veal dishes, assorted shellfish with basil and olive oil, and spinach salad with warm bacon, even a spicy hot version of penne all'arrabiatta. You can also order an aquatic version of saltimbocca made with baby turbot and salmon. Roulade of veal comes with a Gorgonzola sauce. Reservations are necessary.

Tasty, Kurfürstendamm 53 (tel. 030/883-94-44), attracts a sophisticated following among TV people, journalists, and other media-related personalities. Right on the main drag, it offers sidewalk tables in summer; otherwise, guests retreat into a long narrow room with a bar in the center, selecting one of the marble-topped tables with black leather chairs. In this art deco setting, you can peruse the food available on any given day. The specialty is lobster, but you might make other selections from the buffet, including fresh oysters or even caviar if you're feeling flush. Naturally, there's foie gras, along with the freshly prepared specialties of the day, including perhaps herb-flavored veal with spinach pasta. Meals range from 25 DM ($14.85) to 65 DM ($38.60). This is a see-and-be-seen place, and you can do so daily from 11am to 6pm.

Alt-Berliner Schneckenhaus, Viktoria-Luise-Platz 12a (tel. 030/211-20-60), is recommended for old Prussian-style dining. The interior reveals a high-ceilinged Wilhelmian delight, with German Victorian wooden furniture in all its well-oiled, well-polished splendor. The menu is nostalgic, listing many delicacies from appetizers to desserts, with snails a specialty; try, especially, snails Talleyrand style. If you don't like snails, you might begin with a galantine of goose breast or Russian cabbage soup. For a main course, I'd recommend onion steak Alsace. Meals begin at 55 DM ($32.65). The restaurant is open daily from 6pm to 12:30am, but the kitchen stops serving hot food at 11:30pm.

Borbone, Windscheidstrasse 12 (tel. 030/323-83-05), is Italian with an original atmosphere. Small tables are discreetly separated from one another, and the service is efficient. The wine list is extensive, with some legendary expensive bottles, but it also features many reasonable vintages from southern Italy. Notable dishes include a filetto al Pepe and fresh filet of beef in a cream sauce with green pepper and cognac. Pasta courses are invariably excellent. A meal will cost 50 DM ($29.70) to 75 DM ($44.55), and you can order from noon to midnight, closed Sun.

Ernst-August, Sybelstrasse 16 (tel. 030/324-55-76), serves a French and international cuisine to an elite clientele in Berlin. The place is pleasantly overdecorated with dozens of antique pieces of bric-a-brac. Full meals cost 40 DM ($23.75) and might include seven variations of pork filet or two variations of filet of hare. Typical dishes include pork filet with garlic, tomatoes, and cheese; or pork filet with palm hearts and a shrimp sauce flavored with cheese. Rumpsteak comes flavored with herbs in a green pepper sauce or else with raisins, capers, and a cream sauce. The restaurant is open Wed. to Sun. from 6:30pm to 1am. The kitchen stops serving hot food at midnight. Closed from mid-July to mid-August.

Grossbeerenkeller, Grossbeerenstrasse 90 (tel. 030/251-30-64), is an underground Keller in a historic century-old restaurant that escaped the World War II bombings. You'll see people here who have probably been mentioned in the Berlin newspapers in recent months, many of them prominent in politics and the arts. Dozens of beer steins hang from the rafters, their images dimly reflected in the polished paneling of the walls. Specialties are bacon or herring salad with scrambled eggs, a tempting selection of steaming-hot soups (homemade every day), steaks and schnitzels, and enough combinations of Knockwurst, hot or cold, to make any Prussian happy. Meals here begin at a modest 20 DM ($11.90), going up to 40 DM ($23.75). Hours are Mon. to Fri. from 4pm to 2am; Sat. from 6pm to 2am; closed Sun. and holidays. You'll find it most crowded for late-night suppers.

Heinz Holl, Damaschkestrasse 26 (tel. 030/323-29-93), west of the center, has gained a reputation in Berlin as a select dining spot that is somewhat of a social center as well. Your host is Heinz Holl, who has a devoted local following, often among theater and media personalities. Call and reserve a table to savor the recipes that much of Berlin seems to want, including a stuffed cabbage roll so large it could feed a family of four. Other main courses include venison Gulasch, Tafelspitz (a delectable boiled beef), and veal Stroganoff. You might begin with one of the appetizers such as potato soup with wild mushrooms. Meals cost 30 DM ($17.80) to 55 DM ($32.65). All the action takes place in a charmingly cluttered Berlin bistro ambience. The place, which has both a front and a back room (you're exiled to Siberia there), is decorated with kitsch from all over the world, including a 1984 Florida license plate. The restaurant is open from 7pm to 2am, with warm food served continuously until closing. Closed Sun., holidays, and for three weeks in summer.

Weinrestaurant Heising, Rankestrasse 32 (tel. 030/213-39-52). You'll find copies of Gobelin tapestries upholstered onto the backs of the antique chairs here, and a festive atmosphere created partly by the open fireplace and partly by the music provided by the pianist in the corner. The chef is a specialist in French-oriented international cuisine, which seems to find its best expression in the wide range of fresh fish dishes offered, depending on the shopping at the market that day. Fresh snails can be served either as a soup or as a main course with wild mushrooms; or perhaps you'll prefer the filet of lamb or filet of sole (braised or sautéed according to your choice). The wine list contains at least two dozen German wines, each reasonably priced. Excluding the wine, meals will average about 35 DM ($20.80) to 55 DM ($32.65), and they're served daily from 6 to 11pm.

Mundart Restaurant, Muskauerstrasse 33–34 (tel. 030/61-22-061), is a bit of a discovery—a good, honest, straightforward restaurant in the Kreuzberg district. Decidedly informal, the place has a simple but tasteful decor and food that is prepared fresh daily. All the dishes I've sampled have been well made, sauced, and flavored. These include a terrine of venison with mustard sauce and, for a main dish, rumpsteak or Tafelspitz (the famed boiled beef dish so beloved by Franz Joseph of Austria). Meals cost 36 DM ($21.40) to 76 DM ($45.15), with à la carte orders ranging from 55 DM ($32.65). Hours are Wed. to Sun. from 6:30 to 11pm.

Zitadellen-Schänke, Strasse am Juliusturm (tel. 030/334-21-06). You'll find a traditional Germanic decor embellishing this historic restaurant behind the ancient stone walls of Spandau Citadel, in the famous Berlin suburb. The soft candlelight and open fireplace provide a cozy and relaxing ambience. The chefs cook time-honored specialties, yet also experiment with Neue Küche. Some of their better concoctions include wild boar pâté with St. Lucie cherry sauce, Rippenbraten mit Krusten (roast ribs with white cabbage salad), ground filet with steamed dumplings, and Wallenstein grill platter for two persons, consisting of stuffed quails, beef filet, and loin of pork. They're open from 10am to midnight, with warm food available at noon; closed Mon. An average three-course meal will cost 50 DM ($29.70). The weekly special, called Spiesbratenessen, is served as a fixed-price meal every Sun. beginning at 6pm; the cost is 59.50 DM ($35.30). If you go at 6pm on Fri., Sat., or Sun., you can enjoy a medieval banquet, with ballad singing by an open fire.

Zum Lustigen Finken, Alt Lübars 20 (tel. 030/402-78-45), reigns as one of the region's most historic restaurants, with an appreciative daytime clientele who frequently remember meals served here from their childhood. It was originally built in 1680 in what was then the distant outskirts of Berlin. Since 1842 it has welcomed practically everyone of consequence in Berlin, as well as thousands of less visible clients who come for the kind of ambience that their grandparents enjoyed. In summer a large flower-decked terrace provides sitting space. No one minds if you order just a snack, such as Wurst and cheese salad, while you sip your wine or schnapps. Full meals cost from 30 DM ($17.80) and include such dishes as Wiener Schnitzel, roast young pork, Sauerbraten with roast potatoes, and pork cutlets. The place is open all year, Mon., Tues., Wed., Sat., and Sun. from 11am to 7pm; Thurs., hours are 11am to 3pm; closed Fri.

Blockhaus Nikolskoe, Nikolskoer Weg (B-39) (tel. 030/805-29-14), at Am Wannsee und an der Havel, is a holdover from the Berlin of yesterday. The ancestors of present-day Berliners came here on a summer weekend to drink schnapps and beer on the terraces overlooking the Havel River. The elaborate trim on the log cabin that gives this place its name dates from 1819. It's patterned in the Russian style. Historians tell me the house was a present from King Friedrich Wilhelm III to his daughter, Charlotte, on the occasion of her wedding to the man who was later to become Czar Nicholas I. Nicholas, after accepting the gift from his father-in-law, commissioned the construction of a Russian church, Peter-Pauls-Kirche, on a nearby hill. You can choose to sit either on the sun terrace or inside the wooden-walled dining room, with a ceramic stove at one end. Many come here just to order drinks, or to have salads, sandwiches, and Würste on the terrace, averaging about 12 DM ($7.15) for a snack. Or you can order one of the regional meals, attractively priced at 15 DM ($8.90) to 35 DM ($20.80).

The restaurant opens at 10am, closing at 10pm from May to the end of October and at 8pm the remainder of the year. Closed Thurs. To get there, board the S-Bahn to the Berlin suburb of Wannsee. Take bus no. A6 to the Nikolskoer-Weg stop and walk to the restaurant through a forest.

Chalet Corniche, Königsallee 56 (tel. 030/892-85-97), in the Grünewald sector, has a self-styled "much chi-chi" atmosphere with an open fireplace and a view through the panoramic window overlooking the Hallensee. The restaurant is in the "Green Forest," an idyllic retreat. The most prominent artistic feature here is the wall motif of flowers, branches, and twigs painted around a giant book, for a startlingly original ambience. The chef prepares a conservative cuisine moderne, using very fresh but often very expensive ingredients. Menu specialties depend on the shopping and the season. You might, for example, begin with an herb-flavored potato soup with strips of salmon, then follow either with a breast of Barbary goose in a soya sauce or sweetbreads in tarragon butter with a mustard sauce. Try also a saddle of lamb provençal. The *carte* shows 100 varieties of wine. Full meals cost 60 DM ($35.65) to 96 DM ($57), the latter the price of a six-course surprise menu. The chalet is open Mon. to Sat. from 6pm to 1am; Sun. it opens at noon.

Du Pont, Budapesterstrasse 1 (tel. 030/261-88-11), is a restaurant-rôtisserie owned by partners Keuch and Losito. Their modern and stylish restaurant is housed near the Inter-Continental Hotel, within a modern building designed originally as an architects' firm. It is outfitted in a pleasing collection of neutral colors, but the food—based on seasonal produce—is the main allure. The daily specials reflect the availability of choice ingredients at the marketplace that day. Typical listings might include filet of veal stuffed with prunes and served with a cinnamon sauce, filet of Scottish Black Angus with burgundy sauce, or saddle of lamb wrapped with bacon and served with a garlic sauce. Meals range from 50 DM ($29.70) to 84 DM ($49.90) and are served Mon. to Fri. from noon to 3pm and 6pm to midnight; closed Sat. for lunch and all day Sun.

Funkturm, Messedamm (tel. 030/303-829-96). Dining in towers enjoys a vogue in Germany. West Berlin is not without its high-rise cuisine, and the Funkturm in the Charlottenburg district of West Berlin scores by serving good food. At this panoramic restaurant, the local Berlin dishes are notable. Try, for example, braised leg of beef with mixed vegetables and potatoes. A more international offering is the sole meunière. Lobster soup, cream of potato soup, or duck consommé makes a good beginning. Fixed-price meals cost 40 DM ($23.75) to 80 DM ($47.50). Every Fri. a buffet with both hot and cold dishes is served, costing

39.50 DM ($23.45) per person. Food is served daily from noon to 3pm and 6 to 10pm.

BUDGET RESTAURANTS

Of the many budget dining spots in West Berlin, here are the top choices:

Schultheiss-Bräuhaus, Kurfürstendamm 220 (tel. 030/881-70-59), sits diagonally across from the deluxe Hotel Bristol Kempinski. Ever since its appearance on the scene, it has gained admirers, making it one of the leading beerhall restaurants in West Berlin. You can dine on the terrace or go inside to the dark and mellowed tavern. Under the beams and against a background of rustic trimmings, large, hearty portions are served; the prices are low. A fresh soup is made daily. Typical dishes include a thick pork cutlet in brown gravy, with salad and freshly done french fries. A Sülze cotelet with potato salad makes a filling course, and an omelet with bacon is also served. Meals cost 15 DM ($8.90) to 25 DM ($14.85). Hours are 11am to midnight daily.

Hardtke's, Meinekestrasse 27a (tel. 030/881-98-27), right off the Kurfürstendamm, is the best all-around budget restaurant in Berlin. A traditional favorite, it was well known before the war. Restored in the old style after a bombing, with dark beams and wood paneling, Heidelberg steins, and wrought-iron chandeliers, it has many cozy booths for leisurely dining. The prices are low. If you want a filling snack, order a Wurstsalat or Matjesfilet (herring). The restaurant is noted for its homemade sausages. Meals range in price from 15 DM ($8.90) to 30 DM ($17.80). Hardtke's is open daily from 11am to midnight.

Hecker's Deele, Grolmanstrasse 35, D-1000 Berlin 12 (tel. 030/88-90-1), stands about a block from the Kurfürstendamm. The restaurant zealously guards its time-tested recipes, such as its way of preparing venison and wild boar (available only during game season), and keeps its prices down. Meals cost 18 DM ($10.70) to 35 DM ($20.80). With your main course, you are likely to order a stein of one of the six different draft beers, or perhaps a martini made with Steinhaeger gin from Westphalia. Specialties include Sauerbraten with potato, Bratwurst (veal sausage), Knacker (ham sausage), Blutwurst, Leberwurst, and Westphalian ham. Boiled pork knuckles with Sauerkraut and mashed peas is a classic favorite. The kitchen stays open daily from 7am to midnight. The restaurant is part of a modern 50-room hotel with all private facilities and a cozy hotel bar. The hotel charges 180 DM ($106.90) to 220 DM ($130.65) daily for a single, 230 DM ($136.55) to 250 DM ($148.45) for a double.

Reste Fidele, Bleibtreustrasse 41 (tel. 030/881-16-05). Most of its allure and energy are produced by the duet of Yugoslav brothers who run it. They are Ivan (who supervises the dining room) and Vlado (who does everything else), offering a successful and charming re-creation of a French bistro in red-walled rooms whose timbered ceilings evoke a country inn. You can enjoy such specialties as smoked eel, filet of wild goose with cranberries, filet of hare with pepper sauce, filet of beef with Gorgonzola sauce and green noodles, baby salmon in herb sauce, mixed fish platters, and some of the best rumpsteak (prepared in about six different ways) in Berlin. Meals range in price from 35 DM ($20.80) to 60 DM ($35.65). They are open daily from 11am to 2am. The establishment's French name is a translation of the street (Bleibtreustrasse) on which it sits.

Hong Kong, Kurfürstendamm 210 (tel. 030/881-57-56), occupies space on the second floor of a building next to the landmark Paris movie house. Take a small elevator to the restaurant, which is quite stylish, a bit like Raffles in Singapore, with peacock chairs and a version of a Chinese pagoda, with a view of the Ku'damm. The Chinese food here, mostly specialties from the southern provinces, is of fine quality. The menu is large, including such dishes as duckling soup, several shark fin specialties, stewed frogs' legs with green pepper, stewed abalone, and special Hong Kong fare such as fried duckling with sweet and sour vegetables. There is freshly brewed tea, all you can drink. Considering the quality of the food, the prices are fair. It's a fine spot for dinner, which is likely to cost 30 DM ($17.80) to 60 DM ($35.65) for the average repast. Hours are noon to 11pm daily.

Warsteiner Tresen, Uhlandstrasse 195 (tel. 030/312-36-76), on the ground floor of a modern apartment building off the Kurfürstendamm, is typical of the new look of German beer taverns of the '90s. When the weather turns fair, tables are placed outside. The cuisine is not typical beerhall chow, but a well-prepared assortment of German and Continental dishes, made from fresh ingredients. You might begin with a German potato soup (with salmon instead of the traditional sausage), then follow with pork Schnitzel Viennese style, beef Gulasch with buttered noodles, veal Züricher Art (in a cream sauce), and Swabian roast beef. Meals cost from 30 DM ($17.80). The place is open Mon. to Fri. from noon to 1am; Sat. from 6pm to 1am; closed Sun.

Ratskeller Schöneberg, Schöneberg Rathaus, John-F.-Kennedy-Platz (tel. 030/783-21-27). This Ratskeller is on the square that became famous when President Kennedy made his now legendary *"Ich bin ein Berliner"* speech. Many Americans, when visiting the square and the Freedom Bell inside, like to stop here for food. The wines are good, and can be ordered with one of the set luncheons. Among à la carte items, main dishes are fairly ambitious, including such offerings as steak Diane or veal Schnitzel Cordon Bleu, with a fresh salad and french fries. The day's soup is invariably good. A meal averages around 35 DM ($20.80). The Ratskeller is open Mon. to Fri. from 11am to 10pm; Sun. from 11am to 3pm; closed Sat.

Exil, Paul-Lincke-Ufer 44a (tel. 030/612-70-37), is appropriately named. It's in the Kreuzberg sector (see the description under "Modern Berlin" in the sightseeing section). This sector for at least two decades or more has been the haven of guest workers, such as Turks and Yugoslavs, but now is acquiring a different reputation among certain fashionable people who want to avoid tourist haunts. A lot of people connected with the theater come here, and in summer they can sit outside and enjoy a table placed along the canal bank. Of course, the weather has to cooperate before you can dine outside; otherwise, guests retreat inside to order a hearty Austrian cuisine. The portions are extremely generous, and meals cost 50 DM ($29.70) to 60 DM ($35.65). Exil is open from 7pm to 3am; closed Mon. However, the kitchen closes at 1am.

Giraffe, Klopstockstrasse 2 (tel. 030/391-47-17), set in the Tiergarten, derives its name from its location on the ground floor of one of the tallest and narrowest apartment buildings in the city. Situated in a wooded area, it's like a giraffe's neck rising above the plain. Inside, there's a series of dining rooms. You get a hearty Berliner and Germanic fare here, including five different preparations of goose, Eisbein (pork knuckle), or a pot-au-feu with seafood. Set lunches range in price from 18.50 DM ($11) to 65 DM ($38.60), with dinners costing 35 DM ($20.80) to 65 DM ($38.60). In summer, the action spills out onto a terrace. Hours are from 11am to midnight; closed Mon.

Weissbierstuben, Lindenstrasse 14, Kreuzberg (tel. 030/251-01-21). If you're a museum buff, you'll be able to combine a visit to the Berlin Museum with beer and pickles at this restaurant, which is housed in the same building. Rollmops (herring) is a popular snack here for people who often wouldn't otherwise set foot inside a museum. The restaurant is designed in a way that any North German would quickly label "Berliner." In addition to many snacks, it serves a fairly elaborate Sunday breakfast, which includes such specialties as Schweinebraten. Count on spending about 25 DM ($14.85). They serve beer, wine, and food Tues. to Fri. from 11am to 6pm; Sat. and Sun. from 11am to 4pm; closed Mon.

Schwejk-Prager Gasthaus, Ansbacher Strasse 4 (tel. 030/213-78-92). The taste of Eastern Europe is alive and flourishing at this Czech bistro where Bohemian specialties are served in generous portions. You'll find it about two blocks from the Memorial Church, in a kind of neighborhood-tavern ambience of well-scrubbed tables and regular clients. There's a small bar for drinking. Much of the food here tastes better when washed down with a mug of the local Pilsner, and wine is also available. Typical specialties are crackling broiled pork shanks (Schweinhaxen) with salad and Sauerkraut, good-sized bowls of thick borscht or liver-noodle soup, and various kinds of "toasts" piled high with different meats and vegetables, served with flavorful sauces. Table reservations are a good idea, at least during the popular dining hour at 8pm. Full meals turn out to be one of the best bargains in town, priced from 20 DM ($11.90) to 42 DM ($24.95). One of a full range of Czechoslovakian liqueurs might round off a meal. The restaurant is open nightly from 6pm to 1am.

La Maskera, Koburgerstrasse 5 (tel. 030/784-12-27), is a well-known vegetarian restaurant, established near the Schöneberg Town Hall in 1972. It's set within a warmly old-fashioned building whose white walls and exposed wood evoke a turn-of-the-century bistro in Paris or Rome, and, depending on the evening, music may range from Edith Piaf to new wave. Only dinner is served. You can select from an array of antipasti, followed by an al dente version of Mediterranean verduro misto with cream sauce, and several preparations of tofu, including one with a Gorgonzola sauce. The place is especially proud of its ultrafresh vegetables. Meals cost 22 DM ($13.05) to 40 DM ($23.75) and are offered nightly from 4pm to 1am.

Ristorante-Pizzeria San Marino, Savignyplatz 12 (tel. 030/313-60-86), is just one of the many dozens of trattorie spread across Berlin. But this is one of the most central, offering reliable cookery over long hours. Many residents from the neighborhood drop in just for a pizza, costing 8 DM ($4.75). You might begin with an antipasto misto or one of the pasta dishes, ranging from lasagne to spaghetti San Marino (made with peas, mushrooms, ham, and cream sauce). A wide selection of veal and other meat dishes is offered, including grilled rumpsteak, saltimbocca, or Venetian-style liver. Fried squid (calamari) is also popular, as is risotto alla marinara. There's even a children's menu if you have youngsters. Meals cost from 15 DM ($8.90). Open daily from 11am to 1am.

DINING AT EUROPA-CENTER

This 22-story skyscraper, crowned by a revolving Mercedes star, is a virtual culinary United Nations. Many visitors take all their meals in Berlin here and enjoy a widely varied cuisine.

Alt Nürnberg, Berlin Europa-Center (tel. 030/261-43-97), on the ground level, handsomely captures the old style of a German tavern, complete with copper lanterns and wood. It's not expensive either. The house specialty is a plate of Nürnberger Rostbratwürstl. Each day the chefs prepare a different specialty. You might begin with a typical Berlin pea soup with croutons or Hungarian goulash. The Wiener Schnitzel is always reliable, as is the herring salad and the pork filet in a pepper sauce with broccoli. Meals cost 20 DM ($11.90) to 40 DM ($23.75). Alt Nürnberg is open daily from 11:30am to 1am.

Daitokai, Berlin Europa-Center (tel. 030/261-80-99), part of a chain, is considered the leading Japanese restaurant of West Berlin. It lies two floors above street level amid a Japanese-inspired labyrinth of reflecting pools, slate floors that span the water, and low tables. Waitresses appear in kimonos. The chefs are artists with their knives, and each dish is artistically arranged. You might begin with a Samurai cocktail, Japanese whisky, or a Sayonara cocktail, perhaps a small pot of sake. Daitokai offers three set menus, priced at 63 DM ($37.40), 76 DM ($45.10), and 98 DM ($58.20). À la carte meals range from 100 DM ($59.40). The restaurant is open from noon to 3pm and 6pm to midnight; closed Mon.

---

5. The Sights

In the midst of the daily whirl of working, shopping, dining, and entertainment, Berliners along the Kurfürstendamm often glance at a sobering reminder of less happy days. At the end of the street stands the **Kaiser Wilhelm Memorial Church,** destroyed in World War II. Only the shell of the old Neo-Romanesque tower (1895) remains, as a symbol of West Berlin after the war. In striking contrast to the ruins, a new church has been constructed west of the old tower, seating 1,200 people in its octagonal hall, and lit solely by the thousands of colored-glass windows set into the honeycomb framework. Dedicated in 1961, the church has an overall look best described by the nickname given it by Berliners, "the lipstick and powder box." You can wander through the ruins any day from 9am to 7:30pm. Ten-minute services are held in the church daily at 5:30 and 6pm for those going home from work. A Sat. concert is staged at 6pm.

This remarkable combination of old and new is what Berlin is all about. Although there is more new than old in this city, which suffered perhaps more than any other European metropolis during World War II, Berlin offers a multitude of sights for the visitor.

MODERN BERLIN

In World War II, one out of every three Berliners lost his or her home. After the rubble was cleared away—a major problem in itself for this isolated city—the great task of rebuilding began. It took the united effort of many of the world's greatest architects to create contemporary Berlin, which lies just north of the Tiergarten. The **Hansa Quarter** (U-Bahn to Hansaplatz) was a direct result of the great Interbau (international builders' exhibition) of 1957, when architectural designers from 22 nations constructed homes and apartments in this district, along with shops, schools, churches, a cinema, library, and museum. The excitement here is in the variety: each of the nearly 50 architects, including Gropius, Niemeyer, and Düttman, was able to express himself in his own way. Even Le Corbusier submitted a design for an apartment house, but the structure would have been too gigantic for the quarter. You can see it today where it was built in the less congested western section of the city, near the Olympic Stadium. The **Corbusier House,** called Strahlende Stadt (radiant city), is Berlin's largest housing complex, and one of the biggest in Europe. Its 530 apartments (more than 1,000 rooms) can house up to 1,400 people. Typical of the architect's style, this tremendous building rests on stilts.

Berlin's tallest building sits in the heart of the city's activity. The 22-story **Europa-Center,** just across the plaza from the Kaiser Wilhelm Memorial Church, is the largest self-contained shopping center and entertainment complex in Europe. This town-within-a-town opened in 1965 and has been fascinating Berliners and outsiders alike ever since. Besides its three levels of shops, restaurants, nightclubs, bars, and movie houses, it contains dozens of offices, a car park, and an observation roof from which you can view every part of the city.

At the Europa-Center, you can enjoy a show, **Multivision Berlin,** which you might want to view before beginning your exploration of the city. It's like going into a time machine, Berlin in three dimensions. On six screens computers flash the saga of Berlin, everything from the Prussian drill to the Allied airlift. The show can be seen daily from 9am to 5:30am. It lasts 90 minutes and costs 8 DM ($4.75). For information, phone 030/261-79-07.

You may want to venture into **Kreuzberg,** Berlin's most crowded borough, which has been likened to the East Village in New York City. Some people even call it a human zoo. This is the home of the punkers, squatters, skinheads, old and poor people, revolutionaries, struggling artists, what have you. A large part of the population of this 4-mile-square borough with its 19th-century tenements is made up of Greeks, Turks, and Yugoslavs who have come to Berlin to work. You'll see sections that look to be straight from Istanbul, and the buildings everywhere are crowded with boutiques, kebab stands, art galleries, bookshops, pubs, health-food stores, second-hand clothing shops, dingy theaters, and just plain dives. Exercise caution late at night.

THE ZOO AND AQUARIUM

You wouldn't expect to find anything more than a handful of tiny animal cages in the center of a city where space is at such a premium. Yet in West Berlin, where the proportion of green parkland is surprisingly large in comparison to many of the large cities of Europe, you can see the oldest and finest zoo in all of Germany. It's called the **Zoologischer Garten Berlin,** Hardenbergplatz 8, and it was founded in 1844. Just a short walk north from the main street of town, the Ku'damm, it occupies almost the entire southwestern corner of the Tiergarten.

Until World War II the zoo boasted thousands of animals of every imaginable species and description, many of them familiar to Berliners by nicknames. The tragedy of the war struck here as well as in the human sections of Berlin, and by the end of 1945 only 91 animals had survived. For the past 45 years, however, the city has been rebuilding its large and unique collection, until today there are more than 14,000 animals, some of them housed here to prevent their becoming extinct. The zoo has the most modern birdhouse in Europe, with more than 720 different species of birds. Furthermore, great and small cats from all over the world can be seen in the Carnivore House. The zoo's most valuable inhabitant is a giant panda. In the Nocturnal House the visitors can watch the way of life of nocturnal animals. The monkey center is a popular spot, and in the Berlin Zoo you can see breeding groups of apes (no fewer than six gorillas, 13 orangutans, and seven chimpanzees). There are also large open ranges where wild animals can roam in a simulated natural habitat.

In the center of the zoological gardens is a large restaurant where you can dine indoors or out.

The **Aquarium,** on the edge of Budapesterstrasse, is as impressive as the adjacent zoo. Its collection of more than 6,000 fish, reptiles, amphibians, and other animals holds a fascination for every visitor. The second floor is devoted entirely to creatures that live exclusively underwater, with one section for saltwater fish and one for those that live in lakes and streams. Benches are set up along the viewing promenade so you can sit and watch your favorite turtle or octopus for as long as you wish. But even more intriguing is the terrarium on the second floor, with a crocodile collection and a pair of komodo-monitors. You can even walk into the terrarium on a bridge over the reptile pit—but don't lose your balance. Around the outside are several glass cases containing a large collection of snakes, lizards, and turtles, and a large terrarium at the corner with giant tortoises. On the third floor, you can watch the world of insects and amphibians.

The zoo (tel. 030/25-40-10) is open daily from 9am to 7pm (it closes at dusk in winter) and charges 7.50 DM ($4.45) admission. The aquarium, with its separate entrance, is open from 9am to 6pm. Admission here is 7 DM ($4.15), but you can purchase a combined ticket for 11.50 DM ($6.85) that will admit you to both the aquarium and the zoo.

THE DAHLEM MUSEUMS

War is no respecter of persons or objects, and the art collections of Berlin suffered tragically in 1945. Although many smaller paintings were stored in inoperative salt mines during the war, many larger works, including eight paintings by Rubens and three by Van Dyck, were destroyed by fire. Some works that survived are now in East Berlin, where many of Berlin's finest galleries were located before the war. Of the paintings that were relegated to the West and passed from nation to nation in the late 1940s like so many decks of cards, most have now been returned to Berlin and are permanently ensconced in the Dahlem Picture Gallery, Arnimallee 23–27 (tel. 030/83-01-1), making it one of Germany's finest galleries. Of the nearly 1,500 paintings in its possession, more than 600 are on display.

The ground floor has several rooms devoted to early German masters, with panels from altarpieces dating from the 13th, 14th, and 15th centuries. Note the panel of *The Virgin Enthroned with Child* (1350), surrounded by angels that resemble the demons so popular in the later works of Hieronymus Bosch. Eight paintings make up the Dürer collection in the adjacent rooms, including several portraits and a Madonna, with a crown held above her head by two cherubs whose bodies fade into puffs of smoke.

Two contemporaries of Dürer, Albrecht Altdorfer and Lucas Cranach the Elder, are both represented by paintings of *The Rest on the Flight into Egypt*. Note the contrasts between the two works, the former in the Renaissance style, with a town as the background setting and tiny angels playing in an elegant fountain in the foreground. Cranach, on the other hand, chose a quiet pastoral setting and confined the colors and action to the characters themselves, seemingly ready to pose for a family portrait.

Another gallery on the ground floor is given over entirely to Italian painting. Here are five Raphael Madonnas, works by Titian (*The Girl with a Bowl of Fruit*), Fra Filippo Lippi, Botticelli, and Correggio (*Leda with the Swan*). On the ground floor are early Netherlands paintings from the 15th and 16th centuries (van Eyck, van der Weyden, van der Goes, Bosch, and Brueghel).

The floor above is devoted mainly to Flemish and Dutch masters of the 17th century, with no fewer than 21 works by Rembrandt alone. Among the most famous of the great painter's works in the Dahlem is the warmly human *Head of Christ*. One famous painting for years accepted as a priceless Rembrandt, *The Man with the Golden Helmet,* was proved by radioactive testing in 1986 to be by some other painter of Rembrandt's era who imitated the master's style. The subject of doubt for a number of years, the painting has now been called not a phony Rembrandt nor a copy but an independent original, as shown by the latest scientific evidence. Several portraits and biblical scenes make up most of the balance of this excellent collection. Although several works by Rubens were burned during the war, you can still see 19 on display here, including the charming *Child with a Bird* and one of his landscapes, showing milkmaids tending cattle.

In the not-too-distant future the Dahlem will be moving to newer and larger quarters in the southeastern part of the Tiergarten. But until then, we will remain deprived of the more than 800 works packed in the vaults of the museum. The rest of the building is occupied by several other exhibitions, including the **Sculpture Gallery,** with its bas-relief in Carrara marble by Donatello of a serene *Madonna and Child* (1422). The **Prints and Drawings Collection** contains several pen-and-ink drawings by Dürer, including his signed (1511) sketch of *The Holy Family at Rest*. There are 150 drawings by Rembrandt.

The **Ethnographical Museum** houses arts and artifacts from Africa, the Far East, the South Seas, and South America. Many of the figures and ritualistic masks are grotesquely beautiful, presenting a striking contrast in art, especially after a visit to the gallery of paintings. In addition to all the above museums, the Dahlem also houses the **Museums of Far Eastern Art, Islamic Art, and Indian Art.**

You can visit any of the collections at the Dahlem Tues. to Fri. from 9am to 5pm; Sat. and Sun. from 10am to 5pm; closed Mon. Admission to all departments is free. To get there, take bus no. 1, 10, or 17 or the U-Bahn to the Dahlem-Dorf stop.

The museum has a good restaurant where you can have hot meals, including meat, potatoes, and salads, from 11:30am to 2:30pm daily, as well as cold dishes for the rest of the day during museum hours. Meals cost from 12 DM ($7.15), but you may be content with one of the excellent pastries.

CHARLOTTENBURG PALACE

Perhaps Napoleon exaggerated a bit in comparing this palace to the great Versailles when he invaded Berlin in 1806, but in its heyday Charlottenburg, Luisenplatz (tel. 030/32-09-11), was the most elegant residence for the Prussian rulers outside the castle in Potsdam. Begun in 1695 as a summer palace for the friend of the arts, Electress Sophie Charlotte, wife of King Frederick I (Elector Frederick III), the little residence got out of hand until it grew into the massive structure you see today, branching out in long, narrow wings from the main building. When you visit the palace, you should plan on spending the day, since it contains not only the apartments of Prussian royalty but several museums as well.

When you pass the heavy iron gates and enter the courtyard, you'll immediately encounter a baroque equestrian statue of the pompous Great Elector himself, by Andreas Schlüter. The main entrance to the palace is directly behind, marked by the 157-foot-high cupola capped by a gilded statue of Fortune. Inside you'll find a columned rotunda with stucco reliefs depicting the virtues of the Prussian princes in mythological terms.

From this vestibule, you can take guided tours of the **Historical Rooms** Tues. to Sun. from 9am to 5pm. Tours leave every hour. A combined entrance ticket for all the buildings and historical rooms is 6 DM ($3.55) for adults and children over 14; otherwise, children pay 3 DM ($1.80). Unless you know German, you'll have to be content to appreciate the works of art without the running commentary. If you wish to prepare for what you'll be seeing, you can buy the English translation of the guide's lecture in book form at the ticket counter.

Parts of the palace were badly damaged during the war, but most of it has now been completely restored. Many of the furnishings were saved, especially the works of art, and are again on display. The main wing contains the apartments of Frederick I and his "philosopher queen." Of special interest in this section is the **Reception Chamber,** in the left projection of the wing. This large room is decorated with frieze panels, vaulted ceilings, and mirror-paneled niches. The tapestries on the walls (1730) depict men featured in Plutarch's *Lives.* Included are scenes of Pericles in battle and the sacrifice of Theseus on Delos.

At the far end of the west wing is the **Porcelain Chamber,** which is decorated solely by various pieces of Oriental porcelain, hung on the walls, standing on pedestals, some even partly inserted into the walls or suspended by metal rings. The unusual effect is heightened by the profusion of mirrors.

The **New Wing** (Knobelsdorff Wing), built in 1740–46, contains the apartments of Frederick the Great, which have in essence been converted into a museum of paintings, many of which were either collected or commissioned by the king. Most of the ground-floor apartments are galleries of portraits mixed with examples of period furniture, but the treasures are on the upper floor. Here you can see several works by Watteau, including *The Trade Sign of the Artdealer Gersaint,* purchased by Frederick the Great in 1745 for the concert hall of the palace. Another room is devoted to Boucher tapestries depicting love affairs among the gods, including Dionysus and Ariadne on Naxos, and Venus seducing Hephaistus at his forge. In addition to the fine works of art in this wing, it is interesting to notice the decoration on the walls and ceilings of the rooms. Of course, many rooms have been virtually reproduced since the war.

Part of the New National Gallery's collection, the early 19th-century paintings of Caspar David Friedrich, Karl Friedrich Schinkel, Karl Blechen, Karl Spitzweg, and others of their generations, is now housed in the Galerie der Romantik in the Knobelsdorff Wing.

The Charlottenburg Museums

Ägyptisches Museum (Egyptian Museum), Schloss Strasse 70 (tel. 030/320-91-261), is housed in the east guardhouse built for the king's bodyguard. It's worth the trip just to see the famous colored bust of Queen Nefertiti, dating from the Egyptian Amarna period (about 1340 B.C.), discovered in 1912. The bust, stunning in every way, is on the first floor, in a dark room all by itself. It is believed that the bust never left the studio in which it was created, but served as a model for other portraits of the queen. The left eye of Nefertiti was never drawn in. In 1945, in the closing days of the war the bust was mysteriously taken from East Berlin, eventually to turn up here. In addition, look for the ebony head of Queen Tiy and the world-famous head of a priest in green stone.

The museum also contains the monumental Kalbsha Gateway built by Emperor Augustus around 30 B.C., a gift from Egypt. Other displays feature jewelry, papyrus, tools, and weapons, as well as objects relating to the Egyptian belief in the afterlife, including a model complete with all the necessities for the long voyage to the netherworld. The museum is open Mon. to Thurs. from 9am to 5pm; Sat. and Sun. from 10am to 5pm; closed Fri. Admission is free.

Antikenmuseum (Museum of Greek and Roman Antiquities), Schloss Strasse 1 (tel. 030/320-91-215), is housed in the west guardhouse, just opposite the Egyptian Museum. Inaugurated in 1960, it is a great collection of world-famous works of antique decorative art. It is rich in pottery from ancient Greece and Italy; Greek, Etruscan, and Roman bronze statuettes and implements; ivory carvings, glassware, objects in precious stone, and jewelry of the Mediterranean region, as well as gold and silver treasures; mummy portraits from Roman Egypt, wood and stone sarcophagi, and a small number of sculptures in marble. The collection includes some of the finest Greek vases of the black- and red-figured style dating from the 6th to the 4th centuries B.C. The best-known vase is a large Athenian wine jar (amphora) found in Vulci, Etruria, dating from 490 B.C. It shows a satyr with lyre and the god Hermes. As the artist's name is not known, he has been dubbed, after this vase, the "Berlin painter." Of the several excellent bronze statuettes, the Zeus of Dodone (470 B.C.) shows the god about to cast a bolt of lightning. From the sculpture department you can see a rare portrait of Cleopatra (from Alexandria) that is the only known portrait of this famous queen. In the Brandenburg-Prussian art collection, acquired in 1698 in Rome, is an exceptional bronze statue of the goddess Luna descending from the firmament. It is inlaid with silver, and in 1871 the Prussians dubbed it "the pearl of the collection." The museum, charging no admission, is open Mon. to Thurs. from 9am to 5pm; and on Sat. and Sun. from 10am to 5pm; closed Fri.

Museum für Vor-und Frühgeschichte, Langhansbau, a museum of pre- and protohistory, in the western extension of the palace facing Klausener Platz, contains five rooms devoted to art and artifacts discovered mainly in Europe and the Near East. The rooms have exhibits grouped into the ages of man, from 1 million B.C. up to the first millennium A.D. The museum is open Mon. to Thurs. from 9am to 5pm; Sat. and Sun. from 10am to 5pm; closed Fri. Admission is free.

In addition to the exhaustive—and exhausting—collections in the interior of the palace buildings, you can enjoy a relaxing ramble through the palace gardens, where, just a few years ago, lay a field of mud and swampland created by the ravages of war. The gardens have been restored and landscaped much as they were in the days of Friedrich-Wilhelm II. In the formal gardens are two rows of cypresses leading to a lake complete with swans and other waterfowl. To the west of the cypress grove, between the English Gardens and the Prehistory Museum, stands the **Mausoleum,** practically unharmed during the war. Beneath its small temple are the tombs of King Friedrich-Wilhelm II and Queen Louise, sculptured by Rauch, as well as several other interesting funerary monuments of the Prussian royal family.

Charlottenburg lies in the quarter of Berlin of the same name, just west of the Tiergarten. You can get there by a number of routes, including the U-Bahn to either Sophie-Charlotte-Platz or Richard-Wagner-Platz, or by bus no. 9, 54, 62, or 74.

REMEMBER THE BERLIN WALL?

The ideological rift between East and West Berlin, which grew out of the dissolution of the Kommandantura of the Big Four powers in 1948, became a stark reality in August 1961. West Berliners had to adjust to the fact that the wall marked the eastern end of their world. For the visitor, the concrete and barbed-wire barrier held an awe-inspiring, sobering fascination. Then, miracle of miracles, in 1989 the wall started to fall, like Jericho's. By 1990 its demolition—undertaken at night—had continued full swing, much to the delight of souvenir collectors around the world. Collectors purchased pieces of the wall for as much as $100,000 and hauled them off. It was, after all, a piece of history.

Although the dreaded wall is gone, visitors can tour the area where "the wall that was" used to stand. After a bracing cocktail or cup of coffee at the Inter-Continental Hotel, we'll begin. If you follow Budapesterstrasse eastward from the hotel, you'll soon reach the entrance to the **Tiergarten,** Berlin's largest park. The road that enters the park at this point is called Hofjäger (hunter's ground) Allee, reminding us of its 16th-century use by the electors of Brandenburg. When seen by those who trudged into Berlin in 1945, the park was a dreary battlefield laid waste. Children play safely here today amid the young trees planted since the war to replace the ancient forest cut down to supply fuel in the cold winters of 1945–46. If you wander from the main roads, you'll come upon rustic bridges, fishponds, and peaceful, isolated paths and streams.

At the center of the park, where Hofjäger Allee meets the wide avenue called Strasse des 17 Juni (named in memory of those East Berliners who were killed in the unsuccessful uprising against the Soviets on June 17, 1953), is the highest point in the park, the **Victory Column** (Siegessäule). This landmark of West Berlin sits on a traffic circle called the Grosser Stern (Big Star). Erected in 1873, the yellow sandstone column is hollow and you can climb the 290 steps to the observation platform at the top, 210 feet above the street. Towering above the platform is the gilded bronze statue of Victory, 27 feet high, commemorating the German military accomplishments in the Franco-Prussian War. The observation platform is open Tues. to Sun. from 9am to 6pm; Mon. from 3 to 6pm. It is closed during the winter season (November to April). Admission is 1.20 DM (70¢).

If you follow Strasse des 17 Juni eastward from the Grosser Stern, it will take you directly to the site of the old wall. As you proceed, however, you'll pass several attractions worth at least a quick visit. About halfway between the Victory Column and the point where the wall stood, set at the northern edge of the Tiergarten near the Spree River, is the **Kongresshalle,** built as the American contribution to the 1957 Interbau, when the world's greatest architects constructed several buildings in West Berlin. Given to the people of Berlin in the following year, this convention hall is irreverently, but affectionately and perhaps appropriately, called the "pregnant oyster," because of the spans of concrete that curve across the roof and end up in open arches on each side. The auditorium alone seats 1,250, and is equipped with translation equipment and other facilities. In addition, the building houses a 400-seat theater, conference rooms, a garden café, and a restaurant. So big is the hall that it has its own waterworks, which supply not only the building but the pool and fountain below the wide outer staircases as well.

Back on Strasse des 17 Juni, you'll next come to the **Soviet War Memorial.** A little Soviet enclave in the west, it was built in 1946 from the marble of Hitler's former Berlin headquarters. The memorial is surmounted by a large bronze statue of a soldier in battle uniform holding a bayonet. Above the inscription are the dates 1941–45, and a wreath enclosing a hammer and sickle. Once it was a popular spot for demonstrations against the Soviets. It is guarded by Soviet and British soldiers and West German police.

At this point you can see the **Brandenburg Gate,** and beyond it the former main street and promenade of Berlin, **Unter den Linden.** The gate represents a unique act of cooperation between the sectors of the divided city. When the Quadriga (a chariot drawn by four horses) atop the gate was destroyed during the war, and the gate badly damaged, the people of East and West Berlin were anxious to have it restored. The Senate of West Berlin had a new Quadriga hammered in copper and presented it to the administration of East Berlin to place on the newly repaired colonnade.

Just north of this point lies the large square called **Platz der Republik,** only a sand dune until it was developed as the home of the German Parliament in the 18th century. At the eastern side of the square sits the 19th-century **Reichstag,** the Neo-Renaissance Parliament building. The building was destroyed in a mysterious fire in 1933 and badly damaged by bombs in the closing days of World War II, as the Allies moved in on the beleaguered city. A pastiche of styles, mainly High Renaissance, it opened in 1894 as the august Imperial Diet was called to order. At Paul-Löbe-Strasse, you can enter the west wing of the building to see an exhibition devoted to German history since the early 19th century. It is open Tues. to Sun. from 10am to 5pm. The Reichstag lies north of the Brandenburg Gate, at the eastern side of the Tiergarten. The wall used to run right next to the Reichstag, which is used today for political conclaves.

In one wing of this building, a restaurant has been installed, offering moderately priced Teutonic fare, with several regional specialties. It's usually not necessary to make a reservation, but you can do so by calling 030/397-721-72.

Turning to the west side of the square, make for the street called Umgehungsstrasse, which cuts south through the Tiergarten. As you leave the park on the south side, you'll see the wavy roof of the **Philharmonie** (Philharmonic Hall), Matthäikirchstrasse 1, an outstanding example of functional design (1963). Its unusual layout allows the audience to sit on all sides of the orchestra, yet the technical and acoustical aspects of the hall permit them to hear and see well from any point. The Philharmonie is the home of the renowned Berlin Philharmonic Orchestra. In 1987 the architectural ensemble was completed with the opening of the Kammermusiksaal, the chamber music hall.

Opposite the Philharmonie is the **Kunstgewerbemuseum,** Tiergartenstrasse 6 (tel. 030/266-29-11), a museum of applied arts and crafts. Until 1985 it was housed at Charlottenburg, but now has been moved into its new home. Room after room is devoted to domestic and ecclesiastical art from the Middle Ages through the 20th century. Its most outstanding exhibition is the Guelph Treasure, a collection of medieval church treasures in gold and silver. In the basement are rooms devoted to contemporary design from the Bauhaus to Charles Eames and Memphis. Collections of Venetian glass, Italian majolica, and German Renaissance goldsmiths' work, as well as 18th-century porcelain figurines, are outstanding. Some of the treasures are quite delicate, showing superb craftsmanship, including such art nouveau works as a translucent opal and enamel box by Eugène Feuillâtre. The admission-free museum is open Tues. to Fri. from 9am to 5pm; Sat. and Sun. from 10am to 5pm; closed Mon. The cafeteria is open from 10am to 4:30pm.

From Kemper Platz in front of the Philharmonie, follow Bellevuestrasse southeast to **Potsdamer Platz,** a rather dreary square that was once the most active spot in all of Berlin. Along the street leading to the square, you can still see some of the streetlamps that added their nighttime charm to the old city. The square is referred to as the three-sector corner because it is the meeting place of the British, American, and Soviet sectors of the city. The wall used to cut right through the middle of the square. Because most of the buildings around the square have been destroyed, you can glimpse the Reichstag, the Brandenburg Gate, and other important structures from this vantage point. On the East Berlin side, buildings have been cleared away for about 100 yards, creating a deserted sector where a number of daring escape attempts from East Germany were made in the past, many of which failed tragically.

If you don't intend to visit East Berlin, but would still like at least a glimpse of it, you can get your best look from the observation platform near Potsdamer Platz. A photomural here shows the square in its heyday in 1929 and as it looks today. Another mural depicts the near-massacre of the East Germans on June 17, 1953, when they began their unsuccessful revolt against the Soviet oppression of East Germany. A light note is added to the sobering scenes by the souvenir shops and ice-cream stands nearby.

In 1981 the **Martin-Gropius-Bau Gallery** opened at Stesemannstrasse 10 (tel. 030/25-48-6), about a 12-minute stroll from the Tiergarten. The *New York Times* called it one of the "most dramatic museums in the world." It contains the Museum Berlinische Galerie, with works of art, architecture, and photography of the 19th and 20th centuries; the Jewish Museum; and the Werkbund Archiv. On the ground floor are changing exhibitions of different character. The building lies only a dozen or so feet from the site of the former Berlin Wall, and the eastern part of the museum opens onto the leveled former Gestapo headquarters, which were adjoining. It makes for a fascinating stroll to look at this building, whose exterior terra-cotta friezes were not restored. If they were damaged, destroyed, or left intact, that is how they remain today. Hours are 10am to 5pm; closed Mon. Admission is 6 DM ($3.55).

You can visit the **Museum of the Wall**, Friedrichstrasse 44 (tel. 030/251-10-31). This small building houses exhibits depicting the tragic events leading up to and following the erection of the Berlin Wall. You can see some of the instruments of escape used by East Germans, including chair lifts, false passports, hot-air balloons, even a minisub. Photos document the building of the wall, the establishment of es-cape tunnels, and the postwar history of both parts of Berlin from 1945 until today, including the airlift. One of the most moving exhibits is the display on the staircase of drawings by schoolchildren who, in 1961–62, were asked to depict both halves of Germany in one picture. You can also see works by well-known international paint-ers. On the floor above, you can look out toward East Berlin from the observation platform. A further exhibition is called "From Gandhi to Walesa—Nonviolent Struggle for Human Rights." It shows examples of this struggle in the GDR, Po-land, Czechoslovakia, the USSR, and other countries. Admission is 4 DM ($2.40).

NEW NATIONAL GALLERY (NATIONALGALERIE)

In its modern glass-and-steel home designed by Mies van der Rohe, this gallery is a sort of sequel to the art housed at Dahlem. Here are works of 19th- and 20th-century artists, with a heavy concentration on such French impressionists as Manet, Renoir, Monet, and Pissarro. The collection of German artworks starts with Adolph von Menzel's paintings from about 1850.

The 20th-century collection includes a number of works by Max Beckmann, Edvard Munch, and E. L. Kirchner—*Brandenburger Tor* (1929) is among the most popular—as well as a few paintings of Francis Bacon, Dufy, Picasso, Max Ernst, and, of course, Paul Klee.

The National Gallery is a continually growing collection of contemporary art, European as well as American, including such artists as Barnett Newman, Joseph Beuys, and Edward Kienholz.

The standard exhibition is free, although you'll have to pay changing fees for special shows. The gallery is open Tues. to Fri. from 9am to 5pm; Sat. and Sun. from 10am to 5pm; closed Mon. The gallery is at Potsdamerstrasse 50 (tel. 030/266-26-62-3), just south of the Tiergarten. You can get there by taking bus no. 29, 48, or 83, or else the underground (Kurfürstenstrasse Station/U-Bahn). The hours of food service in the café on the ground floor are similar to the opening hours. Hot meals are served only between 11:30am to 3pm. The gallery is closed on January 1, May 1; December 24, 25, and 31; and Tues. after Easter and Whitsunday.

SCHÖNEBERG RATHAUS

Of special interest to Americans, this political center of West Berlin administra-tion and parliamentary life since 1948 was the scene of John F. Kennedy's memorable *"Ich bin ein Berliner"* speech on June 26, 1963, just a few months before he was assassinated. Berliners, taking the speech literally as well as symbolically, have renamed the square around the building the John-F.-Kennedy-Platz. Built in 1911, the facade of the hall is not as outstanding as the interior. Here you'll find many paintings, especially portraits of political leaders of the past, and an exhibition of the history of the Schöneberg quarter of Berlin. Note the eight tinted-glass panels in the vestibule with scenes of various sections of Berlin, each with its own coat-of-arms.

From the 237-foot-high tower of the hall, a replica of the Liberty Bell is rung every day at noon. A gift from the American people in 1950, the Freedom Bell, as it is called, symbolized U.S. support for the determination of West Berliners to preserve their freedom during the days of the Cold War. The document chamber contains a testimonial presented with the bell bearing the signatures of 17 million Americans who gave their moral support in the struggle. You can visit the Liberty shrine on Wed. and Sun. from 10am to 3:30pm.

BOTANICAL GARDEN

In the Dahlem quarter of West Berlin, Königin-Luise-Strasse 6–8 (tel. 030/830-06-0), near the Dahlem Museum, the huge Botanischer Garten contains vast collections of European and exotic plants in the open and in 15 greenhouses, among which the most popular ones are: the big palm house, one of the largest in the world, with its palms, bamboos, and tropical flowers; and the Victoria house, where *Victoria amazonica* and *Victoria cruziana* are in bloom in late summer. In the open, the section representing the vegetation of the temperate regions of the northern hemisphere is most noteworthy. There are also a large Arboretum and several special collections such as a garden for the blind, water plants, and protected plants of Germany. During the summer the garden is open daily from 9am to 8pm. In winter it is closed at dusk. Admission is 2.50 DM ($1.50).

A unique approach to botany is represented in the **Botanical Museum** near the entrance to the gardens. Here you can see dioramas and exhibit cases portraying the history and significant facts of plant life around the world. The museum is open Tues. to Sun. from 10am to 5pm, on Wed. to 7pm. Admission is free.

OLYMPIC STADIUM (OLYMPIA-STADION)

Built in 1936 by Werner March for the 11th Olympic Games, this Olympia-Stadion, Olympischer Platz 3 (tel. 030/304-06-76), seating 100,000 people, was the first in Europe to supply all the facilities necessary for modern sports. Hitler expected to see the "master race" run off with all the awards in the 1936 Olympics, and you can imagine his disappointment when a black American, Jesse Owens, took four gold medals for the U.S. team. The Nazi dictator refused to congratulate him.

The stadium area covers a total of 330 acres, including a swimming stadium, a hockey arena, tennis courts, and riders' exhibition grounds. But the main attraction is the arena, so large that if the seats were laid end to end, they would stretch for more than 25 miles. The playing field in its center lies 47 feet below ground level. You can take the elevator to the top of the 260-foot platform where the Olympic bell hangs. From this point you have a panoramic view of Berlin to the east. It is open daily, costing 1 DM (60¢). The stadium is open from 8am to 5pm in winter and from 8am to 5pm in summer. Since the Olympic Stadium lies northwest of the Radio Tower, you can reach it in a few minutes by a brisk walk. If you come directly via the U-Bahn, take the train one stop past the Radio Tower stop to Olympic-Stadion.

RADIO TOWER (FUNKTURM)

Nearly every sizable town in Germany seems to have a television tower, but this steel-frame construction predates them all—in fact, it predates television. Erected in 1924–26, it sits on a base of porcelain pedestals. Popularly called the "Tall Dwarf," the tower has been converted to a television transmitter, but if you visit here it will likely be either for the restaurant (tel. 030/303-829-96) (at 170 feet) or for the view of Berlin and its environs (as far as Potsdam) from the observation platform at 457 feet. The elevator reaches the top in half a minute. The elevator is in operation daily from 10am to 11pm, charging 3 DM ($1.80) to take you to the restaurant. Admission to the viewing platform is 5 DM ($2.95). The tower sits in the fairgrounds in the same western section of West Berlin. To get there, take the U-Bahn to the Kaiserdamm stop, or the S-Bahn to the Westkreuz stop.

STEINSTÜCKEN

One of the curiosities of the Cold War is this tiny enclave surrounded by East German borders. Steinstücken, only 31 acres, is one of a dozen satellite enclaves, small strips of land cut off from West Berlin under terms of the Big Four agreements. It is under the guardianship of American military police, but doesn't feel so isolated anymore.

Road access to Steinstücken was once denied to the general public unless they were permanent inhabitants. The military police had to fly there in helicopters. That changed in 1977. Any visitor to West Berlin can go there on the bus. A no. 18 double-decker bus (labeled "Steinstücken") will take you there.

Once you get to Steinstücken, there isn't much to see except for a simple monument marking the site of the helicopter run that saved Steinstücken from being absorbed by East Germany. Go here only if you want to see a visible reminder of the long decades of the Cold War.

SCHLOSS TEGEL

To the north of Berlin, Schloss Tegel, Adelheidallee 19–21 (tel. 030/881-40-68), is a two-story building constructed along classical lines with bas-reliefs by Friedrich Tieck on its four towers. It was visited by Goethe in 1778, who wrote of the "ghosts in Tegel." The white-painted castle was erected in 1558 in the reign of Elector Prince Joachim II. It was redesigned in 1822–24 by Karl Friedrich Schinkel, one of the most outstanding architects of Prussia. The work was commissioned by Wilhelm von Humboldt, the philosopher and founder of Berlin University (his descendants own the castle to this day). In the interior, mementos of the family are exhibited, along with works of art. Visits are possible. The address is reached by taking bus no. 13, 14, or 15, or else the U-Bahn, getting off at the Tegel stop. Open only May to September, Sun. from 2 to 5:30pm. Check its status before going there, as it was closed in 1990 for renovations.

BRÜCKE MUSEUM

At Bussardsteig 9 (tel. 030/831-20-29), a considerable proportion of the work of Schmidt-Rottluff is displayed, along with the works of a group of expressionist artists known as *die Brücke* ("the Bridge"), who gathered in Dresden in 1905. One of my favorite German artists, Ernst Ludwig Kirchner, was the leader of "the Bridge." His pictures were sharply patterned and colored, the figures distorted. The Nazi government burned many of his paintings, and before the outbreak of World War II he committed suicide. The one-story museum at the edge of the Grünewald is open from 11am to 5pm; closed Tues. Admission is 3.50 DM ($2.10).

BERLIN MUSEUM

This was once the Court of Justice, built in late baroque style in 1735. These former law courts in Kreuzberg are at Lindenstrasse 14 (tel. 030/2-58-60), and have been converted into a museum of the city of Berlin, with exhibits depicting the life of its citizenry from the 17th to the 20th century. It is open from 10am to 10pm; closed Mon. Admission is 3.50 DM ($2.10). U-Bahn stop is Hallisches Tor.

BAUHAUS MUSEUM

The Bauhaus was founded by Walter Gropius in 1919 at Weimar. (He was later to become a longtime resident of the U.S.) This school was largely responsible for establishing a curriculum for the teaching of industrial design throughout the Western world. The Bauhaus artists were kicked out of Weimar in 1925, moving to Dessau and then to Berlin. This museum, at Klingelhöferstrasse 13–14 (tel. 030/261-16-18), will bring you closer to the ideas and concepts of modern design and architecture and where they originated. Even if you're not a student of architecture or design, you should still be fascinated. The sculptures of Oskar Schlemmer are only one of the many exhibits, which are open from 11am to 5pm; closed Tues. Admission is 3 DM ($1.80).

SPANDAU CITADEL

One of the most popular day trips from the heart of Berlin is to Spandau. Head up Am Juliusturm and you'll eventually reach this suburb, which was incorporated into Berlin in 1920. It is one of the oldest parts of Altmark, receiving its city charter back in 1232. The Hohenzollern electors of Brandenburg turned it into a summer residence, and in time it became the chief military center of Prussia, housing the imperial war treasury.

The Spandauer Zitadelle, or Spandau Citadel (tel. 030/339-12-97), stands at the confluence of both Berlin's rivers, the Spree and the Havel. The Julius Tower (Juliusturm) and the Palas are the oldest buildings still standing, the only remaining parts of the castle, which was built in the 13th and 14th centuries. In the main building, accessible by footbridge, is a local history museum. The citadel is open Tues. to Fri. from 9am to 6pm; Sat. and Sun. from 10am to 6pm. Entrance price is 6 DM ($3.55). The U-Bahn stop is Zitadelle.

The citadel has had a checkered past, and it's been besieged by everybody from the French to the Prussians. It has also been a state prison. However, the remaining leader of the Nazi hierarchy, Rudolf Hess, was not housed there, but at Spandau Prison in Wilhelmstrasse, in the middle of Spandau. Following the death of Hess in 1987, the prison was demolished. Born in 1894, Hess was appointed deputy Führer in 1933, but parachuted into Scotland, where he was arrested and interned until the end of the war. He was sentenced to life imprisonment at Nürnberg in 1946, and thus began his lonely vigil at Spandau. He was guarded—at great expense to all countries—by the Americans, Russians, French, and British. Attempts by the son of the former war criminal to get him released were unsuccessful.

TRANSPORT MUSEUM

Holding an equal fascination for adults and children is the **Museum für Verkehr und Technik,** Trebbinerstrasse 9 (tel. 030/25-48-40). One commentator once wrote, "If it flies, rolls, or floats, you'll find it here." The museum displays models of trains and trams, as well as spacecraft and even a copy of Columbus's *Santa Maria,* which sailed to the New World. The early aeronautical pioneer, Berlin-born Otto Lilienthal, who died in 1896, is also honored. His achievements in "flying models" were said to have been studied by the Wright brothers. Since this museum was bulging with displays, a second wing has opened. It took over the freightyard of the old-time Anhalter Bahnhof, where the fictional Sally Bowles arrived in Isherwood's Berlin stories that were the basis for the musical *Cabaret.* If you want to go there, ask at the main museum for directions. The museum is open Tues. to Fri. from 9am to 6pm; Sat. and Sun. from 10am to 6pm. Admission is 3.50 DM ($2.10), half price for children.

ORGANIZED TOURS

Because of their size, West Berlin and East Berlin can be difficult to navigate on your own. Therefore, you may need the security of an organized tour. The best ones are operated by **Severin A Kühn,** Kurfürstendamm 216 (second floor; tel. 030/883-10-15). Across from the Hotel Bristol Kempinski Berlin, this agency offers a host of tours, including excursions into East Germany.

Their big tour combines East and West Berlin, costs 50 DM ($29.70), and lasts about seven hours. There's an extra 19-DM ($11.30) guidance fee in East Berlin. If you have trouble scheduling your tour of the two Berlins into the same time frame, you take your tours on two different days. In the long run, however, this will cost more than the same-day tour. Each half-day tour, purchased separately, goes for 30 DM ($17.80). Be warned that the East Berlin tour requires presentation of a passport and that only the 2pm tour is given in English; the 10am tour is narrated in German. A visit to the important Pergamon Museum is included, and the tour takes about four hours. The tour of West Berlin takes three hours. For all tours, the company requests that you show up at its headquarters 30 minutes before your scheduled departure.

An even more exotic tour is the one to Potsdam and Sans Souci, leaving on Tues., Thurs. and Sat. from April to October 31, beginning at 9:30am and lasting about nine hours. The cost is 109 DM ($64.70), with lunch included. Reservations must be made in advance to go to Potsdam. You go on a guided visit to the famous Sans Souci Palace. On the full-day tour, you visit not only the New Palace but also the Palace of the Crown Prince, Cecilienhof, where the Potsdam Conference of 1945 was conducted. A lunch break is taken. An abbreviated tour, lasting seven hours, is offered at a cost of 95 DM ($56.40). It is available Wed., Fri., and Sun. from April to October 31, from 9:30am to about 4:30pm, including lunch, and on Tues., Thurs., and Sat. from November 1 to March 31.

BERLIN BOATING

You might not think of a boat as a means of traveling in Berlin, but many operate here, and a boat ride can become quite an outing when you tire of museums and the cafés along the Kurfürstendamm. The lakes of Wannsee (known as "Kleiner" and "Grosser," depending on their size) are the major targets in summer. Sand has been imported from some of the North Sea beaches, and on a hot day the **Wannsee Strandbad** is packed. The lake fills with sailboats.

Berliners can also escape the concrete of the downtown area for a seven-hour boat ride through forests and hills. The best-known boat operator is **Stern und Kreisschiffahrt,** Sachlbernstrasse 60 (tel. 030/803-87-50 or 810-00-40). Among its many boats, it has a lake steamer shaped like a whale, called *Moby Dick.* This or another of the firm's craft departs from a point near the terminus of U-Bahn line no. 6 at Tegel. Walk through the suburb of Tegel to the Greenwich Promenade 10 minutes from the U-Bahn station. Boats operate between March and late September. A four-hour trip leaves from Tegel at 10:30am and at 12:40pm, costing 12.50 DM ($7.40). A longer tour encompasses the Tegelsee, the Hohenzollernkanal, the Ploetzensee locks, the Charlottenburger Lake, the Spree River, Havel Lake, Spandau, and Wannsee. For information, call the numbers listed above. Reservations are usually necessary.

6. Shopping

West Berlin prices are considered more reasonable than those often charged in such cities as Hamburg, Düsseldorf, Cologne, and Munich. The reason, perhaps, is that West Berlin lacks the moneyed class found in these other prosperous cities.

The central shopping destinations for all Berliners are Kurfürstendamm (its Fifth Avenue), Tauentzienstrasse, Am Zoo, and Kantstrasse. You might also want to walk up streets that intersect with Tauentzienstrasse: Marburger, Ranke, and Nürnberger.

Although I'll recommend some specific specialty shops, the average shopper with average requirements will head first for the **Europa-Center** in the heart of Berlin. Here, in addition to the Berlin casino and a number of restaurants and cafés, you'll find a dazzling array of 100 shops. The merchandise is wide-ranging, running up and down the price scale ladder.

Known as KPM, the **Royal Porcelain Factory** is at Wegelystrasse 1 (tel. 030/39-00-90), and it's been in existence since 1763. The Hohenzollern dynasty turned it into Prussia's answer to Meissen in Saxony. Patterns are handmade and hand-painted, and based for the most part on designs from the 18th and 19th centuries.

Prices are royal too. Products from this factory carry a distinctive official signature, an imperial orb and the letters KPM. Guided tours let you look at the beautiful work of the employees, and you can buy exquisite pieces of porcelain here.

Kaufhaus des Westens, Tauentzienstrasse 21–24 (tel. 030/21-21-0), known popularly as KaDeWe, is a luxury department store about two blocks from the Kurfürstendamm. The store, whose name means "department store of the west," was established some 75 years ago in the west end of Berlin. It is the third-largest department store in the world, ranking after Macy's in New York and Harrods in London. Of all the extravagant items on display, it is known mainly for its food department on the sixth floor, which is open Mon. to Fri. from 9am to 6pm and on Sat. from 9am to 2pm. This has been called the greatest food emporium in the world. The finest in German sausages are displayed here. But not only that— delicacies from all the world's continents are shipped in. Sit-down counters are available for sipping Sekt or ordering tasty dishes and desserts. After proper fortification, you can explore the six floors of merchandise. KaDeWe is more than a department store—one shopper called it a "collection of first-class specialty shops."

You might also want to check out the action at Berlin's **Flea Market** at the old U-Bahn station at Nollendorfplatz. Abandoned underground trains have been turned over to sellers who hawk their wares Sun., Mon., and Wed. to Sat. from 11am to 7:30pm. Later you can take a 1920s streetcar that runs every 15 minutes to the next station at Potsdamerstrasse. This place has been converted by guest workers into a **Turkish Bazaar.** You'll think you're in Istanbul, as you wander about, checking over the jewelry, glassware, onyx, and copper items. You can take time out to enjoy Turkish coffee with baklava, perhaps ordering some kebabs if you want to have lunch. If you're a flea market buff, you'll also find a large flea market going strong every Sat. and Sun. on **Strasse des 17 Juni** right in the Tiergarten.

Berlin is one of the world's most fashion-conscious cities, and you can look at a sample of what is au courant for chic women at **Horn's,** Kurfürstendamm 213 (tel. 030/881-40-55).

Sonia Rykiel, Kurfürstendamm 186–187 (tel. 030/882-17-74), is the only outlet in Germany devoted exclusively to this successful French fashion mogul. Ms. Rykiel, in addition to designing some of the most sophisticated hotel interiors in Paris, also designed the interior of this shop, which opened in 1990—a showcase of the most stylish and fashionable wear. Even a Sonia Rykiel T-shirt is expensive, however.

The man who can afford the very best—and to whom price is not a serious roadblock—should head for **Braun & Co.,** Kurfürstendamm 43 (tel. 030/881-34-62), one of the city's leading clothing outlets. This shop is the exclusive outlet in Berlin not only for Hermès neckties and scarves but for the whole Hermès collection. They also stock the well-known Brioni Roman-style collection, with some of the world's more glamorous, but more expensive, suits. A blazer made from the world's finest cashmere is often called a millionaire's cashmere, and when you see the price tag you'll agree. Another line, Chester Barrie, offers first-class English-style fashion for men. Shirts, beautifully designed and made, are imported from Italy and Sweden.

If you're interested in jewelry, you can explore the emporiums along Nürnbergerstrasse. One of the finest stores for jewelry is **Galerie Lalique,** Bleibtreustrasse 47 (tel. 030/881-97-62). The beautifully displayed work here is handcrafted in workshops in West Berlin and West Germany.

Some of the finest leather goods, especially shoes, are sold at the top-rated **Etienne Aigner,** Kurfürstendamm 197 (tel. 030/883-72-33). They also sell stylish clothes for both men and women.

If you're seeking modern design, head for **Rosenthal,** Kurfürstendamm 226 (tel. 030/881-70-51). This store specializes in contemporary Rosenthal designs, each of which is laboriously made in two villages in Bavaria.

Helmut Timberg, Kurfürstendamm 214 (tel. 030/881-91-58), is reputed to feature finer quality Meissen than you'd find in Meissen. An unusual outlet, this store has a license to sell goods manufactured in the state-owned factories in both Meissen and Dresden. Even if a traveler were to go to Meissen and Dresden, these goods would *not* be available. You can buy exquisite, but expensive, Meissen dinner plates here. Dresden ware focuses not so much on plates, but on sculpture, chandeliers, and boxes. The shop offers some stunning three-branch, ceiling-hung chandeliers.

Galerie Lotos, Uhlandstrasse 184 (tel. 030/882-39-81). The Germans, more than most any other nation in Europe, have always had a fascination for the art and antiquities of the near East and India. This unusual shop is richly stocked with hand-crafted treasures that the Lohse family bring back from their twice-annual pilgrimages to India, Tibet, and Nepal. For an insight into the crafts of the Himalayas and their foothills (and perhaps an investment-grade purchase as well), you can browse amid the accumulated treasures of 200 years of East Indian art history. Containing only three medium-size rooms, the place is nonetheless a storehouse of intriguing jewelry, furniture, sculpture, and painting.

The entire Prussian army—that is, in miniature—is for sale at **Berliner Zinnfiguren Kabinett,** Knesebeckstrasse 88 (tel. 030/31-08-02). The army comes in pewter. All figures are hand-molded, hand-painted, and hand-carved, depicting an art form famous in Germany for many, many years. The least expensive soldier always is sold unpainted, but you can pay considerably for a fully rounded, hand-painted figure. These figures depict warriors from the ancient Greek empire up to fashion models in contemporary costume of the 1980s. Students of World War II will also appreciate the depictions of 20th-century German soldiers in both world wars. This business has been owned by three generations of the Schlotz family.

Bric-a-brac and antiques collectors need not leave West Berlin empty-handed. Head for Kantstrasse, which is filled with bric-a-brac stores. Frankly, many items are junk, but perhaps you'll find something appealing.

Ku'damm-Passage, Kurfürstendamm 206–208, contains many little shops in its shopping arcade at the corner of Knesebeckstrasse. Rather than purveying fine antiques, this place is gloriously junk, selling old books, records, household utensils, bric-a-brac, and occasional dusty treasures amid the clutter.

---

7. Kids' Berlin

If you arrive in Berlin with your family, don't worry about small children getting bored. There's plenty for them to do. I will cite only a few examples from among many.

The most exciting place to take them is the **Berlin Zoo** (see previous recommendation). There, the most famous celebrity, among a cast of 10,000 or so, is Bao-Bao, the celebrated panda. His compound is always surrounded by crowds of children. In addition, the zoo has a cliff compound for the monkeys, an open-plan lion precinct, an aquarium, a crocodile house, an underground nocturnal animal center, a reptile collection of cobras and other giant snakes, and even a children's zoo where the animals welcome a cuddle. It also offers playgrounds.

In addition, the tourist office can direct families to certain children's farms where the kiddies can do more than just see the animals: they can actually join in the fun, lending a helping hand and learning farm experience firsthand.

Fun for the whole family is virtually guaranteed at Berlin's many fairs and festivals, including the Spring Festival, the Park Festival at Britz, the Steglitz Borough Festival, the German-American Festival, the Oktoberfest, and the Christmas fairs.

Grips-Theater, Altonaerstrasse 22 (tel. 030/391-40-04), has gained a reputation in Europe for its bright, breezy productions for children of all ages. Consult the *Berlin Programm* for times of shows and price of tickets.

8. After Dark

CULTURAL ENTERTAINMENT

Berliner Philharmonishes Orchester (Berlin Philharmonic), Matthäikirchstrasse 1 (tel. 030/25-48-80), is one of the world's premier orchestras. For many years under the direction of the renowned Herbert von Karajan, it is now directed by Claudio Abbado. You can purchase tickets for performances at the office in the main lobby of the orchestra hall Mon. to Fri. from 3:30 to 6pm, and on Sat. and Sun. from 11am to 2pm. It is not possible to place orders by phone. If you're staying in a first-class or deluxe hotel, you can usually get the concierge to obtain seats for you. Of the 2,218 seats, none is more than 100 feet from the rostrum. The location is in the Tiergarten sector; the hall can be reached from the center of the Ku'damm by taking bus no. 29.

Deutsche Oper Berlin, Bismarckstrasse 35 (tel. 030/341-02-49, or for ticket sales call 030/34-38-1), in Charlottenburg, is one of the world's great opera houses. It was built on the site of the prewar opera house that enjoyed world fame. The present structure is a notable example of modern theater architecture that seats 1,885 persons. The house attracts opera lovers from all over the world. The company is willing to tackle a Puccini favorite, a Janáček rarity, or a modern work, and they have a complete Wagner repertoire. There is a ballet company that performs once a week. Concerts, including Lieder evenings, are also presented on the opera stage.

The lighter muse of the operetta and the musical are at home at the **Theater des Westens,** Kantstrasse 12 (tel. 030/312-10-22). This theater lies between the Berlin Zoo and Kurfürstendamm.

The city's most distinguished theater is the Staatliche Schauspielbühnen Berlin. There are three theaters under this umbrella. The largest is the **Schiller Theater,** Bismarckstrasse 110 (tel. 030/31-95-236). In a separate section is a studio for the **Werkstatt.** Classic plays, as well as modern and experimental drama, are presented; often plays are commissioned. You are likely to see anything from Shakespeare's *Macbeth* to Thomas Bernhard's *Elisabeth II*. The third theater is the **Schlosspark Theater,** Schloss Strasse 48 (tel. 030/793-15-15). Ticket prices range from 8 DM ($4.75) to 53 DM ($31.45) in the Schiller Theater and from 6 DM ($3.55) to 51 DM ($30.30) in the Schlosspark Theater. Ticket prices for the Werkstatt are 15 DM ($8.90) for all seats. The three theaters produce about 25 to 30 shows per season. They are closed from late July until late August.

Peter Stein's **Schaubühne am Lehniner Platz,** Kurfürstendamm 153 (tel. 030/89-00-23), is considered by some to be the most important German-language theater in the country.

CAFÉ LIFE

At its zenith, the mid-19th century, Berlin was famous for its cafés. Max Krell, an editor, once wrote: "Cafés were our homeland. They were the stock exchange of ideas, site of intellectual transactions, futures' market of poetic and artistic glory and defeat." Many of the most famous ones, such as the grand coffeehouses of Unter den Linden in East Berlin, or those celebrated in the post–World War I era among artists and writers—the Café des Westens and the Romanisches Café—didn't survive the Allied air raids of World War II. Some did survive in tattered remains; others fled to such points as Frankfurt; and many relocated from East Berlin to West Berlin. Coffeehouses are still going strong in Berlin. They've changed with the times, however (see below). Every true Berliner has his or her favorite, shunning all the rest. It is said that a person can tell who you are by the café you frequent. So, in your search for self-identity, I'll offer the following selections.

Café Kranzler, Kurfürstendamm 18–19 (tel. 030/882-69-11), was originally established in 1825 on the opposite side of town, near Unter den Linden. About a hundred years later, it packed up its porcelain, busy waiters, and—with its arts-oriented clientele in tow—moved to the (then) less imposing district around the Kurfürstendamm, where it quickly became fashionable. Like almost everything else along the street, it rose from the ashes of World War II ready to thrive in what has become the new center of West Berlin. Today you'll find an unashamedly modern establishment, with striped canopies, sidewalk tables and chairs, and two floors of densely packed tables. Owned by Swiss inventors, the café has a selection of such Swiss specialties as shredded veal Zurich style, which you can eat with such Swiss wines as Fendant; an array of ever-changing daily specials; a pastry buffet; and a wide selection of ice creams. Set meals cost 14.90 DM ($8.85) to 23 DM ($13.65). The place is open daily from 8am to midnight.

Café/Bistro Laysieffer, Kurfürstendamm 218 (tel. 030/882-78-20). A relative newcomer when compared to the venerable ages of its better-established competitors, this family-operated gathering place was established in the early 1980s within the premises of what had been the Chinese Embassy. Some of the ornate moldings and lighting fixtures are still in place from earlier times, not to mention a pair of gilded lions guarding the entrance next door. The street level contains a pastry and candy shop, but most clients climb the flight of stairs to a marble-and-wood–sheathed café with a balcony overlooking the busy Ku'damm. A breakfast served here is one of the most elegant in town: Parma ham, smoked salmon, freshly baked baquette, French butter, and—to round it off—champagne. During the rest of the day, the Leysieffer offers different hot and cold platters, including veal cutlets and beef in horseradish sauce, with meals costing from 40 DM ($23.75). You could also visit just for coffee and a pastry (the Apfelstrudel or the fruit-studded tiramisu would be a good choice), which together would cost about 8 DM ($4.75). The café is open daily from 9am to 10pm; Fri. and Sat. to midnight.

Café Einstein, Kurfürstendamm 58 (tel. 030/261-50-96). Everyone here seems to be either an established musician or an aspiring one. The café is housed in the type of 19th-century neorococo villa that used to be typical of this district. Discreet, sophisticated, and two-sided (it's both a café and a restaurant), it occupies the drawing room of a house that once belonged to Henny Porten, Germany's first cinematic superstar. (Her career endured from 1906 to 1955, though she did not work during the Nazi era because her husband was a Jew.)

Amid a decor of marble and polished wood, you can observe the other clients (by some accounts among the most individualistic in Berlin) and order such dishes as roast pork, spinach tortellini in a cream sauce, Tafelspitz with homemade noodles, mozzarella with tomatoes, as well as pastries and many kinds of wine. Coffee costs from 4 DM ($2.40), and main courses (hot food) begin at 10 DM ($5.95). Hours are 10am to 2am daily.

Café Adlon, Kurfürstendamm 69 (tel. 030/883-76-82). At the turn of the century, the imposing neoclassical decor, overstuffed sofas, and formal waiters made this one of the most prestigious cafés in its neighborhood. (Even Kaiser Wilhelm—when provoked to such frivolity—pronounced it one of his preferred cafés.) Today, only a bit tattered around the edges, with a clientele considerably less formal than in days gone by, it still offers charming summertime vistas from its sidewalk tables, and a view of Berlin kitsch from its interior. You'll find a huge selection of cakes and ice creams, priced at 3.50 DM ($2.10) to 6 DM ($3.55). The Adlon is open daily from 10am to midnight.

Café Buchwald, Bartningallee 29 (tel. 030/391-59-31), originally established in 1852, has passed through the maternal family tree of its founder ever since. One of the few such establishments to have survived the World War II bombings, this café is set within a quiet neighborhood at the edge of the Tiergarten district; its small garden overlooks the Bar-Brücke (Bear Bridge) and the River Spree. Inside, a duet of quiet rooms contains cloth-covered tables, sofas, and comfortable wooden chairs. German-language newspapers are available, and the menu offers coffee, tea, and pastries. A house specialty is Baumkuchen (treecake), a many-layered concoction rich with butter and sugar. Coffee and pastries begin at about 7 DM ($4.20). Open Mon. to Fri. from 8am to 6pm; and Sat. and Sun. from 10am to 6pm.

Café Möhring, Kurfürstendamm 213 (tel. 030/881-20-75). Set behind a belle-époque awning and a bevy of warm-weather outdoor tables, this café is the survivor of a tradition begun in 1898 that welcomed political and literary opinions of all persuasions. From the terrace you'll have a view of the deliberately unrepaired tower of the Kaiser Wilhelm Memorial Church. The fresh flowers and the many older women who linger over their pastries contribute to the strong impression of a bygone era. Cakes cost 4.25 DM ($2.50); a breakfast, 8.50 DM ($5.05); and a main course such as a salad buffet with turkey Schnitzel, 14 DM ($8.30). Hours are 7am to 10pm daily.

A CLASSIC WINE CELLAR

Historischer Weinkeller, Alt-Pichelsdorf 32 (tel. 030/361-80-56), might be the place for your most interesting evening in Berlin. Here, the staff lights a sugarcone and performs the age-old ceremony of "burning the punch," performed three nights a week: Wed., Fri., and Sat. between 10 and 11pm. The punch, a specialty, costs 8.50 DM ($5.05) per glass; as the flame burns, you're supposed to make a wish. On other nights of the week you can select from more than 100 German wines, at prices that begin at 6.50 DM ($3.85) per glass. The 200-year-old cellar vaults are atmospheric. You can also come here to dine, but you should make a reservation. Meals cost 40 DM ($23.75) to 60 DM ($35.65). Hours are from 7pm to 1am; Sun. from 10am to 2am; closed Mon. This little squat inn on a cobbled street has survived wars and all sorts of disasters.

MUSIC AND DANCE

What the Germans call a "ball paradox" is offered at **Café Keese,** Bismarckstrasse 108 (tel. 030/312-91-11). This is a fancy way of saying that the women have a chance to ask the men to dance, instead of the other way around. People go here who actually like to dance the traditional way. The orchestra plays music quite slowly at times, and the place is often jammed, especially on Saturday night. If you're a lone male and fear the women will mob you if you make an appearance on the floor, you can remain perched at the bar. Incidentally, the management reserves the right to kick out any male patron who turns down a female request to dance! The Keese sees itself as something of a matrimonial bureau—always announcing new statistics about the number of people who have met and fallen in love on its premises and later gotten married. Men and women are requested to wear formal attire. No entrance fee is charged. Inside, you can order a beer at 8 DM ($4.75)—the cheapest way to spend an evening here, incidentally—or most whiskies at 12 DM ($7.15) a shot. Café Keese is open daily from 8pm to 4am.

New Eden Revue Night-Club, Kurfürstendamm 71 (tel. 030/323-58-49). One newspaper writer termed this garden "too elegant and expensive for vagabond types." Essentially what you get here is dancing to smooth orchestra music, plus striptease. The carefully selected women strip with flair and style, each having a unique act. The show prides itself on being, in management's own words, "tasteful and elegant—suitable for all viewers, age 20 to 100, including men with their wives." The club is open Mon. to Sat.; closed Sun. Entrance fee is 10 DM ($5.95), and the cost of a first drink is 29 DM ($17.20); after that, each drink goes for 10 DM ($5.95). From Mon. to Thurs., shows are presented at 9:30pm and again at 11:30pm. On Fri. and Sat., show times are 10:30pm and 12:30am.

Big Eden, Kurfürstendamm 202 (tel. 030/882-61-20), bills itself as a dance paradise for 2,000 people. Men dance together, or alone, or with women. The latest electronic gimmicks, all zany, decorate the place, the creation of the fertile mind of Rolf Eden. The strobe system alone may send you into a trance. Here, you'll find a wonderful mélange of Berlin youth, in every conceivable form of dress (or lack of it), dancing to recorded music. As befits the means of most of the clientele, prices are kept low. Big Eden opens daily at 7pm; Sun. to Thurs. it closes at 4am; Fri. and Sat., it doesn't shut down until 7am. Entrance Sun. to Thurs. is 4.50 DM ($2.65), rising to 8 DM ($4.75) on Fri. and Sat. A beer costs 5 DM ($2.95).

Quasimodo, Kantstrasse 12a (tel. 030/312-80-86). Beer and wine—as well as live music—flow nightly in this pub-cum-sound stage. Popular with rockers from 20 to 30, it charges an entrance fee of 10 DM ($5.95) to 20 DM ($11.90), depending on the program. A beer costs from 4 DM ($2.40). The music is rock, jazz, funk, whatever. Hours are from 8pm until at least 1am, sometimes 3am, depending on the crowd.

Metropol, Nollendorfplatz 5 (tel. 030/216-41-22), is one of the leading nightclubs in town, happily blending straights and gays in what used to be a cinema. On Fri. and Sat. nights, it is a standard disco, opening at 10pm and closing at 8am. On those nights, a 10-DM ($5.95) entrance fee is charged and a beer costs from 5 DM ($2.95). On every other night of the week, live concerts are presented at 8pm, lasting 90 minutes, with a total venue, including after-concert time lingering at the bar, of around three hours. The place is usually empty by 11pm. Entrance for the concerts ranges from 15 DM ($8.90) to 35 DM ($20.80). Most clients are in the 18-to-40 age group. Take the U-Bahn to Nollendorfplatz.

Dschungel (Jungle), Nürnbergerstrasse 53 (tel. 030/24-66-98), is considered one of the most fashionable rendezvous points in town, attracting everybody from film personalities to German tennis star Boris Becker. Berlin's beau monde gathers downstairs before heading upstairs to the disco or up a spiral staircase to a favored balcony spot for drinks. The entrance fee is 10 DM ($5.95), and the price of a beer is 5 DM ($2.95). It is open from 11pm to 4am, but no one with any social pizzazz shows up before 1am; closed Tues. Take the U-Bahn to Ku'damm or Wittenberger Platz.

Eierschale, Podbielskialle 50 (tel. 030/832-70-97), means "eggshell" in German. There is live music of one kind or another here nightly beginning at 8:30pm. Possibilities include country and western, rock and roll, and, on Fri. and Sat. only, jazz. The club is open daily from 10am to 2am. There's no cover charge but you pay 5.30 DM ($3.15) for a beer.

CABARET

Most popular among visitors to Berlin is the kind of nightspot depicted in the musical *Cabaret,* with floor show patter and acts full of satire aimed at both the political and the social scene.

La Vie en Rose, Europa-Center (tel. 030/323-60-06), is the major cabaret and revue theater of Berlin, to be found in the cellar of the Europa-Center. The show is a musical revue, including singing, dancing, beautiful costumes, and transvestism. Spoken words are as often in English as in German, because the cabaret attracts a largely international crowd. It is open Tues. to Sun., and a show is presented at 10pm. On Sat., there are three shows: at 8pm, 10pm, and midnight. The doors always open 30 minutes before the evening's first show. Entrance is 25 DM ($14.85), and the minimum drink price is 35 DM ($20.80).

DRAG SHOWS

Ever since the 1920s, when George Grosz was doing his savage caricatures and Greta Garbo, then unknown, was slipping around the town undetected, drag acts have been a staple of Berlin nightlife. Today's scene still goes on, the only problem being that it lacks a Christopher Isherwood to record it.

The show at **Chez Nous,** Marburgerstrasse 14 (tel. 030/213-18-10), has gone on to world fame, attracting an essentially straight clientele. The setting has been called mock Louis XIV. This club books some of the best transvestite acts in Europe, everything from a sultry, boa-draped striptease star from Rio de Janeiro to a drag queen who looks like a gun moll from the 1940s. Shows are nightly at 8:30 and 11pm. Sometimes, but only rarely, a late show at 1am will be offered on a Saturday night (but call about that). Entrance fee is 10 DM ($5.95), and drinks cost from 30 DM ($17.80).

GAY AND LESBIAN BERLIN

On the gay circuit, Berlin has a trio of bars sometimes jokingly referred to as "the Bermuda Triangle." Young men often bar-hop from one to the other.

Tom's Bar, Motzstrasse 19 (tel. 030/213-45-70). Open nightly from 10pm to 4am, it becomes crowded after 11pm. Entrance is free, with a beer costing from 5 DM ($2.95).

Pool Disco, Motzstrasse 90 (tel. 030/24-75-29). Usually very animated and crowded, this is the most popular gay disco as of this writing. It is open nightly from 10pm to 5am. Beer costs 4.50 DM ($2.65).

Knast Bar, Fuggerstrasse 34 (tel. 030/24-10-26). It is the leading leather bar of Berlin. No entrance fee is charged, and beer costs from 5 DM ($2.95). Go after 11pm and stay until dawn if you wish.

Another bar, **Wu Wu,** Kleistrasse 4 (tel. 030/213-63-92), is a place for younger gay men—or, in the words of one client, "blue-jean babies." Of course, older men are always welcome. The club charges an entrance fee of 3 DM ($1.80), plus another 4 DM ($2.40) for a beer, and it is open nightly from 10pm to 7am, just in time for an early breakfast (somewhere else).

For women, **Café-und Kulturzentrum für Frauen,** Potsdamerstrasse 139 (tel. 030/215-43-25), established in 1986, is one of Berlin's most visible headquarters for feminists and the most obvious launching pad for women seeking to meet other women. Within its inner sanctum is a changing array of art exhibitions, poetry readings, German-language discussions, lectures, and social events. You can phone in advance to learn the program. The premises are occasionally transformed into a disco. At the bar, women can order a glass of wine for 4 DM ($2.40) or a cappuccino for 3 DM ($1.80). The center is open Sun. and Thurs. from 6pm to 1am; Fri. and Sat. from 6pm to 4am. Entrance is free.

GAMBLING

One of the biggest attractions for visitors is the **Spielbank** (tel. 030/25-00-89-0) at the Europa-Center (entrance on Budapesterstrasse). It's open daily from 3pm to 3am. Inside you'll find a number of roulette tables, in addition to tables for baccarat, blackjack, and other games. The bar is the longest in Berlin, and it's a watering spot between rounds at the tables. There's also a restaurant serving an expensive international cuisine. There's a 5-DM ($2.95) entrance fee, and minimum bets are 5 DM ($2.95) also. Male guests should wear jackets and ties (no jeans or tennis shoes are allowed). It is important to bring along your passport.

BEER GARDENS

One of the most gemütlich places in Berlin is **Wirtshaus zum Löwen,** Hardenbergstrasse 29 (tel. 030/26-21-02-0), a pub in the city center directly opposite the Kaiser Wilhelm Memorial Church. It is attractively decorated, and even in winter you get the feeling of sitting outside under the chestnut trees although you're snug and warm inside. In summer you can soak up the atmosphere in the beer garden. Every night, a band plays for dancing and singing, with the guests joining in, creating a happy feeling like that found at the Oktoberfest in Munich. The kitchen offers good plain German food, including Bavarian specialties; hot meals start at 12 DM ($7.15). Also served is the Münchener Löwenbrau, typical German beer, costing 4.50 DM ($2.65) for half a liter. The place is open daily from 10am, but the best time to come here to enjoy the atmosphere is from 7pm to midnight. On Fri. and Sat., it is open to 2am.

Loretta im Garten, Lietzenburgerstrasse 89 (tel. 030/882-33-54), a beer garden, is surprisingly rustic for such a midcity location. It offers both waitress service and self-service. It has wooden banquettes and paneling, with a handful of outdoor toys to amuse your children as you drink; there's even a ferris wheel. It also offers live musical acts, including country and western, folk, and rock and roll. Beer costs from 4.50 DM ($2.65). You can also enjoy hearty Berliner and German regional dishes, with meals costing from 15 DM ($8.90). It is open only from May 1 to mid-October, daily from 10am to 3pm and 8pm to 4am.

ELEGANT BARS

One of the special bars of Berlin is the **Times Bar,** Savoy Hotel, Fasanenstrasse 9–10 (tel. 030/311-03-0). It is cozy and intimate, almost like a wood-paneled library in someone's private home. Dedicated to *The Times* (London), whose latest edition is often displayed in the window, this bar is a comfortable rendezvous point. Guests sit in leather upholstered chairs, enjoying the English language newspapers and the style and quiet charm of the place. In addition to drinks, light meals can also be had at the bar, for about 20 DM ($11.90). Perhaps you'd like some lobster soup, or maybe a bowl of velvety ice cream. You can get that and more. It is open daily from 6pm to 1am or "later," depending on the needs and wishes of its patrons.

Harry's Bar, Grand Hotel Esplanade, Lützwufer 15 (tel. 030/26-10-11), is an aggressively stylized bar with a minimalist decor. Entirely sheathed in slabs of polished dark-gray granite, and studded with red leather armchairs, pop art, and photographs of all the American presidents, it models its traditions on the most famous North American watering hole in Paris, Harry's Bar. Its drinks menu is a monument to the oral traditions of the IBF (International Bar Flies) Society, and includes such imbibers' favorites as "Mizner's Dream" (created in 1962 for the Boca Raton Hotel Club in Florida) and the 1964 classic, "The Petrifier" (ingredients unlisted), for two. Frequent visitors consider the "Dirty Harry," "Bill's Knockout Punch," and the "Flying Elephant" far more prosaic. In all, the menu lists almost 200 different drinks—a small library by anyone's standards—as well as a limited selection of food items.

Suitable dress includes everything from leather microskirts with tights to business suits. Beer costs from 3 DM ($1.80), with more elaborate concoctions going for 12.50 DM ($7.45) and up. Open daily from noon to between 2am and 7am, depending on business.

FINDING A KNEIPE

It has long been the custom of a typical Berliner to find a favorite Kneipe, or bar, in which to relax after work or to meet sympathetic friends (or be introduced to new ones). A Kneipe is the equivalent of a Londoner's local pub. Usually (but not always) these places are cozy rendezvous places. There are hundreds of these Kneipen in Berlin. I can only get you started by recommending a handful.

Ax-Bar, Leibnizstrasse 34 (tel. 030/313-85-94), off Kantstrasse, is a hangout for movie people and Berlin literati. The bar is well decorated, but there's no sign on the door. They like to keep it discreet here. You can order Kleinigkeiten or tasty snacks with your beer or wine. Meals cost 25 DM ($14.85) to 40 DM ($23.75). Of course, many come here just to drink, paying from 4 DM ($2.40) for beer. The place is open from 7pm to 3am; closed Sat. The most popular time to eat here is around 9pm, when it's best to reserve a table in advance.

Zwiebelfisch, Savignyplatz 7–8 (tel. 030/31-73-63), has long been a favorite hangout of artists, writers, and newspaper people who find a communicational drinking spirit here. It also attracts U.S. jazz artists after they finish their gigs of the evening in other Berlin clubs. Gossip is easily exchanged, and companions and friends easily met. There is a limited menu in case you want more than libations. Find a seat at one of the spacious wooden tables, where you can order drinks for 2 DM ($1.20) to 8 DM ($4.75); snacks and small platters of food cost from 10 DM ($5.95). Hours are noon to 6am daily.

Gaststätte Hoeck (Wilhelm Hoeck), Wilmersdorferstrasse 149 (tel. 030/341-31-10), lies on a street lined with department stores and shops that are almost deserted after 6pm. Set behind a brightly illuminated facade jammed with slogans for local beers, it is distinctly divided into two very different sections. You (and half of the rest of the neighborhood) can have a drink in the very rowdy, sometimes raucous bar area, where—among other dramas—a clown may be playing the harmonica. The separate dining room serves traditional food. You can choose from more than a dozen kinds of beer (if in doubt, just ask for my favorite, "Pilsner Urguell") and wine by the glass. Meals cost from 30 DM ($17.80), and hot food is served daily from 11am to 11pm. The bar is open daily from 8am to midnight. Co-owners Peter Dahms and Gerd Henselin are genuinely kind hosts.

Lutter und Wegner 1811, Schlüterstrasse 55 (tel. 030/881-34-40). Established just after World War II, the restaurant was named after a gastronomic and social landmark, Lutter und Wegner, which in Wilhelmian days attracted Berlin's leading actors. With the original namesake, dating from 1811, isolated in bombed-out obscurity in East Berlin, its owners set up this very successful grandchild in West Berlin in 1945. The premises are directed by Bavarian-born Justos Robert. No one will mind if you remain in the outermost of the two rooms, at the stand-up bar, with a drink. If you want to dine, however, phone in advance, be on time, and be prepared to wait. Specialties include a soup of smoked trout and salmon with a cranberry cream sauce. Meals range in price from 35 DM ($20.80) to 65 DM ($38.60). The restaurant is open nightly from 7pm to midnight. The bar remains open to 3am.

PART TWO

EAST GERMANY

TRAVELING IN EAST GERMANY

A visit to East Germany today is to see history in the making. It is a land of dynamic change. . . . and problems. But, even so, a visit here in the 1990s will provide stories you can tell your grandchildren. While there's still time, you can even buy souvenir chunks of the Berlin wall. Before the Wall was erected in 1961, some four million East Germans escaped to the West.

East Germany is roughly the size of Ohio, its population less than a third of the Federal Republic's. Yet in the post-war era, East Germany rose to become the number-10 industrial power in the world. Among what was once called "the Eastern bloc nations" in the Cold War era, it was second only to the Soviet Union in industrial production. Its people enjoyed the highest standard of living in Eastern Europe.

But all of what had been widely publicized as "the economic miracle" came apart in 1989, when East Germany stood as the "poor relation" to its economically powerful sister across the border. Shortages of resources had taken their toll, and the economic machinery of the country was revealed to have steadily eroded. Party leaders, notably hard-liner Erich Honecker, were arrested, even as he prophesied, "The wall will last for at least another half century to protect our republic from thieves." Although he and other Communist party bosses preached self-sacrifice to their people, they were exposed as living "high off the hog," enjoying great luxury while literally stealing millions from the treasury.

In the fall of 1989, two-thirds of the country's 16.7 million inhabitants crossed the once-feared border to visit West Germany. For many of them, it was the first time they'd ever set foot in West Berlin, even though they might have lived within a quarter of a mile of the border for 40 years. For an older generation, it was "coming home" again, with memories of a West Berlin that didn't exist any more.

Many stayed to live permanently in the West. Others stocked up on consumer goods and planned to return next weekend. Still others, such as one East Berlin restaurant owner, fled to the West only to return when the Honecker government collapsed under the furtive chants of "We are the people."

As it moves into the 1990s, the big question facing East Germany is how to reinvent itself both economically and politically. With the prospect of reunion with West Germany, the question remains, "How will East Germany retain its separate identity?"

Many East Germans prefer the term "reassociation" instead of reunification. Others fear that even though they may ultimately benefit economically from a more capitalistic system, there will be a period of difficult economic adjustment. East Germans also fear problems may be imported from the West, notably crime and drugs of which they have been relatively free since World War II. It will not be easy to reintegrate the two countries. East Germany has a decaying infrastructure, chronic shortages, and an outmoded technology. But its citizens are an intelligent, educated, hard-working people—even a great people—and they can rebuild a new society, just as they rebuilt after World War II when much of the country lay in ruins.

THE LAND TODAY

As everybody knows, Germany was split into four zones at the end of the war. Russia took the eastern sector, with the exception of West Berlin, which was divided into three zones of occupation by the United States, Great Britain, and France. The rest of the country consisted mainly of the three former states of Saxony, Thüringia, Mecklenburg, and parts of Prussia. The boundaries of East Germany are formed by the Baltic Sea in the north and Poland in the east. Parts of German territory were surrendered to Poland in the aftermath of World War II.

The Deutsche Demokratische Republik (DDR; German Democratic Republic) has a population of almost 17 million people. East Berlin is its capital, and its Länder (states) are Mecklenburg, West Pomerania, Mark Brandenburg, Thuringia, and the Province and Land (state) of Saxony. These divisions, however, were abolished in 1952, and 15 districts (Bezirke) were established, later subdivided into the present 219 small districts.

The head of state is a chairman, with a prime minister as head of government. Legislative power is in the hands of the unicameral Volkskammer (People's Chamber), an elected body.

The DDR has struggled for worldwide recognition. That breakthrough came in 1969 when its existence as a nation was recognized by the nonaligned countries. Today, the U.S. has diplomatic relations with the DDR, and East Germany is a member of the United Nations. By an agreement formulated in Helsinki in 1975, the boundaries of the DDR were given international acceptance.

A NEW FRONTIER IN TRAVEL

Other than its much-visited capital of East Berlin, the land of the DDR remains relatively undiscovered. The people more and more welcome tourists, imposing fewer and fewer restrictions. Tourism, which can be a vital means of bringing Western currency to the country as it rebuilds itself, is given the highest priority.

The truth is, there is much here to see. The cliché image of a grim, gray country of barbed wire is long faded. East Germany has beautiful scenery and monuments, and, perhaps more important, in some of the more remote parts of the country, you will think you've wandered into a time warp, seeing rural Germany as it must have existed in 1928. All that will change, one day, but for the moment, it allows you to wander far off the beaten path of standardized European itineraries.

East Germany is a land of mountainous scenery (one part, in fact, is called "Saxon Switzerland"), heavy forests, and gently rolling plains. The overall average temperature is about 40 to 50 degrees Fahrenheit.

Rural traditions, now largely abandoned in most parts of West Germany, still linger in the east. There are no traffic jams on the roads as you make your way through the Harz Mountains, the Thüringian Forest, or along the Elbe River. Gasoline stations are few and far between, and many of the back roads are in poor condition.

You'll visit cities that rose out of ashes, including Dresden. Many East German cities were collections of bomb-blackened ruins and shell-pocked buildings in 1945. A remnant of once-powerful Prussia, and later a faded piece of real estate left over from the gaudy dream of the Hitlerian Reich, East Germany appeared to face a bleak future. Now, florid baroque palaces are being restored, and hotels of modern comfort are being built to join those that already exist.

East Germany, once a dreaded, feared nation in the West—often connected in our minds with spy novels—is extending a welcome to visitors today as never before.

THE FORMALITIES

If you want to tour East Germany, you should arrange hotel accommodations in advance. That should be done through a travel agent. You can, of course, book directly through the government travel bureau inside East Germany, but that's far more complicated and time-consuming. It's best to have all the arrangements made before you go.

In New York, **Koch Overseas Co.,** 157 E. 86th St., New York, NY 10028 (tel. 212/369-3800), specializes in East German travel, although the agency and its affiliates are a full-service outfit as well. Mr. Koch, however, is a specialist on East German tours, and is an authorized agent for the Travel Bureau of the German Democratic Republic. Born in Leipzig, he was the son of hoteliers there. So at an early age he learned to be sensitive to the needs of travelers.

For purposes of visa applications to the DDR, most tourists fall into one of two categories: those planning on staying in the homes of friends or relatives in the DDR, and those persons planning on staying exclusively in hotels. The entrance requirements are slightly different for each category, but Mr. Koch and his assistants can arrange things smoothly in either case. The Koch agency will arrange all necessary hotel reservations for the tourist. Arrangements will take six to eight weeks after the agency receives a completed reservation request with a down payment of $50 per person. Arrangements by telex can be handled within 10 to 20 days, but if the proposed arrangement is requested by telex, an additional charge of $25 is imposed. Also the DDR will charge $28 for confirmation by telex from the travel bureau there. There is a charge of $15 for any change or cancellation given.

Those tourists who choose to stay in hotels—not with friends or relatives in the DDR—must pay in advance for a specified number of nights, and Mr. Koch will issue vouchers for funds exchanged. In addition, you will be charged a handling fee of $20 per person per arrangement, payable to Koch Overseas. Upon presentation of these vouchers at the frontier, a visa will be issued for 15 DM ($8.90). You then report for registration at your preselected hotel and present your vouchers, at which time the hotel will automatically register you. Visas issued in this way, by the way, are valid only for the number of days for which you present prepaid hotel vouchers.

If you're driving to East Germany from West Germany, refer to the introductory section in Chapter XVII on West Berlin, which explains gasoline purchases and toll fees.

Travel with overnight stays in East Berlin and other parts of the country can also be arranged by the **Reisebüro der DDR,** Augsburgerstrasse 27, 1000 Berlin 30 (tel. 030/219-98-200). You should make arrangements at least one week prior to your planned visit.

CURRENCY

In July 1990, in a historic monetary event, West Germany and East Germany "wedded" their currency system. The East German mark—the *Reichsmark* (M)— faded into the pages of Cold War history. Gone too are the draconian currency controls and the unfair rates of exchange that characterized the 1960s, 1970s, and 1980s.

In East Germany, the West German mark, known as *Deutsche Mark* (DM), now is legal tender and can be brought in and out of East Germany freely.

Headlines had proclaimed "One Currency, One Country," even while the reunification process was still in the talking stage. The merging of the currencies on July 2, 1990, was known as *Tag X* or X-Day. After years of "socialism," this move marked East Germany's entry into the free market system.

Certainly, the East Germans got a good deal, exchanging their battered and tattered East mark for the robust Deutsche mark of West Germany. The Bundesbank, the central bank of West Germany, literally trucked in billions of Deutsche marks to distribute to the people of East Germany in exchange for their old currency. A lot of this new windfall of money was spent by East Germans eager to take a trip. Most foreign travel had been banned for them, and a good part of the population had never been to the West before 1990. Access to Western consumer goods was open for the first time.

Of course, for the foreign visitor, the wedding of currencies will immediately mean a dramatic jump in the cost of a trip to East Germany. The days of the 12¢ subway ticket (likely to rise to $1.62 as in the West) are almost certainly over. The best opera seat in the house, formerly costing $9 in East Germany, will more likely find its way to the $55 high-water mark set in West Germany.

So, while East Germans adjust to the new prices of the West, the foreign visitor to East Germany in 1991 should also prepare for constantly rising prices. This escalation will surely continue until East Germany has "caught up" with West Germany.

Prices in this book are quoted in West German marks, except for some hotel price lists or other tourist data, such as museum entry fees, that appear in U.S. dollars for the convenience of visitors. However, the visitor should be warned again that, as we go to press, all quoted prices are certain to rise. Tourists visiting the East should contact their travel agents for the latest information on hotel and restaurant costs.

CUSTOMS

Restrictions concerning gifts and other articles have been liberalized. As in most other countries, don't bring in weapons, drugs, or pornography. Also, don't bring in any "fascist literature" (such as Hitler's *Mein Kampf*—but chances are you won't be doing that anyway).

However, check with your travel agent, since changes in customs regulations are likely to take place.

GETTING THERE

My suggestion is that you visit West Berlin before venturing into East Germany. Actually, most visitors confine their tour of the DDR just to East Berlin. In any case, West Berlin is likely to be your "gateway" into East Germany. Therefore, I recommend that you refer to the "Getting to Berlin" section in Chapter XVII which details the means of access, including air, rail, and private car.

Airport Arrivals

The national airline of the German Democratic Republic is **Interflug,** D-1189 Berlin-Schönefeld Airport (tel. 00372/67-20). Launched in 1956, the airline operates an extensive network of scheduled services to more than 50 international destinations in Europe, Africa, Asia, and America. Its main long-haul destinations are Beijing and Singapore. Carrying some 1.5 million passengers a year, the DDR airline is linked to international air traffic by more than 240 sales agency agreements. The DDR has air transport agreements with 59 countries.

The main base of Interflug is at Berlin-Schönefeld (perhaps the most modern airport in Eastern Europe), with secondary hubs at Dresden, Erfurt, and Leipzig. At the airport, you'll find an extensive array of services. To call information, dial 00372/672-40-31. Other services include a travel agency (tel. 00372/672-20-17), an Intershop, worldwide car-rental offices (tel. 00372/672-24-18), a restaurant, café, snackbar, left luggage office, duty-free shop, and an airport hotel.

The airport offers a special service for transit or international traffic to West Berlin. The bus terminal for transit passengers is found in front of the airport building. Buses to West Berlin generally run at intervals of 30 minutes, the journey taking about 45 minutes. Fares, including the transport of luggage, are 7 DM ($4.15) for adults and 4 DM ($2.40) for children. The transit visa costs 5 DM ($2.95). To visit the heart of Berlin (East), you can go by electric train (S-Bahn) in 40 minutes or by taxi (30 minutes).

ITINERARIES

Presumably, most Americans visit the DDR on an organized tour; therefore, their itineraries are planned in advance. However, for the independent person visiting East Germany, I have a few suggestions for touring on your own. It takes a minimum of seven days to see just the highlights of East Germany. Of course, it would be desirable to give it far more time if you can afford it, as there is much to see.

Much of your first day in **East Berlin** will be involved in getting there, including border formalities. On your second day you can explore the DDR capital, taking in Alexanderplatz and the Brandenburg Gate, along with the Pergamon Museum and other attractions. Perhaps in the evening you'll attend a performance at the German State Opera House or the Berliner Ensemble. Day 3 (but still with an overnight in East Berlin) can be spent by taking one of the many organized tours to **Potsdam,** where you can visit Sans Souci, the summer residence of Frederick II, as well as other attractions.

On Day 4 you can head south, with **Dresden** as your overnight stopover. If you leave East Berlin on an 8:30am train, you can be in Dresden for lunch. That will leave the afternoon free to explore the city's many attractions, including the Zwinger quadrangle of pavilions and galleries. At night you can attend a performance at the restored Semper Opera House.

If you're driving, you can visit **Meissen** in the northwest of Dresden, touring the famous porcelain factory. Otherwise, Day 5 may see you on a train heading for an overnight stopover in **Leipzig.** The train time from Dresden to Leipzig is less than two hours. Once in Leipzig, you can visit, among other attractions, Thomaskirche, the burial place of its one-time choirmaster Johann Sebastian Bach.

Day 6 can be one of the most interesting in your itinerary, a visit to **Weimar,** that 1,000-year-old town on the edge of the Thuringian forest which for so long has been a seat of German culture. You can visit its principal attraction, the Goethe National Museum, as well as many other famous sights associated with German writers, artists, and composers. The train ride from Leipzig to Weimar takes about an hour. Overnight in Weimar.

Day 7, which will include a final night in **East Berlin,** can be spent by taking a morning trip to **Erfurt,** which lies northwest of Weimar, only a half-hour train ride away. Erfurt is familiar to disciples of Martin Luther, and you can spend a good part of the day exploring the town with memories of the great reformer before returning to East Berlin by either train or private car.

NARROW-GAUGE RAILWAYS

Introduced as the first modern public conveyances in Germany 150 years ago, narrow-gauge railways today have both a certain nostalgia and a practical use. In the most beautiful parts of the DDR they link health and holiday resorts and serve as tourist attractions. Some of them even serve as a part of the railway network of the Deutsche Reichsbahn of the DDR.

Some routes start in Dresden, trains run into the Erzgebirge and Harz Mountains, and still others take passengers on trips in the Baltic coast region, one even serving the island of Rügen out at sea. All of the trains are pulled by steam locomotives, the newest of which was built in 1910. Each of the coaches has a small stove that the conductor will light up if it's cold outside.

The DDR Travel Agency offers 10 tours on the trains, with visits to old track installations, machinery, railway repair and servicing shops, and railway stations.

FAST FACTS FOR EAST GERMANY

There are, of course, differences in visiting East and West, and a few helpful items of information may make your stay in the East more pleasant. However, all data about tourist restrictions are subject to change. All the hotels, restaurants, monuments, and museums described in this chapter will be waiting to receive you when you visit East Germany. What *will* change are the various requirements for travel. Travel conditions and requirements will have to be checked and verified with a travel agent before you go, as there are many, many changes in the air.

Auto requirements: If your automobile does not have the "Blue Card" or "Green Card," **liability insurance** is compulsory. At press time road tolls were assessed as follows. For private cars and minibuses up to nine seats (including driver), for a distance of up to 200 kilometers (125 miles), $1.65 is charged; for up to 300 kilometers (185 miles), $5; for up to 400 kilometers (250 miles), $6.65; and for up to 500 kilometers (310 miles), $8.35. Gas or motor oil can be paid for in U.S. dollars. The requisite coupons can be obtained at all branches of the Reisebüro der DDR, and at international service stations, in the following values: $1.65, $3.35, and $6.45.

Electricity: East Germany operates on 220 volts, AC.

Embassy: In East Berlin, the offices of the U.S. Embassy are at Neustädtische Kirchstrasse 4–5, DDR-108 Berlin-Mitte (tel. 00372/220-27-41). Hours are 8:30am to 5:30pm Mon. to Fri. Canada has no representation in East Germany (in an emergency, you can telephone the Canadian Military Mission in West Berlin at 030/261-11-61). Great Britain Embassy is at Unter den Linden 32–34 (tel. 00372/220-24-31). Australia and New Zealand do not have representatives in East Germany.

Emergency numbers: Call the police at 110; an ambulance at 115. To report a fire, dial 112.

Holidays: Public holidays are as follows: January 1 (New Year's); Good Friday and Easter Sun.; May 1; October 7 (founding date of the DDR); and Christmas (a two-day holiday, December 25 and 26).

Hours of service: In general, the banks conduct business from 8am to 11:30am, excluding Sat. and Sun. Most museums are open from 10am to 6pm, in-

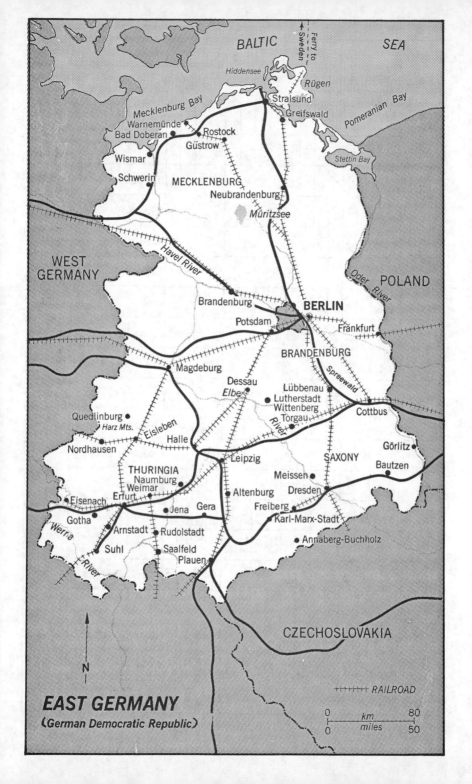

BALTIC   SEA

Ferry to Sweden

Hiddensee

Rügen

Stralsund

Greifswald

Pomeranian Bay

Mecklenburg Bay

Warnemünde

Bad Doberan

Rostock

Güstrow

Stettin Bay

Wismar

Schwerin

MECKLENBURG

Neubrandenburg

Müritzsee

WEST
GERMANY

Havel River

Oder River

POLAND

Brandenburg

BERLIN

Potsdam

Frankfurt

BRANDENBURG

Magdeburg

Dessau

Elbe

Lübbenau

Lutherstadt
Wittenberg

Spreewald

Quedlinburg

Harz Mts.

Eisleben

Halle

Torgau

River

Cottbus

Nordhausen

Leipzig

SAXONY

Görlitz

Bautzen

THURINGIA

Naumburg

Weimar

Meissen

Dresden

Altenburg

Eisenach

Erfurt

Jena

Gera

Freiberg

Gotha

Werra

Arnstadt

Rudolstadt

Suhl

Saalfeld

Plauen

Karl-Marx-Stadt

Annaberg-Buchholz

River

CZECHOSLOVAKIA

N

EAST GERMANY
⟨German Democratic Republic⟩

++++++ RAILROAD

0   km   80
0   miles   50

EAST GERMANY
Mileage Between Major Cities (in Miles)

Wittenberg	Weimar	Waren-Müritz	Suhl	Stralsund	Schwerin	Rostock	Potsdam	Neubrandenburg	Magdeburg	Leipzig	Karl-Marx-Stadt	Jena	Halle	Gera	Erfurt	Eisenach	Dresden	City
76	181	107	233	166	133	143	37	85	109	129	161	167	122	162	201	234	118	BERLIN
84	126	238	167	285	262	273	130	223	145	71	50	111	89	87	136	169		Dresden
164	50	304	46	378	329	339	202	302	128	120	127	67	120	187	39			Eisenach
130	17	270	41	244	295	306	168	268	106	86	93	34	87	53				Erfurt
91	43	231	85	306	257	269	130	229	110	43	47	29	48					Gera
50	61	190	119	265	215	226	89	189	55	22	71	53						Halle
96	14	236	65	311	261	272	135	234	102	53	68							Jena
87	83	247	125	329	272	282	145	267	126	49								Karl-Marx-Stadt
40	67	198	118	273	223	274	96	197	78									Leipzig
53	102	167	142	241	125	202	76	164										Magdeburg
145	249	27	300	63	88	72	102											Neubrandenburg
43	149	104	200	178	129	139												Potsdam
182	286	58	337	45	53													Rostock
171	275	61	237	102														Schwerin
221	325	68	376															Stralsund
162	48	302																Suhl
146	251																	Waren-Müritz
110																		Weimar
																		Wittenberg

cluding Sun. They are closed either Mon. or Tues. Restaurants stagger their hours, and most bars open at 9pm, closing at 4am. Shopping hours vary. In Berlin, shops are generally open Mon. to Fri. from 10am to 7pm, on Thurs. to 8pm. Outside Berlin, hours are 9am to 6pm. On Sat. morning, only large shops and department stores are open (closed Sun.).

Language: The official language, of course, is German, but English is widely understood in Interhotels and major restaurants.

Medical care: For a medical care emergency, inform the police or hospital directly. Expenses incurred have to be borne by the patient (unless special insurance has been taken out). For an emergency, go to the emergency room of the Rettungsamt Berlin, Marienburgerstrasse 41–46 (tel. 00372/282-05-61).

Pharmacy: Try Apotheke am Alexanderplatz, Hans-Beimler-Strasse 70–72 (tel. 00372/212-57-66). The emergency phone number is 160.

Telephone: The charge for local telephone calls is about 6¢. Coin boxes take 20-pfennig coins. You can't make a long-distance call from a pay phone. For that, you must go through your hotel switchboard.

Tips: Follow the Western custom of leaving at least 10%.

Toilets: They are found in major hotels, bars, restaurants, nightclubs, and public buildings such as museums (that is, most museums).

---

1. East Berlin

Even on a rushed visit to West Berlin, you should at least spend a half day in East Berlin, the cultural and political capital of East Germany. For it was here, prior to World War II, that the real cultural center of Berlin lay: the best museums, the finest churches, the most important boulevards. Of course the city you see today is not the exciting, lively city of prewar days, but it still has many attractions, especially its museums.

The old image of a war-torn East Berlin—ripped from the pages of John le Carré's *The Spy Who Came in from the Cold*—is now a cliché. In 45 years, much progress has been made. There are still many reminders of war, such as bullet-pocked buildings, but the blackened rubble of World War II for the most part has been long wiped away. Broad avenues radiate in several directions from the vast and impressive Alexanderplatz, leading to massive housing blocks built for workers.

Actually, East Berliners have accomplished a near miracle since their city was destroyed by the ravages of war in 1945. After the shooting died down, they found nothing but ruins of faded glory about them. With incredibly hard work, they have virtually eliminated poverty. They still don't have enough housing, but that is true virtually all over the world today.

East Berlin became the capital of the Deutsche Demokratische Republik in 1949. It is today a metropolis of some one million industrious people. Believe it or not, it was the dreaded Berlin Wall that stabilized East Berlin by stopping the massive flow of talent to the West, and insured the human energy needed to rebuild the devastated city.

But the wall is gone now, and East Berliners and West Berliners go back and forth across the border as in olden days. More restrictions apply, however, if you are a foreigner (that is, a non–West German passport holder).

CROSSING THE BORDER

A border-crossing point for foreigners can be reached on West Berlin's U-Bahn: Take the train from the Zoologischer Garten station in the direction of Schlesisches Tor. At that station, board the train for Kochstrasse, which is only one stop away toward Tegel. This is the site of the former famous "Checkpoint Charlie."

All you need to take with you is your passport, a few marks, and, if you're driving, your "Green Card." If all goes well, you should be through the Customs inspection within a few minutes. Citizens of the U.S., Canada, and Australia need a visa only if they plan to spend a night in the DDR. Visas are issued free. (Note that visas are issued at Bahnhof Friedrichstrasse and Heinrich-Heine-Strasse but not at Friedrichstrasse-Zimmerstrasse.)

Visitors can also travel to East Berlin on the S-Bahn train. The Friedrichstrasse checkpoint in East Berlin may be reached by taking the West Berlin U-Bahn line (marked "Tegel-Alt-Mariendorf–6") or by traveling the Nordsüdbahn S-Bahn line 2, going between the Frohnan and Lichtenrade stations. This checkpoint can also be reached by using the S-Bahn line 3. You start from S-Bahn station Zoo, going directly to Friedrichstrasse.

Although you must use the same border-crossing point for entering and leaving East Berlin, you are not restricted from choosing which means of public transport you wish to use once you have passed through the checkpoint returning to West Berlin.

If you want to travel to East Berlin by Berlin Transport Authority (BRG), you must buy a special ticket at the ticket window in West Berlin, paying 2.70 DM ($1.60) for a one-way fare. Also, if you take the S-Bahn or U-Bahn back to West Berlin, before entering the checkpoint area at the Friedrichstrasse, be sure to go to the S-Bahn ticket window in the station to buy the return ticket to West Berlin. You can also wait until you've passed through the border checkpoint to buy your ticket. Another way is to use a *Sammelkarte,* by which the price of a single ride is reduced to 2.50 DM ($1.50). You can use both tickets (bought in West Berlin) as a return ticket if the total ride is not longer than two hours.

When you leave the train at the Friedrichstrasse going into East Berlin, follow the signs to the *Grenzübergangstelle* (border-crossing point). Once there, follow the signs saying *Bürger anderer Staaten* (citizens from other countries).

All that is necessary when you desire to enter East Berlin on a one-day visit is to show your passport to the border officer in the booth when you are in the line.

Once in East Berlin, the Friedrichstrasse station is only a block from Unter den Linden. Fares on the S-Bahn, buses, or streetcars begin at the equivalent of 6¢ in East Berlin if you confine your visits to the area. Tickets issued by one system are valid on the other systems as well. A one-day tourist card good for unlimited S-Bahn travel within East Berlin costs only 35¢, and is also available for all public transit in East Berlin for only 65¢. *Warning:* These incredibly low, state-subsidized fares may not last the lifetime of this edition. Higher transportation costs are inevitable in East Berlin.

To return to West Berlin, go back to the station on Friedrichstrasse. Proceed to the customs offices, which are in a station annex across from the taxi stand. Present your passport and card at the entrance marked "Entrance for Foreigners." *Note:* These conditions and restrictions may change. Check before you travel.

ORIENTATION

The Brandenburg Gate, which is technically over the border in West Berlin, is a major landmark in East Berlin. It marks the end of the city's most celebrated street, Unter den Linden (more about this much-traveled Strasse later). This famous street, the heart of historic old Berlin, runs from west to east, cutting a path through the city. Along the way, it passes another major artery of East Berlin, Friedrichstrasse. If you continue south on this street, you'll reach the former location of Checkpoint Charlie. Friedrichstrasse is also the location of the S-Bahn (the surface rail) and the U-Bahn (underground, or subway) stations.

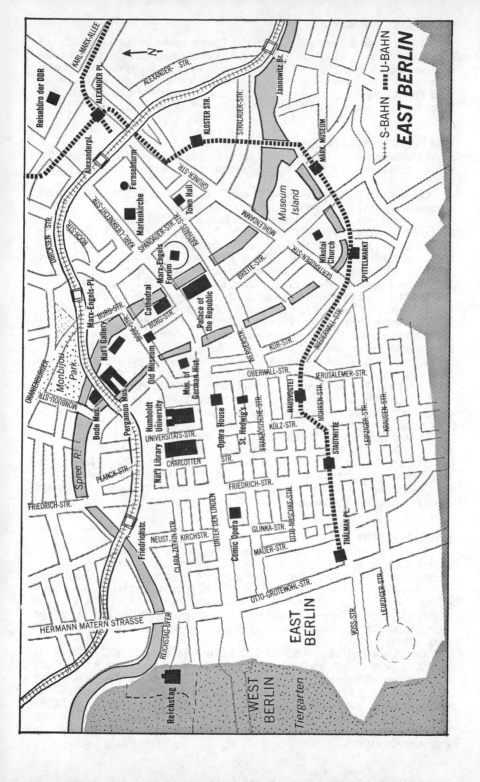

EAST BERLIN

+++ S-BAHN   ■■■ U-BAHN

KARL-MARX-ALLEE

Reisebüro der DDR

ALEXANDER- STR.

ALEXANDERPL.

Alexanderpl.

Fernsehturm

Marienkirche

KLOSTER STR.

STRALAUER-STR.

Jannowitz. Br.

Town Hall

MÄRK. MUSEUM

KARL-LIEBKNECHT-STR.

SPANDAUER-STR.

RATHAUS-STR.

GRÜNER-STR.

Museum Island

MÜHLENDAMM

Nikolai Church

DIRCKSEN-STR.

RÜCH-STR.

Marx-Engels Forum

SPITTELMARKT

GERTRAUDEN-STR.

Cathedral

BREITE-STR.

BURG-STR.

Marx-Engels-Pl.

BÖDE-STR.

Palace of the Republic

BURG-STR.

Nat'l Gallery

Old Museum

Mus. of German Hist.

WERDERSTR.

KUR-STR.

NIEDERWALL-STR.

ORANIENBURGER

Monbijou Park

Pergamon Mus.

Bode Mus.

OBERWALL-STR.

JERUSALEMER-STR.

Humboldt University

Opera House

HAUSVOGTEI

MONBIJOU-STR.

UNIVERSITÄTS-STR.

St. Hedwig's

MÖHREN-STR.

LEIPZIGER-STR.

KRAUSEN-STR.

FRANZÖSISCHE-STR.

Spree R.

PLANCK-STR.

Nat'l Library

CHARLOTTEN

KÜLZ-STR.

STADTMITTE

FRIEDRICH-STR.

STR.

FRIEDRICH-STR.

Friedrichstr.

CLARA-ZETKIN-STR.

KIRCHSTR.

NEUST.

UNTER-DEN-LINDEN

Comic Opera

GLINKA-STR.

OTTO-NUSCHKE-STR.

THÄLMAN PL.

MAUER-STR.

HERMANN MATERN STRASSE

REICHSTAG-UFER

OTTO-GROTEWOHL-STR.

EAST BERLIN

VOSS-STR.

LEIPZIGER-STR.

Reichstag

WEST BERLIN

Tiergarten

Continue walking east along Unter den Linden until you reach Marx-Engels-Platz. On the east of this square is the Palast der Republik, which is filled with restaurants and cafés, and on the north Museum Insel, a "museum island" in the Spree. Unter den Linden continues east (except now it becomes Karl-Liebknecht-Strasse) until it reaches the Alexanderplatz. In the center of this square you can take an elevator up the Funkturm, or television tower, for a panoramic view.

Fast Facts for East Berlin

Besides the points of information pertaining to the entire DDR given in the introduction to this chapter, there are some items that apply more specifically to East Berlin.

Credit cards: American Express, MasterCard, VISA, and Diners Club cards are accepted at a growing number of locations in East Berlin.

Currency exchange: The lowest commissions for cashing traveler's checks are at the **Staatsbank der DDR** (State Bank of the DDR). The branches at the Friedrichstrasse and Ostbahnhof stations are open around the clock daily. Well-known traveler's checks, such as American Express, VISA, and Thomas Cook, are accepted without hassles (not-so-well-known checks may encounter some difficulties). At the Staatsbank, checks can be turned into DM or into U.S. dollars.

Events: A monthly guide to events in East Berlin is available at the Information Center in the TV tower and at many newsstands. Appropriately enough, it's called *Wohin in Berlin* (What's Going On in Berlin). You must be prepared to accept the fact that many museums, restaurants, and other places can be closed without prior notice on "technical grounds." The monthly *Wohin in Berlin* is useful in this regard.

Information: The Information Bureau is called **Informationszenturm am Fernsehturm,** and it's beneath the Television Tower on Alexanderplatz (tel. 00372/212-46-75). It's open Mon. from 1 to 6pm, Tues. to Fri. from 8am to 6pm, and on Sat. and Sun. from 10am to 6pm. In the summer months the staff also opens an information center near the Bahnhof on Friedrichstrasse at the crossing point. This latter one might be even more convenient.

Post office: Postamt Berlin 17, Strasse der Pariser Kommune 8–10 (tel. 00372/430-55-40), Berlin 1017, in the Hauptbahnhof, is open 24 hours a day.

Taxis: If you dial 229-27-17, one will come to you. Otherwise, you can try your luck in hailing one on the street, but they are not as plentiful as one wishes.

Telephones: To call East Berlin from West Berlin, you must use the combined country-city area code, 00372, as from any other country.

WHERE TO STAY

Because there is so much to see in East Berlin, you may want to spend more than a day visiting. If so, you can make arrangements with travel bureaus or the East German tourist office for a proper visa for overnight stopovers. What follows is a rundown of the major hotels of East Berlin. Hotel prices are quoted in U.S. dollars or West German marks, depending on how a particular establishment chooses to advertise its international rates. *Warning:* Because of changes in the currency and the changing political situation there could easily be a significant variance in these prices during the life of this edition.

Grand Hotel, Friedrichstrasse 158, DDR-1086 Berlin (tel. 00372/2-09-20). If the 1930s movie *Grand Hotel,* starring Greta Garbo, were made today, it would have to be set here. Many hotels call themselves grand. This one really is—in fact, not only is it the finest hotel in Eastern Europe, but many say there is nothing in West Germany to equal it. The finishing touches were applied in 1987, just in time for the city's 750th anniversary. Best of all, it's convenient for pedestrian crossing through Checkpoint Charlie. It's also a good location from which to beat a hasty retreat before your visa expires.

Replacing an old and famous landmark, which ended as war rubble, the Grand is today the lavish flagship of the state-owned Interhotel chain. Constructed by a Japanese company at the reported cost of $120 million, the hotel blends belle-époque features with contemporary styling. Its rooms rise, atrium style, above an octagonal lobby whose setting is capped with a lavender-and-pink skylight of intricately crafted stained glass. No one should visit without exploring the public rooms lying at the top of a monumental staircase one flight above lobby level. There's the convivial Peacock Bar (Western currency only), whose backdrop is an oversize oval-shaped window crafted in the form of a peacock. Even more impressive is the Club Diana, a faithful copy of the great room of a Teutonic hunting lodge, with dozens of trophies, a blazing fireplace, Oriental carpets, a coffered and paneled ceiling, and an ornate organ performing daily concerts in the afternoon.

The hotel promises "VIP treatment for everyone," and means it. They arrange visas and can provide chauffeured cars for crossing the border. Rooms come in a wide range of styles, from beautifully appointed standard singles and doubles all the way up to the Schinkel Suite, named to honor the famed early-19th-century architect. In all, there are 350 rooms, each with air conditioning, minibar, and private bath. Even the bed linens are soft, with down pillows and comforters. Other amenities include chrome fixtures, phones, terry-cloth robes, and fresh flowers. Prices are the highest of any hotel in the DDR: 250 DM ($148.45) to 300 DM ($178.15) daily for a single and from 350 DM ($207.85) for a double, the latter a junior suite. Prices include breakfast, plus the use of the fitness club and a multistory car park. Guests can avail themselves of 24-hour room service, patronize the most deluxe hairdressing salon (for both women and men) in East Berlin, and enjoy an impressive marble swimming pool, with its saunas and solarium. Three of the hotel's six restaurants are so exceptional that they'll be reviewed separately.

Metropol, Friedrichstrasse 150-153, DDR-1086 Berlin (tel. 00372/2-20-40), was built with Swedish help and completed in 1977. It lies only a short walk from the Friedrichstrasse station and border checkpoint, and close to Unter den Linden. Many businesspeople choose to stay here because of its location opposite the International Trade Center in Friedrichstrasse. There are 308 units: singles, doubles, apartments, and suites. Many amenities are provided, including refrigerators, direct-dial phones, TVs, and minibars, along with private baths and toilets. A single costs from 200 DM ($118.75) daily, a double from 270 DM ($160.35). The hotel also has a fitness center, with a swimming pool, saunas (unlike in West Germany, the sexes are segregated), solarium, massage service, and bar. There is a Panorama Sauna on the 12th floor, with a terrace attached. The Metropol Club on the premises offers dancing and entertainment. The hotel has good food in its specialty or grill restaurants.

Palasthotel, Karl-Liebknecht-Strasse 5, DDR-1020 Berlin (tel. 00372/24-10), completed in 1979, opposite the Berlin Cathedral, was built in cooperation with Swedish firms. The location is near the Palace of the Republic and conveniently near the S-Bahnhof Marx-Engels-Platz and Museum Island. It offers 585 fully air-conditioned rooms and apartments, with all the modern conveniences, including TVs, radios, direct-dial phones, alarm clocks, private baths, and refrigerators with minibars. A single room costs from 200 DM ($118.75) daily, and a double goes for 270 DM ($160.35). The hotel has eight eating places. You might choose the Märkisches Restaurant, serving international cuisine and specialties of the Mark Brandenburg region; Rôti d'Or, where they offer elegance and French specialties; or Jade, the Asian restaurant. It's the Domklause for home cooking and top-quality beer, served on the banks of the Spree River. Nante-Eck is a Berlin-style pub where you can enjoy good food, good beer, and pub games. For fast service, the Quick lets you serve yourself, and the Grill gives you a view of the boulevard while you eat. At the Café am Palast, a coffeehouse where you can have specialties from the hotel's pâtisserie, musical entertainment is provided, and you can select an inside table or one on the terrace in summer. Three bars include the Sinusbar, a nightclub; the

Kaminbar, adjoining the hotel foyer; and the Pianobar, where you have cocktails to the tune of subdued piano music.

The hotel also has a fitness center with a swimming pool, sauna, solarium, massage service, and a bowling alley. On-site services include a rent-a-car service, a car park, an Interflug city office, an office of the Reisebüro der DDR, a central box office, a hairdressing salon, a souvenir shop, and an Intershop.

Interhotel Unter den Linden, Unter den Linden 14, DDR-1080 Berlin (tel. 00372/22-003-11), stands on the most famous street of Berlin, within walking distance of the S-Bahn station. Handy for visiting the major museums of the capital, it is impersonally modern, containing 301 generously proportioned bedrooms, all with private baths and soft beds. The rate for a single is 115 DM ($68.30) to 145 DM ($86.10) daily; for a double, 160 DM ($95) to 190 DM ($112.80). In the lounge is the Hallenbar and the Hallencafé, open daily from 10am to 3am, where you can order international drinks. The pastries are good. The main restaurant, open until midnight, features international dishes.

In the Environs

Hotel Müggelsee, DDR-1170 Berlin (tel. 00372/65-21-00), lies within an architectural lakeside complex called Müggelseeperle, 15½ miles northeast of Hauptstadt Berlin. You can rent a boat, which is one of the main reasons for staying here, and go sailing on the Müggelsee, Berlin's largest lake. Within 20 minutes by car, you can reach the heart of monumental Berlin, including Museum Island, Unter den Linden, and Alexanderplatz. You can also go by taxi or S-Bahn. If you take the latter, go as far as Köpenick station and from there take bus A-27 in the direction of Muffelheim. The modern hotel is streamlined and efficient, with tables placed outside under umbrellas in fair weather.

Accommodations are attractively furnished and comfortable, with 166 units for rent, costing $97 daily for a single and $134 based on double occupancy. Each unit is equipped with phone, radio, color TV, refrigerator, and private bath. Types of rooms range from studio singles to twin-bedded units to "tourist rooms" and apartments. The hotel is known for its food, served in a number of restaurants. In addition to the main dining room, the Jagdkeller in the basement draws the more discerning diner with its large grill, where chefs prepare meats to order. There's even a Clubnachtbar for late night drinking. Health facilities include a sauna, solarium, massage, and cosmetic treatment. This sports-minded lakeside hotel also offers tennis, horseback riding, surfing, and walks through the surrounding forest.

WHERE TO DINE

East Berlin may represent your introduction to the cooking of East Germany. Meals are hearty and heavy for the most part. Major hotels and restaurants offer an international cuisine, but more and more restaurants feature typically Berliner cooking. Even the fancy Grand Hotel reserves one section of its many menus for Berliner specialties. These include Eisbein (pickled knuckle of pork with Sauerkraut), Kasseler Rippenspeer (spare ribs), Bockwurst (sausage), and Kartoffelpuffer (potato fritter).

Venison, wildfowl, and wild boar appear occasionally, as do carp and trout, along with an infinite variety of sausages and deli-type cold cuts. Each of these dishes is accompanied by the national drink, beer. Wines are served in better restaurants. Ever had Bulgarian wine? You are likely to in East Berlin. No doubt in the future more restaurants will serve the expensive West German wines.

The Top Restaurants

Le Grand Restaurant Silhouette, Grand Hotel, Friedrichstrasse 158 (tel. 00372/2-09-20). By any critic's standards, this posh restaurant is the finest in Eastern Europe. It definitely is the place to go in Berlin if you can afford it. To reach it, take an elevator in the lobby of this previously recommended hotel to the seventh floor. There you'll encounter a maroon-and-white decor with sculpted plaster ceilings, bronze statues, and sinuously paneled window moldings to mask the room's modern construction.

An attentive staff will propose such menu selections as a tempting offering of hors d'oeuvres, including freshly smoked fish straight from the hotel's ovens, thinly sliced salmon from the Baltic, and the hotel's special terrine (made with pike-perch, trout, and smoked eel, softened with a chive mousse). For your soup selection, the choice might be a pheasant pot-au-feu or double duck broth. Main dishes include stewed venison in juniper cream sauce, medallions of veal with lobster slices and oysters, and sliced knuckle of veal au gratin. Desserts are sumptuous, including an ice soufflé with tropical fruits. Meals cost about $60 and up.

The wine list, with some 300 labels, is the most impressive in the country. In addition to an international array, some vintages are from the DDR, made from grapes grown in little vineyards along the Saale and Elbe rivers. Adding to your enjoyment are fine crystal and porcelain, excellent formal service, and both classic and cuisine moderne preparation of dishes. After 10pm, there is live dance music emanating from a piano and occasionally from a small group of stringed instruments as well. Full meals are served daily from 12:30 to 4pm and 6pm to midnight, although the restaurant remains open until 3am. Only hard currency is accepted.

Restaurant Coelln, Grand Hotel, Friedrichstrasse 158 (tel. 00372/2-09-20), is named after the neighborhood in which it sits. (Around 1150, Coelln and Berlin were considered sister towns on both banks of the Spree River.) This is the gracious main dining room of this previously recommended deluxe hotel, a member of that stellar grouping "The Leading Hotels of the World." Accepting only hard currency, the restaurant is open without interruption from 6am to midnight. To reach it, ascend to the second floor. Beneath neobaroque ceilings of sculpted plaster, amid opulently upholstered banquettes and a floral design of taste and beauty, you can order meals priced from $40.

Large windows overlook the street, and white is the dominant shade, supplemented by pastel tones in the furniture, draperies, and carpeting. Valuable china and silver on white damask and Plauen lace table linen give an air of elegance. You can begin here at breakfast and continue through the day, capping the evening with a late candlelight supper served to the sound of soft piano music. The diet-conscious will gravitate to the "bio-corner." Both Berlin specialties and international dishes are offered, enhanced by suggestions from the sommeliers who have wines from the DDR and abroad. Menus are subject to seasonal changes, but could include, for hors d'oeuvres, sautéed calves' brains or Beluga caviar. You might start with seafood soup or a game potage with wild mushrooms, followed by a main dish such as halibut in orange mousse, young pheasant cutlet on wine cabbage, haunch of wild boar braised in burgundy, or medallions of filet of veal in Calvados. An international selection of dishes from all parts of the world is also offered, including lobster Newburg from North America. One part of the menu is reserved strictly for old Berliner cuisine, including the famous Löffelerbsen (yellow split pea soup) and salt knuckle of pork with Sauerkraut. Desserts are elegant and lavish.

Rôti d'Or, Palasthotel, Karl-Liebknecht-Strasse 5 (tel. 00372/24-10), is a restaurant worthy of its international standing, offering refined cuisine in this five-star hotel. The decor of the restaurant, outfitted in shades of black, white, and gold, is a formalized version of art deco. The aproned and jacketed waiters evoke the old days of 1920s Berlin. Glistening silver trolleys go by laden with freshly baked pastries and succulent roasts. Many tables are intimately nestled into curved alcoves, separated one from another with peek-a-boo panels of frosted glass. Open from noon to midnight daily, the restaurant features a 24-page wine list, said to be among the finest in the DDR, complete with vintages from the Atlantic to the Bosphorus. Appetizers and soups include such delights as game ham freshly smoked on the premises or else a terrine of truffled goose liver from Brive. Both freshwater and saltwater fish appear on the menu, including pike-perch from the Havel River. Try the roast cut of veni-son leg or saddle of lamb flavored with thyme. The beef dishes are especially well prepared. For all this elegant service and fine cuisine, you'll pay from $35.

Ganymed, Schiffbauerdamm 5 (tel. 00372/282-95-40), is one of the gourmet temples of the DDR. Lying on the Spree, which runs into West Berlin, in the vicinity of the checkpoint station at Friedrichstrasse, it serves an international cuisine with flair. Rumor has it that back in the 1920s this was the most elegant bordello in Ber-lin, but that memory has certainly been erased. Once Bertolt Brecht, accompanied by Helene Weigel, was a frequent guest here, but nowadays the diners are more likely the cast from one of the productions at the Theater am Schiffbauerdamm in the vicinity. In this plush, genteel environment, you can enjoy such excellently prepared dishes as pork steak Singapore and duck with red cabbage. Your tab, which with wine might come to $40 per head, will be among the highest you'll pay in the entire coun-try. Open Mon. from 5pm to 1am and Tues. to Sun. from 11am to 1am.

Ermeler Haus, Märkisches Ufer 10 (tel. 00372/275-51-03), is a converted 16th-century town house where guests can dine in rococo splendor if they're willing to pay $30 or more, which is considered expensive by East Berlin standards. It's as close as you can come in the capital to dining in an old-world manner. The waiters wear tails. Once the private home of a tobacco merchant, it stands beside a canal on Fischerinsel. Hours are daily from 11am to midnight. The economical section is the beerhall in the cellar. But well-dressed Berliners prefer dancing in the wine restau-rant on Fri. and Sat. from 7pm to midnight. There's an elegant café, and an outdoor terrace as well. However, the wine restaurant is preferred, with its cherubic ceilings and gilt moldings. You might try, for example, rack of venison with a pepper sauce, scallops in a butter sauce, or stuffed filet of beef with oysters.

Spezialitätenrestaurant, Hotel Metropol, Friedrichstrasse 150-153 (tel. 00372/2-20-40), is cosmopolitan, attracting everybody from Japanese industrial-ists to the Western expense-account circuit. They are drawn to the savory viands, which depend on fresh ingredients of better quality than those found in most East Berlin dining rooms. The setting is on the lobby level of this deluxe hotel, an elegant decor with dark modern paneling and polished stone. You might begin with one of the good-tasting soups such as purée of potato garnished with smoked eel. The chef specializes in meats from the charcoal grill, including veal steak Old Viennese style or pepper steak flambéed at the table. Another specialty is smoked sturgeon stuffed with shredded nuts. You can also order, on occasion, venison, roebuck, and wild boar with berries from the woods. For two or more persons, the chef recommends filet of pork in cream sauce flavored with vodka. Beef Stroganoff is prepared at the table. Meals, served daily from 11am to midnight, cost from $22 per person. Reser-vations are essential.

Regional Restaurants

Goldene Gans, Grand Hotel, Friedrichstrasse 158 (tel. 00372/2-09-20), is the "Golden Goose" of this previously recommended deluxe hotel, the greatest in the DDR. In deliberate contrast to the beaux arts glamor of the hotel containing it, this rustic and gemütlich Stube lies one flight above the lobby level of the Grand. It has a wooden ceiling, colorfully embroidered napery, and an open-to-view kitchen. Cuisine is based on Thüringian recipes vividly evocative of old Germany. Although cholesterol counters shun it, the special appetizer of the kitchen (even though it doesn't appear on the menu) is goose fat with mixed pickles and freshly baked rolls. Talk about the good old days. The restaurant's namesake, goose, appears in three different preparations that are very Thüringian and very much of a delicacy here. A host of other regional dishes are also offered. Full meals cost from $25, and must be paid for in Western currency only. Service is daily without interruption from 11am to midnight.

Märkisches Restaurant, Palasthotel, Karl-Liebknecht-Strasse 5 (tel. 00372/24-10), is considered the best place in the city to go for authentic German cookery, including many regional dishes. You get huge portions of food, very farmer's style, served in refined surroundings. The menu reads a lot like a list of recipes cherished by old German grandmothers. You can make your selection while taking in the decor, which includes thousands of the same orange-red bricks that went to build Berlin in the 19th century. The chef's specialties are marinated and braised beef, larded veal roast, glazed knuckle of pork housewife style, salt brisket of beef, and smoked pork steak Kassel style. "From the pan" comes filet of saddle of rabbit, or else you might select tournedos Gypsy style. Lamb specialties from the Schorfheide region include braised leg of lamb wrapped in white cabbage. A few fish dishes, including trout miller style, are also served. Game is also featured, including pheasant with Sauerkraut and roast venison. The availability of many dishes might change depending on the season. Set behind a red-and-white marquee on the lobby level of this previously recommended hotel, the restaurant serves meals costing from $28 daily from noon to midnight.

Other Restaurants

Fernsehturm, Alexanderplatz (tel. 00372/21-042-32), is housed in the Television Tower. If you're visiting just for the view and coffee, see other attractions, under "The Sights." For more serious dining, there is the main restaurant, featuring such regional specialties as herring filets in an apple cream sauce, pork cutlets with ham and cheese, and a fish platter. Adjoining it is a Tagescafé where you can order coffee, cakes, and ice cream. On the ground level is a self-service restaurant. Featured is a Berliner Hackepeter, a generous plate of chopped meat with mix-it-yourself condiments, topped by an egg; you can also order pea soup with Bockwurst, a typical dish of pigs' trotters with Sauerkraut and potato salad. Meals cost from $12. Young Berliners come here for evening dancing to contemporary music. The Tele-Café, which is on the top of the tower (more about this later), is open daily from 8am to 11pm. The main restaurant serves daily from 10am to midnight. Its adjoining café is open Sun. to Thurs. from 10am to 10pm; Fri. and Sat. from 10am to 1am. The self-service restaurant on the ground level is open from 6am to midnight.

Bierschänke-Weinschänke, In der Gerichtsklause, Poststrasse 28 (tel. 00372/21-71-32-45), offers a two-in-one choice of dining spots, both easily accessible if you're walking through the reconstructed Nicholas area (see "The Sights"). Serving from 10am to midnight daily, the Bierschänke is an elegant beer tavern, not unlike the nave of a medieval church. Guests often share tables under vaulted ceilings, the room lit by huge Gothic windows. Food is in the typical beerhall style, including old Berliner soup, a roulade of pork with Sauerkraut, herring Hausfrau style, and, to top it off, wine by the glass (often imported from Hungary or Rumania). The Weinschänke, featuring similar food, is a wine restaurant one floor above street level. It serves daily from 5pm to 1am. Both offer a set menu for $14. On the top landing is a pizza joint popular with young East Berliners.

Palast der Republik, Marx-Engels-Platz (tel. 00372/238-23-64), is a modern building erected on the site of the royal palace of the Prussian heyday. The Hohenzollerns lived here from the mid-15th century until the closing days of World War I. Today, in marked contrast, among other things it's the headquarters of the Parliament of the DDR.

The three major restaurants are on the second floor. The walls of the Palastrestaurant are adorned with a decorative design made of Dresden china, and the Lindenrestaurant and the Spreerestaurant have inlaid walnut parquetry. Multicolored original Gobelin tapestries give these restaurants a warm, inviting atmosphere. The Lindenrestaurant is open from 11am to midnight; closed Wed. The Palastrestaurant is open from 11am to midnight; closed Tues. The Spreerestaurant is open from 11am to midnight; closed Mon. Meals in any of these places cost from $15 per person. Other restaurants in the complex are three small restaurants on the first floor. The Espresso, with daily hours of 10am to midnight, is decorated in warm shades of brown and opens onto Marx-Engels-Platz. The

Milchbar (milk bar), open daily from 10am to midnight, overlooks the Spree River. The Mokkabar, open daily from 10am to midnight, is in the foyer.

The area lying directly alongside the Spree has a special charm. From a terrace paved with granite slabs, near the Jugendtreff and Spree bowling alley, you come to two special restaurants with an intimate atmosphere. These include the Weinstube, open daily from 5:30pm to midnight, which is decorated in a motif of Berlin classicism. It offers an extensive assortment of wines as well as choice menus. A rustic Bierstube, open daily from 10am to midnight, is decorated in a Berlin baroque style and offers special beers and typical Berliner fare. The other restaurants, aside from a Foyer Bar, are reserved mainly for buffets during performances in the Great Hall.

Ratskeller, in the basement of the Rathaus on Rathausstrasse (tel. 00372/212-52-01), near the Television Tower, offers a more traditional German atmosphere, replete with heavy red bricks, stained glass, and dark-wood beams. You'll find hearty fare at a good price: about $10 for a big meal in the Bierstube, which has a traditional German atmosphere. On the opposite side of the building is the Weinstube, with a completely different and more formal setting. It's quieter, with soft recorded music. The waiters are in uniform, and the service is more courteous. The food here is excellent. For the same price you can enjoy such dishes as Ukrainian soup, rumpsteak Hungarian style with potatoes, your selection from the salad bar, and if you wish, a bottle of good Hungarian wine. The hours are 9am to midnight daily.

Klubgaststätte an der Brannernheide, Köthenerstrasse 3 (tel. 00372/332-10-82), is where the East Berliner seeking a night of inexpensive fun heads for festive times. The establishment contains both a restaurant and a less expensive and less formal Bierstube. The ambience is one of paneled walls interrupted with ceramic tiles showing the plant and animal life of an idealized landscape. You get hearty, robust fare here, with meals costing from $15. The restaurant is open daily from 11am to midnight, whereas the Bierstube serves only from 5pm to midnight. Also on the premises is a Nachtbar, which sponsors dance music and a minicabaret show, and serves free-flowing Sekt, wine, and Western-style mixed drinks. The night bar is open Sun. to Thurs. from 8pm to 2am; Fri. and Sat. from 8pm to 4am. Thurs. there is a Berlin Ball; on Sat. the music is live.

Klubgaststätte zum Feldrain, Feidberger Ring 5 (tel. 00372/548-84-14), is paneled in light grain wood and accented with ceramic tiles. This inexpensive mecca for food and drink combines a rather formal restaurant, seating 82, with a less formal Bierstube, holding 45. In summer, however, most guests opt for a place on an outdoor terrace, where 200 imbibers can be seated amid flowers and shrubbery. Food is predictably but appropriately traditional, featuring homemade breads with lots of grainy goodness and such typical plates as filet of herring. An array of grilled meats is prepared in the traditional Berliner style. Meals cost from $15, and you can order both alcoholic and alcohol-free drinks, as well as afternoon coffee and pastries. Hours for the restaurant are 11am to midnight daily, whereas the Bierstube is open Mon. to Fri. only from 4pm to midnight; Sat. and Sun. from 10am to midnight. The subway stop is Kaulsdorf.

Gaststätte Lucullus, Weichselstrasse 35 (tel. 00372/589-23-65), stands at the corner of Frankfurter Allee and Weichselstrasse. Increasingly popular, it caters mainly to local people, often young ones, who gravitate to its inexpensive food and its decor (lots of wood and mirrors). Specialties include fare found in old-fashioned Berliner restaurants, with a scattering of international dishes. Meals cost from $15. In summer the usual capacity (72 seats) is greatly expanded with the use of an outdoor terrace. The restaurant is open daily from 11am to 11pm; Sat. until 1am. Adjacent to the restaurant are a pizzeria and bar.

Want a really good East German Bierstube? Try **Wernesgrüner Bierstuben,** Karl-Liebknecht-Strasse 11 (tel. 00372/282-42-68), overlooking Alexanderplatz. Forget about cuisine moderne here. What you get is typical home-style Berliner cookery. That means knuckle of pork with pickled cabbage, thick pea soups, potato pancakes, various types of smoked Wurst, and an occasional Sauerbraten with dumplings. Prices are cheap. You might get away for about $10 unless you have a lot to drink. The place is open daily from noon to midnight, and reservations aren't necessary.

Zur Letzen Instanz, Waisenstrasse 14-16 (tel. 00372/212-55-28), is reputedly Berlin's oldest restaurant, dating from 1525. In its day it was frequented by everybody from Napoleon to Beethoven, and prisoners used to stop off here for one last beer before going to jail. It is contained within two floors of a baroque building whose facade is ornamented with a row of stone bas-reliefs of medieval faces. The location, just outside the crumbling brick wall that once ringed medieval Berlin, is not far from the historic core of the Nikolai kirche. You push open double doors to reach a series of small, woodsy rooms, one with a bar and ceramic *Kachelofen* (stove). At the back a circular staircase leads to another series of rooms, where every evening at 6, only food and wine (no beer) are served. On both floors you can select from a limited and old-fashioned menu of Berlin staples, including Eisbein (haunch of boiled pork garnished with Sauerkraut); you might begin with Gulasch soup. Meals cost from $8. The restaurant is open Mon. from 4pm to midnight; Tues. to Sat. from 11am to midnight; Sun. from 11am to 4pm.

Turmstuben, Französischen Dom, Platz der Akademie 5 (tel. 00372/229-34-63). In the more southerly of this meticulously rebuilt square's twin domes is a restaurant tucked away under the angles of its roofline. It lies midway up the circular stone staircase of the Französischen Dom. Open daily from 10am to midnight, with a cozy ambience of chunky wooden tables placed in recessed alcoves, it serves a limited menu of uncomplicated food that the Berliners refer to as kleine Gerichte (snacks). Despite its name, many visitors find the portions adequate for a satisfying lunch or supper. You might begin with a mushroom cocktail or a portion of oxtail soup, followed by rumpsteak garnished with fruit. There is a respectable wine list. Meals cost from $8. Before leaving, try for a promenade around the observation platform. Admission to the platform is free daily from 10am to 6pm.

International Restaurants

Jade Restaurant, Palasthotel, Karl-Liebknecht-Strasse 5 (tel. 00372/24-10), is one of the finest Asian restaurants in the DDR. Designed to mimic the best aesthetics of the Far East, this unusual restaurant serves Asian dishes amid bamboo chairs and restful murals—and within an impressive view of the baroque dome of the Berlin Cathedral. To enter, you cross a Japanese-style footbridge and pass a glassed-in garden blossoming from sandy soil. This taste of the Far East lies on the lobby level of this previously recommended hotel. Full meals, costing from $25, are served daily from noon to midnight. The featured specialties are designed only for four persons and include (by advance order only) Indonesian rice dishes and a seafood delight with fish from both the sea and freshwater rivers. Typical dishes include lamb Madras style and duck with ginger and bamboo shoots. Try also slices of fish deep-fried and flavored with sesame. Hours are 11am to midnight daily.

Fioretto, Oberspreestrasse 176 (tel. 00372/657-26-05), is proud of its status as the first Italian restaurant in East Berlin. This tastefully decorated enclave of Mediterranean flavor has done a thriving business as much for its curiosity value as for its cuisine. Local wits have applauded the chefs for improvising last-minute changes whenever important ingredients might not be available. The menu might change by the time of your arrival, but count on Roman-style involtini, seafood salad, and tagliatelle alla bolognese along with several other Italian specialties. Doris Burneleit directs the place with flair, and offers meals only at dinner. Meals cost about $25, most à la carte dishes start at $18. Service is from 7pm to midnight; closed Mon. The restaurant is also closed in June.

Restaurant Moskau, Karl-Marx-Allee 34 (tel. 00372/279-28-69), is a restaurant and café devoted to Russian cuisine. Specialties include a Kiever cutlet, chicken Tabaka, and Bauernteller (a Russian farmer's dish). A meal will cost from $15. Of course, you can order Russian vodka, even Russian champagne (listed as SU-Sekt).

The restaurant is open Mon. to Fri. from 11am to 11pm. A coffee bar, Mokkabar, is on the premises. There are also a Tanzcafé, open from 3pm to midnight, and a Nachtbar, serving from 9pm to 4am. On certain nights of the week, shows are presented.

Weinstube Morava, Rathausstrasse 5 (tel. 00372/210-92-31), is one of eight restaurants in the Gaststättenkomplex Rathauspassagen. It offers a host of Czech dishes in a rustic restaurant and a separate salon opposite the Neptune fountains in front of the tall Television Tower. In summer, tables are set up on the terrace. The specialty here is a filling grill-plate Morava. In addition, you can order typical Czech cuisine, as well as wine and beer from Czechoslovakia. The average tab is about $15. The restaurant is open Sun. to Thurs. from 11am to midnight; Fri. and Sat. from 11am to 1am.

Budapest, Karl-Marx-Allee 91 (tel. 00372/436-21-89), is another leading national restaurant. Offering both a restaurant and Keller, plus a Kleine Bar, it presents the outstanding cuisine of Hungary. However, the dishes lose something in translation from Budapest. The chicken paprika is generally good, and goulash is invariably offered. Prices range from $10 to $15. The restaurant is open daily from 11am to midnight.

Französischer Hof, Otto-Nuschke-Strasse 56 (tel. 00372/229-39-69), a French restaurant, opened its art nouveau doors in 1989. It fills two floors connected by a graceful belle-époque staircase, evoking a turn-of-the-century Parisian bistro. Dishes might include cold fish canapés, ox steak with garlic, and a flambéed filet Stroganoff with almond-studded dumplings. A meal costs from $20. The restaurant is open from 11am to midnight; closed the first Mon. of every month. On the restaurant's upper floor is a disco, open from 7pm to 2am. Admission is free, with drinks costing from $3.50.

The Café Life

Operncafé, Unter den Linden 5 (tel. 00372/20-002-56), is the leading café of East Berlin, a good choice if you're visiting the State Opera next door. The building is a remodeled version of a former structure built for royalty in 1733. The atmosphere is traditional, but the interior is of today. You have a choice of places at which to eat, drink, or dine. In the cellar is a bar, on the street floor a café, and upstairs two restaurants. The café has a small dance floor with a bandstand. An orchestra plays in the evening until 9:30. Lots of green plants and framed theater prints add extra glamor. Tues. to Sat. from 10am, you can order light snacks, Berliner cakes, tea, and coffee. A dinner costs less than $15. The second-floor Weinrestaurant offers more formal dining. Here, specialties include curried pork and a porterhouse steak for two persons. On a lower level, the Nachtbar is open from 9:30pm to 4:30am. At least 70 varieties of drinks are offered. The restaurant is closed Sun. and Mon.

Lindencorso, Unter den Linden 17 (tel. 00372/229-88-41), offers five areas for food, drinks, and entertainment. It is one of East Berlin's most fashionable cafés on a historic street, although its interior is plastic modern. It overlooks the previously recommended Interhotel Unter den Linden. At Das Konzertcafé, open to midnight, you can dance to music. In summer Das Boulevard-café offers 180 guests a chance to sit out and absorb the unique atmosphere of the city. The major spot for dining is the Weinrestaurant, seating 116 guests. Such regional dishes as fried liver with red cabbage and potatoes are offered. A three-course meal is featured for $15. Hours are from 11am to midnight daily. On the Kaffeegedecke you can order pastries and espresso. Finally, the Nachtbar offers entertainment from 7:30pm to 1am (on Sat. and Sun. to 2am).

Offenbach Stuben, Stubbenkammerstrasse 8 (tel. 00372/448-41-06), has a theatrical flair, honoring the creator of the grand opera *The Tales of Hoffmann.* In fact, this is an independently run eatery, reportedly subsidized by two of the leading theaters of the capital, the Berlin Comic Opera and the Metropol Theater. It presents an array of international dishes and Berliner specialties at around $15 for dinner.

The cuisine includes such dishes as veal steak with ham and mushrooms. Reservations are needed, and hours are Tues. to Sat. from 6pm to 1am.

TOURS

For many, an organized tour offered by **Severin + Kühn line,** Kurfürstendamm 216 (tel. 030/883-10-15), in West Berlin, is the best way for you to tour East Berlin. A four-hour English-language tour of the major sights of East Berlin leaves each afternoon at 2pm and costs an inclusive 30 DM ($17.80), plus 19 DM ($11.30) for East German guide fees. Carry your passport. You have the disadvantage, however, of being almost completely confined to your bus seat except for a few quick museum stops. You don't have the opportunity to explore the city as you would on your own.

For a more realistic picture of life in East Berlin, I recommend a follow-up personal tour of the city on foot.

THE SIGHTS

There is no better way to begin your tour of East Berlin than by walking down its world-famous street.

Unter den Linden

The linden trees for which this street was named have been replanted, and many of the old buildings restored, but the prewar gaiety and glamor of Unter den Linden have never returned. The palaces that once lined this street have either been destroyed or turned into lecture halls for Humboldt University, which numbers among its former students the young Karl Marx.

The contrast between the prewar and postwar thoroughfares is obvious from the beginning of Unter den Linden at the **Marx-Engels-Platz.** This large "people's square," built in 1951, was once the site of the 16th-century Imperial Palace. Rather than restore the damaged structure after World War II, the East Germans chose to level it completely and create the square instead.

Beginning at the square, walk down the left side of Unter den Linden, past the Palais Unter den Linden (restored in 1969) to the Opera Café. This former 18th-century palace, complete with gardens and fountains, is used as a nightclub, wine tavern, and concert café, especially popular with the crowds from the adjoining **Deutsche Staatsoper** (German State Opera) at Unter den Linden 7. After 200 years of almost continuous performances, the State Opera company was made homeless in 1941 when bombs almost completely destroyed its hall. In 1955 another opera house, built to the original (18th-century) plans of Knobelsdorff, opened with Wagner's *Die Meistersinger.* The neoclassical hall seats nearly 1,500 persons in its three tiers and box stalls. In addition, it contains smaller concert halls such as the Apollo Hall, a copy of a room in the Sans Souci Palace at Potsdam.

Directly behind the opera house, on Bebelplatz, is the once-magnificent **St. Hedwig's Cathedral,** now the cathedral of the Berlin diocese. The entrance to the building is marked by a series of columns. The copper dome is designed after the Pantheon in Rome. Pictures outside show the Dom as it looked in 1905.

Facing the cathedral on the Bebelplatz is the **Royal Library,** part of Humboldt University. The facade of this building is worth a passing glance because of its rather unusual shape. (The curved wings of the structure have prompted irreverent Berliners to christen it the Kommode, chest of drawers.)

Continuing down Unter den Linden, you'll pass the **Altes Palais** (Old Palace), once the residence of Kaiser Wilhelm but currently in use by Humboldt University. Next are several buildings and administrative facilities of the East German government. Near the end of the street sits the Soviet Embassy, the first of the buildings on Unter den Linden to be restored after the war. The ground floor of this palacelike structure contains shops and travel agencies offering information about holidays within the Soviet Union.

The walking tour brings us within sight of the **Brandenburg Gate,** which forms not only the end of Unter den Linden but also the end of East Berlin. Inspired by the Propylaea of the Parthenon, the gate was constructed in 1789. From this angle, you get the best view of the gate, with its two classical gatehouses flanking the heavy Roman attica. From the East Berlin side you can also approach the Quadriga at its best, since the "best" side of the sculpture does not face west.

The right side (on your left from Brandenburg Gate) of Unter den Linden is mainly taken up by embassies and buildings of **Humboldt University,** the largest university in East Germany since 1949. It dates from the mid-1700s, and in 1810 it became known as Friedrich Wilhelm University. Einstein and Hegel taught here, and famous alumni have included Marx and Engels.

The two sights worth crossing the street for, the Memorial and the Museum of German History, lie at the end of Marx-Engels-Platz.

Memorial for the Victims of Fascism and Militarism

It's much less exhausting to call this neoclassical temple by its older name, the **Neue Wache** (New Guardhouse), Unter den Linden 4. Previous to its current use, the building was a memorial to the dead of other German wars, including World War I. Today, however, it contains the ashes of an unknown soldier (placed there in 1969) to commemorate the heroism of the resistance fighters who fought for the freedom of the German people. The main attraction here, for Westerners at least, is not the memorial but the changing-of-the-guard ceremony in front of the building, Wed. at 2:30pm. The Neue Wache was constructed by the great architect K. F. Schinkel in 1816. A large brick-constructed pile, it is graced with a Doric portico in front, looking like a Greek temple. In 1931 the inside was transformed to honor the dead of World War I; in 1960 it was converted into a monument honoring the victims of Fascism and militarism. In its Hall of Honor, contained within a crystal cube, the eternal flame burns.

The Museum of German History

In what must be the most beautiful arsenal of all time, the **Museum für Deutsche Gerschichte,** Unter den Linden 2 (tel. 00372/200-05-91), gives a politicized view of the history of the German-speaking people. Grouped in exhibits representing various periods of German history from 1789 to 1949, the museum draws contrasts between capitalism and the socialist state. Military uniforms, photomurals, and models show German attempts at colonialism, and documents and photos reveal social inequality. In the room dealing with World War II, you'll see photos of the Krupp armament factories, along with a profit chart for the heavy wartime production of guns and ammunition. In the same room are anti-Nazi posters and photos of Hiroshima. The section devoted to 1945–49 includes pictures of the Nürnberg trials.

The museum building was originally constructed as an arsenal and war trophy museum in 1695 in a subdued baroque style. It is a perfectly square structure, with a large center courtyard, where chamber music concerts are held in the summer. Above the windows are the most outstanding features of the facade, the sculpted heads of 22 dying warriors by Andreas Schlüter (1696). The museum is open Mon. to Thurs. from 9am to 7pm (closes at 6pm from October 1 to March 31). On Sat. and Sun., its hours are 10am to 5pm; closed Fri. Admission costs about $1.65. Built on the Spree, the history museum overlooks Museum Island.

Pergamon Museum

The old Berlin of prewar days was proud of its fine art museums, many of which came under East German control when the boundaries were set up for the divided city. On the island in the Spree, which marks the beginning of Unter den Linden, you'll find the greatest concentration of these. One must remember in visiting the wealth of ancient art and treasures within some of the historical museums that German archeologists of the 19th and early 20th centuries led the way in the studies of ancient civilizations.

The Pergamon Museum complex (tel. 00372/220-03-81) houses several departments. But if you have time for only one exhibit, go straight to the central hall of the U-shaped building to see the **Pergamon Altar.** This Greek altar (180–160 B.C.) is so large that it has a huge room all to itself. Some 27 steps lead from the museum floor up to the colonnade. Most fascinating is the frieze around the base, tediously pieced together over a 20-year period. Depicting the struggle of the Greek gods against the giants as told in Hesiod's *Theogony,* the relief is strikingly alive, with its figures projected as much as six feet from the background. This, however, is only part of the attraction of the **Department of Greek and Roman Antiquities,** housed in the north wing of the museum. Here you'll also find a Roman market gate discovered in Miletus and sculptures from many Greek and Roman cities, including a statue of a goddess holding a pomegranate (575 B.C.) found in southern Attica, where it had lain beneath the ground for 2,000 years wrapped in lead. So well preserved was the goddess that you can still see flecks of the original paint on her garments.

The **Near East Museum,** in the south wing, contains one of the largest collections anywhere of antiquities discovered in the lands of ancient Babylonia, Persia, and Assyria. Among the exhibits is the Processional Way of Babylon with the **Ishtar Gate,** dating from 580 B.C.; these monuments, and also the throne room of Nebuchadnezzar, were decorated with glazed bricks. Cuneiform clay tablets document much of the civilization of the period, which created ceramics, glass, and metal objects while Europe was still overrun with primitive tribes.

The museum's upper level is devoted to the Islamic Museum, the East Asiatic Collection, and the Museum of Ethnography. Although these suffered great losses during the war, the collections contain many noteworthy items. Of special interest are the miniatures, carpets, and woodcarvings in the Islamic Museum.

Hours may vary from day to day in the Pergamon Museum, so it's best to check in advance. In general, they are 10am to 6pm daily. Mon. and Tues. only parts of the museum are open, including the Near East Museum and the three halls of ancient architecture, including the Pergamon Altar. Admission is $1.65.

The Bode Museum

At the end of World War II, West Berliners broke up a set when they secured the bust of Nefertiti from the Egyptian Museum. The head of her husband, King Akhenaton, still remains in the East. Even without the world-renowned queen, the Bode Museum, Monbijou-Brücke, Museuminsel, contains one of the most significant Egyptian collections in the world. Exhibits vary in size from the huge sphinx of Hatshepsut (1490 B.C.) to fragments of reliefs from Egyptian temples. Of special interest is the Burial Cult Room, where coffins, mummies, and grave objects are displayed along with lifesize x-ray photographs of the mummies of humans and animals.

Adjoining the Egyptian Museum is the **Papyrus Collection,** containing about 25,000 documents of papyrus, ostraca, parchment, limestone, wax, and wood in eight different languages. On the opposite side of the staircase is the **Collection of Early Christian and Byzantine Art,** with a rich display of early Christian sarcophagi, Coptic and Byzantine sculpture, icons, and even gravestones dating from the third through the 18th centuries. Also on the lower level is the **Sculpture Collection,** with several pieces from the churches and monasteries, including a sandstone pulpit support by Anton Pilgram (1490) carved in the shape of a medieval craftsman.

Upstairs you'll find the **Art Gallery,** devoted mainly to German and Dutch paintings of the 15th and 16th centuries and Italian, Flemish, Dutch, English, and French masters of the 14th through the 18th centuries, as well as contemporary

German and Dutch paintings. There is also a collection of **Pre-Historic Art.** The museum is open Wed., Thurs., Sat., and Sun., from 9am to 6pm; on Fri. from 10am to 6pm. Admission costs $1.65. Call 00372/220-03-81 for information.

Altes Museum (Old Museum)

This 19th-century building at Lustgarten (Marx-Engels-Platz) would be worth a visit even if it were empty. The facade is supported by 18 Ionic columns. The central vault room was restored in similar style while the rest of the building was modernized and air-conditioned to display prints, illustrations, and drawings. Among the most valuable works here is a sublime illustration Botticelli made for Dante's *Divina Commedia.* Sketches, woodcuts, and engravings by Dutch, German, English, and French masters are supplemented with drawings by 19th- and 20th-century artists, including a number of works by Edvard Munch, whose art Hitler considered scandalous. Propaganda is present here, too, in hundreds of pieces once categorized as "DDR socialist art."

The museum is open Wed. to Sun. from 10am to 6pm. Admission costs $1.65.

The National Gallery (Nationalgalerie)

With an entrance on Bodestrasse, this gallery (tel. 00372/220-03-81) mainly contains 19th- and 20th-century paintings and sculpture. The Nazi campaign against degenerate art depleted this collection during World War II, but you can still see quite a few works by Cézanne, Rodin, Degas, Liebermann, Tischbein, and Corinth. Many of the German works of the 19th century show scenes of court life at Wilhelm I's "Königsberg." The best of these are by Adolph von Menzel (1815–1905), who also is represented in the numerous sketches and drawings included in the museum. You can also see several paintings by one of Germany's greatest portrait artists, Max Liebermann (1847–1935). On the top floor is a large collection of watercolors, many of them satirical. The gallery is open Wed. to Sun. from 10am to 6pm, charging an admission of M 5 ($1.65).

At the **Otto Nagel House,** Am Märkischen Ufer 16-18 (tel. 00372/279-14-02), about 1,100 yards from Museum Island, the Nationalgalerie exhibits works once described as "proletarian revolutionary and antifascist art." Hours from 10am to 6pm; closed Sat. Admission costs $1.65.

Other Museums

Kunstgewerbemuseum (Museum of Applied Art) (tel. 00372/657-26-51), at Schloss Köpenick, shows the history and development of applied art in Europe from the Middle Ages to the present day. In the 36 exhibition rooms, you'll see a wide range of glass, porcelain, faïence, and work by goldsmiths, as well as jewelry and antiques. The museum is open on Wed., Sat., and Sun. from 9am to 5pm; Fri. from 10am to 6pm. Admission costs $1.65 for adults. To reach the museum, catch the S-Bahn to Köpenick. From there, go by tram no. 8.

At the **Märkisches Museum,** Am Köllnischen Park 5 (tel. 00372/279-37-28), the full array of the cultural history of Berlin (maybe more than you want to know) is displayed in one of the most prominent buildings on the banks of the Spree. The museum is operated by the Municipal Council. The 42 rooms contain collections of artifacts from excavations, plus such art treasures as Slav silver items and finds from the Bronze Age. The history of Berlin's theaters and literature, the arts in Berlin and in the March of Brandenburg, and sections dedicated to the life and work of Heinrich Zille, may be seen here. Most visitors like the array of mechanical musical instruments. The museum is open Wed. to Sat. from 9am to 5pm; Sun. to 6pm. Admission costs $1.65.

Postmuseum der DDR (Postal Museum), Leipzigerstrasse and Ecke Mauerstrasse (tel. 00372/231-22-02), provides insight into the historic development of postal service and communications, as shown by original letters that are thousands of years old, postal coaches used in the Middle Ages, modern methods of postal transport, and a modern TV studio, among the exhibits. Philatelists will be attracted to the large stamp collection. The museum also houses radio receivers made by prisoners in Nazi concentration camps with the aim of listening to Voice of Liberty broadcasts. The museum is open Wed. to Sat. from 9am to 5pm; Sun. to 6pm. Admission costs $1.65.

Museum für Naturkunde (Museum of Natural History), Invalidenstrasse 43 (tel. 00372/289-72-0), is attached to Humboldt University. Among the exhibits illustrating evolutionary phases is the original skeleton of the gigantic reptile *Brachiosaurus brancai*, which terrified the world some 125 million years ago. The 25 million–plus natural science objects contained here make this one of the largest museums of its kind in the world. Displays trace the evolution of organic life as well as inorganic matter. Mineralogical, zoological, and paleontological departments make up the vast collections. An arboretum is attached to the museum. You can visit Tues. to Sun. from 9:30am to 5pm; closed Mon. Admission costs $1.65.

Hugenottenmuseum (Huguenot Museum), Platz der Akademie (tel. 00372/229-17-60), in the tower of the French Cathedral, has documents, maps, historic pictures, and objects relating to the spread and status of the Huguenots who were forced to flee France under Louis XIV and found new homes in Berlin and Brandenburg. This relatively small museum contains archives and a Huguenot library. It is open Tues., Wed., and Sat. from 10am to 5pm; Thurs. from 10am to 6pm; Sun. from 11am to 5pm; Mon. and Fri. the museum is closed, but the church and tower can be visited from 10am to 5pm. Admission costs $1.65.

Schinkelmuseum, Werderstrasse (tel. 00372/208-13-23), has been installed in the deconsecrated Friedrichswerdersche Kirche, one of the most famous churches of old Berlin before the war. Right off Marx-Engels-Platz, an easy walk from the Palasthotel, it is at the corner of Niederlagstrasse. The twin Gothic portals of the old church shelter a bronze of St. George slaying the dragon. Inside, the museum is devoted to the memory of Karl Friedrich Schinkel, the architect of the early 19th century. He was responsible for designing many of the great palaces and monuments of Berlin that survived, along with his legend, until 1944 and 1945. In this museum his memory and records of his great accomplishments live on. The museum is open Wed. to Sun. from 10am to 6pm, charging about $1.65 for admission.

The Rebuilt Nicholas Area

You might end your day of exploration by going to the **Nicholas area,** a historic site in East Berlin, which was restored in time for the city's 750th anniversary in 1987. Here, on the banks of the Spree River, is where Berlin was born. Many of the old buildings in the area were totally rebuilt and restored after having been completely destroyed in World War II. The restoration has recaptured some of the old flavor of the city.

The area is named for the **Nikolaikirche** (Church of St. Nicholas) on Spandauerstrasse. The church, built in the 14th century and, as such, the oldest in Berlin, was constructed on the remains of a Romanesque church from the 13th century. In its reconstruction, 800-year-old skeletons were found. No longer a church, the restored building is now used to display the results of archeological diggings following the bombing of Berlin. Since 1982 the church has had two towers again, as it did at the turn of the 20th century. Despite weighing 53 tons each, they were mounted in one day using a mobile crane. The new south tower is topped by a golden weathervane with the Berlin bear and date 1981 to commemorate the start of the rebuilding of the Nicholas quarter. A restoration of the church's old nave with its late medieval vaults was achieved by using relatively simple means. Charging about $1.65 for admission, it is open Mon. from 10am to 5pm, Thurs. from 10am to 6pm, Fri. from 10am to 4pm, Sat. from 10am to 6pm, and Sun. from 10am to 5pm; closed Tues. and Wed.

The **Gerichtslaube,** seat of early jurisdiction, and the 18th-century Ephraim

Palace were also rebuilt. New structures were built in the old style to house apartments, boutiques, shops, cafés, and restaurants, all reflecting the memory of old Berlin.

The historic center was unused for decades, but reconstruction of the old town began in 1981. Around the Nikolaikirche a number of former burgher houses were reconstructed using photographs. Once again old Berlin has such quaint street names as Eiergasse (Egg Alley), Propstrasse (Provost Street), Rosstrasse (Horse Street), Molkenmarkt (Milk Market), and Mühlendamm.

On Church Square, the house in which Gotthold Ephraim Lessing lived from 1752 to 1755 was restored. On Mühlendamm, the famous Ephraim Palace was rebuilt using original parts of the facade and interior. The rounded baroque facade was once popularly known as "Berlin's most beautiful corner." On Mühlendamm, there is also a craftsmen's museum showing the development of Berlin crafts between the 13th and 19th centuries.

In Eiergasse stands Zum Paddenwirt, a restaurant, while the Zur Rippe is on Molkenmarkt, originally the center of the medieval town. Propstrasse proudly shows restored burgher houses from the 17th through the 19th centuries. The Zum Nussbaum restaurant used to be in one of the oldest gable houses on Fischerinsel (Fisherman's Isle). It became famous through its habitués, who included Heinrich Zille and Otto Nagel.

Next to the Spree, a bronze sculpture of St. George slaying the dragon was recently erected. It was made in 1853 by August Kiss, a pupil of Christian Daniel Rauch, for the Castle of Berlin. In Poststrasse, the Kurfürst House and the Grell, the Schubert and Knoblauch Houses have all been reconstructed. Of special interest is the Kaak, a bird with a grinning human face and donkey's ears that symbolizes the insults and ridicule thrown at those once pilloried here.

Other Attractions

Not to be outdone by the cities of West Germany, East Berlin has constructed a massive **Television Tower** (opened in 1969), the second-highest structure in Europe (1,100 feet), second only to the tower in Moscow. It's worth the $1.65 to take the 60-second elevator ride to the observation platform, 610 feet above the city. From this isolated vantage point you can clearly distinguish most of the landmarks of both cities. On the floor above you can enjoy a piece of cake and cup of coffee as the Tele-Café slowly revolves, making one complete turn every hour. By the time the revolution is completed, you'd better be on your way, however, or the guard will throw you out. The tower is open to visitors daily from 9am to 11pm.

At the foot of the tower stands one of Berlin's oldest churches, the brick Gothic **Marienkirche** (St. Mary's), opening onto Karl-Liebknecht-Strasse. Constructed in the 15th century, it is especially notable for the wall painting depicting *The Dance of Death* (1475), discovered beneath a layer of whitewash in the entrance hall of the church in 1860. Also worth seeing is the marble baroque pulpit carved by Andreas Schlüter (1703).

On the opposite side of the Television Tower stands **Alexanderplatz,** center of East Berlin activity. Several modern buildings line the square, including an HO Department Store and the Congress Hall. Information and tickets pertaining to events in East Berlin are available at the Berolina House on the square, open Mon. to Fri. from 9am to 7pm (Sat. to 4pm).

The **Sowjetisches Ehrenmal** (Soviet War Memorial) in Treptower Park, along the Spree, entered from Puschkinallee at the park, is the final resting place of more than 5,000 Soviet soldiers. Entering the park, you pass between two huge red granite pylons in the form of stylized flags, each towering over a bronze sculpture of a kneeling Soviet soldier. The cemetery consists of five large communal graves flanked by 16 raised stone sarcophagi on which bas-reliefs portray the events of World War II. At the end of the Grove of Honor stands the Memorial Statue, atop the Mausoleum, which contains the Book of Honor, listing the victims of the war who are buried here. Much of this memorial was constructed from marble from Hitler's demolished Chancellery.

Incidentally, many readers have asked the way to the **Reichschancellery,** Hitler's bunker, where, on April 30, 1945, the Third Reich came to an end with the suicide of the German dictator. Although the Reichschancellery once stood within walking distance of Checkpoint Charlie, it does not exist today. The Russians bombed the area totally, and bulldozed what was left. The Communists did not want to create a memorial of any kind to Hitler. The site today is an open space. Only a mound of rubble marks the spot where the Nazi nerve center once stood. At one time the building of marble and glass was vast. Art adorned its great halls. The bunker was built 50 feet below ground, following the bombing of Hitler's military headquarters. For persons wishing to visit the site, take the U-Bahn to Thälmannplatz, which is, incidentally, the last stop. The site of the building is at the northwest corner of Vossstrasse and Otto-Grotewohl-Strasse. The mound marking the Führerbunker is located inside the so-called Death Strip. You can get an idea of the grandeur of the building by walking around the Thälmannplatz U-Bahn station or at the Soviet War Memorial in Treptower Park. The walls of the station are lined with red marble taken from the Chancellery.

Theater buffs may also want to seek out the house occupied by **Bertolt Brecht,** the German poet and playwright who lived in the United States during World War II but in East Germany thereafter. It was in East Germany that he created his own "epic theater" company, the Berliner Ensemble, with which he often expressed Marxist, antibourgeois, antimilitarist themes. East Berlin retains the Bertolt-Brecht-Haus as the **Bertolt Brecht Center,** Chausseestrasse 125, in an old tenement house not far from the Berlin-Friedrichstrasse station. This was where Brecht and his lifelong companion, Helene Weigel, lived from 1953 until their deaths. The center contains the artists' living and working rooms and the Brecht and Weigel Archives containing 75,000 manuscripts, typescripts, collections of his printed works, press cuttings, playbills, and sound documents. It's open Tues., Wed., and Fri. from 10am to noon; Thurs. from 10am to noon and 5 to 7pm; Sat. from 9:30am to noon and 12:30 to 2pm.

Kept as a reminder of the Nazi's death grip are the remains of a **synagogue** at Oranienburgerstrasse 28, which was firebombed during Kristallnacht, November 10, 1938. That night, Jewish places of worship throughout the country were devastated by firebombs, and this one has been left standing as a memorial, untouched since the Nazi era. To find it, follow Friedrichstrasse to Oranienburgerstrasse, then turn right for about five blocks. The synagogue is on the left side of the street as you approach. *Warning:* It's a long walk, across the river and past the railway station.

Once the **Gestapo Headquarters** on Prinz-Albert-Strasse was the most feared place in Europe. Many victims who entered it for interrogation never came out alive. Allied bombing reduced it to a heap of rubble (and that is still true today). However, the government has partly excavated some of its cellars to reveal rooms used for torture, which was said to be especially brutal and sadistic. Tourists can visit Tues. to Sun. from 10am to 6pm. There's also an exhibition here called "Topography of Terror."

In one of the suburbs of East Berlin, the famous Jewish cemetery, **Jüdischer Friedhof,** in Weissensee, was opened in 1880. It contains some 110,000 graves of the former Jewish residents of Berlin. Because you may have a hard time finding it on your own, it's recommended that you take a taxi there. The gateway to the cemetery is on Herbert-Baumstrasse. Many of the most distinguished members of Berlin Jewry are buried here, including artists, musicians, and scientists, as well as religious leaders. Some of the tombs are of Jewish soldiers who fought on the German side in World War I. Back then, of course, many Jews were filled with a strong sense of German nationalism and showed great bravery at the front fighting against the Allies. That stands, of course, in marked contrast to the situation in World War II. A memorial honors Jewish victims murdered during the Nazi era. Many graves are of Jews who chose to face suicide in 1942 rather than a long, lingering death in one of the concentration camps. Many visitors from the West visit the cemetery, seeking the graves of long-departed ancestors. The cemetery is open May to September, daily from 8am to 6pm (closes at either 4pm or 5pm in other months).

Boat Excursions on the Spree

Most tourists miss one of the delights of East Berlin, boat excursions on the Spree. For a scenic boat ride through the waterways of the city, check with **Weisse Flotte,** whose white-painted vessels dock at Treptower Park (tel. 00372/271-22-37). They operate daily between late April and early October, usually leaving about eight times a day. After a round trip through the lakes at Luisenhain, I'd suggest you get off in Köpenick, near the Mecklenburger Dorf, which is a reconstruction of a typical 19th-century village in the north of Germany. In the open-air restaurant you can obtain light meals. All Berlin specialties are accompanied by the brew, of course.

AFTER DARK

Cultural Entertainment

If you can get a ticket to a performance at the **Deutsche Staatsoper** (German State Opera), Unter den Linden 7 (tel. 00372/207-13-62), already previewed in our sightseeing attractions, by all means go. It often presents some of the finest opera in the world, along with a regular repertoire of ballet and concerts. Tickets range from $5 (U.S.) to $10. The box office in general sells tickets from noon to 6pm Mon. to Sat.; Sun. from 4 to 6pm. However, if you visit near the end of summer, the opera will be closed.

A visit to another East Berlin performing venue might be in order. The **Komische Oper** (Comic Opera), at Behrensstrasse 55-57 (tel. 00372/229-25-55), lying between the S-Bahnhof Friedrichstrasse and the U-Bahnhof Stadtmitte. Tickets often cost from $4 to $8.

East Berlin, as in legend, has a number of excellent theaters that still flourish. One of the most famous is the **Berliner Ensemble,** Am Bertolt-Brecht-Platz (tel. 00372/282-31-60), which the late playwright, creator of *The Threepenny Opera,* founded in 1948. The box office is open Mon. from 2 to 5pm, Tues. to Fri. from 2 to 7pm, and Sun. from 6 to 7pm. Again, it's closed in late summer.

Tickets to most performances can also be ordered at the government travel agency at Alexanderplatz 5 (tel. 00372/215-44-10).

A Beer Garden

Berlin's largest and oldest beer garden is **Zenner,** Alt-Treptow 14-17 (tel. 00372/272-72-11), which opened in 1727. This pleasure pavilion beside the River Spree in Alt-Treptow, a former fishing village, is housed in a tavern in a classical building. Meals cost from $8, and there are many places for drinking, ranging from an upstairs café to a beer garden under linden trees. It is open Tues., Wed., Thurs., and Sun. from 11am to 8pm; Mon., Fri., and Sat. to 1am. There's dancing on Friday and Saturday, live music on Sunday, and disco action on Monday. You can also rent boats to go for a spree on the Spree.

---

2. Potsdam

Of all the tours possible from both Berlins, the three-star attraction is the baroque town of Potsdam on the Havel River.

From the beginning of the 18th century it was the residence and garrison town of the Prussian kings. Soviet propagandists once called it a "former cradle of Prussian militarism and reactionary forces." World attention focused on Potsdam from July 17 to August 2, 1945, when the Potsdam Conference took place.

The town, 16 miles from East Berlin, can be reached by a short bus or train ride (two local rail lines service it). However, if you plan to spend the night, you must make arrangements in advance for a hotel and a proper visa. You can do this at the offices of American Express in West Berlin.

It is now possible to go to Potsdam on your one-day visa granted to visit East Berlin.

Potsdam is no village. In spite of its historic sights, lakes, and parks, it is a major industrial center. On the main rail line to Magdeburg, the city is known for its beautiful chain of lakes formed by the Havel. Surrounded by a wooded range of hills, the town was beautifully planned architecturally, with large parks, many green areas, and a number of historic buildings. The center of town is Sans Souci Park, with its palaces and gardens, which lies to the west of the historic core. In the northern part of the town is the New Garden, lying on the Heiliger See, a mile northwest of Sans Souci. This garden contains Cecilienhof Palace (see below). The third large garden district of the city lies north of the town district of Bebelsberg.

WHERE TO STAY

One of the best of the high-rise Interhotels, **Hotel Potsdam,** Lange Brücke, DDR-1500 Potsdam (tel. 33/46-31), at the entrance to the city on the route nearest Berlin, rises over the Havel River, on the site of the old winter Cecilienhof Palace. It features a number of amenities, including a sauna and massage, and an Intershop where you can purchase souvenirs. Dancing and entertainment are provided by the nightclub, Bellevue. Its major restaurant is the Sans Souci. It also has a Russian Teestube and a garden restaurant that is popular in summer. There is also a café on the premises. All of the 186 bedrooms are equipped with private bathrooms, along with radios and TVs. The cost is 205 DM ($121.75) to 224 DM ($133) daily for a double, 167 DM ($99.15) for a single. Water-sports facilities are available as well.

Hotel Cecilienhof, Neuer Garten, DDR-1561 Potsdam (tel. 33/2-31-41), will be recommended later as a sightseeing attraction. However, many visitors who pass through here don't realize that it's possible for guests to stay in this lovely tranquil setting. The palace was built from 1913 to 1917 in the style of an English country manor house, and it was the residence of Crown Prince Wilhelm. The government converted a residential wing of the palace into one of the most charming hotels in the country. All 42 rooms have private baths or showers, color TVs, radios, phones, and minibars. Rates are about 110 DM ($65.30) to 150 DM ($89.05) daily for a single, 180 DM ($106.90) to 300 DM ($178.15) for a double. Residents can take their meals in the palace dining room, enjoying a first-class cuisine of both international and regional specialties.

WHERE TO EAT

A reliable, adequate place for lunch is the **Klosterkeller,** Friedrich-Ebert-Strasse 94 (tel. 33/2-15-84), which is often used by tour groups. Here the kitchen turns out presumably the type of cookery enjoyed by Germans before the war. There's no concession to modern taste. Likewise, the prices seem almost prewar, with meals going for $8. Typical fare includes Sauerbraten, rumpsteak, or the inevitable pork steak with french fries and a vegetable salad. Lunch is daily from 11am to 3pm, dinner from 3:30 to 9:30pm.

Bolgar Restaurant, Klement-Gottwald-Strasse 35 (tel. 33/2-25-05), offers some of the tastiest food in the city if your expectations aren't too high. As the name suggests, you get Bulgarian specialties here, but they also turn out regular German fare as well. Meals cost from $6. Open Tues. to Thurs. from 11am to midnight; Sat. and Sun. from 11am to 1am; closed Mon.

THE SIGHTS

At Potsdam, a British air raid on April 14, 1945, destroyed much of the center of the old city, but the major attraction, **Sans Souci Park** and its palace buildings, survived.

With its palaces and gardens, Sans Souci Park was the work of many architects and sculptors. The park covers an area of about a square mile. Information can be obtained at the **Tourist Pavilion,** Yorkstrasse 5 (tel. 33/230-12). You can take a train to Potsdam from East Berlin, with one leaving every 30 minutes. Once at Potsdam, you might consider an organized tour of the park and various palaces. Arrangements can be made at **Besucherbetreuung,** Am Grunen Gitter 02 (tel. 33/238-19). Tours cost $1.20 to $1.70.

Frederick II (called "the Great") chose Potsdam rather than Berlin as his permanent residence. The style of the buildings he ordered erected is called Potsdam rococo, an achievement primarily of Georg Wenzeslaus von Knobelsdorff.

Knobelsdorff built **Sans Souci Palace,** with its terraces and gardens, as a summer residence for Frederick II. The palace was inaugurated in 1747 and called Sans Souci, meaning "free from worry." It is a long one-story building crowned by a dome and flanked by two round pavilions. Of all the rooms, the music salon is the supreme example of the rococo style. The elliptically shaped Marble Hall is the largest in the palace. As a guest of the king, Voltaire lived here from 1750 to 1752. A small bust of Voltaire commemorates that sojourn. Sans Souci is open April to September from 9am to 5pm; November to January from 9am to 3pm; and February, March, and October from 9am to 4pm; closed on the first and third Mon. of every month. Admission is about 35¢.

The **Picture Gallery** (Bildergalerie) was built between 1755 and 1763. Its facade is similar to that of Sans Souci Palace. The interior is considered one of the most flamboyant rooms in the DDR. A collection of some 125 paintings is displayed, including works from both the Italian Renaissance and baroque periods. Dutch and Flemish masters are also exhibited. Such artists as Rubens, Terbrugghen, Van Dyck, Vasari, and Guido Reni, as well as Caravaggio, are represented. Concerts at the Potsdam Park Festival take place here.

To the west of Sans Souci is the **Orangerie,** built between 1851 and 1860. It was based on designs of Italian Renaissance palaces. Its purpose was to shelter southerly plants during the cold months. In the central core, with its twin towers, is the Raphael Hall, with 47 copies of that master's paintings. In addition, you can visit five lavishly decorated salons.

The largest building in the park is the **New Palace,** or Neues Palais, built between 1763 and 1769, at the end of the Seven Years' War. Frederick II called it a *fanfaronade.* Crowning the center is a dome. The three Graces bear the crown on the lantern. The rooms inside were used as a residence for members of the royal family. Filled with paintings and antiques, they were decorated in the rococo style. The most notable chamber is the Hall of Shells, with its fossils and semiprecious stones. At the Palace Theater, also decorated in the rococo style, concerts take place every year from April to November. Keeping the same hours as Sans Souci, the New Palace charges 50¢ for admission. It is closed the second and fourth Mon. of every month.

The **Chinese Tea-House** can be seen through the green of the trees to the south of the hedging on the border of the deer park. It was constructed between 1754 and 1757 in the chinoiserie style popular throughout Europe at the time.

Reached by tram lines 1 and 4, **Charlottenhof Palace** stands south of Ökonomieweg. It was built between 1826 and 1829 to the designs of Karl Friedrich Schinkel, the greatest master of neoclassical architecture in Germany. He erected the palace in the style of a villa, and designed most of the furniture inside. Keeping the same hours as those above, it is open daily except the fourth Thurs. of every month, charging an admission of 35¢.

Neighboring the palace, the **Roman Baths** are on the north of the artificial lake known as "machine pond," or Maschinenteich. This group of buildings was constructed between 1829 and 1835, based in part on designs by Schinkel. The baths were strictly for the romantic love of antiquity, having no practical purpose.

On the Heiliger See, or "holy lake," in the northern part of Potsdam lies the **New Garden,** or Neuer Garten (tel. 33/2-31-41). It is about a mile northwest of Sans Souci. The nephew and successor to Frederick the Great, Frederick William II, ordered the gardens laid out.

To the north of the 200-acre park, **Cecilienhof Palace** (tel. 33/2-31-41) was completed in the style of an English country house and was previously recommended as a hotel. It was ordered built by Kaiser Wilhelm II between 1913 and 1917. The 176-room mansion became the new residence of the then Crown Prince Wilhelm of Hohenzollern. It was occupied as a royal residence until March 1945, when the crown prince and his family fled to the West, taking many of their possessions with them.

Cecilienhof was the headquarters of the 1945 Potsdam Conference. For the conference, 36 rooms had to be quickly reconditioned. Truman represented the United States, and Stalin, of course, represented the Soviet Union. Churchill at first represented Great Britain, but at the time of the actual signing on August 2, 1945, Clement R. Attlee had replaced him. It is possible to visit the studies of the various delegations and to see the large round table, made in Moscow, where the actual agreement was signed. From May to October, the palace is open from 9am to 5:15pm; from November to April, from 9am to 4:45pm; closed Mon. Admission is about 15¢.

---

3. Leipzig

Chances are, your visit to Leipzig will be during one of the annual trade fairs, held around March and again in September. The city is called the "metropolis of fairs," but it also enjoys renown as a center of music. Richard Wagner was born here in 1813, and Johann Sebastian Bach (you'll surely see a statue of him) is closely associated with Leipzig.

Known as "the secret capital of East Germany," Leipzig lies about 111 "rail miles" southwest of Berlin and some 70 miles northwest of Dresden. It stands above the junction of three tiny rivers, the Elster, the Parthe, and the Pleisse.

Because of its strategic value as a rail center, both the R.A.F. and the U.S. Air Force bombed Leipzig heavily in 1943, 1944, and 1945, but it has been rebuilt, more or less well. Leipzig is once again a major rail terminus. From its railway station, with 26 platforms the largest in Europe, lines radiate to all the chief German cities, and from there to the rest of Europe.

Today Leipzig rivals Berlin as the economic and cultural center of the DDR. It still has some narrow streets and houses from the 16th and 17th centuries. However, it's estimated that Allied bombs destroyed nearly a quarter of the city. The heart of Leipzig is encircled by a "ring" road, as in Vienna.

ORIENTATION

For orientation purposes in this city of more than half a million people, you should head first for the **Reisebüro der DDR,** Katharinenstrasse 1, Alte Wagge (tel. 41/7-92-10). It is open Mon. to Fri. from 9am to 12:30pm and 1:30 to 4pm, Sat. from 10am to noon; closed Sun. There you will be given a map pinpointing the major sights. This place becomes a beehive of activity at the time of the annual trade fairs. These fairs are hardly what they were when they rose to fame, first under the margraves of Meissen and later under the electors of Saxony.

Revived by the Communists after the war, today they draw business representatives from more than 50 countries. A lot of people who come to them are concerned with the printing industry, as Leipzig is the principal center of East German publishing. Because of that concentration, the city is also a literary center. Many German authors live in and around Leipzig.

Leipzig is a very spread-out city; however, its historic core is compact enough to be covered on foot (in fact, that's about the only way to explore it). The **Hauptbahnhof** lies directly north of the center, opening onto the Platz der Republik. Some of the streets, such as the Richard-Wagner-Strasse, directly south of the square, are named after artists or composers. Directly south of this square is a green belt with a body of water, called Schwanenteich. The opera house is found at the southern sector of this park, its other side opening onto Karl-Marx-Platz, headquarters of the university. Katharinenstrasse, which was given as the address of the tourist information office, runs west of the heartbeat square, Sachsenplatz. In its southern corner is the restored Rathaus, opening onto Marktplatz. A short stroll west of here will lead to Thomaskirche, the 1,000-year-old Gothic church where Bach is buried. This major attraction of Leipzig will be covered under "The Sights."

WHERE TO STAY

A silver-and-concrete skyscraper, the **Merkur,** Gerberstrasse, DDR-7010 Leipzig (tel. 41/79-90), is near the fairgrounds in the city center. Opened in 1981 and built by Japanese interests, it receives guests from all over the world, maintaining fine international standards. Its 445 rooms and apartments are comfortably furnished and air-conditioned, each unit with a private bath, color TV, radio, and alarm clock, along with direct-dial phone, minibar, and refrigerator. A single costs from 175 DM ($103.90) daily, and a double goes for 245 DM ($145.50). However, at the time of the Leipzig fairs, tariffs go up. The hotel has many dining facilities, including the Brühl restaurant, the Sakura Japanese restaurant, the Arabeske restaurant with its Tiffany nostalgia, and the Milano restaurant—an international array. It will also entertain you in its nightclub, the Club Merkur. If you order drinks at Club 27, you can also enjoy a panoramic view. Also on the premises are a city office of Interflug, a branch office of the Reisebüro der DDR, a rent-a-car service, a hairdressing salon, and many shops. If you're fitness-minded, you'll find a swimming pool, saunas for both men and women, a solarium, a massage room, and a bowling alley. This five-star entry, the foremost address in Leipzig, is definitely a "hard currency" hotel.

Astoria, Platz der Republik, DDR-7010 Leipzig (tel. 41/72-220), stands across from one of the most famous railway stations in Europe. It is given five stars by the government, but it has none of the comfort of the Merkur. However, if the Merkur is fully booked, then many guests are automatically routed to this nearby hotel. During the 19th century the hotel consisted of an elegant corner building with ornate window ledges and lunette windows. In the 20th century someone commissioned the construction of a dignified annex, which extends the hotel another couple of hundred yards from the Platz der Republik. Today the entire mass looks solid and substantial. From the street, you'll notice that most of the ground floor is occupied by the Astoria Bar and Restaurant, well known in Leipzig. The public rooms are divided into a series of salons, conference rooms, cafés, and a nightclub with dancing. Sauna and massage are also available, and it's here that the myth of a middle-aged Valkyrie pummeling your sore muscles can come true. The 305-room hotel has a rent-a-car office on the premises. If you have a choice at all, try to get a room on one of the upper floors and not directly above the Astoria Bar and Restaurant; accommodations are not insulated against traffic noise. The cost is from 130

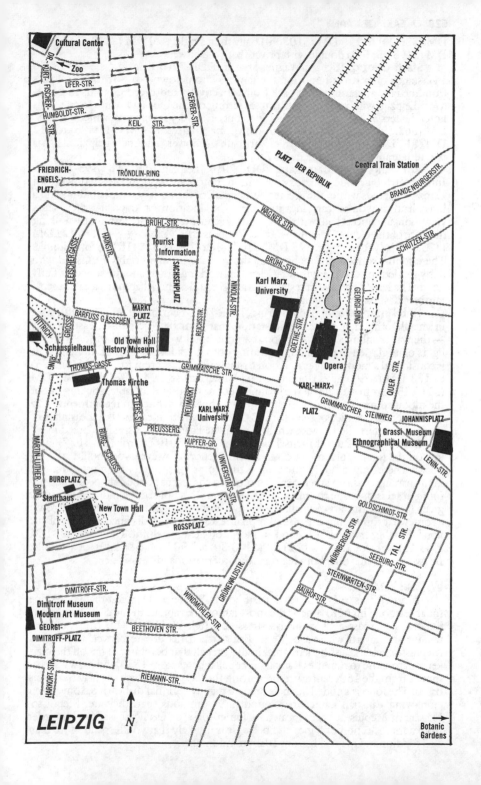

Cultural Center

← Zoo

DR.-KURT-FISCHER-STR.

UFER-STR.

HUMBOLDT-STR.

KEIL STR.

GERBER-STR.

PLATZ DER REPUBLIK

Central Train Station

FRIEDRICH-ENGELS-PLATZ

TRÖNDLIN-RING

BRANDENBURGERSTR.

BRÜHL-STR.

WAGNER STR.

SCHÜTZEN-STR.

FLEISCHER-GASSE

HAINSTR.

Tourist Information

SACHSENPLATZ

BRÜHL-STR.

NIKOLAI-STR.

Karl Marx University

GEORGI-RING

GROSSE

BARFUSS GÄSSCHEN

MARKT PLATZ

REICHSTR.

DITTRICH

RING

Schauspielhaus

Old Town Hall
History Museum

GOETHE-STR.

QUER STR.

THOMAS-GASSE

Opera

Thomas Kirche

GRIMMAISCHE STR.

KARL-MARX-

PETERS-STR.

NEUMARKT

KARL MARX University

PLATZ

GRIMMAISCHER STEINWEG

JOHANNISPLATZ

PREUSSERG.

Grassi Museum
Ethnographical Museum

KUPFER-GR.

UNIVERSITÄTS-STR.

LENIN-STR.

MARTIN-LUTHER-RING

BURG-SCHLOSS

BURGPLATZ

Stadthaus

New Town Hall

ROSSPLATZ

GOLDSCHMIDT-STR.

NÜRNBERGER STR.

TAL STR.

SEEBURG-STR.

DIMITROFF-STR.

WINDMÜHLENSTR.

GRÜNEWALDSTR.

STERNWARTEN-STR.

BAUHOFSTR.

Dimitroff Museum
Modern Art Museum

GEORGI-DIMITROFF-PLATZ

BEETHOVEN STR.

HARKORT-STR.

RIEMANN-STR.

LEIPZIG

↑ N

Botanic Gardens →

DM ($77.20) to 175 DM ($103.90) daily for a single, 220 DM ($130.65) to 330 DM ($195.95) for a double with private bath or shower.

Stadt Leipzig, Richard-Wagner-Strasse, DDR-7010 Leipzig (tel. 41/28-88-14), stands on a street honoring the famous "hometown boy." It too lies across from the railway station, built back from attractively landscaped grounds in downtown Leipzig, with rows of healthy trees setting off the blue-and-white facade. This hotel shelters 341 clean, well-maintained but often very small units, which cost 107 DM ($63.55) to 137 DM ($81.35) daily for a single, 202 DM ($119.95) to 212 DM ($125.90) for a double with private bath or shower. The Stadt Leipzig also has two restaurants, a café, and a nightclub.

Am Ring, Karl-Marx-Platz, DDR-7010 Leipzig (tel. 41/7-95-20), an Interhotel, is big, wide, and boxy, with its monotonous facade of tile. In downtown Leipzig, it stands within the greater "umbrella" of the railway station, but it's still a long haul if you're carrying luggage. The location is opposite the Neues Gewandhaus concert hall, with its legendary acoustics. It is also within easy walking distance of the Neues Opernhaus. Its 277 rooms cost 84 DM ($49.90) to 124 DM ($73.65) daily for a single, 175 DM ($103.90) to 200 DM ($118.75) for a double. These rooms contain private baths or showers and are predictably furnished with fairly modern pieces. Everything is clean, in working order, and the service is fairly good. The hotel boasts such restaurants as L'Preludes and Rhapsodie, a café, a separate breakfast room, and a nightclub.

Hotel International, Tröndlinring, DDR-7010 Leipzig (tel. 41/71-800), is set in a neighborhood, near the railway station, that seemed to escape—at least partially—the war bombings. This 87-room baroque hotel welcomes you inside with the lights of its glassed-in restaurant extending onto the sidewalk in front. In Leipzig, it is considered a moderately priced hotel. Singles with baths rent for 73 DM ($43.35) to 133 DM ($79) daily. Doubles with baths cost 148 DM ($87.90) to 186 DM ($110.45). From the café on the ground floor to the rounded gables sticking out of the modified mansard roofline, the three-star hotel has much to recommend it. In the immediate vicinity of the "Ring," the hotel is within easy walking distance of shopping centers and the zoo, which is renowned for its successful lion breeding.

Zum Löwen, Rudolf-Breitscheid-Strasse, DDR-7010 Leipzig (tel. 41/77-51), low on the totem pole, might do in an emergency. However, you should accept a booking here only in such a situation, as the rooms I inspected were most utilitarian in furnishings, basic in amenities, and often so compact as to be cramped. The 108-room hotel is opposite the main railway station. It is housed behind an eight-story green facade, with pairs of smallish windows grouped together in symmetrical rows; a somewhat forbidding expanse of asphalt extends a long distance in front of the hotel. But the service is fairly good and some of the staff helpful. The cost is 108 DM ($64.15) daily for a single, 174 DM ($103.30) to 190 DM ($112.80) for a double. Its two restaurants offer both regional and international dishes.

WHERE TO DINE

Most visitors to Leipzig eat at their hotels. However, I suggest that you escape for at least one night to dine at the most famous restaurant in the city, **Auerbachs Keller,** Mädlerpassage, Grimmaiscestrasse 2-4 (tel. 41/20-91-31). This is the restaurant and tavern where Goethe in *Faust* staged his debate between Faust and Mephistopheles. It's still there, amazingly, after all that bombing. It lies off the market square, close to the Altes Rathaus. The cellar dates from 1530, and has a series of murals from the 16th century, representing the legend on which the play *Faust* was based. The food is good. The chefs prepare mainly regional dishes of Saxony, often employing Faustian names that sound more ominous than they are: Mephisto-Fleisch, or Mephistopheles' meat, and Teufelstoast, or Devil's toast. You can order from a fine selection of wines and beers. It is unlikely that you'll spend more than $15 for dinner. Open daily from 10am to midnight.

Also historic, **Zum Kaffebaum,** Fleischergasse 4 (tel. 41/2-04-52), is the most famous, and the oldest, coffeehouse in this university town, dating from 1694. It occupies two levels of a building on a wide pedestrian walkway in the oldest part of town in a neighborhood of ornately carved sandstone and splashing fountains. Many visitors consider the relatively quiet upper floor, filled with changing exhibitions of modern paintings, to be the more interesting. In theory at least, it is reserved for artists and writers. Otherwise, you can select from a trio of raffishly decorated dining rooms filled with 19th-century nostalgia. Specialties include Hungarian goulash, onion soup with cheese croutons, and pork steak gypsy style. Full meals cost from $8 and are served daily from 11am to midnight. Everybody from Goethe to Wagner has patronized the café. Leibniz dined here, and Robert and Clara Schumann lived here. In 1848 Robert Blum, a frequent patron, organized the liberal revolution that shook the power structure of Europe.

If you're going to be in Leipzig for another day, you might pay a visit to **Paulaner,** Klostergasse 3-5 (tel. 41/28-19-85), installed in a former bank (you can read about the history of the restaurant on the menu). On a Saturday night, a three-piece band comes in to play romantic songs from the 1940s and 1950s. Soup, a main course, and a large glass of beer cost from $12 per person, including the tip. The menu is in German, and the action is on two floors. The Paulaner is open Mon. to Thurs. from 11am to 3pm and 6pm to midnight; Fri. and Sat. from 11am to 3pm and 6pm to 1am.

Thüringer Hof, Burgstrasse 19-23 (tel. 41/20-98-84), is a long-popular beer cellar in the old town. Young people, especially on weekends, fill up its tables in a fairly elegant setting with carved baroque accents. Waiters in white aprons hurry about, carrying mugs of beer and large platters of food. You get classic German fare here, along with a sampling of dishes from Eastern Europe. Your selection of soups, for example, might come from the Ukraine or else from Hungary. There's even a peppery dash of Mexico in the pork steak platter. One of the most popular dishes is a broiled chicken with apple-flavored red cabbage and potatoes. Meals cost from $6. Warm food is served daily from 11am to 10pm.

Weinrestaurant "Falstaff," Georgiring 9 (tel. 41/29-11-53), is one of the most elegant restaurants in the vicinity of the railway station. More commodious than you'd expect, it sits within a short distance of the opera house. If you'd like a predinner drink, the uniformed maître d' will usher you across Persian carpets to the art nouveau–style, dark-paneled bar in the rear. Afterward, you'll be shown a table in the modern high-ceilinged dining room. There, for about $15, you can select a fine repast that might begin with smoked eel on toast and go on to Thüringian beef with onions or pork steak stuffed with ham and cheese. The Viennese hen is also reliable. Open from 6pm to 1am; closed Mon.

Restaurant Panorama, Karl-Marx-Platz 9 (tel. 41/74-66), is one of the most dramatic restaurants in Leipzig. It lies on the 27th and 28th floors of the University Tower, commanding an impressive view over the rebuilt city. To go up on the elevator, you pay 50¢ during the day and $1.95 at night. The restaurant is open for light meals, snacks, drinks, and coffee from 10am to 6pm. Hot lunches are served from 11am to 2:30pm, costing from $5 and up.

At night it becomes a bar and wine restaurant, often with entertainment and special performances organized by the restaurant's staff. Things get livelier and livelier as the evening progresses. In the evening, meals cost from $6.75 and up. Try, for example, turkey breast with creamed mushrooms and Dutch sauce, crusted potatoes, and various salads; rolls of stuffed beef; or various varieties of steak. Open daily from 8pm to 3am.

Stadtpfeiffer, Neues Gewandhaus (tel. 41/713-20), occupies space in the new concert hall. This restaurant opened in 1982, and for the theme of its decor chose the musical troupes who traveled all over Germany in the 1400s. The name pfeiffe is that of an old woodwind instrument. Such a theatricalized setting attracts many media-related figures who appreciate the good food and service. Meals, costing from $15, are served from 11am to 3pm and 6pm to midnight; closed Sun. The chef uses high-quality ingredients as he prepares such dishes as stuffed loin of pork in a mushroom cream sauce or thinly sliced filet of veal.

THE SIGHTS

Goethe, who was a student at Leipzig, called the city "klein Paris," or Paris in miniature. This city has long been closely linked to the names of eminent personages. A Bach memorial was opened in the reconstructed Bose House on the occasion of the 300th anniversary of the birth of the composer. It was in Gohlis Castle that Schiller wrote his *Ode to Joy.* The historical restaurant Auerbachs Keller was the setting for one of the scenes of Goethe's *Faust,* and there are many productions of Wagner's *Ring* at the Leipzig Opera House. Robert Schumann liked to come to the historical restaurant Zum Kaffeebaum. The German Library, the **Deutsche Bücherei,** is the central archive of German literature, which can be visited only with special permission. It is reputed to possess every item of German literature ever published. It also has a copy of *Iskra,* the Bolshevik newspaper that Lenin came here to print secretly in 1900.

Founded in 1409, the University of Leipzig has contributed greatly to the cultural growth of the city. At the time of Hitler's ill-fated Third Reich, it was the largest university in Germany (today it's the largest in the DDR). The Führer would not have been at all pleased with its new name: **Karl Marx University.**

The **Musikinstrumenten-Museum** (Museum of Musical Instruments), Karl Marx University, Täubchenweg 2 (tel. 41/29-46-58), collects, cares for, and exhibits treasures of musical culture, chiefly Italian, German, and French instruments of the 16th to the 19th centuries. The museum is open Tues. to Thurs. from 2 to 5pm; Fri. and Sun. from 10am to 1pm; and Sat. from 10am to 3pm; closed Mon. Admission 35¢. Perhaps you'll be able to attend one of the concerts that are sometimes played with historical instruments.

A towering figure in the history of music, master of the contrapuntal style, Johann Sebastian Bach (1685–1750) lived in Leipzig from 1723 until his death. Unlike Wagner, he wasn't born in the city. However, he spent the most creative years of his life here. He was a choirmaster at **Thomaskirche** (St. Thomas Church), which has been handsomely restored after World War II damage. It has a high-pitched roof built in 1496. The church grew up on the site of a 13th-century monastery. The city's Thomaner Choir presents concerts (and they're free in this socialist state) every Sunday morning and Friday evening. That is, when they're in residence. The choir is popular all over the country, and often they are on tours, keeping alive the memory of Bach. Bach was buried just in front of the altar. Both Mozart and Mendelssohn performed here, and Richard Wagner was confirmed here in 1813.

Contrary to popular belief, the Thomaskirche isn't the oldest in Leipzig. That distinction belongs to **Nikolaikirche,** Nikolaistrasse, erected in 1165. Many works by Bach, including the *St. John Passion,* were first performed at this church.

The **Paulinerkirche** was erected in 1229 and restored in 1900. It has a grooved cloister, a curiosity, damaged after the Reformation (1556).

The **Altes Rathaus,** dating from the 16th century, stands on the Renaissance Marktplatz, dating from the 12th century. Again, Allied bombs rained down on it, but it has been restored. Inside, you'll find the **Museum für Geschichte der Stadt Leipzig,** Altes Rathaus, Markt 1 (tel. 41/7-09-21), a museum of the city's history, both cultural and political. It is open Tues. to Sun. from 9am to 5pm (closed Mon.), charging $1 admission.

A gateway leads to **Nasch Market,** the city's best-known square; and a short walk nearby takes you to **Königshaus,** which was for many centuries the headquarters of the Saxon monarchs who ruled Leipzig.

The **New Town Hall** (Rathaus) was erected on the site of the old Pleissenburg, the citadel where Martin Luther in 1519 held a momentous disputation.

The **Neues Gewandhaus** (tel. 41/7-13-20) faces the Neues Opernhaus across Karl-Marx-Platz. The famous **Gewandhaus Orchestra,** founded in 1781, saw some of its greatest days under the baton of Felix Mendelssohn, who died in Leipzig in 1847. Its other famous conductors have included Wilhelm Furtwängler and Bruno Walter. Concerts, ballets, and other premier events are staged in this modern structure, which opened in 1981. Recitals are presented on a mammoth organ.

The **Neues Opernhaus** is at Karl-Marx-Platz (tel. 41/75-41). However, you should go to the tourist office for concert information and hard-to-get tickets.

Going out Strasse des 18 Oktober will take you to a memorial honoring the famed 1813 battle. Along the way, see a pre–World War I Russian Orthodox church, built in the Byzantine style as a monument to the 22,000 soldiers killed at Leipzig; and also the fairgrounds, which come alive at the time of the annual trade fairs. At the far end, the memorial, the **Völkerschlachtdenkmal,** was dedicated in 1913 to the combined Prussian, Austrian, and Russian armies who defeated the Grande Armée of Napoleon. It rises some 300 feet in the air. Climb to the top for a view of Leipzig.

Nearby is a museum devoted to the history of Leipzig, including a diorama of the famous 1813 battle fought here. Some historians call this "The Battle of Leipzig," and others more pretentiously refer to it as "The Battle of Nations." At any rate, it's known in all European history books as the battle that led to the defeat of Napoleon and the destruction of his Grande Armée. Tram 15 from the central station runs here.

While in Leipzig, I'd suggest, if the weather is right, an outing to **Wörlitzer Park,** laid out in 1765.

Schillerhaus, a small farmhouse in Gohlis, a suburb of Leipzig, Menckestrasse 42 (tel. 41/58-31-87), is where Johann Christoph Friedrich von Schiller, a friend of Goethe's and, after him, the greatest name in German literature, wrote his *Ode to Joy* in 1785. This was the inspiration for Beethoven's Ninth Symphony. Hours are 9am to 5pm Tues., Wed., Fri., and Sat. Admission is $1.

Gohliser Schlösschen, Menckestrasse 23 (tel. 41/5-29-88), was once a gathering place for Leipzig literati. Today it houses the world's greatest collection of Bach archives and mementos. It is open from 9am to 5pm; closed Sun. Admission is $1.

Nearby is the **Zoologischer Garten Leipzig,** Dr.-Kurt-Fischer-Strasse 29 (tel. 41/29-10-01), where animals—many wild ones, of course—are bred in order to help conserve endangered species. The zoo was founded in 1878 and is internationally known for the breeding of big carnivores. There is also the biggest aquarium in the DDR. In summer it is open daily from 7am to 7pm; in winter from 7am to 5pm. Admission is 55¢. There's a restaurant on the grounds.

If you follow Martin-Luther-Strasse, you'll come to the **Georgi Dimitroff Museum,** Georgi-Dimitroff-Platz 1 (tel. 41/3-30-32). Housed in a building constructed in 1888 as the home of the Supreme Court of the Reich and changed into a museum in 1952, it was given the name of Georgi Dimitroff, head of the Communist party in Bulgaria who was a target for Adolf Hitler. Hitler accused Dimitroff and other Communist leaders of responsibility for the Reichstag fire. They were tried in this building, in what Hitler thought would be a great blow against the Communists and a victory for the Nazis. Dimitroff was interrogated by none other than Hermann Göring. The plan backfired, however, when the Leipzig jury acquitted the defendants. In the carefully preserved courtroom, tapes of the Reichstag trial are played, and you can also hear music in back of the museum. It's coming from the Gewandhaus music center, referred to earlier. Open Tues. to Fri. from 8am to 5pm; Sat. and Sun. from 8am to 2pm; closed Mon.

In the same building, the **Museum der Bildenden Künste** (tel. 41/31-36-17), is a museum of modern art, concentrating mainly on the 19th and 20th centuries.

Open Tues. to Fri. from 9am to 6pm; Sat. from 9am to 5pm; Sun. from 9am to 1pm; closed Mon. Admission is $1.

DAY TRIPS FROM LEIPZIG

While still based at Leipzig, you can branch out in several directions to explore some of the most interesting sights in East Germany. That way, you don't have to go through all the red tape of trying to book another hotel for the night, since you can easily explore the environs and return to Leipzig in time for dinner. Visitors interested in Martin Luther will especially find value in these tours.

Wittenberg

This is the city forever associated with Martin Luther, attracting pilgrims from all over the world. It was the center of the German Reformation. In the Halle district on the Elbe, Wittenberg lies 60 miles southwest of Berlin.

Wittenberg had not one, but two famous sons, and both men are honored with statues in front of the Rathaus. Its other celebrated son was Melanchthon (1497–1560), the German Protestant reformer and scholar who was a friend of Luther's and later of Calvin's (but more humanistic than either).

Both Luther and Melanchthon were buried in the **Schlosskirche,** which dates from the 15th century (but was rebuilt in the 19th century). It was on the Schlosskirche doors that Luther nailed his 95 theses in 1517. The 1858 bronze doors bear the Latin text of the theses.

Part of an Augustinian monastery in which Luther lived has been turned into a **Luther Museum,** and the parish church in which Luther preached is from the 14th century. An oak tree marks the spot outside the Elster gate where Luther publicly burned the papal bull in 1520.

You can also visit the **Stadtkirche,** with an altar by Lucas Cranach the Elder, who used to be the Bürgermeister of Wittenberg.

WHERE TO STAY AND DINE If you're planning to write a paper on Luther or stick around awhile in Wittenberg, you'll find two very basic little hotels, the **Goldener Adler,** Markt 7, DDR-4600 Wittenberg (tel. 451/20-53), and the **Wittenberger Hof,** Collegienstrasse 56, DDR-4600 Wittenberg (tel. 451/25-90). Neither hotel has a room with a bath or shower. Of the two, the Goldener Adler is better, charging from $38 daily for a single and from $56 for a double. The Wittenberger Hof is cheaper, charging from $29 daily for a single and from $50 for a double.

Halle

The town of Halle lies about 21 miles northwest from Leipzig. U.S. forces, in bitter street fighting, destroyed much of the town in 1945. Today Halle is one of the leading industrial cities of the DDR, with a population of some 250,000 residents. It is also a major railway transportation hub.

Georg Friedrich Händel, the composer, was born here in 1685. **Händel-Haus,** Grosse Nikolaistrasse 5, his former home, is a five-minute walk from the Markt. Musical instruments are displayed, some as old as 500 years. Open Tues. to Sun. from 9:30am to 5:30pm; Thurs. until 7pm; small admission fee.

In the center of town is the **Market Square,** dating from the Middle Ages (but restored in the mid-1880s), and the Gothic **Marienkirche** from the 16th century (it has twin towers linked by a bridge). A statue in the square honors Handel.

St. Moritzkirche from the 14th century is still standing, with many woodcarvings and sculpture. The **cathedral** from the 16th century is also worth seeing. All that is left of the **Castle of Moritzburg,** which used to be the headquarters of the archbishops of Magdeburg, is one wing. The rest was burned down at the time of the Thirty Years' War.

WHERE TO STAY AND DINE   The choice is obvious—the **Hotel Stadt Halle,** Ernst-Thälmann-Platz, DDR-4000 Halle (tel. 46/3-80-41). Almost deliberately designed to look forbiddingly massive, this product of state-directed architectural planning sprawls across hundreds of thousands of square yards in downtown Halle. The concrete-and-glass facade is relieved by a Le Corbusier–style concrete parapet extending a welcoming shelter over the pavement in front of the hotel. The hotel has 338 rooms, all of which may not be in use at any one time. The cost is 185 DM ($109.85) to 230 DM ($136.55) daily for a double unit with private bath or shower. Singles go for 109 DM ($64.70) to 145 DM ($86.10). The hotel also has a rather grand restaurant, a comfortable Weinstube, a café, a sun terrace, and a nightclub.

Eisleben

The leader of the German Reformation, Martin Luther, was born and died in this old Prussian town, which lies on the southeastern spurs of the Harz Mountains, about 25 miles northwest of Halle. The town is divided into an old and a new town, the **Altstadt** and the **Neustadt.**

The house at the end of Lutherstrasse, in which Luther was born in 1483, was damaged by fire in 1689 but was rebuilt in its present Gothic Franconian townhouse style and used for a long time as a free school for homeless children. You can see the room in which he was born, as well as exhibits tracing his life story. You can view a woodcarving, the **Luther Swan,** inspired by the statement of the early Bohemian reformer, John Hus, about the swan (taken later to be Luther) who was to follow him.

At the end of his life the ailing Luther returned to his birthplace, and here he died in 1546, in a house near the Market Square, where a memorial statue to him stands. A museum here contains his deathbed, death mask, and coffin shroud, and you can see the room where he died.

In Eisleben you can also see the font where Luther was baptized in the late-Gothic **Peter-Paul-Kirche,** as well as a gigantic statue of Lenin in workingman's clothes. It was presented to the town by the Soviet government when its troops came in in 1945.

Naumburg

If you have unlimited time for the DDR, you might seek out the medieval town of Naumburg, also in the Halle district. A former *Land* of Saxony, it lies 29 miles southwest of Halle. In the 10th century it was a stronghold of the margraves of Meissen.

Built in the Romanesque Transition style, the **Cathedral of St. Peter and St. Paul** dates from the early 13th century and is known for its huge crypt and towers. Look inside for the hand-carved folk figures. In the Town Hall, opening on Wilhelm-Pieck-Platz, is a good **Ratskeller,** serving beer, hearty food, and a local wine that is quite dry.

Altenburg

Some 30 miles south of Leipzig, Altenburg is known as the birthplace of the card game skat. A playing-card museum has been installed in a former ducal castle from the 10th century (much destroyed and rebuilt). Altenburg is still noted for turning out playing cards, which it exports all over the world. The Emperor Barbarossa chose Altenburg as the site of his royal palace, and an Augustinian monastery was also founded here.

---

4. Dresden

Dresden was once called "Florence on the Elbe." Throughout Europe, prewar Dresden, 111 miles south of Berlin by rail, was celebrated for its architecture and art treasures. Then came the night of February 13, 1945. The Allies, presumably in an attempt to crush the morale of the German people, rained down phosphorus and high-explosive bombs on Dresden. If you're interested in the subject, you might want to read the Kurt Vonnegut novel *Slaughterhouse Five*. It is estimated that some 35,000 Dresdeners were sucked into the devastating fire storm that engulfed the historic city. However, because refugees had crowded into the city at the time, no one knows for sure exactly what the body count was. Some sources have claimed as many as 135,000, or even 300,000. However, the 35,000 body count is the figure generally given. By morning the Dresden of legend was but a memory. The bombing of this great city of art is considered one of the major tragedies of World War II, and there are those, especially the Soviets, who have compared its destruction to that of Hiroshima.

For many, many long and dreary years after the war, Dresden no longer resembled the city of baroque paintings on the Elbe, a scene immortalized by Canaletto. Most of it still doesn't, but much of the familiar silhouette has been belatedly restored. Bouncing back from disaster, Dresden, the third-largest city in the DDR, is, outside of Berlin, its major sightseeing target, especially its "centerpiece," the museum-clogged Zwinger (more about this later).

One of the major means of transport in Dresden is the tram, a modern, reliable, low-energy system for getting around. Also, you can take trips on the big paddle-steamers that ply the River Elbe from central moorings below the Brühl Terrace. You can take trips from April to October on one of the ships belonging to the Weisse Flotte (White Fleet). Even if you don't make a river trip, it's exciting to watch as the paddle-steamers lower their funnels to pass under a bridge. One of Dresden's most celebrated bridges is called Blaues Wunder (Blue Wonder), a tribute to the bridge-building genius applied here at the turn of the century. The funicular railway, the first of its kind in the world, built from 1898 to 1900, takes passengers to the viewing site at Loschwitzhöhe.

ORIENTATION

Today, a pedestrian mall, **Pragerstrasse** (Prague Street), once the fashionable Champs-Élysées of Dresden, cuts through the city "that rose from the ashes." The street is lined with modern, heavy, gray commercial buildings—a valley, not a peak, in socialist architecture. However, its severity is relieved by fountains and benches. On those benches you'll find many foreign tourists. Prague Street runs from the Altmarkt to the Hauptbahnhof. The **Altmarkt** itself is the historic hub of the city, with its Palace of Culture, built in 1969.

Dresden consists of both an **Altstadt** and a **Neustadt**. Actually, since the war both terms have been a misnomer. Since it has been rebuilt, the Altstadt is newer than the Neustadt. The old and new towns are connected by four road bridges and one railway bridge, of which the Dimitroff is the best known.

Before tackling Dresden, which is a virtual "museumland," you should head first to the **Information Center,** Ernst-Thälmann-Strasse (tel. 51/486-58), open Mon. to Sat. from 9am to 8pm; Sun. from 9am to 2pm. It stands near the Hauptbahnhof and the Interhotel Newa. You can purchase a map, which you'll definitely need. The **Central Post Office** is at Otto-Buchwitz-Strasse 21 (tel. 51/5-94-40).

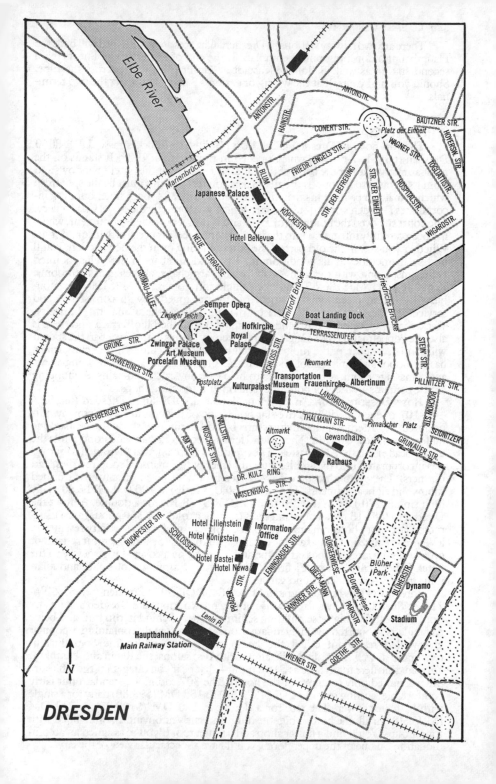

There are two railway stations in Dresden. Chances are your arrival will be at the Hauptbahnhof, opening onto Leninplatz at the end of Pragerstrasse. But there's a second station as well: Bahnhof Neustadt at Dr.-Fr.-Wolf-Platz, across the Elbe. Should you find yourself at the wrong one, trams 3 and 11 connect the two terminals.

WHERE TO STAY

The top hotel of Dresden is the **Hotel Bellevue,** Köpckestrasse, DDR-8060 Dresden (tel. 51/5-66-20), which opened in the spring of 1985. It stands on the most attractive part of the bank of the Elbe, and a look out the hotel's windows and from its terraces to the opposite bank makes you feel as if this must be the spot from which Canaletto painted his magnificent scenes. The 328-room hotel building incorporates Dresden's only double court, which was formerly the Royal Chancellery. The court survived the bombing of 1945 and is now a protected monument, which has been carefully integrated into the hotel, giving a feel of special elegance and style. Whether you stay in the old part of the hotel building or in the new section, you'll find such amenities as air conditioning, TVs, and minibars in the well-appointed bedrooms, along with carpeting, comfortable armchairs, and elegant bathrooms. Rents are 220 DM ($130.65) daily for a single and from 320 DM ($190) for a double. Five eating places offer a variety of cuisine, together with consistent good service. Restaurants are the Palace, the Buri-Buri, the Canaletto Specialty, Wackerbarth's Cellar (recommended separately), and the Elbe Terrace, and there is also the Pöppelmann Foyer Café. Guests can enjoy drinks in the foyer bar, the special wine and beer cellar, or the Jupiter nightclub. Facilities include a fitness club, which has an indoor swimming pool, a solarium, a "bronzarium," saunas, bowling alleys, and a massage room, with therapists to help ease any aches and pains. A shopping arcade contains a variety of boutiques and other interesting shops.

Hotel Dresdner Hof, An der Frauenkirche 5, DDR-8010 Dresden (tel. 51/4-84-10), opened in 1990. A five-star hotel, one of the best in East Germany, it is operated by Interhotel. Its architecture blends harmoniously with the baroque buildings on the Neumarkt. The ground level is decorated with sandstone, while the upper facade is plastered in pastels. The typical high rectangular "Dresden window" was incorporated into the architecture, together with a mansard roof, red tiles, and dormers. The establishment offers 327 comfortably (even elegantly) furnished rooms and eight apartments. The cost is 160 DM ($95) to 190 DM ($112.80) daily for a single, 270 DM ($160.35) to 300 DM ($178.15) for a double. Among the Dresdner Hof's 15 restaurants and cafés (seating a total of 1,360 guests) are a glass-roofed two-story hotel restaurant, a bistro, a Bierclub, a French specialty restaurant, a Viennese coffeehouse, and a wine cellar restaurant. The Sekundogenitur restaurant on Bruhl's Terrace overlooks the Elbe and is linked by a covered passageway to the hotel. Other facilities include a fitness club, with a swimming pool, sauna, and solarium, and a 60-car underground garage.

Interhotel Newa, Leningrader Strasse 34, DDR-8010 Dresden (tel. 51/496-71-12). Surrounded by a flat expanse of green lawn, opposite Dresden's main station, with another high-rise building set immediately behind it, this buff-and-beige rectangle is supported by an even-larger one-story rectangle containing a popular glass-walled restaurant called the Leningrad. There is also the Spezialitäten-restaurant, as well as a Café Baltik, along with two salons, the Repin and Puschkin. You can dine here for as little as $10 a meal—that is, if you can get in (the tables are often assigned only to guests of the hotel). The 307 rooms are standard but fairly comfortable, costing from 134 DM ($79.55) to 158 DM ($93.80) daily for a single with bath or shower. The rate for a double is 170 DM ($100.95) to 213 DM ($126.50). In all, the hotel is big, bustling, and fairly anonymous, often filled with tour groups. You'll find a flower shop and a sauna too. If you're assigned an accommodation on one of the upper floors, you'll have a spectacular view of the city.

Hotel Königstein, Pragerstrasse, DDR-8010 Dresden (tel. 51/4-85-60), stands across from the Newa, also at the main station, of course. It was built near a pedestrian walkway planted with masses of flowers, which change seasonally. It's a big white monster of a building, offering 303 rooms, with an anonymous facade pierced by uninterrupted horizontal lines of glass. The rooms in fair weather are sunny, as well as clean, and they are decorated in a predictably utilitarian modern style. Prices range from 97 DM ($57.60) to 130 DM ($77.20) daily for a single, and from 135 DM ($80.15) to 196 DM ($116.40) for a double, with private plumbing. Other facilities include a restaurant, a roof garden, and a sauna. The restaurant, incidentally, is restricted to residents for most of the day. You'll have to wait for a table, and once you have one, you'll often have to share it.

Motel Dresden, Münzmeisterstrasse, DDR-8010 Dresden (tel. 51/47-58-51), on the outskirts, is built on a more human scale than the monumental hotels within the city. This low-lying establishment is surrounded by green landscaping and a parasoled sun terrace near its glass-and-concrete modern facade. You'll be about 2 miles from the Dresden center here, but there's plenty of parking for your car in this motel arrangement. Rooms—clean, unimaginatively furnished—cost 109 DM ($64.70) to 123 DM ($73.05) daily for a single, 149 DM ($88.50) to 185 DM ($109.85) for a double, with private plumbing. In all, 82 bedrooms are offered, along with a restaurant and a terrace, plus an Intershop selling souvenirs.

WHERE TO DINE

Chances are, you'll be eating in your hotel. If you dine out, Dresden also has some independent eateries, but not as many as are needed. One can only reflect nostalgically about all the restaurants, cafés, and beer gardens of yesterday.

Wackerbarth's Keller, Hotel Bellevue, Köpckestrasse (tel. 51/5-66-20), is perhaps the finest restaurant in Dresden, but it's strictly a hard-currency place. It uses only the best meats and produce, its chefs and service are world-class, and diners (mostly Westerners) enjoy the candlelit setting in the vaulted cellar of this previously recommended hotel. Meals cost from $40, which also makes them the most expensive in Dresden. But you get quality for the price. You might begin with smoked North Sea oysters or else game soup with Pernod-flavored venison quenelles and almond crêpes. For a main course, you can order a gin-pickled venison cutlet garnished with chanterelles and pâté, a peppersteak, or perhaps veal in cream sauce with morels in the style of Zurich. Dinner is offered nightly from 6pm to 1am.

Buri-Buri, Hotel Bellevue, Köpckestrasse (tel. 51/5-66-20), brings the exotic flavors of the South Seas to conservative Dresden. You'll think you're at Trader Vic's as you peruse the menu of lush tropical food and drink. Meals at this hard-currency restaurant cost from $35 and include a selection of Polynesian hors d'oeuvres. You might follow with filet Waikiki or one of the spice meat curries. My favorite, however, is "carpetbag steak." Hours are 6pm to 1am nightly.

Aberlausitzer Töppl, Strasse der Befreiung 14 (tel. 51/5-56-05), is a good place to go for regional specialties of Saxony, accompanied by dark beer. Some of the fare served here is said to be influenced by Lusatia, the home of the Sorbs. There are also many dishes inspired by Bohemia, which is just across the border in Czechoslovakia. Meals cost from $8. Sometimes lines form at the door, and it's hard to get in without a reservation. Open Mon. to Sat. from 10am to 10pm; Sun. from noon to 8pm.

Meissner Weinkeller, Strasse der Befreiung 16 (tel. 51/5-58-14), is perhaps the most popular dining place in Dresden. The location is across from the "golden man" statue near the Hotel Bellevue. In summer it has outdoor tables. An arched stone door leads downstairs to the cellar, and upstairs the place has a modern café decor with a large central bar. It has a devoted following among the young people of town. The chef's specialty is a mixed grill including chicken, pork medallions, and beef medallions. You can also order beef fondue and flambé steak. Meals cost from

$15 and are served daily: Mon. to Fri. and Sun. from 6pm to midnight; Sat. from 6pm to 1am.

Try the **Ratskeller,** in the cellar of the Rathaus, Dr.-Kulz-Ring 19 (tel. 51/495-25-81). Here it's easy to strike up a conversation if there's no language problem. Tables are shared. You can get Sauerbraten and Wiener Schnitzel here, along with plain roast beef and Hungarian goulash. Potatoes—boiled, fried, roasted, mashed, whatever—are always served. Desserts are simple, usually a fruit compote or ice cream. You'll spend about $10 for dinner, if that. The establishment is open daily: Mon. to Fri. and Sun. from 11am to midnight; open Sat. until 1am.

Ungarische Gaststätte Szeged, on the second floor of a building at Ernst-Thälmann-Strasse 6 (tel. 51/495-13-71), is the place to go for food cooked from old Hungarian recipes, as well as latter-day additions inspired by the cuisine of Budapest. If you're hungry for a little paprika, this is the restaurant for you. A la carte meals, costing from $10, include roast pork stuffed with goose liver in a paprika cream sauce, rumpsteak Budapest style covered with a liver ragoût, and roast chicken Hungarian style. There's a coffee bar downstairs in the street-side café. Hours are daily from 10am to midnight.

For my final meal in Dresden, I go to **Luisenhof,** Bergbahnstrasse 8 (tel. 51/3-68-42), where, however good the food is, it takes second place to the magnificent view. Take the funicular railway up to the restaurant site, which has been called "the balcony of Dresden," high above the city. From here you can see the reemerging baroque skyline of the historic, carefully restored buildings and bridges. Try to avoid going here on weekends, when it is sure to be thronged with tourists—some of the 5 million who visit Dresden every year. A meal at Luisenhof will cost $12 and up. Open Mon. to Thurs. from 10am to 11pm; Fri. and Sat. from 10am to 1am; Sun. from 10am to 11pm.

THE SIGHTS

The restoration of old buildings in the "monumental zones" has been tremendous. Ruins from the war can still be seen, most notably in the baroque **Frauenkirche** (Church of Our Lady), built between 1726 and 1743 and once known throughout Europe for its cupola. The blackened hulk remains, supposedly a deliberate decision on the part of the government to remind the passerby of "the horrors of modern warfare." It stands today, a ghostly reminder of what happened to this *Kunststadt,* or city of art.

Some of Dresden's famous churches have been restored, however. The **Hofkirche,** built in the rococo style with a slender clock tower, rises some 300 feet. It was elevated to the status of cathedral by the Vatican following its restoration. The **Kreuzkirche** (Church of the Cross) stands at the Altmarkt. This church is the home of the Kreuzchor, the famous boys' choir of Dresden.

Of Dresden's many parks and gardens, the most visited is the **Grosser Garten,** which lies to the southeast of the Altstadt. The park was mapped out in 1676, and today contains a zoo and a botanical garden. In the center is a Lustschloss (pleasure palace) built in 1670.

As the court of the 17th-century princes of Saxony, Dresden enjoyed renown throughout Europe. Its Palace of Electors and Kings is still in ruins from World War II, but so fascinating are these ruins that they form one of the major attractions of the city. However, the **Zwinger** (palace complex) at Postplatz is a series of beautiful baroque buildings that have been restored and turned into a collection of museums, some 20 in all.

The Zwinger is a large quadrangle of pavilions and galleries. It was here that Augustus the Strong, the elector of Saxony (he was also the king of Poland), staged tournaments that dazzled the townsfolk. He also kept dozens of concubines here, as he was reportedly something of a sexual athlete. His physique was called Herculean, his temperament Rabelaisian, but he had a great love of the arts. It was this monarch who started the collection of paintings that in time was supplemented by his son.

The Zwinger was initially conceived by M.D. Pöppelmann as the forecourt of the castle. In its center are formal gardens, fountains, and promenades, forming a deep curving bay enclosed by pavilions. The Renaissance-style building is from 1846, and the exterior is decorated with sculptures of such celebrated figures as Goethe, Dante, and Michelangelo.

The most important museum is the **Gemäldegalerie Alte Meister** (Gallery of the Old Masters) (tel. 51/495-23-81), open from 10am to 5pm (to 4pm in winter); closed Mon. Admission is $1. The gallery, considered one of the best on the Continent, has as its showpiece Raphael's *Sistine Madonna,* which occupies one entire gallery by itself—and well it should. You'll also see works by Rembrandt, Vermeer, and van Eyck, plus an array of others, including Correggio, Veronese, Rubens, and Titian. For a study in sensuality, seek out one of my favorites, Giorgione's *Sleeping Venus.*

The **Historisches Museum** (tel. 51/495-23-81) displays an ornamental collection of weaponry that is truly stunning, if a bit frightening. It is open March to October, Thurs. to Tues. from 9am to 5pm (closes at 4pm off-season). Admission is $1.

In the **Pewter Museum** and the **Porcelain Museum** (tel. 51/495-23-81), a vast array of two of the best-known crafts of Dresden is exhibited. The collection of porcelain, which was begun by Augustus II, is considered the second biggest on earth. Meissen porcelain tends to dominate the exhibit, but the collection is wide-ranging, even taking in work from China. The museum is open Mon. to Thurs. from 9:30am to 4pm; Sat. and Sun. from 9am to 4pm. Admission is $1.

The glass-domed **Albertinum** (tel. 51/495-30-56), originally from 1559, is another museum complex, this one on Brühl Terrace, housing the state art collection. It's open Tues. and Thurs. to Sun. from 9am to 6pm, charging an admission of $1. Its most famous attraction is the Green Vault, or Grünes Gewölbe, a dazzling exhibition of jewelry and other treasures from the 16th to the 18th century. The museum complex also contains the **Galerie Neue Meister** (Gallery of the New Masters), with paintings by an array of artists from Gauguin to Corot.

The **Museum für Geschichte der Stadt Dresden** (Museum of the City of Dresden), Ernst-Thälmann-Strasse 2 (tel. 51/495-23-02), contains a rich display of Dresden's history. Perhaps no exhibit more fascinates visitors than does the photographs of Dresden following the bombings at the end of World War II. It is open Mon. to Thurs. and Sat. from 10am to 6pm; Sun. from 10am to 4pm. Admission is 35¢.

The **Transport Museum** is also worth visiting.

Sights in the Environs

In the environs, a sightseeing target is **Schloss Moritzburg,** 8 miles northwest of Dresden. It is surrounded by small lakes. From Wed. to Sun. it can usually be visited from 9am to 7pm. Always check with the tourist office before heading there to make sure it's open. Admission is $1. Visitors cross over a bridge to enter this former royal hunting lodge of the Saxon rulers. The lodge is actually a palace. Augustus the Strong built this Schloss in the 18th century, and in it is a collection of furnishings, hunting weaponry, and elegantly baroque porcelain.

A fascination with the American Old West and especially with Native Americans is present in all of Germany, and notably in **Radebeul,** about 5 miles west of Dresden, where the popular German writer Karl May lived until his death in 1912. May wrote about prairies and Indians and frontier villains even though he never visited the United States until after his last book was written. However, he collected Indian artifacts and started the **Indianer Museum,** Karl-Marx-Strasse 5 (tel. 51/731-69), in a log cabin built near his villa in Radebeul, a project completed by his widow in 1928 and opened to the public. Much of the material displayed came from later acquisitions, and today the museum contains peace pipes, tomahawks, totem poles, scalps, moccasins, and many other items of Indian lore. The museum is open daily from 9am to 5pm. Admission is $1. May's restored villa nearby was opened to the public in 1985. It houses many mementos of the writer's life.

One of the most fascinating side trips in the DDR is to the history-rich Sorb country. If you're returning from Dresden to Berlin along the Autobahn, get off at the Lübbenau exit. This section of the country is called **Spreewald,** or forest of the Spree, and it's nearly 100 square miles of woodland, pastures, and a canal network. Drive toward the port (Hafen), where you can usually hire someone, often a woman in national costume, to pilot you in a canoe along these canals. Several waterside cafés are found along the canals, serving food and drink.

The area is still inhabited by the Sorbs, who speak a language similar to Czech and Polish. The Sorbs who live here today are descendants of Slavic tribes who settled here since the 6th century. Over the years, they have faced tremendous persecution, but they always fought hard to preserve their culture. They were particularly persecuted by the Nazis, who outlawed their language and killed many of them. However, since 1949 they have enjoyed equal rights in the DDR. It is estimated that there are still 100,000 Sorbs living in Germany, 30,000 of whom inhabit cottages or other places in the Spreewald. Today they enjoy a protected landscape and are often engaged in growing vegetables and fruit.

CULTURAL ENTERTAINMENT

Between the Elbe and the Zwinger, Dresden's **Semper Opera House,** Theaterplatz 2 (tel. 51/4-84-20), was originally designed by Gottfried Semper, the architect who mapped out the famous picture gallery of Dresden. The opera house, at which both Wagner and Weber conducted, was completed in 1878 in a Renaissance style. What you see today, standing on the western side of Theaterplatz, is the work of restorers who have brought the two-tiered facade and interior of the Italian Renaissance-style building back to life. Careful attention was paid to the replacement of the paintings and decorations used by Semper when the place was built, and the fine acoustics for which the opera house was known have been restored. The stage was altered somewhat to allow for use of modern technology, and fewer seats were designed to allow for more comfort (the old auditorium held 1,700 persons; the new, 1,323). The Semper Opera House was reopened in 1985. The best opera seats can be purchased for $25. The opera company takes a vacation from mid-July to September. Concerts are also performed in summer in the courtyards of the Zwinger. The **Dresden Philharmonic** appears at the **Kulturpalast,** in the Altmarkt (tel. 51/4-86-60).

Your hotel or the tourist office will have a complete listing of these cultural events.

---

5. Meissen

Few Western visitors stay overnight in Meissen, as accommodations are severely limited. The "city of porcelain" is most often visited on a day trip from Dresden. To reach it is inexpensive from the railway station in Dresden. If you're there in summer, the best way to go is to take a boat of the Weisse Flotte (White Fleet), leaving two times a day from Dresden's Brühl Terrace, the fortified embankment on the other side of the Hofkirche. You get to enjoy the scenery along the Elbe.

Since 1710 Meissen has been known around the world as the center of the manufacture of Dresden china. The early makers of this so-called "white gold" were virtually held prisoner within Meissen. The princes who ruled the city didn't want the secret of the porcelain to escape. Of course it did, and rivals imitated it. The city is still known for its factories making porcelain, glass, and pottery.

Meissen lies on both banks of the Elbe, 15 miles northwest of Dresden. The **Altstadt** was built on the left bank. It is a very old town, dating from 920.

WHERE TO DINE

Most visitors in Meissen take lunch there, and there's no better place than one of the little cafés in the castle precincts.

Domkeller, Domplatz 9 (tel. 53/20-34), has been a historic rendezvous point since 1744. Many famous people, both secular and ecclesiastical, have passed through its portals. Today, the tradition continues. Germanic specialties—good, filling, hearty fare—are served in a tavernlike setting. It is open Tues., Wed., and Fri. from 11am to 8pm; on Thurs. from 11am to 3pm; Sat. from 11am to 11pm. Meals cost from $10.

An even more exciting choice, if you don't mind the steep walk down and back, is **Vincenz Richter,** An der Frauenkirche 12 (tel. 53/32-85). Just off the Market Square, this vine-covered restaurant is privately owned. It stands on a terrace in a building dating from 1523 (the present wine tavern was established in 1706). However, here you can sample the famous wines of Meissen and get simple, hearty food—a meal with wine costing from $10. Its hours are 3 to 11pm Tues. to Sat.

THE SIGHTS

Towering over the town is the **Dom** on the Schlossberg, one of the smallest of the German Gothic cathedrals. It's a marvelous early-Gothic building, whose bells are made of porcelain. It was actually built from 1200 to 1450 on the foundation of an even earlier structure. Meissen was the seat of the Saxon bishops, and Saxon kings were buried here, the first interred in 1429. Inside the cathedral, you can see one of the works of Lucas Cranach the Elder. The cathedral, which is now Protestant, is open daily from 9am to 5pm (closes at 4pm off-season), charging $1 admission. The Bishop's Castle is also on the hill.

Sharing the castle quarter with the cathedral and Bishop's Castle is **Albrechts- burg Castle** (tel. 53/29-20), where the first Meissen porcelain was made. The castle construction began in 1471 and went on intermittently until 1525, with restoration in the late 19th century. From 1710 to 1864 it was the site of the Meissen Porcelain Manufactory.

Guided tours go through the **Staatliche Porzellan-Manufaktur,** Leninstrasse 9, from April 1 to October 31, Tues. and Sun. from 8am to 4pm. You can see how the centuries-old manufacture of Dresden china is still carried on, many times using the same designs. On the premises you can visit the **Porcelain Museum,** the oldest in Europe, for about 35¢. The museum is open April 1 to October 31, daily from 8am to 4pm.

The terraces of the nearby vineyards in the Elbe Valley produce fine wines, for which Meissen has been known for 1,000 years, including the hard-to-obtain Meissner Domherr.

---

6. Weimar and Buchenwald

It is with a certain irony that Weimar, which evokes German humanism, should be grouped with Buchenwald, the notorious concentration camp the Nazis built in the 1930s. But that is the nature of geography, as they stand near each other, demonstrating the best and worst of humankind.

WEIMAR

Before World War II, Weimar was a symbol of German culture. Lucas Cranach worked here in the 16th century, and from 1708 to 1717 Bach was court organist. Under the Dowager Duchess Anna Amalia and her son Charles Augustus it reached its peak as a cultural center. In 1775 Goethe came to reside at their court, and he attracted such men as Herder and Schiller. Later on in the 19th century Franz Liszt was musical director, and under his auspices, Wagner's *Lohengrin* had its first performance.

It was at Weimar that the German national assembly met in February 1919, in the aftermath of World War I, and drafted a constitution that created the short-lived "Weimar Republic," a democratic republic that was, regrettably, to dissolve into a dictatorship 14 years later.

After Dresden and East Berlin, the city is the chief target in the DDR for the lover of German culture. The 1,000-year-old town lies on the edge of the Thuringian forest. A 19th-century writer called it "one of the most walkable towns of Europe"—and so it is. A former *Land* of Thuringia in the Erfurt district, its existence goes back to the 9th century.

Unlike many of the cities of East Germany, Weimar still retains much of its old flavor, with its narrow winding streets left over from the Middle Ages and its high-pitched gables and roofs. There is no town in the DDR that has so many important monuments of German classical history that were spared from the bombings of World War II.

Where to Stay and Dine

Hotel Russischer Hof, Goetheplatz 2, DDR-5300 Weimar (tel. 621/23-31), was originally built by Russian aristocrats as a suitable residence for their visits to the court of Weimar during the 19th century. Its dark-green and white facade opens onto one of the most important squares in the center of town. Inside, graceful, pastel-colored rooms, elegant and intimate, form the public rooms. The bedrooms are in a modern annex behind the hotel, each containing a private bath. Of course, the decoration isn't equal to the opulence of the original core, yet each accommodation is suitably furnished and comfortable. The rate for bed and breakfast is $50 per person daily.

The most famous accommodation in Weimar is the **Hotel Elephant,** Am Markt, DDR-5300 Weimar (tel. 621/6-14-71). The elegant facade of this circa 1696 building is set off with stone corner mullions, a beautifully weathered terracotta roof, a series of elongated bay windows stretching from the second to the third floors, and best of all, a frontage onto the old marketplace containing a dried-up fountain dedicated to Neptune. Many celebrities have visited this hotel, including Tolstoy and Bach. The Elephant became famous, however, through the Thomas Mann novel *Lotte in Weimar* (published in English under the title *The Beloved Returns*). A state-run establishment, it has 106 rooms and apartments, some without baths. Singles rent for 122 DM ($72.45) to 157 DM ($93.25) daily, and doubles cost 175 DM ($103.90) to 224 DM ($133).

In the same hotel are the two best places to eat in town, the **Elephantkeller** and the **Belvedere.** The latter, on the main floor, is the more expensive. In this modern, skylit, airy, and spacious room with formal service, meals cost from $18 and feature such dishes as filet Stroganoff, three pork medallions, and beefsteak Cubano with pineapple. Your wine is likely to be from Bulgaria or Rumania. The less formal Elephantkeller, in the cellar of the same hotel, is an elegant, light-colored room whose vaults rest on square columns of travertine. You descend a flight of stone steps from a separate entrance to reach it. Here meals cost from $10. A specialty is Zwiebelmarkt salads, which are made of onions from the famous onion market that is still held in the city each October, a tradition dating from 1653. Food service in both restaurants is Mon. to Sat. from 11:30am to 8:30pm; Sun. from 11:30am to 3pm.

Ratskeller, Stadthaus im Markt (tel. 621/6-13-31). You descend a flight of stairs past the coat-check counter into a pair of dining rooms. The first is vaulted and white, the second more modern and paneled, with a prominent bar. Everything is clean, correct, and proper. You might begin with goose liver on toast, following with a Schnitzel, Gulasch with mixed salad, or pork cutlets prepared four different ways. It is open Tues. to Sat. from 10:30am to 11pm. Meals cost $6.

The town is filled with cafés. One of the most popular is the **Café Esplanade** (also called Konzert-Café), Schillerstrasse 18 (tel. 621/29-10), opening onto a pedestrian street in the center of town. In summer, tables are placed outside, but these tables are reserved only for guests who order ice cream. There are street-level rooms, plus a more formal area one floor above. You can order simple, hearty fare here, with meals costing from $6. The ground floor is open daily from 9am to 5pm, the upstairs level from 2 to 11pm.

The Sights

You may want to head first for the government tourist agency, the **Weimar Informationscentrum,** which is open Mon. from 10am to 5pm, Tues. to Fri. from 9am to 5pm, and on Sat. from 8:30am to 1pm and 1:30 to 4:30pm. You can purchase a map, which will be most helpful in orientation. Have your hotel locate the office on a map, as its new address wasn't known at presstime.

The museums of Weimar are all open from 9am to 1pm and 2 to 4pm (to 5pm between May and October). Each museum shuts down for lunch, but there is always something open and always something to see if you've allowed, as most visitors do, only one day for exploring Weimar. Some museums shut down on Monday; others on Tuesday. Ask at the tourist office for museums likely to be closed during your visit. Entrance prices to museums could only be estimated at presstime, since the government plans to change them for 1991 but had made no decision as of this writing.

The principal attraction of the town is the **Goethe National Museum,** Am Frauenplan 1, where the poet lived from 1782 to 1832. It's an example of a German nobleman's house, a baroque structure built in 1709. There are 14 exhibition rooms, some of them pretty much as Goethe and his wife, Christiane Vulpius, left them. There is much original art in the house, and the library contains more than 5,000 volumes. The writer's mineral collection is here also. At Weimar, Goethe held the post of minister of state, and although his reputation rests today on his writing, the rooms in which he lived reveal his diverse interest in science as well (he was an early advocate of the belief in the common origin of all animal life, for example). He died in Weimar on March 22, 1832. Admission is $1.

Goethe's **"Garden House"** (Goethes Gartenhaus) stands in a park on the Ilm River. This plain wood cottage with a high-pitched roof is where the poet retreated for most of his summers to contemplate nature and anatomy. Goethe selected this house as his first residence when he came to Weimar. Even after he moved to other quarters, he still came here seeking peace and tranquility, describing the park around him as "infinitely beautiful."

The **Schillerhaus,** Schillerstrasse 12, contains the rooms in which this great poet and philosopher lived. A friend of Goethe, he is, after him, the greatest name in German literature. Schiller lived here with his family from 1802 to 1805. A museum has been installed, displaying mementos of his life and work. It also has a collection of costumes from productions of dramas by Schiller. The attic rooms have been refurnished as they were believed to have been in Schiller's day. He wrote his last works here, including *Wilhelm Tell.* Admission is $1.

The Schillerhaus is opposite the **Gänsemännchen,** a statue recalling the legend of the little boy who owned the goose that laid the golden eggs.

The house of yet another famous artist, Franz Liszt (1811–86), can also be visited, as it has been turned into a museum. The **Liszt House,** Marienstrasse 17, is where the Hungarian composer and pianist spent time during the last period of his life. It is said that he "strove to express the deepest romantic emotion in his playing and compositions." His daughter, Cosima, was to become the wife of Richard Wagner. A two-story building, the Liszt House was once the home for the royal gardeners of Weimar. You'll find several mementos, both personal and musical, from the composer's life, including communications between Liszt and his son-in-law. You can also see a piano at which he played and taught his pupils. Admission is $1.

Kunstsammlungen zu Weimar, Burgplatz 4 (tel. 621/6-18-31), contains the state art collections, among other exhibits. Under the guidance of Goethe, the palace was erected in 1789 and completed in 1803 (the previous castle had burned down in 1774; only a tower survived). In one of the wings is a series of galleries dedicated not only to Schiller and Goethe but to two other famous names associated with Weimar: Johann Herder (1744–1803), the German critic and philosopher who was a pioneer of the *Sturm und Drang* movement, and Christoph Wieland (1733–1813), the poet and critic who wrote the satirical romance *The Republic of Fools.* The second floor displays works by Lucas Cranach the Elder. On some of the upper floors you can see art of the famous Bauhaus movement, led by Walter Gropius, which once flourished in Weimar until it was expelled. The school of design, Das staatliche Bauhaus Weimar, was principally responsible for revolutionizing the teaching of sculpture, painting, industrial arts, and architecture throughout the Western world. Followers around the globe may have been impressed, but not the good people of Weimar. They "tolerated" the school until 1925, bombarding it in the press, until it finally moved to Dessau, where it was to survive until the Nazis closed it in 1933, claiming it was a center of "Communist intellectualism." Admission is $1.

Nearby, on the Marktplatz, you can view the **Lucas Cranach the Elder House,** which is decorated with carved bouquets and Neptunian adventures. The painter spent his final years here.

In the **cemetery,** you can see the controversial **Denkmal der Marz Gefallenen,** a monument to the revolutionaries whose slaughter in 1919 hastened the exit of Gropius from Weimar, along with his Bauhaus followers. But most Germans visit the cemetery today to pause in tribute at the grand ducal family vault, where Goethe and Schiller, friends in life, also lie side by side in death. The **Goethe-Schiller Mausoleum,** once the family vault of the Weimar dynasty, is on a terrace above the steps. It was built in 1825–26 according to plans drawn up by Coudray, who consulted Goethe on the design and construction. Schiller was entombed here in 1827 and Goethe in 1832, both in oak coffins. A chapel in Russian church style is on the south side of the mausoleum. It was built in 1859 for Maria Pavlovna, daughter-in-law of Duke Carl August.

The **Kirms-Krackow-Haus,** Jakobstrasse 10, is one of the curiosities of Weimar. A residence with classical furnishings, it also contains exhibits of the *Sturm und Drang* movement.

Follow Rittergasse until the end, when you come upon the **Wittumspalais,** once the residence of Dowager Duchess Anna Amalia. The old ducal dowerhouse is devoted to mementos of the German classical Enlightenment. The admission charge is $1.

Under the Dowager Duchess Anna Amalia and her son, Charles Augustus, Weimar reached its peak as a cultural center.

In a more ecclesiastical vein, you can follow Vorwerksgasse to the Gothic church, the **Herderkirche,** with an altarpiece by Lucas Cranach the Elder. It may be visited daily from 10:30 to 11:30am and 2:30 to 3:30pm, short visiting hours indeed.

In the Goethepark you can see the neoclassical summer residence of Carl August, the **Römisches Haus.** The location is near Belvederer Allee on the other side of the Ilm River. The duke wanted to please Goethe, whose fondness for Roman architecture was well known.

Some 2 miles south of Weimar stands the baroque **Château of Belvedere,** with an open-air theater where stage productions were presented in Goethe's day. This was a favorite retreat of Anna Amalia and the "enlightened" Weimar set, including Carl August. It was a hunting seat and pleasure Schloss in the 18th century. An orangerie was built, along with the open-air theater and an English-style park. A collection of historical coaches is here. In the château are displays of dainty rococo art. It's open Wed. to Sun. from 9am to 1pm and 2 to 5:30pm. From Goetheplatz, take the "Belvedere Express" bus, which leaves about every hour (more buses on weekends). Admission is $1.

You can also visit **Tiefurt Palace,** on the outskirts of Weimar. This was formerly the site of another summer retreat for Duchess Anna Amalia. Guests today can wander through its pavilions and gardens. To reach it, go east along Tiefurter Allee. It can also be visited by a bus that leaves from the main station close to Schillerstrasse. Admission is $1.

BUCHENWALD

The worst for last. A train from the Weimar Hauptbahnhof will take you to Buchenwald, Hitler's concentration camp and death chamber where both Jewish and political prisoners, including the Communist leader Ernst Thälmann, were confined and brutally murdered from 1937 until 1945, when the starving and diseased final prisoners, awaiting extermination, were released by the U.S. Army. On the Ettersberg, 4 miles northwest of Weimar, Buchenwald was the last sight that some 56,000 unfortunate souls saw before their extermination. Officially, it was called a work camp, so Buchenwald did not count the millions dead that Auschwitz did. However, atrocities practiced at this camp have made the name of Buchenwald synonymous with human perversity. For example, Ilse Koch, who has entered history as the notorious "bitch of Buchenwald," was said to have ordered lampshades made from human skin. It is reminiscent of a similar camp, Dachau, outside Munich.

Buchenwald virtually eliminated the Jewish population of East Germany—that is, those who had not already fled. It is estimated that a quarter of a million people were sent here during the camp's reign of terror. A memorial with a cluster of "larger-than-life" people, victims of fascism, was created by Prof. Fritz Cremer to honor the victims of 32 nations who lost their lives at Buchenwald. Hours are 9am to 4:30pm; closed Mon.

---

7. THURINGIA

A famous German *Land,* this heavily forested district lies in the most southwesterly sector of the DDR. Thuringian forest covers most of it, and it also contains some of the most historic cities in the country, including Eisenach. (Other cities in the area, such as Weimar and Erfurt, are previewed separately.)

Beerberg, at 3,225 feet, is the chief elevation, and the principal river is the Saale. The history of the region is long. The 5th-century Thüringians, for example, were vassals to Attila the Hun.

For those rare Westerners who have time to explore it, this is one of the most unspoiled regions in either Germany. Not only are there forests and steep slopes, but clear mountain streams and unusual vegetation. For motorists seeking individual destinations, we'll briefly explore its major centers.

EISENACH

This historic town lies on the northwestern slopes of the Thuringian forest, at the confluence of the Nesse and Hörsel rivers, some 30 miles west of Erfurt, which we'll visit later. This is the home of those little Wartburg cars that you most likely saw during your visit to East Berlin.

It's best known as the site of **Wartburg Castle,** which stands on a hill 600 feet above the town. This ancient castle from 1400 belonged to the landgraves of Thuringia. It has now been turned into a regional museum. Once it was the home of the medieval Minnesänger poets, who were immortalized by Wagner in *Tannhaüser*. Students of Martin Luther will know that it was at this castle that, upon his return from the Diet of Worms in 1521, he hid out until he could complete his translation of the Bible. He is also said to have "fought the Devil with ink" at Wartburg. Hours are 8:30am to 4pm daily. Admission is $1.

Part of the castle has been turned into a hotel and restaurant, opening onto beautiful views of the city.

Eisenach is also associated with Johann Sebastian Bach, who was born here in 1685. The **Bachhaus,** Am Frauenplan 21 (tel. 623/37-14), contains many mementos of the Bach family, along with a collection of musical instruments. It is now a museum, open Mon., Tues., Thurs., and Fri. from 9am to 5pm; Sat. and Sun. from 9am to 12:30pm and 1:30 to 5pm. Admission is $1.

The house where Fritz Reuter lived from 1868 to 1874, known as the **Reuterhaus,** is also a museum, commemorating this German novelist who made *Plattdeutsch* a literary language. Although arrested for high treason in 1833 and condemned to death by the Prussian government, he was later set free in a general amnesty. He died in Eisenbach on July 12, 1874. The museum also has a Wagner collection. Hours and admission charges are the same as for Bachhaus.

You can also visit the **Lutherhaus** of the Cotta family, Lutherplatz 8 (tel. 623/49-83), where the famous reformer stayed as a schoolboy. Hours are 9am to 5pm Mon. to Sat. (2 to 5pm on Sun.). Admission is $1.

While in the city, you might also want to visit the Romanesque **Church of St. Nicholas,** which was restored in 1887, and **St. George's,** which was built in the late Gothic style (it has been restored many times).

Where to Stay and Dine

It's unlikely that you'll spend the night in Eisenach. Most Westerners are booked into hotels in nearby towns such as Weimar. However, Eisenach does have two acceptable hotels. The first is the **Stadt Eisenach,** Luisenstrasse 11–13, DDR-5900 Eisenach (tel. 623/62-33-682), which has modestly furnished rooms, 85 beds in all, costing $38 daily for a single, $65 for a double. The hotel has a restaurant offering hearty Thüringian specialties, a simple meal costing $10.

Parkhotel, Wartburg Allee 2, DDR-5900 Eisenach (tel. 623/62-35-291), is the second choice. It's a good buy, but it is often filled with tour groups. The hotel has a restaurant, plus a state-run gift shop. Rooms are simply furnished without private facilities and cost from $64 nightly for a double, $38 for a single.

SAALFELD

At the opposite extremity of the Thüringer Wald, Saalfeld is another historic city, visited chiefly because it has the most stunning stalactite caves in the DDR (ask at the tourist information office about guided tours).

It lies on the left bank of the previously mentioned Saale River, about 25 miles south from Weimar and some 75 rail miles from Leipzig. It seems a shame the town is so little known by Western tourists, although East Germans visit it, mainly to sample a well-known local beer, Feegrotten, which is consumed in several taverns throughout the town.

Still partially encircled by its medieval bastions and walls, many of its old houses, spared from war damage, evoke the Middle Ages. A palace was constructed here in 1679 on the foundation of St. Peter's Abbey, home of a Benedictine order. Among its historic churches, St. John's was built at the beginning of the 13th century in the Gothic style, and so was the Rathaus, constructed in 1537. The Kitzerstein Palace, on an eminence above the Saale, is believed to have been originally constructed by Henry I, the German king. The present structure, however, dates from around the 16th century.

ARNSTADT

Arnstadt lies about 16 miles southwest of Erfurt (traveling upstream) on the Gera River, at the northern sector of the Thüringer Wald. It is one of the oldest towns in Thuringia, first mentioned in records of the year 704. The most outstanding attraction is the famous "Mon Plaisir" doll collection in the **Neue Schloss Museum,** which also has on display East Asian, Meissen, and Thüringian porcelain as well as Brussels carpets. The town museum, also in the castle, traces the history of Arnstadt and its surroundings.

Two churches are of interest: the double-towered **Liebfrauenkirche,** dating from the 12th and 14th centuries and reflecting the transition from Romanesque to Gothic architecture, and **Bach Church,** which was called the Bonifatiuskirche when Johann Sebastian Bach was organist here from 1703 to 1707. See also the Renaissance **Rathaus**.

To the northwest of Arnstadt is **Drei Gleichen,** a trio of castles on both sides of the Autobahn. Wachsenburg Castle, which has a museum and restaurant within its walls, was built around 900. It occupies a commanding position from the 1,390-foot-high Keuperkegel near Holzhausen, allowing a panoramic view of the countryside of Thuringia. To the west is the Mühlburg, the oldest of the Thuringian castles, which has unfortunately been allowed to fall into decay, except for its tower. Opposite the Mühlburg, north of the Autobahn, is the Schloss Gleichen ruin (Wanderslebener Gleiche) on a 1,220-foot height.

GERA

In the region of the Weisse Elster (White Elster), a river in the Vogtland area, Gera merits a stopover. It stands on the banks of the river some 45 miles southwest of Leipzig. It was first mentioned in records of the year 995 and referred to as a town in 1237. Noted even in its medieval days for the manufacture of cloth and linen, Gera suffered much from invaders. It was sacked by the Bohemians in the mid-15th century and burned by the Swedes in 1639. Some buildings survived one or both of these assaults, with the **Rathaus** dating from the 16th century. There is also a chemist's shop from the 17th century. The **Gera Theater,** still an important cultural institution of the town, has a 350-year-old tradition.

You can visit the orangerie, built between 1729 and 1732, the municipal museum, the Botanical Gardens, and other sites of historic interest and beauty, as well as the three old churches. They are **Marienkirche,** parts of which date from the 12th century, including a carved wooden altar; **Trinitatiskirche,** enlarged in 1611 by incorporating elements from 1323 and with a 1500 pulpit; and **Salvatorkirche,** dating from the 18th century.

A side trip from Gera worth taking is to **Wünschendorf** to see the old **Wehrkirche** (Defense Church) on the Veitsberg, one of the oldest East Thuringian edifices, as well as the 18th-century shingle-roofed wooden bridge and the Pramonstratenser Monastery of Mildenfurth, built in 1193.

Taking the road up the Elster from Gera, you come to Weida, a little town dominated by the 12th-century **Osterburg Castle,** which was once the residence of the princes of Reuss, who took possession of Gera and had the castle built on the site of a 9th-century structure. The castle now houses the district museum and a youth hostel.

Where to Stay and Dine

For overnight stopovers or for dining, you can patronize the **Hotel Gera,** Strasse der Republik, DDR-6500 Gera (tel. 70/2-29-91). In season, you'll find masses of flowers planted densely together on the flat lawn in front of this seven-story, 314-room hotel. The sleek, streamlined architecture of the building itself may not seem inspired, but the windows are large, the rooms bright and clean, and you can enjoy the beerhall, the café, and the sun terrace, along with three restaurants featuring Thüringian specialties; a meal costs about $10. To stay here in a room with private facilities costs 174 DM ($103.30) to 195 DM ($115.80) nightly for a double, 90 DM ($53.45) to 117 DM ($69.45) for a single.

OBERHOF

If you're a worker in Bulgaria, chances are that Oberhof will be as glamorous a vacation destination as St. Moritz is for a West German. This is a resort attracting not only scenery gulpers who want to hike in the mountains in summer but wintersports enthusiasts drawn to its skiing. It has toboggan runs, among many other outdoor activities. You can also visit a botanical garden for alpine flora.

There are a lot of "folkloric" restaurants in the mountains that the tourist office will direct you to. These include the Forsthaus Sattelbach. Many guests who stay at Oberhof take hiking tours along the Rennsteig ridgeway, enjoying the scenery of the Thuringian Forest. The first stage from Oberhof to Frauenwald is a distance of some 12½ miles.

Where to Stay and Dine

Oberhof offers the **Hotel Panorama,** Theodor-Neubauer-Strasse, DDR-6055 Oberhof (tel. 6682/5-01), which is visited mainly by those wanting to stay at least a week. The architect of this resort hotel courageously decided to construct two separate buildings and link them visually by sloping their rooflines in dramatically acute angles. The result is a successful combination of triangles and rectangles, which forms one of the most attractive state-owned hotels in the DDR. The Panorama rents 373 rooms and apartments, and there are five restaurants, along with a café, sun terrace, and nightclub. Sports facilities include a swimming pool, sauna, massage parlor, bowling alley, and minigolf. Bed and breakfast in functionally furnished rooms costs 151 DM ($89.65) to 176 DM ($104.50) daily for a single and 215 DM ($127.65) to 303 DM ($179.90) for a double.

SUHL

This is considered the unofficial capital of the Thüringer Wald. Mainly in the 19th and 20th centuries, it became famous for manufacturing sporting guns. It is one of the most popular tourist regions in the DDR.

The manufacture of hunting and sports guns continues to the present, and you can follow the history of small arms in the **Weapons Museum,** where exhibits and displays trace their development and manufacture from 1535. The museum is in the Malzhaus, a timber-frame structure dating from 1650, beside the River Lauter. The landmark of the city is a sculpture of an armorer on the top of a fountain.

Besides the Malzhaus, Suhl has a number of other timber-frame houses dating from the 16th and 17th centuries, as well as two historic churches. The **Hauptkirche,** originally built in late Gothic style but later extended by adding baroque elements, contains a beautiful rococo pulpit altar. The **Kreuzkirche** (Church of the Holy Cross) is a baroque structure.

From Suhl it's an easy trip to the city of **Meiningen** to see the **Elisabethenburg,** a 17th-century castle; to **Schleusingen,** which has an exhibition center tracing the history of the toy industry; and into the Thuringian Forest.

Where to Stay and Dine

Hotel Thüringen Tourist, Ernst-Thälmann-Platz, DDR-6000 Suhl (tel. 66/56-05), stands on a square named after the Communist leader martyred at Buchenwald, a gloomy note for a resort hotel to sound. Within the city limits, the entrance to this hotel is boldly announced in huge black letters on an aluminum background. The starkness of the sign is relieved somewhat by the parasols at the sun terrace. If you've forgotten your wristwatch, you can always tell what time it is by glancing at the begonias on the front lawn. There, a team of gardeners have laboriously planted a clockface 10 feet across, growing out of miniature shrubs and flowers. A total of 111 bedrooms are available inside, each decorated anonymously, but all clean and comfortable. The charge is 191 DM ($113.40) to 213 DM ($126.50) nightly for bed and breakfast based on double occupancy. Singles cost 123 DM ($73.05) to 150 DM ($89.05). You can buy meal vouchers beginning at $10. The hotel has a restaurant with specialties of the Thüringer Wald, as well as a terrace café and a nightclub. An Intershop on the premises sells souvenirs.

8. Jena and Erfurt

In the vicinity of Weimar, two towns attract two very different types of visitors: Jena the nostalgic-loving devotees of the German Romantic Period, and Erfurt the disciples of Martin Luther.

ERFURT

After a half-hour train ride beginning at the Weimar Hauptbahnhof, you'll be delivered to 1,200-year-old Erfurt. After arriving, head for the government-run information bureau at Bahnhofstrasse 37 (tel. 61/2-62-67), where you can obtain data about what's happening locally and what might be open on the occasion of your visit.

On the Gera River, the city, part of the *Land* of Thüringia, lies right on the Autobahn from Berlin to Frankfurt am Main.

The Augustinian monastery, where the reformer Luther was a monk for some five years, is now used as an orphanage. Gardens originally cultivated by monks just grew and grew, and Erfurt today is world-famous as a horticultural center, known for its wide variety of flowers and vegetables. An international horticultural exhibition is held in Cyriaksburg Park.

One of the curiosities of the town is the **Krämer brücke** (Shopkeepers' Bridge), from the 14th century, with houses on both sides, nearly three dozen in all. Spanning the Gera, the bridge is now filled with bookstalls, cafés, and antique shops, and you'll certainly want to spend some time here browsing.

Well-preserved patrician mansions built in both the Gothic and Renaissance styles are the historic town's dominant features. Many of its narrow streets are lined with half-timbered houses. These houses, for the most part, stood before World War II. Miraculously, Erfurt was the only town of its size in East Germany that wasn't virtually leveled in the bombing raids. The American army liberated it in the spring of 1945 before turning it over to the Russians.

The ecclesiastical center of town is the **Domberg,** where two Catholic churches stand side by side, their 15th-century walls almost closing in on each other at one point. The **cathedral,** begun in the 12th century, was later rebuilt in the 13th century in the Gothic style. It contains many ecclesiastical treasures and some 15th-century stained glass. Its neighbor is the **Church of St. Severus.** The most beautiful churches of Erfurt, "rich in towers," are the Romanesque **Peterskirche,** dating from the 12th and 14th centuries; the **Predigerkirche,** a 13th-century house of worship of the Order of Mendicant Friars; and three churches from the early Middle Ages—**Ägidienkirche, Michaeliskirche,** and **Allerheiligengeistkirche.**

Of special interest is the **Steinerne Chronik** (Chronicle of Stone) in Michaelisstrasse, a combination of architectural styles from different eras.

At the **Museum am Anger,** a splendid baroque structure, you can see exhibits relating to prehistoric times and on up through the Middle Ages, as well as displays regarding the town's history.

The **Museum of Thüringian Folk Art** gives an insight into the history of Thüringian crafts.

In the Renaissance building, Zum Stockfisch, dating from 1607, you'll find the **Natural Science Museum,** with illustrations of the flora and fauna as well as of the geological characteristics of the Erfurt region.

Where to Stay and Dine

Try the **Erfurter Hof,** Am Bahnhofsvorplatz, DDR-5010 Erfurt (tel. 61/5-11-51), an Interhotel. This was at one time a very grand hotel, and over the years it has hosted many famous guests, among them the former chancellor of West Germany, Willy Brandt, who came here in 1970 seeking reconciliation with the DDR. The most expensive hotel in town, it has many tall windows; small wrought-iron balconies embellish a facade done in sculptured limestone. Inside are four restaurants, along with two cafés, a nightclub, and a flower shop. The hotel's 182 rooms are among the best in the DDR, as reflected by the rather high price scale of 142 DM ($84.30) to 260 DM ($154.40) nightly for bed and breakfast in a double unit with private bath or shower. A single costs 90 DM ($53.45) to 150 DM ($89.05). You can dine here for about $10 for a most satisfying meal.

Hotel Kosmos, Juri-Gagarin-Ring, DDR-5010 Erfurt (tel. 61/55-10). The bronze-tinted glass of the low rectangle of the first floor will reflect your image as you try to locate the point where the high-rise ends. This 1981 hotel uses a rare color, orange (not red), highlighting the vertical expanse of the tower. Its 319 rooms are modern, sunny, and clean, decorated in the sterile Interhotel format. The cost is 170 DM ($100.95) to 190 DM ($112.80) nightly for bed and breakfast in a double with private bath or shower. A single goes for 94 DM ($55.80) to 104 DM ($61.75).

JENA

A 12-minute train ride from Weimar, 12 miles away, the university town of Jena conjures up the leaders of the German Romantic Movement. Badly damaged during World War II, the town lies on both banks of the Saale River about 57 miles southwest of Leipzig. As a city, it dates back to the 13th century. The famous Battle of Jena in 1806, in which Napoleon defeated the Prussians, was fought to the north. In spite of war damage, Jena still has a market square from the Middle Ages and many old patrician homes and narrow streets.

Today university buildings take over the site of the old ducal Jena Schloss, where Goethe wrote his *Hermann und Dorothea.* Martin Luther spent a night in the Hotel Schwarzer Bär, Lutherplatz 2, after his flight from the Wartburg. The **University of Jena** dates from 1558; it reached the zenith of its fame when its teaching staff included such great men as Hegel, Schelling, Fichte, Schlegel, and Schiller. Karl Marx wrote his doctoral thesis here. Friedrich von Schlegel, the German poet, critic, and scholar, the younger brother of August Wilhelm von Schlegel, lectured at Jena as a Privatdozent (official but unpaid lecturer). His older brother completed his translation of Shakespeare at Jena (considered one of the best poetical translations in the world). At Jena, these famous brothers were leaders in the new romantic criticism.

In the heart of town, the **Weigel Haus** was the former home of an astronomer of the same name. The building has a deep shaft through which stars can be seen even in daytime.

The most interesting ecclesiastical structure is the Church of St. Michael from the 15th century. The Fuchs-Turm (Fox Tower) was once notorious for its student orgies. Finally, the Zeiss firm of optical instrument makers has its headquarters in Jena, and they have opened a Planetarium.

9. The Harz Mountains

Known for their folklore and traditions, the Harz Mountains, in the southwest sector of East Germany, are also extolled for their scenic beauty. As the last stronghold of paganism in Germany, this is still a land of legends and fanciful names. It is said that the last bear was killed in the Harz in 1705, the last lynx in 1817. The wolf has also become extinct, but there are wildcats, badgers, deer, and foxes. The beech tree that grows in the Harz range has an unusual size and great beauty, and walnut trees abound. The region is also pocked by limestone caves. Much of the Middle Ages remains in old towns, spared from war damage, with their churches and castles.

Of all the many charming towns and "townlets" in the Harz, one of my favorites is Wernigerode.

WERNIGERODE

A romantic hamlet with a castle perched on Agnesberg Hill overlooking it, Wernigerode has many half-timbered houses in its narrow streets left over from medieval days. The town stands on the northern slopes of the Harz in the Magdeburg district. In its earliest days the town was ruled by the counts of Wernigerode, who date back to the early 12th century. They held sway until their downfall in 1429. Wernigerode was absorbed into Prussia in 1714.

Perhaps the most interesting structure in town is the framework **Rathaus,** dating from the 16th century and standing at the junction of Breitestrasse and Markstrasse.

The castle referred to as **Agnesberg** contains a feudal museum, open to the public daily from 10am to 6pm, charging an admission of $1.

For your most exciting adventure, you can take one of the many narrow-gauge steam railways that still exist in the DDR. You can board the train and go up past Brocken, the highest peak in the mountains, which was immortalized by Goethe in the "Walpurgisnacht" section of *Faust.*

NORDHÄUSEN

The southern terminus of the rail trip from Wernigerode is this town, which lies on the Zorge, to the south of the Harz range. A flight of steps connects the upper and lower parts of town. Near the Rathaus, which dates from the Middle Ages, is **Roland's Column,** an ancient landmark symbolizing free trade. Nordhäusen is known today because it has distilleries turning out **Korn Schnapps,** the best-known schnapps in the DDR. Curiously, the drink is not readily available in town, as all of it seemingly is exported because of its popularity and the need to raise hard cash.

QUEDLINBURG

Near the Harz range, **Quedlinburg Castle** was for many centuries the residence of the abbots of Quedlinburg, who ranked among the princes of the empire and had no church superior except the pope himself. They held sway until the secularization of the abbey in 1803.

Spared the destruction of war, the town still basks dreamily in the Middle Ages, with its framework houses, narrow little winding lanes, and Schlossberg, whose tiara is the **cathedral** of Quedlinburg, with towers from the 19th century rising out of a medieval structure. At Marktplatz, the Rathaus is built in the Renaissance style.

Within the castle precincts, you can order a good lunch at the **Schlosskrug,** on Müllerstrasse (tel. 455/28-36), in the forecourt of the castle. The cost is rarely more than $10. Should you arrive too late for lunch, you can stop over here for afternoon coffee and delicious little cakes. The place is open daily from 11am to 8pm.

Accommodations in all of the little towns and hamlets considered so far are extremely limited, and attempting overnight stays might be difficult unless you have relatives there, of course.

For your base in the Harz Mountains, I suggest the city described below.

MAGDEBURG

Razed by Allied bombing in the last year of the war, Magdeburg, the ecclesiastical center of Carolingian royalty (Otto I, 936–973), has been rebuilt. It is the largest inland port in East Germany, as well as the junction of many important rail lines and highways. Standing mainly on the left bank of the Elbe some 90 miles southwest of Berlin, Magdeburg was the capital of the former Prussian province of Saxony. Once a member of the Hanseatic League, the city became known for its *Magdeburger Recht,* or Magdeburg law, a type of municipal administration that was adopted all over Germany and in many parts of Eastern Europe.

The **cathedral** of Magdeburg on Domplatz is dedicated to St. Catherine and St. Maurice. The complex has two 345-foot-high towers, which first saw the light of day in 1209 but were not completed until 1520. Over the years the Romanesque style gave way to the Gothic. There is a three-nave basilica with a polygonal choir-gallery and a ring of chapels.

The oldest church in Magdeburg is the **Liebfrauenkirche,** on Regerungstrasse, a Romanesque structure begun in the 11th century but not completed until two centuries later (the citizens of Magdeburg took a long time on their churches). The Prussians restored it in the closing years of the 19th century. The cloisters may be visited Tues. to Sun. from 10am to 5pm.

The **Rathaus** was built in the Renaissance style in 1691 and expanded in 1866. A copy of the famous equestrian statue of Otto I, erected in 1290, stands on this square. The original, spared from the war, was moved to the **Kulturhistorisches Museum,** Otto-Von-Guericke-Strasse 68, open Tues. to Sun. from 10am to 5pm, charging $1 admission. It has a good collection of art from the Middle Ages.

Where to Stay and Dine

The **Hotel International,** a four-star selection, stands on Otto-von-Guericke-Strasse, DDR-3010 Magdeburg (tel. 91/38-40), named after the most famous citizen of Magdeburg, its former mayor, who lived in the 17th century. Although gargantuan, this 344-room hotel breaks up the monotony of its facade with criss-cross ribs of concrete reinforcing the windows, giving a pleasing checkerboard effect. The expanses of green around the hotel are large enough to keep out the noise of traffic. The rooms themselves are simple but comfortable, doubles with private baths costing 166 DM ($98.55) to 208 DM ($123.50). Singles range from 93 DM ($55.20) to 137 DM ($81.35). You'll certainly enjoy people-watching in the hotel restaurants, one of them called Moskau, or taking coffee in the Café Wien, followed by after-dinner drinks in one of the two salons (the Magdeburg or—test your geography—the Donezk). There's also a nightclub on the premises, along with an Intershop.

---

10. The Erzgebirge

One of the least-visited (by Western tourists) sections of the DDR, the Erzgebirge (Ore Mountains) section lies in the southeast, near the border with

Czechoslovakia. Its roads are virtually free of traffic, except around big cities such as Karl-Marx-Stadt.

It is a land of wooded hills and mountains, suitable for hiking or driving along badly kept roads, discovering some hamlets that seem little changed in 40 years. You'll come upon caves left over from mining days and the ruins of an occasional castle. All in all, the Erzgebirge qualifies as an offbeat adventure in travel.

KARL-MARX-STADT

The district's chief city, Karl-Marx-Stadt was known as the old Saxon city of Chemnitz until 1953. On the River Chemnitz at the foot of the Erz mountain range, it was severely damaged in the Allied bombing raids of World War II, but has been rebuilt, albeit in a rather characterless way.

Originally it was a trading post on the salt route to Prague. Over the centuries it has always been connected to industry, as it is today. For example, it made the first German tools and the first German locomotives. Today its factories turn out everything from underwear to textiles, and are responsible for 15% of the gross DDR output. Because of the availability of hotel accommodations, my suggestion is to use the city as a base for exploring the southeastern part of the DDR.

You can walk from the Hauptbahnhof to the Marktplatz, along the **"Street of Nations."** At Schillerplatz, you'll see a memorial to Engels and Marx.

In the northwest, the **Schlossbergmuseum,** open daily from 10am to 6pm, charging $1 for admission, was formerly a Benedictine monastery established in 1136. Fortified as a castle in 1546, it today contains artifacts of the region, tracing the history of Chemnitz. Seek out the interesting sculpture collection in the Gothic church of the castle.

Once the city had two dozen medieval towers, of which only the **Rote Turm** (Red Tower) stands today (it was originally built as a courthouse).

Where to Stay and Dine

Kongress, Karl-Marx-Allee, DDR 1910 Karl-Marx-Stadt (tel. 71/68-30). Immediately next to the Stadthalle stands this modern hotel complex. Towering over its neighbors, it encompasses 369 rooms between its concrete slabs, which are arranged in vertical lines to emphasize the building's height. Rooms are standardized, costing from 174 DM ($103.30) to 206 DM ($122.30) nightly for bed and breakfast in a double, 126 DM ($74.80) to 151 DM ($89.65) in a single. Meals in one of the hotel's four restaurants, carrying such exotic names as Pasardshik and Irkutsk, begin at $10. There is a wealth of other facilities as well, including two bars, two cafés, and a nightclub. The health facilities include an exercise room, a sauna, a solarium, and massage parlors.

Chemnitzer Hof, Theaterplatz, DDR-1910 Karl-Marx-Stadt (tel. 71/68-40), honors the old name of the city, and this tradition-laden hotel is classified as a historical monument. Breathing an aura of solidity, the massive concrete blocks of the facade of this hotel allow ample room for the oversize windows of the ground-floor restaurants. The windows of the upper stories are rhythmically arranged below the five-foot orange letters announcing the name of the hotel. Once inside, however, you'll find that the hotel is only a third of the size of most of the government-run hotels of the DDR. It offers 109 comfortable bedrooms, costing 85 DM ($50.45) to 95 DM ($56.40) daily for a single and 170 DM ($100.95) to 220 DM ($130.65) for a double. The Chemnitzer has three restaurants, plus a bar and a nightclub popular with businesspeople in Karl-Marx-Stadt.

TOURING IN THE ENVIRONS

A number of interesting excursions are possible from Karl-Marx-Stadt on a daytrip basis. On the town's outskirts, visit **Burg Rabenstein,** a 12th-century castle, and the Rabenstein group of rocks, Felsendome.

At nearby **Pelzmühle,** you can take pleasure steamers for a trip along the river.

Zwickau, the town where composer Robert Schumann was born, has a number of architectural monuments of different eras.

An interesting tour is to the huge **Augustusburg,** a Renaissance castle built in 1572 as the hunting seat of the Saxon electors. It now houses the Erzgebirgian Zoological Museum and a motorcycle museum. The castle chapel has an altar painting by Lucas Cranach the Younger. The well house, which is architecturally interesting, has a 561-foot-deep well.

From the Augustusburg, it's an easy run to the scenically beautiful **Kriebstein Dam,** which is a paradise for lovers of water sports.

Oberwiesenthal is the highest town in the DDR, lying more than 3,000 feet above sea level. This is an important mountain health resort and winter-sports center, lying at the foot of the **Fichtelberg,** some 4,000 feet high. At the summit you'll find an attractive restaurant. A suspension railway takes you up to the Fichtelberg. A magnificent panoramic view of the Upper Erzgebirge is possible from the 132-foot observation tower.

The most famous town in the Erzgebirge is probably little **Seiffen,** widely known for its woodcarvings, its toy museum, and the display workshops of turners and joiners (woodworkers). The Seiffen Toy Museum will acquaint you with the development of Erzgebirge Mountain toys. Nearby in the Sehma Valley is the **Frohnauer Hammer,** an iron-processing center from the 15th and 16th centuries that has been rebuilt as a monument to the history of technology. You can dine here in a restaurant that was a smith's house.

Klingenthal and **Markneukirchen** are known throughout the world for the musical instruments made here for centuries. You can see what may be Europe's largest collection of the instruments in the Markneukirchen Museum.

One of the most impressive towns of the Obererzgebirge is **Annaberg-Buchholz,** about 2,000 feet above sea level, some 22 miles south of Karl-Marx-Stadt and quite close to Oberwiesenthal, just visited. This was once an area known for silver mines. Towering above the town is St.-Annen-Kirche (St. Anne's Church), dedicated in 1520, with beautifully designed reticulated vaulting. Annaberg is known for its bobbin-lace making. The **Erzgebirge Museum** contains a wealth of information on the history of the Upper Erzgebirge and its folk art. Here also are two former homes of prosperous silver-mine owners of the Middle Ages. The mines were closed about 1600 because of low yields.

In the east Erzgebirge lies **Freiberg** (Freyberg), an old Saxon mining town 19 miles southwest of Dresden. Among the sights of interest here is Donats Tower, the remains of the medieval fortifications. You can also see old miners' houses in narrow, twisting little lanes. St. Nicholas Church, a baroque structure, stands on the Buttermarkt. You can also see the town theater, rebuilt from the house of a rich merchant, the Rathaus on the Obermarkt, along with attractive old burgher houses with their colorful painting and gilding. The gem of Freiberg is the late-Gothic cathedral, with wood sculptures on slender pillars and reticulated vaulting, ceiling paintings, a tulip pulpit, and a huge Silbermann organ from 1714. This is the oldest of the 31 organs still extant that were made by the master hand of Silbermann. The Golden Door of the old Marienkirche (St. Mary's Church), from the 13th century, built into the south side of the cathedral, is worth seeing.

11. The Baltic

Part of the DDR opens onto the Baltic Sea, which the Germans call Ostsee. Swept by salty breezes, the atmosphere here is completely different from the rest of East Germany. On any summer day the place is overrun with holidaymakers. Scandinavians often visit here too. In my frankest recommendation, I suggest the DDR Baltic coast not so much for its seaside resorts and beach facilities (there are far more exciting spots in Western Europe for that), but for the remnants that remain of its old Hanseatic towns. That is, what was spared from Allied bombing raids.

ROSTOCK

Largest of the DDR ports, Rostock lies on an estuary of the Warnow, a distance of some 175 miles northwest of Berlin by train and some 80 miles northeast of its more famous neighbor, Lübeck, the hometown of Thomas Mann. Copenhagen lies about 100 miles away to the north.

Rostock joined the Hanseatic League in the 14th century. Because it was the location of one of the largest Nazi aircraft factories, it was blasted by British bombers as early as 1942, which sent the townspeople fleeing to the countryside. Other bombings followed. Its principal street, Langestrasse, or "Long Street," was completely demolished, but has now been rebuilt and modernized. A row of buildings has been restored in the old style as a reminder of the past.

Some noteworthy historic buildings stand on Ernst-Thälmann-Platz, including the Rathaus, a 13th- or 14th-century Gothic brick structure. Early 16th-century Walldiener House and Kerkhof House are also of interest. Among the buildings that survived war destruction is the **Marienkirche** (St. Mary's Church), one of the most outstanding ecclesiastical structures of the Baltic region. Dating from 1398, it is a Gothic building with two towers in the Romanesque style. Look for its clock.

Other churches to be seen are the **Heilig-Kruez-Kirche** (Holy Cross Church), a three-nave Gothic brick hall church from the 14th century, and the **Michaelis Monastery,** a one-nave house of worship of the Order of Mendicant Friars, built between 1480 and 1488.

Rostock also has Zoological Gardens, a sports forum, and an open-air theater, an auditorium, and several restaurants.

You can tour the port of Rostock by boat.

Where to Stay and Dine

Hotel Warnow, Hermann-Duncker-Platz, DDR-2500 Rostock (tel. 81/3-73-81), has a boxy blocklike shape with indented balconies. The entire building, the best hotel in Rostock, containing 336 rooms, is surrounded by an expanse of green lawn dotted with political statues of girls in heroic poses. Inside the hotel you'll find that the rooms are comfortably furnished and appointed, costing 224 DM ($133) to 244 DM ($144.90) daily for bed and breakfast in a double, 139 DM ($82.55) to 149 DM ($88.50) in a single. You'll also find six restaurants, for the most part serving specialties of the Mecklenburg region. There's also the Café Riga (named for another Baltic capital), as well as a sun terrace, bar, nightclub, and Intershop.

Touring in the Environs

Warnemünde is the largest seaside resort in the DDR, with a ferryboat harbor, a 585-yard long pier, a lighthouse, and the big Warnow shipyard on the water. It is about 9 miles from Rostock. A ship serves as an exhibition and cultural center for the town. Warnemünde's beach is good to look at, but going in the cold water can be a chilling experience.

A little more than 10 miles from Rostock is **Bad Doberan,** a spa town surrounded by forested hills. The main attractions are the Doberan Cathedral in a Lower German Gothic brick style; the Zisterziens (Cistercian) Monastery from the 13th to 14th centuries; and the Brewery and Brick House with a water mill dating from 1270.

Some 3 miles on from Bad Doberan lies **Heiligendamm,** the oldest sea resort of the Baltic, founded in 1793. It's called the White Seaside Town. You can go here on the Molli narrow-gauge railway train.

Greifswald, in the east of Rostock County, is the smallest university town in the DDR, known for learning and research, and rich in tradition. The university was founded in 1456. Interesting sights of the town include Kirche St. Marien, with art and historical monuments, such as the pulpit, which has fine marquetry work. It's the town's oldest house of worship. Two other churches worth seeing are Kirche St. Jakobi, started in the 13th century, and Kirche St. Nikolai, a cathedral with a panoramic view from its gallery. The brick burgher's house at Platz der Freudschaft 11, built about 1430, is the best example of houses of this type in Greifswald.

Don't miss seeing the little fishing village of **Wieck,** which has been a part of Greifswald since 1939. You'll see typical fishermen's houses with thatched roofs, whitewashed walls, and tarred framework, all still in good condition. The village, including the wooden drawbridge over the River Ryck, has been taken over as a national monument. Although it has a medieval look, some of it was built as late as 1886.

STRALSUND

A seaport on the Baltic Strait of Bodden, across from Rügen Island, this town dates from the 13th century. Once it was rivaled only by Lübeck in its prominence in the Hanseatic League. Because of its vital importance, it was fought over and has known many masters. Its last conquerors arrived in 1945: they were Soviet troops. Stralsund is about 21 miles from Greifswald, just visited.

Buildings of historic interest are mostly of Lower German Gothic brick construction. They include the **Rathaus,** the oldest parts of which date from the 13th century. This is considered one of the most imposing examples existing of the North German secular brick Gothic architecture. Ecclesiastical buildings predominate among points of interest. The **Nikolaikirche** and **Marienkirche** are 14th-century churches with rich interior decoration. The **Jacobikirche** was transformed into a three-nave basilica in the 14th century. It has a high altar with baroque mounting and paintings by J. H. Tischbein, one of the foremost ecclesiastical artists of his day. The 15th-century **Katharinenkloster** is a significant monastery, and **Heiligengeistkirche** (Church of the Holy Ghost), not far from Katharinenkloster, is noteworthy for its inner courtyard with wooden galleries.

Stralsund has a **Cultural-Historical Museum,** which traces the story of the port and its region from the days of the Vikings to Hanseatic League power and to the present. There is also an **Oceanographic Museum,** the only one of its kind in the DDR.

The Weisse Flotte (White Fleet) not only serves the daily passenger shipping routes of the Baltic resorts with boats from Stralsund, but the harbor here is also the starting point of "Round Rügen" trips, all-day deep-sea excursions, and journeys to Swinoujscie in Poland.

The Baltic island of **Rügen,** opposite Stralsund, is not only the largest in Germany but arguably the most beautiful. It lies just 1½ miles off the northwest coast of what used to be Pomeranian Prussia. Its coastline is dotted with peninsulas and bays. From north to south at its greatest length, it stretches for 32 miles. An excursion from Stralsund takes visitors over the Rügen Dam. The chalk cliffs of Stubbenkammer with the Königstuhl rock, the Granitz hunting lodge, and Kap (Cape) Arkona, the most northerly point of the DDR, can be seen, as well as Spyker Castle with its old walls and dolmens. Try also to visit Jasmund, which is the most beautiful part of the island.

Planned excursions are offered, or you can go on your own, taking a ferryboat from Stralsund to Altefähr on Rügen. From there you can take a narrow-gauge railway train that traverses the island. The old capital of the barony of the princes of Putbus is here, named, appropriately, Putbus.

Another excursion offered by the White Fleet is to **Hiddensee Island,** about 11 miles long. Although it is geologically closely related to Rügen Island, it has a number of characteristics of its own that are worth seeing. It is accessible only by sea, so there are no cars and no streets of any appreciable width. In fact, many of the roadways, such as they are, are not even paved. Botanists find this a good place to study Baltic island flora, and the island's native birds attract nature lovers, birdwatchers, and ornithologists. Parts of Hiddensee are nature reserves.

The former residence of dramatist Gerhart Hauptmann is open to visitors.

Where to Stay and Dine

The best place to stay in Stralsund is the **Hotel Baltic,** DDR-2300 Stralsund (tel. 822/53-81), whose rooms are well kept. Many Scandinavians, especially those from Sweden, favor this place for a holiday. Simply furnished singles cost $61 nightly, and doubles go for $108. The hotel also has the best dining facilities in town, with meals costing from $10. You can get good fresh fish here.

SCHWERIN

Lying inland, this town at the southwest corner of Lake Schwerin is set in a district of "lakelets." It is the industrial and cultural center of an important agricultural district, but it has more to recommend it to visitors than commerce.

Once the seat of the ducal court of Mecklenburg, it has an ancient history. There are not many historic buildings in Schwerin, however, as most of the old structures were destroyed by fire and replaced in the 19th century. Among these is the **Arsenal** beside the Pfaffenteich (an artificial reservoir in the city center), the **Marstall** (royal stables), and the **Kollegiengebäude,** seat of government until 1945.

Schwerin Castle, the seat of the Mecklenburg dukes, was spared by the fire. It stands on Castle Island, a pentagonal structure of many towers and turrets, with characteristics of the Gothic, baroque, and Renaissance styles of architecture. While some of the structural elements are from the 15th to the 16th centuries, the castle's appearance today is in the French Renaissance style of the mid-19th century. It now accommodates a teachers' college and the Polytechnic Museum. Concerts are held in the castle garden, which has terraced waterfalls and a canal running through it. These grounds have been designated as a public park. The baroque castle garden contains valuable sculptures and arcades, and is considered a good example of 18th-century landscape gardening.

Two imposing buildings stand in the former Alter Garten parade grounds, the **Mecklenburgisches Staatstheater** and the **Staatliches Museum Schwerin-Kunstsammlungen, Schlosser und Garten,** Alter Garten 3 (tel. 89/75-81). The museum contains an excellent collection of Dutch paintings and graphic arts of the 17th century, including the two portraits, *Drinking Boy* and *Boy Holding a Flute,* by Frans Hals and *Home Concert* by Frans van Mieris. There are also collections of the German Middle Ages, porcelain (especially Dresden china), and 18th-century court paintings. From May 1 to October 31, the museum is open daily from 9am to 5pm; from November 1 to April 30, from 9am to 4pm. Admission is 40¢.

Schwerin's Gothic **cathedral** is a fine example of medieval architecture. It dates from 1248. The present building is in the Lübeck Baltic Gothic style. The Mecklenburgische Landesbibliothek (regional library) is housed in the cathedral's cloister.

Several interesting trips are possible from Schwerin. You can take boat trips or hikes around the southern shore of Schwerin Lake, where the baths near Schwerin-Zippendorf and Schwerin-Meuss are situated. Of particular interest is the **Television Tower** near Zippendorf, 455 feet high, which offers a panoramic view of West Mecklenburg lakes and hills from its tower café.

Wismar is another seaport town in the country of Mecklenburg. It can be visited by taking a train from Schwerin, a trip of about 20 minutes. Wismar was once ruled by Sweden. World War II bombs wreaked tremendous damage on the town, but it has been largely rebuilt. However, its Marktplatz dates from the Middle Ages.

Where to Stay and Dine

The town has a better-than-average hotel, **Stadt Schwerin,** Grunthalplatz 5, DDR-2700 Schwerin (tel. 84/52-61), which you can book in America, arriving with prepaid hotel vouchers. The rooms are pleasantly furnished, and often they fill up with Danish tourists who take cheap excursions by train, with car-ferry connections, to get a look at life on the other side of the sea. Each of the pleasantly furnished accommodations contains a private bath. Singles go for $51 daily; doubles run $72. The hotel has the best restaurant facilities in town.

GLOSSARY AND MENU TERMS

Glossary

Altstadt old part of a city or town
Apotheke pharmacy
Bad a spa (also bath)
Bahn railway, train
  Bahnhof railway station
  Bergbahn funicular
  Hauptbahnhof main railway station
  Seilbahn cable car
  Stadtbahn (S-Bahn) commuter railway
  Untergrundbahn (U-Bahn) subway, underground system in a city
Burg fortified castle
Dom cathedral
Domplatz cathedral square
Drogerie shop selling cosmetics, sundries
Gasthof inn
Gemütlichkeit (gemütlich) comfort, coziness, friendliness
gutbürgerlich German home cooking
hotel garni hotel that serves no meals, or breakfast only
Kaufhaus department store
Kneipe bar for drinking, may serve snacks
Konditorei café for coffee and pastries
Kunst art
Marktplatz market square
Neue Küche cuisine moderne
Rathaus town or city hall
  Altes Rathaus old town hall
  Neues Rathaus new town hall (currently used as such)
Ratskeller restaurant in Rathaus cellars serving traditional German food
Schauspielhaus theater for plays
Schloss palace, castle
Spielbank casino
Stadt town, city
Tor gateway
Turm tower
Weinstube wine bar or tavern serving meals
Wilhelmian decorative style of the late 19th century

Menu Terms

SOUPS (Suppen)

Erbsensuppe pea soup
Gemüsesuppe vegetable soup
Hühnerbrühe chicken soup
Kartoffelsuppe potato soup

Gulaschsuppe goulash soup
Linsensuppe lentil soup
Nudelsuppe noodle soup
Ochsenschwanzsuppe oxtail soup

MEATS (Wurst, Fleisch, and Geflügel)

Aufschnitt cold cuts
Brathuhn roast chicken
Bratwurst grilled sausage
Deutsches Beefsteak hamburger
steak
Eisbein pigs' knuckles
Ente duck
Gans goose
Hammel mutton
Kalb veal
Kaltes Geflügel cold poultry
Kassler Rippchen pork chops

Lamm lamb
Leber liver
Nieren kidneys
Ragoût stew
Rinderbraten roast beef
Rindfleisch beef
Sauerbraten sauerbraten
Schinken ham
Schweinebraten roast pork
Truthahn turkey
Wienerschnitzel veal cutlet
Wurst sausage

FISH (Fisch)

Aal eel
Forelle trout
Hecht pike
Karpfen carp
Krebs crawfish

Lachs salmon
Makrele mackerel
Rheinsalm Rhine salmon
Schellfisch haddock
Seezunge sole

EGGS (Eier)

Eier in der Schale boiled eggs
Rühreier scrambled eggs
Spiegeleier fried eggs

mit Speck with bacon
Verlorene Eier poached eggs

SANDWICHES (Belegte Brote)

Käsebrot cheese sandwich
Schinkenbrot ham sandwich

Schwarzbrot mit Butter
pumpernickel w/butter
Wurstbrot sausage sandwich

SALADS (Salat)

Gemischter Salat mixed salad
Gurkensalat cucumber salad

Kopfsalat lettuce salad
Rohkostplatte raw vegetable platter

VEGETABLES (Gemüse)

Artischocken artichokes
Blumenkohl cauliflower
Bohnen beans
Bratkartoffeln fried potatoes

Erbsen peas
Grüne Bohnen string beans
Gurken cucumbers
Karotten carrots

Kartoffelbrei mashed potatoes
Kartoffelsalat potato salad
Knödel dumplings
Kohl cabbage
Reis rice
Rote Rüben beets
Rotkraut red cabbage
Salat lettuce

Salzkartoffeln boiled potatoes
Sauerkraut sauerkraut
Spargel asparagus
Spinat spinach
Steinpilze boletus mushrooms
Tomaten tomatoes
Vorspeisen hors d'oeuvres
Weisse Rüben turnips

DESSERTS (Nachtisch)

Blatterteiggebäck puff pastry
Bratapfel baked apple
Käse cheese
Kloss dumpling
Kompott stewed fruit
Obstkuchen fruit tart

Obstsalat fruit salad
Pfannkuchen sugared pancakes
Pflaumenkompott stewed plums
Teegebäck tea cakes
Torten pastries

FRUITS (Obst)

Ananas pineapples
Apfel apples
Apfelsinen oranges
Bananen bananas
Birnen pears

Kirschen cherries
Pfirsiche peaches
Weintrauben grapes
Zitronen lemons

BEVERAGES (Getränke)

Bier beer
Ein Dunkles a dark beer
Ein Helles a light beer
Milch milk
Rotwein red wine

Schokolade chocolate
Eine Tasse Kaffee a cup of coffee
Eine Tasse Tee a cup of tea
Tomatensaft tomato juice
Wasser water

CONDIMENTS AND TABLE ITEMS

Brot bread
Brötchen rolls
Butter butter
Eis ice
Essig vinegar
Gabel fork
Glas glass
Löffel spoon
Messer knife

Platte plate
Pfeffer pepper
Sahne cream
Salz salt
Senf mustard
Tasse cup
Zitrone lemon
Zucker sugar

COOKING TERMS

Gebacken baked
Gebraten fried
Gefüllt stuffed
Gekocht boiled

Geröstet broiled
Gut durchgebraten well done
Nicht durchgebraten rare
Paniert breaded

INDEX

GENERAL INFORMATION

SIGHTS AND ATTRACTIONS

Bavarian Alps

BERCHTESGADEN & ENVIRONS
Berghof, 303–4
"Eagle's Nest" (Obersalzberg), 303
Nonntal, 302
St. Bartholomew (Königssee), 302
Salzbergwerk Berchtesgaden, 302
Stiftskirche, 302

CHIEMSEE
Frauenchiemsee, 313

Neues Schloss (Herrenchiemsee), 313–14

GARMISCH-PARTENKIRCHEN & ENVIRONS
Alspitz, 310–11
Olympic Ice Stadium, 304
Partnachklamm Gorge, 311
St. Anton, chapel of, 305
Ski Stadium, 304–5

Wank, 311
Zugspitze, 310

MITTENWALD
Geigenbau- und Heimatmuseum, 319

OBERAMMERGAU & ENVIRONS
Ettal Abbey, 318
Heimatmuseum, 317
Passionsspielhaus, 317
Schloss Linderhof, 317

Black Forest (Schwarzwald)

East Germany

Franconia & Danube Region

Frankfurt am Main & Environs

Hamburg

The Rhineland

Romantic Road

Schleswig-Holstein

West Berlin

ACCOMMODATIONS

Bavarian Alps

Black Forest (Schwarzwald)

Key to Abbreviations: *A* = Apartments; *B* = Budget; *D* = Deluxe; *E* = Expensive; *M* = Moderately priced; *P* = Pension

East Germany

Franconia & Danube Region

Frankfurt am Main & Environs

Hamburg

Heidelberg/Stuttgart Area

Lower Saxony & North Hesse

Munich & Environs

The Rhineland

Romantic Road

Schleswig-Holstein

SPAS

West Berlin

NOW, SAVE MONEY ON ALL YOUR TRAVELS!
Join Frommer's™ Dollarwise® Travel Club

Saving money while traveling is never a simple matter, which is why the **Dollarwise Travel Club** was formed 31 years ago. Developed in response to requests from Frommer's Travel Guide readers, the Club provides cost-cutting travel strategies, up-to-date travel information, and a sense of community for value-conscious travelers from all over the world.

In keeping with the money-saving concept, the annual membership fee is low —$18 for U.S. residents or $20 for residents of Canada, Mexico, and other countries—and is immediately exceeded by the value of your benefits, which include:

1. Any TWO books listed on the following pages.
2. Plus any ONE Frommer's City Guide.
3. A subscription to our quarterly newspaper, *The Dollarwise Traveler*.
4. A membership card that entitles you to purchase through the Club all Frommer's publications for 33% to 50% off their retail price.

The eight-page **Dollarwise Traveler** tells you about the latest developments in good-value travel worldwide and includes the following columns: **Hospitality Exchange** (for those offering and seeking hospitality in cities all over the world); **Share-a-Trip** (for those looking for travel companions to share costs); and **Readers Ask . . . Readers Reply** (for those with travel questions that other members can answer).

Aside from the Frommer's Guides and the Gault Millau Guides, you can also choose from our Special Editions. These include such titles as *California with Kids* (a compendium of the best of California's accommodations, restaurants, and sightseeing attractions appropriate for those traveling with toddlers through teens); *Candy Apple: New York with Kids* (a spirited guide to the Big Apple by a savvy New York grandmother that's perfect for both visitors and residents); *Caribbean Hideaways* (the 100 most romantic places to stay in the Islands, all rated on ambience, food, sports opportunities, and price); *Honeymoon Destinations* (a guide to planning and choosing just the right destination from hundreds of possibilities in the U.S., Mexico, and the Caribbean); *Marilyn Wood's Wonderful Weekends* (a selection of the best mini-vacations within a 200-mile radius of New York City, including descriptions of country inns and other accommodations, restaurants, picnic spots, sights, and activities); and *Paris Rendez-Vous* (a delightful guide to the best places to meet in Paris whether for power breakfasts or dancing till dawn).

To join this Club, simply send the appropriate membership fee with your name and address to: Frommer's Dollarwise Travel Club, 15 Columbus Circle, New York, NY 10023. Remember to specify which single city guide and which two other guides you wish to receive in your initial package of member's benefits. Or tear out the next page, check off your choices, and send the page to us with your membership fee.

FROMMER BOOKS
PRENTICE HALL PRESS
15 COLUMBUS CIRCLE
NEW YORK, NY 10023
212/373-8125

Date_____

Friends:
Please send me the books checked below.

FROMMER'S™ GUIDES

(Guides to sightseeing and tourist accommodations and facilities from budget to deluxe, with emphasis on the medium-priced.)

☐ Alaska $14.95	☐ Germany $14.95
☐ Australia $14.95	☐ Italy. $14.95
☐ Austria & Hungary $14.95	☐ Japan & Hong Kong $14.95
☐ Belgium, Holland & Luxembourg $14.95	☐ Mid-Atlantic States $14.95
☐ Bermuda & The Bahamas. $14.95	☐ New England. $14.95
☐ Brazil $14.95	☐ New York State $14.95
☐ Canada $14.95	☐ Northwest $14.95
☐ Caribbean. $14.95	☐ Portugal, Madeira & the Azores $14.95
☐ Cruises (incl. Alaska, Carib, Mex, Hawaii,	☐ Skiing Europe $14.95
Panama, Canada & US) $14.95	☐ South Pacific. $14.95
☐ California & Las Vegas $14.95	☐ Southeast Asia $14.95
☐ Egypt. $14.95	☐ Southern Atlantic States. $14.95
☐ England & Scotland $14.95	☐ Southwest $14.95
☐ Florida. $14.95	☐ Switzerland & Liechtenstein $14.95
☐ France $14.95	☐ USA. $15.95

FROMMER'S $-A-DAY® GUIDES

(In-depth guides to sightseeing and low-cost tourist accommodations and facilities.)

☐ Europe on $40 a Day $15.95	☐ New York on $60 a Day. $13.95
☐ Australia on $40 a Day $13.95	☐ New Zealand on $45 a Day $13.95
☐ Eastern Europe on $25 a Day $13.95	☐ Scandinavia on $60 a Day $13.95
☐ England on $50 a Day. $13.95	☐ Scotland & Wales on $40 a Day $13.95
☐ Greece on $35 a Day $13.95	☐ South America on $35 a Day $13.95
☐ Hawaii on $60 a Day. $13.95	☐ Spain & Morocco on $40 a Day $13.95
☐ India on $25 a Day $12.95	☐ Turkey on $30 a Day $13.95
☐ Ireland on $35 a Day. $13.95	☐ Washington, D.C. & Historic Va. on
☐ Israel on $40 a Day. $13.95	$40 a Day. $13.95
☐ Mexico on $35 a Day $13.95	

FROMMER'S TOURING GUIDES

(Color illustrated guides that include walking tours, cultural and historic sites, and other vital travel information.)

☐ Amsterdam. $10.95	☐ New York $10.95
☐ Australia $9.95	☐ Paris $8.95
☐ Brazil $10.95	☐ Rome. $10.95
☐ Egypt. $8.95	☐ Scotland. $9.95
☐ Florence. $8.95	☐ Thailand. $9.95
☐ Hong Kong $10.95	☐ Turkey $10.95
☐ London $8.95	☐ Venice $8.95

TURN PAGE FOR ADDITONAL BOOKS AND ORDER FORM

0690

FROMMER'S CITY GUIDES˙

(Pocket-size guides to sightseeing and tourist accommodations and facilities in all price ranges.)

☐ Amsterdam/Holland $8.95	☐ Montréal/Québec City. $8.95
☐ Athens. $8.95	☐ New Orleans. $8.95
☐ Atlanta $8.95	☐ New York $8.95
☐ Atlantic City/Cape May $8.95	☐ Orlando $8.95
☐ Barcelona. $7.95	☐ Paris $8.95
☐ Belgium $7.95	☐ Philadelphia $8.95
☐ Boston. $8.95	☐ Rio $8.95
☐ Cancún/Cozumel/Yucatán. $8.95	☐ Rome. $8.95
☐ Chicago. $8.95	☐ Salt Lake City $8.95
☐ Denver/Boulder/Colorado Springs. . . .$7.95	☐ San Diego. $8.95
☐ Dublin/Ireland $8.95	☐ San Francisco $8.95
☐ Hawaii. $8.95	☐ Santa Fe/Taos/Albuquerque. $8.95
☐ Hong Kong. $7.95	☐ Seattle/Portland $7.95
☐ Las Vegas. $8.95	☐ Sydney. $8.95
☐ Lisbon/Madrid/Costa del Sol $8.95	☐ Tampa/St. Petersburg $8.95
☐ London $8.95	☐ Tokyo. $7.95
☐ Los Angeles $8.95	☐ Toronto $8.95
☐ Mexico City/Acapulco. $8.95	☐ Vancouver/Victoria $7.95
☐ Minneapolis/St. Paul $8.95	☐ Washington, D.C. $8.95

SPECIAL EDITIONS

☐ Beat the High Cost of Travel. $6.95	☐ Motorist's Phrase Book (Fr/Ger/Sp) $4.95
☐ Bed & Breakfast—N. America $11.95	☐ Paris Rendez-Vous $10.95
☐ California with Kids $14.95	☐ Swap and Go (Home Exchanging). . . .$10.95
☐ Caribbean Hideaways. $14.95	☐ The Candy Apple (NY with Kids). $12.95
☐ Honeymoon Destinations (US, Mex &	☐ Travel Diary and Record Book. $5.95
Carib). $14.95	☐ Where to Stay USA (From $3 to $30 a
☐ Manhattan's Outdoor Sculpture. $15.95	night). $10.95

☐ Marilyn Wood's Wonderful Weekends (CT, DE, MA, NH, NJ, NY, PA, RI, VT) $11.95
☐ The New World of Travel (Annual sourcebook by Arthur Frommer for savvy travelers) $16.95

GAULT MILLAU

(The only guides that distinguish the truly superlative from the merely overrated.)

☐ The Best of Chicago. $15.95	☐ The Best of Los Angeles $16.95
☐ The Best of France $16.95	☐ The Best of New England $15.95
☐ The Best of Hong Kong. $16.95	☐ The Best of New York $16.95
☐ The Best of Italy. $16.95	☐ The Best of Paris $16.95
☐ The Best of London $16.95	☐ The Best of San Francisco $16.95

☐ The Best of Washington, D.C. $16.95

ORDER NOW!

In U.S. include $2 shipping UPS for 1st book; $1 ea. add'l book. Outside U.S. $3 and $1, respectively.
Allow four to six weeks for delivery in U.S., longer outside U.S.
Enclosed is my check or money order for $_____

NAME_____

ADDRESS_____

CITY_____ STATE_____ ZIP_____

0690

AMERICAN EXPRESS CAN DELIVER CASH AND A REPLACEMENT CARD TO YOU WITHIN 24 HOURS, AS LONG AS YOU'RE IN THIS GENERAL AREA.

No matter where you are in the world, if you lose your wallet, we can get a new American Express® Card and cash in your hands usually within 24 hours.*

If you're truly in the middle of nowhere, say the African Outback, it might take a little longer. Depending upon how many wandering hippos and fallen trees our local courier must contend with.

But more often than not, you'll have a new Card and cash the next day. Something you'd expect from American Express.

So carry the American Express Card. And no matter where on earth you go, you'll never leave civilization behind.

For assistance, call your nearest American Express office, or in the U.S. call our 24-hour number 1-800-528-4800; everywhere else call collect 202-554-AMEX. Don't leave home without it®.

MEMBERSHIP HAS ITS PRIVILEGES℠

 TRAVEL RELATED SERVICES

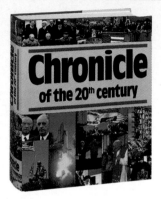
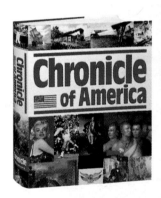

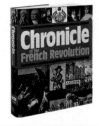